Human Motivation

Third Edition

Robert E. Franken

University of Calgary

Brooks/Cole Publishing Company

Pacific Grove, California

ITP™ The trademark ITP is used under license.

*To all those students who have helped make
my life so wonderful and rewarding*

Sponsoring Editor: Vicki Knight
Editorial Assistant: Lauri Banks-Ataide
Production: Penna Design and Production
Production Services Manager: Joan Marsh
Manuscript Editor: Alan Rockhold
Permissions Editor: Roxane Buck
Interior Design: Detta Penna
Cover Design: Roy Neuhaus
Cover Photograph: John McDermott
Interior Illustration: Pat Rogondino
Photo Researcher: Lindsay Kefauver
Typesetting: Penna Design and Production
Cover Printing: Phoenix Color Corporation
Printing and Binding: Arcata Graphics/Fairfield

Photo credits appear on page xxiv.

Brooks/Cole Publishing Company
A Division of Wadsworth, Inc.
© 1994 by Wadsworth, Inc., Belmont, California 94002

Printed in the United States of America
10 9 8 7 6 5 4 3 2 1

Library of Congress Cataloging-in-Publication Data
Franken, Robert E., [date]
    Human Motivation / Robert E. Franken. — 3rd ed.
        p.   cm
    Includes bibliographical references and indexes.
    ISBN: 0-534-15612-6
    1. Motivation (Psychology)   I. Title.
BF503.F7   1993
153.8—dc20   93-304400
                                                                          CIP

Preface

For centuries scholars have speculated about what motivates humans. In examining the explanations that have been offered, one is immediately struck by their diversity. While there are many ways of conceptualizing motivation, this book is based on empirical research. It is based on the work of researchers who have found there is a genetic or biological basis of motivation, a learned basis of motivation, and a thinking or cognitive basis of motivation.

This book is divided into four parts. In the first part, I talk about some of the past and current issues that motivation theories have addressed and discuss in some detail what I mean when I talk about treating motivation in terms of components. Any time we act, our behavior is the end product of a complex interaction of biology, learning, and thinking/cognition.

In Part 2, I deal with a number of topics that fall roughly under the heading *Deficiency Motivation*. Some time ago, Abraham Maslow made the distinction between deficiency needs and growth needs. I like this distinction and think it is a useful way of thinking about human motivation. I should point out to the sophisticated reader that I conceptualize deficiency and growth motivation somewhat differently than does Maslow, a point that I elaborate in the text. For me, deficiency motivation involves such things as the need to maintain optimal arousal, hunger and eating, the need to sleep and dream, sex behavior, the tendency to use drugs, and why people behave aggressively. I have included a chapter on drugs in this section on deficiency needs because I feel that drugs are often used as a substitute for the real thing. As I point out in this chapter on drugs, most of the recreational drugs people use simply increase or decrease the output of existing chemicals in the body. Most people, I believe, can

learn to achieve the same state without the intervention of drugs.

In Part 3, I discuss emotions. There is a growing movement by motivation theorists to conceptualize motivation in terms of goals and goal-directed behavior. Since there is an abundance of research which show that emotions can undermine or sustain goal-directed behavior it is critical to understand exactly how emotions are aroused and how they can be managed. Some of the main emotion theorists, such as Lazarus, have begun to conceptualize emotions as being goal-congruent or goal-incongruent. According to this conceptualization, emotions can only be understood in the context of goals or goal directed behavior. The reverse is also true. One can only understand motivation by understanding emotion.

I start this section on emotions by talking about the emotion we call stress. Psychologists have done a great deal of work on stress and have shown that the management of stress is perhaps one of the most important things that we need to address if we want to live happy and successful lives. The research on this topic is abundant and the implication are clear. Stress can have devastating effects on success and health if we do not learn how to manage it properly

In addition to stress there are a number of other goal-incongruent emotions that we need to learn to manage. In the chapter *Goal-Incongruent (Negative) Emotions*, I talk about fear and anxiety, which have been shown, over and over, to incapacitate goal-directed behavior. Fear and anxiety often paralyze people into inaction. I also discuss pessimism and depression. It has been shown repeatedly that people who adopt a pessimistic attitude often become depressed and when people are depressed, their motivation virtually stops. Recent work on guilt and shame indicate again that these emotions are highly debilitating and undermine goal-directed behavior.

The main goal-congruent emotions are happiness, hope, optimism, attachment, belongingness, and empathy. When people are happy, hopeful, or optimistic they are inclined to work hard towards their goals. One of the main antecedents of achievement and success, it has been found, is a willingness to persist. In the course of examining goal-directed behavior, researchers have found that people who tend to succeed in achieving their goals are highly social. What I mean is that such people recognize the fact they need to experience a sense of what has been called *relatedness.* While people adopt, from time to time, the view that they do not need other people, research on this topic is quite clear. It is the people who accept and develop their social skills who tend to be successful. Not only are they more successful, but they tend to be physically and psychologically healthier. In this chapter I also talk about the motivation for risk-taking behavior. Risk-taking behavior is a sign of positive health and adjustment, whereas its absence is a sign of neuroticism.

In Part 4, I talk about growth motivation. The idea that organisms are motivated toward development and growth has captured the imagination of many motivation theorists. As more and more research is being done, it is becoming increasing clear to many theorists that humans are not only motivated to develop and grow, but that the mechanisms that guide this tendency are to some degree innate.

If the motivation for growth is innate in humans, and perhaps animals to some degree, then why do people not all grow at the same rate? Why do some people succeed while others do not? Why do some people have big dreams while others do not? The answer is starting to emerge. Not all people are equipped to the same degree with the ability to do at least two things: to manage their emotions and to set goals. It is not enough, as Maslow suggested some time ago, that people merely satisfy their deficiency needs. The new focus in motivation is that people need to learn not only how to manage their emotions (such as the emotion of self-doubt), but they need to learn how to set appropriate goals. The exciting thing is that people can be

taught these skills. This new focus for motivation has been dubbed the self-regulation of motivation.

In the first chapter of this section on growth motivation I talk about the early work on growth motivation that came out of the research on curiosity and exploratory behavior. It was this early work on curiosity and exploratory behavior that led theorists such as Dember and Earl to suggest that organisms are characterized by a tendency towards growth. People are innately motivated to find out all they can about the world in which they live. I also talk about creativity and attempt to show that creativity grows out of the motivation to discover all that life has to offer. I also talk about the sensation-seeking motive. Certain people called sensation seekers appear to be born with a stronger curiosity and exploratory drive. As a result of this strong drive, they tend, among other things, to be more creative and more unconventional.

In the second chapter of this section, *Competence and Intelligence, Achievement and Persistence, Self-Esteem and Self-Worth,* I review research which shows that humans are motivated to become competent and intelligent. It is from their sense of competency and achievements that people develop a sense of self-esteem and self-worth.

Finally, in the last chapter I review a portion of the research on self-regulation of behavior. I call this chapter *Achieving Personal Success: The Self-Regulation of Behavior.* In this chapter, I discuss the principles of goal setting, the principles for managing one's emotions, and the principles for fine tuning one's goal-directed behavior. In this chapter I talk about the need to learn how to manage your thinking so that you can become fully functional and fully self-actualized. I also talk about how you develop a fully-differentiated self-concept. It is out of a fully developed and differentiated self-concept that people learn to dream big dreams. It is from these big dreams that people learn to set difficult goals. In the final analysis, it is from a developing a highly differentiated self-concept that people come to achieve their true potential.

Although this book was written mainly for psychology majors, I have kept in mind that motivation is interesting to just about everyone. Over the years I have had students from business, counseling, education, engineering, nursing, physical education, and social work who took my course because they felt that knowing something about human motivation would help them in their chosen professions. Other students in such field as art, history, and philosophy have said they simply want to know something about their own personal motivation. Because motivation courses often attract a diverse population, I have tried to make the book easily understood by readers with little background in psychology, yet challenging to those who are familiar with the subject.

Many people have contributed directly or indirectly to the preparation of this book. Students in the various motivation classes that I teach have given me the inspiration and the feedback that helped shape the organization and the content. Discussions with colleagues and graduate students have helped sharpen my thinking. To all those people I say thank you.

I thank the four reviewers who gave me many wonderful suggestions. Had I incorporated all their wonderful ideas and suggestions, this book would have been twice its present length. They are: Dr. James Carroll, Central Michigan University; Dr. Sharon Presley, California State University, Fullerton; Dr. Richard Straub, University of Michigan at Dearborn; and Dr. Dean Frost, Portland State University, Portland, Oregon.

I want to thank my editor, Vicki Knight, for her help and support as I struggled with the task of keeping this book from getting too long. I want to thank Colleen Lyle and Jill Petersen who helped in proofing. I also thank Joan Marsh and Detta Penna for their help and support in the production phase.

Finally, I thank my wife Helen, and my children Ryan and Renee, who have given me so much love and support.

Brief Contents

Part 1   History and Organizing Principles

| Chapter One | Past and Current Issues in Motivation | 1 |
| Chapter Two | Components of Motivation | 18 |

Part 2   Deficiency Motivation

Chapter Three	Arousal, Performance, and Attention	49
Chapter Four	Hunger and Eating	78
Chapter Five	Sex Behavior, Love and Sexual Orientation	111
Chapter Six	Wakefulness, Alertness, Sleep, and Dreams	146
Chapter Seven	Drug Use and Drug Addiction	179
Chapter Eight	Anger, Aggression and Compliance	219

Part 3   Goal-Congruent and Goal-Incongruent Emotions

Chapter Nine	Emotions: The Examples of Stress, Distress and Coping	258
Chapter Ten	Goal-Incongruent (Negative) Emotions: Fear and Anxiety, Pessimism and Depression, Guilt and Shame	303
Chapter Eleven	Goal-Congruent (Positive) Emotions: Happiness, Hope and Optimism, Attachment and Belongingness, Empathy	339

Part 4   Growth Motivation

Chapter Twelve	Curiosity, Exploratory Behavior, Play, Sensation Seeking and Creativity	374
Chapter Thirteen	Competence and Intelligence, Achievement and Persistence,Self-Esteem and Self-Worth	409
Chapter Fourteen	Achieving Personal Success: The Self-Regulation of Motivation	442

Contents

Part One   History and Organizing Principles

Chapter One   1

Past and Current Issues in Motivation

What is the Study of Motivation About?   2

Analyzing the Flow of Behavior: A Central Concern of Motivational Theorists   3

Current Focus of Motivation Research   4

Early Conceptions of Human Motivation   4

The Greek Philosophers   4

The Problem of Analogous Behaviors in Humans and Animals   5

Instinct Theories   5

Some Modern Conceptions about
Human Motivation   7

Evolutionary Theory and Charles Darwin   7

Instincts Revised   7

Ethology: The Biology of Behavior   8

Learning Theorists   9

Cognitive Theorists   10

Psychoanalytic Theory   11

Humanistic Theories   12

Abraham Maslow   12

Carl Rogers   12

Some Current Issues in Motivation   14

Environmental Stimuli as Sources of Motivational Arousal   14

Single versus Multiple Determinants of Behavior   14

Persistence of Behavior over Time   15

Interaction of Motive Systems   16

Primacy of Cognition versus Biological Drives   16

Main Points   16

Chapter Two   18

Components of Motivation

A Working Definition of Motivation   19

The Biological Component   20

The Ethological View   20

Open versus closed programs   20

Hardwired versus softwired   21

The Behavioral Neurosciences   21

PRACTICAL APPLICATION 2.1

The Biology of Obsessions and Compulsions   22

Reward centers   23

Reticular activating system   24

Limbic system   24

Constraints Imposed by the Nervous System   24

Summary   25

The Learned Component   25

Acquired Motives   25

PRACTICAL APPLICATION 2.2

Becoming Aware of Your Biological Processes   26

Classical Conditioning   27

Fear as a classical conditioned or respondent conditioned motive   28

Reversing classical conditioning   29

Instrumental learning   29

Achievement as an instrumentally acquired motive   29

Secondary rewards and instrumental learning   29

Intrinsic versus extrinsic rewards   30

The Opponent-Process Model of Acquired Drives   31

Associative learning and connectionism 31

Summary 32

Cognitive Component 32
  Nature of Cognitions 33
  Categories and labels 34
  Beliefs, attitudes, and values 34
  Stereotypes 34
  Cognitive dissonance theory 34
  Implicit theories 35
  Does the external world cause behavior
  or do implicit theories? 35

PRACTICAL APPLICATION **2.3**
  **Becoming Mindful of Your Cognitive
  Processes** 36

  Attribution Theory: Perceiving the Causes
  of Behavior 37

Individual Differences 38
  *Locus of Control Theory: Internal and
  External Causes* 38

Summary 38

The Nature of Theories and Models 39
  *The Search for Critical Variables That
  Govern Behavior* 39
  Testing the Generality of Theories 40
  *Current Focus of Motivation Theory:
  Individual Differences* 40

Summary 41

Some Examples of a Components Approach 41
  Motivation for Running 41
  Motivation for Listening to Rock Music 44

Summary 47

Main Points 47

Part Two   Deficiency Motivation

Chapter Three   49

Arousal, Performance, and Attention

Definition of Arousal 50
Biological Mechanisms of Arousal 50
  The Reticular Activating System (RAS) 50
  The nature and measurement of cortical activity 51
  Positron Emission Tomography (PET) 51
  The Autonomic Nervous System 52
  Routtenberg's Model of Two Arousal Systems 54
Origins of Arousal 54
  Stimulation of the Sensory Systems 54
  Rhythmic Activity of the Nervous System 55
  Cognitive Interpretation 55
  Anticipatory bodily preparation 55
  Cognitive dissonance 55

Summary 55

Performance and Arousal 56
  *Hebb's Model of Arousal, Attention, and
  Performance* 57
  Studies of Sensory Deprivation 57

  Studies of Increases in Arousal 58
  Performance and Sensory Overload 59
  Is Arousal a Unitary Construct? 59
Arousal, The Inverted U-Shaped Function and
  Individual Differences 59
Biological Mechanisms That Reduce Sensory
  Overload 60
  Lacey and Lacey's attention/rejection model 60
  Learned Ways of Dealing with Sensory Overload 62
  Restricted environmental stimulation technique
  (REST) 61
  *Cognitive Ways of Dealing with
  Sensory Overload* 62
  Optimal Stimulation, Hyperactivity, and Autism 62

Summary 63

Arousal and Selective Attention 64
  Arousal and the Reorganization of Attention 64
  *The Interaction of Arousal and
  Selective Attention* 65
  Nonspecific Arousal 65
  The Orientation Reaction and Selective Attention 65

Vigilance: The Ability to Maintain Attention for Long Periods of Time 66

Increasing arousal or taking advantage of rhythmic arousal levels 66

Characteristics of the task 66

Feedback about performance 67

Summary 67

Can We Learn to Control Arousal Levels? 67

PRACTICAL APPLICATION **3.1**
Why Using the Words "Don't" and "Not" Often Fails to Produce Good Performance 68

Learning to Perform Independently of Arousal 69

Summary 69

Individual Differences 70

Eysenck's Theory 70

Extraverts 70

Introverts 70

Background stimulation 71

Reversal Theory: An Alternative Way of Viewing Optimal Stimulation 71

Summary 72

Theories of Emotion that Involve the Concept of Arousal 72

The James-Lange theory 72

Cannon's theory 73

Schachter and Singer's theory 74

Summary 75

Main Points 76

Chapter Four 78

Hunger and Eating

Five Important Issues 79

What psychological mechanism produces hunger? 79

Why do humans have a propensity to obesity? 79

Why do humans have difficulty getting rid of unwanted fat? 79

What produces anorexia nervosa? 79

What produces bulimia? 79

Biological factors in Hunger and Eating 79

Food, Energy and Energy Reserves 79

Fats, carbohydrates, and proteins 79

Energy and energy reserves 80

The need for a balanced diet 80

Insulin and the metabolism of glucose 81

Theories of Hunger 81

The glucose theory of hunger 81

The insulin theory of hunger 81

Reconciling the glucose theory and the insulin theories 81

The fatty acid theory of hunger 82

The heat-production theory of hunger 82

Feedback Systems for Satiety 82

Brain receptors for satiety 82

Signals from the gastrointestinal tract 82

Learned Factors in Hunger and Eating 83

Can we select a balanced diet? 83

Selection of foods based on taste and texture as opposed to nutritional value 85

Cultural preferences 85

Cognitive and Individual Factors in Hunger and Eating 86

Summary 86

The Origins of Overweight 86

Defining Obesity 87

Biological Component 87

The genetic factor 87

Energy Expenditure 87

The three components 87

Age 87

Obesity and Anorexia as Malfunctions of the Hypothalamus 88

Lesions of the ventromedial nuclei 88

Lesions of the lateral hypothalamus 88

What is the exact mechanism? 88

Set-Point Theory 89

The "Yo-Yo" Effect and the Famine Hypothesis 89

The "Yo-Yo" Effect As a Result of Reduced Metabolism 90

The "Yo-Yo" Effect and Health 90

Learned Component 90

The environmental factor 90

Cognitive Component and
  Individual Differences   90
    Rate of Energy Use   90
    Individual differences in metabolism rates   90
    Emotional disorders and obesity   91
Summary   91
Theories of Overweight and Obesity   91
    Internal-External Theory of Hunger and Eating   91
    Stomach contractions and hunger   92
    The Air France study   92
    A further test of Schachter's theory: fear, stomach
    contractions, and hunger   93
    Is Externality Innate or Learned?   93
    Externality and the nonobese   94
    Sensory cues, externality, and the insulin response   94
    Boundary Theory of Hunger, Eating, and Obesity   95
    Restrained and unrestrained eaters   95
    The preloading studies   95
    The disinhibited eater   96
    Binge eating and anorexia   97
Summary   97
Obstacles to Dieting: Why People Can't
  or Won't Lose Weight   97
Biological Factors   97
    *Anabolism (Caloric Thrift) and
    Catabolism (Caloric Waste)*   97
Learned Factors   98
    Increased preference for restricted or
    forbidden foods   98
    Carbohydrates and dieting   98
Cognitive and Individual Difference Factors   98
    Dealing with new expectations   98
Is There Hope for the Dieter?   99
    Short-term weight gains are normally
    not a problem   99
    Behavior modification   99
    Smoking and Weight   99
    Natural Weight Control   99

PRACTICAL APPLICATION **4.1**
  Some Rules for Dieting   100

Other Approaches to Weight Control   100

Summary   101
Disturbed Eating Patterns   102
    Binge Eating   102
    Food deprivation and binge eating   102
    Overweight, dieting and binge eating   103
    Learning of binge eating   103
Bulimia   103
    Definition and prevalence   103
Biological Factors   104
Learned Factors   104
    Sex, age, race, and family history   104
    Psychological dynamics   104
Cognitive and Individual Difference Factors   104
    Binge eating as escape from self-awareness   104
    Treatment   104
Anorexia Nervosa   104
    Definition   104
Biological Factors   105
    Noradregenic system   105
    Serotonergic system   105
Learned Factors   106
Cognitive and Individual Difference Factors   106
    Prognosis   106
Theories and Interpretations of Eating Disorders   107
    *Sociocultural Variables in Bulimia and
    Anorexia Nervosa*   107
    The Spiral Model of Eating Disorders   107
Summary   108
Main Points   108

Chapter Five   111

Sex Behavior, Love, and Sexual Orientation

Motivation for Engaging in Sexual Behavior   112
    The Nature of Human Sexual Arousal (Passion)   112
Sensory and Arousal Factors   112
The Female Sexual Response   113
The Male Sexual Response   113
    Catecholamines and Sexual Activity   115
The Pair-Bonding Hypothesis   115
Summary   116

Learned Component   117
    What is Sexually Arousing to Humans?   117
    Sexual scripts   117
    Sexual arousal   118
    Reward value of sex   118
Summary   119

Cognitive Factors   120
    Liberalism versus conservatism   120
    Beliefs about sex drive in females and males   120
    Meaning attached to sex   120
Individual Differences   120
    Introverts and Extraverts   121
    *Unrestricted Orientation versus Restricted
    Orientation to Sex*   121
Summary   122
Love   122
Biological Component   122
Learned Component   123
    Falling in Love   123
    Attraction and Difficulty of Attainment   124
    Intimacy   124
Cognitive Component   124
Sternberg's Interaction Model   125
    Passion alone = infatuated love   125
    Intimacy alone = liking   125
    Commitment alone = sterile love   125
    Passion + intimacy = romantic love   125
    Passion + commitment = fatuous love   125

PRACTICAL APPLICATION **5.1**
    Striving to Attain Consummate Love   126

    Intimacy + commitment = companionate love   127
    Intimacy + passion + commitment = consummate
    love   127
Summary   127
Sex Differences: What Role Do Hormones
    Play in this Process?   127
Biological Component   128
    Genetics   128
    The Sex Hormones   128
    Three major categories   128
    Origins of the sex hormones   128

    *Sex hormones and differences in physical
    characteristics*   129
    Sex Hormones and Intellectual Functioning   130
Summary   130
    Sexual Dimorphism in the Brain   132
    Some Examples   132
Critical Periods   133
Sexual Dimorphism and Individual Differences   134
The Politics of Sex/Gender Differences   134
Summary   135
The Question of Sexual Orientation   135
    Gender-identity and gender-role   135
Biological Factors—The Question of
    Sexual Orientation   136
    *Sexual Dimorphism of the Hypothalamus and Male
    Sexual Orientation*   136
    Twin Studies and Male Sexual Orientation   136
    Twin Studies and Female Sexual Orientation   136
    *Congenital Adrenal Hyperphasis and Female
    Sexual Orientation*   137
    *DES-Affected Women and Female Sexual
    Orientation*   137
    Animal Work   138
    Changing sexual orientation   138
    Sex-typed behaviors   138
    The Normal Variant Model   138
Learned Component   138
    Psychoanalytic Theory   139
    Chance-Learning Hypothesis   139
    The Kinsey Institute Study   139
    Sex Assignment at Birth   139
    *Experiments of Nature: Rearing Boys as Girls and
    Core Sexual Identity*   140
    Status of the Learning Hypothesis   141
    *Learning and the Expression of a
    Sexual Orientation*   141
Cognitive Factor   141
    Cass's Six Stages of Homosexuality   142
    A Note on Sexual Plasticity in Humans   143
Summary   143
Main Points   143

Chapter Six   146

Wakefulness, Alertness, Sleep, and Dreams

Wakefulness, Sleep, and EEG Activity   147
   Correlates of Sleep and Wakefulness   147
   Jouvet's Model of Sleep   147
   Paralysis During REM   149
   Sleep and Attention   149
   Why We Fall Asleep and Why We Wake Up   149
   Circadian rhythm   150
   Environmental arousal   150
   Sleep deprivation   151
   Individual Differences in Sleep Cycles   151
Why We Periodically Feel Drowsy or Find Our
   Attention Shifting: Other Rhythms   151
   The 12.5-hour ultradian rhythm   151
   The 90-minute ultradian rhythm   151
   BRAC, waking mentation, and dreams   151
   How Much Sleep Do We Need?   152
   Altering Sleep/Wakefulness Cycles   152
The Effects of Sleep Reduction   152
   *Sleep Reduction and Feelings of Sleepiness
   and Fatigue*   152

PRACTICAL APPLICATION **6.1**
   What Is the Best Way to Adjust to Jet Lag?   153

   Sleep Reduction and Performance   153

PRACTICAL APPLICATION **6.2**
   Shift Work, Sleepiness, and Catnaps   154

   Nature of the Task and the Effects of Sleep Loss   156
   Feedback   156
   Complexity   156
   Interaction of Sleep Loss and Circadian Rhythm   156
   Sleep Reduction and Fragmented Sleep   156
   Sleep Deprivation and Mood   156
Summary   157
The Psychological Functions of Sleep   157
   Change in Sleep Patterns   157
Experimental Procedures for Determining the
   Function of Sleep   157

REM Deprivation in Animals   157
REM Deprivation in Humans   158
REM Deprivation and Motivation   158
Ellman's Motivation Theory of REM   158
The REM Rebound Effect   159
REM Sleep Deprivation and
   Psychological Health   159
   Early work   159
   Vogel's research on depression   159
   Vogel's theory   160
REM Sleep, Learning, and Adaptation   160
   REM Sleep and the Consolidation Hypothesis   160
   REM Deprivation and Learning in Animals   160
   REM Deprivation and Learning in Humans   161
   Type of task   161
   Adaptation to stress   161
   Timing of REM sleep   161
   REM Sleep and Divergent (Creative) Thinking   161
   *Individual Differences in the Need
   or REM Sleep*   162
   Field dependence and field independence   162
   Ego threat   162
   Neuroticism   162
   Other Types of Sleep Deprivation   163
Summary   164
Dreaming   165
   Do Dreams Have Any Meaning?   165
   Freud   165
   Neo-Freudians: Jung and Adler   165
   Crick and Mitchison   166
   *Hobson's Activation/Synthesis
   Theory of Dreams*   166
   Do Dreams Have Meaning for Hobson?   167
   *The View that Dreams are a Happening to be Enjoyed
   for their Entertainment Value*   168
   Lucid Dreaming   168
   Lucid Dreaming as Empowerment   168
   Lucid Dreaming and Health   169
Distinguishing Between REM, NREM, and Sleep
   Onset Dreams   169
   REM and NREM Dreams   169

Sleep-onset Dreams 169

PRACTICAL APPLICATION 6.3
Learn How to Become a Lucid Dreamer 170

Equivalence of REM Dreams, NREM Dreams, and Waking Mentation 171

Hartmann's Theory of Sleep 172
  The Function of REM and NREM Sleep 172

  Synchronous versus Asynchronous Electrical Activity During REM and SWS 172

  REM Sleep Restores Catecholamines 172

Summary 173

Sleep Disorders 173
  Insomnia 173

PRACTICAL APPLICATION 6.4
Some Common Reasons for Insomnia

  Drug-related insomnias 174
  Non-drug-related insomnias 176
  Sleep Apnea 176

Summary 176

Main Points 177

Chapter Seven   **179**

Drug Use and Drug Addiction

Current Focus 180
  World Health Organization Definition 180
  Substance Abuse 180

Summary 180

Some Basic Terms and Theories 181
  Psychoactive versus nonpsychoactive 181
  Dependency 181
  Tolerance 181
  Solomon's Opponent-Process Theory 182
  Is There an Addictive Personality? 184
  When drugs become a "crutch" 184

The Motivation to Use Drugs 185

Summary 185

Why Do People Become Addicted to Certain Drugs? 185

Heroin and Morphine—Biological Component 186
  Endorphins: Natural Opiates of the Brain 186

Learned Component 187
  Personal control versus reinforcement 187
  The short-circuiting of biological drives 187
  Needle high and the principles of associative learning 187
  Associative learning and re-addiction in humans 187

PRACTICAL APPLICATION 7.1
Endorphins and Motivation 188

Cognitive Component 188
  Expectations 188
  Psychological/social needs 189
  Social acceptability 190
  Presence of natural rewards 191
  Beliefs about self-control 191

Summary 192

Stimulants: Cocaine and Amphetamines 192

Biological Component 192
  The dopamine system 193
  Dopamine receptors 193
  Dopamine and the self-reward systems 193

Learned Component 194

Cognitive Component 194
  Expectations 194
  Relapse 195

Summary 195

Relaxants: The New Antianxiety Drugs 195

Biological Component 196
  The GABA System 196

Learned Component 196
  Why benzodiazepines are used 196
  Negative emotions are often persistent and pervasive 196
  Becoming benzodiazepene-free 197

Cognitive Component 197
  The tendency to view the world as threatening 197

Summary 198

The Hallucinogenics: Cannabis (Marijuana, Hashish)
and LSD—Biological Component   198
  Cannabis (Marijuana, Hashish)   198
  LSD (Lysergic Acid Diethylamide)   198
Learned Component   199
Cognitive Component   199
  Altered perceptions   199
  Links to antitraditional orientation   199

PRACTICAL APPLICATION 7.2
  **Psychological Health and Adolescent
  Drug Use   200**

Summary   201

Nicotine—Biological Component   202
  Urinary acidity and smoking   202
Learned Component   202
Cognitive Component   203
Summary   204

Alcohol   204
Biological Component   204
  Alcohol and the dopaminergic system   204
  Endorphin hypothesis of alcohol addiction   204
  Depression and alcoholism   205
  Alcohol and the disinhibition effect   205
Learned Component   206
  Multiple determinants of behavior   206
  Alcoholism in France versus Italy   206
  Treating alcoholism using principles of learning   207
Cognitive Component   207
  Beliefs and expectations   207
Alcohol and Myopia   207

PRACTICAL APPLICATION 7.3
  **Why Do Some People Become Addicted While
  Others Do Not? A Theoretical Analysis of How
  an Addiction Develops   208**
  Situational factors   210
  Cultural factors   210
  Beliefs about control   211
  Taking control by cutting down   211

PRACTICAL APPLICATION 7.4
  Factors That Moderate the Use of Drugs   212

PRACTICAL APPLICATION 7.5
  How People Quit Addictions   214

  Beliefs about self-change   214
Summary   215
Main Points   217

Chapter Eight   **219**

Anger, Aggression, and Compliance

Is Aggression Good or Bad?   220
Definition of Aggression   220
  Provoked versus Unprovoked Aggression   220
  Physical versus Verbal Aggression   220

Do North Americans Live in a Violent Society?   221

When Do Humans Become Physically Aggressive?
  Laboratory Analogs   221
  The Teacher-Learner Paradigm   221

Aggression as Obedience to Authority   222

  Shock As Evaluation Paradigm   222
  Retaliation in kind   222
  Massive retaliation   223
  Aggression in the laboratory and the real world   223
The Anger and Aggression Link   223
  *Distinguishing between Instrumental and Affective
  Aggression*   223
Aggression as Control: Gaining Compliance
  over Others   224
Summary   224

**Interpersonal Violence: The Link between
Control and Power   225**

Biological Factors   226
  Genetics and Aggression   226
  Kinds of Aggression   226
  Neurological Structures and Aggression   227
  The hypothalamus   227
  The limbic system   227
  The Klüver-Bucy Syndrome   227

Temporal lobe pathology   228

Social Rank and the Expression of Aggression   230

Hormones and Male Aggression   232

The role of testosterone   232

Estrogen, antiandrogens, and male aggression   234

Hormones and Female Aggression   234

Estrogen, progesterone, and female aggression   234

Androstenedione and Aggression in the Female Hyena   235

Conclusion   236

Summary   236

Learned Component   236

The Reward Value of Aggression: Instrumental Aggression   236

Social Learning Theory   237

Modeling and Imitation   237

Expression   237

Blind Rage: Generalized Anger and Aggression   238

Summary   238

Cognitive Component   239

Internal versus External Locus of Control   240

Attribution Theories   240

Ferguson and Rule's Model   241

Harm and intent   241

Foreseeability   243

Do people tend to be cautious?   243

Weiner's Attribution Model   243

The Process of Deindividuation   243

The Role of Hostility and Anger in Hypertension and Coronary Heart Disease   244

Sex Differences, Anger, and Aggression   244

Summary   246

Sex Differences in Aggression   248

Summary   248

Psychological States that Evoke Aggressive Behaviors   249

Frustration   250

A Persistent Issue: Does Viewing Violence Beget Violence; Pornography and Aggression   250

Some limiting conditions   250

The role of expectancy   251

Negative Evaluation   252

Insults   253

Psychological States and Control Theory   253

Summary   253

Factors that Suppress Aggression   253

Anxiety, Fear, and Social Disapproval   253

PRACTICAL APPLICATION **8.1**
Learning to Manage Anger   254

Empathy   256

Summary   256

Main Points   256

Part Three   Goal-Congruent and Goal-Incongruent Emotions

Chapter Nine   **258**

The Nature of Emotions: The Example of Stress

Why It Is Important to Consider Emotions   259

The Universal Nature of Emotions   259

Core Relational Themes   259

Facial Expression   260

The Role of Appraisal in Emotion   260

Definition of Emotion   261

Classification of Emotions   261

Identifying Dimensions of Emotions   261

Lawfulness of Emotions   261

Summary   264

Use Your Emotions to Identify Your Goals, Motives, and Concerns   265

Stress, Distress, and Coping   266

Definition 266

Conceptualizing Stress as a Fight/Flight Response 267

The Biological Component 267

Distinguishing between the Sympathetic/Adrenal and the Pituitary/Adrenal Responses 267

The Pituitary/Adrenal Response 269

Endorphins and Stress 269

The Work of Hans Selye, the Grandfather of Stress Research 270

Stress and Disease 270

Unpredictability, stress, and disease 271

Summary 271

Learned Factors 271

Discrimination 272

Learning a Coping Response 272

Habituating the Stress Response 273

Automatic and Habitual Behaviors and the Stress Response 274

Learning a Prescribed Set of Rules for Making Decisions under Stress 274

Summary 274

Cognitive Factors 275

Lazarus's Theory 275

Primary Appraisal 275

Secondary Appraisal 275

Problem-focused versus emotion-focused coping 275

Situational Factors and Personal Control 275

Potentially controllable situations 276

Situations unlikely to be controllable 277

Controllability and longevity 277

Summary 277

Stressors of Everyday Life 277

Examination Stress 277

Appraisal and coping strategies 277

Stress, anxiety, and test taking 278

Physiological changes 278

The Workplace 278

Job ambiguity and health 278

Sex differences 279

Conflict-prone and conflict-resistant organizations 279

The individual-environment interaction 280

Summary 280

The Type A Personality, Stress, and Heart Attacks 282

The Type A Personality and Coronary Heart Disease (CHD) 282

Hostility and Heart Disease 282

Suppressed Anger and Coronary Disease 283

Cynical Hostility 283

The interaction of hostility, TABP, and plasma lipids 283

Cortisol and testosterone 283

Nature of Type A Behavior Pattern 284

Desire for control 284

Heritability of Type A Personality 284

Modifying the Type A Response 285

Stress and the Immune System 285

Summary 285

Moderators of Stress 286

Biological Factors 286

Social Support 286

The repressive personality type and social support 286

Learned Factors 286

Coping Skills 286

Breaking events down into manageable units 286

Pet Ownership and Health 287

Epstein's Work and Theory 287

The search for universal principles 287

The question of intelligence and adjustment 287

Constructive versus Destructive Thinkers 289

Origins of destructive thinking 289

Poor constructive thinking and stress 289

Constructive Thinking and Success in Life 289

Emotion-Focused Coping Strategies 289

PRACTICAL APPLICATION 9.1
How Might One Become a Good Constructive Thinker? 290

Relaxation 291

Exercise 291

Biofeedback 292

Cognitive and Individual Difference Factors 292

Talking or Writing About a Trauma: Cognitive Assimilation of Emotions 292

The Hardy Personality 293

Internal versus External Locus of Control 294

Optimism: Having a Positive and Hopeful Outlook 294

Instrumentality 294

Sensation Seeking 295

A Sense of Humor 295

Some Observations and Conclusions about Moderators of Life Stress and Health 295

PRACTICAL APPLICATION 9.2
Some Rules for Dealing with Stress 296

Summary 299

Main Points 300

Chapter Ten 303

Goal-Incongruent (Negative) Emotions: Fear and Anxiety, Pessimism and Depression, Guilt and Shame

Introduction 304

Fear and Anxiety 304

Distinguishing between Fear and Anxiety 304

Definition of Anxiety 304

Antecedents of Anxiety 304

Distinguishing between Fear and Phobia 305

Biological Component 305

Learned Component 306

Conceptualizing Fear and Anxiety as Conditioned Pain 306

Why does the avoidance response occur progressively earlier? 306

Why does the avoidance response persist over time? 306

Treating People Who Experience Excessive Fear and Anxiety 307

Desensitization 307

Flooding 307

Cognitive Component 308

Loss of Control 308

Inability to Make a Coping Response 308

State versus Trait Anxiety 308

Sensitizers and repressors 309

Panic attacks 309

Anxiety as a Person-Environment Interaction 309

Summary 309

Pessimism and Depression 310

Distinguishing Pessimism From Depression 310

Thinking Style and Mood Interaction 310

How Prevalent are Pessimism and Depression in Our Society? 311

PRACTICAL APPLICATION 10.1
Modern Individualism and the Rise of Depression 312

Biological Component 312

Heritability of Depression 312

The Catecholamine Hypothesis 313

Serotonin Hypothesis 314

Using Drugs to Treat Depression 314

Stress and depression 314

Spontaneous remission of depression 314

Depression as an Adaptive Mood 315

Summary 316

Learned Component 316

Seligman's Model of Learned Helplessness 316

Learned Helplessness in Humans 318

Externals and internals 318

Deficits in Learned Helplessness 318

Failure to initiate responses 318

Failure to learn 319

Emotional disturbance 320

Immunization 320

Summary 320

Cognitive Component   320

   Reformulated Theory of Learned Helplessness   321

Three Explanatory Styles for Bad and
   Good Events   321

   1. Permanence: Permanent versus Temporary   321

   2. Pervasiveness: Specific versus Universal   321

The Nature of Hope and Hopelessness   322

   3. Personalization: Internal versus External   322

Caveat About Responsibility   323

Is Depression Ultimate Pessimism?   323

Rumination   324

   *Women, Depression, and the
   Rumination/Distraction Theory*   324

   Beck's Theory   325

   Sociotropic and autonomous subtypes   325

Summary   325

PRACTICAL APPLICATION 10.2
   **Cognitive Theory and Depression: Learning the
   Art of Thinking Constructively**   326

Guilt and Shame   328

   *Why Consider the Emotions of
   Guilt and Shame?*   328

   Definition of Guilt and Shame   328

Biological Component   329

   Guilt and Shame as Adaptive Emotions   329

   Discrete Emotions Theory   329

   Psychoanalytic and Neopsychoanalytic Theories   330

Learned Component   330

   Discipline Techniques   331

   Comparing Love Withdrawal and Induction   331

   *Quality of the Affective Relationship between
   Parent and Child*   331

Cognitive Component   331

   The Guilt-Depression Link   332

Negative Emotions and Goal-Directed Behavior   332

Excessive Guilt and Shame   333

Summary   333

PRACTICAL APPLICATION 10.3
   Managing Excessive Guilt and Shame   334

Main Points   336

Chapter Eleven   339

**Goal-Congruent (Positive) Emotions:
Happiness, Hope and Optimism,
Attachment and Belongingness, Empathy**

Introduction   340

Hedonism and Happiness   340

   Hedonism   340

   Ultimate Hedonism?   341

   Happiness from a Cognitive Perspective   341

   Hedonic Enjoyment and Hedonic Happiness   342

   *Comparing Hedonic Enjoyment and
   Hedonic Happiness*   342

Happiness and Coping Behavior   343

Biological Component   343

Learned Component   344

Cognitive Component   344

Happiness from Confronting Fear
   and Uncertainty   345

Biological Component   345

Learned Component   346

Cognitive Component   346

Analyzing the Motivation for Thrill-Seeking   347

   Hedonistic Interpretations   347

   Opponent-process theory   348

   Arousal theory   348

   Cognitive Interpretations of Thrill-Seeking   348

   *An Interactional Interpretation of
   Thrill-Seeking*   348

   Rock Climbing   348

   Bungee Jumping   350

   Increasing the Level of Risk   350

   Is Risk-Taking Adaptive?   351

   Some Concluding Remarks   351

Summary   351

Optimism and Hope   352

Defining Optimism and Hope   352

   *Are Optimism and Pessimism Two Ends
   of the Same Continuum?*   353

Biological Component   353

   Optimism from an Evolutionary Perspective   353

Learned Component   353

Optimism as an Acquired Thinking Style 353

Seligman's Definition of Optimism and Hope 353

Evidence for Seligman's Theory 354

Success at sales 354

Academic success 354

Optimism and Health 355

Cognitive Component 355

PRACTICAL APPLICATION **11.1**

How to Become an Optimist: The ABCDE Method of Acquiring an Optimistic Explanatory Style 356

Snyder's Definition of Optimism and Hope 360

Empirical Support for the Snyder et al. Hope Model 360

Hope and negative feedback 360

Hope and number of goals 361

Hope and preferred difficulty of goals 361

Hope and goal attainment 361

Personal Control and Optimism 361

Taking an Optimistic versus a Threatening View of the World 362

Summary 362

Belongingness, Attachment, and Community 362

Biological Component 363

Maslow's Need-Fulfillment Model 363

Physiological needs 363

Safety needs 364

Belongingness and love needs 364

Esteem needs 364

Need for self-actualization 364

Learned Component 365

Social Support Systems and Health 365

Attachment Theory 365

Cognitive Component 366

Health and the Commitment to Family and Values 366

Mindfulness and Health 366

Summary 367

PRACTICAL APPLICATION **11.2**

Belongingness and the Immune Response 368

Empathy and Altruism 369

Definition of Empathy 369

Biological Component 369

Learned Component 369

Power and empathy 370

Role playing, modeling, and empathy 370

Cognitive Component 370

Justice Motive and Empathy 370

The justice motive and suffering 370

Summary 371

Main Points 371

Part Four   Growth Motivation

Chapter Twelve   374

Curiosity, Exploratory Behavior, Play, Sensation Seeking, and Creativity

Exploratory Behavior 375

Innate or Learned? 375

The Behaviorist Explanation 375

The reinforcement of random behavior 375

The Challenge of the 1950s 375

Alternation behavior 375

The reactive inhibition model 376

The stimulus satiation model 376

The stimulus change model 376

Other studies of the curiosity drive 376

The Human Tendency to Seek Out Variety and Novelty 377

Cognitive Component 377

Emergence of the Concept of Complexity 377

The tendency to select increasingly complex stimuli 377

Summary 378

Theories of Exploratory Behavior 378

Dember and Earl's Theory   378

Berlyne's Theory   378

Arousal and Esthetics   382

Summary   383

Arousal and Exploratory Behavior   383

Anxiety, Fear, and Exploration   385

Fear as the enemy of exploration   385

Implications for facilitating learning   385

Individual differences   385

Summary   385

Play: Frivolous or Serious?   386

The Functions of Social Play   386

The Functions of Solitary Play   387

Summary   387

PRACTICAL APPLICATION **12.1**

Facilitating Intrinsic Motivation   **388**

Extrinsic Motivation: The Enemy of Exploration   388

Individual Differences and Extrinsic Motivation   390

Summary   390

Sensation Seeking   390

Definition   390

Origins of the Sensation-Seeking Concept   391

Biological Component   391

The Biological Basis of Sensation Seeking   391

Monoamine oxidase and sensation seeking   391

The heritability of monoamine oxidase level   391

PRACTICAL APPLICATION **12-2**

Are you a High or a Low Sensation Seeker?   **392**

Sex and age differences   393

Learned and Cognitive Components   393

Sensation Seeking and Sports   393

Drugs, Sex, Rock and Roll   393

Thinking Styles and Creativity   394

Unconventionality and Delinquency   394

Decision-Making Styles and Sensation Seeking   394

Sensation Seeking and Keeping Your Options Open   395

Summary   395

Creativity   396

Three Reasons why People are Motivated to be Creative   396

Definition of Creativity   396

Biological Component   396

DeBono and Patterns in the Brain   396

Langer and Mindlessness   397

Cognitive Dissonance Theory   397

The Urge to Create   398

Learned Component   399

Creativity as Disinhibition   399

Convention and tradition   399

Rigidity   399

Psychological Climate and Creativity   399

Personality Traits and Creativity   399

Early Experiences and Creativity   400

Later Experiences and Creativity   400

Cognitive Component   400

The Process of Creativity   401

Delineating the Problem   401

Information/knowledge   401

Constructive images and categories   401

Synthesis   401

Suspension of Judgment   402

Learning to Be Creative   403

Remote Associations   403

Major versus Minor Contributions   403

PRACTICAL APPLICATION **12.3**

Motivating Creativity by Adopting the "What If?" Attitude   **404**

Summary   404

Main Points   406

Chapter Thirteen   409

Competence and Intelligence, Achievement and Persistence, Self-Esteem and Self-Worth

Introduction   410

Definition of Competence   410

White's Theory of Competence 411

Piaget's Theory of Competence 411

PRACTICAL APPLICATION **13.1**

Implications for Parents and Teachers 412

Summary 412

Intelligence as a Prototype of Competence 413

Implicit Theories and the Development of Intelligence 413

Implicit Theories about Academic and Everyday Intelligence 414

Sternberg's Triarchic Theory of Intelligence 414

Analytical abilities 414

Synthetic abilities 415

Contextual abilities 415

Dweck's Theory of Intelligence 415

Implicit theories of competency 415

The Consequences of Believing in the Entity Theory versus the Incremental Theory 416

Consequences of believing in the entity theory 416

Consequences of believing in the incremental theory 417

Bandura's Self-Efficacy Theory 417

Outcome expectations 417

Feelings of self-efficacy 417

Three dimensions of self-efficacy 418

Evidence for Self-Efficacy Theory 418

Summary 418

Achievement and Persistence 419

Contributions of Murray 419

McClelland's Contributions 419

Amsel's Theory of Persistence 420

Atkinson's Theory of Achievement Motivation 421

Hope of success 422

Fear of failure 422

Resultant achievement motivation 422

Tests of Atkinson's Theory 423

Vocational choice and achievement motivation 423

Persistence and Achievement Motivation 424

Bernard Weiner's Explanatory Style Theory of Achievement 424

Attribution styles of people high and low in resultant achievement motivation 425

PRACTICAL APPLICATION **13.2**

Getting People to Accept Challenges 426

The Work of J.T. Spence 428

Definition of achievement motivation 428

The Work and Family Orientation (WOFO) Questionnaire 428

Ability of WOFO to predict overall GPA 428

Ability of WOFO to predict annual income 429

Ability of WOFO to predict scientific productivity 429

Summary 430

Self-Esteem and Self-Worth 432

Definition of Self-Esteem and Self-Worth 432

Are People Born with the Need to Experience High Self-Esteem? 432

Competence and Feelings of Self-Esteem 433

Weiner's Theory 433

Coopersmith's Work 433

Self-Esteem and Reactions to Success and Failure 434

Pride, Self-Esteem, and the Self-Concept 434

One's Self-Concept and Self-Esteem 435

Having a Clearly Differentiated (Complex) Self-Concept 435

PRACTICAL APPLICATION **13.3**

Learning to Manage Self-Doubt Following Failure: Using Downward Comparison 436

Self-Perpetuating Quality of Poor Self-Esteem 436

Overgeneralization 437

Compartmentalization of the Self into Positive and Negative 438

Origins of a Good Self-Concept: Coming Full Circle 438

Summary 439

Main Points 439

Chapter Fourteen   442

Achieving Personal Success: The Self-Regulation of Motivation

Introduction   443

From Needs to Goals to Action   443

A Flow Diagram for the Self-Regulation of
   Motivation   443

Defining the Self-Concept   445
   The "I" and the "Me" of Self   445

The Tendency to View the World as Threatening,
   Benevolent, or Benign   446
   *Prototype 1: The World as Threatening or
   Malevolent*   447

   Prototype 2: The World as Benevolent   447

   The Self-Actualized Person   448

   Prototype 3: The World as Benign   450

Self-Theories:
   Individual Strategies/Orientations   451
   The Mastery Strategy   451

   The Performance Strategy   452

   Outcome-oriented versus process-oriented   452

The Relationship between World Theories
   and Self-Theories   452

The Need for a Positive Self-Concept   452
   *Rogers's Concept of Conditional and
   Unconditional Love*   453

Summary   453

Epstein's Cognitive-Experiential
   Self-Theory (CEST)   454
   *Two Semi-Independent Systems for Processing
   Information*   454

   Constructive Thinking Inventory   454

   Constructive Thinking and Coping   454

   *Can People Learn to Become Good
   Constructive Thinkers?*   455

Summary   455

The Process of Self-Motivation:
   Having and Setting Goals   456
   Feedback and self-efficacy   457

Summary   457

Links Between the Self and Goals:
   Possible Selves, Aspirations and Dreams   457
   Possible Selves   458

   The Role of Self-Knowledge   458

   Functions of the Self-Concept   458

   Provide information   458

   Provide context   458

What Kind of Self-Concept Do People Need for
   Developing Diverse Possible Selves?   459

Practical Application 14.1
The Art of Creating Possible Selves   460

*The Self-Concept Is Created/Constructed and So Are
   Possible Selves*   460

Aspirations   462

Dreams and Visualization   462
   *Dreams and Visualization as a Means of
   Personalizing Motivation*   462

   *Dreams and Visualization as a Means of
   Making Goals Real*   462

   *Dreams and Visualization as a Means of Accessing
   Action-Based Motivation Systems*   462

Summary   463

The Self-Regulation of Behavior   463
   *Self-Regulation Process #1:
   Setting Difficult but Attainable Goals*   463

   *Self-Regulation Process #2:
   Making Plans and Making Adjustments*   464

   Designing routes to goals   464

   Adjustment and fine-tuning   465

   Using mental rehearsal   465

Practical Application 14.2
Learning to Become a Risk-Taker   466

   Using Advisors and Coaches   466

   *Self-Regulation Process #3: Managing Your
   Emotions, Moods, and Self-Doubt*   467

   Moods and self-efficacy   467

   Self-doubt as intrusive thinking   468

   Self-doubt and self-efficacy   468

   Three Methods of Dealing with Self Doubt   469

   Self-talk   469

   Cognitive restructuring   469

Practical Application 14.3
   Preparing Yourself for the Setbacks
   and Hard Work Ahead   470

   Substituting other thoughts   470

   Managing Anxiety and Arousal   470

Summary   471

Self-Reflection: The Basis for Self-Change   472

   Behavior Results from Thinking Habits   472

   Reflection and Mindfulness   473

   *Self-Confidence: Harmonizing Feelings of Perceived
   Competency and Optimism   473*

   Self-confidence   473

   Developing your sense of competency   473

   Learn to focus on process   474

   Learned Optimism   474

   Coming Full Circle   474

An Overview: The Key to Personal Success Is
   Becoming a Process-Oriented as Opposed to a
   Goal-Oriented Person   474

   Getting There or Being There   474

Main Points   475

References   478

Author Index   505

Subject Index   514

Photo Credits

Chapter 1: 1, The Bettmann Archive; **6,** The Bettmann Archive; **9,** Photo Researchers, Inc.; **11,** Photo Researchers, Inc.

Chapter 2: 18, Pamela R. Schuyler/Stock, Boston; **45,** Dion Ogust/The Image Works.

Chapter 3: 49, Mac Donald Photography/The Picture Cube; **61,** Roy Bishop/Stock, Boston; **66,** Peter Menzel/Stock, Boston.

Chapter 4: 78, Jeffry W. Myers/Stock, Boston; **83,** George W. Gardner/Stock, Boston; **102,** Michael L. Weisbrot/Stock, Boston.

Chapter 5: 111, Sandra Weiner/The Image Works; **119,** Elizabeth Crews/Stock, Boston.

Chapter 6: 146, Nita Winter/The Image Works; **159,** Michael L. Weisbrot/Stock Boston; **164,** Carrie Boretz/The Image Works.

Chapter 7: 179, Charles Gatewood/The Image Works; **205,** Spencer Grant/Stock, Boston; **216,** Eric Roth/The Picture Cube.

Chapter 8: 219, Akos Szilvasi/Stock, Boston; **242,** Alan Carey/The Image Works; **249,** Hazel Hankin/Stock, Boston.

Chapter 9: 258, Jim Mahoney/The Image Works; **276,** Lionel J-M Delevingne/Stock, Boston; **294,** Cermak/Voller Ernst/The Image Works.

Chapter 10: 303, Jean-Claude Lejeune/Stock, Boston; **324,** Elizabeth Crews/Stock, Boston.

Chapter 11: 339, Michael Siluk/The Image Works; **349,** Lynn R. Johnson/Stock, Boston

Chapter 12: 374, Lee Snider/The Image Works; **398,** John Drysdale/Voller Ernst/The Image Works

Chapter 13: 409, Christopher Brown/Stock, Boston; **435,** Michael Hayman/Stock, Boston.

Chapter 14: 442, Jim Harrison/Stock, Boston; **475,** Elizabeth Crews/The Image Works.

Chapter One

Past and Current Issues in Motivation

- How did early scholars and thinkers conceptualize motivation in humans and animals?

- Why did evolutionary theory change our thinking about motivational processes?

- How does a motivational researcher differ from other psychological researchers?

- What role do biological structures such as the brain play in producing behavior?

- Do past learning and the way we think affect what we do?

- What is the current focus of motivational research?

Consider the following event that occurs with persistent regularity. It is a bright, sunny morning, and a young man is walking briskly across the campus, excited by the prospect of a stimulating lecture from his motivation professor. An attractive young woman crosses his path. His interest is suddenly aroused, and he fixes his attention on her. With obvious practice he quickly examines her face and traces the contours of her body. Satisfied that she meets his critera for a good-looking, if not beautiful, woman, he makes a mental note to find out who she is so he can ask her for a date. He again fixes his attention on finding his way to class. Similarly, a young woman, also on her way to class, notices a man just ahead of her. He is well-dressed and wears a pleasant smile, and she notes that he walks with an air of self-confidence. She quickens her step, hoping he may be going to the same class she is trying to locate.

While these examples appear to have something to do with sexual motivation, there is more to them than first meets the eye. What was it about the young woman that aroused his interest? Why did she want to see more of him? Why didn't each of them merely treat the episode as a pleasant interlude? Is their interest purely sexual? Will they try to arrange an encounter or even a date? To explain such behaviors, we need to know a number of things: We need to know something about the biological factors involved in the sex drive and what sensory factors elicit sexual interest. We need to know how past conditioning affects choice. We need to understand the role of attitudes, beliefs, and self-concept. For example, we need to determine whether the young man or woman is interested in being with this person, being seen with the attractive person, or both.

Through years of research we have come to appreciate that human motivation is complex. It has become clear in recent years that we cannot understand human motivation simply by studying some of the underlying biological mechanisms. Although biological mechanisms are extremely important, the expression of any motive is always due to the interaction of biological, learned, and cognitive factors. It is the purpose of this book to examine how each of these three classes of factors is involved in the expression of a given motive.

What Is the Study of Motivation About?

Texts on motivation typically include discussions of a variety of behaviors because it is thought, for one reason or another, that these behaviors are due to the operation of certain principles of motivation. Inclusion of one topic and exclusion of another therefore implies that there is good agreement on what the term *motivation* means. Unfortunately, there is not. The study of motivation has traditionally been concerned with the arousal, direction, and persistence of behavior. However, the study of arousal, direction, and persistence is not the exclusive domain of motivation theorists. Learning theorists, for example, have also been concerned with what arouses behavior, what gives it direction (choice of one goal object over another or one pattern of behavior over another), and what gives it persistence.

Motivation theorists, in contrast to learning theorists, have been concerned mainly with the question of what arouses and energizes behavior. Therefore, behaviors that most clearly reflect this issue have been of central interest to motivation theorists. For example, sex hormones reduce the threshold for sexual behavior, and therefore sex hormones have become one area of focus for motivational researchers. Similarly, because arousal can increase the intensity of ongoing emotions or reduce the threshold for such behaviors as aggression, factors that produce arousal are of obvious interest to motivation researchers. Because the factors that arouse and energize behavior often give direction to behavior, motivation theorists frequently deal with the question of direction as well. Their main focus, however, is on the dynamic factors that frequently lead to changes in behavior.

Learning theorists, in contrast, are generally more concerned with the question of the stability of behavior. What are the factors that ensure that a person or animal will repeat a behavior at different times or under different environmental conditions or even under different motivational conditions? Their concern is more with the permanence of behavior in a variable environment. As it turns out, many of the factors that lead to stability over time can be found in certain past events that somehow altered the individual in a basic and fundamental way.

The term *energize* applies not only to the immediate behavior but to long-term behavior as well. When I persist toward some long-term goal, what is the motivation that maintains that behavior? Most motivation theorists are not satisfied that future goals (and the rewards that presumably will accompany them) are sufficient in and of themselves to maintain behavior over a long period of time. Nor are they willing to accept the idea that such behaviors are simply due to a strong habit. Consequently, most theorists are interested in identifying the underlying motivational processes they believe are necessary to energize long-term behavior. It has been argued, for example, that the motivational processes underlying the development of competence (or any skill, for that matter) are "feelings of efficacy" (White, 1959) or that what motivates us to develop conceptual systems is the "positive affect" that is associated with the moderate levels of arousal that frequently accompany information processing (Berlyne, 1960). In other words, the motivation theorist is fundamentally concerned with identifying the motivational process that is assumed to be present whenever some behavior occurs.

Most motivation theorists assume that motivation is involved in the performance of all learned responses; that is, a learned behavior will not occur unless it is energized. In other words, although learning can give direction to behavior, a learned behavior will not occur unless there is a motive for engaging in the behavior. Thus, whether events in the environment guide my behavior or I respond out of habit is ultimately linked to the motivational factors. Further, motivation theorists generally assume that motivation affects perception and memory. For example, the motivation theorist is concerned with such questions as whether we are more likely to notice restaurant signs when we are hungry than when we are not, and whether we are more likely to remember the name of a stimulating person than of someone boring. In short, do we ever do something that is not in some way tied to our momentary motivational state?

Analyzing the Flow of Behavior: A Central Concern of Motivational Theorists

One topic of particular interest to the motivation theorist is the question of what gives rise to the flow, or stream, of behavior. As we observe humans and animals, we quickly note that they shift from one activity to another from time to time, systematically altering the direction of their behavior. People who have succeeded or failed in the pursuit of a goal, for example, frequently alter the direction of their behavior or the amount of effort they are willing to exert. How do we account for this process? There are two important questions that the motivation theorist is inclined to ask. First, are such shifts systematic, and second, are such shifts better explained by principles of motivation or by some other principle (such as learning, personality, or perception)? Most motivation theorists have concluded from controlled experiments that shifts in behavior are usually systematic. They have further argued that such shifts are best explained in motivational terms. Motivation theorists have frequently focused their attention on factors that immediately precede a shift in behavior in order to discover some of the antecedents that may predict the stream, or flow, of behavior (Barker, 1963).

One very common example of the flow of behavior is the tendency of humans to shift their attention from one object to another as they explore a new room, visit an art gallery, or view the scenery while driving. The problem for the motivation theorist is to explain this flow. It has been shown that the shifts in attention are typically systematic (we typically respond sequentially to stimuli of increasing complexity or novelty). Further, motivational indicators often show that as we attend to one object, our interest in that object decreases while our interest in other (more novel) objects increases. Both of these points are good evidence that something dynamic as well as systematic is happening. One theoretical orientation postulates that people are inclined (without the benefit of learning) to respond to increasingly complex or novel events (or stimuli) in the environment. According to this view, whenever we respond to a stimulus, we are inclined to process the information it contains, thereby making the stimulus

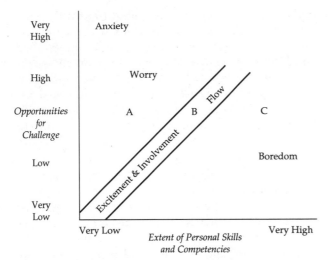

Figure 1–1. Csikszentmihalyi's Model of Flow. ("Model of Flow" adapted from *Flow: The Psychology of Optimal Experiences,*Mihaly Csikszentmihalyi. Copyright © 1990 by Mihaly Csikszentmihalyi. Reprinted by permission of HarperCollins Publishers, Inc.)

familiar and less complex. If other, novel stimuli are present, we will be inclined to direct our attention toward them (Dember & Earl, 1957; Walker, 1980). According to this theoretical orientation, the flow of behavior is the result of a dynamic process governed by a principle that ensures that one behavior systematically gives way to another. This theoretical orientation predicts that, over time, we will process all the information in our environment without having to receive any external rewards.

More recently, it has been suggested that *optimal experiences* that people have can be analyzed in terms of the flow experience. Optimal experiences are those experiences that provide us with a profound sense of excitement and involvement. Csikszentmihalyi (1990) suggests that optimal experience occurs when we undertake challenging tasks with clear goals and immediate feedback. In such situations, he argues, people lose all self-doubt and experience a sense of being in control. The experience is so strong, he maintains, that people are more than willing to put forth the effort that is needed to develop the skills they need.

Current Focus of Motivation Research

In recent years, there has been growing interest in so-called applied questions. People who are overweight want to know why and what they can do about it. Other people want to know why they sometimes have difficulty sleeping or what it is in their lives that produces stress and how they can deal with that stress. Parents want to know why their children take drugs or why they turn up the volume on their stereos. Some want to know why there is so much aggression in our society. Most of us are concerned with whether we can alter the direction of our behavior. Many of these same questions were also of concern to the earliest scholars. Recently, more and more research on these and other questions has produced a wealth of facts and principles that give us some insights into why we do what we do in a number of important areas of our lives.

Early Conceptions of Human Motivation

The Greek Philosophers

Some of the first formal attempts to explain the nature of human motivation were undertaken by the Greek philosophers. Epicurus set forth the proposition that we are motivated to seek pleasure and avoid pain. He believed that pleasure was the only thing worth striving for. It is important to note, however, that many of the Greek philosophers realized that immediate pleasure could, in the long run, bring pain. Therefore, they argued that the goodness of a thing could be obtained only if the intellect was fully developed. The development of the intellect allowed the individual to understand the long-term consequences of a given action. It might be necessary to avoid an immediate pleasure that could, sometime in the future, bring pain to the individual. It might also be necessary to endure pain in order to obtain a greater pleasure. The problem for the individual would be to weigh the various alternatives in order to maximize pleasure.

The position of hedonism has persisted in psychology and philosophy. It reached its peak in the thinking of Jeremy Bentham and John Stuart Mill, and today is the cornerstone of several theories of motivation. In most current theories, however, the concept of hedonism has a much narrower meaning. It typically refers to the human tendency to enjoy immediate pleasure, often from the stimulation of one or more of the sensory systems.

Although the Greek philosophers clearly recognized the human tendency to seek pleasure and avoid pain, they did not address themselves to the question of exactly how the intellect affected the basic motives, such as hunger, sex, and aggression. It appears that they assumed these motives were ultimately the servants of the intellect. Excesses were simply the results of failure to understand the consequences of one's behavior. It is clear from their writings on ethics that they viewed human conflict as a failure in the development of the intellect. Accordingly, the goal of the individual as well as of society was to develop the intellects of all. Conflict would then cease. Conflict and aggression, in other words, were simply the result of ignorance, not the expression of some basic biological urge.

The Problem of Analogous Behaviors in Humans and Animals

The observation that animals and humans engaged in a wide variety of similar behaviors (ate, drank, slept, reproduced, fought) interested thinkers and writers from the earliest times. Was this similarity merely a coincidence, or did it reflect something more? Were these systems homologous—meaning they had a common morphology (structure) or a common origin? The possibility that various behaviors in humans and animals were homologous was rejected outright by most early writers. The Greeks, for example, believed that the essence of humanness was the intellect, something they perceived animals as lacking. The fact remained, however, that the behavior of humans and animals often had a striking similarity.

The concept of *dualism* was developed in part to deal with this as well as other questions. Thomas Aquinas elaborated the dualistic position of earlier writers to reconcile the view of Aristotle with the dogma of the church. According to Aquinas, humans had a dual nature—physical and nonphysical, or body and mind (intellect). Animals, in contrast, were not as-

sumed to have a dual nature. Their behavior was assumed to be the product of physical forces, some external and some internal, acting on the organism. Their behavior, therefore, was assumed to be more or less automatic and mechanical. Although human behavior was also viewed as governed by physical forces, the early position of dualism as advanced by Aquinas did not assume that the laws governing behavior were the same for humans and animals. The reason for this distinction grows out of the position that the behavior of animals was neither good nor bad but that the same behavior in humans could be bad, depending on a variety of things, such as whether it harmed another human or simply whether it was consistent with the will or plan of God.

For example, according to the teachings of the church, the act of reproduction was assumed to be quite different for humans and animals. Animal reproduction was simply a biological or physical act, while human reproduction was assumed to reflect something more. Humans, it was taught, had souls in addition to their bodies—the soul being put there by God. Because the child's soul was assumed to be immature, it was necessary that someone assume responsibility for its development. Although the church took the ultimate responsibility, it delegated part of the duty to the parents, who were joined in marriage—marriage being an act of the church designed to ensure the provision of a family unit in which morality, love, and the will of God would be taught. Not having children ("not being blessed with children") was often believed to represent God's displeasure. Similarly, having children was frequently viewed as a sign that God was pleased. In other words, some people viewed the outcome of the biological act of reproduction as reflecting the direct intervention of God. Such a view was obviously incompatible with the mechanical interpretation of reproduction in animals. Thus, for a period of time, people held that the laws governing certain physical functions were quite different for humans than for animals.

Instinct Theories

It was from the perspective of dualism that human behavior was attributed to the existence of a rational soul while animal behavior was not. The need to explain animal behavior led the Stoics to invent the concept of instinct (Wilm, 1925). The Stoics viewed instincts as "purposive activities implanted in the animal by nature or the creator for the guidance of the creature in the attainment of ends useful to it in its own preservation or the preservation of the species, and the avoidance of the contrary" (Wilm, 1925, p. 40). This idea that instincts are for the preservation of the individual as well as the species has continued to the present. Nevertheless, the problem posed by the similarity of the behavior of humans and animals continued to interest early philosophers and scientists. Many curious scientists wanted to explore this similarity in greater detail but were forbidden to do so because the church considered any such attempt to be blasphemy. That is, because the church held to the position of dualism, to consider otherwise was impious. René Descartes (1596–1650) is credited with resolving this problem by arguing for a slightly revised version of dualism. Descartes's dualism was based on the assumption that the behavior of the body, below the level of willed action, could be explained mechanically. This idea has been referred to as reflexology. More important behaviors that had to do with such things as moral conduct, however, were thought to be directly under the control of the will. By making this distinction, Descartes opened the door for scientists to study the mechanical side of human behavior. They could do so without infringing on the domain of the church, which considered itself the final authority on such matters as the will and the soul. Descartes further assumed that the body and the mind (will, soul) interacted, and he suggested that the site of the interaction was the pineal gland. Certain physical acts, then (presumably including sexual behavior), were under the control of the individual. Therefore, and most important from the church's viewpoint, people could be held responsible for those actions that involved behaviors above the level of reflexes. Animals could, of course, be excused for indiscretions (such as running around naked and doing the unspeakable in broad daylight) because they lacked reason and self-awareness, the elements assumed to be necessary for the existence or the operation of the will.

Charles Darwin

Descartes's position opened the door for scientists to explore an age-old question—the similarity in human and animal behavior. Descartes's position also raised an issue with which psychologists have grappled ever since: Exactly how do the biological and cognitive sides of a person interact? Is it true that our cognitive side has ultimate control? Are there times when the cognitive side loses control? In criminal proceedings, for example, the question of insanity has very important implications. Similarly, a finding of medical abnormalities can dramatically alter the question of whether a person can and should be held responsible for his or her actions.

Although Descartes suggested that humans may share some of the instincts observed in animals, his position clearly argued that we, unlike animals, could control those instincts. It was evolutionary theory that aroused the wrath of the church by suggesting that human behavior was due to the same processes that give rise to animal behavior.

Some Modern Conceptions about Human Motivation

Evolutionary Theory and Charles Darwin

Over the years, several theories of evolution have been advanced. All of these theories have maintained, in one way or another, that the biological structure of organisms has changed over time. Charles Darwin's contribution was not the discovery of evolution, as people often think; rather, it was the description of the mechanism by which evolution operates. Specifically, Darwin suggested that evolution occurs by means of "natural selection." As a young biologist, Darwin traveled throughout the world, studying a variety of species in a variety of environments. Two important principles emerged from his carefully documented observations. First, he noted that each species seemed particularly adapted to its environment. For example, certain species escaped predators because they blended into their environment; that is, their coloration and its patterning acted as perfect camouflage to permit them to elude predators. Second, he noted that some members of a species differed from other members of the same species if they lived in different environments. He reasoned that at one time the species had been more or less uniform, but that each subpopulation had changed over time, adapting to the particular environmental conditions in which it happened to live. Thus, Darwin's observations indicated that species do change.

How did these changes come about? Darwin argued that various members of a species differed in their ability to adapt to their environment. Those that were most adaptable to their environment survived, while the others did not. Consequently, only some members of a species reproduced, resulting in a gradual change in the structure of the species. Characteristics of the species that had survival value were passed on to succeeding members of the species, while characteristics that did not have survival value were gradually lost. Because the environment determined which members of a species survived, only those characteristics that were compatible with survival in that particular environment were retained. Thus, popula-

tions of a species were different in different environments, and yet each was totally adapted to its particular environment.

It has been suggested that Darwin's work in particular caused an intellectual revolution about the causes and origins of human behavior. Darwin argued that what he had observed in animals also held true for humans: the principles governing humans and animals were the same. Further, if human behavior was inherited in the same way that animals' behavior was inherited, the route to understanding human behavior lay through observation of humans in relation to their environment. This was a revolutionary concept because human behavior, before that time, had been thought to be largely independent of physical and biological factors. If human behavior is due to the operation of certain biological structures, it can be argued, the concept of dualism is wrong.

Instincts Revised

Darwin's work renewed interest in the biological and physical determinants of human behavior. Much effort was directed toward identifying behaviors in animals and humans that could be considered instinctive (innate or "hardwired"). For example, William McDougall insisted that the most important determinants of conduct were instincts and their associated emotions. He rejected the essentially rationalistic assumptions of certain philosophers, such as the British associationists, and instead stated that conduct was the result of irrational forces. The main problem, he argued, was to explain why people behaved in a rational and socially acceptable manner rather than to explain why they behaved irrationally (Boring, 1950).

The list of major instincts postulated by McDougall (1908/1950) consisted of flight, repulsion, curiosity, pugnacity, self-abasement, self-assertion, reproduction, gregariousness, acquisition, and construction. McDougall also postulated seven basic emotions, corresponding to the first seven of these instincts. These emotions were fear; disgust; wonder; anger; negative self-feeling, or subjection; positive self-feeling, or elation; and the tender emotion. The remaining three instincts had no major corresponding emotions.

McDougall argued that many emotional experiences were simply compounds of the seven basic emotions. In addition, he suggested that feelings of pleasure and/or pain as well as excitement and/or depression could enter into and thus modify these compounds. It is clear from McDougall's writings that he viewed behavior not only as largely innate but as impulse-driven, and many historians (Boring, for example) believed that this conception of behavior was the forerunner of such concepts as drive.

Ethology: The Biology of Behavior

While the concepts of impulse and drive lived on in psychology, the concept of instinct had a stormy history. A number of psychologists suggested that behavior could be better explained by learning as opposed to instinct. John B. Watson, who later formed the school of behaviorism, concluded that there were only three innate emotional reactions—fear, rage, and love—and that all other emotions were either learned or derived from these three basic emotions (Watson & Morgan, 1917). One of the most compelling reasons for arguing for learning as opposed to instincts as the basis of behavior came from the observation that environmental factors were often linked to certain behaviors. The existence of cultural differences, for example, suggested that environmental factors were responsible, at least to a very large degree, for many of the behaviors observed in humans (Boring, 1950).

Although many of the psychologists of Watson's time tended to reject the idea of innate behaviors, ethologists—students of animal behavior—held to the idea that many important behavior patterns were innate. They engaged in extensive research to identify these behaviors. An important idea held by ethologists was that such behavior patterns tended to occur in response to very specific (and specifiable) stimuli in the environment. These specific stimuli or patterns of stimuli, called "releasers," were thought to be capable of releasing certain responses or patterns of responses if the energy associated with such responses was of sufficient strength. For example, when the female stickleback fish becomes laden with eggs, a releasing stimulus for the male, the male stickleback responds by

preparing a nest. When the nest is finished, the male suddenly turns bright red. The bright red color, together with a zigzag dance, appears to be the releasing stimulus for the female to enter the male's nest. With very little further stimulation, the female deposits her eggs, whereupon the male quickly fertilizes them, thus ensuring the process of reproduction.

What is particularly interesting about the ethologists' position, as viewed from a motivational perspective, is their conceptualization about the source of energy for a particular behavior. Not only do ethologists regard each action as having its own source of energy, but they view this energy source as dynamic. Specifically, they suggest that the energy source is analogous to a reservoir that slowly fills. When the animal engages in a behavior specific to that energy source, such as mating or nest building, the reservoir is depleted or diminished. As a consequence, the probability of eliciting that behavior will be diminished for some period. It has been argued that the more energy available for a given action, the easier it is to release (trigger) that action. That is, there is an inverse relation between the energy level and the threshold for releasing the action specific to that source of energy (Eibl-Eibesfeldt, 1975).

The current position of ethologists is that, although many responses are prewired, animals are capable of modifying these innate responses in the face of environmental obstacles and can even learn certain new responses. For example, an animal might be prewired to retrieve an egg that has rolled from its nest, but the behavior is not so rigid that the animal cannot adjust it in the face of environmental obstacles—for example, if the egg rolls into an area that is on fire. And it is assumed that animals can learn certain new responses, such as locating food hidden under an object that has identifiable features. In other words, so-called releasers may be acquired under certain conditions.

The ideas of the ethologists have parallels in the motivational research of psychologists. For example, the relationship between hormone levels and certain behaviors has been of fundamental interest to psychologists. There is evidence, at least in nonhuman species, that a direct relation exists between sexual motivation and hormone levels. Even in humans, there is good ev-

Ivan Pavlov

idence that hormone levels are important in determining the thresholds for sexual stimuli. Such evidence suggests that certain behaviors may have something like their own energy source and, further, that the energy source operates in a fashion analogous to the reservoir concept suggested by the ethologists.

Ethological work has also played an important role in the work of environmental psychologists. More and more psychologists have come to realize that environmental stimuli, often fairly specific, can elicit certain reactions or behaviors. For example, conditions of crowding have been linked to feelings of distress. The question is whether we can specify the exact nature of the environmental stimuli or events that elicit such feelings. In other words, can we find "releasing stimuli" for certain human behaviors?

There is growing interest among psychologists in using ethological methods to study human behavior. Although psychologists who use the methods of the ethologists do not necessarily adhere to a biological orientation, those methods have helped identify factors in the natural environment that determine behavior. The operating assumption of people who use these methods is that behavior is often controlled by environmental stimuli (learned or unlearned) and that in order to understand behavior we need to understand what elicits and controls it. Such knowledge might allow us to alter the environment or to help people understand what it is about the environment that determines their behavior. The implicit assumption is that we must understand the environment before we can teach people to cope with it.

Learning Theorists

Inspired by the work of Ivan Pavlov (1927), groups of researchers began to study how it was possible to alter the frequency and direction of behavior by applying certain principles of classical conditioning or a subsequent set of laws that came to be called the principles of instrumental learning, or operant conditioning. Since they could show that it was possible to alter the frequency and direction of behavior by applying these rules, they argued that behavior as we observe it is due largely to our past conditioning—our reinforcement history. That is, we are what we are because our environment shaped us in a particular way. Such an argument seemed particularly valid in view of some of the problems with the instinct approach to behavior as outlined by psychologists such as McDougall. In his theory, there was little or no room for environmental input. Also, according to McDougall's theory, motives could not be learned; virtually all behavior and all motivation was assumed to be due to instincts that were present at birth. For many psychologists, that view of behavior was clearly too narrow.

Biological structure, according to the learning theorists, was important because it made learning possible. In addition, it provided the energy base for behavior. The learning theorists did not, however, accept the proposition that biological structures gave behavior direction, nor did they accept the idea that the persistence of behavior was due to the operation of biological systems. They argued that direction and persistence were due to the operation of principles of learning. Direction, they maintained, was due to the process of reinforcement, and persistence was due to the scheduling of reinforcement (Skinner, 1938).

For the most part, learning theorists have tended to regard consciousness, thinking, and perceiving as nonessential phenomena that can be explained by principles of learning. In Chapter 2 I discuss in some detail the principles of classical conditioning and instrumental learning.

Although there is an abundance of evidence that learning plays a major role in behavior, learning theorists have at times taken the position that all behavior is learned. For example, they have argued that such things as curiosity are simply the result of learning and that the desire to develop and exercise skills is merely the result of rewards and punishment. We now know that such a view is too narrow. There are biological and cognitive reasons why people explore or develop new skills. Nevertheless, as we shall see, learning does play a very important role in virtually all behavior.

Cognitive Theorists

Cognitive theorists have, in one way or another, been with us from earliest recorded history. The Greek philosophers emphasized the intellect: they viewed humans as essentially cognitive. It was mainly Darwin, the ethologists, and the learning theorists who challenged this view.

Cognitive theories based on scientific principles are fairly recent. For a long time there was little or no good scientific evidence to show that cognitive processes have anything to do with the way we behave. In fact, there was ample evidence that people often give explanations that have nothing to do with their behavior. There is also ample evidence that different people often give quite different explanations for the same behavior. Thus, when learning theorists were able to show that certain behaviors are indeed explainable and predictable in terms of the principles of learning, there was good reason to accept the position of the learning theorist—namely, that cognitions do not determine behavior but rather reflect the way different individuals explain—often inaccurately—their own behavior.

To show that cognition is a relevant factor governing behavior and not simply something incidental that happens to be associated with behavior, it is necessary to show that there is a direct link between the way a person interprets or labels an event and a subsequent behavior. Finding a consistency between labels and behavior is not an adequate scientific demonstration. One could argue that the behavior was responsible for the label or interpretation.

Recent demonstrations show that how people interpret or label an event has a great deal to do with the future direction of their behavior. For example, if a person believes that his heart is beating fast because he is angry, he will be inclined to behave in an angry fashion; if he believes that his heart is beating fast because he is excited and happy, he will often behave accordingly (Schachter & Singer, 1962; Valins, 1966). Such important demonstrations have forced psychologists to acknowledge that cognitions do play a role in behavior.

Some cognitive psychologists have taken the position that cognitive processes are the most important in governing behavior. In support of their view, they often cite numerous examples to show that many biological processes can be totally subservient to cognitive processes. Evidence comes a variety of sources. There is an abundance of evidence from the research on the relationship between beliefs and attitudes that people hold and the magnitude of stress they experience. When people believe they can control a forthcoming event, for example, they tend to experience far less stress than when they do not believe they can control that forthcoming event (Glass, 1977a). There is also a great deal of research on people's beliefs and attitudes and the amount of anxiety they experience. People who perceive the world as a source of threat, for example, tend to experience more stress and anxiety and tend to be more neurotic than people who see the world as more benign (Watson and Clark, 1984). In the area of health research, there is evidence that have a sense of mastery can enhance the immune system. It has been shown in one study, for example, that rats given mastery training were more likely to die of cancer than were rats given mastery training, Visintainer, Volpicelli, & Seligman, 1982). There is even evidence that having a sense of optimism can decrease the aging process (Petersen, Seligman & Vaillant, 1988). I will be

Sigmund Freud

talking more about these and other studies throughout the book.

As we shall see, however, a great deal of evidence shows that cognitions often do not govern behavior. Take neurotic behavior: no matter how irrational we may regard our guilty or neurotic feelings, we continue to experience these feelings. Extensive relearning is often necessary to free us from these feelings.

Psychoanalytic Theory

Although Sigmund Freud is considered one of the most important figures in the history of psychological thought, his ideas have never been prominent in the mainstream of empirical research on motivation. Most of his ideas grew out of a data base that was quite alien to the empirically based psychologist. While Freud made inferences from the reports of his patients (many of whom were supposedly neurotic), the empiricists

were carefully designing controlled laboratory studies to identify the antecedents of a given behavior. Nevertheless, it is generally agreed that Freud's ideas have had far more influence than one might suppose by counting the times his work has been cited by his empirically based colleagues.

Freud viewed the biological side of humans as providing the energy, or impulse, for behavior (see Freud, 1900/1953, 1911/1949, 1915/1934, 1915/1949, 1923/1947). He posited a group of instincts, each with its own source of energy and its appropriate goal object. Although each of the instincts was hypothesized to have its own source of energy, Freud suggested that they all drew their energy from a general source called *libido*—a term that refers to all life instincts. Unlike the biologists who saw instincts as providing not only the energy but the direction for behavior, Freud viewed instincts as basically an energy source, with the direction of behavior subject to some of the whims of learning and cognition. The process was assumed to work as follows. When the energy associated with one of the instincts built up, it would become a source of tension for the person. To reduce the tension, the person would be inclined to seek out the appropriate goal object. The problem, as Freud conceptualized it, is that in the course of development, certain goal objects have been associated with punishment, and therefore, rather than approach the goal object, the person will tend to avoid it. For example, a child who has been taught that sex is "dirty" or "bad" may be inclined to avoid sex as an adult, or a child who has been taught that it is bad to show anger may inhibit the natural tendency to express aggression.

Two things can happen when goal objects have been blocked. First, the person can learn to make alternative plans for attaining those goal objects, a process that leads to the development of the ego. Second, because it sometimes happens that the ego has not fully developed or the prohibitions associated with the goal object are excessively rigid or strong, the person may redirect the energy along routes that will reduce the tension, even if the appropriate goal object is not attainable by such a path. For example, a person with a strong sex urge may redirect the energy by reading about sex; the person who feels anger toward her boss may redirect that anger through aggression toward her husband and children. Although redirecting energy in this second way may, for a time, reduce the tension associated with the instinct, Freud argued that such methods would never be satisfactory because every instinct had an appropriate goal object. The tension would continue to surface from time to time in the form of neurotic anxiety. Neurotic people, according to Freud, constantly fear that their instincts will get out of control. Freud's goal as a therapist was to help people discover why they had redirected the energy for their instincts—in short, why they felt guilt or fear whenever they considered satisfying their instincts. Freud believed that the instincts were not bad and that the only way to achieve a happy life was to satisfy them. He argued that many young children learn inappropriate ways of dealing with their instincts or learn that the gratification of certain instincts is inherently bad. He believed that people could get rid of the guilt and fear associated with instincts if they gained insight into the conditions surrounding the acquisition of these feelings. Since such feelings were often learned very early in life, it was necessary, Freud argued, for the analyst to help the patient rediscover his or her childhood.

Although Freud believed that insight into the origins of a problem was sufficient to alter the course of behavior, many therapists have concluded that this is often not so. Wolpe (1969), for example, has argued that extensive relearning is often necessary. In other words, Freud's position that cognitions in the form of insights are frequently sufficient for behavioral change has not been corroborated by many therapists.

This is only a brief description of one major part of Freud's theory, but it illustrates how Freud conceptualized the mix of biology, learning, and cognition. We might say that Freud's theory was one of the first interactionist theories. It attempted to explain how certain biological factors interact with principles of learning and cognition to produce behavior.

One of the main problems with Freud's theory has been the difficulty of testing it. In fact, there has been some debate on whether it can be tested at all, since Freud did not view his theory as predictive (Boring, 1950) He felt that the dynamic nature of motivation, combined with the fact that unknown environmental factors could influence the direction of behavior, meant that the best one could produce was an explanatory theory. Current theorists are interested in designing predictive theories—theories that can be tested in the laboratory or in the field. They do not agree with Freud's pessimistic view that it was virtually impossible to construct a predictive theory.

Humanistic Theories

The humanistic approach was originally proposed by Abraham Maslow (1943, 1954) and Carl Rogers (1959). Humanistic psychologists base their theories on the premise that humans are basically good and that they possess an innate tendency to grow and mature. They further believe that each of us is unique. Central to both theories is the idea that humans have a need for self-actualization.

Abraham Maslow

Maslow is perhaps best known for his conception of needs. He argued that needs can be grouped in categories and that these categories of needs are arranged in a hierarchical fashion, with the more basic or primary needs at the bottom of the hierarchy (Figure 1-2). He suggested that only when the needs at the most basic level are satisfied does the next set of needs become relevant. This means that people will be concerned about safety needs only when their physiological needs (food, water, warmth) have been met at some basic level. Before being concerned with their belongingness and love needs, their need to feel secure, safe, and out of danger must be met at some basic level, and so forth. As seen in Figure 1-2, people are ultimately motivated by the need for self-actualization, but only after their other needs have been met at some basic level. Since I will be discussing Maslow in greater detail in Chapter 13, let me turn to the theory of Carl Rogers.

Carl Rogers

Rogers suggested that organisms have one basic tendency, which is to "actualize, maintain and enhance

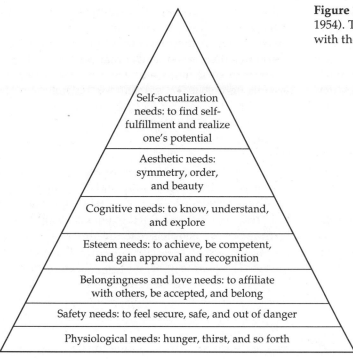

Figure 1–2. Maslow's Hierarchy of Needs (Maslow, 1954). The needs are arranged in the form of a pyramid, with the most basic or primary needs at the bottom.

Self-actualization needs: to find self-fulfillment and realize one's potential

Aesthetic needs: symmetry, order, and beauty

Cognitive needs: to know, understand, and explore

Esteem needs: to achieve, be competent, and gain approval and recognition

Belongingness and love needs: to affiliate with others, be accepted, and belong

Safety needs: to feel secure, safe, and out of danger

Physiological needs: hunger, thirst, and so forth

the experiencing self" (Rogers, 1951). While Rogers recognized that humans have needs, he stressed the inherent tendency of the individual to coordinate those needs in order to develop the self. The self was central to Rogers's theory. He saw the self as constructed from basic sensory experiences and from one's interaction with the world. While the tendency to actualize was seen as innate, he recognized that the route to self-actualization is frequently characterized by pain and suffering. People, he argued, often need to struggle in order to grow and realize their potential.

Rogers believed that people had within themselves the capacity to judge what was good for them and not good for them. Experiences that were perceived as maintaining and enhancing the self would be positively valued and those perceived as regressive and undermining growth would be valued negatively. Thus, what one approached and what one avoided were governed on the basis of how they pertained to the development of the self.

Roger suggested that in the course of interacting with the environment, people come to develop the *need for positive regard*. Positive regard was defined as receiving approval, being accepted, and being loved. The need for positive regard was viewed as the force that guides the individual to seek approval, acceptance and love from others. It was also the thing that makes people sensitive to the criticism and the praise of others. He suggested that positive regard eventually becomes internalized and, as a result, people come to develop *positive self-regard*. Rogers believed strongly that people need to have positive self-regard in order to realize their potential.

Rogers saw an inherent danger linked to internalizing positive regard. If behavior is too closely linked to pleasing others, people lose sight of their own strengths and weaknesses, and they no longer make judgments about what is good for the development of the self. Rogers believed that the movement towards socialized worth and away from inherent worth was antithetical to self-actualization. People need to listen to their inner voices, something he called the *organismic valuation process* (the innate capacity to judge what is good for oneself) in order to ensure they become self-actualized. His advice to parents was to make sure they not embrace conditional love as a philosophy for raising their children (withholding love until the child complied with behaviors they valued) but rather that they embrace unconditional love as a philosophy for raising their children (loving their children for all their choices and behaviors, respecting their inherent ability to do what is best for themselves). In Chapter14 I will talk more about conditional and unconditional love.

While Maslow and Rogers were never part of mainstream empirical psychology, their ideas received wide acceptance outside the mainstream. In recent years there has been a resurgence of interest in the ideas of Maslow and Rogers as psychologists have begun to explore the nature of the self and the role of the self in goal setting. In Chapter 14 I explore some of this work, which has its foundation in the ideas of Maslow and Rogers.

Some Current Issues in Motivation

In recent years there has been a renewed attempt to integrate information about the biological, the learned, and the cognitive sides of human beings. The new theories are more empirically based than Freud's. Starting with existing knowledge about the biological, learned, and cognitive factors that determine our behavior, current theorists are trying to specify exactly how these factors interact. As these new theories have developed, many issues have arisen that need to be carefully understood and, ideally, resolved through controlled studies. Five such issues are fundamental to a number of important topics discussed in this book.

Environmental Stimuli as Sources of Motivational Arousal

There has been growing interest in understanding how the environment affects behavior. How do noise, high population density, the need to use public transit or drive on crowded roads, sharing offices, and any number of other factors in our daily lives affect the way we function? Do such events cause stress or fatigue, and if so, how does that affect our performance? Do such

daily experiences change thresholds for aggression? What are the effects of such factors on mental health?

There seems to be little question that the environment does affect behavior in a variety of ways. The motivation theorist tends to view the environment as a source of arousal. The problem for the motivation theorist is to describe and explain how this source of arousal affects behavior: does arousal produced by the environment alter our threshold for experiencing stress, acting aggressively, or feeling helpless?

An issue that is central to this work is whether our responses to these environmental sources of arousal are innate or learned. Do all or most people react similarly to such environmental events in the absence of learning, or are people's reactions the result of learning? Since human behavior is frequently modified as the result of learning or of changing cognitions, another way of stating the issue is to ask: "To what degree are these reactions, if innate, modified by learning or by the way we perceive the situation?" Psychologists interested in helping people cope with their environments are particularly concerned with the second part of the issue: they want to know whether and to what degree people can learn to deal with certain factors in the environment.

Single versus Multiple Determinants of Behavior

Historically, psychologists have tended to look for single causes or antecedents of behavior. It may seem natural to assume (or at least proceed on the assumption) that a given behavior is due to a single antecedent, but there is no logical reason it should be. For example, it is possible that one person smokes a cigarette to relax while another person smokes a cigarette to experience a "lift." We tend to assume that people smoke cigarettes to get just one thing, the nicotine, and we assume that nicotine has the same effect on all people. It is possible, however, that people smoke cigarettes for other reasons and that nicotine affects people differently, depending on whether they are experiencing fatigue, stress, or any number of other internal states.

It is becoming increasingly clear that people may engage in the same behavior for different reasons. If several factors can lead to the same behavior, then the important question is whether the probability of observing the behavior will be greater if two or more of these factors (antecedents) are present. For example, is a person who is anxious and experiencing stress more likely to smoke a cigarette than a person who is not anxious but just experiencing stress? This line of argument has become critical in attempts to explain the etiology of alcohol addiction, for example (Sadava, 1978).

Historically, people have argued that the failure to reduce the antecedents of a behavior to a single one simply reflects our failure to go back far enough in the chain of events that determine behavior. That is, if we reconceptualized the antecedents, we would discover that they are merely aspects or dimensions of the same antecedent. For example, stress and anxiety might be viewed as aspects of something more global, such as sensitivity to stimulation. The question of single or multiple antecedents is an important issue in current motivational research. Only history will tell us whether it is necessary to hold that there are multiple determinants of behavior or whether this approach grew out of our inability to perceive or construct appropriate organizing concepts.

Persistence of Behavior over Time

Some time ago, Gordon Allport (1937) noted that behavior often continues in the absence of the factors (motives) that initially elicited it. He called this phenomenon "the functional autonomy of behavior." Today the issue is somewhat different. Instead of viewing behavior as occurring in the absence of motivation or simply out of habit, psychologists are assuming that some motivation or other is maintaining the behavior, and they are asking whether it is the same as the motivation that initially elicited the behavior or whether the motivation has shifted over time. For example, can we be satisfied that the motivation that maintains the attachment between a married couple is the same as the motivation that initially led the two persons to be attracted to each other?

There is an appealing simplicity in assuming that a behavior that recurs is due to the operation of the same motivational system, but there is no logical reason to assume so. We may initially go to the theater because we want to circulate with a certain "in crowd" and then discover to our surprise that we like the experience provided by live performances. This issue is important in drug addiction. There is good evidence that the motivation that initially led someone to try drugs may be quite different from the motivation that maintains such behavior. This issue is by no means limited to addiction. It has been considered by people investigating obesity (Rodin, 1980), altruism (Cialdini & Kenrick, 1976), and aggression (Berkowitz, 1974), among other things.

Just as with the question of single versus multiple antecedents, the fact that the motivation underlying a given behavior appears to shift does not necessarily mean that the behavior has different determinants at different times. Rather, our level of analysis or our understanding of the variables may still be somewhat immature or incomplete. Quite possibly, as we become more sophisticated in our understanding, we will discover that in fact a given behavior is governed by a single underlying motive.

Interaction of Motive Systems

In recent years we have come to realize that the brain and the rest of the central nervous system are not in a constant state of readiness. It has been shown, for example, that an area at the top of the spinal column called the reticular activating system can both increase and decrease electrical activity in the cortex. Because we are more likely to detect and process information or respond to events in the environment when the cortex is active, the reticular activating system plays an important role in mediating (controlling) our behavior. Other brain systems have also been implicated in various forms or states of arousal (see Chapter 3 for a more complete discussion). While it is important to know that arousal can facilitate some ongoing activity, it is fascinating to note that these general states of arousal often lower the threshold for other activities. For example, it has been shown that running not only produces arousal but will lower the threshold for provoking an aggressive response from us (Zillmann,

Katcher, & Milavsky, 1972). If increased arousal can lower the threshold for other behaviors—and there is ample evidence that it often does—the question arises whether all motive systems may be interdependent. Can we increase our sensitivity to food by engaging in an arousal-producing activity? For example, alcohol in moderate amounts increases arousal. Is that why people often have a cocktail before dinner? Does the arousal produced by alcohol increase our sensitivity to the pleasurable qualities of food? Similarly, why do we like to have company when we eat? Social interactions reliably increase arousal. Does the arousal from such interactions actually make our food taste better?

There is good reason to hypothesize that humans have learned, probably by accident, that combining one activity with another can increase the pleasure of the second activity. Some of us may have come to realize that after a tense (high arousal) day, our threshold for loud noises—among other things—is low. Therefore, we may warn people that we are not in the mood for certain activities or simply that we are in an irritable mood.

Primacy of Cognitions versus Biological Drives

To what extent is our behavior under cognitive control? The fact that people frequently have difficulty losing weight, stopping smoking, abstaining from the use of a drug such as a tranquilizer or alcohol, and so on, shows that good intentions are often not sufficient to alter the course of behavior. The fact remains, however, that people frequently do lose weight, stop smoking, or abstain from drugs on which they had become dependent. Sometimes such changes are abrupt and dramatic. Further, the fact that people can learn not only to tolerate stress but to find it challenging seems to indicate that attitudes can change a potentially noxious event into a rewarding one. Therapy that alters people's perceptions of themselves or their environment often produces dramatic long-term behavioral change.

Although evolutionary theory suggests that the biological side of humans should have ultimate control of behavior, it must be remembered that behavior is a product of our interaction with our environment. The environment motivates people to develop the rich repertoire of responses that makes it possible for them to deal effectively with an environment that is not only complex but also changing. The issue remains, nevertheless, whether humans are truly as plastic (malleable) as we might gather from some of the research on learning and cognition. The important question is whether learning and cognition can produce long-term behavioral change when such change is inconsistent with the biological structure of humans. Can we learn to ignore our hunger drive, our sex drive, or our tendency to retaliate when provoked, or is all learning simply guided by our biological structure? That is, what limitations does our biological structure impose? What are the consequences of overriding these biological tendencies? Is there a price we must pay?

This book takes what I call a "components approach" to motivation. I attempt to point out what we know about several important areas of human motivation. I deal with questions that concern most of us at various times in our lives. In the next chapter I will spell out precisely what I mean by a components approach.

Main Points

1. Traditionally, the study of motivation has been concerned with the arousal, direction, and persistence of behavior.

2. Current motivational research is more concerned with the arousal and energizing of behavior. It is also concerned with explaining the stream, or flow, of behavior.

3. Some of the earliest formal attempts to explain human motivation were undertaken by the Greek philosophers, who proposed that the purpose of life was the pursuit of happiness.

4. The route to happiness, according to the Greeks, was the development of the intellect (reason).

5. A recurring problem for early thinkers was the analogous behaviors (and motives) of humans and animals.

6.   The position of dualism suggested that humans have a dual nature—physical and nonphysical, or body and soul—and that their behavior is due to nonphysical forces, such as the will, whereas animals' behavior is due to physical forces, such as instincts and reflexes.

7.   Descartes modified the original position of dualism, arguing that the behavior of the body, below the level of willed action, could be explained mechanistically (reflexology) while all other behaviors were under the control of the will.

8.   Darwin challenged the traditional dualist view when he suggested that human behavior was the product of evolution.

9.   Darwin's position encouraged the study of instincts in humans. McDougall's theory is a good example of this approach.

10.   Although psychologists rejected the instincts approach to behavior, a form of this position was revived and elaborated by the ethologists.

11.   The reservoir model of energy has been of particular interest to psychologists, especially in their interpretation of the relation between hormone levels and behavior.

12.   The neurosciences are concerned with identifying the mechanisms that govern, at least in part, the nature of various behaviors.

13.   Learning theorists argued, at least for a time, that all behaviors could be explained by the principles of classical and instrumental learning.

14.   Freud suggested that the source of all energy was the libido and that the direction of behavior was due to learning and cognition.

15.   Freud's goal as a therapist was to help people discover why they had redirected the energy for their instincts in inappropriate ways and to help them feel comfortable with satisfying their natural instincts.

16.   Although Freud stressed the idea that people could be "cured" simply by gaining insight into the origins of their problems, other psychologists have argued that a great deal of relearning is often needed in order for people to be "cured."

17.   Humanistic theorists start with the position that humans are basically good and possess an innate tendency to grow and mature.

18.   Maslow is perhaps most famous for his work on the hierarchy of needs.

19.   Rogers was one of the early psychologists to talk about the importance of the self in understanding human behavior and human growth.

20.   Current motivational research is characterized by efforts to resolve several issues. Five of these issues were briefly discussed.

Chapter Two

Components of Motivation

- What are the components of motivation?

- Why is it necessary to talk in terms of components?

- Why have scientists tended to study behavior from a single perspective?

- What assumptions are involved when one takes a single perspective?

- What are some of the implications of viewing behavior from multiple perspectives?

- Why do scientists construct theories and models?

- How does a multiple-perspective (components) approach help us understand such things as why people run or why people listen to rock music?

A Working Definition of Motivation

The main question asked by motivation theorists today is "What creates action?" In the past it was thought that needs lead directly to action (e.g., Murray, 1938). Thus, all the motivation theorist needed to do was understand the nature and origins of needs or motives. This point of view no longer dominates motivational psychology. The current view is that motivations need to be viewed as *dispositions* (Atkinson & Birch, 1978; de Rivera, 1982; Raynor, 1974; Weiner, 1974). There is a great deal of research showing that two different people can have the same underlying motive or need, such as the motive or need to achieve, but one person acts while the other does not (Markus & Nurius, 1986). Action, it turns out, depends on a number of things including biological readiness (being hungry, for example), whether or not we have a specific goal, whether or not we believe that we can achieve our goal, whether our actions will be socially appropriate, how much pain we will have to endure, and so forth. In short, there are a number of intervening variables between motives and actions. Unless we can understand the nature of these variables, we cannot understand action.

In this book we will examine a number of behaviors (actions) in order to understand what leads to those behaviors. We need to examine biological factors, learned factors and cognitive factors because each of these classes of factors has been found to determine why some people act and others do not. I refer to these factors collectively as the "components" of motivation. Typically, all three are involved to varying degrees in any motivated behavior. They somehow interact to produce organized and, ideally, adaptive behavior. Behavior, therefore, is not due solely to a biological, a learned, or a cognitive process but rather to the interaction of the three (Kleinginna & Kleinginna, 1981a).

An interaction is, by definition, complex. Even though scientists are dedicated to the task of making things simple and understandable, no one has yet been able to account for the complexities of human motivation by a single set of principles, be they principles of biology, learning, or cognition. Nevertheless, our understanding of motivation is growing daily; the pieces

of this complex puzzle are slowly falling into place. It is becoming clear that human motivation is the joint product of these three components working together in a surprisingly smooth fashion. Before examining this process, we will look at each component separately. As we shall see, each operates according to a quite different set of principles.

From time to time, people have tried to explain motivation from only a single perspective such as a biological perspective or a learned perspective or a cognitive perspective. For the most part, this approach leaves a very incomplete picture of what is truly taking place. After spending a year in England, I found it interesting to discover that North Americans tend to have a bias towards learning explanations whereas the English tend to have a bias towards biological explanations. There is great power in both types of explanations. And in recent years we have come to realize the importance of cognitive factors as well.

The working definition of motivation that I use, therefore, is that motivation is concerned with understanding how dispositions lead to action through the interaction of biological, learned and cognitive processes. One of the key concepts in contemporary motivation theory is that people can learn to create action (manage their own motivation) through self-regulation (Bandura, 1990). The process of self-regulation depends on understanding the role of biological, learned, and cognitive factors. It is because people often fail to understand the role of each of the factors that they are unable to fully self-regulate their actions. One of the most exciting things to emerge in recent years has been the demonstration, in a wide number of areas in psychology, that people can self-regulate their behavior including their biology.

Biology is not something that works independently of learning and cognition; rather, it works in conjunction with learning and cognition. The idea that biology can be regulated or controlled is not new. Many years ago we were honored to have the Nobel prize winner Nikko Tinbergen visit our campus to deliver a "distinguished" lecture on his work on aggression. During a conversation, he recounted the following story.

Just before coming to our campus he was in Vancouver where he was unable to give his talk because he was "shouted down" by a group of dissenters. Later that evening he met with a delegation of the dissenters in order to try to understand their motives. They said that if aggression was biologically based, then there was no hope for mankind. Thus, they had to ensure he was unable to deliver this message. Tinbergen pointed out to them that they completely misunderstood the whole point of science and of his work, and that by shouting him down, biology would not disappear. They argued, in reply, that his fame would carry such weight that people would believe his message that aggression was natural—and then assume aggression to be right. He said that just because there is a biological basis for something does not make it right or correct. What is important, he argued, is to recognize that we are influenced by biology but also to recognize that because we have a large cortex we have a greater capacity to learn how to control (inhibit) our aggression than many animals. The first step in learning to control something, he concluded, is knowing what it is that you need to control.

It always perplexes me when people attempt to deny there is a biological basis to our behavior under the misguided idea that to deny it will make it go away or somehow lessen its impact. Nothing could be further from the truth. Like Tinbergen, I believe that if we ever are to achieve self-regulation we need to understand the biological basis of behavior. It is then that we will have the knowledge necessary to control it.

The Biological Component

The Ethological View

The principles of biology assume that behavior is the product of our genetic structure. We behave as we do because our genetic structure not only sets a behavior in motion but gives direction to that behavior.

The biological position does not necessarily assume that behavior is either stereotyped or totally prewired. Ethologists such as Tinbergen and Konrad Lorenz

(1969) have acknowledged that learning can play an important role. Nevertheless, they and others have argued that what is learned is guided by the genetic structure of the individual. For example, Lorenz has stated that "all learning is very specifically innately programmed" (1969, p. 21). According to this position, humans (as well as animals) are equipped to take advantage of certain experiences. Several articles and books have clearly shown how the genetic structure we inherit makes it possible for us to learn certain things and not others. The tendency to acquire language appears to have a genetic basis (Chomsky, 1972; Lieberman, 1984), as does our tendency to form social groups or behave altruistically (Wilson, 1975). Numerous constraints on animal learning have been reported (Hinde & Stevenson-Hinde, 1973), all of which can be readily understood from an evolutionary perspective (Barash, 1977). It has been shown, for example, that it is virtually impossible to teach an animal that normally flees when threatened to attack or to teach an animal that normally attacks to flee. On the other hand, it is very easy for humans to learn to avoid substances that make them ill. Genetics often play a central role in behaviors related to our ability to survive.

Open versus closed programs. Mayr (1974) has distinguished between open and closed genetic programs. A genetic program that cannot be modified appreciably during its translation into behavior is called a "closed program." A genetic program that is open allows additional input during the translation of the program into behavior. Most programs are neither completely open nor completely closed. A good example of this can be found in the work done with song learning in male birds. Songs in a territorial male bird serve to advertise his species membership, his sexual maturity, and his ability to defend an area against other males of his species. In attempting to determine to what extent songs in birds are the product of open versus closed programs, researchers have studied white-crowned sparrows that had been raised under natural conditions versus a group of hand-reared white-crowned sparrows that had not been permitted to hear the songs of white-crowned sparrows or allowed to hear them only at certain times in their development. The results of these studies indicate that the white-crowned sparrows are tuned to imitate only the song of their species, suggesting they have a template that is selective to certain sounds of their species. The results also indicate that they need to listen to the song at certain critical stages (10 to 50 days old) to learn a full song, and that if they are allowed to listen later instead (4 months of age), they never learn a full song, suggesting that there is a critical stage for them to learn.

One interesting feature of the sparrows' song learning is that at about 150 days after hatching they begin singing what is called a subsong. Through a process of trial and error, they match this subsong to the song template they stored while young. If they did not hear the song during the critical period because they were raised in isolation, they never learn to sing the full song. In other words, the critical feature of song acquisition in white-crowned sparrows is learning the template during a critical stage of development. The function of this highly selective program is to ensure that the white-crowned male can communicate with other members of his species and attract a female. While the program is closed for the most part (there is a template that is only responsive to sounds of the same species) it is open to the degree that additional input is needed for it to be translated into behavior (Alcock, 1979; Marler, 1970).

Human behavior is often the result of programs that have both open and closed elements. The acquisition of language in humans is a good example. The fact that all languages have the same underlying grammatical structure suggests that humans have closed programs that govern the acquisition of language (Chomsky, 1972). It can be shown, however, that exposure to language is very important. Many of the finer features of language come from being exposed to models that provide the words and other features of language essential to effective communication.

Hardwired versus softwired. It is important to note that writers often use the words hardwired and softwired to distinguish between behaviors that result largely from some genetic predisposition versus those that re-

sult mainly from learning. In the case of sexual orientation, for example, hardwired would mean that there was a biological disposition towards heterosexuality, homosexuality or bisexuality, whereas softwired would mean that sexual orientation was mainly learned (see Chapter 5). The term hardwired not only implies that there is a genetic predisposition but also that it cannot be modified. If homosexuality is hardwired, as a great deal of evidence suggests, it means that homosexuality is not modifiable. Therefore, sexual orientation is the product of a closed program.

The expression of a homosexual orientation, however, tends to be highly variable. Like heterosexuals, homosexuals have a diversity of interests and skills and can be found in a variety of occupations. The expression of one's sexual orientation appears to be largely if not completely the product of an open program.

Prewired is also used to denote that a behavior is largely due to biology but that learning can and often does play an important role. In the case of sickness, for example, it has been shown that people are prepared (prewired) to associate sickness with taste but not with visual or auditory stimuli (see section on Learned Component in this chapter). This means that it is virtually impossible to get people to associate sickness with visual or auditory stimuli but that they can be taught to associate sickness with a number of different types of tastes.

The Behavioral Neurosciences

Although the ethological position has proved to be a very productive framework for analyzing behavior, there are other ways of viewing the biological system. A more popular view among psychologists is that human evolution favored general activation and reward systems rather than specific innate responses. According to this view, a behavior is acquired because of a reward mechanism that increases the likelihood of a response. For example, obtaining food for performing a certain response, or eliminating a noxious stimulus by making an avoidance response, is assumed to produce an internal reinforcing event. This reinforcing event is thought to be triggered by some

PRACTICAL APPLICATION 2.1

The Biology of Obsessions and Compulsions

In her book, *The Boy who Couldn't Stop Washing*, Judith Rapoport (1989) talks about Sergei, a 17-year-old who was transformed almost overnight into a loner outsider, incapacitated by his psychological disabilities. Haunted by the idea that he was dirty—in spite of evidence to the contrary—Sergei began trying to cleanse himself from imaginary dirt. At first his ritual was confined to weekends and evenings, but eventually it began to consume all his time and he was forced to drop out of school. His condition was diagnosed as obsessive–compulsive disorder (OCD).

Obsessive–compulsive disorders have been a major challenge to psychologists because they have proved to be so resistant to various forms of psychological therapy, including attempts to extinguish these behaviors using principles of learning. Judith Rapoport has proposed a biological (ethological) model for the origins of OCD. This intriguing example of Sergei illustrates how it is possible to view OCDs in terms of biology. It may well be that not all OCDs can be explained in terms of a biological model; however, the example of Sergei is a compelling one and indicates why it is important to consider the role of biology in explaining behaviors such as OCDs.

The central element of Judith Rapoport's theory is that certain behavioral "subroutines," related to grooming and territory, have been programmed into the brain over the course of evolution. Ordinarily, the senses tell the individual that he is clean or that he is safe, and this is sufficient to suppress those subroutines that have to do with cleaning or taking measures to ensure that one is safe. If higher brain functions fail to suppress these subroutines due to some type of malfunction, the subroutines are replayed over and over, making the individual a slave to behaviors such as washing or checking to see if the door is locked, even when he knows that he is clean or that the door is locked. One patient that Judith Rapoport treated was a woman who felt compelled to pull out her hair, one strand at a time, a behavior that would presumably come from the subroutine associated with grooming.

While obsessive–compulsives often know their behaviors are irrational, they feel helpless to control them. Because they understand their rituals and thoughts are senseless, they often go to great lengths to hide them. When they can no longer conceal them, they often retreat from public view or public encounters. Howard Hughes is a good example of a person who became a recluse following the development of his obsession that contact with other people was a source of germs (Rapoport, 1989).

Approximately 2% of the population suffers from OCD. While OCD is resistant to psychotherapy, it seems to be treatable by antidepressants. Judith Rapoport has argued that the reason such drugs as clomipramine alleviate OCD symptoms is that they affect the production/regulation of the neurotransmitter serotonin. Neurotransmitters are important in governing behavior because they carry messages across the synapse (the gap between two nerve cells) in the brain. Whenever their concentration levels change, they can dramatically affect the way people think, feel, and act.

While drugs have proved effective, I should point out that learning principles have also been used to deal with OCD. Specifically, it has been shown that these behaviors can be extinguished. While it may seem contradictory to claim, on the one hand, that a behavior is biologically based and to simultaneously accept, on the other hand, the fact that behavioral conditioning can reverse it, ethologists have come to accept the idea that many fixed action patterns, which stem in part from hardwiring, can be altered through the principles of learning.

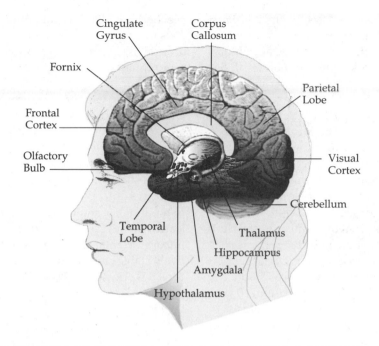

Cingulate Gyrus
Corpus Callosum
Fornix
Frontal Cortex
Olfactory Bulb
Parietal Lobe
Visual Cortex
Cerebellum
Temporal Lobe
Thalamus
Hippocampus
Amygdala
Hypothalamus

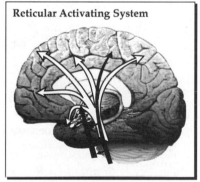

Reticular Activating System

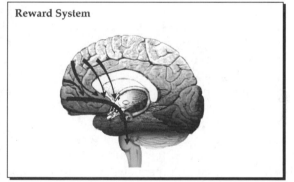

Reward System

Figure 2-1. Major structures of the human brain and their relationships to two important systems.

innate reward mechanism or mechanisms. When a reinforcing event occurs it is assumed to have the capacity, according to the principles of learning, to increase the likelihood (probability) of that response occurring again in the future. Since learning is generally considered to be a gradual process, it is assumed that the reinforcing event must occur several times before learning is complete (before the response will occur with a high probability). In other words, what makes learning possible is the existence of some type of innate reward mechanism or mechanisms.

Reward centers. A great deal of evidence supports the view that the reward mechanisms that evolved were general rather than specific. Olds (1955, 1956), for example, discovered that animals will learn a wide variety of responses in order to receive electrical stimulation in certain areas of the brain that have come to be called the "reward centers" (see Figure 2.1.) Such centers also exist in the human brain. The fact that the brain contains structures that are capable of reinforcing a wide range of behaviors raises questions. If all significant behaviors are prewired, as strict biological determinism holds, the existence of these centers is difficult to explain. Why would such centers exist unless they had an adaptive function? The existence of reward centers does not, of course, cause any problems for those who maintain that general reward mechanisms evolved to ensure the survival of organisms. According to this view, such mechanisms serve to reward long-term adaptive behaviors (Glickman & Schiff, 1967). The problem here is to explain what mechanism or structure tells the reward system that an adaptive response has been made. As these reward centers are activated by certain drugs, such as amphetamines (see Chapter 7), there is good reason to believe that they are indeed very general mechanisms that may not be tied exclusively to adaptive behaviors. They may, in fact, be capable of rewarding short-term maladaptive behaviors.

Reticular activating system. In 1949, Moruzzi and Magoun discovered that the energy for a wide variety of behaviors came from a general rather than a specific activation system. They found that an area at the top of the brainstem (the reticular formation) is capable of activating the entire cortex. They found that if they directly stimulated the upper part of the reticular activating system with a mild electrical current when an animal was asleep, the entire cortex would suddenly become active (aroused). Simultaneously, the animal showed all the normal signs of awakening from sleep, such as opening its eyes and stretching. On the basis of their work, Moruzzi and Magoun decided that the reticular formation acted as a center for arousing the cortex and therefore named it the "reticular activating system" (RAS)(see Figure 2.1). They suggested that the incoming sensory signals activate the reticular activating system, which in turn activates the cortex.

Moruzzi and Magoun's discovery stimulated a great deal of research that suggested not only that humans perform best at moderate levels of activation or arousal (Hebb, 1955), but that they have a preference for moderate levels of activation or arousal (for exam-

ple, Berlyne, 1960). This finding led a number of theorists to propose that moderate levels of activation or arousal have reinforcing properties. Thus, people learn to do things that will raise a low level of arousal and to do other things that will lower a very high level of arousal. As a variety of external stimuli will increase arousal, the existence of such a mechanism can explain why people who are bored (experiencing too little stimulation or too little arousal) may like to travel or to listen to certain types of music. Similarly, the existence of such a mechanism can explain why people will seek out a quiet place when they feel stressed (exposed to too much stimulation or too much arousal) or will learn to avoid certain situations that cause arousal to be uncomfortably high. The concept of seeking a relatively stable state of equilibrium is commonly referred to as the principle of *homeostasis*.

Limbic system. The limbic system is a structure deep within the brain which regulates many of our emotions, such as fear, love, and anger. We all know from experience that emotions are a source of pleasure as well as pain. For this reason, many behavioral neuroscience researchers have proposed that the limbic system is still another area of the brain that is involved not only in the activation of behavior but also in its reinforcement.

Constraints Imposed by the Nervous System

These various reward mechanisms do not, however, make human behavior infinitely flexible. It is limited or constrained by a variety of factors. Our ability to activate the brain's reward centers appears to be limited by, among other things, the availability of certain chemicals in the brain which are released only under certain conditions. There is a great deal of evidence that these chemicals are released only when we find ourselves in a situation that requires us to make an adaptive response. It has also been found that our supply of these chemicals can become depleted. Thus, even when the environment provides the appropriate conditions, these structures will not provide the same level of reward as they would had the supply of these chemicals not been depleted.

Similarly, not all stimulation will increase arousal. As we tend to become habituated to stimulation (used to or familiar with that stimulation), we often need to find new forms of stimulation to increase our arousal.

The way we express our emotions is determined to a very large degree by the cortex. According to MacLean (1975), the cortex plays an important role in modifying (inhibiting) the expression of emotions. MacLean notes that there are many interconnections between the cortex and such structures as the limbic system. Frustration, for example, is often but not always followed by aggression.

The question of whether or not an emotion can be aroused by some specific environmental event is affected by such things as hormones. The sex hormones, for example, play a very important role in determining whether or not an organism will be sexually aroused. When the levels of sex hormones are low, it becomes difficult to arouse sexual motivation. The implications of this finding are far-reaching. If certain drugs suppress the sex hormones, then they will also suppress sexual behavior.

Still other structures in the brain place constraints on the functioning of these reward mechanisms. While the hypothalamus has traditionally been regarded as the energy base for all motivation (Stellar, 1954), more recent researchers (for example, Valenstein, Cox, & Kakolewski, 1970) have argued that the hypothalamus is the locus of species-specific behaviors. This means that, at least to some degree, certain adaptive behaviors are prewired.

While it is not particularly important to remember all these details, as we will be examining many of these concepts more closely later, it is important to remember three things. First, the brain contains general reward mechanisms that make possible great variation in the way we behave. Second, our behavior is nonetheless constrained by the requirement that certain conditions (both physical and psychological) must be met before these reward mechanisms can operate. Chemical or hormonal levels must be right, for example, or the situation might threaten our life. Third, there is evidence that certain behaviors are not governed by these general reward mechanisms. We know, for example, that sleep/wakefulness cycles are controlled by

biological rhythms, and that despite our best efforts, we cannot modify them.

Summary

Motivation is concerned with understanding how dispositions can lead to actions through the interaction of biological, learned and cognitive processes. These processes are referred to collectively as "components of motivation." There is ample evidence from a variety of sources that human behavior is not infinitely flexible, as some learning theorists have argued, nor is it totally preprogrammed. The existence of general reward systems and arousal systems suggests that humans are capable of learning a number of new behaviors not specifically dictated by their genetic structure. Not all new behaviors are adaptive. Nevertheless, it can be argued that these behaviors exist because the biological structure of humans allows them to exist and in some instances ensures that they persist. Biological processes, however, can be regulated. People can learn to become aware of their biological processes. For at least some of these biological processes, becoming aware of them is the first step to learning how to control and regulate them.

The Learned Component

Learning plays a very important role in motivated behavior. The term *acquired motives* (or *acquired drives*) is often used to refer to the type of learning that we will be talking about in this book.

Acquired Motives

At birth we have such primary drives or needs as hunger, thirst, sleep, temperature regulation, curiosity, and even tactile stimulation (we need to be held or touched). Certain primary drives are not full-blown at birth but emerge as the organism matures. The sex drive, for example, while present in infants, develops in strength when the sex hormones become more active.

Some drives or motives, however, do not seem to be present at birth or do not seem to be tied directly to any specific biological system. The need to achieve, the

PRACTICAL APPLICATION 2.2

Becoming Aware of Your Biological Processes

People can become aware of many of their biological processes. Peter Suedfeld (Chapter 3), has found that people who had spent long periods of time under conditions of sensory deprivation often became aware of some of their physiological responses, such as their heart rate and respiration. He suggests that when people are under conditions of sensory isolation they begin attending to their physiological responses because they have nothing else to arouse their attention. More important, perhaps, he found that as a result of their sensory isolation experience they were less affected by stress at a later time. The reason they experienced less stress, he argued, was that they had learned to control those responses. In short, they had learned the basic techniques of relaxation, one of the main ways to alleviate stress.

There is a great deal of research showing that one of the first steps in learning to control your physiological responses is to become aware of them. In relaxation training, for example, people are often first taught to contract a certain set of muscles (such as in their arm) and then relax them. In the process of contracting and then relaxing a group of muscles, people typically become aware of those muscles and how to control them. As a result, when they become tense they can focus on those muscles and relax them at will. People can even learn to monitor and control their brain waves. People hooked to a machine that records brain waves (electroencephalograph or simply EEG) and allowed to monitor their brain waves by viewing them on a screen can learn to produce Alpha waves that have been linked to "being relaxed" or something called "relaxed awareness." In order to produce Alpha waves at will, people can learn to recreate the psychological state that is linked to Alpha waves. Thus, when people are in a state of "relaxed awareness" they know, based on past learning, that their brain is likely producing Alpha waves.

While people can become directly aware of such things as their heart rate, respiration, and tenseness of their muscles, there are a number of biological processes that people can only become aware of indirectly. Take, for example, the reward pathways in the brain. These pathways have been linked to moods. When people are experiencing a positive mood or positive affect, it is likely due to the activation of this pathway. Research has shown that when this pathway is activated we experience positive moods or feelings of euphoria, and when it is not active we tend to experience negative moods or even feelings of depression. One way to become indirectly aware of your reward pathway is to monitor how positive or negative you feel.

Chemicals called neurotransmitters carry messages across synapses in the brain. Without them it would be impossible to think or process information.

need for power, the tendency to take drugs, the tendency to avoid enclosed places (claustrophobia)—all are patterns of behavior that have no specific biological antecedent; that is, no biological state that needs to be satisfied. Hunger is satisfied by food, thirst is satisfied by water, sleepiness is satisfied by sleep, curiosity is satisfied by exploration, and sex is satisfied by engaging in a sexual act that leads to orgasm.

If there is no specific biological antecedent for such motives as achievement and power, then how do we explain the existence of these motives? What activates the tendency to achieve or the tendency to search for power or the tendency to take drugs? It is important to note that when we talk about acquired motives, we assume that some people will acquire these motives and others will not, and that those who acquire them

As a result of such things as intense mental activity, stress, and even drinking alcohol, these neurotransmitters often tend to become depleted. When this happens, thinking often becomes sluggish. By monitoring your ability to think clearly, you can indirectly monitor the release of neurotransmitters in your brain. At various times throughout the day estimate how well you can think or process information. This will give you some idea of the level of your neurotransmitters.

Since you tend to fire neurons in your brain when you create visual images (Crick & Koch, 1992), try creating a variety of visual images. The more detailed they are the more neurons you will fire in your visual cortex. Try creating images or fantasies and then observe what happens to such things as your heart rate, your respiration, and your moods. Create an image that you find very relaxing, such as sitting on the bank of a creek in summer, and then monitor such things as your heart rate, your respiration, and your mood. Next, imagine a situation that would cause a stress response, such as seeing a spider walk across your arm or leaning over the balcony on the fortieth floor of an apartment building. Again, monitor your heart rate, your respiration and your feelings. Try alternating between a relaxing and a stressful image to see how your reactions change. In this exercise you are not only firing neurons in your brain, you are causing a variety of chemicals to be released that have been linked alternatively to relaxation and to stress. The more you practice doing this the more you will become aware of your own biology.

It has been argued that people raised in the western hemisphere have been raised to ignore their biological processes or treat them as distinct from mental processes—something called dualism (Langer, 1989). When we begin to see that our biological responses are directly linked to our mental processes and that our mental processes are directly linked to our biological processes, we start to become more aware of the biological processes that many of us have learned to ignore.

There is a great deal of research suggesting there are many health benefits from becoming aware of our biological processes. Research in the field of health psychology provides overwhelming evidence for the idea that how we think about things (especially adversity) affects not only our moods but also such things as our immune system (Seligman, 1989). Perhaps one of the most powerful tools we have to affect our physiology and our health is humor (Carroll & Schmidt, 1990; Carroll, 1992). When you learn to put on a happy face you can change your entire physiology (see Chapter 9). Try experimenting with humor to see what humor does to some of your biological processes.

will do so to varying degrees. The net result is that when we talk about acquired motives, there will often be significant individual differences.

Classical Conditioning

Ivan Pavlov (1927) discovered classical conditioning when he found that dogs could be taught to salivate at the sound of a bell if the bell was rung whenever food was presented. According to Pavlov's analysis, food is an unconditioned stimulus (UC) that naturally leads to the unconditioned response (UR) of salivation. When the bell (which does not naturally elicit salivation) is paired with food (preferably a half-second before the food is presented), it acquires the ability to elicit salivation because it is a reliable predictor that food is

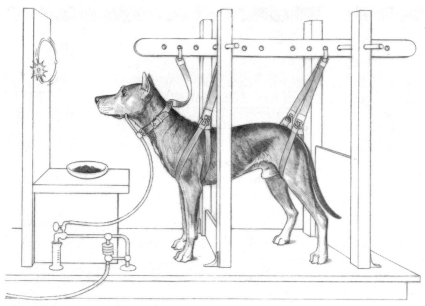

Figure 2–2. A typical Pavlovian setup.

forthcoming. Pavlov found that after several pairings of bell and food, the bell elicited salivation even when no food was presented. In such circumstances we say that the bell has become a conditioned stimulus (CS). When the CS has acquired the capacity to elicit the response it is called the conditioned response (CR). In general the CR is never as strong as the UR. If the bell (CS) is repeatedly presented in the absence of the US (with no accompanying food), it will eventually lose its ability to elicit the response. The procedure of repeatedly presenting the CS in the absence of a reward or the US is called extinction.

Fear as a classical conditioned or respondent conditioned motive. The discovery of classical conditioning was a great help to psychologists in their efforts to understand such things as human fears. Since many fears such as the fear of enclosed places (claustrophobia) or the fear of flying are not universal among humans, it has been suggested they are learned. Claustrophobia may be the result of some traumatic experience early in life. As a child you may have been locked in a closet as a prank or by accident. While you were in that closet you prob-

ably experienced some very negative emotions. You may have thought that whoever locked you in that closet had forgotten about you, and you were doomed to starve to death. Or you may simply have been afraid of the dark, and after a time began to imagine that some monster was surely going to get you. According to the principles of classical conditioning, your emotional state was likely to become conditioned to that closet. Whenever you reentered the closet, you would again experience the same emotion. But that emotional experience would not be limited to that particular closet. Humans are inclined to generalize. That is, we are inclined to react in the same way to any situation we perceive as similar to the one that originally elicited a particular emotion. This tendency serves to explain why a person might exhibit claustrophobia in an elevator, for example, even though that person had never had any aversive experience in one. Fear, according to the theory of classical conditioning, is simply a conditioned emotional response that has generalized to a variety of situations that the individual, for one reason or another, perceives as similar to the original situation that elicited the negative emotional state.

Reversing classical conditioning. It is important to note that, according to the theory of classical conditioning, it doesn't matter if you are aware of the conditions that have led to the conditioning of the aversive emotion. The only way to get rid of your fear is to extinguish the response or to use some kind of counterconditioning procedure. If the response is to be extinguished, the CS must be presented to you repeatedly in the absence of the US. This procedure should, according to the theory of classical conditioning, lead to a weakening of the fear response. In many cases it doesn't, for reasons that we needn't go into here. Alternatively, the CS could be paired with a more favorable response, such as relaxation or feelings of security. If the new response is strong enough, it should cancel out or replace the previously acquired response. This procedure is called counterconditioning.

Instrumental Learning

A second kind of learning that is often involved in acquired drives or motives is instrumental learning. In instrumental learning, a response that occurs at some natural rate (often called the operant rate) can be made to occur at a higher rate if the receipt of a reward is made contingent on a higher rate of responding. If a reward is to work, an appropriate motivational system must be activated. Certain foods can be rewarding (reinforcing) to an animal if it is hungry or if the food stimulates one of the sensory systems associated with food intake. What is particularly interesting about rewarded behavior is that often the behavior will continue at a high rate even if the reward is removed. A nonrewarded response will eventually diminish in rate or strength; this process is called extinction. One way to make a response continue in the absence of reward is to offer partial reinforcement of the behavior. That is, instead of rewarding the behavior on every trial, you reward the behavior on only some of the trials. In Chapter 12 we will discuss why this procedure works.

Achievement as an instrumentally acquired motive. According to the principles of instrumental learning, the strength of any response can be increased if a reward is made contingent on the occurrence of the re-sponse. If a child were to come home with a score of 9 out of 10 on a math quiz, for example, and if her father were to reward her in some way, a likely outcome is that she would strive to do well on other math tests. If her father then rewarded other good outcomes in the same way, she might strive to do well in a variety of other subjects. Over time, the child might develop a tendency to strive to do well in all her school subjects. This tendency might even generalize beyond school and become a much more general characteristic. At this point we might refer to this behavior pattern as achievement motivation.

Secondary rewards and instrumental learning. If a reward is to be effective, it must be applied as soon as possible after the desired behavior has occurred. While primary reinforcers, such as food, are often very effective as rewards for behavior, especially in the training of animals, primary rewards are not very practical as reinforcers of many human behaviors. The word primary means that the thing or event has the capacity to increase responding independent of any previous learning. The reason food is a primary reward is because we do not have to learn to experience the reward value that comes from eating food, particularly when we are hungry. It's hard to imagine a university professor offering little pieces of candy to a student each time the student does well on a test. It has been shown that symbolic or secondary rewards, such as "Very good" or a big "A" on a paper, are often even more effective than primary rewards. The question is why these symbolic or secondary rewards actually work. There are at least two lines of thinking. One is that various forms of praise acquire reward value because they have been associated with the presentation of a primary reward (thus the term secondary). When your dog sits up and you give him a little piece of meat, for example, you are likely to say something like "Good dog." After a time the phrase "Good dog" acquires reinforcing properties, through the principles of classical conditioning, because it has been paired with the presentation of the primary reward. When you were a child, your parents did the same thing when they fed you. As a result, when they express praise for you now, it makes you feel good, just as the food you ate as a child made you

---

Classical Conditioning

Teaching a dog to salivate to a bell

UCS (food)   ➔   UCR (salivation)
CS (bell)   ➔   CR (salivation)

1. The optimal conditions for producing conditioning is to present the CS (conditioned stimulus) about .5 sec. before the UCS (unconditioned stimulus).
2. In this type of learning the CS becomes a signal that the UCS is about to be presented. The UCR (unconditioned response) is automatically elicited by the UCS. The CR (conditioned response) is typically weaker but it is the same response.
3. If the UCS (food) is not presented, the response will eventually extinguish.

Instrumental Learning

Teaching a dog to sit on command

S ("Sit")   ➔   R (reward) (dog sitting)

1. The optimal conditions for producing instrumental learning is to present the reward immediately after the desired R (response) is made.
2. In this type of learning the stimulus S (stimulus) becomes the signal to perform an R (response). Getting the R to occur may require shaping (e.g., putting the dog into a sitting position).
3. If the reward is not presented, the response will eventually extinguish.

Figure 2-3. Comparison of classical conditioning with instrumental learning.

feel good. The second line of argument is simply that since humans can think and reason, you know that "Very good" or an "A" at the top of your paper means that you are acquiring a skill that has value. This skill can be used to earn money or simply to earn the love and respect you want from people who matter to you.

Intrinsic versus extrinsic rewards. A distinction is often made between intrinsic and extrinsic rewards. When an activity itself provides the reward, we say that the activity is intrinsically rewarding; when an activity is performed in order to obtain a reward that is unrelated to it, then we say that the activity is extrinsically rewarding. A child who does well in school simply to gain approval from his parents or to acquire a skill that he can then use to earn money or acquire fame is engaging in the activity for extrinsic reasons (rewards). If, however, he finds the activity motivating even in the absence of approval or some other form of gain, then we say that he is engaging in the activity for intrinsic

reasons (rewards). Some people have argued that one reason people become strongly achievement-oriented is not to obtain extrinsic rewards (as I suggested above) but rather because achievement motivation is linked to more intrinsic forms of motivation. Robert White (1959), for example, has suggested that achievement or mastery is linked to what he calls "effectance motivation," whereas David McClelland (1985) has argued that it grows out of curiosity or exploratory motivation; both are viewed as intrinsic forms of motivation. We will talk more about such motivation in Chapter 12.

Both intrinsic and extrinsic rewards play an important role in shaping such complex motives as the need for achievement. The rewards and punishments that we experience modify not only the strength but the direction of the initial motivation on which complex motives are built. Throughout this book we will examine how both intrinsic and extrinsic rewards affect the way motives are shaped and expressed. Sometimes we may start to do something for extrinsic reasons and end up doing them for intrinsic reasons. At other times, we start to do something for intrinsic reasons and end up doing them for extrinsic reasons.

The Opponent-Process Model of Acquired Drives

Richard Solomon (Solomon, 1980; Solomon & Corbit, 1974) has advanced a very different kind of model to account for such acquired drives as fear, achievement, power, drug taking, and other complex motives. According to the opponent–process model, reinforcers are viewed as affective states (ranging from positive to negative feelings) that are aroused or elicited by stimuli in the environment. Jumping off a high building, for example, typically produces negative affect (fear). Taking drugs produces positive or negative affect, depending on the drug. The appearance of an attractive person of the opposite sex elicits positive affect (attraction and arousal). In other words, according to Solomon's model, every event naturally elicits some state that may range from very satisfying to very aversive.

We all know that events that elicit positive affect typically lose their power over time. For example, after repeated exposure to a song that we initially found very exhilarating, we tend to lose interest in it. Similarly, events that produce negative affect can also lose their power over time. We may find it very aversive to drive in heavy traffic, for example, but after a time we grow accustomed to it if we have to do it every day.

In order to account for the fact that events lose their ability to reinforce us and that affective states often undergo some sort of change, Solomon has proposed a two-process model called the opponent–process theory. Initially, an environmental event arouses or elicits a process that is experienced as an affective reaction (process a). According to the theory, process a automatically elicits process b, an affective reaction that is opposite in direction to process a. Process b, the opponent process, counteracts process a and brings the organism back to its normal operating state.

While process a is always the same, process b changes as the result of experience. With repeated exposure to process a, process b begins earlier, has greater magnitude, and lasts longer. People who parachute from a plane for the first time typically experience fear and then relief when they hit the ground. After many jumps the fear gets weaker and the relief is experienced as joy or exhilaration, which often lasts for a considerable period of time. According to Solomon's theory, process b has strengthened and become long-lasting. Experienced parachutists typically report that they experience great exhilaration during their descent. According to the theory, process b has started to occur earlier.

Solomon's theory is a very powerful one because it can explain why some activity that is initially aversive can come to motivate behavior. It seems to make little sense, for example, that people get hooked on something like work, yet we know that many people do. According to Solomon's theory, work, often a boring or even painful experience, is capable of triggering an opponent process that is experienced as joy and even exhilaration. I will discuss Solomon's theory in more detail in Chapter 7, when I talk about drug addiction.

Associative Learning and Connectionism

Many current learning theorists think that the distinction between classical conditioning and instrumental learning is forced and unnecessary. They argue that all learning can be conceptualized as associative learning or the learning of relations among events (Rescorla, 1988). Organisms not only learn to associate a stimulus with a response but they also learn to associate a stimulus with another stimulus. In the case of multiple determinants of behavior, a powerful way of conceptualizing addictive behaviors, it has been suggested that a particular behavior, such as smoking or drinking, can become associated with a wide range of stimuli and, as a result, a particular behavior can be elicited by a wide range of stimuli or their combination.

The word connectionism has recently been used to refer to the fact that learning often involves, among other things, the connection of neurons in the brain into "neural networks" or "patterns" (Bechtel & Abrahamsen, 1991). Neural networks and patterns are sometimes viewed as the neurological equivalent to categories.

One example of why the concept of connectionism is important comes from the observation that humans often "parallel process" different aspects or dimensions of the same stimulus (McClelland & Rumelhart, 1986; Rumelhart & McClelland, 1986). It has been shown, for example, that different dimensions of a stimulus (color, form, movement) activate different areas in the brain (Zeki, 1992). The more dimensions of the stimulus that are present, the more likely it is that a person will fully see or comprehend (recognize) the stimulus. The reason this is so important is that it suggests that humans must learn to connect (integrate) a number of different dimensions or aspects of a stimulus before they have a clear image or perception. Once these dimensions have become connected, it has been argued, they are then stored as some type of image or schemata in memory. As a result, an incomplete stimulus can be recognized because it elicits an image that has been stored in memory. The reason that the presence of more dimensions is likely to lead to recognition is that with more dimensions there is a greater likelihood that a given neural network or pattern will be activated (Crick & Koch, 1992).

In many ways, connectionism is the bridge between what we commonly call learning and what we call cognition (Bechtel & Abrahamsen, 1991). I won't deal explicitly with connectionism in this book. The closest I will come is when I discuss images. Our ability to create images is very important and undoubtedly comes from the tendency of the brain to form neural networks and patterns. When we create images in our mind we actually activate neural networks in the brain. Thus, the images we create may form the basis for action. When someone sees him- or herself hitting a golf ball onto the green, that image may activate several systems including the motor system that is necessary to ultimately guide the ball to its desired location. While there are many other things that can also affect the outcome, the image seems to be central to this process. As we will see later, people often develop images of what it means to be beautiful, for example. If part of that image is being thin, that image can be a powerful source of motivation for not eating even when other mechanisms tell you that you are hungry. In short, images are important for understanding a wide range of motivated behaviors. Images often provide the standards that guide our actions.

Summary

Acquired motives or drives are often linked in some very basic way to the biological side of human behavior. Fears, for example, are thought to be linked in some way to unlearned reactions, such as those that occur when we are presented with a painful stimulus, such as a loud noise or an enclosed space, which may seem to threaten our survival. Similarly, achievement motivation may be linked in some fundamental way to such basic biological drives as the need to be loved or simply the need to accommodate the environment. According to the opponent–process model, some underlying biological mechanism gives rise to the opponent process.

Even though these new motives or drives may be linked to some underlying biological need, they differ from the original motive that gave rise to them. In many cases they seem to have become autonomous. That is, they seem to have their own source of energy. Even though we may not always be able to specify what that new source of energy is, it is important to recognize that without the occurrence of learning, that new drive or motive would not exist. What makes the opponent–process theory so attractive is that it spells out where the new energy comes from.

For some time it has been assumed that all learning can be conceptualized as either classical conditioning or instrumental learning. More recently researchers have suggested this distinction is forced and arbitrary, and that all learning can be thought of as simply associative learning. The concept of connectionism has grown out of the idea that people tend to form neural networks or patterns which may be the basis of the images that we create.

Cognitive Component

Psychologists use the term *cognitive* to refer to processes that have to do with knowing. Cognition, therefore, involves thinking, perceiving, abstracting, synthesizing, organizing, or any other process that allows the individual to conceptualize the nature of the external world and the nature of self. The self has been conceptualized as both agent and repository (a storage place) of society's values. The repository part of the self involves values (e.g., family, justice, sharing) and regulatory processes (e.g., persisting, following rules, abstaining from aggression), whereas the agent side is the autonomous side of the self that needs to be in control (James, 1890; Deci & Ryan,1991). We internalize both values and regulatory processes because, as social beings, we have a need for relatedness. When the autonomous side of the self is allowed to develop skills and competency by mastering the environment, the individual gains a sense of self-determination. In Chapter 14 I discuss the self in some detail.

Nature of Cognitions

What I will be talking about in this section are some of the things that psychologists have discovered about the nature of cognitions, many of them inferred from the behaviors of people in different situations.

Categories and labels. The brain has evolved to identify the main features or identifying characteristics of incoming stimulation. It is the process, for example, by which infants learn to recognize the faces of their parents. In order to make sense out of the complex world in which we live, the brain has been designed or organized not only to isolate features (figure as opposed to background, for example) but to identify abstract qualities that define a thing or group of things. Take, for example, the category called animals. Animals belong to a category because they share a number of similar defining attributes such as legs, body, life, and so forth. Horses, cows, and dogs are subcategories of the comprehensive category called animals. Behavioral neuroscientists suggest that when a distinct set of neurons are repeatedly fired, they form an interconnection (or a pattern in the brain) to which we attach names. These distinct patterns are not just the product of the external environment, but involve memories as well. When we can't see something—perhaps because something is in the way and therefore blocking our view—we "fill in" the missing information, presumably drawing upon our generic memory (sometimes called schemata) to supply what is missing. Generic memory contains the essential or defining features of a category

(Crick & Koch, 1992). Categories, in other words, allow us to summarize complex information into more generic forms, thereby freeing us from the necessity of having to keep track of endless pieces of specific information. We often give these categories names or labels such as house, dog, mountains.

Not only do we have categories and labels that help us identify objects or things, but we also have categories and labels that help us identify dispositions, emotions, or behaviors such as anger, happiness, sadness, aggression. Think for a minute how important it is that we are able to do this. Let's say that I am standing in the hallway and someone steps on my toe. The question I am inclined to ask myself is, how should I classify and label this behavior? If I label it "clumsy" I can forget it, but if I label it "aggressive" it is quite a different matter. Humans for the most part feel that they must retaliate for an aggressive act. Therefore, if I label the behavior as aggressive I probably should retaliate, and if I don't I may be forced to regard myself as a victim. Thus, how I label someone else's behavior has important implications for how I react to them. If I were to perceive and label the behavior of another person as selfish rather than altruistic, I might be more inclined to provide a poor job recommendation for that person, especially if the job involved helping handicapped children. If that same person were applying for a job as a construction worker, however, my perception of the person as more selfish than altruistic might have no effect on my recommendation.

Even more important, perhaps, is how I categorize and label my own behavior. Stanton Peele (1989) has argued that when people label themselves as "alcoholic" they begin to behave like one (they lose control of drinking, for example). It is the label, he argues, and not the alcohol, that creates, in large part, the behavior. Research has shown that people who drink as heavily but do not label themselves as "alcoholic" do not behave like alcoholics (they do not lose control of their drinking, for example). Peele argues that in our culture there is an association between being an alcoholic and the tendency to lose control when drinking alcohol. Thus the label I use to describe myself can be very important because labels carry with them a wide range of prescribed behaviors that I will unwittingly follow.

Beliefs, attitudes, and values. Many of our beliefs, attitudes, values are often initially copied from our parents. We come to believe, for example, that a certain political party is best for us and our country because we have listened to the arguments of our parents and observed how they voted. We develop the attitude that it is generally good to give to the poor because our parents did or, alternatively, that it is generally not good to give to the poor because we came to accept their idea that giving too much makes people dependent. We may come to value the family or the church because our parents valued them.

Many beliefs, attitudes, and values, however, are constructed based on our experiences and our own desires. Take, for example, the question of values. Values pertain to things we believe are important for achieving such things as success, happiness, health, fulfillment. As we experiment with the values of our parents, we may be inclined to change them. We might come to adopt the belief, principle, or rule, for example, that it is more important to live a full life than a long life. As a result of our new rule/principle, we treat new situations in very different ways.

There is a considerable amount of evidence to suggest that children and adolescents are indeed producers of their own development (Lerner, 1982, 1984). An adolescent might, for example, come to appreciate the fact that his or her behavior is leading to the destruction of the environment, which in turn will eventually reduce the length or quality of life. As a result, he or she decides to adopt a different lifestyle, one that will have less negative impact on the environment. The adolescent might decide, for example, to recycle bottles and cans, buy only products from companies that are environmentally sensitive, or eat foods that cause no negative impact on the environment. By changing values (rules or principles) he or she hopes to achieve new goals, not only on a personal level but for society at large.

Stereotypes. Stereotypes such as "blacks are good dancers," "men are aggressive," "women are complainers," "Italians are criminals" arise when we try to generalize from a limited number of examples in which a certain pattern of attributes was observed.

Because Michael Jackson is a good dancer doesn't mean that all blacks are necessarily good dancers, or because we read in the paper several accounts of men killing other men does not mean that all men are violent, or because we watch a television show in which the women are complaining doesn't mean that all women are complainers, or because the Mafia is made up of Italians doesn't mean all Italians are criminals. Stereotypes, in other words, are a special type or class of categories.

Stereotypes also arise because we have no personal knowledge and, in the absence of such personal knowledge, we simply adopt beliefs and attitudes of other people. Many of our stereotypes come from parents, teachers, and other significant people in our lives. We have stereotypes about many things, including how people should or will act at different ages, how people will act if they are religious, how people will act if they are rich or poor, and so forth.

Like beliefs, attitudes and values, stereotypes are often relatively stable. However, there is research which indicates that they can and often do change. The research has shown, for example, that stereotypes often tend to disappear when we encounter new examples that do not fit the expected category. When this happens, we are forced to make finer and finer distinctions. As this happens, the original stereotype (category) is hopelessly inadequate and the brain rejects it (see Langer, 1989, for a good description of what happens).

Cognitive dissonance theory. Cognitive dissonance theory has its roots in the idea that people need to experience cognitive consistency. Cognitive dissonance theory helps to explain why such things as categories, beliefs, attitudes, values and stereotypes are highly resistant to change. According to cognitive dissonance theory, humans are inclined to process information in such a way that it will be consistent with existing categories, beliefs, attitudes, values, stereotypes and behavior. The theory proposes that humans are inclined to ignore information that does not fit with existing beliefs and to seek out information that is consistent. What this means is that if we have a stereotype about old people, for example, we will be inclined to ignore exceptions and to process only those examples that are consistent with our beliefs.

Leon Festinger's work on cognitive dissonance had an enormous impact on how psychologists came to think about certain cognitive processes and especially about how to change behavior as well as cognitions. In a variety of experiments and situations, Festinger and others have shown that people are inclined, at least under certain conditions, to make their cognitions consistent with their behavior. This was a radical idea at one time because people felt that it was clear that cognitions control behavior and not the reverse. While it is true that cognitions do control behavior, what Festinger was able to show is that you can change cognitions and thereby behavior by first getting people to change their behavior. Often what you had to do was to "trick" people into changing their behavior. Once their behavior changed they would change their cognitions.

Implicit theories. It has been suggested that people have personal theories about the world and about themselves, something called "implicit theories" (Epstein, 1990; Dweck, 1991). These implicit theories are hypotheses, models, beliefs, that we have about the nature of the external world (world theories) and about what we need to do to satisfy our desires in this world (self-theories). They are called implicit theories because they often exist at the preconscious level. In psychology, the word *conscious* typically means we are fully aware of the reasons for our actions, and the word *unconscious* means we are not aware of the reasons for our actions. Preconscious means that we could become conscious of the reasons for our actions given the right guidance or perhaps the right set of circumstances (Epstein, 1990). Self-knowledge pertains to becoming aware of the reasons for our actions. It means becoming aware of the respository and agent side of the self.

Unlike scientific theories that are more rational and designed to make sense out of an existing body of facts, implicit theories often involve more irrational and intuitive thinking. Epstein has proposed that implicit theories often come out of a different system for processing information, a system that he calls the experiential system.

In the past, psychologists talked a great deal about expectations. The concept of expectations was employed to explain why different people with different desires, needs, or experiences would see things differently (Bruner, 1992). In recent years, it has become more and more apparent that the concept of expectations is often too narrow to explain the rather complex patterns of thought that link people's actions to their perceptions of the external world and their conceptualizations of their skills and abilities. As a result, the concept of implicit theories has begun to emerge as a major new theoretical concept.

While implicit theories can be learned, at least in part, from modeling the behaviors of others, listening to the views of others, and reading what others have to say, implicit theories are for the most thought to result from our own experiences, our own interactions with the world, our own successes and failures. In short, they are very personal.

Does the external world cause behavior or do implicit theories? It has been suggested from time to time that such things as happiness depend on whether or not the environment is providing us with satisfying rewards. According to this view, the way to increase happiness in the world is to create a perfect environment. This has been one of the basic assumptions of the learning theory put forth by Skinner. But what is a perfect environment? To answer that question, you simply need to ask people what would make them happy. Unfortunately, when you do this, people do not agree on the answer. Cognitive theories do not see the environment as the appropriate place to focus. They argue that while the environment is obviously important, it is often very difficult or even impossible to change the environment. The best thing to do under such circumstances is to change the way you view the environment. Further, they argue, what makes people happy is highly subjective and depends on what people believe makes them happy. This idea was summarized centuries ago by the emperor Marcus Aurelius who said: "If you are pained by the external things, it is not they that disturb you, but your own judgment of them. And it is in your power to wipe out that judgment now."

Cognitive theories typically subscribe to the idea

PRACTICAL APPLICATION 2.3

Becoming Mindful of Your Cognitive Processes

In her book *Mindfulness*, Ellen Langer (1989) makes the case that our behavior is often mindless. We set out for work without thinking about how to get there, yet we arrive safely and on time. While mindless or automatic behavior is useful because it frees our conscious mind to think about other things, mindless behavior often means we get into ruts. That is, even when we should change our habits we don't, and as a result, we keep doing the same things over and over. If we want to change we need to become mindful of our cognitions. When we become mindful we gain the power to change and control things. As we shall see later, the ability to control or simply the belief that one can control his or her destiny is important for physical and psychological health.

How does one become mindful of one's cognitions? There are a number of things you can do. Each time you decide to do something, ask yourself if there is something else you might do instead. Several things happen when you do this. First, you learn to generate alternatives. If you are going to make a decision you obviously need to have alternatives. Generating alternatives is a creative act and is the basis for all behavioral change. When you generate alternatives you learn to appreciate the fact that life is always made up of alternatives. Second, you gain a sense of control. When you make decisions you become aware of the fact that life is not just happening to you but you are making it happen. Third, you learn not only to make decisions but you learn *how* to make decisions. Decision making is something that people need to practice. If you learn to make decisions about simple things, you will develop the ability to make decisions about important things. Fourth, you learn

to take control of your thinking process. The more you think about your thinking, the more you will become aware of your thinking/cognitions and the more you will be able to control your thinking. By forcing yourself to make a conscious decision about things that you do, you slowly become aware of the fact that you often do things for reasons. The next time you turn on the television ask yourself: "Why am I turning on the television? Is there something else I could do?" You can use this technique for almost everything you do. If you find yourself making a value judgment such as "I hate living in this climate, this city, working with these people," ask yourself exactly what it is you don't like and if you want to do something about it. This forces you to make finer and finer distinctions. In doing so, you learn to isolate or identify what it is that you don't like. You might discover, using this approach, that it is not the city you are living in that you dislike but rather the neighborhood in which you live, the house, or even some particular thing such as traffic. If you come to realize that it is your neighborhood and not the city, you have gained a great deal of power. Now, instead of having to quit your job and leave your friends in order to be happy, you only have to move to a new house or apartment. What you have done is turned what appeared to be an insurmountable problem into a very manageable one. You discovered that you can become happier without having to quit your job and leave your friends. As a result, you have gained a great deal of power and control over your life. It all happened because you learned to become aware of your cognitions.

that what you see or feel depends to a very large degree on your beliefs (or, more simply, on your implicit theories). In our society we often hold the view (an implicit theory) that we cannot be happy unless our stomachs are full. Yet in cultures where there is a chronic shortage of food, people learn to be happy in spite of the fact their stomachs are not always full. They take pleasure, for example, in being with their families or in laughing when their children make faces to tell jokes.

Happiness, in other words, is highly subjective. It depends on what you have decided it is that brings happiness. People often erect barriers that limit their ability to experience happiness. They say to themselves: "I will be happy when I retire" or "I will be happy when I have a sports car" or "I will be happy when I get a gold medal" or "I will be happy when I am married." When you erect barriers that do not allow you to be happy, you can tell your brain that the emotion called happiness cannot surface until a certain set of conditions is met.

There are many people who have decided that happiness is something they want to experience as often as possible. As a result, they can find happiness in simple things such as a cat chasing its tail, a wild flower, a compliment they receive from another person. Some of the happiest people in the world are people who have come close to death because of an accident or an illness. As a result of this event, they come to appreciate simply being alive and being capable of experiencing the world in which they live.

According to this view, being happy is a state of mind. It is the result of decisions we make. We know, for example, that optimists tend to be happy people whereas pessimist do not. Optimists see what is good while pessimists see what is bad or malevolent. Research points to the fact that optimism can be learned. Martin Seligman (1991), one of the leading psychologists in the world, has written a book entitled *Learned Optimism*, a book that tells people how to become more optimistic. It may well be, as Seligman and others have argued, that optimism is the result of learning to adopt a new way of viewing the world, a new implicit theory of life.

Does this mean the external world is not important? Quite the contrary. We gain happiness through our senses, through exercising skills, through exercising competency in the external world, and through interacting with people in the external world. There is no question about that. But what you decide will make you happy in the external world is a matter of personal choice. There are many ways to stimulate our senses, to exercise competency, and to experience the joys of so-cial relations. If you accept the message of the advertising industry that happiness is found in wearing the right clothes, driving the right car, or drinking the right beer, you will cut yourself off from other means of experiencing happiness. Many people have found that happiness does not require an abundance of material things. They have learned that happiness can be found in such things as the environment, in developing friendships, in helping other people. In short, it can be found in the things that are constantly around us, things that do not require money.

Attribution Theory: Perceiving the Causes of Behavior

In recent years, a great deal of research has been done on the question of how humans come to perceive the causes of behavior. This issue falls under the heading of "attribution theory." To what cause does a person attribute a given behavior? How does he account for the fact that he failed? How does he account for the fact that he succeeded? When a person notices her heart is beating faster, how does she account for this fact? Will her interpretation affect her subsequent behavior? If someone's perceptions (interpretations) about the cause of behavior affects subsequent behavior, then we have good evidence that cognitive factors are not just secondary or incidental but are in fact fundamental to behavior itself. That is, cognitive factors play a central role in the arousal, direction, and persistence of behavior.

An experiment by Nisbett and Schachter (1966) illustrates how cognitive factors can affect behavior. They showed that humans could be made to tolerate high levels of shock by persuading them that their autonomic responses, such as fast heart rate, were due not to the shock but rather to a pill they had taken. In their experiment, Nisbett and Schachter asked subjects to take a series of electric shocks of steadily increasing intensity, telling them to indicate (1) when the shocks became painful and (2) when the shocks became too painful to tolerate. Before receiving the shocks, the subjects were given a pill. Some were told that the pill would produce hand tremors, palpitations, and other autonomic responses. Others were told that the pill would produce a variety of symptoms that were not autonomic. Actually, the pill was a placebo (it had no physiological effects).

If attribution theory is correct (that people are inclined to look for reasonable explanations for their behavior, including autonomic responses), then the subjects who thought the pill would increase autonomic activity would be inclined to attribute their autonomic responses to the pill, while the other subjects would be inclined to attribute their autonomic responses to the shock. Subjects who did not perceive their autonomic responses as due to the shock should not be as sensitive to it. As a result, they should be willing to tolerate higher levels of shock. Nisbett and Schachter found that, indeed, subjects who were told the pill would produce autonomic responses tolerated shock levels four times as great as the other subjects. These results indicate that cognitive factors play an important role even in something as basic as the perception of pain.

Individual Differences

Because people come from different backgrounds, because they have different experiences, and because they learn to think differently, they react very differently to the same event. Whether they are optimists or pessimists, for example, has important implications for how people will react. In this book, I will repeatedly address the question of individual differences. Let me introduce you to individual differences by talking about the distinction between people whom we call internals and people whom we call externals.

Locus of Control Theory: Internal and External Causes

Heider (1958) proposed that ordinary people, in their concern with knowing the causes of behavior, differentiate between two types of causes: internal and external. People who are internals perceive that the cause of behavior lies within themselves, whereas people who are externals believe that the cause of behavior lies outside themselves. One difference between external and internal determinants of behavior is that only

sources of action attributed to the person (internal) can be labeled "intentional." For example, if someone were to step on your toe, you might arrive at two different conclusions: that she did it intentionally (internal) or that it was an accident (external). How you assess the situation will, of course, affect how you will respond to the situation. "Should I ignore the fact that she stepped on my toe, or should I retaliate?" Interestingly, some people are more likely to use an external frame of reference to label an event, while other people are more likely to use an internal frame of reference. Because of this difference, "internals" often react somewhat differently than "externals" to the same environmental event. We will return to this difference later. For the moment it is sufficient to note that humans are inclined to look for causes and in the process to label events in some systematic fashion.

Summary

Cognition involves thinking, perceiving, abstracting, synthesizing, organizing, or any other process that allows the individual to conceptualize the nature of the external world and the nature of self. The self has been conceptualized as both agent and repository (a storage place) of society's values. The repository part of the self involves values (e.g., family, justice, sharing) and regulatory processes (e.g., persisting, following rules, abstaining from aggression) whereas the agent side is the autonomous side of the self that needs to be in control.

Cognitive processes give rise to categories to which we attach labels. Cognitive processes also give rise to beliefs, attitudes, and values. Stereotypes are a special type of category that often develops out of limited information or the tendency to adopt the beliefs and attitudes of other people, especially people who serve as role models. Beliefs, attitudes, values, and stereotypes are often very resistant to change. One explanation for this can be found in cognitive dissonance theory which suggests that humans are inclined to process incoming information so that it is consistent with existing cognitions.

Implicit theories are hypotheses, models, beliefs that we have about the nature of the external world

(world theories) and about what we need to do to satisfy our desires in this world (self-theories). People are often not fully aware of them, but they guide behavior nevertheless. Implicit theories can, for example, play an important role in such things being happy or contented.

According to attribution theory, human have a natural tendency to look for the causes of their behavior. Nisbett and Schachter illustrated the importance of the attribution process in the study of pain (shock)discussed earlier. They showed that misattribution (mislabeling) of the source of increased autonomic activity was sufficient to decrease a person's sensitivity to pain (shock). Subjects who thought that their elevated arousal level was due to a placebo pill, not to the shock itself, tolerated shock levels four times as high as other subjects.

Humans tend to differ along a continuum that goes from perceiving the causes of things as due to internal factors to perceiving the causes of things as due to external factors. This tendency accounts for the wide range of individual differences that we observe. The labels people use frequently provide a clue to the way they interpret, perceive, or think about the cause of an event. Research has shown that the way we label an event—be it an internal event, such as a change in arousal level, or an external event, such as having someone step on our toe—can affect not only how we feel but how we react.

The Nature of Theories and Models

The Search for Critical Variables
That Govern Behavior

In the past, psychologists have tended to construct models and theories of motivation that are based solely on principles of biology, principles of learning, or principles of cognition. Often these models can explain a limited body of facts but are unable to explain other facts. In short, these models are useful but limited in scope.

Exactly why scientists have tended to base their theories and models exclusively on biological, learning, or cognitive principles is not altogether clear. One reason may be that it is difficult to integrate principles derived from different approaches. The language and assumptions of biology, learning, and cognition are quite different. For example, biological principles typically assume that the reason for a behavior is laid down in the genetic structure. Thus, a person behaves aggressively because his or her genetic structure determines which responses will be made. Learning theory, in contrast, tends to view aggressive behavior as a learned pattern. Sometime in the person's past, he or she was rewarded for behaving aggressively. Cognitive theory might view aggression as a means of regaining control over the environment or exercising power. Therefore, a person behaves aggressively to avoid losing everything he or she has worked so hard to get, or simply because exercising power is satisfying. It would be difficult for any theorist to reconcile these differences by means of a single set of assumptions.

Another possible reason theorists have tended to explain behavior according to a single set of principles is that one of the goals of science is to simplify—to use the fewest number of concepts or assumptions required to account for phenomena. One obvious way of attaining this goal is to adopt only a single set of principles and stretch these principles rather than add new ones.

Still another reason may be that the nature of scientific analysis leads scientists to study very limited phenomena. That is, since it is necessary to control all variables in a scientific study, the scientist is forced to deal with only parts or aspects of a larger problem. It follows that scientists tend to select those parts of problems that they are most competent to analyze. The biologically oriented psychologist will focus on behaviors that appear to be determined biologically; the learning theorist will tend to focus on those that appear to be the result of learning. Thus, although all are working on the same global problem, the behaviors they select are quite different. A problem arises, therefore, when the theorist attempts to construct general principles on the basis of a limited set of observations. A biologically oriented psychologist interested in understanding aggression, for example, might focus his or her research on the relationship between hormone levels and aggression, while a learning theorist might focus on the repetition of aggression following rewards and no rewards. The biologically oriented psychologist would discover, as we shall see, that hormones do affect aggressive behavior; the learning-oriented psychologist would discover, as we shall also see, that rewards also affect it. If each of these scientists were to construct a theory on the basis of his or her limited set of observations, we would have two very different theories about aggression.

In recent years, more and more attempts have been made to integrate divergent data and principles into a single theory. Pribram (1976), for example, has integrated both learning and cognitive principles into his basically biological view of human behavior. This approach appears to have its origin in the productive interaction of three scientists who initially came together with somewhat divergent views of human beings (Miller, Galanter, & Pribram, 1960).

Testing the Generality of Theories

The goal of science is to find general principles rather than specific ones. The discovery of general principles permits a wide variety of specific facts to be organized and understood. Often quite diverse facts can be integrated by certain general (typically abstract) principles. When a theory has been formulated, usually on a limited set of observations, the next step is to see how general the theory is. Can it predict a variety of behaviors other than those on which it is based? If it can, then it is assumed that the principles discovered from a limited set of observations are general principles. Darwin's theory of evolution is a theory that grew out of a limited set of observations. When Darwin applied his ideas to a wide variety of species, he concluded that the idea of natural selection was a general one that could explain the changes in all species.

Although it is desirable to see whether a theory is generally applicable, the tendency to generalize must be treated with caution. For example, there is considerable evidence that many behaviors are learned, but there is also considerable evidence that learning is constrained by the structure of the nervous system. Accordingly, before we try to use principles of learning—often derived from research with animals—to modify human behavior, we need to consider carefully

such things as the structure of the human nervous system and the way humans interpret events. Although there are many similarities between the nervous systems of humans and animals, there are also differences. There also appear to be major differences in the cognitive structures of humans and animals. The exact implications of this fact are still not totally understood. Nevertheless, we must constantly remind ourselves that these differences are probably not an evolutionary accident: they presumably arose for a very good reason. Humans are different from other animals, and it is our job to understand the exact nature of the differences.

Current Focus of Motivation Theory: Individual Differences

The main problem with most of the early theories of motivation was their failure to account for individual differences. Many of the theories of the 1950s were about so-called average humans. (A notable exception was Atkinson's theory of achievement motivation, to be discussed in Chapter 13.) Data averaged from random samples of rats, pigeons, and humans were used to tell us how the average person learned. Since then we have come to realize that most of us don't behave in this way. Humans differ because of sex, age, temperament, past conditioning, cognitive structures, momentary stress, goals, and recent failures and successes. Each of these factors can cause us to respond in distinctive ways to our environment. It is these often-dynamic factors that we need to understand if we are to explain why different humans do quite different things under the same environmental conditions.

Current studies of motivation are trying to come to grips with the question of individual differences. Why is it that some people become obese while others do not? Why do some people take drugs while others do not? Why do some people like to jump from planes while others do not?

At one time, psychologists operated on the assumption that all motivational systems (hunger, thirst, sex, and so on) could be described by the same set of general laws, but there is now good reason to believe that each system is more or less unique, being both similar and dissimilar to other systems. Further, there is reason to believe that a given system (such as hunger) is not the same in all people. That is, basic individual differences are associated with each system. Therefore, the current focus is on explaining how different people will react when a given motivational system is activated. If these systems are more or less unique, are they also independent? There is good reason to believe they do interact. The question then arises of what happens when two or more systems are activated simultaneously. Do they tend to compete for control of behavior, or is the person so constructed that one system always takes precedence over another? What are the implications of having different motive systems that need to be satisfied? Does this ever lead to stress and unhappiness? What role do our cognitions play in controlling the simultaneous activation of different motive systems?

Although explanations of individual differences are important, any theory worth its salt should be able to predict individual behavior patterns. At least, that is our goal. As we all know, it is easy to explain at the end of a game why a team won or lost. It is far more difficult to predict ahead of time whether it is going to win or lose. If we know the critical variables, we should be able to predict. Therefore, the best criterion for determining whether we have identified the important variables—the best criterion for a good theory—is to take some behavior we think we understand and predict whether it will occur given that certain variables are present, absent, or combined in certain ways. In short, good explanations of behavior are based on studies that have shown that certain variables are truly antecedents of a given behavior.

Summary

In their attempts to account for behavior, scientists have based their approaches on different sets of assumptions, all of which have proved partly true. The biologically oriented researcher found there was evidence for a genetic basis to behavior. The learning theorist was able to demonstrate that learning is important. The cognitive psychologist has been able to demonstrate that cognitions are important. Today we

realize that evidence that supports one set of assumptions does not invalidate the others. Most psychologists accept the position that each of these approaches can tell us something about why we do what we do. The present goal, therefore, is to understand the nature of the interaction of biological, learned, and cognitive factors. In accepting the idea that behavior may be the product of an interaction, we have also had to accept the possibility that the nature of the interaction may vary from person to person. We have had to recognize that important individual differences exist, be they biological, learned, or cognitive.

Some Examples of a Components Approach

I started this chapter by arguing that it is necessary to adopt what I call a components approach to the analysis of motivation. To illustrate this approach, I have selected two common behaviors to analyze, to see whether we can devise some hypotheses about why people engage in them. These hypotheses (as opposed to explanations) are based on the assumption that behavior is the product of biological, learned, or cognitive factors or of some combination of these three basic classes of behavioral determinants. Let us start by examining the current craze for running.

Motivation for Running

On the surface, running appears to be a straightforward activity. People state that they decide to run in order to "get into shape," to "lose weight," or to "improve their health." No doubt these are some of the reasons that people initially run, but there are also less obvious reasons. Some people run, they confess, in order to get away from their spouses or to avoid having lunch with their colleagues or to escape from the close confines of their office or house. So far, all the explanations I have listed are couched in avoidance terms. People run to escape from "being fat," "a noxious spouse," "an unpleasant environment," or something else. What are some of the positive reasons? The positive reasons for running often emerge when people have engaged in running for a while. It is hard for most people to see that puffing and sweating on a hot day or freezing on a cold day can be pleasant. It is only when they have had a chance to experience the effects of running that they honestly say they do it because it makes them feel good or look good or because the act of running is itself pleasant and satisfying. The immediate question is how an activity that appears to demand so much effort (and sometimes pain) can be pleasant.

Before we try to answer this question, we need to understand that why people do something initially and why they continue to do it may be unrelated. This simple fact is very important. Most of us are aware that we often have good intentions that somehow fail to get translated into long-term behavioral change. I call this "the New Year's resolution phenomenon." People often change their behavior for a day, a week, sometimes even a month, but more often than not the change turns out to be transitory. Once the initial motivation fades, there is nothing to maintain the behavior.

What, then, is the motivation that maintains running, as distinct from the motivation for taking up running? We should start by noting that not all people who try running continue to do it. Some, however, develop signs of being addicted. If they stop running for a few days, they experience a negative physiological or psychological state that is analogous to withdrawal from a drug. They have a compulsion to engage in the activity on a regular basis, just as a drug addict feels a compulsion to take a drug regularly. The obvious question that needs to be answered is whether running produces in this group of people some kind of chemical output that has motivating and possibly addicting properties.

The answer is a qualified yes. It appears that running (and aerobic exercise in general, such as swimming, cycling, walking, rowing, and cross-country skiing) does stimulate the output of several chemicals. Norepinephrine, for example, will increase to as much as four and one half times normal (Davis, 1973; Howley, 1976). Since increased norepinephrine levels have been implicated in feelings of elation and euphoria, whereas low levels have been implicated in feel-

ings of depression (Post et al., 1978; Schildkraut & Kety, 1967), there is reason to argue that people may run in order to experience increased outputs of this or related chemicals. Can people become addicted to norepinephrine? Again, the answer is a qualified yes. Addiction to amphetamines, which produce arousal and euphoria, has been documented for some time. Among other effects, amphetamines stimulate the output of norepinephrine and dopamine, and it has been hypothesized that people take amphetamines specifically for this purpose. It makes sense, therefore, that people will continue to perform a response, such as running, that stimulates the output of one of these rewarding chemicals.

A number of studies have shown that aerobic exercise alleviates anxiety (for example, Morgan & Horstman, 1976) and depression (Greist et al., 1979). Although these studies must be considered preliminary because several alternative explanations have not been completely ruled out, the results are consistent with a number of other physiological findings (Ledwidge, 1980). Concerning anxiety, exercise has been shown to be a muscle relaxant (Baekeland, 1970; Baekeland & Lasky, 1966) and to reduce lactate, an acid that has been found to play a key role in anxiety symptoms (Clarke, 1975; Larson & Michelman, 1973; Pitts, 1969). In fact, there is evidence that aerobic exercise produces a general decrease in the adrenocortical response to stress (Tharp, 1975; White, Ismail, & Bottoms, 1976). This means that a person who engages in aerobic exercise will experience a less severe reaction to physical stress. Concerning depression, we have the evidence already discussed above implicating low levels of norepinephrine in depressive disorders. The fact that running increases norepinephrine output offers a compelling argument that exercise can alleviate feelings of depression. Further, there is evidence that chronic fatigue, a common complaint of depressives, is alleviated by aerobic exercise (Kraines, 1957). The fact that depressives exhibit less slow-wave sleep (Gresham, Agnew, & Williams, 1965), together with the fact that aerobic exercise increases slow-wave sleep (Griffin & Trinder, 1978), suggests another important link between exercise and depression (Ledwidge, 1980). Finally, there is evidence that running improves short-term performance on mental tasks (Tomporowski & Ellis, 1986). The implication is that for people who want to improve their cognitive functioning, running would have obvious reinforcing effects.

It is frequently observed that people who run tend to increase the amount they run. Returning to the analogy between running and drug addiction, we might say that these people are showing a tolerance effect. That is, they are increasing their dosage level in order to experience the same effect. If people run to experience the effects of norepinephrine or some other chemical, it makes good sense that they should tend to increase the amount of time they devote to running, for two reasons. First, as their bodies become conditioned, it is likely that they will have to run longer to get the same output of norepinephrine and dopamine. Second, and not unrelated to the first, human motivation appears to have the character of an "opponent process" (Solomon & Corbit, 1974). For every process set in motion, as we have seen, the body develops an opposing process to return itself to its original state. Thus, when a drug stimulates one type of reaction, the body initiates another reaction that opposes the action of the drug. Norepinephrine and dopamine appear to produce arousal and euphoria; the opposing process of the body would be one that reduced arousal and counteracted euphoria. People who take amphetamines often experience fatigue some time after they have taken the drug. According to the opponent process model of drug addiction, this reaction is due in part to the operation of the opponent process. It is assumed that the opponent process occurs more quickly and becomes stronger each time it is activated as the result of taking a drug, and a person would need to take larger doses of the drug to override this opponent process. In other words, because the opponent process becomes stronger each time it is activated, the person develops a tolerance for the drug. Using the same line of reasoning, we could argue that the body develops a tolerance for the chemicals produced by running, and so a runner needs to run more to get the same reaction.

If running is analogous to an addictive drug, why doesn't everybody who tries running become addicted to it? The most plausible explanation is that not everybody finds the chemical changes reinforcing.

According to Schildkraut and Kety (1967), some people (such as those who experience depression) have a deficit of norepinephrine. Such people, according to their hypothesis, would be inclined to find running rewarding. Hans Eysenck (1967) has argued that certain people (extraverts) tend to have subnormal arousal levels and that these people are more inclined to pick out situations or take drugs that increase their arousal level. Thus the failure of some people to become addicted is not altogether unexpected.

Our explanation of why people run is, at this point, a hypothesis. Further research is needed to verify all facets of this explanation. Moreover, even if some people run for the reasons given above, it does not mean that all do. Psychologists have been inclined to assume that there is one and only one reason for a given behavior. It may well be that some people run simply to lose weight and do not find running rewarding, aside from its results. I have talked to many people who run. Most of them say they enjoy the activity, but a number state that they do not and that they do it only for extrinsic reasons. They say that their doctor told them they must exercise to control their blood pressure or that they want to get in shape for another sport, such as skiing or racquetball. If it is true that some people do not find the activity intrinsically rewarding while others do, it may well be that these two groups differ in resting arousal levels, resting norepinephrine levels, or even something else that has not yet been suggested as a mechanism that mediates the rewards associated with running.

When people say they run because they want to lose weight or because their doctor told them to, we label such motivation as cognitive. Remember that I suggested that all motives probably reflect the interaction of biological, learned, and cognitive components. It seems quite possible that people run not only because it makes them feel good but because they enjoy the attention they get when they look younger and sexier and can wear more stylish clothes. Also, people sometimes feel virtuous when they have done something they perceive required effort, discipline, and determination. These would be cognitive factors. What about learning? If a person performs a response, such as running, at the same time each day, time of day could become a sufficient cue to elicit that response. Learning theorists have shown that once a response has become a habit (usually because it has been rewarded for a period of time), that response will often be emitted for some time in the absence of a reward. Even if it is rewarded only occasionally, it will often continue at a steady and predictable rate for long periods. Therefore, it seems reasonable to suggest that sometimes a person runs out of habit. A person might run also because other rewards, not directly linked to running, are contingent upon it. The opportunity to enjoy the company of friends might induce some people either to run in the first place or to continue running. Because the activity of running itself would then not be providing the reward but would only be instrumental in its acquisition, the behavior would be viewed as being governed by the principles of learning.

It should also be noted that the rewards for a given behavior may shift over time. It is quite possible, for example, that after a runner has become trim and sexy, or when tolerance has increased until the activity provides little biological reward, other rewards come along to maintain the behavior. Enjoying the company of other runners could, for example, come to act as the primary source of motivation for this activity. As such, running would be viewed as occurring for learned rather than cognitive or biological reasons.

Before we leave the topic of running, it should be mentioned that there is a great deal of concern about the high rate of divorce and marital problems among runners (Lowther, 1979). Some therapists have noted that running often leads to a change in personality, which may contribute to marital breakdown. For example, people who take up running often gain self-confidence. Such a change might motivate someone to extricate himself or herself from an already unhappy relationship. Why self-confidence should increase as a result of running is not altogether clear. It could be due to chemical changes or to changes in one's self-image. There are several other reasons that running might lead to marital breakdown. The addictive properties of running might leave one spouse alone and neglected for long periods. Or it may be that a person took up running to escape his or her spouse. Thus the marital breakdown might have begun long before the running,

so that running was the result, not the cause, of the marital problem.

Although this discussion is interesting in itself, it was included here to make several points. First, what appears to be a simple behavior may be due to a complex set of processes working together. Second, the reason someone initially engages in a behavior may be quite different from the reason he or she continues that behavior. For example, we noted that a person may initiate a behavior for cognitive reasons (doctor's recommendation), come to do it for biological reasons (norepinephrine and/or dopamine output) or psychological reasons (to reduce anxiety and/or depression), and finally maintain it out of habit or learning (to be with friends). In the final analysis, probably all three components are jointly responsible for maintaining the response over a long period. People run for a variety of reasons. The same person may run for different reasons at different times. One cannot infer motivation from simply seeing the behavior. The reasons that each individual runs can be uncovered only when we understand the individual.

Although running may be maintained to a large degree by chemical outputs, it must be emphasized again that this is a hypothesis. It is a good hypothesis because the converging data all seem to point to chemicals (such as norepinephrine) as a possible common mediating variable. That is, we can explain the relationship between certain events because we have identified an underlying common variable. Frequently in the field of psychology, converging data are used to formulate possible explanations about behavior. When more and more data point to the same mediating variable (such as norepinephrine), we tend to view that variable as a good candidate to explain the behavior. An important question for the motivation theorist is whether such common mediating variables are motivational. That is, can they be considered important in the arousal, energization, and persistence of behavior?

Motivation for Listening to Rock Music

Music is one of the most important sources of thrills that people report they experience. Table 2.1 shows what a sample of people have said gives them "thrills."

What motivates people to go to rock concerts?

Table 2.1 Some Things That Give People Thrills

Stimulus	Percent Respondents
Musical passages	96
Scenes in movie, play, ballet or book	92
Great beauty in nature or art	87
Physical contact with another person	78
Climactic moment in opera	72
Sexual activity	70
Nostalgic moments	70
Watching emotional interactions between other people	67
Viewing a beautiful painting, photograph or sculpture	67
Moments of inspiration	65
Something momentous and unexpected happening	63
Seeing or reading about something heroic	59
Sudden insight, understanding, solution to a problem	57
Particular moments in sports event	52
Success in a competitive endeavor	49
Particular fragrances	39
Physical exercise	36
Parades	26

(From A. Goldstein, "Thrills in Response to Music and Other Stimuli.," *Physiological Psychology*, 1980, *8*, 126-129. Copyright © 1980. Reprinted by permission of the Psychonomic Society, Inc.)

It is interesting to note that on such a list, musical passages ranked highest. Music is very pervasive in our lives and thus becomes a challenge to explain. Why is it that people will do such things as buy musical recordings, go to concerts, learn to play instruments, sing?

Presumably we come to appreciate music, at least in part, because of cognitive processes. We listen to new records because they have different lyrics, different melodies, and different combinations of notes and instruments. Hunt (1963) has argued that we are motivated by newness or incongruity—that is, the difference that exists between what we already know and what we have just experienced or are about to experience. Walker (1974) has suggested that a new piece of music can provide the psychological complexity that we seek after we have become familiar with other pieces. In his book *Emotion and Meaning in Music,* Leonard Meyer (1961) argues that when we listen to music we generate expectations about how things will proceed, based on our past experience with music. When the music conforms to our expectations we relax, but the more it deviates the more we become tense. He goes on to argue that it is the artful juxtaposing of tiny expectations, frustrated and then fulfilled, that is the basis of our emotional reaction to music. Others have extended this argument to suggest that the link between how we cognitively process music and the emotions we experience are, in part, unlearned reactions that can be understood in terms of the link between cognitions and such areas in the brain as the limbic system (Rosenfeld, 1985).

In addition to the motivating properties arising from cognitive variables, there are motivating properties that come as a result of previous learning. We may like a piece of music because it stimulates pleasant memories or evokes pleasant fantasies. The voices of certain singers appear to be able to conjure up images of romance or just plain sex. Under certain conditions, a piece of music could conceivably evoke feelings of well-being or even self-confidence if in the past the music had been associated with this psychological state. All of us have probably at one time or another suddenly remembered a pleasant experience that was associated with a particular piece of music. We may even deliberately play a piece of music in order to evoke the pleasurable state that it elicits.

For a number of people, mainly adolescents, rock music is best appreciated when it is played loud. What makes loudness an integral quality of rock music for some people? We know from several sources that sounds above a certain loudness level (approximately 80 decibels, abbreviated dB) tend to produce certain reliable physiological changes. Live rock music is often played at well over 100 dB in a closed room. If you happen to sit near a speaker, it may be as high as 120-140 dB—a level that can produce permanent hearing loss (see Dey, 1970; Fern, 1976; Mills, 1975, 1978). The main physiological change produced by high noise levels is increased arousal. As we have already noted, arousal has to do with the level of activity in the central nervous system. A structure in the brain, the reticular activating system, appears to govern arousal levels. As sensory input bombards the arousal system, the system responds by activating the brain. From a motivational point of view, moderate levels of arousal are experienced as pleasurable. In fact, humans will often seek out stimulation in order to experience moderate to high levels of arousal. We might ask, therefore, whether listening to rock music is motivated, at least in part, by the desire to experience increases in arousal.

Given what we know about the relationship of noise, arousal, and pleasure, this explanation of why people like to listen to loud music seems to be grounded in basic science. A problem arises, however, if we try to explain why people often like to listen to loud rock music with friends as well as to dance to rock music. The problem comes from the knowledge that social interactions and exercise also produce arousal. If a person is listening to rock music to experience moderate arousal, then dancing and social interactions will increase arousal beyond a moderate level. Since high levels of arousal have been hypothesized to be aversive (Hebb, 1955), why do people seem to enjoy listening to rock music while dancing and socializing? Why do some people, in fact, actively seek out such situations? Perhaps adolescents need a great deal of stimulation in order to experience moderate arousal, or it may be that there are times when very high levels of arousal can result in pleasure (Berlyne, 1960). Schachter and Singer (1962) have shown that relatively high levels of arousal can intensify an already pleasurable reaction. If a person is already enjoying the company of friends, rock music together with dancing may enhance this already pleasurable state. Music and dancing are often an integral part of festivals and celebrations and have been for thousands of years. Obviously there is something about music and dancing that makes one feel good or possibly enhances an already festive mood.

Like running, the activity of listening to rock music demonstrates that a common behavior can have several components that vary from time to time. Research clearly indicates that some type of biological factor is involved in listening to rock music played at noise levels above 80 dB. The fact that people listen to rock music when they could more readily obtain the same arousal level by running around the block indicates that something more is involved. Obviously, the structure of the music and the associations it elicits are important factors in the total reaction to it. Somehow all these factors interact to produce a particular sensation.

Given that all these factors may contribute to the final motivation, can we ever know exactly which factors are involved in a particular person's motivation, and in what proportions? Is it possible that one person is motivated mainly by biological components, another mainly by cognitive components, and yet another mainly by learned components? The answer is yes to both questions. It is possible, within limits, to determine whether one of these factors is more important for one person than for another. We could make this determination by designing a series of controlled experiments to compare the reactions of several people. It would be a good exercise for the student in experimental psychology to design just such an experiment. Whether it would be worth the time and the effort required to carry it out is another question.

Before leaving this example, let me summarize why I included it. Like the previous example, it demonstrates that motivation, even esthetic appreciation, involves the interaction of three basic components. In addition, the example demonstrates that the motivation for a particular activity may be enhanced or even changed by other activities that also have motivational properties. Specifically, rock music is often used in social situations that themselves are arousal-producing. Further, people often dance to music in social situations, and dancing has been implicated not only in arousal but in the output of norepinephrine. The joining together—or, more precisely, the pooling—of motivation is a fascinating thing to note about human behavior. It is a phenomenon that characterizes much of daily human motivation. Rarely does one motive arise in isolation from other motives. For that reason, we need to understand not only what components are involved in each motive system, but how different motive systems interact.

Summary

The two examples discussed in this section—the motivation for running and the motivation for listening to rock music—illustrate why it is necessary to consider biological, learned, and cognitive factors when we try to explain a particular behavior. Although most, if not all, behaviors have a biological component, biological factors can never be viewed as the sole determinants of human behavior. Humans are subjected to a wide variety of external rewards, which we know have a profound effect in modifying the direction of their behavior. Further, we must recognize that biological factors frequently find their expression because humans have learned a response that stimulates a biological mechanism. This pattern appears to reflect the fact that many human responses are not prewired but can be acquired because we possess general reward mecha-

nisms. People who run, it can be argued, have learned to perform a response in order to experience a feeling of euphoria—a feeling that all people are inherently capable of experiencing—provided they find a means of tapping that system by making a response that will activate it. Cognitions, too, play a profound role in human behavior. Our ability to appreciate music, for example, appears to be mediated to a very large degree by our ability to respond to the pattern of stimulation that music provides.

Main Points

1. The working definition of motivation is that motivation is concerned with understanding how dispositions can lead to action through the interaction of biological, learned and cognitive processes or components.

2. Three basic components are involved in all motivational systems: a biological component, a learned component, and a cognitive component.

3. The biological approach to motivation has traditionally assumed that behavior is ultimately tied to genetic structure.

4. Open and closed programs have been proposed as a means of accounting for the varying amounts of learning that are involved in the development of a behavior.

5. It has been suggested that obsessive-compulsive disorders (OCDs) may be due to the activation of subroutines that evolved for grooming and territory.

6. The behavioral neurosciences have favored the idea that general reward systems evolved as opposed to innate response patterns.

7. Even though reward centers have been located in the brain, behavior is nevertheless constrained by the nature or structure of the nervous system.

8. The learning approach to motivation has traditionally assumed that behavior is the result of a person's reinforcement history and is governed by principles of learning.

9. There are two types of learning: classical conditioning and instrumental learning.

10. Psychologists distinguish between two classes of rewards: intrinsic and extrinsic.

11. In order to account for the fact that events lose their power to reinforce behavior, Solomon has proposed the opponent-process theory.

12. Psychologists use the term *cognitive* to refer to processes that have to do with knowing. Cognition, therefore, involves thinking, perceiving, abstracting, synthesizing, organizing, or any other process that allows the individual to conceptualize the nature of the external world and the nature of self, or that thing called "person."

13. Implicit theories that humans use to guide their behavior can be thought of as hypotheses, models, beliefs that they have about the nature of the world.

14. Stereotypes often emerge because we have no personal knowledge and simply model the behavior or adopt the categories of other people.

15. Many of our beliefs, attitudes, values are often initially copied from our parents; however, they are also constructed based on our own experiences and our own desires.

16. Cognitive dissonance theory has its roots in the idea that people need to experience cognitive consistency. According to cognitive dissonance theory, humans are inclined to process information in such a way that it will be consistent with existing categories, values and beliefs.

17. Implicit theories are hypotheses, models, and beliefs that we have about the nature of the external world (world theories) and about what we need to do to satisfy our desires in this world (self-theories).

18. We can, however, learn to become aware (mindful) of our cognitive processes by doing such things as thinking about why we make the decisions we do as well as considering the alternatives available to us.

19. Attribution theory proposes that humans are inclined to look for the causes of their behavior.

20. It has been suggested that there are two types of people, those who see the cause of behavior as due to themselves (internals) and those that see the cause of behavior as due to things outside themselves (externals).

21. The idea that all motivational systems can be explained by a single set of principles based on a single set of assumptions has, to this point, failed. An abundance of research shows that each system operates according to somewhat distinctive principles.

22. Theorists are now being forced to account for the interaction of the three components—a task that has forced them to question some of the early ideals that guided theory construction.

23. Current motivation theorists are concerned with the question of individual differences.

24. No matter how well a theory can explain behavior after the fact, the most important criterion of a good theory is its predictive ability.

25. Analysis of why people run and why they listen to rock music indicates that all three components—biological, learned, and cognitive—can be important in motivating a behavior.

Chapter Three

Arousal, Performance, and Attention

- Why do we suddenly get a burst of energy when we are faced with an emergency?

- Why do even little changes in the environment sometimes make us feel alert and energetic?

- Why can we sustain our alertness for long periods of time when we become intellectually involved in something?

- Why are we more efficient at some times than at others?

- Why do we feel stressed and tend to make mistakes when we become flooded with information?

- How can we learn to maintain our attention to boring tasks?

- Why do we like our environment to be sometimes very stimulating and at other times more monotonous and restful?

When we are suddenly confronted by an emergency, such as a car accident, our whole body prepares itself to deal with that event. Mentally, we attempt to make sense of the situation. Is anybody in danger? Is there anything we can do? What alternatives are available to us? At the same time that our mind is attempting to grasp what has happened, our body is preparing to expend enormous amounts of physical energy. When people are confronted by emergencies, they often do things that they never thought they were capable of doing—lift enormous weights or swim several miles, for example. People who have never before delivered a baby will undertake this formidable task. People who normally feel faint at the sight of blood will administer first aid to a bleeding victim.

Not all emergencies are matters of life and death, but the body responds as though they were. The mind becomes active while the body prepares for the increased demand for energy. When we compete in a sports event, for example, our mind searches for things we can do to beat our competitor. At the same time, our body prepares to deal with the energy requirements of the competition. Our heart rate speeds up, we breathe more quickly, and we begin to sweat. Even the prospect of having to give a speech can increase our heart rate and breathing and make our palms sweat.

What we are experiencing under such conditions is an increase in arousal. As we shall see, arousal involves physiological as well as psychological changes. The interaction between them is fairly complex. On the one hand, the physiological changes produce psychological changes. When arousal increases, we think differently, process information differently, and act differently. Some of these psychological changes we cannot control. That is, certain changes in the way we think, process information, and act are often automatic.

But this is a two-way street. The way we think, process information, and act can and often does produce physiological changes; just as the body influences the mind, the mind influences the body. In the course of adapting to a new situation, a kind of back-and-forth process produces changes in the way we think and act and alters certain brain chemicals and body secretions. These changes further alter the way we think and act.

In this chapter we examine some of these interactions between the mind and the body. (In Chapters 10 & 11, we will look at this question again as it pertains to the emotions.) We will start by examining one of the most basic physiological reactions, the arousal response.

Definition of Arousal

Arousal is the activation of the brain and the body. When we are aroused, the brain and the body are in a state of readiness, preparing us to engage in adaptive behaviors. Electrical activity in the brain increases, the heart beats more rapidly, and blood is redirected to the brain and muscles. Muscle tonus increases in preparation for quick and efficient response. The activation or arousal of the brain and the body can be viewed as a state of energization. When we are aroused, the brain and the body are prepared to make use of various chemicals (stored in various places in the body) that facilitate the processing of information, planning, and the expenditure of physical energy.

Biological Mechanisms of Arousal

We generally speak of two primary mechanisms of arousal: the reticular activating system (RAS) and the autonomic nervous system. As we shall see, these two systems are not the only ones involved in arousal, but they are the two primary ones.

The Reticular Activating System (RAS)

Each of the various sensory receptors (visual, auditory, tactile, and so on) is connected to a sensory area in the brain via an afferent nerve pathway that ascends to the cortex via a specific projection system. Fibers branching from these pathways ascend to the reticular formation (Figure 3-1). As indicated in the previous chapter, until 1949, it was assumed that the the reticular formation was some type of relay station. We now know that this system is also an activating system that puts the individual is in a state of physical and psychological readiness. As a result of being put in this state of readiness several things happen. Among other things, people are able to process not only more infor-

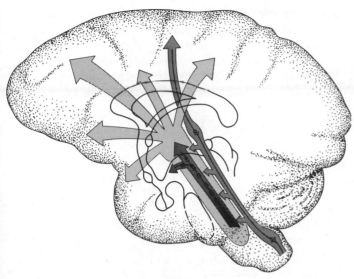

Figure 3–1. Ascending reticular activating system (reticular formation) schematically projected on a monkey brain (From D. B. Lindsley, *Handbook of Physiology: Neurophysiology, Vol. 3,* 1960. Copyright © 1960 by the American Psychological Society. Reprinted with permission.).

mation (visual, auditory, tactile etc.) but are able to process it better, they are able to better identify important features in the environment and integrate that information with memories or schemata that are stored in the brain, and finally because the motor cortex has been activated, they are prepared to make an appropriate or response or responses both rapidly and accurately.

The nature and measurement of cortical activity. The brain is composed of many interconnecting nerve pathways. Electrical impulses are generated by chemical processes and travel along these pathways. There are many gaps in these nerve pathways, and these gaps are called "synapses." In order for an electrical impulse to move from one part of the brain to another, it must cross several synapses. One of the main chemicals that facilitates passage of nerve impulses across synapses is norepinephrine (von Euler, 1956). When norepinephrine is secreted at various sites in the brain, move-

ment of electrical impulses across synapses in those sites is facilitated.

The electroencephalogram (EEG) was designed to amplify these impulses so that a permanent record could be made of the activity of various brain structures. It is technically possible to obtain records of activity in any brain structure, but EEG recordings on humans are typically taken from the structures on the outer perimeter of the brain. Surface recordings can be made by means of electrodes attached to various locations on the skull with a high-conductance glue. These electrodes can measure the activity of the visual cortex, auditory cortex, motor cortex, or other areas near the surface of the brain, depending on the location of the electrodes. Since the electrodes cannot readily measure the activity of deeper brain structures, such as the hypothalamus, it is often necessary to use animals in order to learn about these deeper structures. In general, therefore, when we talk about EEG activity in humans, we are talking about the activity of the cortex. The cortex, the outer layer of the brain, mediates, at least in part, our ability to see, hear, smell, taste, and experience tactile stimulation, and to perform a wide variety of motor responses, including speech. We say the cortex is involved "in part" in these activities because other brain structures also play a fundamental role in these functions. Whatever the exact role of the cortex, we know it plays some role in the processing of sensory information so that the external world appears to be organized and predictable.

EEG readings have shown that changes in brain activity are characterized by abrupt rather than gradual changes in the amplitude and frequency of the impulses ("brain waves"). In general, as a particular brain structure becomes more active, the amplitude (height of a wave) decreases and the frequency (number of peaks per second) increases. Figure 3-2 shows some examples of cortical activity corresponding to various behavioral and mental states.

Positron Emission Tomography (PET)

For about 100 years, it has been known that the regulation of blood supply to the brain is tightly coupled to local neuronal activity in the brain. About 40 years ago researchers began tracing circulation by infusing radioactive material. PET is a refinement of this technique. A PET scanner is composed of hundreds of detectors that circle the brain. Using mathematical averaging techniques, the distribution of an isotope in the tissue can be measured. The image that results is a very plastic and changing image that reflects neuronal activity in various regions in the brain (Raichle, 1988).

This technique has allowed scientists to establish a number of important facts. The following is a sampler. Semir Zeki (1992) has used PET to explore which areas of the brain become active when people are exposed to various forms of visual stimulation. His work shows, among other things, that different regions in the brain become active in response to different dimensions of a stimulus such as color, form, or movement. The brain tends to break down images into their component parts. Through a series of converging experiments, it has been established that the right prefrontal cortex is part of an attentional system that is engaged when a subject is looking for a particular signal (e.g., Petersen, Fox, Posner, Mintun, & Raichle, 1988; Posner, Petersen, Fox, & Raichle, 1988). Richard Gur (1991) of the University of Pennsylvania has noted that men and women use different parts of the brain when solving problems, and that men have difficulty detecting emotions in facial expressions, especially the facial expressions of women.

This work complements the work on the RAS. Not only does the brain as a whole become generally more active in response to external stimulation, but different areas of the brain selectively become more active in response to specific task demands. Perhaps even more important is the finding that as people operate on information in certain ways, different areas of the brain become involved (e.g., Petersen, Fox, Posner, Mintun, & Raichle, 1988; Posner, Petersen, Fox, & Raichle, 1988).

The Autonomic Nervous System

Although cortical activity has frequently been used as a measure of arousal, many other physiological changes occur when a person is in a state of arousal. The autonomic nervous system is responsible for these changes. A wide array of stimuli trigger activity in the autonomic

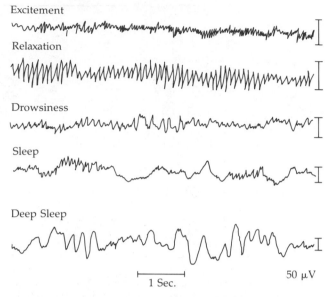

Figure 3-2. EEG patterns ranging from sleep to wakefulness to excitement (From H. H. Jasper, "Electroencephalography." In W. Penfield and T. C. Erikson (Eds.), *Epilepsy and Cerebral Localization*, 1941. Copyright © 1941 by Charles C. Thomas, Publishers. Reprinted with permission.)

nervous system. For example, physical exertion, exposure to a loud noise or novel stimulus, injury to the body, anxiety, apprehension, or certain drugs will elicit a rather predictable pattern of responses. Heart rate increases and blood vessels constrict. Together, these two reactions produce an increase in the flow of blood. The liver releases glucose for immediate energy, and the spleen releases red corpuscles, which are important for carrying oxygen. Digestion halts; however, fats are released into the bloodstream for conversion to energy. Perspiration increases, which is important for cooling when the person is expending great amounts of energy. Secretion of saliva and mucus decreases, giving the "dry mouth" feeling. The muscles tense, the pupils dilate, and the senses are improved.

This pattern of responses is generally accompanied by increased cortical activity, and is due mainly to the action of the hypothalamus, which triggers two paral-

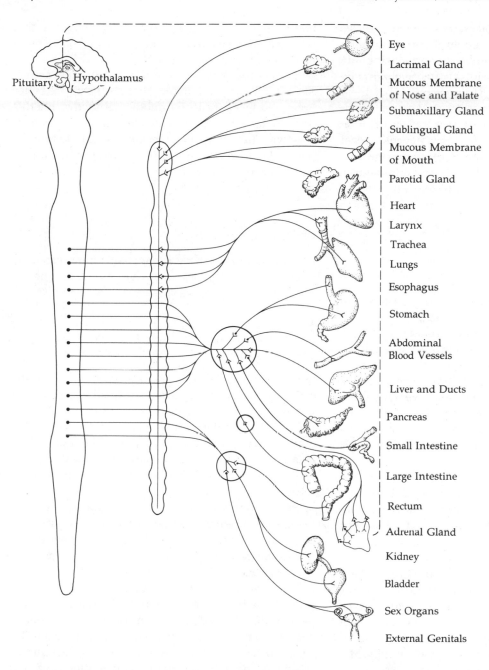

lel and complementary reactions: it stimulates activity in the autonomic nervous system and in the endocrine (glandular) system (Levine, 1960). Figure 3-3 shows the pathways in the sympathetic nervous system, a divi-sion of the autonomic nervous system. Most of the physiological changes noted above can be traced to the activity of the sympathetic nervous system. In addition to producing these changes, the autonomic nervous system stimulates the adrenal medulla, which then secretes various amounts of epinephrine or norepinephrine. Both epinephrine and norepinephrine are involved in a number of physical and psychological reactions. They both produce RAS arousal. RAS activity is often associated with general arousal, which mediates sensory thresholds, muscle tonus, and the other responses mentioned above. It has been suggested that the release of epinephrine and norepinephrine provides a long-lasting chemical backup for the immediate action of the sympathetic nervous system. Epinephrine and norepinephrine have also been implicated in human emotional reactions.

Routtenberg's Model of Two Arousal Systems

Routtenberg (1968) noted that often there is a lack of correlation among behavioral arousal, EEG activity, and RAS activity. This fact immediately raised the question whether the RAS is the sole brain structure responsible for cortical and behavioral arousal. Routtenberg found that when lesions are made in the RAS, EEG desynchronization will still occur. (The term *desynchronization* is typically used when the normal alpha rhythm changes abruptly into an activation pattern—a phenomenon that occurs, for example, when a new or novel stimulus is presented.) However, no EEG desynchronization occurs if lesions are also made in the limbic system (a complex system of the brain that involves certain subcortical structures, the hypothalamus, and part of the cerebral cortex, which has been implicated in emotion and related activities). Thus it appears that the limbic system can, under certain conditions, take over for the RAS when it has been damaged. This finding seems to provide evidence that the RAS is not the sole structure responsible for cortical arousal. Routtenberg has argued that this fact, along with a number of others, can be explained by the assumption that the RAS is arousal system 1 and the limbic system is arousal system 2.

Why two systems? Following the lead of others, Routtenberg has suggested that the RAS is concerned mainly with the neuronal organization involved in responding, whereas the limbic system is concerned mainly with rewards. There is ample evidence that when the limbic system is active, a person is more likely to repeat a response, but that this does not happen when the reticular system is moderately active. There is also ample evidence that responses are better organized when the RAS is moderately active, but this does not appear to be the case when the limbic system is active. Thus the evidence seems to indicate that the two systems serve different functions. The limbic system is concerned with rewards and the RAS system is concerned with responding.

Origins of Arousal

Arousal is produced by three basic phenomena: (1) stimulation of the sensory systems, (2) biological rhythms, and (3) our interpretation of an event.

Stimulation of the Sensory Systems

Stimulation of any of the sensory systems (visual, auditory, olfactory, tactile) is accompanied by an increase in arousal. From the point of view of survival, it is important that the individual be prepared to deal with any sudden change in the environment. Often, an increase in sensory input from the environment requires the individual to make some adaptive responses, and quickly. We obviously make our best adaptive responses when we are functioning at some optimal level, that is, when the brain is fully active and the body is prepared to deal with enormous energy demands. Since an adaptive response to change involves the entire body, it is important that the entire brain become active, not just that area of the brain that must process the incoming stimulation. Similarly, it is important that the body be put into a state of readiness so that no matter what the demand on it, it will be ready to respond. If we hear a window break in the middle of the night, for example, it is important that the entire brain should become active, not just that area of the brain that processes auditory stimulation. If the window has been broken by an intruder, all our senses must be prepared to deal with the event.

Rhythmic Activity of the Nervous System

Arousal, especially cortical arousal, is also under the control of certain biological rhythms. Michel Jouvet's (1967) work suggests that the alternating activity of the raphe nuclei (which secrete serotonin) and the locus coeruleus (which secretes norepinephrine) governs arousal and alertness in humans. Jouvet found that serotonin is associated with reduced cortical activity (reduced arousal) while norepinephrine is associated with increased cortical activity (increased arousal). All of us are more alert at some times than at others. Not only do all normal people experience these involuntary changes in arousal (alertness), but they often experience them at certain predictable times of the day. So-called morning people, for example, experience greater alertness in the mornings, while night people experience greater alertness at night. Still others have a mixed pattern—they experience a period of alertness in the morning followed at midday by a drop in alertness, which is followed in turn by another period of increased alertness. Not surprisingly, such people are more likely than others to take a nap.

Cognitive Interpretation

Anticipatory bodily preparation. The third major source of arousal is our interpretation of the environment. Whenever we interpret an event as threatening or potentially exciting, we are likely to experience an increase in arousal, both cortical and autonomic. When we are threatened, it is important that the body be prepared to deal with that threat, both mentally and physically. Similarly, when we select some activity that is capable of providing excitement, the body must be prepared for that event. If we are going to engage in some sport such as scuba diving, for example, we need to be both physically and mentally prepared for it. An increase in arousal, in other words, is associated with a wide variety of activities.

The important point to remember about this kind of arousal is that it is anticipatory. That is, the arousal typically occurs before some event or anticipated event takes place. Because it is based on our cognitive interpretation, it may be inappropriate. I may anticipate that I am going to be fired, for example, when in fact nothing of the sort is about to happen. Sometimes it is the magnitude of the arousal we experience that is not appropriate. While I may have good reason to experience a very high level of arousal if I am asked to address a large audience, it would be inappropriate to experience that same high level of arousal if I were asked to introduce a friend to someone else I know.

Cognitive dissonance and arousal. One of the interesting features of experiencing cognitive dissonance (see Chapter 2) is the finding that cognitive dissonance leads to increased arousal. Getting people engage in behaviors that go against their feelings and/or beliefs is a common way for inducing cognitive dissonance in people. Robert Croyle and Joel Cooper (1983) induced cognitive dissonance using this procedure by asking students who had previously indicated their disagreement with the statement "Alcohol use should be totally banned from the Princeton campus and eating clubs" to write forceful arguments in support of a ban on alcohol. Their findings indicate that cognitive dissonance can indeed produce increases in arousal. If one is going to think clearly and form rational arguments it would, of course, be important that the brain be in a state of optimal arousal. What this and other research show is that cognitive demands or cognitive activities can and does have a direct effect on the underlying biological processes.

Summary

Arousal is the activation or energization of the brain and the body. Arousal has two primary mechanisms: the reticular activating system (RAS) and the autonomic nervous system. The RAS, located at the top of the brainstem, is primarily responsible for the activation of the brain. Studies focusing on the electroencephalograph (EEG), a recording device designed to measure and record brain activity, have shown that changes in brain activity are abrupt rather than gradual. The autonomic nervous system produces a number of bodily changes that prepare the individual to expend great amounts of energy. Most of the bodily changes are produced by a branch of the autonomic nervous system called the sympathetic nervous system. The adrenal glands are activated by the pituitary gland. The chemicals secreted by the adrenal glands, epinephrine and norepinephrine, provide the long-term backup for the more immediate action of the sympathetic nervous system. There are three basic phenomena that elicit arousal: stimulation of the various sense systems, rhythmical activity of the nervous system (alternating activity of the raphe nuclei and locus coeruleus), and cognitive interpretation.

Performance and Arousal

Research on the RAS has shown that unless the cortex is aroused, sensory signals going to the cortex will not be recognized or processed. If the cortex is optimally aroused, it will quickly recognize signals and efficiently process incoming information. In one study (Fuster, 1958), rhesus monkeys were required to learn to discriminate between two objects (learn which object had a food reward hidden under it) when the objects

Table 3-1. Psychological states and their EEG, conscious, and behavioral correlates (From D. B. Lindsley, "Psychological Phenomena and the Electroencephalogram." *Electroencephalography and Clinical Neurophysiology*, 1952, 4, 443-456. Copyright © 1952 by Elsevier Publishing Company. Reprinted with permission.)

Behavioral Continuum	Electroencephalogram	State of Awareness	Behavioral Efficiency
Strong, excited emotion (fear, rage, anxiety)	Desynchronized: low to moderate amplitude; fast mixed frequencies	Restricted awareness; divided attention; diffuse, hazy; confusion	Poor (lack of control, freezing up, disorganization)
Alert attentiveness	Partially synchronized: mainly fast, low-amplitude waves	Selective attention, but may vary or shift; concentration, anticipation, "set"	Good (efficient, selective, quick reactions); organized for serial responses
Relaxed wakefulness	Synchronized: optimal alpha rhythm	Attention wanders—not forced; favors free association	Good (routine reactions and creative thought)
Drowsiness	Reduced alpha and occasional low-amplitude slow waves	Borderline, partial awareness; imagery and reverie; dreamlike states	Poor (uncoordinated, sporadic, lacking sequential timing)
Light sleep	Spindle bursts and slow waves (larger); loss of alphas	Markedly reduced consciousness (loss of consciousness); dream state	Absent
Deep sleep	Large and very slow waves (synchrony but on slow time base); random, irregular pattern	Complete loss of awareness (no memory for stimulation or for dreams)	Absent
Coma	Isoelectric to irregular large slow waves	Complete loss of consciousness (little or no response to stimulation); amnesia	Absent
Death	Isoelectric: gradual and permanent disappearance of all electrical activity	Complete loss of awareness as death ensues	Absent

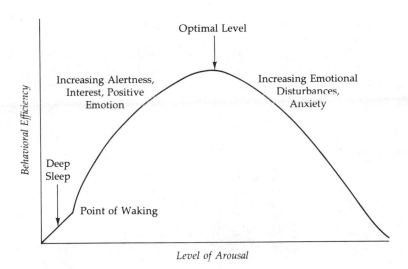

Figure 3-4. Hypothetical relation between behavioral efficiency and level of arousal (From D. O. Hebb,"Drive and the C. N. S. (Conceptual Nervous System)." *Psychological Review*, 1955, 62, 243-254. Copyright © 1954 by the American Psychological Association.).

were presented tachistoscopically (that is, for a fraction of a second at a time). In the experimental condition, the animals were electrically stimulated in the RAS through a permanently implanted electrode. Control animals received no stimulation. Not only did the experimental animals learn faster, but they had faster reaction times.

The RAS also has a descending tract, which influences motor functions. Since reactions are faster and more finely coordinated under higher levels of arousal, there is good reason to believe that the descending tract of the RAS may be in part responsible for this improvement.

Table 3-1 summarizes some of the data relating psychological states, EEG, and behavioral efficiency. Note that behavior is most efficient not when arousal is at its highest level but when it is more moderate.

Hebb's Model of Arousal, Attention, and Performance

After reviewing all the data relating behavioral efficiency to arousal, Donald Hebb (1955) proposed that the relation between arousal and performance could be represented by an inverted-U-shaped function (Figure 3-4). This inverted U-shaped function is also commonly referred to as the Yerkes-Dodson principle, first named so in 1908 based on the observations of Yerkes and his student Dodson.

Studies of Sensory Deprivation

One of the major contributions of Hebb and his students was the study of sensory deprivation (Bexton, Heron & Scott, 1954; Heron, 1957). According to Hebb's model, people should find it difficult to maintain their attention or to think clearly under conditions of sensory deprivation. That is because sensory deprivation should produce a state of low arousal. As shown in Figure 3-4, behavioral efficiency is very poor under low arousal.

In order to study sensory deprivation, Heron paid male college students a substantial sum of money to lie on a bed for as many days as they could. Several things were done to restrict forms of potential stimulation. In order to restrict visual stimulation, the students had to wear special translucent visors. In order to restrict auditory stimulation, they had to rest their heads on rubber pillows that were next to an air conditioner that put out a steady hum. In order to reduce tactile stimulation as much as possible, the students were required to wear cotton gloves together with cardboard forearm cuffs. The fingers are a rich source of stimulation and can be used to stimulate the body, such as when one rubs his hands together or rubs his head with his hands. The experimental setup is shown in Figure 3-5.

The effects of sensory deprivation began to show up after about a day in sensory deprivation. Subjects

Figure 3-5. Sensory deprivation chamber used by the McGill University group. See text for details. (Adapted from Eric Mose, "The Pathology of Boredom," by Woodburn Heron. *Scientific American*, January 1957, 52. Copyright © 1957 by Scientific American, Inc. All rights reserved. Used by permission.)

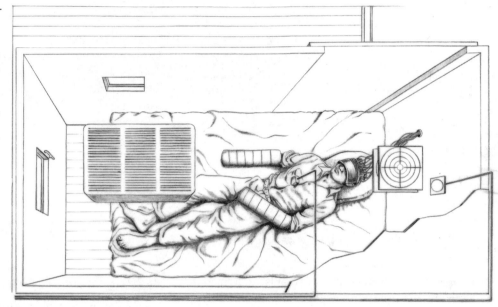

indicated that they had trouble thinking clearly. Many indicated they simply ran out of things to think about and that when they did try to think about something, they had trouble concentrating on any one thing for any length of time. After 48 hours, most of the subjects found they were unable to do even the most basic mathematical computations ($12 \times 6 = ?$).

Many subjects found that they began to see "images," and nearly all reported they had dreams or visions while awake. Hallucinations were common and were likened to those produced by drugs. Most subjects tried to entertain themselves by thinking about certain things or activities, but many found it difficult to concentrate. Most of the participants welcomed activities that normally held no interest for them (recording for stock market reports, for example). Such findings are consistent with Berlyne's view that when people are underaroused they will attempt to generate stimulation as best they can or focus on what is available.

All of the subjects found the experience very aversive. Even though they were being paid a substantial sum of money for each day they stayed in the experiment, most left after the second or third day. These findings underline the importance of having continual stimulation. In subsequent work, Zubek (1969) clearly showed that humans need a moderate amount of incoming stimulation to maintain not only their performance but their sense of well-being. Berlyne (1960) has pointed out that when people are deprived they are inclined to seek out stimulation in order to increase their arousal level. He has argued that people are motivated to maintain a moderate level of arousal which is optimal not only for performance but for feeling good (experiencing positive affect).

Studies of Increases in Arousal

A number of investigators have examined in some detail just what happens when arousal increases. In order to study the relationship between arousal and performance, they began to manipulate arousal systematically. While it is possible to manipulate arousal by means of drugs, the ethical considerations associated with the use of drugs caused investigators to look for other ways to achieve the effects they sought. Noise increases autonomic arousal, and many investigators began to use noise in laboratory studies. The results of these studies clearly showed that as autonomic arousal increases with noise level, performance increases (Takasawa, 1978). Up to a point, then, there is a direct relationship between noise and arousal. As autonomic arousal increases beyond some point, however, performance tends to fail (Kahneman, 1973) or responsivity may simply decline (Alexander & Epstein, 1978). The problem is to account for such failures and loss of responsivity. What are the mechanisms by which increases in arousal produce these effects?

Performance and Sensory Overload

It makes a great deal of sense that performance should increase as arousal increases. When the brain is more active, it should be able to process information better; similarly, when the body is in a state of readiness, it should be able to execute responses better. But why should performance decrease when the brain and body still have not reached their peak of arousal? It has been proposed that even though the body appears to be attaining ever greater levels of preparedness, something limits the individual's ability to respond with greater efficiency. G. A. Miller (1956) suggested that the body is able to handle only a limited amount of information input. Thus, whenever a given amount of information input is exceeded, the individual becomes overloaded and the orderly processing of information simply breaks down. Various people have suggested that in conditions of overload the RAS may limit information input by blocking certain sensory signals or by reorganizing the incoming stimulation in some way (Easterbrook, 1959; Lacey & Lacey, 1978; Pribram & McGuinness, 1975). According to this view, the RAS is more than a simple activating system. It is, in a very basic sense, an executive that controls not only how much but what we see in the environment.

Is Arousal a Unitary Construct?

Arousal theory is based on the idea that arousal is a unitary construct. Indeed, it is often possible to find a positive correlation among various indicators of arousal such as cortical activity, heart rate, and skin conductance. There is a great deal of data, however,

which indicates that under certain conditions these various indicators of arousal are independent. It has been shown, for example, that subjects who were trained to control cortical arousal showed increased heart rate when they were threatened with electric shock but not a corresponding increase in cortical activation (Orne & Paskewitz, 1974). Even studies with untrained subjects have shown that the threat of being shocked does not necessarily lead to increases in cortical arousal even though it does lead to increases in such things as heart rate and skin conductance (Frost, Burish, & Holmes, 1978). If different systems do not act in unison, it either means that there is more than one arousal system, an idea that various people have suggested, or that humans can learn to control these systems in some way.

Arousal, The Inverted U-Shaped Function and Individual Differences

Hebb's model of the relationship between arousal and performance has been criticized on the grounds that it fails to adequately describe the wide range of individualized differences that result from people having different cognitive styles or interpreting arousal differently (e.g., Neiss, 1988, 1990). Different athletes, it has been noted, often interpret high arousal alternatively as "being psyched up" or "being anxious or scared." As a result, one athlete performs at a high level, consistent with being highly motivated or "psyched up," while the other performs poorly, consistent with being anxious, even though they are at the same level of arousal. It has been pointed out by others (e.g., Anderson, 1990) that Hebb's model was not designed to exclude the role of other variables such as cognitive style, but rather was designed to account for the curvilinear relationship that results when arousal goes above some optimal level.

I agree with the position that arousal is a useful way of organizing a wide range of diverse behavioral data. I also take the position, however, that it is essential to understand each of the underlying motivation systems and the role of individual differences in order to predict behavior. As I indicated in the previous chapter, I view behavior as an interaction of biological, learned, and cognitive factors. Arousal is merely one of many factors that interact to produce behavior.

Biological Mechanisms That Reduce Sensory Overload

Lacey and Lacey's attention/rejection model. Beatrice and John Lacey (1970, 1978) have proposed a model that suggests that the heart acts as the mediator for controlling excessive stimulation (sensory overload). For many years they have been interested in the fact that about a third of the nerve pathways connecting the reticular system and the heart are feedback pathways (they provide information about the state of the heart to the RAS). Until this discovery by the Laceys, it was assumed that all the nerve pathways merely carried information from the reticular system to the heart; that is, the pathways existed so that the reticular system could instruct the heart to beat faster or slower. The Laceys' discovery suggested that the heart provided information to the reticular system. The question was, why? When the Laceys began to study the relationships between the activity of the heart and the activity of the reticular system, they found that there is a correlation between acceleration of the heart and inhibition of the RAS and, conversely, between deceleration of the heart and excitation of the RAS. Because acceleration of the heart produces pressure on the receptors in the heart (in the carotid sinus and aortic arch), and because this pressure has been shown to reduce RAS activity (Bonvallet & Allen, 1963), Lacey and Lacey have suggested that changes in heart rate determine reticular activity, at least in part. Their position is quite different from that of most arousal theorists, who have proposed that the RAS controls heart rate, not the reverse.

Lacey and Lacey have suggested that such a feedback system has important psychological significance. The reduced activity of the RAS resulting from heart-rate acceleration would, according to their model, block a certain portion of the incoming stimulation and thereby reduce cognitive overload. Similarly, when the person was not working to capacity, the RAS, signaled by deceleration of the heart, would allow an increase in the amount of incoming stimulation.

In one test of Lacey and Lacey's model, subjects had to do three tasks (Lacey et al., 1963). In one task the subjects had to pay close attention to external stimulation. In another they had to do mental problem-solving that presumably would be disturbed by external stimulation. The third task involved both internal and external stimulation. The results showed that when the task called for careful attention to external stimulation, the heart decelerated, and when the task called for the momentary rejection of external stimulation, the heart accelerated. In the combined task, there was no change. The Laceys and their colleagues argued that when the subject had to concentrate on both external and internal information simultaneously, there was a conflict, which would, of course, have resulted in no change.

Further evidence consistent with the Laceys' view comes from the work of Nancy Israel (1969). It has been known for some time that people's responses to external stimulation vary. Some people, called "levelers," tend to respond to the overall organization of the external environment, ignoring detail or differences between situations. "Sharpeners," in contrast, seem to focus on detail, readily noting differences between situations. According to Lacey and Lacey's model, since sharpeners are more open to and accepting of external stimulation, they should show greater cardiac deceleration than levelers in response to new situations that involve the processing of information about the external environment. This is, in fact, what Israel found. Thus it appears that different people may have different cognitive styles that are mediated by the heart.

There are several questions that Lacey and Lacey's model does not answer. For example, what signals the heart to accelerate or decelerate? Does cognitive overload stimulate the heart directly, or do people learn to accelerate the heart in response to overload? Further, what gives rise to different cognitive styles? Is it because people differ in their ability to process information that they adopt different cognitive styles, or are cognitive styles learned and then generalized to a wide variety of situations? As we shall see, there is evidence that people can learn to control input and that fundamental differences in cognitive style do affect arousal levels.

When we encounter natural beauty like this, we often feel the need to stop everything we are doing in order to give our brain the time it needs to fully comprehend the significance of such a complex, awe-inspiring, sensory event.

Learned Ways of Dealing with Sensory Overload

Young children have a very easy way of dealing with sensory overload; they simply cover their eyes or their ears with their hands. As adults, we learn similar ways of dealing with sensory overload. We seek out a nice quiet place or we put on some soothing music. Realizing that many people often arrive for work already too highly aroused to work efficiently, some companies have instituted brief periods of relaxation at the beginning of the day. Coffee breaks often serve a similar function.

In Chapter 9 we will deal with a variety of procedures, such as biofeedback, relaxation, and meditation, that are very effective in reducing arousal. One such technique is restricted environmental stimulation technique (REST).

Restricted environmental stimulation technique (REST). It has been suggested that many people in our society suffer from excessive environmental stimulation. When environmental stimulation is excessive on a regular basis, it can produce physical as well as psychological disorders (Suedfeld, 1975; Suedfeld & Kristeller, 1982). Because excessive environmental stimulation increases arousal, it can lead to hypertension (high blood pressure), for example. And because people are inclined to avoid excessive stimulation, exposure to it may lead to withdrawal, which in turn can lead to loneliness and other psychological problems.

One technique that has been devised to deal directly with problems that seem to be related to excessive environmental stimulation is the restricted environmental stimulation technique (REST). Two basic methods have been used in the REST research. One method involves secluded bed rest in a completely dark, soundproofed room for 24 hours. A second method is to have the individual float for approximately an hour in a shallow tank filled with a solution of Epsom salts and water.

The REST technique can increase the power of more standard stress-management techniques, such as biofeedback (Plotkin, 1978). When REST was used as a component in the treatment of essential hypertension, clinically significant drops in systolic and diastolic blood pressure were found (see Suedfeld & Kristeller, 1982). REST has also been used successfully to help people stop smoking, to lose weight, and to reduce drug dependency.

Why does REST work? Studies have shown that REST has not only an immediate but a long-term effect. Peter Suedfeld and Jean Kristeller (1982) have suggested that REST may help people to shift their attention away from external cues to internal cues. High arousal, as we shall see shortly, often directs attention to survival-related cues. As survival-related cues are often external (because our survival is typically threatened by things outside ourselves), it follows that people exposed to excessive environmental stimulation may acquire the habitual tendency to attend to the external environment. REST may help such people to shift their attention to internal cues. As a result, they tend not only to monitor those cues more closely but to deal with them before they produce serious health problems.

Cognitive Ways of Dealing with Sensory Overload

As humans are capable of anticipating events, they often experience a form of anticipatory arousal (Spinks, Blowers, & Shek, 1985). Anticipatory arousal is simply the arousal that will be required to deal with some forthcoming event. If, on a particular day, we realize

that we have a great deal to accomplish and little time, we may experience anticipatory arousal that exceeds some optimal level. One way of reducing this kind of arousal is to break down the tasks that face us into manageable units and then proceed to deal with each unit without thinking about the others (Horowitz, 1979). The idea is to prevent the system from becoming overloaded. When we fail to break down activities into manageable units, we experience anticipatory sensory overload.

Optimal Stimulation, Hyperactivity, and Autism

It has been suggested that two syndromes, hyperactivity (currently referred to in the research literature as Attention Deficit Disorder) and autism, can be accounted for by optimal stimulation theory (Zentall & Zentall, 1983). The syndrome called hyperactivity consists of excessive displays of a variety of related behaviors that include high general activity, impulsivity, short attention span, aggression, and variability (Davids, 1971). According to optimal arousal theory, hyperactivity results from a chronic state of underarousal. In order to experience optimal arousal, hyperactive children engage in activities that will increase momentary arousal. Motor activity is a very good way of increasing momentary arousal. Motor activity stimulates arousal not only of the autonomic nervous system but of the cortex. Feedback from the muscles stimulates the RAS, which in turn activates the cortex. The impulsivity and short attention span that characterize hyperactive children are also believed to result from the tendency of such children to seek out new and different experiences. When we are confronted by new stimuli or new information, the brain automatically becomes aroused in order to process it. Once the information has been processed, the brain can then relax. Therefore, in order to maintain momentary arousal at an optimal level, the hyperactive child must continually seek out new stimulation. Consistent with this interpretation, it has been shown that hyperactive children become habituated very rapidly to novel stimuli (see Rosenthal & Allen, 1978, for a review). One of the consistent findings in the arousal literature is that low arousal results in faster habituation. It has been argued that speed of habituation is one measure of how fast or how much information people are processing. According to arousal theory (e.g., Berlyne, 1960), people are motivated to experience optimal arousal and will seek out information if they are underaroused and avoid information when they are overaroused. The greater the need for arousal, therefore, the faster people should habituate to a new or novel stimulus. The aggression and variability of hyperactive children seems to be characteristic of a delinquent antisocial behavior pattern. It has been suggested that both delinquency and antisocial behavior grow out of a tendency to seek stimulation (Quay, 1977).

Autism is a syndrome characterized by stereotyped movements, gaze avoidance, echolalia (repetition of words or phrases), lack of responsiveness to sound, minimal variation in facial expression, withdrawal, resistance to change, fears, inappropriate social behavior, and inability to play (Wing, 1971). According to optimal arousal theory, autistic children are in a state of chronic overarousal. Since any form of environmental stimulation would produce further increases in arousal, the autistic child is motivated to keep environmental stimulation to a minimum. Because social interactions, change, play, and sound reliably lead to increases in arousal, these things must be avoided. Repetition is the opposite of change. It seems to make sense, therefore, that these children should be inclined to engage in stereotyped movements and to repeat things they have heard (echolalia).

There are symptoms associated with hyperactivity and autism that cannot be accounted for by optimal stimulation theory. Self-inflicted injury in autistic individuals, for example, is one of those symptoms. It may be that the reason autistic individuals bang their heads is to stimulate the release of endorphins, a chemical that can produce a sense of well being (see Chapter 7). As I have indicated before, it is often necessary to look for the interaction of different factors to explain such complex behaviors as hyperactivity and autism. The fact that optimal stimulation theory can explain a major portion of these two behavior disorders provides us with an illustration of the power of optimal stimulation theory to explain a wide range of other behaviors.

Why are hyperactive children chronically underaroused and autistic children chronically overaroused? It has been shown that levels of blood serotonin are abnormally low in hyperactive children (Coleman, 1971) and abnormally high in autistic children (Geller et al., 1982). When you read about Jouvet's model in Chapter 6, it may appear that these findings are inconsistent with Jouvet's finding that sleep onset (reduced cortical activity) is due to elevated levels of serotonin in the reticular activating system. Let me simply point out that serotonin is a neurotransmitter that performs many different functions depending on where it is found in the brain. Also, it may well be that the behavior of the autistics and the hyperactives in the above research was responsible for producing these chronically different levels of serotonin. That is, more activity may lead to more serotonin. The point I want to make here is that there are biological differences and these biological differences can be linked to a chemical that has itself been linked to arousal.

Summary

Hebb has concluded that humans process information best when arousal is moderate, so that the relation between arousal and performance can be best represented by an inverted U-shaped function. Various researchers have argued that when humans experience sensory overload, arousal levels can be adjusted to deal with this problem. There is growing evidence that people can learn to control arousal so that even if the body is highly aroused, the cortex is not. Further, there is growing evidence that how one interprets arousal plays an important role in whether or not high arousal will disrupt or improve performance. Lacey and Lacey have argued that the heart can act as a mediator when there is sensory overload. This suggestion is based on the fact that when the heart accelerates, the activity level of the RAS is reduced, whereas when the heart decelerates, the activity level of the RAS increases. Further support for Lacey and Lacey's position comes from the finding that "sharpeners" show greater cardiac deceleration than "levelers" in response to new situations.

The restricted environmental stimulation technique (REST) is one way to help people learn to deal with the effects of excessive environmental stimulation. REST has been successful in helping people to reduce hypertension, stop smoking, lose weight, and reduce drug dependency, among other things. According to one theory, REST teaches people to switch their attention from external to internal cues. Cognitive approaches to the management of sensory overload suggest that people can reduce overload by breaking down incoming information into manageable units. According to the theory of optimal stimulation, hyperactive children are chronically underaroused while autistic children are chronically overaroused.

Arousal and Selective Attention

Selective attention is a tendency to orient oneself toward, attend to, or process information from one part of the environment to the exclusion of others. There is an abundance of evidence that selective attention is governed, at least in part, by arousal level. One of the persistent questions is whether the shifts in attention that accompany changes in the arousal level are automatic (you don't have to plan them or think about them) or purposeful (you must engage in some active planning or thought process in order to decide your best course of action). The general consensus seems to be that these changes are more or less automatic. That does not mean that rational thought plays no part in the process, only that much of it occurs in the absence of active or purposeful thought. Are these so-called automatic processes learned or innate? Some researchers (Hamilton, Hockey, & Rejman, 1977) view the link between arousal and attention as learned (people learn to use the most optimal set of cognitive operations for a given level of arousal); other researchers have argued that shifts in attention need not be learned but may be innate. The tendency of birds to avoid gardens in which there are snakes, for example, is assumed to be an unlearned or innate response. On the other hand, the tendency of a soldier to pick up a gun when he hears some noise in the adjacent undercover would be regarded as mainly learned. Both responses, nevertheless, can be automatic.

Arousal and the Reorganization of Attention

James Easterbrook (1959) hypothesized some time ago that high arousal tends to make one concentrate on the dominant aspect of the stimulus or on cues closely related to survival. Let me relate a personal experience to illustrate this point.

Several years ago I was attending a convention in a large city in the United States. My parents were in the same city, staying at the apartment of some friends who were away on vacation. I wanted to join them for dinner and decided to use the subway to get there. As I was unfamiliar with the routes, I bought a map of the subway system and proceeded to locate what I thought was the right train. As the train proceeded, I kept track of the street numbers that periodically appeared in the stations that we passed. When I arrived at a station that corresponded to the approximate street I wanted, I got off the train and proceeded up the stairs to find myself in a very rough area of the city. After consulting my map again, I realized I had taken the wrong train. As I was already late, I didn't want to return to the city center, so I decided I could walk the few blocks to get to the address I wanted. After all, I thought, it would take at least another hour to go back downtown. After I had walked a little more than a block, it began to dawn on me that not only did I look very much out of place but people were watching me very closely. I could feel my heart begin to pound. I accelerated my pace. I wanted to walk fast enough so that I would know if anybody was following me but I didn't want to run because I thought that might betray my fear. At this point I found my attention beginning to shift. I remember looking for safety signs, such as a police car, another person who looked like me, or simply a reassuring smile from someone. I remember thinking about how I should respond if someone blocked my path. Would I defend myself? Would I run? If I ran, how far could I get? Could I climb that chain-link fence that I saw in the distance? When I did get to that chain-link fence, I found a hole in it and proceeded up a steep bank to a very different-looking neighborhood. I had made it without incident. A wonderful feeling of relief came over me and I continued to do what I normally do when I go for a walk. I looked at the architecture, I thought about what I would like to eat that night and what I would do the next day.

What caused my attention to shift? Laboratory research provides considerable evidence that such shifts in attention are governed by arousal. In the laboratory it is possible to manipulate arousal and then study what happens to attention. Such studies provide evidence that changes in arousal are sufficient to produce changes in attention.

The Interaction of Arousal and Selective Attention

Daniel Kahneman (1973) has suggested that Easterbrook's hypothesis can account for the failure of experimental subjects to perform well on certain tasks that demand fine discriminations or response to less dominant cues. In a more elaborate development of such an idea, Peter Hamilton, Bob Hockey, and Mike Rejman (1977) have argued that arousal alters the "control hierarchy." They suggest that our cognitive operations are affected directly by our arousal state. According to their model, we may learn to use one set of cognitive operations at one arousal level and another set of cognitive operations at another arousal level. They maintain that attention is systematically redirected to achieve the goals that are associated with each specific arousal level. In this sense, arousal serves an executive function.

In the example I provided above, I pointed out that when I entered a rough neighborhood my arousal level increased (I became fearful for my safety), and when that happened my attention shifted (I began to search for safety cues). In that sense, arousal served the executive role of directing my attention toward safety cues.

Nonspecific Arousal

According to various models of selective attention, arousal that has not been elicited by the situation (nonspecific arousal) can come to influence our attention in that situation. If I happen to be more aroused than you because of a drug I recently took or because of some immediately preceding event or simply because I tend to have a higher base-line level of arousal, I will attend to different cues than you will. One implication of this idea is that I may overreact. That is, I may attend to safety cues when in fact the situation does not call for such a reaction. People frequently behave inappropriately when they enter new situations, probably because new situations tend to be highly arousing, and the resultant high level of arousal makes them involuntarily attend to cues they would otherwise ignore. Some people have suggested that we attend to survival cues when we are highly aroused. Such a tendency would of course be highly adaptive. It can at the same time be very maladaptive.

The Orientation Reaction and Selective Attention

Novel stimuli typically elicit a pattern of physiological responses that has been called the "orientation reaction." These responses include EEG desynchronization, autonomic arousal (sympathetic nervous-system activity), increased galvanic skin response, and dilation of the pupils (Lynn, 1966). Of particular interest to psychologists is the fact that the orientation response habituates—it diminishes with repeated presentation of a novel stimulus. Because altering a stimulus in certain ways will typically reelicit the orientation reaction, we can be fairly certain that the person continues to monitor that stimulus. It would appear, however, that the stimulus no longer has the same motivational qualities. That is, it is no longer capable of holding the person's attention.

The fact that the orientation reaction can be elicited by a new or novel stimulus, or when the person is deliberately searching for a significant stimulus from some stimulus array, suggests that the orientation reaction is intimately tied up with selective attention (Bernstein, 1973, 1979; Bernstein, Taylor, & Weinstein, 1975; Maltzman, 1979). Specifically, it appears that the orientation reaction occurs whenever we are confronted with new or unassimilated information or whenever we happen to locate an important stimulus in our environment. We have all experienced the phenomenon of seeing something new in our environment. Such an event may simply grab our attention for a brief moment or literally stop us in our tracks. Similarly, we have all experienced the effect of spotting someone we know in a crowd. Typically our scanning stops, at least momentarily, as we fixate the person carefully as though to confirm our initial detection.

The fact that the orientation response tends to habituate to a stimulus suggests that attention is no longer being focused on that stimulus. It has been suggested that the habituation of the orientation response is a type of gating mechanism that underlies selective attention. That is, habituation serves to shift our attention (Waters, McDonald, & Koresko, 1977). It can be argued that once we have processed the necessary information a stimulus contains, we no longer need to continue focusing our attention on that stimulus. We are free, so to speak, to turn to new stimuli or to process other information in our environment. In this sense, it can be argued that arousal in general and the orientation response in particular in some way control the processing of all the information in our environment.

Vigilance: The Ability to Maintain Attention for Long Periods of Time

It is extremely difficult for humans to maintain their attention in a situation that involves little change. It has been found, for example, that the performance of people who must attend to a radar screen and identify certain signals (such as the appearance of a blip that signifies an enemy aircraft) declines significantly after as little as 30 minutes (Mackworth, 1948). Since many jobs require people to maintain attention under similar conditions, it is important that we understand not only the source of the decline in performance but how we might reverse this decline.

What is it that makes it difficult for people to maintain their attention? Part of the problem appears to be linked to the lack of change or the absence of complexity. Repetition and monotony lead to a reduction in arousal. People whose vigilance declines often show signs of low arousal, such as low levels of adrenaline in the urine and blood and brain wave patterns that signify sleepiness (Warm & Dember, 1986). What can be done to restore vigilance? Several strategies have been devised.

Increasing arousal or taking advantage of rhythmic arousal levels. Since arousal tends to be subject to rhythmic

The ability to maintain attention for extended periods of time is difficult for most people. Feedback about performance tends to enhance one's ability to maintain attention.

fluctuation, we can take advantage of those periods of the day when arousal is highest. If this suggestion proves impractical, we can turn to mild physical exercise and other forms of sensory stimulation, such as music, which can stimulate arousal and therefore help us to remain attentive. Even the stress that comes from working in an uncomfortably warm environment can help people remain attentive. Students who study for long periods might be well advised to take a walk or change the background stimulation in order to increase their arousal. Since social interactions can increase arousal, brief social encounters (provided they do not become too distracting) can be a useful means to maintain attention. Coffee breaks have long been regarded as a very practical means of helping people maintain attention.

Characteristics of the task. Not surprisingly, the task itself is an important source of arousal. Tasks that are too repetitive or boring tend to result in reduced vigilance. On the other hand, tasks that are too complex or demanding can also lead to reduced arousal and attention. One study showed that a reduction in the rate at which bottles passed before inspectors improved their performance (see Warm & Dember, 1986). Obviously, excessive demands produce sensory overload. Again, students may be well advised to gauge their reading rate to match the difficulty of the material they are trying to digest.

Feedback about performance. Providing people with immediate feedback about their performance has been shown to be a very effective procedure for maintaining performance. In one study, people were asked to watch lines that appeared on a video screen and indicate which lines they thought were longer. Some people heard a tone when they were correct (hits), some when they were wrong (misses), and still others when they said they saw a long line when the line was in fact short (false alarm). Feedback about hits and false alarms improved performance, whereas feedback about misses did not (Warm & Dember, 1986). One practical application of this research would be the practice of programming into a boring or repetitious task the opportunity to receive feedback on hits and false alarms.

How might students make use of this information to improve their efficiency in studying? I remember hearing many years ago that it was a good idea to spend time periodically reciting the ideas that one has just read. When you do that, your memory of the material typically improves. Your recitation gives you immediate feedback about whether or not you have actually processed the material.

Summary

Work on the orientation reaction indicates that when we are exposed to new or novel stimulation, we respond with increased arousal together with a tendency to orient our sense receptors toward the source of that stimulation. After repeated exposure to the new or novel source of stimulation, we tend to become habituated to it. Individual differences in autonomic arousal affect such things as rate of habituation. Several theorists have argued that arousal serves an executive function in that it often redirects or reorganizes attention. According to one theory, arousal alters the "control hierarchy."

One of the basic problems associated with attention is that of maintaining attention (vigilance), especially in situations that involve repetition. Research has identified several things that tend to maintain arousal and thereby help to maintain attention under boring and repetitive conditions.

Can We Learn to Control Arousal Levels?

According to Easterbrook's (1959) theory our attention changes (reorganizes) as a function of arousal level. Specifically, at low levels of arousal our attention is broad (leading us to attend to many things) and inclusive (leading us to process a great deal of information), but when it gets high (beyond the optimal level) it narrows our attention (leading us to attend to few things) and is exclusive (leading us to ignore everything but survival-related stimuli). According to this position, arousal governs attention and information processing. We are prewired, so to speak, to do and perceive certain things when arousal is low and other things when it is high. This idea has been pursued by Herbert Benson, who has spent years studying the "relaxation response" by using relaxation procedures to reduce muscle tension and lower sympathetic arousal. Benson (1987) has concluded that people's lives often change dramatically when they learn to relax. He notes, among other things, that they begin to experience greater positive affect, that they shift from a more negative view to a more positive view of the world, and that they find life more rewarding. These changes do not occur overnight, so to speak, but rather occur over several months or even years once people learn to habitually relax. How can we understand these findings? It can be argued, using Easterbrook's ideas, that when people begin to relax they naturally shift their attention to new and different things. As a result, they begin to see the world from a new perspective, much like a child sees the world for the first time. The new perspective they would adopt in this relaxed state would be one that was less focused on potential threats and dangers and more on novelty and harmony. As a result, they would find life more enjoyable and rewarding.

PRACTICAL APPLICATION 3.1

Why Using the Words "Don't" or "Not" Often Fails to Produce Good Performance

It has been suggested that our brain tends to be highly visual. This means that when we give it a verbal instruction to do something, such as hit a golf ball 250 yards, it creates some kind of visual mental image of what that looks like. In the case of golf, it would create an image of how the golf club needs to be swung in order to accomplish that goal. When we tell our brain not to do something, it cannot completely visualize this process so it simply ignores the word "not." That means if I tell my brain "not" to hit the ball in the water, there is a very good chance that I will hit it into the water. All my brain really knows at that point is that I am interested in the water and therefore the best it can do is send the ball in that direction.

Sometimes the brain tries to form an image that incorporates the concept of "not," but the results are not what we might intend. In the 1988 Winter Olympics, Brian Orser of Canada told himself before he went onto the ice, "Don't fall." When he skated he nearly fell several times and ended up winning the silver medal. Try to visualize not falling. The best I can come up with is an image of just about falling and then correcting myself. That is what Brian Orser 's

brain seems to have done. In contrast, Brian Boitano, the gold medal winner, said to himself that this was the day he had spent his whole life training for and told himself to go for it.

You don't have to think of the brain as being visual to come to the conclusion that the word "not" is a poor way to get good performance. Think of going down the road and coming to a junction in which there are four alternatives marked with the numbers 1 to 4. If someone tells you not to take alternative 3, you are still faced with choosing between the three remaining alternatives. There are often numerous alternatives at each junction in our lives.

Research has shown that knowing what to do when you get to a decision point (e.g., having a clear mental image or having overlearned a response) can be a better strategy than trying to control your arousal level. For athletes as well as others, knowing what to do will ensure that even if your attention might be inclined to wander as a result of shifts in arousal, the response is so well learned or so well planned that it will run exactly as you intended no matter what your arousal level at the time.

Can people learn to relax the brain while the body is active? For some time, researchers have been aware of the fact that cortical measures of arousal do not correlate that highly with sympathetic measures of arousal such as heart rate or respiration. This fact has led people to question the idea that arousal is a unitary concept (see discussion above). Instead, people have suggested that cortical arousal and sympathetic arousal are controlled by different systems. We know from the work on relaxation (see Chapter 9) that people can learn to control cortical arousal and they can learn to control sympathetic arousal, and that learning to control one does not automatically teach them to con-

trol the other. In other words, there is a great deal of evidence to suggest that these two systems need to be viewed as independent but also as perhaps linked to some degree.

According to RAS theory, all regions of the brain are assumed to become aroused more or less simultaneously. With new technology, however, it is becoming increasingly clear that this view of the brain is oversimplified. Using PET, researchers have shown that different areas of the brain become active quite independent of other areas (e.g. Zeki, 1992). Which areas become active depends on whether or not that area of the brain is involved or necessary for a particular task. In the field of sports psychology, there is growing evidence that athletes can learn to achieve what Easterbrook would call "broad attention" (attending to many things) and "inclusive attention" (processing a great deal of information) while their bodies are in a state of high arousal (Cratty, 1989). While there is considerable evidence that most of the brain can be in a relaxed state while the body is in a highly aroused state, just how dissociated are they? This question still needs to be explored more fully. What we can conclude at this point is that these systems are not nearly as closely linked as people previously thought. Among other things, this means that it should be possible to control them independently, at least within some limits.

There are a number of important implications that follow from the idea that people might be able to learn to relax one part of the body while some other part of the body is in a state of readiness. One implication for business people is that they can learn to perform at a high level without experiencing the debilitating effects of stress (see Chapter 9) that often accompany the need to perform under pressure. After work, these same people might engage in vigorous physical exercise to condition their bodies while their brain is allowed to relax. There is no point in running all the systems at a high level when only one needs to be operating at that level. Learning to control arousal in various parts of the body, therefore, could be important for all of us.

Learning to Perform Independently of Arousal

There is also growing evidence that we can learn to perform quite independently of our arousal state. The best examples of this come from our knowledge about how performers and athletes have learned to maintain consistently high levels of performance across a wide variety of conditions. The main problem that performers and athletes face is losing control of their ability to focus their attention because of competing stimulation that comes from the environment (e.g., weather, noise, distractions) or internal states (e.g., arousal, personal conflict, fatigue). One of the most sophisticated methods that performers and athletes use to control

their attention is mental imagery. In mental imagery one creates a mental picture or image of how a response should look and then rehearses this over and over until it forms a clear image in the mind, much like a color video. The image is then synchronized with the actual performance of the response so that the image and the response become one. Once this has been well practiced, the person will feel as if they are executing the response even when they are only running the mental image in their mind. As a result of having mental images, people do not depend on having a certain level of arousal in order to execute a response. The beauty of mental images is that they tend to block out all other stimulation, thereby eliminating the distracting effects that often come from such stimulation. Greg Louganis, the 1988 Olympic diving champion, used mental images to win the gold medal in diving. According to his account of the process, he rehearses a given dive in his mind several times before ever climbing to the high board. When it is time to execute the dive, he simply begins to run the mental image and lets it take him through the dive. Jack Nicklaus uses mental imagery in golf. As he gets ready to swing, he begins to visualize the ball flying through the air and landing at a specific location on the fairway or on the green. Like Greg Louganis, he typically rehearses the drive before actually stepping up to the ball to take his swing.

Performers also make extensive use of mental images to achieve the precision of performance that is currently demanded of professionals. The idea of using visual images in other fields has yet to be fully exploited.

Summary

There is growing evidence that people can learn to perform quite independently of their momentary level of arousal. This suggests that arousal does not cause behavior, at least under certain conditions. Evidence suggests that people learn to control or focus their attention, often by employing some type of mental process. One of the most effective mental processes is mental imagery, a process that often involves visualizing a desired outcome.

Figure 3-6. Relation between level of sensory input and hedonic tone as a function of personality (From H. J. Eysenck, *Experiments with Drugs*, 1963. Copyright © 1963 by Pergamon Press Ltd. Reprinted with permission.).

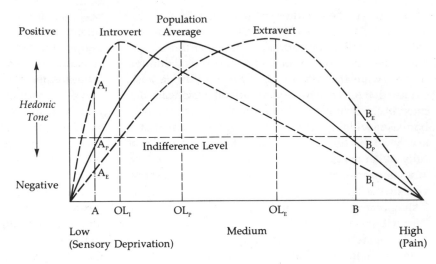

Level of Stimulation

Individual Differences

Eysenck's Theory

Do people differ in their levels of motivation? The obvious answer is yes. Given that they do differ, how can this difference be explained? Eysenck (1963, 1967) believes that the difference can be traced to the biological roots of personality. He has attempted to explain why most experimental approaches to the study of personality have found that there is an underlying factor, or continuum of factors, on which a population of people can be reliably differentiated. Specifically, he has suggested that the main continuum on which people can be differentiated is that of arousal, or activation. Some people, he has suggested, have an arousal level that is relatively low (extraverts), while others have an arousal level that is moderate to high (introverts).

Extraverts. The key to understanding the difference between extraverts and introverts, according to Eysenck, is understanding how these two types of people maintain optimal stimulation. Eysenck assumes that people are motivated to maintain an optimal level of arousal. Since extraverts require external stimulation in order to raise their normally low arousal to an optimum level, they fill their lives with behaviors designed to increase

arousal. For example, the highly social nature of extraverts can be understood if it is recognized that social situations typically produce increases in arousal. Similarly, the impulsive nature of extraverts, their tendency to do new and different things, can be understood if it is recognized that behaviors directed toward producing change increase arousal. Even behaviors such as drug use can, according to Eysenck, be explained, at least in part, by the structure of personality. Since nicotine is a stimulant, it is not surprising that extraverts are more likely to smoke than introverts (Eysenck, 1973).

Introverts. Because introverts tend to have a moderate to high arousal level, they are motivated either to maintain existing arousal levels or to reduce arousal levels. Therefore, in contrast to extraverts, who seek out social stimulation, introverts tend to avoid social contacts in order to prevent any further increase in arousal. Similarly, since sudden changes would increase arousal, introverts maintain more orderly, less impulsive lives. Even the kinds of drugs and how they are used should be different for the introvert. Introverts should use drugs for sedation rather than stimulation. Thus the introvert should tend to use barbiturates (tranquilizers) rather than stimulants.

Figure 3-6 shows the relation between level of sensory input and hedonic tone (affect) as a function of personality. The optimum level of sensory input for the introvert (OL_I) is toward the left of the continuum called "level of stimulation." The optimum level of stimulation for the extravert (OL_E) is to the right. The optimum level for the combined groups (the average, OL_P) lies in the middle. When we compare points A and B, we see that low levels of sensory input (A) produce positive hedonic tone (are pleasurable) for the introvert and produce negative hedonic tone (are unpleasurable) for the extravert, whereas high levels of sensory input (B) produce positive hedonic tone for the extravert but negative hedonic tone for the introvert.

Background stimulation. Since extraverts prefer more stimulation than introverts, one implication of Eysenck's theory is that extraverts may tend to select environments with greater background stimulation. Various tests of this idea have demonstrated that extraverts do indeed prefer environments that provide greater background stimulation. In one study, extraverts and introverts were asked to select a level of noise that they preferred for a paired-associates learning task. Extraverts selected a higher level of noise than introverts (Geen, 1984). Another study showed that extraverts are more inclined to select a location for studying that provides greater external stimulation. Not only do extraverts prefer higher noise levels, but they like environments that provide a greater opportunity to socialize (Campbell & Hawley, 1982). Both noise and social interactions are excellent sources of arousal.

Reversal Theory: An Alternative Way of Viewing

Optimal Stimulation

Reversal theory assumes that rather than preferring some moderate level of arousal, people sometimes prefer high arousal and at other times they prefer low arousal. That is, sometimes people like to experience excitement and at other times they like to relax. According to this theory, people tend to swing back

and forth between these two states. Even though all people are assumed to swing back and forth, some people are assumed to be dominated by the high arousal state while others are dominated by the low arousal state (Apter, 1982).

People also shift between two other motives. At certain times, people are motivated by a desire to achieve goals (telic goals). They not only carefully plan their activities but tend to complete those activities in order to receive the satisfaction that comes from achieving a goal. Their behavior is marked by efficiency rather than pleasure. In this state they are serious-minded and future-oriented; they plan. At other times, the same individuals are motivated by a desire to experience pleasure in the here and now (paratelic goals). They are inclined to prolong activities as long as they are producing high levels of pleasure. They tend to be playful and spontaneous (Svebak & Murgatroyd, 1985).

The crux of the theory is that the hedonic tone associated with arousal can shift abruptly, depending on which of the two motives is currently active. In other words, satisfaction comes not from high or low arousal but from the interaction of these two motives with the appropriate level of arousal (see Figure 3-7). When we are in the achievement state, low arousal can be pleasant; we call it "relaxation." When we are in the pleasure-seeking state, we call the same low level of arousal "boredom." Similarly, high arousal can be very unpleasant ("anxiety") in the achievement state and very pleasant ("excitement") in the pleasure-seeking state.

Since preference for arousal shifts with the motivational state, it follows that the individual may at one time want to increase arousal (arousal-seeking state) and at another time may want to decrease arousal (arousal-avoidance state). In one test of this theory, subjects were asked to indicate their preference for certain colors under various motivational states (such as states corresponding to achievement versus pleasure-seeking). Colors that are more arousing (red, yellow) were selected more often in the pleasure-seeking state, whereas less arousing colors (green, blue) were selected more often in the achievement state. The study also showed that within a given experimental session, subjects tended to shift between the achievement and pleasure-seeking states (Walters, Apter, & Svebak, 1982).

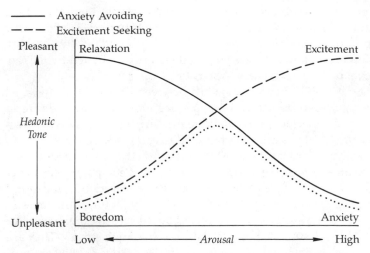

Figure 3-7. The hypothesized relationship between arousal and hedonic tone for the anxiety-avoidance and the excitement-seeking systems (From M. J. Apter, "One Commonly Occurring Sequence of Changes between Different Types of Experimental Arousal." *The Experience of Motivation*, 1982. Copyright © 1982 by Academic Press. Reprinted with permission.).

Summary

Eysenck hypothesizes that some people have a chronically low level of arousal (extraverts) while others have a chronically high level of arousal (introverts). In order to produce an optimal level of arousal, extraverts seek out stimulation in an effort to increase their arousal level, whereas introverts seek out a nonchanging environment in an attempt to avoid being flooded with more stimulation than they want. Reversal theory, in contrast, suggests that people sometimes like high levels of arousal and at other times like low levels of arousal. Some people, according to this theory, are dominated by the high arousal state while others are dominated by the low arousal state. Whether or not people enjoy high or low arousal depends, however, on which of two other motive states is active: the achievement motive or the pleasure-seeking motive. According to this theory, the hedonic tone we experience (positive or negative) depends on the interaction of the appropriate arousal level with one of the two motive states.

Theories of Emotion that Involve the Concept of Arousal

The James-Lange theory. William James (1884) and Carl Lange (1885/1922) first questioned the traditional assumption that affect was cognitive. They independently suggested that the basis of emotional experience was to be found in peripheral physiological sensations, such as those resulting from increased heart rate and blood pressure and from contractions of visceral and skeletal muscles (all indicators of arousal). For example, a man who runs at the sight of a bear will experience a number of sensations resulting from running, and those sensations will serve as the basis for the emotion called fear. Why does the man run from the bear? He runs, according to the James-Lange theory, because it is adaptive for humans to engage in some kind of "flight or fight" response when confronted with an event that threatens their survival. This reaction, according to James and Lange, occurs not because of an emotion, but rather because it is necessary to react appropriately to a wide

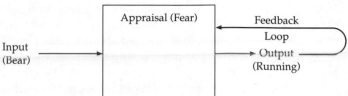

James-Lange Theory of Emotions

The emotion of fear depends on the appraisal of one's responses to the input.

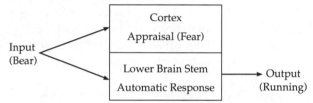

Cannon's Theory of Emotions

The emotion of fear occurs quite independent of the feedback from one's responses.

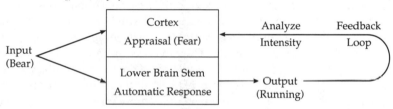

Schachter-Singer Theory of Emotions

The emotion of fear is independent of one's responses but the intensity of that emotion is dependent on one's responses.

Figure 3–8. Comparison of the James-Lange, Cannon, and the Schachter-Singer Theories of Emotions.

variety of stimulus events. Different events might require slightly different responses. Emotions, they believed, are synonymous with the physiological changes that accompany each of these different reactions. If there were no physiological changes, there would be no emotions. It should be noted, however, that it is not necessary to have an overt reaction before one feels an emotion. Physiological changes may occur without any overt response. Just before we engage in a flight response, for example, a number of physiological changes occur to prepare us for this reaction. Clearly, we experience an emotion under such conditions.

Cannon's theory. William Cannon (1927) criticized the James-Lange theory on the basis of a series of experiments showing that visceral changes are nonspecific reactions that accompany diverse emotions. If visceral changes are nonspecific, Cannon argued, they cannot provide the basis for different emotions. Therefore, the diverse emotions we experience must be cognitive. Some theorists have argued that certain motivational systems (for example, eating, aggression, and sex), together with their accompanying affects, have their bases in more primitive parts of the brain (Arnold, 1960, 1970); however, the importance of the cerebral cortex in directing the behaviors associated with these systems has repeatedly been emphasized (for example, Hebb, 1949). That is, in the final analysis, the label we give to an emotion is determined by the way we perceive the event that prompts it.

Schachter and Singer's theory. According to Schachter and Singer (1962), emotions are essentially cognitive; however, since emotions are accompanied by physiological responses, such as rapid heart rate and a flushed face (arousal), the person is confronted with the task of accounting for arousal. They assume that the person will interpret the physiological reactions in such a way as to be consistent with his or her cognitive appraisal of the stimulus events evoking the physiological responses. If a person has already labeled a situation as producing a particular emotion, such as euphoria, anger, or fear, then how should the person account for differences in arousal? Because emotions are perceived to vary in intensity, it seems reasonable to hypothesize, as Schachter and Singer do, that the person will infer that differences in physiological activity accompanying a particular emotion reflect differences in intensity. Thus, the greater the magnitude of the physiological activity, the greater the intensity of the emotion. The three theories are summarized in Figure 3-8.

To test their theory experimentally, Schachter and Singer manipulated physiological responses by using epinephrine (an arousal-producing drug) under the guise of studying how vitamin supplements affect vision. Epinephrine, of course, produces autonomic arousal, whose symptoms include increased heart rate, hand tremors, and flushing of the face. To evaluate the joint effects of autonomic arousal and cognitive activities, Schachter and Singer used four conditions, three of which are of interest here. In one condition, participants were given injections of epinephrine but were told it was a vitamin compound that could be expected to produce some side effects—heart palpitations, tremors, and so on. This was the "epinephrine informed" group. In a second condition ("epinephrine ignorant"), subjects were also given injections of epinephrine and told it was a vitamin compound, which most subjects would not associate with symptoms of autonomic arousal; they were

not informed of any side effects. A third group ("placebo") were given injections of saline solution, an inert substance that does not produce autonomic arousal. (In the fourth condition, subjects were given epinephrine and misinformed about its side effects— they were told it would cause numbness and itching.)

Since the subjects in the epinephrine-ignorant condition were not told about the side effects of epinephrine, they would experience physiological changes for which they had no explanation. Subjects who were informed about the side effects would experience the same physiological responses but would have an explanation for them. Schachter and Singer's theory predicts that the participants who were not informed would be motivated to find an explanation for these reactions, while the informed participants would not.

In a clever design to test whether unexplained physiological reactions contribute to the intensity of a cognitively manipulated emotion, Schachter and Singer exposed the subjects to a variety of situations that were designed to elicit particular emotions. For example, they exposed some subjects to a situation involving some tomfoolery by a confederate in order to elicit euphoria. They insulted other subjects in order to elicit anger. According to their theory, subjects who had not been informed about the side effects of their injections would experience more intense emotions than subjects who had been informed, regardless of the type of emotion aroused.

Observations of the participants and data obtained with a questionnaire supported Schachter and Singer's hypothesis. As predicted, the uninformed participants were angrier in the anger-inducing situation and more euphoric in the euphoria-inducing situation than either the informed group or the placebo group. These findings support Schachter and Singer's theory that physiological reactions contribute to the magnitude of the emotion under conditions in which such reactions are unlabeled. The fact that arousal level, when labeled, does not contribute to the intensity of the emotion is consistent with their view that both the direction and the intensity of an emotion are mediated by cognitive factors.

In a later experiment, Schachter and Wheeler (1962) demonstrated the generality of the previous findings.

Participants were injected with epinephrine, a placebo, or chlorpromazine (a drug that inhibits autonomic arousal). Then they were shown a brief comedy film. Their reactions to the film indicated that the level of expressed amusement was greatest under epinephrine and lowest under chlorpromazine.

Recently, several attempts have been made to replicate Schachter and Singer's work. Erdmann and Janke (1978) obtained results that are consistent with those originally reported by Schachter and Singer (1962). That is, they found that epinephrine enhanced happiness and anger. Two other papers, however, have reported failures to replicate (Marshall & Zimbardo, 1979; Maslach, 1979). Whether these are truly failures to replicate remains unanswered at this point, because there are several important procedural differences between these studies and Schachter and Singer's. Schachter and Singer (1979) argue that these differences are critical and therefore it is impossible to compare the two sets of experiments. Rainer Reisenzein (1983) has reviewed the research evidence relevant to Schachter's theory of emotion and has concluded there is good support for the idea that misattributed arousal intensifies emotions.

What about individual differences? Do all people attempt to account for physiological arousal? The answer is no. It appears that people who are more "unemotional" do not respond the same way as people who are "emotional" (Valins, 1967). In a study, Valins gave fraudulent heart-rate feedback to men while they were shown pictures of seminude women. He found that the feedback had a greater effect on emotional than unemotional men. It may be that the reason some people are more "unemotional" is that they have, for whatever reason, become insensitive to their own physiological reactions. Possibly through such mechanisms as denial (see Lazarus, 1966), they have come to ignore this source of information. Failure to consider this information would, according to Valins, result in a lowered emotional reaction. Hirschman and Hawk (1978) and Liebhart (1977), using aversive slides and fraudulent heart-rate feedback, found results similar to those reported by Valins. Hirschman and Hawk found, in addition, that resting autonomic levels affect reactivity: people with higher resting autonomic levels showed larger electrodermal responses (increases in electrical conductivity of the skin, typically accompanying increases in autonomic arousal) to the heart-rate feedback/slide combination and reported the experience to be more unpleasant. This finding suggests that emotional reactivity is not just a cognitive event but is mediated as well by resting physiological activity.

Summary

According to the James-Lange theory, emotions are intimately linked to peripheral physiological sensations. Cannon's position, in contrast, is that emotions are purely cognitive. Schachter and Singer have argued that while emotions are essentially cognitive, the intensity of emotions is determined to a very large degree by the feedback that comes from our peripheral physiological responses, such as heart rate and breathing.

General Summary

In this chapter I have discussed data which show, on the one hand, that arousal is a type of executive, controlling our attention which indirectly controls our behavior, and on the other hand, that people often behave quite independently of arousal. How can we make sense out of these apparently contradictory data? The key, I believe, lies in acknowledging that learning and cognition come to play an increasingly important role in our daily lives. If we start with the proposition that at birth it is important that some system be in place to guide our behavior, then it makes sense that the arousal system would be that system. Evidence suggests that the arousal system helps protect us against threats on the one hand and encourages us to learn on the other. What the data seem to suggest is that we can learn to take control of attention. In doing so, the arousal system has less and less control. It is interesting to note that performance on exams, an event that produces wide differences in arousal (anxiety) and therefore is a good place to study whether or not arousal affects performance, is best predicted by grade point average (GPA) and scholastic aptitude test (SAT). In fact, when you partial out GPA and SAT, anxiety is a nonsignificant predictor of performance (Sewitch, 1984) . The general rule of thumb for ensuring that arousal will not disrupt performance is to overlearn the material, a technique that stage performers have used for years to help them deal with stage fright. Many performers who win standing ovations report their heart was beating so fast at some point they thought they might pass out or have a heart attack. One of the themes that I decided to develop in this book is the idea that humans have a great deal of ability to gain control over themselves and their environment. We have a great deal of evidence in this chapter that humans can gain control over some very basic processes.

Main Points

1.   Arousal is the activation or energization of the brain and the body.

2.   Arousal is produced by two primary mechanisms: the reticular activating system (RAS) and the autonomic nervous system.

3.   Chemicals secreted by the adrenal glands, epinephrine and norepinephrine, provide the long-term backup for the more immediate action of the sympathetic nervous system.

4.   Three basic phenomena elicit arousal: stimulation of the various sense systems, rhythmic activity of the nervous system, and cognitive interpretation of events in the environment.

5.   The relationship between arousal and performance appears to be best described as an inverted U-shaped function.

6.   There is growing evidence that arousal is not a unitary construct.

7.   How a person interprets arousal plays an important role in determining whether or not high arousal improves or disrupts performance.

8.   According to Lacey and Lacey's attention/rejection model of sensory overload, the heart provides feedback that affects activity in the reticular activating system (RAS).

9.   Restricted environmental stimulation technique (REST) has proved to be a useful way of helping people deal with excessive environmental stimulation. It is hypothesized to work by helping people to focus their attention on internal rather than external cues.

10.   People can also deal with excessive environmental stimulation by breaking information down into manageable units.

11.   According to optimal arousal theory, hyperactivity results from a chronic state of underarousal, whereas autism results from a chronic state of overarousal.

12.   Both hyperactivity and autism may be linked to abnormal levels of serotonin.

13.   It has been proposed that arousal may automatically control or direct the attention process. Under higher levels of arousal, our attention tends to shift to cues that have to do with our safety, whereas under low levels of arousal, our attention shifts to facilitate the processing of new information.

14.   Studies of the orientation response have provided evidence that new or novel stimuli elicit arousal.

15.   People become habituated to new or novel stimuli more slowly at high levels of arousal than at low levels of arousal.

16.   Vigilance is the ability to maintain attention for long periods of time.

17.   It is very difficult for people to maintain their attention in a situation that involves little change.

18.   Feedback is a very good procedure for maintaining arousal during vigilance tasks.

19.   There is evidence that people can learn to control their arousal levels.

20.   There is also evidence that people can learn to perform independent of their arousal level.

21.   Eysenck's theory to account for individual differences is based on the concept that different people have different arousal levels. The low arousal level that presumably characterizes extraverts motivates them to seek out stimulation, including social situations. The

moderate arousal level that presumably characterizes introverts motivates them to keep external stimulation to a minimum.

22.   Reversal theory assumes that rather than preferring some moderate level of arousal, people sometimes prefer high arousal and at other times prefer low arousal.

23.   Also according to reversal theory, people are sometimes motivated by a desire to achieve goals (telic goals) and at other times they are motivated by a desire to experience pleasure in the here and now (paratelic goals).

24.   The James-Lange theory of emotions suggests that emotions depend on peripheral physiological sensation; Cannon's theory suggests that emotions are purely cognitive; the Schachter-Singer theory suggests that only the intensity of the emotion is dependent on physiological response (arousal).

Chapter Four

Hunger and Eating

- What makes us feel hungry?
- What makes us feel satisfied or full after we eat?
- Why are certain foods more appealing to us than others?
- Are people biologically equipped to select foods that are good for them and to avoid foods that are bad for them?
- What factors are involved in the rate of energy use?
- Why do so many people tend to become obese?
- Why do people who have become overweight have difficulty shedding those extra pounds?
- Why do some people binge?
- Why do some people starve themselves to the point of emaciation?
- Why is it so important for women in our society to be thin?

Thousands of articles have been written about various aspects of hunger and eating and about the relation between them. The abundance of articles and research reflects the difficulty that has been encountered in providing a clear picture of the mechanisms involved in hunger and eating. Several persistent issues have stimulated research in this field. We will be dealing with five of the more important issues.

Five Important Issues

What psychological mechanism produces hunger? From a biological perspective, it seems that we should eat when we need to replenish depleted metabolic fuels, just as we fill the fuel tank of a car when the gauge nears the empty mark. Humans and animals store two types of fuel—food in the gastrointestinal tract (which is immediately available) and reserves of fat. The problem is that we often feel hunger even though we have ample fat reserves (Friedman & Stricker, 1976). Researchers have therefore focused on the glucose level in the bloodstream, only to find that overall blood glucose levels do not correlate with reports of hunger (Mayer, 1955), even though glucose injections inhibit eating (Mook, 1963) and even though injections of insulin, which lower glucose levels, lead to reported feelings of hunger as well as stomach contractions (Goodner & Russell, 1965). Therefore, the reason that people report they are hungry must be more complex. In this chapter we will examine other data that suggest exactly what stimulus conditions give rise to hunger.

Why do humans have a propensity to obesity? An abundance of anecdotal and experimental data indicates that organisms (humans in particular) often eat too much. The by-product of overeating is overweight. The extra food is simply converted to fat. The fact that obesity can be induced in the laboratory by lesions in certain areas of the brain (parts of the hypothalamus) has led to the idea that naturally occurring obesity is due to some failure in a *satiety center*. Current research has tended to rule out such a simple explanation. The reasons for obesity, as we shall discover, are very complex. Several biological systems in addition to the hypothalamus are involved in hunger and eating. Learned habits and cognitions have also been clearly identified as part of the obesity syndrome. We must consider all of these factors together if we are to account for obesity.

Why do humans have difficulty getting rid of unwanted fat? People who are obese often wish they were not. As a consequence, many of them pursue some form of dieting. The fact that people often have difficulty in curbing the amount they eat has provided us with a wealth of data about the role of learning and cognition in hunger and eating.

What produces anorexia nervosa? Although the number of people who fail to eat enough to maintain a normal weight is small compared with the number who overeat, the phenomenon is so dramatic that it has aroused wide attention. Why do some people restrict their food intake to such a degree that they become emaciated? Is there a biological explanation, or is this disorder psychological?

What produces bulimia? Bulimia involves binge eating followed by purging. It is typically a very secretive activity. Bulimics tend to plan their binges carefully so that no one will know what they are doing. After they have binged, bulimics deliberately vomit the food they have eaten to avoid gaining weight. Why are some people so unable to control their eating that they must resort to purging to control their weight?

Biological Factors in Hunger and Eating

Food, Energy and Energy Reserves

Fats, carbohydrates, and proteins. When we ingest food, our stomach and intestines (the gastrointestinal [GI] tract) break down that food into more basic units that can be used for energy as well as for the rebuilding of the body cells and the manufacturing of the chemicals that are needed to run the body. *Fats* that we get from such foods as meats, milk products, and cooking oils are broken down into fatty acids and glycerol; *carbohydrates*, also referred to simply as starches and sugars (that we get from eating such foods as bread, pasta, cakes, desserts, and fruits), are broken down into glucose and fructose; and *proteins* that we get from such foods as meats, beans, and vegetables are broken down into amino acids. Once broken down into these more basic units or molecules, they are absorbed into the bloodstream. Most of the absorption of these basic units into the blood takes place in the small intestines. Very little absorption takes place in the stomach except for such things as aspirin and alcohol, which pass more or less directly through the stomach walls into the bloodstream (Sherman & Sherman, 1989). The absorption of alcohol across the stomach wall accounts for the rapid effects that come from drinking it. The intestines are an excellent storehouse for energy. After a big meal, it typically takes several hours for all the food in the intestines to be digested (Friedman & Stricker, 1976).

Energy and energy reserves. Part of the glucose that is absorbed into the blood remains in circulation to be used as energy, but most of it is transported across the cell membranes and is stored in the cells as glycogen, thereby providing an energy reserve. If we do not use all the glucose that is generated by the digestive process, the liver converts some of it to fat, which is then stored as an energy reserve in our fat cells (also called adipose tissue). Fats are considered a quick form of energy, and in the days of our ancestors were likely burned off before they could be stored in any great quantities in the adipose tissue. Even today, when people engaged in manual labor need a steady source of energy, fats play an important role in supplying that energy. For people who do not engage in intense physical activity, however, weight gain is an inevitable byproduct of a high-fat diet.

Amino acids and sugars go directly to the liver. This gives the liver the first choice of nutrients before passing them along to the rest of the body. The level of amino acid in the blood is regulated by the liver. Amino acids are used by the body for growth, repair and energy. There are 20 different amino acids that are derived from proteins. The best source of amino acids is meat. Most plants are low in amino acids and many do not contain the full complement of the 20 amino

acids the body needs to function normally. The net result is that if you do not eat meat, it is important to eat a variety of vegetables. While beans (a protein) are a good source of amino acids, it is important to remember that they often do not contain the full complement of amino acids. Therefore, a mixture of beans and vegetables is generally recommended if one decides to become a vegetarian.

The need for a balanced diet. A balanced diet should consist of protein (15%), carbohydrates (65%) and fats (15% to 20%), together with vitamins and minerals, trace elements and water. Vitamins, minerals and trace elements are normally found in sufficient quantities in the foods we eat. The reason we need to be concerned with having a balanced diet is that too little or too much of one type of food can cause problems. For example, too much fat has been linked not only to heart disease but to cancer. Complete absence of fat, on the other hand, means that we do not have one of the important foods that supply us with energy. The absence of protein is also problematic. While we can get along without carbohydrates and fats (which are stored in the body), we cannot get along without proteins. The amino acids contained in proteins provide the basic components that our body needs to manufacture such things as the neurotransmitters (e.g., norepinephrine and serotonin) that our brain needs to function (Wurtman, 1982). Amino acids also contain the components necessary for the repair of cells. Too much protein, on the other hand, is not only unnecessary but can indirectly lead to high fat levels. Red meats in particular (especially those cuts that contain high fat levels) have been linked to the high levels of fat in our diet.

Carbohydrates are one of our main sources of energy. They are also important because they supply us with many of our vitamins, minerals and trace elements. Since many junk foods are often low in vitamins, minerals and trace elements, they are sometimes referred to as "empty calories." Alcohol is a carbohydrate that is high in calories but low in vitamins. While it can lead to weight gain, it is often referred to as a product characterized by empty calories.

Since carbohydrates are necessary to properly digest other foods (they act as a catalyst), the absence of carbohydrates in the diet can prevent other foods from being fully digested and will eventually result in a dangerous toxic reaction in which ketone levels become very high. In order to lose weight, people sometimes cut down on carbohydrates or avoid them altogether. Because carbohydrates are an important source of energy—an important source of vitamins and minerals— and because they are important in the digestive process, people should not avoid them when trying to lose weight but rather select ones that are low in calories, such as potatoes. Any successful dieter should make an active search for low-calorie carbohydrates in order to help reduce caloric intake while simultaneously maintaining a balanced diet.

Insulin and the metabolism of glucose. When glucose levels in the blood rise, the pancreas responds by secreting insulin. Insulin is important for converting glucose into energy as well as for transporting glucose to the cells. Without insulin, a condition arises called diabetes. As glucose levels continue to rise, the kidneys draw water into the urine, resulting in an excessive output of diluted urine. To compensate for the lack of available fuel (glucose) and energy for brain functioning, fat is mobilized, fatty acids are released, and protein is used as a source of energy. As a result, repair of injured tissue is slowed and resistance to infection is low. Diabetics have particular difficulty breaking down carbohydrates, a condition that can be easily treated by daily injections of insulin and restricted intake of carbohydrates (Sherman & Sherman, 1989).

Theories of Hunger

The glucose theory of hunger. Since we tend to get hungry when the food in our intestinal tract is depleted, it seems to follow that the reason we eat is that our blood glucose level is low. Indeed, early research on this topic provided good support for this idea. Researchers manipulated the level of available energy by transfusing blood from a starved dog to a satisfied dog and vice versa. They found that a recently fed dog had stomach contractions when it received blood from a starving one (Luckhardt & Carlson, 1915; Tschukitschew, cited in Templeton & Quigley, 1930). Similarly, a transfusion of blood from a recently fed dog to a starving dog terminated stomach contractions (Bash, 1939). It has been suggested that the stomach, liver, and hypothalamus contain glucoreceptors that provide feedback on the available glucose in the system (Russek, 1963).

The insulin theory of hunger. In general, the correlation between hunger and low blood glucose levels has not been very close. For this reason, researchers have continued to search for other explanations for hunger. One theory is that insulin plays an important if not the primary role in producing feelings of hunger. Since food (in and out of the GI tract) stimulates the secretion of insulin, the level of insulin is highly correlated with the level of glucose: either both are high or both are low. In other words, it could be insulin rather than glucose that actually triggers those feelings of hunger. In order to find out which is more important, the levels of glucose and insulin have to be manipulated independently. Researchers inserted catheters into a vein so that they could administer insulin and glucose directly into the blood. They found that insulin was a better predictor than glucose not only of hunger and eating but of the pleasure people derived from sweet-tasting foods (Rodin et al., 1985).

The insulin theory is attractive because it can explain phenomena that are hard to explain by other theories. It can explain, for example, why people who are overweight have higher basal levels of insulin than people of normal weight (Rabinowitz & Zierler, 1962). It can also explain the frequent finding that insulin administered to humans and animals leads to overweight. While the insulin theory is appealing, it should be pointed out that there is other evidence that high levels of circulating insulin may result in decreased food intake (see Rodin et al., 1985).

Reconciling the glucose theory and the insulin theories. The glucose theory and the insulin theory are not easy to reconcile. Later in this chapter, I will discuss evidence that the insulin response can be conditioned. In this work, it has been shown that merely presenting food (stimulating the senses with the sight and smell of food) while not allowing people to actually eat the food, is sufficient to trigger the insulin response, at least in some people. This work shows that people in whom the insulin response has been triggered eat more. If the amount people eat is taken as an indicator of how hungry they are, the obvious conclusion is that insulin causes hunger. In another series of studies, it was shown that glucose (starches and sugars) triggers a larger insulin response (one that persists longer) than does fructose (fruits). According to the insulin theory, if there are higher levels of circulating insulin when one eats, one would be inclined to take more food (presumably reflecting greater hunger caused by the higher levels of insulin). Indeed, it was found that people who had eaten foods that produced higher glucose levels took more food at a later meal than people who had eaten foods that produced higher fructose levels. The argument is that, after a period of time, the insulin levels in people who had eaten fructose was lower, and that if insulin is linked to hunger, it follows they would eat less. Such results provide highly convincing data for the insulin theory. Nevertheless, there is also strong evidence for the glucose theory. It may be that both theories are correct. That is, we tend to respond to glucose levels under certain conditions and to insulin under other conditions.

The fatty acid theory of hunger. When we have used up the food in our gastrointestinal tract (GI tract) and have depleted the glucose that is circulating in our blood, our body will begin to release fatty acids and glycerol from the adipose (fat) tissue. Because these free fatty acids are deposited in the bloodstream, the level of free fatty acids should be closely related to hunger. Various researchers have proposed that the body may have receptors that are designed to detect an increase in the level of fatty acids, and that their activation triggers the subjective feeling we call hunger (Dole, 1956; Klein et al., 1960).

The heat-production theory of hunger. John Brobeck (1960) has suggested that a drop in body and blood temperature, as sensed by brain cells, will lead to increased feelings of hunger, while a rise in body and blood temperature will lead to decreased feelings of hunger. This theory can explain findings that pose difficulties for other theories. Since one of the by-products of activity

is heat production, it can explain why various activities lead to a decline in hunger. It can also explain why we feel hungrier in a cold environment than in a warm one.

Feedback Systems for Satiety

Various theorists have argued that humans not only have receptors that can tell them when they are hungry, but that they have receptors that tell them when they have eaten enough (satiety receptors). Two very different lines of research have identified two very different mechanisms; one of these is located in the brain while the other is located in the lower end of the gastrointestinal tract.

Brain receptors for satiety. Amphetamines have been used for some time to control appetite. Apparently, amphetamines and their derivatives work by binding to receptors in the brain. This finding has led to speculation that the body must produce its own amphetamines that normally control appetite. Tricyclic antidepressants, on the other hand, lead to increased food intake. Tricyclic antidepressants are known to alter such things as norepinephrine, a neurotransmitter that is produced and stored in the brain. Exactly why tricyclics lead to increased food intake is not clear. They may suppress, in some way, the normal functioning of the satiety receptors. Alternatively, they may stimulate receptors that trigger the hunger response. Taken together, these findings suggest that receptors in the brain play an important role (Kolata, 1982). What this research fails to tell us is why this mechanism fails to control weight in some people.

Signals from the gastrointestinal tract. When glucose is injected slowly into the gastrointestinal tract (the duodenum) it can produce a decline in eating, whereas when it it is injected quickly it can produce an increase in eating (Geiselman & Novin, 1982). The implication is that one could decrease feelings of hunger by slowing the rate at which food arrives at the duodenum. Henry Koopmans (1985) has provided direct evidence of the existence of satiety signals from the stomach that control short-term eating and other satiety signals from the

Junk food is a relatively new phenomenon. The attraction to junk food has been linked to the tendency of humans to select food based on taste and texture as opposed to nutritional value.

lower small intestine that appear to be involved in the control of long-term eating. How can we make use of these mechanisms to control eating in people who are obese? Would it be possible, for example, to devise harmless pills that contain nutrient-rich foods that dissolve when they reach these receptors and thereby shut down the eating response? It is important to remember that for many people the real culprit in overweight is not the initial desire to eat but rather not experiencing the sensation of being satisfied or satiated when they have eaten enough food to satisfy their nutritional needs.

Learned Factors in Hunger and Eating

Can we select a balanced diet? Do we instinctively know what foods we should eat in order to meet our nutritional needs, or do we learn to select a balanced diet?

From time to time it has been suggested that humans are indeed born with this capacity. A now classic and often-quoted study (Davis, 1928) has been offered as evidence. In the Davis study, children were given a wide range of foods from which they could select what they wanted to eat. His studies showed that over a period of time young children presented with an array of food items will select a nutritionally balanced diet (they don't just select sweet foods, for example). While the Davis study has been offered as evidence that humans can select a nutritious (balanced) diet, critics have pointed out that all the foods that Davis presented to the young children were nutritious and therefore his study fails to provide clear evidence that humans can select between foods that are nutritious and those that are not. It is noteworthy that junk foods as we know them today were not available at the time Davis did his study.

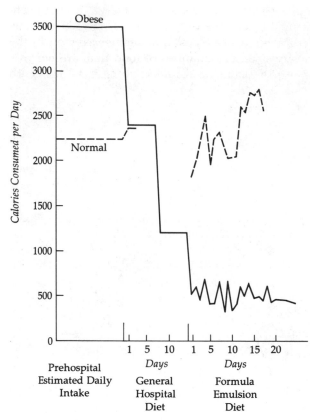

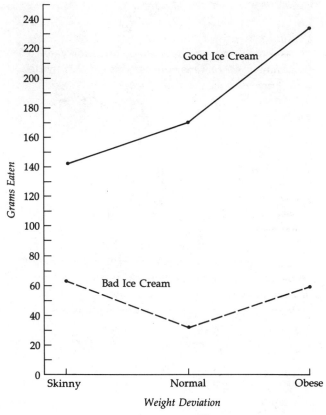

Figure 4–1. Effect of a formula emulsion diet on the eating behavior of an obese and a normal subject. (From S. Schachter, Emotion, Obesity and Crime, 1971. Copyright © 1971 by Academic Press. Reprinted with permission.)

Figure 4–2. Amount of good-tasting and bad-tasting ice cream eaten by subjects of different weights. (From S. Schachter, Emotion, Obesity and Crime, 1971. Copyright © 1971 by Academic Press. Reprinted with permission.)

Although we have evidence to suggest that humans may select balanced diets under certain conditions, we also have an abundance of evidence to the contrary. In many isolated instances, people both individually and in groups have developed food preferences that have led to various forms of malnutrition, even when nutritious foods have been readily available. Our own society seems to be enamored of the so-called junk foods, which have an appealing taste but are low in essential nutrients.

There is also evidence that people at the lower socioeconomic levels of American society eat foods with less nutritional value than people at the higher socioeconomic levels (Adelson, 1968). Some people have er-

roneously argued that this difference simply reflects the fact that poor people cannot afford nutritious foods. A more careful analysis has shown that people at the lower socioeconomic levels buy more prepared foods and more snack foods, both of which tend to be low in nutritional value. Interestingly, these foods are generally more expensive. Therefore, although such people spend more money on food, they select foods that are not so good for them. It has been suggested that the reasons people at the upper socioeconomic levels of society tend to buy more nutritious foods is that they are more knowledgeable about the nutritional value of food and more willing to spend time preparing it.

Selection of foods based on taste and texture as opposed to nutritional value. There is an abundance of data indicating that humans are inclined to select foods based on taste and texture rather than on nutrition value (e.g., Schachter, 1971a). One consequence of this tendency is that people will often select junk foods which taste good and have appealing texture but fail to provide the basic nutrients that people need. In some cases junk foods, including some of the popular breakfast cereals, not only fail to provide basic nutrients but load the body with salt and sugar. These are often the primary ingredient in many so-called nutritious breakfast cereals, and if it were not for the milk that people pour on these cereals, they would meet few of our basic nutritional needs.

As I indicated earlier, one of the main criticisms of the Davis study is that in 1928 there were no junk foods as we know them today. The cakes and other sweets of which children are so fond were made from basic food products, not from the synthetic materials used to manufacture some of the current junk foods.

The tendency towards overweight and obesity has been linked to the tendency of some people to select foods based on their sensory qualities. Probably one of the most dramatic demonstrations that the obese person's eating is often highly dependent on sensory cues is a study that compared grossly obese men and women with nonobese controls (Hashim & Van Itallie, 1965). The researchers prepared a bland, homogenized liquid diet similar in taste and composition to the vanilla flavors of such commercial preparations as Nutrament and Metrecal. The subjects (who were confined to a hospital) were allowed to eat as much of this diet as they wanted, but consumption was in a situation totally devoid of any social trappings. Normals continued to consume their daily average of about 2400 calories, but obese subjects diminished their intake to 500 calories a day, about 3000 calories less than their daily average before admission to the hospital (Figure 4-1).

Although other studies have not shown so dramatic an effect, the same general finding seems to hold even in very tightly controlled studies. In an experiment that asked subjects to evaluate taste (Nisbett, 1968), obese subjects ate significantly more than normals and skinny subjects when it tasted good, but ate about the same amount when it tasted bad. Again, this indicates that obese people are influenced more by the positive sensory qualities of food than are normals (Figure 4-2). Similar results have been obtained with cake and milk (cited in Schachter, 1971b).

Cultural preferences. The different eating preferences of different ethnic groups provide compelling evidence that learning plays an important role in what we eat. The Italians are known for their love of pasta, the East Indians for their love of curry, the French for their garlic, the Mexicans for their hot peppers, the Japanese for their raw fish, and so forth. Where do these different preferences come from?

It can be argued from an evolutionary perspective that it would be highly adaptive if humans could learn to eat different foods depending on what was available. To do this they would need not only to be able to identify which foods were nutritious but which ones were toxic. There is considerable evidence that indeed humans as well as other organisms can learn to avoid foods that are lacking in nutrition and are toxic (make you sick). While avoiding foods which make you sick is learned quickly, learning to select foods which are nutritious takes considerably more time. The research of John Garcia and others suggests that in order to detect that a food is not providing nutrition, the organism must develop a general malaise. In other words, food selection comes from learning to avoid all those foods that produce some type of aversive state in the organism, a state that results from not having the right nutrients in one's diet (see Nachman, 1970; Garcia & Koelling, 1966; Garcia et al., 1968). In order to ensure that individuals would not have to learn this for themselves, the development of taste preferences in the early stages of food intake would be highly adaptive. Specifically, modeling one's parents and thereby developing preferences would eliminate the need to go through some type of long trial-and-error learning process, a process that is fraught with dangers.

Since the availability of certain foods changes, it would be important that this learning not be too rigid, thereby preventing the individual from trying new foods in the absence of his or her preferred diet. The fact that people develop new tastes, albeit over a considerable period of time, is consistent with this idea. Again, it can be shown that many of these new preferences are linked to taste and texture rather than to nutritional value.

Cognitive and Individual Factors in Hunger and Eating

Today, many people are learning to eat different foods based on knowledge of what is healthy for them. Even though they might prefer a juicy hamburger, they slowly learn to eat foods that contain less fat, sugar, salt, and so forth. What is interesting is that people often report that after a time they do not have to actively think about what they should or should not eat because their preferences have changed. People who have learned to eat less red meat or leaner cuts of red meat, for example, often report that after a time they come to prefer smaller amounts and that fatty cuts often elicit an aversion sometimes bordering on revulsion. Such reports are encouraging, because they mean that with time we will develop taste and texture preferences that are in line with what we know in our heads is healthy for us.

Summary

When the three basic food types (fats, carbohydrates, and proteins) are ingested, they enter the gastrointestinal tract where they are broken down into more basic chemical units and used as energy to rebuild cells and to manufacture the chemicals that are needed throughout the brain and body. One of the main sources of energy is carbohydrates, which are broken down into glucose and fructose. While some of the glucose circulates in the blood, providing a source of immediate energy, much of it is transported across the membrane walls of the small intestines and is stored in the cells as glycogen. Since carbohydrates are also our main source of vitamins, minerals, and trace elements, it is important for humans to ensure that their diets contain 65% carbohydrates. Fats can be an important source of energy, but when there is excess in the diet, much of it is transported to the fat cells (adipose tissue) where it is

stored for future needs. Excess fat in the diet has been linked not only to heart disease but also to cancer. Nevertheless, 15% to 20% of our diet is fat. Amino acids are important for rebuilding cells and for manufacturing many of the chemicals—such as the neurotransmitters in our brains—that our body and brain need to function. Even though proteins are important, only 15% of our diet should be in the form of proteins. Insulin plays an important role in the conversion of glucose to energy. Without insulin a condition arises which is called diabetes.

Several theories of hunger have been proposed, including the glucose theory which suggests hunger is linked to decreased glucose levels, the insulin theory which suggests that hunger is linked to increases (possibly sudden increases) in insulin levels, the fatty acid theory which suggests that we have receptors that are designed to detect increases in fatty-acid levels, and the heat-production theory which suggests that drops in blood temperature are detected by the brain and trigger hunger.

Various researchers have suggested from time to time that we not only have mechanisms that trigger hunger but that we have mechanisms that trigger satiety (when we have had enough to eat). Since various drugs, such as the amphetamines, reduce feelings of hunger, it has been suggested that the body produces its own amphetamines to control hunger. Also, since stimulating the lower end of the gastrointestinal tract with nutrient-rich food can shut down eating, feedback mechanisms in the gastrointestinal tract may help control the amount we eat.

There is a great deal of evidence that humans are inclined to select what they eat on the basis of taste and texture of food. Further, it appears these preferences for taste and texture are learned, probably in childhood. There is growing evidence that people can learn to change these preferences. In time, selection of food based on knowledge of what is healthy for us can become habit.

The Origins of Overweight

If we continue to eat after we have ingested sufficient food to last us until our next meal, the extra food will be stored as fat in the adipose tissue. This is as certain as that the sun will rise tomorrow. Should we repeat this practice regularly, we not only will tend to gain weight but eventually will become obese (severely overweight). The question is why many people eat more than they need. As we shall see, there are several possibilities. At least three of the explanations assume some abnormality in the biological structure of obese people.

Defining Obesity

Who are the obese? Unfortunately, there is no easy way to define obesity. The term has been used to refer to people who have a very moderate amount of fat and to those who are grossly overweight. In many of the studies I will be discussing, *obese* is defined simply as exceeding the average weight for one's height, build, age, and sex by a given percentage, for example 20% or 30%. This means that a person who should weigh 150 pounds would be classified as obese if he or she weighed 180 pounds. Thus, we are not talking about the fat lady at the circus sideshow but about people with whom we interact daily. Many of us have experienced or will experience excessive weight gain sometime during our lives. Therefore, within many of us there lives the potential obese person, ready to emerge if given half a chance. It is interesting to note that in recent years the tables for normal weight have been revised, allowing for more leeway than in earlier tables.

Biological Component

The genetic factor. In order to separate what is inherited from what is acquired through experience, it is necessary to control for either the environment or our genes. Since it is often difficult to control the environment, scientists have traditionally liked to study adopted versus natural children and identical versus fraternal twins. These studies have shown that adopted children tend to resemble their biological parents in weight far more than they resemble their adoptive parents (Stunkard et al., 1985) and that identical twins, even when reared apart, are more similar in weight than are fraternal twins or other siblings (for example, Stunkard, Foch,

& Hrubec, 1985). One of the things that may be inherited is metabolism rate. A person who has a high metabolism rate tends not to become obese.

The resemblance of children to their parents in weight may be due to factors other than metabolism rate. In one study, it was found that children of overweight parents not only preferred sweeter solutions but were more responsive to external cues in their environments (Milstein, 1980). The externality theory of why people eat will be discussed in some detail later in this chapter. For now let me simply say that people who are external are highly susceptible to such things as the taste and texture of food.

Energy Expenditure

The three components. Energy expenditure has three main components: *basal metabolism rate* (BMR), *physical activity*, and *specific dynamic action* (SDA) of food. About one-third of our energy use is attributable to exercise and about two-thirds to our BMR (Rodin, 1981). SDA is the increase in energy expenditure following the ingestion of food. SDA can increase the BMR by up to 20% for a few hours after a meal. Certain foods, such as proteins, produce the greatest increase (Powers, 1982). The actual proportions of energy expended in exercise and metabolism obviously depend on individual exercise patterns. The basal metabolism rate is the amount of energy we use in a given period of time in relation to our body size. Specifically, it is measured as the number of calories we burn per square meter of body surface in an hour when we are resting. What is interesting about basal metabolism is that it changes with age, varies markedly from individual to individual, and is affected by how large we are, what we eat, and how long we have gone without food.

Age. From birth to about age 18 to 20 in females and a little later in males, the metabolism rate declines rapidly. As Figure 4-3 shows, at about age 20 the rate levels out, and from then on it declines much more slowly. This means that the amount of food we need to function at resting levels, in proportion to body size, declines rather sharply, starting shortly after birth, until age 20 or so. From then on we need approximately the same amount of energy to operate on a day-to-day basis. There is a sharp increase in food intake around puberty because food is needed to build bones and muscles that are developing rapidly at that time as well as to supply the energy for the high level of activity that frequently occurs then.

Although obesity can occur at any age, humans often first encounter problems of overweight around age 20 or shortly thereafter. If the amount we eat is controlled more or less by habit, it is not surprising that overweight first shows itself at this age. First, because we have stopped growing, we no longer require as much food. Second, the reduction in metabolism rate means our bodies burn up fuel more slowly. The extra food will be converted to fat. Finally, any reduction in exercise would further make us prone to overweight. The slow but continuous decline in basal metabolism rate with increasing age and the tendency to exercise less with increasing age are important factors in the tendency for humans to become overweight in their later years.

Obesity and Anorexia as Malfunctions of the Hypothalamus

Two areas of the hypothalamus have been linked to the two behavioral phenomena of overeating and failure to eat. Lesions of the ventromedial nuclei of the hypothalamus produce overeating, which leads to obesity (see Teitelbaum, 1961), and lesions of the lateral hypothalamus lead to a failure to eat, a state called *anorexia*.

Lesions of the ventromedial nuclei. Philip Teitelbaum (1961) noted that animals with lesions of the *ventromedial nuclei* (VMN) show the following characteristics.

1. They are unresponsive to normal satiety cues that are presumably mediated by glucose.

2. They will not work as hard as normal animals to obtain food.

3. They will stop eating "adulterated" foods (such as food laced with quinine) sooner than normal animals.

4. They will eat large amounts of highly palatable foods.

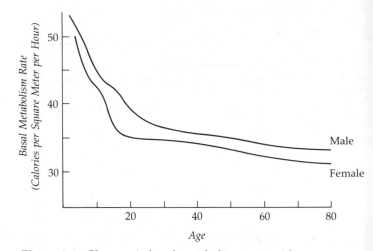

Figure 4–3. Changes in basal metabolism rates with age (From R. B. Stuart and B. Davis, *Slim Chance in a Fat World*, 1972. Copyright © 1972 by the Research Press Company. Reprinted with permission.)

Lesions of the lateral hypothalamus. Lesions of the *lateral hypothalamus* (LH) have been shown to produce an effect analogous but complementary to those in the VMN. Specifically, it has been shown that lesions of the LH result initially in the cessation of eating. After such animals have lost considerable body weight, they begin to eat again, but at a much reduced rate. This reduced rate of eating tends to be very stable. While palatable foods tend to result in increased eating and weight gain, just as they do in normal and obese animals, animals lesioned in the LH continue to maintain their weight well below the normal level. The degree of anorexia that the animals display is related to the size of the lesion (Keesy & Powley, 1975).

What is the exact mechanism? Does the hypothalamus simply regulate the amount we eat or does it act as a monitor of, say, the level of body fat? The most widely held view is that the hypothalamus is involved in monitoring the store of adipose tissue. There is considerable evidence that VMN lesions produce a disruption in fat metabolism, which increases the amount of glucose that is converted to lipids, which are then transferred to adipose tissue for storage (Frohman, Goldman, &

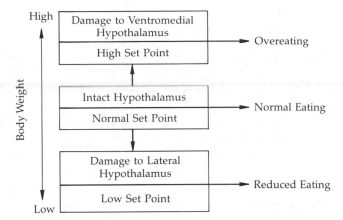

Figure 4–4. Damage (or lesions) to the ventromedial hypothalmus raises the set point, while damage (or lesions) to the lateral hypothalmus lowers the set point. (Based on R. E. Keesy and T. L. Powley, "Hypothalamic Regulation of Body Weight," *American Scientist,* 1975, *63,* 558-565.)

Bernardis, 1972; Goldman et al., 1970, 1972a, 1972b; Haessler & Crawford, 1967). It could be argued that the obesity resulting from the VMN lesion is due to the disruption of the normal metabolism process—that is, the lesion produces overeating because of the abnormally low glucose level that results from this disruption.

Set-Point Theory

Richard Keesy and Terry Powley (1975) have proposed that the findings from studies of the hypothalamus provide evidence for a set-point theory of weight level. Specifically, they have proposed that the hypothalamus sets our weight. Some of us will have normal weight, some of us will tend toward obesity, and still others will tend toward anorexia. This hypothesis is summarized in Figure 4-4.

Keesy and Powley argue that their theory of weight level can readily account for the tendency of people who are inclined to overweight to fall off their diets. Because such people have a high set point they would feel hungry, and in order to satisfy their hunger they would be inclined to overeat. Over time their weight

would match their set point and at that time their food consumption would level off. Only by deliberately restraining their eating would they be able to keep their weight down. Any failure to restrain their eating would immediately result in a tendency to overeat.

The "Yo-Yo" Effect and the Famine Hypothesis

People who diet in order to achieve the slim figure that society has come to favor often experience a phenomenon labeled the yo-yo effect. Once they have achieved their desired weight they find it virtually impossible to keep the weight off and after a short time are again overweight, at least according to their standards. Obsessed with the desire to be slim, they again diet but again they put on weight after achieving their desired weight. To their dismay such dieters often find that each time they put on weight following a diet they not only regain all the weight they lost but they put on a little more. Slowly but surely they get heavier on each upswing. Why do they put on more weight each time they diet? No one is certain, but one explanation comes from the famine hypothesis.

According to the famine hypothesis, obesity can be understood as an adaptive mechanism gone awry because we are no longer faced with periodic food shortages. David Margules (1979) theorizes that the adipose tissue evolved to protect humans against food shortages, and now that such shortages are rare, we tend to continue adding to an already adequate reserve. In short, people are inclined to progress from a comfortable reserve to a state of obesity. Extending this hypothesis to account for the yo-yo effect goes something like this. When people lose weight the body responds to the weight loss as though it just went through a famine. If the weight loss due to the diet pushed the body below the person's set point, the body says to itself at the end of the diet: "I didn't have enough fat reserves to handle this last famine, so I must put on more weight than before so I will be prepared for the next famine." When the person diets again and achieves his or her desired weight (again pushing the body below its set point) the body says: "The last time I put on extra weight it wasn't enough so next time I will have to put on even more." As a result, each time the individual pushes his or her weight below set point the body responds with even greater determination to prevent this from happening again and works even harder to protect the individual against the next, inevitable famine by increasing the fat reserves even more. Obviously, the body doesn't talk to itself. There has to be some type of mechanism that has yet to be identified that could signal the body to put on more weight.

The "Yo-Yo" Effect As a Result of Reduced Metabolism

It is possible that the yo-yo effect is simply the result of decreased metabolism that is typically associated with dieting. In other words, it may simply be that people tend to eat the same amount following a diet, but because metabolism has gone down, returning to normal eating habits results in greater weight gain.

The "Yo-Yo" Effect and Health

Not only is the yo-yo effect frustrating for the dieter, it is bad for one's health. In a recent study of 3,130 men and women age 30 to 62, it was found that so called yo-yo dieters ran a 70% higher risk of dying from heart disease than did people whose weight stayed relatively steady, even if they were overweight. The effect on health is greater for men than for women. The exact reasons are not clear. One explanation is that fluctuating weight may stress the body, producing elevated blood pressure and cholesterol. The good news is that the number of dieters is leveling off, dropping from 65 million in 1986 to 48 million in 1991 (Kramer & Williams, 1991) (Time, July 8, 1991).

Learned Component

The environmental factor. Statistics indicate that overweight children are likely to have overweight parents (Garn & Clark, 1976). Further, there is evidence that overweight children tend to become overweight adults (Eden, 1975; Hirsch, Knittle, & Salans, 1966). Although these findings provide support for the idea that obesity may be genetically determined, there are reasons for questioning this conclusion. First, if a separate correlation is calculated between a child's weight and the weight of each parent, the child's weight tends to be more highly correlated with the mother's weight than with the father's (Garn & Clark, 1976). If the cause were purely genetic, the correlations should be equal. Second, the resemblance in weight of siblings, even identical twins, decreases in later life. This decreasing resemblance suggests that factors other than genetics must be responsible for weight patterns.

How do we account for these findings? The fact that a child's weight tends to be correlated with the mother's can be accounted for by the likelihood that the mother controls to a large degree the eating behavior of her children or simply the availability of food. Because of her own tendency to overeat, for example, the mother may fill her children's plates with more food than they require or simply make food available. If they are encouraged to eat all the food on their plates or to snack, the children will eventually convert the extra food into fat. If this tendency to take more food than is needed becomes a habit, it could help to explain their tendency to overeat in later life.

Another possibility is that fat mothers like to prepare appealing foods. Children who learn to eat such foods when they are hungry may learn to associate eating with certain cues. Thus, foods that had a particular taste, texture, or smell would tend to elicit the eating response. The presence or availability of such foods would determine whether such a person became obese. If, in later life, he found himself in an environment where such foods were readily available, he would be likely to overeat.

Cognitive Component and Individual Differences

Rate of Energy Use

Individual differences in metabolism rates. There are large individual differences in basal metabolism rates. In one study, subjects who had wide differences in caloric intake were matched for height, weight, and level of activity. Even though their weights did not change over a period of weeks, it was often found that one member of the matched pair ate twice as much as the other (Rose & Williams, 1961). Such differences in basal metabolism rate obviously play an important role in determining who will be prone to obesity and who will have difficulty dieting.

Emotional disorders and obesity. Do we eat more when we are depressed, anxious, or stressed? No direct link has been established between emotional disorders and overeating. Typically, depression is characterized by weight loss rather than overeating. It has been shown, however, that when a depressed state was induced in subjects high in self-restraint, they ate significantly more than similarly depressed subjects who were low in self-restraint (Frost et al., 1982). This finding makes a great deal of sense if we assume that the ability to control eating is greater in people who have more self-control and that when people become depressed they lose their ability or desire to exercise control. One of the things that happens when people become depressed is that they feel they have lost control of their lives.

A recent study examined the effects of stress on eating. In one condition a group of men and women were shown a film about industrial accidents (stress condition) or a pleasant travelogue (control condition) while they had access to sweet, salty, and bland snack food. While stress markedly decreased food consumption in men, women ate nearly twice as much sweet food and more bland food under stress than did their control counterparts (Grunberg & Straub, 1992). As in the study reported above, there is some reason to suspect that the reason women ate more was that more women than men tend to be restrained eaters.

It has been suggested periodically that the reason some people tend to eat more when they are emotionally upset or when they are experiencing stress is that they have been taught to eat under these conditions. If a mother tries to comfort her children with food when they are upset, for example, the child may learn to eat under these conditions. Later in life, such people turn to food just as they turned to mother in the past.

Summary

Obesity is commonly defined as weight in excess of some norm, usually by approximately 25% or more. There is good evidence that the tendency to obesity is at least partly genetically determined. First, people who are overweight often come from overweight parents. Second, twin studies show that adopted children are more likely to resemble their biological parents in weight than their adoptive parents. Two possible explanations are: they inherit a similar metabolism rate and/or they inherit a propensity to eat in response to external cues.

Energy expenditure may also be a contributing factor to overweight. Energy expenditure has three main components: basal metabolism rate (BMR), physical activity, and specific dynamic action (SDA). Our basal metabolism rate, which accounts for about two-thirds of our energy expenditure, decreases as we age. It slows fairly abruptly at around age 20. This change can explain why some people tend to put on weight around that age.

Set-point theory suggests that we have a set point that governs our weight. This theory grows out of research that has shown that lesions in the hypothalamus can produce obesity and anorexia in animals. Margules has argued that obesity is an adaptive mechanism gone astray: we prepare for a famine that never comes. The famine hypothesis can account for the yo-yo effect. Each time individuals bring their weight below their set point the body responds as though the famine has come. If food is available, as it tends to be in North America, individuals will be motivated to eat and prepare for the next famine.

There are several factors which suggest overweight is due, at least in part, to learning. Since a child's weight is more likely to resemble the mother's weight than the father's, it has been argued that fat mothers probably have fat children because in a variety of ways they encourage their children not only to overeat but to eat foods high in calories.

One of the individual difference factors that can account for differences in weight is metabolism. BMR varies widely among individuals so that some people can eat considerably more than others without putting on weight. Emotional disorders have also been linked to obesity.

Theories of Overweight and Obesity
Internal-External Theory of Hunger and Eating

One of the major theories about why people are overweight is linked to the observation that some people seem to eat in response to *external* cues, such as the sight and smell of food and the time of day, whereas other people seem to depend on *internal* cues to tell them when to eat, such as stomach contractions, glucose levels, fat levels, and so forth. This led Stanley Schachter to propose the Internal-External Theory of overweight and obesity. This theory generated a great deal of research and has been the cornerstone for more recent research.

Stomach contractions and hunger. One of the first systematic demonstrations that obese and nonobese people respond to different cues was made by Albert Stunkard (1959). He arranged for both obese and nonobese subjects to enter the laboratory at 9:00 in the morning, having gone overnight without food. Each volunteer was asked to swallow a gastric balloon (filled with water) that was attached to a mechanical device to record stomach contractions. Every 15 minutes for four hours, the volunteers were asked to report whether they were hungry. It was found that the nonobese were more likely to report hunger when the stomach was active than the obese. This finding suggests that feelings of hunger are associated with internal stimuli for the nonobese but not for the obese. Since we would expect hunger to be associated with internal cues, the question is why the obese fail to respond to these cues. If they are not responding to internal cues, what cues are eliciting their reports of hunger?

Stanley Schachter (1971a) demonstrated that whereas the nonobese person tends to respond to internal cues such as stomach motility or hypoglycemia (low blood glucose level), the obese person tends to respond more to external cues. An obese person who is accustomed to eating at a certain time, for example, will feel hungry when the clock indicates mealtime. The nonobese person will be less influenced by the time on the clock unless it happens to coincide with his or her internal cues or biological clock. To test this prediction, Schachter had volunteers come to the laboratory under the pretense of studying "the relation between physiological reactions and psychological characteristics which require base level measurements of heart and sweat gland activity" (Schachter & Gross, 1968, p. 99). Electrodes were attached, presumably to

Table 4-1. Amount of crackers eaten (in grams) by Schachter's subjects in four conditions. (From S. Schachter, *Emotion, Obesity and Crime*, 1971. Copyright © 1971 by Academic Press. Reprinted with permission.)

	Time	
Weight	Slow	Fast
Obese	19.9	37.6
Normal	41.5	16.0

measure heart rate and galvanic skin response. Half the obese and half the nonobese subjects were then left for a period of time (presumably to establish a baseline) with a rigged clock that over 50 minutes would be 15 minutes slow. The other half were left for the same period with a rigged clock that would be 30 minutes fast. The first group finished this phase of the study when its clock said 5:20 P.M.(normal), the second when its clock said 6:05 P.M.(normal). The experimenter returned at this point with a box of crackers from which he was snacking and offered some to the volunteer. The experimenter also asked the subject to fill out an irrelevant questionnaire. If the obese person is more affected by clock time than real time, he should eat more in the *fast clock time* condition than in the *slow clock time* condition, since in the fast-time condition the apparent time was either near or past his normal eating time. The results (Table 4-1) supported the hypothesis. On the average, obese subjects ate more crackers in the fast-time condition than in the slow-time condition— just the reverse of the nonobese subjects, who ate more in the slow-time condition. Why was there a reversal for the nonobese? Schachter notes that when the nonobese in the fast-time condition refused crackers, they said "No, thanks, I don't want to spoil my dinner." Apparently, cognitive factors were responsible for the tendency to eat less in this condition.

The Air France study. These findings are consistent with those obtained by more naturalistic methods (Goldman, Jaffa, & Schachter, 1968). An airplane crosses several time zones when it flies from Paris to New York,

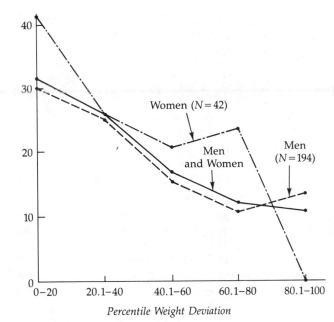

Figure 4–5. Relation of weight deviation among Air France personnel to complaining about the effect of time-zone changes on eating. (From S. Schachter, *Emotion, Obesity and Crime,* 1971. Copyright © 1971 by Academic Press. Reprinted with permission.)

so that a passenger's internal cues will fail to correspond with clock time after a flight. Because obese people respond to clock time rather than internal cues, they should adjust quickly to the local eating time; the nonobese, in contrast, should find it much more difficult to adjust their eating habits to local time. Interviews with Air France personnel assigned to transatlantic flights indicated that those who were overweight had less trouble adjusting to local eating time than those who were average in weight (Figure 4-5).

A further test of Schachter's theory: fear, stomach contractions, and hunger. To determine more precisely whether nonobese people respond to an internal state—namely, stomach motility—a study was designed in which stomach cues would be suppressed or eliminated (Schachter, Goldman, & Gordon, 1968). Because it has been found that fear will suppress gastric movement, and because researchers find it easy to manipulate fear by informing

subjects that they will receive a shock, it was relatively easy to design a study in which nonobese subjects would experience little or no gastric movement. Subjects were told that the purpose of the experiment was to evaluate the effects of tactile stimulation on taste and that electrical stimulation would be used to stimulate the skin receptors. In the low-fear condition, subjects were told the electrical stimulation would produce a mild tingling sensation; in the high-fear condition, subjects were told the shocks would be painful but would cause no permanent damage. They were further instructed that the experimenters wanted to get measures of taste before and during tactile stimulation. Hence the subjects started the tasting part of the experiment with the belief that they would shortly be experiencing shock in the next phase of the study. Actual shock was not given; the instructions were used merely to induce fear. The tasting task involved judging some crackers in terms of several dimensions (salty, cheesy, garlicky, and so on). However, the actual behavior of interest was the number of crackers obese and nonobese volunteers ate. Subjects were told they could eat as many crackers as they wanted in order to make their judgments. If the fear manipulation worked and if it is true that nonobese subjects' tendency to eat is determined by gastric motility, the nonobese volunteers should have eaten less under the high-fear than the low-fear condition. This was, in fact, what occurred (Figure 4-6). The obese volunteers were not sensitive to the fear manipulation: they ate almost equal amounts under high- and low-fear conditions. This finding is consistent with the view that obese people are insensitive to internal cues.

Is Externality Innate or Learned?

As I have already indicated according to Schachter's theory, some people come to depend on external cues to tell them when to eat whereas other people come to depend on internal cues to tell them when to eat. Whether or not this is an innate or learned pattern of behavior has never been clearly established. Many diet clinics encourage people to listen to their bodies' needs (internal orientation) rather than allowing themselves to be controlled by the sensory qualities of food (external orientation). Despite this common-sense sugges-

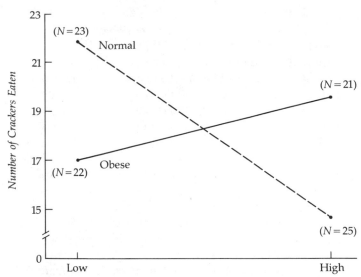

Figure 4–6. Effects of fear on number of crackers eaten by normal and obese subjects in Schachter, Goldman, and Gordon's study. (From S. Schachter, *Emotion, Obesity and Crime,* 1971. Copyright © 1971 by Academic Press. Reprinted with permission.)

tion, there is evidence that if you are an external, it is very difficult to learn to become an internal.

Externality and the nonobese. One might conclude from Schachter's work on the relation between obesity and externality that only obese people are sensitive to cues in the environment that are associated with eating. Some recent work by Judith Rodin and her colleagues indicates that this is not true. They have shown that many nonobese people are sensitive to such environmental cues and that many obese people are not (for example, Rodin, 1981; Rodin & Slochower, 1976). Further, they have shown that losing weight is not accompanied by a decrease in responsiveness to those cues (Rodin, Slochower, & Fleming, 1977). If a steak made an obese person's mouth water when she was obese, it would also make her mouth water after she had lost considerable weight. Rodin's work indicates that although externality may be associated with the motivation to eat, there is no one-to-one correspondence between that motivation and a person's weight. This lack of correspondence is undoubtedly due to

three factors: differences in metabolic rates, differences in self-control, and differences in availability of food, especially palatable foods.

Sensory cues, externality, and the insulin response. In a series of studies, Rodin (1981) has explored the hypothesis that sensory cues such as taste and smell are sufficient to stimulate the release of insulin in externals. As we noted earlier, Rodin has argued that an elevated insulin level produces feelings of hunger. If, indeed, sensory cues are capable of triggering the release of insulin in externally responsive people but not in internally responsive people, then we have a mechanism that can explain why externals tend to become obese. In order to determine whether this hypothesis was correct, Rodin first determined the subjects' degree of externality by using a battery of noneating measures. Next she asked the subjects not to eat anything for a period of 18 hours. When they arrived at the laboratory at noon, having eaten nothing since the previous night, a steak was in the process of being grilled. They could see it, smell it, hear the crackling sound of it. At the same time, a blood sample was drawn in order to measure their insulin levels. The externally responsive subjects, whether they were of normal weight or overweight, showed the greatest insulin response to the sight, smell, and sound of the grilling steak. In another study, Rodin examined whether the insulin response would increase as a function of palatability. As expected, the insulin response was greater in externally responsive subjects.

Rodin's work suggests that it is possible to condition the insulin response to the sight and smell of food. All of us can probably attest to the fact that certain sights and smells make us want to eat the food that we have just seen or smelled.

Boundary Theory of Hunger, Eating, and Obesity

Janet Polivy and Peter Herman (1983; Herman & Polivy, 1984) have proposed a boundary model of hunger and eating. According to this model, two separate mechanisms control hunger and eating, one for *hunger* and one for *satiety* (see Figure 4-7a). Both mechanisms are assumed to have a physiological basis.

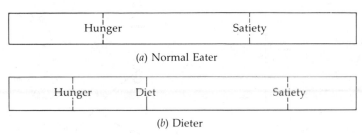

(a) Normal Eater

(b) Dieter

Figure 4–7. Hunger and satiety boundaries of normal eaters and dieters. (The diet boundary is purely cognitive.) (Adapted from C. P. Herman and J. Polivy,"A Boundary Model for the Regulation of Eating." In A. J. Stunkard and E. Stellar (Eds.), *Eating and Its Disorders,* 1984. Copyright © 1984 Raven Press, New York. Reprinted with permission.)

Following the lead of other theorists, Polivy and Herman assume that if we fail to eat or if we eat too much, we will experience an aversive state. Between these two boundary points is a range that is not under direct physiological control. Once we become hungry and begin to eat, the amount we eat will be controlled by such factors as social expectations and the taste and texture of the food. They argue that within these boundaries eating is under cognitive rather than biological control.

They further suggest that the upper and lower boundaries vary from person to person. The lower hunger boundary is lower in dieters than in nondieters, they suggest, and the upper satiety boundary is higher (compare Figures 4-7*a* and *b*). They further argue that because dieters want to control their weight, they impose on themselves an upper boundary that is well below the biological satiety boundary. This is a purely cognitive boundary. This particular idea is an outgrowth of work on dieters and nondieters, which led Polivy and Herman to distinguish between restrained and unrestrained eaters.

Restrained and unrestrained eaters. Dieters, Polivy and Herman have found, tend to be *restrained eaters.* That is, while they often feel hungry, think a great deal about food, and are readily tempted by the sight and smell of food, they consciously attempt to control their impulse to eat, and if they do overeat or eat high-calorie foods (a no-no for dieters), they feel guilty. Nondieters, in contrast, tend to be unrestrained eaters. They do not experience persistent feelings of hunger, do not think about food as much as restrained eaters, and are not so readily tempted by the sight and smell of food. More important, as far as this distinction is concerned, they

are not constantly trying to control their food intake, nor do they feel guilty when they do overeat.

Polivy and Herman have developed a scale to determine whether or not people are restrained or unrestrained (normal) eaters. They argue that the ideal of normal weight, as prescribed by society, is often below the lower limit of a person's natural range. If such people are to achieve this ideal weight they must constantly restrain themselves from giving in to their natural urges. In other words, the problem for the restrained eater is the need to deal more or less constantly with hunger and attraction to food. To see if you are a restrained eater, take the test in Table 4-2. The higher your score, the more restrained an eater you are.

The preloading studies. One of the most convincing lines of evidence for Polivy and Herman's theory comes from studies that I will simply refer to as the preload studies. They gave dieters and nondieters either one or two milkshakes (preloading) and then asked them to judge the tastes of three varieties of ice cream; some subjects got no milkshake. The subjects were told that the purpose of the preloading was to determine how a previous taste affected subsequent taste perception, but the real purpose was to determine if preloading would affect the amount of ice cream that dieters and nondieters would eat. As dieters are restrained eaters who avoid such foods as ice cream, would they feel guilty and consequently make fewer taste tests (that is, eat less) than nondieters? The initial study showed that as the size of the preload increased, the amount of ice cream the dieters ate in the course of the taste test also increased (Herman & Mack, 1975; see Figure 4-8). In a subsequent study subjects were told that the caloric content was high or low. When they were told that the

Table 4-2. Eating restraint scale (From J. Polivy and C. P. Herman, *Breaking the Diet Habit: The Natural Weight Alternative*, 1983. Copyright © 1983 by J. Polivy and C. P. Herman. Reprinted with permission.)

1. How often are you dieting?
Never; rarely; sometimes; often; always.
(Scored 0–4)

2. What is the maximum amount of weight (in pounds) that you have ever lost within one month?
0–4; 5–9; 10–14; 15–19; 20+. *(Scored 0–4)*

3. What is your maximum weight gain within a week?
0–1; 1.1–2; 2.1–3; 3.1–5; 5.1+. *(Scored 0–4)*

4. In a typical week, how much does your weight fluctuate ?
0–1; 1.1–2; 2.1–3; 3.1–5; 5.1+. *(Scored 0–4)*

5. Would a weight fluctuation of 5 pounds affect the way you live your life?
Not at all; slightly; moderately; very much. *(Scored 0–3)*

6. Do you eat sensibly in front of others and splurge alone?
Never; rarely; often; always. *(Scored 0–3)*

7. Do you give too much time and thought to food?
Never; rarely; often; always. *(Scored 0–3)*

8. Do you have feelings of guilt after overeating?
Never; rarely; often; always. *(Scored 0–3)*

9. How conscious are you of what you are eating?
Not at all; slightly; moderately; extremely. *(Scored 0–3)*

10. How many pounds over your desired weight were you at your maximum weight?
0–1; 2–5; 6–10; 11–20; 21+. *(Scored 0–4)*

caloric content was high, the effect was even greater (Polivy, 1976). That is, contrary to what one might intuitively expect, dieters ate more than nondieters.

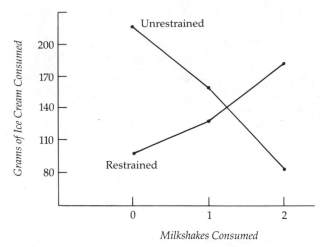

Figure 4-8. Unrestrained eaters, having consumed one or two milkshakes, show appropriate compensation when asked to taste and rate the flavors of three kinds of ice cream. Restrained eaters, however, eat more ice cream the more milkshakes they have already consumed. Herman and Polivy (1984) hypothesize that the suspension of their self-imposed restraint (in this case, in the form of the milkshakes) causes dieters to capitulate to internal (hunger) and external (taste) cues. (From J. Polivy,"Perception of Calories and Regulation of Intake in Restrained and Unrestrained Subjects." *Addictive Behavior*, 1976, *1*, 237-243. Reprinted by permission` of the author.)

The disinhibited eater. Herman and Polivy have suggested that when dieters fail to restrain their eating (in this case because they had agreed to serve in an experiment that required them to break their normal strict rules), they adopt a what-the-hell attitude. That is, they say to themselves "As long as I've already lost control, I might as well eat as much as I want." What has happened, Herman and Polivy suggest, is that having for the moment abandoned their diet boundary, they are left with only their biological satiety boundary, which is higher than the nondieter's. The fact that the effect increases when they are told that the preload is high in calories provides compelling evidence that the diet boundary is indeed cognitive rather than biological. How long does the dieter remain in this disinhibited

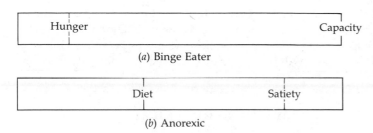

(a) Binge Eater

(b) Anorexic

Figure 4-9. Failure of satiety and hunger boundaries in binge eaters and anorexics. (The diet boundary is purely cognitive.) (Adapted from C. P. Herman and J. Polivy, "A Boundary Model for the Regulation of Eating." In A. J. Stunkard and E. Stellar (Eds.), *Eating and Its Disorders*, 1984. Copyright © 1984 Raven Press, New York.)

(what-the-hell) state? Many dieters consider the next day a new beginning and restrained eating is again the rule. It has also been shown, however, that the what-the-hell effect can be markedly reduced if their attention is called to their behavior (either by themselves or by someone else) (Polivy et al., 1986).

While the boundary theory appears to be able to explain the behavior of dieters (especially the characteristic disinhibition effect) and of bingers as well, it has been criticized on the grounds that it fails to contribute to a better understanding of why people actually become obese (Ruderman, 1986).

Binge eating and anorexia. Herman and Polivy's theory can also account for binge eating and anorexia. Figure 4-9 depicts these two types. Note that the binge eater is not responding to the satiety boundary (or the satiety boundary is inoperative) whereas the anorexic is not responding to the hunger boundary (or the hunger boundary is inoperative).

Summary

Internal-external theory grew out of the observation that obese people often eat in response to external cues whereas nonobese people eat in response to internal cues. Several studies have been done to show that obese people tend to respond to such things as time of day, palatability of food, and other external cues, whereas the nonobese tend to respond to internal cues. In a fascinating study, Judith Rodin has shown that the insulin response to the sight and smell of food is greater in externally responsive people than in internally responsive people.

Boundary theory proposes that we have two boundaries, one for hunger and one for satiety. Polivy and Herman suggest that restrained eaters are people who have a very high satiety boundary and as a result tend to overeat. In order to maintain their weight, they set a cognitive boundary. If circumstances should induce them to exceed their cognitive boundary, they tend to become disinhibited eaters for a time, usually the remainder of the day. Boundary theory can also account for binge eating and anorexia.

Obstacles to Dieting: Why People Can't or Won't Lose Weight

It is important to note that 70% of women say they feel fat but only 23% are truly overweight. In other words, many people who are dieting are trying to achieve body weights that are below what is probably good and natural.

Biological Factors

Anabolism (Caloric Thrift) and Catabolism (Caloric Waste)

The metabolism rate tends to slow down during food deprivation (Apfelbaum, 1975; Garrow, 1978). The deceleration of metabolism is referred to as *anabolism* or *caloric thrift*. This mechanism is generally viewed as adaptive. If people begin to run out of food, one good way of conserving energy is to reduce one's metabolism. A large weight gain, on the other hand, is often accompanied by an acceleration of metabolism, which is referred to as *catabolism* or *caloric waste*. In this state, energy is spent more freely (Polivy & Herman, 1983). Further, overweight people tend to have higher levels of insulin than people of normal weight, a condition referred to as hyperinsulinemia (Rabinowitz & Zierler, 1962). In this condition, fat storage is enhanced because insulin accelerates the conversion of sugar into fat. As we noted earlier, an excess of insulin tends to increase feelings of hunger (for example, Williams, 1960). The net effect is that fat people tend to get fatter.

While caloric thrift may be adaptive in a world where food is scarce, it comes to haunt the overweight person who decides it is time to diet. When the overweight person begins to cut down on food, the body responds with a reduced metabolism rate, thus frustrating the dieter's attempt to lose weight. To overcome this counter-regulatory mechanism, the dieter must cut down still further. And again the body responds by further reducing the metabolism rate.

Learned Factors

Increased preference for restricted or forbidden foods. One way to make a diet more efficient is to stop eating foods high in calories. The problem with this strategy is that the more one restricts one's intake of these restricted or forbidden foods, the more one craves them (Striegel-Moore, Silberstein, & Rodin, 1986). Why should an individual have an increased desire for sweets? Polivy and Herman (1983) have suggested that the body has a memory of the amount of food it normally gets. When an individual begins to eat fewer calories, the body responds by signaling the need for more food, especially foods high in calories, which would bring the caloric intake back to normal.

Carbohydrates and dieting. Interestingly, our basal metabolism rate depends on the type of food we eat. When our diet includes an excess of carbohydrates in proportion to saturated fats, our basal metabolism is higher (Goldman et al., 1975). Thus the popular low-carbohydrate diets actually reduce the metabolism rate. Further, because over time the metabolism rate tends to stabilize at a lower level, the person on a low-carbohydrate diet is almost certain to gain weight after terminating the diet (Beller, 1978). Relatively long periods of food deprivation also lower the basal metabolism rate (Wooley, Wooley, & Dyrenforth, 1979). Therefore, trying to lose weight by selecting a low-carbohydrate diet or by dieting can eventually be counterproductive (Rodin, 1981).

Cognitive and Individual Difference Factors

Dealing with new expectations. Some fat people acquire a variety of behaviors that center on their fatness—spending a great deal of time cooking and preparing foods, reading cookbooks, hunting out good restaurants. At the same time, they shun sports and avoid thinking or worrying about fashion; they may even take on the stereotyped "jolly fat person" style. The problem for the obese person who does lose weight is to find new activities that will help maintain the weight loss. Such people have to learn to redirect some of their energy toward things other than food. Another problem is learning how to deal with other people's assumptions that a loss of weight indicates a change in character. Since it is common in our society to view fatness as a sign of self-indulgence and inability to control oneself, people who do lose weight often find that people begin to treat them as having suddenly acquired willpower and the ability to control events. As a result they expect more of the formerly fat person—more achievement, more success, more drive. This is a tall order. Perhaps a more serious problem is the need to deal realistically with one's own expectations. Fat people tend to feel that if only they were thin, all their problems would disappear. They would be admired and respected and sought after. They would get the job, get the raise, get the guy or the girl. When at last they really are thin and find that they still have problems—other problems, perhaps, but still problems—they wonder if a fashionable figure is worth the self-control that they did in fact exert and are still exerting. Some people decide it's easier to be fat. It has even been suggested that some people become fat in order to solve problems. A woman who finds sex distasteful, for example, may become overweight in order to avoid it. Unless this problem is treated first, it would be pointless to urge her to go on a diet.

Is There Hope for the Dieter?

Short-term weight gains are normally not a problem. In view of the many factors that work to make us gain weight and the equally numerous obstacles to losing it, is there any room for optimism? Most people working on the problem believe that the average person can be optimistic. First, there is good evidence that many of the regulatory mechanisms do work reasonably well in most individuals. In a classic study, short-term obesity was induced in 15 volunteers who came close to the goal of a 25% weight increase by eating high-calorie diets. At the termination of the study all but two had returned to control values within a few weeks (Sims et al., 1968). These results, however, do not tell us how obese people can achieve normal weight; they only tell us that short-term weight gains are normally not a problem.

Behavior modification. The most popular and probably the most successful approach to weight control for the average person has been the application of the principles of learning. According to this approach, the main problem for the overweight person is to learn new patterns of eating that will not only lead to an immediate weight loss but will also maintain the new weight. Many diets can result in weight loss; the problem is to keep from gaining the weight back again. Weight Watchers, probably the most famous behavioral program, was developed out of the belief that the best way to treat overweight is to teach people new eating habits.

To illustrate this approach, I have constructed a series of rules that a person in such a program might be required to follow. The rules in Practical Application 5-1 are merely logical extrapolations from the research literature on hunger and eating and are similar in some respects to rules that can be found in books on how to alter eating habits (for example, Jeffrey & Katz, 1977; Mahoney & Mahoney, 1976; Stuart, 1978). I have briefly summarized the reasons that these rules not only should lead to weight loss but should, over time, also lead to a new set of eating habits that will maintain that weight loss. There is nothing magical about these rules; they simply show how we may use our current knowledge base to keep our weight under control. I should caution the reader, however, that our knowledge about dieting and weight control is still incomplete. Not all overweight people are overweight for the same reason, a point that Rodin (1981) and others have repeatedly emphasized. Nevertheless, there is a great deal of agreement that whatever the exact cause of the problem, it is important for overweight people to learn to reorganize their lives if they are to lose their unwanted weight and keep it off.

Smoking and Weight

There is considerable evidence that nicotine inhibits hunger and eating. It has been shown that smokers weigh less than nonsmokers, that those who quit smoking gain weight and that those who start smoking lose weight (Klesges, Meyers, Klesges & La Vasque, 1989). At least one study has shown that nicotine reduces the insulin response, consistent with the insulin theory which has hypothesized that insulin plays a central role in hunger and eating. Given that smoking is bad for one's health, the question is how to prevent postcessation weight when one decides to quit smoking. While studies have shown that with proper intervention it is possible to reduce or delay such weight gains, more research is needed to deal with this vexing problem. While nicotine gum has proven to be a useful intervention strategy it must be viewed as only a short-term strategy, since people who are weaned from such gum show weight gains (Gross et al., 1989).

Natural Weight Control

Can people control their weight and not feel hungry by carefully selecting the foods they eat? Many people find that the effort to maintain some desired weight level is a constant battle. Not only do they feel hungry most of the time (they are restrained eaters) but they find they must avoid exposing themselves to food cues because they are prone to eat whenever they are exposed to food, especially very palatable foods. For these people life is very unnatural.

Very encouraging research suggests that it may be

PRACTICAL APPLICATION 4.1

Some Rules for Dieting

Rule 1: *Eat in only one place and at regular times.* This rule is intended to help you stop snacking by limiting the number of places where you eat and ensuring that you eat at appropriate intervals rather than by impulse. Remember that people are typically not good at monitoring their food intake and that many overweight people have become overweight because they snack. If you eat at regular times, your body will have the necessary calories and nutrients to keep you going. Eat *nothing* between meals.

Rule 2: *Use small plates.* Overweight people tend not only to fill their plates but to eat what is on them. Therefore, when you use a smaller plate, you tend to eat less.

Rule 3: *Eat slowly.* You should accomplish three things by eating slowly. First, the pleasure you get from eating will be maximized. Second, since the mouth provides feedback about the amount we have eaten, we can signal the brain that we have eaten a great deal by carefully chewing our food and making the eating process last as long as possible. Third, when we eat slowly, our digestive system has time

to absorb some of the food, and this process should help to stimulate our satiety mechanism. I call this the *fondue phenomenon.* A meat fondue is made at the dining table, not in the kitchen. Each diner immerses little pieces of meat, one at a time, in a pot of near-boiling oil. When one piece is eaten, another goes into the pot. The process often takes a couple of hours. People often report that they feel full long before all the meat is gone, even when the quantity of food eaten is quite small.

Rule 4: *Eat in the company of others.* People tend to eat slowly and to eat less when they are in the company of others. Besides, conversation tends to extend the eating time, an important factor in reducing food intake (see rule 3).

Rule 5: *If you eat alone, don't read or watch television.* The purpose of this rule is to help you learn to respond to internal cues as well as to help you monitor what and how much you are eating. When you are doing something else, you not only fail to monitor your intake but tend to eat quickly.

Rule 6: *Limit the availability of fattening foods.* If

possible to control one's weight by carefully selecting the foods one eats at various times of the day. In a study by Spitzer (cited in Rodin, 1984) subjects were asked to drink lemon-flavored water that contained either fructose, glucose, or glucose that was made to taste as sweet as fructose. Two and one-quarter hours later, subjects were presented with a buffet containing a very large variety of foods and asked to eat whatever they liked until they were comfortably full. Subjects in both glucose conditions ate significantly more than subjects in the fructose condition. Extrapolating to what might happen if subjects ate as they had done during the experiment over the course of a year, Rodin calculated that a given individual

would gain (or lose) up to 50 pounds. What mechanism is involved here? Since fructose triggers the release of much less insulin than glucose does, Rodin suggests that this may be the mechanism. Remember that there is good evidence that an elevated insulin level is associated with increased feelings of hunger. Therefore, if we are offered food when our insulin level is still relatively high, we will tend to eat less simply because our feelings of hunger are less intense at the time.

Other Approaches to Weight Control

Several other approaches to the treatment of obesity

you can't resist cookies, candy, cake, and other high calorie foods, limit the amounts that are available. Remember that overweight people are often externals, and the mere sight of such food can stimulate the output of insulin.

Rule 7: *Allow for variety.* When we eliminate from our diet certain foods that we normally eat, we often develop a craving for those foods. When the craving becomes strong, we have a tendency to eat large quantities of those foods if they are available. So if you are accustomed to eating pastas, for example, don't try to eliminate them altogether, just cut down.

Rule 8: *Don't try to lose weight too fast.* When we do, our body often responds with a reduced metabolism rate. This response not only interferes with our ability to lose weight but may cause problems for us when we have reached our ideal weight. Another problem with trying to lose weight very quickly is that when we fail to meet our short-term goal, we tend to give up.

Rule 9: *Eat a balanced diet.* The goal of dieting should be not only to lose weight but to keep that weight off. Sometimes you can lose weight very rapidly by following a diet that requires you to eliminate certain types of food. Not only do such diets often precipitate health problems, but they fail to teach us how we should eat after we have reached our desired weight. The goal of dieting is simply learning to eat less while staying healthy.

Rule 10: *Combine your diet with exercise.* Since basal metabolism can account for a third of our energy expenditure, and exercise increases the BMR, exercise is useful not only for getting rid of excess fat but for maintaining our desired weight. The most effective program calls for at least 20 minutes of exercise three times a week and involves an activity that uses 300 calories and raises the heart rate to 60% or 70% of its maximum (McCardle, Katch & Katch, 1991). Ideal activities are running, swimming, bicycling, walking upstairs, or any other aerobic activity that induces us to take in large amounts of oxygen (oxygen is required for the burning of calories).

are currently being taken (Leon, 1976). Various forms of psychotherapy, including group therapy, have been devised on the assumption that the problem has a psychological origin. Drugs, wiring the mouth shut, surgery to remove fat, and bypass surgery have also been used. Despite all these techniques, however, dieting is the most commonly accepted approach to the problem of obesity.

Summary

There are several obstacles to dieting. First, the metabolism rate tends to slow down when the body is deprived of food, thereby frustrating the dieter's attempt to lose weight. Second, dieting often produces a craving for restricted foods, often high-calorie foods. Third, dieting is often accompanied by a set of new expectations, both the dieter's own and those of other people.

Despite all the obstacles, there is hope for the dieter. One of the most successful approaches to weight loss is behavior modification, which has grown out of learning theory. Also, there is growing evidence that as we learn more about the characteristics of certain foods, we can learn to control our weight naturally by carefully selecting what we eat. Foods that do not produce a high insulin response, such as fruits, may reduce the constant feelings of hunger that some dieters experience.

Binge eating is a serious problem for many people in out society. The tendency
to binge occurs mostly in people who are chronic dieters.

Disturbed Eating Patterns

Binge Eating

Binge eating is a session of extreme overeating in which
the individual typically eats until the stomach can tolerate no more food. It is a fairly prevalent syndrome
that occurs among the overweight, the underweight,
and people of normal weight (Crowther, Lingswiler,
& Stephens, 1984). A typical binge episode lasts less
than two hours, according to the third edition of the
Diagnostic and Statistical Manual of Mental Disorders
(DSM-III, 1980; DSM-IIIR, 1987) of the American
Psychiatric Association. Other surveys have reported
binge eating ranging from 3% to 90% in the female
population and 1% to 64% in the male population
(Conners & Johnson, 1987). The reason for the great

variability in the rates is probably that what some people consider a binge others call simply pigging out.

Food deprivation and binge eating. There is considerable
evidence that the tendency to binge is triggered by food
deprivation. It has been shown, for example, that rats
who have been deprived of food develop a tendency to
overeat, especially if they are presented with palatable
foods (Coscina & Dixon, 1983). Another piece of compelling evidence comes from the work of Ancel Keys
and his associates (1950). During World War II a group
of conscientious objectors volunteered to serve in an experiment on the effects of semistarvation on behavior.
These men starved themselves down to 74% of their
original body weight. When unlimited food was later
made available, they exhibited a tendency to binge.

Table 4-3.   Criteria for a diagnosis of bulimia

Recurrent episodes of binge eating

At least three of the following:

   Consumption of high-caloric, easily ingested food during a binge

   Termination of binge by abdominal pain, sleep, or self-induced vomiting

   Inconspicuous eating during binge

   Repeated attempts to lose weight

   Frequent weight fluctuation greater than 10 pounds

Awareness of abnormal eating pattern and fear of not being able to stop eating voluntarily

Depressed mood after binges

Cause not anorexia nervosa or any physical disorder

Adapted from DSM-III.

Polivy and Herman (1985) have argued that dieting is one of the factors that often leads to binge eating. The tendency to binge, they suggest, may represent the body's attempt to restore one's weight to a level that is more biologically appropriate. If there is a set point for weight, as Nisbett (1972) and others have argued, then even people whose weight is well above normal may tend to binge when their weight drops below their set point as the result of dieting. As Polivy and Herman (1985) point out, the precise mechanism for this tendency has not yet been identified. Perhaps, as they suggest, chemical changes in the body result in increased hunger, increased sensitivity to food, and/or lowered inhibitions.

Overweight, dieting, and binge eating. Overweight people tend to binge (Loro & Orleans, 1981). But binge eating is not limited to overweight people. Binge eating often occurs among people who are of normal weight and even underweight. The common factor may be the tendency to diet. In North American society, dieting has become a way of life (see Polivy & Herman, 1987 and Conners & Johnson, 1987). In one study it was found

that 80% of girls (but only 10% of boys) reported having been on a diet before age 13 (Hawkins, Turell & Jackson, 1983). In another study, 77% of college females described themselves as dieters (Jakobovits, Halstead, Kelly, Roe, & Young, 1977). If you tend to view yourself as overweight, you may be inclined to diet; this then triggers the tendency to binge.

Learning of binge eating. There is evidence that binge eating does not have to be triggered by food deprivation. It may simply be learned or modeled under certain conditions. In one study it was shown that as friendships in two different sororities developed their eating behaviors became more similar. This study also found that binge eating was not only acceptable among the women studied but was highly valued. In one sorority, for example, the more one binged the more popular one became (Crandall, 1988). The implication is that if you live with people who are binge eaters you, too, may develop this tendency.

Bulimia

Definition and prevalence. Bulimia (literally "ox hunger") is often referred to as the binge-purge syndrome. People who are bulimic periodically eat so much that they experience abdominal pain. Then they force themselves to vomit or take a laxative to rid themselves of the food; after it is gone, they often sleep (Schlesier-Stropp, 1984). Bulimia has been referred to as the "secretive syndrome." People who are bulimic tend to plan these episodes to ensure that they will not be discovered, and they rarely share their secret with other people (Herzog, 1982a). Bulimics tend to be preoccupied with food and the urge to eat. At the same time, they are concerned with their weight and often alternate between dieting and gorging (Schlesier-Stropp, 1984).

While binge eating may be fairly prevalent, bulimia, as defined by DSM-III, is not. The true rate for bulimia is most likely 4% to 8% of females (in their late teens or early twenties) and 2% or less of males (Heatherton and Baumeister, in press).

The diagnostic criteria for bulimia are presented in Table 4-3.

Biological Factors

Numerous neurochemical changes have been linked to bulimia. Since many of these changes are very close to those found with anorexia, I will discuss these biological factors when I deal with anorexia.

Learned Factors

Sex, age, race, and family history. It seems fairly clear that bulimia is a woman's disease. It has been suggested that about 90% of all bulimics are women (see Striegel-Moore, Silberstein, & Rodin, 1986). Most studies have found bulimics to be in their 20s—the mean age is between 21 and 25.3—and white (Schlesier-Stropp, 1984). Self-report data indicate that bulimics' families have a high incidence of alcoholism and weight problems (for example, Herzog, 1982b). While we cannot completely rule out that some of these differences are due to biology, most researchers believe that we can best understand these as the products of learning. For example, it has been suggested that young women develop the belief that it is important to be thin in order to attract men, to succeed, to be accepted, and so forth.

Psychological dynamics. Bulimics tend to be characterized by depression and anxiety. While bulimia has been linked to anxiety and depression, there is little evidence that it is an affective disorder. That is, there is little evidence that depression causes bulimia (Hinz & Williamson, 1987). Rather, it seems that bulimia is due to their perceived lack of control in regulating their food intake (Fairborn & Cooper, 1982; Herzog, 1982b). It has been suggested, for example, that eating, especially binge eating, elicits anxiety and that vomiting reduces it (Rosen & Leitenberg, 1982). (In Chapter 10 we will examine in more detail the link between feelings of lack of control and depression.) Further, it appears that bulimics tend to suffer a great deal of guilt, shame, and self-contempt following a binge (see Schlesier-Stropp, 1984). If the bulimic, having binged, is prevented from vomiting by an unexpected interruption, she feels extreme anxiety together with overwhelming guilt and self-contempt. Purging may be a kind of safety valve that helps the bulimic to deal with her tendency to binge (her lack of self-control).

Cognitive and Individual Difference Factors

Binge eating as escape from self-awareness. Heatherton and Baumeister (in press) have argued that binge eating is motivated by a desire to escape from self-awareness. They argue that when we are in a state of high self-awareness, we are acutely sensitive to the demands of others, even if these demands are unreasonable, as they seem to be in the case of weight expectations. When we fall short of these perceived standards we experience emotional distress, often including anxiety and depression. To escape from this aversive state we narrow our attention to the immediate stimulus environment such as our body sensations. The process of narrowing one's attention serves to block out thoughts about the broader standards and society's demands and expectations. In the process of narrowing our attention, that part of our brain or mind that would normally inhibit us from eating becomes disengaged. As a result we can become disinhibited eaters—individuals who are momentarily free of societal standards and controls. For those moments we can experience the pleasurable sensations that come from eating.

Treatment. The most appropriate treatment for the bulimic is still an open question. Since cognitions appear to play an important role in this disorder (bulimics are obsessed with thoughts of weight, food, eating, and ridding themselves of food they have eaten), cognitive therapy seems an obvious treatment model. Cognitive therapy attempts to change the bulimic's maladaptive thoughts about such things as ideal body image and self-control without focusing on the vomiting. The need to vomit, it is assumed, will diminish once the individual has gained control of the eating process (Fairborn, 1980, 1981). Behavior therapy has focused more on breaking the link between the anxiety produced by eating and the need to vomit (Rosen & Leitenberg, 1982). The data available are still insufficient to permit evaluation of the adequacy of this approach.

Anorexia Nervosa

Definition. According to DSM-III, *anorexia nervosa* is

Table 4-4.   Criteria for a diagnosis of *anorexia nervosa*

Intense fear of becoming obese, which does not diminish as weight loss progresses.

Disturbance of body image, e.g., claiming to "feel fat" even when emaciated.

Weight loss of at least 25% of original body weight or, if under 18 years of age, weight loss from original body weight plus projected weight gain expected from growth charts may be combined to make the 25%.

Refusal to maintain body weight over a minimal normal weight for age and height.

No known physical illness that would account for the weight loss.

Original Source: DSM-III (Based on P. E. Garfinkel and D. M. Garner, Anorexia Nervosa: A Multidimensional Perspective, *1982.)*

characterized by refusal to maintain body weight above minimum norms, weight that is 25% below expected body weight, intense fear of gaining weight or becoming fat, disturbance of body image, and, in females, the absence of at least three consecutive menstrual cycles. The diagnostic criteria for anorexia nervosa are presented in Table 4-4.

Biological Factors

There is growing evidence for the role of neurochemical factors in anorexia as well as bulimia. It has been suggested that the onset of anorexia and bulimia may produce changes in the neurochemistry of the body which then perpetuate these disorders as well as produce many of the psychological symptoms that have been linked to these disorders (Fava, Copeland, Schweiger, & Herzog, 1989). It is important to note that while anorexia nervosa and bulimia nervosa are considered distinct entities, stringent attempts by patients with anorexia to limit food intake are interrupted by episodes of bulimia. Therefore, one might expect to find both similarities and differences in the biological

factors associated with these two disorders (Fava et al., 1989).

Noradrenergic system. The noradrenergic system releases norepinephrine and is known to be involved in the regulation of eating. Anorexics and bulimics are characterized by lower than normal norepinephrine levels, often as much as 50% below normal. It has been suggested that under conditions of starvation, norepinephrine output may be lowered, leading to lowered metabolism (anabolism), a condition that protects the individual from further weight loss. According to this theory, the body makes a highly adaptive response to conditions of starvation. While norepinephrine levels initially return to normal when anorexics begin to put on weight, they tend to return to previous low levels, thus perpetuating the condition of anorexia. While it has not been unequivocally demonstrated that this is an acquired state in anorexics, the animal research makes it quite clear that it is. It has been shown in animals, for example, that repeated alterations between caloric deprivation and overfeeding have a cumulative metabolic effect resulting in progressively slower rates of metabolism on each occurrence of refeeding (Brownell, Gennwood, Stellar, & Shrager, 1986).

The noradrenergic system has also been implicated in anxiety and depression. Lower levels of norepinephrine would result in lower anxiety but increased depression, thus accounting for the symptoms of depression that are often associated with both anorexia and bulimia.

Antidepressant drugs, known for their ability to increase levels of norepinephrine and dopamine in the brain, have been found to be useful in the treatment of bulimics but not anorexics. Not only do these drugs help control binge eating in bulimics but they tend to reduce symptoms of depression (Fava et al., 1989).

Serotonergic system. The serotonergic system inhibits eating by acting on the ventromedial hypothalamus, that part of the brain considered a satiety system. Interest in the serotonergic system grows out of the fact that the neurotransmitter serotonin has been implicated in depression, obsessive-compulsive disorders, and anxiety. While no clear relationship has been

found between serotonin levels and anorexia, there is evidence of a link to low serotonin turnover and bulimia. Moreover, there is evidence that drugs which increase serotonin turnover (e.g., flenfluramine) can be effective in treating bulimia (Fava et al., 1989).

Learned Factors

It has been suggested that the North Americans' preoccupation with slimness may be a cause of anorexia nervosa, at least in its milder forms (Bliss & Branch, 1960; Bruch, 1973). According to this view, *any* fat may be perceived as excessive, and this perception may lead to a pattern of constant and excessive dieting. The incidence of anorexia nervosa tends to be greater in middle and upper socioeconomic groups (for example, Bruch, 1973; Dally, 1969) and in college and university populations (Bemis, 1978). Because such groups are typically concerned with slimness, the learned origin of anorexia nervosa is a tenable position. The best evidence to support the learning model, however, comes from research showing that behavior modification techniques can produce substantial weight gains (for example, Banji & Thompson, 1974; Halmi, Powers, & Cunningham, 1975). Bruch, however, has argued that although behavior modification techniques may produce gains, such techniques often fail to get at the primary cause. In a follow-up study of anorexia nervosa patients who had been successfully treated by behavior modification, Bruch (1975) found that some of them had undergone physical and emotional deterioration that sometimes included suicidal behavior. Thus there is evidence that learning alone is not responsible for anorexia nervosa.

Cognitive and Individual Difference Factors

It has been argued that the drive to be thinner is secondary to a need for control and/or fears about the consequences of achieving a mature shape. The individual pursues thinness in order to feel a sense of mastery over her body (Garfinkel & Garner, 1982). While all of us from time to time may be concerned about losing control, such as when we "pig out," anorexics are obsessed with this fear and spend a great deal of time and effort controlling anything related to eating. They are inclined, for example, to use appetite suppressants, such as amphetamines and other diet pills, or drink large quantities of fluid in order to feel full (Garfinkel & Garner, 1982).

Anorexia nervosa patients almost always have distorted body images: they tend to overestimate their weight even when they have become extremely emaciated (for example, Askevold, 1975; Ben-Tovim, Whitehead, & Crisp, 1979; Crisp & Kalucy, 1974; Garfinkel et al., 1978; Gomez & Dally, 1980; Slade & Russell, 1973). Their failure to recognize their emaciation is difficult to explain in view of the fact that the patients have frequent opportunities to see their own reflections and the reactions of other people to them. Despite an abundance of evidence to the contrary, they continue to maintain that they are either normal or overweight. Such irrational behavior has led many people to conclude that these patients are suffering from a profound psychological disturbance.

Considerable evidence indicates that anorexia nervosa may be due, at least in part, to disturbed family relationships. Numerous reports depict mothers of anorexics as dominant and intrusive (for example, Bruch, 1973; Goodsitt, 1974; Katz, 1975).

Not all researchers agree that the problem arises from a dominant mother or a pathological family organization (for example, Katz, 1975; Sours, 1974), and some have argued that no consistent pattern is to be found among the families of anorexics (for example, Bliss & Branch, 1960; Dally, 1969).

Prognosis

Whatever the exact origins of anorexia nervosa, the prognosis for complete recovery is not good. It is likely, according to some authors' estimates, that 25% to 50% of patients will experience a recurrence of the symptoms after successful treatment (Moldofsky & Garfinkel, 1974), and that as many as 38% will require readmission for anorexia nervosa within two years (Dally, 1969). These figures emphasize the chronic nature of the disease.

Theories and Interpretations of Eating Disorders

Sociocultural Variables in Bulimia and Anorexia Nervosa

Throughout our society, women are told that thin is in. Fashion magazines link beauty with thinness. Studies of bulimics and anorexics yield an abundance of evidence that they are motivated to diet by the belief that fat is ugly and must be gotten rid of. One study found that by age 13, 80% of girls (but only 10% of boys) have already been on weight-loss diets (Hawkins, Turell, & Jackson, 1983).

Slenderness is also linked to femininity. Several studies have supported the observation that physically attractive women tend to be perceived as more feminine than unattractive women (for example, Unger, 1985; Heilman & Saruwatari, 1979). And what does that ideal woman look like? She is a thin, nonathletic type (Guy, Rankin, & Norvell, 1980). The ideal man, in contrast, is muscular and athletic. In view of such widely held perceptions, it is not surprising that many women become obsessed with thinness.

To be feminine is to behave in certain stereotyped ways. Feminine women are presumed to eat sparingly. When they eat heartily, others see their behavior as masculine (Chaiken & Pliner, 1984). But not all women subscribe to the stereotyped view of women. Are these women just as vulnerable? Various people have suggested that being a feminist or simply being ambitious does not free the average woman from pursuit of a thin figure. An image of femininity may give a woman a competitive edge (Brownmiller, 1984). Also, as we have noted, failure to control one's weight is often viewed as indicating a lack of control or willpower. It is not to the advantage of the ambitious woman to be viewed as weak-willed and self-indulgent. It has been suggested that weight loss in our society is often viewed as a sign of maturity (Steele, 1980), and therefore a concern with dieting may be a symbol both to oneself and to others that one is indeed mature. Finally, there is growing evidence that self-esteem is linked to body image. Because society says that women should be thin, the achievement of thinness can be a source of self-esteem. In her book *Perfect Women*, Colette

Dowling (1988) argues that many women with eating disorders have an overwhelming desire to achieve perfection. She argues that the drive to be perfect comes out of a feeling of inferiority. She goes on to argue that the reason women are more likely to feel inferior than men, and therefore suffer more from eating disorders, is the result of women being disparaged by society for "eons." This particular gender feeling, she believes, is handed down from mother to daughter. In order to break this cycle, therefore, the communication between mother and daughter needs to be changed.

What is the solution? Since bulimia and anorexia nervosa seem to be related to our cultural values or practices, the real solution lies in coming to grips with our cultural values. Values change. People not yet old can remember when women as thin as today's ideal were spurned as too skinny. Such women tried as desperately to gain weight as contemporary women try to lose it. The answer to eating disorders, therefore, may lie in or waiting for the pendulum to swing back in actively creating a new, more realistic ideal for women to emulate.

The Spiral Model of Eating Disorders

In order to account for some of the diverse findings surrounding bulimia and anorexia nervosa, Heatherton and Polivy (in press) have developed the *spiral model*. This model starts with the finding that we live in a society in which a great deal of value is placed on being thin, especially for women. In order to match those societal standards, people become restrained eaters. Among other things, this means that there are large numbers of people constantly depriving themselves of food (restraining their food intake). Since the body has a natural tendency to maintain a normal weight or normal set point, the individual finds himself or herself in an endless struggle to control the body's natural tendency to maintain normal weight. One by-product of this struggle is what has been labelled the yo-yo weight effect; weight loss followed by large weight gains, often weight gains that surpass previous high levels. According to this model, when the body begins to win the battle (and we begin to put on weight), the individual's self-esteem begins to suffer or decrease. With lowered self-esteem comes a *disinhibition effect*. A disinhibition effect can be thought of as loss of control. The cortex of our brain normally inhibits behavior that we consider socially unacceptable (such as aggression) but when disinhibition occurs (such as when we drink alcohol), the cortex loses that capacity for a period of time. In the case of restrained eating, when our self-esteem falls we lose our ability to control our food intake. One of the things that may happen as a result is binge eating. According to this model, the obvious way to break out of the downward spiral is to abandon the unrealistic standards that we perceive we must meet.

Summary

Binge eating is a fairly prevalent syndrome that occurs among people who are overweight, underweight, and of normal weight. There is considerable evidence that binge eating is an acquired syndrome. One of the antecedents of binge eating is prior deprivation. Polivy and Herman suggest that it may represent the body's attempt to restore weight to a point that is more biologically appropriate. Bulimia, a condition characterized by episodes of binge eating followed by purging, is now considered to be a clinical eating disorder. There is good evidence that it is an acquired syndrome. It is found predominantly in young white women whose families have a history of alcoholism and weight disorders. Bulimics tend to experience both anxiety and depression. It has been suggested that binge eating is motivated by a desire to escape self-awareness. Cognitive therapy has proved to be effective with some bulimics.

Anorexia nervosa is characterized by refusal to maintain body weight above minimum norms, a weight level that is 15% below expected body weight, intense fear of gaining weight and a disturbance of body image. Anorexia nervosa has been linked to changes in noradrenergic and serotonergic systems. Evidence that anorexia is learned comes from the observation that at least in some cases the disorder is treatable with learning principles. Also, because anorexia nervosa is more common among middle and upper socioeconomic groups, there is good reason to believe that the disorder has a learned component. The fact that anorexics almost always have a disturbed body image has led to the belief that such patients are suffering from a cognitive disorder. One group of researchers has argued that the disorder is the result of disturbed family relationships.

In view of the fact that our society tends to equate thinness with beauty and femininity, it is not surprising that many women strive to achieve a thin figure. Given that there are serious consequences associated with trying to be thin, the question is whether or not the best solution might be to change society's attitudes. According to the spiral model of eating disorders, when a dieter's self-esteem begins to suffer, often in response to the inability to control weight, he or she binges. This tendency to binge can be viewed as motivated by the desire to escape from self-awareness.

Main Points

1. Carbohydrates, fats, and proteins are broken down into more basic units that can be used as energy, to rebuild body cells and to manufacture chemicals to run the body and brain.

2. Most of the glucose that is absorbed by the blood is transported across cell walls and is stored in the cells as glycogen; the remaining glucose is used for energy.

3. Unused glucose is converted into fat and stored in the adipose tissues.

4. Some of the proteins are converted into amino acid, which is important in the rebuilding of muscle and the manufacture of essential chemicals.

5. A balanced diet should consist of protein (15%), carbohydrates (65%), an fats (15% to 20%.)

6. When glucose levels rise in the blood, the body responds by secreting insulin.

7. According to the glucose theory of hunger, hunger is due to lowered glucose levels.

8. According to the insulin theory of hunger, hunger is due to elevated insulin in our blood.

9. According to the fatty acid theory of hunger, when we begin to make use of stored fat, we become hungry.

10. It has also been suggested that we become hungry when the blood and body temperatures begin to fall.

11. Receptors in the brain and the gastrointestinal tract provide feedback about when to stop eating.

12. There is no evidence that humans are equipped at birth to select a balanced diet.

13. Animals and humans tend to select foods based on taste and texture.

14. Cultural differences suggest that food preference is, at least in part, learned.

15. Both animals and humans can learn to avoid foods that cause a general malaise.

16. Obesity is defined as weight about 25% or more in excess of normal.

17. Twin studies suggest that genetics plays an important role in determining weight. What we may inherit is our metabolism rate.

18. Environmental factors also play an important role in overweight.

19. About two-thirds of our energy expenditure is due to basal metabolism rate and one-third to exercise.

20. Basal metabolism rate decreases from birth until about age 20, when it tends to level off.

21. Lesions in the ventromedial nuclei of the hypothalamus lead to overeating, which leads to obesity.

22. Lesions in the lateral hypothalamus cause the individual to reduce food intake.

23. Set-point theory suggests that the hypothalamus sets our weight.

24. According to Margules, the tendency to store fat is an adaptive mechanism that evolved to prepare us for periodic famines. Obesity, therefore, follows from the fact that we no longer have to endure famines.

25. The yo-yo effect can be explained by the famine hypothesis. People who experience the yo-yo effect are 70% more likely to experience heart problems than people whose weight remains relatively stable.

26. A child's weight tends to be correlated more highly with the weight of the mother than with that of the father. This asymmetrical correlation, combined with the fact that the mother tends to be the person who controls the availability of food, has led to the assertion that obesity may be due in part to the availability of food.

27. The number of fat cells is a good predictor of whether or not a person will put on weight.

28. Internal-external theory suggests that one of the reasons people become overweight is that their food intake is controlled by external cues, such as the sight and smell of food, rather than by internal cues, such as stomach contractions, the glucose level, or other internal mechanisms.

29. Externals show an increase in insulin output when palatable foods are available.

30. Boundary theory proposes that two separate mechanisms control our eating, one for hunger and one for satiety.

31. Dieters tend to be restrained eaters; people who often feel hungry think a great deal about food and find it necessary constantly (and consciously) to control their food intake. It has been suggested that in order to control their weight, they set a *cognitive boundary*.

32. Preloading studies have shown that when this cognitive boundary has been overstepped, restrained eaters tend to become disinhibited eaters.

33. Metabolism tends to slow down during deprivation (anabolism).

34. Metabolism tends to increase after weight gain (catabolism).

35. Increased desire for forbidden or restricted foods often accompanies weight loss.

36. People often spontaneously develop new expectations in regard to people who are successful at dieting, as do the dieters themselves.

37. Short-term weight gains are typically not a serious problem.

38. Behavior modification has been used to help people lose weight. This approach focuses on helping people to modify their eating habits.

39. Smoking tends to inhibit appetite which may explain why smokers are inclined to gain weight when they quit.

40. There is some evidence that careful selection of the foods one eats can result in natural weight control.

41. While binge eating is fairly prevalent in our society, the condition of bulimia (binge eating and purging) is less so.

42. Bulimics have lower than normal norepinephrine levels and low serotonin turnover.

43. Deprivation has been found to be one of the primary antecedents of binge eating.

44. It has been suggested that binge eating is motivated by a desire to escape from self-awareness.

45. Anorexia nervosa and bulimia are disorders primarily affecting young white women.

46. Anorexia nervosa is characterized by a weight level that is 15% below expected body weight, an intense fear of gaining weight, disturbance of body image, and the absence of at least three consecutive menstrual cycles.

47. Anorexia nervosa has been linked to changes in noradrenergic and serotonergic systems.

48. There is considerable evidence that the family relations of anorexia nervosa patients are disturbed.

49. The prognosis for a permanent cure of anorexia is poor.

50. North Americans' preoccupation with thinness has been suggested as a major determining factor in both bulimia and anorexia nervosa.

51. The spiral model was developed to account for some of the diverse findings that are associated with eating disorders.

Chapter Five

Sex Behavior, Love, and Sexual Orientation

- From a biological or physiological perspective, what constitutes sexual arousal or passion?

- Is sexual arousal the same or different for females and males? What produces sexual arousal in females and males?

- In what ways are orgasms the same and different for females and males? What role do hormones play in secual behavior and sex differences?

- What role does learning play in achieving satisfying sexual behavior?

- Do attitudes play any role in determining whether or not people enjoy sex?

- Is variety in sexual intercourse normal?

- How is love different from sexual arousal or sexual passion?

- Why do people fall in love?

- Can we learn to fall in love or is that beyond our control?

- Why do some people fall in love suddenly while others fall in love gradually?

- Is homosexuality biologically determined, is it learned, or does it comes from choices that people make? Can people change their sexual orientation?

The study of sex behavior and sex differences has and continues to be a controversial topic. The controversy arises from such basic issues as the appropriateness of discussing the topic of sex openly. It involves the question of how males and females are being presented: Is one sex being presented in a better light than the other? It involves the question of traditional values: Is sex only for reproduction? Is sex only for marriage? Or perhaps, is sex merely to have fun? The controversy has to do with women challenging the old male dogma and introducing their own dogma. It has to do with the role of biology as opposed to the environment. It has to do with the question of how to deal with the problem of stereotyping females and males when in fact females and males are perhaps more similar than they are different.

In this chapter I will examine some of this controversy by addressing four major topics. First, what is the underlying motivation for engaging in sexual behavior? Second, what is the basis of love? Third, what role do hormones play in sexual behavior and in creating sexual differences? Fourth, what is the origin of sexual orientation? That is, why are some males homosexuals and some females lesbians?

Motivation for Engaging in Sexual Behavior

The Nature of Human Sexual Arousal (Passion)

It was not until the pioneering work of Masters and Johnson in their book *Human Sexual Response* (1966) that we had any solid scientific information about the nature of human sexual arousal, something that people commonly call passion. This seems an extraordinary

fact in view of the vast number of books and articles that had been and were being published purporting to inform the professional and the lay person about the nature of human sexual motivation. For example, a leading medical text stated unequivocally that not only were women nonorgasmic, but they rarely, if ever, had sexual feelings and certainly had little sexual interest (cited in Masters & Johnson, 1966). Two books by Alfred Kinsey and his associates, *Sexual Behavior in the Human Male* (1948) and *Sexual Behavior in the Human Female* (1953), caused a storm of controversy. In these books, Kinsey objectively reported the results of interviews he and his associates had conducted with male and female volunteers. Kinsey's books indicated not only that women enjoy sex (as do men) but that both sexes seem to enjoy a wide variety of sexual practices. That is, they like to have sex in different locations and in different positions. At the time (and even today), many people regarded as perverse the whole idea of variation in the sexual response. Among other things, Kinsey was attacked for the procedures he followed to obtain his sample. The basic argument was that his volunteers were not representative of the general population. It was suggested as evidence for this idea that anybody willing to talk to strangers about their sexual practices was deviant or abnormal. Although there were problems with Kinsey's sampling procedures, time has more or less vindicated him. People are no longer arguing about whether his figures are correct because current information about human sexual practices supports his basic findings. Not only do humans enjoy sex, but a large number of them enjoy variations in their sexual behavior.

Sensory and Arousal Factors

The consensus that has emerged from the work of Masters and Johnson is that human sexual behavior occurs in two major stages. These consist of a nontactile stage followed by a tactile stage. First, the person becomes interested in a member of the opposite sex because of visual, auditory, olfactory, or even cognitive cues. A woman, for example, may arouse the interest of a man by the shape of her body, her clothes, the way she smiles, the quality of her voice, the way she smells, or what she says. If she in turn finds the man attractive, she may agree to spend some time in proximity to him. They may go to a movie, have dinner together, walk together, and so on. If this first stage of proximity is satisfying for both, they move on to the second stage, which involves tactile stimulation. It usually begins with touching or holding hands and proceeds to petting, gradually becoming more intimate provided there are no inhibitions to prevent the natural progression. Those areas of the body that not only are highly sensitive to touch but are regarded as belonging to the sexual response will become involved in a mutual attempt to bring pleasure to the other person. The eventual aim is usually to have intercourse with accompanying orgasm.

Masters and Johnson focused their research on the stages that characterize the tactile phase of sexual behavior. In general, they held that human sexual behavior can be described as a sensory event. To understand the nature of the sexual system, therefore, it is critical to understand exactly how this system is designed to provide the sensory events that are assumed to be the reason we, as humans, engage in sexual behavior.

It should be noted that there is remarkable similarity between the female and the male sexual response. In other words, from a biological perspective, the sex response seems to be organized in much the same way for males and females. What differences there are seem to be due largely to learned and cognitive factors.

The Female Sexual Response

Until fairly recently there were a number of misconceptions about the female sexual response. One was that women do not experience any pleasurable sensation from sex. Another was that they do not experience orgasm. Masters and Johnson (1966) have found not only that women experience a variety of pleasurable sensations but that they experience orgasm. In fact, they have never found a case in which a woman who was properly stimulated did not experience an orgasm. It is likely that some of the misconceptions about female sexual response have resulted from men's ten-

dency to compare this with their own. There are some differences, but the differences do not necessarily make a woman's response less intense or less satisfying than her partner's.

Masters and Johnson have divided the female sexual response into four stages in order to describe the patterning of physiological and psychological responses. These stages, or phases, are called (1) the excitement phase, (2) the plateau phase, (3) the orgasmic phase, and (4) the resolution phase.

The female sexual response involves physiological changes that can be classified roughly under three headings: (1) those that are outside the genital area, (2) those that are specific to the clitoris, and (3) those that occur in the vagina. Figure 5-1, on page 115, is a schematic representation of the female pelvic area and should be used as a reference in the following discussion.

It is beyond the scope of this chapter to describe all the varieties of stimulation that will produce a female orgasm; it should simply be noted that the most effective stimulation for most women is some form of tactile stimulation in the genital area.

Stimulation of the female genital area produces a more or less uniform pattern of physiological and psychological responses. Table 5-1 summarizes the reactions in a form that makes it possible to compare those associated with the various phases.

It should be noted that, according to Masters and Johnson (1966), the clitoris is unique among organs in the human body in that its only function is pleasure. They argue that it exists solely for the purpose of receiving and transforming sensual information. Although no one denies that stimulation of the clitoris produces pleasure, some have argued that it is analogous to the penis (for example, Morris, 1969). Masters and Johnson maintain that it is unique because it has nothing to do with reproduction and may not be necessary for orgasm, although it obviously plays some role in the pleasure associated with sex and is usually involved in orgasm.

The Male Sexual Response

The sexual responses of males and females are very similar. Figure 5-2 shows a lateral view of the male

Table 5-1. The human female sexual response (Based on W. H. Masters and V. E. Johnson, *Human Sexual Response*, 1966.)

Phase	Extragenital	Clitoris	Vagina
		Site of reaction	
Excitement	Nipple erection Enlargement of breasts Sex flush (breasts) Involuntary muscle contractions Contractions of rectal sphincter	Size of clitoris increases (wide variation among individuals)	Vaginal lubrication Lengthening and distention of vagina Retraction of cervix and corpus of uterus into false pelvis
Plateau	Nipple erection continues Breasts enlarged Sex flush may spread to lower abdomen, thighs, buttocks Involuntary muscle contractions (hands and feet) Hyperventilation Increased heart rate Increased blood pressure	Entire clitoris retracts from normal overhang position	Marked vasocongestion near vaginal opening
Orgasm	Nipple erection continues Breast enlargement continues Sex flush terminates abruptly Involuntary muscle contractions Continued hyperventilation Peaking of heart-rate increase Peaking of blood pressure increase	Clitoris remains in retracted position	Rhythmic contractions near vaginal opening (area of vasocongestion)
Resolution	Decrease in all the above; also perspiratory reaction	Clitoris returns to normal overhang position	Rapid dispersal of vasocongestion Relaxation of vagina

anatomy; Table 5-2 summarizes the male's reactions at various stages.

The penis is not an organ totally parallel to the clitoris, although both serve as important receptor systems for sensual stimulation. The penis is also an integral organ for reproduction; the clitoris, as we have noted, is not necessary for reproduction. Further, the penis serves an important role in stimulating the female, while the clitoris has no similar role in stimulating the male.

One of the first signs of sexual arousal in the male is penile erection, which results from vasocongestion in the penis. The tissue structure of the penis is such that

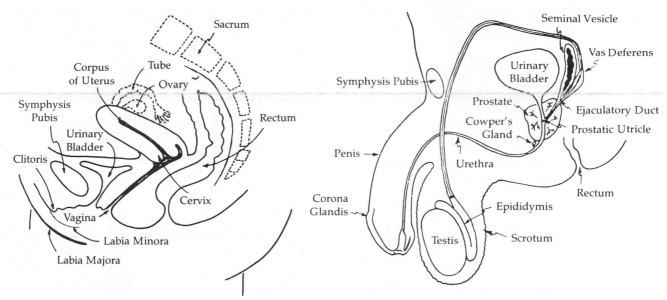

Figure 5–1. Female pelvis: normal anatomy. (From W. H. Masters and V. E. Johnson, *Human Sexual Response*, 1966. Copyright © 1966 by Little, Brown and Company. Reprinted with the permission of the publisher [and authors.)

Figure 5–2. Male pelvis: normal anatomy . (From W. H. Masters and V. E. Johnson, *Human Sexual Response,* 1966. Copyright © 1966 by Little, Brown and Company. Reprinted with the permission of the publisher and authors.)

the increased supply of blood results in elongation and distention of the penis. Continued stimulation of the penis typically produces ejaculation.

Norepinephrine and Sexual Activity. Although, as Masters and Johnson have noted, sexual activity is pleasurable because stimulation of the sex organs produces a rewarding sensation, sexual pleasure may involve something more. Specifically, sexual activity may stimulate the output of certain catecholamines, which, as we have seen in Chapter 2, have been implicated in various affective reactions. For example, there is evidence not only that norepinephrine is greatly elevated during male sexual activity (100% to 1,200%) but that it is closely correlated with amount of activity and degree of erection (Wiedeking, Lake, Ziegler, Kowarski, & Money, 1977). Dopamine was not found to be highly correlated with sexual activity. Animal research provides evidence that norepinephrine and dopamine levels may be related to fluctuations in ovulation and therefore to mating behavior in

female animals (Crowley, O'Donohue, & Jacobowitz, 1978).

The Pair-Bonding Hypothesis

While the male members of many species have orgasms, it has been suggested that only the female of the human species has orgasms (Symons, 1979), although some data indicate that females of some of the higher primate species may occasionally have orgasms as well (Goldfoot et al., 1980). Why is there this difference? According to the sociobiologists (e.g., Morris, 1969), the female orgasm evolved to facilitate pair-bonding. Because both parents were needed to raise the human offspring, it was important that some mechanism evolve to facilitate such pair-bonding. Masters and Johnson (1975) use the term *pleasure bond* to refer to the intimacy that develops from two people sharing a common satisfying sensory experience. As I will discuss in the section on love, intimacy plays a central role in love.

Table 5-2. The human male sexual response(Based on W. H. Masters and V. E. Johnson, *Human Sexual Response*, 1966.)

	Site of reaction		
Phase	*Extragenital*	*Penis*	*Scrotum and testes*
Excitement	Nipple erection (60% of males)	Penile erection (vasocongestion)	Localized vasocongestion
	Some sex flush	Urethra lengthens	Contraction of smooth-muscle fibers
	Involuntary muscle contractions		Thickening of scrotal skin
	Involuntary contraction of rectal sphincter		Testicular elevation
Plateau	Nipple erection	Vasocongestive increase in penile diameter	Continues as above, plus greater elevation of testes and increase in testicular size
	Greater sex flush (25% of males)	Penile urethral bulb enlarges	
	Involuntary muscle contraction		
	Involuntary contraction of rectal sphincter		
	Hyperventilation		
	Increased heart rate		
	Increased blood pressure		
Orgasm	Continued nipple erection	Ejaculatory reaction (regular contractions of muscles)	Continues as above
	Continued sex flush	Seminal fluid expelled through involuntary muscle contractions	
	Involuntary contraction of rectal sphincter	Urethra contracts in rhythm	
	Hyperventilation		
	Increased heart rate		
	Increased blood pressure		
Resolution	Very gradual retraction of nipples	Penile detumescence (two stages): rapid decrease in vasocongestion followed by slow decrease in vasocongestion	Either rapid or delayed return to normal state
	Rapid disappearance of sex flush		
	Perspiratory reaction		

Summary

The pioneering work of Masters and Johnson has provided us with a scientific description of the physiological events that result from sexual stimulation. The sexual response of both females and males can be divided into four phases: excitement, plateau, orgasm, and resolution. We have known for some time that there are important differences in the reactions of females and males. The work of Masters and Johnson has shown that there are many similarities.

Masters and Johnson acknowledge that pleasurable sex can occur without love and that a person can enjoy love without sex. They take the position that one of the best ways to achieve pleasurable sex is to have the right nerve receptors stimulated. In short, sex is rewarding because sex stimulates certain receptors that provide pleasurable sensory stimulation. Recently it has been shown that sexual intercourse will increase the output of norepinephrine by as much as 1,200%. Because running increases norepinephrine by only 300%–400%, we may have an explanation of why some people prefer sex to running.

The pleasure associated with sex is not only important for encouraging reproduction, but it is also important for encouraging and maintaining pair-bonding. Ultimately, pair-bonding is important, according to the sociobiologists, for ensuring that both parents will work as a team in the rearing of the offspring. Masters and Johnson suggest that orgasm plays an important role in the development of intimacy.

Learned Component

What Is Sexually Arousing to Humans?

For some time there has been a great deal of interest in the question of what is sexually arousing. It is perhaps not surprising that researchers have found that pictures of nude members of the opposite sex can elicit sexual arousal. Furthermore, it is perhaps not surprising that researchers have also found that pictures that show a member of the opposite sex in a state of sexual arousal or two persons engaged in sexual acts are more potent elicitors of sexual arousal (for example, Griffitt, May, & Veitch, 1974; Mosher & Abramson, 1977). Several studies have shown that the stimulus material does not have to be in pictorial form. Verbal descriptions of sexual behavior are sufficient to elicit sexual arousal in the majority of volunteer subjects (for example, Heiman, 1977). The ability to fantasize may be an important mediator of this phenomenon, because subjects can become sexually aroused through fantasy (for example, Heiman, 1975, 1977; Masters & Johnson, 1966). Fantasy-prone people as well as those with greater sexual experience find it easy to produce sexual fantasies (Carlson & Coleman, 1977).

Romantic themes and lust themes apparently produce the same amount of arousal (for example, Fisher & Byrne, 1978; Heiman, 1977; Osborn & Pollack, 1977). It has long been held that women are not aroused by explicit erotic material whereas men are (for example, Abelson et al., 1971). It has further been suggested that women are more sexually aroused by romantic themes. The failure to find evidence for this generally held opinion may be explained by the cultural expectations for women with respect to pornography. It appears that women are not expected to be aroused by pornography, and as a result they have been reluctant to admit they are (Gebhard, 1973).

Although romantic and lustful themes have not produced differences in sexual arousal, the theme of chance encounter appears to increase sexual arousal in response to pornographic material. This finding is consistent with the literature on romantic attraction (a topic that I will discuss later).

Why are pictures of nudity, themes of romance, themes of chance encounter so arousing? It has been suggested by Gagnon that this is learned, and learned specifically through the creation of sexual scripts. According to Gagnon's analysis, all human sexual behavior is governed by sexual scripts.

Sexual scripts. Sexual scripts refer to one's mental representation or schemata of how an interpersonal sexual episode should be enacted (Gagnon, 1974, 1977; Simon & Gagnon, 1986). A sexual script can be conceptualized as analogous to a movie script in which there are actors who have motives and feelings. Part of this movie script requires the actors to say certain things and to engage in certain nonverbal actions (Gagnon, 1974). Thus, each time a person engages in a sexual encounter, he or she has a script to guide them through that encounter to a successful conclusion.

Simon and Gagnon argue that sexual scripts initially arise out of information to which children are exposed, from rewards and punishment they receive, and from the process of imitation and modeling. Up until adolescence, they mainly involve gender-appropriate behaviors. Sexual scripts tell young boys and girls how they should react to and treat each other in a nonsexual encounter.

With the onset of adolescence, these scripts begin to incorporate sexual feelings. It has been suggested that during masturbation, males coordinate or integrate their sexual feelings and activities with their gender roles. This coordination leads them to develop a sexual script that tells them how they should respond in actual sexual intercourse. It is suggested that as they experience each of the phases of the sexual response (excitement, plateau, orgasm and resolution), they see themselves engaging in certain sexual behaviors (certain physical activities) and communicating (engaging in appropriate verbal and nonverbal responses). As the sexual script becomes more sophisticated, each phase becomes more clearly differentiated, so that the appropriate sexual behaviors (physical activity) and appropriate communication pattern coincide more closely to each of the phases of the sexual response.

It has been suggested that females have more difficulty learning to coordinate or integrate sexual feelings into the their sexual scripts because fewer females masturbate in early adolescence. Also, the female sexual scripts in early adolescence contain less information that is purely sexual (as least when compared to a male perspective). Female scripts tend to focus on falling in love as opposed to engaging in sexual intercourse or some other sexual act, while male scripts tend to focus mainly on engaging in sex. While falling in love may involve the excitement phase of the sexual response, it typically does not involve the other phases which are more closely linked to engaging in sexual intercourse. Later in adolescence, female sexual scripts do incorporate the entire sexual response and, at that time, their sexual scripts become similar to the four-stage sexual response. In short, their sexual script comes to parallel that of the male.

Gagnon (1974) suggests that when adolescents begin to date, the script begins to shift from a fantasy-based masturbatory script to a more interpersonal and interdependent sexual script. In the course of petting, young couples begin to explore sexual arousal through the process of touching each other while they are fully clothed. While the behavior is experienced as exciting, it does not typically produce orgasm. What is learned at this stage is to coordinate the feeling of being touched by another person with the excitement phase of the sexual response. In other words, the fantasy gives way to interpersonally instigated sexual excitement that comes largely through touch. Eventually the female begins to adjust her script to include sexual arousal. This lays the groundwork for eventual sexual intercourse.

As dating continues, a number of other skills are acquired such as learning mutual disrobing, learning how to obtain privacy, learning how to better focus attention on the other person. Gagon points out that at this stage sexual performance is often awkward, clumsy and anxiety ridden. With repeated practice and with greater sensitivity to each other, couples learn to coordinate their sexual scripts so that both can achieve sexual pleasure. Once a satisfactory solution has been worked out, sexual behavior often becomes semi-ritualized (Simon & Gagnon, 1986).

Sexual arousal. Because sexual scripts play such an important role in achieving mutual sexual pleasure, it can be argued that heterosexual and homosexual sexual pleasure is the result of an interaction of biological (sensory) and learned factors. The pleasure that originally came only from self-stimulation eventually is shifted to the other person. According to this interpretation, sexual arousal comes to depend on the sensory awareness of the sexual partner. Characteristics of the other person—including the sight, smell and touch of that person—come to act as the source of sexual arousal. Through the process of generalization, other people can also act as sources of sensory arousal. Since images, fantasies, and scripts have also become linked to sexual arousal, the degree to which another person elicits these images, fantasies, and scripts will determine, in part, their potential for eliciting sexual arousal in another person. In that respect, sexual arousal is in the eye of the beholder. It is what people perceive will happen that arouses them.

Reward value of sex. While perceiving what might happen can be sexually arousing, the reward value of sex seems to come from participating in a sexual script that is satisfying. Women and men show a great deal of agreement on the typical sequence of sexual behaviors that lead to coitus. Fourteen behaviors have been identified as part of this script including such things as kissing, caressing, manual stimulation, oral stimulation and penetration. Where the sexes differ is in the degree of arousal they experience from each of the fourteen behaviors in the script. While male arousal tends to build linearly with each subsequent step (behavior) in the sequence, culminating with the greatest arousal at penetration, female arousal does not show this pattern. It does not build, as it does with males, but rather is highly variable. What females found most arousing was being stimulated by males, not penetration. Thus, even though they agree on the script, females tend to react to the same sexual behaviors differently (Geer & Broussard, 1990). This could account for the finding that females tend to show less interest in sex than do males (Hite, 1976; Zilbergeld, 1978).

Over the years there has been a great deal of speculation about the nature of the female orgasm, and conjecture as to why there are differences between the sexes when it comes to sexual arousal. According to the learning interpretation, differences in sexual arousal are linked to one's focus. Since females tend to focus on being stimulated by the male rather than on penetration, it follows that their greatest feelings of sexual arousal would not be linked to orgasm associated with penetration, as it is in the male, but to being stimulated.

Summary

A variety of material has been found to be sexually exciting in both males and females, including pictures of nude members of the opposite sex, people engaged in sexual acts, and verbal descriptions of sexual behavior. The ability to fantasize plays an important role in determining the degree to which various types of material will be sexually arousing.

It has been suggested that human sexual behavior is largely the result of sexual scripts. These mental representations or schemata help guide the individual through a sexual episode. It has further been suggested that during masturbation, males and females coordinate or integrate their sexual feelings and activities

As the sex drive increases in adolescence, interest in sexual material also increases. Males have been found to be particularly interested in visual material.

with their gender roles. This coordination leads them to develop a sexual script that tells them how they should respond during actual sexual intercourse. With the onset of dating, the fantasy-based script eventually undergoes a transition or transformation that leads to a more interpersonal and interdependent sexual script. It is suggested that this transition is often characterized by awkwardness, clumsiness, and anxiety. To put it in learning terms, this transition is characterized by much trial and error behavior. Because sexual scripts play such an important role in achieving mutual sexual pleasure, it can be argued that heterosexual and homosexual sexual pleasure is the result of an interaction of biological (sensory) and learned factors. According to this analysis, mature sexual arousal (sexual arousal that comes from others as opposed to the self), results from an increased awareness of the sensory characteristics of a sexual partner.

Cognitive Factors

The sexual scripts that people come to use as adults are influenced by the beliefs and attitudes they hold. Where do these beliefs and attitudes come from? They come in part from the society at large, from one's peer group, and from the values and ideals that one has internalized. It is impossible to review all the data here, so I will simply illustrate the role of belief systems by examining a few topics.

Liberalism versus conservatism. From the 1950s to the early 1980s, North American society became more sexually permissive, especially towards premarital intercourse (D'Emilo & Freedman, 1988). Since then, sexual attitudes have become somewhat more conservative, perhaps reflecting a concern over sexually transmitted diseases and a general return to conservatism (Gerrard, 1987). In addition, the sexual double standard declined between the 1950s and 1980s (Brooks-Gunn & Furstenburg, 1989). The result, despite the return to conservatism, is that couples are having sex earlier and more frequently. They no longer believe that it is necessary to be married to enjoy sex, and consequently people have become more open in their attitudes about sex.

Beliefs about sex drive in females and males. One of the persistent beliefs shared by both males and females is that males have a stronger sex drive than females (e.g., Byrne, 1977). As a result, sex is perceived by both females and males as being more important and enjoyable for men than women. The implications of this belief need to be more fully explored. Among other things, this belief may account, in part, for the double standard our society has with respect to sexual promiscuity of females and males. As an exercise, you might try to think of some further implications of this particular belief.

Meaning attached to sex. Perhaps one of the strongest differences between males and females is the meaning they attach to sex. While females tend to connect sex with feelings of affection and closeness, males tend to perceive sex as an achievement, an adventure, a demonstration of control and power, or a purely physical release. While women generally have their first sexual experience with someone with whom they are romantically involved, this is not always the case for males. Women value intercourse because it gives them a sense of shared feelings, emotional warmth and being wanted. Men, in contrast, often isolate sex from other aspects of the relationship. They are more inclined to focus on the arousal rather than the shared feelings, emotional warmth and being wanted (Basow, 1992). While these are general tendencies that can be identified in the general population, it is important to remember that, like women, men often connect sex with feelings of affection and closeness and that, like men, women may perceive sex as an achievement, adventure, a demonstration of control and power, or a purely physical release.

It is also important to note that we are talking about statistical differences. Most men prefer that love and sex go together. In fact, men, like women, value love far ahead of sex in terms of overall importance in their lives (Chassler, 1988: Pietropinto & Simenauer, 1977). As men get older, love and intimacy become the main motivators of sex (Sprague & Quadagno, 1989). The fact that males sometimes indicate that sex is for adventure, control and power, or physical release may simply reflect the male tendency to present themselves as the stereotyped macho male.

Individual Differences

While sex differences are important, merely talking about differences between the sexes can be misleading because it leaves the impression that males as a group are homogeneous and females as a group are homogeneous. That is clearly not the case, a point I made in the section above on the meaning attached to sex. There are large differences among males just as there are large differences among females. In fact, when the focus is on individual differences as opposed to sex differences, males and females are often more similar than they are different.

My preference is to focus on individual differences whenever possible. This helps to circumvent the problem of stereotyping females and males. The following two theoretical approaches illustrate the fact that it is possible to talk about individual differences without necessarily falling into the trap of stereotyping females as doing one thing and males as doing something else. In these two approaches, we can see that males and females often work from a common set of principles.

Introverts and Extraverts

As already noted, Eysenck has delineated two major types of people: introverts and extraverts. Extraverts are characterized by a high degree of sociability, impulsiveness, physical activity, liveliness, and changeability. Introverts tend to be less sociable, less impulsive, less active, and more stable in their responses to the external environment, and they can generally be characterized as more fear/anxiety-prone.

Questionnaires administered to introverts and extraverts have found several differences in the sexual behavior of these two types of people. For example, Giese and Schmidt (1968), in a study of German students, found that extraverts petted more and had intercourse more often, while introverts tended to masturbate somewhat more often. Eysenck's study of English students (1976) produced similar findings. He found in addition that extraverts tended to engage in a greater variety of sexual behaviors (such as cunnilingus, fellatio, and varied coital positions). A summary of these findings, broken down for males and females, is presented in Table 5-3.

Probably the most important finding from both Eysenck's study and Giese and Schmidt's is that extraverts tend to express more satisfaction with their sexual behavior. In fact, Eysenck reports that introverts are dissatisfied with their patterns of sexual behavior. Eysenck has suggested that this dissatisfaction results from inhibitions, worries, and guilt feelings that prevent introverts from fulfilling their desires. The introvert, Eysenck notes, tends to endorse the orthodox Christian approach to sex, in which virginity and fidelity are emphasized while the sensory aspects of sex are downplayed. In sharp contrast, the extravert endorses the unorthodox permissive and promiscuous approach, in which frequency of sex and different partners are important to sexual satisfaction. Similar results

Table 5-3. Sexual practices of extraverts and introverts among unmarried German students (From H. J. Eysenck, "Introverts, Extraverts and Sex." *Psychology Today*, January 1971, 4(8), 48-51. Reprinted from Psychology Today Magazine. Copyright © 1971 American Psychological Association. Reprinted with permission.)

	Males		Females	
Practice	Extraverts	Introverts	Extraverts	Introverts
Masturbation at present	72%	86%	39%	47%
Petting	78	57	76	62
Coitus	77	47	71	42
Long precoital sex play	28	21	18	21
Cunnilingus	64	52	69	58
Fellatio	69	53	61	53
More than three different coital positions	26	10	13	12

were obtained in a study of Canadian college students (Barnes, Malamuth, & Check, 1984).

Unrestricted Orientation versus Restricted Orientation to Sex

People whose orientation to sex is considered to be unrestricted indicate that they have had many sex partners and plan to have many more, have had one-night stands, and endorse casual sex as a comfortable experience. In contrast, people whose view of sex is considered to be restricted indicate that they have had few sex partners, anticipate having few in the future, do not have one-night stands, and endorse the idea that commitment is a necessary prerequisite for sex. Incidentally, it has also been found that an unrestricted view is more prevalent among men than among women (Snyder, Simpson, & Gangestad, 1986).

What produces this difference? A person who holds an unrestricted orientation is a personality type that has been called a high self-monitor, while a person who has a restricted orientation is a personality type that has been referred to as a low self-monitor. Low self-monitors are people whose actions are based on underlying dispositions and attitudes (e.g., sex is only for marriage). High self-monitors tend to be responsive to the social and interpersonal cues of the situations in which they find themselves; that is, these people make decisions on the basis of their personal analysis of situational variables, and so their behavior tends to vary with the situation to which they are responding. While we do not know the precise factors that cause variations in self-monitoring, it seems clear that the degree of promiscuity displayed by an individual is related to relatively stable personality factors (Snyder, Simpson, & Gangestad, 1986).

It appears that low self-monitors tend to associate sex not only with love and romance but with commitment to a long-term attachment. High self-monitors, in contrast, tend to view sex as a romantic encounter that does not necessarily imply any long-term commitment. If one associates intimacy with long-term commitment, then low self-monitors are the people who form truly intimate relationships.

As we will see in the section on love, intimacy and commitment are probably best viewed as independent processes. What that means is that one does not necessarily have to be commited to experience intimacy and that being commited does not necessarily ensure intimacy.

Summary

The sexual scripts that people have are influenced by beliefs, attitudes, and values. It is not surprising that as people came to adopt a more liberal attitude towards sex, such things as premarital sex increased. One persistent belief is that males have stronger sex drives than females, a belief that may help account for the double standard our society has with respect to sexual promiscuity of females and males.

One of the strongest differences between males and females is the meaning they attach to sex. While females connect sex with feelings of affection and closeness, males tend to perceive sex as an achievement, adventure, a demonstration of control and power, or a purely physical release. It is important to note that

these are statistical differences and do not reflect individual differences. Like females, most men prefer that love and sex go together. Like women, most men value love far ahead of sex in terms of overall importance in their lives.

The fact that the sexual practice of extraverts differs from that of introverts indicates that cognitive factors play a basic role in sexual behavior. The finding that extraverts petted more, had intercourse more often, and tended to engage in a wider variety of sexual behaviors is consistent not only with Eysenck's theory but with the position of Masters and Johnson. According to Masters and Johnson, sex can be viewed as a sensory experience. According to Eysenck, extraverts tend to seek out more stimulation than introverts, a theory that would explain why they tend to have sex more frequently and to engage in more varied practices. It is interesting that people who tend to let the situation determine their behavior (high self-monitors) are more likely to hold an unrestricted view of sex, whereas people who tend to let their beliefs and attitudes govern their behavior (low self-monitors) hold a more restricted view of sex. These findings seem to indicate that low self-monitors are the more inhibited.

Love

Numerous writers have argued that it is important to distinguish between lust and love. Lust has to do more with short-term sexual attraction, whereas love has more to due with long-term psychological intimacy. Love involves lust, or what we commonly call passion, but it is more. Robert Sternberg (1991) of Yale University suggests that love involves three components: passion, intimacy and commitment. Figure 5-3 presents Sternberg's love triangle. I will talk more about Sternberg's model shortly. First, let me discuss the biological, learned and cognitive components of love.

Biological Component

One of the things that characterizes love is the euphoria that comes from being in love. While there has been considerable speculation about why people fall in love, there is little question that when people are in love they experience a certain psychological state that is perhaps closest to euphoria. In this regard, it is perhaps not surprising that love has been linked to dopamine and norepinephrine, since both have been implicated in feelings of euphoria. In addition, it has been found that love is especially linked to phenylethylanine (PEA). This chemical, Walsh (1991) suggests, "gives you that silly smile that you flash at strangers. When we meet someone who is attractive the whistle blows at the PEA factory." It is worth noting that there is frequently a chemical backup for many of the emotions. It appears, however, that phenylethylanine does not last forever. After two or three years it begins to fall. One might expect, therefore, that people would separate after two or three years. Consistent with this observation is the findings of Fisher (1992) that in 62 different cultures, the divorce rate peaks around the fourth year of marriage.

How does one explain, therefore, how many marriages last? It has been suggested that the initial attraction stage gives way to an attachment stage which, it is hypothesized, is mediated by the chemical endorphin (Fisher, 1992). I will discuss endorphins in greater detail in Chapter 7. For the present let me simply say that endorphins are the equivalent of the body's own morphine. Endorphins not only reduce pain but they produce feelings of well-being. There is growing research showing that endorphins are released under a wide variety of conditions, not just pain or fear as the original research clearly established. There is growing evidence that endorphins are released by other emotions (e.g., humor), and that endorphins play a critical role in maintaining the immune system (see Chapter 7). Thus, it is perhaps not surprising that the immune system tends to drop quite dramatically following the death of a spouse (see Chapter 11).

Oxytocin is another chemical that has been implicated in love. This chemical is produced by the brain and sensitizes nerves and stimulates muscles. It has been suggested that this chemical may promote cuddling on the one hand and enhance orgasm on the other hand. In a study of men, it was found to increase three to five times its normal level during climax.

Helen Fisher suggests that oxytocin produces feelings of relaxed satisfaction and attachment.

Learned Component

Falling In Love

The phrase *falling in love* is frequently used in our society to describe the emotional attachment that members of the opposite (or sometimes the same) sex develop toward each other. "Falling in love" can be fairly sudden or gradual. Can we identify some of the factors that contribute to two persons' falling in love? Everyone, of course, seems to look for certain physical and psychological variables in a mate. Nevertheless, it has been found that we frequently fall in love with somebody other than our ideal. In one study, only 40% of the subjects reported that their most intense experience of love was with a person close to their ideal (Averill & Boothroyd, 1977). In other words, falling in love depends on factors other than those we think we are looking for.

Certain common elements are associated with the process of falling in love. Thoughts about the other person and dating frequency seem to be important factors (Kleck & Rubenstein, 1975; Tesser & Paulhus, 1976). Obviously, if one person is attracted to another, thinking about and wanting to be with that person would be normal and expected; it is consistent with the idea of sexual scripts. Interestingly, chance meeting appears to be among the conditions most conducive to falling in love (Averill & Boothroyd, 1977). It may well be that because we implicitly believe in our society that people fall in love, we are inclined to look for situations in which there is an unexpected or unplanned quality. The word "falling" denotes an accidental quality, and if we believe that something is going to be accidental we need to find a situation that roughly approximates that.

Sternberg (1991) argues that whether or not we fall in love is to a very large degree under our control. It has to do with our cognitive set. If we are set or prepared to fall in love, we will. According to Sternberg's position, love does not have to be accidental. It can be planned. You fall in love through your actions. You can stay in love through your actions.

Attraction and Difficulty of Attainment

One good illustration of the importance of our own actions comes from research on attraction and difficulty of attainment. The question asked in one study was: "Are so-called easy-to-get women as attractive as hard-to-get women?" The results indicate that neither easy-to-get nor hard-to-get women are as attractive as women who are moderately hard to get. Apparently, when a woman is perceived as hard to get, men simply feel that the possible reward is not worth the time or the effort required to pursue it. In other words, they fail to become motivationally aroused. Easy-to-get women, it appears, also fail to arouse motivation. Very simply, it is not necessary to be highly motivated to win the easy-to-get woman. Moderately hard-to-get women, on the other hand, are perceived as potentially attainable goals if a reasonable amount of time and effort are devoted to the pursuit. Under these conditions, men appear to experience a high level of arousal, a condition that is assumed to enhance the attractiveness of the goal (Wright, Toi, & Brehm, 1984).

Why are goals that require some effort to attain more attractive to us than those we can have for the asking? There is no obvious answer. Apparently, the process of working towards a goal can be just as important as reaching the goal itself, perhaps even more so. The opportunity to experience a high level of arousal, as we have seen, can be reinforcing. One reason the romance goes out of marriage may be that the element of pursuit is lost. We value those things in which we invest time and energy. As Sternberg argues, we can stay in love if we are willing to work at love.

Intimacy

Intimacy has to do with feelings of closeness, connectedness, and being bonded. It pertains more to the social/psychological aspects of love. Intimacy is something that people must learn in order to fully experience a sense of closeness, connectedness, and being bonded. In the intimacy literature, long-term commitment is often used as one of the defining characteristics of whether or not people are truly intimate.

Sternberg has wisely separated intimacy from commitment as distinct components. Commitment is a decision; it is a cognitive activity. Intimacy, on the other hand, is a skill; it is something that you learn.

While some people have suggested that intimacy takes time to develop, there is evidence that this need not be the case. One of the ways people establish intimacy is to engage in self-disclosure. In self-disclosure, a person discloses something personal/private about themselves, expecting in return that the other person will self-disclose something personal/private about themselves. In this process, the more one engages in self-disclosure the faster intimacy can be established.

There is research that indicates that the willingness to self-disclose can be linked to the personality attribute called sensation seeking. Zuckerman (1979) has suggested that people in the general population can be differentiated in terms of the degree to which they need novelty and complexity in their lives and their willingness to take risks in order to experience such change. Research from a variety of sources has shown, among other things, that high sensation seekers are people who tend to have more sexual partners than low sensation seekers. One interesting question, therefore, is to what degree do high sensation seekers engage in self-disclosure. Do they use self-disclosure or do they use some other strategy? In a study we did on this question, we found that high sensation seekers are inclined to self-disclose information about their sexual motivation and behavior (Franken, Gibson, & Mohan, 1990). We interpreted this finding to indicate that sensation seekers not only use self-disclosure to establish intimate relationships, but they use a form of self-disclosure that signals their motives to the other person early in their relationship.

Cognitive Component

Love, or more precisely, staying in love has to do with the decision that you love someone and as a result you are willing to invest the time and energy that is necessary (Sternberg, 1991). According this position, it is ultimately your decision whether or not you stay in love or fall out of love.

Commitment involves, among other things, the realization that love involves satisfying the needs of two distinct individuals. It also involves, suggests Sternberg, coming to accept the fact that there are going to be differences or problems and that if love is to endure, these differences or problems must be resolved to the mutual satisfaction of both parties. In the final analysis, commitment is not just a desire or wish but rather the willingness to invest the time and energy to ensure that love will endure.

For Sternberg, the investment of time and energy should be devoted to developing problem-solving skills that enable people to deal with their differences. I will return to this question when I talk about how to develop consummate love (see Practical Application 5-1 on page 126).

Sternberg's Interaction Model

As I indicated in the introduction for this section, Sternberg views love as involving three primary components, passion, intimacy, and commitment. Sternberg's model of love is a true interaction model. One of the interesting things about his theory is what happens if people are lacking one or even two of the three primary components.

Passion alone = infatuated love. Infatuations often arise unexpectedly simply as the result of a look, a touch, a word. They are characterized by bodily sensations, a tingling feeling, a heightened heart rate, a warm sensuous feeling. Sometimes people act on their infatuations (sometimes called attractions) and sometimes they do not. They can and often are the grist for fantasies that people have.

Sometimes infatuations become obsessive. Teens, for example, sometimes become so infatuated with a movie star or a rock star that they are unable to pursue a real relationship. Infatuations are, by their very limited nature, unfulfilling. Unless one can get beyond infatuation, one can never be truly happy.

Intimacy alone = liking. Liking occurs when you feel close and connected but you do not experience a need for passion or a need to make a commitment. Relation-

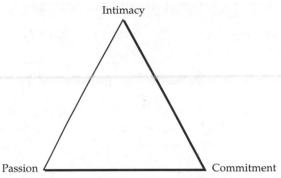

Figure 5–3. Sternberg's love triangle. (From R. J. Sternberg, *Love the Way You Want It*, 1991. Copyright ©1991 by Bantam Books. Reprinted with permission.).

ships at work can be of this type. They are important for the work setting but are not important outside the context of work. Many of our friendships are of the liking variety. We enjoy sharing our ideas and feelings with someone because it gives us a sense of being in tune with another person.

Commitment alone = sterile love. We often see commitment alone at the end of a long-term relationship when partners are no longer physically attracted to each other and when they have lost their emotional involvement with each other. In societies where marriages are arranged, sterile love often comes at the beginning of a relationship followed by the development of passion and intimacy.

Passion + intimacy = romantic love. Romantic lovers experience more than just physical attraction. They enjoy the emotion that comes with being together, experiencing the same feelings, sharing in their closeness. They do not, however, have any sense that this will last or that they particularly want it to last. Sometimes romantic love starts with passion and the partners become close. Sometimes it starts with a friendship that over time it grows into passion. It is something that happened and they are quite prepared to leave it that way. It could be a shipboard romance or summer fling.

Passion + commitment = fatuous love. Fatuous love is like

PRACTICAL APPLICATION 5.1

Striving to Attain Consummate Love

Sternberg argues that people can learn to attain consummate love. The first thing they need to recognize is that consummate love is like any other goal that people set for themselves. Among other things, that means that people must consciously decide it is a goal that they want to attain and that they are willing to work towards attaining it.

It is important to remember that many people in our society are not willing to commit themselves to this goal. For various reasons they may decide, for example, that they do not want intimacy or are incapable of intimacy or that commitment to another person is inconsistent with their desire to be free or to be an individual. As a result they may decide that they will pursue endless sexual relationships in order to satisfy their passion. As one relationship fades, as they are bound to when passion is the only focus, they look for another sexual encounter.

Sternberg points out that if people commit themselves to the goal of consummate love they need to recognize that the road to consummate love is filled with obstacles and challenges. First, people have different tastes, different beliefs, and different habits. As a result there are bound to be conflicts and problems. In order to deal with such differences people need to learn problem-solving skills. One of the first things they need to learn is how to identify a problem. A good starting place is to simply identify the category to which it belongs. Does the conflict have to do with money, running the household, sexual preferences, friends, religion, political beliefs and so forth? Identifying the category helps to define the problem. Unless two people both agree on the problem, there is no point in trying to find the solution. Identifying the problem helps focus communication on the problem and prevents people from bringing in unrelated arguments such as, "And furthermore, you never put the cap back on the toothpaste." Sometimes it may be important to seek the help of other people. If a goal, such as consummate love, is important, then people need to get the best help they can to achieve that goal. When people learn to focus on the problem and treat it as a mutual problem, they are less likely to blame each other, a common problem in relationships.

Sternberg argues that people who have made the decision to attain consummate love need to learn to recognize the pitfalls or what he calls "love villains" in relationships. All of us, he argues, hide behind a mask from time to time. When we feel vulnerable or afraid, we may try to hide our feelings. In order to hide, we often put forth an image that is opposite of what we really feel. When we do this we are prone to cause problems in the relationship. Sternberg has identified ten villains or masks: *the controller, the typecaster, the pious fraud, the procrastinator, the conflict avoider, the yes-sayer, the expert, the righteous accuser, the pretender, the blamer.*

People who wish to attain true consummate love must take a growth orientation. By that I mean they must learn to accept that relationships are never perfect and are never cast in stone. People change and we need to learn to accept such change. People make mistakes and we need to learn to forgive. In the final analysis, we need to see obstacles as challenges and see the future in terms of optimism and the possibility for growth.

---

the proverbial Hollywood Marriage. After a whirlwind courtship, the couple gets married, never taking the time to develop intimacy. After a glorious honeymoon, they go their separate ways, committed to the idea that their love will cross continents. But because there was no intimacy, true commitment never develops. When the passion fails there is nothing left to hold them together.

Intimacy + commitment = companionate love. Companionate love might best be described as a long-term committed friendship. Sometimes, as the passion in marriage subsides, people retain a strong sense of intimacy and commitment. Family relationships are often characterized by both intimacy and commitment, just as are cherished friendships.

Intimacy + passion + commitment = consummate love. Consummate love is the combination of intimacy, passion, and commitment. It is something that is hard to initially attain and harder still to keep. It is what people strive for but what often eludes people at the same time. (See Practical Application 5-1.)

Summary

Love has been linked to dopamine and norepinephrine because both have been implicated in feelings of euphoria. In addition, it has been found that attraction may be due, at least in part, to phenylethylanine (PEA). It has been suggested that this initial attraction stage gives way to an attachment stage which, it is hypothesized, is mediated by the chemical endorphin. Oxytocin (a chemical that sensitizes nerves and stimulates muscles and seems to produce feelings of relaxed satisfaction and attachment) has also been implicated in love and intercourse.

Chance meeting has been found to be a major determinant of why people fall in love. It appears that many people take the phrase "falling in love" literally and, as a result, when they meet an attractive person by chance they are predisposed to fall in love with that person. Difficulty of attainment also plays a role, suggesting that investing energy to attain a goal governs, in part, the dynamics of love feelings associated with another person.

According to Sternberg, love (consummate love) has three major components: passion, intimacy and commitment. Passion has to do with the physical and emotional aspects of love. It has to do with being attracted to another person and a desire for romance. Intimacy has to do with feelings of closeness, connectedness and being bonded. Intimacy is a skill that people can and must learn if true love is to be achieved.

Commitment involves making a decision that the person with whom you have chosen to share your life is worth the time and effort to make it work. Having made that decision, it is then necessary to put forth the effort to acquire the problem-solving skills that are necessary for resolving conflict and differences. Sternberg shows that when one or more of these components are missing, you have something less than consummate love. He argues that people can attain consummate love and offers several ideas on how to do it.

Sex Differences: What Role Do Hormones Play in this Process?

Males and females have the same sex hormones but in different amounts. They play a critical role in ensuring that we have two sexes, male and female. They have also been implicated in a wide range of behaviors. Thus is it is critical that we address the question of hormones. A great deal of controversy has arisen out of this work. While no one disputes the fact that hormones have the capacity to alter development in dramatic ways, two important issues have arisen out of the work on hormones. First, are they responsible at least in part for sexual orientation? Second, do they give rise to differences in abilities between the sexes? These are two distinct issues but, interestingly, grow out of a common line of research that shows hormones affect brain development. I will treat them as distinct issues, but before I do that, I want to briefly put this research into a context that will help you understand its significance.

Some of the research on hormones grows out of work that has been going on for more than 25 years but is still in its infancy. It is a tremendously exciting line of research that may help us to eventually come to a better understanding of individual differences. Right now, much of the focus is on sex differences because sex differences (at least in animals) are very stereotypical and therefore relatively easy to quantify. One should not be misled, however, by this choice of dependent measures. While this work does indicate that there are sex differences, I believe that its significance relates to the more basic question of how the brains of male and female develop.

It is unfortunate that some of this research has been used, at times, to argue that one sex (male) is superior to the other and even to justify the status quo ("keeping women in their place," for example) (see Tavris, 1992). Just as unfortunate is the attempt to trivialize this work because it has been misused. To fully appreciate this research one needs to keep an open mind. That does not mean that people shouldn't attack methodological and conceptual problems. Keeping an open mind simply means this is a potentially very important area of research that has slowly but surely been giving us an idea of how our brains develop, the complexity of our brains, and the subtlety with which the brain differences can affect our behavior.

Biological Component

Genetics

Males and females are genetically different. There is no question about that. The question is, how genetically different are the two sexes? In 1990, British scientists identified a single gene of the Y chromosome that determines maleness. It is this gene that activates a host of other genes to the complex task of turning a fetus into a boy. Without this gene all embryos would develop into females. Let me explain this process and, in doing so, let me talk about the sex hormones.

The Sex Hormones

Three major categories. The major category of hormones that govern male sexual behavior consists of androgens. The most important of the androgens is testosterone. The two main categories of hormones that govern female sexual behavior consist of estrogens and progestins. The major estrogen is estradiol and the major progestin is progesterone. Though we speak of androgens as "male" sex hormones, and of estrogens and progestins as "female" sex hormones, this distinction is not entirely accurate. Androgens can be converted into estrogens and progestins, just as progestins can be converted into androgens. Estrogens and pro-

gestins circulate in the blood of men as well as women, and androgens circulate in the blood of women (Hoyenga & Hoyenga, 1979). Estrogen levels in males have been found to range from 2% to 30% of the level found in females, while the androgen levels in females has been found to range from 6% to 30% of the level found in males (Money, 1980). The main difference between the sexes, therefore, is simply the degrees of concentration of these hormones. One reason that the range is so large is the fact that the levels of all hormones change constantly. As we shall see, both internal and external factors can dramatically alter these levels.

Origins of the sex hormones. The sex hormones are produced by the adrenal glands and the gonads. The male gonads are the testes and the female gonads are the ovaries. The male gonads produce mainly androgens, whereas the ovaries produce mainly estrogens and progestins. The adrenal glands produce mainly androgen. It has been estimated that about half of the androgen found in females is produced by the adrenal glands and about half by the ovaries.

The amount of each sex hormone that is present at any given moment is governed by the pituitary gland, which is ultimately controlled by the hypothalamus. The pituitary releases as many as ten hormones that act in various ways to excite, inhibit, and generally modulate the complex patterns involved in the arousal and direction of the sexual response (Whalen, 1976). Most research has focused on the two gonadotropic hormones: FSH (follicle-stimulating hormone), which induces maturation of the ovarian follicles in the female and stimulates production of sperm in the male, and LH (luteinizing hormone), which induces ovulation in the female and stimulates the output of androgen by the testes of the male. Androgen influences the mating response of male animals and is generally regarded as one of the hormones that governs the arousal of sexual interest in the human male.

Androgen is produced more or less continuously in males. The amount produced increases suddenly in early adolescence (thus accounting to a large degree for the sudden awakening of sexual interest in adolescent boys) and declines gradually through adulthood and old age. It has been suggested that the decline in sexual interest with increasing age is due to the decrease in androgens (Bancroft, 1987). It may also be due to a variety of other factors such as lack of variety and even a self-fulfilling prophecy (e.g., when you get older you lose interest in sex).

The female hormones, in contrast, are produced in accordance with a 28-day cycle that is linked to the production of the egg. It should be noted that the ovaries have a dual function: they produce both egg cells and hormones. The beginning of a cycle is initiated by an anterior-pituitary hormone (follicle-stimulating hormone) which stimulates an ovarian follicle—an ovum and the surrounding cells—to grow. This growth continues for half the cycle. Because it is the follicle cells that secrete the hormone estrogen, the amount of estrogen produced increases with the growth of the follicle. About halfway through the cycle, the ovum breaks through the wall of the follicle and the ovary. This phenomenon is called "ovulation," and the few days surrounding it are the period of the cycle when the female is fertile (that is, the ovum is capable of being fertilized by the male spermatozoa). In many lower animals, the female is at her peak of receptivity at this time, and therefore copulation generally occurs at the point in the cycle when conception is most likely. It appears on the basis of research in which estrogen has been injected at various times in the cycle that estrogen is responsible for female receptivity. Since the production of estrogen corresponds to the development of the ovum, it is no accident that the female is receptive when conception is most likely. Once the ovum breaks through the wall of the follicle and the ovary, estrogen production diminishes quickly, but it continues to circulate in the bloodstream for some time.

In humans, ovulation ceases in the late 40s and early 50s, on the average. Simultaneously, of course, estrogen production dwindles. This change in physiological functioning is called "menopause." Although estrogen is closely tied to receptivity in lower animals, it does not appear to be tied to receptivity in humans. Many women do report a decline in sexual interest at 40 to 50 years, but just as many report no decline or even an increase.

Sex Hormones and Differences in Physical Characteristics.

For about one month after the egg has been fertilized, the male and female embryos cannot be differentiated. In the second month sex differences begin to appear. If the egg has been fertilized with an X chromosome, the gonads (the two collections of germ cells) begin to develop into ovaries. As the male ducts disintegrate the female ducts thicken and become the womb, the fallopian tubes, and the upper two-thirds of the vagina.

If the egg has been fertilized with a Y chromosome, the process of development moves in a very different direction during the second month. H-Y antigens, believed to be produced by the Y chromosome, change the ovaries into testicles. The testicles produce various hormones: one that absorbs the female parts, such as the womb; testosterone, which thickens the spermatic cord; and still another, dihydrotestosterone, which promotes the formation of the external male genitals (Goy & McEwen, 1980; Haseltine & Ohno, 1981; Wilson et al., 1981; see also Durden-Smith & de Simone, 1983, for a very readable discussion of the material presented in this section).

To demonstrate that hormones are indeed responsible for the development of sex organs, female rats have been injected with the male hormone testosterone. Their female offspring are then found to be modified in several ways. They are born with an external vagina, often have a penis, and exhibit few mating responses in adulthood (see Beach, 1976).

It is obviously impossible to perform such manipulations with humans, but a great many data indicate that the human hormones work in the same way. One line of evidence comes from observations of people who have undergone a voluntary sex change. Candidates for sex-change operations are injected with either testosterone (for a female-to-male change) or estrogen (for a male-to-female change). A male transsexual who receives estrogen (the family of hormones related to estradiol) can expect to grow breasts and add fat at the hips and thighs. Conversely, if androgen (the family of hormones related to testosterone) is given to a female transsexual, she develops an enlarged clitoris and grows facial hair, her voice deepens and her musculature becomes more masculine (Rubin, Reinisch, & Haskett, 1981; Ciba Foundation Symposium, 1979).

Sex Hormones and Intellectual Functioning

While men and women do not differ in terms of intellectual functioning (e.g., I. Q.), they do seem to differ in terms of certain specific problem-solving abilities. Doreen Kimura (1992), who studies the neural and hormonal basis of human intellectual function, indicates that, on the average, men perform better than women on certain spatial tasks (rotating an object or manipulating it in some way), mathematical reasoning tasks, navigating their way through a route, and guiding or intercepting projectiles, while women do better than men on a perceptual speed tasks (identifying and matching items), show greater verbal fluency (including the ability to find words that begin with a specific letter), perform better in arithmetic calculation, and are better at recalling landmarks. Kimura concludes that many of these differences occur long before puberty, at least based on studies conducted in her laboratory.

Not only has she been able to find a number of differences, but she has been able to relate at least some of these differences to testosterone levels. For example, she found that women with high testosterone perform better on a spatial task (rotating figures) than women with low levels of testosterone, and that men with low levels outperform men with high levels (see top panel of Figure 5-4). On tests of mathematical reasoning, men with low levels of testosterone perform better than men with high levels, but in women mathematical reasoning is unrelated to testosterone level (see middle panel of Figure 5-4). On perceptual speed tasks—tasks in which women are typically superior—there is no relationship between testosterone and performance (see bottom panel of Figure 5-4).

Doreen Kimura has not been able to find any differences on vocabulary tests and tests of verbal reasoning. This is consistent with the work of Hyde and Linn (1988), who did a meta-analysis of 165 studies involving about 1 million subjects and found no differ-

ences between the sexes. Doreen Kimura has, on the other hand, found sex differences in mathematical abilities. There is a great deal of controversy about sex differences in mathematics. In a meta-analysis of 100 studies, Hyde, Fennema and Lamon (1990) concluded that "gender differences in mathematics are small" (p.139). What is particularly interesting about their work is the finding that this difference has decreased quite dramatically over the past two decades, suggesting that the environment has played a role in producing these differences. The largest sex differences in mathematical ability tends to be found at the upper end of the of distribution (a gifted population) with males outnumbering females 13 to 1 (Benbow and Stanley, 1980, 1983). Even small differences can result in large differences. The place where one would expect to find those differences would be at the upper end of the distribution. Hyde, Fennema and Lamon (1990) have argued, however, that it is inappropriate to generalize from such samples as studied by Benbow and Stanley. Benbow herself has recognized this point.

Summary

While males and females share the same basic sex hormones, they produce them in different amounts. It is the different concentrations of the sex hormones that appear to be responsible not only for many of the physical differences between males and females but some of the psychological differences as well. On the physical side, testosterone has a masculinizing effect. Among other things, testosterone is responsible for such things as the development of the male penis, the growth of facial hair, and depthe of the voice. Injections of testosterone in females tends to produce an enlarged clitoris. conversely, estrogen tends to have a feminizing effect. Among other things, estrogen produces female breasts and stimulates the body to store fat on the hips and thighs. Injections of estrogen in males (such as in transsexual operations) produce the corresponding effects in males—enlarged breasts and a tendency to store fat on the hips and thighs.

It has also been shown that testosterone is involved in a number of specific problem-solving abilities. Doreen Kimuraa has shown that performance on cer-

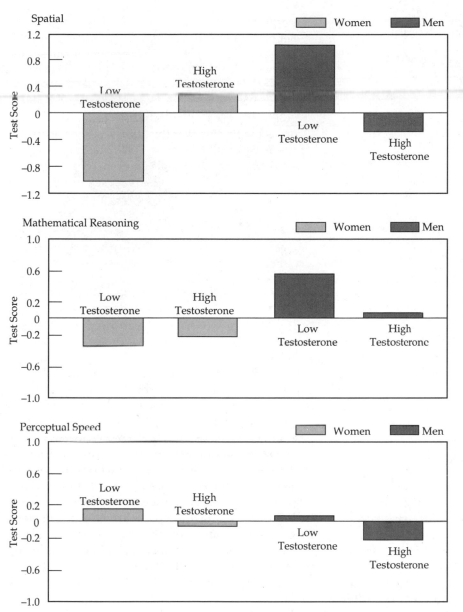

Figure 5–4. Testosterone levels can affect performance on some tests. Women with high levels of testosterone perform better on a spatial task *(top)* than do women with low levels; men with low levels outperform men with high levels. On a mathematical reasoning test *(middle)*, low testosterone corresponds to better performance in men; in women there is no such relation. On a test in which women usually excel *(bottom)*, no relation is found between testosterone and performance. (From Doreen Kimura,"Sex Differences in the Brain." *Scientific American,* 1992, *267,* 118-125. Copyright © 1992 by Scientific American. All rights reserved.)

tain spatial tasks and mathematical reasoning tasks is linked to testosterone levels. Women with high levels of testosterone tend to perform better on certain spatial tasks (tasks in which men tend to outperform women) than women with low levels of testosterone. On mathematical reasoning tasks, men with low levels of testos-terone tend to outperform those with high levels. On mathematical reasoning tasks, men with low levels of testosterone tend to outperform those with high levels whereas no relationship was found between testos-terone levels and mathematical reasoning in women. While this research is very new and needs to be repli-

Figure 5–5. Cross-section of the human brain showing some of the structures in which sexual dimorphism has been found.

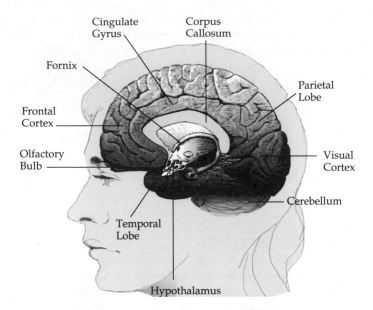

cated, it indicates that the study of hormones may be important in order for us to fully understand sex differences. As I will show in the next section, hormones have been strongly implicated in sexual orientation, a topic that has recently generated a great deal of interest in the media.

Sexual Dimorphism in the Brain

The word dimorphism is defined as crystalizing into two distinct forms. Evidence for sexual dimorphism comes from the observation that a particular structure in the brain is often different for females and males in terms of such things as size, number of neurons, and dendritic branching (see Gorski, 1991).

Many researchers believe that these structural differences may account for certain behavioral differences. What is particularly noteworthy is that these structures can often be altered by pre- or post-natal administrations of sex hormones, suggesting that sex differences in the brain are due, at least in part, to the effects of sex hormones. There is also evidence, however, that the environment often alters these structures as well, suggesting that there is a complex interaction of hormones and the environment.

Some Examples

1. The Hypothalamus. There is considerable research indicating that the hypothalamus is involved in sexual and reproductive behavior. In an area of the hypothalamus that has been dubbed the "sexual dimorphic nucleus," male rats have more neurons than female rats. These nuclei are five to seven times larger in the male than in the female. It has been shown that prenatal injections of testosterone will increase the number of neurons in a nucleus of the female rat's hypothalamus, making the hypothalamus more similar to that of the male, and that anti-testosterone drugs prenatally administered to a male rat will make his hypothalamus more similar to that of the female (Gorski, 1974, 1985, 1991; Haseltine & Ohno, 1981; Wilson et al., 1981).

Research with humans has also shown that such differences can be found in the human brain (Swaab & Fliers, 1985). The location of the hypothalamus in the human brain is shown in Figure 5-5, together with some of the other structures in which sexual dimorphism has been found. Recently it has been found that an area of the human brain that is known to be linked to sexual behavior (and is more than twice as large in men as in women) is smaller (half the size) in homo-sexual men than in heterosexual men (LeVay, 1991). Because the sample size was small and because the sample came from an AIDS population, further work needs to be done to verify this finding. It is consistent, however, with research which indicates that if new-born male rats are castrated and deprived of testos-terone, they never try to mate with females as adults and allow other males to mount them.

2. The Cerebral Cortex. It has been found that the right cortex is thicker than the left in male rats but not in female rats (Diamond, Dowling, & Johnson, 1981). It has been suggested that the right hemisphere is involved in spatial abilities. We know that these dif-ferences are due, at least in part, to sex hormones be-cause it is possible to produce these differences artificially by an injection of testosterone in the female infant rat at a critical stage—usually around birth or shortly thereafter—or by castration of the male infant rat at the time of birth (see Beach, 1976; Haseltine & Ohno, 1981; Wilson et al., 1981). The work of Stewart and Kolb (1988) indicates that androgens suppress de-velopment of the left cortex. There is good evidence that the environment also affects the development of these structures in rats (Diamond, 1988). Animals that have been provided with an enriched environment will show an increase in certain structures of the cortex.

A similar pattern of results has been obtained in human fetuses, with the right hemisphere larger than the left in males but not in females (LaCoste et al., cited in Kimura, 1992). In other words, the right and the left hemispheres do not appear to be equally asymmetri-cal in males and females. Despite such reports, the ev-idence for humans is still meager and therefore needs to be treated with caution.

3. The Corpus Callosum. The corpus callosum is thought to be involved in the coordination of the two sides of the brain. It has been reasoned that if there are more connecting fibers in one sex, that sex should be able to communicate between the two hemispheres more fully (e.g., Kimura, 1992). In humans, the corpus callosum, or more precisely the posterior portion, is larger and more bulbous in females than in males (Allen, Richey, Chai, & Gorski, 1991). Recently it was found that verbal fluency correlated positively with the size of a region of the corpus callosum (mainly defined by the splenium) and that another region of the cor-pus callosum (the posterior callosum) correlated nega-tively with language lateralization (Hines, Chiu, McAdams, Bentler, and Lipcamon, 1992). Such evi-dence is consistent with the suggestion that the corpus callosum does, indeed, play some role in the ability of the two hemispheres to communicate. It is notewor-thy that this research makes use of a new method of measuring the intact (living) brain called magnetic res-onance imaging (MRI). Before the development of this technique, it was necessary to rely on patients with neural lesions, a method that is highly limited. There is also evidence that not only can sex hormones alter this dimorphism but that early experience can do so as well (Berrebi et al., 1988; Juraska & Kopcik, 1988).

As yet there is no clear evidence at what stage in de-velopment the corpus callosum becomes sexually di-morphic, nor has it been clearly shown to be affected by sex hormones. Since all sexually dimorphic struc-tures examined thus far have been shown to be influ-enced by prenatal hormones, Gorski (1991) suggests there is reason to expect such effects will be found for the corpus callosum.

3. Other regions. Another sexual dimorphism can be found in the the the anterior commissure, which is larger in human females than in males (Allen & Gorski, 1991). It has also been shown that there are differences in subregions of the amygdala (Hines, Allen & Gorski, 1992), a region in the brain that has often been linked to sex, aggression, gonadotropic secretion and integration of olfactory information. In other words, there is evi-dence for sexual dimorphism in the brain for a num-ber of functions that differentiate the two sexes.

Critical Periods

There has been a great deal of interest in the question of when sexual dimorphism occurs. There is much re-search to suggest that these structures can be "mas-culinized" only at certain stages of brain differentiation and that to reverse them at a later stage is impossible. Remember that without testosterone, the brain would tend to develop as a "female" brain. The word "mas-culinized" is an unfortunate word because females also produce small amounts of testosterone, and the research with both animals and humans suggests that even small amounts of testosterone can and do alter the development of the female brain. In other words, one reason why various structures of the female brain differ from those of the male brain is that the female brain was exposed to testosterone at some critical stage of development. Until someone suggests a better word, I will use the term "masculinized."

Masculination can occur before birth, after birth, or over a fairly long period bridging the time before and after birth. There is evidence, for example, that after a certain critical period, injections of testosterone will no longer alter the hypothalamus (see Haseltine & Ohno, 1981; Wilson et al., 1981). There is considerable evidence that this critical period occurs either shortly before birth or shortly after birth. If the hypothalamus governs sexual orientation, as some people have suggested, the idea of critical periods means that once sexual orientation has been established in the brain, it is very difficult if not impossible to alter that orientation. In practical terms, this means that attempting to change the sexual orientation of a person at some later point in time would be very difficult and perhaps impossible.

In the case of the cerebral cortex, on the other hand, there is a great deal of evidence that sexual dimorphism can and often does occur much later and perhaps over a longer period of time. This suggests that there may be a greater potential for environmental input to some structures than to others.

Sexual Dimorphism and Individual Differences

One of the things that Gorski and others often point out in connection with their work on sexual dimorphism in the brain is that there are large individual differences. It is important to emphasize in this context that individual differences are generally larger than group differences. In practical terms, the fact that there are larger individual differences than group differences (differences between males and females) means that many female brains look more like male brains than female brains and, similarly, that many male brains look more like female brains than male brains.

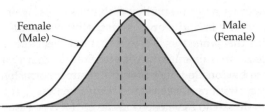

Figure 5–6 Normal distribution curves representing the differences between males and females. In most cases the differences between males and females is small. These curves show that when there are small differences, the vast majority of males and females tend to be alike rather than different (shaded area). Thus when people talk about differences, they are talking about a very small proportion of the general population (unshaded area).

Figure 5-6 shows how such differences in the brain and abilities can be conceptualized. While differences between the sexes may be larger or smaller depending on what we are talking about (brain differences or abilities differences), the general finding is that most differences between the sexes are normally quite small compared to the large individual differences within the sexes. In some cases, such as the hypothalamus, these differences can be and often are quite large.

The Politics of Sex/Gender Differences

The work on sex differences in the brain is highly charged with emotion. The reason is that biological difference between the sexes can and sometimes has been used to argue for the superiority of one sex over the other (see Tavris, 1992). If it can be show, for example, that males are superior in some way to females in certain areas, such data may be used to argue for the status quo. That is, male dominance in certain occupations should be accepted and should remain because that is the way nature intended it or that males should be allowed to express themselves in certain ways. Many women scholars have taken issue with this line of argument and have argued that most of the differences are small and further that many of these differences may be due to the environment/experience rather than biology. In other words, the argument for maintaining the status quo is based on very weak data or no data at all. What about findings that show women are superior to males in certain skills and abilities? This, again, is problematic. It has been suggested by some female scholars that when this happens those skills or abilities are sometimes devalued by males (see Tavris, 1992). The net result is that males can claim superiority in the face of a difference that seem to favor females.

Scholars who have been critical of the work on sex differences, have often been particularly critical of the animal research on sex differences. The main argument is that you cannot generalize from animals to humans. While this is true, the work on animals has allowed researcher to study the role of various sex hormones under precisely controlled conditions, research that would be impossible to do with humans for ethical reasons. This research has shown unequivocally that hormones do indeed produce a wide range of sex differences. This research has permitted researchers to speculate about the origins of certain sex differences in humans, drawing upon experiments of nature to help them establish if such findings do indeed generalize to humans. What we can conclude from all this research is that, indeed, much of what has been found with animals often does generalize, however the magnitude is often much smaller.

Since the sex differences in humans are small, some scholars have argued that they can be ignored because they have no practical significance. That may or may not be true. Often small biological differences are responsible for creating large individual differences. By aiming the organism in one direction versus another, they influence what an organism sees, hears, experiences, thinks, and even the self-schemas they construct.

While sex differences are, indeed, often small, individual differences, by contrast, are relatively large. If we are ever going to understand people at the level of the individual person we must keep an open mind to this research. Each of us has difference skills and abilities. Many of these differences may have their roots in brain differences, differences caused by sex hormones.

As I will discuss in the next section on sexual orientation, the significance of brain differences appears to be very important at the level of the individual. It makes a big difference to a person who feels drawn to a member of the same sex or the opposite sex.

Summary

There is a great deal of research indicating that certain structures in the brains of males and females are different—something called sexual dimorphism of the brain. Much of this research shows that such sexual dimorphism is due to the hormone testosterone. It has been shown, for example, that prenatal injection of testosterone will increase the number of neurons of the female rat's hypothalamus, making her hypothalamus more like that of a male, or that injections of testosterone will increase the thickness of the right hemisphere of the female brain, making it more like that of the male. Interestingly, it has been shown that the environment can produce these differences as well. Recent evidence indicates that there may be sexual dimorphism of the corpus callosum. There is also evidence that these differences may be linked to brain lateralization. Further, there is ample evidence that such sexual dimorphism occurs during critical periods of brain development.

The Question of Sexual Orientation

Gender-identity and gender-role. It has been suggested that all human beings have a sense of being female, male or some ambivalent position between the two and that humans are inclined to publicly present themselves as female, male, or ambivalent. The combination of private inner experience and public outward expression are collectively termed our *gender-identity/role* (Money, 1987). Traditionally, the words "gender-identity" and "gender-role" are treated as distinct concepts because there is good reason to believe that gender-identity and gender-role come about in different ways. In the following section I will be talking mainly about gender-identity.

Where do feelings about femaleness and maleness come from? The work on sexual dimorphism of the brain suggests that such differences may have a biological origin, but that appears to be too simplistic. Hormones do not biologically crystalize humans into feelings of femaleness and maleness, but rather appear to aim them more in one direction than another.

Whether or not we come to see ourselves as females or males depends as well on learned and cognitive factors. In this section I want to address the question of sexual orientation and, more specifically, the subject of homosexuality.

Biological Factors— The Question of Sexual Orientation

Sexual Dimorphism of the Hypothalamus and Male Sexual Orientation

Recently, Simon LeVay (1991), a neurobiologist at the Salk Institute in San Diego, published an article which provides evidence that homosexuality is determined, at least in part, by biological factors. The study involved examining a speck of neurons in the hypothalamus that is known to be linked to sexual behavior and is more than twice as large in men as in women. Since the area is very small—too small to study in living humans—he used the autopsied brains of 19 homosexual men and 16 heterosexual men. He found the oval cluster in homosexual men to be half the size of that found in heterosexual men, and sometimes was even missing. The decision to look at the hypothalamus grew out of the knowledge that when the hypothalamus is damaged in male monkeys, they lose interest in females but they do not lose their sex drive, as evidenced by their continued tendency to masturbate.

LeVay's research is consistent with other research which indicates that if newborn male rats are castrated and deprived of testosterone, they never try to mate with females as adults and allow other males to mount them (Gorski, 1974, 1985, 1991). It is also consistent with the research which indicates that testosterone may be the hormone that is responsible for the development of the hypothalamus (Haseltine & Ohno, 1981; Wilson et al., 1981; Gorski, 1988). It is important to point out, however, that the nuclei that LeVay found that was larger were not the same nuclei as those in the rat research. The significance of this difference needs to be clarified.

Despite LeVay's findings, neurobiologists do not believe this is the sole cause of homosexuality. First, there is other research which indicates that the anterior commissure, a nerve network that connects the two hemispheres, is larger in females than in males, and is larger in homosexual than in heterosexual men (e.g., Allen & Gorski, 1991). Further, we have a great deal of evidence that the environment is also important, an issue I will deal with shortly.

Twin Studies and Male Sexual Orientation

Recent evidence indicates that genetic factors are important in determining individual differences in sexual orientation; heritability estimates range from 31% to 74% (Bailey & Pillard, 1991). Using 110 fraternal and identical twins and 46 adoptive men and their brothers, this study found that if one of the brothers was already homosexual, the more similar they were to their brother the more likely they too would be homosexual.

The study advertised for homosexual and bisexual men who had a male twin or an adoptive or genetically unrelated brother with whom they started living by age 2. Fifty-two percent of the 56 sets of identical twins were both gay, 22% of the 54 fraternal twins sets were both gay, and 11% of the adopted brothers were both gay. Since identical twins have the same genes, fraternal twins only share some of the same genes, and the adopted should have virtually none of the same genes, the evidence points to the role of genetics in homosexuality.

Twin Studies and Female Sexual Orientation

Similar resutls have been found for lesbians (Bailey, Pillard, Neale & Agyei, 1993). In a study of 71 sets of identical twins, 37 sets of fraternal twins, and 35 sets of adoptive sisters, it was found that 48% of the identical twins who said they were homosexual or bisexual had twins who were also lesbian, as did 16 % of the fraternal twins, and 6% of the adopted sisters. Heritability estimates ranged from 27% to 76%. These results closely parallel those found for gays reported above.

Congenital Adrenal Hyperphasis and Female Sexual Orientation

Research with rats in which male rats were deprived of testosterone (e.g., by castration) and female rats were given estrogen (a drug that can have a masculinizing effect), indicated that genetic males behaved like females and the genetic females behaved like males (Williams, as cited in Kimura, 1992). Since it is impossible to do this same research with humans, researchers have to depend on experiments of nature to determine whether or not hormones affect sexual orientation. By experiment of nature, I simply mean that there is a manipulation in the study, much like a laboratory manipulation, except that it was not planned but occurred by accident. Because of a genetic defect, some women produce abnormally high levels of adrenal androgens—a condition called congenital adrenal hyperphasia (CAH). In order to assess whether these women tend to be more bisexual or homosexual, their responses to erotica have been examined. The reason for using responses to erotica grows out of the idea that erotica is perhaps less governed by social pressure to conform than is something like gender identity. Ehrhardt & Meyer-Bahlburg (1981) reported that in studies using such measures, approximately half the dreams of CAH-affected women were bisexual (none were homosexual). However, since there were no control groups, the researchers said they could not draw any definitive conclusions from this measure. Their conclusions were undoubtedly affected by the fact they also found that CAH-affected women tend to adopt the gender identity they were assigned at birth; that is, they saw themselves as female. In a more highly controlled study, evidence was found for the idea that CAH-affected women tend to be more bisexual or homosexual (Money, Schwartz & Lewis, 1984). In a sample of 30 CAH-affected women, 37% rated their sexual imagery and activity as bisexual or homosexual, 40% as heterosexual, and 23% were noncommittal. In a control group of 27 women with other endocrine disorders, 7% rated their erotic imagery and activity as bisexual whereas the remainder rated it as heterosexual.

Because CAH-affected girls often have more masculinized genitalia, it has been suggested that the effects may be due to CAH-affected girls being raised as more male-like (Quadagno, Brisco & Quadagno, 1977). This point has been contested by Ehrhardt and Meyer-Bahlburg (1981), who have noted that if anything, parents of such children tend to encourage femininity. That is, they tend to encourage stereotypical sex-typed female behavior in their CAH-affected daughters. One additional point is worth mentioning here. Ehrhardt and Meyer-Bahlburg (1981) also found that CAH-affected girls showed: (1) "a combination of intense active outdoor play, increased association with male peers, long-term identification as a "tomboy" by self and others, probably all related to high energy expenditure" and (2) "decreased parenting rehearsal such as doll play and baby care, and a low interest in the role of rehearsal of wife and mother versus having a career" (p. 1314).

DES-Affected Women and Female Sexual Orientation

There is also data from women who were exposed prenatally to diethylstilbestrol (DES), a synthetic estrogen (formerly used to maintain pregnancy) that can have masculinizing effects on the brain but does not produce masculinizing effects on the genitalia (Dohler et al., 1984; Hines et al., 1987). In a sample of 30 DES-exposed women, 21% rated themselves as having bisexual or homosexual responsiveness compared to none in a control group (Ehrhardt et al., 1985). Since 12 of the DES-exposed had unexposed sisters, it was possible to compare them with their sisters. Whereas 42% of the DES-exposed rated themselves as bisexual or homosexual, only 8% of their sisters rated themselves similarly. Since DES does not masculinize the genitalia, it is difficult to argue that the effects are due to the parents' decision, based on the size of the genitalia, to raise their daughter more male-like (see section on sex assignment at birth for a more complete description of this hypothesis). The work on the CAH-affected and DES-exposed is not without critics. Fausto-Sterling (1985) has offered a detailed critique of the work on congenital-adrenal hyperphasia as well as other work that has been put forth as evidence for a biological basis for sex differences. Barinaga (1991) has offered an alternative to homosexuality, arguing that behavior can change chemistry.

Animal Work

Because it is difficult to study the effects of hormones in humans, a great deal of work has been done with animals. I want to briefly refer to this work because it has shown that it is possible, at least in animals, to alter sexual orientation by injecting hormones at a certain critical period of brain development.

Changing sexual orientation. If male rats are castrated the day they are born, they tend to show what Günter Dörner (1983) calls heterotypical behavior; that is, these animals show "a significant preference of sexual responsiveness to male partners, following estrogen or even androgen treatment in adulthood" (p. 205). The higher the androgen level during brain differentiation, the stronger the male and the weaker the female sexual behavior in adulthood, irrespective of sex. Even complete sexual inversion (male sexual behavior in place of female sexual behavior or vice versa) has been observed when androgen has been deficient in the male and in excess in the female. In other words, it can be shown that early alterations in the hormone levels will create a predisposition for lowered sexual motivation, bisexuality, and homosexuality (see Dörner, 1983).

Sex-typed behaviors. Sex hormones play an important role in a wide variety of sex-related behaviors. Work at the University of Wisconsin indicates that the style of play adopted by males and females is linked to the sex hormones. Goy and McEwen (1980) have noted that the behavior of young male rhesus monkeys differs from that of females in four ways: they initiate play more often, they roughhouse more often, they mount their peers of both sexes more often, and they mount their mothers more often. When pregnant mothers were given injections of testosterone for various periods of time during the critical period of fetal development, their female offspring not only had masculinized genitalia but adopted a male style of play. Goy and McEwen also observed that male rhesus monkeys usu-

ally occupy the dominant position in a mixed-sex troop. When pregnant female monkeys were given injections of testosterone, they were more likely than other females to assume the dominant position in mixed-sex troops.

The Normal Variant Model

Without specifying the mechanism, a large number of theorists and researchers believe that homosexuality is a normal variation within the continuum of human sexual behavior. Animal research has shown that among mammals sexual contacts between the same sex are quite common (Ford & Beach, 1951). Homosexuality has been found to be prevalent in all cultures at about the same rate (Whitam & Mathy, 1986). Also, it has been found there are many similarities in their behavior (Whitam & Mathy, 1986). Researchers who have examined the question of whether or not homosexuality is the result of poor psychological adjustment have generally come to the conclusion that homosexuality is within the normal range of psychological functioning (Bell & Weinberg, 1978).

In summary, the normal variant model emphasizes the fact that there are wide individual differences and that such differences do not appear to be due to such things as culture or even psychological functioning. Now let me turn to the question of learning.

Learned Component

For a long period of time there has been a bias towards viewing sexual orientation as acquired. One of the main hypotheses of homosexuality was that homosexuality was the result of pathology. When researchers began to investigate this hypothesis they could find no evidence for this idea. In his study of 30 homosexual and 30 heterosexual men, Hooker (1957) concluded: "Homosexuality as a clinical entity does not exist. Its forms are as varied as those of heterosexuality" (p. 30). It is noteworthy in this context to point out that, lacking any evidence for the pathology hypothesis, the American Medical Association and the American Psychological Association no longer list homosexuality as a clinical disorder.

As more and more research begins to show that there is a strong biological component, other learning interpretations have come under much closer scrutiny. It is no longer sufficient to say that it is self-evident that homosexuality is acquired or that homosexuality is the result of choice. If homosexuality is acquired, as some people argue, what are the conditions that lead to homosexuality? In the following section I will examine some of the hypotheses that have been advanced over the years.

Psychoanalytic Theory

According to psychoanalytic theory, the cause of homosexuality in males grows out of an family constellation characterized by a close-binding overprotective mother and a detached, absent, or openly hostile father (see Bieber et al., 1962). Such parents inhibit the expression of heterosexual feelings in the son. In addition, the absence of an effectual father means the child does not have a good role model for learning appropriate heterosexual behavior. The general consensus is that there is not good support for the psychoanalytic interpretation. In short, there is no research which has been able to clearly link domineering mothers and ineffectual fathers to homosexuality.

Chance-Learning Hypothesis

According to this hypothesis, if a young person were seduced by someone of the same sex he or she would learn to associate the pleasures of sex with the gender of the seducer. Not only has no evidence been put forth in support of this hypothesis, but recent work in which young females and males who have been sexually seduced (or, perhaps more properly, "sexually abused") indicates that if anything it often has the opposite effect. The following study by the Kinsey Institute suggests there is little or no evidence to support the chance-learning hypothesis.

The Kinsey Institute Study

One of the most extensive studies of the origins of homosexuality was undertaken by a group of researchers at the Kinsey Institute (Bell, Weinberg, & Hammersmith, 1981). They interviewed 979 homosexual men and women and 477 heterosexual men and women, asking them a number of questions from a variety of theoretical orientations. On the basis of their research, they drew the following conclusions concerning the origins of sexual preferences.

1. Sexual preference occurs prior to adolescence even when youngsters have not been particularly sexually active. (There are numerous other studies which have shown that most homosexual males become aware of their same-sex orientation during childhood or adolescence) (Dank, 1971; Reiche & Dannecker, 1977; Whitam, 1977).

2. Homosexual behavior emerges from homosexual feelings—feelings that occur about 3 years on the average before any overt homosexual experience.

3. Homosexual women and men tend to have a history of heterosexual experiences in childhood and adolescence but found these experiences not to be satisfying.

4. Identification with either parent played no significant role in the development of sexual orientation.

5. There was no evidence for the hypothesis that any particular type of mother produces homosexual children. A slightly higher proportion of homosexuals had a poor relationship with their fathers, but it was impossible to determine if this was a causative factor or simply a reflection of the fact that sexually different sons and daughters had more difficulty relating to their fathers.

Sex Assignment at Birth

One of the main hypotheses that has been put forth concerning gender identity is the role of sex assignment at birth. This model is presented in Figure 5-7.

According to this hypothesis, boys and girls are treated differently as they grow up. This starts by dressing girls in pink and boys in blue, for example, and then follows a pattern in which boys are given toy cars and trucks and rewarded for boy activities while girls are given dolls and rewarded for girl activities.

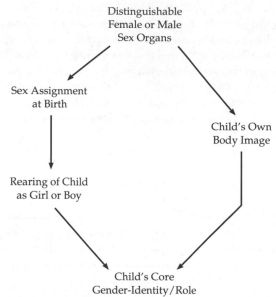

Figure 5–7. This details the environmental and cultural factors that influence the development of the child's gender-identity/role. (From G. F. Kelly, *Sexuality Today: The Human Perspective, Third Edition* , 1992. Copyright ©1992 by The Dushkin Publishing Group, Inc., Guilford, CT. All rights reserved. Reprinted with permission.)

According to this hypothesis, sex assignment is the key to sex differences because the process of sex assignment determines how children are rewarded (Tavris & Wade, 1984). While there is considerable evidence for the idea that boys and girls are rewarded differently, the studies are correlational, a criticism that can be leveled at numerous other studies. Let me examine one study which is not a correlational study but rather is an experiment of nature.

Before I discuss some of this work, it is important that I make a distinction between sexual orientation and *core sexual identity*. Whereas sexual orientation has to do with preference for a sexual partner, core sexual identity has to do with the sense of being male or female. In the studies that I will discuss, I will be talking mainly about core sexual identity (see Hines & Green, 1992).

Experiments of Nature: Rearing Boys as Girls and Core Sexual Identity

Because of a genetic deficiency of enzyme 5-alpha-reductase, there is a decreased production of dihydrotestosterone from testosterone that begins in utero. This leads to female-appearing genitalia because dihydrotestosterone is necessary for the prenatal development of male genitalia. In a sample of 18 such individuals, all raised as girls, 17 of the 18 professed male identity in adolescence. It should be noted that at puberty their genitalia developed under the influence of testosterone. Thus, at puberty they all possessed appropriate sex organs (Imperato-McGinley et al., 1979). According to the sex-assignment-at-birth hypothesis, they should have adopted the identity of the sex they were assigned.

An enzymatic deficiency (17-beta hydroxysteroid dehydrogenase) produces female-appearing genitalia at birth that is followed by considerable phallus growth and excessive hair growth in adolescence. In a study of 25 such individuals it was found that these persons generally adopted a male identity during adolescence despite having been raised as females (Rosler & Kohn, 1983).

Critics of these studies have suggested that the individual may not have been raised unambiguously as females since the genitalia were not identical to those of normal females (e.g., Money, 1976). One often-quoted study that is often offered in support of the idea that, indeed, sex assignment at birth is what determines sexual orientation and perhaps core sexual identity, involves the unfortunate case of a young boy whose penis was severely injured during circumcision. Because doctors determined that reconstructive surgery had a low probability of succeeding, they recommended the boy be given an artificial vagina instead and that he be raised as a girl. Since the boy had an identical twin brother, it was an ideal situation to assess the effect of sex assignment on various sex-typed behaviors. Follow-up studies at age 5 to 6 showed the two children were clearly differentiated in terms of activities, toy preferences, and mannerisms (Money, 1986). In fact, these two children were more clearly differentiated than most boys and girls, indicating that the parents perhaps had treated the children quite differently. With the onset of adolescence, however, things did not progress as the learning hypothesis would suggest. A report by the "girl's" psychiatrist indicated "she" was experiencing a great deal of gender confusion (Diamond, 1986). (I agree with one of my reviewers that this study probably doesn't prove anything. I decided to include it because it is one of those studies that people keep dragging up to "prove" that humans are completely plastic when it comes to gender identity.)

What these studies seem to indicate is that, indeed, biology likely does plays an important role when it comes to sexual orientation and core sexual identity but perhaps not when it comes to sex-typed activities (such as playing with dolls versus trucks, etc.). It is a rather common error for people to confuse sexual orientation with being masculine or feminine (engaging in sex-typed behaviors). There is considerable evidence that these two attributes vary independently. Homosexual men, like homosexual women, show the whole range of attributes ranging from masculine to feminine sex-typed behaviors. As Bell and Weinberg (1978) point out, it is impossible to predict the nature of one's personality, social adjustment, and sexual functioning on the basis of one's sexual orientation.

Status of the Learning Hypothesis

While there is still relatively little evidence for any of the three main hypotheses that I discussed above, there is evidence from another source that does indicate learning plays an important role. This comes from the work with twins (both male and female) that I discussed earlier. If biology is the main thing that leads to homosexuality, then one would expect that if one identical twin was a homosexual the other would also be a homosexual. That is clearly not the case. Only 30% to 70% of the variance in the study of male twins can be directly attributed to heredity, leaving a great deal of room for the role of learning or cognition (Bailey & Pillard, 1991). Perhaps the only thing we can conclude at this point is that none of the learning hypotheses by themselves provide a very complete explanation. Perhaps there is some truth in all of them. That is that under certain conditions, a domineering mother cou-

pled with an ineffectual father, or a chance homosexual experience, or being treated as a member of the opposite sex can and does does push one in the direction of homosexuality. What is clearly needed are studies which do not simply pit learning theories against each other or even learning against biology, but rather experiments that attempt to elucidate the different kinds of learning experiences that might push one in that direction.

Learning and the Expression of a Sexual Orientation

Even if it were established that sexual orientation was completely biologically determined (which it isn't), it would still be important to consider the role of learning. There is a great deal of evidence that gays and lesbians are like anyone else in that they select different role models. One consistent complaint from the gay community has been that the media do not offer them a range of role models. When gays are presented in the media they are often shown as stereotyped effeminate individuals who are passive and often promiscuous. Similar arguments come from the lesbian community which complains about the presentation of lesbians as very masculine, aggressive and anti-male.

One can express a particular sexual orientation in many different ways. I assume that what determines its expression is the same for homosexuals as it is for heterosexuals. In other words, I assume that learning plays just as important a role in the expression of a homosexual orientation as it does in the expression of a heterosexual orientation.

Cognitive Factor

Is homosexuality a choice? Do people decide that they want to become homosexuals because it offers them a lifestyle they find more attractive and self-fulfilling? Do people make the decision—perhaps at some unconscious or preconscious level—that they want to pursue a homosexual lifestyle even if they do not consciously come to that conclusion?

In researching this question I could find little or no evidence that homosexuality is actively chosen except perhaps under unusual circumstances such as when people are imprisoned. In fact, much of the evidence points in the opposite direction. Many homosexuals say that when they finally came to accept the possibility they were gay or lesbian they became very distraught and experienced a wide range of psychological symptoms including anxiety, depression (together with suicidal ideation) and stress.

While there is little evidence that people choose homosexuality because it offers them a lifestyle that they find attractive, there is, nonetheless, a great deal of evidence that cognitive factors play an important role in how homosexuals come to think about themselves and express themselves. I decided to present Cass's six stages of homosexual identity formation which illustrates the role of cognitive factors in the expression of homosexuality. His theory does not exhaust what we know about cognitive processes, but it does provide a good summary of many of these processes.

Cass's Six Stages of Homosexuality

Cass's description of the six stages of homosexual identity formation provides an indication of the role of cognitive factors in the expression of homosexuality (Cass, 1990). This theory suggests that in order for the process of homosexual identity formation to begin, an individual must experience some degree of sexual attraction or interest in someone of the same sex. As you can see from the following description, several cognitive processes are at work involving such diverse things as changes in attitudes, the development of new expectations, the construction of a gender schema, and so forth.

Stage 1: Identity confusion. In this stage the individual begins to realize that information about homosexuality may somehow relate to them. They often experience persistent dreams and fantasies about members of the same sex but typically avoid homosexual behavior.

Stage 2: Identity comparisons. In this stage the individual begins to examine the broader implications of what it means to be a homosexual. They deal with the question of how the acceptance of such an identity might affect their relationships with their family and their friends and how will they fit into society. They often experience a profound sense of loss as they come to realize their alienation from the stereotyped heterosexual society. While some may devalue the importance of heterosexuality, others may turn their sexual identity confusion into antihomosexual attitudes and even exaggerated heterosexual behavior while still entertaining homosexual fantasies.

Stage 3: Identity tolerance. As they come to accept their homosexuality, they begin to realize that sexual, social, and emotional needs go with being a homosexual. The typical pattern is for the individual to become more involved with other homosexuals at this stage. As they become more involved with other homosexuals and as they come to accept that they have special sexual, social, and emotional needs, they develop a greater tolerance of their homosexual identity.

One of the questions that the individual must face at this stage is how openly they wish to become about their sexual orientation. The process of allowing oneself to acknowledge that one is homosexual and communicating that to others has been called "coming out of the closet."

Stage 4: Identity acceptance. The main thing that characterizes this stage is the acceptance of the homosexual self-image as opposed to merely tolerating it. In this stage there is typically greater involvement with the gay and lesbian subculture and the development of a positive attitude towards other homosexual individuals.

Stage 5: Identity pride. As individuals come to accept the accomplishments of the gay community and come to realize that there are standards of comparisons other than those of the heterosexual community, they develop a sense of pride and abandon attempts to hide their homosexuality from the community. This stage is often characterized by anger. As they begin to realize there is discrimination and homophobia that is preventing them from living a full life, they often become politically active in an attempt to change laws and perceptions that people have about them.

Stage 6: Identity synthesis. In this last stage the homosexual begins to accept the idea that the world is not divided into homosexual and heterosexuals and that all heterosexuals need not be viewed negatively. The anger that characterizes Stage 5 gives way to a greater acceptance of the self as an individual who not only has a sexual orientation (is gay or lesbian) but also has other personality attributes that need to be satisfied.

A Note on Sexual Plasticity in Humans

There is considerable evidence from cross-cultural work that the sexual behavior of humans can be and often is highly plastic. What I mean by that is that humans can adapt themselves to a wide range of conditions when they do not find themselves in ideal conditions. The high rate of homosexual behavior in prisons is an example. When confined to prisons, many men will engage in homosexual behavior even though they regard themselves as heterosexual. Money and Ehrhardt (1972) offer many examples of this, pointing out that in some cultures young males go through a period in which they adopt a homosexual orientation, for example. This plasticity should not be confused, however, with what has been called core sexual identity.

Summary

Evidence from a wide variety of sources indicates that sexual orientation (at least in homosexuals) has a biological basis. Specifically, it appears that sexual dimorphism of the hypothalamus is likely responsible. That is not to say that homosexuality in men or women is hardwired. Perhaps the best model is one that suggests biology points the individual in a certain direction. Consistent with this idea is the fact there is considerable evidence for the role of learning and cognition in the development of the homosexual orientation. The selection of role models undoubtedly plays as important a role in homosexual lives as do value systems. There is also evidence that female homosexuality has a biological basis. The work on CAH-affected and DES-exposed women suggests that exposure to androgens during critical stages of brain differentiation may be responsible, at least in part, for female homosexuality.

While it has been suggested that sexual orientation and core sexual identity are the result of sex assignment at birth, there is only modest evidence for that position. There is good evidence that core sexual identity has a biological basis. That is not to say that learning does not play an important role. Heritability estimates account for anywhere from about 30% to 70% of the variance, leaving considerable room for learning and cognition.

Perhaps one of the most compelling arguments that male homosexuality does not come from a rational choice but rather has a biological basis, comes from the homosexual community itself. It makes no sense, they argue, for people to select a lifestyle that is characterized by a job discrimination, attacks from homophobics, where there is a high probability of becoming a drug addict, where there is a high risk for contracting AIDS, not being able to marry and raise a family, and being generally rejected by friends, family, and society.

Main Points

1. Masters and Johnson have identified four more or less distinct phases in the sexual response of males and females.

2. Masters and Johnson suggest that the main motivation governing human sexual behavior is the pleasure derived from various forms of tactile stimulation.

3. Masters and Johnson point out that the clitoris is unique among humans in that its only function is pleasure.

4. Masters and Johnson have found there is remarkable similarity between the sexual responses of males and females.

5. Sexual intercourse will increase norepinephrine by as much as 1,200%.

6. It has been suggested that sexual behavior in humans is largely the result of sexual scripts.

7. With the onset of adolescence, sexual scripts become coordinated with sexual feelings that are self-aroused through masturbation.

8. It has been suggested that the reason females have more difficulty coordinating sexual feelings with sexual scripts arises out of the tendency of fewer females to masturbate.

9. While males and females agree on the sexual script that leads to intercourse, females focus more on being stimulated by the male than on penetration.

10. Guilt feelings can reduce the arousal typically produced by erotic or pornographic material.

11. The sexual scripts that people come to use are influenced by the beliefs and attitudes they hold. Three beliefs that influence sexual scripts are: beliefs pertaining to the desirability of being permissive, beliefs about the sex drive of females and males, and the meaning the two sexes attach to sex.

12. It has been suggested that women value intercourse because it gives them a sense of shared feelings, emotional warmth and being wanted, whereas men often focus more on the arousal aspect of sex rather than on the shared feelings that sex can provide.

13. Extraverts tend to pet more and have intercourse more often than introverts.

14. Also, people with an unrestricted orientation to sex have more sex partners.

15. Variety and change tend to enhance sexual arousal.

16. It has been suggested that attraction is due, at least in part, to phenylethylanine (PEA) whereas attachment is due, at least in part, to the chemical endorphin.

17. Oxytocin (a chemical that sensitizes nerves, stimulates muscles, and seems to produce feelings of relaxed satisfaction and attachment) has been implicated in love and intercourse.

18. According to Sternberg, love (consummate love) involves three components: passion, intimacy and commitment.

19. Perhaps because we implicitly believe in our society that people fall in love, we are inclined to look for situations in which there is an unexpected or unplanned quality.

20. While people often take the position that love is accidental (you fall in love), Sternberg argues that you can make love happen.

21. Interestingly, moderately difficult-to-get women are perceived by men as more attractive than easy-to-get women.

22. It appears that intimacy is something people can learn.

23. Intimacy is not to be confused with commitment in Sternberg's model. There is evidence that people can be intimate without having a sense of long-term commitment.

24. Sternberg's model provides an interesting way of conceptualizing the complexity of love, as well as providing an explanation of why people who do not share a common definition of love may find it difficult to maintain a long-term relationship.

25. There are three main categories of sex hormones: androgens (mainly male), estrogens (mainly female), and progestins (mainly female).

26. Both males and females produce hormones associated primarily with the other sex; thus their behavior is governed by the joint action of male and female hormones.

27. Two important gonadotropic hormones are luteinizing hormone and follicle-stimulating hormone.

28. If an egg has been fertilized by a Y chromosome, H-Y antigens change the embryo's ovaries into testicles.

29. Testosterone, produced by the testicles, produces a variety of changes in the embryo, including the development of the penis.

30. While men and women do not differ in IQ, they have been found to differ in a variety of problem-solving abilities.

31. While men tend to be better at such tasks as rotating things in space and mathematical reasoning, women tend to be better at perceptual speed tasks, arithmetic calculations, and have greater verbal fluency.

32. Much of the sexual dimorphism of the brain has been linked to the presence of sex hormones during critical stages of development.

33.   Three examples of sexual dimorphism of the brain can be found in the hypothalamus, the cerebral cortex, and the corpus callosum.

34.   There is considerable evidence that sexual dimorphism occurs during certain critical periods of development.

35.   In many cases, individual differences tend to be larger than sex differences.

36.   There is evidence that sexual orientation may be due in part to an area in the hypothalamus that has been linked to sexual behavior. The cluster of neurons in this area of the hypothalamus was found to be half the size in homosexual men than in heterosexual men.

37.   Twin studies have provided further evidence for the biological basis of homosexuality.

38.   CAH-affected and DES-exposed are more likely to have a homosexual orientation.

39.   A number of theorists and researchers believe that homosexuality is a normal variation within the continuum of human sexual behavior.

40.   The Kinsey Institute study collected evidence that is inconsistent with the psychoanalytic and the chance-learning interpretation of homosexuality.

41.   It has yet to be demonstrated that one can change the core sexual identity of an individual merely by rearing him or her as the opposite sex.

42.   The major role that learning plays in homosexuality is in the expression of homosexuality.

43.   Cass has described six distinct stages of homosexual identity formation: identity confusion, identity comparisons, identity tolerance, identity acceptance, identity pride and identity synthesis.

Chapter Six

Wakefulness, Alertness, Sleep, and Dreams

- Why do we fall asleep?
- Why do we wake up?
- Why isn't it possible for us to fall asleep any time we want to?
- Why do we have difficulty falling asleep when we are under pressure or when we are excited?

- How should people deal with jet lag when they fly long distances?
- Why can't people learn to do without sleep?
- Why do we dream?
- What is the significance of dreams?
- What causes insomnia?

Why do we feel tired and drowsy at some times but rested and alert at others? We all know from experience that these states are related, at least in part, to how long ago and how well we slept. As our normal sleep time approaches, we typically feel somewhat tired. Usually, shortly after waking we feel rested and alert (sometimes with the aid of a cup of coffee) unless, of course, we did not sleep well. We also know from experience, however, that feelings of drowsiness and alertness can be somewhat independent of how long and how well we slept. We sometimes feel drowsy even though we have slept recently, and we sometimes feel alert even though it is well past our normal sleep time. We also know from experience that it is difficult to shift our normal sleep pattern. Anyone who has tried to get up earlier than usual can attest to the fact that such a shift requires more than just going to bed earlier. People who cross several time zones in their travels often have difficulty adjusting to a new clock time. Such experiences seem to suggest that humans have an internal clock that can be reset only with some difficulty. There is also the question of dreams. What is the function of dreams? Are they important for mental health, processing information, or what?

Years of controlled laboratory research have begun to provide answers to these and other fascinating questions about wakefulness and sleep. As we shall see, wakefulness and sleep involve physiological and psychological mechanisms that work together in a complex manner. The states of wakefulness and sleep are not so distinct as one might think, yet we cross a very important line when we pass from wakefulness to sleep: we lose consciousness—awareness of the external environment. Typically, loss of consciousness is fairly abrupt, although at times we seem to enter a detached intermediate state that may reflect what Gerald Vogel (1978) calls *sleep-onset mentation*.

Wakefulness, Sleep, and EEG Activity

Correlates of Sleep and Wakefulness

The best index of wakefulness, drowsiness, and sleep in humans is cortical activity (Webb, 1975). Figure 6-1 shows EEG activity during the various stages of sleep.

A typical night of sleep consists of gradual progress from stage 0 (wakefulness) through stages 1, 2, 3, and 4 and then backward through stages 3, 2, and 1 into what is called stage 1-REM. This cycle, which takes about 90 to 120 minutes, then repeats itself. In the course of seven to eight hours of sleep we go through this cycle about five times. The regularity of the pattern I have described comes from the averaging of EEG data from several individuals. Typically it is not quite this regular for a given individual. Figure 6-2 shows the EEG pattern of a typical individual. The important thing to note is that while an individual may bypass certain stages from time to time, a rhythm (pattern) can nevertheless clearly be observed.

REM is an acronym for rapid eye movement. In studying electrical recordings of eye movements, Eugene Aserinsky and Nathaniel Kleitman (1953) found that rapid eye movements occurred in conjunction with low-voltage mixed brain-wave frequencies, and that when people were awakened on such occasions they regularly reported vivid dreams. Four years later, Dement found that dreams and REM were, indeed, related. Since then it has been common to refer to this pattern as REM sleep and to all other patterns as NREM (non-REM) sleep. Figure 6-2 identifies periods of REM sleep. Although it was initially thought that REM sleep was synonymous with dreaming, it has since been shown that humans dream during the other stages of sleep as well. For example, dreaming often occurs at the onset of sleep, in the absence of REM (Vogel, 1978).

Periods of REM typically occur in conjunction with stage 1 sleep. REM—or REM bursts, as they are sometimes called—occur about 90 minutes after one goes to sleep and then recur on an average of every 90 minutes (the time varies between 70 and 110 minutes). Interestingly, REM sleep tends to lengthen as the night progresses until it lasts as long as an hour at a time. As a result, an adult who sleeps 7.5 hours generally experiences 1.5 to 2 hours of REM sleep (Dement, 1972).

Jouvet's Model of Sleep

Why do EEG patterns fluctuate during sleep? Probably the most widely held view is that EEG activity during

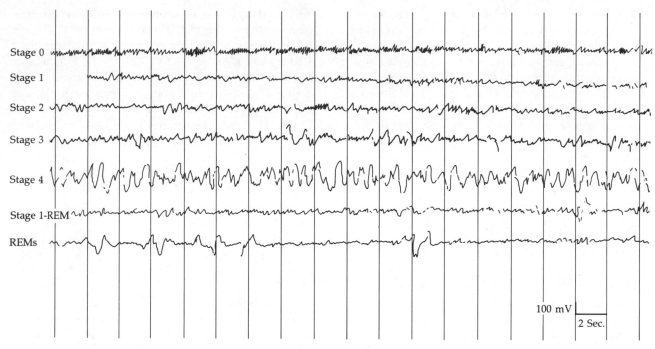

Figure 6–1. EEG tracings of the sleep stages. Stage 0 is wakefulness. (From W. B. Webb, *Sleep: The Gentle Tyrant,* 1975. Copyright © 1975 by Prentice-Hall, Inc. Reprinted by permission of the author and the University of Florida Sleep Laboratories.)

the sleep state is governed by the reticular activating system (RAS). Michel Jouvet (1967) has shown that changes in EEG activity during sleep are due to alternating activity of two sites in the RAS. The raphe nuclei, which secrete serotonin when active, have been shown to increase NREM sleep in cats (sleep characterized by low levels of EEG activity). Jouvet has suggested that the onset of sleep is due to the increased activity of the raphe nuclei. The locus coeruleus, which secretes norepinephrine when active, has been shown to increase REM sleep. Since increased EEG activity during REM sleep is typically associated with dreaming in humans, Jouvet has suggested that the onset of dreams is due to increased activity of the locus coeruleus. Because the activity of these two sites tends to alternate, Jouvet's model can readily account for the rhythmic nature of sleep—its fluctuation between deep and light sleep. Exactly why these two sites alternate in

activity is not altogether clear. One good possibility is that the activity in one center, after a period of time, stimulates activity in the other center, producing the alternating pattern (see also Siegel, 1979). Morgane and Stern (1975) agree that serotonin and norepinephrine play a role in the generation and maintenance of sleep. They suggest, however, that these biogenic amines only trigger processes that actually control the onset of waking or the onset of sleeping. That is, other chemical circuits may actually induce sleep or waking.

It should be noted that the biogenic amines are a group of chemicals that mediate and/or regulate biological activity. The word "amine" simply means that hydrogenated nitrogen is the common chemical signature of this group of chemicals. Mood, level of arousal, and the rate of metabolism are governed, at least in part, by biogenic amines. Many substances interact with biogenic amines and in so doing disrupt or some-

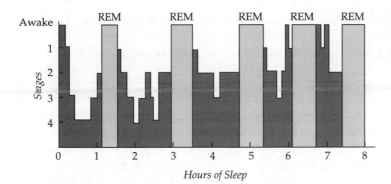

Figure 6–2. A plot showing the pattern of REM sleep, NREM sleep, and the four stages of NREM sleep over the course of one entire night of sleep. (From *Some Must Watch While Others Must Sleep* by William C. Dement. Copyright © 1972, 1974, 1976 by William C. Dement and the Stanford Alumni Association. Reprinted with permission.)

times enhance their normal regulatory action. LSD, for example, can block serotonin and cause hallucinations, whereas amphetamines can increase the sympathetic arousal normally caused by the presence of norepinephrine. I will talk more about how various drugs people use interact with biogenic amines in Chapter 7.

Jouvet's model can account for fluctuations in EEG activity at night (and possibly during the day). It is not altogether clear, however, why a given center should become active at a particular time. Specifically, why do people wake up at a given hour, and why is it difficult to shift periods of wakefulness and sleep?

Paralysis During REM

Since the brain and the entire central nervous system tend to become very active during REM, the question is why people don't walk, talk, and engage in other motor responses when they begin to dream. The answer is very simple. In each period of REM sleep the action of the motor neurons of the spinal cord that cause skeletal muscles to contract is inhibited. As a result, the muscles are atonic (without tone): they are paralyzed. The mechanisms that control this inhibition and the release from it are located in the reticular formation (Morrison, 1983). One reason researchers have been so interested in understanding these mechanisms is that some people experience a condition called narcolepsy, which causes them suddenly and unexpectedly to pass from wakefulness to REM sleep without losing consciousness. As a result, these people experience paralysis but can do nothing to control

it. If they are sitting they may find they will fall and can do nothing to stop themselves. This condition typically is not only stressful but dangerous, for a narcoleptic who suddenly slips into REM sleep could, for example, topple over and be injured by the fall.

Sleep and Attention

It has been suggested that sleep can be considered a state of extremely low attention (Glaubman et al., 1979). When we are asleep, our threshold for detecting incoming stimulation is very high, and as a result, information input is low. It has also been suggested that some type of filter allows only intense or specific forms of stimulation (such as a baby's cry) to reach the brain. This filter may be very important for maintaining the sleep state; without it we might tend to awaken periodically.

Since the learning of new material involves the ability to process information, it is not surprising that people show little if any new learning when they are asleep (Aarons, 1976). This does not mean that during sleep we may not be able to engage in important cognitive activities that involve information we processed when we were awake. As we shall see later in this chapter, it appears that we in fact do just that.

Why We Fall Asleep and Why We Wake Up

At least three sets of factors determine when we fall asleep and when we wake up. As we shall see, each set of factors interacts with the others.

Circadian rhythm. One of the prime factors that determines when we fall asleep is our circadian rhythm. The word *circadian* comes from the Latin *circa diem,* "about a day." People who have been left to establish their own routines in caves, bunkers, or specially designed laboratories tend to adopt a 25-hour cycle as opposed to the 24-hour circadian rhythm (Aschoff, 1965). It appears that the tendency to follow a 24-hour cycle is due largely to the synchronizing effects of events in our environment. Because we generally have regular times for eating, watching TV, going to bed, and so on, we tend to constantly reset our biological clocks so that they are attuned to the 24-hour day. When we free ourselves from the normal synchronizing effects of the environment, such as on a weekend or vacation or when we stay up late, "sleep in," and eat when we like, we often experience great difficulty getting back into our normal routine. The Monday-morning blues may be a direct result of letting ourselves shift to our natural 25-hour biological rhythm. If we allow ourselves to follow our internal biological clock on the weekends (going to bed one hour later each night), we might find that when Monday morning comes around we are not only sleep deprived when the clock says it is time to get up, but that we don't become alert until two hours later than normal. Wilse Webb and H. W. Agnew (1975a) have argued that our society may produce a state of chronic sleep deprivation because we sleep according to clock time rather than according to our need for sleep. They found that subjects who were allowed to awaken spontaneously after three nights of controlled sleep (11 P.M. to 7 A.M.) slept an additional 126 minutes, on the average.

What produces this rhythm? There is evidence that not only the time we fall asleep but the soundness of our sleep and the length of time we sleep are linked to the output of adrenaline (also called epinephrine) by the adrenal glands. When the epinephrine level declines, we tend to fall asleep, and when it rises, we tend to wake up (Nishihara et al., 1985). Going back one step further, researchers have suggested that the rhythm of the adrenal glands is controlled by the hypothalamus. Ultimately, in other words, the circadian rhythm is due to some rhythmical activity of the hypothalamus.

It should also be noted here that there is a correlation between body temperature and sleep. Our temperature tends to fluctuate one to two degrees in the course of a day. When we fall asleep, our temperature drops rather suddenly. The lowering of body temperature may be an important factor that not only induces sleep but helps to maintain it. Anybody who has tried to stay up late to study or work on a project can attest to the feelings of coldness that often occur during those prolonged vigils. During the course of the night our temperature tends to rise gradually. It has been suggested that the rise in temperature (which is linked to our daily arousal rhythm) may signal us to wake up (Gillberg & Åkerstedt, 1982). Our inability to maintain sleep during the day may simply be due to the fact that our underlying arousal level (presumably due to the secretion of the adrenal glands) maintains our temperature at a level that is inconsistent with sleep. Several studies have confirmed that there is a positive relation not only between temperature and wakefulness but between temperature and performance on a vigilance (attention-demanding) task (Moses et al., 1978; Taub, 1977). Consistent with this finding is the observation that most athletic records are broken in the evening when our body temperature is highest. P. L. Parmeggiani (1977) has suggested that the link between temperature and sleep is governed directly by the hypothalamus. His reasoning is based largely on research showing that the hypothalamus appears to govern the link between temperature, sleep, and conservation of energy in hibernating animals.

Environmental arousal. When we are under stress, our body moves into a state of high arousal. Under these conditions, we often find that we cannot go to sleep or that we have trouble staying asleep. Drugs that increase arousal, such as stimulants, also disturb sleep onset and interfere with the ability to stay asleep. An exciting event can and often does produce increases in arousal. Not surprisingly, therefore, exciting events often tend to interfere with sleep onset and good sleep. Since environmental arousal is situational, sleep disturbance caused by it tends to disappear when the event that produces the arousal disappears or is removed.

Sleep deprivation. One of the important factors that determines if and when we go to sleep is the length of time that has passed since we last slept. When people are deprived of a night's sleep, they tend to go to sleep sooner and to stay asleep longer, even if they have recently experienced environmentally induced arousal. We will return to this topic shortly.

Individual Differences in Sleep Cycles

There is evidence that personality variables may predict the rhythm of daily patterns. Extraversion and introversion measures, for example, may predict fluctuations not only in body temperature but in performance on vigilance tasks (Taub, Hawkins, & Van de Castle, 1978). Extraversion is associated with higher body temperature and better performance in the evening, introversion with higher body temperature and better performance in the morning. It has been suggested that these two personality types grow out of biological differences. It is the underlying biology, in other words, that is ultimately responsible for this effect.

Why We Periodically Feel Drowsy or Find Our Attention Shifting: Other Rhythms

The 12.5-hour ultradian rhythm. Studies have shown that when subjects are first deprived of sleep and then allowed to sleep for an extended period of time, there is a significant return of SWS (slow-wave sleep) after 12.5 hours of sleep (Gagnon, De Koninck, & Broughton, 1985). These findings are consistent with the observation that people tend to become not only less alert but sleepy around noon (Richardson et al., 1982). In many cultures it is the norm to take an afternoon siesta. The phenomenon of afternoon napping, according to Pierre Gagnon and his colleagues, "may reflect a biological propensity to re-enter the psychological state that accompanies SWS" (1985, p. 127) (also called stage 4 sleep).

The 90-minute ultradian rhythm. There is a basic rest/activity cycle (BRAC) that lasts about 90 to 120 minutes. This cycle has been found in such waking activities as performance on various sensory tasks, vigilance tasks, and fantasy tasks. The ability to fall asleep during the day is determined by this cycle. That is, it is easier to fall asleep when we are in the rest part of the cycle.

The regularity of REM sleep every 90 minutes raises the interesting possibility that REM is somehow controlled by BRAC. It has been shown, for example, that people tend to dream at the same time every night (McPartland & Kupfer, 1978). Some researchers have supplied evidence that seems to contradict this conclusion. They have shown, for example, that REM tends to occur 90 minutes after sleep onset (McPartland & Kupfer, 1978; Moses, Naitoh, & Johnson, 1978). If sleep onset controls REM, then it cannot be controlled by some natural BRAC rhythm that is independent of sleep onset. This apparent inconsistency disappears when we recognize that people often don't go to sleep until they are in a certain phase of their BRAC. In other words, not only our overall circadian rhythm but our BRAC rhythm affects our inclination to go to sleep.

BRAC, waking mentation, and dreams. The brain has two hemispheres, each of which performs slightly different functions. The right hemisphere tends to be involved in fantasy and intuitive thought, while the left hemisphere tends to be involved in verbal and intellectual thought. What is fascinating is that each hemisphere has a 90- to 100-minute cycle that is 180 degrees out of phase with the other hemisphere. Thus we tend to swing back and forth between fantasy/intuitive thought and verbal/intellectual thought (Klein & Armitage, 1979). REM dreams tend to be more fantasy/intuitive in character whereas NREM dreams tend to be more verbal and intellectual. It may well be that before I can have REM dreams or NREM dreams I need to be in the right mental state—that state being determined by my BRAC.

How Much Sleep Do We Need?

The fact that some people seem to need very little sleep has intrigued both the lay person who would like to get along on less sleep and the scientist who is interested in the function of sleep. In a study of long and short sleepers, it was observed that short sleepers tended, on the whole, to deny personal or interpersonal problems, to have a greater need to be accepted, and to be more socially skilled and more socially dominant. Long sleepers tended to be more shy, more depressed or anxious, and more inhibited sexually and in expressing aggression (Hartmann, Baekeland, & Zwilling, 1972). In a similar study, Webb and Friel (1971) found no differences. These results may be due to differences in sampling techniques. A more recent approach to the question of whether length of sleep is related to personality functioning has been to expose people to gradual sleep reduction to see what, if any, effects are observed.

Voluntary sleep reduction to 4.5-5.5 hours a night has not been shown to reduce performance or to produce significant personality changes, but it tends to produce persistent feelings of fatigue (Friedman et al., 1977). As sleep time is reduced, the pattern of sleep undergoes several changes. Although there is no reduction in the amount of stages 3 and 4 sleep (see Figure 6-1), there is a significant reduction in REM and stage 2 sleep (Mullaney et al., 1977; Webb & Agnew, 1975a). When the regimen of partial sleep deprivation is maintained, it appears that REM sleep begins to occur earlier in the sleep period, thus attenuating the REM deficit. It rarely, however, replaces stage 4 in order of appearance, and it never achieves normal levels.

The fact that people tend to make up for certain types of sleep when their sleep time is curtailed is probably one of the important reasons that lack of sleep does not have a greater impact on their normal functioning. As we shall discuss in more detail shortly, stage 4 and REM sleep seem to serve specific functions that help to maintain physiological and psychological integrity. If they are important, it would make sense for the system responsible for sleep to give priority to them when total sleep time is reduced. As a result of this priority design, humans are able to function when sleep is shortened, even if that functioning may be less than optimal. Since shortened sleep regimens tend to lead to persistent fatigue, it appears that some mechanism tells us to return to more normal sleep patterns.

Interestingly, subjects who voluntarily reduced their total sleep time for experimental purposes maintained their total sleep time 1-2.5 hours below base-line. The fact that none of the subjects ever went below 4.5 hours of sleep per night while on this voluntary program suggests that there may be biological limits to sleep reduction (Mullaney et al., 1977).

Altering Sleep/Wakefulness Cycles

If we assume for the moment that adults need about 7 to 8 hours of sleep each 24-hour period, the question arises whether we can redistribute our sleeping time in some way. Studies of this question have found that adjustment to new schedules is possible but difficult. Since the best predictor of sleep onset is elapsed time since last sleep, and since the best predictor of sleep termination is how long we have slept, it is not surprising to find that people tend to lose sleep in new schedules because they have difficulty getting to sleep or they wake up too soon. Finally, circadian rhythms make it difficult to adapt to schedules that do not follow the approximately 24- to 25-hour cycle (Webb & Agnew, 1975b).

The Effects of Sleep Reduction

Sleep Reduction and Feelings of Sleepiness and Fatigue

Lack of sleep often produces feelings of sleepiness and fatigue. We use *sleepiness* to indicate a craving or desire for sleep, while *fatigue* refers to a general lack of motivation or energy. Sleepiness is generally viewed as the converse of alertness (Dement & Carskadon, 1982). While the belief is widespread that sleepiness (lack of alertness) will impair performance, it has sometimes been hard to document this effect in the laboratory by means of various psychomotor and intellectual tests (see Dement & Carskadon, 1982). There is also little evidence that sleepiness resulting from a reduced sleep regimen produces any physiological abnormalities (see Hartse, Roth, & Zorick, 1982). After several days of sleep reduction, most people show full recovery after a single night of sleep (Carskadon & Dement, 1981). It appears that REM sleep is more important than NREM as far as reversing sleepiness is concerned (Carskadon & Dement, 1977).

PRACTICAL APPLICATION 6.1

What Is the Best Way to Adjust to Jet Lag?

Let's say you left New York on a plane bound for Paris at 6 P.M. Eastern Standard Time. Flight time is about eight hours. Therefore, when you arrive in Paris it's 10 A.M. Paris time, but your circadian clock is telling you it's 2 A.M.(two hours past your bedtime). What should you do—take a nap or stay up till midnight Paris time? The answer depends on whether you want to see Paris nightlife or be a "regular tourist." If you go to your hotel and sleep, you're likely to sleep for seven to eight hours, so you will wake up at 6 P.M. That will give you plenty of time to have a leisurely dinner, close down the last nightclub, and sip a brandy with or after breakfast before retiring for eight hours. But, if you want to be a regular tourist, then you should stay up until midnight. By midnight you will be experiencing the effects of sleep deprivation and you should have little or no difficulty getting to sleep and sleeping most of the night, even though you are not synchronized with your circadian rhythm. A night's sleep will help to reset your circadian rhythm. Remember that one of the factors that determines when you will next be sleepy is the time that has elapsed since you last slept. Even a short nap is not a good idea because it will reduce some of the effects normally associated with sleep deprivation, and as a result you will not be able to sleep as long when you do go to sleep.

Sleep Reduction and Performance

Despite the fact that lack of sleep does not seem to do any harm, people report difficulty in performing when they feel sleepy. Field studies have shown that people who work at night not only complain of sleepiness but perform more poorly than they do when they work during the day (Ånkerstedt, Torsvall, & Gillberg, 1982). Interestingly, older subjects seem to be affected more by sleep loss than younger ones (Webb & Levy, 1982). Here are some of the basic changes that occur as a result of sleep loss (Dinges, 1989; Dinges & Kribbs, 1991).

1. **Lapsing.** Lapsing refers to the *unevenness* in performance with sleep deprivation. Instead of responding immediately to a signal or a crisis, as people normally do when not sleep deprived, people who are sleep deprived sometimes respond quickly while at other times their reaction times are quite slow. As people become more and more sleep deprived, lapsing become more and more of a problem, to the point where it can be shown that performance gradually deteriorates with increased sleep deprivation. In situations where people need to react quickly, lapsing is a major source of concern for safety (Dinges & Kribbs, 1991).

2. **Cognitive slowing.** Cognitive slowing refers to the observation that when people are sleep deprived and in a self-paced task, there is a reduction in the number (speed) of cognitive responses. While it was thought at one time that this effect was due to lapses, it is now thought that this effect is due to *microsleeps*. Microsleeps are very short sleep episodes that are interjected into an otherwise wakeful state. Microsleeps appear to increase in number as sleep deprivation increases. As a result, people tend to show greater cognitive slowing as the length of sleep deprivation increases (Dinges & Kribbs, 1991).

3. **Memory problems.** Reduction in immediate recall often occurs during sleeplessness. It has been suggested that the problem may be due to a combination of factors including the failure to encode information properly and to lapse. In many of the studies on memory loss, the problem does not seem to arise to any significant degree until wakefulness has exceeded 30 hours (Dinges & Kribbs, 1991).

4. **Vigilance decrements and habituation.** As a general rule, the longer the task duration the greater the likelihood that performance will show the impair-

PRACTICAL APPLICATION 6.2

Shift Work, Sleepiness, and Catnaps

Shift work is a major problem in our society. The problem is worst for people who work night shifts (somewhere from 11 P.M. to 7 A.M.). Catastrophes such as those at Three-Mile Island and Chernobyl took place in the early hours of the morning. Later afternoon shifts (4 P.M. to 12 P.M.) are also a problem but to a lesser degree.

There are two basic problems. First, people who work night shifts and later afternoon shifts are often out of phase with their normal circadian rhythms. As a result, even though they are awake they are not alert. As I indicated earlier, temperature and alertness are correlated. It has been found that people who work night shifts often show a drop in temperature in the early hours of the morning (3 A.M. to 5 A.M.), a time when many accidents occur (Dinges, 1984).

People can and often do learn to shift their circadian rhythms, but that often takes a considerable period of time for many people. It is still not clear why some people can shift to a new circadian rhythm relatively fast while others cannot. When people cannot adjust they experience feelings of sleepiness. This leads us to the second problem, which is sleep deprivation. There is considerable evidence that people who work night shifts are also experiencing chronic sleep loss, which also leads to feelings of sleepiness. Many find it difficult to sleep during the day and as a result they are chronically sleep deprived.

Pilots often find themselves in a particularly difficult situation because they often must make a return after as little as 8 to 12 hours of rest. Even if they could sleep, many find they cannot. As a result, when they make their return flight they are experiencing sleep loss.

What Is the Best Way to Deal with Shift Work?

Many companies are concerned with the question of shift work because people who work later afternoon and night shifts often perform poorly and are acci-

dent prone. In the case of such occupations as pilot, train engineer, doctor, or nuclear plant operator, there is the question of safety to the public. As a result, a great deal of research has gone into the question of how best to help people deal with shift work or with jobs that require them to perform at times other than when they are normally at their peak.

Since people who work later afternoon and night shifts are often chronically sleep-deprived, the question is how best to help them get the amount of sleep they need. There is no easy answer to this question because one of the reasons people are chronically sleep-deprived is that they attempt to maintain their social relations or family obligations. Because they are out of sync with other people, they often find it necessary to design a sleep schedule that allows them to maximize their social relations. One byproduct of this is a chronic loss of sleep. People who work late afternoon shifts and night shifts are often not aware of the fact they are sleep-deprived (Dinges, 1989). Thus one of the things that is necessary is to educate people about their sleep needs and help them plan a sleep schedule that will enable them to get enough sleep as well as satisfy their other needs. Even when people know they should get more sleep they sometimes find it difficult to do so because their circadian rhythms tell them it is time to be awake.

The question of how to get people to adjust their circadian rhythms to the demands of the task has received considerable attention. The formal name for this area of study is Chronobiology (which can be defined as the branch of science that studies rhythms of life that are an outgrowth of biology). There are several important considerations.

First, because it takes time to adjust circadian rhythms, a general rule of thumb is that people should not be required to change their shifts too often. This will allow them to settle into a shift and synchronize their biological rhythms with the demands of the task (Coleman, 1986). Since there are wide individual differences, the amount of time this takes varies greatly between people. Sleep deprivation is a good way to speed up this process (such as I suggested in how to adjust to jet lag). In the case of businessmen flying to Europe or vice versa, they should allow themselves a few days to adjust as best they can. Coleman (1986) has suggested that under certain conditions, sleep deprivation combined with sleeping pills might be justified as a means of speeding up the adjustment time.

Second, if people are put on shifts, they should be moved from morning to afternoon to night and not in the reverse direction. Studies have found that people find it much easier to move in this direction than in the reverse (Coleman, 1986). The reason for this is that there is a natural tendency for the circadian rhythm to drift to a later time (i.e., we are inclined to go to bed later and get up earlier because our circadian rhythm is 25 hours as opposed to 24 hours on the average).

Third, it might be advisable that people doing shift work take catnaps (see below).

Making Up for Loss of Sleep with Catnaps

There is a great deal of evidence that people not only can but should make use of catnaps to make up for loss of sleep. Most people can go without one night of sleep without much loss in performance. Any attempt to go beyond one night of sleep loss typically results in significant performance drops. Research has shown that people can achieve complete or virtually complete recovery after one full night of sleep, young or old (Bonnet & Rosa, 1987). In the absence of being able to get a full night of sleep, a catnap of any length is highly effective in helping to restore full functioning. If one knows ahead of time that they will need to forego sleep for a long period, such as for an entire night, they can prepare themselves for it with a catnap (the longer the better, but any length will help) (Dinges as reported in Saltus, 1990).

If people need to get a lot of work done over a short period of time, they might consider changing their sleep regimen so that they break up what sleep they can get into short naps. During his creative period, Leonardo Da Vinci would reduce his sleep regimen to 6 catnaps of 15 minutes each. Many famous people are reported to have survived on catnaps including Winston Churchill, Napoleon and Thomas Edison. Laboratory studies have shown that it is indeed possible for people to survive for up to two weeks on such a schedule. In the animal world, catnapping is widespread and thought by some to be more normal than the sleep/wakefulness cycle that modern humans attempt to maintain. It has been suggested that the industrial revolution forced us into a sleep cycle that is not consistent with our history as humans. In many cultures the afternoon "siesta" is common, allowing people to get up early on the one hand and party late on the other.

People who cannot get adequate sleep because of jet lag (e.g., pilots), interrupted sleep (e.g., combat soldiers, medical doctors), the need to be on alert (e.g., combat pilots), might learn to use catnaps as a means of making up for the losses they experience because of their jobs. It has been shown that elderly people who find it difficult to sleep for 8 hours straight can benefit greatly from learning to take catnaps. Since many researchers believe that most people in North America, if not the industrialized world, do not get enough sleep, all of us should consider using catnaps as a way of getting more sleep. There is considerable evidence that people who have good sleep regimens are not only healthier but live longer (Hoth, Reynolds, Houck, Hall, et al., 1989).

While there are strong arguments for catnaps, they can also contribute to sleep disturbances such as insomnia if they begin to replace normal sleep. I discuss this problem in Practical Application 6.4 (later in this chapter).

ment of sleep deprivation. In other words, when peo-ple first arrive at work they often do not show the decrement of sleep loss, but they are likely to show them as their work shifts progresse (Dinges & Kribbs, 1991). This has important implications for people who must monitor devices in dynamic plants (plants where there need to be periodic adjustments) such as nuclear reactor plants and gas plants.

   5.   **Optimum response shifts.** In many situations there is a limited time period in which people must re-spond with *sustained attention* before some adverse consequence will occur. While it was thought for some time that people could rise to these occasions, there is now data which suggest they may not (Dinges & Kribbs, 1991). This has important implications for peo-ple such as pilots and even doctors who often experi-ence sleep loss in the course of doing their jobs.

Nature of the Task and the Effects of Sleep Loss

The extent to which any of these changes will be observed depends to some degree on the task characteristics.

Feedback. For some time it was thought that feedback would override the effects of sleep loss. There is evi-dence that, while it may help, it often does not remove the effects. The best feedback is that which judges whether or not the subject is succeeding or failing as opposed to feedback that merely provides information about speed and accuracy (Dinges & Kribbs, 1991).

Complexity. While there is considerable data that the ef-fects of sleep loss are greater on complex as opposed to simple tasks, there is also evidence that sleep loss also affects performance on simple tasks that involve sustained attention.

Interaction of Sleep Loss and Circadian Rhythm

To complicate matters, sleep loss interacts with circa-dian rhythm. People who work night shifts are the ones who are most susceptible to this effect. Since night shift workers are often chronically sleep-deprived, and since many of them have not completely adjusted their cir-cadian rhythms to coincide with the demands of their

tasks, they are the ones most likely to show perfor-mance decrements. These decrements are likely to arise, as I suggested before, from about 3 A.M. to 5 A.M.

   Probably the reason it is more difficult to demon-strate an association between sleepiness and poor per-formance in the field than in the laboratory is that humans are capable of "rising to the occasion" for short periods when the situation requires them to do so. The implication is that while we may perform more poorly following reduced sleep, probably because of lack of motivation, we can nevertheless perform well if we have to.

Sleep Reduction and Fragmented Sleep

It should be noted that the loss of one night of sleep not only can produce sleepiness but can impair perfor-mance as well. Recently it was shown that when peo-ple were repeatedly awakened in the course of a night's sleep (after every minute of sleep), the severe reduction in SWS and REM led to a decline in perfor-mance and indexes of sleepiness equivalent to those found after a loss of 40 to 64 hours of sleep, even though the subjects had been sleeping a great deal of the time (Bonnet, 1985). Later we shall see why the loss of SWS and REM is believed to be so devastating. As I have already mentioned, when people go on reduced sleep regimens, they typically compensate for the loss of sleep by increasing REM and SWS at the expense of other states of sleep.

Sleep Deprivation and Mood

Roth and his colleagues (Roth, Kramer, & Lutz, 1976) found that sleep deprivation adversely affects certain moods (friendliness and aggression) but not others. In a carefully controlled study, David Cohen (1979) tried to determine whether REM deprivation was particu-larly important in the control of mood. All he could find was that when people are awakened during ei-ther REM or NREM, they experience increases in ag-gression and decreases in friendliness.

   Studies conducted in clinical laboratories suggest that mild to moderate antidepressant effects can follow just one night of sleep deprivation in 30% to 60% of endogenously depressed individuals (those whose depression cannot be linked to a specific life event) (Gerner et al., 1979). It has been suggested that the neurophysiological effects of sleep deprivation are similar to those produced by antidepressant medication (Buchsbaum, Gerner, & Post, 1981).

Summary

EEG activity has a rhythmic pattern during sleep. Jouvet has suggested that these rhythms are controlled by the RAS. But why do people fall asleep in the first place? Various biological rhythms (circadian, 12.5-hour cycle, and BRAC) play important roles in our sleep patterns. In addition, the time that has elapsed since we last slept and the level of our arousal at the time we try to go to sleep are further determining factors in our ability to sleep. Why do we wake up? Rhythmic increases in temperature and arousal seem to be the main reason. While it is possible to get along with as little as 4.5 to 5 hours of sleep per day, reduced sleep produces feelings of sleepiness and fatigue. Performance of some tasks is affected by sleep reduction, but not all—only those tasks that require sustained interest and attention. While people can learn to get along on reduced sleep, it is important that their bodies maintain a certain minimal level of SWS and REM.

This research emphasizes what sleep consultants have said for some time: in order to go to sleep, maintain sleep, and have quality sleep, it is important to have a routine. Routines not only synchronize our biological rhythms with our daily performance demands but allow us to have reasonably continuous sleep. A routine is important even when sleep must be reduced because it enables SWS and REM to occur soon after we fall asleep, thereby ensuring that we will get enough SWS and REM in the course of a night's sleep.

One very good way to make up for lost sleep is with "catnaps." People who do not get adequate sleep because of their occupations or because of situation demands, such as the need to complete an important task, often learn to use catnaps as a means of making up for lost sleep.

Table 6-1. Change in Sleep Patterns

	Sleep	REM	Absolute
Infancy (3 months)	14.0	40%	5.6
Maturity	7.5	20%	1.5
Old Age (70s)	6.0	20%	1.2

The Psychological Functions of Sleep

Humans differ greatly in terms of the amount of REM they show at different stages of development. Infants, for example, have twice as much REM sleep as adults.

Change in Sleep Patterns

Infants spend a greater percentage of time in REM sleep than either adults or the elderly. While the percentage stays the same for adults and elderly, the absolute amount of REM goes down in the elderly. Table 6-1 summarizes some of these findings. It is interesting to note that during REM the flow of blood goes up by 40%, metabolism increases, spontaneous firing of nerve cells increases beyond the level of waking, and the kidneys make less but more concentrated urine.

Experimental Procedures for Determining the Function of Sleep

Both animals and humans have been studied to determine the function of sleep. To date, the majority of studies have focused on REM sleep deprivation; however, there is a growing interest in other types of sleep deprivation (Webb, 1979). We will begin by examining some of the effects of REM sleep deprivation.

REM Deprivation in Animals

All mammalian species that have been studied have REM sleep. In addition, a sizable percentage of avian predators (e.g., hawks, eagles) have REM. Only a negligible amount of REM occurs in other birds, and reptilian species show no REM (Ellman & Weinstein, 1991).

The main technique for depriving small mammals, such as rats, of REM sleep is to place them on a small elevated platform above a tank of water. Since a rat will become paralyzed when they go into REM sleep and consequently fall off the platform into the water, the use of this procedure ensures that the rat gets very little REM sleep. Either the rat learns to avoid REM sleep in some way or it falls off into the water when it goes into REM sleep. The experience of falling off the platform into the water and then needing to climb back on the platform appears to be a powerful source of motivation for rats to learn to avoid the REM sleep stage. Not surprisingly, there has been some controversy about whether this technique produces stress in addition to depriving rats of REM.

REM Deprivation in Humans

By continuously monitoring the EEG of a sleeping person and waking that person whenever a particular sleep pattern such as REM appears, it is possible to study the effects of certain types of sleep deprivation, such as REM, on various activities. In these studies, one group of subjects is typically awakened after they enter REM in order to disrupt REM and thereby reduce REM, while another group of subjects is awakened during NREM. Using such a procedure we can be assured that the effects are not simply due to being awakened.

REM Deprivation and Motivation

The research with animals has been important because it is possible to monitor what is happening in more central as well as peripheral parts of the brain. This research has shown that the thresholds for sexual aggressive behaviors and eating are lowered. That means these behaviors are easier to arouse with the appropriate arousing stimuli. Dement (1969) has suggested that REM sleep provides a type of periodic drive discharge. This means that if you are REM-deprived there will be less discharge and, therefore, greater motivation (lower thresholds for such things as eating and aggression).

Ellman and Steiner (1969a, 1969b) have put forth a similar hypothesis in which they postulate that during REM sleep some elements of the network for positive reinforcement (the reward pathways in the brain) are activated. The activation, they suggest, makes the brain ready (primes the brain) for motivated behaviors. Obviously, if the brain is in a ready state for motivated behaviors, the threshold for motivated behaviors will be lowered.

Ellman's Motivation Theory of REM

The essence of Ellman's theory is that during both sleep and wakefulness the positive reward system—intracranial self-stimulation (ICSS)—system needs to be periodically fired. It is assumed the ICSS system maintains motivation when we are not involved in consummatory behaviors such as eating, drinking, sex, and aggression, and is turned off when organisms are involved in these behaviors. During sleep the REM state is assumed to be responsible for periodically firing the ICSS system.

How can this be related to the content of REM dreams? Implicit in Ellman's theory is the idea that the environment is a rich source of stimulation for periodically firing the ICSS (although it may also be fired in part by one of the ultradian rhythms). In sleep, the body needs to generate similar simulation that will fire the ICSS. This stimulation needs to be vivid and compelling like the environment, it is argued, in order for the ICSS to become activated. In order to produce such vivid and compelling stimulation, Ellman further argues, it is necessary for humans to momentarily set aside self-reflection. The net result of setting aside self-reflection is that REM dreams have a vivid and compelling quality, like that of the external environment, but also may have some strange organizational characteristics (bizarreness) when we reflect on them in a waking state (Ellman & Weinstein, 1991).

One of the fascinating features of Ellman's theory is that it can explain why infants spend so much time in REM. In the absence of external stimulation, they need to generate stimulation that will keep the ICSS in a state of motivated readiness. If organisms are not in a state of readiness their threshold for motivated behav-

This infant seems to be having a good REM dream, but because infants can't verbalize their mental processes we cannot assess the contents of their REM dreams.

ior would increase, a highly nonadaptive state much like that observed in depressive individuals. Ellman and Weinstein (1991) go so far as to argue that the lack of REM in infancy may slow down the maturational process. In other words, REM in infancy is critical for the maturational process to take its natural course.

The REM Rebound Effect

Early studies of REM deprivation showed that people who are deprived of REM sleep for one or more nights show what is called REM rebound. That is, when people are allowed to sleep without interruption for a whole night following at least one night of deprivation, they spend more total time in REM sleep than they normally do. This observation led researchers to conclude that REM must indeed be important for normal functioning. This finding is consistent with the study of Carskadon and Dement (1977), who studied the sleep

patterns of subjects who were permitted to sleep for 30-minute periods separated by 60 minutes of forced wakefulness. Sleep-onset REM periods occurred frequently during the 30 minutes of sleep, an indication that although REM sleep may be subject to some biological clock that normally programs REM to begin 90 minutes after sleep onset, the lack of REM for any significant period will trigger some other mechanism to override the first in order to ensure that the body gets adequate REM sleep.

REM Sleep Deprivation and Psychological Health

Early work. Probably the main reason people have focused on REM sleep deprivation grew out of the reports of Dement (1960). He noted not only that people who were awakened from REM sleep reported vivid dream content but that interruptions of REM sleep (REM deprivation) produced anxiety, irritability, and difficulty in concentrating. People have for some time been interested in the function or purpose of dreams, and Dement's findings suggested that the REM deprivation technique might uncover their function. As we have noted, people later realized that dreams also occur in other stages of sleep (Foulkes, 1962; Foulkes & Vogel, 1965). Nevertheless, the impetus for REM deprivation studies had been well established by that time.

Vogel's research on depression. Following Dement's initial reports of the effects of REM deprivation, researchers freely speculated on the relation between the absence of REM sleep and psychological health. It was suggested that absence of REM sleep could produce such disturbances as schizophrenia and depression (Fisher & Dement, 1962; Snyder et al., 1968). These speculations, it turns out, were not well founded. Vogel (1975) has deprived people of REM sleep for up to three weeks without serious side effects. In fact, he has shown that REM deprivation can be beneficial in depressives. He has offered a motivational theory of REM deprivation that not only can account for this effect but has some important implications for understanding the function of REM sleep.

Vogel's theory. Vogel (1979) has suggested that neural activity is heightened during REM sleep and prevented or inhibited by REM deprivation. As a result, REM deprivation leads to greater neural activity or excitability during the waking state. (Neural excitability is a hypothesized state of neural readiness necessary for efficient and effective response to events in the environment. It is generally assumed to be due to some chemical process that readies the cells to fire.) Because there is evidence that greater neural excitability increases such drive-motivated behaviors as sex, aggression, pleasure seeking, food seeking, and grooming, Vogel argues that under certain conditions REM sleep can have a detrimental effect on certain waking behaviors. It is possible, he argues, that depression results from excessive neural disinhibition during REM sleep. That is, REM sleep dissipates too much accumulated neural excitability. As a result, depressives lose interest in or fail to engage in those activities that provide the positive rewards that normally accompany "healthy" behavior. According to this view, it is easy to understand why REM deprivation would lead to improved mood in depressed persons. Since such deprivation would prevent the discharge of neural excitability, depressed persons would again become more sensitive to their drive states. As a result, they would engage in behaviors that produced rewards associated with these drive states. In short, they would experience the positive affect that typically flows from adaptive behaviors.

It should be noted that Vogel's theory of depression is essentially a theory of endogenous, rather than reactive, depression. Endogenous depression is depression that occurs for unknown reasons, whereas reactive depression is typically precipitated by some traumatic event, such as the loss of a spouse, a child, or a job. According to Vogel's theory, endogenous depression occurs when, for still-unknown reasons, there is excessive neural disinhibition during REM sleep. Normally, he argues, neural activity is not allowed to dissipate completely. He believes that some inhibitory mechanism exists to prevent complete discharge and serves an important survival function by ensuring that the person is in a stage of readiness to respond to drive stimuli.

Vogel (1975) has reviewed some of the research showing that drugs can frequently alleviate symptoms of depression. The most effective drugs, he notes, are those that produce a dramatic and sustained reduction of REM sleep—the major antidepressants (monoamine oxidase inhibitors and the tricyclics). In other words, he maintains, these drugs work because they block REM sleep, which is assumed to be responsible for the dissipation of neural excitability.

Ellman's theory, discussed above, says essentially the same thing and is essentially an extension of Vogel's theory. Ellman (see Ellman et al., 1991) suggests the reason REM deprivation alleviates depression is that REM deprivation ensures motivation remains high.

REM Sleep, Learning, and Adaptation

REM Sleep and the Consolidation Hypothesis

One of the most actively pursued hypotheses concerning sleep is that REM sleep is important for the consolidation of memory. According to the consolidation theory, it takes time for recently learned material to be transferred from immediate or short-term memory to long-term memory. The question is whether the REM state facilitates this transfer. There is indeed very good evidence that REM does facilitate the consolidation of memory (see McGrath & Cohen, 1978; Grosvenor & Lack, 1984). There is further evidence that REM may be involved not simply in the consolidation of memory but in the active integration of complex information (Scrima, 1982). The emphasis here is on *active.* Apparently, previously acquired information or knowledge is somehow involved in the consolidation process to ensure that the newly acquired material is integrated with material that has already been learned.

REM Deprivation and Learning in Animals

There is considerable data from animal studies that indicates REM deprivation interferes with learning and retention (Ellman et al., 1991). Shuttle box avoidance learning, for example, depends on REM sleep (Smith & Young, 1980; Smith & Butler, 1982). Other studies have shown that whether or not REM deprivation disrupts learning depends on whether or not animals were emotional. If they were emotional when training took place, REM deprivation disrupts learning, whereas if they were not emotional when training took place, REM deprivation has no effect (Koridze & Nemsadze, 1983; Oniani, 1984).

REM Deprivation and Learning in Humans

Type of task. While REM sleep seems to facilitate most kinds of learning, it is particularly beneficial for certain kinds of tasks. In general, the REM deprivation literature shows consistent benefits from REM sleep on the learning and retention of more complex and/or emotionally loaded tasks. In one study that demonstrated beneficial effects of REM sleep (Cartwright et al., 1975), subjects were required to "Q-sort" adjectives as descriptive of themselves and of their ideal selves and were then tested for immediate and delayed (seven hours) recall of the words. A Q-sort task requires the subject to place cards bearing descriptive words into stacks corresponding to how well they describe the thing specified. In this case, subjects were required to order the items in accordance with how well they described their actual and ideal selves. During the retention interval, subjects were treated in one of four ways: (1) were maintained awake day or night, (2) were allowed undisturbed sleep, (3) were allowed to sleep but were REM-deprived, or (4) had their REM sleep reduced by 25%. After the retention intervals, subjects were asked to recall as many of the adjectives as they could. For our purposes, there were two important results: the REM-deprived subjects tended to recall more self-affirming items, whereas the normal-sleep subjects tended to recall more items indicating personal dissatisfaction. That is, REM sleep facilitated memory for items related to personal dissatisfaction. In contrast to this study, subjects have also been asked to learn to associate two neutral words (paired-associate learning). Such studies have consistently failed to show that one or two nights of REM deprivation affect retention of paired associates (for example, Castaldo, Krynicki, & Goldstein, 1974).

Adaptation to stress. That REM sleep can increase adaptation to a stressful or noxious stimulus has been clearly demonstrated by Greenberg, Pillard, and Pearlman (1972). They exposed subjects to a stressful film and then allowed the subjects (1) undisturbed sleep or (2) REM-deprived sleep or (3) NREM-deprived sleep. After sleeping, the subjects were shown the film again and their reactions to it were assessed. REM-deprived subjects showed the greatest anxiety, suggesting that the opportunity to experience REM sleep had produced some adaptation to the stressful events in the film. This finding is consistent with the animal data I just discussed in which I noted that REM deprivation interfered with learning if the animals were emotional.

Timing of REM sleep. The research on REM deprivation does not show that REM sleep is necessary for good processing or storage of information, only that if a person must sleep, REM is the best form of sleep. Whether it is better to sleep or stay awake during the retention interval is another question (McGrath & Cohen, 1978). Studies on this question suggest that it is better to stay asleep, presumably because when awake we learn new material that interferes with our ability to recall the target material. It should be noted in this regard that the benefits of REM sleep are directly proportional to its proximity to learning. That is, deprivation of early REM (that which occurs closest to sleep onset) disrupts retention of the target material more than deprivation of late REM (that which occurs some time after sleep onset) (Hockey, Davies, & Gray, 1972).

REM Sleep and Divergent (Creative) Thinking

If REM sleep facilitates the processing of information, especially information that must be integrated with existing information, the mental activity of REM sleep should be consistent with such a task. Indeed, there is evidence for such a position. Lewin and Glaubman (1975) have found that REM sleep is characterized by extremely flexible and divergent thinking. They have argued that mental activity during REM sleep is not integrative and consolidating but rather divergent and exploratory; however, this does not rule out the possibility that the flexible and divergent aspects of REM mental activity are involved in the integration of new, complex, emotional, or unusual information. In fact, it could be argued that such divergent mental activity during REM sleep would facilitate the integration of such information. In a replication of Lewin and Glaubman's original study with somewhat different procedures, it was again shown that REM sleep does indeed facilitate divergent thinking (Glaubman et al., 1978). Subjects were assigned a divergent-thinking task in the evening and told they would have to perform the task in the morning. The task required them to tell what the consequences would be "if gravity disappeared," for example, or "if all people went blind." During the night, subjects were deprived of either REM or NREM sleep. NREM-deprived subjects gave not only more original responses but numerically more responses (both are indexes of degree of divergent thinking). Interestingly, the NREM-deprived subjects gave more positive consequences than the REM-deprived. For example, to the question "if all people went blind" they were more likely to say "Wars would be abolished" than "All people would die."

Individual Differences in the Need for REM Sleep

Do all people need the same amount of REM sleep? If amount of REM sleep under nondeprivation conditions is used as a measure, then there is only meager evidence that different people have different needs. Although most studies have found equivocal results, it has been shown that retardates with lower IQ scores need less REM sleep (for example, Castaldo & Krynicki, 1973) and that elderly people with lower IQ scores also need less (Feinberg et al., 1973). Because of the samples, these results must be treated with caution. It should also be noted here that schizophrenics show little or no increase in REM sleep following REM deprivation (for example, Gillin & Wyatt, 1975). Because schizophrenia is a complex topic and because there is some question about whether this lack of REM rebound is well established (Vogel, 1975), I will not speculate on the significance of this phenomenon.

Field dependence and field independence. If increased REM sleep following REM deprivation (REM rebound) is used as a measure of need, then there is good evidence for individual differences. For example, it has been shown that field-independent people exhibit greater REM rebound than field-dependent people (Cartwright, Monroe, & Palmer, 1967). Field dependence/independence is an aspect of cognitive style. Field-independent people tend to use an internal frame of reference in organizing incoming information. This means the person is inclined to relate information to the self, and this style is therefore regarded as a very active form of information processing. Field-dependent people, in contrast, tend to use external frames of reference. This means they are not likely to involve the self and thus take a more passive approach to information processing (Goodenough, 1978). The terms field-independent and field-dependent have their origins in studies on visual perception. Some people, it was found, used themselves (their bodies) as reference points for making judgments, for example, about the direction a light is moving (field-independent), while other people make judgments, for example, about the direction of a moving light by using some feature of the environment as a reference point (field-dependent). Thus the distinction between these two types of individuals pertains to the degree to which they involve themselves while processing information. Many people feel that is takes more time or effort when you involve yourself when processing information, especially if it is a cognitive activity.

That field-independent people require more REM sleep fits with the consolidation hypothesis of learning—the hypothesis that it takes a period of time for information initially stored in some type of temporary memory storage system to be transferred into a more long-term storage system. Dealing actively with information (organizing it according to some internal scheme or the self) would not only be a more difficult or complex task, but one that would take more time. As a consequence, field-independent subjects would tend to need more REM sleep.

Ego threat. Greiser, Greenberg, and Harrison (1972) showed that ego-threatening manipulations affect memory. In their study, subjects were given anagrams preselected to ensure that about half of them could be solved in the allotted time. To threaten the subjects' concept of themselves (ego), they were told that the task was a measure of intelligence. The subjects were then exposed to sleep manipulation. The results showed that REM sleep deprivation (compared with NREM sleep deprivation) disrupted recall of failed anagrams but did not affect recall of solved anagrams. These results suggest that REM sleep facilitates the processing of material that draws one's self-concept into question or material that is inconsistent with one's self-concept.

Why would a person be inclined to have better recall of material inconsistent with or threatening to his or her self-concept? One obvious explanation is that the person is motivated to resolve the discrepancy. We know from other work that this form of dissonance (discrepancy or conflict) tends to produce arousal and that people are motivated to reduce such dissonance (Kiesler & Pallak, 1976). If a person fails to reduce the dissonance before sleep onset, REM sleep may offer an opportunity to accomplish this task.

Other researchers have threatened the egos of subjects by giving them a difficult test (they intimated that it measured intelligence) that could not be completed in the allotted time. Control subjects were given an easier version of the test that they could complete in the time allowed. The study found that ego threat did produce stress and that one night of uninterrupted sleep resulted in significant adaptation to the stress (Koulack, Prevost, & De Koninck, 1985). Further, subjects who recalled more of the presleep stressful event in their dreams showed less adaptation upon awakening. These findings suggest that the adaptive value of sleep is the resolution or partial resolution of the stressful presleep event (ego threat). When subjects did not resolve the stressful event, as indicated by their failure to show the same adaptive effects as other subjects, they continued to have elements of the presleep stressful event represented in their (REM-state)dreams.

Neuroticism. People who score high on neuroticism (sensitizers) show less REM rebound following deprivation than low-neuroticism people (repressors) (see, for example, Nakazawa et al., 1975). The terms *sensitizer* and *repressor* are used in connection with the neuroticism scale to differentiate the general way these two groups of people deal with threat. The person who

tries to deny or minimize a threat or avoids thinking about its consequences is called a *repressor.* The person who tries to control the danger by dwelling on its potential consequences is called a *sensitizer* (Bell & Byrne, 1978). In one study, subjects were deprived of either REM or NREM sleep early in the sleep period to determine the effects on REM episodes later in the period (Pivik & Foulkes, 1966). Repressors showed increased dreamlike fantasy during these later REM periods, while sensitizers did not. Finally, consistent with these results, Cohen (1977) showed that repressors have a greater need for REM sleep.

Why the greater need for REM by repressors? A repressor tends to deal with threat by denying it. A great deal of cognitive activity will be required to resolve the dissonance associated with such a strategy. In that sense, the repressor may be behaving like Greiser's subjects (Greiser et al., 1972) who were subjected to ego-threatening manipulations.

Greenberg and Pearlman have suggested that REM sleep is necessary for the consolidation of learning that involves the "assimilation of unusual information" (1974, p. 516). Such a view explains why personality interacts with the nature of the task. Remember that the field-independent person tries to organize all incoming information in terms of an internal (and personal) frame of reference. Understanding how all external information relates to this frame of reference may require the testing of several hypotheses. The repressor has a different problem: how to rationalize the fact that he or she is denying the existence of a threatening event. A good or adequate solution may involve the generation of hypotheses. The need to generate hypotheses would, of course, require divergent thinking.

Other Types of Sleep Deprivation

As we noted in connection with the question of how much sleep we need, reduction of total sleep produces a proportional increase in stage 4 sleep but not in REM sleep. Studies that have combined total sleep deprivation with selective deprivation of stage 4 and REM indicate that deprivation of stage 4 produces stage 4 rebound, just as REM deprivation produces REM rebound. Further, it appears that stage 4 sleep takes

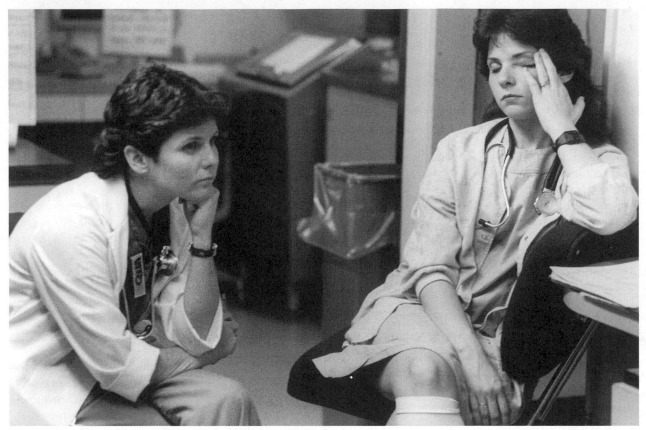

Shift work often leads to feelings of sleepiness and fatigue. Nurses are one of those groups of workers that need to deal with chronic sleep deprivation.

precedence over REM sleep. That is, any lack of stage 4 sleep will always be satisfied before a lack of REM sleep is made up (Moses et al., 1975). It has also been shown that when sleep regimens are varied in length, stage 4 and REM are maintained (Webb & Agnew, 1977). In a review of the research on sleep requirements and stages, Hartmann (1974) has concluded that there are two separate requirements for sleep—for slow-wave and desynchronized sleep (such as REM)—and that the need for slow-wave sleep is more constant than the need for desynchronized sleep. Andrew Tilley (1985) has suggested that "obtaining a daily stage 4 quota acts as the primary drive mechanism of the sleep system" (p. 129).

Summary

All mammalian species that have been studied and a sizable portion of avian predators (e.g., hawks and eagles) have REM. The research with animals has been important because it has allowed researchers to establish, under controlled laboratory conditions, that REM is linked to the lowering of the threshold for motivated behaviors such as sex and eating. According to Ellman's theory, REM sleep is important for periodically firing the ICSS system. The function of REM dreams is to create the stimulation that can fire this system. According to Ellman's theory, the reason infants have so much REM is because, in the absence of external stimulation, the brain creates the necessary stimulation needed for the development of the brain. Although some early studies found that deprivation of REM sleep produced anxiety, irritability, and difficulty in concentrating, more recent studies have failed to replicate these findings. In fact, Vogel has found that REM deprivation often alleviates symptoms of endogenous depression. Although lack of REM sleep may not drive a person insane, it frequently leads to feelings of sleepiness and affects certain moods, such as friendliness and aggression. Considerable evidence indicates that REM sleep facilitates learning, especially learning that is complex or emotionally loaded. There is also evidence that REM sleep increases adaptation to stressful and noxious events. The timing of REM has been found to be important in this regard. REM sleep has been characterized as extremely flexible and divergent, qualities that would facilitate storage of complex and emotionally loaded material. Greenberg and Pearlman (1974) have argued that REM sleep is necessary for the consolidation of learning that involves the "assimilation of unusual information"(p. 576).

Not all people have the same need for REM sleep. Field-independent people, people who are ego-threatened, and repressors tend to need more. These findings are consistent with the hypothesis that certain cognitive styles or certain habitual ways of dealing with problems or events require a divergent approach that can be augmented through REM sleep.

Dreaming

Do Dreams Have Any Meaning?

From the lay person's point of view, probably the most important or interesting question is: "Do my dreams have any meaning?" Over the years some theorists have argued they do, others that they don't, and still others that they may have some meaning but that the content of dreams needs to be viewed in terms of the larger question of the neurophysiology of the brain.

Freud. Freud argued that dreams can be important in understanding unconscious motivation. He viewed all dreams as being motivated by unfulfilled needs that expressed themselves as wishes. These wishes, often sexual wishes, were assumed to be a product of the id (the more biological part of the personality) and buried deep in the unconscious. Since many of these motives were assumed to be in direct conflict with the conscience or the superego (the social/moral part of the personality), there was a strong counterforce from that part of the personality to push them back into the unconscious. According to Freud's theory, these motives would continue to grow in strength and eventually force their way into the conscious where they could find expression. In order to avoid this conflict, Freud hypothesized that the ego transformed the unacceptable images that arise from needs into more acceptable images. The method the unconscious used, according to Freud, was to employ "universal" symbols to replace the actual image. Thus, if one were motivated to view a man's penis, the ego might transform the image of a penis into a pencil or a telephone pole (presumably depending on how large a penis one might be motivated to see). Similarly, if someone was motivated to have sex they might have an image of themselves engaged in an up and down motion, such as being in an elevator, riding a horse, jumping over things, to replace the actual image of intercourse. The idea that there were universal images for things meant they if you knew the symbols that the unconscious used, anyone would be able to understand the contents of their dreams.

Freud did not believe that universal symbols existed for all manifest dream content. As a result, he often found it necessary to have patients free-associate to the manifest content of their dreams in order for them to identify the underlying real or latent content. The point I want to emphasize here is that Freud believed that dreams were highly meaningful and that it was possible to analyze even the most minute detail of a dream in order to find meaning. The reason I emphasize this point is that more recent theorists do not believe that dreams have the same degree of meaning as Freud did.

Neo-Freudians: Jung and Adler. Many of Freud's followers did not agree with all of Freud's ideas, and as a result they set out to revise them, thus the term neo-

Freudians. One of the first to split with Freud was Carl Jung, who quarreled with Freud over his emphasis on sexuality and eventually created a theory that put less emphasis on the early years of life. Jung made extensive use of dream analysis in his therapy. He did not interpret dreams as clues to past experience or feelings as did Freud, but rather saw dreams as providing signs that the person was neglecting certain aspects of personality and thus causing disequilibrium.

Jung is perhaps best known for his concepts of *collective unconscious* and *archetypes*. The collective unconscious was conceived as a storehouse of memory traces inherited from ancestral past, a past that included not only racial history of humans but of prehuman animals. It suggested that these memories are not inherited intact but rather the predisposition to revive them is inherited. As a result of these memories, people are predisposed to fear such things as snakes, spiders or even dark places because in the past these things were a source of threat. Archetypes refer to universal thoughts that are associated with a great deal of emotion. Archetypes that Jung identified in his writing were birth, death, power, the earth mother, the wise old man/woman, and the animal. Jung also saw the collective unconscious together with archetypes as a source of dream content. To make sense out of dreams, Jung argued, it was necessary to view their content as being determined, at least in part, by the collective unconscious, specifically the archetypes housed in the collective unconscious. Like Freud, he saw dreams as symbolic and disguised. By analyzing dreams in terms of archetypes, Jung felt that it was possible to identify major sources of concern and emotion for people.

Jung's theory has often attracted the interest of artists. Because artists are often interested in communicating universal emotions and/or concerns, many have looked to Jungian dream analysis as a way of identifying the visual nature of those symbols, hoping to use those symbols in their art to communicate more directly and perhaps unconsciously universal concerns.

Another neo-Freudian who was interested in dreams was Alfred Adler, who insisted that humans are basically social beings motivated by interpersonal needs. Adler is perhaps best known for his theory that humans are *striving for superiority*, something that is motivated by feelings of inferiority (feelings that arise from conscious or unconscious recognition of one's physical, psychological and social imperfections). Striving for superiority does not refer to superiority in society but rather to a need for perfection or self-actualization. Dreams, according to Adler, reflect the human need to maintain good self-esteem. Thus to understand dreams, they need to be interpreted in terms of people striving to maintain a sense of positive self-regard.

Crick and Mitchison. According to Crick and Mitchison, the content of dreams has little or no meaning. They maintain that dreams are simply the utilization of stored memories to make sense of random activation. They argue that the random activation accounts for the bizarreness, discontinuity, and the incoherence of dreaming. While the content of dreams is assumed not to be important, they believe that REM sleep is, nevertheless, an important process that is "designed to make storage in an associative net more efficient" (Crick & Mitchison, 1983). They proposed that the function of sleep

> is to remove certain undesirable modes of interactions in network of cells in the central cortex. We postulate that this is done in REM sleep by a reverse learning mechanism, so that the trace in the brain of the unconscious dream is weakened, rather than strengthened.

In a second paper they suggested that dreams were important to reduce fantasy and obsession in the waking state (Crick & Mitchison, 1986). The reason I have made reference to their work here is simply to point out that there are fundamental differences among theorists when it comes to whether or not there is any value in studying dream content.

Hobson's Activation/Synthesis Theory of Dreams

In Hobson's (1988) Activation/Synthesis theory, the activation of dreams is linked to the giving up of control by a group of neurons in the brain stem called the aminergic cells. While most cells of the brain do not rest during sleep, the aminergic cells—a group of cells related to attention and memory—do, especially during REM sleep. Other cells—sensorimotor neurons—are disinhibited when this happens, leading to the REM state. The REM state makes dreams possible but does not determine the the content of dreams. It is the synthesis phase that determines the content. In order to understand dreams it is necessary, argues Hobson, to explain five important features of dreams: (1) their hallucination quality, (2) their delusional quality, (3) the distortions of time, place, and person, (4) the strong emotion that accompanies REM dreams, and (5) the failure of people to remember dreams.

1. Dreams as Hallucination. While external sensory input and motor output produce our sensory experiences, the mental activity we experience in sleep arises out of a special excitatory signal that activates the higher neurons in the visual system. The net effect is that the visual system responds to memories as though the signal came from the outside world and we "see" memories as though they were produced from external sensory input and motor output. Fantasy, in contrast, does not involve this excitatory process and, as a result, fantasies lack that vivid and compelling quality that dreams have.

2. Dreams as Delusions. What makes these hallucinations so fascinating is that we tend to accept them as reality. Hobson argues that the internally generated signals grow out of memories that are synthesized into extraordinary stories. These stories which link the vivid and compelling sensory experience (the hallucinations) allow the past to be experienced as present. Like Ellman, Hobson believes the extraordinary stories can occur because the synthesis system bypasses or momentarily sets aside the self-reference system.

3. Distortions in Time, Place and Person. In REM sleep, multiple sensory channels are simultaneously activated by multiple memories. This is very unlike the waking stage, in which attention is focused sequentially on different sensory inputs. Hobson argues that despite the great difference from the waking state, the brain still attempts to synthesize this information. In order to accomplish this feat it must allow for distor-

tions in time and place and people. In other words, it sets aside certain fundamental rules that would govern perceptions in the waking state. If it did not set aside such distortions, it would not be able to create a unifying story or theme to unite the various elements. Hobson has referred to this tendency of the forebrain to synthesize information differently in dreaming and waking as *mode switching.*

4. Intensification of Emotion. Hobson argues that the activation produced by the brain stem is responsible for physiological changes such as increased heart rate or increased activity in some part of the limbic system (that system linked to emotions). In the synthesis stage, the brain attempts to account for the physiological activity by ascribing the physiological response to an emotion such as anxiety, surprise, fear, or elation. In other words, the brain creates an emotion that accounts for the increased physiological activity of the body and, at the same time, helps link the the various memories into a unified theme or story.

5. The Failure of Memory. Hobson accounts for this as follows:

> In dreaming, the brain-mind follows the instructions: "Integrate all signals received into the most meaningful story possible; however farcical the results, believe it; and then forget it." The "forget" instruction is most simply explained as the absence of a "remember" instruction.

According to this interpretation, we can learn to remember our dreams by training the mind to remember. Many dream researchers have trained their brains to remember by keeping a journal of their dreams.

Do Dreams Have Meaning for Hobson?

According to Hobson dreams are transparent and unedited. He suggests they are also meaningful, undisguised, and often rich in conflictual impulses. This conceptualization is very different from that of Freud, who conceptualized dreams as obscure and disguised, the result of a censor that transformed unacceptable wishes (often sexual wishes) into symbolic dream content whose meaning was unavailable to the naive dreamer. Hobson believes that dreams are a mirror of our inner stories. In order to understand dreams we need to look at the narrative that holds the diverse content together. He also believes that dreams are creative; during sleep, new ideas and new solutions are derived consciously or unconsciously from our inner mental world. Finally, Hobson believes that dreams are there to entertain us. We therefore need to accept them and enjoy them.

The View that Dreams are a Happening to Be Enjoyed for their Entertainment Value

Freud conceptualized dreams as growing out of unfulfilled needs. This meant that the occurrence of dreams, the sensory experience of dreams, and the story were created from an unfulfilled need. The purpose of dreams was to solve fundamental problems. Modern theorists such as Hobson start from the position that dreams are caused by a neuronal state (REM state) and that the content of REM dreams is something that occurs once the individual enters this REM state. The sensory experiences or hallucinations initially "happen" as the result of memories, and then the brain attempts to make sense out of them with a story or narrative. These narratives are viewed as creative story telling. While the stories may resemble other stories used in the past, they are typically unique even though the underlying theme of different stories may be the same. When I use the word "happen," I do not mean to imply these memories are completely random occurrences. Some memories may be more dominant because they are recent or they are associated with some underlying need state and, therefore, may be more likely to trigger a hallucination. According to this approach, nevertheless, dreams are to be viewed more as a happening, an expression of the brain's natural tendency to make sense out of nonsense and to be a creative story teller. While this position acknowledges that dreams can be useful in the consolidation of information, in helping to solve problems, and in providing us with a mirror of our waking life, dreams are to be appreciated for their creativity and entertainment value (Hobson, 1988).

Lucid Dreaming

While the individual is typically a passive observer in dreams, there is now evidence that people can learn to actively participate in their own dreams. That is, they can learn to participate in the dream state as though they were awake and aware (the definition of lucid dreaming). It is like being fully conscious in the sensory world that characterizes dreams. In this state of being awake and aware, people can make decisions about what they want to do with the hallucinations they are experiencing. If they are walking down a hall, for example, they can make a decision to turn right as opposed to turning left, or open a door to see what is inside. They can talk to people and ask them to do things, they can leave if they don't like what is happening, or they can do battle with a threatening figure (Gackenbach & Bosveld, 1989; LaBerge, 1985) .

One of the most interesting things about lucid dreaming is that people can engage in extraordinary physical and psychological feats because they are not bound by the laws of physics. They can do such things as fly, jump over skyscrapers, throw trucks through the air, jump from one continent to another with no loss of time. It is not surprising that once people have learned to become lucid dreamers they look forward to going to sleep so they can enter the world in which they can take complete control. It is also not surprising that one of the things people like to do best is to experience the exhilaration that comes from flying from one place to another. To sleep is to explore and be entertained.

While studies of lucid dreaming emphasize the entertainment value associated with becoming a lucid dreamer, one can also use lucid dreams to achieve self-discovery and self-mastery.

Lucid Dreaming as Empowerment

One of the interesting features of lucidity is that people, situations and things are less threatening. As a result, people can confront threatening people, situations, and things, and learn how to deal with them. If, for example, people are unable to confront one of their parents in normal waking life, they can use lucidity to deal with them. Once they have learned to deal with their parents in their dreams, it appears they can transfer that learning to the waking state.

Because it is possible to manipulate dream content, it is possible for people to actively get in touch with places, times, situations, or persons that are a source of anxiety or conflict. They can then use lucidity to resolve the anxiety or the conflict. It is even possible for people to get a new perspective on a situation by occupying another person's body. There are clinical reports of people detaching themselves from their own body and floating over to another person's body and occupying it (see Gackenbach & Bosveld, 1989).

Lucid Dreaming and Health

It has been suggested that there is great potential for lucid dreaming as a vehicle to improved health. Some of the things that have been linked to good health are such things as self-confidence, feelings of control, optimism. All of these, it seems, could be enhanced with the aid of lucid dreaming. There are numerous reports in the lucid dreaming literature that when people learn to conquer their anxieties and fears they are more confident, more in control and more optimistic about life (LaBerge, 1985). While there is anecdotal evidence for the link between lucid dreaming and health, more controlled laboratory work needs to be done before we can definitively conclude that lucid dreaming is an avenue to better health.

Distinguishing Between REM, NREM, and Sleep Onset Dreams

While the majority of work has focused on REM dreams, it is interesting to note that we also experience other types of dreams.

REM and NREM Dreams

While there are fewer NREM dreams, in many ways REM and NREM dreams are the same. They tend to be of similar lengths, occur throughout the sleep period, and be equally identified as having dreamlike qualities (Cohen, 1979; Foulkes, 1966). Nevertheless, they dif-

fer in some basic ways. NREM dreams tend to reflect greater conceptual thinking. Their content is often a re-creation of some recent psychologically important event. In contrast, REM dreams are more perceptual and emotional. Unrelated scenes and people are frequently brought together. Strong feelings often accompany these dreams, such as feelings of anxiety, hostility, and violence (Foulkes, 1966). It has been suggested that in Freudian terms REM dreams are more like primary-process thinking, which is frequently unrealistic and emotional, whereas NREM dreams are more like secondary-process thinking, which is more realistic (Vogel, 1978).

An interesting property of REM dreams is that they tend to become more intense throughout the sleep period (Czaya, Kramer, & Roth, 1973; Kramer et al., 1974); NREM dreams apparently do not (Tracy & Tracy, 1974). For example, Czaya's subjects rated 12 aspects of their dreams on a 5-point scale: recall, activity, emotion, anxiety, clarity, pleasantness, violence, hostility, degree of distortion, how frightening, how related to personal life, and sensibleness. Of these, emotion, recall, anxiety, and pleasantness showed a significant linear increase throughout the sleep period. What does this mean? In Freudian terms, it might mean that the subjects were giving greater expression to primary-process thinking. To the degree that there is a need for this type of mental/emotional activity, it might be argued that people tend to satisfy this need more in later than in earlier sleep cycles. It might be hypothesized, for example, that some kind of inhibitory mechanism, such as that proposed by Vogel, is more operative in the early stages of the sleep period, and that with time the inhibition on this type of mental activity is reduced, leading to increases in the length and intensity of REM sleep. This idea is consistent with the finding that as a person is deprived of REM sleep, attempts to compensate for it increase. Presumably, as the need for REM increases, the mechanism that inhibits this type of activity finds it more and more difficult to block the activity.

Sleep-onset Dreams

Some people are more inclined to dream at sleep onset than others (Vogel, 1978). The dreams of these people,

PRACTICAL APPLICATION 6.3

Learn How to Become a Lucid Dreamer

It does not appear that difficult to become a lucid dreamer. If you are willing to persist and are willing to exercise a bit of patience, you probably can become a lucid dreamer. When I have sampled my classes I have found that about 15 to 20 percent of them have experienced lucid dreams without deliberately having tried to become a lucid dreamer. I assume that means it is not that difficult. The five rules I have listed below may help you to become a lucid dreamer. There are no guarantees, however, since we do not fully understand the nature of lucid dreams. In any event, good luck.

1. Practice dream recall. First thing every morning you should record your dreams in a "Dream Journal." The act of recording your dreams instructs the brain-mind that you want it to store your dreams in memory. The natural tendency of the brain-mind is to *not* store dreams in memory. What you will discover when you start recording your dreams is that you will remember more and more dreams. Learning to remember your dreams is the first step toward recognizing that you are dreaming. It is the ability to recognize that you are dreaming that will make you a lucid dreamer.

When you get up in the morning you should ask yourself "What did I dream?" Even if the answer to the question does not come immediately, don't give up. After a short time you will likely find that you can recall some fragments. As time passes, these frag-

ments will evolve into complete dreams. It takes time for the brain-mind to clearly understand that you want to be able to record your dreams in some detail as opposed to simply having some indication that you did dream.

One way to help trigger your dream memories is to ask yourself how you are feeling and what you are thinking about. Often the feelings and thoughts that you have first thing in the morning are linked to the dreams you had during the night. By focusing your attention on these thoughts and feelings you may be able to trigger the memory.

Make sure that you do not let other things get in the way of recording your dreams in the morning. If you don't record them immediately you won't remember them in as much detail, and there will be a tendency for you to record your dreams into a more waking-like form. These dream records are important not only because they teach you to remember, but because they will provide you with the information you need to recognize when you are dreaming.

2. Teach yourself to recognize that you are in a dream. Start by asking yourself five to ten times a day "Am I dreaming?" This will help you ask the question at night. Before going to bed, make it your intention to recognize dreams. If you wake up in the night, use LaBerge's (1985) MILD (Mnemonic Induction of Lucid Dreams) technique. That simply involves saying to yourself "Next time I am dreaming I want to re-

sleep-onset (SO) dreamers, tend to resemble waking fantasy. To understand why certain people are more likely to dream at sleep onset, Foulkes, Spear, and Symonds (1966) gave a variety of psychological tests to SO dreamers and SO nondreamers. From tests, they were able to identify profiles of these two types. They found SO dreamers were more self-accepting, less rigidly conforming to social standards, and more so-

cially poised. SO nondreamers were more rigid, intolerant, and conformist. Since some people do not tend to dream at sleep onset, it is not surprising that studies of the relation between REM dreams and SO dreams have found no correlation (Foulkes et al., 1966). For this reason, Vogel (1978) has argued that the mechanisms responsible for REM dreams and for SO dreams differ. In effect, this means the two kinds of

member to recognize I am dreaming." LaBerge suggests that you generate this intention either immediately after waking from a REM period or following full wakefulness. In his research he has found this a particularly good technique for triggering the recognition of dreams.

Learn to ask the question "Am I dreaming?" whenever you experience a strong emotion or when something seems strange, bizarre, or has any of the characteristics associated with dreams. Since dreams are characterized by strong emotions and such qualities as strangeness and bizarreness, learning to ask this question whenever you detect something that is similar to a dream in the waking state will increase the probability that you will ask this question when you are dreaming. In short, that will lead to recognition.

Read your Dream Journal so that you will become familiar with the characteristics of your dreams. This will help train your mind to recognize when you are in a dream. Identify any unique characteristic about your dreams so that you will be able to more readily recognize that you are in a dream. Actively practice linking these and other characteristics of dreams to the idea that you are dreaming. Say to yourself, for example, such things as "When two people from two different parts of the country are talking as old friends it means I am probably dreaming." The more you become aware of the characteristics that differentiate dreams and the waking state, the better you will be at recognizing that you are dreaming.

3. Learn to confirm to yourself that you are dreaming. One of the easiest tests to use to see if you are dreaming is to see if you can violate the laws of gravity by floating, flying, or jumping six feet in the air. Sometimes people suspect they are dreaming, but in the absence of direct evidence they fail to fully make use of the fact they are dreaming. In short, they fail to become fully lucid when they are on the threshold of lucidity.

4. Plan ahead of time what you intend to do when you become lucid. There are two reasons why this is a good practice. First, when you make plans you give your brain-mind the message that you want to know when you are in a dream so you can carry out some goal. Second, while lucid dreams can be highly entertaining, they are useful to deal with specific problems or to achieve goals. In order to make sure you will fully exploit lucidity, you need to make plans in advance.

5. Practice the skills you need as often as possible. Like any learned skill, you need to practice as often as possible. The more you practice the better you will become. Lucidity is a skill that anyone can acquire. Whether or not you acquire this skill is completely determined by your motivation.

dreams have different functions. Vogel (1978) has offered a psychoanalytic interpretation of the difference between SO dreams and REM dreams. According to Vogel, REM dreams reflect the operation of the subconscious as directed by the id. SO dreams, in contrast, reflect the operation of more volitional processes as directed by the ego. According to this explanation, SO dreams are more controllable than REM dreams.

Equivalence of REM Dreams, NREM Dreams, and Waking Mentation

Different kinds of dreams probably satisfy different needs. This conclusion is based on the fact that depriving people of one type of dream (such as that associated with REM sleep) does not increase the frequency or length of other types, nor does it change the nature of dream mentation (Arkin et al., 1978). There is some evidence, however, that depriving people of REM sleep does affect waking mentation. The extent to which REM deprivation affects waking mentation appears to be related to individual differences. Cartwright and her associates initially found that REM-deprived subjects, when given the opportunity for REM rebound, show one of three basic response patterns: "disruption," "compensation," or "substitution." In subjects showing the disruption pattern, stage 2 intrusions occur during REM sleep. In the compensation pattern, REM time increases, and the first REM period after REM deprivation begins sooner after sleep onset than usual. In the substitution pattern, subjects do not show the normal REM rebound effect that characterizes the compensation pattern (Cartwright, Monroe, & Palmer, 1967). In a later study, Cartwright and Ratzel (1972) found that substituters were more likely than compensators to have dreamlike fantasies while awake. They interpret this finding to mean that for substituters, dreamlike fantasy can take the place of a dream during sleep, thus removing the need to make up for REM deprivation. The lack of this tendency or ability in compensators means that the compensator will have to make up for lost REM sleep through increased REM sleep (REM rebound). Responses to tests both before and after REM deprivation were consistent with the idea that REM deprivation affects mental activity during the waking state.

The work of Cartwright and her associates suggests that one reason some people can get along with less sleep is that they are able to compensate in some way through waking activity for the lack of REM sleep that typically occurs when sleep is restricted. To test this explanation, it is necessary to analyze waking activity more thoroughly in order to assess the relation between waking and sleeping mental activity (Hoyt & Singer, 1978). Since people on restricted sleep regimens tend to compensate for lack of sleep by increased stage 4 sleep, there is a good possibility that stage 4 sleep may not be related to waking behaviors in the same way that REM seems to be. Future research will undoubtedly answer this question.

Hartmann's Theory of Sleep

The Function of REM and NREM sleep

Ernest Hartmann (1973) has offered a theory of sleep that suggests that REM sleep and NREM sleep serve two distinct and important functions. He proposes that NREM sleep serves a general physiological restorative function and REM sleep serves a more specialized "reprogramming" function. Because of the complexity of our daily lives, he argues, we have much unfinished business, such as stress, conflict, and unorganized information. REM not only helps deal with this unfinished business but plays a general role in maintaining the systems that underpin the processes of alertness and attention.

Synchronous versus Asynchronous Electrical Activity During REM and SWS

In a study involving patients with implanted electrodes that monitored the activity of 13 deep subcortical structures, it was found that changes in electrical activity in the various areas were asynchronous (not related to activity in other areas) during SWS (NREM) sleep but were highly synchronous during REM (Moiseeva, 1979). This finding is consistent with Hartmann's theory that during SWS each of the various areas of the brain is undergoing "repair," whereas during REM the various areas work together to reprogram the individual so that the individual will be prepared for the following day.

REM Sleep Restores Catecholamines

Hartmann has specifically argued that information processing depletes catecholamines and that REM sleep serves to replenish them. According to his theory, when we are awake we are able to maintain our attention because of subtle feedback systems that allow us to block out irrelevant information or focus on relations that make the situation meaningful. These feedback-modulated guidance systems weaken with extended use (because of catecholamine depletion), and REM sleep restores these systems to their proper level. In effect, Hartmann argues that these systems are bypassed while they are under repair. From this perspective, he suggests, we can understand the nature of dreams. During dreams, he notes, we often are unable to focus attention; we simply experience a pattern of environmental events that sometimes may even violate laws of time and space. That is, we sometimes put two things together that normally don't go together, or we perceive two events occurring simultaneously when in fact they occurred at different times. For example, we may dream of two persons who have never met (but whom we happen to know) talking to each other as though they were old acquaintances. It is because the feedback systems are not operative that this can happen.

In a test of this theory, Hartmann and Stern (1972) deprived rats of desynchronized (REM) sleep, thus producing a decrement in acquisition of an avoidance task. When the rats were then injected with a drug that increased the availability of catecholamines, this deficit was reversed. That is, the rats learned normally when the catecholamine level was raised.

Summary

According to Freud, dreams are the result of unfulfilled wishes. In order to avoid a conflict with the conscious, the ego transforms unacceptable images into more acceptable images. Dreams, therefore, are both disguised and symbolic. Crick and Mitchison have argued that the content of dreams is random and, therefore, they have no meaning. According to their theory, REM sleep serves to reverse learning. According to Hobson's activation/synthesis theory, dreams are meaningful, undisguised and often rich in conflictual impulses. Hobson suggests that the brain has a natural tendency to synthesize the images (i.e., create a story) produced by the random firing of memories. The meaning of dreams, therefore, is to be found in the story that our brain creates.

In lucid dreaming, individuals participate in the dream as though awake and aware. Some researchers view lucid dreaming as a means for attaining empowerment and health.

Most dreaming occurs during REM sleep, but dreams also occur during NREM sleep. Although REM and NREM dreams have many similarities (length, dreamlike qualities, periodic occurrence), their contents differ. NREM dreams tend to reflect greater conceptual thinking, whereas REM dreams are more perceptual and emotional. Further, REM dreams become more vivid as the sleep period goes on; NREM dreams do not. A separate class of dreams, called sleep-onset (SO) dreams, have been found to occur more for some people (SO dreamers) than others (SO nondreamers). Vogel has suggested that REM dreams reflect the operation of the id, SO dreams the operation of the ego. Research on the question of equivalence of REM dreams, NREM dreams, and waking mentation has led to the conclusion that lack of REM sleep affects waking mentation. The extent of this effect is affected, however, by individual differences. Hartmann has proposed that REM and NREM sleep serve two distinct functions, a "reprogramming" function and a restorative function, respectively.

Sleep Disorders

The best way to determine the exact nature of a sleep disorder is to take EEG measures during one or more nights of sleep in a sleep clinic. Often people who complain of a sleep disorder are unable to explain its exact nature, or they perceive a problem that in fact doesn't exist. With objective data, it is possible to chart a course of action that may alleviate the problem (Dement, 1972).

Insomnia

One of the most common categories of sleep disorders is insomnia. Insomnia is any failure of sleep. It may involve inability to get to sleep, inability to stay asleep, periodic awakenings, or "light sleep," a condition in which the person has difficulty staying asleep and tends to have a high proportion of stage 1 sleep and a low proportion of stage 4 sleep (Webb & Agnew, 1975b). Large-scale surveys have found that about 14% of the population feel they have some difficulty with sleep. These studies indicate that difficulties with sleep are independent of racial origin, socioeconomic status, and nationality (Webb & Agnew, 1975b). Age, however, has been found to be a major predictor. Up to half

PRACTICAL APPLICATION 6.4

Some Common Reasons for Insomnia

Many of us suffer from insomnia from time to time. There are at least four common reasons for difficulty in going to sleep.

Sleeping In

If we have stayed up late or if we have not been getting enough sleep, we are often inclined to sleep in. Also, since the duration of our circadian rhythm tends to be 25 hours rather than 24 hours, we have a natural tendency to go to bed later on succeeding nights and so to get up later and later in the morning. According to Kleitman, the grandfather of sleep research, one of the best predictors of the time we will go to sleep is the length of time we have been awake, because the body tends to alternate between sleep and wakefulness in a very orderly fashion. Because our circadian rhythm lasts 25 hours, the body will quickly adjust to any new pattern that puts us to bed later and gets us up later. In order to maintain a 24-hour rhythm, then, we must constantly reset the cycle by getting up at the same time each day. When we interrupt the pattern by sleeping in, our body adopts a new arousal (alertness) pattern that finds us staying alert longer in the evening and being less alert in the morning. Alertness (arousal) in the evening makes it very difficult to get to sleep. The Monday-morning blues that many people experience may sim-

ply be the result of having let their bodies get out of synchrony with the 24-hour world in which they live. When they try to get to sleep on Sunday night, they discover that they cannot readily fall asleep. When they finally do fall asleep, they simply do not have enough time to get the necessary amount of REM and stage 4 sleep. And since they have not reset their alertness cycle, they tend to be out of synchrony with the 24-hour working day.

Engaging in an Activity that Produces High Arousal before Sleep

I find that if I lecture for three hours in the evening, say from 7:00 to 10:00, I have a great deal of difficulty getting to sleep. The reason is fairly simple. In order to sleep, our arousal level needs to decline to a level that makes sleep possible. Certain activities, such as lecturing for three hours, tend to produce a fairly high level of arousal (at least for me), which takes time to diminish. The bottom line is that even moderately high levels of arousal are incompatible with sleep. That is why people who win lotteries or suffer the death of a loved one typically cannot sleep. Students who must take an exam the following day often have difficulty sleeping. When we think about some forthcoming activity, especially one that is challenging, we often experience fairly high levels of arousal.

---

of the older people questioned indicated they experienced troubled sleep from time to time.

Drug-related insomnias. One of the most common treatments for insomnia has been barbiturates. Although barbiturates will initially increase sleep time, larger and larger doses are typically required to maintain this pattern. Eventually most people who use barbiturates develop a very disturbed sleep pattern. They can initially go to sleep (with the aid of barbiturates), but they have difficulty staying asleep. The reason has become

clear. Initially, barbiturates suppress REM sleep. In larger and larger doses, barbiturates suppress not only REM sleep but stages 3 and 4 sleep. Because the absence of REM and stage 4 sleep produces deficits that need to be made up, people who take barbiturates are put into a state of continuous REM and stage 4 sleep deprivation. The many bursts of cortical arousal observed among barbiturate users during sleep can be interpreted as attempts to enter stage 3, 4, or REM sleep (Dement & Villablanca, 1974).

The effects of alcohol on sleep are similar in many

Irregular Bedtime

People who do not go to bed at the same time each night often experience insomnia, especially on a night when they try to go to bed early. The reason is linked to the fact that while we can get along with less than eight hours of sleep, we tend to thrive on regularity. That is, our body attempts to synchronize itself with certain demands or expectations that we place on it. When we stay up late, our body attempts to accommodate that demand. When we suddenly go to bed early expecting to sleep, we find that our body is still operating at a higher level of arousal than is compatible with sleep. The net effect is that we lie awake waiting for our body to shut down.

It should be noted that while our body tends to respond to internal clocks (rhythms), we can reset those clocks by adopting a new pattern of waking and sleeping. While some people can adjust their rhythms quickly, others find the task difficult. Most researchers agree that the best way to produce a good internal rhythm is to adopt a set schedule. When you do not stick to a schedule, the body fails to develop a consistent rhythm. As a result, you are likely to have occasional difficulty getting to sleep.

Napping

Since the ability to fall asleep is determined to a very large degree by the time that has passed since you last slept, a relatively long afternoon nap can make it very difficult for you to fall asleep at your regular bedtime. Napping as I refer to it here is different from catnapping which is generally not more than 30 minutes. People who are inclined to nap in the evening can also suffer a form of insomnia. Sometimes naps in the evening (naps that are longer than 30 minutes, for example) are treated by the body as part of the sleep cycle. Since awakening is determined to a very large degree by the length of time we have slept, people who nap in the evening tend to wake up very early. Not surprisingly, they then have difficulty getting back to sleep. The best way to cure this problem is to discontinue the evening naps. This is often very difficult to do because people who are in the habit of taking such naps often fall asleep involuntarily while they are reading or watching television. A nap serves to maintain the pattern they have established: early to sleep and much too early to wake. Not all people have trouble with naps. The body can learn to accommodate naps in the daily waking/sleeping cycle. This fact indicates that the sleep/wakefulness pattern can to some degree be trained.

respects to those of barbiturates. In single doses alcohol reduces REM sleep while sometimes slightly increasing slow-wave sleep. Chronic alcohol use typically produces fragmented sleep characterized by a reduction of REM and slow-wave sleep. Withdrawal of alcohol following chronic use often results in hallucinations. It has been suggested that delirium tremens ("DTs") may result when REM sleep breaks into the waking state (Webb & Agnew, 1975b).

Mild stimulants such as caffeine (found, for example, in coffee, tea, some soft drinks, and NoDoz) produce a mild disruption of sleep. The equivalent of three to four cups of coffee before retiring lengthens the time it takes to get to sleep, produces more awakenings, and generally leads to the subjective evaluation of "poor sleep." Strong stimulants such as amphetamines have a much more pronounced effect. They not only increase the time it takes to get to sleep and the number of awakenings, but they also reduce REM and slow-wave sleep. Withdrawal from chronic use results in REM rebound and associated nightmares.

Antidepressants and some tranquilizers also decrease REM sleep, as do some nonprescription sleeping pills. The ultimate benefit of these drugs as far as sleep is concerned is therefore questionable.

Non-drug-related insomnias. Webb and Agnew (1975b) have suggested that there are basically five categories of non-drug-related insomnias: situational, benign, arrhythmic, sleep anomalies, and secondary sleep disorders.

Situational insomnias are those produced by a response to some event in the waking world. Excitement about a new business opportunity or a new love, the death of a loved one, guilt, or failure may all create a temporary sleep disorder. Often the passage of time will resolve a situationally induced sleep disorder.

Benign insomnias are those in which people perceive they have "poor sleep" although in fact their sleep patterns are well within normal limits. For example, the person who feels she is not sleeping enough or has difficulty trying to get to sleep may not need to sleep as long as she thinks she should. Such a person may simply need to be made aware that there are great variations not only in the length of sleep but in its timing.

Arrhythmic insomnias are those caused by irregular sleep patterns. Going to bed or getting up at irregular hours eliminates some of the cues that normally control sleep. As a consequence, a person may have difficulty going to sleep or may not get enough sleep because of the tendency to wake up early. Following a regular sleep pattern will usually control if not eliminate such forms of insomnia.

There are several types of *sleep anomaly.* One kind involves the intrusion of sleep into the waking state (narcolepsy and hypersomnia). These disorders are frequently disruptive but can be treated by sleep clinics. A second kind involves the presence of wakelike behaviors during sleep (sleepwalking, night terrors, nightmares, enuresis). These sleep disorders are age-related. Typically they disappear by mid-childhood.

Sometimes sleep disorders occur because of some form of pathology. Treatment requires an attack on the primary cause. Once the primary pathology has been removed, sleep typically returns to normal—hence the term *secondary sleep disorder.* For example, a person who has difficulty sleeping because of feelings of guilt must learn how to deal with the guilt before normal sleep can be achieved.

Sleep Apnea

A person who suffers from sleep apnea stops breathing for about ten seconds 30 or more times during the course of one night. Some sufferers stop breathing as often as 500 times a night. While this condition is reasonably rare (Bixler et al., 1982), it is nevertheless considered life-threatening because it can cause severe hypoxia (deficiency of oxygen in the body tissues), and cardiac arrhythmias (irregular heartbeat). Although it has been considered a common cause of insomnia in adults, controlled laboratory studies have not confirmed this belief (Kales et al., 1982). Insomnia occurs for a wide variety of reasons other than sleep apnea. Because cessation of breathing typically causes one to awaken, such people tend to suffer fragmented sleep, which typically leads to daytime sleepiness (Stepanski et al., 1984; see also the earlier section on fragmented sleep). The mechanism by which this disorder is produced is not completely understood. The condition has been successfully eliminated by plastic surgery. Consumption of alcohol before bedtime can increase sleep apnea (Scrima et al., 1982).

Summary

One of the most common sleep disorders is insomnia. A wide variety of chemicals including barbiturates, alcohol, and caffeine can produce this condition. Insomnia can also be produced by environmental conditions. In some cases the person believes he or she is suffering from insomnia but is not—a condition called "benign insomnia." Sleep apnea, characterized by cessation of breathing, is a life-threatening disorder. There are several kinds of sleep anomaly, such as intrusion of sleep into waking state or the presence of wakelike behaviors during sleep. Though disruptive, many of these disorders can be treated.

Main Points

1. The best index of wakefulness, drowsiness, sleep, and dreams is cortical EEG activity.

2. In the course of a night an individual goes through approximately five sleep cycles, involving four states of sleep plus what is called stage 1-REM.

3. Sleep has been divided into two general categories called REM and NREM.

4. Dreaming is typically associated with REM sleep.

5. REM sleep episodes lengthen as the sleep period continues; the total is about 1.5-2.0 hours of REM sleep a night.

6. According to Jouvet's model of sleep, serotonin controls the onset of sleep and norepinephrine produces REM sleep.

7. Paralysis experienced during REM sleep is controlled by mechanisms in the RAS.

8. Sleep can be considered a state of extremely low attention in which the individual's threshold for detecting stimulation is high.

9. If people are left to establish their own sleep/wakefulness cycles (circadian rhythm), they tend to adopt a 25-hour cycle.

10. We tend to have more difficulty going to sleep when we have been aroused by some environmental event.

11. One of the factors that most strongly determines the time we go to sleep is the length of time that has elapsed since we last slept.

12. It has been shown that we have a 12.5-hour rhythm, which explains why many people like to nap in the afternoon.

13. The basic rest/activity cycle (BRAC) lasts from 90 to 120 minutes.

14. The tendency to shift from fantasy and intuitive thought to verbal and intellectual thought and back again follows a 90-minute cycle.

15. People who reduce the total time they sleep to 4.5-5.5 hours experience less REM and stage 2 sleep than normal but the same amount of stages 3 and 4 sleep.

16. People typically experience difficulty alternating their sleep/wakefulness cycles.

17. Although reduced sleep may lead to feelings of sleepiness and fatigue, it does not seem to produce any serious psychological disturbances.

18. People typically recover fully from sleep deprivation after a full night of sleep.

19. Sleep reduction tends to reduce performance in tasks that demand persistence and attention but not in tasks that demand precision and cognitive functioning.

20. Fragmented sleep, defined as sleep from which the individual is awakened repeatedly, can produce deficits similar to those that accompany total deprivation of sleep.

21. Loss of sleep reduces friendliness and increases aggression.

22. A good way to make up for lost sleep is to learn to take catnaps.

23. Infants have about twice as much REM as adults.

24. All mammalian species that have been studied and a sizable portion of avian predators (e.g., hawks and eagles) have REM.

25. According to Ellman's theory, REM sleep is important for periodically firing the ICSS system.

26. Lack of REM sleep typically leads to REM rebound.

27. There has been some controversy as to whether lack of REM sleep produces serious psychological disturbances.

28. Vogel has provided evidence that REM deprivation may in fact benefit people experiencing endogenous depression.

29. Vogel's theory is that too much REM sleep leads to too much dissipation of neural energy.

30. There is convincing evidence that REM sleep is involved in the consolidation of memory.

31. Further, REM may be involved in the integration of recently learned material with previously learned material.

32.   There is evidence that REM facilitates the learning not only of complex tasks but of emotionally loaded ones.

33.   REM sleep appears to play a particularly important role in dealing with material that is threatening to the ego.

34.   Field-independent people and repressors have a greater need for REM sleep.

35.   REM sleep has been characterized as a form of divergent thinking.

36.   Deprivation of stage 4 sleep reliably produces stage 4 rebound.

37.   It appears that people need a daily quota of stage 4 sleep.

38.   According to Freud, dreams are both disguised and symbolic.

39.   Crick and Mitchison have argued that dreams have no meaning.

40.   According to Hobson's theory, dreams are meaningful, undisguised and often rich in conflictual impulses.

41.   In lucid dreaming, individuals participate in the dream as though awake and aware.

42.   People dream during several stages of sleep, but the dreams differ in nature in the various stages.

43.   NREM dreams tend to be conceptual and logical; REM dreams tend to be perceptual and emotional.

44.   Sleep-onset (SO) dreams are similar to waking fantasy.

45.   Because REM dreams and NREM dreams differ somewhat in content, it has been suggested that they have different functions.

46.   Hartmann has suggested that NREM sleep has a restorative function and that REM sleep has a reprogramming function.

47.   Up to 14% of the population suffers from insomnia.

48.   One major cause of insomnia is the use of drugs, including sleeping pills.

49.   There are three categories of insomnia in addition to the kind related to drugs: situational, benign, and arrhythmic insomnia.

50.   Sleep apnea is characterized by the cessation of breathing.

Chapter Seven

Drug Use and Drug Addiction

- What is drug addiction?
- Is there an addictive personality? Why do some people fail to become addicted?
- What is the difference between drug abuse and drug addiction?
- What are some of the biochemical explanations of the effects of drugs?
- What role does learning play in the addictive process? What role do cognitive processes play in addiction? Do our expectations about what drugs do have any effect?
- Is abstinence the only cure for addiction, or can people who have become addicted learn to use drugs responsibly?
- Does alcohol increase sexual arousal?
- Is having a couple of drinks a good way to relax?
- How do people quit addictions?

Although the term *addiction* is typically used in connection with the use and abuse of drugs—alcohol, barbiturates, stimulants, heroin, marijuana, nicotine, even caffeine—there is a growing tendency to extend the term to such activities or behaviors as meditation, running, and work (Glasser, 1976).

In this chapter I will focus my attention on the use and abuse of drugs. I will try to answer a number of questions, such as "Why are people more likely to become addicted to some drugs than others?" "Why is it that some people become addicted and others do not?" "Can the addiction process be reversed? If so, how?" As we shall see, the answers to these questions are complex. There is no single determinant of drug addiction, nor is there a single route to drug addiction. Nevertheless, certain principles appear to describe the process, at least in part.

Current Focus

World Health Organization Definition

The World Health Organization has defined drug addiction as "a state of periodic or chronic intoxication produced by repeated consumption of a drug" (Swinson & Eaves, 1978, p. 56). Characteristics of drug addiction described by the World Health Organization are presented in Figure 7-1.

The World Health Organization has recognized that there are many problems with this definition, and, as a result, has suggested that the term may be counterproductive and should be dropped (Worick & Schaller, 1977). The term has gained such wide currency, however, that it is unlikely to fade from use.

The main problem with this definition is that it identifies only the final stages of addiction. Often in the final stages, such as confirmed alcoholism, serious health problems have set in, making it virtually impossible to reverse the process. Further, serious psychological dependency on the drug often exists in the final stages. Years of use can dramatically alter a person's ability to cope with the real world: years of failing to exercise normal coping responses can leave the person without any. In short, the drug may have changed the person both physically and psychologically. To understand drug addiction, we need to know the motivation for drug use, not just its effects. What we need to know is why people initially take drugs and, further, why they continue to take drugs. What roles are played by biological factors, the environment, and personality?

Substance Abuse

The one common factor in most, if not all, instances of drug addiction is drug abuse or what has come to be called *substance abuse* (Worick & Schaller, 1977). Substance abuse refers to the tendency to use a substance to excess, either more than was prescribed by a doctor or more than the person can handle without physical and psychological ill effects. It also refers to any tendency to use substances indiscriminately without regard for one's need to function as a member of society. The question that we need to answer, therefore, is why some people are able to use a drug or substance in moderation so that it does not markedly affect their health, their performance, or their interpersonal relationships, while other people use the drug or substance to excess so that it causes problems in these areas of their lives.

It is interesting to note that the DSM-III diagnostic criteria (1980) defines substance abuse differently for each of the various drugs/substances that we will be discussing in this chapter. It appears that the exact nature or pattern of abuse depends on the nature of the drug or substance in question. In other words, abuse depends on the interaction of the drug with the needs of the individual.

Summary

The term addiction is typically used in connection with the abuse of such drugs as alcohol, barbiturates, stimulants, heroin, marijuana, nicotine, and even caffeine. In recent years, research has focused on attempts to determine what motivates people to use drugs rather than merely on the effects of drugs. This shift in emphasis grows out of the perception that it makes more sense to prevent addiction than to devise methods for treating it.

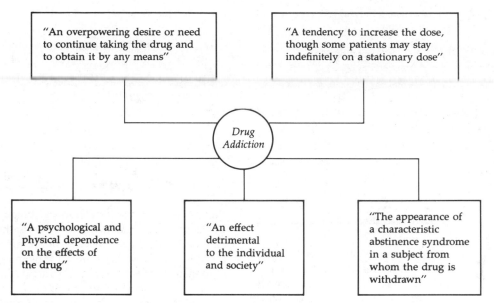

Figure 7–1. Characteristics of drug addiction as defined by the World Health Organization (Based on R. P. Swinson and D. Eaves, *Alcoholism and Addiction*, 1978. Copyright © 1978 by Macdonald and Evans, Ltd., Estover, Plymouth.)

Some Basic Terms and Theories

Psychoactive versus nonpsychoactive. A psychoactive drug is one that affects mood and/or consciousness. It may be a prescription drug such as Valium or it may be a nonprescription drug such as marijuana. This distinction is generally viewed as important in the drug abuse literature because people tend to abuse psychoactive drugs but not nonpsychoactive drugs. In short, it is because a drug can alter psychological functioning that people tend to use and abuse certain drugs.

Dependency. It can readily be shown that most drugs produce a variety of physiological and chemical changes in the body. It is assumed or can be shown that a drug that produces addiction has altered normal body functions to such a degree that further doses of the drug are required to maintain a state of normal well-being. This state of drug dependency is generally assumed to be physiological, even though the main symptoms associated with the absence of the drug are

often psychological. For example, a drug may produce a very pronounced feeling of euphoria or general well-being. Once a dose of the drug has run its course, the person may suffer intense depression or anxiety. Because more of the drug is required to return the person to a normal psychological state, let alone a state of euphoria, the person is regarded as having a physical dependency on the drug even though the main indicator is psychological.

Tolerance. The term *tolerance* is typically used in the drug literature to refer to the fact that people often need to use increasing amounts of a particular drug in order to obtain the same psychological effects. There is evidence that tolerance to many if not all drugs is due to the physiological changes they produce. Solomon and Corbit (1974) have argued that tolerance is due to the development of an "opponent process" that tends to return the organism to its normal resting or operational level. According to their model, the person needs to take increasingly larger amounts of the drug to overcome the sluggish but powerful opponent

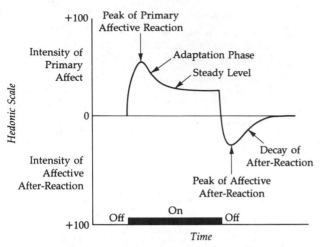

Figure 7–2. The standard pattern of affective dynamics, showing the five distinctive features: the peak of the primary affective reaction, the adaptation phase, the steady level, the peak of the affective after-reaction, and finally the decay of the after-reaction. (The heavy black bar represents the time during which the affect-arousing stimulus is present. The ordinate represents two hedonic scales, each departing from neutrality, one for the primary affect, the other for the affective after-reaction.) (From R. L. Solomon, "The Opponent-Process Theory of Acquired Motivation." *American Psychologist,* 1980, *35,* 691-712. Copyright © 1980 by the American Psychological Association. Reprinted with permission.)

process. Whatever the exact mechanism, the fact that people tend to develop a tolerance for drugs has been taken as clear evidence that drug addiction is due to physiological changes that result from repeated use of a drug.

Solomon's Opponent-Process Theory

Solomon (Solomon & Corbit, 1974; Solomon, 1980) has noted that whenever a person experiences an increase in positive affect, he or she is likely to experience a sharp increase in negative affect a short time afterward. Similarly, an increase in negative affect is likely to be followed shortly by a sharp increase in positive affect. He argues that the human is designed so that whenever affect departs from a baseline, an opponent

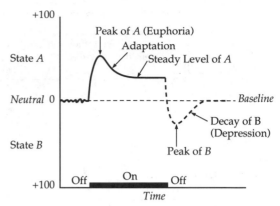

Figure 7–3. The manifest temporal dynamics generated by the opponent-process system during the first few stimulations. (The five features of the affective response are labeled.) (Adapted from R. L. Solomon, "The Opponent-Process Theory of Acquired Motivation." *American Psychologist,* 1980, *35,* 691-712. Copyright © 1980 by the American Psychological Association. Reprinted with permission.)

process is triggered that returns the person to baseline. He suggests that the opponent process is rather sluggish and requires time to exert its full effect. When it does exert its effect, it produces for a time the affective state opposite to the one that initially triggered it. This sequence is illustrated in Figure 7-2.

Solomon holds that the opponent process is strengthened by use and weakened by disuse. He suggests that because the opponent process tends to increase in strength each time it is triggered, the initial affective reaction will be shortened and the opponent affective reaction will get stronger. This change with repeated use is shown in Figures 7-3 and 7-4. Figure 7-3 shows a typical affective reaction to a drug when a person initially uses it. Figure 7-4 shows the reaction after repeated use. Note that state *A* diminishes in strength while state *B* increases in strength. In the case of amphetamine use, state *A* would correspond to feelings of euphoria that typically accompany the use of amphetamines, while state *B* would correspond to its opposite, something akin to feelings of depression. With repeated use of amphetamines, the euphoria would diminish and negative feelings (depression) would increase.

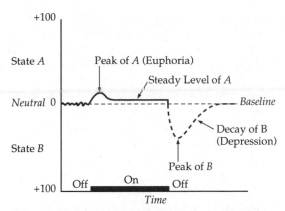

Figure 7–4. The manifest temporal dynamics generated by the opponent-process system after many stimulations. (The major features of the modified pattern are labeled.) (Adapted from R. L. Solomon,"The Opponent-Process Theory of Acquired Motivation." *American Psychologist*, 1980, 35, 691-712. Copyright © 1980 by the American Psychological Association. Reprinted with permission.)

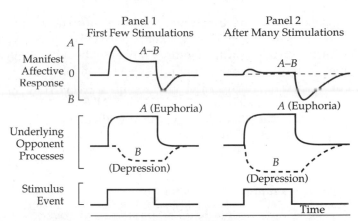

Figure 7–5. The comparison of the effects of *B* processes for relatively novel unconditioned stimuli and for unconditioned stimuli that are familiar and have frequently been repeated (Adapted from R. L. Solomon,"The Opponent-Process Theory of Acquired Motivation." *American Psychologist*, 1980, 35, 691-712. Copyright © 1980 by the American Psychological Association. Reprinted with permission.)

Figure 7-5 illustrates, in a slightly different way, what is happening. With repeated stimulations, process *B* (depression) occurs more quickly and with greater intensity (panel 2). If the affective reaction is *A* minus *B* (*A* – *B*), then as process *B* increases, the affective reaction (euphoria) decreases, as shown in Figure 7-4.

According to Solomon, this change accompanying repeated use of a drug accounts for the tolerance effects often observed when people use opiates, barbiturates, amphetamines, and a number of other drugs. When people take a drug, the body sets up an opponent process that tends to neutralize its effects. As the opponent process strengthens, greater quantities of the drug will be required to provide the same initial reaction.

Solomon suggests that the development of tolerance may play a fundamental role in making a person an addict rather than a casual user. Consider what happens when someone starts to use an opiate. If the person finds the elation and euphoria produced by the opiate rewarding, he or she will be inclined to use the drug again. The problem begins to occur, according to Solomon, when the tolerance for the drug begins to build. At this point the person tends to increase the dose of the drug in order to experience the same effect, and as a result will experience greater negative aftereffects—pain, fatigue, and depression. If the person should find the aftereffects intolerable, he or she tends to take the drug in order to reduce or eliminate the aftereffects. At this point the motivation for using the drug has shifted. The person is no longer seeking merely to experience a positive affective state but wants rather to reduce a negative affective state. It is at this point that the person is gripped by compulsion. This, of course, would account for the dependency effect.

Numerous examples demonstrate that the opponent process is not restricted to drugs (see Solomon, 1980). It is common for people who worked hard to achieve a goal to report that they experienced a letdown after they attained their goal. Athletes frequently report a letdown after winning an exciting and hard-fought game. Performers often report that they feel emotionally down or even depressed the day after what they felt was an exciting performance. In contrast, skydivers, who often experience high levels of anxiety before and sometimes during a jump, often talk of the exhilaration that follows a jump. Combat soldiers frequently return from the front lines cheerful and optimistic. After a difficult examination, students will often party into the small hours of the morning. All these examples illustrate that whenever positive affect is triggered, it will be followed more or less automatically by negative affect, and vice versa.

Is There an Addictive Personality?

For some time people have attempted to discover whether there is an addictive personality. That is, is there a constellation of physical or psychological characteristics that make some people more prone to become addicted to all drugs or simply to a single drug, such as alcohol or heroin? Assessment of alcoholics (Vaillant, 1983) and narcotics addicts (Robins et al., 1980) has yielded essentially negative results.

It is important to distinguish between the tendency to use drugs and the tendency to become addicted. There is evidence, for example, that college students drink for a variety of reasons. Some drink to avoid aversive situations, some to socialize, some to satisfy a need for sensation, and some for pure enjoyment. Problem drinkers tend to drink for all of those reasons (McCarty & Kaye, 1984). Various studies have found that people who score high on Zuckerman's sensation-seeking scale (see Chapter 12) are more prone to use drugs than people who score low (Huba, Newcomb, & Bentler, 1981). This does not necessarily mean that these people are more prone to become addicted. At this point, there is no evidence that high sensation seekers are more likely than low sensation seekers to become addicted.

It is possible that when such traits as sensation seeking are linked to a more maladaptive behavioral style, an individual may be more susceptible to drug abuse and addiction. It has been shown, for example, that sensation seeking contributes to the addiction process when it is part of a more general trait called "antisocial personality." McCarty and Kaye (1984) found a link between sensation seeking and a tendency toward alcohol abuse only when sensation

seeking was part of a constellation of factors that included "avoidance," including the need to avoid failure.

Consistent with this idea, there is evidence from a variety of sources that people who have a poor self-concept may be prone to alcohol abuse and perhaps drug abuse. Alcohol is known for its ability to reduce negative aspects associated with the self or with performance in a particular task. Banaji and Steele (1989) have shown, for example, that when there is a discrepancy between the ideal self and the real self, alcohol tends to reduce this conflict by allowing people to see only their more positive qualities. As a result, it has been argued, people may learn to use alcohol whenever there is such a discrepancy. Similarly, it has been shown that people who find being evaluated as aversive are inclined to use alcohol in order to lessen the impact of potentially negative evaluation. If people are not threatened by evaluation there is not the same motivation to use alcohol, according to this hypothesis, and thus the likelihood of abusing alcohol is much less (Steele & Josephs, 1990).

When drugs become a "crutch." In order to understand why people become addicted, motivation theorists have come to focus on the question of why people use drugs (e.g., Eysenck, 1963; McClelland et al., 1972). Is the drug used to reduce boredom? To ward off fatigue? To facilitate social contacts? To gain a sense of power and well-being? To provide altered sensory input? To escape from painful experiences? As a substitute for love, sex, feelings of adequacy? There is considerable evidence that if people use drugs to avoid a noxious or aversive situation they are more likely to become addicted than if they merely use drugs for entertainment purposes (e.g., Nathan & Lisman, 1976). That is, when drugs become a crutch for dealing with life's problems, then addiction is more likely to occur.

The suggestion that people are more likely to become addicted when they use drugs to escape a noxious or aversive situation (e.g., anxiety, depression) is consistent with Kolb's (1962) finding that there are two more or less distinct types of people who take drugs. On the one hand is the hedonist, who takes drugs to obtain a euphoric effect; on the other hand is the psychoneurotic, who takes drugs to obtain relief from anxiety. This is consistent with the findings reported above that while sensation seekers are prone to use drugs, they are not more prone to become addicted. It may be due to the fact that sensation seekers are more likely to use drugs for entertainment than to escape a noxious or aversive situation. Kolb's hypothesis is also consistent with the findings reported above that people who experience negative feelings linked to the self are more likely to use alcohol.

The Motivation to Use Drugs

Evidence from a wide variety of sources suggests that the motivations to use drugs include curiosity (seeking out new and varied experiences), modeling (following the behavioral example of parents, friends, or a portion of society, such as an ethnic group), group pressure (requirement for admission to a gang, a challenge to prove one is not a "chicken"), or medication (prescribed either by a doctor or by oneself). Curiosity, modeling, group pressure, and medication not only dispose people to use drugs but often dictate which drug they will use (for example, Roebuck & Kessler, 1972; Sheppard et al., 1972). For example, young people are more likely to use alcohol if their parents or peers do (Braucht et al., 1975; Gorsuch & Butler, 1976). These factors, however, do not tell the whole story. There tend to be large individual differences. The problem is to account for these differences.

Summary

Drug dependency is generally thought to be physiological even though the main symptoms associated with the absence of the drug are often psychological. The term *tolerance* is typically used in the drug literature to refer to the fact that people often need to use increasing amounts of a particular drug in order to obtain the same psychological effects. Solomon's theory can account not only for the dependency and tolerance in connection with drug use, but for the observation that a marked mood shift, either very positive or very negative, is likely to be followed by the opposite mood. According to Solomon, an opponent process is triggered whenever there is a marked shift in mood. The

opponent process is sluggish, but when it does exert its effect it can be powerful, depending on past experience, and can push the mood not only back to baseline but in the opposite direction.

Researchers have attempted for some time to discover whether there is an addictive personality, but virtually all attempts have yielded negative results. While such personality traits as sensation seeking have from time to time been linked with drug abuse, it appears that such traits by themselves do not necessarily lead to drug abuse or addiction. When sensation seeking is linked with other, antisocial traits, however, or with the fear of failure, it may then lead to addiction.

It has been suggested that whether or not people use drugs to escape a noxious or aversive situation is one of the main factors involved in addiction. When people use drugs as a crutch as opposed to using drugs for entertainment, they increase their chances of becoming addicted, regardless of who they are.

Evidence from a wide variety of sources suggests that curiosity plays an important role in initial drug use.

Why Do People Become Addicted to Certain Drugs?

While the general theories about the addictive process are useful in helping to conceptualize at a general level some of the factors involved in the addictive process, in order to understand why people become addicted to a specific drug we need to understand something about the nature of that drug and how that drug interacts with situational and personality variables. Some people do become addicted to several different drugs simultaneously, but, as far as we can tell, becoming addicted to one drug does not automatically make one addicted to all drugs or even a wide variety of drugs. To become addicted to a certain drug one needs to use that drug within a certain context.

In this section I will look at some of the more common drugs to which people become addicted. Some of these drugs are called recreational drugs and some are called prescription drugs. Some of the so called recreational drugs are legal, such as alcohol and tobacco, while others are not, such as marijuana and cocaine.

Some of the prescription drugs can be bought on the street and are often sold by the same people who sell marijuana and other illegal drugs.

I will start with heroin and morphine and leave alcohol towards the end of this list. Alcohol is a complex drug that involves several different systems including some of those that are involved in such drugs as heroin and cocaine.

Heroin and Morphine— Biological Component

Heroin rapidly breaks down to morphine in the body. The most common mood change associated with heroin is euphoria, although panic and anxiety are not uncommon. The maximum effect is reached in about two hours, and the effect begins to wear off in five hours. One of the main medical reasons for administering morphine is to reduce pain. Secondary uses of morphine are for the treatment of diarrhea and the relief of cough. It appears that morphine does not reduce pain (the sensation) so much as it reduces the aversive qualities that people normally report when presented with a painful stimulus (Julien, 1975).

Opioids, such as heroin and morphine, are thought to produce their effects though a number of different neurotransmitter systems including norepinephrine, serotonin, and Substance P (Jaffe & Martin, 1990; Dykstra, 1992). Substance P is important in the transmission of pain whereas norepinephrine and serotonin have been implicated in elevated mood.

Endorphins: Natural Opiates of the Brain

In 1973 it was discovered that the brain has specific receptors for opiates (Snyder, 1977a, 1977b). In subsequent research it was discovered that the body manufactures its own opiates which are called *endorphins* (from *endogenous morphine*). Not only do endorphins kill pain, but they alter mood and remove symptoms of stress. Their more subtle effects are to slow respiration, induce constipation, constrict the pupils, lower body temperature, and alter the functioning of the pituitary (Fincher, 1979). The fact that humans and animals show a marked tolerance to mor-

phine suggests that an opposing metabolic process or antagonist is at work to counteract the effects of morphine.

Researchers have found several antagonists to endorphins. Antagonists neutralize or counteract a given chemical and thereby make it possible to determine the effect of a chemical when it is present and when it is absent. Antagonists are often used to determine if, indeed, the chemical is producing a certain behavior. If you give a patient an antagonist and there are no differences or no changes then you can assume the chemical is not present, but if you give an antagonist and there are significant differences or changes then you can assume that the differences or changes are due to the presence of the chemical.

One of the main antagonists used to study endorphins is naloxone. Naloxone has been used to demonstrate that endorphins are involved in a wide variety of behaviors including stress (Bandura, Cioffi, Taylor, & Brouillard, 1988). In one study it was shown that people who believe they are in control in a stressful situation experience less stress and therefore do not show endorphin output, whereas those who do not believe they are in control show marked endorphin output. In this study, subjects were asked to perform mathematical operations under stressed and nonstressed conditions. Following this treatment they were given saline or naloxone and then subjected to a pain measure. If the endorphin system had been activated during the stress, those subjects given saline would be less able to bear pain than their counterparts who had been given naloxone. As expected, the result indicated that the endorphin system was not activated under the nonstress conditions. Further, the results indicated that for people who believed they could control the situation, the endorphin system was not activated. Only those subjects who did not believe they were in full control showed the endorphin system had been activated. As I will discuss more fully in the chapter on stress, beliefs about control are important in controlling stress, attesting to the importance of our thinking processes.

The discoveries of opiate receptor sites and of endorphins have provided us with a much clearer idea of why people become addicted to opiates such as morphine, heroin, and methadone. The fact that there are natural opiates (endorphins) suggests that somehow it was necessary for vertebrates to evolve these chemicals—that they were important for survival. (Endorphins are found only in vertebrates and the ancient hagfish.)

Learned Component

Personal control versus reinforcement. A person who initially uses a drug typically believes his or her behavior is under his or her conscious control. The individual uses the drug and obtains an effect, and presumably that is the end. If, however, the drug produced a strong reinforcing effect (by producing a pleasant feeling or reducing an unpleasant feeling, such as anxiety), there is a strong probability that the person has been subtly changed. Years of research with strong reinforcers have shown that positive reinforcers tend to increase the probability that the same response will occur in the future. Because each subsequent reinforcement tends to produce an additional increase in the probability of repeating that response, a person who begins to use a drug on a regular basis is likely to develop a strong habit of doing so. Once a habit has been established, it is very difficult to break.

The short-circuiting of biological drives. Because heroin will effectively reduce a variety of discomforts, including hunger, fatigue, anxiety, and pain (Martindale, 1977), the possibility exists that the heroin addict may have fortuitously learned to use heroin to reduce such discomforts. For example, a person who used heroin at one point to eliminate withdrawal symptoms might learn, through continued use, that heroin is an effective way of coping with anxiety. Nichols (1965) originally suggested this possibility when he pointed out that morphine can short-circuit many biological drives (such as hunger, thirst, and sex). It is worth noting that the relapse rate for heroin addicts is 90% (Dole, 1980). This finding is consistent with Nichols' suggestion that heroin use becomes a habit that is probably triggered by a wide variety of stimuli in the environment.

Needle high and the principles of associative learning. *Mainliners* (people who inject opiates intravenously) report a *rush* (intense pleasure) shortly after an injec-

tion. According to the principles of classical and instrumental conditioning, if a drug that produces reinforcing effects is used in the presence of certain stimuli, those stimuli will come, over time, to be associated with the internal state that those drugs produce and will come to control drug-taking behavior (S. Siegel, 1979; Wikler, 1980). It has been suggested that the reason some addicts can get a high simply by inserting a needle into their arm (in the absence of any drug effect) is that they associate the insertion of a needle with the euphoric feeling that typically follows an injection of heroin.

Associative learning and re-addiction in humans. Habits appear to be controlled by stimuli. The stimuli governing a habit may be external, internal, or a combination of both. A given habit may be controlled by external stimuli for some people and by internal stimuli for others. According to the principles of associative learning, a former addict who returns to the sort of environment in which he originally became addicted is likely to relapse. During the Vietnam war a number of soldiers used heroin. Based on the then-current re-addiction data for addicts who had been treated for heroin addiction, it was assumed that even with a good treatment program, there would be a relapse rate close to the existing figure of 85% to 95%. As it turned out, only 15% re-addicted themselves. Those that re-addicted themselves after returning home typically were those who had abused drugs before they went to Asia (Siegel, 1983). In other words, it can be argued that environmental cues previously linked to drug use elicited the drug-taking response.

If it is assumed that the aversive or noxious state associated with withdrawal is what motivates relapse, then principles of associative learning can also account for the re-addiction of some Vietnam veterans who were addicted in Asia. According to associative learning theory, if a veteran returned to an environment that bore similarities to the Asian environment in which he became addicted, the similarity of the two situations would be sufficient to trigger a conditioned withdrawal response, and that response would automatically lead to the tendency to take a drug that would reduce those withdrawal symptoms (O'Brien et al., 1980; Wikler, 1980).

PRACTICAL APPLICATION 7.1

Endorphins and Motivation

Many of the things we like to do trigger the release of endorphins. The release of endorphins is often linked to a defensive reaction of our body. It has been suggested that the release of endorphins is nature's way of rewarding us for doing things that are important for our survival. Lionel Tiger (1979), for example, has suggested that the release of endorphins played an important role in sustaining our ancestors' hunting behavior. The fact that people often learn to do things that will trigger the release of endorphins suggests that humans can learn to tap into this system. What this means, among other things, is that we may learn to do things which are sometimes neither healthy nor adaptive. In other words, by learning to tap into this system we can gain immediate self gratification which may or may not be healthy for us in the long term. One thing is clear: endorphins play an important role in a wide variety of behaviors in which we engage.

   1. Relief of pain. Dennis Hough had three of his vertebral discs ruptured by a patient while he was working in a psychiatric unit of a hospital. Bed-ridden, suffering constant pain, with little hope after two failed operations, Hough was depressed to the point of suicide. In response to the intense pain that the patient was experiencing, doctors decided to implant electrodes in a tiny area in the brain known to release endorphins, called periaqueductal gray (PAG). After the operation Hough could, by using a radio transmitter, stimulate the PAG to release endorphins. His recovery was dramatic. He not only returned to work, taking an office job, but he became engaged to be married (Hopson, 1988). Most scientists now agree that acupuncture (a treatment often used to reduce pain or induce relaxation) works by triggering the release of endorphins (Hopson, 1988).

   2. Self-Injury. Pain, even self-inflicted pain, can release endorphins. It has been suggested that one reason autistic children bang their heads may be to produce an endorphin release. While this is hardly adaptive it may be one way that autistic children have learned to gain pleasure from an otherwise painful life.

   In the pursuit of the sometimes elusive *runner's high*, runners may push themselves too hard. Basking in the glow of an endorphin high and reduced sensitivity to pain that comes with that high, runners may fail to draw back and continue to push themselves when the body needs to rest. One reason athletes may push themselves to the point of pain in a wide variety of endeavors may be to trigger an endorphin release.

   3. Self-Deprivation. It has been shown that food deprivation in anorexics enhances the release of opiates in the brain. It has been suggested that like the autistic self-injury, the anorexic's self-starvation may be rewarding (Hopson, 1988).

   4. Exercise. The positive mood that often accompanies exercise (such as running) can be blocked with naloxone, providing evidence that the exercise mood link is due to the release of endorphins (Hopson, 1988). It should be noted in this context that running has been linked to two very distinct moods: a *high* and a *calm*. While some people talk about running to get high, others talk about running to relax. It may

Cognitive Component

Expectations. It has been repeatedly demonstrated that placebos can be just as effective as an active drug. In one study it was shown that a placebo killed pain as effectively as morphine (Lasagna et al., 1954). It has also been shown that whether or not people experience withdrawal symptoms, the symptoms they do experience depend to a very large extent on knowing that heroin can produce withdrawal symptoms and on knowing what these symptoms are (Peele, 1985).

well be that running does produce these two distinct moods and that they come from different chemical processes (e.g., endorphins and norepinephrine). The question that needs to be answered is, if that is the case, what are the exact conditions that lead to a *high* emotional state and what leads to a *calm* emotional state? Perhaps the answer will be found in whether people focus on pushing themselves (to get high) or on the repetitive nature of running (to calm themselves). It may even be that people can learn to trigger both these chemical process simultaneously, thereby producing an emotional state that is an interaction of these two chemical processes, something that might be described as *relaxed awareness*. (This term has been used to describe how people feel when they take amphetamines.)

5. Health. One of the byproducts of exercise is better health. This might be due in part to the fact that the release of endorphins has been linked to an increase in the activity of the immune system.

6. Risk-taking. There is considerable evidence that endorphins are released when we experience fear. One reason people may take physical and psychological risks is to trigger an endorphin release (Bolles & Fanselow, 1982). Rock climbers, parachutists, hang gliders all talk about the *high* they get when they engage in these sports

7. Eating. It has been argued that the presence of opioids tends to facilitate eating. Drugs that increase levels of opioids (e.g., butorphanol tartrate) lead to increased food intake, whereas drugs that block opioids (e.g., naloxone) lead to decreased food intake (Fava et al., 1989). Evidence from animal research indicates that injections of small amounts of beta endorphin will trigger the eating of fats, proteins or sweets in satiated rats. It has been suggested that opiates increase the hedonic pleasures linked to food, and this would account for why naloxone decreases food intake in the obese (Hopson, 1988).

8. Alcohol. It has been shown that alcohol releases endorphins. It has been suggested that one reason people drink is to get the high that comes from alcohol consumption (Volpicelli, 1987).

9. Music. People who get a get spine-tingling thrill from their favorite music get less of a thrill when they are given naloxone versus a placebo (Hopson, 1988).

10. Laughter. There is a great deal of circumstantial evidence that laughter triggers an endorphin release which, it has been hypothesized, somehow enhances the immune system. However, confirmation of this link is still lacking.

11. Love and Attachment. Panksepp (1986) has suggested that when humans fall in love their body secretes endorphins and therefore they literally become *addicted to love*. When separated, he argues, they go through withdrawal that people often characterize as being a painful experience. This link between attachment and the secretion of endorphins would account for the fact that separation, not just between lovers but with any close relationship, often leads to stress and disease. As I pointed out above, endorphins have been linked to activity of the immune system.

Psychological/social needs. Although animals are sometimes used to study addiction, Vincent Dole (1980) states that "it is noteworthy that most animals cannot be made into addicts" (p. 142). This fact suggests that it is not the drug itself that is the cause of addiction. Indeed, it is important to note that often special conditions need to be met in order to produce addiction in animals. Specifically, animals need to be deprived of the opportunity to express basic needs or drives.

Consistent with this suggestion, a comprehensive research program at Simon Fraser University has shown that it is necessary to house rats under very restricted conditions (very little space, no social interaction, virtually nothing to explore) in order to produce morphine addiction (see Alexander et al., 1985). In one study, rats were trained to ingest large amounts of morphine. This technique was devised by Nichols (1965) to produce withdrawal symptoms, one of the conditions that has been hypothesized to motivate drug use. As expected, this technique did produce increased morphine consumption but, interestingly, the effect was much greater in the animals housed under restricted conditions than in those housed under more natural conditions (more space, opportunity for social interaction, and availability of objects to explore). In other words, the tendency to select morphine, even under conditions of withdrawal, is modified by housing conditions. One interesting finding was that female rats tended more than male rats to prefer morphine under restricted conditions. This effect was magnified after the rats were trained with Nichols's procedure. Why the sex difference? It may, as we shall see, have something to do with the female rat's greater need for social contact and/or opportunity for activity.

Subsequent studies have attempted to separate out the social opportunities of the more natural environment and the opportunity for activity. These studies have shown that it is the combination of space and social contact rather than either space or social contact alone that produces the results.

How can we account for these effects? It has been suggested that the reason rats in the more natural environment fail to use morphine is that morphine interferes with complex rodent activity. If we assume that these activities are rewarding for rodents, it makes sense that rats in an environment that provided those rewards might tend to avoid morphine. Rats' sexual behavior, too, is affected by their environment. If rats are to mate, they need ample space because their normal procedure consists of a series of chases and mounts. After a female has been mounted, she runs away from the male; he pursues her and mounts her again.

Social acceptability. Until the Vietnam war the only data we had on human addiction to morphine (heroin) came from the study of street users. There are numerous problems with relying on data from street users. First, they do not represent a cross-section of society. Many are on the street because they are disturbed, they have been abused as children, they lack basic skills which would allow them to be employed, they are constantly having to deal with lack of shelter, they are often subjected to threats from other street people as well as from the police, they are not eating properly, they are exposed to disease, they do not have access to proper medical treatment, they are stressed, and so forth. When you study street people, in other words you do not know if you are studying the effects of a drug they might be using or the effects of all the other things that characterize their existence. Attempts to locate other users failed because people would not admit they were users for fear of losing their jobs, being harassed by the police, and so forth. Think about it: would you admit that you were using heroin if a researcher came to your door and asked you?

When it became apparent that soldiers were using heroin, the conditions necessary for obtaining good data were met. First, since the soldiers were a captive group who could be tested at will by the army to see if they were users, it proved to be a relatively easy task to identify a group of so-called *heroin addicts*. What alarmed the army was the fact there was a very large group of users. Given the statistics on readdiction (85% to 95%) even following good treatment programs, there was a concern about turning loose such a large group of potential addicts into the population. As I have already indicated, only 15% re-addicted themselves, and those who did were mainly men who had used heroin before going to Vietnam.

Even though the low re-addiction upon returning to the United States can be explained at least in part by the principles of associative learning, many who have looked at these data have given it a more cognitive interpretation (e.g., Davis, Goodwin, & Robins, 1975; Robins, Davis, & Goodwin, 1974; Peele, 1989). In order to understand this interpretation it is necessary to tell the story a little more fully.

The Vietnam war was a very unpopular war.

Many of those serving were not fully committed to the official reason given for fighting (e.g., to stop the spread of communism in Asia), and many were critical of the way the war was being waged (e.g., too much dependence on ground forces and not enough emphasis on striking at the source with air power). Many soldiers felt they were not there to win but rather to force a stalemate. As a result of all this, many felt this was a stupid and pointless war. Many experienced constant stress from the ability of the Viet Cong to infiltrate and selectively kill U.S. soldiers. While the war was technically between North and South Vietnam, it was virtually impossible to recognize the enemy from so-called friends. The lack of family and friends also made it a lonely experience for many soldiers. In short, the conditions for becoming addicted were ideal, at least according to the model which suggests that one must be in an avoidant condition. This would help explain the high rate of addiction to heroin, since nothing like this had ever been observed before by the army. It is interesting to note in this context that 70% or more of the Vietnam soldiers experienced an anxiety disorder called *Post Traumatic Stress Disorder*.

One of the interesting things about the Vietnam war was that it was conducted at a time in history in which the use of drugs such as marijuana by young people, especially university students, was the norm rather than the exception. In other words, the prohibitions against using drugs, at least certain drugs, were more or less absent for this group of soldiers. It has been shown that one of the things which prevents or inhibits people from using drugs or a particular drug in the first place is lack of social acceptance. Further, heroin was readily available, and availability has repeatedly been shown to be a factor in drug use. The combination of availability and lack of social prohibitions against drug use thus set the stage for using heroin. Despite the fact that all the conditions were present to motivate people to use drugs and to become addicted to them, only 15% re-addicted themselves after they returned home. It has been suggested that one of the reasons most did not re-addict themselves was that they returned to environments in which drug use was not generally accepted. Even though some of

their peers might have accepted smoking marijuana, they would not likely have accepted heroin. And, as I have already indicated, those 15% who did re-addict themselves returned to environments in which drug use was accepted and often the norm. In other words, it was the cognitive assessment of the situation that was responsible for the lack of re-addiction in one case and the tendency to re-addict in the other case.

Presence of natural rewards. The research of Alexander et al. reported above suggests that an additional factor may have been operating. It may well be that one of the reasons most of the Vietnam war veterans did not resume taking heroin in the United States was that they returned to an environment that provided them with natural rewards. But what about those who did resume using heroin? It has been suggested that many of them were users before they went to Vietnam, and the rest simply did not have or could not find a rewarding environment after their return. As John Falk (1983) has said, drug abuse "depends on what behavior opportunities are available in life's situations, and whether the individual is prepared to exploit those opportunities" (p. 390).

Beliefs about self-control. There is a growing body of data which suggests that people are most likely to give up an addiction because they have made the decision to do so (Peele, 1985; Peele & Brodsky, 1991). That is, when they say to themselves that they can control their behavior they do in fact change. The success rate is typically much higher for self-initiated change as opposed to other-initiated change. That is, when people are placed in programs designed to educate and train them, but they do not make the decision or the commitment for themselves that they can or will change, they often fail. Success in beating addictions seems to start with the belief that "I can control my behavior" on the one hand, and the decision that "I want to change my behavior" on the other hand. Unless you believe you can change your behavior, you can't, and if you don't want to change your behavior, you won't. The Vietnam findings indicate that once we're addicted to a drug does not mean we have to stay addicted. It is a choice.

Summary

Heroin and morphine are referred to as opioids and typically produce feelings of euphoria as well as suppress the aversive qualities of pain (analgesic properties). Opioids are thought to produce their effects through a number of different neurotransmitter systems as well as through Substance P which transmits pain signals. Receptor sites for morphine led scientists to conclude that the body produces its own morphine (endorphins). Naloxone, an antagonist to endorphins, has been used widely in research to establish whether or not morphine is mediating certain moods or reactions to pain.

Many habits that humans acquire come to be controlled by internal or external stimuli. As a consequence, certain behaviors are performed in the absence of the motivating state that was originally necessary to establish that habit. Nichols's research shows that even animals will learn to use a drug out of habit. Because morphine has the capacity to short-circuit various biological drives, people sometimes use morphine when they should be doing such things as eating, drinking, and establishing social relationships. It has been suggested that the failure of most Vietnam veterans to re-addict themselves can be explained in terms of learning.

Endorphins have been implicated in a wide range of phenomenon including self-injury, exercise addiction, risk-taking and even music.

Rats can be induced to become addicted to morphine if they are subjected to very restricted living conditions. The reason, it has been suggested, is that under restricted living conditions the rats are unable to experience natural rewards. One implication of this research is that people will have a tendency to become addicted or re-addicted when they live in an environment that prevents them from experiencing natural rewards. Although it has been suggested that the failure of the Vietnam veterans to re-addict themselves can be explained in terms of principles of learning, a more cognitive interpretation of this finding is that social acceptability may have played an important role not only in the initial addiction of the Vietnam veterans but in the failure to re-addict themselves. Others have argued that the presence of more natural reinforcers might account for the failure of most Vietnam veterans to re-addict themselves upon returning to the U.S.

Stimulants: Cocaine and Amphetamines

Although heroin and cannabis have been reported to induce feelings of euphoria, controlled studies comparing heroin and cannabis with amphetamines and cocaine have shown that not only do amphetamines and cocaine more reliably produce euphoria, but the euphoria is far more dramatic (intense) than the euphoria associated with heroin or cannabis (see Grinspoon & Hedblom, 1975).

Two of the best known stimulants (or euphoria-producing drugs) are cocaine and the amphetamines. Both work in a very similar way.

Biological Component

Cocaine is a naturally occurring chemical that can be found in significant quantities in the leaves of two species of the coca shrub. Cocaine reliably produces positive feelings in many people. Researchers have found that people have difficulty discriminating small doses (less than 10 milligrams) of cocaine from a placebo. At moderate to high levels (25 to 100 milligrams), people who take cocaine intranasally reliably report euphoria within 15 to 30 seconds. Some people may experience anxiety, depression, fatigue, and a desire for more cocaine 45 to 60 minutes after taking a 100-milligram dose. There is often a crash period of extreme discomfort after a large amount of cocaine is smoked or injected. This effect is less common when cocaine is taken intranasally. As is the case with many other drugs, it appears that the adverse effects (discomfort or disturbing thoughts) are associated with higher doses (Van Dyke & Byck, 1982).

Amphetamines generally reduce feelings of fatigue while increasing feelings of efficiency, endurance, and perseverance. It is important to note that although people under the influence of amphetamines may experience feelings of reduced fatigue or of greater efficiency, their behavior may not be consistent with those feelings. They may, in fact, behave in a very inefficient manner,

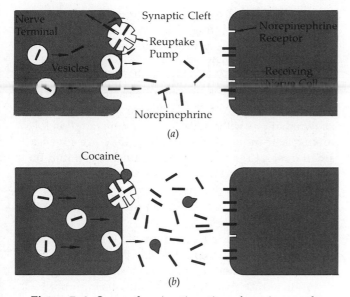

Figure 7–6. Sympathomimetic action of cocaine results when the reuptake of such neurotransmitters as norepinephrine is blocked at synapses of the sympathetic nervous system. (The sympathetic nervous system controls such functions as heart rate and blood pressure.) When the molecules of the neurotransmitter are released from vesicles in the nerve terminal (*a*), the molecules cross the synaptic cleft and stimulate the succeeding nerve cell. Ordinarily, some of the neurotransmitter molecules in the cleft are pumped back into the nerve that released them. In the presence of cocaine the action of the reuptake pump is blocked (*b*) and the stimulation by the neurotransmitter molecules increases as their concentration in the synaptic cleft builds up. (From C. VanDyke and R.I. Byck," Cocaine." *Scientific American*, March 1982, *246*, 128-141. Copyright © 1982 by Scientific American, Inc. All rights reserved.)

and their movements may suggest fatigue rather than energy. Under certain conditions, amphetamines can nevertheless lead to more energetic and efficient behavior. For example, amphetamines have been shown to facilitate such physical and intellectual activities as swimming, running, and cognitive problem-solving tasks. Faster conditioning and decreases in reaction time have also been reported (Barr, 1969; Grinspoon & Hedblom, 1975; Kalant, 1973; Swinson & Eaves, 1978).

There is considerable evidence that amphetamines produce their effect in much the same way as cocaine. That is, they stimulate the output of dopamine.

The dopamine system. There is a great deal of evidence that the effects of cocaine are due to its action on the brain. It has been suggested that cocaine produces at least some of its effect by blocking the reuptake of dopamine and other monoamine transmitters such as norepinephrine and serotonin (Spealman, Madras & Bergman, 1989). Figure 7-6 conceptualizes what happens when cocaine blocks the reuptake pump; concentrations of monoamines such as norepinephrine and dopamine increase at the synapses. Because we have evidence that an increase in norepinephrine or dopamine at the synapses is associated with feelings of euphoria and a decrease is associated with feelings of depression, it follows that the feelings of euphoria are probably linked directly to these concentration levels. It should be noted that tricyclic antidepressants also block the reuptake of norepinephrine. In other words, it is believed that tricyclics work because they alter such monoamines as norepinephrine, dopamine levels, and serotonin.

The current evidence suggests that cocaine's main effect is by way of the dopamine uptake system. When antagonists to dopamine are administered to animals, they reduce the reinforcing effects of cocaine, whereas antagonists to norepinephrine and serotonin do not reduce the reinforcing effects of cocaine (Bergman, Kamien & Spealman, 1990).

Dopamine receptors. There is considerable evidence that there are recognition sites for dopamine. It is believed that the dopamine antagonists work by selectively blocking the recognition sites, thus not allowing dopamine to bind to these sites. Thus, even if cocaine is creating artificially high levels of dopamine at these sites by interfering with the uptake system, cocaine has no effect because these sites are being blocked.

Dopamine and the self-reward systems. Research has shown that drugs that elevate catecholamines facilitate self-stimulation and drugs that block catecholamines block self-stimulation (Routtenberg, 1978;

Wise & Stein, 1969). The direct link between the presence of certain catecholamines and the operation of the self-reward systems suggests that the experience of certain pleasurable moods, such as euphoria, may be due to the activation of one or more of these systems by the catecholamines.

Catecholamines can be activated in a variety of ways other than by means of drugs. Many natural activities affect catecholamine level. For example, the work of Davis (1973) and Howley (1976) clearly shows that running increases the level of norepinephrine. Zuckerman's work indicates that all forms of sensation-seeking behavior may increase norepinephrine levels (Zuckerman, 1978a; Zuckerman, Buchsbaum, & Murphy, 1980).

Learned Component

A series of experiments provided evidence for the hypothesis that dopaminergic activity can be conditioned (Schiff, 1982). In these studies, rats were administered amphetamine or apomorphine (drugs known to affect dopamine metabolism) and placed in a novel environment. These drugs produced certain predictable behavioral changes in head bobbing, sniffing, activity levels, amount of rearing and so forth. After ten training trials they were given a test trial in which a placebo was administered. It was found that when the animals given the placebo were placed in the novel environment (the CS), they showed the distinctive pattern of behaviors that tend to be produced by injections of amphetamine or apomorphine, while the controls (given drug treatment but not placed in the distinctive novel environment) did not. To determine if this pattern of responses was mediated by changes in dopamine metabolism, the animals were sacrificed so certain chemicals in the brains could be carefully analyzed. The results of this analysis provided support for the idea that the conditioned responses to cues previously associated with amphetamine and apomorphine (the novel environment) were mediated by increased dopamine turnover.

The results have important implications for understanding addiction. There is an abundance of data which show that medically *cured addicts* (people who

have gone through a drying-out period and have received drug counseling) will often re-addict themselves upon returning to an environment in which drugs were previously used. This may be due to conditioning. If the environment stimulates dopaminergic activity, this may be sufficient to reinstate the habit of taking a drug (Schiff, 1982). Research with rats has shown that rats will reinitiate drug administration following self-induced abstinence if they are given a small dose of the drug (Pickens, 1968). It should be noted in this context that a basic tenet of incentive motivational theory is that reinforcers have response-instigating as well as response-reinforcing effects (Bindra, 1974).

Using this same line of argument, Wise (1988) has argued that a person could reinstate a craving for a particular drug after he or she has been *cured* or gone through withdrawal by self-administering another drug that activates the common brain system that mediates positive reinforcement for that drug. For example, since cocaine and heroin activate the same underlying system, a person "cured" or who has gone through withdrawal from heroin could activate a heroin craving by taking cocaine.

The fact that people are often inclined to re-addict themselves to a drug when a particular mood is elicited (e.g., stress, anxiety, depression) can also be understood in terms of conditioning. If that mood has been linked to the habit of taking a drug, then there will be a tendency for that habit to be evoked whenever that particular mood arises.

Cognitive Component

Expectations. What do people say they experience when they take amphetamines or cocaine? Some people claim it produces a wonderful sense of euphoria, some claim it gives them a sense of control, some claim it makes them experience a sense of power, some claim it improves their sexual prowess, some claim it makes them more creative, some claim they experience nothing, and so forth. Amongst all these claims the most common is that people say they experience a sense of euphoria. The diverse feelings and thoughts that people experience when they take such drugs as amphetamines or cocaine depends to a very large degree on their expectations (Peele, 1985). If they were led to believe before they took the drug that something would happen, it seems to happen. While there is little evidence for withdrawal symptoms for cocaine, some people do report negative withdrawal symptoms. Some people show tolerance effects even though the research demonstrates that cocaine sensitizes rather than desensitizes the dopamine system (Vezina, Kalivas, & Stewart, 1987). There is even some data which show that the magnitude of the reaction, whatever it is, is linked to how much you paid for the drug; the more you paid the better the effect you report.

Relapse. One of the central issues in all drug research is the problem of relapse. Why do we relapse? It has been suggested that one of the main components of relapse is linked to our memory of the effects of the drug. What we may experience is a craving for the experience that we remember we had with the drug (Wise, 1988). According to this interpretation, we are not compelled to take the drug, rather we have some control over the process. We may, for example, be able to become mindful of the consequences of giving in to our craving. Alternatively, we may learn to substitute other memories of good experiences that we had participating in non-drug-related activities.

Summary

Both cocaine and amphetamines are known for their ability to produce feelings of euphoria, their ability to reduce feelings of fatigue, and their ability to increase feelings of efficiency. They are sometimes used to enhance both physical and mental performance. Cocaine and amphetamines appear to work by increasing the concentration of neurotransmitters such as norepinephrine and dopamine at the synapses. The general consensus is that the dopamine system activates the self-reward system in the brain and that it is this system that produces the euphoria that has been linked to cocaine and amphetamines. While cocaine and amphetamines do not produce a tolerance effect nor do they produce symptoms of withdrawal, they are habit-forming.

There is evidence that the dopaminergic system can be conditioned. One implication of this fact is that when a particular mood is elicited it may prime the dopaminergic system and lead to re-addiction.

People experience a wide range of emotions in connection with using cocaine and amphetamines. It has been suggested that the diversity of reactions is due in large part to expectations that people have. The main explanation for relapse with cocaine is the memory that people have about what the drug does.

Relaxants: The New Antianxiety Drugs

Estimates indicate that 7% of the U.S. population experience anxiety to the degree that it becomes debilitating (Katz, 1990). Anxiety is a common emotion and thought to be normal as long as it does not become completely debilitating. It becomes a disorder when it has no known cause and when it is completely out of proportion to the danger. Panic attacks, phobias and obsessive compulsive disorders are all examples of anxiety that is debilitating. It is interesting to note that on the average twice as many females as males experience debilitating anxiety (11.0 % for females and 5.1% for males). Most of that difference is due to the higher incidence of phobias in women (8.0% of the females and 3.4% of the males).

Because there are so many people who experience debilitating anxiety, there has been a great deal of interest in producing drugs that will help them to cope. The two most common antianxiety drugs are chloriazepoxide (Librium) and diazepam (Valium). While these drugs have proved to be highly effective, they also turned out to be highly addictive. Statistics indicate that about 15% of the U.S. population is addicted to Valium (Ledwidge, 1980). This is with a drug that was supposed to be nonaddictive and vastly superior to the barbiturates. The reason so many people are addicted is that these drugs have not only been prescribed for debilitating anxiety, but have also been prescribed for a wide variety of complaints including such things as inability to sleep, inability to relax, inability to cope, short-term as well as chronic stress. They have even become a popular *street drug* that is handled by pushers.

Biological Component

Librium and Valium belong to a class of drugs called benzodiazepines. The effects of these drugs come from their action on the central nervous system. The main effects are decreased anxiety, sedation, muscle relaxation and anticonvulsant activity. While they initially produce drowsiness, the effect tends to wear off in a couple of days. When combined with alcohol, however, sedation is a serious problem. In addition, the diazepines produce substantial memory impairment, motor incoordination, ataxia and confusion in some people. Even though it has been suggested that a large number of people are addicted, it appears that the majority of patients who use benzodiazepines do not abuse the drug (Woods et al., 1987).

The GABA System

The general consensus is that the effect of the benzodiazepines is due to the actions of Gamma-aminobutyric acid (GABA) system. GABA is a naturally occurring inhibitory neurotransmitter (Cooper, Bloom, & Roth, 1982; Tallman et al., 1980). That means that GABA somehow reduces the flow of neural transmission. There are GABA receptor sites to which GABA will bind and produce the effects indicated above. The ability of GABA to bind, however, does not appear to be fixed but rather is dependent on the presence of benzodiazepines. Benzodiazepines themselves have receptor sites, and when they bind to these receptor sites they increase the ability of GABA to bind. The net effect is that the potency of GABA is momentarily enhanced. The fact that there are receptors for such drugs as Librium and Valium suggests that the body probably produces its own benzodiazepines, though naturally produced benzodiazepines have not yet been isolated. This whole process is presented graphically in Figure 7-7, which shows that the shape of the GABA site changes when Valium has itself binded with its receptor site. By changing the shape of the GABA site (like making it possible for a key to fit a lock), more GABA is allowed to exert its effect. In other words, in order for GABA to be maximally effective, benzodiazepines must be present. When they are not present

the amount of GABA remains the same, but they lose their ability to bind and thereby lose their ability to effect a change.

GABA itself is not the final part of this chain of events. GABA receptors are themselves thought to trigger the opening of chloride channels, and it is these chloride channels that lead to the decreased firing rate of critical neurons in many parts of the central nervous system (Dykstra, 1992).

One of the main antagonists for GABA is biuculline. Such antagonists completely block the effects of benzodiazepines and thus allow researchers to establish if a benzodiazepine is mediating a particular behavior.

Learned Component

Why benzodiazepines are used. It is important to remember that benzodiazepines are typically prescribed to help people deal with a wide range of aversive or noxious situations such as anxiety, death of a friend or relative, and all types of stress such as job stress, loss of a job, divorce, financial crises, and so forth. As suggested earlier, when people use a drug that will allow them to escape a noxious or aversive situation (a negative reinforcer), they become very susceptible to the reinforcing effects of that drug. Thus, it is not surprising that it has been found that addiction to the benzodiazepines is relatively high in the general population. Even though the benzodiazepines may not produce physical symptoms of withdrawal, that does not mean people are not addicted. Nor does the fact that people do not abuse benzodiazepines mean that they are not addicted (Woods et al., 1987).

Negative emotions are often persistent and pervasive. The thing about anxiety and stress which is so important to remember is that these emotions are not only aversive and noxious, but once triggered they tend to be very persistent and pervasive. That is, it is very hard to ignore them or to distract oneself from them. As a result, these emotions tend to take complete charge of our attention. In terms of what we know about the principles of learning, this fact is very important. While

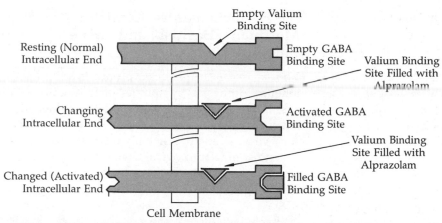

Figure 7–7. Valium/GABA receptor. This simplified schematic drawing shows three stages in activation of the receptor complex: (1) The receptor, lodged in a cell membrane, has unfilled binding sites for GABA and a benzodiazepine (Valium, alprazolam, etc.) molecule. (2) When alprazolam binds to its site, like a key in a lock, it may open (activate) the GABA site, allowing it to bind a GABA molecule. (3) Once both alprazolam and GABA are bound and active, the intracellular end of the receptor may change its shape, setting off a "chemical domino effect" that can transmit a message inside the cell. (From S. M. Fishman and D. V. Sheehan, "Valium/GABA Receptor." *Psychology Today*, 1985. Reprinted from Psychology Today Magazine. Copyright © 1985 American Psychological Association. Reprinted with permission.)

people might be able to distract themselves from cues that might elicit cocaine consumption (assuming people are using it for recreational reasons), it would be very difficult for them to distract themselves from the fact that their heart is pounding because they are anxious. As a result, if people have learned to associate the reduction of one or more of these emotions with the self-administration of benzodiazepines, the probability of their doing so again should be very high. Further, if people have no other alternatives available to them for dealing with these emotions (which is often why they have been prescribed the drug in the first place), the likelihood of their using benzodiazepines should be high.

Becoming benzodiazepine-free. In order for people to wean themselves off drugs such as the benzodiazepines, people must either learn how to better cope with the events that elicit these emotions or learn how to reduce the emotions. Learning how to cope, unfortunately, is not that easy because people normally need

to acquire coping without the support of the drug that enables them to function. While it is possible to teach people how to reduce emotions such as anxiety and stress by teaching them relaxation techniques, this is not the best long-term strategy. In the long run we need to be in control of those events that elicit our emotions.

Cognitive Component

The tendency to view the world as threatening. There is considerable evidence that while some people view the world as threatening, others tend to view it as more benign (Franken, Gibson, & Rowland, 1992). Those who view the world as threatening are people who are characterized by high anxiety. While it can be argued that anxiety causes people to view the world as threatening, there is growing evidence that we can break this causal chain by teaching people to either be habitually more relaxed or by teaching them to habitually view the world as less threatening. It is clear from the work of

Benson that when people become habitually more re-laxed they change their view of the world. Among other things, they tend to see the world as offering more alternatives and opportunities. It is also clear from a variety of sources that when people learn to think about the world in more positive terms they are less anxious, more in control of their emotions, and tend to accomplish more (Seligman, 1990). In the final analysis, a central feature of being in control has to do with our beliefs about our ability to effectively deal with the world. In the chapter on Optimism, I will discuss in more detail how you can learn to change the way you think. In the last chapter I will talk about how you can learn to change the way you think about the world and your ability to deal with the world. The point I simply want to emphasize here is that addiction to benzodiazepines must be viewed in the larger context of how people think about themselves. People use benzodiazepines because they are experiencing powerful negative emotions. The reason they are experiencing such strong negative emotions is due, among other things, to their view of themselves and their ability to cope with the world in which they live.

Summary

Two of the most well-known antianxiety drugs are Librium and Valium. They exert their influence by making it possible for GABA to bind at the receptors. GABA reduces anxiety by reducing the flow of neural transmission. What GABA seems to do is trigger the opening of chloride channels which lead to decreased firing of critical neurons in many parts of the central nervous system.

Benzodiazepines have the power to reduce a number of noxious or aversive psychological states. As *avoidant drugs*, they are believed to be highly addictive. Since negative emotions are highly aversive, the occurrence of a negative emotion is often sufficient to trigger a relapse.

Since people who are anxious tend to view the world as threatening, it has been suggested that the way to make people less dependent on such drugs as the benzodiazepines is to train people to see the world as less threatening and having more alternatives.

The Hallucinogenics: Cannabis (Marijuana, Hashish) and LSD—Biological Component

Cannabis (marijuana, hashish) produces a number of rather mild physical symptoms, including increased pulse rate, rise in blood pressure, dilation of the pupils, redness of the eyes (due to dilation of the conjunctival blood vessels), and occasionally breathlessness, choking, and some neurological changes reflected in unsteadiness, muscular twitches, tremors of the tongue, and changes in the deep reflexes (Swinson & Eaves, 1978).

Psychologically, cannabis produces a wide variety of reactions. Naive subjects often experience anxiety and apprehension. These reactions, however, may not reflect the action of the drug so much as fear of the unknown. Generally, the effects of the drug are agreeable. Besides a general feeling of euphoria, there are distortions of time and space, together with illusions and even hallucinations. Often there are changes in body image, together with a feeling of depersonalization (Joyce, 1970; Paton & Crown, 1972; Swinson & Eaves, 1978).

LSD (lysergic acid diethylamide) produces a number of changes, including a rise in blood pressure, sweating, dilation of the pupils, increase in muscle tension (sometimes accompanied by nausea), headaches, and lightheadedness (Swinson & Eaves, 1978). These changes are due to the stimulant action of the drug on the reticular activating system (RAS). In addition, LSD often produces changes in perceptual processes associated with all sense modalities. The most dramatic changes typically occur in connection with visual perception. Objects appear to change in color, shape, and size. Two-dimensional objects may suddenly appear to be three-dimensional. Under certain conditions, people will experience fully formed hallucinations of objects, events, or even people. There are typically alterations in perception of time or the ability to gauge time. The ability to reason is often disturbed, as is the ability to plan ahead.

There is evidence that LSD acts to depress the activity of the serotonin-containing neurons in the raphe nuclei. According to this explanation, serotonin normally inhibits certain kinds of visual and other activities of the brain. The net effect is that LSD disinhibits activity of the neurons in the visual system, the limbic system (the area of the brain linked to emotions), and other brain areas (Jacobs & Trulson, 1979; Jacobs, 1987). It has been shown that drugs that increase the level of serotonin in the human brain reduce the effects of LSD, while drugs that block serotonin magnify the effects of LSD. It should be noted that psilocybin (the active component of *magic mushrooms*) seems to work by the same mechanism.

Learned Component

Addiction to cannabis and LSD does not appear to be a major problem. It is interesting to note that in reviews of addiction to drugs, cannabis and LSD often receive only passing attention (e.g., *Journal of Abnormal Psychology, May, 1988*; Special Issues: Models of Addiction). That is not to say that people cannot and do not become addicted. Rather, in our society, the number of people who have become dysfunctional because of cannabis or LSD addiction is relatively small in comparison to many of the other drugs people use such as alcohol, heroin and cocaine. Of the two drugs, cannabis seems to be the one that people are more likely to use habitually. That is likely due to the fact that it is used less often. In general, people rarely become addicted to drugs they use infrequently. One reason LSD is used less often or habitually is because it becomes virtually impossible to do other things while under the influence of LSD. In other words, in order to use LSD people need to devote large blocks of time to the activity . Cannabis, in contrast, can be used more casually and in the context of normal living. This means, among other things, that it can be used more often, one of the things that has been linked to addiction.

Cognitive Component

Altered perceptions. Cannabis and LSD are mainly known for their ability to alter perception, especially visual perception. *Psychedelic designs* came from the

1960s and represented the visual experiences that people had when they used cannabis and LSD. Many of these designs were actually made while under the influence of one of these drugs. Other sensory systems are also altered including auditory and tactile. Many artists and musicians in the 1960s used cannabis and LSD because they felt it increased their ability to be creative by allowing them to see the world differently.

Links to antitraditonal orientation. In the 1960s, both cannabis and LSD were extensively used by people called *hippies*, a throwback to the phrase *being hip* that was used by earlier generations. This group of people were characterized by such things as their rejection of traditional values (e.g., work ethic) and their attempts to create a more communal way of life to replace the traditional family. Many of these people came from homes in which both parents worked in order to achieve what has come to be called a *materialistic lifestyle,* a lifestyle characterized by such things as a large and comfortable home in the suburbs, fancy cars, designer clothes. In order to achieve this lifestyle, people had to work long and hard, often neglecting their children and friends in the process of achieving the much-valued materialistic goals. It is not surprising in this context that a group of young people asked themselves the obvious question "Does this make any sense?" From their vantage point they perceived their parents as well as other adults as having lost the meaning of life. Life, they argued was to have friends, experience love, be creative. Using this as their focus they began to share apartments and look for work that would provide for the basic necessities but at the same time allow them to do other things such as create, make love, and develop friendships. The term *free love* came to characterize this movement. Free love meant, among other things, that you did not have to be engaged in some type of social contract such as marriage to enjoy sex nor did you have to purchase sex on the street. Sex was something that was to be freely given and enjoyed. Free love was also highly symbolic of this movement because many believed that the only way for humans to heal their differences was through love. Bumper stickers such as *Make Love Not War* were popular. Not only did this group reject the materialistic view of their

PRACTICAL APPLICATION 7.2

Psychological Health and Adolescent Drug Use

Drug use among adolescents is a growing problem in our society today. Who uses drugs and why? In a recent longitudinal study of adolescent drug use, it was found that adolescents who engage in some drug experimentation (primarily marijuana) were the best adjusted. Frequent drugs users, on the other hand, were maladjusted and showed a distinct personality syndrome characterized by interpersonal alienation, poor impulse control, and emotional distress. Those adolescents in the sample who by age 18 had never experimented with any drug tended to be anxious, emotionally constricted and lacking in basic social skills (Shedler & Block, 1990).

Differences among the groups were evident in early childhood. Observations of parent-child interactions indicated that frequent users and abstainers were judged to have relatively poorer maternal parenting than experimenters. As compared with mothers of experimenters, mothers of frequent users and abstainers were judged to be cold, critical, pressuring and unresponsive to their children's needs. While there was nothing noteworthy about the fathers of the frequent users, fathers of the abstainers (as compared to the father of experimenters) were relatively unresponsive to their children's needs, authoritarian, autocratic and domineering.

The results can be understood if it is recognized that adolescence is normally a time of questioning the traditional values and beliefs of society. Adolescents who feel secure, therefore, feel comfortable in experimenting with drugs. While society may say it is wrong, drugs are readily available to adolescents from their peers. There would be a natural curiosity to experiment and find out for oneself the effects of taking drugs. Because they are reasonably well-adjusted they are not using drugs to escape or avoid and therefore do not get hooked. Frequent users, in contrast, feel alienated and distressed, two conditions that have repeatedly been linked to drug abuse. Because drugs can reduce stress and because frequent users do not feel inhibited to use drugs, they would quickly discover the reinforcing properties of drugs. As a result they would be inclined to get hooked. The abstainers, it appears, do not feel comfortable with the idea of even experimenting with drugs. To experiment would be equivalent to challenging the traditional values that typically characterize authoritarian parents. With authoritarian parents there is always the risk that if they do not approve of your behavior, they are likely to withhold their love and support. Therefore, experimenting is too risky. As a result, they hold in check their natural impulses to question and experiment with drugs. It appears they even hold in check the natural tendency of adolescents to develop new and varied friends. The net result is they develop a personality syndrome characterized by anxiety, emotional restraint, and the absence of social skills.

It should be noted in this context that sensation seekers, known for their curiosity and their desire for new experiences, are characterized by their tendency to experiment with cannabis (Zuckerman, 1979).

parents but they argued that wars were being fought for purely materialistic reasons. Weapons, they argued, were a tremendous source of revenue that made many influential people rich and thus the main motive for wars was not ideological but material.

What started out as a demonstration to the world of what could be achieved if one adopted a more loving and communal approach to life turned sour. The increase in cases of sexually transmitted disease severely limited the practice of *free sex* and many of these communities were infiltrated by drug dealers who saw this as an opportunity to make large sums of money. They brought with them not only crime (e.g., theft) but a sense of mistrust. The experiment with an open and communal society fell on hard times. Many moved away to more isolated locations in an attempt to keep alive their dream of a cooperative society. Nonetheless, the 1960s represented an open challenge by youth to the old guard who held such traditional values as sex only within marriage, the importance of the traditional patriarchal family, the importance of work, and so forth.

Even today, cannabis is often used by people who feel alienated from traditional values (Kandel, 1984). Soldiers in Vietnam used cannabis extensively. As I mentioned earlier in connection with heroin, the Vietnam war was an unpopular war that many soldiers viewed as a political war. Cannabis use tends to be higher in such places as California, where a large number of people tend to hold more antitraditional values. Cannabis use is also higher in young people, an age when traditional values are carefully examined for their worth. During the 1960s, cannabis use on university campuses was very high and coincided with students' challenging the relevance of the university curriculum and the paternal practices that often characterized universities in the 1960s.

Exactly why cannabis has been linked to antitraditonal values is not immediately clear. People who used cannabis and LSD in the 1960s were interested in the whole question of seeing life from different perspectives. In addition to altering visual and auditory perceptions, cannabis and LSD alter perceptions of time. We live in a society that is run by the clock. If you disagree with or would like to challenge the concept of linear time, then you might start by using a drug that itself alters time. Under cannabis and LSD, time can stand still or race ahead. It all depends on the activity in which you are engaged.

It is probably not surprising that when people come to accept more traditional values as they get older, they also tend to stop using cannabis and LSD. Whether these drugs are mere symbols of rebellion or have the capacity to help people see things differently is not clear. We do know that if people believe that a drug can produce certain effects it *will* produce this effect. Clearly, cannabis and LSD are more than mere placebos. They can and do show people that reality as we normally know it can be altered. Time and space can be perceived differently under the influence of these drugs. If time and space can be seen differently, then what else can be seen differently? This desire to see the world differently may be one of the motivating forces for using these drugs. Clearly, it is the motivating force for sensation seekers (Zuckerman, 1979).

Summary

Cannabis has stimulant or euphoric properties but is best known for its ability to distort perceptions of time and space. LSD also has stimulant or euphoric properties and, like cannabis, is known for its ability to alter perceptions. Not only are time and space typically altered, but the sense modalities are usually affected—especially vision. While there is some evidence that cannabis and LSD are addictive, they typically are viewed as drugs which are not a major source of concern. The use of these drugs has been linked to an antitraditional orientation. It is also a drug that has been linked to curiosity and experimentation.

Nicotine — Biological Component

It appears that heavy smokers smoke in order to obtain the effects of nicotine. In a carefully controlled study, Stanley Schachter (1977) showed that when nicotine levels are varied, smokers tend to adjust the number of cigarettes they smoke in order to maintain a constant (preferred) nicotine level.

Nicotine produces a number of physiological changes. One of the primary effects is arousal (Eysenck, 1973). In small doses, nicotine increases arousal, but in larger doses it paradoxically decreases arousal (Armitage, Hall, & Sellers, 1969; Gilbert, 1979). The arousal elicited by nicotine appears to be very similar to the arousal elicited by a variety of agents including amphetamines, caffeine, and LSD (Eysenck, 1973). Unlike other stimulants, however, nicotine produces arousal that is of short duration and is followed by three distinct phases: "a period of EEG alternations between sedation and excitation, a period of behavioral and EEG sedation and sleep, and, finally, a frequent occurrence of paradoxical or activated sleep" (Eysenck,

1973, p. 123). In other words, the effect of cigarettes varies with time after intake.

Wise and Bozarth (1987) have argued that nicotine, like such drugs as caffeine, barbiturates, alcohol, benzodiazepines, cannabis, and phencyclidine, activates the dopaminergic system. Recent research by Susan Wonnacott (1992) indicates nicotine improves learning and memory. It does so, she argues, by mimicking one of the brain's natural signaling molecules: acetylcholine.

Urinary acidity and smoking. People not only smoke more when they are stressed, they tend to smoke more at parties (Silverstein, Kozlowski, & Schachter, 1977). If people smoke for nicotine, then why would they be inclined to smoke more when stressed or when at a party? Is this effect due to stress or perhaps learning? The reason, it turns out, is that there is a link between urinary acidity and the urge to smoke, as well as a link between urinary acidity levels and such things as stress and attending a party.

This is what happens. When people are put under stress or even when they attend a party, their urinary acidity levels increase. This effect appears to be due to changes in metabolism. As metabolism increases so do acidity levels. The interesting thing is that smoking tends to track with urinary acidity levels. But why are people inclined to smoke more when acidity levels are high? It appears that when acidity levels are high nicotine is excreted in the urine at a high rate, thus lowering nicotine levels in the body (Silverstein, Kozlowski, & Schachter, 1977). Since stress is one of the easiest ways to change acidity levels and since stress can also increase smoking, how can we be sure that the increased smoking is really due to urinary acidity levels and not simply to stress?

In a study designed to examine this question, students were studied on days in which one group was required to make class reports (*reporters*) while a second group was not, but would simply be *listeners*. Since giving reports has been found to be a reliable source of stress, it was expected that those students who would be required to give reports would show high urinary acidity levels while those not required to give reports (listeners) would show low urinary acidity (high alka-

line levels). This is in fact what was found (see Figure 7-8). When these same students were tested on a day when there were no class reports, they had almost identical but relatively high acidity levels. The relatively high acidity levels on the no-report day were expected because class participation would normally be expected on such a day, an event that normally elicits a stress response (Schachter, Silverstein, & Perlick, 1977). To separate out the effects due to stress and acidity, some of the students were given bicarbonate of soda in order to reduce acidity levels. As predicted, subjects given the bicarbonate of soda smoked less. Thus, even though they had been stressed, they did not increase their smoking to the same degree as those who were not given bicarbonate of soda.

The bottom line is that people smoke to maintain nicotine levels in the blood. Events that lower nicotine levels increase smoking because they deplete nicotine levels. What is interesting is that a wide range of activities can lead to the depletion of nicotine levels, which can account for why people are inclined to smoke under a wide variety of conditions.

Learned Component

There is considerable evidence that smoking behavior is controlled to a very large degree by cues in the environment, both external and internal. Interestingly, cigarette smoking appears to be governed by internal cues (nicotine levels) in heavy smokers and by external cues in light smokers (Herman, 1974). Herman has shown that light smokers can be made to smoke as much as heavy smokers if the external cues for smoking are made prominent.

It is fascinating that people will often report they didn't enjoy the cigarette they just smoked or they will put out a cigarette shortly after lighting it. In other words, there is evidence from a variety of sources that people often smoke even though they did not experience a *craving*. Conversely, when people do experience a craving they will go to great lengths to have a cigarette. Since it has become common for buildings to be designated as nonsmoking, you will now find people standing in a snowstorm outside their office building puffing on a cigarette. What all this means is that while

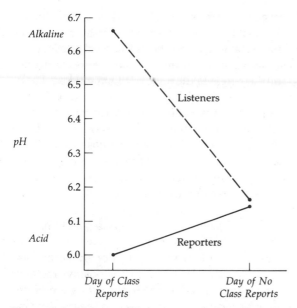

Figure 7–8. Urinary pH among students assigned to give class reports ("reporters") and among their classmates ("listeners"). (From S. Schachter, B. Silverstein, L.T. Kozlowski, C. P. Herman, and B. Leibling, "Effects of Stress on Cigarette Smoking and Urinary pH." *Journal of Experimental Psychology: General*, 1977, *106*, 24-30. Copyright © 1977 by the American Psychological Association. Reprinted with permission.)

smoking is often the result of a habit, there is also a biological basis for smoking.

For most smokers there are many cues which elicit smoking, a fact which creates problems for some people when they attempt to quit. Even if they have successfully weaned themselves from their nicotine dependence, the urge or desire to smoke is often triggered by the presence of one of these cues. Because people come to smoke in the presence of so many cues (until recently it has been widely accepted to do so in our society) the tendency to relapse is very high for smokers. A single cigarette can and often does reestablish the smoking habit in ex-smokers. Not many other drugs are used in such a wide range of cues and therefore, according to learning theory, the relapse rate for them should be much lower than for nicotine.

People report that even after months or even years of not smoking they will suddenly get the urge to smoke when they find themselves in a situation that was previously linked to smoking. According to Wise, the situation elicited a memory for the pleasure that people once experienced (Wise, 1988). In other words, even in the absence of a biological need, the desire or urge to smoke can be triggered.

Cognitive Component

One of the things people are often asked to do when they enter a smoking program is to keep track of when they smoke so that they can become aware of the cues that control their smoking. Habits by their very nature are automatic, which means that we do not have to make a conscious decision each time we do something. That decision is made for us by a program that often operates at an unconscious level of our brain.

The idea behind making things conscious is to force people to make a conscious decision each time they engage in a particular behavior. The theory is that if people are forced to make conscious decisions they will gain control over their old habits (Langer, 1989). In the process of gaining control, people can then replace old behaviors with new behaviors. For example, if I was inclined to have a cigarette each time I had a cup of coffee, I might decide not to do this and instead have a piece of gum after each cup of coffee. One of the unfortunate byproducts of such substitution procedures is that I may develop a new habit which is to chew gum after drinking coffee. Indeed, I have a friend who has successfully quit smoking but is now a habitual gum chewer. Eventually gum chewing should disappear because gum does not have the same reinforcing properties of nicotine (at least as far as we know).

One of the important ideas behind this approach is that people learn to deal with the wide range of cues that elicit their behavior. Even if they relapse, they have acquired an important set of skills related to a particular aspect of their addiction that will eventually help them deal with their total addiction. In other words, relapse, which is so common in drug addiction (Niaura, Rohsenow, Binkoff, Monti, Pedraza, & Abrams, 1988), is not to be viewed as starting from scratch. Rather, relapse is something that happens on the way to acquiring not just a single skill but a number of skills that are necessary for eventual success. A common problem for many smokers who are also drinkers is relapsing when drinking alcohol (probably because of the disinhibition effect that comes with alcohol consumption). Eventual success, therefore, demands that they learn how to deal with this situation.

Summary

Nicotine in small to moderate doses typically acts as a stimulant. In larger doses it can have a calming effect. The fact that smoking often increases in stressful situations suggests that some people smoke to reduce stress. Like many other drugs, it has been suggested that nicotine works by activating the dopaminergic system. There is also good evidence that urinary acidity mediates the tendency to smoke. When urinary acidity levels go up, so does smoking. Stress leads to increases in urinary acidity levels which may trigger the desire to smoke.

There is considerable evidence that smoking is triggered by cues in the environment. The fact that people smoke in so many locations means their smoking behavior is often conditioned to a diverse and extensive set of environmental cues. Teaching people to become aware of the cues that trigger their smoking habit and encouraging them to learn other ways of responding to these cues has been suggested as an important method of capitalizing on the power of cognition.

Alcohol

Without question the drug which has received the most attention by researchers is alcohol. Alcohol is not only widely used but is widely abused in our society and many parts of the world. People often find it very difficult to quit drinking, and numerous programs have been developed to help people to control their drinking or stop drinking altogether.

Biological Component

In low doses, alcohol stimulates the central nervous system. In moderate doses, it depresses activity of the brain by direct action on the brain. This leads to a disinhibition effect that will be discussed shortly. The heart rate rises with moderate doses, and the mechanical efficiency of the heart as a pump is reduced. In large doses, alcohol temporarily increases the level of blood glucose. Later, the blood glucose level falls, often to disastrously low levels. Alcohol tends to decrease the formation of glucose in the liver and accelerate the deposition of fat in the liver, a condition giving rise to cirrhosis of the liver. Large amounts of alcohol affect the cerebellum, producing the motor impairment typically associated with large alcohol intake (Swinson & Eaves, 1978).

Alcohol and the dopaminergic system. Wise (1988) has argued that alcohol produces its pleasurable effect largely through the activation of the dopaminergic system. Thus, like many other drugs, the positive feelings that people experience are due to the activation of the dopaminergic system and its effect on the positive reward systems of the brain. To understand alcohol, however, it is necessary to understand some of its other effects.

Endorphin hypothesis of alcohol addiction. There is considerable evidence that alcohol increases endorphin activity (Blum, Hamilton, & Wallace, 1977; Davis & Walsh, 1970; Vereby & Blum, 1979). This can provide a ready explanation for the sense of euphoria that drinkers often experience. This finding also offers an explanation as to why people become addicted to alcohol. If alcohol can stimulate endorphin output, it could eventually produce a marked reduction in the concentration of endorphins circulating in the body. When this happens a person experiences a negative mood state together with other symptoms of withdrawal. Through the learning process, a person would learn to drink alcohol in order to further stimulate endorphin activity. In other words, the person would become addicted to alcohol.

What is not clear from this explanation is how alcohol can stimulate endorphin activity if the stores of endorphins are depleted or markedly reduced. It may be that alcohol produces metabolites that can stimulate the receptors directly, thereby acting as a substitute for endorphins, or that alcohol somehow increases the

Alcohol is readily available in our society and is often used in a social context. Whether or not people become addicted depends to a large degree on whether or not they use alcohol to avoid an aversive or negative state.

opiate receptors' sensitivity to endorphins, or that when the stores are reduced alcohol is still capable of triggering the output of still more endorphins. For a discussion of the evidence related to these hypotheses, see a review by Joseph Volpicelli (1987).

Depression and alcoholism. Researchers have repeatedly found a link between alcohol abuse and depression. Until recently it was concluded that people drink to reduce their depression. In other words, depression somehow leads to drinking. There is now good evidence that the cause/effect relationship is just the reverse. Vaillant (1983) started tracking a group of 600 adolescents before any drinking problems had arisen. He concluded, among other things, that a difficult life was rarely a major reason for developing alcohol dependence. In a *Nova* segment broadcast on public television, Vaillant said, "I found to my surprise that alcoholics are depressed because they drink; they don't

drink because they are depressed." This finding, of course, is consistent with the observation that alcohol leads to the depletion of dopamine/norepinephrine.

Alcohol and the disinhibition effect. Because one of the main functions of the cortex is to inhibit behavior (Eysenck, 1973), the depressant action of alcohol on the cortex (and the reticular activating system) produces a state of disinhibition. That is, behaviors that are normally inhibited are freely expressed under the influence of alcohol. There have been several demonstrations of this phenomenon. It was first shown by Masserman and Yum (1946). Cats that showed no inclination to drink alcohol were trained to obtain food from a closed feeding box. Once this habit was well learned, the cats were given an air blast when they opened the box. This noxious stimulus not only disrupted the cats' normal feeding pattern but produced a number of emotional responses that Masserman and Yum labeled *experimen-*

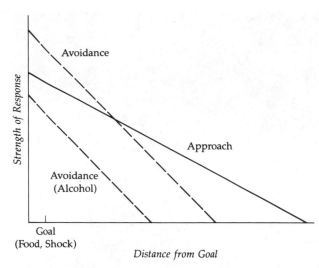

Figure 7–9. Approach and avoidance gradients for appetitive and aversive goal stimuli. Alcohol produces a general reduction in the tendency to avoid while leaving the tendency to approach unaffected. (Based on J. J. Conger, " Reinforcement Theory and the Dynamics of Alcoholism." *Quarterly Journal of Studies on Alcohol,* 1956, *17,* 296-305.)

tal neurosis. When the cats were given alcohol, they approached the food box and persisted in spite of the noxious air blast. Many of these cats came to prefer a milk-alcohol mixture over plain milk. Other work has confirmed that alcohol tends to reduce anxiety in the type of situation that Masserman and Yum created (Smart, 1965).

Since Masserman and Yum's situation is a classic approach/avoidance conflict, Conger (1956) decided to determine whether alcohol was increasing the tendency to approach or decreasing the ·tendency to avoid. Conger first taught rats to eat at a particular location and then introduced shock at the feeding site. After measuring the rats' tendency to approach the food site under normal and alcoholic states, Conger concluded that alcohol reduced the avoidance gradient. His findings can be summarized in the form of a general model that includes approach and avoidance gradients (Figure 7-9). It has not always been possible to confirm these findings (for example, M. Weiss, 1958). There is considerable evidence, nevertheless, that alcohol does reduce emotional

reactivity in frustrating situations and does lead to a greater persistence of goal-directed behavior in such situations (Barry, Wagner, & Miller, 1962).

Alcohol is frequently used in connection with sex. In small amounts, alcohol seems to facilitate sexual interest and performance. This effect presumably is due to the fact that many people experience inhibitions in connection with sex, inhibitions which are reduced when alcohol is consumed. In large amounts, alcohol lowers testosterone output in males, thus often reducing sexual interest or performance or both (Farkas & Rosen, 1976).

Learned Component

Multiple determinants of behavior. According to the principles of learning, any time a behavior occurs in the presence of a stimulus, that behavior will tend to come under the control of that stimulus. In other words, an association tends to develop between a stimulus and a behavior. In this way, a given behavior can come to be controlled by a wide variety of stimuli. If a person tends to drink alcohol when he is anxious, for example, he will develop the habit of drinking alcohol whenever he feels anxious. Similarly, if he tends to drink with dinner, after a time he will develop a habit of drinking with dinner. If he learns to drink in social situations, a tendency will develop to drink whenever he is part of a social gathering. The high alcoholism rate in France becomes understandable in light of this fact.

Alcoholism in France versus Italy. Since France has a good climate for grapes, one of the main industries of France is wine making. Hence, wine is so easily available that it has been customary in many households to drink it throughout the day. Wine is often drunk with breakfast, lunch, and dinner, and between meals too, either to quench thirst or to lubricate social occasions (Swinson & Eaves, 1978). Thus the French tend, from a very early age, to drink wine extensively under a wide variety of stimuli, or cues. As we have noted, alcohol tends to reduce such aversive states as stress and anxiety and to produce feelings of well-being, power, and arousal. The average French citizen has ample opportunity to experience the wide range of reinforcing effects that alcohol produces in various situations, and so to form multiple associations of alcohol intake with internal and external cues.

Italy also has a good climate for grapes and has also developed an extensive wine industry, yet its rate of alcoholism is relatively low (Swinson & Eaves, 1978). The reason for this difference can be found in the fact that most Italians drink wine only with the evening meal. Therefore, drinking is restricted to a particular time and a particular setting. Drunkenness is not condoned. Accordingly, when Italians drink, they tend to drink moderately (Swinson & Eaves, 1978). Since alcoholism usually results from the abuse of alcohol (too much and for the wrong reasons), Italians have less opportunity than the French to learn to associate alcohol with a wide variety of internal and external cues.

Treating alcoholism using principles of learning. There has been growing interest in using the principles outlined above to treat addicts, especially alcoholics (Miller & Muñoz, 1976). The basic aim is to teach the person to restrict his drinking to particular situations and then to limit the amount he drinks in those situations. If the person associates with people who drink excessively, he is encouraged to find new friends; if he goes to a place where alcohol is readily available, he is encouraged to seek out places where it is more restricted. In essence, the goal of such programs is to put drinking under external control, as the very nature of alcohol seems to make it difficult for the alcoholic to learn internal control.

Cognitive Component

Beliefs and expectations. People's beliefs and expectations about the positive effects they can expect from drinking alcohol are an important predictor of drinking behavior (Stacy, Widaman, & Marlatt, 1990). It has been suggested that while these positive expectations can come from a variety of sources, the main source of our expectations is our own past experiences with alcohol (Cox & Klinger, 1988).

When people are given a placebo in place of alcohol they often experience a wide range of not only voli-

tional behaviors (ones they want and can control) but nonvolitional behaviors (ones they do not want or can't control) (Kirsch, 1985). Many of the expectations people hold are a part of our cultural heritage. That is, we have come to believe that certain things will happen when we use a drug such as alcohol. It has been shown, for example, that people become more aggressive and sexually aroused when they erroneously believe that they have been drinking alcohol (Wilson, 1981). Alcoholics even *lose control* when they have been misinformed that they have been drinking alcohol (Engle & Williams, 1972). One of the criteria often used to determine whether a person is an alcoholic is whether the individual can stop drinking after a single drink. The fact that alcoholics lose control in the absence of alcohol intake suggests that it is the belief about what alcohol does when they are addicted (it makes them lose control) rather than the alcohol itself that leads to loss of control. After reviewing studies on the role of expectancy, Hull and Bond (1986) concluded: "Expectancy increases the incidence of illicit social behaviors and has few effects on nonsocial acts. Such a pattern of behavior is consistent with the hypothesis that expectancy provides an attributional excuse to engage in desired but socially prohibited acts" (p. 358).

It is interesting to note that as a source of antisocial behavior, alcohol has been implicated in 70% of fatal automobile accidents, 65% of murders, 88% of knifings, 65% of spouse batterings, 55% of violent child abuse and 60% of burglaries, to mention a few (National Commission on the Causes and Prevention of Violence, 1970).

Alcohol and Myopia

While expectation seems to play an important role in the effects people experience, Steele and Josephs (1990) have argued that expectations alone do not explain the effects. They point out that, under the influence of alcohol, the same person can be aggressive and belligerent one night, amiable and generous another night, and morose and withdrawn a third night. If expectation alone were responsible, one would expect greater consistency.

They argue that alcohol causes *myopia*. Myopia is characterized by short-sighted information processing

PRACTICAL APPLICATION 7.3

Why Do Some People Become Addicted While Others Do Not?
A Theoretical Analysis of How an Addiction Develops

To understand why one person might become addicted to a drug while another might not, it is necessary to chart a typical addiction pattern. The term *addiction* is used here to refer to the development of a psychological dependency or strong psychological need. In the course of taking a drug, a person can experience a variety of effects, depending on his or her ongoing motivational state. If a person takes morphine when he is tired, for example, one of the main feelings he will experience is a lessening of fatigue. If he takes morphine when he is anxious, he will experience a lessening of anxiety together with a general feeling of well-being. If he should take morphine when he is lonely, he will experience a reduction in loneliness. Because each of these psychological states is more or less distinct, one can learn to use a drug for a wide variety of reasons. Any or all of these states could, therefore, come to control the tendency to use a particular drug.

When people first use drugs, they typically do so under rather well-defined conditions. For example, they may drink alcohol on Friday nights with friends, or they may smoke marijuana late in the evenings, again with friends. When a drug is used under very limited conditions, the person has very limited opportunity to learn the full extent to which the drug can alter various motivational states. Many of the popular drugs have very pervasive effects. Heroin in particular can reduce a number of negative psychological states in addition to producing a general state of euphoria. Over time, many people begin to use drugs under a wider range of stimulus conditions. For example, someone might start having a beer after work. Because alcohol in small to moderate amounts is a stimulant, the person might learn to use beer as a means of warding off the fatigue that she experiences after a hard day of work. Because alcohol can reduce feelings of anxiety experienced in social situations, she might also start to use alcohol as an aid to enjoying social gatherings. Thus, as she uses a drug under

in which people come to ignore certain pieces of information that would normally inhibit their behavior. Instead of attending to all the relevant cues they attend to only the most salient cues. Take, for example, a situation in which one encounters his boss at a cocktail party the same day he had a negative encounter with that boss. Still reeling from this encounter, the most salient thing in his life at this moment is his feelings of injustice and anger. Normally he would decide not to "chew out" the boss because this could result in embarrassment for both of them, it could provoke a further negative encounter, and it could even lead to the loss of his job. In other words, normally we are able to deal with the complexity of the situation and act appropriately, which in this case means to avoid the impulse to chew out the boss. Under alcohol, however, as Steele and Josephs argue, we are limited in our ability to deal with the complexity or the amount of information and, as a result, we focus only on what is most salient, which in this case would be our feelings of anger. As a result we do not consider other things such as the presence of other people, the possible negative implications of expressing our anger, and the fact that we were not entirely without blame.

What makes their theory so appealing is that it can explain not only why alcohol is often linked to increased aggression but also why it can lead to such things as a self-inflated ego (conceit). When most of us think about ourselves we think not only about our ideal self but about our real self as well. The fact that we often do not measure up to our ideal is a source of conflict for most of us and as a result, we tend to show a certain amount of modesty. Under the influence of alcohol, however, people often show what we

more and more varied conditions, she has more opportunities to discover that the drug has diverse reinforcing properties.

A person who continues to use a drug under a wide range of conditions is likely to discover that the drug's reinforcing properties are associated with internal states rather than external stimuli. For example, a person might discover that alcohol reduces anxiety in a wide variety of situations or that heroin will reduce a variety of aversive psychological states, including anxiety and depression. We have already seen that many of the commonly used drugs have a variety of effects and are used for a variety of reasons. Presumably, each person discovers what property of the drug is reinforcing for him or her as a result of experimenting with it under a variety of conditions. The person slowly learns to use drugs to produce certain internal states. The more the person uses drugs in this way, the more his or her behavior will shift from external to internal control.

People generally are inhibited from using drugs extensively because of fears for health or social norms. Their behavior therefore remains, at least in part, under external control. A businessman who is concerned that he may be fired if he drinks on the job may restrict his drinking to evenings or weekends. By restricting his drinking to particular times and locations, he is forced to continue exercising coping responses to a number of daily stressors. When a person fails to restrict his intake to particular situations, the stage is set for him to use a given drug in more and more situations and, as a result, to develop a generalized dependency on it.

According to this model of addiction, it is not surprising that high rates of alcoholism are found among people in alcohol-related occupations, such as bartending. If a person is in a setting where there is little reason to restrict intake, there is a greater opportunity to learn about the extensive reinforcing properties of alcohol.

call an inflated ego. They brag, for example, that they are more than they really are. According to Steele and Josephs, when we drink we are inclined to focus only on the more salient cues, one of which in this case is our ideal self. No longer plagued by the reality of negative or limited attributes, we are free to talk about our ideal self. Figure 7-10 shows the effects of alcohol versus a placebo on the changes in ratings of the real self by level of conflict. In this study by Banaji and Steele (1989), subjects rated the importance of 35 traits pertaining to their *real* and *ideal* selves before and after they drank alcohol or a placebo. Since the differences between the real and the ideal self could be minimal or very large, they decided to group the differences into two groups: large differences that were viewed as important by the individual (*high inhibition conflict*) and small differences that were viewed as not

important by the individual (*low inhibition conflict*). It was found that alcohol had a very significant effect on self-ratings but only for the *high inhibition conflict* condition. Specifically, it was found that self ratings were significantly bettered after drinking alcohol (see right hand side of Figure 7-10). Banaji and Steele concluded on the basis of these results that alcohol has a myopic effect which can result in a form of self-conceit. Instead of considering relevant information pertaining to their limitations, the participants in this study ignored that information after drinking alcohol and saw only their strengths. In short, they lost their ability to *temper* or *inhibit* their optimistic feelings about themselves based on a realistic assessment of their weaknesses.

To summarize, according to this model, the pharmacological effects of alcohol restrict people's attention

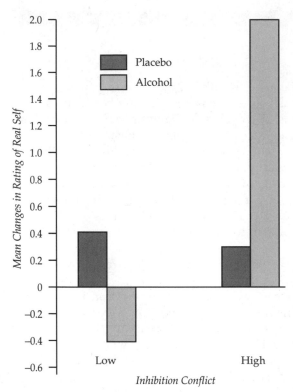

Figure 7–10. Changes in rating of the real self by conflict level of the trait dimension and alcohol. (From C. M. Steele and R. A. Joseph, "Alcohol Myopia: Its Prized and Dangerous Effects." *American Psychologist* , 1990, *45*, 921-933 (Figure 3). Copyright © 1990 by the American Psychological Association. Reprinted with permission.)

to the most salient cues. The greater the amount of alcohol that is consumed, the greater the restriction of attention (the greater the myopia). It is assumed that what is salient is determined by cognitions that are linked to people's current thinking, attention, and motivation. Whether or not there will be marked behavioral changes is assumed to depend on the amount of conflict in people's cognitions. The greater the conflict, the greater the tendency for people to see those qualities that are central to their thinking, attention and motivation. Since people seem to be motivated to see themselves in the best possible light, it is not surprising, for example, that they are inclined to see only their

good qualities and ignore their limitations when intoxicated.

Situational factors. Studies have shown that the tendency not only to use a drug but the amount of a drug that we use and where we use it are governed by situational factors. Situational factors, in this context, are such things as our perceptions of the appropriateness or social desirability of a behavior in a specific situation. The tendency to develop a drinking problem can be predicted from the amount one's companions drink and the extent to which one's life revolves around drinking (Cahalan & Room, 1974). It has been shown that the tendency to use a narcotic is governed to a very large degree by such things as the appropriateness of the response in a given social situation. Many addicted Vietnam veterans, for example, stopped using heroin for good when they returned to friends and family who did not use it or condone its use (see Robins et al., 1974; Robins, Helzer, & Davis, 1975). Conversely, addicts who had gone through a treatment program but then returned to an environment in which their friends not only condoned the use of drugs but used them themselves tended to show very high re-addiction rates (for example, Nichols, 1965, 1972). If drug use were a disease or a biological drive, one could not predict its occurrence on the basis of environmental factors. It has even been shown that the tendency to experience withdrawal symptoms is related to the social acceptability of demonstrating such symptoms. When it is expected that they will occur, they do; when it has been made clear that such symptoms are not only not expected but unacceptable, they do not occur (for example, Zinberg & Robertson, 1972). Such findings have led people to question the whole idea that withdrawal—the pain and discomfort that come when people stop using a drug—is one of the primary reasons that people re-addict themselves.

Cultural factors. Stanton Peele (1984, 1985) has reviewed some of the data on the role of cultural factors in drug use. He points out that the Zuñi and Hopi Indians used alcohol in a ritualistic and regulated manner until the coming of the Spanish, after which they used it in a destructive and generally addictive manner. Peele further points out that the use of alcohol in certain cultures (American Indian, Eskimo, Scandinavian, Eastern European, and United States) leads to antisocial aggressive behaviors but fails to do so in other cultures (Greek, Italian, American Jewish, Chinese, and Japanese). It has been suggested that these and other differences relate to the beliefs that people hold about what drugs do.

Beliefs about control. Several important implications follow from the idea that cognitions play an important role in addiction. People often have a great deal of information, correct and incorrect, about what happens to people when they become addicted to a drug. Much of this information comes from conversation, newspapers, and television. You may have read, for example, that alcoholics are people who lose control once they start drinking, or have a drink every day, or show a tendency to become aggressive when they drink, or find that it is impossible to quit drinking, or drink progressively more as time goes on. All of these various pieces of information then provide the basis for your belief system. There are two important things to note here. First, few people share precisely the same belief system. Second, two people may have basically the same drinking pattern yet one may fit the criteria of addiction while the other does not.

If belief controls behavior, then it follows that people who come to the conclusion that they are alcoholics will begin to behave in a manner consistent with the label they have applied to themselves. They will tend, that is, to lose control when they drink, or to find it virtually impossible to quit drinking, and to exhibit the other behaviors they associate with alcoholism. People who do not label themselves as alcoholics, on the other hand, may drink just as much but manage not to lose control and find it less difficult to quit. Indeed, data suggest that people who do not perceive themselves to be alcoholics (or who perceive themselves as having at least some control) respond much better to rehabilitation programs that involve control of alcohol rather than total abstinence (for example, Skinner, Glaser, & Annis, 1982). Conversely, people who perceive themselves to be alcoholics (or as having no control) do not fare well in such programs but do benefit

from programs that focus on abstinence (Miller, 1983). That makes sense; if you think you can't control your drinking, then the best solution is to not drink.

It is interesting to note that the program of Alcoholics Anonymous (AA) is based on the principle that certain people can never learn to control their drinking and that if they are ever to live a normal life, they must recognize this fact. The requirement that AA members must openly identify themselves as alcoholics serves to make them admit to themselves that they have lost control. It further reinforces the idea that they can never drink again. The message that they have lost control could be very damaging if they were to generalize it to other parts of their lives. Labeling alcoholism as a *disease*, however, helps to reduce the tendency to generalize. At this time there is no clear evidence that alcoholism is a disease. I point this out not because AA is not an effective organization, but rather to emphasize AA's message: if you have absolutely no control over your drinking, then your only alternative is abstinence. There is also a danger of relapse for people who label themselves alcoholics. If being an alcoholic means you are unable to control your drinking, then the more you endorse the concept "I am an alcoholic," the more you will tend to lose control when you drink (Heather, Winton, & Rollnick, 1982; Peele, 1985). It is interesting to note that abstinence programs have success rates of only 5% to 10% (Emrick & Hansen, 1983).

Taking control by cutting down. In recent years research has been launched to determine whether people who are abusing alcohol (drinking too much) can learn to cut down on the amount they drink (e.g., Miller & Muñoz, 1976; Sobell & Sobell, 1976). While this research has come under vigorous attack, evidence mounts that some people who have been classified as alcoholics (that is, uncontrolled drinkers) can learn to drink in moderation. In fact, Miller (1983) has reported that 23 of 24 studies on this question have found the reduced drinking technique superior to other treatment techniques for a range of alcohol abuse problems, and that no study has shown that abstinence is more effective overall than moderation. It is important to note that we still do not know what determines whether a person can return to a pat-

PRACTICAL APPLICATION 7.4

Factors That Moderate the Use of Drugs

Commitment to other activities. In *The Meaning of Addiction*, Peele (1985) argues that while there is very little evidence for an addictive personality per se, there is considerable evidence that the addiction process is linked to social, cultural, and parental influences, together with a desire to satisfy certain needs. He has argued that lack of commitment to non-drug activities often plays an important role in the process. If drugs interfere with activities that people value, they will limit their drug use or abstain in order to maximize the rewards of the non-drug activity. In their therapy program, Cox and Klinger (1988) attempt to help people to develop nonchemical goals as a means of developing a satisfying way of life.

Social class. A strong relationship has been found between socioeconomic level and alcohol addiction. Subjects of lower socioeconomic backgrounds are three times more likely to be addicted to alcohol than middle-class subjects (see Vaillant, 1983). The question arises as to the origins of these differences. As we shall see, they may be traceable not to socioeconomic class per se but rather to other characteristics associated with the various classes. The values that one holds, for example, may be the important factor.

Peer and parental influences. Peers have consistently been found to play an important role in initiating drug use. Research studies have shown that the effect of peer pressure is greatest in regard to marijuana, somewhat less in regard to alcohol, and least in regard to hard drugs (Kandel, Kessler, & Margulies, 1978). While peers may be influential in the initial experimentation with drugs, it is questionable whether peer pressure can account for the tendency of a given individual to abuse drugs. In fact, it has been suggested that peers may provide role models for moderation. It has been found, for example, that groups that encourage controlled use of heroin tend to stress limiting the use of drugs to certain specific occasions while simultaneously encouraging the maintenance of social, scholastic, and professional interests (Jacobson & Zinberg, 1975, cited in Peele, 1985).

Culture and ethnicity. Membership in a particular ethnic group seems to exert an influence on the likelihood of drug abuse. Several studies in this area point to the fact that cultures or ethnic groups vary widely in the attitudes they foster, and that these attitudes influence drinking patterns. There are wide cultural and ethnic differences in regard to the acceptability of drunkenness, the tolerance of aggression in a drunken person, the idea of drinking as an expression of masculinity, and so forth. Jews as a group tend to be moderate drinkers, whereas the Irish tend to drink to excess (Vaillant, 1983). It has been suggested that this difference is linked to the Jewish tradition of high regard for rationality and self-control (Keller, 1970) and an Irish ethos that is both magical and tragic (see Bales, 1946). The Irish, that is, treat drinking not as something that one may choose to do or not do, but rather as something that

tern of moderate drinking. Values, beliefs about control, and stress are just some of the factors that need to be explored further in the context of controlled drinking.

It has been suggested that perhaps not everybody can learn to control their drinking. In a 10-year follow-up of the subjects treated by Sobell and Sobell (1976), a group of researchers found that of the 20 subjects treated, only one was drinking without problems, eight were drinking excessively, six were abstinent, four were dead for reasons related to alcohol consumption, and one could not be located (Pendery, Maltzman, & West, 1982). While Pendery, Maltzman & West were highly critical of the Sobells, suggesting that the Sobells were promoting a life-threatening procedure, they

can bring magic into one's life. The Japanese and Chinese tend to be very moderate drinkers, whereas the North American Indians and the Eskimos tend to be excessive drinkers (Klausner, Foulkes, & Moore, 1980). As excessive drinking is incompatible with a commitment to achievement, it has been suggested that this factor may be responsible for the moderate drinking of the Japanese and Chinese (Peele, 1983).

Moderation as a life value. Drug abuse, it has been suggested, reflects a tendency to excessive behavior (Gilbert, 1981). Conversely, it has also been suggested that people for whom moderation is the central organizing principle will be less inclined to develop drug dependence (Peele, 1983). One important factor that may underlie the adoption of the moderation principle is the placing of a high value on health, which may be learned from one's parents or from members of one's social group (Becker, 1974).

Achievement motivation and fear of failure. There is evidence from a variety of sources that people characterized by strong achievement motivation are less likely to become addicted than people who lack such motivation. People with strong achievement motivation tend to work hard and generally have good opinions of their abilities. People with a strong fear of failure tend to have a low opinion of their abilities, and so tend to avoid situations that may demonstrate their ineptitude. In order to avoid looking bad, they look for easy problems or problems that are so difficult that no one would reasonably ex-

pect them to succeed. In short, their lives revolve around attempts to escape the need to perform (to test their skills). One means of escape is to take drugs, often a highly ritualized activity that requires little skill and therefore offers no threat to one's low self-esteem. Birney, Burdick, and Teevan (1969) have suggested that the rise in drug use in the 1960s grew out of this learned fear of failure. Peele (1982) has included this kind of drug use among the coping strategies he calls *magical solutions*. While such a coping strategy enables the individual to escape the immediate problem, it has no long-term survival value, for it keeps the individual from facing reality.

Commitment as opposed to alienation from society. When people become alienated from their society, they have an increased tendency to become addicted. It has been found, for example, that the use of marijuana is associated with alienation from social institutions (Kandel, 1984) for several reasons. When people become alienated from their society, they no longer feel bound by its rules. As a consequence, they see no value in the principle of moderation or the standards by which other people judge the appropriateness of behavior. The lack of activities designed to lead to achievement or other rewards valued by the society makes these people susceptible to the drug experience (Jessor, 1979). It makes sense that when people experience no rewards from the society in which they live, they might look elsewhere for a rewarding experience.

failed to do a follow-up on the control group used by the Sobells. When the Sobells did that follow-up, they found that while the mortality rates were 20% for the controlled drinking subjects they had treated, the rate for the control group was 30%. The long and the short of this is that while controlled drinking does not work for some, there is no evidence that people are worse off

for having tried such a procedure. It has been suggested that the reason for the low success rate in the Sobells's study was due to the fact they were attempting to treat people who had been abusing alcohol for some time. Studies in which people have been treated earlier in their pattern of abuse consistently find higher rates of success.

PRACTICAL APPLICATION 7.5

How People Quit Addictions

Data from people who quit addictions indicate that most people do it on their own. The success rate from formal treatment programs tends to be very poor. Survey data about smoking, for example, indicates that millions of people quit smoking and most of these (as many as 95%) do so on their own (Cohen et al., 1989). In fact, 30% of adult Americans are now ex-smokers (Peele, 1989). Abstinence rates from formal treatment programs tend to cluster around 20% (Cohen et al., 1989). The same patterns have been found for alcohol. George Vaillant (1983) found (*The Natural History of Alcoholism*) that most alcohol abusers overcame their alcohol problem by either cutting back or quitting altogether. Very few of those who licked their drinking problem had sought formal treatment. Of those who chose to abstain, 60% had no contact with AA. Those who simply cut back did not contact AA, an organization which is based on the concept that the only way to deal with alcohol abuse is through abstinence. It is interesting to note that abstinence programs have success rates of only 5% to 10% (Emrick & Hansen, 1983). Even when it comes to losing weight, doing it on your own is more likely to work than if you join a formal program. Schachter and Rodin (1974) found in a study of two different populations that 62% of those who had tried to lose weight had succeeded. Not only had they succeeded in losing weight (the average weight loss was 34.7 pounds) but they had kept if off (11.2 years). What data there are with heroin and cocaine suggest again

that doing it on your own works best (Steele, 1989).

How do people do it? They seem to do it by designing their own programs. But before you can design your own program you need to believe that you can quit and you need to have a reason to quit. After that, it is often a trial-and-error procedure that eventually results in success. It has been described as a dynamic process, not a discrete event (Cohen, et al., 1989).

1. Belief that one can quit. Believing you can quit on your own is one of the most important factors. If you believe that you can only quit through a formal program, you give responsibility to an external agent. Should you fail, it is the program's fault and not yours. The formal programs that work best seem to be those that convince the individual they can succeed, and then put the responsibility on the individual (Peele, 1989).

2. Developing self-efficacy. When people take responsibility for designing their own program and succeed, their self-efficacy improves. Even small successes can improve feelings of self-efficacy. If someone tells you what to do and you succeed, you cannot take responsibility and, as a result, your self-efficacy will not improve. When people's self-efficacy improves it reinforces their initial belief that they can quit (Bandura, 1991).

3. Learning how to interpret failure. Since it is common for people to relapse, one might expect that self-efficacy would be undermined following failure.

Beliefs about self-change. There are numerous accounts of people who, after drinking heavily for years, have suddenly altered their drinking patterns. A father who one day notices that his son is modeling his drinking suddenly stops drinking; a mother who realizes that she is slurring her speech at the dinner table abruptly stops having her usual three or four cocktails before dinner.

Peele (1983) has noted that people frequently alter their drinking pattern when it begins to interfere with things they value. While some people may indeed be unable to control their drinking, it is obvious that many people can. George Vaillant (1983) has presented data that show that alcohol problems regularly reverse themselves without medical intervention. In other words, the inevitable pro-

Whether or not it is undermined depends on how people interpret failure. If they interpret failure as a flaw in the design they have created, and not in themselves or their ability to quit, they learn how to focus on the design and improve it. For example, if they find they are inclined to drink too much, they might set a limit beforehand and then resolve to quit when they reach that self-imposed limit. Some people learn to drink one beer and then fill the bottle with water and drink that before having a second beer. When you begin to ask people how they have learned to succeed, you get literally hundreds of different answers. Different things work for different people. Each person needs to find out what works for him or her. It is important to note in this context that the number of previous unsuccessful attempts is unrelated to future success in quitting (Cohen et al., 1989).

4. Valuing health. When people value health they are less inclined to use drugs such as alcohol and nicotine because of the negative health implications. As people get older they often come to realize that if they are going to live a long productive life they need to take care of their health. There are many examples of people who drank heavily or used drugs in their younger years and then suddenly cut down or quit altogether (Peele, 1989).

5. Developing interests in new activities or coming to value activities. When people value their work, their family, the various activities they do, they often refrain from drinking or taking drugs in order to better appreciate those things. It is common to hear someone say that they have had enough to drink or they are not going to take drugs tonight because tomorrow they want to get up early to engage in a cherished activity. It is when people have no other reason for living they fill their lives with drugs. One reason for the high addiction rate in the slums has been linked to the fact that many of these people do not have positive things on which they can focus their attention. One of the primary reasons athletes abstain from drugs is that virtually all drugs interfere with high-level athletic performance. It is only those athletes who do not value doing their very best who will typically fall prey to drugs. When people's lives are filled with activities they cherish, they have little reason for taking drugs (Cox & Klinger, 1988; Peele, 1985).

6. Maturing out. As a general rule, people tend to cut down or quit using drugs altogether as they get older (Peele, 1989). This reduction in drug use or quitting has been explained in many ways, ranging from the loss of reinforcing powers that drugs have on people as they get older (a biological explanation) to conscious control that results from such things as health concerns (a more cognitive explanation). Whatever the explanation, the idea that the longer you use drugs the more likely it is that you will become addicted is not the general rule. Quite the contrary, the general rule is that people seem to give up drugs after years of use. Quitting, in other words, is very natural.

gression that some people say characterizes alcoholics and other drug users does not hold for all people.

Summary

Alcohol, though a stimulant in small to moderate amounts, is probably best known for its disinhibiting properties at moderate to high levels. The euphoric effect often associated with alcohol may be due to its ability to stimulate the dopaminergic system and the endorphin system. That alcohol creates depression and is not the result of depression is consistent with the idea that alcohol stimulates the release and eventual depletion of such chemicals as dopamine and endor-

Alcohol is a disinhibitor. As a result of this disinhibition effect, people tend to let go, often engaging in behaviors they would never dream of doing if they were sober.

phins. When these chemical are at a low level people experience depression, since these chemicals seem to be the source of positive feelings. One important characteristic of alcohol is its disinhibition effect which results in a reduced tendency to avoid without affecting the tendency to approach a goal in an approach/avoidance conflict.

According to the learning model, if a drug is used in the presence of many different stimuli, all those stimuli will come to control that behavior. The different addiction rates for the French and Italians illustrates this principle.

Cognitive factors play an important role in alcohol use and abuse. Beliefs about what drugs do seem to play a large part in determining the effects of drugs. According to Steele and Josephs, expectation alone cannot account for many of the effects observed with alcohol. They argue in their interaction model that the pharmacological effects of alcohol produce restricted attention in which people under the influence of alco-

hol attend to only the most salient cues. As a result, when people come to react to a situation, they often neglect considering certain important pieces of information and, as a result, demonstrate what Steele and Josephs call a *myopic* approach to the world. Situational factors, too, such as whether a behavior is perceived to be appropriate, determine to a very large degree the way people behave when they use drugs. As beliefs about the effects of drugs and about appropriate behaviors vary from culture to culture, it is not surprising to find that drugs have quite different effects on people of different cultures. The disease model of alcoholism links loss of control directly to the "disease of alcoholism," not to cognitive variables.

Several factors moderate the use of drugs. These include commitment to other activities, social class, peer and parental influences, culture and ethnicity, a respect for the value of moderation, the need to achieve, the fear of failure, and degree of alienation from society.

It appears that the best way to give up an addiction is to do it on your own. At least six things have been linked to self-quitting: belief that one can quit, developing feelings of self-efficacy, learning how to interpret failure, valuing health, developing interest in new activities, and maturing out.

Main Points

1. The World Health Organization has defined drug addiction as "a state of periodic or chronic intoxication produced by repeated consumption of a drug."

2. Because drug addiction is usually preceded by drug abuse, the current strategy for studying addiction is to identify the factors that lead to drug abuse.

3. Dependency refers to the need to take drugs to maintain normal feelings of well-being.

4. Tolerance refers to the fact that people need to take increasing amounts of a drug to achieve the same feelings of well-being.

5. Solomon's opponent-process theory suggests that addiction is due, at least in part, to the strengthening of an opponent process. People need to increase drug intake to overcome the opposing reaction.

6. There is no evidence for the idea that there is an addictive personality, although there is evidence that certain personality types may be more inclined to use drugs.

7. There is good evidence for the position that people who use drugs to escape noxious or aversive situations are more likely to become addicted.

8. The tendency to initially use a drug is often motivated by curiosity, modeling, group pressure or medication.

9. The discovery of opiate receptors in the brain has led researchers to suggest that the use of opiates is a means of tapping into certain naturally occurring reward/survival mechanisms.

10. Nichols has argued that morphine can short-circuit many biological drives.

11. It has been shown that placebos can be effective pain killers if the person thinks such placebos are indeed pain killers.

12. Considerable evidence points to the idea that humans, as well as animals, only become addicted to such drugs as heroin if basic psychological and social needs are not being met.

13. It has been argued that social acceptability often plays an important role in the addiction process, especially to such drugs as heroin.

14. Beliefs about control play an important role in one's ability to recover from an addiction such as heroin.

15. Current evidence suggests that cocaine's main effect is by way of the dopamine system.

16. The fact that such drugs as amphetamines activate the self-reward systems of the brain suggests that one reason people take drugs is to experience the positive affect that occurs when such centers are activated.

17. While amphetamines do not produce tolerance or withdrawal, they can become habit-forming.

18. The reaction that people get from amphetamines depends to some extent on their expectations.

19. Antianxiety drugs such as Librium and Valium belong to a class of drugs called benzodiazepines. The general consensus is that the effect of the benzodiazepines is due to the actions of Gamma-aminobutyric acid (GABA) system.

20. It is generally thought that antianxiety drugs work by regulating neural transmission.

21. Benzodiazepines are very addictive due to the fact that this class of drugs is a powerful negative reinforcer (reduces negative affect).

22. There is considerable evidence that people who are anxious tend to view the world as threatening.

23. In order to get people off benzodiazepines it is necessary for them to develop the confidence that they can effectively cope with the world in which they live.

24. Research indicates that LSD works via the serotonin-containing neurons in the raphe nuclei.

25. Hallucinogenics produce what people have referred to as an altered state of consciousness.

26. Numerous studies have found the use of hallucinogenics as linked to what has been called an *antitraditional orientation*.

27. Adolescents who have experimented with marijuana but who have not become users tend to be well-adjusted.

28. Nicotine appears to produce its effect by activating the dopaminergic system.

29. There is considerable evidence that smoking behavior is controlled to a very large degree by cues in the environment, both external and internal.

30. In low doses, alcohol stimulates the central nervous system. In moderate doses, it depresses activity of the brain by direct action on the brain. This leads to a disinhibition effect.

31. Evidence points to the idea that alcohol produces its pleasurable effect largely through the activation of the dopaminergic system.

32. There is also evidence that alcohol produces its pleasurable effect by increasing endorphin activity.

33. The link between alcohol and depression can be explained by the tendency of alcohol to produce depression through the depletion of dopamine/norepinephrine stores.

34. It has been shown that alcohol reduces the avoidance gradient in an approach/avoidance conflict.

35. The different rates of alcohol addiction in France and Italy illustrate the idea that drinking can be elicited by a wide range of stimuli.

36. It has been suggested that the effects of alcohol can be explained to a very large degree by people's expectations.

37. According to Steele and Josephs, alcohol produces restricted attention which, in turn, leads to a myopic view of the world.

38. The fact that people's reactions to drugs vary with the situation and with the drug taker's culture raises serious questions about the disease model of addiction.

39. There are considerable cultural differences in how people respond under the influence of alcohol.

40. Beliefs about both control and self-change play an important role in determining whether a person becomes addicted.

41. According to the interaction model of addiction, the extent of a drug's reinforcing properties depends on environmental conditions. An environment that is the source of positive reward tends to reduce the reinforcing properties of the drug.

42. The use of drugs is moderated by such factors as commitment to other activities, social class, peer and parental influences, culture and ethnicity, adoption of the principle of moderation, a strong need to achieve and a weak need to avoid failure, and commitment to the values of the society in which one lives.

43. There is considerable evidence that when people quit on their own they are more likely to succeed.

Anger, Aggression, and Compliance

- Is aggression in our genes? Are brain structures involved in aggressive behavior?

- How does our body respond when we become angry?

- Do we use aggression to control people in our environment?

- Does testosterone make males aggressive? What about females?

- To what degree is aggression learned?

- Can we learn to control our aggression?

- Is it true that much of human aggression is due to frustration?

- Does viewing aggression on television and in movies lead to aggressive behavior?

- Can people learn to control their anger?

Is Aggression Good or Bad?

The term *aggression* is used to refer to a wide variety of behaviors, of which some are considered socially desirable and others socially undesirable. A person who works long and hard to win a business contract or a person who competes with others to obtain the top position in a large company or an athlete who manages to become the top scorer on the team is typically viewed in our society as being aggressive in a socially acceptable and desirable way. However, a driver who honks his horn at an elderly lady entering a line of fast-moving traffic or a person who challenges another person to a fight in order to settle an argument is typically regarded as being aggressive in a socially unacceptable or undesirable way. Psychologists use the term aggression to refer to socially unacceptable behaviors.

Definition of Aggression

Aggression is defined as the intention to harm another person (Geen, 1990). In general, we draw a rather fine distinction between behaviors intended to harm and those not intended to harm (Baron, 1977). The emphasis here is on *intended*, since it is not uncommon in the course of competitive behavior for one person to harm another unintentionally. A person who competes for a top executive position and obtains that position causes others to lose. The very nature of competition means that some will succeed and others will fail. A football player may injure another player while blocking for a teammate, but if it was not his intention to injure but rather to provide a needed opening for his teammate, the injury is typically regarded as unintentional. Unintentional harm may occur in a variety of situations. A driver might accidentally hit another car, a clerk might inadvertently short-change a customer, or a professor might err in grading a student's essay. The fact that these acts were unintentional means they were not acts of aggression.

In contrast, the driver who honks his horn at the elderly lady is directing his behavior specifically at the lady whom he perceives as the source of his immediate problem. His horn-honking is intended to prod an obviously unsure person into entering a line of fast-moving traffic, and forcing her to make a bad decision could be fatal.

Provoked versus Unprovoked Aggression

Our daily papers are filled with examples of violence. Not only do humans inflict physical harm on other humans, but they vandalize public and private property to the tune of millions of dollars annually. Many people are concerned that they too might become victims of violence. What alarms people in particular is that there seems to be a great deal of unprovoked violence in our society. Many people are afraid to leave their homes for fear they will become victims of unprovoked violence in the streets or that their property will be vandalized or burglarized in their absence.

Although unprovoked violence may be a very real possibility for most of us at some point in our lives, the actual probability of being a victim of unprovoked violence is relatively low. Most violence can be classified as provoked. By words or actions, a person provokes another person to behave aggressively. We are probably all aware that calling someone stupid is likely to elicit anger accompanied by some form of retaliatory aggression. Shoving or elbowing to get to the front of a line is almost certain to provoke a retaliatory shove, an elbow, or a sharp verbal rebuff. Imagine what your neighbor might think and feel if you deliberately threw a rock through her window or tripped her as she walked in front of you. Such behavior would be an obvious act of provocation.

Physical versus Verbal Aggression

Most of us provoke other people in one way or another, although rarely do we do anything as extreme as throw a rock through a neighbor's window or trip someone as she passes by. Certain forms of aggression are almost sure to result in severe retaliation. Most people try to avoid doing things that will precipitate physical aggression. Children may resort to physical aggression, but our culture tends systematically to discourage it. By the time humans have reached their adult years, most aggression is limited to verbal exchanges (Patterson, 1976).

Do North Americans Live in a Violent Society?

Each year, approximately 3 million people are victims of violent crimes in the United States, representing 3% of the population (Langan & Innes, 1985). Violent crimes such as murder, rape, robbery, and aggravated assault occur nearly every 20 to 25 seconds. Interestingly, many of the violent crimes are committed by people who know each other and live with each other. For example, 1.2 million acts of violence were among relatives (U.S. Department of Justice, 1980). Thirteen percent of all marriages are characterized by severe violence (Straus, 1977, cited in Widom, 1989). One survey found that between 1.4 and 2.3 million children have been beaten by their parents some time during their childhood (Straus, Gelles, & Steinmetz, 1980), while another survey found that 1200 children died as a result of abuse and neglect (see Eagly & Steffen, 1986).

Can one lead a life free of violence? Many people do. Random acts of violence are relatively rare. Why are some people, therefore, more prone to be victims of violence while others live lives relatively free of violence? The answer lies in understanding the biological, learned and cognitive factors that lead to aggression and violence. Aggression and violence are not inevitable. They are behaviors that humans can and do learn to control.

When Do Humans Become Physically Aggressive? Laboratory Analogs

The Teacher-Learner Paradigm

It is relatively easy to produce physical aggression in the laboratory if certain conditions are met. Researchers have often elicited physical aggression by creating some condition that justifies the release of aggression under the guise of punishment, presumably as a means of understanding how punishment can be used to help people. This procedure is called the teacher-learner paradigm. In the teacher-learner paradigm, the participant is led to believe that the shocks he or she is administering may help the recipient learn certain arbitrary associations between words, for example, and that this will help science understand how punishment can be used to facilitate learning. In the teacher-learner paradigm, the teacher (a confederate of the experimenter) shocks the learner (the subject or participant) whenever the learner fails. At the end of this training session, the learner is allowed to evaluate the quality of the teacher by delivering no shocks, a few shocks, or many shocks to the teacher (usually 1 to 10). In most studies based on this paradigm, the teacher is given no chance to use another form of feedback (control) to assist the learner, since the main point of the study is ostensibly to understand how punishment affects learning. As we will see, some learners, especially women, will choose other forms of feedback if they are given a choice.

The fact that physical aggression is observed under these conditions is probably not surprising. The question is whether these results should be taken as evidence that humans have a high tendency to be physically aggressive, in view of the fact that they have not been given a choice (Baron & Eggleston, 1972). A study by Rule and Nesdale (1974) clearly demonstrates that physical aggression, at least in the laboratory, may not necessarily reflect a desire to harm. Rule and Nesdale used the teacher-learner paradigm with two sets of instructions. One group of teachers was told that higher-intensity shocks would help the learner's performance, while another group was told that such shocks would interfere with performance. Another manipulation was to have the teacher, who was a confederate of the experimenter, either insult or not insult the learner. Rule and Nesdale reported that learners who had been told the shocks would interfere with perfor-

Aggression as Obedience to Authority

Using the teacher-learner paradigm Stanley Milgram (1963, 1974) has shown that people will administer high levels of shocks when they are instructed to do so by an authority figure. In his study, subjects were seated in turn in front of a machine and told that it could deliver shocks of up to 450 volts. They were instructed to depress the levers in ascending order when the "learner" in the next room made a mistake, a procedure they were told would deliver progressively intense shocks.

In actuality, the machine never did shock the other person. The "learner" was a confederate of Milgram and made errors deliberately, thus requiring the subjects to deliver more and more intense shocks. In order to convince the subjects that shocks were indeed being delivered and were painful, the confederate cried out in pain as the shock intensity supposedly increased and even pounded on the wall and pleaded with the subject to stop.

Many of the subjects indicated that they wanted to stop, but Milgram, in an increasingly authoritative voice, told them they had no choice, they must continue. Most subjects followed the instructions. In fact, 65% of the subjects administered 450 volts even after the learner had ceased to respond, giving the impression that the shocks had seriously incapacitated him.

It has been suggested that these results provide evidence that humans will give up personal control or personal morality when they are placed in a situation in which they perceive that another person is in charge and knows what he is doing. The laboratory situation may be considered analogous to war, in which an officer orders soldiers to act in an aggressive manner. The fact that people will obediently carry out acts of aggression ordered by an authoritarian figure has caused a great deal of concern among social scientists. This concern typically involves the potential misuse of authority and the bloodshed that it may precipitate. The problem for the individual is to guard against falling prey to the tendency to obey all authority, yet at the same time to respect the need for appropriate authority.

---

mance chose more intense shocks for the insulting than the neutral teacher. Subjects who had been told the higher-intensity shocks would facilitate learning delivered more intense shocks to the neutral than to the insulting teacher. These findings suggest that the learners were trying under one condition to assist the teacher and under another condition to disrupt the performance of or even punish an insulting teacher.

Shock As Evaluation Paradigm

Retaliation in kind. Another procedure that effectively elicits physical aggression from participants in the laboratory is to initially administer physical punishment to the subject under the pretext that it is some form of evaluation. For example, a participant may be given a certain number of shocks to indicate the adequacy of his performance on a required essay. The evidence seems to show that the recipient is likely to respond in kind and number to the punishment if given the chance. That is, if the recipient is given a certain number of shocks, he is likely to return the same number (for example, Borden, Bowen, & Taylor, 1971; Dengerink & Bertilson, 1974; Dengerink & Myers, 1977; Taylor, 1967). Again, it is unclear whether such studies show that humans tend to avoid the use of physical aggression except when provoked to do so.

It is interesting to note that subjects could easily escalate or de-escalate levels of counteraggression by either increasing or decreasing the level of the attack (Borden, Bowen, & Taylor, 1971; Dengerink & Myers, 1977; O'Leary & Dengerink, 1973; Taylor, 1967). I will examine some studies later in this chapter which show that when subjects feel that the instigator cannot retaliate at some later point in the future (they are anonymous or somehow protected from future retaliation), they are inclined to escalate as opposed to retaliate in kind.

Massive retaliation. It has been suggested that counter-aggression often serves the function of terminating the aggressive attack. Patterson (1976) has observed that aggressive behavior within the family setting is often used by one member of the family to stop the attacks of another member. He has further observed that when one family member suddenly increases the intensity of the aggressive exchange, the other person is likely to terminate his or her attack. Thus, although gradual escalation of the attack may increase an aggressive exchange, a sharp increase (massive retaliation) may serve to decrease or stop that exchange. Evidence from other sources is consistent with this observation. For example, when the threat of retaliation for aggressive behavior is high, the tendency to initiate an attack is lowered (Baron, 1973; Dengerink & Levendusky, 1972; Shortell, Epstein, & Taylor, 1970). There is one important exception. It appears that when a person is strongly angered, the threat of retaliation does not reduce the tendency to initiate an attack. Thus, even if the person believes that retaliation not only will be forthcoming but will be severe, he or she will not inhibit an aggressive attack (Baron, 1973).

Being angered is, of course, one of the most fundamental conditions evoking aggressive behavior in humans. Being angered does not, however, necessarily lead to physical aggression. A person may engage in a variety of aggressive verbal behaviors before resorting to physical aggression. It appears that humans often stop short of evoking a physical attack. In diplomatic exchanges, great care is often taken to allow the other party (nation) to "save face" in order to avoid evoking a physical counterattack. The aggressor may escalate the attack to such a high level that the recipient of the attack may feel he or she has no choice but to resort to a physical counterattack. Under these conditions the attacker may be forced to use physical aggression as well.

Aggression in the laboratory and the real world. When I have informally asked students how long it would take them to provoke (anger) another person, they have indicated that it would take only a matter of seconds. Despite this ability to anger other people at will, most people do not engage in such behaviors. First, they have no reason to behave aggressively. Second, they are well aware of the principle of retaliation. Third, there is a general norm for not being physically aggressive. Thus, when students come to serve in experiments involving shock, the experiments often need to be disguised as something else. It is the fact that they are disguised, often as experiments with lofty goals (such as helping people to learn), that has made some people question the degree to which we can generalize from these studies. In many instances, the participants think, just as doctors do when they take out your appendixes, that they are doing something good and beneficial. Additionally, because participants are often not given other alternatives for dealing with a provocation, we have no way of estimating how aggressive people really are. In other words, just because we can get people to behave aggressively in the laboratory (shock other people) does not mean that humans have a propensity to act aggressively. One of the themes I want to emphasize in this chapter is that while humans can behave aggressively, they are very restrained in their tendency to do so. It is often the media that give us the impression that humans are very aggressive.

The Anger and Aggression Link

Distinguishing between Instrumental and Affective Aggression

While there is a strong positive correlation between anger and aggression, people often become angry without becoming aggressive and people often engage in aggressive behavior without experiencing the emotion of anger. For example, people often experience the emotion of anger when they become sick, when they are frustrated in their attempts to achieve a goal, or when a relationship fails but they do not strike out at someone else. Similarly, without feeling angry, people will sometimes act aggressively simply to achieve a desired goal such as to win in a sporting event, to gain an advantage in a political contest, or to exercise power. In the Milgram study, the subjects who administered high levels of shock did so without experiencing anger.

It has been suggested that when aggression is not provoked by anger it is instrumental aggression (Geen, 1990). That is, the behavior is motivated by the desire to achieve a desired goal, such as a political office, or to help someone learn, and is not motivated by the desire to hurt or harm another person. When anger is not followed by an aggressive act towards another person, we say the person is simply in an affective or emotional state. Since no one caused the behavior, it is not considered to be provoked. Therefore, it would make little sense to strike out aimlessly, although at times people do. When anger is linked to aggression it is called affective or angry aggression (Feshbach, 1964). The main goal of this aggression is to injure or harm the provocateur.

This chapter will focus, for the most part, on affective or angry aggression. It is our goal to understand under what conditions people will attempt to harm another person.

Aggression as Control: Gaining Compliance over Others

The wish or need to exert control over events or people seems to be a fundamental human characteristic (Rotter, 1972). It is not surprising, therefore, that humans develop a wide range of skills for exerting such control. Aggressive behaviors can be viewed as a subclass of control behaviors. Can we specify the conditions under which this subclass of control behaviors is used? Further, can we specify when physical—in contrast to verbal—aggression is used in an attempt to control events and people in the environment?

There is evidence from a variety of sources that humans will often resort to more immature forms of behavior when other behaviors fail. If this idea is applied to aggressive behavior, it suggests that humans will resort to physical aggression if other methods of control fail. Thus, physical aggression may be viewed as a last resort (Shortell, Epstein, & Taylor, 1970). For example,

a person may try to use positive rewards to control behavior. When these efforts fail, he may move to some form of verbal attack. And finally, if this strategy fails, he may resort to physical aggression. Abuse of children and spouses is often an outgrowth of the motivation to control.

Hans Toch (1969), who has extensively studied the violent criminal, has pointed out that the violent criminal often lacks the basic social skills that would allow him to control people and events in the environment. He therefore tends to use force as a means of compensating for his immature and underdeveloped social skills. Physical violence is often used by young children but eventually gives way to more socially acceptable methods of control (Patterson, 1976). If a person has failed to develop such skills, the only methods of control available to him are these more childlike methods. That is, he is prone to use physical aggression. Toch believes that the physically aggressive criminal needs to learn the appropriate social skills for controlling events in the environment. Learning such skills would, he suggests, help eliminate some of the situations that often precipitate acts of assault against others.

Summary

Psychologists typically use the word *aggression* to refer to those behaviors that are intended to harm another person. The word *intended* is the key, because one can accidentally harm another person out of negligence or in the normal course of competitive behavior, as in an athletic contest. Although some acts of aggression are unprovoked, most aggressive acts are provoked. Psychologists have, for the most part, focused their research on provoked aggression. Although children will frequently use physical aggression when provoked, adults tend to avoid physical exchanges and to retaliate verbally to acts of provocation. Even though we read or hear a great deal about violence in our society, only 3% of the population is involved in violent crimes.

Two of the most commonly used procedures to study aggression in the laboratory are the teacher-learner paradigm and the evaluation paradigm. While these two procedures have been used extensively in

Interpersonal Violence: The Link Between Control and Power

One of the main themes that has emerged from the feminist literature on male-female violence is that violence towards women reflects a need by men for control over women. According to the feminist political gender analysis, men have been socialized into believing they have the right to control women in their lives, even through violent means (e.g., Walker, 1989).

While violence towards women has been identified as a serious problem and linked to male aggression, numerous studies have found that in certain situations, females may be more aggressive and violent than men (e.g., Eagly & Steffen, 1986). In the case of interspousal abuse, for example, it has been shown that wife-to-husband violence sometimes prevails over husband-to-wife violence (e.g., Brinkerhoff & Lupri, 1988). Because of male strength, however, it is the women in these violent exchanges who often suffer the most physical harm and who are therefore the more likely to need protection.

There are also many examples of both men and women being violent towards their children in our society (e.g., Reid, 1983). One of the common themes of these studies is the desire to control and the belief in the right to control through force. There is also a great deal of violence towards minorities and people with different sexual orientations, such as gays and lesbians. Again, it has been suggested that people in our society have been socialized to believe that they have the right to engage in violence to control such minorities.

The feminist scholars, minority scholars, and gay and lesbian scholars have suggested that the attempts to control others through violent means can often be understood in terms of the link between power and control (e.g., Walker, 1989). A common theme in that literature is that when people have power or perceive they have power, they will be inclined not only to exercise it on their own behalf, but will attempt to maintain their power base. Walker argues that it is the perception of having power that gives people the idea that they have the right to control and exclude others, even to the extent of using violent means.

What triggers acts of violence? According to psychological control theory, it is the threat that one is going to lose power (control). The father and mother who abuse their children do so because they want to retain power. Lacking the skills to control their children's behavior through more socially accepted means, they resort to physical violence. Similarly, the husband who beats his wife or the wife who abuses her husband is motivated by the desire for power. Again, lacking the skills to maintain control, they resort to physical abuse.

It has been suggested that much of the violence we see towards minorities, gays, and lesbians reflects, in one way or another, a struggle for power. To gain power (or to become empowered) has become the goal of all those who wish to escape from the violence that is perpetrated on them by others. Often it is the very attempt to gain power, however, that triggers acts of violence. As people try to free themselves from the control of those in power and take charge of their lives, they threaten the status quo and existing power structures. According to this analysis, it is necessary to demonstrate to people that when one group gains power it does not necessarily mean that others will lose their power.

the laboratory, people have questioned whether or not these paradigms truly reflect the expression of aggression in the real world. There is reason to argue that when people retaliate to an aggressive act, especially when angry, their desire is to terminate the aggression rather than harm the other individual.

While there is a strong positive correlation between anger and aggression, people often become angry without becoming aggressive and often engage in aggressive behavior without experiencing the emotion of anger. It has been suggested that in order to understand these differences we need to distinguish between instrumental aggression (characterized by aggression without anger) and affective aggression (characterized by both aggression and anger).

Aggressive behaviors can be viewed as a subclass of control behaviors. Often when people lack the skills to control others through socially acceptable means, they resort to physical aggression.

It has been suggested that one source of violence in our society—such as violence towards women, men, children, minorities, gays and lesbians—grows out of a need or desire for power. The way people maintain their sense of power is by controlling others, often through violent means.

Biological Factors

Although aggressive behavior in humans differs in many respects from aggressive behavior in animals, work with animals has had a great impact on the understanding of human aggressive behavior. The work with animals shows, in a rather pure form, the biological roots of aggressive behaviors. Although humans share these biological roots, cultural influences have modified, to a very large degree, the expression of aggression. In order to appreciate the nature of the biological roots of aggression, we will briefly review some of the work on genetics and some of the conclusions reached by ethologists from their studies of animal behavior.

Genetics and Aggression

There is no doubt that animals can be bred specifically for aggression. There are numerous examples of fighting cocks, fighting dogs, and other animals that have been selectively bred for that characteristic (McLearn, 1969). In a very extensive study of the genetics of aggression, mice were selectively bred for both high and low aggression (Lagerspetz, 1964). While many people feel that it would be possible to breed humans for aggression, there is no record of anyone attempting this, and hopefully no one will ever try.

Kinds of Aggression

The physiological basis of aggression has turned out to be quite complex. Not only have several brain centers been identified as being involved in aggression, but the activity or sensitivity of these systems seems to vary among individuals and in accordance with the levels of certain chemicals circulating in the blood (Moyer, 1976). The complexity can be understood if we recognize that the term *aggression* is used as a broad category covering a number of behaviors that share certain common properties. At least eight types of aggression can be identified (Moyer, 1976):

1. *Predatory*. Attack behavior that an animal directs against its natural prey.

2. *Intermale*. Threat, attack, or submissive behavior by a male in response to a strange male.

3. *Fear-induced*. Aggressive behavior that occurs when an animal is confined. Attack behavior is usually preceded by an attempt to escape.

4. *Territorial*. Threat or attack behavior when an intruder is discovered on home-range territory or submissive and retreat behavior when an animal is confronted while intruding.

5. *Maternal*. Attack or threat directed by the female toward an intruder when her young are present.

6. *Irritable*. Attack or destructive behavior directed toward any object as the result of frustration, pain, deprivation, or any other stressor.

7. *Instrumental*. Aggressive behavior that has previously resulted in some kind of reward.

8. *Sex-related*. Aggressive behavior elicited by the same stimuli that elicit sexual behavior.

Though some of these forms of aggression are more relevant to behavior in animals than in humans, all have at one time or another been treated as aggressive behaviors. Moyer (1976) has pointed out that somewhat different neural systems are involved in each of these types of aggression. A full discussion of the various types of aggression and the neural systems that support them is beyond the scope of this chapter. I will confine my discussion to some of the basic neural systems and the general principles that have emerged from research on such systems.

Neurological Structures and Aggression

Several brain structures have been implicated in various kinds of aggressive behavior (Mark & Ervin, 1970). Figure 8-1 is a cross section of the brain, showing several of the structures that have been implicated in aggressive behavior.

The hypothalamus. The hypothalamus was one of the first brain centers to be implicated in aggressive behaviors. Bard (1928) showed, for example, that the posterior hypothalamus is important for producing a rage response. In the same year, Hess (1928) published data showing that another area of the hypothalamus is also implicated in a well-integrated rage response. Still other studies have shown that the hypothalamus is involved in attack or predatory behaviors (Egger & Flynn, 1963; Hess & Brugger, 1943) and defensive behaviors (Roberts & Kiess, 1964; Roberts, Steinberg, & Means, 1967). The fact that different areas of the hypothalamus are involved in different types of aggressive behavior provides rather clear evidence that there is no single mechanism for all aggressive behaviors. Rather, it appears that each one must be treated as distinctive, at least at the neurological level.

The limbic system. At least three major circuits within the limbic system (hippocampus, amygdala, and septum) have been implicated to some degree in aggressive behaviors (see Figures 8-1 and 8-2). Stimulation of the amygdala and the septum often causes attack and defensive behaviors; lesioning produces a marked calming effect. The septal area seems to be additionally involved in feelings of pleasure, often with sexual overtones (Grossman, 1967).

In reviewing the animal studies on the relation between the amygdala and aggression, Moyer (1976) has concluded that different areas of the amygdala appear to control different types of aggression, even though these areas overlap to some degree. He has noted, for example, that the amygdala contains separate locations for fear-induced, irritable, and predatory aggression. Septal

lesions in rats can produce a temporary increase in the tendency to make irritable, as opposed to predatory, attacks on a mouse. Similarly, lesioned rats show an increase in fighting when shocked (Moyer, 1976). This research suggests that the septum may exert an inhibitory function, so that lesioning increases aggressive behavior.

Although lesions in rats have been shown to reduce shock-induced fighting, such lesions have also been shown to increase rats' tendency to attack the prod used to shock them (Blanchard, Blanchard, & Fial, 1970). The differences in the reactions suggest that different neural systems mediate responses in these two situations. The role of the limbic system is still not totally understood, but it seems to be important in the instigation and organization of aggressive behaviors that are elicited by a variety of environmental conditions.

The Klüver-Bucy syndrome. In a now-famous series of studies, Heinrich Klüver and Paul Bucy (1937, 1938, 1939) produced a striking behavioral change by removing the tips of the temporal lobes of normally aggressive rhesus monkeys. The operation removed the amygdala, the anterior hippocampus, and much of the temporal lobe (see Figure 8-2). Monkeys that had been very difficult to manage suddenly became tame, friendly, and easy to handle. They began to approach and explore normally feared objects, such as a snake or a burning match. Further, they showed unusual oral behavior. They would mouth everything within reach, including snakes, a burning match, nails, dirt, and even feces. The male monkeys became hypersexual, masturbating constantly or attempting to copulate with male and female monkeys that were unreceptive, or even with dogs and cats if they were available. Finally, the monkeys tended to be abnormally restless and active.

Since Klüver and Bucy discovered this unusual pattern of behavior, other research with animals has shown that the fear and anger reduction observed by Klüver and Bucy can be produced by lesioning of the amygdala (for example, Karli & Vergnes, 1965; Siegel & Flynn, 1968). Cutting the tops of the temporal lobes has been shown to control aggressiveness in schizophrenics (Terzian & Ore, 1955) as well as psychopaths (Vallardares & Corbalan, 1959). Most surgical attempts to control aggression in humans, however, have in-

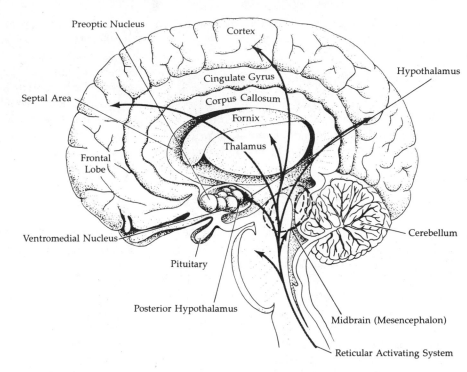

Figure 8–1. Cross section of the human brain. (From K. E. Moyer, *The Psychobiology of Aggression*, 1976. Copyright © 1976 by K. E. Moyer. Reprinted with permission of Harper & Row, Publishers, Inc.)

volved selective lesions to the amygdala. The results of this research are unequivocal: amygdalectomy in humans produces a marked reduction in destructiveness, hostility, aggressiveness, and even excitability (for example, Heimburger, Whitlock, & Kalsbeck, 1966; Narabayashi, 1972). Many patients who had been difficult to manage became model patients after the operation.

Temporal lobe pathology. One of the most widely publicized cases of extreme hostility that may have resulted from temporal lobe pathology was that of Charles Whitman. He was an introspective young man with no previous history of violence who one night killed his wife and his mother. The next morning he went to the University of Texas administration building, where he killed the receptionist and barricaded himself in the tower. From the top of the tower, he used his high-powered rifle equipped with a telescopic lens to shoot anyone he could bring into view with his powerful sights. During the next 90 minutes, he killed 14 persons and injured another 24. His shooting spree ended only

when the police were able to kill him. The autopsy showed a tumor whose exact location was difficult to pinpoint because of the wounds inflicted by police bullets; the evidence seemed to indicate, however, that the tumor was located on the medial part of the temporal lobe.

Whitman's case is particularly interesting because he kept notes on his feelings and had consulted with a psychiatrist about them several months earlier. He revealed to the psychiatrist that he sometimes became so angry that he would like to go to the top of the university tower and start shooting people. The letter he wrote just before he killed his wife and mother provides some insight into his tortured mental state.

I don't quite understand what it is that compels me to type this letter. Perhaps it is to leave some vague reason for the actions I have recently performed.

I don't really understand myself these days. I am supposed to be an average, reasonable and intelligent young man. However, lately (I can't re-

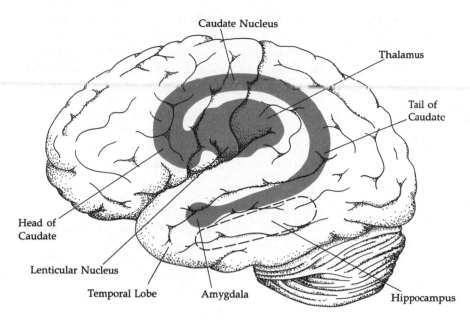

Figure 8–2. Relation of the caudate nucleus and amygdala to the rest of the brain. (From K. E. Moyer, *The Psychobiology of Aggression*, 1976. Copyright © 1976 by K. E. Moyer. Reprinted with permission of Harper & Row, Publishers, Inc.)

call when it started) I have been a victim of many unusual and irrational thoughts. These thoughts constantly recur, and it requires a tremendous mental effort to concentrate on useful and progressive tasks. In March when my parents made a physical break I noticed a great deal of stress. I consulted a Dr. Cochrum at the University Health Center and asked him to recommend someone that I could consult with about some psychiatric disorders I felt I had. I talked with a doctor once for about two hours and tried to convey to him my fears that I felt overcome (sick) by overwhelming violent impulses. After one session I never saw the doctor again and since then I have been fighting my mental turmoil alone, and seemingly to no avail. After my death I wish that an autopsy would be performed on me to see if there is any visible physical disorder. I have had some tremendous headaches in the past and have consumed two large bottles of Excedrin in the past three months.

It was after much thought that I decided to

kill my wife Kathy, tonight after I pick her up from work. . . I love her dearly, and she has been a fine wife to me as any man could ever hope to have. I cannot rationally pin-point any specific reason for doing this. I don't know whether it is selfishness or if I don't want her to have to face the embarrassment my actions would surely cause her. At this time though, the prominent reason in my mind is that I truly do not consider this world worth living in, and am prepared to die, and I do not want to leave her to suffer alone in it. I intend to kill her as painlessly as possible. . . .

After he had killed his mother and wife, he wrote:

I imagine it appears that I brutally killed both of my loved ones. I was only trying to do a good and thorough job.

If my life insurance policy is valid please see that all the worthless checks I wrote this weekend are made good. Please pay off all my debts. I am 25 years old and have never been financially independent. Donate the rest anonymously to a mental health foundation. Maybe research can prevent further tragedies of this type.*

Social Rank and the Expression of Aggression

Although aggressive behaviors may be controlled by a number of neurological structures, it is clear from research that the tendency to express aggression is also affected by certain social factors. Specifically, social rank seems to be important in determining whether aggression will be inhibited. A study by José Delgado (1967) clearly illustrates this point. An electrode was

*From K. E. Moyer, *The Psychobiology of Aggression*, 1976. Copyright © 1976 by K. E. Moyer. Reprinted with permission of Harper & Row, Publishers, Inc.

permanently implanted in the thalamus (nucleus ventralis posterior lateralis) of a monkey called Lina, and she was stimulated by means of a radio transmitter when she was low, moderate, or high in dominance. Delgado altered her dominance position by changing the composition of the group of monkeys living with her in a large cage. He found that if Lina was stimulated when she was high in the dominance hierarchy, she initiated a relatively large number of attacks; if she was stimulated when she was moderate or low in the hierarchy, however, she initiated very few attacks, as Table 8-1 indicates. Table 8-1 also reveals that Lina was the recipient of many attacks when she was low in the dominance hierarchy and received no attacks when she was high. These results indicate that the social structure plays an important role in determining whether aggressive tendencies are expressed (see also Delgado, 1963, 1966, 1975).

Figure 8-3. Dominance hierarchy in a colony of monkeys before any operation. (From K. Pribram,"Self-Consciousness and Intentionality." In G. E. Schwartz and D. Shapiro (Eds.), *Consciousness and Self-Regulation: Advances in Research (Vol. 1),* 1976. Copyright © 1976 by Plenum Publishing Corporation. Reprinted with permission.)

Dave 1
Dominant, Self-Assured, Feared

Zeke 2
Aggressive, Attacker

Riva 3
Aggressive, Active

Herby 4
Placid, Unaggressive

Larry 8
Submissive, Cowering, Frequently Attacked

Shorty 7
Submissive to Others, Aggressive toward Larry

Arnie 6
Noisy, Eager

Benny 5
Alert, Active Food Getter

Work by Pribram further illustrates this point (see Pribram, 1976). In one study, Pribram and his colleagues set out to determine whether bilateral amygdalectomies would affect fighting and how this might in turn affect the position of a dominant monkey in a colony (Rosvold, Mirsky, & Pribram, 1954). As expected, the lesions resulted in a shift in the dominance hierarchy, as shown in Figures 8-3 and 8-4. The dominant monkey, Dave, became totally submissive. When they subjected the newly dominant monkey, Zeke, to the same operation, he too became submissive, sinking to the bottom of the dominance hierarchy. To their surprise, when they attempted to do this a third time, the newly dominant monkey, Riva, did not become submissive or drop in the hierarchy. This unexpected finding can be understood, Pribram explains, if we note that the number 2 monkey in the dominance hierarchy (Herby) did not challenge Riva. His nonag-

Table 8-1. Number of attacks initiated and received by Lina as a function of dominance. (Adapted from J. M. R. Delgado, "Social Rank and Radio-Stimulated Aggressiveness in Monkeys." *The Journal of Nervous and Mental Diseases*, 1967, 144, 383-390. Copyright © 1967 by the Williams and Wilkins Co., Baltimore. Reprinted with permission.)

Lina's dominance status	Attacks initiated by Lina	Attacks received by Lina
Low	1	15
Moderate	6	1
High	40	0

Note: Numbers are based on 120 experimental sessions at each dominance level.

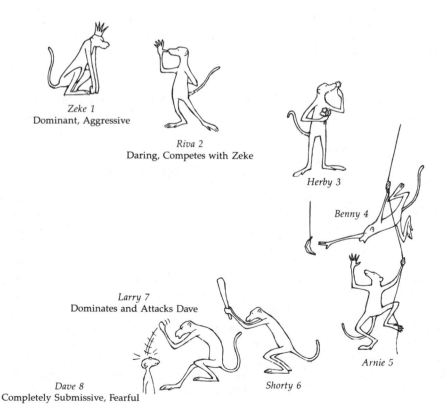

Zeke 1
Dominant, Aggressive

Riva 2
Daring, Competes with Zeke

Herby 3

Benny 4

Larry 7
Dominates and Attacks Dave

Arnie 5

Dave 8
Completely Submissive, Fearful

Shorty 6

Figure 8-4. Dominance hierarchy after bilateral amygdalectomy in Dave, formerly the dominant monkey. (From K. Pribram,"Self-Consciousness and Intentionality." In G. E. Schwartz and D. Shapiro (Eds.), *Consciousness and Self-Regulation: Advances in Research (Vol. 1)*, 1976. Copyright © 1976 by Plenum Publishing Corporation. Reprinted with permission.)

Figure 8-5. Dominance hierarchy after bilateral amygdalectomy in Zeke. (From K. Pribram,"Self-Consciousness and Intentionality." In G. E. Schwartz and D. Shapiro (Eds.), *Consciousness and Self-Regulation: Advances in Research (Vol. 1),* 1976. Copyright © 1976 by Plenum Publishing Corporation. Reprinted with permission.)

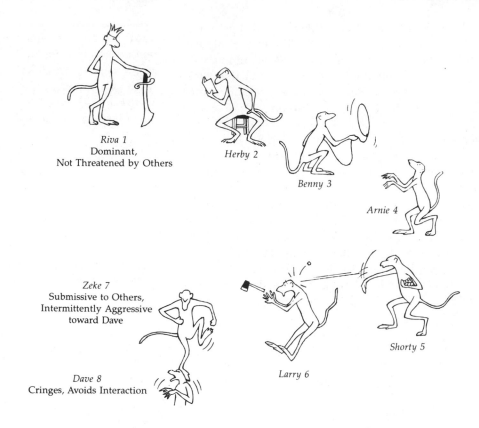

Riva 1
Dominant,
Not Threatened by Others

Herby 2

Benny 3

Arnie 4

Zeke 7
Submissive to Others,
Intermittently Aggressive
toward Dave

Shorty 5

Dave 8
Cringes, Avoids Interaction

Larry 6

gressive personality allowed Riva to remain in the top spot. This finding is illustrated in Figures 8-5 and 8-6.

These results show, Pribram (1976) argues, that the amygdala, like other structures that have been implicated in aggression, may have to do not with aggression itself but rather with some brain process that mediates an organism's sensitivity to the social environment. Perhaps the amygdala somehow mediates the way an organism gains or maintains control in the social environment. Therefore, when the amygdala is lesioned in some way, the ability to gain or maintain control is lost or disrupted. If aggressive behavior is a means of gaining control, then it too should be lost or disrupted. Thus, when Herby failed to challenge Riva, Riva remained in the top position by default. As we shall see, there is good reason to argue that humans and animals have a need or tendency to control events or other people or animals, and that aggression is simply a means of obtaining that control. If this is true, it

could be argued that the bilateral amygdala lesions disrupted the means or behavior necessary to gain or maintain control, not the basic motive to control.

Hormones and Male Aggression

The role of testosterone. A large body of research has been able to link male aggression to testosterone. At about age 9, human males show a dramatic increase in testosterone level, which rises about tenfold by age 10-15 (Hamburg, 1971). This increase has been suggested as an explanation for the increase in aggressive behavior that adolescent boys tend to manifest at this time (Moyer, 1976). Although further research is needed to verify this hypothesis, other research tends to provide some converging evidence that testosterone is, at least in part, responsible for the greater amount of aggressive behavior in young adolescent males. It has been suggested that testosterone may be related to the *dis-*

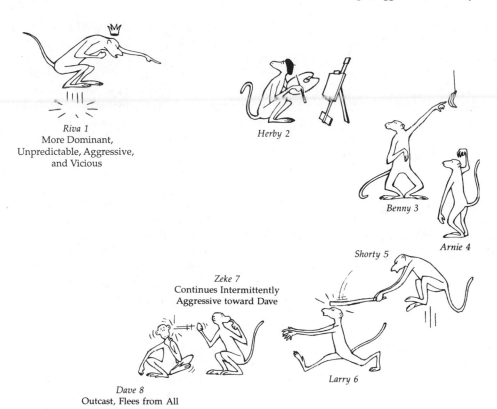

Riva 1
More Dominant,
Unpredictable, Aggressive,
and Vicious

Herby 2

Benny 3

Arnie 4

Shorty 5

Zeke 7
Continues Intermittently
Aggressive toward Dave

Larry 6

Dave 8
Outcast, Flees from All

Figure 8-6. Dominance hierarchy after bilateral amygdalectomy in Riva. (From K. Pribram,"Self-Consciousness and Intentionality." In G. E. Schwartz and D. Shapiro (Eds.), *Consciousness and Self-Regulation: Advances in Research (Vol. 1)*, 1976. Copyright © 1976 by Plenum Publishing Corporation. Reprinted with permission.)

position to aggress (Olweus, Mattsson, Schalling, & Low, 1980). That is, it does not cause people to be aggressive, but rather lowers the threshold for aggressive behaviors if provoked. This is consistent with the finding that testosterone levels are positively correlated with lack of tolerance for frustration.

Though testosterone levels vary widely among males, they tend to decrease on the average during the twenties. Persky, Smith, and Basu (1971) found that the average testosterone level of a group of men aged 30-66 was half that of a group of men aged 17-28. If testosterone is at least partly responsible for aggression, then aggressive behaviors would be expected to decrease after the twenties. This is exactly what Persky and his colleagues found. Older men were less inclined to be aggressive than younger men, as measured by the Buss-Durkee Hostility Inventory.

Further evidence that androgen (testosterone) plays an important role in aggression has been ob-

tained from studies of the effects of castration. Castration has been used primarily to treat sex offenders. Follow-up studies of castrated sex offenders have indicated that castration not only reduces the sex drive but reduces hostility and aggressive tendencies (Bremer, 1959; Hawke, 1950; Sturup, 1961). Injections of testosterone in castrated males have been shown to restore the previous aggressive tendencies (Hawke, 1950). Therefore, the reduction of aggression was very likely due to a decrease in testosterone level, not simply a by-product of the obvious trauma associated with being castrated.

Several studies have reported a link between testosterone and acts of aggression and violence. In a study of a young criminal population, it was found that 10 prisoners with a history of violent and aggressive crimes in adolescence had significantly higher levels of testosterone than a comparable group of 11 prisoners who did not have such a history (Kreuz & Rose,

1972). Similar results have been obtained in other studies (e.g., Ehrenkranz, Bliss, & Sheard, 1974; Rada, Laws, & Kellner, 1976; Dabbs, Frady, Carr, & Besch, 1987). A study of hockey players has also found positive correlations between degree of aggression, response to threat, and serum testosterone (Scaramella & Brown, 1978).

A recent study that used a self-report instrument that measure both physical and verbal aggression, the *Aggression Inventory*, found that blood samples taken to assess levels of testosterone and estradiol were positively linked to indices of aggression in men but negatively related to those same measures in women (Gladue, 1991). Animal work has shown that aggressive behavior can be established and induced by estrogen as well as androgens, presumably because testosterone can be metabolized into estradiol (Simon & Whalen, 1986). When the data were examined with the purpose of establishing what percentage of the aggressive behavior could be linked to hormones, only 20% to 25% of the variance could be explained by endocrine factors. Thus, it was concluded that endocrine factors are only partially responsible for self-reported aggression.

Estrogen, antiandrogens, and male aggression. Stilbestrol, a synthetic drug that has been shown to have the effects of natural estrogen, has often been used to control aggressive tendencies of adolescent boys (Foote, 1944; Sands, 1954; Whitaker, 1959). Like estrogen, stilbestrol depresses the anterior-pituitary gonadotropic function. In addition to stilbestrol, there are a number of substances that block androgenic activity and in doing so reduce aggressive behavior.

Hormones and Female Aggression

Attempts to link female aggression with hormones has been elusive at best. As I indicated above, Gladue (1991) was able to link male aggression to testosterone but found no links to aggression in females. One line of research suggests that female aggression may come from an imbalance of progesterone and estrogen.

Estrogen, progesterone, and female aggression. Just before

menstruation and during the initial stage of menstruation, some women experience increased irritability and hostility, part of a larger syndrome called premenstrual syndrome (PMS) (see, for example, Ivey & Bardwick, 1968; Shainess, 1961). Not only are they more irritable and hostile, but there is evidence that they tend to act out their feelings and so to get into trouble. For example, one study found that schoolgirls tend to break more rules—and, as a consequence, receive more punishment—during their menstruation, while older girls who are responsible for discipline are likely to mete out more punishment during their own menstruation (Dalton, 1960). Women prisoners are also more likely to get into trouble during this phase (Dalton, 1961), and many frequently ask to be isolated because they recognize that their behavior is likely to get them into trouble (Dalton, 1964). There is further evidence that more crimes are committed during this period (Dalton, 1961; Morton et al., 1953). Dalton suggests that the fall in progesterone level, together with the rise in the ratio of estrogen to progesterone, is associated with these symptoms. Figure 8-7 shows the levels of estrogen and progesterone during a 28-day menstrual cycle.

Several studies indicate that the administration of progesterone will alleviate the symptoms (for example, Dalton, 1964, 1977; Greene & Dalton, 1953; Lloyd, 1964). Katharina Dalton (1977) has done extensive work on the question of using progesterone to alleviate these symptoms and has concluded that progesterone not only will reduce the more common symptoms (irritability and hostility), but will alleviate a number of other symptoms that also increase during this part of the menstruation cycle, including asthma, herpes, tonsillitis, baby battering, epileptic seizures, and alcoholic bouts.

The work of Dalton and others has been criticized on both methodological and conceptual grounds (Parlee, 1973; Fausto-Sterling, 1992). On methodological grounds, it has been noted that many of the studies do not have adequate controls, that there has been a failure to use double-blind testing procedures (critical in this type of study), that sample sizes are small, that the method for measuring moods are poor or nonexistent, and that there has often been a failure to check for testosterone levels. The reason it is important to

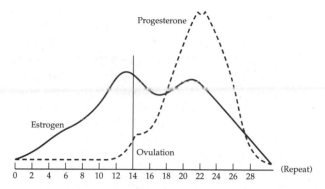

Figure 8–7. Hormone levels during a 28-day menstrual cycle. (From S. A. Basow, *Stereotypes and Roles, Third Edition.* Copyright © 1992 by Wadsworth, Inc.)

check for testosterone levels is that there is considerable evidence that both estrogen and progesterone tend to mask the effects of testosterone. If these levels are low, any increase in aggression could be due to this fact. According to Figure 8-7, if aggression were linked to hormones, aggression would be highest at the beginning of the cycle.

On conceptual grounds it has been noted that PMS may be due to a variety of other factors including Vitamin A and Vitamin B deficiency, hypoglycemia, disturbances in prolactin metabolism, and so forth (see Abplanalp, 1983; Reid & Yen, 1981). Finally, it should be noted that women in North America and Western countries tend to believe that they should experience negative moods and feelings of aggressiveness during menstruation (see McFarland, Ross, & DeCourville, 1989). Future studies will need to control for this factor if they are to clearly show that aggression in females is due to imbalances in estrogen and progesterone, as Dalton and others believe.

Androstenedione and Aggression in the Female Hyena

While there is no clear evidence for a link between hormones and aggression in humans, there is evidence that hormones are linked to aggression in the female spotted hyena. Female spotted hyenas not only look and act like males, but they force their dominance over males through their size and aggression. Researchers have found, for example, that a single female will dominate the pecking order along with a dozen or more adult females. When researchers have examined the testosterone levels of this dominant female they have found testosterone and related androgens to be higher than the average male and six times higher than the average female.

What has particularly intrigued scientists about the female spotted hyena is the enlarged clitoris which looks strikingly like the male penis. How and why did this happen? The answer, it turns out, is linked to a "prehormone" called *androstenedione*. Androstenedione is produced in the ovaries (if female) or in the testes (if male), and in the adrenal glands (both sexes) of all mammals. It is one of the chemicals that is produced in a chain of chemical reactions. What makes this chemical so special is that it is the last chemical in a chain of chemical reactions before the chain splits into the production of either male hormones or female hormones. As a result, it was hypothesized that this chemical has the capacity to determine gender. Indeed, it has been shown that this chemical induces bisexuality in male rats. When male rats were castrated to remove their normal source of testosterone and then injected with androstenedione, they displayed both female posturing and male mounting. When pregnant female rats were injected with androstenedione their offspring were born with a phallus and exhibited male-type sexual activity.

Researchers have suggested that the aggressive pattern of behavior evolved to give the female hyena and her offspring an evolutionary advantage. They suggest that the masculine genitals may have been an accidental byproduct of this evolutionary process (Hopson, 1987).

Studies with humans have found that higher levels of androstenedione in both male and female adolescents is related to a variety of problem behaviors including lying, disobedience, tendency to explode, talking back to parents and teachers (in boys), and taking an angry and dominating attitude towards parents (in girls) (see Hopson, 1987). In other words, according to an evolutionary position, it appears that there is potential for the human female to evolve in this direction since humans have the same prehormone *an-drostenedione* and it has been shown that this prehormone is linked to aggression in humans.

Conclusion

While there is no question that both males and females are aggressive (as measured by self-report indices), one of the consistent findings is that males tend to be more aggressive than females (Gladue, 1991). Since there is not a great deal of data clearly linking female aggression to the hormone testosterone, could this difference between males and females be due to a greater contribution of testosterone to male aggression than to female aggression? One cannot be sure. In the study I just reported, resting levels of testosterone and estradiol were measured, not increases that often occur as a result of engaging in aggressive behavior. One thing that we can conclude from the work attempting to link female aggression to hormone levels is that if there is a link, this relationship is much more complex in females than in males. Because other hormones are present in females that can mask the effects of testosterone, for example, it is important to demonstrate that this is the case. If it can be clearly demonstrated, then we need to have a explanation of the significance of this fact. Why, from an evolutionary perspective, for example, would it be desirable that the hormones in the human female be organized in such a way as to generally reduce female aggressiveness relative to male aggressiveness, yet allow it to occur at very precise times or conditions? In short, why isn't the human female more like the female hyena?

How important is it for us to understand the role of hormones? The fact that 20% to 25% of aggression may be due to endocrine factors suggests that hormones are indeed important to consider. According to the components approach, however, biological factors are just one of the things likely to give rise to a particular behavior. Thus, we need to look to learned and biological factors as well to get the complete answer.

The work on the female hyena suggests that scientists need to do more work on the prehormone androstenedione. Using that as their focus may help to clarify the role of hormones in aggression.

Summary

The fact that animals can be bred for aggression indicates that there is a genetic component for aggression in animals. Moyer has identified eight kinds of aggression, which he argues are mediated by different brain structures or combinations of brain structures. The main structures implicated in aggression are the hypothalamus, the limbic system (hippocampus, amygdala, and septum), and the temporal lobes. The hypothalamus, it has been shown, is involved in the rage response, attack and predatory behavior, and defensive behaviors. The amygdala and septum have been implicated in attack and defensive behaviors. The temporal lobes have been further implicated in acts of hostility and aggression. The behavior of Charles Whitman has been offered as an example of hostility traceable to an abnormality of the temporal lobe. Research on various brain structures implicated in aggression and dominance hierarchies shows that social factors play an important role in modifying (inhibiting) behaviors that have a neurological basis. The question raised by Pribram is whether such structures as the amygdala are specifically structures that mediate aggression or are more general structures that may mediate a more general class of behaviors.

While there is a large body of data linking male aggression to testosterone, there is little conclusive data linking female aggression to testosterone or to changes in the ratio of estrogen and progesterone. The research with hyenas suggests that testosterone may be one of the main sources of aggression in females as well as males. Research, however, does not support the idea that testosterone governs aggression in human females. We are left with the question of why female aggression is organized so differently from that of males in the human species.

Learned Component

The Reward Value of Aggression: Instrumental Aggression

If aggressive behavior is adaptive, it should also be rewarding. If it is rewarding, it will be repeated. There is, in fact, evidence that it will be, at least under certain conditions. Specifically, it appears that an aggressive act will be repeated if it achieves some desired goal. If aggressive behavior stops the aggressive behavior of an attacker, for example, it is likely that the tendency to engage in similar aggressive acts will increase (Hokanson & Edelman, 1966). Severe punishment for aggressive behaviors, however, tends to decrease such behaviors in animals (Ulrich, Wolfe, & Dulaney, 1969), and less severe punishment in the form of "time out" has been used to control severe, long-standing behavior problems in humans (for example, Allison & Allison, 1971; White, Nielsen, & Johnson, 1972). Clearly, engaging in aggressive behavior can lead to a reward, which will increase the tendency to be aggressive. The key is whether the aggressive behavior achieves a goal.

Social Learning Theory

According to social learning theory, the environment often plays an important role in the acquisition, expression and maintenance of aggressive behavior (Bandura, 1973).

Modeling and Imitation

One of the main way children learn aggression is through observation and imitation. We know, for example, that how people discipline their children is often very similar to how they were disciplined as children (Patterson, 1980). If they were raised with strict discipline they often employ strict discipline with their children. If they were raised in a more lenient way they tend to be lenient with their children. On the darker side, we now know that abuse and violence, both physical and sexual, can be and often is passed on from generation to generation. This so-called "cycle of violence" has been identified as a major problem in our society. While parents who abuse their children often know that it is wrong by the standards of society, they engage in abuse just the same. It is as if they acquired a habit which they find hard to break. The consensus among experts in this field is that unless the pattern is broken, it will continue into succeeding generations, truly an amazing example of the power of learning in the acquisition and maintenance of an aggressive behavior pattern.

A recent review of the "cycle of violence" research literature indicates that not all children who grow up in violent homes (also characterized by neglect) become violent or abuse their children (Widom, 1989, 1991). Unfortunately, at this point we do not know why this cycle of violence tends to break in some cases and not in others. As DiLalla and Gottesman (1991) point out, there are important biological and genetic factors which have been implicated in the transmission of violence from generation to generation. That is, while learning may play an important role, it may be that the individual must possess a certain biological temperament, for example, before such learning takes place. As we have seen before, certain types of learning only take place if the individual is biologically prepared. If we are going to break this cycle of violence we need a clearer understanding of the genetic factors and how they interact with learning.

Expression

Even though aggression is viewed by most psychologists as a universal phenomenon among humans, there are wide variations in how aggression is expressed. Whether aggression remains at a verbal level or progresses to a physical level, for example, is very different between cultures as well as in our various subcultures.

One of the most widely accepted notions about aggression is that we learn to inhibit aggression (see Zimbardo, 1969). According to this position, the tendency to act aggressively is simply a characteristic of humans. It has been suggested that aggression was important for our survival and as a result the tendency to act aggressively is something which has come to characterize humans (e.g., Lorenz, 1966). According to this position, humans must learn to inhibit their natural aggressive tendencies.

What motivates them to inhibit such natural tendencies? According to social learning theory, we learn to inhibit those behaviors which result in punishment. As a child, for example, if I hit another child and am punished for such an act, I will tend not to do that again for fear of being punished.

Blind Rage: Generalized Anger and Aggression

There are some people who respond to a wide variety of negative situations with anger and aggression. What makes their behavior so difficult to understand is that no one provoked their behavior and, in the course of expressing their anger and aggression, they lash out at anything and everything in sight.

Berkowitz (1990) has offered an explanation for aggressive behavior that is not provoked. His analysis starts with the observation that a wide variety of unpleasant feelings give rise to anger and aggression. Foul odors, high temperatures, exposure to pain, cold water, disgusting scenes, getting sick, getting caught in an elevator or a traffic jam, have all been linked to feelings of anger and the tendency to aggress. Sometimes when people become sad, such as with the death of a close friend, or when they become depressed, such as after losing one's job, they also become angry as well. Berkowitz suggests that the tendency to become angry and aggressive in response to this wide range of stimuli is largely learned. He suggests that people learn to associate a wide range of negative feelings with anger and aggression and, as a result, whenever they experience such negative feelings they become angry and may become aggressive. Specifically, he suggests that negative affect activates ideas, memories, and actions associated with anger and aggression. As a result, when we begin to experience such negative feelings we are put in a state of readiness to experience the emotion of anger and to engage in a variety of aggressive acts.

While cognitive theorists maintain that certain kinds of beliefs are necessary before the emotion of anger can arise, Berkowitz argues that this is not the case. He maintains, for example, that even when a negative event is viewed as a personal threat or cannot be blamed on someone else's unjustified action, people nevertheless experience feelings of anger. Take, for example, a person who develops a toothache and as a result becomes angry. They may say to themselves something like "Why me?" as they kick the door in front of them. Berkowitz argues that when an individual experiences pain it elicits memories of previously negative feelings, such as anger, and of the actions that one used to deal with that anger, such as aggression. Through the process of association, the feeling of pain that comes from a toothache becomes linked not only to the emotion of

In our society there are a number of norms that guide what aggressive acts are acceptable (e.g., verbal versus physical aggression). Should I overstep the boundaries set by those norms, I can expect to be punished, either by the legal system or by my peers through the process of social ostracization. It is not surprising, therefore, that the presence of other people often inhibits the expression of aggression.

Summary

The fact that aggression can be increased with rewards demonstrates that it is governed, at least in part, by the principles of learning. According to social learning theory, the environment often plays an important role in the acquisition, expression, and maintenance of aggressive behavior. One of the main ways children learn aggression is through observation and imitation. This may be why there is the phenomenon called the "cycle of violence" in which aggression seems to be passed on from generation to generation. Whether or not violence is passed along from generation to generation has also been linked to biological and genetic factors. It may be that biological and genetic factors affect temperament—something that seems to play an important role in the transmission of violence. There are wide variations in the expression of aggression. It has been shown that these differences are often linked to cul-

anger but to the actions that one used in connection with the emotion of anger. As a result, people come to express their emotion anger and engage in acts of aggression whenever they experience pain (even when it comes from a toothache). It is important to note that in this theory, the common mediator of the two distinct emotions is "negative feeling." It can readily be seen, according to this conceptualization, that a wide range of negative emotions might, over time, come to elicit aggression.

Berkowitz makes provision in his theory for the role of cognitions. In fact, he calls his theory a cognitive-neoassociationistic approach. Most people, he argues, have a rudimentary idea (prototype) of the primary emotions and what factors are involved in these emotions (sensation, thoughts, memories, etc.). As a result, there is a limit on the degree to which negative emotions can become linked to anger and aggression. According to his theory, the better one has learned to differentiate emotions (the more clearly defined prototypes one has) the less generalization there will be. As a result, while one person may come to express anger and aggression to the sensation of pain, someone else may not show this at all.

The strength of Berkowitz's theory lies in its ability to account for two things. First, it can account for why certain negative emotions can come to elicit anger and aggression even though, at least from a biological perspective, it would not be adaptive to respond to emotions such as pain with anger and aggression. Second, it can account for why people who have learned to differentiate their emotions do not show this "maladaptive" tendency. It is clearly maladaptive to respond to something like a toothache by kicking the door and possibly hurting oneself in the process. We also know from the work linking health to anger and aggression that to act aggressively is not good for one's overall health, a topic we will turn to in more detail later.

According to this theory, it should be possible to reduce generalized aggression in our society by teaching people how to better differentiate their emotions. According to the biologists, emotions evolved to make us adaptive. In order for us to maximize our adaptiveness as humans, then, we need to learn to better differentiate our emotions so that we engage in the right action for each of the emotions we experience.

ture. It has been suggested by various studies that we learn to inhibit our aggression using the norms of society to guide our behavior. If the norms are aggressive (such as in gangs) we will be inclined to act aggressively.

Berkowitz has suggested that one of the main things that leads to anger and aggression is negative affect. He argues that negative affect activates ideas, memories, and actions associated with anger and aggression. As a result, when we begin to experience such negative feelings we are put in a state of readiness to experience the emotion of anger and engage in a variety of aggressive acts. Berkowitz points out that people who learn to better differentiate their emotions are

less likely to engage in this "maladaptive" tendency to respond to all negative affect with anger and aggression.

Cognitive Component

In humans, cognitive processes play a very important role in aggressive behaviors. How we interpret an event may mean the difference between deciding to retaliate or not retaliate to a provocation. Whether or not we have the means for effectively retaliating (being capable of injuring the other person) also may influence our decision to retaliate. Because we can evaluate the consequences of our actions, we may decide to inhibit our aggression altogether or use a more socially acceptable means of retaliation. In short, most human aggression is not blind; it involves making decisions that determine whether or not we will hold the person who made the provocation responsible.

Internal versus External Locus of Control

Julian B. Rotter (1972) has suggested that there are two types of people, internals and externals, who differ in their beliefs about their ability to control their own destinies. At one extreme, internals feel they can influence events in their environment; at the other extreme, externals feel powerless to do so. According to Rotter, internals are more likely to respond with aggression than externals if, for example, the aggression will help them achieve a goal or remove a barrier or noxious stimulus. In other words, internals are more likely than externals to engage in instrumental aggression.

In an experiment to test this hypothesis (Dengerink, O'Leary, & Kasner, 1975), a large group of male undergraduates—210 subjects—was given Rotter's Internal-External Locus of Control Scale (Rotter, 1966). Two groups of subjects were selected— those scoring high on the scale (externals) and those scoring low (internals). Both groups served in an experiment based on a reaction-time paradigm originally designed by Taylor (1967). In this paradigm, the subject is informed that he will be competing in a reaction-time task with a second subject (in actuality, a confederate of the experimenter) and that the person who is slower on any trial will receive a shock that was set by the competitor in advance of that trial. The subject is then made to lose on a predetermined proportion of the trials. Subjects in both groups served in one of three experimental conditions. In the increasing-attack condition, the partner began by setting low shocks and gradually increased the intensity over trials. In the decreasing-attack condition, the partner began by setting high shocks and decreased the intensity over trials. In the constant-attack condition, the partner set a moderate-level shock throughout the experiment.

Dengerink and his colleagues predicted that internals would be more sensitive to the partner's behavior than externals. Specifically, it was predicted that sub-

jects exposed to increasing attacks would become increasingly aggressive, that subjects exposed to decreasing attacks would reduce their level of aggressiveness, and that subjects exposed to a constant level of attacks would maintain a constant level of aggression.

Figure 8-8 shows the results. As predicted, internal subjects were far more sensitive to their partners' behavior than externals. This is particularly noticeable in the Decrease condition in Figure 8-8. If people are going to de-escalate aggression, it is important that they be sensitive to the behavior of the aggressor, especially when the aggressor provides any sign that they are willing to de-escalate the aggressive exchange. Presumably, the reason externals are less likely to de-escalate aggression is that they have a generalized belief that their behavior will have no effect on people or events in the environment. According to Rotter, they feel they are powerless and as a result simply accept harsh treatment because they believe they have no ability to control it. As we have noted, people can often stop aggression by escalating the attack. Just why certain people (externals) do not respond in this adaptive way will be examined in the next chapter.

Attribution Theories

Ferguson and Rule's Model

The process by which people deal with provocation has been summarized by Ferguson and Rule (1983), who suggest that people tend to ask three questions after being harmed by someone:

1. *What was the act of harm that was done and was it intended?* The purpose of this question is to establish if there was harm and if the intent was to harm. Generally, harm without intent does not justify retaliation.

2. *What ought to have been done under the circumstances?* The purpose of this question is to identify the norms and values that should have guided the presumed aggressor's actions.

3. *Does a discrepancy exist between what has been done and what ought to have been done?* The purpose of this

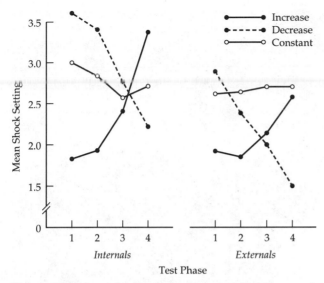

Figure 8–8. Mean shock settings by internal and external subjects for opponents decreasing, increasing, and not changing shock levels during four blocks of testing. (From H. A. Dengerink, M. R. O.'Leary, and K. H. Kasner, "Individual Differences in Aggressive Responses to Attack: Internal-External Locus of Control and Field Dependence-Independence," *Journal of Research and Personality*, 1975, *9*, 191-199. Copyright © 1975 by Academic Press. Reprinted with permission.)

question is to decide whether or not the discrepancy was of such a magnitude that retaliation is justified.

According to Ferguson and Rule, there are three separate attributions that people are inclined to make before they will retaliate: intent, foreseeability of harm, and motive.

Harm and intent. The first thing a person must do is establish whether or not there was harm. If there was no harm, then the justification for retaliation does not exist or is low even if there is suspicion of intent. If there was harm they must then ask themselves if the harm was intentional. Harm without intent is typically viewed as an accident. Only when there is harm and intent do we have clear grounds for retaliation. These various attributions can be summarized in a two-by-two classification (see Table 8-2).

Table 8-2. Attributional outcomes from a two by two classification of harm/no harm and intentional/unintentional. (From "An Attributional perspective on Anger and Aggression." In R. G. Geen and E. Donnerstein (Eds.), *Aggression: Theoretical and Empirical Reviews, Vol. 1: Theoretical and Methodological Issues*, 1983, 41-74. Copyright © 1983 by Academic Press. Reprinted with permission.)

	Harm	*No Harm*
Intentional	Aggressive act	Possibly aggressive act
Unintentional	Accident	Benign

Whether or not an outcome is classified as aggressive, possibly aggressive, accidental, or benign is often a fine distinction that may involve making a further judgment about the nature or character of the possible aggressor. Let me illustrate the difficulty that people sometimes experience when they attempt to make these distinctions and how we often need to make inferences about the nature or character of the individual before we can be fairly certain an act was truly aggressive.

In baseball, pitchers often throw what is called an inside ball (a ball that when thrown properly often forces the batter to step back from the plate in order to make a good hit). Keeping the batter off guard is one of the goals of a good pitcher, and pitchers often use the inside ball to keep batters back from the plate. In other words, their intention is to keep the batter off guard and back from the plate but not hurt or injure them. Since batters may be inclined to crowd the plate and pitchers are not always accurate, there is a good possibility that a batter can get hit from an inside ball. From time to time they do get hit, in which case they are automatically awarded first base. How does one know, however, that the pitcher did not intentionally throw the ball at the batter? From time to time the charge has been made that pitchers often deliberately throw the ball at certain players, such as at the pitcher of the op-

A collision in baseball may or may not lead to an acto of aggression. Research suggests itis harm together with the perception of intent that triggers an aggressive act.

posing team, in order to deliberately harm them and put them out of the game. From time to time fights will break out when a batter is hit by an inside ball.

Let's say that you are a pitcher who is up to bat and you get hit every time or almost every time you come up against a certain pitcher. Since other pitchers also get hit when they face this pitcher, you may have good justification to conclude this was an aggressive act. That is, it harmed you, the pitcher could foresee the consequences of his actions, and there is good reason to believe his intentions were to harm. What happens, however, if the ball just misses you? Was that an aggressive act or simply a possible aggressive act? Let's say you get hit by someone who rarely hits a batter. Was this simply an accident? The decisions that people make under these conditions often involve their beliefs about the character of the other person. If we believe they are aggressive people, we are more likely to make the attribution that the outcome was an aggressive act. If we do not believe they are aggressive people, we are more likely to dismiss the incident or wait for further evidence before we make an attribution.

The point I want to emphasize with this example isthat in the real world it is often very difficult to decide when a person has behaved aggressively (that is, they not only harmed you but they intended to harm you). Additionally, it should be noted that we are sometimes more likely to make the attribution that it was an aggressive act because of the person's race, the subculture from which the person comes, or even gender. The reason we often make different attributions for different subgroups is that we have stereotypes about the aggressiveness of various subgroups.

Foreseeability. Pitchers are fully aware of the consequences of their actions. They know that a ball travelling 90 miles per hour can injure the person it hits. Often people are not fully aware of the degree to which their actions may inflict harm. Sometimes young athletes imitate professional players without realizing the consequences of their actions and inflict irreversible harm on another person. A young skier, for example, while fantasizing about being the world's fastest downhill skier, runs into an innocent bystander and injures her back in the process. In general, we believe that when people are fully cognizant of the possible consequences of their actions they should be held more responsible than if they did not realize the consequences. If two different people caused a similar accident because their brakes were faulty, and one acknowledged the problem while the other said he believed he merely needed new brake linings in the near future, we would tend to hold the person who knew more responsible (Arkkelin et al., 1979).

Do people tend to be cautious? What Ferguson and Rule's model suggests is that people tend to be cautious in their decisions whether to interpret an act as aggressive. As we will see later, some people view the world with suspicion while others view it as more benign, and this can affect how they label an act.

Weiner's Attribution Model

According to Weiner (1985) people do not become angered by unpleasant events unless these events can be attributed to someone's intentional and controllable misdeeds. According to Weiner's formulation, harm and intent are not sufficient to elicit anger and aggression; it must also be clear that the person was in complete control of his or her actions. A person who engaged in an aggressive act because he was under the control of another person would not be judged as responsible as someone who had complete control. A gang member who acted aggressively towards another person, for example, because he feared he might be viewed as weak by other gang members, or even ostracized if he didn't act, might be judged as not being in complete control. As a result, society is not inclined to hold that person as responsible as a person who acted solely on his own. As the victim of that person's aggression, we are less inclined to feel the same degree of anger and aggression.

There are many instances in our society in which we do not perceive people as being in complete control of their actions and, as a result, we do not experience the same degree of anger towards them. For example, when people belong to groups (religious or political) that advocate severe discipline, we sometimes (but not always) judge them as less responsible for such things as child abuse in the course of disciplining their children. Even the children who are the victims of their aggression are often inclined to excuse them. In the case of police work, excessive force by individual police officers is sometimes justified and excused as due to police training procedures (external control) rather than as an individual decision process (internal control). As a result, the victims of excessive police force often respond with anger and aggression towards those they perceive are responsible or in control.

The Process of Deindividuation

Philip Zimbardo (1969) has argued that a normal precursor of physical aggression is deindividuation. Deindividuation, according to Festinger, Pepitone, and Newcomb (1952, p. 382), is a state in which the inner re-

The Role of Hostility and Anger in Hypertension and Coronary Heart Disease

Research has shown that when fear is induced in a laboratory setting it produces a physiological reaction similar to that elicited by epinephrine, and when anger is induced it produces a physiological reaction similar to a mixed epinephrine-norepinephrine response (Ax, 1953; J. Schachter, 1957). Whether or not one expresses anger (anger-out) or holds it in (anger-in) plays an important role in this process (Figure 8-9). While anger-out subjects show increased diastolic blood pressure with little change in heart rate, anger-in subjects show increased systolic blood pressure and increased heart rate (Funkenstein, King, & Drolette, 1974). Since this early work, it has been shown that repressed anger (anger-in) is linked to hypertension and cardiovascular problems (Dembrowski & Costa, 1987). In other words, people who express anger (anger-out) seem to be at less risk for cardiovascular problems than those who do not express their anger. The evidence indicates that anger-out as opposed to anger-in leads to a greater reduction in systolic blood pressure (in some studies), diastolic blood pressure (in some studies), as well as decreased heart rate.

In addition to the finding that anger suppressors are at greater risk than anger expressors, it has been found that men are at greater risk than women, that blacks are at a greater risk than whites, and that people living in high-stress neighborhoods are at greater risk than those in low-stress neighborhoods (Gentry et al., 1982; Johnson et al., 1987). Coping style plays an important role in reducing risk. People who let their anger out, both in their jobs and in everyday life situations, show less hypertension (Gentry, 1985).

Also at risk for hypertension, as well as coronary heart disease, are people who have a personality style that is characterized by hostility (Dembrowski & Costa, 1987). It has been suggested that people who are hostile tend to be suspicious and mistrustful of others, and that it is this view of the world that underlies their hostile orientation (Weidner et al., 1987). When this orientation is combined with highly competitive behavior (the Type A personality) the risk for coronary heart disease becomes even greater (Weidner et al., 1987).

It has been suggested that the best way to deal with interpersonal anger is neither to express it

straints are lost when "individuals are not seen or paid attention to as individuals." In developing his theory, Zimbardo has stated that deindividuation is characterized by low self-awareness and self-evaluation and a lesser concern for how others evaluate one. In other words, when people do not regard themselves in a good light, they are more likely to resort to physical forms of control.

Zimbardo has proposed that anonymity can lead to a state of deindividuation, which in turn will increase the tendency toward physical aggression. Feelings of anonymity occur, Zimbardo has shown, when people perceive that they cannot be identified as distinct individuals. For example, when a person wears a mask or a

uniform, his or her identity is often hidden (at least in part) by it. Under such conditions, Zimbardo suggests, people no longer feel constrained by social values and practices. As a result, they are more likely to behave in a more primitive, less inhibited fashion. Such behavior is typically characterized by its aggressive qualities. People who experience feelings of anonymity are more likely to give harsh punishment than people who see themselves as distinct and identifiable entities.

In a classic experiment, Zimbardo (1972) simulated a jail to examine the whole question of how humans respond in power-related situations. Paid volunteer university men were randomly assigned to play the roles of guards or prisoners. To make the situation as real

(anger-out) nor hold it in (anger-in). When you express anger before allowing yourself to calm down, you run the risk of making the situation worse. Often when people are angry they say things that they later wish they had not said. On the other hand, if you let anger smoulder inside you, it also takes its toll. As we dwell on it, our blood pressure remains elevated. The best way to deal with anger, it has been suggested, is to calm down or engage in "anger control," (Spielberger, Krasner, & Solomon, 1988) and then try to reason with the other person (Tavris, 1989). Anger often involves a conflict that needs to be resolved. Unless people work at resolving the conflict they will be prone to re-experience that anger again and again. One of the things people need to learn to do is to *reflect* on their anger (Harburg, Blakelock, & Roeper, 1979) so they can understand what it is that makes them angry. If people can do this, they are in a better position to change the way they think and respond.

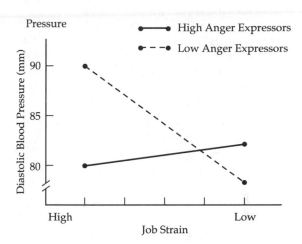

Figure 8–9. Relationship between anger expression, potential for hostility, and incidence of coronary occlusion. (From W. D. Gentry, "Relationship of Anger-Coping Style and Blood Pressure Among Black Americans." In M. A. Chesney and R. H. Rosenman (Eds.), *Anger and Hostility in Cardiovascular and Behavioral Disorders*, 1985, 139-147. Copyright ©1985 Hemisphere Publishing, Washington, D. C. Reprinted with permission.)

as possible, Zimbardo arranged for the "prisoners" to be picked up and booked by the local police department before being brought to the university, where a makeshift jail had been constructed. Dressed in jail-style uniforms, this group of students began to "serve time" in the improvised jail. The students acting as guards were dressed in appropriate uniforms and carried out the functions normally served by guards in a jail. That is, they transferred prisoners from one section to another and ensured that the rules were obeyed.

The prisoners were required to engage in various activities designed to emphasize or enhance the theme of subservience (prisoner to guard). For example, at one point they were required to wear bags over their heads while they marched in columns linked by a chain attached to their feet. The guards, of course, were responsible for ensuring that the prisoners carried out this subservient behavior in an organized and proper manner.

Zimbardo found that after six days it was necessary to terminate the experiment. In that short time, very dramatic changes had taken place in the behavior of the participants. About a third of the students who were acting as guards began to act in a very cruel and debasing fashion toward their fellow participants who had been assigned the role of prisoner. Those students acting as prisoners began to act as very "servile" and "dehumanized robots," "thinking

Sex Differences, Anger, and Aggression

One of the methods that has been used to study anger and aggression is to monitor the rise and fall in blood pressure. It has been found in a variety of studies that when people express aggression their systolic blood pressure will drop. In a series of studies, Jack Hokanson has shown that heightened systolic blood pressure dropped faster in angered subjects who responded aggressively than in those who did not respond at all (Hokanson & Burgess, 1962a, 1962b; Hokanson, Burgess, & Cohen, 1963; Hokanson & Shetler, 1961).

When sex was examined as a variable using the Hokanson paradigm it was found that this general pattern held only for men (Baker & Schaie, 1969; Gambaro & Rabin, 1969; Holmes, 1966; Vantress & Williams, 1972). In a study designed to examine sex differences, Hokanson and Edelman (1966) introduced a condition in which subjects could provide a reward to the anger instigator. In this study, the subject was seated in one room and his or her partner in another room. Subjects were told the study had to do with interpersonal behavior. The experiment was designed, they were told, to examine how they might behave in a real-life situation if they didn't like someone or didn't like what the person was doing. The subject was led to believe, through instructions, that shocks would come from the partner. In actuality, however, the experimenter delivered the shocks and the partner was never involved. The experiment was set up so that the partner always responded first. The subject then had the choice of giving the partner a shock, a reward, or not responding. Men's responses coincided with those found in previous research; that is, systolic blood pressure dropped faster after an aggressive (shock) response. Women's responses differed considerably: their systolic blood pressure dropped more quickly after they had rewarded their partner.

To explain these and other findings, Hokanson has suggested that men and women have learned different ways of turning off the aggressive behavior of their peers. Men have learned to counter aggression with aggression, while women have learned to behave nonaggressively (Hokanson, 1970). One study designed to examine sex differences (Hokanson, Willers, & Koropsak, 1968) showed that when women are rewarded for behaving like men in order to counter aggression, they tend to show a faster drop in systolic blood pressure when they use aggression as a means of stopping aggression. Similarly, when men are rewarded for behaving like women, they tend to show a faster drop in systolic blood pressure after a

only of escape," "their own survival," and "their hatred for the guards." In short, Zimbardo had to terminate the study because of the growing hatred and aggression emerging between guards and prisoners.

Zimbardo's study demonstrates that when humans are given the opportunity to control the behavior of other people, they tend to resort to very basic forms of control: in short, they will act aggressively. According to Zimbardo, feelings of anonymity can act as a disinhibitor of behavior. In Zimbardo's study, belonging to a group called "guards" and wearing a uniform symbolizing that group identity were sufficient to provide this sense of anonymity. Under these conditions, Zimbardo argues, a person no longer feels compelled to behave according to his or her personal standards acquired in the process of socialization. Rather, the person tends to resort to more primitive forms of control.

Summary

Internals are more inclined than externals to use aggression to achieve a goal or remove a barrier (instru-

nonaggressive response. This study indicates that the normal response styles used by men and women to turn off aggression are probably learned. When given new training, not only will they shift their response style, but the physiological reaction will follow the new response style. Thus the differences between men and women are not due to their sex per se but rather to the fact that in our culture the sexes learn to behave differently.

In a study by Frodi (1978), some subjects were required to give a "stream of consciousness" (SOC) report while they responded in an aggression-eliciting competitive task, and others were not required to give a report. Frodi found no sex differences among the subjects not required to give a SOC report but did find the usual sex differences among the subjects required to give one. That is, she found that men were more aggressive than women in the SOC condition. Using the SOC reports, ratings, and other measures, Frodi concluded that men tend to stimulate themselves into more aggression whereas women adopt a nonhostile strategy for coping with stress.

Other studies have also found sex differences in the expression of aggression. One study exploring the use of physical and verbal aggression (based on a teacher-learner paradigm) found that women tended to aggress in the verbal mode whereas men aggressed in both the verbal and physical modes. The teacher-learner paradigm is a commonly used procedure in which the subject is involved in a learning task. Feedback for performance comes in the form of a shock for incorrect responses. Afterward the learner is asked to evaluate the teacher either verbally or with shock. The number of aggressive verbal responses or the number of shocks given to the teacher is used as a measure of aggression. Using this paradigm, researchers found that men tended to use the physical mode more frequently under two conditions: when the teacher was female and the experimenter was male, and when the teacher was male and the experimenter was female (Shope, Hedrick, & Geen, 1978). It is likely that men's greater tendency to use physical aggression can be explained by the different social norms for men and women.

There are a number of reasons why females may be inclined to turn off aggression rather than retaliate in kind. The two main reasons that have been offered are: 1) women may be taught not to use aggression to deal with provocation or conflict, and 2) the fact that it may be dangerous for women to use physical aggression, especially with physically stronger males.

mental aggression), a finding that is consistent with the proposition that internals have a strong belief that they can control events in their lives.

Ferguson and Rule suggest that people need to make three attributions before they will retaliate to a provocation: intent to harm, foreseeability of harm, and motive to harm. If there was no harm, if the individual could not foresee there would be harm, or if there was no motive to harm, then retaliation is unlikely.

According to Weiner (1985), people do not become angered by unpleasant events unless these events can be attributed to someone's intentional and controllable misdeeds. Zimbardo has argued that a normal precursor of physical aggression is deindividuation. Zimbardo's simulated jail study demonstrates that when humans are given the opportunity to control the behavior of other people, they tend to resort to very basic forms of control: they become aggressive. He notes that deindividuation is characterized by low self-awareness and self-evaluation and a lesser concern for how others evaluate one: a state of disinhibition.

Sex Differences in Aggression

In view of the positive correlation between testosterone and male aggression, one might jump to the conclusion that males, because of their higher levels of testosterone, are more aggressive than females. While such things as crime statistics clearly show that males commit most crimes, research studies that directly compare male and female aggression suggests there is little differences between the sexes.

Many studies reported in the research literature have been conducted comparing male and female aggression using many different measures of aggression. In a review of these studies, it was concluded that while males, on the average, were found to be more aggressive than females, the magnitude of the difference was quite small (Eagly & Steffen, 1986), In addition, there was a preponderance of studies that used the teacher-learner paradigm, a design that involves physical harm. In a meta-analysis of 143 studies, Hyde (1986) found the size of the difference between males and females was about one-half a standard deviation in scores (d = .50). This means that 63% of the males were above average in aggression and 38% of the females were above average. Her meta-analysis indicated that gender accounted for only 5% of the difference. A recent comparison of males and females using "The Aggression Questionnaire" found that men scored slightly higher on Verbal Aggression and Hostility, much higher on Physical Aggression, and were equal on Anger (Buss & Perry, 1992).

There is a fundamental problem when using averages to attempt to decide whether males or females are more aggressive. The preponderance of one type of measure to assess aggression (physical versus psychological, for example) can skew the data. In the studies that were reviewed by Eagly and Steffen (1986), there was a preponderance that used a particular design that is more likely to elicit aggression in men than women and to elicit greater aggression towards men than women. Eagly and Steffen point out in their review that when you break down studies into those where aggression involves physical harm and pain and those where aggression produces psychological or social harm, the magnitude of the differ-

ence between the males and females is related to their tendency to use physical harm. It appears that women are much more cautious than males about using any form of physical aggression, largely because they seem to be more cognizant of the perceived consequences of their actions. Further, it appears that women experience more guilt and anxiety in connection with the decision to retaliate. Finally, there is considerable evidence that females may be more motivated to turn off or de-escalate aggression as opposed to engaging in retaliation, especially in aggressive exchanges with males. But this is not always the case. As I indicated before, in the cases of interspousal abuse, it has been found that wife-to-husband violence sometimes prevails over husband-to-wife violence (Brinkerhoff & Lupri, 1988).

Summary

Persistent sex differences have been found using a variety of measures of aggression. Males tend to be slightly higher on such measures as verbal aggression and hostility and much higher on measures of physical aggression. It appears that females are more inhibited when it comes to expressing aggression, especially physical aggression, and experience more guilt and anxiety with expressing aggression.

Hokanson has found that men tend to use aggression in response to an anger instigator, whereas women in the same situation tend to use rewards. Further, Hokanson found that men's heightened systolic blood pressure dropped faster when they used aggression (as opposed to not responding or using rewards) and that women's heightened systolic blood pressure dropped faster when they used rewards (as opposed to not responding or responding aggressively). The difference in behavior, it appears, is tied to cultural expectations about how men and women should deal with aggression. It is interesting that the same physiological response follows the two different response styles. These results have important implications for understanding not only why there are sex differences in cardiovascular disorder, but also how people can learn to reduce the likelihood of developing cardiovascular disorders.

It has been shown that anger-out subjects show in-

Does viewing violence on television beget violence? Research indicates parental attitudes towards violence play a much greater role than does viewing violence on television.

creased diastolic blood pressure with little change in heart rate, while anger-in subjects show increased systolic blood pressure and increased heart rate. This finding is important because anger suppressors are at greater risk for cardiovascular disorders than anger expressors. It has also been found that men are at greater risk than women, that blacks are at greater risk than whites, and that people living in high-stress neighborhoods are at greater risk. This finding suggests that other factors—likely including stress—are operating as well. Hostility and a competitive orientation are prime culprits in hypertension and cardiovascular disorders. This is moderated, however, by coping style.

Current research emphasizes the idea that it is neither good nor bad to express anger. Rather, it is important to solve the conflict or problem that produces the anger. In this way people can find a long-term answer to the question of anger.

Psychological States that Evoke Aggressive Behaviors

A number of psychological states evoke aggressive behaviors in humans. Frustration, negative evaluation, and insult are some of the more widely studied of such psychological states.

Frustration

For some time, frustration has been held to be one of the main causes of aggression. According to the frustration hypothesis, the tendency to become aggressive increases when goal-directed behavior is blocked (Berkowitz, 1962, 1969; N. E. Miller, 1941). Finding that a favorite restaurant is closed, not being able to find the shoe one wants in the right size, having to wait in line to see a movie, not getting a certain grade on a test—all are examples of everyday events in which goal-di-

A Persistent Issue: Does Viewing Violence Beget Violence; Pornography and Aggression

A great deal of research has focused on the question of whether aggression in pornographic films leads to increasing violence toward women, especially rape (see Donnerstein & Linz,1986; Malamuth & Donnerstein, 1984). The primary effort of this research has been to distinguish the effects of erotica that involves no violence or force from those of pornography that does portray violence and force. A film showing a woman being raped or tortured, for example, differs substantially from a film depicting two lovers engaged in intercourse. This research has shown that erotica per se does not seem to lead to an increase in male aggression toward women, but that violent pornography, involving scenes of rape, may lead to an increase in the tendency to rape. The reason I use the word *may* is that these studies have not shown that men who have volunteered to participate in them have actually raped as a result of watching scenes of rape; they have shown rather that men who have watched such films tend to develop a somewhat relaxed attitude toward rape. Such men tend to see rape as having no serious or harmful effect on women. A possible reason for this attitude is that pornographic films often portray the rape victim as offering only token resistance before she is swept away by passion for her attacker. Men who fail to understand that rape is a terrifying and traumatic experience for a woman may be misled by these portrayals. In view of the fact that attitudes and information affect our behavior, the finding that vio-

lence in pornographic films leads to attitude changes is an important demonstration of the power of pornography. Clearly, such films are not in the best interests of men, of women, or of society at large.

If it is not the depiction of sexual activity that is producing the attitude changes but rather the way women are portrayed in pornographic films, it is important to consider how the media in general portray women. A great deal of violence toward women is shown on television, in films, and in advertising. At this point, very little work has been done to evaluate the effects of these portrayals of violence toward women.

In 1987 the Attorney General's Commission on Pornography concluded that there is a causal relationship between exposure to many forms of pornography and several antisocial behaviors, including violence towards women (Linz, Donnerstein, & Penrod, 1987). They have called for more stringent law enforcement. Scientists whose work was used by the commission to make various extrapolations have argued that some of the extrapolations are unwarranted and that some of the findings of the commission are incongruent with research data. They argue that we should be concerned with violent images not just in pornography but elsewhere. Rather than calling for stricter legal control of pornography, these scientists have argued for educational programs to mitigate the effects of sexual violence in the media and not just in pornography (Linz, Donnerstein, & Penrod, 1987).

rected behavior has been blocked. According to the frustration hypothesis, each of these events might produce frustration, which in turn would increase the tendency to engage in aggressive behavior. Although a fairly large number of studies have obtained results consistent with the frustration hypothesis (for example, Berkowitz & Geen, 1966; Burnstein & Worchel, 1962; Geen, 1968), other studies have failed to find that

frustration facilitates the expression of aggression (for example, Buss, 1963, 1966; Kuhn, Madsen, & Becker, 1967; Taylor & Pisano, 1971).

Some limiting conditions. Robert A. Baron (1977) has carefully examined the conflicting results and has concluded that "frustration can indeed facilitate later aggression" (p. 91). He points out, however, that

Television Violence and Aggression

Does watching television violence promote real violence? Although there has been extensive research on this question, the answer is still not clear. Research has shown that television may increase the tendency of some people to engage in aggressive behaviors, provided they are provoked. This does not mean, however, that television causes aggressive behavior in the absence of provocation. It may be that television acts indirectly to increase aggressiveness (for example, Fenigstein, 1979). At least four explanations have been offered: (1) modeling and imitation of aggression, (2) release, or disinhibition, of aggressive impulses, (3) elicitation of aggressive actions that have been previously learned, and (4) an increase in arousal produced by watching aggressive activities (Bandura, 1973; Geen, 1976).

It has been found that a large proportion of the children who watch violence on television do not show increased aggressiveness, and it is necessary to account for this fact. One important factor is how the parents view violence. If the parents do not endorse violence as a means of settling disputes, achieving goals, and so on, children who watch violence on television tend not to be affected by it (Dominick & Greenberg, 1971). Another factor that needs to be considered is whether a given child prefers violence. Not all children, it appears, like to watch violence. Those who do prefer violence on television tend to be more aggressive (Eron et al., 1972; Fenigstein, 1979). The fact that viewing television violence is correlated with later aggressiveness is therefore not surprising. The aggressiveness, however, is not necessarily due to TV violence. Rather, it appears to be due to an underlying tendency to be aggressive. Again, parental attitudes may play an important role in facilitating or inhibiting this tendency. Finally, since the tendency towards aggression is mediated by anger, whether a child is angry may play a role in determining whether TV violence will have an effect. As we saw earlier in this chapter, certain environmental factors will increase aggressiveness only if the person is angry. It appears that TV violence can be a very powerful contributor to aggression, at least for a short time, when a person is angry (Doob & Climie, 1972). This finding suggests that TV violence has a general arousal effect that facilitates aggressiveness, as opposed to a specific modeling effect.

More recently, Freedman (1984, 1986) has argued that there is little evidence for a link between television violence and aggression. He points out that if you exclude the laboratory studies indicating there is a causal link between television violence and aggression, the link is weak and often inconsistent. He goes on to argue that there are good reasons for not generalizing from the laboratory studies. The debate goes on.

---

frustration is likely to produce aggression only when frustration is (1) "quite intense" and (2) "when it is unexpected or arbitrary in nature" (p. 91). Thus, having to wait in line may fail to facilitate aggression, because waiting in line is not intense enough. In fact, most of us learn that at times we will have to wait, and as a result of that expectation we often experience little or no frustration. Whether a student's failure to receive the grade he or she expected will facilitate aggression might be affected by the student's perception of whether the grading was fair or arbitrary.

The role of expectancy . The role of expectancy in a frustrating situation is illustrated in a study carried out by Worchel (1974). Worchel offered students one of three incentives for their participation in an experiment: (1)

an hour of experimental credit, (2) $5 in cash, or (3) a bottle of men's cologne. Initially the participants were required to rate these incentives for attractiveness. The rankings allowed the experimenter to manipulate degree of frustration. For example, if a subject was given his first choice, he should experience no frustration; if given his second choice, mild frustration; if given his third choice, the greatest frustration.

To examine the role of expectation, Worchel gave participants different information. A third of the participants were told that after their participation in the experiment the prize they received would be whatever the experimenter's assistant wished to give them. This was called the "no-expectancy" condition, because the participants had no idea what they could expect from the assistant. Another third of the subjects were told they would receive the prize they had rated as most attractive. This was called the "expectancy" condition. The final third of the subjects were told they would have the opportunity to choose their prize after participating. This was called the "choice" condition.

After these expectations had been established, the participants were involved in some activities under the supervision of the experimenter's assistant. To determine the effects of frustration, the experimenter had manipulated the distribution of prizes so that some subjects in each condition (no expectancy, expectancy, choice) did not receive or were not allowed to select their favorite prize. Each subject received either his most-preferred, second-most-preferred, or least-preferred object in a manner consistent with the experimental condition. Then the subjects were asked to rate the performance of the experimenter's assistant. The results of interest were their ratings of the assistant. As expected, subjects who were frustrated most (received the least-preferred prize) showed the greatest tendency to aggress verbally toward the experimenter's assistant. This occurred, however, only under the choice and expectancy conditions. When subjects had no expectancy, they did not show greater aggressive tendencies when they failed to receive their most-preferred prize. In other words, frustration alone, at least in this experiment, did not increase the tendency to aggress.

Worchel's study illustrates how cognitive factors affect the expression of aggression. Specifically, to the degree that we learn not to expect certain consequences, we will not become frustrated. In our society, standing in line may or may not be frustrating, depending on whether we are cognitively prepared for this event. There are probably many other potentially frustrating events that, as a result of our daily experiences, fail to elicit feelings of frustration and consequently do not increase the tendency toward aggression.

In a recent re-examination of the research pertaining to the frustration-aggression hypothesis, Berkowitz (1989) has suggested that frustration generates aggressive inclinations to the degree that it arouses negative affect. There are numerous reasons people often fail to act aggressively when frustrated and, according to Berkowitz, this is because they fail to arouse negative affect. One reason many situations fail to arouse negative affect is because of various thought processes that are at work. When people perceive, for example, that they have been blocked deliberately or accidentally, they react quite differently. If they perceive they have been deliberately blocked by someone else from reaching their goal they are more likely to react with anger and aggression.

Negative Evaluation

Being evaluated tends to produce a state of apprehension or anxiety in a large part of the population (Mandler & Sarason, 1952). The physiological changes that accompany this state may be summarized as a mild to moderate stress reaction. Anyone who has faced a difficult examination can attest to the fact that tests can cause increased anxiety, increased heart rate, increased perspiration, and other reactions. Being evaluated does not, by itself, increase aggression. However, when the evaluation appears to be arbitrary, harsh, or negative, anger and aggressive behaviors are increased (for example, Donnerstein & Wilson, 1976; Geen & O'Neal, 1969).

The laboratory procedure for showing the effect of negative evaluation typically involves two steps. First, the participant is asked to write an essay or engage in some other activity that involves submitting to a judgment. Next, the participant is given feedback that his or her essay is poor, silly, or unacceptable. Since participants typically try to cooperate by doing their best, arbitrary or harsh feedback generally angers them (Berkowitz, 1962, 1964). The problem for the psychologist has been to delineate exactly why these procedures evoke anger and, further, why anger leads to aggression.

The research on this question seems to indicate that the perceived intent of the person doing the evaluating may be the main determinant of whether anger is evoked. If the evaluator's actions are perceived as just and fair, there appears to be little anger. However, if the evaluator's actions are perceived to be arbitrary, unfair, or harsh, the participant is likely to become angry and behave aggressively (for example, Greenwell & Dengerink, 1973). In many instances, the participant perceives the evaluator as being deliberately provocative (Greenwell & Dengerink, 1973). In such circumstances humans are inclined to retaliate (for example, O'Leary & Dengerink, 1973; Schuck & Pisor, 1974): they evaluate the evaluator (typically the experimenter's assistant) as harshly as or more harshly than they were evaluated.

Insults

Insults have been used fairly extensively in laboratory research to elicit anger. The experimenter or a confederate will act in a rude manner toward the subject, questioning his or her intelligence, desire to cooperate, or promptness, for example (Ax, 1953; Baron & Bell, 1973; J. Schachter, 1957). Insults, of course, are often used in our society when we are frustrated. When a referee calls a personal foul on our favorite football player, we might respond with phrases like "Stupid," "Moron," "Are you blind?" When a sales clerk gives us the wrong item, which we must then return, we may (if the clerk is not present) refer to the clerk as "stupid" or "retarded." Such behavior can be provocative. Indeed, most of us are careful not to call a muscular, 300-pound sales clerk "stupid" directly to his face.

Psychological States and Control Theory

It is not surprising that people will often react aggressively when insulted or when given negative evalua-

tions, because both events question whether we are in control. They are threats to our self-esteem. Frustration results when a goal is blocked. Such an event would immediately challenge my perception that I am in control of events in my environment.

Summary

Several psychological events will evoke aggression in humans. Frustration, provided it is quite intense and unexpected or arbitrary, is likely to evoke aggression. Negative evaluation will often lead to retaliation if an appropriate opportunity is made available. Insults, such as questioning a person's intelligence or his or her willingness to cooperate, have often been used in the laboratory to provoke aggression.

Factors that Suppress Aggression

Many people are concerned about the level of aggression among humans, not only in North America but throughout the world. Animal data indicate that humans are not uniquely aggressive. Both animals and human data indicate that we are equipped with inhibitory mechanisms that enable us to selectively use aggression as a strategy or suppress it altogether when it is in our interest to do so (Lore & Schultz, 1993). In this section I will explore some of the research that pertains to the conditions under which humans suppress aggression.

Anxiety, Fear, and Social Disapproval

In our society, certain forms of aggression, especially physical aggression, are not socially acceptable ways of dealing with people or events in the environment. People who experience a strong need for social approval or people who have anxiety about the use of physical aggression should, therefore, show less tendency toward physical aggression when provoked. Laboratory research has confirmed that in fact, people who have greater anxiety (of any kind, not just anxiety about aggression) show less aggression (for example, Dengerink, 1971) as do people who have a strong need for social approval (for example, Dorsky & Taylor,

PRACTICAL APPLICATION 8.1

Learning to Manage Anger

Anger has been found to be the emotion that is the bridge to both physical and verbal aggression and hostility (Buss & Perry, 1992). Given that this is the case, we need to learn how to manage anger if we are to learn to reduce aggression and hostility.

While a great deal has been written on how to deal with anxiety and how to deal with depression, little has been written on how to deal with anger. This is because we often think that anger is something we cannot or should not control (Tavris, 1989). There is growing evidence, however, that it is an emotion that we can and should learn to manage in the same way that we can and should learn to manage such emotions as anxiety and depression.

Anger is an emotion that can be a very powerful source of positive energy if it is properly channeled. The black movement and the feminist movement both grew out of a strong sense of injustice combined with feelings of anger. While there were people in both movements that allowed their anger to turn to aggression and violence, many if not most people directed their anger towards changing the system. Martin Luther King summed up what happens when anger is properly directed.

> When I am angry I can write, pray, and preach well, for then my whole temperament is quickened, my understanding sharpened, and all mundane vexations and temptations gone.

All of us, I am sure, can think of times when our anger gave us not only direction but energy. A critical comment from a professor on a paper you wrote may have angered you but at the same time it also may have stirred you to think more clearly and argue more precisely. That has been true for me.

When not properly directed or managed, however, anger can be a very destructive emotion. If we allow it to fester inside us, for example, it can lead to such physical problems as hypertension. On the other hand, if we ventilate it (strike out at the source of our anger) we often make matters worse. While there is a school of thought that argues that ventilation is a good way of draining off hostile energy, there is little evidence to support that idea. Many people who do ventilate experience shame and loss of control. In the heat of an angry exchange they say or do things that they regret later. Instead of solving the problem, they make matters worse. In addition, the act of yelling or shouting escalates the negative bodily reactions. Anger turns to rage and people are left in a state of heightened negative emotion. There is considerable evidence that if we learn to control our anger (cool down), we are less likely to fall prey to this problem.

While learning to cool down by counting to ten, for example, is one way of controlling anger it may not be the best long-term solution, especially for people who are chronically angry. People who are chronically angry often view the world in a very different way. Many chronically angry people see the acts of others that are directed towards them as motivated by anger and aggression. As a result, they perceive they are constantly being provoked by others. When a person on a bus rings the bell twice, for example, the chronically angry bus driver might interpret the response as insulting to his or her intelligence or as a deliberate act of provocation. It may be, however, that the person who rang twice is merely anxious about missing their stop and wants to communicate that fact to the driver.

How does one learn to change their perceptual habits without becoming totally passive and helpless? It is a fine line between allowing oneself to become a victim and overreacting with rage to events that we think should not have happened to us. The following are a few things that you might do. For more on this topic I would recommend Carol Tavris's book, *Anger: The Misunderstood Emotion*.

1972). In both studies it was found that the tendency of these groups to inhibit aggression lessened as the strength of provocation increased. Under strong provocation, people high and low in anxiety tend to be

1. Look for another explanation. Sometimes when people are critical or they act in ways that violate the norms or our expectations, it may be they were distracted or under some type of stress. I remember on one occasion when I had to slam on my brakes to avoid a car that ran a stop sign. Even though the car that ran the stop sign only sliced off my front license plate, I was angry. When the elderly driver apologized and explained that he just discovered his wife had cancer, my anger quickly subsided and I felt relieved and thankful.

2. Distract yourself. One of the best ways to cool down is to do something that will not allow you to dwell on your anger. Some people find exercise works, others find reading or watching TV works, still others find that becoming involved in their favorite hobby works.

3. Look for the humor. Humor is a way of recasting a situation to find the incongruity or the absurdity in something. When we can do that our anger will subside because humor is an emotion that is incompatible with anger. Learning to laugh at our reactions not only helps us relieve our anger, it communicates to others that we understand our reactions were not appropriate.

4. Determine what triggers our anger. It has been suggested that we should keep a diary of our anger so that we can discover what types of situations make us angry. Different things make people angry, but there is usually an individual pattern. Once people know what makes them angry they are in a better position to deal with their anger. There are some people, for example, who find that any form of criticism makes them angry, while other people find that certain behaviors of others makes them angry and so forth. Once people understand what triggers their anger, they can make plans for how to deal with such situations (Novaco, 1985).

5. Create an inner dialogue that reduces rather than escalates anger. Most people carry on inner dialogues with themselves. While some people have dialogues that reduce anger, others have dialogues that escalate or maintain their anger (Jacobs, see Tavris, 1989, p. 303). Often in divorce, couples will stay angry with each other for years. When people analyze their inner dialogues, they often find that the inner dialogue is responsible for much of their anger. They may, for example, spend all their time dwelling on one thing, such as an affair their spouse had, and they may discover that they are still trying to extract the kind of apology they thought they deserved but never got.

6. Learn to recognize that life is not always fair. When people don't allow for the fact that the world is less than perfect, they find endless things to make them angry. Not being treated politely, breaking their leg because they tripped on a broken sidewalk, finding they were not invited to a party, having a flat tire on their way to work, all become reasons to get angry. Whether to become angry or not can be a decision. It is a decision that we can learn to make both consciously and unconsciously. We can develop the habit of accepting the fact that life is unfair.

7. Learn to talk it out. When there is conflict, anger is often present as well. Since conflict comes from viewing things from different perspectives, one way to decrease anger is to engage in a dialogue that will enable us to see how the other person or persons view the situation. While we may not always agree with the other person, talking with them provides the basis for negotiating some kind of solution or compromise. Most of us do not like to compromise, but once we can learn that a compromise is better than the continuing presence of anger, we can learn to value the fine art of compromise as a means for living a happier and more stress-free life.

equally aggressive, and people who are high and low in need for social approval are approximately equal in ag-

gression. This finding indicates that as anger increases, personality variables, at least those mentioned here, tend to play a less important role in the expression of aggression. This finding is consistent with studies that have shown that the threat of strong retaliation is effective when anger is at a low level but is almost totally ineffective when anger is very strong (Baron, 1973). It makes sense from a survival point of view that a person should retaliate more severely when strongly threatened. It may be desirable for the society to establish prohibitions against aggression, but for the individual it could be fatal, either physically or psychologically, to fail to respond in the face of a strong provocation.

Empathy

There is considerable evidence that people who tend to be more empathetic as indicated by self-report are less inclined to be aggressive (Miller & Eisenberg, 1988). While there is a persistent myth that females are more empathetic than males, there is no research evidence to support that idea.

As might be expected, abusive parents tend to score lower on measures of empathy compared with a "normal" population (N. D. Feshbach, 1987). Further, children who were abused tend to exhibit less empathy than nonabused children. In fact, there is considerable evidence that this lack of empathy by abusive parents has long-term negative implications for the socio-emotional development of these children. The lack of empathy and generally poor emotional development may account for the cycle of violence that I referred to earlier. It has been suggested that empathy training may be one way of helping break this cycle of violence (Miller & Eisenberg, 1988).

Summary

Anxiety, fear and social disapproval all tend to inhibit the expression of aggression. This tends to weaken, however, when the strength of provocation increases. People who are inclined to empathize are less likely to act aggressively.

Anger, when properly directed, can be a positive source of energy, but when not positively directed it can be a very disruptive emotion. People can learn to do at least six things to manage their anger: (1) look

for another explanation, (2) distract themselves, (3) look for the humor, (4) determine what triggers their anger, (5) create an inner dialogue that reduces rather than escalates anger, (6) learn to recognize that life is not always fair, and (7) learn to talk it out.

Main Points

1.   Human aggression has frequently been defined as the intent to harm another human. Ethologists do not view aggression as good or bad; rather, they view it as an expression of the self-preservation motive.

2.   Even though newspapers and television report numerous violent crimes, only about 3% of the population is involved, and most of these are between people who know each other.

3.   Most people attempt to avoid acts that might provoke physical aggression.

4.   In the teacher-learner paradigm, physical aggression by participants (the teacher) towards others (a learner) is justified as a means of understanding how punishment can be used to help people to learn.

5.   Research suggests that physical aggression, at least in the teacher-learner paradigm, may not necessarily reflect a desire to harm.

6.   In the evaluation paradigm, physical aggression is elicited by administering physical punishment to the subject under the pretext that it is some form of evaluation and then allowing the subject to retaliate. People typically retaliate in like kind.

7.   Massive retaliation, according to Patterson, is designed to inform the attacker that the aggressive exchange should stop.

8.   When an aggressive act is motivated by the desire to achieve a desired goal, and is not motivated by the desire to hurt or harm another person, it is called instrumental aggression.

9.   When anger is linked to aggression it is called affective or angry aggression.

10.   Often aggressive behavior grows out of a need to control other people.

11.   It has been suggested that violence towards

men, women, minorities, gays, and lesbians grows out of a need to maintain existing power structures.

12.   The fact that it is possible to breed animals for aggressive behavior suggests that aggression in animals is determined in part by genotion.

13.   Moyer has suggested that there are at least eight kinds of aggression.

14.   Several brain structures have been identified as mediating different kinds of aggressive behavior (hypothalamus, amygdala, septum, hippocampus).

15.   These brain structures have been shown to interact with social dominance in the expression of aggression.

16.   The male sex hormone testosterone has been shown to augment aggression under certain conditions.

17.   In women, the fall in progesterone level just before menstruation, together with the relative rise in estrogen level, has been associated with aggression.

18.   While self-reported aggression in human males has been linked to testosterone and estradiol, self-reported aggression in human females has been negatively linked to high levels of testosterone and estradiol.

19.   It has been shown that aggressive behavior can be both punished and rewarded.

20.   One of the main ways children learn aggression is through observation and imitation.

21.   There are wide variations in how aggression is expressed.

22.   Whether or not people behave aggressively is often governed by norms.

23.   People sometimes respond to a wide variety of negative situations with anger and aggression.

24.   Internals are more likely to respond with aggression than externals if the aggression will help them achieve a goal or remove a barrier or noxious stimulus.

25.   According to Ferguson and Rule, there are three separate attributions that people are inclined to make before they will retaliate: intent, foreseeability of harm, and motive.

26.   According to Weiner, people do not become angered by unpleasant events unless these events can be attributed to someone's intentional and controllable misdeeds.

27.   Deindividuation is a state in which the inner restraints are lost when "individuals are not seen or paid attention to as individuals."

28.   While males, on the average, tend to be more aggressive than females, the magnitude of the difference is quite small.

29.   Women are more likely than men to behave in a nonhostile fashion when provoked.

30.   In addition to the finding that anger suppressors are at greater risk than anger expressors for hypertension and cardiovascular disorders, it has been found that men are at greater risk than women, that blacks are at greater risk than whites, and that people living in high-stress neighborhoods are at greater risk.

31.   Also at risk for hypertension as well as coronary heart disease are people who have a personality style that is characterized by hostility.

32.   Intense and unexpected frustration, negative evaluation, and insult are some of the more common psychological states that evoke aggression.

33.   Pornography that portrays violence toward women can alter attitudes or beliefs that may lead to increases in aggression by men against women.

34.   There is evidence that watching TV violence is correlated with increased aggression. However, children who are already aggressive are more likely to watch violence on TV.

35.   Most people inhibit the tendency to retaliate physically when provoked. Such inhibition seems to be greatest among people who are sensitive to the evaluations of others and who value an orderly society. It is not surprising, therefore, that people who are alienated in some way from society are more prone to physical violence and destructiveness.

36.   People who are empathetic are less likely to behave aggressively.

37.   Learning to control anger is not only possible, but seems desirable.

Chapter Nine

The Nature of Emotions: The Example of Stress

- Why is stress viewed as an emotion? What causes stress?
- Why is stress often referred to as the fight/flight response?
- How are arousal and the stress reaction related?
- What chemicals are released when we are under stress and what do these chemicals do?

- Is it true that our learning is altered when we are experiencing stress?
- Why do people often fail to experience pain when they are injured?
- Why does stress often lead to disease?
- Why is it important to consider emotions in a text on motivation?

- What is the nature of emotions?
- What are some of the things that give rise to stress in humans?
- Why are people doing research on stress so interested in the Type A personality?
- What are some of the moderators of stress?
- What can people do to cope with stress?

Why It Is Important to Consider Emotions

Researchers have argued that you cannot think about emotions without considering motivation and that you cannot think about motivation without considering emotion (Frijda, 1988; Lazarus, 1991). This has not always been the case. Not until quite recently have psychologists incorporated the concept of emotions into their theories of motivation or the role of motivation into theories of emotion. In the 1930s and 1940s, motivation was conceptualized in terms of needs. Needs were thought to provide the impetus (energy), the direction, and the persistence of behavior. Little was said about the role of emotions. In the 1950s and 1960s, motivation was conceptualized as due the existence of *drives*. In these early theories, drives provided the energy or impetus for behavior while learning provided the direction (Hull, 1943). According to the drive theorists, emotions were thought to be mainly a by-product of motivation but not integral to motivation. Berlyne (1960), for example, conceptualized motivation as the drive for *optimal arousal* and viewed *affect* as a by-product of satisfying that drive. Persistence-within-drive theory was conceptualized as largely learned. According to Amsel's (1958, 1972) theory, for example, persistence was largely due to the counterconditioning of stimuli that had come to be linked with frustration, and frustration was a very limited concept of emotion, an emotion that grew out of the failure to receive a reward.

In the later 1960s and early 1970s, psychologists began to talk about motivation in terms of action. Motives and needs were central in this conceptualization, but needs were conceptualized very differently than they had been in the 1930s and 1940s. Instead of viewing needs as causing action, psychologists began to view needs as merely *dispositions* to action. What created action were goals and threats; goals were conceptualized as positive incentives and threats as negative incentives (Atkinson & Birch, 1978; de Rivera, 1982; Raynor, 1974; Weiner, 1974).

While conceptualizing motivation in terms of goals proved to be a powerful theory (Locke & Latham, 1990; Pervin, 1989; Snyder et al., 1991), it became apparent to a number of theorists that while goals and threats were perhaps the impetus to immediate action, they often failed to account for long-term action. While some people persisted in their goal-directed behavior, others did not. What seemed to differentiate people in terms of their persistence was their emotions. While some people found they could remain optimistic in the face of threats and difficulties, others would develop feelings of pessimism and self-doubt which often resulted in their abandoning their goals (Seligman, 1990). While the exact nature of the emotions was often different for different theorists, they all agreed that emotions played a critical role.

This observation led a variety of psychologists to argue that people need to learn to self-regulate their emotions. As Albert Bandura pointed out, "Talent is only as good as its execution" (Bandura, 1991). In order for people to achieve goals, he argued, they need to learn how to manage these emotions, especially the emotion of self-doubt.

In this section on emotions, I discuss some of the basic emotions that have clearly been implicated in goal-directed behavior. The major focus of this section is to understand how people can learn to develop those emotions that can sustain goal-directed behavior on the one hand, and neutralize or deflect those emotions that tend to undermine goal-directed behavior, on the other hand.

The Universal Nature of Emotions

Core Relational Themes

All emotions, it has been argued by various theorists, arise out of our interactions with the environment and result from our attempts to adapt to the environment.

Evidence from a variety of sources suggests that there are a common set of emotions that all humans experience. These emotions can be described by their "core relational themes" (Lazarus, 1991). Table 9-1 presents a list of some core relational themes for various emotions. Lazarus uses the term *relational* to emphasize the idea that emotions grow out of our interactions with the environment. He uses the term *theme* to emphasize the idea that emotions are highly cognitive and involve interpretation. Finally, he uses the term *core* to emphasize the idea that emotions are often complex, involving two or more emotions operating simultaneously. Therefore, it may be necessary when examining an emotional response to identify the various core themes and define the emotional response in terms of those core themes. This would obviously help us reduce the complexity that results when various core emotions interact.

Facial Expression

People who have studied facial expression have found that certain basic emotions such as happiness, anger, distress, disgust, can be identified in a wide range of cultures. This gives credence to the idea there are core relational themes underlying emotions. Some researchers who have studied facial expression have even argued that most if not all emotions are a product of heredity. Whether or not this is true is still being hotly debated, since other researchers view emotions as largely the product of learning and culture (see Ekman, 1989).

One thing that seems quite clear is that when people experience an emotion they are inclined to wear that emotion on their face. Further, there is evidence that when people deliberately put on a happy or a sad face they tend to trigger that subjective emotion that corresponds to the facial expression (e.g., Izard, 1990). Based on the observation that emotions and facial expression are closely linked, Izard has suggested that people can learn to regulate their subjective feelings by learning to control their facial expressions (Izard, 1990). The bottom line is that if you want to be happy, you put on a happy face.

Table 9-1. Core Relational Themes for Various Emotions (From R. S. Lazarus, *Emotion and Adaptation*, 1991, 122. Copyright © 1991 by Oxford University Press, New York. Reprinted with permission.)

Anger	A demeaning offense against me and mine.
Anxiety	Facing uncertain, existential threat.
Fright	Facing immediate, concrete, and overwhelming physical danger.
Guilt	Having transgressed a moral imperative.
Shame	Having failed to live up to an ego-ideal.
Sadness	Having experienced an irrevocable loss.
Envy	Wanting what someone else has.
Jealousy	Resenting a third party for loss or threat to another's affection.
Disgust	Taking in or being too close to an indigestible object or idea (metaphorically speaking).
Happiness	Making reasonable progress towards the realization of a goal.
Pride	Enhancement of one's ego-identity by taking credit for a valued object or achievement.
Relief	A distressing goal-incongruent condition that has changed for the better or gone away.
Hope	Fearing the worst but yearning for better.
Love	Desiring or participating in affection, usually but not necessarily reciprocated.
Compassion	Being moved by another's suffering and wanting to help.

The Role of Appraisal in Emotion

While there are a common set of emotions that seem to characterize all humans (core relational themes), whether or not we experience a certain emotion depends on how we appraise a situation (Lazarus, 1991). We might ask ourselves, for example: "What emotion is appropriate for this situation, given my goals, my motives and my concerns?" The idea that appraisal plays an important role in our emotions suggests, of course, that the cognitions are central to emotions. If cognitions (ways of thinking) are important, then the implicit theories that people hold are also important. That means, for example, that if people tend to view the world optimistically versus pessimistically, they will experience a very different pattern of emotions; they will be happier if they think optimistically versus pessimistically. As we will see, how much stress people experience depends to a very large degree on whether they appraise a situation as a threat or a challenge. Since people are inclined to appraise situations differently, for reasons that we will discuss in more detail later, large individual differences in emotion often occur.

Definition of Emotion

Probably because emotions are so complex, a wide variety of definitions has been proposed over the years. In an attempt to arrive at a consensual definition, Paul Kleinginna and Anne Kleinginna (1981b) examined the definitions in use and proposed a definition that incorporated the key elements of existing definitions. According to this consensual definition, emotions occur as a result of an interaction between subjective factors, environmental factors, and neural/hormonal processes. In support of this definition, they point out that emotions *(a)* give rise to affective experiences (such as pleasure or displeasure), *(b)* stimulate the individual to generate cognitive explanations (to attribute the cause to oneself or to the environment, for example), *(c)* trigger a variety of internal adjustments (such as increased heart rate), and *(d)* elicit behaviors that are often, but not always, expressive (laughing or crying), goal-directed (helping or avoiding), and adaptive (removal of something that may threaten the individual's survival). It is worth noting here that this definition acknowledges that emotions result from the interaction of biological, learned and cognitive processes.

One very important additional function of emotions is to reward and punish behavior. When people experience a very positive emotion, they are likely to engage in behaviors that will produce that emotion again. Similarly, when people experience a very negative emotion, they will avoid behaviors that will cause them to feel that emotion again.

Classification of Emotions

Many researchers have focused their efforts on how to classify emotions so that it is possible to understand and make rational sense of the the wide range of emotions that people exhibit. So many classification systems have been put forth that it would be impossible to review them all here. Since this approach has not proved to be that successful, many researchers have taken another approach, which is to try to identify some of the common underlying dimensions of emotions.

Identifying Dimensions of Emotions

If you ask people to characterize various emotions—fear, anger, sadness, happiness, disgust—they typically use three basic dimensions: *(a)* pleasant/unpleasant, *(b)* active/passive, and *(c)* intense/not intense (Daly, Lancee, & Polivy, 1983). The emotion of sadness, for example, is typically characterized as unpleasant and passive. The intensity of sadness varies with the situation, from extreme to slight. Sadness is usually experienced as a very intense emotion if it has been precipitated by the death of a loved one. Sadness is typically viewed as a passive emotion because there often is little one can do about the situation. Besides, when people are sad, they often lack the motivation to do anything. The emotion of happiness, on the other hand, is characterized as pleasant and active. If we are very happy, as we might be if we won a lottery, we are likely to be very active. We might, for example, want to have a party. While various researchers agree that emotions can be described in terms of a limited number of dimensions, they have reached no consensus on the names or numbers of those dimensions (for example, Russell & Steiger, 1982).

Lawfulness of Emotions

It has been suggested that emotions are a lawful phenomena and thus can be described in terms of a set of

Table 9-2. Laws of Emotions.(Adapted from on N. H. Frijda, "The Laws of Emotion." *American Psychologist*, 1988, 43, 349-353. Copyright © 1971 by the American Psychological Association. Adapted with the author's permission.)

1.   Law of Situational Meaning. The situation must match or be congruent with the cognitive structure that people have for a given emotion.

Example 1. *Falling in love*. If you believe that in order to fall in love, the other person must be a stranger, the situation must be romantic, and you must be alone and not otherwise occupied, then meeting someone on a cruise ship would provide the perfect set of circumstances in which to fall in love.

Example 2. *Experiencing sadness*. If you believe that the death of a politician you admired but never met is an irrevocable loss, you will likely experience sadness, but if you do not see this person's death as an irrevocable loss you may experience little or no sadness.

2.   Law of Concern. Emotions are *subjective experiences* that arise in response to events that are important to the individual's goals, motivations, or concerns.

Example. *Experiencing pride versus shame*. An individual whose life-long ambition is to become a medical doctor might experience shame upon receiving a B on a test because that event could be viewed as an obstacle that might prevent him or her from getting into medical school. An individual whose ambition was to get a degree might experience pride because they performed above average.

3.   Law of Apparent Reality. Emotions are elicited only to the degree that the eliciting situation seems real or is appraised as real, with the intensity of the emotion corresponding to its apparent reality. According to this law, vivid imagination can act as a substitute for reality.

Example. *Maintaining the desire to train through vivid imagination*. Mark Tewksbury, who was on our university swim team and won a gold medal in the 100-meter backstroke at the 1992 Olympics, said that one of the things that helped him maintain his desire to train was the image he created of what it would be like to win. He said he vividly imagined not only hearing the crowd applaud when he won but that he could see an official putting the gold medal around his neck. (Note in this example how emotion leads to action readiness.)

4.   The Law of Expected Change. Emotions are elicited not so much by the presence of favorable or unfavorable conditions but by *actual or expected changes in favorable or unfavorable conditions*.

Example. *Winning a handsome contract*. Winning a contract to supply half the furniture for a new office building could make one salesperson euphoric (because she had never won such a big contract before) and another sad or dejected (because he was accustomed to winning the whole contract, not just half).

5.   The Law of Habituation. Continued pleasures wear off and continued hardships lose their painfulness.

Example 1. *Performing a skill*. People who experience exhilaration at performing a skill, such as climbing a mountain, need to find new and more challenging mountains in order to overcome the loss of emotion that comes from habituation.

Example 2. *Love*. People will eventually get over a lost love, but unfortunately their present love may also lose its magic.

6. The Law of Comparative Feeling. The intensity of an emotion depends on comparing the current outcome with previous outcomes.

Example 1. *Experiencing stress.* If you have always found that you could cope or deal with a certain situation, your unexpected inability to cope or deal with that or a similar situation would result in great stress, perhaps overwhelming stress.

Example 2. *Experiencing a breakthrough.* If you suddenly and unexpectedly solve a problem that you have been working on for some time, the joy you would experience would be greater if you had failed on many similar attempts. Discovering how to increase the gas mileage of a standard car engine after years of failure would likely result in a state of true euphoria.

7. The Law of Hedonic Asymmetry. While pleasure is always contingent upon change and disappears with continuous satisfaction, pain may continue under persisting adverse conditions.

Example. *Praise versus criticism.* A rock star may habituate to the applause of fans but never get used to the jibes and taunts of music critics.

8. The Law of Conservation of Emotional Momentum. Some events retain their power to elicit emotions indefinitely, unless counteracted by repetitive exposures that permit extinction or habituation. This law grows out of the observation that time often does not soften emotion or heal old wounds. This law can be viewed as a further restriction on the law of habituation (#5).

Example. *War and the loss of a loved one.* People who have suffered tragedy and adversity, such as the loss of a child in a fire, or have experienced the stark brutality of war, often cringe with the same intense emotion that they experienced when the event took place. Often professional help involving repetitive exposure is needed to deal with such stubborn emotions.

9. The Law of Absoluteness. Emotions tend to be absolute and not influenced by other needs and concerns. This law is intended to capture the observation that when people fall in love, for example, their feelings are absolute, or when they are angered their desire for revenge is often absolute.

Example 1. *Falling in love.* People fall in love even though the other person lives 10,000 miles away and would be rejected by their family.

Example 2. *Wanting revenge.* People want revenge even though they know they could lose their job or be severely punished.

(continued on next page)

laws of emotion (Frijda, 1988). Frijda use the word law to emphasize the idea that there are empirical regularities. He suggests that by understanding these regularities, we can better grasp what is meant by emotions and how they arise. Frijda's laws of emotion are based on the idea that emotional experiences consist of two components: appraisal and action readiness (Frijda, Kuipers, ter Schure,1989). Frijda's laws are summarized in Table 9-2.

Table 9-2. Laws of Emotions *(continued)*

10. The Law of Care for Consequences. "Every emotional impulse elicits a secondary impulse that tends to modify it in view of its possible consequences" (Frijda, 1988, pp. 355). Frijda notes that emotions are not always characterized by the attribute of absoluteness as suggested by the above law. In fact, he argues, there is a tendency for humans to reflect on their emotions, which may lead to the termination of an action or even to an opposite action.

Example. *The urge for massive retaliation.* Since massive retaliation may lead to further negative consequences, a person may decide to inhibit his or her desire to retaliate massively or perhaps decide not to retaliate at all.

11. The Law of Lightest Load. When people are experiencing a negative emotion (causing load), they are inclined to look for alternative ways of interpreting that event in order to reduce the negative emotion (lighten the load).

Example. *Reducing pain and stress.* Defensive denial, denial, avoidant thinking, entertaining illusionary hopes, are some of the ways that people reduce pain and stress.

12. The Law of Greatest Gain. When people are experiencing a positive emotion, they are inclined to look for alternative ways of interpreting that event in order to maximize the positive emotions. This law is based on the idea that emotions can produce gains and that humans attempt to get whatever gain they can from their positive emotions.

Example. *Maximizing the pleasure one gets from putting someone in their place.* Having enjoyed putting someone down, a person may justify his or her angry and aggressive behavior by taking the high moral ground and saying that, "It was time this person was put in their place and I took the responsibility upon myself of doing so." In doing so, they can relish in their success.

Summary

While early theorists conceptualized motivation in terms of *drives*, current theorists conceptualize motivation in terms of needs, which are viewed as *dispositions*. While goals are often the impetus for action, sustained action appears to come from positive emotions such as optimism. It has been suggested that people can learn to regulate their emotions and thus sustain goal-directed behavior.

Evidence from a variety of sources suggests that there is a common set of emotions that can be described in terms of their "core relational themes." Further evidence for the existence of a common set of emotions comes from the work on facial expression. While there are a common set of emotions that seem to characterize all humans (core relational themes), whether or not we experience a certain emotion depends on how we appraise a situation. According to the definition of emotion, emotions give rise to affective experiences, stimulate the individual to generate cognitive explanations, trigger a variety of internal adjustments, and elicit expressive, goal-directed, and adaptive behaviors. When people are asked to characterize emotions, they tend to view them in terms of three dimensions: pleasant/unpleasant, active/passive, and intense/not intense.

Use Your Emotions to Identify Your Goals, Motives, and Concerns

Since emotions reflect our goals, motives, and concerns (Frijda, 1988), we can use our emotions to help identify our goals, motives and concerns. At first, this may sound like an odd exercise since most people believe they have a good knowledge of what they want and what is important to them. What they often fail to understand, however, is that they have goals, motives and concerns in their more primitive/unconscious system of which they are largely unaware (Epstein, 1991). This system often houses the goals, motives and concerns that our parents gave us early in life. The ones that we are aware of are largely housed in the so-called rational/conscious system. In order to get at one or both of these systems, we can systematically keep track of our emotional responses in a variety of situations and then analyze our reactions to see if we can discover the meaning structures that would explain our reactions. The situations that I like to analyze are those in which I find my reactions were inappropriate, exaggerated, or inhibited. In other words, I like to analyze my reactions when they do not fit with my perceptions of how I think I should have reacted or how I should behave (my ideal-self).

Let me describe a person I will call Jane. Upon hearing that her brother had won a scholarship, she immediately called her mother to find out more details. As she talked with her mother she felt hurt that her mother expressed such admiration for her brother's achievement. Jane began to denigrate his accomplishment by belittling the magnitude of the achievement, saying that a lot of people got that award and suggesting that he had "buttered up" the right people to win it. After hanging up the phone, she felt guilty about what she had done. She loved her brother and wished him the best. Why, therefore, had she done this? She would be mortified if her brother ever found out what she had said to their mother. Now she began to experience a sense of shame.

When Jane began to analyze her response she realized that this was not the first time she had done this. As she thought about other situations, she began to realize that she often felt hurt when she was not the center of her mother's attention. As she thought about it more and more, she realized that the emotion she was experiencing was envy or perhaps jealousy (see Table of Core Relational Themes). She had always been envious of her brother even though her mother often praised her for her accomplishments. Jane found she couldn't go any further with discovering the meaning of her emotions until some time later when she heard about conditional love—the concept that some parents give love only when their children have done something they value. When she realized this she immediately understood why she was envious of her brother. Because he had accomplished so much, he was the recipient of more love. She felt left out and, like any child who believes there is a scarcity of something he or she wants, she tried to convince her mother that he didn't really deserve the praise, hoping to get some of that same praise for herself.

Identify an emotional response to a situation, either a positive one or a negative one, and see if you can explain why you experienced that emotion. Why did you feel so proud or why did you feel so mortified? One of the reasons why people experience a sense of rage is that they have failed to clearly differentiate their emotions. You may not be able to totally explain your reactions the first time, but the more you do this the better you will become at specifying why you tend to experience the emotions that you do. When you can explain why, then you have discovered the meaning structure for that emotion in that situation. It is important to remember that emotions are situation specific. Therefore, you need to keep track of the situation in order to discover your "meaning structure" for a certain emotion.

Frijda's laws of emotion are based on the idea that emotional experiences consist of two components: appraisal and action readiness. Each emotional experience is viewed as determined by cognitive structures that represent our goals, motives and concerns. Whether or not an emotion is elicited depends on our cognitive structure (law of situational meaning) and on the degree to which we perceive the situation as real (law of apparent reality). What elicits an emotional experience is not the presence of favorable or unfavorable conditions per se, but changes (actual or expected) in favorable or unfavorable conditions (law of expected change). When things go as expected (favorable) we experience pleasure, but when they go against us (unfavorable) we experience pain (law of comparative feeling). Repeating an activity, either one that produces pleasure or pain, typically results in habituation (law of habituation), emphasizing the idea that change is important in order for us to experience emotions (law of change). There are limitations, however, to the law of habituation, especially as it pertains to certain painful events. There are some painful events to which we never habituate (law of hedonic asymmetry). Still a further limitation of the law of habituation is the law which states that certain emotional events retain their power to elicit emotions indefinitely, unless counteracted (often in a therapeutic setting) by repetitive exposure (law of conservation of emotional momentum). The observation that emotions often tend to be absolute as opposed to relative illustrates the idea that the action-readiness component of emotions can and often does dominate the cognitive side of emotions (law of absoluteness). A limitation to this idea is the proposition that every emotion elicits a tendency (impulse) to consider the consequences, which may lead us to modify or inhibit our actions (law of care of consequences). Finally, according to Frijda's theory, people are inclined to appraise situations in such a way as to maximize their pleasure and minimize their pain (law of greatest gain).

Stress, Distress and Coping

Definition

Stress has to do with *adapting to threat*, or to use a more positive word, it has to do with *adapting to challenge*

(Friedman, 1992). We often use the term *stress* in our daily lives in connection with a variety of events, including taking examinations, the breakup of a marriage or other close relationship, the difficulty involved in not having enough money to pay our bills, the annoyance and frustration of having to drive on congested roads, the conflict that occurs when we have to deal with someone we dislike or with whom we disagree.

People have come to use the word stress to describe a diverse set of negative feelings and reactions that accompany threats and challenges. Failing an examination can be experienced as a highly aversive event that produces feelings of humiliation and shame, but it is also experienced as stress. The breakup of a close relationship may lead to a deep sense of loss and remorse which, too, is often experienced as stress. Not being able to pay our bills can be frustrating and irritating and for many is referred to as one of those stresses of life. Driving on a crowded road may produce both frustration and anger, and again is often described as a daily stressful event. Interpersonal relationships that are marked by conflict can lead to contempt and disgust. For many people this is yet another example of daily stress.

The lay person, then, generally uses the term *stress* to describe negative feelings. But the scientist uses it somewhat differently. Stress is generally viewed as a set of neurological/physiological reactions that serve some ultimate adaptive purpose, a process I will describe shortly. How the individual responds to those reactions determines whether they produce feelings of *distress* (a negative feeling) or produce feelings of *eustress* (a positive feeling). In general, when people view an event as threatening they experience distress, but when they view a situation as challenging they experience eustress.

What the current research indicates is that when people interpret an event as challenging versus threatening, the effects on health are quite different. When an event is interpreted as challenging people, their health is not adversely affected, whereas when they interpret an event as threatening, their health can be adversely affected. In general, when people interpret an event as challenging they engage in coping responses, and it is believed by some researchers that the differences in health may be due to these coping responses. Among other things, that means that merely learning to make appropriate coping responses will lead to improved health (Cohen & Williamson, 1991; Friedman, 1991). In the second half of the chapter I will talk about the links between stress and health.

Conceptualizing Stress as a Fight/Flight Response

When people talk about the stress reaction, they frequently refer to it as the fight/flight response. This label grows out of an evolutionary analysis of the origins of the stress response. Animals have two basic ways of dealing with threats: they fight or they flee. A rabbit depends on its ability to flee in order to stay alive. A lion, in contrast, depends on its ability to fight to stay alive as well as to obtain the food supply that it requires. Whether one fights or flees, certain basic requirements must be met. First, one needs to expend a great deal of energy. Second, one has to keep one's head. Third, one frequently has to deal with injury. Stress can be viewed as a reaction that maximizes the expenditure of energy (see Figure 9-1). Blood rushes to the sites where it is needed (the muscles and brain), fats are released into the bloodstream, we perspire to cool ourselves, and so forth. The high level of arousal we experience helps us to focus our attention on survival cues. Our blood thickens, and chemicals are released that will enable our body to deal with injury, should it occur.

From a stress-management point of view, the problem is that we live in a world where we do not have to expend the same amount of physical energy as our foraging ancestors did, nor are we normally threatened with injury when we experience stress. We no longer need to have so much fat released in our blood, we do not need to perspire, it is not necessary for our blood pressure to skyrocket, it is not necessary for our blood to thicken to guard against an injury, we do not need to have chemicals circulating in our blood ready to attack some foreign body that might enter our system.

Even though it is not necessary for any of these things to happen, each time we experience stress our body prepares itself as though we were still living as our ancestors lived.

The Biological Component

Distinguishing between the Sympathetic/Adrenal and the Pituitary/Adrenal Responses

When people are challenged, they tend to mobilize a great deal of effort in order to deal with that event. Similarly, when people lose control, they may try to reassert their control. Under these conditions the body makes what is called a sympathetic/adrenal response. The sympathetic system allows us to respond to the immediate demands of the situation by activating the body. Our heart rate accelerates, our blood pressure rises, we become more alert, and so forth. In short, we become aroused (see Chapter 3). Two main chemicals, epinephrine and norepinephrine, are released by the adrenal glands (see Figure 9-2) to provide a chemical backup to the immediate action of the sympathetic system. These two chemicals are released from the adrenal medulla (the inner part of the gland; see Figure 9-3). Epinephrine and norepinephrine are also referred to as adrenaline and noradrenaline, respectively, especially when those chemicals are released to the periphery of the system rather than to the brain. As this distinction is often ignored, however, we will call them by the names most commonly given them: epinephrine and norepinephrine.

The pituitary/adrenal system is more closely associated with what is traditionally called the stress response. The adrenal cortex (the outer part of the gland) secretes two main hormones, mineralocorticoids and glucocorticoids. It is important to understand that the release of these two hormones is linked to the release of other chemicals. I will discuss this pattern of responses shortly. The point I want to make here is simply that when people are faced with stress, they often engage in behaviors that are designed to eliminate or control the stress. Thus, the sympathetic/adrenal and the pituitary/adrenal responses typically occur together. These two systems, however, can and fre-

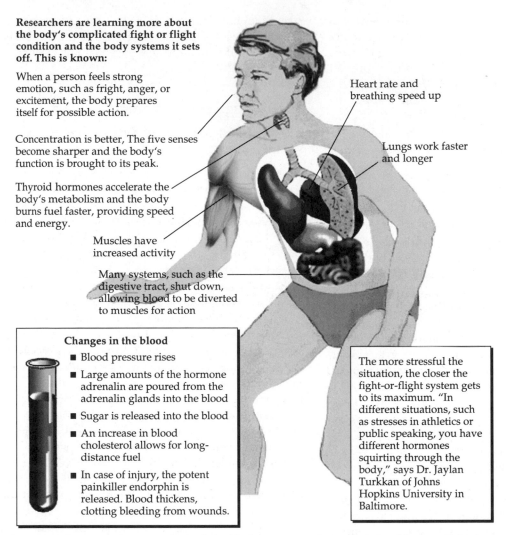

Researchers are learning more about the body's complicated fight or flight condition and the body systems it sets off. This is known:

When a person feels strong emotion, such as fright, anger, or excitement, the body prepares itself for possible action.

Concentration is better, The five senses become sharper and the body's function is brought to its peak.

Thyroid hormones accelerate the body's metabolism and the body burns fuel faster, providing speed and energy.

Muscles have increased activity

Many systems, such as the digestive tract, shut down, allowing blood to be diverted to muscles for action

Heart rate and breathing speed up

Lungs work faster and longer

Changes in the blood
- Blood pressure rises
- Large amounts of the hormone adrenalin are poured from the adrenalin glands into the blood
- Sugar is released into the blood
- An increase in blood cholesterol allows for long-distance fuel
- In case of injury, the potent painkiller endorphin is released. Blood thickens, clotting bleeding from wounds.

The more stressful the situation, the closer the fight-or-flight system gets to its maximum. "In different situations, such as stresses in athletics or public speaking, you have different hormones squirting through the body," says Dr. Jaylan Turkkan of Johns Hopkins University in Baltimore.

Figure 9–1. Stress can be viewed as a fight/flight response. Stress is defined by psychologists as a set of neurological/physiological reactions that act are ultimately adaptive. (Adapted from Rob Struthers, "Stress Reaction." Copyright © The Calgary Herald. Adapted with permission.)

quently do operate separately, generally when an individual gains control over stress by engaging in some kind of adaptive behavior. As one gains control, the cortisol level frequently drops while the epinephrine level remains high (Frankenhaeuser, Lundberg, & Forsman, 1980). Cortisol is frequently used as a mea-sure of the action of the pituitary/adrenal system, whereas urinary epinephrine is a measure of the activity of the sympathetic/adrenal system. As we have already explored the nature of the sympathetic/adrenal system in Chapter 3, let us turn now to the pituitary/adrenal system.

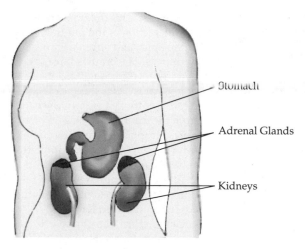

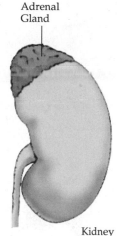

Figure 9–2. The location of the adrenal glands in the body. (From K. B. Hoyenga and K. T. Hoyenga, *Motivational Explanations of Behavior.* Copyright © 1984 by Wadsworth, Inc.)

The Pituitary/Adrenal Response

Figure 9-3 is a schematic representation of the pituitary/adrenal system. The hypothalamus initiates activity in the endocrine system by secreting corticotropin-releasing factor (CRF), which stimulates the pituitary. The pituitary, in turn, secretes adrenocorticotropic hormone (ACTH).

Experimental findings suggest that ACTH plays a central role in our ability to respond to threatening stimuli. Curiously, ACTH stimulates another hormonal reaction that is responsible for terminating the secretion of further ACTH. Specifically, ACTH stimulates the adrenal cortex, which then secretes glucocorticoids. When the glucocorticoid level is elevated, the central nervous system shuts down the processes that lead to the secretion of the stimulating hormone ACTH (de Wied, 1967, 1980; Vernikos-Danellis & Heybach, 1980).

Animal research indicates that ACTH is released approximately 10 seconds after a stressful event. The slowness of this reaction in comparison with the immediate action of the central nervous system suggests that the endocrine system is probably not responsible for the immediate survival responses of fight and flight, but is probably involved in longer-term survival reactions. For example, ACTH stimulates the release of fatty acids and the utilization of glucose, which provide the energy to deal with a threat (White, Handler,

& Smith, 1964). It takes between 15 minutes and 1 hour before glucocorticoids are elevated to a level sufficient to terminate secretion of ACTH (Vernikos-Danellis & Heybach, 1980). Thus, once the stress reaction has been set in motion, it continues for a time. The glucocorticoids remain active much longer than ACTH. It has been suggested that the continued presence of glucocorticoids in the blood accounts for some post-stress reactions such as weight loss, changes in body temperature, and increased secretion of stomach acid (Weiss, 1968).

A somewhat different pattern of events occurs when a stressor is present for a long time. It appears that prolonged stress results in a breakdown of the adrenal system, making the person susceptible to a wide variety of diseases. This question will be dealt with a little later under the heading "Stress and Disease."

Endorphins and Stress

It has been observed that beta-endorphin is mobilized from the pituitary during stress in approximately the same quantities as ACTH (Rossier, Bloom, & Guillemin, 1980). The main significance of this fact may be its ability to explain why stress tends to induce analgesia (Akil et al., 1976). In addition, it has been shown that endorphins produce feelings of euphoria. It appears that endorphins produce these feelings by alter-

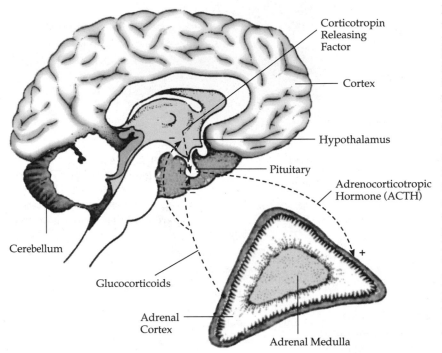

Figure 9–3. This diagram shows the interaction of the pituitary, hypothalamic, and adrenal cortical hormones. The brain is illustrated in a so-called midsagittal section—that is , as if sliced down the middle, halfway between the ears, from the front to the back. Corticotropin-releasing hormone from the hypothalamus stimulates secretion of ACTH from the pituitary. ACTH stimulates the secretion of the corticosteroids from the adrenal cortex into the bloodstream. In turn, the glucocorticoids inhibit both the hypothalamic and pituitary secretion of hormones. This process is an example of a negative feedback loop. (From K. B. Hoyenga and K. T. Hoyenga, *Motivational Explanations of Behavior.* Copyright © 1984 by Wadsworth, Inc.)

ing concentrations of neurotransmitters that activate the reward pathways in the brain (J. E. Smith et al., 1980).

Laboratory studies of endorphins indicate that the endorphin response can be triggered not only by physical stressors, such as shock, but by fear (see Bolles & Fanselow, 1982). This finding may explain why people frequently expose themselves to situations that elicit fear, such as parachuting and mountain climbing.

The Work of Hans Selye, the Grandfather of Stress Research

Hans Selye, the person who has had the greatest impact on our understanding of stress, published an article in 1936 suggesting that a wide variety of diseases are associated with a common reaction that has come to be called the stress reaction or the general adaptation syndrome (G.A.S.). This general reaction was and is viewed as a set of reactions that mobilize the person's resources to deal with an impending threat. Over

the years Selye has published many articles and books arguing that this general reaction is produced not only by diseases but by a wide variety of psychological situations as well (see Selye, 1974, 1976). He has argued that people need not experience distress whenever they experience a stress reaction. Feelings of distress or eustress are, to a large degree, results of people's attitudes toward events and/or their own physiological responses (Selye, 1978).

Stress and Disease

Although the stress response is very important for mobilizing the organism's defensive reactions to deal with such threats as diseases, there is considerable evidence that the stress reaction can precipitate diseases. Hans Selye has spent a lifetime analyzing this paradox. His work seems to indicate that the negative side of stress occurs only when stress is prolonged.

Selye (1974) has noted that a person who is subjected to prolonged stress goes through three phases. The first stage is the *alarm reaction*. I have already discussed the various physiological and psychological responses that occur when a person is initially confronted with a stressor. When the stressor continues, the person enters what Selye has called the *stage of resistance*. A number of important physiological reactions characterize this phase. The pituitary secretes ACTH, which is mainly responsible for energy metabolism and also stimulates the adrenal cortex. The adrenal cortex secretes glucocorticoids, which are important for resistance to stress. The two most important glucocorticoids are cortisone, which inhibits tissue inflammation, and mineralocorticoids, which promote inflammation. As Selye notes, "These hormones allow the body to defend its tissues by inflammation or to surrender them by inhibiting inflammation" (1969, p. 26). There is evidence from animal research that the adrenal glands actually increase in size during the resistance stage, presumably a reflection of their increased activity. If the stress is prolonged, the adrenal glands stop functioning or collapse. The collapse of the adrenal glands is often the precursor to death and is called the *exhaustion stage*.

Selye has noted that many of the diseases precipitated or caused by stress occur in the resistance stage. These *diseases of adaptation* seem to be due to some form of derangement in the secretion of the adaptive hormones. For example, Selye notes that excessive production of a proinflammatory hormone in response to some local irritation could damage organs in other parts of the body. Many "diseases of adaptation" have been identified, including emotional disturbances, headaches, insomnia, sinus attacks, high blood pressure, gastric and duodenal ulcers, certain somatic or allergic afflictions, and cardiovascular and kidney diseases (Selye, 1974).

Although Selye's *generality model* has dominated thinking about the relation between stress and disease, evidence is growing in support of a *specificity model*. There is increasing evidence that different physical stressors produce different hormonal profiles—a finding that is inconsistent with Selye's general adaptation syndrome theory (Mason et al., 1976).

Unpredictability, stress, and disease. While aversive events can elicit the stress reaction, it is important to distinguish between events that are predictable and those that are not. It has been shown repeatedly that exposure to aversive events is much more likely to produce stress and disease if the events are unpredictable than if they can be foreseen. In comparison with predictable stress, unpredictable stress produces higher levels of corticosterone (Weiss, 1970, 1971a), more severe stomach ulceration (Caul, Buchanan, & Hays, 1972; Weiss, 1971a), greater weight loss (Weiss, 1970), alterations in levels of glucose and free fatty acids (Quirce, Odio, & Solano, 1981), and myocardial dysfunction (Miller et al., 1978). Thus it is not the experience of an aversive event per se that causes stress and disease. As we shall see, when people know an aversive event is coming or when they can make some kind of coping response, stress and the diseases that accompany it are often dramatically reduced.

Summary

When an individual is threatened or challenged physically or psychologically, a characteristic pattern of responses called the stress reaction occurs. A series of chemical reactions set in motion by the hypothalamus alter, in a predictable way, an individual's response to events in the environment.

Selye has identified three stages of the stress reaction: the alarm reaction, the stage of resistance, and the exhaustion stage. In animals subjected to prolonged stress, the adrenal cortex increases in size during the stage of resistance but eventually collapses. The collapse is typically the precursor of death.

Although the stress response is important in mobilizing the organism's defensive reactions to deal with threats, Selye has shown that stress itself can precipitate diseases. This outcome tends to occur in the second stage of the stress reaction, when stress is prolonged. Specifically, it appears that the glucocorticoids begin to attack the very system they initially were mobilized to protect.

Learned Factors

The nature and magnitude of the stress reaction are also affected by factors that relate to principles of learning. One of the most important things that can help us deal with stress is to know when the stressor will come. That process is called discrimination.

Discrimination

Research has shown that if an organism experiences intermittent stress, knowing when that stress will come could be important in helping the organism to prepare for the stress just before onset and to relax after the stress has ended. The problem for the organism, therefore, is to learn to discriminate the cues that predict the onset of stress. Laboratory research has shown that, indeed, this is an important factor. In one study (Weiss, 1970) rats were given a warning signal that they were about to receive a tail shock. A yoked control group received the same duration and pattern of shocks but without a warning signal. Intermittent shocks produce not only a reliable stress reaction but lesions in the stomach (thought to be a precursor to ulcers). The question was whether signaled or unsignaled shock would produce more lesions. The results are shown in Figure 9-4. Clearly, unsignaled shocks are more stressful than signaled shocks. The analogy with humans is obvious. Scheduled tests are difficult enough at the best of times. Unscheduled tests are even more stressful because they do not allow the person to relax.

Several studies have failed to show that signaled shock leads to less stress (see Averill, 1973). Commenting on these studies, Averill notes that signaled shock seems to work only if the signal tells the subject not only when shock will come but also when the subject can relax. The key, in other words, is knowing when to relax. In the office, knowing when the boss is scheduled to arrive, or when things normally go wrong, can have important implications for learning to deal with stress.

Learning a Coping Response

Monkeys in a shock-avoidance situation show somewhat different patterns of catecholamine output when they can and cannot avoid shock (Brady, 1975). Weiss (1968, 1971a) found that animals that learn an avoidance response not only experience less lesioning of the

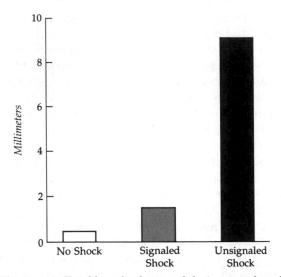

Figure 9–4. Total length of stomach lesions produced by shocks that are signaled so that rats can learn a discrimination and shocks that are unsignaled so that no discrimination is possible. (From J. M. Weiss, "Somatic Effects of Predictable and Unpredictable Shock." *Psychosomatic Medicine*, 1970, *32(4)*, 397-408. Copyright © 1970 by Elsevier North-Holland, Inc. Reprinted with permission.)

stomach but show less stress (as measured by level of plasma corticosterone) than yoked control subjects that do not have the opportunity to make an avoidance response. Exactly why coping responses reduce stress is not altogether clear. Studies have ruled out the possibility that their effectiveness is due to the greater activity (exercise) that accompanies active avoidance (Weiss, Glazer, & Pohorecky, 1976). As we shall see in the next section, there is good evidence that the effect is, at least in part, cognitively mediated.

The coping response must be fairly easy as well as free of conflict if it is to be effective. In one study, rats had to perform either an easy coping response (a single bar press) or a more difficult response (several bar presses) to avoid shock. Animals with an easy response had fewer stomach lesions than their yoked partners (Tsuda & Hirai, 1975). In another experiment rats had to experience a brief shock while making an avoidance response that prevented a longer train of shocks. In this

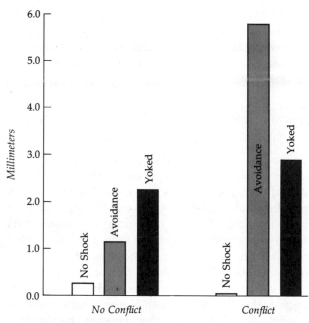

Figure 9-5. Total length of stomach lesions produced by an avoidance task when the avoidance response involves conflict and when it does not. The "executive" rat that learned the avoidance (coping) response suffered fewer stomach lesions than yoked control subjects when the task was simple and clear-cut but considerably more when the task involved conflict. (From J. M. Weiss, "Effects of Punishing the Coping Response (Conflict) on Stress Pathology in Rats." *Journal of Comparative and Physiological Psychology,* 1971, *77,* 14-21. Copyright © 1971 by the American Psychological Association. Reprinted with permission.)

situation, the coping group developed more stomach lesions than the yoked control subjects (Weiss, 1971b). These latter results are presented in Figure 9-5, together with the results for a no-conflict control condition.

In everyday life we learn to experience less stress if we know what to do. Say, for example, that your job is to deal with customer complaints. Since you are going to be the brunt of a lot of anger, how can you learn to deal with it? Many training programs have been designed to deal with this and similar situations. After people have been trained in these situations they often experience very little stress. What most of these

programs teach is how to diffuse the anger and solve the problem. This involves two steps. First, they need to learn to accept the fact that people have been inconvenienced, and therefore have a right to be angry, but that such anger is not directed at them personally. In accepting the anger, they communicate to the customer the fact that indeed they understand how the customer feels and they sympathize with the customer. Second, they need to turn their attention to solving the problem. Once people see that someone is willing to help them, which is why they are there, their anger often subsides and they too become involved in helping to solve the problem. People who have learned this technique well often can turn a bad situation in a neutral and even a positive situation for both themselves and the customer.

In the section on moderators of stress, I will talk more about the role of coping.

Habituating the Stress Response

Various studies have shown that an acute stress reaction depletes norepinephrine (see N. E. Miller, 1980). Animals are slow to learn after an acute stress reaction, and it has been hypothesized that the failure to learn is due to the depletion of norepinephrine.

In one study designed to determine if the stress response can be habituated, rats were exposed to acute stress for 15 consecutive days. Control rats were exposed to acute stress on only one day, with no prior exposure. The rats were examined in order to determine the effects of repeated exposure on norepinephrine metabolism in the brain. The prior-exposure animals had higher levels of enzymes involved in norepinephrine synthesis than the no-exposure animals (Weiss et al., 1975).

Marianne Frankenhaeuser (1980) has argued that repeated exposure to a stressor will reduce the stress reaction (particularly the activity of the adrenal medulla) only if there is a decrease in psychological involvement. For example, she notes that parachute jumping never becomes routine. Catecholamine secretion during jump periods tends to remain high even after several jumps (Bloom, von Euler, & Frankenhaeuser, 1963). Probably the reason is that parachute jumping demands constant attention and concentration. In other words, when a high degree of readiness is required for psychological reasons, the stress reaction remains high.

Prior exposure is often used as a training procedure to help people in a variety of situations deal more effectively with certain forms of stressful stimulation. Training soldiers for combat typically involves exposing them to acute stress over a period of time prior to any combat duty. Mountain climbers train extensively, exposing themselves to as many as possible of the conditions that they will encounter in an important climb, such as cold, rain, wind, and simply physical exertion. Pilots are trained in simulators to react to a wide variety of emergencies. In all these situations, the goal is not only to train the stress reaction but to teach the person to correctly evaluate the nature of the stimulus that is a potential stressor. Certain patterns of stimulation should elicit the stress reaction and others should not.

Automatic and Habitual Behaviors and the Stress Response

One curious thing that stress does is disrupt much of that behavior which we consider automatic or habitual. As a result of being told his wife has cancer, a man drives through a stop sign on his way home from her doctor; after being refused a loan by her banker, a woman forgets to pick up her purse; after learning from a friend that her boyfriend was just arrested, a young woman walks home leaving her mother's car in the mall parking lot; after opening the mail and reading that he has not been accepted at medical school, a young man completely forgets to pick up his girlfriend from work. Evidence from a wide variety of sources indicates that under stress even automatic and habitual responses no longer operate in a predictable manner.

Why do a wide variety of behaviors deteriorate under stress, including both motor and intellectual behaviors? Many theorists attribute the deterioration in performance to alterations in attention (for example, Easterbrook, 1959). It has been suggested, for example, that under stress our attention is distracted from

what we were in the process of doing and shifts to the source of the threat (Lazarus, 1991). Often, the greater the stress the greater the distraction and thus the greater the disruption of automatic and habitual behaviors.

Learning a Prescribed Set of Rules for Making Decisions under Stress

The reason people are deficient in making decisions under stress is a fascinating example of what stress does. In one study it was found that the reason people often make bad decisions is due to a significant extent to their failure to fulfill an elementary requirement of the decision-making process, which is to systematically consider all the relevant alternatives (Keinan, 1987). This failure to follow such mundane rules is both surprising and perplexing to those who must deal with the aftermath of people who make decisions under stress. In order to ensure this does not happen, such as when controllers are guiding planes into an airport for a landing, people are carefully trained to make sure they follow a carefully prescribed set of rules. Sometimes people are required to actually check off each function as they complete that function so there won't be any "screw-ups" (as people often say).

Summary

Both the nature of the stress reaction and the way a person or animal tends to respond under stress can be modified by learning. Learning to predict when a stressor will come allows the individual to relax when the stressor is absent. Short periods of relaxation appear to help ward off the effects of stress. Learning a coping response seems to reduce some of the adverse effects of stress, such as ulcers. Habituating a response under stress seems to mobilize the body to provide the necessary physiological base for good performance. Evidence from a wide variety of sources indicates that under stress, automatic and habitual responses deteriorate. The failure to make good decisions under stress is an example of how stress disrupts performance, probably by disrupting attention.

Cognitive Factors

Lazarus's Theory

One of the most comprehensive theories about the role of cognitive factors in stress has been developed by Richard Lazarus and several of his colleagues (Coyne & Lazarus, 1980; Folkman, 1984; Folkman et al., 1986; Folkman, Schaefer, & Lazarus, 1979; Lazarus, 1981; Lazarus & Launier, 1978). According to this theory, the way an individual appraises an event plays a fundamental role in determining not only the magnitude of the stress response but the kind of coping strategies that the individual may employ in efforts to deal with the stress.

Primary Appraisal

According to this theoretical formulation, a stressful event may be appraised as representing either harm/loss, threat, or challenge. *Harm/loss* refers to injury or damage that has already taken place, such as loss of a limb, loss of a job, or simply loss of self-esteem. *Threat* refers to something that could produce harm or loss. *Challenge* refers to the potential for growth, mastery, or some form of gain. As we shall see, a variety of factors, both personal and situational, are involved in an individual's appraisal of a situation. From this perspective, we cannot assess the origins of stress by looking solely at the nature of the environmental event that precipitates it. Rather, stress is a process that involves the interaction of the individual with the environment.

Secondary Appraisal

After assessing a stressful event as a situation of harm/loss, threat, or challenge, we evaluate our coping resources and options. We ask "What can I do?" The coping resources available to any individual are classified as physical, social, psychological, and material. Physical resources include such things as health and energy; social resources include family and friends; psychological resources include such things as self-esteem and problem-solving abilities; and material resources include such things as money and equipment.

Problem-focused versus emotion-focused coping. According to Lazarus's theory, *coping* refers to cognitive and behavioral efforts to master, reduce, or tolerate the internal and/or external demands that are created by the stressful transaction (Folkman, 1984, p. 843). One of the important things to note about this definition is that coping refers to efforts to manage rather than the outcome of those efforts per se. In other words, having or developing a positive attitude is a form of coping even if that positive attitude ultimately fails to resolve the situation.

The theory makes an important distinction between two ways of reducing stress. One way, termed *problem-focused coping*, is to engage in some kind of problem-solving behavior designed to resolve the stressful transaction. If an individual is experiencing stress on the job because of another person, for example, it may be possible to reduce that stress by asking to be transferred to another department, arranging for the other person to be transferred, or devising some strategy to change the other person's behavior. Another way of reducing stress, *emotion-focused coping*, is to focus on controlling the symptoms of stress. If it is impossible to avoid the other person, for example, one might deliberately take time out after every encounter to relax and think about the positive aspects of the job or to talk with some other person who might provide sympathy.

Situational Factors and Personal Control

Whether an individual tends to focus on the problem or on the emotion in an attempt to reduce stress depends to a very large degree on whether the individual appraises the situation as controllable and on whether the situation is, in fact, controllable. Some situations are basically uncontrollable—living near a nuclear reactor, perhaps, or working as a police officer, or having a friend who is dying of cancer. Other situations are subject to control—having an examination scheduled next week, perhaps, or having a tire on your car that has a slow leak, or having no money but having a job that permits you to work overtime. I say "perhaps" because circumstances may make what appears to be an uncontrollable situation controllable and vice versa.

Natural disasters are typically unpredictable and uncontrollable. At times like this people often seek out the support of others—an emotion-focused coping strategy for dealing with stress.

But more important for our present purposes, people sometimes appraise as uncontrollable a situation that is really under their control and, conversely, may perceive themselves to have control when they do not.

Potentially controllable situations. When people are faced with a forthcoming examination, they tend to appraise that event as both challenging and threatening (Folkman & Lazarus, 1985). When people appraise an event as challenging, two things typically happen. First, they engage in problem-solving behaviors. Second, they develop a positive emotion (excitement, eagerness, hopefulness) that acts as a motivational support for their problem-solving behavior. In other words, two complementary processes emerge that lead

to effort. When people appraise an event as threatening, however, something quite different happens. It is important to note that people tend to appraise a situation as threatening when they perceive that it may not be altogether controllable. A negative emotion typically accompanies this kind of appraisal. Negative emotions are indicators that something is wrong; at least, that is the traditional way of viewing negative emotions. Whatever the exact reason, it appears that humans experiencing a negative emotion tend to focus on that emotion. The time and effort devoted to coping with the negative emotion distract the individual from activities better calculated to solve the problem.

Getting a promotion or simply having a high-level job can be perceived as both challenging and threatening. What makes a promotion threatening is the possibility that one may not succeed in the new job. As long as the job is perceived as challenging, the individual is likely to handle it effectively. When feelings of threat arise, however, the individual is likely to spend a great deal of time and effort coping with those feelings. Management systems that use threats to motivate people obviously undermine the motivation of those people.

Situations unlikely to be controllable. When people are faced with events over which they are unlikely to gain much control, it may be prudent to accept this fact rather than treat the situation as potentially controllable. Inasmuch as viewing a situation as a challenge leads to such a positive psychological state, this may seem like bad advice. But what happens when people make repeated attempts to control a situation that in fact is not controllable? A study of residents of Three Mile Island, the site of a nuclear accident (Collins, Baum, & Singer, 1983), suggests that people who engage in problem-focused coping to deal with such an uncontrollable situation develop more psychological symptoms than people who rely on more emotion-focused coping. When we are faced with a problem that is truly beyond our control, it seems to make more sense simply to deal with our emotions.

Controllability and longevity. Apparently, perceived controllability even promotes longevity. In a long-term study of a group of institutionalized aged, Rodin and Langer (1977) studied the effects of giving people more options for control and responsibility. They found that those given more control not only became more active but reported being happier. Reduced levels of corticosteroids provided further empirical data suggesting that these subjects were experiencing less stress. After two years, this group was significantly more healthy than a comparison group. A dramatic finding was that half as many people died in this group as in a comparison group.

Summary

Primary appraisal, according to Lazarus's theory, involves classifying or labeling a stressful event as representing either harm/loss, threat, or challenge. Secondary appraisal involves the evaluation of the coping resources and options available, given the initial labeling of the event. In general, coping strategies are either problem-focused or emotion-focused. According to Lazarus's theory, whether an individual tends to use problem-focused or emotion-focused coping depends on two additional factors: whether the threat is potentially controllable and, if it is, whether the individual perceives that he or she has the skills to deal with it.

Stressors of Everyday Life

The stress reaction is elicited by a wide variety of psychosocial stimuli—stimuli associated with our jobs, our residences, our social interactions, the activities we engage in. Because they are part of our daily lives, they can elicit a prolonged stress reaction, which may precipitate a variety of *adaptive diseases*.

Examination Stress

Appraisal and coping strategies. A forthcoming examination is typically a source of stress. As we have noted, students tend to respond to the prospect of an exam with feelings of threat and challenge. How do students deal with this threat? Typically they use a combination of problem-focused and emotion-focused coping strategies. During the anticipatory stage they tend to prepare for the examination. During this stage of problem-focused coping they experience positive emotions, such as hopefulness. Just before the exam, during the final waiting stage, their emotions begin to turn negative. Having reviewed the material to be covered by the exam, they are no longer actively preparing (at least to the same degree as before) and they have time to appraise the adequacy of their efforts (Folkman & Lazarus, 1985).

Social relationships have been shown to decrease the stress connected with taking a major exam but only if they are discretionary and not obligatory (Bolger & Eckenrode, 1991). In the section on moderators of stress, I will talk more about the importance of social relations.

It is important to note that there are large individual differences in the amount of stress experienced in connection with examinations. This is not surprising, as the outcome has different implications (stakes) for different individuals. Students who need a certain grade to get into graduate school, for example, may perceive the stakes as very high indeed. Individuals differ, too, in the amount of control they feel as they prepare for the exam, wait for the day to arrive, and finally take the exam. Their perceptions of the exam's difficulty vary as well. We will look at the effects of perceived difficulty in Chapter 13.

Stress, anxiety, and test taking. For some time now, we have had evidence that stress and anxiety tend to interfere with the ability to perform on tests. Why should this be the case? Sarason (1984) has argued that the problem with stress and anxiety is, to a very large degree, a problem of *self-preoccupying intrusive thinking* (p. 929). A preoccupation with one's own thoughts interferes with task-focused thinking. What kinds of thoughts? They seem to fall into a general category of responses that arise from a self-assessment of personal deficits in the face of certain situational demands. Neurotics are particularly prone to engage in such thinking. In one study it was found that the trait of neuroticism increases pre-examination anxiety. The study found that neurotics are prone, among other things, to engage in wishful thinking and self-blame (Bolger, 1990).

Can an individual learn to reduce the interference that comes from such thinking? Sarason has shown that self-preoccupying intrusive thinking is reduced when one focuses on the task. He argues that helping people to focus on the task is a much better way of helping them to deal with this type of situational stress than simply attempting to reassure them. In other words, problem-focused coping is a better way of dealing with this kind of stress than emotion-focused coping.

Physiological changes. A variety of physiological changes have been shown to take place as one prepares for and takes an examination. It has been shown, for example, that glucose levels rise before an exam and decline significantly during the course of the exam. Lactic acid, too, was found to be elevated before an exam, but unlike glucose, it continued to increase during the course of the exam (Hall & Brown, 1979); both of these responses are indicative of the stress level. It has also been shown that norepinephrine levels rise while immunoglobin A levels (a measure of B-cell immune function) decline, especially in people with a strong power motive (McClelland, Ross, & Patel, 1985). McClelland has argued that the power motive reflects, among other things, the need to control. People with a strong power motive tend to be most highly aroused by situations in which they fear loss of control, such as examinations. Following an examination (or loss of control), this research suggests, an individual might be more susceptible to various kinds of infection.

The Workplace

Job ambiguity and health. Researchers who studied the relationship between the ambiguity of the job and various emotional reactions found that tension was highest when the situation was ambiguous (Kahn et al., 1964). Both job satisfaction and self-confidence were found to be significantly lower when the job was ambiguous. Finally, people in ambiguous situations perceived their attempts to cope with the environment as futile. These findings are summarized in Table 9-3. Since a foreman must deal with the demands of management as well as the demands of the workers, his job may well have all the qualities that produce ambiguity.

There is evidence that peptic ulcers are negatively related to self-esteem. The lower the self-esteem, the more likely the person is to have ulcers (Kahn, 1969). Although a person's self-esteem tends to be relatively stable over time, there is evidence that self-esteem on the job is affected by people's perceptions of their role in the organizational structure. If they perceive themselves as occupying an important role (more responsibilities, more subordinates, higher pay), they tend to experience good self-esteem. If they do not perceive themselves as occupying an important role, they tend to suffer from low self-esteem.

The feedback people receive on how well they are doing their jobs also affects self-esteem. Negative job appraisal not only lowers self-esteem but leads to a lower level of performance. Positive job appraisal leads

Table 9-3. Correlations between measures of experienced ambiguity and various emotional reactions in 53 subjects. (From R. L. Kahn, D. M. Wolfe, R. P. Quinn, J. D. Snoek, and R. A. Rosenthal, *Organizational Stress: Studies in Role Conflict and Ambiguity*, 1964. Copyright © 1964 John Wiley & Sons, Inc. Reprinted with permission.)

| | Experienced-ambiguity measures | | |
Emotional reaction	Ambiguity index	Role expectations	Evaluations
Tension	.51*	.44*	.40*
Job satisfaction	−.32[†]	−.33[†]	−.17
Futility	.41*	.34[†]	.20
Self-confidence	−.27[†]	−.20	−.44*

*p <0.01, [†]p <0.05

to improved self-esteem and a corresponding output in performance (French & Meyer, cited in Tanner, 1976).

Air-traffic controllers seem to experience not only high stress but a high incidence of ulcers. The question asked in one study (Cobb & Rose, 1973) was whether they have a higher rate of ulcers (as well as high blood pressure and diabetes) than pilots. The study showed that air-traffic controllers had a significantly higher incidence of ulcers, diabetes, and high blood pressure than pilots. This result parallels the finding that foremen have a higher incidence of ulcers than executives. What mechanism is responsible for the higher ulcer rate? Epinephrine has been implicated in ulceration in rats (Phillip & Boone, 1968); however, whether epinephrine is responsible for ulceration in humans remains to be demonstrated. As I have already noted, epinephrine tends to be secreted when the organism is unable to make an adaptive response. It is interesting to note that most experiments on stress-induced ulceration have used situations that prevent active coping (Weiss, 1968).

It is likely that the reason pilots and executives experience less stress than some other people who work at related jobs has to do with the availability of coping responses. The foreman's job is particularly difficult because he is caught between an executive whom he cannot afford to offend and workers for whom he must assume responsibility. Similarly, the air-traffic controller must assume responsibility for the safe landing of an aircraft he is not flying.

Sex differences. Sex differences have been found in studies of the relationship between job demands and cardiac heart disease. In one study of 548 men and 328 women, it was found that men were at a much higher risk than women (La Croix & Haynes, 1987). What make this study so interesting is that the jobs were broken down in terms of job demands (high versus low) and supervision clarity (high versus low). It can be seen from Figure 9-6 that the men showed a higher incidence of coronary heart disease than did the women. In view of the research reported above, the fact that men showed such high levels of coronary heart disease under conditions of high supervision clarity is somewhat surprising.

Several conflicting explanations have been put forth. While it could be argued that men are more susceptible for perhaps biological reasons, there are many other explanations that need to be considered. Perhaps the environments were different for men and women, a factor that needs to be carefully controlled as you can see from the next section on the effects of working in a conflict-prone versus a conflict-resistant organization. Also, men and women may come to the workplace with different dispositions. Men tend to be more competitive and they also may be more hostile and angry. These dispositional qualities could account for these differences. In addition, there could be an interaction of certain dispositions with the environment, something that needs a great deal more work.

Conflict-prone and conflict-resistant organizations. It has been suggested that the physical arrangements and the social conditions of an organization can predispose their members towards chronic conflict and resultant health problems (Stokols, 1992). Table 9-4, on page 280, presents the qualities of conflict-prone and conflict-resistant organizations. The characteristics of these two organizations are broken down into three general categories: (1) social-psychological qualities of groups,

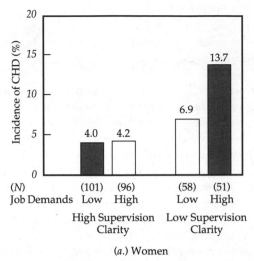

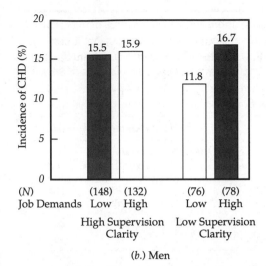

Figure 9–6. (a) Ten-year incidence of CHD by job demands and supervision clarity among currently working women. **(b)** Ten-year incidence of CHD by job demands and clarity of supervision among currently working men. (Reprinted with permission of the Free Press, a Division of Macmillan, Inc. from *Gender and Stress* by Rosiland C. Barnett, Lois Biener, and Grace K. Baruch. Copyright © 1987 by Rosiland C. Barnett, Lois Biener, and Grace K. Baruch.)

(2) organizational structure, and (3) environmental conditions. Stokols argues that the conflict-prone organization is often a major source of stress and illness in people.

The individual-environment interaction. In his work on organizations, Stokols argues that more attention needs to be paid to the physical environment and the sociocultural environment. In the past, researchers have focused on the individual's ability to adapt as the main source of difficulty, putting the blame more or less on the individual for his or her stress. While there is no question that one's personal disposition is important (having a disposition towards optimism, hardiness, high self-esteem, for example), these factors alone may not be sufficient to eliminate work-related stress. If the environment plays havoc with people who have relatively positive dispositions, then how much more havoc will that same environment play with people who have more negative dispositions (towards hostility, anger, and low self-esteem). As yet we do not have any direct estimates, but from what researchers can extrapolate based on other research, there is good rea-son to be concerned. Indeed, some people's jobs are killing them and it is worse for those people who have more negative dispositions.

Summary

Students tend to appraise a forthcoming exam as both threatening and challenging, and they respond with both emotion-focused and problem-focused coping. Positive emotions tend to be associated with problem-focused coping. It has been argued that the reason anxiety tends to interfere with performance on exams is that anxiety produces self-preoccupying intrusive thinking. Problem-focused coping can reduce the negative effects of anxiety on test performance. It has been shown that the stress associated with taking an exam can produce a reduction in immunoglobin A.

A job can be a significant source of stress, especially if it is characterized by ambiguity or if it fails to provide self-esteem. Perceived control also affects whether or not a job will produce stress. Finally, it has been suggested that organizational structure can be a major source of stress and illness.

Table 9-4. Qualities of Conflict-Prone and Conflict-Resistant Organizations. (From D. Stokols "Conflict-Prone and Conflict-Resistant Organizations, " In H. S. Friedman (Ed.), *Hostility, Coping and Health*, 1992, (Table 5-1). Copyright © 1992 by the American Psychological Association. Reprinted with permission.)

| | *Tendencies Toward Conflict or Cohesions* | |
| | *Organizational Profiles* | |
Levels of Organizational Analysis	*Conflict-Prone*	*Conflict-Resistant*
Social-psychological qualities *(norms, goals, and role expectations)*	Absence of shared goals among group members	Presence of and commitment to shared goals among group members
	Incompatible styles and role assignments among group members	Compatible style and role assignments among group members
	Presence of rigid ideologies; low tolerance for diverse points of view	Absence of rigid ideologies; high tolerance for diverse points of view
Organizational structure *(interrelations among roles and resources)*	Existence of competitive coalitions	Absence of competitive coalitions
	Nonpartcipatory organizational processes	Participatory organizational processes
	Overstaffed organization;	Adequately staffed organization;
	pervasive competition among members for scarce roles and resources	minimal competition among members for roles and resources
	Ambiguous organization of space and territory among group members	Clear-cut territorial organization and use of space among group members
	Relatively unstable role structure and membership	Relatively stable role structure and membership
	Absence of formal and informal dispute-resolution mechanisms	Availability of formal and informal dispute-resolution mechanisms
External environmental conditions	Local and remote environmental resources for meeting organizational goals are inadequate	Ample environmental resources for meeting organizational goals are available
	Environment external to the organization is anomic and turbulent	Environment external to the organization is cohesive and nonturbulent

The Type A Personality, Stress, and Heart Attacks

The Type A Personality and Coronary Heart Disease (CHD)

Because physiological indicators are only moderately good predictors of heart disease and, further, because people who experience coronary heart disease tend to have a distinct personality style, Friedman and Rosenman (1974) decided to see if they could measure the personality style that they found in their clinical work and see if it was a predictor of heart disease. In their landmark studies, they established that there is indeed a distinct personality style that leads to coronary heart disease which they labeled the Type A Personality. This pattern has subsequently come to be called the coronary-prone behavior pattern (TABP). The Type A person, as originally described by Friedman and Rosenman, is characterized by three qualities: a competitive striving for achievement, an exaggerated sense of time urgency, and a tendency towards aggressiveness and hostility in interpersonal behaviors. The Type B person, in contrast, is less competitive and more easygoing but not necessarily less effective. The Western Collaborative Group Study, a study of men in the San Francisco area, found that the Type A person was three times as likely to have a heart attack as the Type B person (Rosenman et al., 1966, 1970, 1975).

In recent years several studies have not been able to find the link between Type A pattern and heart attacks. While some of this may be due to the fact that other researchers have moved away from the structured interview first devised by Friedman and Rosenman to measure the Type A personality and instead have used paper and pencil tests such as the Jenkins Activity Survey, there is an abundance of research which shows that at least one component of the Type A, hostility, is linked to heart disease.

Hostility and Heart Disease

Since the early work of Rosenman and Friedman, it has repeatedly been shown that the component of the TABP most clearly related to coronary heart disease is hostility (e.g., Dembroski & Costa, 1987). Some researchers have used the phrase *potential for hostility* to

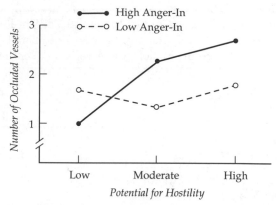

Figure 9–7. Relationship between anger expression, potential for hostility, and prevalence of coronary artery disease. (From T. M. Dembroski, J. M. MacDougall, R. B. Williams, T. L. Haney, and J. A. Blumenthal, "Components of Type A , Hostility, and Anger-In : Relationship to Angiographic Findings." *Psychosomatic Medicine*, 1985, 47, 219-233. Copyright © 1985 by the American Psychosomatic Society. Reprinted by permission.)

describe this quality (e.g., Matthews et al ., 1977). Some researchers have found that independent measures of hostility are better predictors than the TABP. This reinforces the idea that hostility is one of the main factors—if not the dominant factor—in coronary heart disease (Barefoot et al., 1983). The best predictor of coronary heart disease seems to be having a high TABP score and a high hostility score. In other words, it is the interaction of TABP (which measures other things than just hostility) and hostility tests (tests that focus mainly on hostility) that is most likely to lead to coronary heart disease (Matthews, 1988). It has been suggested that the tendency to be hostile (to be suspicious and to mistrust others) may not lead to heart disease unless it it combined with a competitive motive (Weidner, Sexton, McLellarn, Connor, & Matarazzo, 1987). Dembroski and Costa (1987) point out that potential for hostility is a multidimensional construct. In order to better identify the nature of this construct they did ratings using established dimensions of personality (McCrae and Costa, 1987). Their research led them to the conclusion that potential for hostility is highly related to low agreeableness or antagonism. When they examined potential for hostility in terms of style of interaction they found that high potential for hostility identifies individuals who are uncooperative, antagonistic, rude, disagreeable, unsympathetic, callous, and the like.

More recently Dembroski and his colleagues (Dembroski, MacDougall, Costa, and Grandits,1989) found that hostility, especially an antagonistic interaction style, but not global TABP, is an independent risk factor for CHD in a younger population (47 or less) but not an older population (greater than 47). These results are consistent with the growing evidence that the main predictor of heart disease is hostility as opposed to TABP. The fact that these results were only found in the younger population is consistent with with other data indicating such measures have diminishing predictability with increasing age.

Suppressed Anger and Coronary Disease

There is considerable evidence that anger-hostility plays a role in cardiovascular diseases (Siegel, 1992). Hostility has been linked not only to coronary heart disease but also to hypertension (elevated blood pressure). The work on hypertension has shown that hostility only leads to hypertension when people are characterized by anger-in. The same thing has been found for coronary heart disease (e.g., Dembroski et al., 1985). Figure 9-7 shows the number of occluded vessels for high anger-in and low anger-in patients. It can be seen from Figure 9-7 that as the *potential for hostility* goes up, the number of occluded vessels also goes up for high anger-in but not for low anger-in.

As I indicated in the chapter on aggression, learning to deal with anger in a constructive way is important not only for physical but for mental health. Anger is one of those emotions that people can learn to manage and, from a health perspective, *should* learn to manage.

Cynical Hostility

Not just hostility but cynical hostility has been suggested to be an important predictor of heart disease (Smith & Frohm, 1985; Fischman, 1987).The general picture of a person who is cynically hostile has been described by Geen (1990) as:

someone who carries around a great deal of anger,

and resentment, often over little daily problems, but who possesses poor adaptive skills or adjustive mechanisms. The anger therefore tends to become expressed in hostile and irritating ways that alienate other people and lead to social rejection and lack of support. Aversive social feedback simply reinforces the bleak expectations of the cynical person and helps to maintain his or her hostile behavior (Geen, 1990; p. 178).

The high level of anger, the high arousal, the poor ability to cope, and the low level of social support all keep the person in a chronic state of stress. As we will see shortly, good coping skills and good social support go a long way towards helping reduce stress reaction. What we can conclude from all this is that stress plays a key role in heart disease and that people with a personality style that leads to a lower stress response will experience less heart disease.

The interaction of hostility, TABP, and plasma lipids. Consistent with the argument that coronary heart disease is produced by the interaction of hostility and TABP, it has been shown that when these two factors are high, plasma lipid levels (cholesterol and triglycerides) are also elevated but that neither high hostility or nor high TABP alone reliably leads to elevated plasma lipids (Weidner et al., 1987). It has been suggested that only when both hostility and TABP are high are people put into a psychological state of being constantly vigilant, which in turn produces a chronic stress reaction. The general consensus seems to be that chronic stress, which can result from such things as being constantly vigilant, is what triggers the release of high levels of catecholamines. The high levels of catecholamines, in turn, mobilize the plasma lipids (both of which are physical risk factors). These in turn have been implicated in blood platelet aggregation, which is also a risk factor for coronary heart disease (Carruthers, 1974; Simpson, et al., 1974).

Cortisol and testosterone. One of the hormones that is released under stress is cortisol. In fact, cortisol is often used as an indicator of the amount of stress people are experiencing. It has been found that the cortisol response is higher in Type As, consistent with the idea that TABP results in levels of stress. It has been suggested that cortisol may be one of the hormones that produces coronary heart disease (Williams, 1989). It has also been found that in those Type As who scored high in cynical hostility, the testosterone response was large (Williams, 1989). Animal research has shown that extra testosterone increases arteriosclerosis in animals.

Nature of Type A Behavior Pattern

Even though hostility may, at least under certain conditions, be a better predictor of heart disease than the Type A pattern, people have been and continue to be interested in the Type A pattern for its own sake. This is likely because it is often a source of conflict in the work setting and a source of curiosity by those who are not Type As. One of the fascinating things about Type As is their almost universal irritation and even hostility with standing in line, their explosive speech, and the frequency of their anger (e.g., Matthews et al., 1977). What are the origins of such behaviors?

Desire for control. Hypothesizing from a wide array of evidence, that As and Bs may differ in their need to control their environments, Glass and his associates conducted a series of experiments to examine this question. One common way to study the question of whether a person has a need to control is to present the person with a controllable or an uncontrollable event and then observe his or her behavior (this issue is dealt with in more detail in Chapter 11). In a series of experiments, Glass and his associates used noise as an aversive and stressful stimulus. Some subjects could control the noise by engaging in some instrumental response, such as pushing a button; other subjects were unable to control the noise. In general, the results indicate that Type As are more motivated by the uncontrollable condition. For example, when Type As were unable to control a loud noise, they worked harder than Type Bs. This finding, that Type As are more motivated than Type Bs to master a task, is consistent with the earlier findings that Type As tend to rise to a challenge, work hard at tasks when time is important, are upset when they are interrupted while working at such tasks, and

tend to retaliate against people who degrade their efforts.

Heritability of Type A Personality

There is considerable evidence that the Type A pattern may be inherited. A study of 93 monozygotic and 97 dizygotic middle-aged male twins provided evidence for a heritability factor in Type A behavior (Rahe, Hervig, & Rosenman, 1978). Recently, a study was conducted in which a group of 72 pregnant women were given the Jenkins Activity Survey (a test that measures Type A traits such as competitiveness and impatience) a month prior to the birth of their children. Using amount of crying and the Brazelton as indicators of an intense behavioral style, these researchers concluded Type A mother are more likely to have children with an intense style (Parker & Barrett, 1992). While it might be concluded that these results lend support to the idea that there is a genetic component, it cannot be ruled out that the high amounts of stress hormones normally produced by Type As crossed the placenta and caused a momentary or long-term change in the offspring.

Further evidence for heritability of the Type A pattern comes from animal research which has shown that it is possible to breed animals (gerbils) for behaviors that are analogous to that observed in humans (Straub, Singer, & Grunberg, 1986). In addition to being more aggressive or dominant, it has been noted that Type As exhibit greater time urgency than Type Bs. Consistent with this observation is the finding that Type As are more accurate at estimating relatively short intervals, but less accurate than Type Bs at estimating longer intervals. A common procedure for assessing time estimation in animals is the DRL schedule (differential reinforcement of low rate of response). In this schedule, reinforcement for the animal is contingent on being able to delay responding. By selecting animals that have difficulty delaying their responses as well as being more dominant (as measured by a dominance test), and then breeding these animals and retesting them in subsequent generations, it has been possible to show that it is possible to breed animals for both these characteristics.

Modifying the Type A Response

There has been considerable pessimism about the ability to modify the Type A response (Fischman, 1987). Many attempts have met with failure. The fact that the pattern is hard to modify is not surprising in view of the fact that it is established early in life (Matthews, 1982). As such, it has become a pervasive feature of the person's approach to the world. When people do change the change is often short-lived. One of the problems encountered in attempting to modify the behavior of Type As is to get Type As to realize that their behaviors are bad for them. Since many of them are successful and receive a great deal of enjoyment from their competitive style, they see no reason to change. Further, many do not realize that they are obnoxious to others. Interestingly, one of the best techniques that has been found to modify the Type A pattern is to put 10 Type As into a room together. As they all compete and interrupt each other they soon see how obnoxious this behavior pattern is (Fischman, 1987). For many this becomes the motivation to change.

Redford Williams has argued that the Type A pattern characterized by cynical hostility has grown out of a disturbed thinking process (Williams, 1989). He argues that these people have developed a tendency to view the world from a cynical and hostile perspective in which they mistrust other people. The first thing they must do is to learn to reduce their cynical mistrust of others. He takes an optimistic view of their ability to change, although he admits that it can be difficult. He suggests that they should start by monitoring their thinking so they can identify these cynical and hostile thoughts. Having learned to do this, the next step is to attempt to reduce this mistrust. Listening, attempting to see the world from the other person's point of view, practicing trust, learning to be assertive, learning to laugh at oneself, and learning how to forgive are some of the things that can help people change their thinking.

Since it is often difficult to change how people think, most researchers have suggested that learning how to relax is a skill that all Type As need to master, irrespective of whether or not they attempt to change their basic approach to the world.

Stress and the Immune System

In recent years, a direct link has been found between stress and the immune system. It has been argued that under increased stress the immune system loses its ability to deal effectively with infectious and noninfectious diseases, from the common cold to cancer. Research has shown that the psychological factors that help an individual to maintain control also alleviate stress and so make people healthier. Further, social support has been found to play an important role in helping restore the immune system. This research emphasizes the importance of controlling or managing stress if we want to remain healthy. In reducing stress, we reduce disease (Maier & Laudenslager, 1985; O'Leary, 1990).

Summary

The Type A personality (more recently referred to as the Type A behavior pattern or TABP) is characterized by a competitive striving for achievement, an exaggerated sense of time urgency, and a tendency toward aggressiveness and hostility. The Type A person is inclined to rise to a challenge, to experience annoyance and impatience when interrupted, and to retaliate when provoked. While early studies found a strong link between the Type A personality and coronary heart disease, some recent studies have not found this link. Suppressed anger and cynical hostility, however, have been clearly linked to coronary heart disease.

It has been shown that people who score high in TABP and hostility tend to have high plasma lipids, two physical risk factors that have been implicated in coronary heart disease. It has also been shown that cortisol and testosterone levels tend to be higher in certain Type As.

It has been suggested that the need or desire for control may be one of the underlying motives or needs that characterize the Type A personality. While there is evidence for the heritability of the Type A personality, it still has not been ruled out that this behavior pattern is, at least in part, acquired.

There has been some controversy over whether it is possible to modify the Type A pattern and whether or not it is desirable. The fact that the pattern may be inherited suggests that it may not be modifiable. Some researchers have shown, however, that it can be modified, at least in some people. One current approach is to get people to change the way they think about the world.

There is considerable evidence that increased stress results in a lowered immune response.

Moderators of Stress

Moderators of stress can be broken down roughly into biological, learned and cognitive. While the fit is not perfect, I decided to use this breakdown to emphasize the idea that moderators work in different ways to achieve their final common goal, which is to reduce stress.

Biological Factors

Social Support

One factor that has consistently emerged as a moderator of life stress is social support—the sympathy and help provided by one's family and friends, particularly in times of trouble (B. R. Sarason, Sarason, & Pierce, 1990). Three dimensions of social support have been identified: emotional support (intimacy and reassurance), tangible support (the provision of aid and service), and informational support (advice and feedback) (Schaefer, Coyne, & Lazarus, 1981). Whether or not social contacts are beneficial depends, it has been been shown, on whether or not social contacts are discretionary as opposed to obligatory (Bolger & Eckenrode, 1991). Having an irritating relative visit and offer advice in times of stress may increase rather than decrease stress, a fact of which most of us are painfully aware.

It is interesting to note that when people are lacking good social relations they often become depressed and unhealthy (Seligman, 1990). In other words, it makes sense that when we experience social support we not only experience less stress but are healthier.

The repressive personality type and social support. It has been suggested that certain people who resist seeking out social support are susceptible to a number of physical diseases, particularly cancer (Eysenck, 1988). This personality type has been loosely called the *repressive* type. People of this type are characterized by their tendency to chronically defend themselves against negative affects, particularly anger and anxiety, and to deny they are distressed (Emmons, 1992). Several mechanisms have been offered to explain why repressive individuals are more susceptible to disease, but I won't go into them here (Weingberger,1990). Of particular interest for our purposes is the research literature which indicates that repressors tend to experience difficulties in interpersonal functioning. They seem to be preoccupied with issues of relatedness and are troubled by feelings of dependency and ambivalence in their relations to others (Bonanno & Singer, 1990). The bottom line, it appears, is that people tend to be healthier when they have good social support systems and need to feel related.

Learned Factors

Coping Skills

Breaking events down into manageable units. One of the main theoretical explanations that has been offered as to why people experience stress from serious life events is based on the idea that people need to be in control of events in their lives (Geer, Davison, & Gatchel, 1970; Krantz & Schulz, 1980). Horowitz (1979) argues that in order to deal with life stressors, the person must avoid becoming overwhelmed. To do this, the person engages in a variety of control operations that allow him or her to keep the stress within bounds. For example, a person might use denial in order to regain composure or might break up the stressful information into a series of micro-intervals to reduce its impact or might focus on only one aspect of the event. Horowitz uses the term *micro-interval* to capture the idea that information can be broken down into a series of units. The size of the unit (or the interval containing that unit) would be determined by the person's ability to deal with that information. In this way the person would be able to master a stressful event by sequentially attacking each of its parts, or units. Failure to put

Pet Ownership and Health

As people get older their health often deteriorates and they seek out doctors to help them. This puts a great burden on the medical system. Since there has been a great deal of anecdotal lore about how pets can improve the psychological outlook of patients and can even help sustain life in times of physical and psychological stress, the need to examine pet ownership is not only important from a financial perspective but from a psychological perspective as well (Siegel, 1990). Because people often have difficulty recalling the past, Judith Siegel did a prospective study of 938 Medicare enrollees in a health maintenance organization over the span of one year. The results of her study indicated that not only did people with pets visit their physicians less, but that pets helped them to deal better with stressful events. People with pets, for example, experienced less stress associated with the loss of companionship. Loss of companionship was common in this sample (26% experienced the death of a close friend) and, as noted earlier, is a major source of stress for most people. Over 75% of the pet owners mentioned that their pet provided them with companionship and comfort, while 25% indicated they felt more secure with their pets and 21% said they felt loved as a result of owning a pet. In other words, owning a pet seems to help meet people's companionship needs. Judith Siegel suggests that one reason people may go to see their doctor is to satisfy their need for companionship.

Which is the best pet to own? The results indicated that owning a dog is a stress buffer while owning other pets is not a stress buffer. Finer analysis of the data indicated that dog owners reported spending more time outdoors with their pet and talked more with their pets. Once again, this provides evidence for the companionship idea. Since Judith Siegel controlled for health status in all of her data analyses, it appears that pet ownership influences social and psychological processes rather than physical health per se. Nonetheless, we know that psychological health is often a good predictor of physical health. In two studies of the elderly, it was found that the greater the owners' attachment to their pets the better their physical health (Garrity et al., 1989; Ory & Goldberg, 1983), indicating that there is a positive relationship between psychological variables and physical variables.

---

the stressful information under tight control, Horowitz says, might lead to information overload, which could precipitate a total breakdown. In computer language, we might say the system would crash.

Epstein's Work and Theory

Epstein's theory is largely a cognitive theory, but it is important to note that the way people think is habitual. As I point out in this section, it is because we learn to think about things in certain ways that we experience stress. By learning to think differently we gain control over stress.

The search for universal principles. For some time, coping has been suggested as one of the main moderators of stress. Despite a great deal of anecdotal evidence linking individual coping strategies to reduction in stress, psychologists have had difficulty identifying universal coping principles or styles of coping that underlie these diverse individual strategies. The work of Folkman and Lazarus (described earlier) and the work of Seymour Epstein of the University of Massachusetts and his associates have moved much closer to identifying such universal strategies. In a nutshell, Epstein's theory is that people who are effective in dealing with stress tend to think more *constructively* when faced with problems, whereas those who tend to experience stress think more *destructively* (Epstein & Meier, 1989).

The question of intelligence and adjustment. Epstein's the-

Table 9-5. Examples of Items From Constructive Thinking Inventory Scales. (From S. Epstein and P. Meier, "Constructive Thinking: A Broad Coping Variable with Specific Components. " *Journal of Personality and Social Psychology*, 1989, *57*, 332-350. Copyright © 1989 by the American Psychological Association. Reprinted with permission.).

Emotional Coping

I worry a great deal about what other people think of me. (–)
I don't let little things bother me.
I tend to take things personally. (–)

Behavioral Coping

I am the kind of person who takes action rather than just thinks or complains about a situation.
I avoid challenges because it hurts too much when I fail. (–)
When faced with upcoming unpleasant events, I usually carefully think through how I will deal with them.

Categorical Thinking

There are basically two kinds of people in this world, good and bad.
I think there are many wrong ways, but only one right way, to do almost anything.
I tend to classify people as either for me or against me.

Superstitious Thinking

I have found that talking about successes that I am looking forward to can keep them from happening.
I do not believe in any superstitions. (–)
When something good happens to me, I believe it is likely to be balanced by something bad.

Naive Optimism

If I do well on an important test, I feel like a total success and that I will go very far in life.
I believe that people can accomplish anything they want to if they have enough willpower.

Negative Thinking

When I am faced with a new situation, I tend to think the worst possible outcome will happen.
I tend to dwell more on pleasant than unpleasant incidents from the past. (–)
I get so distressed when I notice that I am doing poorly in something that it makes me do worse.

ory has grown out of his work on practical intelligence. Like others before him, he has observed that academic intelligence does not predict adjustment. Specifically, he has noted that academic intelligence does not predict mental health, physical health, good family relations, good social relations, satisfactory romantic relations, or success at work. According to his cognitive-experiential self-theory (CEST), people have three semi-independent systems that help them deal with daily life: a rational system (roughly corresponding to academic intelligence), an experiential system (which I will describe momentarily) and an associationistic system (observed in altered states of consciousness). It is the experiential system, according to his theory, that gives rise to good mental and physical health, good relationships, and success at work. It should be noted in this context that while academic intelligence predicts such things as grades and therefore is indirectly related to success at work, there are many people who are successful at work who do not have high academic intelligence. In short, academic intelligence does not predict such things as who makes the most money, who gets promoted, and other indicators of success at work (Epstein, 1990).

In order to test his theory, Epstein created an inventory to measure experiential abilities called the *Constructive Thinking Inventory* (CTI). This inventory provides an index of the degree to which people tend to be constructive thinkers versus people who are destructive thinkers when dealing with daily life problems. This inventory contains a global measure of coping plus six specific measures or scales: emotional coping, behavioral coping, categorical thinking, superstitious thinking, naive optimism and negative thinking. The first two scales, emotional coping and behavior coping, are not only the best predictors of coping but correspond to Folkman and Lazarus' emotional-focused coping and problem-focused coping. Often the best way to understand what a scale measures to examine some of the items. I have provided some examples in Table 9-5. Scales such as that created by Epstein typically contain positively and negatively worded items. The absence of a negative sign (–) indicates the item is a direct measure of the construct indicated by the heading (Epstein & Meier, 1989).

Constructive versus Destructive Thinkers

Work with the scale (especially the global scale) has provided some indication of how people who are good constructive thinkers differ from poor constructive thinkers. The main difference, it appears, relates to how good and poor constructive thinkers deal with negative outcomes. While both groups tend to respond favorably to good outcomes (they remain positive and optimistic about future performance), poor constructive thinkers tend to overgeneralize about the self after negative outcomes. Among other things their self-esteem plummets, they feel depressed, and they assume a helpless attitude about future performance. Interestingly these are some of the symptoms that characterize depressed individuals.

Origins of destructive thinking. Why do some people develop such a profound negative self-view following poor performance while others do not? Epstein (1992) speculates that this may be linked to self-schemata that are part of our implicit self-theory that we developed as children. He suggests, like many others before him, that when love is withdrawn for poor performance or when love is made conditional on good performance, we tend to develop as part of our implicit self-theory the idea or belief that making mistakes or performing

poorly will result in the withdrawal of love. Since the withdrawal of love is one of the most profound and devastating experiences that a child can experience, making mistakes or performing poorly takes on much greater significance than it should. Even though we may come to the conclusion as adults that our reactions are inappropriate, we often have difficulty learning how to respond more appropriately. Why we have difficulty unlearning this belief and replacing it with a more rational or reasonable one is not altogether clear. Among other things, it has been suggested that the experiential system does not work by rules of reason or logic and therefore to change requires something more than just understanding the source of our problem (Epstein & Meier, 1989).

Poor constructive thinking and stress. In laboratory studies of stress (where stress was induced by having subjects engage in subtracting 7s from 300 and constantly told of their errors and in mirror-tracing in which errors were again constantly announced), poor constructive thinkers reported more negative thoughts (both related to the experiment and unrelated to the experiment) and experienced more negative affect (Katz & Epstein, 1991). Physiological measures of poor constructive thinkers also indicated they experienced greater stress than good constructive thinkers. It was concluded that poor constructive thinkers contribute to the stress they experience by spontaneously generating negative thoughts in the absence of external stressors and that they appraise external stressors as more threatening.

Constructive Thinking and Success in Life

It is not surprising that Epstein's theory is relevant not only to managing stress but to achieving success. In the chapter on achieving personal success, I will talk more about the importance of learning how to develop the kind of thinking that has been used by successful people.

Emotion-Focused Coping Strategies

A wide variety of strategies has been advocated to deal with stress. They include exercise, relaxation, meditation, and even biofeedback training. In recent years

PRACTICAL APPLICATION 9.1

How Might One Become a Good Constructive Thinker?

From the work of Epstein it appears that poor constructive thinkers not only focus their negative thinking on the self but that they focus their negative thinking on the outside world as well. As a result, not only do they see themselves as inadequate or lacking, they see the world as threatening. Whether these two characteristics are distinct or merely two sides of the same coin is not completely clear at this time. Existing research suggests they are different but highly related and probably have a common origin which can be found in the implicit theories that people have constructed about such things as their ability to deal with the external world. In other words, while some people may tend to focus their negative thinking more on the self, others focus their negative thinking more on the environment. All behavior involves, at least to some degree, an attempt to interact with the environment. To interact successfully involves an assessment of one's abilities (the self) and the challenge offered by the environment. If making a mistake is serious business in one implicit theory, then interacting with the outside world is clearly dangerous and one needs to be cautious. It could be dangerous because one lacks skills or because the environment is difficult and threatening.

How does one learn to deal successfully with the external world? First, you need to believe that you can succeed and then you need to learn the skills that will enable you to succeed. Many people never put forth the effort to develop the skills they need because they don't believe they can succeed. The first step,

therefore, is to develop a more positive attitude about one's ability to deal with the environment—to see the external environment as something which can be successfully subdued or managed. The second thing, of course, is to see the world in terms of opportunity—a source of pleasure as opposed to pain. I will talk about how to develop such thinking when I discuss optimism in the next chapter and again in the last chapter. Let me simply point out at this time that many psychologists are moving towards conceptualizing thinking styles (constructive versus destructive, for example) as habits that people have developed. If they are habits, people can learn to change their habits through the principles of reinforcement and thereby develop new and better ways of thinking about themselves and the world. In other words, we have reason to be optimistic that we can all become constructive thinkers.

Conceptualizing thinking in terms of habits makes a great deal of sense to me because it helps me understand more clearly why I often have difficulty changing the way I think. Even though I know at some rational level that it makes sense to think differently, I often find myself falling back into my previous mode of thinking. It seems easier and more natural—more me. Eventually, however, I come to feel very comfortable with my new way of thinking.

It has been my experience that when I do change the way I think, often after repeated attempts to do so, that the world looks very different to me; it is often a better world.

---

much research has been done on some of these techniques in an effort to assess their ability to reduce stress. We will briefly examine a portion of that research.

Meditation. Transcendental meditation (TM) was introduced to North America by Maharishi Mahesh Yogi

in the 1960s. More than half a million people have already been trained, and their numbers continue to grow. There has been a virtual explosion of books and articles advocating the use of meditation to overcome stress and *increase inner energy* (for example, Bloomfield et al., 1975; Schwartz, 1974).

There are several techniques for meditation. All

seem to be equally effective in lowering anxiety and countering the effects of stress. According to Daniel Goleman, who has compared several techniques, each retrains attention in some way. Goleman (1976, p. 84) has offered the following brief procedure that anyone can follow to learn to meditate:

> Find a quiet place with a straight-back chair. Sit in any comfortable position with your back straight. Close your eyes. Bring your full attention to the movement of your breath as it enters and leaves your nostrils. Don't follow the breath into your lungs or out into the air. Keep your focus at the nostrils, noting the full passage of each in- and out-breath, from its beginning to its end. Each time your mind wanders to other thoughts, or is caught by background noises, bring your attention back to the easy, natural rhythm of your breathing. Don't try to control the breath; simply be aware of it. Fast or slow, shallow or deep, the nature of the breath does not matter; your total attention to it is what counts. If you have trouble keeping your mind on your breath, count each inhalation and exhalation up to 10, then start over again. Meditate for 20 minutes; set a timer, or peek at your watch occasionally. Doing so won't break your concentration. For the best results, meditate regularly, twice a day, in the same time and place.*

The evidence showing that meditation does reduce the stress reaction is fairly impressive. It has been shown, for example, that meditation will reduce high blood pressure (Benson & Wallace, 1972) as well as the frequency of such complaints as headaches, colds, and insomnia (Wallace, Benson, & Wilson, 1971). One series of studies showed that transcendental meditation practiced by volunteer subjects produced a decrease in oxygen consumption (Wallace & Benson, 1972). These results are presented in Figure 9-8. This study is particularly impressive because oxygen consumption reflects metabolism rate—a

---

* From "Meditation Helps Break the Stress Spiral," by D. Goleman. In *Psychology Today*, February, 1976, *9*, 82-86. Copyright © 1976 American Psychological Association. Reprinted by permission.

physiological response that cannot be altered through voluntary efforts. Of particular interest is the question of whether meditators can reduce the activity of the adrenal cortex. In general, there is evidence that meditation does reduce adrenocortical activity, as indicated by reduced cortisol levels (Jevning, Wilson, & Davidson, 1978).

Goleman has noted that rapid recovery from stress is a typical trait of meditators. He has suggested that this fact is the key to understanding why meditators are successful in resisting the effects of stress. If a person can relax after each stressful event, the aversive effects associated with stress are kept to a minimum, giving the person greater reserves of energy to deal with future stressful events. Rather than letting each stressful event add to the previous one, the person treats each event more or less separately. As we have noted, stress seems to have a damaging effect only if it is prolonged. It appears that the meditator's rapid recovery from stress serves to circumvent this possibility.

Relaxation. Researchers have attempted to determine whether relaxation is as effective as meditation. The hypothesis guiding this research is that the beneficial effects of meditation are due to the increased relaxation produced in the course of meditation—in other words, that there is nothing mystical or unique about meditation. Indeed, several lines of research have shown that relaxation is just as effective as meditation (Beary, Benson, & Klemchuk, 1974; Cauthen & Prymak, 1977; Fenwick et al., 1977; Holmes, 1984; Morse et al., 1977). Several studies have shown that relaxation is effective in reducing both systolic and diastolic blood pressure (for example, Fey & Lindholm, 1978; Mount et al., 1978). In his book *The Relaxation Response* Herbert Benson (1975) tells how relaxation can be readily learned and used.

Exercise. The effects of exercise have been examined mainly in connection with anxiety. As anxiety is often associated with stress, however, the results of this research are highly relevant. A study comparing the effects of exercise and meditation found that although exercise reduced certain somatic aspects of anxiety, it

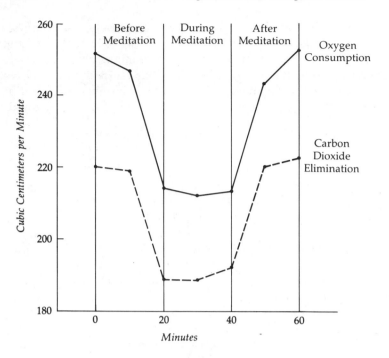

Figure 9–8. Effect of meditation on subjects' oxygen consumption (solid line) and carbon dioxide elimination (dashed line), recorded in 20 and 15 cases, respectively. After the subjects were invited to meditate, both rates decreased markedly. Consumption and elimination returned to the premeditation level soon after the subjects stopped meditating. (From R. K. Wallace and H. Benson, "The Physiology of Mediation." *Scientific American,* February 1972, 84-90. Copyright © 1972 by Scientific American, Inc. All rights reserved.)

did not necessarily reduce the cognitive aspects (Schwartz, Davidson, & Goleman, 1978). These researchers argue that exercise has a more specific effect. If exercise were combined with relaxation, exercise could enhance the beneficial effects of relaxation. In other words, exercise cannot be substituted for relaxation. Nonetheless, there is considerable evidence that simply being physically fit, even when one is under psychological stress, does moderate against the health effects that often come from life stress (Brown, 1991).

Biofeedback. Ever since it was first shown that involuntary responses mediated by the autonomic nervous system can be altered through operant conditioning procedures, there has been a great deal of interest in using these procedures to reduce the stress reaction. After reviewing the research on this question, Tarler-Benlolo (1978) concluded that there is no evidence that biofeedback is better than relaxation for dealing with a variety of stress-induced disorders, including migraine headaches and elevated blood pressure. Each of these two techniques may be particularly suited to

certain people or certain disorders, but as yet there is no clear indication which technique is preferable for particular persons or ailments. There may, in fact, be reason to use both techniques at the same time (Cuthbert et al., 1981; Fey & Lindholm, 1978).

Cognitive and Individual Difference Factors

Talking or Writing About a Trauma: Cognitive Assimilation of Emotions

Individuals who have suffered from a variety of traumas in childhood are far more likely to become ill if they never talk about the traumas (Pennebaker, 1992). Working on the hypothesis that getting people to talk about their traumas might have health benefits, several studies have confirmed the idea that talking or writing about a trauma leads to health benefits. Among other things, it has been found that people who wrote about their traumas visited the doctor less and had an improved immune response (Pennebaker, 1990).

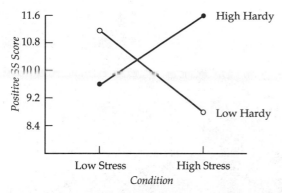

Figure 9–9. Effects of stress and hardiness on positive self-statements (SS). (From K. D. Alfred and T. W. Smith, "The Hardy Personality: Cognitive and Physiological Responses to Evaluative Threat." *Journal of Personality and Social Psychology*, 1989, *56*, 257-266. (Figure 1, p. 262) Copyright © 1989 by the American Psychological Association. Reprinted with permission.)

Pennebaker argues that while inhibition is normally highly adaptive because inhibition allow us to control such things as our thinking and behavior (such as in goal-directed behaviors), inhibition of traumatic events is very harmful. Over time, he argues, the constant inhibition to not think about the trauma creates stress. In order for people to reduce this stress they need to deal with the trauma and put it to rest. Various theorists have argued that when people actually translate an experience into language they can *assimilate* that event (Horowitz, 1976). Whatever the actual process, talking and writing seem to serve the function of reducing the tension that comes from constantly having to inhibit something that affected us deeply.

The Hardy Personality

It has been suggested that the personality profiles of people who remain healthy after experiencing high degrees of life stress differ from those of people who sicken under stress. This sort of personality, which has been referred to as the hardy personality, is distinguished by three main characteristics: control, commitment, and challenge (Kobasa, 1979a, 1979b, 1982; Kobasa, Maddi, & Kahn, 1982). *Control* refers to the be-

lief that it is possible to influence the course of life events; *commitment* refers to the belief that life is meaningful and has a purpose; and *challenge* refers to the attitude that difficult or onerous events are normal and can provide an opportunity for mastery and development. It has been suggested that the concept of hardiness may account for other moderators of stress, such as the internal/external dimension and sensation-seeking (Kobasa & Puccetti, 1983). Suzanne Kobasa has shown that people who have a hardy personality profile are less likely than others to become ill after experiencing stress. The work of Hull, Van Treuren and Virnelli (1987) suggests that hardiness is not a unitary phenomenon and should be treated as three separate phenomena. They found that only commitment and control were significantly related to health outcome.

The concept of a hardy personality has generated a great deal of interest and has led to a number of studies that have been designed to determine exactly how and why the hardy personality leads to lower rates of illness. The bulk of the evidence seems to indicate that the effects have to do with their cognitions. Specifically, it is the way they appraise themselves and their interactions with the environment. Hardy people not only see the world as less threatening but they see themselves as more capable of dealing with stressful events. Evidence that they see themselves as more capable comes from studies which have found that hardy individuals offer more positive self-statements and fewer negative self-statements when confronted with stress (Allred & Smith, 1989), and from studies which show higher frustration tolerance (Wiebe, 1989). Figure 9-9 shows the number of positive and negative self-statements of high and low hardy people under high and low stress.

Since illness is often precipitated by high stress, one might expect that various indicators of stress such as blood pressure would be lower in hardy people. The evidence on this is equivocal (e.g., Wiebe, 1989). Some studies have found that hardy individuals often have higher levels of systolic blood pressure when presented with a stressful event. It has been suggested that this may reflect the tendency for hardy individuals to cope with the stress (Allred & Smith, 1989). Since it has been suggested that chronic stress, not momentary stress, leads to greater illness, this finding should not necessarily be viewed as inconsistent with the idea that hardiness does not ultimately exert its influence through the reduction of chronic stress.

Internal versus External Locus of Control

Internals' belief that the environment is essentially controllable has been shown to be an important factor in the reduction of stress (Lefcourt et al., 1981). But what happens when an event is in fact not controllable? Lundberg and Frankenhaeuser (1978) have shown that internals give evidence of greater stress when in such situations than they do when a task is controllable, whereas externals show less stress when the situation is uncontrollable than when it is controllable. In other words, stress is related to the consistency of one's cognitive orientation with the outcome of one's effort to control the stressor. Inconsistency leads to greater stress.

One particularly interesting finding is that internals derive greater benefits from social support than those who have a more external orientation (Lefcourt, Martin, & Saleh, 1984). This finding may help to clarify why some studies have not been able to demonstrate that an internal orientation does not always lead to the amelioration of stress. Apparently, the internal orientation interacts with such variables as social support and cognitive appraisal. One study demonstrated that internals appraise situations in a more adaptive fashion than externals (Parkes, 1984).

Optimism: Having a Positive and Hopeful Outlook

There is considerable evidence that people who adopt a positive and hopeful outlook (take an optimistic view of the world) are healthier than people who adopt a more pessimistic view. In her book entitled *Positive Illusion*, Shelly Taylor (1989) makes the case that people who see things from an optimistic point of view tend to show better recovery from a wide range of illnesses including cancer. Pessimists, on the other hand, tend to have a poor prognosis for recovery from illness. The current evidence suggests that when people take a pessimistic outlook in response to a stressful event, their catecholamines become depleted, triggering the endor-

When we are experiencing stress, we often feel like we have the weight of an elephant holding us back. But that doesn't stop an optimist.

phin response. The endorphin response, in turn, shuts down the immune system (see Seligman, 1990).

Since I will be talking at some length about the role of optimism in Chapter 11, I will leave this fascinating subject for now.

Instrumentality

In both cross-sectional and longitudinal studies it has been shown that instrumentality is a significant stress-buffer (Shaw, 1982; Roos & Cohen, 1987). Instrumentality is a measure, among other things, of problem-solving behavior that has been implicated in adjustment. Consistent with previous work, Roos and Cohen

(1987) found that instrumentality was negatively related to psychological distress. Interestingly, it was found that androgynous individuals (those who scored high on both instrumentality and expressiveness on Spence and Helmreich's scale) showed the greatest resilience to recent life stress.

The finding that instrumentality is linked positively to health is congruent with the conceptualization that active coping is important for good health. When people take charge of their lives, they are less likely to fall prey to the the debilitating effects of stress.

Sensation Seeking

Sensation seeking has also been found to be a moderator of stress (Cohen, 1982; Smith, Ptacek, & Smoll, 1992). Like people with a hardy personality, sensation seekers tend to view the world as less threatening (Franken, Gibson, and Rowland, 1992). Like hardy people, they tend to engage in more active coping (Smith, Ptacek & Smoll, 1992). Like optimists, they tend to view the world in positive (optimistic) as opposed to negative (pessimistic) terms and they tend to be highly instrumental (Franken, 1992).

As I point out in more detail in Chapter 14, sensation seekers are people who see the world as benevolent. They take the view that life is a happening, something to be embraced and enjoyed. They are people who are ready to disclose their feelings to others (Franken, Gibson, & Mohan, 1990). They are not perfectionists but rather people who can accept imperfection. They like people and they have a great deal of tolerance for other people's values and points of view. In short, they have many of the qualities that we have discussed that make them resistant to the effects of stress. They also have a good sense of humor.

A Sense of Humor

Initial work on humor showed that humor helps to reduce stress (Martin & Lefcourt, 1983). In a follow-up study it was shown that humor reduces stress, but only for depressed individuals and not for individuals with anxiety symptomology (Nezu, Nezu, & Blissett, 1988). Why does humor reduce stress? One possible interpretation is that people with a sense of humor appraise stressful situations differently than people who do not. Another possibility is that a sense of humor leads to responses that are incompatible with the stress reaction. It has been shown, for example, that putting on a happy face is sufficient to produce the changes in heart rate and other physiological reactions that would be expected if one were actually experiencing a happy mood. Even thinking about an emotion produces the reactions that accompany the emotion when it is actually being felt (Ekman, Levenson, & Friesen, 1983). This latter research study strongly suggests that some sort of feedback mechanism helps to reduce stress. Whatever the exact mechanism, it seems to make a lot of intuitive sense that humor should be an effective means of reducing stress. It remains to be seen why it fails to work with people experiencing anxiety.

Some Observations and Conclusions about Moderators of Life Stress and Health

The current research seems to indicate that seeing the world as less threatening and believing in one's capacity to cope are two very important attributes for good health. When people see the world as less threatening, they do not experience the same magnitude of stress. Further, if they perceive they have the capacity to cope they do not experience the same magnitude of stress. These two moderators seem to have their roots in the implicit theories that people have about the world and about themselves; about how threatening the world is and how good they are at coping with the world. This may be the basis for why some people become constructive thinkers and others become destructive thinkers. If people grow up with the idea that they live in a world filled with opportunities and that they have the potential for interacting or coping successfully with the world, they would naturally act constructively in their interactions with the world. If, on the other hand, they grow up with the belief that there is a scarcity of opportunities and that they are lacking in potential to deal or cope with the world, they would be inclined to think more destructively in their interactions with the world.

Some Rules for Dealing with Stress

A wide variety of organizations, agencies, and educational institutions are offering courses or seminars designed to help people deal with unwanted stress. Some of the courses and seminars teach methods for reducing the magnitude of the stress reaction. Meditation, relaxation, exercise, and biofeedback are some of the more commonly used methods. Other courses and seminars help people plan their lives so that they either encounter fewer stressors or arrange for the stressors to come at times when they are both physically and psychologically prepared to deal with them. Below are seven rules that one may follow to deal with unwanted stress.

1. Plan activities to reduce or eliminate stressors

The daily routine of many people exposes them to a wide variety of events that produce stress. Traffic snarls on the way to and from work, periodic interruptions, noise, the need to make quick decisions, requests for assistance in areas that are not one's responsibility, criticisms relating to quality or quantity of work, and involvement in hostile exchanges are some of the events that can increase stress. Although some of these events are unavoidable, it is often possible to reduce the number or magnitude of such stressors. Arranging to go to work earlier and leaving earlier could, for example, allow one to avoid traffic jams, work at least for a period of time without interruptions, experience less noise, limit the opportunity for people to make unwarranted requests, and reduce hostile exchanges. If it is possible to do at least part of one's job before the rest of the employees arrive, there may be more time to make decisions and to respond tactfully to criticisms and requests. The resulting reduction in stress may decrease irritability and arousal and thus make one less sensitive to potential stressors. Finally, the overall reduction in stress could lead to improved performance, which not only would reduce

criticism (another potential source of stress) but could lead to rewards and promotions.

2. Plan activities so that stressors come at times when they are psychologically easier to handle or tolerate

An event can induce a more intense stress reaction if it occurs at certain times rather than others. For example, one of the most common sources of stress for many people is interruptions that occur when they are trying to complete a task—a ringing telephone, a person dropping by to ask questions or simply to chat, certain unexpected or distracting noises. It is often possible to reduce or eliminate this source of stress by some planning. Turning off the telephone bell, telling one's secretary that one will return the call, putting up a "Do not Disturb" sign, and moving to a location where such interruptions are unlikely are some possible solutions. People often find that after an important task is completed, such events are less stressful or possibly not stressful at all. Alternatively, one might take care of details early in the day so that a block of time will be available later in the day to work at certain tasks.

3. Learn to relax between activities

Stress-resistant people tend to experience less stress in the course of a demanding or rigorous schedule than other people. Although constitutional differences may account for some of this difference, there is evidence that it is due in part to the way people pace themselves. Shutting down the stress reaction periodically by relaxing appears to be one way to keep the stress reaction under control. Research from a variety of sources suggests that stress becomes distressful when it is allowed to become intense. When a person fails to shut down the stress reaction periodically, the stress of one activity tends to add to the stress of another. At some point stress becomes the person's enemy. It is likely to have an adverse affect not only on one's health but on one's performance. Intense stress, therefore, not only can interfere with one's ability to cope but can become an additional source of stress. If one can learn to relax between activities, there is much less chance that stress will either become distressful or adversely affect health and performance. It has also been suggested that it may be easier to reduce a little stress than a lot. When the stress reaction becomes very intense, it frequently provokes a psychological state of helplessness. That is, one perceives that one no longer has control over the events that are capable of inducing stress. Such a feeling can, of course, act as a primary source of stress. Because stress can interfere with a person's ability to cope, which would remove this state of helplessness, the person is caught in a vicious circle in which the experience of stress becomes a stimulus for further stress.

4. Learn to recognize the early signs of stress

Because humans are dynamic, their reactions to events are always affected by previous activities and events. This means that at certain times an event may cause only mild stress, while at other times it may cause intense stress. Since there is reason to believe that we need to gain control of the stress reaction before it becomes too intense, we must be able to recognize when stress is starting to exceed some *safe limit*. For many people this is not an easy task. Many people can recognize stress only when it has reached a high level of intensity. Biofeedback training can help such people understand the nature of the stress reaction and teach them how to intervene when it starts to exceed some safe limit.

5. Learn to treat stress as a challenge

Stressful events often demand that we react. We can react with fear and helplessness, or we can rise to the challenge. If we treat a stressor as a challenge and attempt to control it, we will create norepinephrine. Norepinephrine not only helps supply us with energy but provides us with positive affect. In other words, it appears that norepinephrine has evolved to help us cope with stress. To tap that adaptive chemical, we must rise to the challenge. We must view stress as an opportunity to exercise our adaptive responses or to develop such responses. Failure to rise to the challenge will only undermine our self-concept and our natural tendency to control stressful events in our environment.

6. Learn to prevail by becoming problem-focused

There is a great deal of research which emphasizes the idea that it is important for people to learn how to manage self-doubt because when you learn to manage self-doubt you have learned an important aspect of how to prevail. As Bandura (1991) points out, everybody experiences self-doubt from time to time, especially when they are faced with a negative life event. The thing that differentiates people who manage to prevail and succeed versus give up and fail is how they deal with such self-doubt. The people who fail typically allow themselves to ruminate on their self-doubts, rehearsing all their past failures and counting all their inadequacies. Those who succeed, in contrast, engage in a very different type of thinking. They learn to rehearse their past successes and to enumerate their strengths.

The key to managing self-doubt is learning to become problem-focused. When attention is focused on the problem, as opposed to the self, something productive can happen. That is the basis for hope and optimism. When people become self-focused, they tend to focus on the negative, emphasizing the idea that nothing can change because the source of their difficulty lies in their personal inadequacies. The more

(continued on next page)

PRACTICAL APPLICATION 9.2

Some Rules for Dealing with Stress (continued)

they ruminate the more distressed they become and the harder it is for them to think about a solution to the problem they are facing (e.g., Wood, Saltzberg, Neale, Stone, & Rachmiel, 1990).

In order to become more problem-focused, it is important to start by thinking of how you succeeded in the past under similar circumstances. In other words, give yourself a little pep talk. Next, look for ways that other people succeeded under similar circumstances. This will get your thinking off yourself. Finally, ask people to help you find a solution. This is a good way to establish social relations and make use of the considerable skills that other people have.

7. Actively develop those personality characteristics that will ward off stress

Personality is to a very large degree a matter of attitude towards the world and oneself. People who are healthy are people who are positive, optimistic, accept themselves, take charge of their lives, have a sense of humor, and have good social relations. Most people cannot change their personality overnight. But people can and often do change. Personality is not carved in stone. It is something that one can construct (see Chapter 14). One of the most powerful reasons I can think of for wanting to change is to be physically healthier and as a result live longer. Stress is not inevitable. It is something that people can keep to a minimum if they are willing to create an environment that is conducive to harmony, cooperation, and support.

The interesting thing about holding positive views (and thinking constructively) is that people do not have to immediately succeed in order to experience the beneficial effects that come from engaging in positive thinking. There is a great deal of research to show that when people think positively they begin to cope and they feel less stressed. In a study of HIV-positive men it was found that those characterized by dispositional optimism engaged in more positive health-related coping behaviors and experienced less distress even though the virus they were carrying would almost certainly kill them in due course (Taylor, Kemeny, Aspinwall, Schneider, Rodriguez, & Herbert, 1992). The ability to think positively is what seems to be important. It produces the tendency to cope and it leads to a reduction in stress. But which of these two factors is more important, the coping response or the reduction in stress?

While it has been assumed for some time that stress is the cause of a diminished immune response, there is

now good reason to challenge that assumption. It may well be that the stress reaction is not the cause but that negative cognitions are. Seligman (1990) has noted with respect to depression that depletion of the catecholamines (a condition that occurs when there is depression) triggers an endorphin response which then shuts down the immune system. While stress often depletes the catecholamines, it is important to note that the immune system often shuts down without there being a stress response. In other words, the immune system can and does shut down in the absence of stress. If negative cognitions are the cause of a diminished immune response, this would explain why researchers have not be able to consistently show that stress markers, such as high blood pressure, consistently predict poor health and why indicators of negative cognitions often predict poor health.

One study which provides evidence that a pessimistic outlook is responsible for health was a study examining the links between optimism, aging and health. In this study, optimists and pessimists were compared on various health measures. While these two types did not show any differences in health at age 25 as a result of being pessimistic versus optimistic, after about age 45 the health differences begin to emerge (Peterson, Seligman, & Valiant, 1988). Specifically, people who were more pessimistic begin to show more health disorders, while people who remained optimistic often showed little deterioration. It is at age 45 when the aging process begins to take its toll. In other words, many researchers feel that people who are more negative and pessimistic will ultimately pay the price for their pessimism. We still don't know the full ramifications of why positive thinking is so important, but we do know it is important. Perhaps it is because positive thinking leads to coping. In other words, the key to good health can be found in doing the right things, something that people seem to do quite naturally when they are optimistic. Ellen Langer (1989), in her book entitled *Mindfulness*, has talked extensively about the aging process and has suggested on the basis of her research that one of the moderators against both physical and psychological aging is remaining mindful—staying in touch with the world by being an active decision-maker and an active learner. She stresses that it is important not only to think positively but to engage in coping behavior.

What about the evidence that relaxation is the route to good health? Herbert Benson (1987) has pointed out that relaxation not only reduces the stress response but that it alters people's perceptions of the world. He has found, for example, that as a result of learning to relax people often come to see the world as less threatening and see themselves as more in control. It may well be that the beneficial effects of relaxation come not from shutting down the stress response but rather from changing the way people view the world and themselves. In the chapter on positive emotions we will explore in more depth the whole question of how our outlook affects such things as our health and our success.

Since all of us at one time or another will be troubled by stress, Practical Application 9.2 summarizes some of the things we can do to reduce it.

Summary

One of the most fundamental moderators of life stress is social support. It has been suggested that certain people who resist seeking out social support (repressive types) are susceptible to a number of physical diseases, particularly cancer. Interestingly, owning a pet, especially a dog, has significant health benefits.

Coping has for some time been suggested as a major moderator of stress. Epstein's theory is that people who are effective in dealing with stress tend to think more *constructively* when faced with problems, whereas those who tend to experience stress think more *destructively*. The "Constructive Thinking Inventory" (CTI) contains a global measure of coping plus six specific measures or scales: emotional coping, behavioral coping, categorical thinking, superstitious thinking, naive optimism and negative thinking. Work with the scale indicates that constructive thinkers tend to deal effectively with negative outcomes. It has been suggested that the destructive thinking style emerges early in life and may result from the withdrawal of love for poor performance. To become constructive thinkers, people need to learn how to change the way they think about themselves and the world

Several emotion-focused coping strategies have been suggested to help people deal with stress. Transcendental meditation has been shown to be effective; however, researchers such as Goleman have concluded that all forms of meditation are equally effective. It appears that meditation teaches people to relax following a stressful event. Relaxation is important in reducing the adverse effects that often accompany a prolonged stress reaction. Some researchers have suggested that meditation is not a necessary condition to obtain the effects of relaxation. Relaxation can be taught directly. Exercise has also been advocated as a way of reducing stress. Although exercise reduces certain somatic components, it does not appear to be a substitute for relaxation. Biofeedback has also been used. It is effective, but it appears to be no better than relaxation. Exactly why relaxation is so effective is not altogether clear. Research is needed to determine whether relaxation affects only bodily reactions or whether it also affects cognitive reactions.

Another moderator of life stress is the hardy personality, characterized by control, commitment, and challenge. The bulk of the research on hardiness suggests that the effects are due to the way hardy people appraise their interactions with the environment. Specifically they see the world as less threatening and themselves as more capable of dealing with stressful life events. It has been shown that internals are more stressed by uncontrollable situations, whereas externals are more stressed by situations they feel they can control. Taking a positive and hopeful outlook has been found to be a major moderator of stressful life events. Instrumentality has also been implicated, indicating that people who are highly instrumental are more resilient than those who are low. Sensation seeking has also been implicated, not surprising in view of the fact that sensation seekers tend to view the world as less threatening, tend to be optimistic, and tend to be highly instrumental.

Not surprisingly, it has been demonstrated that a sense of humor can reduce stress. Even putting on a happy face can be an effective way of reducing stress.

While stress has traditionally been viewed as one of the—if not the main—psychological causes of a reduced immune response and thus poor health, there is growing evidence of a direct link between negative (pessimistic) thinking and a reduced immune response. This suggests that there needs to be a major shift from the strategy of teaching people to reduce stress to teaching people to think positively.

Some rules for dealing with stress, all the way from avoiding stressors to changing the way you think about stressors and about yourself, are offered as a way of using the information discussed in this chapter to live a more stress-free and healthier life.

Main Points

1.   While early motivation theorists conceptualized motivation in terms of drives that lead directly to action, current theorists conceptualize motivation as dispositions. Whether or not these dispositions will result in action often depends on emotions which can undermine or sustain goal-directed behavior.

2.   Emotions arise out of our interactions with the environment and result from our attempts to adapt to the environment.

3.   The study of facial expression suggests that all humans experience a common set of emotions.

4.   Lazarus has suggested that appraisal plays a critical role in determining the emotions we experience.

5.   Various theorists have suggested that the emotions we experience come from two independent systems.

6.   According to the Kleinginnas' definition, emotions give rise to affective experiences, stimulate the individual to generate cognitive explanations, trigger a variety of internal responses, and elicit behaviors that are expressive, goal-directed, and adaptive.

7.   Three basic dimensions of emotions have emerged: (a) pleasant/unpleasant, (b) active/passive, and (c) intense/not intense.

8.   It has been suggested that emotions are lawful phenomena that can be described in terms of a set of "laws."

9.   Stress is frequently conceptualized as the fight/flight response.

10.   Stress can be elicited by a variety of physical and psychological stimuli called stressors.

11.   Two separate systems, the sympathetic/adrenal and the pituitary/adrenal, are involved in the stress response.

12.   The sympathetic system is a fast-acting system that produces, among other things, a general increase in arousal.

13.   In the case of the pituitary/adrenal response, the hypothalamus initiates activity in the endocrine system by stimulating the pituitary, which secretes ACTH (adrenocorticotropic hormone).

14.   Engaging in adaptive behavior reduces the stress response.

15.   Endorphins are mobilized from the pituitary and are important for their analgesic properties.

16. Stress itself does not cause diseases but rather makes the person more susceptible to diseases.

17. The *general adaptation syndrome*, as Selye calls it, is characterized by three stages: alarm reaction, resistance, and exhaustion.

18. It is during the resistance stage that the adrenal glands first increase and then decrease in size. When the adrenal glands lose their capacity to resist, people become susceptible to disease.

19. Generally, unpredictable events are more likely than predictable events to elicit the stress response.

20. Being able to discriminate (predict) the onset of stress can reduce the magnitude of the stress response.

21. Exercising and coping can reduce the stress.

22. Under certain conditions it is possible to habituate the stress response.

23. Stress can alter certain attentional processes, thus undermining performance. However, training methods can teach the organism to resist these effects.

24. There are three types of primary appraisal: harm/loss, threat, and challenge.

25. Secondary appraisal involves the evaluation of coping resources and options and may be either problem-focused or emotion-focused.

26. The tendency to use a problem-focused or an emotion-focused approach depends on whether the situation is perceived to be controllable and on whether one feels one has the ability to control the event.

27. Students facing an examination typically use both problem-focused and emotion-focused strategies. Discretionary social relationships can moderate pre-examination stress.

28. It has been argued that the stress and anxiety associated with taking a test produces *self-preoccupying intrusive thinking*.

29. Job-related stress is greatest when the job situation is characterized by ambiguity. Job satisfaction is lowest when ambiguity is high.

30. While men tend to show greater incidences of coronary heart disease in the workplace, the reasons for this are not clear.

31. It has been suggested that some organizations are more conflict-prone than others and that more conflict-prone organizations are likely to lead to health problems.

32. Although early research found the Type A personality prone to heart attacks, more recent research has had difficulty replicating this finding.

33. The hostility component of the Type A pattern has, nevertheless, been found to be a good predictor of coronary heart disease.

34. Suppressed anger and cynical hostility has also been linked to coronary heart disease.

35. The level of catecholamine output associated with the Type A behavior pattern (TABP) may mediate, in part, coronary disease.

36. Both cortisol and testosterone have not been ruled out as a possible contributing factor in coronary heart disease.

37. The interaction of hostility and TABP has been shown to increase plasma lipids, two physical markers for coronary heart disease.

38. Type As are sensitive to loss of control, which may account for their increased susceptibility to coronary disease.

39. There is considerable evidence for the heritability of Type A personality.

40. There is considerable evidence that the Type A pattern characterized by cynical hostility arises from a disturbed thinking style.

41. Although it may be difficult to modify the Type A pattern, people can reduce stress associated with the Tape A pattern by learning to relax and to restructure their environment.

42. There are several moderators of stress that can be classified as biological (social support), learned (breaking information down into manageable units, a constructive thinking style, and emotion-focused coping strategies) and cognitive/personality (hardiness, external locus of control, an optimistic outlook, instrumentality, sensation seeking, and a sense of humor).

43.   Repressive types are susceptible to a number of physical diseases, particularly cancer.

44.   Owning a pet has been found to be an important moderator of stress and has been implicated in health.

45.   Epstein has identified *constructive thinking* as one of the universal coping styles that can lead to a reduction in the stress reaction.

46.   Emotion-focused strategies for coping with stress include meditation, relaxation, exercise, and biofeedback.

47.   Studies have confirmed the idea that talking or writing about a trauma can lead to health benefits.

48.   The personality profile of people who remain healthy after experiencing high degrees of life stress has been referred to as the hardy personality, which is distinguished by three main characteristics: control, commitment, and challenge.

49.   While stress has traditionally been viewed as one of—if not the main—psychological causes of a reduced immune response and thus poor health, there is growing evidence for a direct link between negative (pessimistic) thinking and a reduced immune response.

Chapter Ten

Goal-Incongruent (Negative) Emotions:
Fear and Anxiety, Pessimism and Depression, Guilt and Shame

- What are goal-incongruent emotions?
- What is the difference between fear and anxiety?
- Can people learn to become less fearful and less anxious?
- Why are some people more fearful and anxious than others?

- What is the relationship between pessimism and depression? How prevalent is depression in our society?
- Is there a biological basis for pessimism and depression?
- Do antidepressants cure depression or do they simply remove the symptoms?

- When people become depressed, why do they often feel helpless?
- Can people get rid of depressed feelings by changing the way they think?
- Do attitudes we hold about ourselves have anything to do with depression?
- What is the difference between guilt and shame?
- Why do some people experience more guilt and shame than others?
- Can people learn to get rid of guilt and shame?
- Is it desirable to experience no guilt or shame?

Introduction

Certain emotions facilitate or sustain goal-directed behavior behavior while others tend to inhibit or undermine it. Goal-incongruent emotions are those emotions that thwart the attainment of personal goals, whereas goal-congruent emotions are those emotions that facilitate the attainment of personal goals (Lazarus, 1991). Goal-incongruent emotions are often referred to as negative emotions, whereas goal-congruent emotions are often referred to as positive emotions. This way of classifying emotions is consistent with the recent approaches to motivation in which goals are central to conceptualizing the motivation process (Locke & Latham, 1990). In addition to the emotions that I will be discussing in this chapter, there is the emotion of anger and hostility which I have dealt with to some degree in the chapters on aggression and stress. Let me start by talking about two related emotions, fear and anxiety, which have over the years been viewed as both adaptive and pathological emotions.

Fear and Anxiety

Distinguishing between Fear and Anxiety

It is not altogether clear that we should make a distinction between fear and anxiety. Some theorists have suggested that the two are basically the same (Izard & Tomkins, 1966); others have suggested that the goal object of fear is fairly specific while the goal object of anx-

iety is more vague or ambiguous (Miller, 1951). For example, we may fear snakes or high places or failing a test. Anxiety, on the other hand, is an emotion that we experience when it is not possible to specify the exact reason. We might, for example, experience anxiety in connection with the prospect of giving a speech. While we have no good reason to think that anything will go wrong, we nevertheless have a feeling that something terrible may happen. Images flit through our mind: we open our mouth to speak and nothing comes out or we speak all too clearly and everyone laughs at us.

Some theorists have suggested that anxiety is a more powerful emotion than fear. When we are afraid, we know what is causing our emotion. When we are anxious, however, the emotion is so unfocused that we have difficulty dealing with it (see Epstein, 1972).

Definition of Anxiety

Rollo May (1983) has proposed the following definition of anxiety:

> Anxiety is the apprehension cued off by a threat to some value that the individual holds essential to his existence as a personality. The threat may be physical (the threat of death), or to psychological existence (the loss of freedom, meaninglessness). Or, the threat may be to some other value that one identifies with one's existence: patriotism, the love of another person, "success," etc. [p. 205].

Antecedents of Anxiety

Seymour Epstein (1972) has argued that three primary conditions elicit anxiety: (1) overstimulation, (2) cognitive incongruity, and (3) response unavailability. These three conditions produce not only feelings of anxiety (apprehension) but high arousal as well. When we are anxious we may experience such physical symptoms as an increased heart rate, flushed skin, and a general state of muscle tension. Mentally, we may feel confused and unable to deal with the environment around us. In the following sections we will be dealing with these and other conditions that elicit anxiety.

Distinguishing between Fear and Phobia

A word that often comes up in the context of fear and anxiety is phobia. Phobia is viewed as an anxiety disorder and is defined by Mineka (1985) as a persistent and recognizable irrational fear of an object or situation that is characterized by distress and a compelling desire to avoid that object or situation. The thing that differentiates phobias from fear is the irrational aspect of phobias. People often come to fear such things as spiders or snakes even when they know they are harmless.

It has been suggested that phobias can be viewed as the product of classical conditioning. But that explanation alone does not account for why people are inclined to become fearful of certain things and not others (Mineka, 1985). It has been suggested that somewhere in our evolutionary past it was important for us to avoid such things as spiders and snakes and, as a result, the fear of spiders and snakes has become innate. Even if a phobic reation is not elicited when spiders and snakes are initially presented, research has shown that it is very easy to condition a fear reaction to these stimuli. This suggests that we are biologically prepared to learn to avoid certain stimuli but not others (Seligman, 1970). Within this context it is not too hard to understand why people might develop a wide variety of phobias such as *claustrophobia* (fear of enclosed places) or *acrophobia* (fear of heights). According to the evolutionary hypothesis, we may be prepared to learn to avoid a number of things that could threaten our survival. It may even be that we have a generalized tendency to develop phobic reactions to anything that we perceive might somehow threaten us. A particularly interesting phobia that has recieved a great deal of media attention is *agorophobia* which is defined as the fear of having an anxiety attack and losing control in public places or unfamiliar situations; a fear of leaving home or a familiar place. The need to be in control is important to humans, a topic that I will discuss in more detail shortly.

Biological Component

I have already discussed to a very large degree the biology of anxiety in the chapter on drug addiction. Let me briefly review what I said earlier. The drugs used to treat anxiety are the benzodiazepines. These drugs (Valium, Librium, alprazolam) seem to work by making it possible for GABA (gamma-amino butyric acid) to perform one of its functions. GABA is a naturally occurring transmitter inhibitor (Cooper, Bloom, & Roth, 1982; Tallman et al., 1980). That means that GABA somehow reduces the flow of neural transmission. In other words, the biology of anxiety is being overwhelmed by information.

From a subjective point of view, when we are flooded with stimulation or information (experience overstimulation), or when we have difficulty reconciling some event such as the loss of a loved one, with a deeply felt belief in a just world (cognitive incongruity), or when we simply do not know how to handle a difficult situation such as meeting new people (response unavailability), we often experience anxiety together with high arousal. People who parachute for the first time often report anxiety attacks that some describe as pure panic. The reason we think that people who are new to parachuting experience anxiety attacks is that the first time they jump they are suddenly faced with a totally new event that requires them not only to process information but to make decisions. They find themselves overloaded (or overwhelmed). There are simply too many demands being placed on the system, and the novice skydiver responds subjectively with feelings of anxiety.

What we think the antianxiety drugs do in such situations is regulate neural transmission. There is considerable evidence that when some optimal level of stimulation or arousal is exceeded, we not only experience anxiety but lose a large measure of our ability to think, act, and perform (Hebb, 1955). GABA appears to be one of those substances in the body that helps to maintain an optimal flow of stimulation or information. But as we have noted, GABA may perform this function only in association with another substance, such as benzodiazepine. Perhaps people who experience more anxiety than others fail to produce or release either the benzodiazepines that are necessary to keep anxiety under control or the amount of GABA needed to regulate neural transmission.

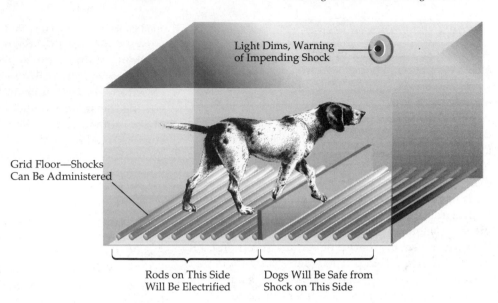

Light Dims, Warning
of Impending Shock

Grid Floor—Shocks
Can Be Administered

Rods on This Side
Will Be Electrified

Dogs Will Be Safe from
Shock on This Side

Figure 10-1. Shuttle box used to study avoidance learning in dogs. (From Neil R. Carlson, *Discovering Psychology*, 1988. Copyright © 1988. Reprinted by permission of Allyn and Bacon.)

Learned Component

Conceptualizing Fear and Anxiety as Conditioned Pain

According to such neobehaviorists as Neal Miller (1951) and O. H. Mowrer (1939), fear is a conditioned response to pain. If a person experiences pain in a specific situation, the stimuli associated with that situation acquire the ability to elicit the same emotional reaction that the pain originally elicited. An example would be parents who see their child die in a hospital. Each time they pass the hospital they re-experience the pain they experienced the day their child died.

Many of the early studies of fear and anxiety involved the use of pain and an avoidance-learning paradigm. Animals, often rats or dogs, were administered a painful shock to the feet in an enclosure called a shuttle box. In the type of shuttle box used with dogs, a barrier divides the space into two areas. The dog can *escape* the shock by jumping over the barrier when the shock comes on. In order to see whether the animal can learn to *avoid* shock, a light or tone is typically presented before the shock to signal the animal that shock is forthcoming. If the animal jumps over the barrier when the signal is turned on, it indicates the animal has learned to avoid the painful stimulus. The procedure can then

be repeated in reverse: the side of the box that was safe is now electrified and vice versa. In the course of several trials the animal jumps back and forth; thus the name *shuttle box*. The type of shuttle box used with dogs is presented in Figure 10-1.

It is important to note that in the course of learning, the animals show a great deal of emotionality. Rats, for example, urinate and defecate. Dogs often yelp or whine. As learning progresses, however, these signs of emotionality decrease (Amsel, 1962).

According to Miller, the main difference between fear and anxiety is whether the stimuli eliciting the fear are identifiable or vague. When they are clearly identifiable it is fear and when the stimuli are vague it is anxiety. The parents who saw their child die in a hospital may also experience or sense pain in other situations such as when it is Christmas, when they pass a playground filled with children, or when they see children on television. It is no longer the exact situation of the hospital that elicits that feeling of pain. Rather, it is any situation that reminds them of their loss.

Why does the avoidance response occur progressively earlier? A number of important things have been learned from studies of avoidance learning (Solomon & Wynne, 1954). First, with experience animals learn to respond progressively earlier until they are responding as soon as the signal is presented. As their response time shortens, the emotionality associated with this kind of learning decreases. The behavior, in fact, looks quite routine after extensive training. What we believe is happening is that the signal triggers the emotional response, which would normally increase in strength as time passes. The animal learns that it can reduce the aversive emotion triggered by the signal by making a quick response. One important finding that provides converging evidence for this interpretation is the fact that when animals are prevented from making their responses quickly, they show a great deal of emotionality. Humans react in much the same way. When we have to wait for an hour in a dentist's reception room, we tend to experience more anxiety than we do when we are ushered immediately into the chair. Performers often say that having to wait to go on stage is one of the things that causes them the most anxiety.

Why does the avoidance response persist over time? The second thing that we have learned from the avoidance-conditioning studies is that the avoidance response tends to persist for a long time in the absence of any reinforcement. Normally, a learned response will diminish in strength with time. The explanation that has been offered is that when the response is made early, any anxiety that occurs is immediately reduced. The reduction in anxiety comes to act as a reinforcer of the avoidance response. Thus the avoidance response is being continually reinforced. This finding is consistent with the clinical observation that certain kinds of anxiety reactions (especially phobic reactions) persist and even become stronger despite the absence of any recent experience that would explain why someone would continue to maintain that response.

Treating People Who Experience Excessive Fear and Anxiety

Desensitization

Further evidence in support of this explanation comes from work pertaining to the elimination of fear and anxiety. Two procedures have been successfully used to reduce fear and anxiety. The first is called desensitization. Since humans show less fear in response to symbolic forms of the fear stimulus than to the actual object of fear, it is possible to rank-order stimuli along a continuum ranging from those that elicit only mild fear (usually symbolic stimuli) to those that elicit extreme fear (usually concrete stimuli). People who are afraid of spiders, for example, usually respond with only mild fear to the word *spider*, with greater fear to pictures of spiders, and with intense fear to an actual spider. In desensitization training, the therapist starts by presenting a stimulus that elicits only mild fear under conditions in which the client feels relaxed and in control. Under these conditions, the mild fear stimulus often loses its ability to elicit the fear reaction. The therapist then moves to a stronger stimulus and repeats the procedure. Eventually the therapist moves to the strongest stimulus. The idea behind this procedure is that some kind of counterconditioning is occurring. That is, the client is conditioning a feeling of relaxation/control to the stimulus or stimuli that originally elicited fear.

Flooding

A second procedure that has been successful in reducing the fear response is called flooding (Kazdin, 1978). In this procedure the individual is typically presented with a fear-producing stimulus and the full emotional reaction is allowed to run its course. The key to success with this procedure is to make sure the client remains in the presence of the eliciting stimulus. This is a sink-or-swim procedure. The explanation for its effectiveness is again counterconditioning. When the emotional reaction subsides, a new reduced emotional response is conditioned to the stimulus. Over repeated experiences, that emotional response dwindles away.

The important thing about both procedures is that the subject is not allowed to make an avoidance response. The fact that an avoidance response interferes with the effectiveness of the treatment lends additional support to the idea that persistence of the avoidance response is linked in some way to the anxiety reduction that accompanies it.

Cognitive Component

Cognitive factors play an important role in the fear/anxiety response. We will limit our discussion to a few of the major cognitive components.

Loss of Control

Losing control, or simply the fear of losing control, often leads to feelings of anxiety. Martin Seligman (1975) has suggested that when events are unpredictable, we develop feelings of helplessness. Feelings of helplessness are sufficient, it is argued, to produce not only anxiety but depression. One of the reasons people experience anxiety in connection with having to give a talk, for example, is the fear that they may lose control. Uncertainty and unpredictability are associated with such a task, and it is the uncertainty or unpredictability that makes people anxious.

Inability to Make a Coping Response

Lazarus (1991) has argued that the inability (or the perceived inability) to make an adaptive response to a threatening event, or the fact (or perception) that no such response is available, will lead to feelings of anxiety. Lazarus points out that ambiguity is the key consideration here because it prevents the elaboration of clear action patterns (coping strategies) that would allow the individual to deal with the threat.

Larazarus suggests that transforming anxiety into fear might be a useful way of getting people to cope with a threat. The reason is that when people know what it is that is threatening them, they can devise a pattern of action to deal with it. When they don't know what the threat is, they are left in limbo, experiencing anxiety but not knowing what to do about it.

Evidence for Lazarus's idea can be found in the work on *self-certainty*. It has been shown that people who have explored and come to know both their weaknesses and their strengths (self-certain people) like themselves better than people who have only come to explore and know their strengths (Baumgardner, 1990). Among other things, self-certain people have better self-esteem. As a result, Baumgardner points out, self-certain people can take action to maximize

their outcomes because they know what they can and cannot do. They can make plans, for example, on how to get around their weaknsses. In contrast, people who lack knowledge about their weaknesses are not in a position to take action because they are not fully aware of the nature of their weaknesses and therefore not in a good position to make the appropriate plans for dealing with their weaknesses. What they experience instead is a sense of insecurity. This work is consistent with Lazarus's suggestion that people who cannot make a coping response (in this case because they lack knowledge) experience anxiety. It is also consistent with Lazarus's suggestion that one way for people to learn to deal with their anxiety is to transform their anxiety into something specific, such as a fear or perhaps incompetency. For the person who lacks knowledge about his or her weaknesses and therefore experiences insecurity, the route to security is to become aware of weaknesses. It is then that they can engage in planning, something that Lazarus calls coping. It is then that they can experience a sense of security.

State versus Trait Anxiety

Is anxiety caused by events in the environment or is it a characteristic of the individual? There is no question that certain events in the environment are a source of threat. Venturing into a rough neighborhood or being caught in a snowstorm while driving on the highway may cause us to fear for our personal safety. But should we experience a threat to our personal safety when we are sitting at home on a nice sunny day or simply driving down the highway? Some people feel much more threatened than others. Some people spend considerable time making sure the doors are locked and making sure they have enough food in the house in case of a snowstorm. These people are said to experience *trait anxiety*.

State anxiety has been defined as a transitory emotional response involving feelings of tension and apprehension (Spielberger, 1983), whereas *trait* anxiety has been defined as a personality trait that determines the likelihood a person will experience anxiety in stressful situations (Spielberger, 1983). According to this distinction, some people are more inclined to experience more anxiety in all stressful situations. Because they feel more anxious in all situations, we assume that they bring that anxiety with them to the situation. What they likely bring with them is a perception that the world is threatening as opposed to benign.

Sensitizers and repressors. It has also been suggested that people can be differentiated in terms of whether they are sensitizers or repressors. Sensitizers are people who dwell on the potential consequences of a threat; repressors avoid thinking about the consequences. Sensitizers, not surprisingly, tend to experience more anxiety than repressors. Yet, while repressors may experience less stress in a moment of threat, there is some question as to whether this is truly an adaptive way of dealing with a threat. Generally, we believe it is more adaptive to deal objectively with a threat. Most psychologists would probably agree that dwelling on a threat is not adaptive, either.

If you tend to experience stress in certain social situations, such as meeting new people, it probably would not be a good idea to dwell on what might go wrong. Such thoughts are likely to increase your natural tendency to avoid social situations in which you would have to meet new people. On the other hand, avoiding thinking about those situations might not be adaptive either. A more adaptive approach might be to recognize that you do indeed have a problem and then think of ways you might improve your ability to handle those situations.

Panic attacks. Panic attacks are relatively rare in the general population, but for those who experience them they are highly debilitating. In the case of agoraphobics, the fear of having a panic attack in public is often sufficient to make them prisoners in their own homes (Chambless & Gracely, 1989). When patients believe their attacks represent an immediate medical crisis, for example, convincing them otherwise is often sufficient to stop them from having a full-blown attack. For the agoraphobic, it is the fear of having the attack that seems to actually precipitate the full-blown attack. When they are convinced this fear is unjustified, they do not have a full-blown attack (Salkovskis, Clark, & Hackmann, 1991). These and other studies are exciting

because they indicate that by changing peoples belief systems, the emotions they experience can be modified.

These studies are consistent with the idea that people's emotional reactions can be understood, in part, through a *normative approach* (What is perceived to be normal or expected). The fact that normative arguments can affect anticipated emotions, such as a panic attack, indicates that people are inclined to bring their emotional response in line with what they believe to be appropriate or normal (Baron, 1992).

Anxiety as a Person-Environment Interaction

It has been suggested that while some people are inclined to be more anxious than others in all situations, different people tend to show different amount of anxiety in different situations. This has led to the suggestion that anxiety can be conceptualized as a person-environment interaction. Consistent with this idea, it has been shown in factor analytic studies that there are four distinct situations that elicit anxiety: *social evaluation, physical danger, ambiguity,* and *daily routines* (Endler, Parker, Bagby, & Cox, 1991). According to the person-environment interaction hypothesis, anxiety arises out of an individual's perception of how well he or she can cope with certain situations. If a person perceives they have greater coping skills for certain situations than others they will experience less anxiety in that situation.

As we have already seen with the distinction between sensitizers and repressors, there is a great deal of evidence that people do develop cognitive styles that lead them to interpret events in different ways. Further, it appears that these different ways of interpreting the environment may underlie differences in levels of anxiety that people experience in different situations. As we have seen, people who are inclined to see the world as threatening experience greater anxiety than people who see the world as more benign (Watson & Clark, 1984).

Summary

The general consensus is that the goal object of fear is fairly specific, while the goal object of anxiety is more vague or ambiguous. It has been suggested that three basic conditions elicit anxiety: overstimulation, cognitive incongruity, and response unavailability. Current knowledge indicates that GABA normally controls anxiety by reducing the flow of neural transmission. The benzodiazepine family of drugs (antianxiety drugs) is believed to help reduce anxiety by assisting GABA in performing its function.

According to the neobehaviorists, fear and anxiety are conditioned responses to pain, and the only difference between them is the stimulus to which they respond: an identifiable stimulus elicits fear, an ambiguous one anxiety. Two important things happen in the course of learning to avoid an aversive stimulus: first, the avoidance response tends to occur progressively earlier, and second, it tends to persist over time. Desensitization and flooding are two treatment techniques that can reduce fear and anxiety. Both procedures are assumed to work according to principles of counterconditioning.

Loss of control and the inability to make a coping response are two very important cognitive antecedents of fear and anxiety.

Individuals vary widely with respect to the amount of anxiety they experience. State anxiety is thought usually to be learned; the origin of trait anxiety is less clear. It may result from a low threshold of arousal, which makes people unusually responsive to all forms of stimulation, or it may result from the way one has learned to view the world. Some people, for example, tend to dwell on the consequences of a threat (sensitizers), while others tend to avoid thinking about such consequences (repressors). It has been suggested that trait anxiety reflects a general disposition toward negative affectivity. Finally, there is considerable evidence that the emotion of fear and anxiety that people experience is governed to a very large degree by their belief systems.

Pessimism and Depression

Distinguishing Pessimism From Depression

The concepts of pessimism and depression are closely linked. The study of depressed individuals shows that most tend to use a *pessimistic explanatory style*. There is also considerable data which indicate that people who use a pessimistic explanatory style are more likely to become depressed (Seligman, 1991). Nevertheless, it is important to note that there is a difference. While people who are depressed are characterized by loss of motivation (loss of interest in such things as food, sex, work, social relationships, achievement) and loss of interest in life (often they are suicidal), pessimistic people often remain motivated even though they might be characterized as inhibited in their tendency to embrace and interact with the outside world.

In this section I will be examining depression not so much from a clinical perspective as from the perspective that depressed individuals provide us with a clear example of what it means to be ultimately pessimistic. According to Seligman, pessimism can and often does lead to depression. It is often a matter of the degree to which people use an *explanatory style* that characterizes depressed individuals.

Thinking Style and Mood Interaction

Pessimism, like optimism, is more than just an explanatory thinking style; it is also a mood. To be precise, pessimism is a negative mood state that tends to undermine goal-directed behavior, whereas optimism is a positive mood that tends to facilitate goal-directed behavior. The more pessimistic the mood the more negative one feels and the more optimistic the mood the more positive one feels. The fact that it is a mood has a number of important implications. Research has shown that there tends to be a rather strong correlation between various biochemical states, mood, and thinking style. Which is first in the chain is, of course, the perennial chicken-and-egg question. While the traditional position has been that biochemistry produces mood, which in turn governs thinking style, there is reason to believe that thinking style can directly change or cause biochemical states and that these biochemical states cause mood. The first position is consistent with the observation that when people are given mood elevating drugs or antidepressants, they often think more positively. The second position is consistent with the evidence which shows that when people think in a pessimistic style they experience negative mood and when they think in an optimistic style they experience positive mood (e.g., Seligman, 1991). According to the latter position, mood may simply act as a chemical backup for maintaining a given thinking style. In other words, thinking optimistically or pessimistically can be conceptualized as stimulating the body to manufacture those chemicals necessary to maintain a positive mood state or a negative mood state. Further, according to this position, if you change your thinking style, the chemistry of your body will change to match it. Indeed, there is a great deal of data to support such a position. People who go to motivational speakers often report that after hearing an inspirational talk they experience a positive mood state and they think positively, but that the effect wears off after a period of time (often a few days). Presumably, what happens is the inspirational talk momentarily changed how they think about themselves and/or the world and this led to a change in their biochemistry. Because their thinking has only been changed momentarily and not permanently, the effects would tend to wear off. What people need to do is to make a permanent change in the way they think about themselves and the world. Research indicates that antidepressant drugs often fail to effect a long-term change unless people learn to change their explanatory style. In a study that compared drugs alone with drugs plus therapy as treatment of depression, it was found that antidepressant drugs were significantly more effective if they were used in conjunction with therapy. People who were treated only with drugs tended to drift back into their negative mood states (see Seligman, 1990).

To summarize, there is growing evidence that moods do govern the way we think and act (Carlson, Charlin, & Miller, 1988; Forgas & Bower, 1987). There is also growing evidence that thinking styles (what Seligman calls explanatory styles) cause moods, presumably by changing our body chemistry. If this is the case, then the route we must follow for finding happiness is learning how to think optimistically. We shouldn't, however, rule out other ways. If the key is mood, then we would be open to a variety of things that have been shown to affect our moods including such things as the foods we eat, getting good sleep, exercising, developing good social relations, and so forth.

How Prevalent Are Pessimism and Depression in our Society?

Since there is no clear benchmark for labeling a person as "too pessimistic" unless they are depressed, we need to turn to the research literature on depression to get some idea about the role of pessimism in people's lives and who in our society is troubled by pessimism. Some years ago, Aaron Beck and J. Young (1978) conducted a survey to determine how prevalent depression was among university students. They found that 78% of the students questioned reported that they had experienced depression at some time during the course of the academic year. Forty-six percent of those who reported depression indicated that their symptoms had been severe enough to warrant psychiatric help. When people are depressed, they frequently entertain thoughts of suicide, and a significant number of people actually *do* kill themselves. Of the 9 to 10 million people who suffer from depression yearly in the United States and Canada, upwards of 150,000 (about 15%) eventually commit suicide (Rosenfeld, 1985). When people are depressed, their motivation typically declines. They often lose their appetites, lose interest in sex and in social interaction generally, have no interest in achieving goals, are unable to concentrate, tire easily and have little energy, and are overwhelmed by feelings of hopelessness, worthlessness, guilt, or self-reproach.

Beck and Young reported that depression is generally twice as high among university students as in a comparable group of nonuniversity students. Women are two to five times more prone to depression than men. In the past, depression tended to occur more frequently at midlife (the 40s or 50s), but recently it has been occurring earlier. Many people in their 30s, 20s, and even teens are experiencing depression. The elderly, too, are susceptible to depression. Suicide is becoming increasingly common among these groups. Depression is not new. It hounded many famous figures of history, from Saul and Nebuchadnezzar of biblical times to Abraham Lincoln, Winston Churchill, and Ernest Hemingway of more recent times.

What is the cause of depression and why is it occurring earlier and earlier? We have no clear answer.

PRACTICAL APPLICATION 10.1

Modern Individualism and the Rise of Depression

The rate of depression has increased 10 times in the United States over the last two generations. Amidst this alarming increase there are a group of 10,000 Amish farmers who have not shown this increase. The Amish are a closely knit religious community that use no electricity, have no cars, and use no drugs or alcohol. Examination of depression in other parts of the world has led to the conclusion that depression is found to be highest in technologically advanced countries. In less technologically developed countries depression is almost nonexistent. In a study of one primitive tribe, the Kaluli of New Guinea, scientists were unable to find any signs of depression (Seligman, 1988).

Why is the increase taking place in technologically advanced countries? Martin Seligman has suggested that a new form of individualism has emerged that is highly susceptible to depression. There is a long history of describing Americans in terms of individualism, and there have been many forms of individualism over the years (Alex de Tocqueville,1969; Bellah, Madsen, Sullivan, Swidler, & Tipton, 1985). In recent years a form of individualism has emerged that is called *modern individualism*. Two of the basic qualities or characteristics of this modern individualism are autonomy and self-reliance. While individualism has served North Americans well, it has

recently been suggested by Seligman and others that perhaps some people have taken it too far. What does it mean to push it too far? It means pursuing individualism at the expense of such things as obligation (e.g., family), commitment (e.g., marriage), involvement (e.g., community). In short, it means not being responsible for, obligated to, or involved in anyone or anything but the self.

In addition to embracing autonomy and self-reliance, the modern individual has been encouraged to embrace "consumerism." People have been and are being told they can find happiness by owning objects. Just pick up any magazine and you will find this as a major theme. Things can provide pleasure, people are told, and they do not demand commitment, obligation, or feeling. Also, they do not threaten autonomy and self reliance. Drugs and sex have also been marketed as part of this new consumerism. To be happy you simply need more drugs or more sex, or different drugs or variety in sex.

If the complete focus on the "me-self" is causing people problems, why don't they return to a more traditional life style? It has been suggested that the thought of returning to a more traditional life style triggers a concern or fear that to re-embrace such a lifestyle we would have to give up our autonomy and self-reliance—two attributes which many of us have

---

Depression is often referred to as a mood disorder. It is certainly a profound mood disorder, but it is much more than that. It involves biological changes in the neurotransmitters, and it has been shown that it can be learned. While various researchers have emphasized biological over learned factors or learned over cognitive, it seems obvious that if we are to have a full understanding of depression we will have to understand the interaction of its biological, learned, and cognitive components.

Biological Component

Heritability of Depression

There is a long line of evidence that depression runs in families (Weissman, Lear, Holzer, Meyers, & Tischler, 1984). Perhaps the best data come from twin studies. It has been shown that identical twins are four to five times more likely to show concordances for major depressive disorder than fraternal twins (Kendler, Heath, Martin, & Eaves, 1986; Wender, Kety, Rosenthal, Schul-

come to value (see *Habits of the Heart*). What, then, is the answer or solution to the growing problem of depression? For many writers the answer lies in recognizing that as humans we are, by nature, social animals. This is an old theme but one which seems, nevertheless, to be timely. Among other things, being a social animal means that humans need other humans to experience certain basic emotions (Izard, 1977). They need other people, for example, to experience love and worth. Unless these emotions are satisfied there will be a void or a lack of meaning. Going to another palmist, trying a new drug, trying another diet, or trying to think oneself into a state of happiness cannot, according to this line of reasoning, ever provide that same sense of well-being that comes from belonging or being committed to the group. While belonging to a group brings with it certain obligations, the group is viewed as the source of love and worth. When people attempt to by-pass the group, they lose the means by which a sense of worth is ultimately found. The result for many is the "empty-self" feeling, and here lies the paradox: to find the self demands that we become part of a group or groups; it demands that we learn cooperation and trust. That may not be an easy task for those of us who have been raised to be competitive.

Going back to the group and recognizing our so-cial side does not necessarily mean that we have to give up individualism. We merely have to give up the extreme form of individualism that stresses complete self-reliance. Some of the major current theories of the self have their roots in a form of individualism. The theory of Deci and Ryan (1991), for example, is based around the concepts of autonomy and self-determination as opposed to the concepts of autonomy and self-reliance. While self-reliance and self-determination may sound similar, there is a subtle and important difference. Self-reliance has been interpreted to mean that people do need other people (as I suggested above in connection with modern individualism), whereas self-determination means something quite different. Self-determination means to take charge of one's life. It involves making choices, developing competencies, and adapting to one's social environment (see Deci & Ryan, 1985). Deci and Ryan clearly acknowledge the need for relatedness within their theory. They suggest that people have three needs: the need for autonomy, the need for competence, and the need for relatedness (Deci & Ryan, 1991). It is the satisfying of these needs that brings happiness.

singer, Ortmann, & Lunde, 1986). It has been suggested that the genetic loading for childhood and adolescent depression may be greater than for depression that occurs in adulthood, and that earlier onset is predictive of more frequent and severe episodes (Petersen, Compas, Brooks-Gunn, Stemmler, Ey, & Grant, 1993). It should be noted, however, that most family studies have failed to disentangle genetic and environmental influences. As a result, it is still not clear to what degree learning and cognition play in this whole process. The only thing we really know is that there is a significant genetic component.

The Catecholamine Hypothesis

After analyzing the relationship between affective disorders and catecholamines, Joseph J. Schildkraut and Seymour Kety (1967) formulated the catecholamine hypothesis of affective disorders. Because drugs that deplete or block norepinephrine and dopamine (especially norepinephrine) produce sedation and depression, whereas drugs that increase norepinephrine relieve depression and produce elation and euphoria, they concluded that norepinephrine and dopamine are the chemicals primarily involved in the mood changes that characterize various affective disorders. According to their hypothesis, excessive amounts of norepinephrine and dopamine produce the manic state—the high end of the manic-depressive continuum—and that a deficiency of norepinephrine and dopamine produces the depressive state at the low end.

Serotonin Hypothesis

Glassman (1969) noted that while the catecholamines had received a lot of attention, there was also evidence that the indolamines were also implicated, especially serotonin (also called 5-HT). The evidence for this theory is similar to the evidence offered for the catecholamine theory. Resperine was known to deplete stores of norepinephrine and serotonin, leading to depression, and monoamine oxidase inhibitors (MAOI) were known to prevent the breakdown, leading to a reduction in depression. Which theory is correct? To get some idea we need to examine the research literature which shows how various drugs affect depression.

Using Drugs to Treat Depression

Depression is often initially treated with drugs. It has been concluded that 60% to 80% of patients treated with drugs experience significant short-term improvement. The question of long-term improvement is a different matter. As I have already indicated, research suggests that unless cognitive therapy is combined with drug therapy people often fall back into a negative mood state together with negative thinking (Hollon, DeRubeis, & Evans, 1990).

Tricyclic antidepressants, such as Tofranil and Elavil, are preferred for the initial treatment of symptoms of depression. They take about two weeks to take effect and can have some unpleasant side effects. The tricyclics work the same way that cocaine works: they help to block the reuptake of norepinephrine and serotonin at the receptors, thereby increasing the concen-

tration of norepinephrine and serotonin at the receptor sites. Another set of antidepressants that is often used, especially if the tricyclics fail to work or if their side effects are severe, consists of the monoamine oxidase inhibitors (MAOI), such as Narplan, Nardil, and Parnate. Monoamine oxidase is an enzyme that is important in the regulation of such catecholamines as norepinephrine and serotonin. When the monoamine oxidase level is high, it somehow reduces the level of norepinephrine and serotonin. As the MAOI inhibits monoamine oxidase, the norepinephrine and serotonin levels rises.

The world's top-selling antidepressant is Prozac, which blocks the reuptake of serotonin. While it may not be as effective as the tricyclics, the fact that it does seem to work, at least under certain conditions, has led some researchers to speculate that serotonin is one of the key regulators of mood and that depression represents a shortage of serotonin. It may well turn out that there is more than one neurotransmitter involved in depression (see Figure 10-2).

Stress and depression. Numerous studies have found a link between stress and depression. One of the laboratory techniques for inducing stress is to expose humans or animals to uncontrollable shock. When animals are exposed to uncontrollable shock, norepinephrine is released at a high rate from the locus coeruleus, an area in the brainstem that we discussed in connection with sleep and dreams in Chapter 6. Apparently, the receptors in the brainstem do not use all of the available norepinephrine, and the unused norepinephrine is reabsorbed by the neuron and destroyed. The store of norepinephrine is then depleted, and once the body cannot synthesize norepinephrine as quickly as it is being released, the norepinephrine level in the locus coeruleus is lowered. This lowered level of norepinephrine is believed to result in feelings of depression (Weiss, 1982, cited in Turkington, 1982).

Spontaneous remission of depression. One of the fascinating things about depression is the suddenness with which many depressives spontaneously recover without therapy. Can their recovery be traced to a restoration of physiological/neurological functioning or to

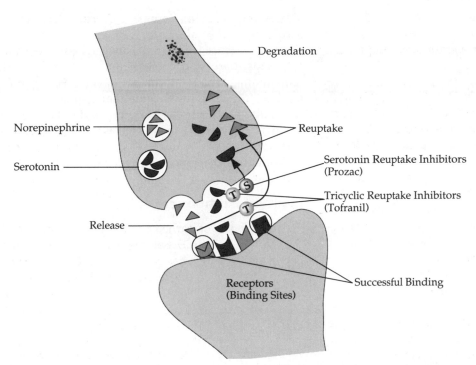

Figure 10–2. Serotonin and norepinephrine are neurotransmitters that carry messages across the synapses from one nerve cell to another. While some bind, others are reabsorbed through a process that is called reuptake. It has been suggested that these chemicals plug the reuptake pump, which is responsible for the reabsorption. While *Tricyclics* appear to block the reuptake of both norepinephrine and serotonin, *Serotonin Inhibitors* (such as Prozac) simply block the reuptake of serotonin. The net result is that concentrations of norepinephrine and serotonin are high at the synaptic gap, a phenomenon that has been linked to elevated mood. The *Monoamine Oxidase Inhibitors* (MAOI) work in a very different way. They block the action of the enzyme *Monoamine Oxidase* (MAO), an enzyme that is involved in the regulation of these neurotransmitters. It has been found that when MAO is high, norepinephrine and serotonin are low. By blocking the action of MAO, norepinephrine and serotonin are allowed to rise. When the levels of these two transmitters are high, mood is elevated. Note that for the purposes of this diagram I have ignored the role of dopamine that some people have suggested is involved in depression.

some cognitive process or to learning? At this point we do not know.

Depression as an Adaptive Mood

The fact that so many people experience depression has led scientists to ask "Is depression adaptive?" (Costello, 1976). If it is adaptive, the next question is "What function does depression serve?" The fact that depression often disappears spontaneously suggests that something is happening at some biological level. One possibility is that depression is a protective mechanism that allows the body to rebuild or reprogram itself after one has been exposed to a set of conditions that prevent one from exercising control. Once the rebuilding or reprogramming has taken place (which may take quite a long time), the depressive symptoms disappear. The lack of motivation or simply the lack of initiative that accompanies the mood disorder prevents the individual from engaging in new activities, so that the rebuilding or reprogramming can proceed without interruption.

Another possibility is that depression helps the individual to abandon goals that are unattainable (Klinger, 1975). When people find that events are uncontrollable, they tend to become depressed. When they become depressed, they tend to disengage themselves from ongoing activities. Having abandoned activities that are not adaptive, they can eventually switch to new activities. In the interim they may engage in cognitive activities that will help prepare them to deal again with the environment. The cognitive activities may lead to the setting of new goals or simply to experimentation with new behaviors that eventually lead to the development of new skills. The net effect is an individual who is better prepared to interact with the environment.

What these explanations don't tell us is why people develop self-destructive feelings. Thoughts of suicide hardly seem adaptive for a person in the process of reorganizing for the future or of disengaging from some activity that is causing grief. If we do not view depression as adaptive, however, we are faced with the conclusion that depression somehow represents evolution gone astray, a concept that is difficult to reconcile with other information we have about the adaptive nature of human motivation. Obviously, we still have much to learn about this mood disorder.

Summary

Depression is a fairly common mood disorder that has been found to be particularly prevalent among the young, women, and the elderly. Studies of twins indicate that depression can be inherited. There is strong evidence that depression is linked to the catecholamines, especially to norepinephrine. When the norepinephrine level is low, one tends to experience depression; when it is high, one tends to experience euphoria. Data in support of this hypothesis come from the finding that antidepressant drugs elevate the norepinephrine level at the synapses, and this results in a mood change from negative to positive. Serotonin has

al been implicated in depression. Drugs that elevate serotonin levels alleviate feelings of depression. Further evidence for the link between neurotransmitters and depression comes from work done with monoamine oxidase inhibitors (MAOI). Monoamine oxidase (MAO) is an enzyme that regulates neurotransmitters in the brain. Various people have argued that depression should be viewed as an adaptive mechanism that can be of value to us in our continuing need to deal with a changing environment.

Learned Component

The main model of learned helplessness has come from the work of Martin E. Seligman and his colleagues. Because his research has occupied such a central place in the research on depression, I will deal with it in some detail.

Seligman's Model of Learned Helplessness

While doing research on the relation between fear conditioning and instrumental learning, Seligman and two colleagues discovered a striking phenomenon that came to be called "learned helplessness" (Overmier & Seligman, 1967; Seligman & Maier, 1967). Initially, they restrained dogs in a harness in order to administer moderately painful but not physically damaging shock (see Figure 10-3). Although their original intent had not been to study inescapable shock, that is in fact what they had fortuitously arranged for the dogs. Nothing the dogs did could affect the onset, the offset, the duration, or the intensity of the shocks. The shocks were therefore uncontrollable from the perspective of the dogs.

The second phase of the experiment was designed to study how these dogs behaved in a shuttle box, something I described earlier in this chapter (see Figure 10-1). Normally, when naive (untrained) dogs are placed in the shuttle box and the shock is turned on, they frantically jump about the box and accidentally scramble over the barrier to the safe (no-shock) side. In a very few trials, these dogs learn to jump as soon as the shock begins, thereby drastically limiting the amount of shock they experience at any given trial. Typically it

Figure 10–3. Experimental apparatus used used to study the effects of inescapable/ uncontrollable shock in dogs. (From Neil R. Carlson, *Discovering Psychology*, 1988. Copyright © 1988. Reprinted by permission of Allyn and Bacon.)

takes several more trials before the dogs will begin to avoid the shock by jumping at the onset of the signal rather than the onset of the shock. They eventually learn this very important adaptive response, which enables them to avoid the painful stimulus altogether.

Much to the surprise of Seligman and his colleagues, the dogs given the inescapable-shock training showed a markedly different pattern of responses to the shock. Initially, they behaved like naive dogs: they frantically ran around the shuttle box when the shock was turned on. After 30 seconds, however, their behavior suddenly changed. They stopped jumping and running, lay down on the shock grid, and whined. When the animals failed to make any further responses for 60 seconds, the shock was turned off. They had, of course, failed to make an escape response. The same pattern of behavior occurred in the next trial. The animal struggled at first and then gave up, passively accepting the shock. On succeeding trials the behavior followed a similar pattern, with increasing passivity toward the shock. On none of the trials did the animal attempt to escape.

To make sure the effects observed were due to lack of control over the shock, not merely to the shock itself, Seligman and his colleagues designed an experiment to isolate the effects of controllability from the effects of shock. The design involved three groups.

The first group of dogs received pretreatment shock that they could control by some response. In one

study, the dog was able to limit the duration of the shock by pressing a panel with its nose (Seligman & Maier, 1967); in a second study the dog was able to limit the duration of the shock by not moving (Maier, 1970). A second group consisted of yoked controls. These dogs received the same pattern of shock but had no way of controlling it. Thus the second group experienced exactly the same amount of shock as the first without the critical factor of control. In both the first and the second conditions, the animals were restrained by a hammock to prevent them from jumping or running. A third group was given no pretreatment.

After 24 hours, the dogs were given escape-avoidance training in a shuttle box. The no-pretreatment group and the group allowed to control the shock during pretreatment readily learned the task. They jumped over the barrier at the onset of shock and then learned to avoid the shock. The group given uncontrollable shock performed much more poorly. Most of the dogs failed to jump the barrier at the onset of shock. These results clearly show that it was not the shock itself that produced the deficit but rather the inability to control the shock. The fact that not moving in Maier's (1970) study was as effective a procedure as nose pressing in Seligman and Maier's (1967) study shows that the important variable was control. Maier's study makes it impossible to argue that the animals were simply learning to be active. In Maier's study the animals were learning not to be active.

Learned Helplessness in Humans

The phenomenon of learned helplessness is by no means restricted to dogs. Learned helplessness has been demonstrated in cats (for example, Thomas & Balter, cited in Seligman, 1975), in fish (for example, Padilla et al., 1970), in rats (for example, Maier, Seligman, & Solomon, 1969; Seligman, Maier, & Solomon, 1971), and in primates (for example, Seligman, 1975). The main interest in learned helplessness, however, has focused on humans.

Numerous studies have been reported on learned helplessness in humans. In one study, Hiroto (1974) used human subjects and replicated almost exactly the findings obtained by Seligman and his colleagues. Subjects in his controllability group were exposed to a loud noise which they could turn off by pushing a button. His lack-of-controllability group received the same loud noise but could not control it. After this pretreatment, the subjects were tested in a finger-shuttle box that simply required them to move their hand from one side to the other to escape the noise. Just as in the dog experiments, the no-pretreatment and controllability groups quickly learned the escape problem, but the lack-of-controllability group failed to learn it. Most of the subjects in the lack-of-controllability condition sat passively and accepted the noxious noise.

Externals and internals. Hiroto's study included two additional variables that indicate that the subjects' perceived ability to control the events governed their responses. Half of the subjects in each of the three groups were told their performance in the shuttle box was a test of skill; the remaining half were told their scores were governed by chance. As expected, subjects who received the "chance" instructions tended to respond more helplessly in all the conditions. Hiroto also decided to examine personality differences. Using a personality inventory measure, he divided his subjects into two groups corresponding to "externals" and "internals." Externals, according to Rotter (1966), are people who *believe* that events in their lives are governed to a large degree by chance. Internals believe that events can be controlled and that the application of skills can bring about positive outcomes. As predicted,

externals were more inclined to become helpless than internals.

The results of Hiroto's study not only confirm that humans react to lack of control in the same way animals do, but emphasize the cognitive nature of helplessness in humans. This is consistent with Seligman's suggestion that helplessness reflects a belief about the effectiveness of responding. The helpless person *does not* believe that his or her responses will have any effect on aversive or noxious events, whereas the person who has not learned to be helpless *does believe* that his or her responses will be effective in terminating such events.

Deficits in Learned Helplessness

Seligman has concluded from these and other studies that learned helplessness is characterized by three deficits: (1) failure to initiate responses, (2) failure to learn, and (3) emotional disturbance.

Failure to initiate responses. Adaptive behavior is generally characterized by repeated attempts to achieve a goal. In the course of initiating responses, the individual typically tries a wide range of responses. Sometimes these behaviors are highly systematic, suggesting that the individual may be systematically testing all possible alternatives in some hierarchy of adaptive responses. Aggressive behavior, as discussed in Chapter 8, may be a class of behaviors that falls within the hierarchy of adaptive responses. That is, aggressive responses may enable the individual to regain control of the environment.

There is evidence indicating that certain adaptive responses are inherited (unlearned) or at least that the predisposition to make these responses is inherited (Bolles, 1970). Other adaptive responses, however, are clearly learned. According to the principles of learning, a response will be repeated if it results in reinforcement. For example, an escape response is learned in the shuttle box because jumping over the barrier reduces the duration of a noxious event, and that is reinforcing. In human terms we might say termination of a noxious event produces relief. We feel relief when we turn off a noxious TV program or when the neighbor's dog stops barking after we yell at the dog or its owner. We know from studies of learning that it is likely that these responses will be repeated because the responses produced a desired effect: relief from the noxious or aversive stimulus. Within learning theory, the presentation of an aversive or noxious stimulus is called a negative reinforcer.

It can happen that certain aversive events in our environment come and go and we can do nothing about them. For example, our next-door neighbor may play the stereo into the early hours of the morning. We complain, but nothing happens, and then unexpectedly the person moves. A neighbor may have a dog that, despite our pleas, is allowed to bark throughout the night. One day the neighbor sells the dog. In such cases, the relief we experience is independent of our responses. According to the principles of learning, the fact that there is no predictable association between a response and the occurrence of a reward means there can be no learning. Seligman has argued, however, that we do in fact learn something. We learn that relief is sometimes independent of our responses. He further suggests that this cognitive set, or belief, can then generalize to other situations. As a result, we may fail to initiate responses in the presence of aversive or noxious stimuli.

Failure to initiate responses of any kind is very nonadaptive. Noxious stimulation not only is aversive but in some cases may threaten our very survival. It is critical, therefore, for us to try to remove or stop the noxious event. We can do so only if we initiate a response, no matter how poor or inappropriate that response may be. Even random behavior may result in termination of the aversive event. Given that most of us have some previous experience dealing with noxious events, we have at our disposal a hierarchy of responses that may help us deal with such events. Failure to initiate responses of any kind reflects, therefore, a loss of basic survival motivation.

Failure to learn. Another striking characteristic of learned helplessness is inability to learn that one can control certain events in one's environment. In an experiment very similar to that of Hiroto (1974), Miller and Seligman (1975) studied three groups of students who received escapable, inescapable, or no loud noise in the prelearning phase and were then confronted with a task involving skill and a task involving chance. The skill task required subjects to sort 15 cards into ten categories with a time limit of 15 seconds. The experimenter arranged to have them succeed or fail on a given sorting trial by saying the time was up either before or after they had finished. The subjects were unaware that the experimenter was ignoring clock time. At the end of each trial, the subject was asked to estimate his chances of succeeding on the next trial. Subjects who had previously been exposed to the inescapable noise (the helpless condition) showed little change in their expectancy after each new success or failure. The escape group and the no-pretreatment group, in contrast, showed large changes in their expectancy of success after each new success or failure. In other words, the helpless subjects did not perceive that the outcomes were related to their actions, while the escape and no-pretreatment groups did. When the three groups were exposed to a chance task, they showed no difference in expectancy change following success and failure. All three groups responded as though the outcome were independent of their actions—an appropriate way of responding to a chance event. Other studies have replicated this basic finding (for example, Hiroto & Seligman, 1975).

Seligman (1975) has pointed out that evidence from a variety of sources indicates that experiencing two events as independent (noncontingent) makes it very difficult at some later time to learn that they are dependent, or related, when they have been made contingent (for example, Kemler & Shepp, 1971). To explain this fact, Seligman has argued that organisms acquire information about what events are and are not dependent in the environment. He suggests that once two things are perceived as independent, it is just as difficult to alter this perception as it is to alter the idea that two things are dependent. The confirmation either that two things are related or that they are unrelated seems to retard further information processing. As a result, the helpless person fails to learn that two events have become dependent. He or she has, according to Hiroto (1974), become an external type of person. As we shall see, the internal person is like the external in that he or she also fails to respond to certain types of new information. Whereas externals fail to respond to information that their responses are producing changes in the environment, internals fail to respond to information that their responses are not producing changes in the environment.

Emotional disturbance. Numerous studies have shown that lack of controllability produces a variety of emotional responses. As we noted in Chapter 9, uncontrollable shocks are associated with high outputs of epinephrine (for example, Brady, 1967) as well as ulceration (for example, Weiss, 1968, 1971a, 1971b, 1971c). In contrast, being in control is associated with high outputs of norepinephrine (Brady, 1967, 1975) and the absence of ulcers (Weiss, 1968, 1971a, 1971b, 1971c). Higher blood pressure has also been found to characterize people who are exposed to uncontrollable situations (for example, Hokanson et al., 1971).

In addition to these and other physiological changes, there are at least two distinct psychological changes. Lack of controllability produces increases in anxiety and depression (Seligman, 1975). Both anxiety and depression are complex psychological states that have been shown to have a very debilitating effect on humans. I will discuss these effects in more detail later. What is clear is that some very basic and important emotional changes are produced when aversive stimulation becomes uncontrollable.

Immunization. If exposure to uncontrollable events is sufficient to produce learned helplessness, then is it possible to immunize people against learned helplessness by teaching them that events are often controllable. Early work showed that it is possible (Maier & Seligman, 1976). More recently it has again been shown that giving people a controllable experience produces a proactive interference against attempts to induce helplessness (Ramírez, Maldonado, & Martos, 1992).

Summary

According to Seligman's model, when animals or humans are presented with an aversive stimulus such as shock, and are unable to escape that stimulus, they develop a sense of helplessness. In contrast, when animals or humans are presented with an aversive stimulus they can learn to escape (and thereby control its duration), they do not develop a sense of helplessness. When they develop a sense of helplessness they fail to initiate behaviors that will allow them to learn how to escape an aversive situation. When they fail to develop a sense of helplessness they are inclined to initiate behaviors that will allow them to learn how to escape an aversive situation. Seligman has pointed out that evidence from a variety of sources indicates that experiencing two events as independent (noncontingent) makes it very difficult at some later time to learn that they are dependent, or related, when they have been made contingent. As a result, the individual who has experienced noncontingency will tend to behave as though there is no contingency.

From his studies of helplessness, Seligman suggested that learned helplessness is characterized by three deficits: failure to initiate responses, failure to learn, and emotional disturbance.

Although Seligman suggests that experiencing noncontingencies is the basis for learned helplessness, not all experiences of noncontingencies will necessarily lead to feelings of helplessness. If, for example, an individual has previously learned that two events are contingent, suddenly making them noncontingent will not result in feelings of helplessness. It appears that the previous contingency training is sufficient to "immunize" the individual against helplessness training.

Cognitive Component

For a decade Seligman's theory seemed to be a plausible explanation of why some people get depressed when placed in situations where they were unable to control the outcomes. The major problem with the theory, as John Teasdale of Oxford pointed out, was that the helplessness training procedure that had been used to demonstrate the validity of the theory seemed to work on two out of three people; a third of the people resisted the training procedure and showed no inclination to become helpless. This observation, together with doubts expressed by two of his own graduate students, lead Seligman, together with his critics, to recast the theory in more cognitive terms.

Reformulated Theory of Learned Helplessness

One of the main contributing forces behind the reformulation of the learned helplessness theory came from the work of Bernard Weiner of the University of California at Los Angeles, who had been studying people's explanatory styles (attributions) in achievement situations. Weiner found, among other things, that whether people are inclined to persist or not persist at a task in the face of failure is linked, for example, to whether or not they concluded that the failure they were presently experiencing was simply a lack of effort on their part or was due to something over which they had no control (see Weiner, Frieze, Kukla, Reed, Rest, & Rosenbaum, 1971). The reformulated theory drew upon some of Weiner's ideas, expanding them to help explain why some people become depressed and others never do (Abramson, Seligman, & Teasdale, 1978; Miller & Norman, 1979). The reformulated theory suggests there are three basic reasons why some people fail to become depressed when they experience bad events (Peterson & Seligman, 1984).

Three Explanatory Styles for Bad and Good Events

1. Permanence: Permanent versus Temporary

Explaining bad events. People who give up and become helpless believe that the causes of bad events that happen to them are permanent. People who do not give up, in contrast, believe that bad events are temporary. If you believe that something is temporary versus permanent, then there is reason to persist. Here are some examples.*

Permanent (Pessimistic):	Temporary (Optimistic):
"I'm all washed up."	"I'm exhausted."
"Diets never work."	"Diets don't work when you eat out."
"The boss is a bastard."	"The boss is in a bad mood."

Failure tends to make almost everyone momentarily helpless. The people who succeed, however, are those who pick themselves up and try again. One of the major characteristics of success is persistence. It is such a consistent finding that it might be called "the law of success." It might be phrased something like, "People who persist will eventually succeed." Unless you persist in the face of difficulty you will never learn how to do something correctly and thus attain a goal. That is not to say that you should persist blindly. You need to alter your responses systematically so that you can discover how to reach a goal.

Explaining good events. Pessimists and optimists treat good outcomes just the reverse of how they treat bad outcomes. When good things happen to pessimists they see that outcome as temporary whereas optimists see that outcomes as more or less permanent.

Permanent (Pessimistic):	Temporary (Optimistic):
"I'm always lucky."	"It's my lucky day."
"I'm talented."	"I try hard."
"My rival is no good."	"My rival got tired."

It is interesting to note that people who believe that good events have permanent causes try harder after success, whereas people who believe good events are due to temporary causes tend to give up. If you believe good events are temporary you think what happened was a fluke. You gambled and won so take your earnings and quit.

2. Pervasiveness: Specific versus Universal

Explaining bad events. While permanence is about time, pervasiveness is about space. When pessimists experience a bad event, they allow that bad event to affect all parts of their life. When a relationship breaks up, for example, they are inclined to stop eating, stop seeing their friends, stop working or studying and so forth. While all of us might be affected by such events for a few days, pessimists tend to wallow in their sadness, allowing their sadness to affect every other part of their life, eventually allowing themselves to become to-

---

* (Based on M. E. P. Seligman. *Learned Optimism*, 1991. Copyright ©1991 by Alfred Knopf, New York.)

tally depressed. The optimist, in contrast, may experience initial reaction, something like "Life is not worth living," but then after a few days they begin to bounce back. They decide that life has many rewarding aspects. As a result, they make a special effort to see their friends, they bury themselves in their work, they decide to learn how to prepare a new recipe. It is as though the optimist has the ability to compartmentalize life, seeing life as made up of many little boxes, each of which contains a little treasure they need to preserve. Pessimists, in contrast, seem to see life as one big box where everything is mixed together. When one little treasure gets broken, all the treasures in the box get broken as well.

In my description of the pessimist, I suggested that they allow themselves to wallow in their misery. I did this deliberately to emphasize one of the most exciting new ideas that has come out of therapy in some time. That is the idea that people can learn to stop themselves from sinking deeper and deeper into depression. Optimists, it seems, have learned to do this on their own. I will talk more about how to become an optimist in the next chapter.

Here are some examples of how pessimists and optimists explain bad events.

Universal (Pessimistic):	*Specific (Optimistic):*
"All teachers are unfair."	"Professor Franken is unfair."
"I'm repulsive."	"I'm repulsive to him."
"Books are useless."	"This book is useless."

Explaining good events. The way pessimists and optimists explain good events is just the opposite of how they explain bad events.

Specific (Pessimistic):	*Universal (Optimistic):*
"I'm smart at math."	"I'm smart."
"My broker knows oil stocks."	"My broker knows Wall Street."
"I was charming to her."	"I was charming."

While pessimists explain good causes in terms of *transient* events, such as mood and effort, optimists explain good events in terms of *permanent* causes, such as traits and abilities. While one says *sometimes* the other says *always*.

The Nature of Hope and Hopelessness

Hope and hopelessness in Seligman's theory grow out of the two dimensions of pervasiveness and permanence. In order to be characterized as hopeful, people need to respond to bad events in terms of *specific* and *temporary*. People who are hopeless, in contrast, are characterized as *permanent* and *universal*.

3. Personalization: Internal versus External

Explaining bad events. When bad things happen, people are inclined to either blame themselves (internalize) or blame someone else (externalize). When my son backed our car into my sailboat, which I left in the driveway, causing some minor damage to the sailboat, my son blamed me for not putting it back where we normally keep it while I blamed him for not having watched where he was going. Further, I argued, he should have remembered that I had gone sailing to which he replied, "Why am I supposed to keep track of what you are doing?" The positive side of this story is that people with low self-esteem blame themselves when something goes wrong, whereas people with good self-esteem tend to blame others. I guess we are both on the right track for good self-esteem even if the sailboat had to pay the price.

Here are some examples of how low self-esteem and high self-esteem people are inclined to respond to bad events.

Internal (Low self-esteem)	*External (High self-esteem)*
"I'm stupid."	"You're stupid."
"I have no talent at poker."	"I have no luck at poker."
"I'm insecure."	"I grew up in poverty."

Interestingly, children often learn this explanatory style very early and very well. Getting children to admit it was their fault is a formidable task for any parent and one that we as parents need to think about carefully. Teaching children to take responsibility is important, but destroying a powerful mechanism for maintaining good self-esteem is another issue. There needs to be a balance.

Explaining good events. Again, the style for explaining good events is the opposite to that of explaining bad events. Here are some examples.

External (Pessimistic):	Internal (Optimistic):
" A stroke of luck . . . "	"I can take advantage of luck . . . "
"My teammates' skill . . ."	"My skill . . . "

When people believe they cause good things to happen to themselves they like themselves, whereas when they believe that good things come from other people or some circumstances over which they have no control, they are less inclined to like themselves.

Caveat about Responsibility

Seligman is careful to point out that while there are clear benefits to adopting an external belief system, he does not advocate that people should necessarily switch from being internals to externals. Individual responsibility is important; it gives a person a sense of control that has been shown to be important. There are times, however, when people assume too much responsibility. A wife, for example, who takes responsibility for the fact that her husband did not get a promotion because of something she said may be going too far. When we take too much responsibility we do not allow ourselves to make mistakes or to forgive ourselves when we do. Perhaps instead of blaming others, we need to learn to forgive ourselves and then forget. When we don't allow ourselves to forgive and forget, we carry with us excess baggage that is unnecessary and unhealthy.

Is Depression Ultimate Pessimism?

There are three kinds of depression: normal, unipolar, and bipolar. Bipolar depression is also called a manic-depressive disorder because people with this disorder experience both manic episodes and depressive episodes. Bipolar depression is much more heritable than unipolar and is very responsive to lithium carbonate. There is good reason to believe that bipolar depression is not the result of pessimistic thinking but rather due to a genetic disorder (Seligman, 1991).

The prevailing medical view is that normal depression is simply a passing demoralization, and that unipolar depression is a chemical/clinical disorder and needs to be treated with drug and/or psychotherapy. Seligman (1991) takes exception to this view, pointing out that the two cannot be distinguished on the basis of their symptomology. He argues that the reason normals are more likely to recover is that they are not as severely depressed. The diagnostic criteria for depression using the DSM-III-R is the following:

1. Depressed mood
2. Loss of interest in usual activities
3. Loss of appetite
4. Insomnia
5. Psychological retardation (slow thought or movement)
6. Loss of energy
7. Feelings of worthlessness and guilt
8. Diminished ability to think and poor concentration
9. Suicidal thought or action

How can one demonstrate that pessimism is the cause of depression? One way is to take people who tend to think more pessimistically and see what happens when they experience bad events. In at least two studies, it has been shown that people who think more pessimistically are more likely to become depressed. In one case Seligman studied students who did not perform as well as they expected on an examination, and he found that people with a more pessimistic thinking style were more likely to demonstrate the symptoms listed above. In another case he studied prisoners. The interesting thing about prisons is that they consistently produce depression in people who tended not to show depression before they were sentenced. Seligman found that pessimists sentenced to prison were inclined to develop deeper depression than those who had a more optimistic thinking style (Abramson, Metalsky, & Alloy, 1989; Sweeney, Anderson, & Bailey, 1986; Seligman, 1991).

When people become depressed, they lose their motivation, they develop feelings of worthlessness and guilt, and frequently entertain thoughts of suicide.

A second way to demonstrate that a pessimistic thinking style is the cause of depression is to show that it is possible to alleviate the symptoms of depression by changing the pessimistic thinking style of people to a more optimistic one and observing whether or not their symptoms of depression then wane. There is a great deal of research which shows that teaching people to think more optimistically does result in the lessening of depression, often curing people completely of their depression. Since antidepressant drugs often reduce depression, is there any difference between people treated with drugs and those who have learned to think differently? The general finding is that while drugs will often work for a period of time, people who have been given only drug treatment tend to relapse, whereas people who have been given drugs plus taught how to think differently are much less inclined to relapse (Hollon, DeRubeis, & Evans, 1990).

Rumination

One of the main characteristics of depressed people is they tend to engage in excessive analysis, a process called "rumination" (after the original meaning of "chewing cud"). Since depressed people tend to use a pessimistic thinking style, when they ruminate they tend to create a highly negative world for themselves. A person who ruminates can be an optimist, but when optimists ruminate they create a highly positive world for themselves.

Research shows that people who tend to be pessimists but not ruminators are less likely to become depressed. In other words, being pessimistic and being a ruminator are two independent qualities which, when they come together, are likely to produce depression (Kuhl, 1981; Nolen-Hoeksema, 1990).

Women, Depression, and the Rumination/Distraction Theory

Women tend to show depression at about twice the rate of men. Various theories have been advanced to account for this difference, including theories that say that women, because of their sex roles, have learned to be more helpless than men. If this were the case, it would be expected that women would be more pessimistic than men, but there is virtually no evidence to support this idea. Most studies show that men and women tend to be about the same. The theory which can best account for this difference is the rumination/distraction theory. Whereas women tend to be ruminators, men tend to be distractors. When bad things happen to women they are more likely to engage in excessive analysis, whereas when bad things happen to men they are more inclined to engage in some activity, such as sports, that takes their mind off the bad event. As a result, those women who tend to have a more pessimistic thinking style tend to become depressed while men who have a pessimistic thinking style are not as inclined to become depressed. Why men and women have different styles remains an intriguing question that future research needs to elucidate (Nolen-Hoeksema, 1987, 1990).

Beck's Theory

Aaron Beck (1967, 1976, 1991), a pioneer of cognitive approaches to depression, has proposed that the thinking patterns of depressed people play a critical role not only in initially producing depression but in maintaining it. He has pointed out that depressed people tend to view their current and future situations in negative terms. Such thinking is characterized by three tendencies. First, depressed people tend to view situations as negative even when a positive interpretation is possible. Second, they view interactions with the environment in terms of deprivation, disease, and defeat. Third, they tend to tailor facts to fit their negative conclusions. They may even ignore external input that is not consistent with their conclusion that life is essentially bad.

Beck argues that depressed people tend to develop an organized and stable "schema," or representation of themselves, and they process information on the basis of this schema. They screen, differentiate, and code the environment in accordance with the representation they have formed of themselves.

Beck emphasizes that the thinking process of depressed people often leads to "cognitive distortions." Because depressed people have a systematic "bias against the self," so that they compare themselves unfavorably with other people, they develop feelings of deprivation, depreciation, and failure. These cognitive distortions can be viewed as "errors in thinking." Beck identified four kinds of errors of thinking: exaggeration (exaggerating the negative aspects of their experiences), dichotomous thinking (viewing a partial failure as complete failure), selective abstraction (seeing only the negative aspects of an experience and using that information to make an inference about one's ability), and overgeneralization (using one outcome to make inferences about one's ability). In exaggeration, people are inclined to say to themselves something like "I made a complete fool of myself," when in fact they simply made a social error in the midst of an otherwise impeccable social performance. In dichotomous thinking, people are inclined to say something like "My talk was a total bomb," when in fact the only problem with their talk was they simply did not have a good ending. In selective abstraction, people are inclined to say something like "Nobody liked my performance," when in fact there was only one person who raised an objection while more people voiced their approval. In overgeneralization, people are inclined to say something like "I have no ability whatsoever to do that kind of thing," when in fact they do have a great deal of ability but they didn't do so well in one situation.

Sociotropic and autonomous subtypes. Beck (1983, 1991) has suggested there are two types of individuals—*sociotropic* and *autonomous*—who are prone to become depressed after a negative experience congruent with their personality. The autonomous type, who is motivated by the need for independent achievement, mobility, and solitary pleasures, is prone to become depressed after an "autonomous stressor" such as failure, immobilization or enforced conformity. The sociotropic type is motivated by the receipt of acceptance and attention from others and is prone to become depressed by "sociotropic traumas" such as social deprivation or rejection.

According to this distinction, not having good social relationships would have very different implications for these two types. Specifically, while the lack of good social relationships would not affect the autonomous type, it would affect the sociotropic type. Indeed, this is what has been found (Hokanson & Butler, 1992).

Summary

According to the reformulated theory of learned helplessness, the reason some people get depressed when exposed to helplessness training procedures while others do not is linked to their explanatory style. People who are inclined to see bad events as temporary, specific, and external are less inclined to become helpless and depressed. There is considerable evidence to support the idea that depression is the result of a pessimistic explanatory style. One piece of evidence is the

PRACTICAL APPLICATION 10.2

Cognitive Therapy and Depression: Learning the Art of Thinking Constructively

Cognitive therapy is based on many of the ideas that I have just discussed. It can be summarized in terms of five tactics that people can use to take charge of their thinking (Beck, 1983; Seligman, 1991). The tactics used to help depressives are tactics that anyone who is prone to pessimism and depression can use.

1. Learn to recognize destructive automatic thoughts. When things go bad, people often hear themselves repeat short phrases or sentences. A mother who has lost her temper, for example, may hear herself say "I'm a terrible mother." A student who has done poorly on an exam might hear himself say "I should be shot, I am such an idiot." A teenager who has made a social blunder and as a consequence feels embarrassed may hear herself say "I wish I were dead." The curious thing about such fleeting thoughts is they seem to come from somewhere inside us and yet we know that we haven't consciously created them. They just seem to happen. They have, therefore, come to be called *automatic thoughts*.

2. Learn to dispute destructive automatic thoughts. Most people fail to challenge their automatic thoughts. They accept them as coming from somewhere deep inside themselves and therefore they are treated as fair and valid commentary. At the same time, most people find these thoughts to be disturbing and are perplexed by their occurrence. Why they arise is not clear. Most people in cognitive therapy argue that these thoughts are not fair commentary and that it is critical that we learn to dispute them. The best way to dispute them is to *marshall contrary evidence.* Just because a mother has lost her temper does not mean that she is a bad mother. She likely does a number of good things, and to deal with such disturbing thoughts she needs to enumerate her good qualities. Similarly, the student who has performed

poorly needs to say to himself that while I didn't do as well as I expected, you don't shoot people for doing poorly. In addition, he needs to recount the number of times he performed admirably.

3. Learn to avoid using destructive explanations. Many of the fleeting comments that people experience are characterized by permanence and pervasiveness. What people need to learn to do is change the explanation to one that is more temporary and situation-specific. The mother might learn to say something like, " I tend to be a good mother most of the time but later in the afternoon when it gets hot (or when I am tired) I tend to become irritable. And that little rascal is not in such a great mood when it gets hot either." The student might say something like, "I had a bad day. The exam was different than I expected and I guess I ended up studying the wrong thing." The teenager who made a social blunder might say, "I was thinking about something else and as a result, I slipped up. If someone had videotaped that one it would get a lot of laughs on television."

4. Learn the art of distracting yourself from depressive thoughts. Becoming involved in another activity is a very good way of distracting oneself from depressive thoughts. As I indicated above, there is a great deal of evidence that men are more inclined to do this than women. There are numerous activities that one can identify which will work. Some of these are reading a book, going for coffee with a friend, becoming involved in a hobby, going to a movie, or simply imagining yourself in some activity that you like or might like.

5. Learn to create less self-limiting "happiness self-statements." Many people have difficulty being happy because they have put limits on what will allow them to be happy. When they talk to themselves about what will make them happy they say such things as:

"I won't be happy until I have a new car."

"I will be happy when I fall in love."

"I can't be happy unless I know that everybody likes me."

"I will be happy when I am retired."

If you examine each of these statements you will immediately realize that each of them puts severe limits on when or how you can be happy. As a result, they are inclined to set you up for depression. There is nothing wrong with wanting a new car or wanting to be in love or looking forward to retirement; the problem lies in saying that you can't be happy until those conditions have been met. The thing to remember is that when people engage in this form of inner dialogue, the statements they make to themselves become rules or principles. As a result, they find themselves unable to experience the emotion of happiness until the conditions set by these self-imposed rules have been met. Unfortunately, when the conditions set by the rule are met, people often experience only momentary happiness because happiness is rarely found in end-goals; it tends to be found in the process of attaining goals.

Assessing your inner dialogue. Take some time to analyze your inner dialogue to see if you are setting limits on your happiness. Give yourself a little time so that you can become aware of your automatic thoughts. Each time you become aware of one, write it down so that you can analyze it rationally.

Redesigning your inner dialogue. Here is how you might redesign each of the above statements so they remain as goals but do not prevent you from achieving happiness in the interim.

"This is a good car for now but my goal is to one day buy a new one."

"I am enjoying dating and look forward to falling in love."

"I would like to be viewed as a sensitive and considerate person, but since I have values that are different from those of other people, I need to learn that people may not always understand or appreciate where I am coming from."

"It is great to be healthy and earning a good living, both of which are going to make retirement rewarding."

6. Learn to make your inner dialogue process-oriented. You might go one step further and turn each of your happiness statements into more of a process-goal as opposed to an end-goal. A process-goal is one that capitalizes on the underlying process and less on the actual end-state. Most people seem to get their happiness out of the process as opposed to the end-state. Perhaps the reason for this is that we are inclined to become habituated to static emotions very quickly (Frijda's [1988] Fourth Law of Emotion). Here are some examples of how to turn the original happiness statements into process statements.

"I get a great deal of enjoyment out of cars and I hope to own several fine cars in my lifetime."

"Love and being loved is a skill. I am going to work hard at making love a central focus of my life."

"My goal is to gain the respect and admiration of many people in my life. It is a skill that others before me have nurtured and developed, and I am determined to see if I can emulate them."

"To be truly happy in retirement takes a great deal of work and planning. I am going to study people who are happy in retirement so that when I retire, I can be truly happy."

demonstration that people who are more pessimistic are more likely to become depressed. Another convincing piece of evidence is that which shows that people given antidepressant drugs plus cognitive therapy are more likely to recover from depression than people given only drugs.

People who engage in excessive analysis (rumination) are more likely to become depressed. Interestingly, women are more likely to ruminate and also more likely to become depressed. Men, in contrast, are more likely to distract themselves.

Beck has noted that depressed people tend to view the present and future in negative terms. This negative style of thinking grows out of a stable internal representation, called a "schema." Depressed people, Beck argues, have a "bias against the self" that leads to errors in thinking, such as the tendency to overgeneralize and to make inferences without consideration of alternative points of view.

Beck has suggested there are two type of people who are prone to become depressed—the sociotropic and the autonomous. Among other things his theory predicts that good social relationships are important for the sociotropic type but less so for the autonomous type.

The five tactics that people can use to take charge of their thinking are: (1) learn to recognize automatic thoughts, (2) learn to dispute destructive automatic thoughts, (3) learn to avoid using destructive explanations, (4) learn the art of distracting yourself, (5) learn to create less self-limiting "happiness self-statements," and (6) learn to make your inner dialogue process-oriented.

Guilt and Shame

Why Consider the Emotions of Guilt and Shame?

Guilt and shame are usually treated as overlapping emotions. Until recently, they had been the object of much theorizing, but there was little empirical data on the nature and origins of these emotions (Zahn-Waxler & Kochanska, 1990). As more work is being done on these emotions, the growing consensus is that these emotions are important to consider because they are implicated in a wide range of human motivated be-

haviors. There are at least five points worth mentioning in this regard.

First, guilt and shame are uniquely human emotions (although some have argued that canines are capable of guilt). Second, guilt and shame have been found to play a role in a wide variety of behaviors including sexual abuse, rape, holocaust survivors, eating disorders, stress-related physical disorders, alcoholism, divorce, and emotional illness. There is reason to believe that these emotions are involved in many more motivated behaviors but have not as yet been studied. Third, these two emotions (guilt in particular) have been linked to pessimism and depression. People who are more depressed experience more guilt and shame. Some researchers believe that guilt and shame are not simply correlates of depression but that they cause depression (Zahn-Waxler & Kochanska, 1990). Since pessimism and depression are central to this chapter, a full understanding of guilt is important. Fourth, it is widely held that the capacity for these emotions is innate (evolved to be adaptive), but that their mode of expression is learned (Zahn-Waxler & Kochanska, 1990). Among other things, this means that there are wide individual differences in the expression of these emotions as a result of the complex interaction that children have with their parents and their environment. Moreover, if the mode of expression is learned it means we can redirect it into more adaptive ways. Fifth, while these emotions may have evolved to be adaptive, they can become maladaptive. Like virtually all other negative emotions, when they become excessive they tend to disrupt rather than sustain adaptive behavior. One immediate implication is that if people wish to achieve goals they need to learn how to manage these emotions, something that many researchers now feel is a distinct possibility (Thompson, 1990).

Definition of Guilt and Shame

It is important to recognize that guilt and shame can elicit and sustain certain behaviors (e.g., achievement, cooperation) while inhibiting others (e.g., anger, aggression). From an adaptive perspective, this is very important. The proper execution of any response typically demands some complementary process of excitation and inhibition of various response systems. In order to "win a contract," for example, it may be necessary to inhibit expressions of anger or dislike.

It is also important to distinguish between acts of commission (e.g., becoming angry and aggressive, belittling someone's achievements, criticizing) and acts of omission (failure to achieve a goal, failure to provide for one's family, failure to live up to a family value). Lazarus's distinction between guilt and shame seems to address this issue. Lazarus (1991) has suggested that the core relational theme for guilt is "having transgressed a moral imperative," while the core relational theme for shame is "having failed to live up to an ego-ideal." It is interesting to note in this context that Beck's view of depression is consistent with Lazarus's definition of shame. Beck suggests that depressed people tend to view their interactions with the environment in terms of failure, an explanatory style that leads to depression.

It has been suggested that the opposite emotion of guilt is empathy (Zahn-Waxler & Kochanska, 1990). Whereas guilt often comes from being insensitive to the feelings or needs of others (acting in one's own self-interest), empathy involves being sensitive to the feelings and needs of of others. In the next chapter we will deal not only with empathy but with worth, two important emotions that seem to play a fundamental role in helping and acts of altruism.

Both guilt and shame are clearly involved in goal-directed behavior. In our desire to achieve our goals we may do various things that cause us to feel guilty such as when we take short-cuts, hoard information to prevent others from finding the solution, take the ideas of others and pass them off as our own, undermine the attempts of others, and so forth. Similarly, we may experience shame for not having achieved the level we think we should have, for not having worked as hard as we might have, for not having won the praise that we thought we should have, and so forth.

Biological Component

Guilt and Shame as Adaptive Emotions

Numerous writers agree that guilt and shame are basically adaptive emotions. A common underlying theme is that guilt and shame serve to ensure good social relationships and that this process is "built-in" (Kagan, 1984). From an evolutionary perspective, it is important that good social relations are maintained because the survival of the individual is often dependent on the larger group to which the individual belongs.

It has been suggested that maintaining good social relations depends on two complementary processes: being sensitive to the needs of others and being motivated to make amends or make reparations when a transgression does occur. In short, one needs to have the capacity for guilt. Hoffman (1982) has focused on the guilt that comes from harming others and has suggested that the motivational basis for this guilt is *empathetic-distress*. Empathetic-distress would occur when people realize their actions had caused harm or pain to another person. Motivated by feelings of guilt, they would be inclined to make amends for their actions. Making amends would serve to repair damaged social relations and restore group harmony.

Discrete Emotions Theory

Guilt is viewed in Izard's (1977) theory as a discrete emotion. Discrete emotions are viewed as the primary constituents or component of motivation. According to this theory, discrete emotions involve three basic elements: a neural substrate, a characteristic facial pattern (or neuromuscular expressive pattern), and a distinct subjective feeling. Other systems are also involved (and presumably governed by the neural substrate) including cardiovascular, endocrine, and respiratory systems. According to the theory, emotions evolved to serve an adaptive function and the communication of emotions is hypothesized to take place via the recognition of facial expression.

The main adaptive function of guilt, according to Izard, is to prevent waste and exploitation. According to this view, taking responsibility and making amends for wrongdoing have survival value for individuals and relationships—which ultimately ensures the survival of societies and civilization. Guilt is suggested by this theory to be a major component of conscience that serves to inhibit aggression and to encourage people to make reparations—a key method for restoring harmony. It is worth noting that according to this evolutionary view, it is the survival of the group that is emphasized as opposed to the survival of the individual.

Psychoanalytic and Neopsychoanalytic Theories

In Freudian theory, guilt was thought to emerge as a result of restraints that parents imposed on expression of sexual and aggressive impulses. In the course of attempting to express these impulses, it was argued, children often found that they were in conflict with their parents and this resulted in feelings of anger and hostility towards the parents. Because they feared being punished or because they feared their parents might withdraw love, children learned to inhibit their impulses and to eventually internalize proper standards of conduct. A central theme in the Freudian analysis of guilt is the concept of anxiety. It is argued that whenever children are confronted with the possibility of losing the love of their parents, there are intense feelings of anxiety. These feelings serve to suppress, at least at the conscious level, feelings of anger and hatred that the children normally have towards their parents.

These internal standards or rules served, it is argued, to help protect the child from engaging in behaviors that would result in punishment or loss of love (the basis for anxiety). More specifically, it was argued that whenever the children felt the urge to indulge their impulses, they would experience a complex set of feelings or emotions that anticipated how they would feel if they actually did indulge these impulses. These anticipatory feelings or emotions, therefore, were thought to act as a powerful source of motivation for inhibiting sexual and aggressive impulses.

While Freudians often talked about guilt as growing out of the need to learn to inhibit certain impulses, guilt is something that can also be experienced after a so-called *misbehavior*. Again, the source of the guilt is the fear that, having engaged in a misbehavior, an individual will eventually be rejected or punished. It is simply a matter of time before the misbehavior will be recognized and understood.

In Freudian theory, it was thought that children learned proper conduct by identifying with the same-sex parent. The idea behind this assertion is that standards of conduct are somewhat different for the different sexes and that the best way for a child to learn proper conduct for his or her sex was to pattern behavior after the same-sex parent.

The neopsychoanalytic theorists (see Friedman, 1985) questioned Freud's emphasis on hostility, fear, anxiety, and threat of punishment as the driving force behind guilt. They argued that guilt grew out of the need or desire to establish good relationships. Guilt, it was argued, arose when there was an imbalance between the needs and goals of the self and those of significant others. In other words, whereas the psychoanalytic theorists tended to view humans as highly selfish or self-centered, neopsychoanalytic theorists tended to view people as more socially oriented.

Learned Component

The social-learning theorists have also been interested in the question of social conduct and good social relations, but have avoided using such mentalistic terms as guilt and shame to explain the existence of these behaviors. They prefer to talk about the origins of such behaviors in terms of such things as rewards, punishment, extinction, discrimination, generalization. According to the social-learning theorists, good social behavior—including such things as the expression of aggression—have their origins in our social interactions, especially those with our parents. They argue that when our parents show disappointment and disapproval we experience a negative emotion (punishment) that we then connect, through the process of association, to that event that elicited their disappointment and disapproval. Whenever we find ourselves engaging in the same behaviors, these feelings are automatically elicited. Engaging in these behaviors may even trigger memories so that when we engage in those same behaviors we actually experience images of our parents. When we feel guilty for some "transgression," for example, we see our mother frowning in disapproval, or when we experience shame for not having lived up to some ideal, we may see our father's face bathed in disappointment. Guilt, in this analysis, does not involve any mentalistic or cognitive elements. Guilt is simply a conditioned negative feeling and nothing more (Zahn-Waxler & Kochanska, 1990).

The learning theorists have focused mainly on affectively driven guilt (empathetic-guilt and anxiety- or fear-based guilt). In their approach to guilt they have examined such things as the timing and severity of punishment, the specific techniques used, and the quality of the affective relationship between parent and child (Zahn-Waxler & Kochanska, 1990). In the following section I will review a small portion of their research—that which focuses on discipline as a technique for teaching social conduct together with the larger role of parental love and warmth.

Discipline Techniques

The study of discipline techniques has been a central focus of the social-learning theorists. Discipline techniques can be classified in three groups or types: power assertion, love withdrawal, and induction (Hoffman, 1970a, 1982). Power assertion refers to physical punishment, threats, deprivation of privileges or objects, and direct control. Love withdrawal refers to nonphysical expressions of dislike and anger in which the parent shows disapproval by using such love withdrawal techniques as turning away, refusing to communicate, and threatening separation. Induction refers to providing explanations so the child can understand why their behavior is a cause for concern (e.g., "that makes Sally unhappy when you tease her").

Naturalistic studies of children have shown that power assertion leads to low levels of moral development as measured by such things as being able to resist temptation, feelings of guilt, or confession. Induction, in contrast, has been linked to high levels of moral development. Love withdrawal has been found to be related to moral development but less consistently than induction (Hoffman, 1970a).

Comparing Love Withdrawal and Induction

Some studies have shown that love withdrawal and induction lead to different kinds of guilt. Hoffman (1970b), for example, distinguished between two types of children representing two types of guilt: *humanistic-flexible*, who were concerned about the harm they had done to others, and *conventional-rigid*, who were more concerned with whether or not they had violated institutionalized norms. Hoffman suggests that the humanistic-flexible children are motivated by feelings of empathy whereas the conventional-rigid are motivated more by their lack of impulse control. It should be noted that the conventional-rigid type corresponds closely to the psychoanalytic conceptualization of guilt. When Hoffman examined the socialization of these two types, he found that the humanistic-flexible had been socialized more by the process of induction, while the conventional-rigid had been socialized more by the process of love withdrawal.

Quality of the Affective Relationship between Parent and Child

In general, it has been found that there is a positive relationship between parental warmth and the development of conscience and guilt in children. It has been suggested that one of the reasons for the inconsistent effects of love withdrawal on guilt is linked to whether or not parents tend to be warm and affectionate. There is some evidence that withdrawal of love may only be effective if the parent tends to be warm and affectionate to begin with.

Cognitive Component

According to the cognitive theorists, guilt is a conscious process that involves a well developed self-structure. Feelings of guilt occur when the process of self-reflection (also called self-judgment) lead one to conclude that one's behavior fails to meet some internal standard of conduct. As we saw earlier when we defined guilt and shame, Lazarus (1991) clearly views shame as growing out of the self-concept. He prefers the word "ego" to "self" and suggests that shame can be defined, as I indicated earlier, as "having failed to live up to an ego-ideal."

Where do internal standards of conduct come from? Most cognitive theorists take the position that they are due in part to learning or role taking (e.g., we accept the beliefs and values of our parents, or we accept norms) and in part to rational construction that grows out of a process called self-reflection. Rational construction would come from our analysis of the external world or a body of facts and our belief about those facts. We may decide after reading several articles on the state of the environment, for example, that proper conduct should involve recycling of waste. We may decide on this conduct even though our parents and friends do not share our view that recycling is important.

It is important to keep in mind the distinction between acts of commission (guilt) and acts of omission (shame). While acts of commission often grow out of transgressions against others, acts of omission grow more out of our failure to work towards goals that we have set for ourselves. These goals may be goals that have been given to us by our parents ("You should become an engineer") and those that we have decided on ourselves ("I don't want to become an engineer because I hate math" or "I think I should become a doctor because I like the life sciences and I like helping people"). While we are inclined, in everyday language, to use the word "guilt" for both of these situations, it would be more appropriate if we learned to use different words to give distinct meaning to these two situations.

Cognitive theorists hold the view that we not only construct standards but change standards through a process of self-reflection. We may, for example, decide to alter our goals when we reflect on the fact that our talents do not match up with our goals. I have a friend who entered a university with the ultimate goal of becoming an engineer like his uncle. When he reflected on the fact that he was not particularly interested in engineering but found economics fascinating, he decided to abandon his previous goal (one that had largely been given to him by his parents) and set a new goal for himself. In due course, his parents were able to come to terms with his new goal and give him their wholehearted support. Self-reflection, as I will discuss in greater detail in Chapter 14, involves carefully analyzing our interactions with the environment to see how our talents best harmonize with the environment.

The fact that we can construct new and different standards of conduct for ourselves has a number of important implications. It means, among other things, that the amount of guilt and shame we experience may be due in part to the standards we have set for ourselves (see Practical Application 10-3 entitled *Managing Excessive Guilt and Shame*).

The Guilt-Depression Link

Guilt and depression have been explicitly linked to depression in both the theories of Beck and Seligman. In Beck's (1967) model it is suggested that depressives are likely to assume personal responsibility for events with negative outcomes which result in feelings of guilt, self-blame, self-deprecation and dejection. In Seligman's reformulated model, the self is also held responsible for negative outcomes and these self-attributions of responsibility are permanent, pervasive and consistently internal. One obvious conclusion is that guilt comes from taking far too much responsibility for negative outcomes.

Negative Emotions and Goal-Directed Behavior

All of the negative emotions we have discussed in this chapter tend to undermine goal-directed behavior. When people see the world as threatening, as in the case of fear and anxiety, they are less inclined to initiate goal-directed behaviors. Rather, they tend to pull back, focusing their energies on protecting themselves from what they perceive is a world that is hostile to their intentions. In contrast, as we will see in the next chapter, people who view the world as more benign or more benevolent are more willing to explore and interact with the world, mastering and shaping the environment so that it can provide them with pleasure. Similarly, when people interpret any failure in their attempts to master and shape the world as evidence that they are helpless victims—as in the case of pessimists and depressives—they are inclined to discontinue their goal-directed efforts. They assume, instead, a helpless-victim attitude that prevents them from putting forth effort and overcoming obstacles. In contrast, as we will see in the next chapter, optimists are not debilitated by failure and carry on in the face of obstacles. Finally, there are people who set excessively high standards for themselves and, as a result, often experience either guilt or shame. In contrast, as we will see in the next chapter, there are people who have a strong sense of self-worth and who take joy in their encounters and can forgive themselves for their shortcomings.

Excessive Guilt and Shame

The question of excessive guilt has fascinated psychologists for some time. One of the paradoxes they have attempted to explain is why people who realize that their feelings of guilt and shame are excessive continue to experience these excessive negative feelings. It has been suggested that there may be two parallel systems: a sensory based system or an experientially based system and a rational system, and that these unwanted feelings have their origins in such systems. It has been argued that the reason these feelings fail to extinguish is that people engage in behaviors that quickly reduce these feelings, thereby preventing them from becoming full blown—a condition that may be necessary for habituation to take place. Further, it has been argued that the the act of terminating these negative emotions is positively rewarding. The net effect is that people learn to maintain behaviors that prevent them from being put into situations that would result in habituation.

It may not be altogether desirable to extinguish feelings of guilt and shame, since they seem to serve an adaptive function. The problem may not be with having such feelings but rather with our cognitive reactions to such feelings. The goal for most people may not be to get rid of these feelings but rather to learn how to correct one's behavior without ruminating. For many people, guilt feelings tend to result from an explanatory style in which failure is viewed as permanent and pervasive. By learning a new explanatory style, people should be able to view failures to meet standards as temporary and specific—an explanatory style that may also reduce the tendency to ruminate.(See Practical Application 13.1.)

Summary

Guilt and shame are usually treated as overlapping emotions. The biological theorists have argued that guilt is innate and universal and that its modes of expression are learned. The biological theorists have worked from an adaptive framework in which they argue that guilt is designed to maintain good social relations. According to Izard, the main adaptive function of guilt is to prevent waste and exploitation—a function which has survival value not only for the individual but for the larger group. Psychoanalytic theorists view guilt as growing out of a conflict between the biological and social parts of the personality and serving to protect children from engaging in behaviors that would result in punishment or loss of love. While the psychoanalytic view is based on the concepts of hostility, fear, anxiety, and the threat of punishment, the neopsychoanalytic position emphasizes the social function of guilt.

The learning theorists have focused on affectively driven guilt (empathetic-guilt and anxiety- or fear-based guilt). The study of discipline techniques has shown that the highest level of moral development comes from the technique called *induction*, while the worst comes from the technique called *power assertion*. *Love withdrawal* has been found to be inconsistently related to moral development. The work of Hoffman suggests that love withdrawal leads to two different kinds of guilt: *humanistic-flexible* and *conventional-rigid*, each of which has been linked to different socialization processes.

Cognitive theorists have focused on symbolic and representational skills such as role-taking and self-reflection in their analyses of guilt. The cognitive theorists have argued that guilt and shame come from the internal representation of norms (often through the process of role-taking) and through rational construction of standards (through the process of self-reflection). It is through the process of self-reflection that people can change their standards.

Guilt and shame have been explicitly linked to depression in the theories of Beck and Seligman. Learning to deal with excessive guilt and shame plays an important role in reducing depression.

PRACTICAL APPLICATION 10.3

Managing Excessive Guilt and Shame

There are many people who experience what can be called "excessive guilt and/or shame." By that we mean they experience guilt and shame totally out of proportion to the situation. Take, for example, a man who feels guilty when two member of his family get into an argument. Because he knew that they are prone to conflict he blames himself for not having done something to avert the situation. Children sometimes feel guilty when their parents break up and divorce. They reason that it was something they did that provoked the split. A woman may feel guilty when her husband is fired. She reasons that if she had been more friendly towards her husband's boss, even though she found his off-color jokes offensive, her husband would not have been fired.

A similar thing happens in the case of shame. When a student receives a B+ instead of the A he expected, he reasons that he has failed not only himself but his family. A mother who takes great care to teach her children honesty experiences sharp pangs of shame each time she remembers the day the principal called her into his office to explain that her son had copied someone else's work. The head of a company feels a sense of despair as the company he heads loses money in the middle of a recession. He reasons that he should have been better prepared to deal with the recession.

Often, people realize that the guilt and shame they experience are unwarranted but still find they are unable to do anything about their feelings. They feel trapped and unable to escape. The fact that people can come to the conclusion that their feelings are not in line with their behavior has perplexed psychologists for some time. Frijda (1988) recognizes this paradox in the two laws of emotion, the Law of Habituation and the Law of Conservation of Emotional Momentum. Because people fail to habituate, Frijda suggested that under certain conditions, "emotional events retain their power to elicit emo-

tions indefinitely, unless counteracted by repetitive exposures that permit extinction or habituation, to the extent these are possible." As I indicated earlier, this law was proposed as a restriction on the law of habituation.

In order to explain this paradox, various writers have suggested there are two parallel systems: one that is conscious and one that is unconscious. The conscious system is generally conceptualized as more abstract and rational, involving such things as logical explanations, whereas the unconscious system is generally conceptualized as more sensory based, operating by way of images, memories, and the principles of associative learning (e.g., classical conditioning) (e.g., Lazarus, 1991), or more experientially based, operating by way of concrete images, metaphors, narratives (e.g., Epstein, 1990). In the more sensory-based system described by Lazarus, images and memories are thought to become linked to feelings so that when certain images are elicited, they automatically trigger certain feelings. Guilt, according to the sensory-based system, might be elicited by something as simple as a frown. Because one's mother frowned in the past when she disapproved of some transgression, the mere presence of a frown on anyone's face might be sufficient to elicit pangs of guilt. Presumably, the precise feeling that one would experience would depend on the feeling that one experienced when caught for a transgression. That feeling could be loss of love, pain that comes from punishment, or simply the negative emotion that people experience when there is a social conflict. In short, the feeling component may be somewhat different for different people.

What about the feelings that come from the more rational system? Are they the same as those we experience from the sensory based system? While there is no "yes" or "no" answer to this question, some theorists have taken the position that indeed the feelings may be very different. Hoffman suggests, for example, that the rational system is more likely to be based on *empathetic-distress*. Rather than re-experiencing our own pain, we learn to experience the pain or distress of others.

In general, most theorists seem to believe that the feelings that come from the sensory-narrative based system are much harder to alter than the feelings that come from the rational-based system (e.g., Epstein, Lipson, Holstein, & Huh, 1992; Epstein, 1990). While it should be theoretically possible to extinguish (habituate) these feelings by repeatedly exposing an individual to the stimuli that cause the guilt feelings, the problem seems to lie with the fact that people often do things that remove in some way the stimuli that caused their guilt feelings. When a person frowns, for example, they may alter their comments or stop doing what they were doing, so that the frown disappears. As a result of their attempts to repair the situation, the guilt feelings never become full-blown and therefore cannot extinguish or habituate (Frijda, 1988). Most theorists seem to agree that in order for habituation to occur, a response must be allowed to run its course; it must be allowed to wear out, so to speak. Also, acts of reparation are positively reinforcing because they reduce or remove the negative feeling of guilt. As a result of this repeated positive reinforcement, people are inclined to perpetuate acts of reparation and thus never put themselves in a situation that would allow the emotions to habituate. To put it very simply, the reason people continue to experience guilt when their parents are present is that they often work hard to ensure that their parents are not upset. Only by allowing their parents to become upset can they hope to allow habituation to take place. One can readily see from this example how guilt serves to minimize conflict even though it may cause a great deal of internal stress. The question of excess might best be conceptualized as a problem of rumination: people who feel guilty or who experience shame often ruminate about their feelings. It is in the course of ruminating that people become debilitated.

It is important to note in this context that people are often reinforced for their feelings of guilt and shame in our society. We tell people how important it is for them to be considerate of the feelings and wishes of other people, especially their parents, even when it undermines their own ability to deal with important events in their lives. We also praise people for taking full responsibility for their actions. The problem, therefore, is that people have difficulty dealing with excess guilt and shame because our society constantly reinforces them for harboring these two emotions.

Is there any hope for the person who feels he or she is experiencing too much guilt? Probably the best solution is to tackle the problem at the rational (thinking) level. Both Beck and Seligman suggest that people need to be equipped with an explanatory style that will confine the problem to a specific situation and to a specific time. Epstein argues that when people operate out of the experiential system they tend to overgeneralize. Often people need to learn that the reactions of other people, such as their parents, are not ones they have thought through rationally but rather are ones they have adopted from their parents.

If people arm themselves with a better way of viewing situations so that they do not give rise to feelings of permanence and pervasiveness, they can better manage and control feelings of guilt. According to such an approach, people do not attempt to get rid of these emotions (habituate them) but rather make them more situation- and time-specific. It should be remembered that most people experience pangs of guilt from time to time. Further, it should be remembered that there is nothing wrong with being sensitive to social conflict and wanting to make amends for our acts of transgression (sins of

(continued on next page)

PRACTICAL APPLICATION 10.3

Managing Excessive Guilt and Shame (continued)

commission) or lapses in sensitivity or empathy (sins of omission). It is psychopaths who tend to be lacking in their desire to maintain good social relations or to experience feelings of empathy. Also, the problem of modern individualism may have its roots in our failure to maintain good social relations. People need to view feelings of guilt and shame as simple reminders that we are social beings. Making quick

and simple corrections or reparations has always been the mark of socially sophisticated people. The key is not to expect perfection in ourselves or to think that we can please everybody. It is when people think they cannot make mistakes or that they must be loved by everybody that they come to suffer from shame and guilt. Such thinking is almost bound to lead to negative rumination.

Main Points

1.   Some theorists have suggested that fear and anxiety are basically the same. Others have suggested that the goal-object of fear is fairly specific while the goal-object of anxiety is more vague or ambiguous.

2.   It has been suggested that three primary conditions elicit anxiety: overstimulation, cognitive incongruity, and response unavailability.

3.   GABA appears to be one of those substances in the body that helps to maintain an optimal flow of stimulation.

4.   Benzodiazepines help reduce anxiety by either stimulating GABA output or making it possible for GABA to do its job.

5.   Neobehaviorists have argued that both fear and anxiety are conditioned pain.

6.   Two important things take place in avoidance learning: the response occurs progressively earlier and tends to persist.

7.   Feelings of loss of control, unpredictability, and the inability to make a coping response can give rise to feelings of anxiety.

8.   State anxiety is specific to a given situation, whereas trait anxiety is not situation-specific.

9.   Sensitizers dwell on the consequences of a threat, whereas repressors tend to avoid thinking about the threat.

10.   Some people seem to be predisposed to experience aversive emotional states.

11.   People who become depressed tend to use an explanatory style that is characterized by pessimism.

12.   While there is evidence that moods govern the way we think and act, there is also evidence that the way we think and act governs our moods.

13.   Depression is very prevalent in our society and is characterized by a lack of motivation.

14.   When depression is very severe it leads to thoughts about self-destruction (suicide).

15.   *Modern individualism* has been linked to increases in depression.

16.   The solution to modern individualism may be relearning the importance of the group and the importance of cooperation.

17.   It has been suggested that all depression involves a reduction in certain catecholamines, especially norepinephrine.

18.   More recently, it has been suggested that depletion of serotonin is a major cause of depression. One of the newest antidepressants is Prozac, which blocks the reuptake of serotonin.

19.   Various drugs used in the treatment of depression work by elevating norepinephrine levels or serotonin levels.

20. Stress appears to cause depression by lowering norepinephrine levels.

21. It has been suggested that depression is an adaptive mood. Depression may play a role in reprogramming. For example, it may help people abandon goals that are unattainable.

22. Seligman has suggested that depression is learned helplessness, where learned helplessness is defined as "a psychological state that frequently results when events are uncontrollable."

23. Experiments with both animals and humans have shown that exposure to an aversive stimulus event that is both inescapable and uncontrollable is often sufficient to produce learned helplessness.

24. According to Seligman, learned helplessness is characterized by three deficits: (1) failure to initiate responses, (2) failure to learn, and (3) emotional disturbance.

25. The reformulated model of learned helplessness suggests that people are inclined to become depressed if they use an explanatory style characterized by permanence (permanent versus temporary), pervasiveness (universal versus temporary), and personalization (internal versus external).

26. Hope and hopelessness grow out of two dimensions: pervasiveness and permanence.

27. Evidence for the idea that pessimism causes depression comes from research which shows that people who tend to use a pessimistic explanatory style are more likely to become depressed when they experience bad events.

28. Rumination refers to excessive analysis. When pessimists ruminate they create a negative world for themselves, whereas when optimists ruminate they create a positive world for themselves.

29. Whereas women tend to be ruminators, men tend to be distractors.

30. According to Beck's theory, depression results from a negative thinking style that alters the way people screen, differentiate, and code the environment. Their "bias against the self" leads to "cognitive distortions" or "errors in thinking."

31. Beck has suggested there are two subtypes of depression. The sociotropic type is motivated by the receipt of acceptance and attention from others, while the autonomous type is motivated by the need for achievement, control and the avoidance of interpersonal impediments.

32. There are five basic tactics that people can use to change their thinking: (1) Learn to recognize destructive automatic thoughts, (2) learn to dispute destructive automatic thoughts, (3) learn to avoid using destructive explanations, (4) learn the art of distracting yourself from depressive thoughts, and (6) learn to create less self-limiting "happiness self-statements."

33. Lowered catecholamines may be responsible, in part, for the way people think.

34. Beliefs about control may lead to adaptive behaviors that trigger catecholamine release.

36. Guilt and shame are involved in a wide range of adaptive and maladaptive behaviors.

37. Guilt and shame can sustain certain adaptive behaviors (e.g., achievement, cooperation) while inhibiting others (e.g., anger, aggression).

38. One way of thinking about guilt and shame is to think of guilt as acts of commission and shame as acts of omission.

39. According to the Izard's discrete emotions theory, guilt evolved to prevent waste and exploitation.

40. According to Freudian theory, guilt was thought to emerge as a result of restraints that parents imposed on their children.

41. Neopsychoanalytic theorists view guilt as facilitating social interactions.

42. Guilt, according to the social-learning theorists, is simply a conditioned negative feeling.

43. Parents are inclined to employ one of three discipline techniques: power assertion, love withdrawal, and induction.

44. Induction tends to produce a *humanistic-flexible* type, whereas love withdrawal tends to produce a *conventional-rigid* type.

45.   Cognitive approaches to guilt and shame have emphasized the role of self, and view guilt as coming from the process of self-reflection.

46.   Because excessive guilt and shame tend to undermine goal-directed behavior, people often need to learn how to manage these emotions.

47.   Getting rid of guilt and shame may not be altogether desirable.

48.   The difficulty that some people experience in their attempts to manage these emotions may be due to the fact there are two parallel systems—one at the unconscious level (sensory-based system) that is difficult to access, and one at the rational level (rational-based system) that is accessible through rational thought.

Chapter Eleven

Goal-Congruent (Positive) Emotions:
Happiness, Hope and Optimism, Attachment and Belongingness, Empathy

- What are goal-congruent emotions?
- Is happiness a state of mind or is happiness simply a sensory/chemical experience?
- Can people learn to create happiness?
- Do people who take risks do it to experience elation and euphoria or do they have a death wish?
- What role do cognitions play in happiness?

- What is the difference between optimism and hope?
- Are some people born optimists or can anybody learn to be an optimist if they want to?
- Is hope something that comes from inside us or is it triggered in us by our environment?
- Are there any particular chemicals that have been linked to optimism and hope?

- How do the emotions of belongingness and attachment affect my physical and psychological health?

- What role do cognitions play in the emotions of belongingness and attachment?

- Why are empathy and altruism viewed as positive emotions?

- Are people born with empathetic feelings or are such feelings learned?

- Is altruism a selfish motive or are people truly motivated to help others?

- Why do people sometimes tend to blame victims for their misfortunes rather than empathize with them?

Introduction

Goal-congruent emotions are those emotions that facilitate and sustain the attainment of personal goals (Lazarus, 1991). In addition to the emotions that I will be talking about in this chapter, there is the emotion of pride, which I will deal with in the chapter on competence, and love, which I will discuss under the heading of attachment and belongingness (and which I have already covered to some degree in the chapter on sex behavior). While I cannot do full justice to these emotions in this text, my desire is to provide the reader with an appreciation of the power of goal-congruent emotions in our daily lives.

Hedonism and Happiness

In this section I am going to provide an explanation of why some people are inclined to engage in certain activities, especially thrill-seeking activities. I begin with the assumption that they do it to make themselves happy. But exactly what is happiness? According to the hedonists it is one thing and according to the cognitive/emotional theorists it is something very different. Let me start by distinguishing between these two approaches.

Hedonism

According to the principles of hedonism, organisms are motivated to seek pleasure and avoid pain. Hedonism is typically conceptualized in terms of those feelings that result from stimulation of the different sensory systems (vision, hearing, taste, smell, and touch) or those feelings that come from being bombarded with stimulation (arousal). According to the principles of hedonism, our feelings can be represented by a continuum that ranges from positive affect at one end to negative affect at the other end. Happiness involves maximizing positive affect.

Perhaps one of the best-known of the hedonists is Paul Young (1975), who did extensive research on food preferences. His work, together with that of Carl Pfaffman (1960), showed that organisms are motivated to avoid certain substances (such as bitter substances) and approach other substances (such as things which are sweet). Their work indicates that organisms select foods based on their sensory qualities rather than their nutrition or energy values as with artificial sweeteners or various seasonings. Harry and Margaret Harlow (1969) demonstrated the importance of tactile stimulation in infant-mother bonding. Infant monkeys, they showed, prefer mothers that can provide them tactile stimulation over mothers that just provide food. Mothering, in short, is more than just providing for the nutritional requirements of their offspring. Daniel Berlyne (1960) demonstrated that organisms are motivated to seek out and obtain optimal levels of stimulation. When stimulation is very low, organisms are motivated to increase stimulation, often by engaging in exploratory behavior; when it is high, they are motivated to decrease stimulation, often by seeking out familiar and predictable stimulation. According to Berlyne's theory, when levels of stimulation are optimal, people experience positive affect, and when stimulation is either low or very high it is experienced as aversive.

In recent years, a popular term that has often been used to describe the motivation linked to seeking pleasure is *getting high*. This term is used in connection with a variety of activities that people freely select without regard to their ultimate survival value. These activities, often called thrill-seeking activities (Farley, 1986), seem

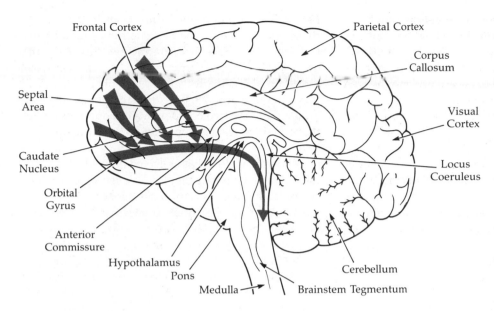

Figure 11-1. The reward system of the human brain has been roughly localized in the shaded regions. These areas correspond to the parts of the rat brain that support self-stimulation behavior (Routtenberg, 1978). (From A. Routtenberg, "The Reward System of the Brain." *Scientific American*, November 1978,160. Copyright © 1978 by Scientific American, Inc. All rights reserved.)

to have little or no short-term or long-term survival value. Hang gliding, bungee jumping, parachuting, skiing fast, driving fast, and rock climbing are just a few of the activities that fall into the category called thrill-seeking or sensation-seeking (Zuckerman, 1979).

Ultimate Hedonism?

The discovery of reward pathways in the brain provided the mechanism that many people felt gave the concept of hedonism a sound scientific basis. More than 30 years ago, James Olds discovered that rats with electrodes implanted in certain areas of the brain would learn to press a bar in order to receive electrical stimulation that activated those areas (Olds, 1956; Olds & Milner, 1954). He confirmed that laboratory animals stimulated themselves in this way only when the stimulation activated particular brain areas. It should be noted that self-reward systems have also been found in humans (Heath, 1963). The reward systems of the human brain are seen in Figure 11-1.

Can people activate the reward pathway without engaging in any goal-directed behavior? One way of activating those areas of the brain is to take certain drugs. It appears that when certain neurotransmitter

substances are elevated, this pathway becomes active. Aryeh Routtenberg (1978) has demonstrated, for example, that the amphetamines facilitate self-stimulation, whereas chlorpromazine reduces self-stimulation. It should be noted that amphetamines do not themselves activate the reward centers but rather stimulate the output of two brain chemicals, dopamine and norepinephrine, which activate the reward pathways (Stein, 1980).

Is the reward pathway activated when we engage in goal-directed behavior? There is good evidence that norepinephrine is released when people engage in a variety of coping behaviors as well as thrill-seeking behaviors. There is evidence from work with race-car drivers that norepinephrine is released in the course of competing (Taggart & Carruthers, 1971). They are also elevated in the course of parachuting (Hansen, Støa, Blix, & Ursin, 1978). In other words, there is good reason to believe that engaging in a variety of coping behaviors can activate the reward pathways.

Happiness from a Cognitive Perspective

While the affect in theories of hedonism is viewed as an emotion, cognitive theorists argue that in order for affect to be called an emotion must meet the criteria of having a core relational theme. Core relational themes result from our appraisal of our interactions with the world. The world *relational* in the phrase "core relational theme" is intended to draw attention to the idea that emotions are the result of person-environment interaction. In the case of happiness, the core relational theme is defined as "Making reasonable progress towards the realization of a goal" (Lazarus, 1991, p. 121). Thus, it is a person-environment interaction that denotes the existence of an emotion and not simply the occurrence of affect. It is important to note in this context that there are a number of common synonyms for happiness which are *joy, overjoyed, satisfied, contented, gratified, pleased, carefree, jubilant, exuberant, exultant, enthusiastic, blissful, cheerful, playful, amused, glad, gay, gleeful, jolly, jovial, delighted, euphoric, ecstatic, elated, enraptured,* and *triumphant* (Lazarus, 1991).

If the affect referred to in theories of hedonism and the affect referred to by the cognitive theorists are conceptualized as arising out of different or distinct processes or systems, are they the same affect or are they different? I am going to operate on the assumption that these are, indeed, two distinct kinds or forms of affect that arise out of different systems but that often merge, resulting in a new emotion or feeling. Lazarus (1991) has noted that when two or more core relational themes are aroused simultaneously, a new emotion emerges that reflects their combination. Unlike Lazarus, however, I am going to make the case that we have emotions that reflect the combination or merging of sensory and core relational themes.

Hedonic Enjoyment and Hedonic Happiness

The idea that there are different types of forms of happiness has been made before (Tefler, 1980). Tefler has argued that some activities are characterized only by their ability to produce hedonistic feelings (*hedonic enjoyment*) while others are characterized by their ability to produce both hedonic feelings and feelings of self-satisfaction that come from realizing one's potential (called self-actualization within Maslow's theory). Those activities that help people to realize or develop their potential have been called *personally expressive activities* (Waterman, 1993). It has been suggested that these activities give rise to something called *hedonic happiness*, which has been defined as "the belief that one is getting the important things one wants, as well as certain pleasant affects that normally go along with this belief (Kraut, 1979, p. 178). According to this definition, there are two components of happiness: beliefs that pertain to what is important to the individual, and affect.

Waterman (1993) has collected data which support the idea that activities that involve self-realization are sufficient to produce happiness but that people need not realize their potential to necessarily experience happiness. As expected, Waterman found that *hedonic happiness* (feelings of personal expressiveness) was more strongly associated with a feeling of being challenged, experiencing competence, putting forth effort, concentration, feeling assertive and having clear goals, whereas *hedonic enjoyment* was more strongly associated with feeling relaxed, excited, content, happy, losing track of time, and forgetting one's personal problems.

Comparing Hedonic Enjoyment and Hedonic Happiness

The discovery of reward pathways in the brain together with the demonstration that organisms are motivated to seek out sensory stimulation has provided compelling data for the concept of hedonism. This work suggests that one does not have to achieve a goal, overcome obstacles, or satisfy a basic drive (such as hunger) in order to experience positive affect. The discovery that various drugs can stimulate the release of chemicals that activate these pathways provides converging data for the idea that activities such as using recreational drugs are often motivated by the desire to experience pleasure in the absence of any other goal or the realization of any potential, and are not necessarily motivated by the need or desire to escape an aversive or noxious state.

Lazarus, on the other hand, assumes that positive emotions such as happiness exist to facilitate or sustain goal-directed behavior. It is clear from Lazarus's definition of happiness that some goal other than just pleasure is involved in happiness. Thus, the main distinction between hedonism and happiness pertains to whether or not the goal is simply pleasure or something else. While happiness has been conceptualized by cognitive theorists as a means to an end (goal), hedonism has been conceptualized as an end (goal). Happiness for the cognitive theorists is something that you experience on the way to a goal.

As I have already indicated, the reason I am interested in making this distinction is that I want to talk about why people engage in various activities, especially thrill-seeking activities. While many of these activities can be interpreted as goal-directed activities that demand the use of coping skills (e.g., rock climbing), other activities do not fit this classification. In the case of bungee jumping, for example, there are no clearly defined goals nor is there a clearly defined set of skills that one must have to engage in this activity. Yet in both cases the motivation is often described as the motivation to *get high*. I am going to argue that while they both are motivated by the same end state (to get high) they represent different ways that people have learned to get high. In some cases people have learned to make use of goals as a means of getting high (hedonic happiness), while in other cases they have learned to tap into their sensory systems in order to get high (hedonic enjoyment).

Happiness and Coping Behavior

If happiness comes from making reasonable progress towards the realization of a goal (or the realization of potential), how does one know if one is making reasonable progress? It has been suggested by a number of different researchers that coping with the demands of the immediate task provides the basis for making such a judgment (e.g., Bandura, 1991; Lazarus, 1991). It is important to emphasize that the use of the word "coping" does not imply that people have attained the goal, solved the problem, or that they are performing without error. Rather, it means they are dealing with it as effectively as can be expected given their present state of competency. Implicit in many of the theories of coping is the idea that people believe they can improve their competencies which will enable them to

deal more effectively as time goes by. In this section I want to examine the nature of coping and responding in terms of the three basic components that I have used to organize this book.

Biological Component

There is considerable evidence that when people make a coping response various chemical changes take place in the brain and body that reflect this fact. It has been shown, for example, that norepinephrine is released when animals learn an avoidance response. Before we look at a study that measured norepinephrine in a situation that demanded coping, let me point out that norepinephrine plays a very primary role in determining our emotions. It has been found that when concentrations of norepinephrine are high at the synapses, we tend to feel optimistic or euphoric. As I indicated in the chapter on drug use, the reason cocaine produces feelings of euphoria is that it increases the concentrations of norepinephrine at the synapses (see Chapter 7). When concentrations of norepinephrine are low, we tend to feel depressed (a topic I covered in Chapter 10).

A series of studies by Joseph Brady (Brady, 1967, 1975) clearly illustrates that norepinephrine is released when animals make a coping response, which in this case was an avoidance response (see also Mason, 1975; Mason, Brady, & Tolson, 1966). Brady and his colleagues measured epinephrine and norepinephrine output in monkeys during a shock-avoidance task. In such a task the monkey is presented with a signal (such as a horn) which is followed several seconds later by shock. The point of the task is for the monkey to learn that it can avoid the shock by making some adaptive response, such as pressing a lever. When the monkey makes that response, the shock does not occur. Being fairly intelligent animals, monkeys quickly learn what they must do to avoid the shock. In order to determine whether the levels of these two catecholamines change as the result of learning, the investigators measured them both before and after the monkeys had learned to avoid the shock. As the first two panels in Figure 11-2 illustrate, the levels of both epinephrine and norepinephrine were quite low before learning had occurred

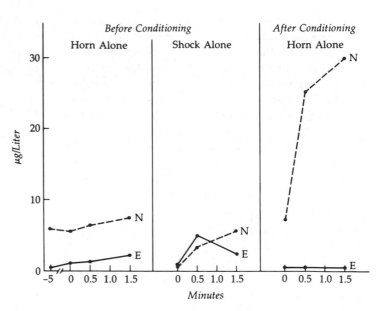

Figure 11–2. Plasma norepinephrine (N) and epinephrine (E) responses in monkeys before and after shock-avoidance conditioning. (From J. W. Mason, J. V. Brady, and W. W. Tolson,"Behavioral Adaptations and Endocrine Activity." In R. Levine (Ed.), *Endocrines and the Central Nervous System: Proceedings of the Association for Research in Nervous and Mental Diseases,* 1966, 43, 227-248. Copyright © 1966 by the Association of Research in Nervous and Mental Diseases. Reprinted with permission.)

when either the horn or the shock was presented alone. After learning, however, norepinephrine levels rose quite dramatically when the horn was sounded.

Learned Component

Evidence from a wide variety of sources indicates that when people make a coping response they experience a wide range of feelings or emotions. They may, for example, feel gratified, pleased, elated, euphoric or triumphant (Lazarus, 1991). If they had to acquire a new skill in the process of exercising control, they may even experience a sense of pride or feelings of self-efficacy (a sense of being able to deal effectively with the demands of the task). In addition to experiencing these feelings, their body releases a number of chemicals. The typical finding is that when people engage in behavioral coping, norepinephrine levels increase.

In the case of dealing with a feared object, people often experience a sense of *relief*, an emotion that has not received a great deal of attention in the research literature but one that is potentially important for understanding behavior (Lazarus, 1991). In the study reported above, it was found that after the monkeys had acquired an avoidance response (exercised a well-prac-

ticed coping response), the level of plasma 17-OH-CS (17 hydroxycorticosteroids) declined. Because 17-OH-CS has been associated with anxiety, the decline in 17-OH-CS suggests that the ability to make a coping response reduces anxiety (Brady, 1967, 1975). This finding, of course, is consistent with our general impression that when we gain control over events in our lives, anxiety is lessened. Further evidence in support of Brady's position comes from the work of Jay Weiss and his colleagues (Weiss, Stone & Harrell, 1970). They subjected rats to shock under conditions in which it was possible to escape and avoid the shock and under conditions in which it was not. Animals that could escape showed a significant elevation in brain norepinephrine, whereas animals in the "inescapable" condition showed a significant decrease in brain norepinephrine. What this and other studies show is that norepinephrine levels are elevated when the situation is predictable and controllable.

Cognitive Component

The work of Albert Bandura suggests that when people develop the skills they need to cope with a given situation, they develop strong feelings of self-efficacy for

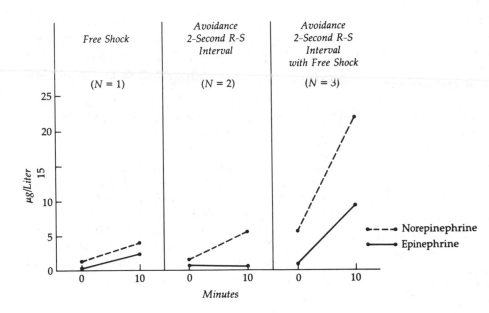

Figure 11–3. Plasma epinephrine and norepinephrine responses to "free shock" alone, "regular" nondiscriminated avoidance, and avoidance with "free shock." N = number of animals in sample. (From J.W. Mason, J.V. Brady, and W. W. Tolson, "Behavioral Adaptations and Endocrine Activity." In R. Levine (Ed.), *Endocrines and the Central Nervous System: Proceedings of the Association for Research in Nervous and Mental Diseases,* 1966, 43, 227-248. Copyright © 1966 by the Association of Research in Nervous and Mental Diseases. Reprinted with permission.)

that and similar tasks (Bandura, 1990). Thus, when they approach a new task that is similar to the one they just encountered, they will likely have strong feelings of self-efficacy in that new task as well. Within Bandura's theory, feelings of self-efficacy are a powerful cognitive/emotion state that determines whether or not people will decide to put forth energy. In short, feelings of self-efficacy are the basis for action.

I will talk more about these feelings. First, let me discuss the effects of uncertainty on people's behavior.

Happiness from Confronting Fear and Uncertainty

Often tasks that we undertake have an element of uncertainty associated with them. By that I mean we do not know exactly what is required in order to achieve a particular goal. As a result, we may not feel fully prepared to meet the challenge and we experience a sense of apprehension. If I am giving a talk on something that is relatively new for me, for example, I may not be completely certain that I can answer all the questions that might arise. As a result I might feel somewhat apprehensive.

Biological Component

What happens to the chemicals in our body when there is an element of uncertainty? To examine this question, Mason, Brady, & Tolson (1966) introduced random shocks in a shock-avoidance task, using monkeys as subjects. Introducing random shocks means introducing uncertainty. Introducing random shocks for the rat can be viewed as analogous to introducing risk for the rock climber (increasing the chances of making a mistake). As a result of introducing uncertainty, they found that both epinephrine and norepinephrine levels were elevated (see Figure 11-3). These and other findings indicate that epinephrine may be elevated when the situation becomes only potentially controllable or when there is an uncontrollable element. Compare this figure with Figure 11-2. Whereas epinephrine remained fairly low in the highly predictable situation, it was relatively high in the unpredictable or uncertain situation.

After examining this and other experimental evidence, Schildkraut and Kety suggested that

increased epinephrine excretion seems to occur in states of anxiety or in threatening situations of uncertain or unpredictable nature in which active coping may be required but has not been achieved. In contrast, norepinephrine excretion may occur in states of anger or aggression or in situations which are challenging but predictable and which allow active and appropriate behavioral responses to the challenge. Under various conditions, increase of either epinephrine or norepinephrine or of both of these catecholamines may represent specific adaptive responses [1967, p. 23].

It is interesting to note that men respond to such diverse things as injections, the threat of an examination (Frankenhaeuser, Dunne & Lundberg, 1976), and the prospect of jumping from a mock-training tower (Hansen et al., 1978) by releasing more norepinephrine and epinephrine as measured by levels in the urine. It appears that whenever we find ourselves in a situation that involves a certain degree of unpredictability, these two chemicals are reliably released.

Learned Component

There is a great deal of evidence that people get significantly more self-satisfaction from exercising a coping response when the task is difficult than when it is easy (Bandura, 1991; Locke & Latham, 1990). In learning terminology, this means that being able to control the outcome in a very demanding situation has a higher reward value than being able to control the outcome in a less demanding situation. There is much evidence that personal control over threatening events is a powerful source of motivation for humans, and that inability to control such events is often a source of stress (Bandura, Cioffi, Taylor, & Brouillard, 1988). It is perhaps not surprising that when people perceive their coping behavior to be high in effectiveness, they experience less stress than when they perceive their coping behavior to be low in effectiveness.

It is important to note in this context that there is generally a positive relationship between the difficulty of coping and the magnitude of the norepinephrine response (Frankenhaeuser & Johansson (1976). This relationship may be due to the fact that when the response is more difficult to make people must put forth more effort. As a great deal of research has shown, when situations become uncontrollable organisms are inclined to redouble their efforts. Effort aimed at controlling a situation has typically been linked to high outputs of norepinephrine as long as the response is potentially adaptive (see stress chapter). From a human perspective, when we get feedback that we can control a situation at least part of the time, we are inclined to attribute our lack of control to lack of effort. As a result we put forth more effort. Thus, it can be argued that the reason for the high output of norepinephrine in the above study is that the monkeys had feedback that their efforts were working at least part of the time. They were, in effect, coping as best they could.

Why the high levels of epinephrine? It is important to remember that the situation is only partly controllable. In general, epinephrine levels tend to increase when the situation is characterized by threat or uncertainty.

Cognitive Component

Bandura (1991) has suggested that people do not avoid potentially threatening situations because they experience anxiety and arousal, but rather because they fear they will not be able to cope either behaviorally or cognitively. In behavioral coping, people engage in behaviors that will prevent or at least curtail the threat. In cognitive coping, people operate under the belief that they can manage their thinking or cognitions. One of the greatest sources of threat at the cognitive level is the inability to deal with perturbing thoughts that often arise when one is confronted with fear and threat. For people engaged in potentially life-threatening activities such as bungee jumping, it would be dealing with such perturbing thoughts as being killed, hurt, or even being humiliated because they might have to back out at the last minute. It is interesting to note in this context that one of the reasons people with agoraphobia have a fear of leaving their homes is because they are afraid they will have a panic attack in a new or strange situation. It is the fear of not being in control in that new or strange situation that terrifies them.

Evidence for the idea that both *perceiving that one has behavior coping skills* and *perceiving that one can control one's thinking* determine whether one will choose to

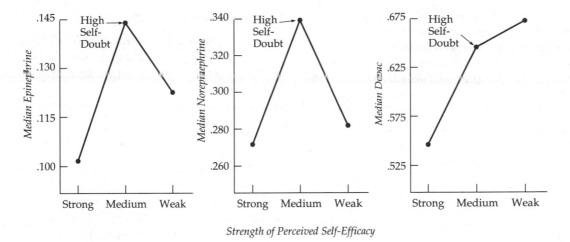

Figure 11-4. Median level of plasma catecholamine secretion (epinephrine, norephinephrine, and dopamine) as a function of perceived coping self-efficacy. (From A. Bandura, C B. Taylor, S. L. Williams, I. N. Mefford & J. D. Barchas, "Catecholamine Secretion as a Function of Perceived Coping Self-Efficacy." *Journal of Consulting and Clinical Psychology*, 1985, 53, 406-414. Copyright © 1985 by the American Psychological Association. Reprinted with permission.)

engage in a particular activity comes from a variety of sources but is perhaps best illustrated in a study of women who were fearful of being assaulted (Ozer & Bandura, 1990). In this study, women were taught how to fend off potential attackers. To assess the effects of this training on feelings of self-efficacy women were asked to indicate to what degree they felt their feelings of self-efficacy had changed as a result of the training. The results indicated that not only did this training lead women to perceive that they could better cope behaviorally with an assault, but that they were less fearful of going to places that previously aroused a great deal of anxiety. In short, they felt less constricted and less threatened as they went about their daily activities.

It is important to note in this context that there is a strong link between feelings of self-efficacy and catecholamines such as norepinephrine and epinephrine. When feelings of self-efficacy are high, catecholamines are typically low. As self-doubt begins to increase, the level of these two catecholamines increases markedly. When people reject participating in a potentially threatening activity, the level of these two catecholamines goes down (Bandura, Taylor, Williams,

Mefford, & Barchas, 1985). It is important to note that Figure 11-4 reflects cognitive coping as opposed to behavioral coping. Typically, behavioral coping leads to an increase in norepinephrine (as shown in Figure 11-3) while cognitive coping leads to a decrease in norepinephrine (Figure 11-4).

Analyzing the Motivation for Thrill-Seeking

Before I offer an interpretation of thrill-seeking based on the interaction of biological, learned, and cognitive factors, let me briefly summarize the two hedonistic theories that are frequently offered as an explanation of why people engage in thrill-seeking behaviors.

Hedonistic Interpretations

Hedonistic theories emphasize the role of sensory processes or simply affect in their theories. Two theories that have been offered are the opponent-process theory of Richard Solomon and arousal theory.

Opponent-process theory. It is important to note in this context that Richard Solomon (1980) proposed the opponent-process theory that can account for this kind of behavior (see Chapter 2). There are a number of thrill-seeking activities that are preceded by fear and followed by exhilaration. Solomon argues that people can learn to expose themselves to stimuli that elicit an emotion that is opposite to the one they eventually want to experience. As I indicated earlier, Solomon has suggested that whenever people experience negative affect they are likely to experience positive affect a short time afterward (or vice versa). He argues that the human is designed so that whenever affect departs from a baseline, an opponent process is triggered that returns the person to baseline.

Arousal theory. According to optimal stimulation theory, the reason people are inclined to engage in thrill-seeking activities is that they have a chronically low level of arousal. In order to increase their level of arousal, they engage in activities designed to raise their arousal level (Eysenck, 1967). While this idea can explain thrill-seeking to a certain degree, Zuckerman (1979) has argued that thrill-seeking is mediated by the catecholamine system as opposed to the arousal system. I will deal with Zuckerman's work in the next chapter when I talk about curiosity and exploratory behavior.

Cognitive Interpretations of Thrill-Seeking

It is not as easy as the opponent-process theory suggests or as optimal stimulation theory suggests for people to engage in thrill-seeking activities. If engaging in thrill-seeking means confronting one's fears and anxieties in some way, why are some people able to do this better than others? Lazarus (1991) has suggested that people need to turn their anxieties into fears so they can develop coping responses. Anxieties are too vague, he argues, for people to deal with. You cannot make coping responses to anxiety but you can make coping responses to fear. In other words, according to the cognitive theorists, the key to understanding behaviors such as thrill-seeking behaviors is to understand how people come to deal with their fears and anxieties.

An Interactional Interpretation of Thrill-Seeking

In my view, the cognitive theorists often fail to adequately acknowledge the role of the sensory and chemical factors in the emotions that we experience. In short, they tend to ignore the role of biological factors such as the release of norepinephrine and epinephrine. I believe that if these findings are integrated with the findings that have come out of learned and cognitive approaches, we get a much clearer picture of what motivates the choice of a wide variety of activities. In order to make this point, let me discuss the motivation for thrill-seeking activities. These are particularly interesting activities to analyze because people suggest that their goal for engaging in these activities is to get high.

Rock Climbing

Let me start by addressing the question of why some people are motivated to engage in an activity such as rock climbing. Rock climbing demands that people make coping responses. As a result it is an activity that is likely to produce feelings of self-efficacy (a sense of being able to deal with the demands of the task) that would also likely lead to changes in the catecholamine levels. Despite a great deal of research on norepinephrine and epinephrine, we cannot be certain whether increases are experienced as more rewarding than decreases or vice versa. Some people have suggested that when they are high they reflect distress (a negative state), while others have suggested that when they are high they reflect eustress (a positive state). Research suggests that increased arousal is rewarding for thrill-seekers and that decreases are rewarding for people who are plagued by anxiety (Zuckerman, 1979). It is important to remember that both epinephrine and norepinephrine are arousal-producing chemicals and, according to Schachter and Singer's theory of emotions, they can lead to an increase in the intensity of any ongoing emotion. Therefore, if people are experiencing a strong positive emotion (good feelings of self-efficacy, for example) increases in the level of these two chemicals would be highly rewarding. That is, it would simply increase their already positive feelings. Contrast this with a person who tends to be plagued by constant

Rock climbing is an objectively risky activity that demands good coping skills. It is this combination that likely produces the high that climbers typically experience.

feelings of anxiety or who constantly feels threatened. In order to allay their feelings of anxiety, they would be inclined to select an activity in which their feelings of self-efficacy would be high. This in turn would result in a reduction in the level of their catecholamines and for them this would be experienced as highly rewarding.

The problem for the thrill-seeker is to find an activity in which he or she can experience a high level of self-efficacy on the one hand, and a high level of catecholamines on the other hand. One strategy would be to select an activity in which he or she experienced self-doubts, because catecholamine levels increase when people have self-doubts (see Figure 11-4). The problem with that strategy is that you would be undermining your motivation for engaging in that activity; that

would be counterproductive. A much better strategy would be to find some other way to increase these catecholamines, such as by exposing oneself to fear or uncertainty. That is, choose an activity at which you are good (you have good feelings of self-efficacy) but where there are elements of uncertainty. For rock climbers that would mean selecting a rock face that was highly challenging.

It is important to remember that there is a great deal of evidence that catecholamines are also involved in activating the reward pathways in the brain (Stein, 1980). This line of research suggests that the motivation for rock climbing may involve another element which is to get the *high* that comes when norepinephrine levels are elevated. But why doesn't everybody want to climb rocks if this is the case? It is perhaps, as Zuckerman has suggested, that some people (sensation seekers) are biologically prepared to experience a high when they climb rocks while others are not. His research indicates that low sensation seekers have high monoamine oxidase levels while high sensation seekers have low monoamine oxidase levels (Zuckerman, 1979). Monoamine oxidase is an enzyme that reduces concentrations of norepinephrine. As I indicated in the previous chapter, one type of antidepressant is a monoamine oxidase inhibitor. By inhibiting monoamine oxidase, norepinephrine levels are allowed to go up, creating a positive mood state. Thus it follows that if you have high MAO levels, it would be difficult to experience a high because the high level of MAO would keep the norepinephrine level low. Because sensation seekers have a low MAO level, on the other hand, they have the capacity to experience a high.

Finally, it is important to remember that many thrill-seeking activities involve fear. Fear, as I have noted previously, is a good way of triggering the endorphin response. It is perhaps not accidental that rock climbers often select rock faces that are characterized as highly vertical. While this typically makes them more difficult to climb, when you look down as you climb a rock wall the sensation can be quite overwhelming. Part of what people feel is an endorphin rush.

The thing that I am stressing in this interpretation is the idea that people make use of the fear or uncertainty component to trigger the chemicals that ultimately give them their high. Because they have good coping skills, they do not in fact experience that much fear but rather experience a sense of self-satisfaction that comes with exercising their highly developed coping skills in the face of uncertainty. As I pointed out earlier, this type of self-satisfaction should lead to hedonic happiness, happiness that involves both a hedonic component and a personal expressive component.

It is interesting to note that climbers report they normally do not experience fear as an emotion except when something draws their attention to the fact that they might hurt or kill themselves such as when a rock they are holding on to gives way.

Bungee Jumping

How can we explain bungee jumping? Is it completely different from rock climbing or are these two activities analogous? I believe they are analogous but that the feelings of self-efficacy come from different sources. Whereas feelings of self-efficacy for rock climbers arise out of people's perceptions relating to their behavioral coping skills, I think the feelings of self-efficacy for the bungee jumper come from perceptions relating to their cognitive coping skills. As I suggested earlier, if you cannot control your thinking you will be plagued by a variety of perturbing thoughts (such things as being killed, getting hurt, or being humiliated should you decide to back out at the last minute). It is these kinds of thoughts that keep people from entertaining the idea of engaging in such activities as bungee jumping. Therefore, the real problem for most people is to make the decision to actually engage in the behavior. Like climbing a rock face, making the decision to bungee jump would result in strong feelings of cognitive self-efficacy. It is hard to imagine somebody not being proud of themselves for doing something that other people are afraid to do. By eliciting strong feelings of self-efficacy, a person would trigger the release of catecholamines. Couple this with the endorphin rush that would come from being hoisted to the top of a tower. To top things off, there would be a wonderful emotion of relief that often comes when people have faced threatening situations and turned them to their favor.

The thing that I am stressing in this interpretation is the idea that people need good cognitive coping skills to deal with their fears. It is the use of these skills that enables them to deal with their perturbing thoughts. At the same time they make use of the fear component to trigger the chemicals that ultimately give them their high. Thus the main difference between rock climbing and bungee jumping involves whether their focus is on behavioral coping skills or cognitive coping skills. This is not to say that rock climbers do not make use of cognitive coping skills. As Ozer and Bandura have shown, giving people good behavior coping skills can result in their having fewer perturbing thoughts—thoughts that might prevent them from engaging in an activity they perceive will give them a high. While bungee jumping can certainly be labeled as an example of *hedonic happiness* because it involves confronting and coping with one's fears, it seems to me that it is also a good example of *hedonic enjoyment*. By that I mean it is not characterized as much by its personal expressive qualities as it is by the hedonic rush that comes from throwing oneself into space.

Increasing the Level of Risk

Once a person has mastered the adaptive responses associated with a particular type of activity, he or she tends to increase the risk level. This tendency cannot be readily handled by traditional drive-reduction theory. Rewards, in traditional drive-reduction theory, result in a stereotyped response to a given set of stimulus events. Thus the theory does not predict a shift in the level of risk. According to opponent-process theory, the reason that people need to increase the level of risk is that they habituate to fear. It is the fear that eventually triggers the opponent process of exhilaration. Thus, in order to maintain a high level of exhilaration they need to increase fear. According to arousal theory, it would be due to habituation that comes with learning to deal with a certain level of arousal. According to self-efficacy theory, the reason people are inclined to increase risk is that positive affect ultimately comes from the existence of a discrepancy. It is meeting a challenge that provides people with feelings of self-satisfaction. As competency improves, people need to set new goals to maintain an optimal level of discrepancy.

Dealing with uncertainty is clearly a form of discrepancy. It is perhaps one of the greatest challenges.

Is Risk-Taking Adaptive?

It may well be that risk-takers have learned how to tap mechanisms that evolved to reward adaptive behaviors. In selecting tasks that not only are risky but require an adaptive response, they are able to get the high feeling that evolved to reward adaptive behaviors. Richard Lazarus and Raymond Launier (1978) have noted that some people treat *threats* as *challenges*, thus causing negative affect to shift to more positive affect. Hans Selye (1974) has argued that attitudes do indeed alter the subjective experience of stress. A positive attitude, Selye suggests, can reduce the distressful feeling that often accompanies the stress reaction. Suzanne Ouellette Kobasa (1979a) has found that executives who experience high stress but do not tend to become ill have a clearer sense of their values, goals, and capabilities than their stressed colleagues who are more susceptible to illness, and they have a strong tendency toward active involvement in their activities. When faced with challenge, they tend to react positively and adaptively. Such findings seem to indicate that positive emotions have a basic survival function, promoting both psychological and physical well-being.

Some Concluding Remarks

I have tried to make the case in this section that it is possible to understand why people take risks by viewing risk-taking activities as a means to triggering a variety of chemical reactions. In short, I am arguing that hedonism is a useful way of conceptualizing why people engage in certain behaviors which do not seem to have any particular adaptive function. Goals are also important; it is setting and achieving goals that gives rise to feelings of self-efficacy. Also, it is through setting goals that people can trigger certain chemicals to be released. My criticism of the cognitive theorists is their failure to recognize that we are biological creatures and that our feelings come from such things as the chemicals our body releases. My criticism of the hedonists is their failure to deal with the very important

question of how people deal with their perturbing thoughts. It is our perturbing thoughts which so often stop us from doing many things. People obviously cannot learn to enjoy an activity if their thoughts will not allow them to even entertain the idea.

Summary

According to the principle of hedonism, organisms are motivated to seek pleasure and avoid pain. Over the years hedonism has been concerned with the question of the relationship between our sensory systems and the feelings we experience. Not only do our senses produce qualitatively different feelings, but the amount of stimulation we experience is important. The discovery of reward pathways in the brain suggests that there is a structure in the brain that produces the positive feelings we experience in connection with a wide variety of behaviors. It has been shown that these reward pathways are activated by the release of dopamine and norepinephrine.

According to the cognitive theorists, happiness is defined as "making reasonable progress towards the realization of a goal." It has been suggested that some activities are characterized only by their ability to produce hedonistic feelings (*hedonic enjoyment*), while others are characterized their ability to produce both hedonic feelings and feelings of self-satisfaction that comes from realizing one's potential (*hedonic happiness*).

The work of Brady and his associates indicates that when organisms make an adaptive response, norepinephrine is released. These studies suggest that we may be able to learn responses that lead to the release of norepinephrine, a chemical that has been implicated in positive feelings. It is interesting to note that when events are made unpredictable, the chemical released is epinephrine, which has been linked to feelings of anxiety.

Brady's work also indicates that after learning has taken place, the release of norepinephrine is associated with exercising a coping response. Since norepinephrine tends to produce positive affect, the reward that people experience as a result of having made a coping response is due to the release of this chemical.

According to self-efficacy theory, people develop strong feelings of self-efficacy in connection with making a coping response. It has been shown that feeling of self-efficacy are one of the main factors that lead to action. It is when people have goals and strong feelings of self-efficacy that they are likely to engage in an activity and put forth effort.

According to the cognitive theorists, one of the important questions that needs to be addressed in order to understand thrill-seeking activities is how people learn to deal with their fears and anxieties. Having good behavioral coping skills appears to be one way for people to deal with their fears. In the absence of good behavioral coping skills, people need to have good cognitive coping skills.

Optimism and Hope

When people see desired outcomes as attainable, they are inclined to continue to exert efforts to attain those outcomes; however, when people see outcomes as unattainable, whether it is due to something they lack or to external constraints, people reduce their efforts and eventually give up (Scheier & Carver, 1988). In other words, outcome expectancies play an important role in determining whether or not people are inclined to continue or give up.

The interesting thing about optimists as well as hopeful people is that they have the tendency to view all desired outcomes as attainable, even in the midst of failures and setbacks. They tend to persist, and even put forth more effort, when things are presently going against them. Some people have suggested they tend to be very unrealistic (e.g., Alloy & Abramson, 1979) or that they live in an illusionary world (e.g., Taylor, 1986) because they fail to accept the fact that things are not going well. They refuse to accept the fact that the best predictor of the future is how things are going right now. Why can't these people accept this fact and get on with their lives?

The paradox, of course, is that people who refuse to give up often end up accomplishing great things. Even though the idea of a light bulb was not new when Edison began his work, it took him and a staff of scientists nearly three years before they finally found the right combination of features that would make the light bulb a viable commercial product.

While there is not a great deal of difference between optimists and pessimists—hopeful and hopeless people—when things are going well, there are big differences when things start to go badly. While pessimistic and hopeless people tend to give up in the face of adversity, optimists and hopeful people tend to persist. What we will examine in this section is why some people refuse to give up when things go badly.

It should be noted that giving up is not all that bad. There is both a blessing and a curse of being too hopeful. As Tillich (1965) said:

> Hope is easy for the foolish, but hard for the wise. Everybody can lose himself in foolish hope, but genuine hope is something rare and great.

Defining Optimism and Hope

There are a wide array of approaches to optimism and hope. Some take a more biological focus and define optimism and hope in terms of biological variables. Others such as Seligman have taken a learning approach, treating optimism as the result of having acquired a particular explanatory style. Still others, such as Snyder, Harris, Anderson, Holleran, Irving, Sigmon, Yoshinobu, Gibb, Langelle, & Harney (1991) take a more cognitive approach, conceptualizing optimism more in terms of the self-concept that people have. While these approaches overlap in certain ways, they are, nonetheless, distinctly different ways of thinking about the concepts of optimism and hope.

For a working definition of optimism, let me use that offered by Scheier and Carver (1985), which simply states that *optimism is a generalized expectancy that good, as opposed to bad, outcomes will generally occur when confronted with problems across important life domains.* Using their Life Orientation Scale (LOT), Scheier and Carver (1985) have been able to demonstrate a positive relationship between optimism, health and recovery from surgery (Scheier, Matthews, Owens, Magovern, Lefebvre, Abbott, & Carver, 1989).

Hope has been defined in a variety of ways that I

will discuss in more detail after I have reviewed some of the work related to optimism. In general, optimism is used to denote a positive attitude or disposition that good things will happen independent of one's ability, whereas hope is used in connection with goal-directed behavior. The concept of hope implies that one can find the path or route to a goal, often by using one's skills or ability or perhaps by persisting (e.g., Snyder et al., 1991).

Are Optimism and Pessimism Two Ends of the Same Continuum?

If they are two ends of the same continuum, then there would be little reason to have separate measures of these two constructs. Recent research indicates they are not (Marshall, Wortman, Kusulas, Hervig, & Vickers, 1992). Pessimism seems to be principally associated with neuroticism and negative affect, whereas optimism is principally linked with extraversion and positive affect. Among other things, this seems to indicate that while optimists tend to be open to new experiences or new stimulation, pessimists tend to be more withdrawn and inhibited in their interactions with the world.

Biological Component

Optimism from an Evolutionary Perspective

In *Optimism: The Biology of Hope*, Lionel Tiger (1979) argues that when our ancestors left the forest and became plains animals, they were faced with the task of having to obtain food by killing other animals. In the course of hunting, he argues, they doubtless experienced many adverse circumstances. Many of them must have suffered a variety of injuries. The principles of learning tell us that humans tend to abandon tasks that are associated with negative consequences. So why did hunters carry on in the face of such adverse conditions? Tiger argues that it was biologically adaptive for our ancestors to develop a sense of optimism. Optimism would carry them through adverse circumstances, even injury.

By what mechanism or mechanisms did optimism develop? Tiger suggests that one of the mechanisms

that evolved consisted of endorphins. When we are injured, our bodies typically release endorphins. Endorphins have at least two important qualities (as I indicated in Chapter 7). First, they have analgesic properties (the ability to reduce pain). Second, they produce feelings of euphoria. Sometimes people talk about their ability to reduce feelings of fatigue. Tiger argues that it was adaptive for our hunting ancestors to experience a positive rather than a negative emotion when they were injured because it would reinforce rather than punish their tendency to hunt in the future. It would have been disastrous, he argues, if our ancestors had abandoned the tendency to hunt.

Tiger points out that it is important to have a sense of optimism in general. When things go wrong, it is important not to give up. He points out that optimism is not only a very positive emotion but a very active one as well. Optimism makes us look to our environment with the view that it can provide us with the resources we need. Such an attitude, he argues, was very important for our ancestors' survival, especially in the face of hardships and setbacks.

Learned Component

Optimism as an Acquired Thinking Style

A number of researchers are beginning to conceptualize the thinking styles as habits. As it turns out, this has proved to be a very powerful way to conceptualize the behavior of optimists and hopeful people. If these thinking styles are merely ways that people have learned to think about the world and do not reflect deep underlying personality attributes, it should be relatively easy to change such thinking styles. Indeed, this is the premise on which Seligman's thinking program is based.

Seligman's Definition of Optimism and Hope

As I indicated in the previous chapter, Seligman (1990) has taken the approach that optimism grows out of people's explanatory style. Optimists are people who view (explain) setbacks, failures, adversity, and the like as *temporary*, as *specific to a given situation*, and due to *external* reasons or causes. Hope, within Seligman's system, involves an explanatory style that is *temporary*, and as *specific to a given situation*. In other words, optimism within Seligman's system is the more inclusive concept (it contains three elements or components whereas hope contains only two). We will see later that some people tend to see hope as the more global or superordinate of these two concepts.

Evidence for Seligman's Theory

There is considerable support for Seligman's theory in the research literature. In this section I will review a few examples that illustrate the diverse areas in which the theory has proven to be applicable.

Success at sales. One of the toughest jobs is selling life insurance because salespeople are faced with repeated rejections. What typically happens is that after a period of time, many salespeople give up and quit. Over the years, insurance companies have developed a variety of tests to assess the suitability of applicants for selling life insurance because it is very expensive to train new salespeople. To determine whether measures of optimism might be good or even better predictors of sales success, Seligman undertook one study in which he compared his test of optimism with the "Career Profile" tests that had been developed by Metropolitan Life to select their sales staff. The control group (the Regular Group) for this study was a group of salespeople who were hired using the Career Profile (the normal way of hiring). The Special Force Group, as they were called, was hired using two criteria; they had to have high optimism scores (they had to be in the top half) and they had to have failed the Career Profile.

The Regular Group was also given Seligman's ASQ test (which measures optimism and pessimism) so that it would be possible to simply look at the role of optimism independent of the Career Profile. At the end of the first year, the optimists in the regular force outsold the pessimists by only 8 percent. At the end of the second year, however, the optimists had outsold the pessimists by 31 percent.

What about the Special Force Group? They outsold the pessimists in the regular force by 21 percent in the first year and 57 percent in the second year. They even outsold the average of the regular force over the two years by 27 percent. As a result of this study, Metropolitan Life began to use optimism scores as their main hiring criteria, a less costly procedure for increasing their sales staff (Seligman, 1990; Seligman & Schulman, 1986).

Academic success. Although academic intelligence (I.Q.) is a reasonably good predictor of success in school, educators have argued for some time that intelligence scores by themselves fail to account for the wide range of achievement that teachers observe daily. Clearly, many educators have argued, motivation plays a critical role. It is those children who persist that get the top marks. More recently, educators have observed that one reason performance in the classroom dives is because children get depressed.

In one study to examine the role of failure on the behavior of school children, they were divided into two groups based on their explanatory style: helpless (pessimists) and mastery-oriented. Each group was given solvable and then unsolvable problems to examine how they reacted to failure. Before failure was introduced, the two groups showed no difference in their problem-solving skills. After failure, however, the problem-solving skills of the pessimistic children deteriorated to the first-grade level. When the mastery-oriented students failed, their problem-solving skills stayed at the fourth-grade level (Dweck & Licht, 1980).

In a longitudinal study to examine the role of optimism and pessimism on depression and intellectual achievement, it was found that there were two major risk factors for poor achievement: pessimism and bad life events (parents separating, family deaths, family job loss). Not only are these factors predictors of poor achievement, but they are predictors of depression in children (Seligman, 1990).

To assess whether optimism plays any role in success at a university, first-year students were given the ASQ (Seligman's Attributional Style Questionnaire). Since they had submitted grades and their SAT (Scholastic Aptitude Test) scores as part of the admission procedure, it was possible at the end of the first semester, when the grades were submitted, to determine if optimism played any role in their performance. The question asked in this study was: Are optimism scores a better predictor of success than previous grades or SAT scores? The results showed that students who did better than expected as predicted by their grades and their SAT scores were optimists. It appears that being optimists prepared many of the students to deal with this new environment and to overcome the adversity and setbacks that are common for students entering a university setting.

Optimism and Health

There is considerable evidence that optimistic people are healthier than pessimistic people. In an early study, Chris Peterson (1988) followed the health of a group of 150 students for a year. He found that pessimists had twice as many infectious illnesses and made twice as many visits to their doctors than optimists. Since then there have been numerous studies, including studies which have shown that optimists survive cancer longer than pessimists (Seligman, 1990).

That explanatory style can influence not only the progression of a disease but the recovery from a disease such as cancer has, over the years, been greeted with a great deal of skepticism. There has been a tendency, at least in our society, for people to view disease as being quite independent of any mental process. If anything, disease should produce a deterioration in mood, not the reverse.

In order to determine if a disease such as cancer can be affected by psychological states, Madelon Visintainer (1982) decided to produce helplessness in rats using the helplessness training procedure that Seligman had used with his dogs (the procedure that led Seligman to conclude that depression can be and often is linked to the psychological state of "helplessness"). The main difference in her study was that she used rats that had been implanted with a few cells of sarcoma under each flank the day before she began her helplessness training procedure. The tumor she selected was one that invariably leads to death if it grows and is not rejected by the animal's immune system.

At the end of a month, 50% of the rats not given helplessness training (not shocked) had died while the other 50% had rejected the tumors. She had determined ahead of the experiment just how much of the cancer cells needed to be implanted to produce a 50% death rate. Of the rats given mastery-training, 70% rejected the tumor compared to only 27% of those given helplessness training. What Visintainer showed conclusively in this well-controlled study is that helplessness training causes cancer (Visintainer, Volpicelli & Seligman, 1982).

Can immune activity be increased through cognitive therapy? Preliminary results indicate that it is indeed possible to increase the immune activity of cancer patients using cognitive therapy (see Seligman, 1990). If these preliminary results can be replicated in other studies the implications for health-care delivery in humans may be dramatically altered.

There is a currently a great deal of interest in whether or not various forms of visualization may enable people to ward off diseases such as cancer. There have been numerous reports, for example, of people who have been cured of cancer (and other disorders) by visualizing "good" or "friendly" cells attacking the cancer cells in their body. What is needed at this point are controlled studies to show that indeed is visualization can reliably cure various disorders, perhaps via enhancing the immune system, and further to show that this effect is not simply another form of optimism.

Cognitive Component

Although Seligman's theory of optimism is written in the language of thinking and cognition, I decided to cover it under the heading of learned component because Seligman views explanatory style as something that people learn and something that becomes habit with continued practice. As I indicated before, the most exciting part of Seligman's theory is that part which deals with how people can learn this explanatory style. In this section I am going to look at the work of Snyder et al. who suggest that optimism contains a proactive component called planning. It is this aspect of their theory that mainly differentiates it from that of Seligman and others and the reason why I have chosen to cover their work here.

PRACTICAL APPLICATION 11.1

How to Become an Optimist: The ABCDE Method of Acquiring an Optimistic Explanatory Style

There is considerable evidence that people who are inclined towards depression (that is, use an explanatory style characterized by *permanent, pervasive and personalized*), can learn to change to a more optimistic style. The method that has been developed by Seligman, in conjunction with Dr. Steven Hollon of Vanderbilt University and Dr. Arthur Freeman of University of Medicine and Dentistry of New Jersey, is called the ABCDE method. It is based on the ideas and work of Albert Ellis, an early pioneer in cognitive therapy. This method is designed to help people think more accurately when they are faced with adversity.

In order to understand and use this method, I will break this method down into two parts: the ABC part and the DE part. Let me start with ABC part.

Step 1: Identifying Adversity, Belief, and Consequences (ABC)

As I indicated before, what differentiates optimists from pessimists is how they deal with adversity. The reason optimists are more successful is that they do not fall apart, as pessimists do, when they encounter adversity. Instead of giving up they tend to persist. Thus, the focus of this method is how to help people better deal with adversity by analyzing the inner dialogue that typically accompanies that adversity.

We are just beginning to fully appreciate that humans tend to engage in *perpetual dialogue* that is often just below our level of awareness. We can, it seems, access that dialogue if we focus our attention on it, something that we are not normally inclined to do. What Ellis, Beck, Seligman, and others have discovered is that by asking the right questions it is possible for people to become fully aware of their inner dialogues. They start by pointing out that it is common for people to encounter setbacks, failures, obstacles, and frustrations, which fall under the general

heading called adversity (A). Next they point out that such adversities tend to trigger interpretations or explanations that fall under the general heading of belief (B). Finally, they point out that feelings result from our interpretations, which fall under the heading of consequences (C). Let me show you what I mean by providing some examples of adversity and the thinking process that follows.

Example 1: Jeff's attempt to develop a new friendship. Jeff left his small hometown to attend a large university in the city and wanted very much to develop some new friends. He missed his old friends and was feeling lonely as he began his studies. He suggested to Chris, a student he had just met in one of his classes, that they might go hiking on the weekend and Chris seemed to be genuinely interested. They agreed to go on Saturday. When he stopped by to pick up Chris on Saturday morning, he learned from Chris's roommate that Chris had decided to go home for the weekend. As Jeff walked down the sidewalk towards his Jeep he said to himself: "It is going to be a very lonely year for me. I'm never going to make any friends. I should never have decided to come to this university. I come from a small town and people probably think I'm a hick. Maybe I should pack my bags and go home." When Jeff was asked to analyze this adversity into the three components described above, he offered the following.

Adversity: "I want to develop some friendships but I haven't been able to do so."

Belief: "I lack the ability to make friends."

Consequence (feeling): "I am feeling more lonely than ever."

If we look carefully at his inner dialogue we see that it contains all the elements of a pessimist. The failure has led to an explanatory style that is *perma-*

nent (I can't make friends), *pervasive* (I will never make friends), and *personal* (I lack the ability to make friends).

Example 2: Mary's failure to get an A on a paper she had written. Mary was one of the top students in her high school and had no difficulty being admitted to a top university. When she began her university studies, she thought she should get As as she had in the past. When she got her first essay back it was only a B+. As she returned to her room she found herself engaged in the following dialogue: "I really blew this one. I thought I was bright but maybe I have been fooling myself. Now I am in the big leagues and that's what counts. Probably the reason I got the grades I did in high school was because I was one of those polite kind of people who teachers reward for being nice. With those grades I will never be able to get into Med school. I probably shouldn't even be here. All these people are much smarter than I am. Maybe I should quit at the end of this year."

When Mary was asked to analyze her adversity into the three components described above she offered the following.

Adversity: "I want to go into medicine but I don't think I will be able to get into Med School."

Belief: "I am not as smart as I thought I was."

Consequence: "I feel awful and wish I could drop out of the university."

If we look carefully at her inner dialogue, we see that it too contains all the elements of a pessimist. The failure leads to an explanatory style that is *permanent* (I can't get the grades I think I need), *pervasive* (I will never get those grades), and *personal* (I lack the ability to get good grades).

Keeping a Record of Your Adversities

If you want to determine if you are prone to pessimistic thinking and might like to change your think-ing style, you should collect some examples of adversity for the next couple of days or until you have at least five examples of adversity. There are many examples that all of us experience from time to time such as: someone not returning your phone call, someone not returning something you loaned them, discovering that you lost your parking stall because your check was misplaced, discovering that someone dented your car and did not leave a note or contact you, getting a poor mark on a test, not being able to get a course that you need to graduate, finding your bicycle has been stolen, discovering that the dry cleaner damaged your favorite coat, finding that your bank made a mistake and as a result one of your checks bounced.

Once you have collected your examples, write down your interpretation or explanation (beliefs), followed by your feelings (consequences). Analyze these examples to see if they reflect a pessimistic thinking style. You may discover from your analysis that your style is not completely pessimistic but that it has elements of pessimism.

I deliberately chose two examples in which the two people responded to an adversity with a pessimistic thinking style. You may well find that you are inconsistent, which is the way most people respond.

Step 2: Distraction and Disputation (D) and Energization (E)

Although Jeff's and Mary's stories are fairly dramatic, they are not that unusual. Having friends is important to people and doing well in college is important to people. As a result, people often respond quite dramatically to adversities when these domains of their lives are threatened.

Seligman suggests there are two ways of dealing with pessimistic thinking: distraction and disputation. If we don't distract ourselves or if we don't dis-

(continued on next page)

PRACTICAL APPLICATION 11.1

How to Become an Optimist: The ABCDE Method
of Acquiring an Optimistic Explanatory Style (continued)

pute our thinking, we are inclined to ruminate. As I indicated in the previous chapter, one of the worst things that people can do is allow themselves to ruminate about such events.

Distraction means you try to think of something else or simply get involved in something else. Some time ago, Ellis suggested that people should simply say "No" or "Stop" when they do not want to think about something. This has proven to be a fairly effective way of eliminating unwanted thoughts. You should feel free to say "No" or "Stop" out loud or to write these words in bold letters on a card and put it in front of yourself. After you have practiced saying "No" or "Stop" you will find that you can indeed stop some of this negative thinking.

Disputation involves learning how to argue with yourself. I have found on many occasions that when I start to tell people my interpretation of an adversity, I realize I have blown things out of proportion. Even when I don't immediately recognize that I am overreacting (taking an unduly pessimistic view), my friends will point this out to me. Disputation means learning how to argue with yourself. There are four questions that you need to learn to ask yourself.

1. What evidence do I have for my interpretation? When Jeff was asked what evidence he had that he couldn't make friends, he could only cite this one example. The same thing for Mary. This was a one-shot deal.

2. What alternative interpretations are there? As it turned out, the reason Chris was not there when Jeff arrived was that he left in a hurry because his mother was ill. Chris's roommate failed to pass that information along, thinking that Jeff knew that Chris's mother had been ill. Mary found out that the best mark for that particular paper was a B+. It had been standard practice of this particular professor to give low grades on the first paper to get rid of the cockiness that he perceived characterized new students.

Often there are other explanations, and before you jump to a conclusion you should investigate this possibility.

3. What are the implications for me if I take this position? Another way of saying this is to ask the question "Even if my belief is correct, what does it mean?" The point of asking this question is to *decatastrophize*. People need to ask themselves, "Is it really that important?" When Jeff was asked to think about the implications he began to realize that life was not over just yet. So what if Chris is irresponsible? Surely there are a lot of people out there like the ones he knew in his hometown. He always had people who would jump at the chance of going with him in his Jeep. When Mary was asked to consider the implications of her adversity, she too decided things weren't as bad as they initially looked. Indeed, she knew she had worked as hard as she could have. Further, she had from time to time thought she might like to pursue her interest in the arts. She had often thought that pursuing a career in arts would be far more exciting, even if she would likely be poor.

4. How useful is my belief? Life is not always fair, nor does it always work out as we plan. It would be nice if things were perfect, if people always did what we wanted them to do, if life worked out just as we had planned. But how realistic is that? Much of the excitement in life comes from the unexpected. Jeff began to realize as the year progressed that people were more competitive at the university than at his high school. They were also less tolerant or less interested in some of his more rural ways of having fun. Others found him fresh and sincere. When asked about Jeff, one person said "Jeff's a genuine article." The friends he developed turned out to be far more interesting and diverse than Jeff had anticipated. Chris, he discovered, was a nice person but someone who lacked imagination. Mary learned that good grades were tougher to get than she had thought.

"Everybody is smart here," she concluded. She began to discover that by using her social skills she could get the help and guidance she needed to rise to the top. By the end of the year she was close to being a straight-A student. Because she asked so many questions she was offered a summer job as a research assistant by one of her professors. Her professor said to her, "I like you because you aren't afraid to ask tough questions."

Energization (E)

Energization involves summarizing your thoughts and actions and planning where you will go next. It is important that you gain some degree of closure so that you can put this event behind you and move ahead. This will help to close the door to further rumination as well as set the stage for further adaptive actions. You might like to view energization as an internal pep talk in which you are your own coach.

Let me return to the two people we discussed earlier so you can see what their finished ABCDE records look like. In telling their stories I went beyond the particular incident so you would have a better feel for these people. Therefore, remember that the record that I am showing you occurred shortly after they experienced their adversity. I want you to pay particular attention to their disputation because this is where you learn to change your thinking.

Jeff's ABCDE Record

Adversity: "I want to develop some friendships but I haven't been able to do so."

Belief: "I lack the ability to make friends."

Consequence (feeling): "I am feeling more lonely than ever."

Disputation: "I was disappointed when I found out that Chris had gone home and was upset that he hadn't called me (evidence). He probably didn't realize how important it was to me (alternative). The fact that he didn't call was inconsiderate of him, but there may be some explanation (alternative). I really shouldn't let one event get me so upset (usefulness). It is not as though this is the last person in the world (implications). I think I have a pretty good record for making friends (implications)."

Energization. "There will undoubtedly be more opportunities for making friends this coming week. Who knows, I might be able to meet someone tonight if I go to the local coffee house or possibly the bar. I hate going by myself but maybe it is time to put aside my pride and admit that I am lonely. I can't be the only person at this university who is feeling lonely tonight. Surely there is nothing wrong in admitting that you are lonely."

Mary's ABCDE Record

Adversity: "I want to go into medicine but I don't think I will be able to get into Med School."

Belief: "I am not as smart as I thought I was."

Consequence: "I feel awful and wish I could drop out."

Disputation: "It was a real shock for me to receive a B+ because I always did very well on papers in high school (evidence). I guess I thought that I could put forth the same effort I did in high school and get the same grades (implication). I wonder if I really understood the assignment (alternative). Perhaps the professor was looking for something different (alternative). If worse comes to worse I can pursue one of my other strengths (alternative/usefulness). I really should stick it out a little longer before I decide I don't have the ability (implication). I may be working myself into a 'snit' over nothing (usefulness)."

Energization. "The first thing I must do is make an appointment with my professor so I can get his honest appraisal. I have heard for years that it is much tougher to get As at the university than in high school. I know I can put forth more effort if that is

(continued on next page)

PRACTICAL APPLICATION 11.1

How to Become an Optimist: The ABCDE Method
of Acquiring an Optimistic Explanatory Style (continued)

what's required. I've always been good at asking questions, so now it is time to make use of those skills."

Catastrophize versus decatastrophize

These two examples illustrate how people often jump to conclusions or *catastrophize*. When we catastrophize we see the worst case scenario. Disputation serves, among other things, to *decatastrophize*. This is important because it allows us to think about other al-

ternatives and eventually to think about positive ways of producing the results we want. The world is not always as we would like it to be or as we planned it. Armed with a sense of openness and a willingness to learn, we can often succeed in ways that we had not expected or planned.

For a more detailed discussion of how to become an optimist, read Martin E. P. Seligman's book entitled *Learned Optimism*.

Snyder's Definition of Optimism and Hope

Snyder et al. (1991) define hope as being based on two major elements. First, they argue that hope is fueled by the perception of successful *agency* related to goals. That is, people have a sense they can attain future goals, perhaps by using good goal-setting procedures or perhaps through new learning, because they were able to attain goals in the past using those means. Note that this is a very generalized belief. In fact, it all boils down to a belief in oneself. This belief might be summarized by the saying "Where there is a will there is a way." Second, they argue that hope is based on the perception that there are *pathways* available to attain those goals. You can believe in yourself but you need a sense that there are pathways. More specifically, they argue that people who are characterized by hope believe they can generate those paths. They may believe, among other things, in their own creativity. In Chapter 12 I will present a motivational interpretation of creativity.

Snyder et al. conceptualize the relationship between *agency* and *pathways* as reciprocal. On the one hand there is the self-belief that one can attain goals (agency) and on the other hand there is the belief that one can generate the alternatives (pathways) that are needed to achieve those goals. In their theory, these two elements are interdependent because without one

you cannot have the other. They feed on each other, so to speak. Thus, to talk about hope and optimism you need to talk about these reciprocal elements.

They contrast their theory with that of Scheier and Carver whom I discussed briefly in the introduction to this section. Scheier and Carver (1985) argue that outcome expectancies are the best predictors of behavior. They define optimism as a generalized expectancy that good, as opposed to bad, outcomes will generally occur when confronted with problems across important life domains. Snyder et al. argue that putting all the emphasis on outcomes fails to adequately account for behavior.

Empirical Support for the Snyder et al. Hope Model

Hope and negative feedback. According to their position, hope is something that sustains people in the midst of a stressor, such as an obstacle to a goal. This prediction is captured in the saying "When the going gets tough the tough get going." The study involved having subjects imagine themselves having experienced a setback to their efforts to reach a goal (Yoshinobu, 1989). For purposes of this study, subjects were divided into three hope groups (high, medium, and low) and told in the negative feedback conditions that:

Although you have set your goal of getting a B, when your first examination score worth 30% of your final grade is returned, you have received a D. It is now one week after you have learned about the D grade.

After imagining themselves in that situation they were asked to respond to five agency questions on a 7-point scale:

1. How much effort are you exerting to reach your goal (no effort to extreme effort)?
2. When I think about this goal, do I feel energized (not at all to extremely)?
3. How confident are you of reaching your goal (not at all to extremely)?
4. How important is receiving this grade goal to you (not at all to extremely)?
5. What is the probability of reaching this goal (0% to 100%)?

Subjects were also asked five pathways questions which involved listing potential strategies for reaching the grade goal of B.

With respect to the agency measure, the results showed that both medium- and low-hope subjects (especially low-hope students) reported less agency in the negative feedback condition (compared to a no-feedback position). With respect to the pathways measure, the high-hope subjects reported more pathways than medium-hope subjects who in turn reported more pathways than the low-hope students. To summarize, when confronted with a setback or an obstacle, high-hope subjects sustained agency and pathway behaviors whereas low-hope subjects showed decreased agency and pathway behaviors.

Hope and number of goals. The hope model of Snyder et al. (1991) also predicts that people with enhanced goal agency and a sense of pathways to goals would pursue a greater number of goals in their lives. A study of people in their 20s, 30s and 40s found that indeed people who are high in hope tend to have more goals (Langelle, 1989).

Hope and preferred difficulty of goals. The theory of Snyder et al. (1991) also predicts that because high-

hope people have a stronger sense of agency and pathways, they should set more difficult goals. This hypothesis has been tested in two studies (Harris, 1988; Sigmon & Snyder, 1990), and both studies provided clear support that high hope people are more inclined to select difficult tasks. Scheier and Carver's LOT scale was not as good a predictor, consistent with the idea that goal-directed behavior is mediated by the interaction of agency and pathways.

Hope and goal attainment. Do high-hope people actually meet the more difficult goals they set for themselves? This was examined in a study in which students were asked to set a realistic goal for their final grade. The results of this study indicated that: 1) high- as compared to low-hope students said they would get higher grades, 2) they were more successful at attaining those higher grades even when early feedback suggested they might not, and 3) actually did obtain the higher grades they set for themselves (Anderson, 1988).

Personal Control and Optimism

Various psychologists have argued that a sense of personal control is central not only to adjustment but to goal attainment (e.g., Abramson, Seligman, & Teasdale, 1978; Bandura, 1991). Scheier and Carver (1985) have distinguished between personal control and optimism, and have provided considerable data showing that optimism by itself is highly predictive of such things as health. The idea that optimism independent of personal control is a good predictor has not gone unchallenged. It has been suggested that a sense of personal control is critical. To assess this idea, both the optimism scale of Scheier and Carver (1985) and the self-mastery scale of Perlin and Schooler (1978) were examined in a study of symptoms of depression in women. It was concluded from this study that while these two scales are empirically distinct, there is considerable overlap. It appears, on the basis of regression analysis, that the predictive power of the optimism scale comes from its overlap with self-mastery (Marshall & Lang, 1990). In other words, personal control is important.

Taking an Optimistic versus a Threatening View of the World

When I discuss competence (Chapter 13), I will argue, as the cognitive theorists have done, that while optimism is important, feelings of competency, both general and specific, are also important in the achievement of goals. In my view, Scheier and Carver (1985) have done an excellent job of demonstrating the importance of seeing the world as positive. In the previous chapter I pointed out that when people see the world as threatening they are inclined to become fearful and anxious, conditions that are not conducive to positive goal setting. What Scheier and Carver have demonstrated is that when we view the world in positive terms we are inclined to persist. In the chapter on competency I will show that our view of ourselves is also important. When we view the world as positive and ourselves as competent we have reason to not just be optimistic but hopeful. If we only view the world as positive but fail to have a strong sense of competency, we are only optimists. It is no longer enough, I believe, to be just optimistic. We need to have a sense of hope. That can only come from developing our competencies. I will attempt to show how all this fits together in the last chapter.

Summary

Scheier and Carver define optimism as a generalized expectancy that good, as opposed to bad, outcomes will generally occur when we are confronted with problems across important life domains. According to Tiger, optimism not only provides the motivation for acting (engaging in adaptive behavior) but rewards behaviors that have an adaptive function. According to the learning theorists, optimism can be viewed as an acquired thinking style. Seligman has suggested that optimists are people who view (explain) setbacks, failures, adversity, as *temporary, specific to a given situation*, and due to *external* reasons or causes. Evidence for Seligman's theory is extensive. Among other things, the theory has been successful in predicting the success of life insurance salespeople, academic success, and health. Seligman, together with Hollon and Freeman,

had developed a program simply called the ABCDE program, which is designed to change pessimistic thinking styles into more optimistic thinking styles. The center of this program involves getting people to dispute their negative thinking by asking four questions: (1) What evidence do I have for my interpretation? (2) What alternative interpretations are there? (3) What are the implications for me if I take this position? (4) How useful is my belief?

Cognitive theorists such as Snyder et al. have argued that hope involves both a sense of agency and a sense of pathways. They have offered a series of convincing studies to show that, indeed, there is a reciprocal relationship between *agency* and *pathways*. They have shown that their measure of hope, which taps into both agency and pathways, predicts behavior in response to negative feedback, number of goals that people set for themselves, the difficulty of goals they select for themselves, and the attainment of goals. Consistent with the position of Snyder et al., it has been shown that self-mastery is a better negative predictor of depressive symptoms than the LOT measure of optimism.

Belongingness, Attachment, and Community

Maslow argued some time ago that one of the basic needs of humans is the need to love and to belong. In recent years, people have begun to use such words as being attached and even the word community, arguing that humans need to be part of some type of social support system in which they can reach out for help in times of difficulty. The term "community" has come to replace, in many respects, the concept of family. In the past, people lived and grew up in close proximity to their family and could reach out to their families in times of difficulty. Now, as people move away to seek better jobs or to find a better climate, they do not have families nearby. The word "community" is a more inclusive term than "family"; it is a term that includes other support groups such as the church, friends, neighbors, or any other organization that can provide support in times of difficulty (e.g., Peck, 1988).

There is considerable evidence that people who

have good social support systems are less prone to depression and tend to be healthier than people without such social support systems (Sarason, Pierce, & Sarason, 1990). It can be argued that the low depression rate among the Amish, for example, is due to the existence of a highly developed community, and that the high depression rate that has been linked to modern individualism is due to the lack of such a community.

Community has also been linked to self-worth. We know that a sense of self-worth plays an important role not only in people's health but in their achievement strivings. Having a sense of worth seems to come largely from the effects of our efforts on the lives of other people. Mother Teresa, for example, has a strong sense of self-worth which seems to come largely from her efforts to benefit others. Many retired people get a strong sense of self-worth through volunteering their efforts to help others. It has even been shown, as I indicated in Chapter 9, that when people have a pet they are healthier and experience a stronger sense of self-worth.

In this section I want to review some of the results that pertain to the emotions that come from experiencing belongingness, attachment, and community. My purpose is to show that these emotions can, when present, help sustain goal-directed behavior, and when absent can result in depression, poor health, and the absence of motivation to persist. For people who have not yet learned this lesson, it is time to teach them the values of community.

Biological Component

Before discussing Maslow's theory I should point out why I am including it under biological component and why under this section on belongingness. Let me start by pointing out that Maslow's theory is a very global one that covers a wide range of behaviors. It is a theory, nonetheless, which is conceptualized as being based on a set of innate needs. What distinguishes Maslow's theory from other needs theories is the idea that they are organized, without the benefit of any particular experiences, in a hierarchical fashion. Although parts of his theory could be presented more appropriately under one or more of the other headings in this chapter or

even other chapters, I decided to include much of it here because Maslow was one of the first psychologists to emphasize the importance of belongingness and love needs. Since his theory makes more sense, at least to me, when it is presented as whole rather than in parts, I have decided to include it here.

Maslow's Need-Fulfillment Model

Abraham Maslow (1970) posits that humans are born with a set of needs that not only energize but direct behavior. He argues that these needs are organized in a hierarchical fashion whereby needs lowest in the hierarchy must be satisfied first. (The hierarchy is upside down in the sense that the needs at the bottom have first priority. Maslow diagrams the need hierarchy as a pyramid in which emergence of "higher," more sophisticated needs, such as esthetic needs, rests on the base provided by the fulfillment of "lower" needs, such as hunger and thirst.) These needs dominate the person's attention until they are satisfied. When these "basic" needs have been satisfied, the next set of needs in the hierarchy comes to exert its influence. As before, these needs come to dominate the person's attention. And so the process continues. Eventually, if all the basic needs have been satisfied, the person will reach the top of the hierarchy. Let's begin, however, by starting at the bottom of the hierarchy.

Physiological needs. Humans must satisfy a number of basic physiological needs. For example, they must eat, drink, control their temperature, and ingest certain nutrients in order to live and function normally. Since failure to remedy an imbalance in any of these areas would disrupt normal functioning and eventually result in death, it is critical for the person to attend to such states of imbalance as soon as possible. From an evolutionary point of view, therefore, it makes good sense that a person should become preoccupied with such need states. That humans do become preoccupied with such physiological need states has been well documented. For example, in Chapter 5, I referred to research that clearly showed that men on semi-starvation diets spent much of their waking and sleeping time thinking about food. In a very fundamental sense, all other needs were secondary. These men showed little interest even in such basic motives as sex, let alone in improving their cognitive skills.

Safety needs. Maslow says that once these basic physiological needs have been satisfied, the person comes to focus on another class of needs—"safety needs." Safety needs, it can be argued, are also basic in that failure to take adequate measures to guard one's safety could result in harm or even death. However, safety needs are secondary to the basic physiological needs. If safety needs took precedence over the physiological needs, we might not venture forth to find the food and water necessary to our survival. For many animals, the satisfaction of physiological needs entails risks. Venturing into unknown territory in pursuit of food or venturing to the watering hole has obvious risk qualities.

For humans, safety comes from knowing about our environment and making it predictable. Although children may look to their parents for their own safety, safety for adults comes from making the environment as orderly, predictable, and lawful as possible. In such an environment one can then pursue one's other needs without constant fear that something or someone will threaten one's safety. Children, Maslow argues, have a strong need for things to be orderly and predictable within their environment. It is within such an environment that they can explore and learn.

Neurotic people are in many ways like the fearful child. They are typically anxious, always afraid that something dreadful will happen to them. Because they are preoccupied with the vague feeling that something dreadful will happen, they are preoccupied with making the world safe. It appears that they have adopted a strategy, Maslow argues, of using rigid and often stereotyped behaviors as a means of assuring themselves that the world is indeed orderly and predictable and therefore safe. Because of this preoccupation with safety, they cannot respond to the new or novel in their world. They are "fixated," to use a psychoanalytic term, at the level of satisfying safety needs.

Belongingness and love needs. If both the physiological and safety needs are fairly well gratified, Maslow says, love, affection, and belongingness needs will emerge.

Although there is little scientific information about belongingness needs, they are a common theme in books, poems, songs, and plays. One need only look around to see how many humans gather into groups at coffee breaks or lunchtime. Maslow theorizes that the tendency to join organizations is often motivated by the desire to belong. When people have been separated from other people for some time, they often have a strong need to engage in some type of social exchange. The family unit seems to be held together, in large part, by a need to belong. If that unit is broken by divorce, for example, all members of the unit seem to suffer stress. Bouts of loneliness and depression are common not only for the spouses but for the children as well.

That belongingness needs are not as fundamental as safety and physiological needs has been shown in a variety of contexts. There are many examples of people risking their lives for people they love and even for people who are complete strangers. There are many examples of people who give money or work hard to preserve organizations that provided them help, support or a sense of community at one time in their lives—organizations such as universities, churches, social clubs, and community organizations. Attempts to maintain the family or to maintain family relationships have characterized humans from the beginning of history. It is in their relationships to other people that many people find meaning in life.

Esteem needs. All people have a need or desire to have a good opinion of themselves. Maslow suggests that there are two subsidiary sets. First, there are the desires for strength, achievement, adequacy, mastery, and competence. Second, there is the need for reputation and prestige, status, fame, glory, dominance, recognition, attention, importance, dignity, or appreciation. Satisfaction of the esteem needs, Maslow argues, leads to feelings of self-confidence, worth, strength, and capacity, together with the feeling of being useful. Failure to satisfy the esteem needs leads to feelings of inferiority, weakness, and helplessness.

Need for self-actualization. Even if all these needs have been satisfied, Maslow says, we will still experience feelings of discontent and restlessness. Each of us, he argues, is a unique person with unique skills and abilities. To be truly happy, we must do that for which we are uniquely suited. The artist must paint; the musician must make music. Although we may not all be artists, each of us is nevertheless unique and each of us can be creative in our own way. Therefore, Maslow argues, each of us must search for and find that uniqueness so that we may experience satisfaction in knowing and doing that which we as individuals are specially equipped to do.

I will talk more about the need for self-actualization in Chapter 14 when I talk about the importance of the self in the regulation of motivation.

Learned Component

Belonging to a group not only seems to fulfill a fundamental human need, but it helps to promote and sustain a number of important behaviors including health and exploration. Many theorists argue, therefore, that people need to learn to develop friendships and to establish communities in order to assist them in gaining the most happiness they can from their lives. In this section I will review two lines of research which show the importance of belongingness and community. In Practical Application 11.2, I discuss the links between "belongingness" and the immune response.

Social Support Systems and Health

The social support research is analogous to the research on pessimism. When things are going well, the role of social support systems does not seem to be that important. It is when people encounter adversity that social support systems seem to be important (Cohen & McKay, 1984, Taylor, 1990). Specifically, the research shows that people who have a strong social support system (e.g., family and community) tend to recover more quickly than those who do not have that social support system.

Social support is a multifaceted thing. It involves such diverse things as emotional support, informational support, tangible assistance, and appraisal support. It has been argued that different types of support are needed in different types of situations. In tightly knit communities, such as the Amish community, there is a comprehensive network system in which different people within the community provide different types of support when they are needed by the individual.

In this work, David McClelland (1989) has found that affiliative trust, together with a sense of agency, is linked to a strong immune response and good health. In this work, McClelland has examined the role of power, which he has consistently compared with affiliative trust. His research indicates that people with a strong power motive are very susceptible to a decreased immune response and subsequent health disorders, whereas people with a strong affiliative trust have a much stronger immune response and fewer health disorders. While it is not altogether clear why the power motive leads to a lowered immune response, his findings that strong affiliative trust leads to a stronger immune response is consistent with a growing body of data which indicates that people with good social support systems tend to be healthier.

Social support can be conceptualized as the backup system that people can turn to in times of adversity. The interesting thing about social support systems is that simply perceiving that one has such a system in place is often sufficient to ward off the negative effects that often come with adversity. It has long been suggested in the health literature that beliefs about one's ability to control play a significant role in averting or buffering the effects of adversity. The belief that one has a support system in place may give people that sense of control that would explain why they bounce back from adversity even when they do not fully access or make use of that support system. Attachment theory addresses this question more directly (Taylor, 1990).

Attachment Theory

Attachment theory suggests that the degree of security and confidence that we feel determines such things as our willingness to explore, learn, and take on new challenges. Attachment theory suggests that when people develop secure attachments (mainly with their mothers) they see the world as less threatening, less hostile, and as a result they are less vulnerable to adversity (Ainsworth, Blehar, Waters, & Wall, 1978; Bowlby 1969, 1973, 1980).

Some adherents of attachment theory have suggested that we need to have someone believe in us in order for us to believe in ourselves. According to this idea, we do not simply develop self-confidence on our own and through our own accomplishments, but we also need some form of external (social) validation.

Attachment theory has addressed the question of where individual traits such as self-confidence come from and how they are maintained. While attachment theory emphasizes the role of parents in the development of such traits, it acknowledges that other attachments later in one's life can provide the basis for feelings of security. It may be, for example, that in later childhood we develop a strong attachment to a teacher or perhaps to a coach, and that from such an attachment we develop a sense of security. In this regard, mentors can and often do provide a secure home base for people venturing out into the world. In times of difficulty the mentor often provides the emotional and informational support that people need to carry on in the face of adversity. The bottom line is that people are important to us in times of adversity.

Cognitive Component

There is an extensive body of research which shows that how we think about life, our beliefs, our attitudes, and our values play an important role in determining such things as our physical and psychological health. In this section I will confine my discussion to a couple of lines of research that have had a great deal of impact on how we think about the role of belongingness, attachment, and community.

Health and the Commitment to Family and Values

Suzanne Kobasa's work on the hardy personality has received a great deal of attention in the psychological literature because the hardy personality enjoys good health and is resistant to stress. The majority of the ev-

idence seems to indicate that the effects are due to their cognitions. Specifically, it is the way hardy people appraise their interactions with the environment. Hardy people not only see the world as less threatening but they see themselves as more capable of dealing with stressful events.

As I indicated earlier, people with a hardy personality are characterized by control, commitment, and challenge (Kobasa, 1979a, 1979b, 1982). When people refer to Kobasa's work they often fail to emphasize the fact that her definition of commitment goes beyond just commitment to self and work, as people often like to emphasize, but it also encompasses commitment to family and values. As I have already indicated, we know that the family can and often is a source of social support that buffers stress (see Taylor, 1990). Values, perhaps more than anything else, provide people with a sense of belongingness and community. Values are at the heart of being part of something that is larger than oneself, something that has meaning and purpose.

Many health psychologists are beginning to recognize the importance of creating an environment in which people can experience a sense of community (e.g., Kaplan, 1990; Stokols, 1992). While such health psychologists acknowledge that an individual's attitude (e.g., being positive and optimistic) plays an important role in promoting good health, they also emphasize the role community plays in creating a climate for health. In particular, they emphasize the importance of creating environments in which there is strong *social cohesion* (Stokols, 1992).

Mindfulness and Health

Ellen Langer (1989) has don ? a great deal of work on health, especially health in older people. Her work emphasizes the importance of becoming more mindful. She has shown that when you make people more mindful, they enjoy better psychological and physical health. Becoming mindful means, among other things, becoming actively involved in making plans and making decisions. It means creating new distinctions so that it is possible to think more clearly about what is happening. It means breaking out of old ways of thinking (stereotypes and traditions) and developing new ways of thinking (generating new alternatives). It means being open to new information and new experiences. It means increasing awareness of what one needs to do to become happy and hopeful.

Many older people live their lives mindlessly. They continue to do the same thing they have done for years. They do things out of habit rather than asking "why?" or "what other alternatives are there?" As the world changes, they continue to do the same things or think the same way. It is important for people to become aware of what makes them happy and what they can do to make their lives more interesting and challenging. I know a woman in her nineties who is a very mindful person. Her guiding phrase is "to savor every moment of life." In order to realize that goal she works very hard to make each day a very special one. She starts by asking herself what she can do to make that day a special day. It may be going for a walk, talking with friends, reading a new book or savoring a poem, cooking something special, or writing a letter to her family or friends. Often she spends several days in advance planning how to make a special day happen. It may be making plans to have a group of people over for tea or coffee. It may be reading a book that she plans to discuss at her reading club. It may be setting aside some time to attend her painting class to improve her painting skills. It may mean calling to volunteer for a luncheon at her church. She does not wait for things to happen. She makes things happen.

In the chapter on stress, I referred to a study by Langer and Rodin (1976) that bears directly on the relationship of being mindful and health. Based on the observation that staff in nursing homes tend to make virtually all the decisions for the residents and assume responsibility for routine things as watering plants, cleaning rooms, telling the residents where to entertain their family and friends, and what movies to watch, it occurred to them that this would be an ideal place to study what happens when people are forced to become more mindful and responsible. When the residents were evaluated eighteen months later, having been given responsibility for routine activities, they found that residents forced to make decisions were more ac-

tive, vigorous, and sociable. More compelling perhaps, was the finding that the health of the experimental group improved, while the health of the control group worsened. Not only was the experimental group more healthy, the death rate was half that of the control group. Clearly, making the residents more mindful had a powerful effect on their well-being.

Summary

Maslow argued some time ago that one of the basic needs of humans is the need to belong and the need to be loved. Attachment and community are two other words often used to describe these needs. The need to belong and the need to be loved was viewed by Maslow as a need that was in the middle of a hierarchy of needs—above physiological and safety needs and below esteem and self-actualization needs.

There is a great deal of evidence that people with strong social support systems (e.g., family and community) tend to get sick less often and recover more rapidly than people without such a support system. Social support is a multifaceted thing. It involves emotional support, informational support, tangible assistance, appraisal support. David McClelland has found that affiliative trust, together with a sense of agency, is linked to a strong immune response and good health, whereas strong power needs are associated with a decreased immune response and health disorders.

Attachment research suggests that the degree of security and confidence people feel determines such things as their willingness to explore, learn, and take on new challenges. When we develop secure attachments (mainly with our mothers) we see the world as less threatening, less hostile, and as a result we are less vulnerable to adversity. Attachment theory emphasizes the role of parents in the development of traits such as self-confidence, although it also acknowledges that other attachments later in life can also provide the basis for feelings of security. The theory suggests that people are particularly important to us in times of adversity.

Research has indicated that how we think about life, our beliefs, our attitudes, and our values play an important role in determining physical and psychological health. Kobasa has suggested that commitment is

PRACTICAL APPLICATION 11.2

Belongingness and the Immune Response

When humans experience adversity several powerful neurohormones are released, including catecholamines, corticosteroids, and endorphins. These chemicals in turn alter the immune function. Corticosteroids exert a powerful immunosuppressive effect. In order to counteract this effect, steroids are often used—especially in connection with allergic reactions like asthma and hay fever, auto-immune disorders like rheumatoid arthritis, and to suppress rejection of transplanted organs. Endorphins also lead to an immunosuppressive effect. In one study with rats it was shown that when rats were delivered brief electrical shocks to trigger endorphin release, their tumor fighting ability was reduced. In another study it was shown that exposure to uncontrollable shock suppressed the ability of the T-cells to multiply when they were later stimulated to do so (see Maier, Laudenslager, & Ryan (1985). How are the catecholamines involved? It appears that when the catecholamines get depleted, endorphins are released. This means that when people get depressed and their catecholamine levels go down, endorphin activity goes up, which in turn shuts down the immune system (Angell, 1985). This research suggests that anything which leads to a reduction in the catecholamines, such as drugs, could make us susceptible to disease.

Several studies have linked the onset and course of virus infections to stress-altered immune function. A study that examined the incidence of oral herpes found that recurrence of oral herpes was linked to increased stressful life events, daily hassles, and anxiety. It has also been shown that loneliness and mild-life stress can trigger decreased immune cell activity (see Ornstein & Sobel, 1985).

There is growing evidence that people can learn to improve their immune function and thereby prevent disease. It has been shown, for example that relaxation training can improve immune function.

There is even some evidence that hypnosis together with imagery may help to increase immune function (see Taylor, 1990).

Some of the most striking evidence, however, is that which links immune function to the emotions of belongingness and community. There is considerable data which show that stressful life events, especially the death of a spouse, result in an impaired immune response that has been linked to death. People who have good social support systems when they experience a stressful life event, however, often show fairly rapid recovery. In commenting on the idea that the immune system shuts down when people perceive they are no longer a viable or useful part of a social system, Ornstein and Sobel (1987) state:

> And conversely, a solid and stable connection to a larger social group, or to humanity in general, may have the opposite result: improved resistance because the person is probably more valuable as a member of a group. From our speculative viewpoint this may be one reason why almost all societies have developed conventions emphasizing the same virtues and why there is such an emphasis in most religions upon caring for others, being generous to others and serving them. Perhaps one of the many reasons is that doing so is not only helpful to the entire community but also to the health of the donor (p. 52).

The subtitle of their article states: "People with a strong sense of belongingness have minds that are better adaptive to preventing disease" (p. 48). Many of us who have been raised in a society that promotes individualism characterized by self-reliance need to become more aware of the value of belongingness, not only for our psychological health but for our physical health.

important, not only to work and the self but to family and values. Health psychologists are beginning to recognize the importance of creating an environment in which people can experience a sense of community. Ellen Langer has done a great deal of work on health which emphasizes the importance of becoming more mindful.

Recent research indicates that the mind triggers the release of certain chemicals which affect the immune function. Experiencing adversity, for example, triggers the release of several powerful neurohormones including catecholamines, corticosteroids, and endorphins. These chemicals alter the immune function. People can improve their immune function and thereby prevent disease by engaging in stress reducing activities such as relaxation training. Hypnosis together with imagery has been shown to help increase the immune function. It has been suggested that "Individuals with a strong sense of belongingness have minds that are better adaptive to preventing disease."

Empathy and Altruism

The emotions of empathy and altruism are often treated together because feelings of empathy often lead to helping. While psychologists have assumed for some time that caring grew out of an egocentric orientation, there is now a great deal of evidence to suggest that when we feel empathy for others we are capable of caring for them not just for our own sake but for theirs (Batson, 1990). As I have indicated elsewhere, there is a growing trend in psychology to acknowledge that we are social animals living in a social arena. We not only need other people for our own health and survival but we need them for the survival of our children. Moreover, if we don't care for others, the likelihood of our species becoming extinct could increase markedly. The study of empathy and altruism is beginning to emphasize more and more the degree to which we are social beings who need each other for a wide variety of reasons, including physical, psychological and survival-related reasons. It has been suggested, for example, that without others our lives often seem meaningless and incomplete. In other words, we are psychological beings who find meaning in our rela-

tionships with others. Because fo space considerations, I will deal only with empathy.

Definition of Empathy

While the literature on empathy has failed to agree on a single definition, there are three important qualities that various lines of research in this area have identified as characterizing empathy: 1) knowing what another person is feeling, 2) feeling what another person is feeling, and 3) responding compassionately to another person's distress (see Levenson & Ruef, 1992). The third characteristic implies that this is an active as opposed to a passive emotion. That is, people are inclined to behave prosocially when this motive is aroused.

Biological Component

Various writers have argued that because empathy was important for our survival, not only as individuals but as a species, we had to learn to communicate rapidly and accurately. As a result, it has been suggested that our central nervous system evolved a neural system or neural substrate that made it possible for us to quickly and effectively communicate (e.g., Brothers, 1989). While some writers have emphasized the role of facial expression to make this communication possible (e.g., Izard), others have suggested that there is a shared physiological substrate for empathy that involves more than just facial expression. Recent evidence, for example, indicates that the ability to accurately detect empathy is linked to physiological characteristics of the organism. It has been shown in one study that accuracy ratings of another person's positive emotions were correlated with low cardiovascular arousal (Levenson & Ruef, 1992). This suggests that we can become sensitized to the feelings of others when we are not ourselves threatened.

Learned Component

Despite the fact that people can be and often are very accurate in determining the emotions of other people under certain circumstances, there are wide individual differences when it comes to this ability. While some of these differences may be due to physiological states such as arousal, it has been suggested that other factors need to be considered. One of these is competing motives and the other is learning.

Power and empathy. Kenneth Clark (1980), in discussing the question of empathy, has argued that power drives tend to block empathy. The person loses the ability to feel the experiences, joys, anxieties, hurt, or hunger of others as though they were his or her own. This, Clark argues, is the basis of social tensions, conflicts, violence, terrorism, and war. He maintains that humans can be trained to become more empathetic. Such training, he suggests, will tend to counteract the mere animalistic determinants of behavior, such as the tendency to dominate and control people.

Role playing, modeling, and empathy. People often learn what it means to suffer when they or someone close to them have experienced some misfortune themselves. As a result of such experiences they are more sensitive to the feelings of others and seem to automatically react with greater care and concern to similar plights.

It has been suggested that people can and need to learn to become more prosocial (e.g., Kanfer, 1979). How might you train someone to be more empathetic in the absence of inflicting harm on them or their friends? One fairly simple way would be to get people to model or role-play. By modeling or assuming the role of victim, for example, people can often learn to experience what it feels like to experience pain, a hardship, adversity, and so forth. Humans have a remarkable capacity for simulating emotions. Simply assuming the facial expression often seems to be sufficient. This is consistent with the theory of Izard, who has argued that there is a positive feedback loop between facial expressions, a neural substrate for that facial expression, and the emotion that accompanies the activation of that neural substrate. The whole process of sensitization is thought to result from periodic activation of a sensory or neural system. By simply simulating a facial expression we can trigger that system. Like any other part of our body that we expect to work properly, we need to use (exercise) it periodically. Otherwise it will react like a muscle that we haven't

used for some time; it won't work very well. As a general rule, whenever we fail to activate a system, it becomes harder to activate that system in the future. It is simply the law of disuse. With repeated activation, on the other hand, the system will react quickly and consistently when the situation is appropriate (see Cacioppo, Uchino, Crites, Snydersmith, Smith, Berntson, & Lang, 1992).

Cognitive Component

Justice Motive and Empathy

In recent years there has been growing interest in the question of why a person will at one time exhibit deep compassion for someone who is suffering and at another time be indifferent to equal or greater suffering (Lerner, 1977). One of the themes that has emerged is that people perceive that certain forms of suffering are deserved and others are not. This *deserving*, or *just world* hypothesis suggests that people are, under certain conditions, responsible for their own fate. Curiously, one of the byproducts of that thinking style is to sometimes not be empathetic.

The justice motive and suffering. If people have a need to believe that they live in a world where people generally get what they deserve, how will they respond to other people's suffering? The justness of any person's fate has implications for one's own fate. If other people can suffer undeservedly, then the possibility arises that I, too, can suffer undeservedly. One way of dealing with this problem is to compensate the victim. Another way is to convince oneself that the victim deserves to suffer (Lerner, 1970). Even though we may believe in a just society, we generally acknowledge that there are exceptions. A person can have a "bad character" or can make a mistake. As a consequence, the suffering he or she might experience would simply be due to factors that lie outside the realm of justice.

Extensive research has been carried out to examine how people respond to the suffering of others (see Lerner & Miller, 1978). In the original study, Lerner and Simmons (1966) had subjects view a videotape of a person showing pain who, they were led to believe, was being shocked for making errors. In one condition (compensated condition), subjects could compensate the person by reassigning her to a condition in which she would receive money instead of shocks. In another condition (uncompensated condition), they were simply informed that the shocks would continue. In a third condition (martyr condition), they were told she had allowed herself to be talked into being shocked. When the subjects were asked to rate the person, they tended to rate the compensated subject as most attractive and the martyr subject as least attractive. According to justice theory, the reason a person tends to degrade a victim who is suffering is the person's need to reassure himself or herself that the world is just. Unattractive people can be considered to have brought on their own problems. Therefore, if a person is suffering, he or she is perceived to be unattractive.

Several conditions modify the tendency to *derogate* a victim (Lerner & Miller, 1978). First, if the victim can be viewed as behaviorally causing his or her own suffering (making a mistake, exercising poor judgment), there is not the same tendency to derogate the victim. In other words, no injustice has occurred. Second, if the victim is highly attractive or enjoys high status, there is a greater tendency to find fault with the victim's actions rather than derogate the victim's character. Third, if the observer expects to be in a situation similar to that of the victim, the tendency to derogate the victim is decreased. Empathy appears to emerge under this condition. Fourth, if the victim was in a situation in which the chances of escaping were equal for two persons, the tendency to derogate is also decreased. Apparently, the observer feels that someone had to be the victim, and since self-interest prevailed, the victim's suffering was not his or her fault. This is related to the third condition, in which the prospect of being a victim tends to elicit empathy.

Summary

While for many years psychologists assumed that caring grew out of an egocentric orientation, there is now a great deal of evidence that when we feel empathy for others we are capable of caring for them not just for our own sake but for theirs.

It has been argued that empathy is important for our survival and that at one point in our evolutionary history we needed to evolve ways of communicating rapidly. To this end, it has been suggested that we evolved the ability to communicate via facial expression as well as through other physiological indicators of emotion.

It has been suggested that competing motives, such as the power motive, can block the empathy response. It has also been suggested that people can become sensitized to certain emotions by periodically triggering that emotion. According to Izard's theory, it should be possible to trigger that emotion merely by simulating the correct facial expression.

The *deserving* or *just world* hypothesis suggests that people are, under certain conditions, responsible for their own fate. Within this framework it is possible to explain why people sometimes derogate victims and at other times show care and concern.

Main Points

1. Goal-congruent emotions facilitate and sustain the attainment of personal goals.

2. According to the principles of hedonism, organisms are motivated to seek pleasure and avoid pain. Happiness is defined by hedonists as maximizing pleasure.

3. The discovery of reward pathways in the brain provided the mechanism that many people felt gave the concept of hedonism a sound scientific basis.

4. Reward pathways are activated by the release of norepinephrine and (probably) dopamine.

5. Cognitive theorists argue that what differentiates emotions is not affect but core relational themes that result from our appraisal of our interactions with the world.

6. Lazarus suggests that the core relational theme of happiness is "Making reasonable progress towards the realization of a goal."

7. While happiness has been conceptualized by cognitive theorists as a means to an end (goal), hedonism has been conceptualized as happiness as an end (goal).

8.   Some activities are characterized only by their ability to produce hedonistic feelings (*hedonic enjoyment*), while others are characterized by their ability to produce both hedonic feelings and feelings of self-satisfaction that comes from realizing one's potential (*hedonic happiness*).

9.   Research suggests that norepinephrine is released when organisms make coping responses and that epinephrine is often released together with norepinephrine when the situation is characterized by unpredictability or uncertainty.

10.   Thrill-seeking often involves activities that are characterized by uncertainty or unpredictability.

11.   When people develop the skills they need to cope with a given situation they develop strong feelings of self-efficacy for that and similar tasks. Self-efficacy refers to the sense that a person has that they can effectively deal with an task.

12.   Evidence suggests that people experience more self-satisfaction from making a coping response in a difficult versus an easy task.

13.   Bandura has argued that people do not avoid potentially threatening situations because they experience anxiety and arousal but rather because they fear they will not be able to cope either behaviorally or cognitively.

14.   Both *perceiving that one has behavior coping skills* and *perceiving that one can control one's thinking* play an important role in governing peoples choices of activities and whether or not they will engage in a particular activity.

15.   Both opponent-process theory and arousal theory can account for why people learn to engage in thrill-seeking activities but they fail to deal with the question of how people come to deal with their fears.

16.   Cognitive theorists have argued that in order to understand thrill-seeking behaviors it is necessary to understand how people come to deal with their fears and anxieties.

17.   In certain thrill-seeking activities such as rock climbing, the way people deal with their fears is through the development of behavioral coping skills.

18.   In other thrill-seeking activities such as bungee jumping, people learn to deal with their fears by developing cognitive coping skills.

19.   Optimists and hopeful people have the tendency to view all desired outcomes as attainable.

20.   While pessimists and hopeless people tend to give up in the face of adversity, optimists and hopeful people tend to persist in the face of adversity.

21.   Tiger has argued that optimism not only provides the motivation to act but rewards adaptive behaviors. He has suggested that endorphins are the chemical basis of optimism, and that is from this emotion that hope develops.

22.   A number of researchers conceptualize thinking styles as habits that can be changed.

23.   Seligman has taken the approach that optimism grows out of people's explanatory style. Optimists are people who view (explain) setbacks, failures, adversity, and the like as *temporary, specific to a given situation*, and due to *external* reasons or causes.

24.   Hope, within Seligman's system, involves an explanatory style that is *temporary*, and *specific to a given situation*.

25.   It has been shown that one of the best predictors of success for life insurance salespeople is optimism.

26.   It has been shown that the two major risk factors for poor achievement are pessimism and bad life events (parents separating, family deaths, family job loss).

27.   One study showed that students who did better than expected as predicted by their grades and their SAT scores were optimists.

28.   It has been shown that helplessness training can cause cancer in rats.

29.   Optimists do not age as quickly as pessimists.

30.   In order to become an optimist it has been suggested that people should adopt the ABCDE method. This method involves first identifying *adversities, beliefs*, and *consequences*. Next, people must learn to *distract* and *dispute* their thinking and then to act, which will result in *energization*.

31.   Snyder and associates have defined hope as being based on two reciprocal elements: *agency* and *pathways*.

32.   Support for the theory of Snyder and associates comes from research which has shown that high-hope people sustained both agency and pathways when confronted with a setback or an obstacle, that high-hope people had more goals, that high-hope people set more difficult goals for themselves, and that high-hope people tended to actually meet the more difficult goals they set for themselves.

33. There is good reason to believe that the predictive power of optimism scales may be due to the fact that optimism scales not only measure one's positive outlook, they also measure some aspect of personal control.

34.   Maslow argued some time ago that one of the basic needs of humans is to be loved and to belong.

35.   There is considerable evidence that people who have good social support systems are less prone to depression and tend to be healthier than people without such social support system.

36.   When humans experience adversity several powerful neurohormones are released, including catecholamines, corticosteroids, and endorphins, which have been linked to the immunosuppressive effect.

37.   Belongingness and love needs are one of five groups of needs that Maslow has argued are hierarchically organized.

38.   Research shows that people who have a strong social support system (family, community) tend to recover more quickly than those who do not have that social support system.

39.   Social support is a multifaceted thing. It involves such diverse things as emotional support, informational support, tangible assistance, appraisal support.

40.   Attachment theory suggests that when we develop secure attachments (mainly with our mothers) we see the world as less threatening, less hostile, and as a result we are less vulnerable to adversity.

41.   Many health psychologists have recognized the importance of creating an environment in which people can experience a sense of community or a sense of *social cohesion*.

42.   Three important qualities characterize empathy: knowing what another person is feeling, feeling what another person is feeling, and responding compassionately to another person's feelings.

43.   It has been suggested that because our ancestors needed to communicate quickly and accurately, they evolved facial expression as a means of communicating.

44.   It has been suggested that the power drive blocks empathy.

45.   Various psychologists have suggested that prosocial behaviors can be learned. One method for increasing empathy might be through modeling and role playing.

46.   According to the *just world* hypothesis, there are two ways to deal with injustice: compensate people or convince yourself they deserve what they get. The latter may involve derogation.

47.   Failure to derogate a victim's character occurs when the victim is attractive, when the victim can be viewed as having done something that brought on his or her own suffering, when the person believes he or she might be in a similar situation, and in situations in which the chances of two persons' escaping were equal.

Chapter Twelve

Curiosity, Exploratory Behavior, Play, Sensation Seeking, and Creativity

- What motivates people to explore a new city?
- Is this exploratory behavior learned or unlearned?
- Why do people believe that exploratory behavior is motivated by the curiosity drive?
- What activates the curiosity drive?
- Is the curiosity drive always active, or is it activated only under certain conditions?
- Is play a frivolous activity or is it important for learning and development?
- What is sensation seeking?
- Is the trait of sensation seeking learned or acquired, or is it something we are born with?

- What motivates people to be creative?

- Why is it that people sometimes feel creative and other times they do not?

- Do people have to be inspired in order to be creative or can people be creative at will?

- Are younger people more creative than older people?

Exploratory Behavior

Innate or Learned?

Children in particular like to explore their environment. It is common to see young children taking the pots and pans out of the kitchen cupboard, rummaging through a book of old photos they found in a box in the basement, or to find only the remains of a watch they disassembled but couldn't put back together. Parents often complain that if they left their young children alone, they would empty every cupboard or closet in the house. Many parents find that they must lock certain cupboards, closets, or rooms because children like not only to see and touch but to taste. As our homes are usually filled with all kinds of toxic chemicals, it is necessary to ensure that these chemicals are kept away from children too young to understand that there are dangers associated with exploring the environment.

As children grow up, they begin to explore other areas, such as the neighborhood in which they live. They develop friendships and learn to play games. All of this seems to occur without very much encouragement from their parents. In fact, parents often try to discourage their children from their interest in the contents of closets and cupboards and from wandering too far from home. What motivates this behavior? We often say that such behaviors grow out of a strong curiosity drive. The question that we will deal with in this chapter is what motivates this curiosity drive and what function it ultimately plays in our development. Interestingly, people have not always believed that there is such a thing as a curiosity drive, or that if it did exist, it was not very important. Until fairly recently, people tended to view all important behaviors as developing from such basic drives as hunger and

sex. That is, they believed that the curiosity drive was learned.

The Behaviorist Explanation

The reinforcement of random behavior. How do we come to learn about our environment? Before the 1950s, the behaviorists argued that primary drives, such as hunger, energized the organism to engage in random behavior. When the appropriate goal object was found in the course of such random movements, the drive would be reduced and the behavior that had just preceded the reduction of that drive would be reinforced. The organism would then become more and more efficient at finding the appropriate goal object when a given drive state had been activated. That is, through learning, the organism would come to engage quickly and efficiently in a pattern of movements that would result in the finding of an appropriate goal object.

According to this explanation, exploratory behavior was assumed to be random in the first instance. It became systematic only as a result of learning (reinforcement). Note that according to this explanation, a different pattern of exploratory behavior should occur for each drive state. That is, when you are hungry, you engage in one pattern of responses; when you are thirsty, you engage in another pattern of responses; when you are sexually motivated, you engage in still another pattern of responses; and so forth. In other words, according to the behaviorists of the 1950s, there was no such thing as a generalized curiosity drive. You did not learn for learning's sake. You learned only in order to help you satisfy a more basic (biological) motive system.

The Challenge of the 1950s

Alternation behavior. The behaviorists' explanation of exploratory behavior was challenged in the 1950s by many studies. One group of such studies involved the phenomenon called *alternation behavior*. If you place a rat in a T-maze and allow it to select one of the two arms of the maze, the probability of its selecting either of the two arms of the maze is 50%. If you then remove that animal and immediately give it a second choice, you find that it tends to select the arm of the maze it did not enter on the first trial. This tendency to choose the previously unvisited alternative on the second trial has been referred to as alternation behavior.

The reactive inhibition model. Clark Hull (a behaviorist) attributed alternation behavior to something he called reactive inhibition. Hull (1943) argued that when organisms make a response, some kind of inhibition to that response builds up. For a time, then (until the inhibition wears off), the animal is unlikely to repeat that response. Thus if an animal made a right-turn response on trial 1, it would not be inclined to make that same response on trial 2. Since the only other response it can make in the T-maze is a left-turn response, it would tend to make that response.

The stimulus satiation model. An alternative model suggested that on trial 1, the animal became satiated for the stimulus to which it had just been exposed (Glanzer, 1953). Satiation is like inhibition except that the inhibition is not limited to responses. You could become satiated visually or auditorially or olfactorily and so forth. When we're talking about humans, we tend to use the word *bored*. Murray Glanzer demonstrated that if you changed the color of the walls of the arm of the maze that the animal visited on trial 1, the animal tended to repeat a right-turn or left-turn response, as Figure 12-1a indicates. The dotted lines show where the animal went on trial 2.

The stimulus change model. Were the animals in Glanzer's experiment avoiding a stimulus for which they had become satiated or were they simply approaching a new or different stimulus? William Dember and R. W. Earl (1957) suggested that animals are motivated by change or by stimulation that is novel. In order to determine whether this was the case, Dember (1956) designed an ingenious experiment: he made one of the arms of a T-maze white and the other black, and at the entry to each arm he put a glass panel that prevented the animal from entering. As it could turn neither right nor left, it could not develop reactive inhibition. As the animal saw one white arm and one black arm, it would be satiated equally for black

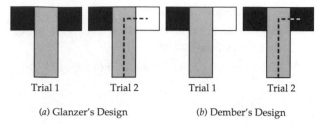

Trial 1   Trial 2   Trial 1   Trial 2

(a) Glanzer's Design   (b) Dember's Design

Figure 12–1. (a) Glanzer's design to test his stimulus satiation hypothesis; **(b)** Dember's design to test his stimulus change hypothesis.

and white at the termination of trial 1. As we shall see, this was an important manipulation. After 10 minutes in the maze the animal was removed, the glass panels were removed, and one of the arms was changed so that both arms were now either black or white. On trial 2, Dember watched to see if the animal entered the changed arm or if its behavior was random. According to the reactive inhibition model, since the animal made no response on trial 1, the probability of entering one of the arms on trial 2 should be 50%. According to the satiation model, since the animal was equally satiated to black and white, the probability of entering one of the two arms should also be 50%. According to the stimulus change model, on the other hand, the animal should enter the changed arm. Dember found, as he had predicted, that his animals entered the changed arm (see Figure 12-1b).

These studies, as well as others that I will discuss shortly, changed forever the way psychologists thought about curiosity and exploratory behaviors. As the animals used in these studies were deprived of neither food nor water, their exploratory behavior had occurred without the activation of some more basic primary drive. The general conclusion, therefore, was that these animals explored because it is the nature of organisms to explore. The motivation for this tendency was assumed to be a curiosity drive that motivates organisms to investigate novel things in their environment.

Other studies of the curiosity drive. Many studies have been conducted to investigate the curiosity drive. At the University of Wisconsin, Robert Butler and Harry Harlow did a number of studies that showed that monkeys have a very strong exploratory drive that is motivated by the visual, auditory, and manipulatory properties of the objects they encounter. Harlow (1953) showed, for example, that monkeys will learn to solve various kinds of mechanical puzzles when no motivation is provided other than the presence of the puzzles. Moreover, the monkeys had a persistent tendency to carry out the solution in a flawless manner. Butler (1953) put monkeys in a room with four windows that they could open to see a toy train, various other objects, or other monkeys. These monkeys spent a great deal of time simply looking at things. The monkeys learned which window provided which kind of stimulation. Thus Butler demonstrated that the curiosity drive could reinforce learning—something that is not surprising now but was important to demonstrate at that time because the behaviorists tended to dismiss the curiosity drive as weak, transient, and not very important in the overall functioning of the individual.

The Human Tendency to Seek Out Variety and Novelty

Children in particular like to seek out new and varied stimulation. If a child is presented with an object he has not previously encountered, for example, and he is in a familiar and secure environment, he will tend to approach the object, visually inspect it, and then begin to interact with it by touching it, holding it, picking it up, tapping it, turning it over, and so on. If there are parts that can be moved or removed, the child is almost certain to discover this fact. After the child has thoroughly investigated the object, his interactions with it begin to wane.

Corinne Hutt (1966) gave children a novel object that had a lever connected to a set of counters so that the child could see the numbers change as she moved the lever. In one condition the children could see the counters move; in another condition the counters were covered. As expected, when the counters were visible, the children spent more time pressing the lever. Also as expected, their interest in the counters diminished with repeated trials.

When a person stops interacting with a novel object, we say that he or she has become satiated. The term *satiated* implies that the person has had enough, that the object is no longer a source of motivation, and that the person has exhausted all the information or entertainment value of the object. Since children often return to objects previously abandoned, it appears that satiation dissipates with time. This is one of the important facts that need to be explained by a theory of curiosity and exploratory behaviors. When children abandon an object, it is usually because they have shifted their interest and attention to other objects, usually objects that are new or ones they have not encountered for a while. Thus, children have a tendency to interact constantly with more and more of the environment.

Cognitive Component

Emergence of the Concept of Complexity

As the studies of the curiosity drive continued, it became very apparent not only that organisms tend to explore things that are novel or different but that they are attracted to things that are complex. One of the important questions that arose out of this research was whether humans are simply attracted to the most complex things in the environment or whether there is some optimal level of complexity that falls short of the greatest complexity possible.

If you assume that organisms are processing the information contained in the stimuli they select, then from an information-processing viewpoint it would make sense for people to attend only to stimuli that provided information they had the cognitive capacity to process. Such an interpretation suggests that children would probably choose less complex stimuli than adults, simply because children have had less experience than adults and therefore they do not have the backlog of knowledge, skills, or cognitive structures to deal with very complex stimuli.

The tendency to select increasingly complex stimuli. One of the first demonstrations of the tendency of humans to respond to increasingly complex stimuli was reported by Robert Earl (1957). He first had children work on block-design puzzles of moderate complexity and then gave them the opportunity to select a new block-design puzzle. The children could choose either more complex or simpler designs. Most selected a design that was somewhat more complex than the design they had just been working on. They did not, for the most part, select either a design that was simpler or a design that was much more complex. This very systematic tendency to select a slightly more complex puzzle indicates that human exploratory behavior is highly systematic. Humans do not, it appears, explore their environment haphazardly.

Earl's findings have been duplicated by Richard May (1963). May had preschool children look at checkerboard designs of moderate complexity. Then they were given the opportunity to look at a pile of simpler or more complex checkerboard designs. May found, as did Earl, that most of the children selected the more complex designs. Arkes and Boykin (1971) have further shown that children who participated in a Head Start program came to prefer more complex stimulation. There have been numerous demonstrations that animals also tend to select more complex stimulation after being exposed to moderate complexity. The fact that a wide variety of animals respond in the same way as humans provides evidence that this tendency is a biological characteristic, not a learned behavior pattern.

Age differences also play a role in the preference for complexity. If humans tend to seek out more and more complex stimulation, it follows that older people should prefer more complex stimulation than younger people. To test this hypothesis, various experiments have used geometrical figures that vary in complexity, as defined by the number of angles and sides. Examples of such figures are shown in Figure12-2. In general, it has been found that older people tend to prefer stimuli of greater complexity (Munsinger & Kessen, 1964; Thomas, 1966).

Summary

Research with animals has indicated that the tendency to explore is motivated by novelty or stimulus change. In fact, a great deal of research indicates that animals are motivated by the opportunity to explore the visual, auditory, tactile, and olfactory properties of objects and that they will learn to do things that make it possible for them to experience the stimulation that comes from interacting with various objects. Work with humans indicates that, like animals, we are motivated by the variety and novelty of objects we encounter. There is considerable evidence that animals and humans are motivated by the complexity of objects. It has been shown that children tend to select increasingly complex objects. Apparently, as children's ability to handle more complex forms of stimulation increases, they have a natural tendency to select more complex stimuli.

Theories of Exploratory Behavior

Dember and Earl's Theory

The results of the studies that I have just reviewed can be readily accounted for by the Dember and Earl theory. Dember and Earl (1957) assume that organisms are motivated to experience optimal complexity. One special and important feature of their theory is their concept of a pacer stimulus or a pacer range. They suggest that an organism becomes accustomed, or habituated, to a certain level of complexity (called an *adaptation level*) and is motivated to explore stimuli that are slightly more complex than this adaptation level. This part of the theory is illustrated in Figure 12-3. The pacer concept is intended to explain why exploratory, curiosity, and play behaviors tend to be systematically directed towards more complex levels of stimulation. Further, the pacer concept is intended to explain why individuals prefer certain stimuli to others. The appeal of the theory is its simplicity. It predicts that individuals will always select slightly more complex stimuli (given that they have had time to adapt to a given level of complexity) and that over time individuals will come to prefer more and more complex stimulation.

The measure of any theory, however, is how well it can account for the research findings. Several tests of the theory have shown that, indeed, many forms of stimulation can be ordered in terms of their psychological complexity and, further, that preferences are systematically related to psychological complexity. For

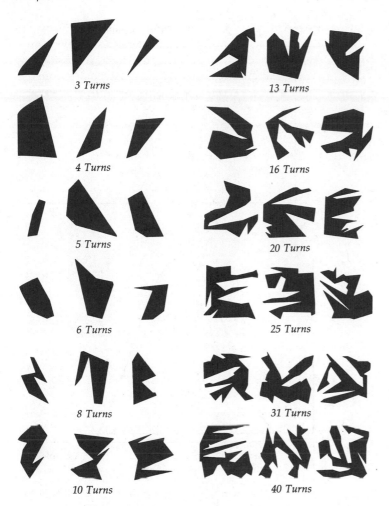

3 Turns

4 Turns

5 Turns

6 Turns

8 Turns

10 Turns

13 Turns

16 Turns

20 Turns

25 Turns

31 Turns

40 Turns

Figure 12–2. The 12 sets of three asymmetrical shapes used by Munsinger and Kessen. (From H. Munsinger and W. Kessen, "Uncertainty, Structure, and Preference." *Psychological Monographs*, 1964, *78*, 1-23. Copyright © 1964 by the American Psychological Association. Reprinted with permission.)

example, preference for auditory stimuli appears to be determined by their complexity (Vitz, 1966a, 1966b), as does preference for visual stimuli (for example, Munsinger & Kessen, 1964; Smith & Dorfman, 1975). In addition, a number of studies have shown that preference for complexity shifts upward as a result of experience with a certain kind of stimulation. For example, Vitz (1966b) found that subjects with greater musical experience rated complex auditory stimuli as more pleasant than other subjects did. Munsinger and Kessen (1964) found that art students preferred more variability than other students. Sackett (1965) found that rhesus monkeys raised in more complex environments preferred more complex stimuli. As I mentioned

earlier, Arkes and Boykin (1971) found that children in a Head Start program significantly increased their preference for complexity.

Berlyne's Theory

Probably the most influential of the theories of exploration was proposed by D. E. Berlyne (1960, 1971). Berlyne's theory is based on the assumption that exploration and play are directed toward the processing of information. He suggested that through exploration and play the individual becomes knowledgeable about its environment. Berlyne further theorized, drawing on a large body of data, that such behaviors are highly

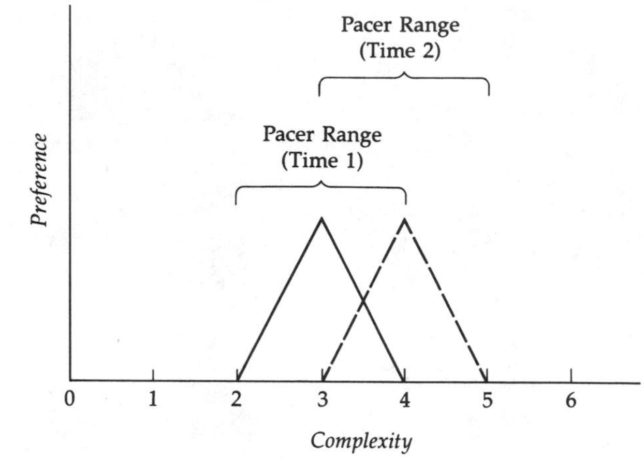

Figure 12–3. According to Dember and Earl's theory, an organism that has adapted to the level of complexity represented by point 2 on the complexity dimension will be inclined to respond only to stimuli enclosed by points 2 and 4, maximum attention being directed toward stimuli at point 3. Interacting with stimuli at point 3 will lead to a new adaptation level corresponding to point 3. As a result, there will be a new pacer range, enclosed by points 3 and 5. Thus, as long as there are stimuli corresponding to those in the pacer range, over time the individual will systematically interact with all stimuli in its environment.

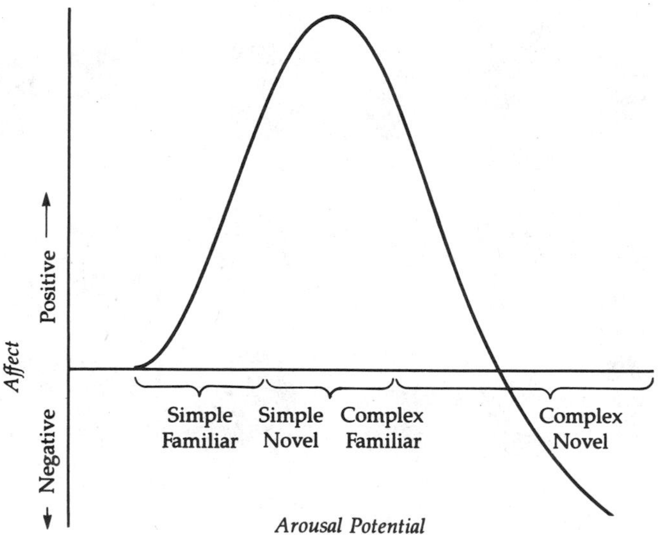

Figure 12–4. The hypothesized relation between affect and the arousal potential of a stimulus as proposed by Berlyne. Note that positive affect is greatest when a stimulus is moderately complex or moderately novel. (From D. E. Berlyne, "Novelty, Complexity and Hedonic Value." *Perception and Psychophysics*, 1970, 283. Copyright © 1970 by the Psychonomic Society, Inc. Reprinted with permission.)

systematic. Animals as well as humans, he thought, respond systematically to events, especially novel events (Berlyne, 1958). The questions to which Berlyne addressed himself were (1) "What motivates the tendency to process information?" and (2) "What governs the tendency to respond systematically to certain stimuli and not others?"

Berlyne (1960) suggested that the basic mechanism underlying exploratory and play behaviors is level of arousal. He proposed that the relation between arousal and hedonic tone can be described as an inverted U-shaped function, such that hedonic tone is greatest

when arousal is moderate (Figure 12-4). He argued that either very low levels of stimulation or very complex stimulation produces low affect, and that high complexity or novelty can even lead to negative affect. According to Berlyne's theory, organisms are motivated to seek out positive affect and avoid negative affect. Therefore, a person who is experiencing low arousal (is in a situation that has low arousal potential) will seek out situations that will increase arousal, while a person who is experiencing high arousal (is in a situation that has high arousal potential) will seek out situations that will lower arousal.

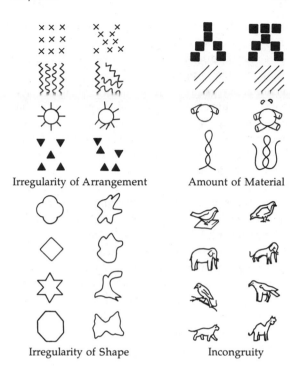

Irregularity of Arrangement   Amount of Material   Heterogeneity of Elements

Irregularity of Shape   Incongruity   Incongruous Juxtaposition

Figure 12–5. Materials of the type used by Berlyne to study collative variables and arousal. (From D. E. Berlyne, "The Influence of Complexity and Novelty in Visual Figures on Orientating Responses." *Journal of Experimental Psychology*, 1958, 55, 289-296. Copyright © 1958 by the American Psychological Association. Reprinted with permission.)

Berlyne's theory assumes that arousal comes from interacting with external stimulation or by exercising internal processes, such as imagining, fantasizing, and thinking. Much of Berlyne's research focused on identifying and classifying those forms or characteristics of stimulation that could produce arousal. After carefully analyzing a large body of research, Berlyne concluded that there is a class of variables associated with arousal, which he called *collative variables*: novelty, degree of change, suddenness of change, surprisingness, incongruity, conflict, complexity, and uncertainty. Figure 12-5 presents examples of stimulus materials illustrating certain collative variables used in Berlyne's research.

Berlyne used the term *collative* to describe these variables because their ability to produce arousal is assumed to depend on the person's comparison of a given stimulus with some "standard" stimulus. Berlyne conceptualized the standard stimulus as some form of memory representation. He suggested that when a person attends to a stimulus, he or she compares that stimulus with other stimuli represented in memory. If the stimulus departs in some way from

other stimuli represented in memory, it should elicit arousal.

How does a standard develop? Berlyne theorized that humans tend to process all the information contained in a stimulus. Processing information, he maintained, is as natural as seeing. He proposed that humans do not simply store a detailed icon but tend rather to abstract essential features of the stimulus. These essential features make up the "standard." Berlyne argued that once all the essential features have been abstracted, the stimulus loses its ability to elicit further attention. The standard then becomes the backdrop against which all new information is processed. When a person attends to a new stimulus, he or she compares its essential features with those of the standard.

The tendency to process new information is assumed to be governed by the ability of the new stimulus to elicit arousal. When a person encounters a new stimulus that departs in some way from the standard, it is assumed that the discrepancy will elicit arousal. The greater the discrepancy, the greater the arousal. If the discrepancy is moderate, it will elicit moderate arousal, and since moderate arousal is pleasurable, the person will, according to the theory, try to maintain contact with the stimulus. However, because organisms are inclined to process the information contained in a stimulus, it is simply a matter of time before the essential features of the new stimulus will be abstracted. As a result, a novel stimulus becomes familiar, a surprising stimulus will lose its ability to elicit surprise, and an incongruous stimulus will become ordinary and predictable. Because it is assumed that organisms are motivated to maintain moderate arousal, the theory predicts that they will be inclined to seek out new stimuli that depart from the standard in order to experience moderate arousal once again. In this way, the organism tends, over time, to learn more and more about different parts of its environment.

According to Berlyne's theory, a stimulus could evoke too much arousal and thus become aversive. Rather than explore such a stimulus, the theory predicts, the individual would tend to terminate contact with the stimulus in order to avoid or reduce negative hedonic tone. This motivational tendency, Berlyne argues, serves an important function. If it is assumed that the ability to process information depends on the existence of certain cognitive structures, then certain stimuli may exceed the individual's ability to abstract the information they contain. Therefore, until the individual has developed the appropriate structures (presumably as a result of interacting with stimuli that can be processed), there is no point in interacting with such stimuli. In short, it is a waste of the individual's time.

To summarize, Berlyne's theory predicts that people and animals are motivated to explore stimuli that contain a moderate amount of new information (novelty). Such stimuli are defined as having a moderate amount of "arousal potential." If an individual attends to them, they will evoke a moderate amount of arousal, which, according to Berlyne's theory, is the optimal level of arousal for producing positive hedonic tone.

Berlyne recognized that organisms could, for a variety of reasons, experience a chronically high level of arousal. Anxiety, for example, is often characterized by high arousal. Such an individual, according to Berlyne's theory, would be less inclined—or not inclined at all—to seek out new and different stimulation. In fact, such an individual might be inclined to seek out very common and familiar stimuli to keep arousal from increasing further.

The idea that external stimulation will simply add to the existing arousal level is an intriguing one that has been subjected to a number of experimental tests. In one experiment, Berlyne, Koenig, and Hirota (1966) initially had rats learn to press a bar in order to experience a certain pattern of light onset/offset. After the animals had become familiar with this pattern, some of them were injected with methamphetamine to increase arousal and some were injected with saline solution (a control condition). In the test phase, the animals had the choice of bar-pressing for the familiar pattern of light onset/offset or for a new pattern. As predicted, the animals given a drug to increase arousal barpressed more for the familiar pattern. These results provide excellent support for the idea that external stimulation adds to the pool of existing arousal and can decrease the exploratory tendency.

Arousal and Esthetics

Berlyne (1971) has suggested that esthetics can, in part, be understood within his arousal framework. He pointed out that art often contains elements of novelty, surprise, incongruity, conflict, complexity, and uncertainty. Accordingly, he set out on a program of research designed to analyze esthetic experiences in terms of the collative variables. A large number of studies have tested Berlyne's ideas. The work of Dorfman (1965) and Smith and Dorfman (1975) illustrates how Berlyne's conceptual framework can account for some esthetic preferences.

Dorfman (1965) constructed six visual stimuli that differed in complexity. Each subject was asked to rank all six in order of preference. Although different subjects preferred different levels of complexity, Dorfman found that preferences systematically decreased on each side of the most preferred stimulus. In other words, he obtained evidence consistent with Berlyne's suggestion of an inverted U-shaped function. The fact that preferences for stimuli differing in complexity could be related to an inverted U-shaped function provides support for Berlyne's suggestion that esthetic preferences are mediated by collative variables.

In a somewhat more complex study, Smith and Dorfman (1975) measured liking for visual stimuli as a function of complexity and number of exposures. According to Berlyne's theory, when a person is exposed to a stimulus, he or she is likely to process the information it contains. As a result, his or her liking for that stimulus should decrease. A simple stimulus contains less new information than a complex stimulus, and therefore it should take less time to process all the information a simple stimulus contains. It follows that interest in a simple stimulus should diminish more rapidly with repeated exposures than interest in a complex stimulus. Further, with experience a person might develop the structures necessary to process a complex stimulus. It would be predicted, therefore, that interest in a complex stimulus might increase rather than decrease with repeated exposures. Both of these predictions were confirmed. These results are shown in Figure 12-6. In addition, Smith and Dorfman found that a stimulus of medium complexity initially elicited very little interest or liking. With repeated exposure, liking grew and then declined. Presumably, after 20 exposures the subjects had processed the information in the medium-complexity stimulus but still had not exhausted the information in the high-complexity stimulus.

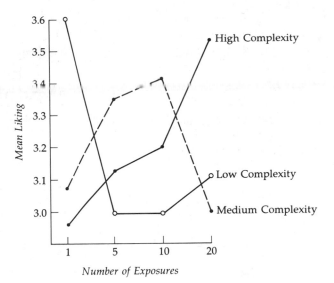

Figure 12–6. Mean likability ratings at each level of stimulus complexity as a function of number of exposures to the stimulus . (From G. F. Smith and D. D. Dorfman, "The Effect of Stimulus Uncertainty and the Relationship between Frequency of Exposure and Liking. " *Journal of Personality and Social Psychology*, 1975, *31*, 150-155. Copyright © 1975 by the American Psychological Association. Reprinted with permission.)

Summary

Dember and Earl argue that organisms are motivated to interact with a level of complexity slightly above their current level. According to Dember and Earl, only a range of stimuli (the pacer range) will be acceptable. Berlyne has suggested that the mechanism underlying exploratory and play behaviors is arousal. He has suggested that when arousal is low, organisms are motivated to increase arousal by interacting with novel stimuli in their environment. Stimuli that can provide optimal arousal will become the objects of attention. According to Berlyne's theory, attention to an object is sufficient to produce information processing. Once all the information has been processed, the individual will be inclined to seek out new stimuli.

Arousal and Exploratory Behavior

Berlyne has argued that organisms are motivated to seek out optimal levels of stimulation. According to his theory, arousal produces positive affect (Figure 12-4). Since it is assumed that organisms are motivated to maximize positive affect and to minimize negative affect, the theory assumes that when arousal is high, organisms will not explore. Exploration would lead to further increases in arousal and would be experienced as negative affect.

In one experiment designed to determine whether high levels of arousal will lead to decreased exploratory behavior, Franken and Strain (1974) used a large multi-unit maze that permitted certain sections to be changed from white to black or black to white between the two daily trials. Figure 12-7 shows the arrangement of the maze, together with the changes made in it between trials 1 and 2. If exploratory behav-

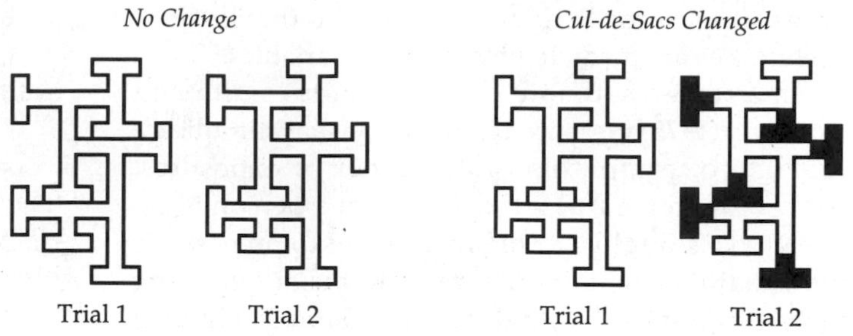

No Change   Cul-de-Sacs Changed

Trial 1   Trial 2   Trial 1   Trial 2

Figure 12–7. The maze used by Franken & Strain (1974), showing the changes that occurred between trials 1 and 2.

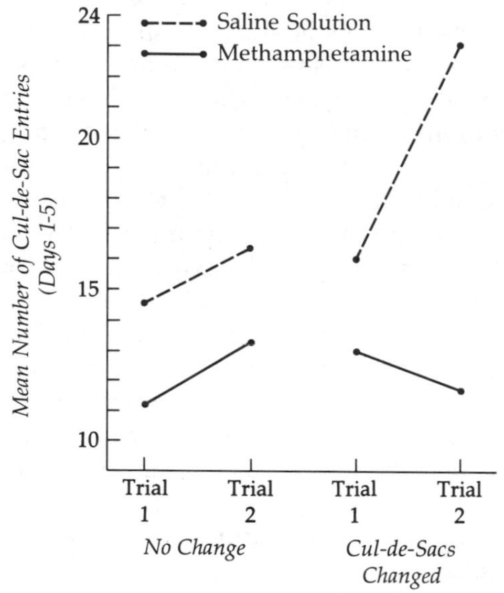

Figure 12–8. Number of cul-de-sacs entered by rats injected with methamphetamine and by rats injected with saline solution when cul-de-sacs were changed in color between trials and when they were not. Methamphetamine reduced exploration (number of cul-de-sacs entered) as well as the tendency to approach the changed cul-de-sacs on the second trial. (Reproduced with the permission of the publisher from: R. E. Franken and A. Strain, "Effect of Increased Arousal on Response to Stimulus Change in a Complex Maze." *Perceptual and Motor Skills*, 1974, 39, 1076-1078. Copyright © 1974 Perceptual and Motor Skills.)

ior is motivated by the tendency to seek out new stimulation, animals high in that tendency should select and respond to the changed parts of the maze. To determine whether this tendency might decrease when an animal was highly aroused, half of the animals (rats) were injected with methamphetamine (an arousal-producing drug) between the two daily trials, and the other half were injected with saline solution (an inert substance).

As expected, the animals injected with saline solution (low-arousal animals) responded to the changes made in the maze. These animals entered somewhat more cul-de-sacs on trial 2 than on trial 1, even when the cul-de-sacs were not changed, but when they were

changed, the animals entered many more of them. The results for the methamphetamine-injected animals (highly aroused) were almost opposite to those of the saline animals but are exactly as predicted by Berlyne's theory. When the cul-de-sacs were changed, the animals tended to avoid them (they entered fewer cul-de-sacs on trial 2 than on trial 1). These results, summarized in Figure 12-8, clearly show that arousal does mediate the tendency to respond to new stimulation. Berlyne has performed similar experiments, manipulating arousal with drugs, and has obtained results consistent with his theory (Berlyne, 1969; Berlyne, Koenig, & Hirota, 1966).

The fact that arousal mediates something as basic

as exploratory behavior means that arousal indirectly governs what and how much we come to know about our environment. Most developmental psychologists argue that through the process of exploration, children come to be knowledgeable about and competent in dealing with their environment (for example, Piaget, 1952; White, 1959).

Anxiety, Fear, and Exploration

Fear as the enemy of exploration. Various researchers have noted that people are less inclined to explore when they are fearful or anxious. White (1959) suggested that fear is the enemy of exploration. People's lack of interest in exploration when they are anxious can be readily explained by Berlyne's theory. According to his theory, fear and anxiety produce high levels of arousal, and when arousal is high, exploration will be low or nonexistent.

Animals often fail to show exploratory behavior in the laboratory. In order to see if their apathy was due to emotionality (anxiety), experimenters devised procedures to reduce the emotionality of these animals. One procedure that has been used extensively, called "handling" or "taming," calls for the experimenter to spend some time each day playing with the animals (handling them). After a couple of weeks, animals that have been treated in this way show much less emotional behavior. It has repeatedly been shown that this taming or handling produces increases in exploratory behavior (Denenberg, 1967).

Implications for facilitating learning. This research points the way to methods of facilitating learning in children and adults as well. If we expect people to learn by interacting with their environment, then it is important that we make them feel as comfortable and relaxed as possible. An "anxious environment" will simply produce increases in arousal that will get in the way of this kind of learning. Good teachers are typically aware of this fact and work hard to give the environment a relaxed atmosphere.

Individual differences. Eysenck's (1947) theory predicts that introverts will prefer simpler stimuli and ex-

traverts will prefer more complex stimuli. Although there are some data to support this theory (Eysenck, 1947), there are also conflicting results (for example, Bryson & Driver, 1972). Because complexity preferences change as a function of contact with stimuli, it is not surprising that the relation between personality and complexity preferences is at best unstable. Munsinger and Kessen (1964) found that art students prefer more complex visual stimuli. This would, of course, be expected because art students presumably have considerable contact with a wide variety of visual stimuli. Unfortunately, we do not know whether art students are more extraverted than the average person. Further work is needed to determine just how personality affects the tendency to experience complex stimuli. There is good evidence (Thomas, Chess, & Birch, 1970) that children with a relatively stable ("easy") temperament are more receptive to new situations. Children who are less receptive to new experiences ("slow to warm up") will eventually come to respond to new experiences, to explore, and to adapt to new situations once they have become secure in their environment. They are like the anxious person who becomes less anxious or the highly aroused person who experiences a lowering of arousal. When the anxiety and arousal lessen, they readily respond to new and varied stimulation.

We all know from experience that there are times when we are more open to novel and complex stimulation and times when we are less open to it. Presumably these variations are related to whether we are already overloaded with information and are therefore experiencing high levels of arousal.

Summary

There are several things that reduce the tendency to explore. High levels of arousal, such as those produced by drugs, have repeatedly been shown to reduce the tendency to explore. Another thing that reduces the tendency to explore is fear. The reason fear may reduce the tendency to explore is that it often produces high levels of arousal. Because people often differ in terms of arousal levels and fear, it is not surprising that there are great individual differences associated with the tendency to explore. It may be possible for teachers and parents to increase a child's tendency to explore by creating an environment that is relaxed (low in arousal properties).

Play: Frivolous or Serious?

Exploration appears to be a very serious activity with the obvious function of making the person or animal familiar with the environment; play seems to be less serious. Further, it often appears that play is not systematic. For these reasons, the research on play has been designed to determine whether in fact play serves an important function and, if so, what that function is.

Humans, especially during their so-called formative years, spend a great deal of time engaging in activities collectively called "play." For example, a child may build a tower out of blocks, skip rope with a friend, pretend that he or she is a nurse or doctor, make up a game, draw a picture. Because these activities are quite diverse, it is difficult to decide why they all have come to be called play.

Historically, people have treated certain activities as important and others as frivolous. Work has typically been regarded as important because of its obvious relation to survival needs. School learning has also been regarded as important, at least in certain societies, because it also has a long-term relation to survival needs. Within such a framework, activities that do not have an immediate or future survival function are regarded as frivolous or, in the case of children, as simply playful. They are assumed neither to help nor to hinder preparation for the important activities involved in survival. According to this view, the activity of children during the preschool years is often frivolous. It is assumed that during these years children are simply putting in time until they are ready for the "real" learning that occurs in school.

In recent years we have come to appreciate just how much learning occurs in these early years. Current theories of child development typically regard all forms of play as contributing to the optimal development of the child. Thus, play in the formative years is no longer regarded as frivolous. The question remains, of course, whether adult play is frivolous or whether it serves an important function in the physical or psychological well-being of adults. At this point we can only assume that it serves an important function and is not simply a way to pass the time. For the present we will confine our discussion to the play of children and young primates.

A great deal of research on the relation between play and development has been done with monkeys. One advantage of using monkeys for this research is that it is possible to impose a number of experimental controls that would not be possible with humans. Further, since monkeys develop faster than humans, it is possible to study the role of play in development in a relatively short period. Although the results with monkeys may not completely explain the role of play in human development, such research can help indicate the direction that research with humans should take.

The Functions of Social Play

Research by Harry Harlow and his associates has uncovered a number of important relations between play and development. By comparing monkeys that have been raised in various states of isolation and therefore deprived of social play, Harlow has concluded that social play is very important for normal development. A paper by Suomi and Harlow (1971) succinctly summarizes some of these findings:

> We think that play among monkey infants serves two general, but important, functions. First, it provides a behavioral mechanism by which activities appropriate for adult social functioning can be initiated, integrated, and perfected. Play repertoires of monkeys under a year of age contain rudimentary forms of virtually all behaviors that characterize adult social life. Patterns of social grooming, aggression, sex, and dominance are clearly evident in infant monkey play activity. When they first emerge, these patterns are not exhibited at adult levels of competence. Rather, they are clumsy and unsophisticated. It is only after months, even years, of "practice" that the behaviors become truly adult in form. The practice comes through peer play.
>
> It is primarily through play that young mon-

keys learn to interact in a social world. In the months of early play development the infant progresses from a recognition that social objects differ from the rest of the environment to a state of living with and loving fellow monkeys. Presence of peers is sought, rather than avoided, as with isolate-reared monkeys. Furthermore, the infants pick up social graces, such as how to behave in the presence of a dominant, as opposed to a lower status, peer. Dominance hierarchies established among peers early in life persist, unchanged in form, throughout adulthood. In these respects, the function of play for monkeys closely parallels the role of play among human children.

The second function of play in monkey social development is to mitigate aggression when it emerges in the monkey's behavior repertoire. Aggressive behavior, absent in very young monkeys, seems to manifest itself spontaneously at about seven months of age, independent of rearing conditions. For this reason we believe aggression to be genetically predisposed in the rhesus monkey. All monkeys show aggressive behavior of some form, beginning at seven months of age. However, the situations in which aggressive behavior is exhibited are controlled, not by genetic, but rather by social variables. Monkeys permitted to play exhibit their aggression in their play activity. Because it is part of the play repertoire, it is of relatively mild form. Through play, the control of aggression is achieved [p. 75].*

The Functions of Solitary Play

Harlow's research clearly shows that early social play is important for several related adult behaviors. What about nonsocial—solitary—play? Here again, the research indicates that play serves an important function. In a study by Sylva, Bruner, and Genova (1976), children aged 3-5 were exposed to materials (sticks and

* From S. J. Suomi and H. F. Harlow "Monkeys at Play." *Play: A Natural History Magazine Supplement*, December 1971. Copyright © 1971 by The American Museum of Natural History. Reprinted with permission.)

clamps) that were involved in a later problem-solving task. The task required the child to retrieve a piece of chalk that could be reached only by joining the shorter sticks together with the clamps. In one condition, the child was allowed to play for 10 minutes with the sticks and clamps. In a second condition, the child was simply shown how the sticks could be joined together with one of the clamps. In a third condition, a control condition, the child was not given any treatment. Using several indices to evaluate the children's performance, the investigators concluded that those who played before attempting the solution did better for three reasons:

1. They were more self-initiated in their approach. Self-initiation is, of course, a primary requirement for problem solving.

2. They had learned more about the various ways the sticks could be joined; that is, they had learned alternative ways of solving the problem.

3. They were less frustrated by failure. When one attempt failed, they could modify their approach or start over. Children without the prior play experience were more likely to give up.

These results suggest that play tends to breed intrinsic motivation. Children who experienced prior play seemed to find the process of solving the problem rewarding. They were not preoccupied with finding a solution quickly, nor did they give up when one of their attempts failed. The shift away from goals (success and failure) to the process is, of course, what distinguishes intrinsic from extrinsic motivation.

Summary

Although people historically tended to view play as frivolous, educators and psychologists today take the position that all forms of play are probably important for development. Given this assumption, the question is what function play serves in the developmental process. At this point, there is reason to distinguish between social play and solitary play. Social play in monkeys, according to Suomi and Harlow, serves two important functions: it initiates, integrates, and perfects behaviors important for adult social functioning, and it mitigates aggression when it emerges. Because aggres-

PRACTICAL APPLICATION 12.1

Facilitating Intrinsic Motivation

What factors facilitate the development of intrinsic motivation? It appears that one of the main factors is being free to learn whatever there is to be learned. To put it another way, it is freedom from constraints or external demands, such as having to finish a task quickly, to do it in a certain way, or to please someone else. It has been shown, for example, that when goals are imposed by someone else, intrinsic motivation decreases (Manderlink & Harackiewicz, 1984; Mossholder, 1980). Before looking at why freedom and personal choice may lead a person to become intrinsically motivated, let us examine what happens when there is no freedom.

When there are constraints on behavior, such as the need to finish a task quickly or to find a particular solution, behavior is characterized as answer-oriented and shallow (Condry, 1977; Sylva, Bruner, & Genova, 1976). That means the person is not trying to discover the underlying structure or the relation between elements. Rather, the person is simply generating a series of more or less random responses, often to external cues either from the environment or from other people, such as the experimenter. Why does the person not try to understand the nature of the elements and their relation? There are two lines of argument.

According to one argument, extrinsic demands increase anxiety or arousal level or simply increase drive level. Increases in anxiety, arousal, or drive, it is argued, alter the way a person processes information.

They narrow attention (Bruner, Matter, & Papanek, 1955) or somehow shift attention in some way that interferes with the learner's ability to deal with the more subtle aspects or relations in the situation (Easterbrook, 1959). If learners cannot deal with all the information, they cannot generate a series of systematic responses. They will be forced to respond with only strategies that worked or simply try to proceed on the basis of limited information.

The other line of argument to explain why external constraints lead to stereotyped or trial-and-error behavior is based on the idea that such learning teaches responses and not rules or understanding. The person merely imitates another person's behavior or learns a sequence of responses that somehow works. Although such responding may work in certain situations, it often does not work when the task demands are shifted.

When there is freedom and personal choice, something quite different happens. A person who has freedom appears to learn about relations between elements. Studies such as that by Sylva and his colleagues (1976) have shown that a person who has had the freedom to interact with the materials to be used in a later problem can generate a wide variety of approaches, suggesting that the person is testing a series of hypotheses. Why should freedom from constraints facilitate intrinsic motivation? Although a complete answer is not possible at this time, several factors are likely to be involved.

---

sion emerges more or less spontaneously, Suomi and Harlow believe that it may be genetically based, at least in the rhesus monkey. However, aggression is controlled by social variables. It is important that monkeys acquire such control, and play can facilitate this achievement. Solitary play is important in breeding intrinsic motivation.

Extrinsic Motivation: The Enemy of Exploration

In an article titled "Enemies of Exploration: Self-Initiated versus Other-Initiated Learning," John Condry (1977) concludes that in certain contexts, extrinsic incentives undermine not only performance but

First, there is evidence that when people are free from anxiety, emotionality, or any form of excessive arousal, information processing not only is highly motivating but takes a much different form than when people are anxious, emotional, or highly aroused. It appears that when people are free from anxiety, emotionality, or arousal, they are more inclined to explore systematically all the various elements and the relation of those elements. Such learning, obviously, would prepare the person to deal with problems based on some or all of the relations contained in that material.

Second, there is considerable evidence that the opportunity to process information is highly motivating for humans as well as animals. Humans, it appears, tend to abstract principles and laws from the information they encounter. This information then becomes the backdrop for the processing of other information. Not only are humans good at fitting together the pieces of a cognitive puzzle, but they find the activity pleasurable. As Leon Festinger (1957) noted some time ago, reducing dissonance is rewarding.

If information processing is rewarding, it follows that activities offering this opportunity will be valued. Further, if exercising one's skill at a task increases one's ability, then a person with more practice will have more opportunity to engage in this highly valued activity. Thus, the more one processes information, the more likely this activity is to occur in the future. The key, therefore, is to free the person from the constraints that block or interfere with the natural tendency to process information.

Deci and Ryan (1985) have offered a theory of intrinsic motivation in which the concept of *self-determination* plays a central role. Self-determination, within their theory, involves two things: becoming aware of one's needs and then setting goals so that those needs can be satisfied. They argue that reaching a goal typically involves learning or mastery. *Automatic* or *non-self-determined* behaviors, in contrast, simply involve engaging in behaviors that terminate external forces often without having mastered anything. The important thing is that in learning to set and achieve goals, people learn to become self-determined, which is the essence of what it means to be intrinsically motivated. It is important to note in this context that when people set goals for themselves they typically set more difficult goals which, of course, means they are going to learn more (Locke & Latham, 1990). It is also important to note that when other people set the goals, people follow the path characterizing non-self-determined behavior. That path involves a very different kind of learning which is motivated by the need to terminate an external force. In the case of other people setting the goals, the motivation is to please the other person as opposed to the self.

interest in the activity. Why do extrinsic incentives undermine performance and interest? Before we attempt to answer this question it is important to look briefly at some of the research on this problem.

An obvious extrinsic incentive, or reward, is money. In a series of studies to examine whether money would increase or decrease subsequent interest in a task, Edward L. Deci (1972) used a game called SOMA®. This game includes a number of blocks that can be arranged into different patterns. Participants in the study were asked to play the game and in different conditions were offered (1) nothing, (2) a monetary reward, or (3) a social reward (praise) for every configuration they produced. In the middle of each of three experimental sessions, the experimenter left the room and the subjects were viewed surreptitiously to determine whether they continued to play at the game. The amount of time they played with the blocks during these "free sessions" was used as a measure of interest, or intrinsic motivation. Deci found that intrinsic motivation was less when subjects were given an external reward but greater when they were given verbal praise.

The important point about these and other studies is that it is not the receipt of the reward itself that affects subsequent interest but whether the subject undertakes the task in order to receive a monetary reward. For example, if a subject unexpectedly receives a reward, it does not affect his or her performance (for example, Greene & Lepper, 1974; Lepper & Greene, 1975; Lepper, Greene, & Nisbett, 1973). It appears that the promise of a reward alters the person's approach to the task. Several sources (for example, Haddad, McCullers, & Moran, 1976; McGraw & McCullers, 1974, 1975; Miller & Estes, 1961; Spence, 1970) indicate that rewarded children learn less than nonrewarded children. Further, Condry and Chambers (1978) and Maehr and Stallings (1972) have found that rewarded children attempted easier problems and were more answer-oriented. Thus, as Condry (1977) points out, there is evidence that extrinsic motivation leads subjects to adopt different strategies in a learning or problem-solving situation—strategies that do not breed intrinsic motivation.

Individual Differences and Extrinsic Motivation

In view of the fact that achievement motivation is typically regarded as an example of intrinsic motivation, it is interesting to note that subjects high in need achievement (nAch) are more likely to volunteer for difficult tasks when evaluation is internal and for easy tasks when evaluation is external (Maehr & Stallings, 1972). This finding clearly demonstrates that external factors modify the normal tendency of high achievers to select tasks of moderate difficulty. Switzky and Haywood (1974) have also shown that external factors tend to override the natural tendency of intrinsically motivated behavior. Using a personality test to identify

intrinsically and extrinsically motivated types (Haywood, 1971), Switzky and Haywood found that under conditions in which a child could reward his or her own performance, intrinsically motivated types maintained their performance longer than extrinsically motivated types. When the rewards were externally administered, extrinsically motivated children maintained their performance longer than intrinsically motivated children.

Summary

Considerable evidence shows that extrinsic motivation not only is the enemy of exploration but leads to incomplete learning or at least a different kind of learning. Extrinsic motivation may alter attentional processes, which in turn affect what is learned. Alternatively, extrinsic motivation may simply teach a series of responses that are not based on an understanding of the task. Intrinsic motivation seems to be tied to the motivation to process information. When a person is free from constraints, he or she is inclined to learn about relations between elements in a given situation. Such learning not only can facilitate later problem solving but can breed intrinsic motivation.

Sensation Seeking

Definition

Sensation seeking, according to Marvin Zuckerman (1979), "is a trait defined by the need for varied, novel and complex sensations and experiences and the willingness to take physical and social risks for the sake of such experiences" (p. 10). The important thing to note here is that one of the key elements of sensation seeking is the willingness to take risks. The work on exploratory behavior has typically suggested that organisms tend to avoid exploration (the seeking of new sensations and new experiences) when it entails risks. It has been suggested that risks often arouse fear, and fear is incompatible with exploratory behavior. Several of the theories of exploratory behavior assume that such emotions as fear produce high levels of arousal. Since many of these theories assume that organisms explore in order to increase arousal, it follows that the reason that organisms experiencing fear do not explore is that they are already at an optimal level of arousal. Alternatively, it has been suggested that high arousal tends to shift attention to more survival-related cues (see Chapter 3), behavior that is assumed to be incompatible with exploratory behavior. It is interesting, therefore, that Zuckerman has been able to identify people who are willing to take risks (experience fear) in order to explore. In order to see if you are a high, medium, or low sensation seeker, take the test in Practical Application 12.2.

Origins of the Sensation-Seeking Concept

As we have seen, people normally find restricted environmental stimulation quite aversive. In the course of doing work on restricted environmental stimulation, Zuckerman (1979) found that some people are more inclined to volunteer for such experiments and are much more likely to enjoy the effects of environmental stimulation. In order to see if he could actually identify these people, he began to develop a paper-and-pencil test. This test came to be known as the Sensation Seeking Scale (SSS). People who score high on this scale are typically referred to as high sensation seekers, while those who score low are referred to as low sensation seekers or sensation avoiders. (Most people score somewhere in the middle of the scale, and so tend to have characteristics of both the high and the low sensation seeker.)

Zuckerman found that it is the high sensation seekers who are attracted to restricted environmental stimulation. This is not what anyone would expect on the basis of the findings that I reported above. Normally we think that people who prefer change and novelty would prefer more rather than less stimulation. The reason the high sensation seekers said they enjoyed restricted environmental stimulation was that it provided them with a new experience. Under restricted environmental stimulation it is much easier to become aware of bodily functions—the heart beating, the blood rushing through the arteries, food digesting, and so forth. To the sensation seekers, this was a novel experience. If you keep this in mind, together with the idea that these people are willing to take risks in order to

have novel experiences, you have two of the basic keys to this personality type. In the following sections I will point out some of the interesting things that characterize sensation seekers. Obviously I can only scratch the surface of this fascinating subject.

Biological Component

The Biological Basis of Sensation Seeking

Monoamine oxidase and sensation seeking. What is the origin of the sensation-seeking trait? It has been shown that sensation seeking is negatively correlated with monoamine oxidase levels (see Zuckerman, 1979). That is, the level of monoamine oxidase is low in high sensation seekers and high in low sensation seekers. Monoamine oxidase is an enzyme that is important in the regulation and therefore the ultimate availability of such neurotransmitters as norepinephrine. When the monoamine oxidase level is high, little norepinephrine is available; when it is low, norepinephrine is highly available. What makes this fact so important is the additional fact that the level of norepinephrine in the brain is linked to whether or not the "reward centers" of the brain can be activated. One reason that sensation seekers are hypothesized to use such drugs as cocaine is that the effects of these drugs may depend on the activation of these reward centers. If your reward centers are activated or can be activated to a high degree, then it should be possible for you to experience greater pleasure or greater reward as the result of engaging in such activities as using drugs. In other words, it is suggested that high sensation seekers receive more reward value when they use certain drugs and therefore are more prone to use drugs in the future. Conversely, low sensation seekers are thought to be prevented from experiencing the same level of reward value when they use those drugs and therefore are less likely to use drugs in the future.

The heritability of monoamine oxidase level. Where do these differences in monoamine oxidase level come from? Zuckerman (1979, 1983) has argued that they are inherited. Twin studies have indeed supported the hypothesis that the monoamine level has a genetic component.

PRACTICAL APPLICATION 12.2

Are You a High or a Low Sensation Seeker?

To test your own sensation-seeking tendencies, try this shortened version of one of Marvin Zuckerman's earlier scales. For each of the 13 items, circle the choice, A or B, that best describes your likes or dislikes or the way you feel. Instructions for scoring appear at the end of the test.

1. A. I would like a job that requires a lot of traveling.
   B. I would prefer a job in one location.
2. A. I am invigorated by a brisk, cold day.
   B. I can't wait to get indoors on a cold day.
3. A. I get bored seeing the same old faces.
   B. I like the comfortable familiarity of everyday friends.
4. A. I would prefer living in an ideal society in which everyone is safe, secure, and happy.
   B. I would prefer living in the unsettled days of our history.
5. A. Sometimes I like to do things that are a little frightening.
   B. A sensible person avoids activities that are dangerous.
6. A. I would not like to be hypnotized.
   B. I would like to have the experience of being hypnotized.
7. A. The most important goal of life is to live it to the fullest and experience as much as possible.
   B. The most important goal in life is to find peace and happiness.
8. A. I would like to try parachute-jumping.
   B. I would never want to try jumping out of a plane, with or without a parachute.
9. A. I enter cold water gradually, giving myself time to get used to it.
   B. I like to dive or jump right into the ocean or a cold pool.
10. A. When I go on a vacation, I prefer the comfort of a good room and bed.
    B. When I go on vacation, I prefer the change of camping out.
11. A. I prefer people who are emotionally expressive even if they are a bit unstable.
    B. I prefer people who are calm and even-tempered.
12. A. A good painting should shock or jolt the senses.
    B. A good painting should give one a feeling of peace and security.
13. A. People who ride motorcycles must have some kind of unconscious need to hurt themselves.
    B. I would like to drive or ride a motorcycle.

Scoring. Count one point for each of the following items that you have circled: 1A, 2A, 3A, 4B, 5A, 6B, 7A, 8A, 9B, 10B, 11A, 12A, 13B. Add up your total and compare it with the norms below.

0-3	Very low on sensation seeking
4-5	Low
6-9	Average
10-11	High
12-13	Very high

Although the test gives some indication of a person's rating, it is not a highly reliable measure. One reason, of course, is that the test has been abbreviated. Another is that the norms are based largely on the scores of college students who have taken the test. As people get older, their scores on sensation seeking tend to go down.

Frank Farley (1986) has pointed out, however, that sensation seeking has also been linked to testosterone level. Whatever the exact mechanism, he also endorses the hypothesis that sensation seeking is inherited.

Animal research has shown that exploratory behavior is inherited. Since exploratory behavior has been linked to the need for variety and change, such data provide converging evidence that the sensation-seeking need, or the need to experience novelty and change, may indeed be inherited.

Sex and age differences. For reasons that are not altogether clear, sex differences have been found in sensation seeking. Men tend to be higher in this trait than women. It has also been shown that the sensation-seeking trait tends to diminish with age. One of the things that may account for both sex differences and the tendency for sensation seeking to diminish with age is that one of the scales to measure sensation seeking contains a large number of sports interest items.

Zuckerman's sensation seeking scale is based on four related but independent factors that were derived through factor analytic procedures. These four factors denote slightly different aspects of sensation seeking.

1. Thrill and adventure seeking. People differ in their desire to seek excitement through risky but socially acceptable activities such as parachuting or driving fast, even if they haven't engaged in such activities.

2. Experience seeking. Some people desire to seek sensation by engaging in activities outside the normal middle-class lifestyle. They may travel, seek out unusual friends, engage in artistic endeavors, experiment with drugs and in general lead less conventional lives.

3. Disinhibition. Those who choose to follow the middle-class lifestyle may periodically escape by engaging in social drinking, gambling, or pursuing a variety of sexual partners. They drink to free themselves from the social inhibitions that are part of their middle-class lifestyles.

4. Boredom susceptibility. Some people have a much lower tolerance for repetition and sameness. They tend to seek out stimulation and change in order to escape the monotony of everyday life. These are people who are inclined to engage in sensation seeking activities.

Learned and Cognitive Components

Sensation seekers learn to satisfy the sensation-seeking motive in a wide variety of ways. In the following section I briefly review some of the diverse ways in which the sensation-seeking motive is satisfied. As you will see, the sensation-seeking motive can and often is satisfied through learned and cognitive channels.

Sensation Seeking and Sports

Sensation seekers tend to get involved in sports, especially sports that are regarded as risky. It's the high sensation seekers who climb mountains, hang-glide, scuba dive, go in for downhill skiing, and so forth. Are the sensation seekers attracted to such activities because they are dangerous? There is no evidence that they are attracted to danger. It appears rather that the sensation seeker does not let risk stand in the way of new experiences. Rowland, Franken, and Harrison (1986) found that high sensation seekers more quickly get bored with a given sport and so try something new. Over a period of time, then, they are likely to participate in more sports than low sensation seekers. If you are constantly trying new sports, you are likely sooner or later to get involved in high-risk activities. Since high sensation seekers are not put off by risk, it is not surprising that more high than low sensation seekers tend to get involved in the more risky sports.

Drugs, Sex, Rock and Roll

In the movie *The Rose*, Bette Midler shouts a rhetorical question to her adoring audience: "How do I keep this tired old body in shape?" Without waiting for a reply, she shouts: "Drugs, sex, rock and roll! Drugs, sex, rock and roll! Drugs, sex, rock and roll!" The audience—sensation seekers all—respond with obvious delight: "Drugs, sex, rock and roll! Drugs, sex, rock and roll!"

There is an abundance of evidence that sensation seekers tend to use alcohol, marijuana, and cocaine (for example, Huba, Newcomb, & Bentler, 1981). It has been suggested that their interest in drugs can be explained by their biological constitution. As far as sex is concerned, an abundance of data indicates that sensation seekers not only like to have sex frequently but like to have a variety of partners (see Zuckerman, 1979). Finally, there is a great deal of evidence that sensation seekers like parties, especially parties that can be called uninhibited. The general picture that emerges is that the sensation seeker likes new experiences, especially ones that involve new people, and likes the feeling of being disinhibited (not bound by the normal constraints of society). The uninhibited party is the perfect place to satisfy such desires.

Thinking Styles and Creativity

It would be not only unfair but incorrect to depict the sensation seeker merely as a jock or a party animal. Sensation seekers often become entrepreneurs, artists, educators, entertainers, scientists, adventurers. They can be found at the leading edge of many fields. One of the things that enables these people to advance beyond safe boundaries is their creativity, which grows out of their thinking style.

In order to be creative, you need to be able to view things in new ways or from a different perspective. Among other things, you need to be able to generate new possibilities or new alternatives. Tests of creativity measure not only the number of alternatives that people can generate but the uniqueness of those alternatives. The ability to generate alternatives or to see things uniquely does not occur by chance; it is linked to other, more fundamental qualities of thinking, such as flexibility, tolerance of ambiguity or unpredictability, and the enjoyment of things heretofore unknown. Sensation seekers have all of these qualities (Farley, 1986; Franken, 1987), and it is these qualities that enable them to become productive.

Unconventionality and Delinquency

Sensation seekers describe themselves as being open, unconventional, and undependable. If you are going to experience what is new, it is important not to erect barriers between yourself and the new. That means, among other things, that you cannot let what other people think or say interfere with your choice of activities. Sensation seekers indicate that they often do things they know their friends and relatives would not approve of. It is also important that they not let previous decisions prevent them from taking advantage of new experiences. Sensation seekers are quite willing to break a commitment if they find something more interesting to do (Franken, 1987). This tendency not to let the feelings of other people interfere with what they want to do often puts sensation seekers in conflict with authority as well as with convention. Thus the sensation seeker is prone to delinquency (Farley, 1986). If this unconventional way of thinking is channeled into beneficial activities, however, it can lead to creativity and productivity. Being a sensation seeker, in other words, does not make you successful or unsuccessful. Rather, it provides you with qualities that can make you either an idol or an outcast.

Decision-Making Styles and Sensation Seeking

In their book *In Search of Excellence*, Thomas Peters and Robert Waterman (1982) describe the planning and decision-making styles of the top executives of the best-run companies in the United States. They point out that these executives like to make decisions, like to make them quickly, can make them without having complete information, and are willing to abandon plans that are not working. The general picture that emerges is that these executives have the capacity to stay on the cutting edge of their fields by following their hunches. Sensation seekers tend to behave very much like these executives. That is, they like to make decisions, they like to make them quickly, they can make them on the basis of incomplete information, and they can abandon plans that are not working (Franken, 1988). Sensation seekers' personality style makes them particularly adept at working in environments where change is a way of life.

Sensation Seeking and Keeping Your Options Open

If the need for variety and change is a fundamental or primary need, it follows that the sensation seeker cannot afford to become involved or committed to any one activity because in doing so they would cut themselves off from taking advantage of new and more interesting opportunities. In order to ensure that they can take advantage of change, therefore, they need to be vigilant about *keeping their options open*. Evidence that high sensation seekers do keep their options open comes from a study in which it was found that sensation seekers are inclined to make decisions at the last minute, make only short-term commitments, do not feel guilty when they break commitments because something more interesting came up, do not make plans but rather let things happen, do not carefully consider the consequences before they act. They even indicate that keeping their options open is more important than being viewed as dependable. In other words, it appears that sensation seekers do not ascribe to the idea that it is important to make long-term commitments (Franken, 1993).

It is interesting to note in this context that while sensation seekers are inclined to self-disclose (a quality that has been linked to intimacy), they are not inclined to commit themselves to long-term relationships (Franken, Gibson, & Mohan, 1990). While there is evidence that high sensation seekers are inclined to marry high sensation seekers and that low sensation seekers are inclined to marry low sensation seekers, it has been found that sensation seeking has a negative impact on marital satisfaction in high sensation seeking women (Gibson, Franken, & Rowland, 1989). We suggested that there may be more pressure for high sensation seeking women to conform to the traditional role of wife in a marital relationship than for high sensation seeking men to conform to the traditional role of husband and that this is the source of the problem. That is, because high sensation seeking women are motivated by a more unconventional lifestyle, they find marriage to be highly restrictive even though their husbands themselves are high sensation seekers. In short, it may be the expectations that society has for women that is the source of the marital dissatisfaction.

Summary

Sensation seeking "is a trait defined by the need for varied novel and complex sensations and experiences and the willingness to take physical and social risks for the sake of such experiences" (Zuckerman, 1979).

Twin studies provide considerable evidence that the sensation-seeking trait may be inherited. Zuckerman has argued that the mechanism that governs sensation seeking is monoamine oxidase. High sensation seekers have low monoamine oxidase levels while low sensation seekers have high monoamine oxidase levels. Farley has suggested that testosterone may play an important role in motivating sensation seeking. Consistent with this interpretation is the finding that men score higher than women on Zuckerman's Sensation Seeking Scale. The sensation-seeking trait, as measured by Zuckerman's scale, has been shown to decline with age. Factor analytic studies have identified four distinct factors that characterize the sensation seeking motive: Thrill and adventure seeking, experience seeking, disinhibition and boredom susceptibility.

High sensation seekers are inclined to get involved in a variety of sports activities. Their tendency to get involved in risky sports appears to be motivated by their interest in new experiences rather than by an attraction to risk per se. High sensation seekers also tend to use drugs, have a variety of sex partners, and seek out situations, such as parties, at which they can behave in an uninhibited manner.

High sensation seekers tend to be open and unconventional people. This trait can lead to creativity, but if it is not properly channeled it can also lead to delinquency. The tendency to be undependable may grow out of an urge to take advantage of every opportunity for a new experience, even if that means one must break promises or commitments. High sensation seekers like to make decisions, like to make them quickly, and are willing to make them with incomplete information. In addition, they are willing to abandon plans that are not working.

High sensation seekers tend to keep their options open. This tendency means, among other things, an unwillingness to make long-term commitments.

Creativity

Three Reasons why People Are Motivated to Be Creative

There are at least three reasons why people are motivated to engage in acts of creativity. First, creativity is motivated by our *need for novel, varied, and complex stimulation.* One way to experience novel, varied and complex stimulation is to create new things or find new things that will stimulate our senses (e.g., new recipes, new art, new buildings, new cars) or challenge our intellect (e.g., books, computers, movies). As I have already indicated, Berlyne (1960) suggested that the creation of beauty or the appreciation of beauty (esthetics) grows out of the need for novel, varied and complex stimulation. Second, creativity is often motivated by the *need to communicate* ideas and values. Concerned with the fact that children are dying of starvation, a photographer triggers our sense of compassion with a picture of a wide-eyed innocent child whose body is nothing but skin and bones. Alternatively, a politician wanting to make a difference writes a book or gives a speech that is designed to challenge our beliefs and stimulate us to action. Third, creativity is often motivated by the *need to solve problems.* As we encounter new diseases or as our business begins to fail, we search for answers that can give us hope and health.

Definition of Creativity

There has been a great deal of controversy surrounding exactly what should be called creative and what should not (see Mumford & Gustafson, 1988). Some writers have argued that creativity should be defined in terms of problem-solving ability (Cattell, 1971). Such a definition would exclude some of the world's most famous paintings or novels as creative products. Some writers have suggested it is a personality trait (MacKinnon, 1962). Such a definition suggests that some people are creative and others are not. Some people have suggested that it be defined in terms of the production of ideas (Guilford, 1967). Such a definition excludes people who themselves may not be good at producing ideas but can recognize a creative

idea or product when they encounter it. Some people have suggested it should, indeed, involve the recognition of ideas (Tyler, 1978). This means that a movie producer or the owner of a publishing company plays a creative role in making available to the public truly creative products.

I take the position that all of these various definitions are a useful way of thinking about creativity. For our purposes, creativity is defined as *the tendency to generate or recognize ideas, alternatives, or possibilities that may be useful in solving problems, communicating with others, and entertaining ourselves and others.* While I accept the idea that there are individual differences, I think that all people have the innate capacity to act creatively when the situation demands or when they are properly motivated. For me, creativity is more an expression of motivation than it is of talent.

Biological Component

DeBono and Patterns in the Brain

Edward DeBono (e.g., 1970, 1987) has written extensively on the topic of creativity and has taken the position that the brain evolved to isolate predictability and consistency. In other words, like the theorists that have attempted to account for curiosity and exploratory behavior, he believes that the main function of curiosity and exploratory behavior is to ensure that we learn to make sense out of the complex array of stimulation that falls on our receptors. DeBono conceptualizes this process in terms of patterns being formed in the brain, an idea that has its roots in neurobiology. As organisms explore their environment, certain groups or patterns of cells are fired. When this same group or pattern of cells is fired repeatedly they become connected. As a result, when only a portion of the cells forming this pattern is fired, the entire pattern is fired. This enables us, for example, to recognize an object, such as a chair, by seeing only a leg of that chair, or to see the image of a person merely by hearing their voice.

For our ancestors, this ability to form patterns enabled them to do a number of things quickly and automatically. Instead of attempting to escape from their enemies by trial and error (which is not a very good method when threatened), they could simply execute a series of responses that had been previously connected together by a brain pattern.

While the ability to form patterns may have helped our ancestors to both function and survive, DeBono has argued that patterns can and often are the enemy of creativity. In order to be creative we need to break out of existing patterns and form new ones. That is something that is more easily said than done. Instead of enabling us to see things differently, our brain is designed to help us see things in the same way time after time.

How, then, do we break out of these patterns? Often it is in times of crisis that we look at things differently, do things differently, or reorganize our thinking. For our ancestors, encountering a fallen tree in the middle of their escape route would likely have triggered them to act creatively. We are reasonably certain of this fact because we are here today. Had our ancestors not been creative individuals who could adapt to new demands, we likely would have gone the way of the dinosaurs.

Does this mean that we can only act creatively when there is some type of crisis? DeBono believes that people can act creatively at will. They do not need some type of crisis. He believes that we can create new patterns at will by learning techniques that force the brain to form new patterns, something the brain is designed to do. In other words, DeBono believes that humans are inherently creative beings. In order to access their creativity, people simply need to become motivated to do those things that will make the brain form new patterns.

Langer and Mindlessness

Ellen Langer (1989) has used a similar line of reasoning to account for the lack of creativity that often characterizes people. She argues that many of our behaviors become habitual or automatic. When that happens they also become unconscious. As a result, we behave in a "mindless" (thoughtless) as opposed to a "mindful" (thoughtful) way. Like DeBono, she argues that it is highly adaptive for us to be able to do

things without actively thinking about them. Among other things, it frees our brain to focus on other things while we are engaging in routine behaviors. There is a downside, however, to having well-ingrained habits. We can and often do become their servants. Instead of actively deciding what we should do in a certain situation, our decisions are controlled by our habits. As things change in our environment, we continue to engage in the same responses even though they are no longer adaptive. In order to break out of our mindless behavior patterns we need to become "mindful," but how do we do this? Langer suggests that the first thing we need to do is become aware of the fact that we have the choice to behave differently. The next thing we need to do is become aware of what those alternatives are. That involves the process of generating possibilities and alternatives based on our assessment of the situation.

Langer believes that people can become mindful at will, an idea that parallels that of DeBono, who argues that people can become creative at will. It is, to a very large degree, simply a matter of motivation. Motivation, however, needs to be supplemented with techniques that can help people to generate new alternatives or possibilities. For Langer that means learning to make new distinctions and create new categories.

Cognitive Dissonance Theory

Cognitive dissonance theory also suggests that humans are motivated to avoid making new distinctions and creating new categories. When people encounter information that is not consistent with existing beliefs, they are inclined to reject that information in order to preserve existing belief systems. This tendency to maintain the status quo can and often does cause us problems.

Like DeBono and Langer, cognitive dissonance theory suggests that this tendency to maintain the status quo is unlearned. According to cognitive dissonance theory, the best way to change the way we think about things is to change our behavior. When we change our behavior, our cognitions will change so that they are congruent with our behavior (Festinger, 1957).

Some people create, not to solve a problem, but rather to entertain themselves and others. Often such creative acts are highly esthetic.

The Urge to Create

Does this mean that humans have no urge to break out of the status quo? Alternatively, does this mean that all acts of creativity are motivated by our need to adapt to the environment and nothing more? Many writers have argued that, indeed, we have an urge to create that is not driven by our need to adapt. Most of these theorists who have addressed this point have argued, however, that people need to be in the right state of mind or emotion before they are inclined to create. Maslow (1970), for example, suggests that creativity (typically described as being more or less synonymous

with the need for self-actualization) is at the top of the hierarchy of needs. That means that before we are inclined to engage in acts of creativity we need to satisfy all the motives that are below that need. Zuckerman's (1979) research has addressed this question as well. People high in the sensation seeking motive tend to be more creative than people low in this motive. This suggests that sensation seekers satisfy, at least in part, their need for variety and change through acts of creativity.

The need or urge to create is often driven by problems that we encounter on a daily basis. In that sense, it can be said that the need to create is often driven by our need to adapt.

Learned Component

Creativity as Disinhibition

Convention and tradition. Researchers have suggested that people often have a tendency to act creatively but inhibit such tendencies because they fear they will be rejected by society (Franken, 1990). Such people may be motivated more by the need to be accepted or to belong than by a need to experience variety and change. As a result they become conventional and traditional in their views, molding their ideas to fit with those espoused by society. Instead of questioning the values of society, as do people who are more creative, they go along. The research on creativity suggests that in order to be creative people need to be able to *let go* of conventional ways of looking at things (Strickland, 1989). Letting go means becoming disinhibited. We need to say to our unconscious, "Feel free to recombine things in new and different ways even if such combinations may seem silly or even wrong."

Rigidity. Many people are afraid of change or simply motivated to avoid it. They may be anxious, fearful, or simply highly aroused, and in order to manage their anxiety, fear, or high arousal they look for consistency and predictability in their environment, conditions that can reduce anxiety or arousal. When people are chronically anxious or chronically aroused, they often develop a behavior pattern that is characterized by excessive rigidity. The rigidity serves the function of ensuring that nothing new or unexpected will happen to them. In order for these people to become creative they need to throw off their rigidity, something that is more easily said than done if they are experiencing anxiety or high arousal (e.g. Berlyne, 1960).

Rigidity can also occur simply because we have allowed ourselves to become creatures of habit, as Langer suggests in her book on mindfulness. Whatever its origins, being rigid is inconsistent with creativity and therefore blocks creativity.

Psychological Climate and Creativity

Consistent with the idea that all people are potentially creative, it has been shown that, under the right condi-

tions, people who often fail to be creative will suddenly demonstrate creativity (Mumford & Gustafson, 1988). It has been shown, for example, that when it is made clear to people that creativity is expected, they will perform better on divergent-thinking measures (Harrington, 1981; Torrence, 1965). Divergent thinking has frequently been used as an indicator of creativity. Studies indicate that when the organizational climate provides physical support for creative efforts and encourages independent action, scientific productivity is enhanced (Taylor, 1972; Andrews, 1975). Finally, there is considerable data which show that support and recognition of creative effort, particularly in the early stages of a project, lead to innovation (e.g., Lind & Mumford, 1987). Virtually all the research on climate points to the idea that removal of impediments that normally inhibit the expression of creativity, such as "This is the way it has always been done," as well as rewarding people for creativity, can unleash creativity in virtually all people. Again, it appears that creativity is often being actively inhibited.

There is also data which indicate that affect plays an important role in creativity. When affect is positive people tend to be more creative. It has been suggested that positive affect plays a facilitating role in cognitive organization. Specifically, it has been argued that positive affect increases the tendency to combine things in new ways and to see relatedness among divergent stimuli (Isen, Daubman, & Nowicki, 1987).

Personality Traits and Creativity

Barron and Harrington (1981) have concluded there are a set of personality characteristics that can be linked to creativity. These include *intellectual and artistic values, breadth of interests, attraction to complexity, high energy, a concern with work and achievement, independence of judgment, autonomy, intuition, self confidence, ability to tolerate and resolve conflict, and creative self-image.* More recently, people have talked about *openness to experience* as a characteristic of creative people (McCrae, 1987). While it has been suggested that some people are born with these traits, it can also be argued that people learn these traits, often through the process of modeling. Because they admire someone, for example, they adopt the traits of that person. Still others view the development of these traits as the outgrowth of the desire to be creative. According to this position, people learn to adopt certain orientations to the world and themselves (which might be also called beliefs and attitudes) because they have discovered that certain orientations increase the likelihood of their being creative. The assumption underlying this position is that because some people find creativity so rewarding, they are more inclined to create an orientation or approach to the world that will maximize their chances of being creative (Franken, 1993).

How does this work? If you value creativity you might learn to become more tolerant of ambiguity in your life or you might become more inclined to keep an open mind because you have learned that these are key elements of the creative process. Similarly, in order to be more creative you might learn to see yourself as *autonomous, independent*, and *creative*. In order to buffer yourself, or simply make yourself less sensitive to the criticism that creative people often experience, you might adopt a more *unconventional* or even an *questioning-of-tradition attitude*. Because creativity demands that you become highly involved with your materials, you might develop an *achievement orientation*. According to this interpretation, the traits that characterize creative individuals emerge over time. They emerge out of the creative individual's desire to maximize his or her own creativity.

According to this interpretation or model, there are two interdependent and opposing forces at work. On the one hand there is the reward that comes from acting creatively. On the other hand there is punishment that sometimes come when one does act creatively. Teenagers are often acutely aware of the punishment (criticism) that comes when they attempt to dress differently or when they invent a new vocabulary to communicate their view of themselves and the world in which they live. Similarly, academics are acutely aware of the punishment (criticism) they often experience when they attempt to put forth a new theory (e.g., Seligman, 1990). In order for people to become truly creative and enjoy the rewards that come with creativity, they need to learn how to reduce the punishment (criticism) they often experience. They do this by downgrading the importance of another person's view.

They may even adopt an unconventional or antitraditional orientation that serves to buffer them from such inevitable criticism.

Early Experiences and Creativity

The work on early experiences suggests that learning plays an important role in developing the kinds of personalities that make people more prone to be creative as adults. First, it has been shown that the intellectual values that characterize creative individuals seem to come from their families. It has been shown that families that foster intellectual development tend to produce more creative individuals than those who do not (see Mumford & Gustafson, 1988). Second, it has been shown that the *autonomy* and *independence* that characterizes creative individuals also comes from their early upbringing. It has been shown for example that creative scientists were subjected to less structure and less discipline (Stein, 1968), that their parents were less controlling and more likely to encourage *openness to experience* (Getzels & Jackson, 1962), and that the family environment gave children a firm *sense of self as a creative entity* (Trollinger, 1979). All of this research is consistent with the idea that creativity is, to a very large degree, learned.

Later Experiences and Creativity

Considerable evidence points to the idea that creativity is often fostered later in life through mentors and teachers. This research suggests that what teachers and mentors do (at least in the case of scientists) is help novices internalize exacting *professional standards* along with a *sense of excellence, achievement* and *self-confidence* (Zuckerman, 1974). In much of the research on later influences, the themes of excellence, achievement and self-confidence repeatedly emerge. What mentors seem to do is teach, often through their example, the conditions that are necessary for creativity to emerge.

Cognitive Component

In this section I want to focus on the process of creativity in order to show that it is possible to increase creativity by doing certain things. By understanding the conditions that lead to greater creativity we can learn how to motivate people to become more creative.

The Process of Creativity

Creativity involves several important ingredients including: delineating the problem, knowledge, the ability to construct images and/or categories, the ability to synthesize, and the willingness to withhold judgment.

Delineating the problem. Delineating or defining the problem is necessary because it gives direction to our thinking. Movie producers, publishers, and CEOs of large companies often depend on others for the solutions they require. Unless they know what the problem is they are unable to determine which of the various solutions that are constantly being offered to them are worth considering. When we know the problem, we can immediately recognize which of the various patterns that our brain generates are potentially important or useful. Often, the more time one spends on delineating or defining the problem the faster the creative process. That is not surprising because in the process of delineating and defining we tell the brain what is and is not important. Obviously the less it has to deal with the faster it can arrive at a solution.

Information/knowledge. In order to generate new alternatives or new ideas, people need to have a well-developed information or knowledge base. Ideas do not arise spontaneously. They are typically the product of synthesizing information (Langley, Simon, Bradshaw, & Zytow, 1986). It is not surprising, therefore, that creativity is moderately related to intelligence. One needs a certain basic level of intelligence in order to acquire a knowledge base. Given that people have the intelligence, the thing that differentiates those who are creative from those who are not is their motivation to gather that information or acquire the knowledge base they need. I have become very skeptical in recent years of the trend to teach people how to be creative but not bother to provide them with the information or the knowledge that will enable them to become truly creative. Many people operate on the misconception that creativity is something that occurs independent of knowledge. They encourage children to write creative stories or they hire a facilitator to help them solve problems. Unfortunately, if there is no depth to their knowledge base their creativity will blossom and then die much like a flower that is planted where there is no soil to nourish it.

Constructing images and categories. Pieces of information or knowledge can be thought of as involving groups of patterns or, simply *components.* This means that when I think about the sky, for example, a group of cells fire that correspond to the sensory experience I get when I look at the sky. While sensory experiences tend to occur in sequence rather than simultaneously, I can ask my brain to superimpose different images and thereby create a new image out of a set of distinct memories. What I am asking my brain to do is activate several memories or patterns simultaneously. I can, for example, superimpose some clouds, perhaps add an airplane, and even insert a funnel of a tornado into my image of the sky. In each step, my image of the sky abruptly changes. The interesting thing about this whole process of constructing images is that I can create images that people have never seen before by activating different patterns or combining unusual ones. I can, for example, insert a flying elephant into my sky image if I wish. Dreams, it has been suggested, are nothing more than several patterns in the brain being activated simultaneously (Hobson, 1988).

A verbal category, such as the category "dog" or the category called "silverware," can also be viewed as a pattern, even if I don't get a visual image. When I think about the word "dog," a group of cells fire that correspond to the attributes that define the category "dog." If I try to think simultaneously of several different animals, such as dogs, cats, bears, wolves, I would likely activate the superordinate category called "animals" or perhaps "mammals."

Synthesis. Synthesis involves putting together parts or components in order to create a whole. How does this happen? It can happen spontaneously, through what we normally call insight or creativity, or it can be approached in a very logical way, at least according to Edward DeBono, perhaps one of the best known gurus of how to become more creative. DeBono conceptualizes the brain as a highly sophisticated information/problem solver that looks for redundancy. When it finds that redundancy, a pattern emerges in the brain that corresponds to that redundancy. This conceptualization is consistent with the way behavioral scientists conceptualize the emergence of distinct images.

According to DeBono, we can deliberately activate various patterns in the brain and the brain will look for redundancy among those patterns. It will look to see what all those patterns have in common. Thus, rather than waiting for various patterns in the brain to become active simultaneously—perhaps by chance—we can deliberately activate a variety of patterns. The whole method of deliberately activating various patterns in the hopes of speeding up the process of finding redundancy has been called *lateral thinking* by DeBono (1987). According to him, we do not have to learn how to see new patterns when they emerge. He suggests that as soon as a new pattern emerges it will be seen immediately as something that is new and distinct. It is worth noting in this context that the early writers described creativity as the "aha" or "insight" experience. It happened when people suddenly discovered that two things they never thought belonged together were related because they shared certain common features.

What precisely is *redundancy*? Redundancy is the basis for perception and meaning. When we can see something as distinct from the background, for example, we have a perception. It might be something as simple as seeing a chair as a distinct object that exists independent from the background. Meaning typically involves intention. Thus, when someone takes another person by the arm and leads them across the street, we say the act has meaning. It was meant or intended to help or assist. Patterns are the basis for categories. The only thing left for us to do when a pattern emerges is to assign a verbal name to the new pattern so that we can retrieve that category at will.

Presumably, the reason that creativity has been linked to the willingness or ability to tolerate ambiguity (the willingness to simultaneously entertain various pieces of information that do not seem re-

lated) is that the brain is designed to search for *redundancy* when two or more patterns are simultaneously activated. Presumably, the reason that being open to new information has been linked to creativity is that new information provides the brain with yet another piece of information that it can make use of to find redundancy.

The process of generating alternatives is an example of using lateral thinking. Instead of waiting patiently for an idea to emerge we actively generate possibilities, often using past experience. If someone asks me how I might get a ball off a roof, I might think of various possibilities, the most obvious being to get a ladder. In the absence of a ladder, I might become more creative and begin to think of such possibilities as throwing rocks at it, using the force of the water from a garden hose to spray it off, climbing up a tree near the house and jumping over to the house to get it, hiring a helicopter and so forth. Obviously, some of these ideas are better than others and I could simply select from among the alternatives. Another example of lateral thinking is to use analogies or to even open the dictionary at random and start reading words in the hopes that one of the words I read will stimulate me to come up with an answer. The words in this example are intended to activate patterns.

Hobson (1988), whom we discussed in Chapter 6 in connection with dreaming, has suggested that the brain has a natural tendency to link these different patterns by creating a story. Other people have suggested that the brain creates categories that allow us to summarize the essential features contained in a body of information (Langer, 1989). Still others have argued that some types of reorganization or reintegration occur that allows us to make sense out of information or gain insight into it (Kaha, 1983). Realizing that it is *Mardi Gras*, for example, would make it possible for you to understand why some of the people you are encountering on the streets during your visit to New Orleans are wearing costumes. Story-telling, categories, reorganization, or reintegration all imply that some type of synthesis is taking place.

Suspension of judgment. One of the things that will stop the creative process (stop synthesis) is making judgments (Strickland, 1989). People with strong views often have difficulty being creative because they are inclined to short-circuit the creative process by making premature judgments. Langer has argued that premature judgments are one of the things that cause mindlessness or characterize mindlessness. Hobson (1988) has suggested that in order to dream (which reflects creative story-telling), people need to set aside their self-referent or self-reflection systems. Some researchers have suggested that being introspective or self-focused can interfere with making good decisions. It has been shown, for example, that making people aware of the reasons for their choices is not a good way for people to make decisions (Wilson & Schooler, 1991). When you make people focus on their reasons they appear to shift their attention away from the more global problem at hand, resulting in the adoption of a nonoptimal strategy. In order for categories to emerge spontaneously, we need to free the brain from constraints. We need to learn to suspend judgment long enough for the creative process to run its course.

Adopting a playful attitude is a very good way of suspending judgment. The very nature of play is to have fun without having to achieve a goal or find closure. Play allows us to deal with uncertainty and ambiguity. It allows us to incorporate such things as fantasy. In its purest form, creativity involves the complete suspension of judgment.

Learning to Be Creative

If it is correct that the brain is designed to synthesize, then it should be possible to promote creativity by simply juxtaposing certain pieces of information in our brain. Indeed, there is a great deal of data to support this idea.

Remote Associations

One of the most interesting studies on this point is one which showed that giving people moderately remote associations as opposed to highly remote associations produced greater creative achievements (MacKinnon, 1962; Gough, 1976). According to the patterns analogy,

if things are moderately remote they would overlap and thus a distinct pattern would emerge, but if they were highly remote they would not overlap and therefore a distinct pattern would not emerge.

DeBono (1987) has often suggested that in order to trigger creativity in people it is necessary to get them to engage in the process of making remote associations. To that end, he has invented a number of exercises that get people to make remote associations (see Practical Application 12.3). To the degree that these techniques become habitual, it should be possible to train people to be creative. Consistent with this idea is one study that found that the dreams of professionals were more implausible and unrealistic than were the dreams of less creative people (Sladeczek & Domino, 1985). Perhaps some people learn, as DeBono has suggested, to make more remote associations. It becomes a style of thinking, so to speak.

Major versus Minor Contributions

It has been found that major contributions tend to be made by people in young adulthood whereas minor contributions tend to peak at middle age (Lehman, 1966). There are at least three possibilities: creativity declines with age, motivation changes with age, or younger people are more likely to make remote associations.

Most people feel there is not good data to support the idea that the capacity for creativity decreases with increasing age. Often, middle-aged people have an excellent knowledge base and, therefore, there is no reason why they shouldn't be able to make major contributions. Further, the fact that they often make good minor contributions suggests they have the capacity for dealing with complex material. Finally, there is a great deal of data showing that many older people remain highly creative throughout their lives.

There is good data, however, to argue that motivational concerns shift from young to middle age. It has been noted, for example, that as people reach middle age they value pragmatic achievements, perhaps because they are more concerned with career development than are younger people (e.g., Valliant, 1977). There are also data to indicate that *idea generation* is

PRACTICAL APPLICATION 12.3

Motivating Creativity by Adopting the "What If?" Attitude

One of the central themes in the creativity literature is that the brain tends to resist forming new ideas. What this means is that when people try to think creatively their minds or unconscious (whatever you want to call it) only generate solutions that are consistent with what is accepted by society as being true or correct. As a result, people find that when they attempt to be creative, their brain only offers them a rehash of everything they already know. The problem, therefore, is to get the brain to break out of existing patterns and entertain new ones.

There are at least three conditions that are necessary for triggering the emergence of new patterns (see DeBono, 1970). First, it is necessary to *juxtapose* two seemingly unrelated ideas so the brain will look for new ways of relating that information. While juxtaposing two pieces of unrelated information is not that difficult, the brain's initial tendency is to ignore such juxtaposing. If they haven't been perceived as related in the past, for example, the brain is inclined to make the judgment that they are unrelated and should remain so. In order to get the brain to actually look for relationships it is necessary to get the brain to withhold its natural tendency to make such judgments. Thus, the second thing that people need to learn to do

is actively employ techniques that force the brain to withhold this kind of premature judgment. Sometimes, simply telling the brain to withhold judgment is sufficient to increase creativity.

If we can get the brain to withhold such judgments, then the third thing that people must do is to allow the brain *time* to do its job. There is a great deal of evidence to indicate that when the brain is given time, it will find areas of similarity no matter how remote those similarities might be. In order to give the brain time it is important to withhold judgment. To withhold judgment means, among other things, learning to tolerate ambiguity and uncertainty. If we should demand certainty or predictability at all times, we will certainly short-circuit this process. During this time of incubation, as it is often called, the brain appears to ruminate (look at ideas from many perspectives), and it is this process of rumination that allows the brain to discover relationships. Sometimes people have access to this process via their inner dialogue. They will hear themselves, for example, say such things as, "If I did X then maybe Y would occur, and perhaps if I did Y then Z would happen."

In his book entitled *Lateral Thinking*, DeBono suggests a number of techniques that people can use to

---

more important to younger than to older individuals (Macon, 1987).

What about ability to make remote associations? Again, this may simply be a matter of motivation. It has been observed that although young adults often produce a number of highly creative solutions (e.g., to a mechanical ingenuity problem), middle-aged adults produce more workable solutions. It may well be that with experience people learn which types of associations have a higher payoff (Owens, 1969). Alternatively, it may be that with experience people tend to rely more on tried and true procedures that may inhibit reinte-

gration by virtue of their stability, prior use and automaticity (Barsalou, 1983). In Practical Application 12.3, I discuss one technique developed by DeBono that people can use to increase their creativity.

Summary

There are at least three reasons why people engage in acts of creativity: to satisfy their *need for novel and varied stimulation*, to improve their ability to *communicate* ideas and values, and to help them to *solve problems*. Many different definitions of creativity have been of-

enhance juxtaposing while simultaneously inhibiting their brain's natural tendency to reject such juxtapositions, especially of information that seems highly unrelated. One technique he suggests, for example, is the random-word method. When people get stuck on a problem, for example, they simply learn to pick up a dictionary and randomly read out words. The idea behind this technique is to stimulate the brain to activate patterns that were previously inactive in the hopes they will provide the bridge that is necessary to ultimately find the relationship or link that will connect two remote or semi-remote ideas that can provide the solution to the problem. In addition, the random-word technique seems to elicit a playful attitude which can help people withhold or inhibit the judgment process. As I have already indicated, the key to creativity is getting people to withhold the judgment process, because in doing so, the brain will naturally look for similarities or links between those patterns that have been simultaneously activated.

DeBono emphasizes the idea that solutions to problems often involve a series of steps, an idea contrary to the popular myth that the correct solutions to problems emerge suddenly and in their final form.

He argues that the key to problem-solving and creativity is getting the brain to do what it does naturally—finding relationships or links between things that initially may not seem, for various reasons, to be related or linked.

By forcing the brain to look for these relationships and links, and learning to tolerate ambiguity in the process, we should be able to become more creative. It should happen, according to DeBono, when we learn to withhold judgment, when we learn to accept as many divergent views as possible, and when we no longer feel uncomfortable with ambiguity. It should happen when people learn to approach life with a "what if?" attitude.

The "what if?" attitude is an attitude of playfulness. When we adopt the "what if?" attitude, we free ourselves from the rules of convention, the rules of tradition, the rules of closure, the rules of consistency, the rules of logic, the rules of time, or the rules of place. In short, we put ourselves in a position to juxtapose anything we like in any way we like. When we do this, we provide the brain with the ideal set of conditions for doing what it has been designed to do: generate new possibilities, new alternatives, new realities.

fered over the years, each of which has been useful in helping us to understand the nature of creativity.

DeBono takes the position that the brain evolved to isolate predictability and consistency and, as a result, is highly resistant to forming new patterns. Langer has taken a similar position, arguing that many behaviors become automatic (habitual) and that as a result we tend to become mindless. Like DeBono, she argues that it is highly adaptive for us to be able to do things without thinking about them. Unfortunately, as things change in our environment, we continue to do the same things even though they are no longer adap-

tive. In order to break out of our mindless behavior patterns we need to become "mindful." Cognitive dissonance theory also suggests that humans are motivated to avoid making new distinctions and creating new categories.

Various writers, such as Maslow, have argued that we have an urge to create that is not driven wholly by our need to adapt. In Maslow's theory, this need is called the need for self-actualization. Zuckerman's research suggests that sensation seekers may satisfy, at least in part, their need for variety and change through acts of creativity.

Numerous researchers have suggested that, while many people are potentially creative they are strongly motivated by the need or desire to inhibit creative behavior because it may conflict with the conventional or traditional views of society. People characterized by rigidity may inhibit creativity because they have a strong need for predictability. Consistent with the idea that all people are potentially creative is the observation that when the right conditions exist, people who often fail to be creative will suddenly demonstrate that they can be creative.

There are a number of personality characteristics that have been linked to creativity, including artistic values, breadth of interests, attraction to complexity, high energy, a concern with work and achievement, independence of judgment, autonomy, intuition, self-confidence, tolerance for ambiguity, a willingness to resolve conflict, creative self-image, openness to new experiences and/or new ways of viewing things.

It can be argued that people learn to adopt certain orientations to the world and themselves (which might be also called beliefs and attitudes) because they discover that certain orientations increase the likelihood of their being creative. The assumption underlying this position is that because some people find creativity so rewarding they are more inclined to create an orientation or approach to the world that will maximize their creative output. Consistent with this position is the work on the effect of early and later experiences.

Creativity involves at least five important steps: delineating or defining the problem, gathering information and knowledge, constructing images and/or categories, synthesizing, and withholding judgment. Many writers on creativity have suggested that we can learn to be more creative. One of the most interesting studies on this point is a study which showed that giving people moderately remote associations as opposed to highly remote associations produced greater creative achievements.

It has been found that major contributions tend to be made by people in young adulthood, whereas minor contributions tend to peak at middle age (Lehman, 1966). The evidence suggests that motivation changes with age, leading younger people to make more remote associations and older people to make fewer remote associations.

According to DeBono, people can learn to be more creative: 1) by learning to juxtapose information or ideas, 2) by learning to withhold their natural tendency to reject the juxtaposition of two things because past experience suggests they are unrelated, and 3) by giving ourselves time.

Main Points

1. The early behaviorists thought that exploratory behavior was learned.

2. The tendency of animals to alternate in a T-maze has been shown to be motivated by the tendency to respond to change.

3. Research has shown that monkeys are motivated by the visual, auditory, and manipulatory properties of stimulus objects.

4. Humans are motivated to seek out variety and novelty.

5. Various studies have shown that humans are motivated to seek out optimal complexity.

6. According to an information-processing interpretation of curiosity and exploratory behavior, people will be motivated to attend to stimuli that are consistent with their abilities. Consistent with this interpretation, it has been shown that humans prefer increasingly complex stimulation with increasing age.

7. The Dember and Earl theory suggests that all stimulation varies in complexity and that optimal complexity motivates exploration.

8. According to Berlyne's theory, arousal will increase when a person or animal processes new information. Therefore, the environment is always a source of potential arousal.

9. Berlyne suggests that there is a class of variables associated with arousal, which he has labeled "collative variables." These include novelty, degree of change, suddenness of change, surprisingness, incongruity, conflict, complexity, and uncertainty.

10. Berlyne has suggested that esthetics can be partially understood within the arousal framework. Indeed, there is empirical evidence that esthetic preferences are governed by those collative variables that are important in eliciting arousal.

11. A variety of studies have shown that when arousal is too high, organisms are not inclined to explore novelty.

12. Emotionality or anxiety can be considered a state of high arousal that reduces the tendency to explore.

13. One implication of the research on arousal and exploration is that to promote exploratory behavior, it is important to make people relaxed and free from anxiety.

14. Art students tend to prefer more complex forms of stimulation. This preference may reflect their greater experience with collative variables that Berlyne has identified as a source of arousal.

15. The need for consistency governs, in part, what information is processed.

16. In recent years, psychologists have begun to appreciate the fact that a great deal of important learning occurs in the course of play.

17. Through play, monkeys learn the social skills necessary for adult social interactions.

18. Through play, monkeys learn to control aggression.

19. Solitary play tends to breed intrinsic motivation.

20. Extrinsic motivation not only reduces the tendency to explore but undermines intrinsic motivation.

21. We can facilitate intrinsic motivation by giving people the freedom to organize tasks as they want and by reducing or eliminating competing motives.

22. High sensation seekers are motivated by a need for novel and complex sensations and experiences.

23. High sensation seekers are willing to take physical and social risks in order to experience varied, novel, and complex sensations and experiences.

24. High sensation seekers tend to be involved in a wide range of sports over a period of time.

25. High sensation seekers tend to use drugs, to have a variety of sex partners, and to like situations that allow them to behave in an uninhibited manner.

26. High sensation seekers tend to have a thinking style that is characterized by flexibility, tolerance of ambiguity, and unpredictability. These qualities of thinking are probably what make the sensation seeker more creative.

27. High sensation seekers' tendency to be open and unconventional can result in delinquency, but if it is properly channeled it can lead to creativity and productivity.

28. High sensation seekers like the responsibility to make decisions, like to make them quickly, and are willing to make them with incomplete information.

29. High sensation seekers have low monoamine oxidase levels while low sensation seekers have high monoamine oxidase levels.

30. There are at least three reasons why people are motivated to be creative: the need for novel, varied and complex stimulation, the need to communicate, and the need to solve problems.

31. Creativity is defined as the tendency to generate or recognize ideas, alternatives, or possibilities that may be useful in solving problems, communicating with others, and entertaining ourselves and others.

32. DeBono has suggested that the tendency to create patterns in the brain tends to make our brains resistant to creativity.

33. Langer suggests that we have a natural tendency to become mindless, and that in order to act creatively we need to become more mindful.

34. Cognitive dissonance theory suggests that humans are motivated to see things the same way, which means, among other things, that we are inclined to reject new information.

35. Despite the fact that we tend to be motivated towards predictability and consistency, it has been suggested that humans have a creative urge.

36. Learning theories suggest that creativity can be viewed as disinhibition.

37. The tendency towards rigidity may be motivated by the desire to reduce anxiety or arousal.

38. Personality characteristics that can be linked to creativity include intellectual and artistic values, breadth of interests, attraction to complexity, high energy, a concern with work and achievement, independence of judgment, autonomy, intuition, self-confidence, ability to tolerate and resolve conflict, creative self-image, and openness to new experiences and new ways of viewing things.

39. It has been suggested that people learn to adopt certain beliefs and attitudes because they increase the opportunity to act creatively, an experience that people find rewarding.

40. People who are creative tend to come from families that value intellectual development and encourage autonomy and independence.

41. There are four important elements or components of creativity: knowledge, the ability to construct images and/or categories, the ability to synthesize and the willingness to withhold judgment.

42. Moderately remote associations are more likely to lead to creativity than highly remote associations.

43. Major creative contributions tend to be made by younger people, whereas minor creative contributions are more likely to be made by older people.

44. DeBono has offered a number of techniques that can help people overcome their natural tendency to be uncreative.

Competence and Intelligence, Achievement and Persistence, Self-Esteem and Self-Worth

- What is competence and where does it come from?

- What are some of the factors that lead to the development of competence?

- What is intelligence and why are humans so interested in intelligence?

- Is intelligence innate or do we acquire intelligence?

- What role does thinking play, if any, in the expression of intelligence?

- Are more intelligent people better able to cope with life?

- Why do people vary in their tendency to achieve goals?

- Why are people with a strong tendency to achieve goals more likely to persist than people with a weak tendency to achieve goals?

- Can people develop the motivation to achieve?

- How do success and failure experiences affect the tendency to achieve?

- Why do some people set difficult goals while others do not?

- Does our perception about ability and intelligence influence what goals we set for ourselves?

- Where do our feelings of self-esteem and self-worth come from?

- Is it good for us to take pride in our achievements or does pride make us vulnerable?

- Is it normal for people to experience self-doubt when they fail?

- Why is it so difficult to people with poor self-esteem to change their view of themselves?

- What kind of self-image does one need to have to experience positive self-esteem and positive self-worth?

Introduction

Even in the early years of life, children need to feel they are competent. As they play with other children they need to have a sense that they can do things that other children can do. If they don't possess the skills needed to effectively interact with other children, they often withdraw from social interactions. Similarly, when they cannot effect changes in their environment because they lack skills, their self-esteem drops and they give up.

In order for people to feel good about themselves throughout their lives, they need to develop and maintain a strong sense of *agency*. Agency means that people believe they can do things, that they can control things, that they can make things happen, that they can adapt, that they can learn. Agency should not be confused with having an optimistic attitude, where people have a positive outlook but no clear idea of how they might achieve a goal or deal with adversity. Agency comes from a sense of possessing skills or possessing the ability to acquire and develop skills. Agency, in short, involves having a sense of *pathways*.

While some theorists tend to view *agency* as distinct from *pathways*, most theorists tend to view agency and pathways as closely linked or even interdependent (as we noted in Chapter 11 with the Snyder et al. definition of hope). The concept of mastery, for example, suggests that people not only have a sense of agency but a sense of pathways. People with a strong mastery motive are inclined to say, for example, "I believe I can learn what I need to know in order to achieve my goals."

While love and acceptance by parents and significant others play an important role in creating an initial sense of self-worth and self-esteem in people, that is typically not enough to sustain their belief that they are worthy and significant people. Take, for example, what happens when people get older. As people age it is often communicated to them in various ways that they are no longer needed or useful. As a result, their sense of self-worth and self-esteem suffers, often resulting in feelings of loneliness and depression.

In this chapter I will explore the links between competency, self-esteem, and self-worth. I will show that by taking pride in their accomplishments, people develop a strong sense of agency, and it is from this sense of agency that they are motivated to set goals, persist in the face of failure, and eventually succeed. In the process of coping with life, they ward off feelings of helplessness and hopelessness that often emerge when people no longer feel competent or able to cope effectively.

Definition of Competence

Competence is skill, ability, capacity, proficiency, or fitness. It is something we all have in varying amounts. It is something we strive to attain. It is what parents encourage their children to develop. Everyone has specific skills that enable him or her to deal with specific situations. Seeing ourselves as having competencies means we see ourselves as having strengths. Seeing ourselves lacking in competencies, on the other hand, means we see ourselves as having weaknesses.

In this chapter we will not be examining the origins of specific skills, capacities, or proficiencies; rather, we will be examining the motivation that underlies the development of all competencies. Our focus will be more on the general question of what leads one person to persist or select difficult goals while another person gives up or selects easy goals. Since none of these theories clearly falls under biological, learned, or cognitive, I will not use this organizational structure in this section.

White's Theory of Competence

One of the most influential articles on the nature of competence was published by Robert White in 1959. He drew heavily on the work of the early 1950s, which showed that curiosity and exploratory behavior are not tied to such primary drives as hunger, thirst, and sex. He suggested that the tendency to explore is based on a more general motive which he called *effectance motivation*. This motive, White suggested, is directed towards understanding the nature of the environment and the order inherent in it. Feelings of *efficacy* occur when the individual comes to understand or know that he or she is able to affect the environment. Such feelings, White argues, can act as a reward. An infant who discovers that whenever she kicks her feet, the mobile hanging above her head moves, for example, would experience feelings of efficacy. She might smile, laugh, or show some other outward sign of her internal state. Most important, she would gain a sense of mastery.

White suggests that effectance motivation subsides when the situation has been so thoroughly explored that it no longer presents new possibilities. Thus, unlike primary (biological) rewards, which tend to produce a highly repetitive behavior, feelings of efficacy lead to the persistence of a behavior only so long as that behavior can produce new stimulation or knowledge. This idea is very similar to Berlyne's idea that arousal potential subsides as the individual processes all the information contained in a stimulus, and to Dember and Earl's idea that the motivational incentive of a stimulus wanes as the individual's complexity level shifts upward to match that of the pacer stimulus.

White notes that effectance motivation often fails to be aroused when the individual is anxious or when other motive systems are engaged. He suggests that this arrangement is biologically adaptive. It means that when survival motives are engaged, the individual fully attends to the task at hand, and that when survival needs are not pressing, the individual can spend the time necessary to explore all the possibilities in the situation. The point to emphasize about effectance motivation is that it takes time to exhaust the possibilities of a situation. The individual must not feel pressured or try to take shortcuts. Doing so would result in incomplete knowledge.

Piaget's Theory of Competence

For several decades, the Swiss psychologist Jean Piaget wrote about the development of competence (for example, Piaget, 1952; Piaget & Inhelder, 1969). His impact on developmental psychology and education has been enormous. His basic tenet is that competence develops naturally when a child interacts with his or her environment. The environment, Piaget says, forces the child to develop structures that will allow him or her to interact with that environment. This process is called *accommodation*. Equipped with certain cognitive structures, the child is then prepared to integrate the information contained in his or her environment. This process is called *assimilation*. The degree of assimilation is always limited by existing structures. Thus, when the child encounters new information that is discrepant from existing structures, he or she will be unable to process that information adequately. The child is therefore forced to develop new structures or, in Piagetian terms, to accommodate. Development is characterized by periods of assimilation followed by accommodation followed by further periods of assimilation, and so on. In Dember and Earl's terms, development may be thought of as cognitive adaptation in which the cognitive structures become increasingly complex as the child has contact with stimuli of increasing complexity. Ability to assimilate is limited by the complexity of the child's cognitive structures.

The motivation to develop new structures (to ac-

PRACTICAL APPLICATION 13.1

Implications for Parents and Teachers

What are the implications of this research for parents and teachers? The theories of Berlyne, Dember and Earl (Chapter 12), White, and Piaget all suggest that children are biologically equipped to develop competence provided certain conditions are met. First, it is important that a stimulating and varied environment be available. Without such an environment, the motivation to develop competence will be lacking. Children need to be exposed to stimulation that will create moderate incongruity or a moderate discrepancy. Such stimulation, it appears, elicits the intrinsic motivation necessary for developing new cognitive structures, raising the adaptation level, or abstracting new principles. Second, it is important that the child be freed from competing motives. Survival motives (such as hunger and thirst) appear to take precedence over the motivation to develop competence. Anxiety appears to be particularly debilitating. White (1959) has suggested that anxiety is one of the enemies of exploration. Dember and Earl theorize simply that organisms fail to be motivated by a

discrepancy between their complexity level and that of the environment when they are anxious. Third, it is important that the child be free to respond as he or she sees fit. Because it is impossible for the parents or teacher to know the exact state of a given cognitive structure, it is best to let the biological process take its natural course. There is good reason to believe that if a child is left to his or her own ways, he or she will eventually exhaust all the possibilities. The fact that children do this in different ways should not be surprising if we remember that the motivation for processing information comes from the environment, which, as we know, is highly varied. Fourth, it is important that a child not be pressured by time. The development of cognitive structures appears to be a complicated process. If we accept the idea that the development of cognitive structures is essentially an abstracting process, then it follows that the child must differentiate relevant from irrelevant information. This can be a very time-consuming process, even for a computer.

---

commodate) is assumed to come from the discrepancy that exists when a child is confronted with a situation that he or she is unable to assimilate adequately. This idea is very similar to Hunt's idea that the motivation to process new information results when we encounter incongruity (that is, when present information deviates from our expectations). Thus Piaget, like Hunt, believes that the motivation for developing competence is inherent or intrinsic. It is not necessary for the parent or the teacher explicitly to reward such behavior.

Summary

Competence has to do with skill, ability, capacity, proficiency, or fitness. Several theories have been ad-

vanced to explain why some people have more of it than others. White has proposed that competence grows out of curiosity and exploratory behaviors, which are based on a general motive he has called effectance motivation. This motive is directed towards understanding the nature of the environment and the order inherent in it. Feelings of efficacy occur, he suggests, when a person comes to understand or know that he or she is able to affect the environment. Piaget has argued that the person is motivated to integrate the information contained in his or her environment. Integration occurs by a process called assimilation. When no structures exist to assimilate information, the person must develop new cognitive structures. This process is called accommodation.

Intelligence as a Prototype of Competence

In this section I want to discuss intelligence as a prototype of competence. Intelligence is, to a very large degree, a competence that is acquired as a result of our interactions with the environment. While Piaget talks in general terms about how and why certain intellectual structures are acquired, the theory that I will be discussing talks more about the specific nature of those structures and the implications for coping and adjusting as a result of having different kinds of mental structures.

Implicit Theories and the Development of Intelligence

Different people have different implicit theories of intelligence. For example, some people believe that if you have a good memory you are intelligent, some people believe that if you are good at solving problems you are intelligent, and some people believe that if you can deal effectively with people you are intelligent. Because people value intelligence, they are inclined to work at those things that they believe reflect intelligence. Obviously, if people have different implicit theories of intelligence they will work at different things. The net result is that some people develop one set of skills while others develop other sets of skills.

How can we conceptualize this process? For some time psychologists have used an attentional model. According to this model, when people are motivated to do or learn one thing as opposed to another they are are inclined to attend to examples in the environment that will provide them with the information they need. Initially they may imitate another person, for example, and in the process of imitating they extract the information or rules that will allow them to perform that same response. Eventually they come to develop cognitive structures that summarize and organize that information so they can produce the response they need with ease.

As these cognitive structures become more and more refined or differentiated, people find it easier to make sense out of the world using those cognitive structures. As a consequence, they develop a prefer-ence for viewing the world using those structures. They develop what might be called a bias for viewing the world in a certain way. They see it from a certain perspective that is governed by their new cognitive structures. These structures eventually come to control, at least in part, the attentional processes of the individual. Thus, we come full circle. By first attending to certain things in the environment we come to develop cognitive structures, and then with these new cognitive structures in place we have a bias for seeing certain things as opposed to others.

The concept of attention is based on the idea that we cannot process all the information that we encounter because it leads to sensory overload. As a result, we develop mental structures that allow us to "chunk," group or categorize information so that we can deal with large quantities of information. Instead of having to deal with all the individual pieces of sensory information impinging on our receptors, we simply represent all that sensory information by a label or a name that we give to the "chunk," the group, or the category (Miller, 1956). By using abstract labels or names we can increase our ability to deal with large amounts or complex arrays of information. The more labels or categories that we have the more information we can handle at any one time. We can even learn to chunk "chunks" or group groups or develop superordinate categories in order to handle still larger amounts of information.

There are many different ways that we can "chunk," group or categorize sensory information. Some ways of chunking information are better for certain tasks than for others. Ideally, we should learn to chunk information in different ways so that when we are faced with a particular task we can use the organization most suitable for dealing with that task. It appears that most of us do not do that; we come to develop a preferred way of chunking information and, as a result, we have a preferred way of thinking and problem solving.

Robert Sternberg (1988) suggests that people learn to process information differently and therefore can solve certain problems better than others. Just why people come to process information differently is not clear. Perhaps our genes play a role in this process.

How people are taught to approach tasks no doubt makes a difference. As a result of this tendency to process information in different ways, some people can deal with certain tasks or situations better than others. While some are good at academic tasks or tasks that involve logic and the sequential organization of information, others are good at dealing with tasks that involve a more holistic organization or tasks in which information must be processed more rapidly, or tasks where information must be integrated. By examining how people process information or how they solve problems, it is possible to classify people as having different kinds or types of intelligence that enable them to deal with certain types of tasks better than others.

As you read about Sternberg's theory, which I discuss next, you might ask yourself what might lead people to develop their intellects differently. What happened, perhaps early in life, that motivates them to attend to one thing as opposed to another?

Implicit Theories about Academic and Everyday Intelligence

Intelligence tests were originally designed to predict academic success. It is not surprising, therefore, that such tests often do not predict success in other areas such as business, politics, sports, and the arts. Recognizing this fact, Sternberg has set out to identify and describe those competencies that predict success in other areas of life.

As a starting point, Sternberg asked experts (university professors who work in the area of intelligence) and lay persons to describe characteristics of people who are academically intelligent versus everyday intelligent. What Sternberg discovered is that lay persons have well-defined, implicit theories of intelligence. From their rating he found they view intelligence as made up of three components: *problem-solving ability* (e.g., reason logically, identify connections among ideas, see problems as a whole, and get to the heart of the problem), *verbal ability* (e.g., ability to speak clearly, fluently, and to articulate well, read with high comprehension), and *social competence* (e.g., acceptance of others, admit mistakes, display interest in the world, and is prompt). When he compared the experts' rating of

these qualities with the lay persons', he found that lay persons tend to stress *interpersonal* skills in a social context ("acts politely, displays patience with self and others, gets along well with others, is frank and honest, and emotions are appropriate to the situation") whereas experts stressed *intrapersonal* skills in an individual context ("shows flexibility in thought and action, reasons logically and well, displays curiosity, learns rapidly, thinks deeply and solves problems well") (Sternberg, 1990, pp. 120-121).

Sternberg's Triarchic Theory of Intelligence

The theory of intelligence that Sternberg eventually proposed is called the *triarchic theory of intelligence* and was heavily influenced by this early research examining the implicit theories of academic and lay persons. In the final analysis, he decided that intelligence has to do with problem-solving abilities. The question he needed to answer is what factors or components give rise to good problem-solving behavior. From his work with academics he saw the need to incorporate the idea that analytical skills play an important role in problem-solving. As a result, one of the components he included in his theory was *analytical abilities*. Since problem-solving involves the ability to generate alternatives, he decided to also include *synthetic abilities*. The ability to generate alternatives to a problem means that people need to be able to synthesize material in new and different ways. In short, they need to be creative. One of the main things that Sternberg learned from his early research into intelligence and competence is that lay persons tend to value the importance of being able to deal with everyday situations. As a result, one of the main components that he incorporated into his theory was *contextual abilities*. As I will discuss shortly, these have to do with the complexities of everyday living. Let me define each of these abilities more precisely.

Analytical abilities. Analytical abilities involve making use of both memory and analytical reasoning skills. People with good memory and analytical reasoning skills are good at criticizing and finding flaws. They can logically get from one point to another. It is those abilities or competencies that have traditionally been used to measure academic intelligence. People with analytical skills typically do well on university entrance tests which emphasize the ability to think critically and logically. They often end up in jobs—such as engineering, law, or medicine—where certain types of knowledge are important.

Synthetic abilities. Synthetic abilities have to do with one's ability to synthesize information. Among other things, synthetic abilities involve the ability to see things in new ways, to create new categories, to be creative. People with good synthetic ability are often good researchers, good story-tellers, inventors, designers, artists. Synthetic abilities can be acquired. As I indicated in Chapter 12, one of the things that often prevents people from generating new alternatives or new categories is their rigid adherence to familiar, traditional or conventional ways of doing things. In order to break out of this pattern, people need to recognize that change and creativity involve entertaining new and different ways of viewing things. People who teach creativity like to show that when people are given the set to be creative (it is the thing to do at that moment) they can become very creative. What often prevents people from being creative is a judgmental atmosphere in which people feel that making a novel suggestion will result in some form of negative judgment or even ridicule.

Contextual abilities. Contextual abilities have to do with everyday practical reasoning. People with good contextual abilities are good at figuring how to get through the complex demands of everyday living. They can quickly determine what is expected of them and how to meet those expectations. People who have contextual abilities are often referred to as "streetwise." When they make mistakes they correct them quickly. People with good contextual abilities are good at surviving when things change. They know how to adapt to new demands quickly and effectively.

An interesting exercise is to assign yourself percentages for each of these three components: Are you mainly analytical with a bit of synthetic and contextual, or are you mostly synthetic or contextual? Or what?

Sternberg has questioned the tendency of univer-sity admissions procedures to rely mainly on analytical skills to admit students. As the competition becomes even greater, there may be a bias towards admitting only those students who have analytical intelligence. What are the implications of not admitting people who are high in synthetic and contextual intelligence?

Dweck's Theory of Intelligence

Implicit theories of competency. People view themselves and their competencies in different ways. Some people view competency in terms of the skills and knowledge they now possess. They say to themselves "This is what I am and therefore this is what I can do." Other people view competency in terms of their ability to acquire skills and knowledge. They say to themselves "Look what I have accomplished so far. That's a good indication of what I can do in the future." The first type of individual ascribes to an *entity* theory (they see intelligence as fixed) whereas the second type ascribes to an *incremental* theory (they see intelligence as changeable) (Dweck, 1991; Dweck & Leggett, 1988). For reasons that are still not completely clear, some people hold the view that learning stops at a certain age or their capacity to learn is limited. Therefore, no matter how hard they work, there is little hope for real change. For such people possibilities are limited. People who believe in the incremental theory, on the other hand, believe that the only thing that limits their ability to learn and develop new skills is their willingness to work. The possibilities are virtually unlimited for such people. The important thing to note here is that how much you learn is linked to how much you think you can learn. There are limits, of course, that are placed on you by your nervous system. There are also better ways to learn than you may have discovered up to this point in your life. Nonetheless, one of the major components determining how far you go is how persistent you are, and how persistent you are is linked to your beliefs about whether you can learn and develop.

Research with people who perceive they have ability and ascribe to an entity theory versus an incremental theory indicates that when given a choice among tasks of various levels of difficulty, people who hold an

Table 13.1 Dweck and Leggett's Theory of the Relationship Between Implicit Theories of Intelligence and The Behavior Patterns of Mastery and Helpless Types. (From C. S. Dweck and E. L. Leggett, "A Social-Cognitive Approach to Motivation and Personality." *Psychological Review*, 1988, *95*, 256-273. Copyright © 1988 by the American Psychological Association. Reprinted with permission.)

Theory of intelligence	Goal orientation	Perceived present ability	Behavior pattern
Entity (Intelligence is fixed)	Performance (Goal is to gain positive judgments/avoid negative judgments of competence)	High	Mastery (Seek challenge; high persistence)
		Low	Helpless (Avoid challenge; low persistence)
Incremental (Intelligence is changeable)	Learning (Goal is to increase competence)	High or Low	Mastery (Seek challenge that fosters learning; high persistence)

incremental theory tend to choose challenging tasks, tasks that will challenge them to stretch themselves, whereas people who ascribe to an entity theory tend to choose tasks that are more in line with their abilities. Since humans are motivated to see themselves in a positive way, people who perceive themselves to be low in ability and who hold to an entity theory are inclined to choose relatively easy tasks. They are likely to succeed in such tasks, which means they can avoid judgments about their lack of competency. Should they fail, of course, it would be devastating to their already low perception of their competency. The net result is that people with low perceived ability who hold to an entity theory are inclined to avoid challenges and to choose easy tasks.

Dweck and Leggett (1988) argue that the tendency to avoid a challenging activity is a maladaptive strategy, whereas the tendency to select challenging tasks is adaptive. The reason, they argue, is simple. Most achievement involves overcoming obstacles, acquir-

ing skills and persisting in the face of setbacks. Therefore, it is important to be dispositionally disposed to always select challenging tasks. Table13.1 summarizes Dweck and Leggett's theory. Note that people with low perceived ability are prone to helplessness, a condition that we have already discussed in some detail in Chapter 10.

The Consequences of Believing in the Entity Theory versus the Incremental Theory

Consequences of believing in the entity theory. According to Carol S. Dweck's model, people who believe in the entity theory are motivated to select goals that will indicate they do have intelligence and to avoid goals that might provide evidence that they lack intelligence. Consistent with the theory, research indicates that when these people experience failure, they tend to attribute it to lack of intelligence (for example, Elliott & Dweck, 1985, cited in Dweck, 1986). If I believe I lack intelligence, why should I put forth effort? It makes no sense to put forth effort if I have already come to the conclusion that I lack intelligence. People who reason this way have to select their tasks very carefully. Even a single encounter with failure can be damaging because it confirms their lack of intelligence. After reviewing the research literature on the way children react to success and failure, Dweck has suggested that even a single encounter with failure can make a person helpless.

The important thing to note here is that failure can be devastating to people who hold to the entity theory. For this reason they learn to set their goals with an eye to avoiding failure. They tend to avoid challenges, especially challenges to new ventures in which they cannot be certain of avoiding failure. These people may become low achievers in order to avoid the failure they fear.

Consequences of believing in the incremental theory. According to Dweck, people who believe in the incremental theory tend to select goals that will enable them to increase their competence (for example, Nicholls, 1984). Since intelligence is something that you can acquire, it is important to select goals that can maximize learning. Learning, in other words, becomes synonymous with competence and intelligence. How do you maximize learning? One thing you must be careful not to do is to select goals on the basis of certainty of success. Sometimes you can learn a great deal in situations in which failure is likely. Take the ring-toss task. You can't learn the skills needed to be good at this task by simply standing next to the post and dropping the ring over it. While this may seem obvious, it is not always clear to the person who is obsessed by the need to avoid failure.

Since the development of competence at any task usually requires persistence, belief in the incremental theory of intelligence turns out to be very adaptive in the process of setting and attaining goals. Both rewards and failure simply provide feedback to the individual. Belief in the entity theory is not at all adaptive. To a person who holds to the entity theory, failure is feedback about a lack of competence or intelligence. When you lack intelligence, it no longer makes sense to put

forth effort. The reason some people do not select challenging goals for themselves, then, is that they view each new task as a potential threat to their self-esteem.

Bandura's Self-Efficacy Theory

Bandura's self-efficacy theory is a very powerful theory that is designed to explain conditions that lead people to put forth effort and learn. There are two main constructs within his theory: outcome expectations and feelings of efficacy.

Outcome expectations. According to Bandura's (1986) theory, when people consider or reflect on a certain outcome as being desirable or undesirable, such as to stop smoking or to continue smoking, they make a judgment about what they can expect if they change their behavior or they don't. Will they live longer, feel better, save money, for example, if they stop smoking? As a result of their reflections or considerations, they form an *outcome expectation.* They might say to themselves, for example, "I will have more money, feel better, and live longer if I quit smoking." Outcome expectations are defined, therefore, as "a person's estimate that a given behavior will lead to certain outcomes."

Feelings of self-efficacy. The next thing they need to consider is whether or not they have the competence, the motivation, or whatever it takes to achieve that outcome. Again, as a result of reflection, they will make some judgment about their confidence or, to use Bandura's concept, they will experience feelings of *self-efficacy.* If I have strong outcome expectations and have strong feelings of self-efficacy, I will be inclined to put forth the effort that is necessary to achieve the desired outcome. Self-efficacy is defined as "the conviction that one can successfully execute the behavior required to produce the outcomes."

Consider another example. Let's say that I decide I would like to become an actor and, as a result, I think about whether or not I should try out for a part in a play. I decide as a result of reflection that this would be a good idea. I decide that if I could prove myself in this role I could launch my career. In other words, I form a strong outcome expectation that getting this part will help me achieve my ultimate goal to become an actor. Next I consider whether or not I have the talent to get this part. Let's say I come to the conclusion that I do not have the skills I need, at least not at this time. As a result I have poor feelings of self-efficacy. Will I try out or will I not? According to the self-efficacy theory, the thing which best predicts performance is perceived self-efficacy. As the theory predicts, I do not bother to schedule a tryout even though I know being successful could launch my career.

The concept of self-efficacy refers to personal judgments and beliefs about capabilities of performing a specified behavior in a particular situation. These feelings of self-efficacy are assumed to be stable not only across situations but across time, but they are *not* stable across different situations. Unlike having global feelings of competency, self-efficacy is situation-specific. Self-efficacy is not a feature of personality. That is, it is not a broad trait such as optimism. Thus, according to Bandura's theory, it is necessary to measure feelings of self-efficacy for each and every situation.

Three dimensions of self-efficacy. There are three dimensions of self-efficacy that need to be evaluated in order to predict behavior: magnitude, strength, and generality. Magnitude is measured by observing which level of difficulty a person selects from a graded series. People who have low-magnitude feelings believe they can only perform the simpler or easier tasks of a graded series of tasks, while people with high-magnitude feelings believe they can perform the most difficult or hardest of a series of tasks. Strength refers to probabilities, judgments about how certain one is. People who are highly certain they can perform at a particular difficulty level would indicate so by selecting high probabilities, say 98%, while people who are low in certainty would select low probabilities, say 25%. Generality refers to the extent to which efficacy expectations will generalize to other situations. Even though the theory is situation-specific, a certain set of skills should generalize to similar situations. Acting ability, for example, should generalize to different plays.

Evidence for Self-Efficacy Theory

Self-efficacy theory has proved to be very powerful in predicting a wide variety of behaviors such as adherence to exercise programs, stop smoking programs, complex decision-making (Bandura & Jourden, 1991), and even empowering people (Ozer & Bandura, 1990). The theory was originally proposed to account for the effectiveness of various intervention programs in the treatment of anxiety. The key to all these programs was to give people the skills they need to deal with various anxiety-provoking or fearful situations. As a result of learning specific skills, people experienced much less anxiety.

The theory focuses on teaching people the specific skills they need to effectively deal with a specific situation. If a person is anxious or fearful about public speaking, for example, the general procedure would be to provide such people with the skills that would enable them to effectively handle such a situation. This might include a variety of things including, how to structure a talk, practice at speaking, managing the inevitable anxiety that accompanies public speaking. When people are given the skills they need, it has been found their self-efficacy typically increases correspondingly. In short, when people perceive they have the skills necessary to deal with a specific situation, they not only feel empowered but self-confident. I will talk more about self-efficacy theory in Chapter 14.

Summary

Intelligence is, to a very large degree, a competence that is acquired as a result of our interactions with the environment. The general model that underlies Sternberg's theory might be conceptualized in terms of an attention model. When people learn to attend to different things they are inclined to develop different cognitive structures or simply different ways of organizing information.

Recognizing that intelligence tests often do not predict success in everyday life, Sternberg has set out to identify and describe those competencies that predict success in other areas of life. Using various ratings he found that people view intelligence as made up of three components: *problem-solving ability, verbal ability,* and *social competence.* Sternberg has proposed that intelligence can and should be conceptualized as being made up of three components, each of which plays an important role in problem-solving: analytical, synthetic, and contextual. It is important to note that according to Sternberg's theory, intelligence is largely acquired; it involves the development of skills. Because the acquisition of skills is often due to motivation, Sternberg's theory can properly be viewed within the context of motivational processes. That is, people learn to develop those skills they value.

According to Dweck's model, people who believe in the entity theory are motivated to select goals that will indicate they do have ability and to avoid goals that might provide evidence that they lack ability. People who believe in the incremental theory tend to select goals that will enable them to increase their competence. Since ability (intelligence) is something one can acquire, it is important to select goals that can maximize learning.

What are the consequences of believing in the entity model or the incremental model? People who believe in the entity model of intelligence are motivated to select goals that will put them in a favorable light. Should they fail, they tend to attribute their failure to lack of ability (intelligence). This perception tends to undermine any future desire to put forth effort. People who hold to the incremental model of intelligence tend to set a goal that will increase their competence. When these people fail, they tend to interpret failure not as lack of ability but as feedback that tells them how well they are performing. They often interpret failure as an indication that they did not put forth the necessary effort, so they are motivated to work harder.

According to Bandura's theory, there are two important things to consider when predicting behavior: *outcome expectations* and *feelings of self-efficacy.* Outcome expectations are defined as "a person's estimate that a given behavior will lead to certain outcomes." Self-efficacy refers to personal judgments and beliefs about capabilities of performing a specified behavior in a particular situation. They are assumed to be stable not only across situations but across time. Self-efficacy is not a feature of personality but rather is specific to situations. Self-efficacy is defined as "the conviction that one can successfully execute the behavior required to produce the outcomes." The three dimensions of self-efficacy that need to be evaluated in order to predict behavior in specific situations are: magnitude, strength, and generality.

Achievement and Persistence

Again, it is not easy to clearly break down the various theories into biological, learned and cognitive. I have arranged the theories, however, in terms of those that are more biological to those that are more learned and finally to those that are more cognitive.

Contributions of Murray

The initial impetus for work on achievement motivation came from Henry Murray, who recognized that people vary in their desire or tendency to "overcome obstacles, to exercise power, to strive to do something difficult as well as and as quickly as possible" (Murray, 1938, pp. 80-81). Murray called this tendency the "need to achieve."

The Thematic Apperception Test (TAT) was created by Chrishana Morgau and Henry Murray to measure variations in human motivation. The test consists of a series of pictures about which people are asked to write stories. The theme of the story is analyzed to obtain a measure of the motives that people have projected into the story. The basic assumption underlying the TAT is that when a particular motive is aroused, people tend to incorporate ideas pertaining to that motive in the stories they write.

McClelland's Contributions

For over four decades, David McClelland has been doing research related to the achievement motive. His contributions are so extensive that it is impossible to do justice to them here. His book *Human Motivation* (1985) provides an excellent summary of his work. In order to measure the achievement motive with more precision, McClelland and his colleagues (1953) adapted the TAT and developed a precise method for scoring the achievement motive. A number of studies have been done to assess the validity of the TAT measure they devised. These studies show that a generalized motive does exist and that it can predict behavior in a wide variety of situations (for example, Atkinson, 1953; French, 1956; Lowell, 1952; Mischel, 1961).

McClelland has not been able to identify an obvious biological link to a brain center or a neurotransmitter. He argues, however, that the achievement motive grows out of a more basic incentive to "do something better"—not to gain approval or any other kind of external reward, but "for its own sake" (McClelland, 1985, p. 228). McClelland points out that the environment plays an important role in the development of this natural incentive. He argues, for example, that parents play an important role, often by providing the kind of environment that allows the achievement motive to develop naturally.

Amsel's Theory of Persistence

In a period spanning more than 20 years, Abram Amsel (for example, 1958, 1962, 1972) systematically developed a general theory of persistence. This theory has its origins in animal research but readily explains a number of important phenomena relating to human persistence. The theory assumes that persistence is learned in rather specific situations but tends to generalize to other situations that share certain common properties. The basic process or mechanism that is assumed to be responsible for persistence is the counterconditioning of disruptive stimuli.

To illustrate the theory, we will examine some problems associated with a novice swimmer learning to become a competitive swimmer. Let's assume that our swimmer has already learned to swim but has never engaged in competitive swimming. According to Amsel's analysis, when a person exercises a response in the presence of new or different stimuli, it is likely that these stimuli will have a disruptive effect on the response. For example, if a person has never engaged in a competition before, the anticipation of the competition could produce a state of high arousal that might disrupt the response of swimming. Fear of failing might cause anxiety, which could also disrupt performance. Similarly, noise, the presence of spectators, the turbulence of the water, or other aspects of the competition could prove distracting and thereby cause a swimmer to perform poorly.

To perform well, a swimmer must adapt to these stimuli. In learning theory, this process is called "habituation." The best way to learn to ignore or adapt to these stimuli is to exercise the desired response in their presence. A good coach will typically take great care to ensure that an athlete is systematically exposed to all potentially distracting stimuli prior to any important competition. The coach will, for example, have teammates compete against each other, enter the swimmers in local competitions where spectators and the press are present, make them aware of the importance of winning, and finally introduce them gradually to more and more competitive events.

Amsel suggests that the process of habituation involves counterconditioning. It is assumed that if a person exercises a response in the presence of potentially disrupting stimuli, these stimuli will become conditioned to the response. As a result, the stimuli lose their ability to disrupt the desired response. Further, and more important, Amsel argues, these stimuli come to *support* the desired response. The idea that disruptive stimuli could become supportive stimuli may not be intuitively obvious. Years of research, however, have shown that this does in fact happen. Not only do the stimuli not disrupt behavior, but in many cases their presence becomes a necessary condition in order for the response to occur—or at least to occur at a very high level. We have probably all heard of athletes who perform better when they begin to lose or an entertainer who performs best when he has a large or hostile audience or a singer who does her best when she is anxious. A famous baseball pitcher, when asked whether it bothered him when he was booed, said that he always did his best when the crowds were hostile. He pointed out that he had learned to pitch under these conditions.

What does this have to do with persistence? According to Amsel's analysis, persistence involves learning to exercise or perform a response in the presence of disruptive cues. As we all know, achieving a goal often involves a great deal of time, effort, and, most of all, frustration. Amsel's theory specifically addresses the question of how people come to deal with frustration.

Amsel (1958, 1962) noted some time ago that when an animal fails to receive a reward for a response that is normally rewarded, the animal becomes highly emotional, a reaction that Amsel labeled frustration. For example, Amsel noted that when laboratory rats failed to receive a reward for a response they had learned, they would urinate and defecate (involuntary responses that have been used as indicators of high emotion in certain animals), become aggressive, and tend to run faster on the next trial. Amsel argued that the faster running on the next trial reflected the increased arousal that normally accompanies frustration. Amsel further noted that if an animal experienced several nonrewards interspersed with rewards, the animal eventually persisted longer in the absence of all rewards than animals that had been continuously rewarded. This is known in the learning literature as the partial reinforcement effect (PRE).

According to Amsel, the reason an animal will persist longer in the absence of all rewards when it has previously experienced nonrewards interspersed with rewards is that it has learned to perform in the presence of frustration cues. Specifically, Amsel has suggested that frustration cues are conditioned to the ongoing response. Thus, rather than disrupting performance, frustration tends to support, or facilitate, performance.

It is important to note that in order to condition frustration cues to the ongoing response, the frustration must never be too great. If it becomes too great, it will totally disrupt performance. When this happens, the frustration cues become conditioned to "not responding." A good swimming coach is careful not to push a swimmer into competitions that might totally disrupt the swimmer's ability to perform. Typically a good coach will gradually introduce the athlete to potentially disrupting stimuli in order that such stimuli can be conditioned to the desired response.

In summary, Amsel's theory suggests that persistence is acquired over a period of time. It is necessary for a person to be exposed gradually to cues that may

disrupt a desired response in order to countercondition those cues. By being exposed to more and more frustrating cues—or any cue, for that matter, that might interfere with performance—the person becomes more or less immune to such disruptive cues. A surgeon working for hours may fail to realize just how tired she has become until she finishes an operation. A long-distance runner may be oblivious of fatigue until she finishes a race. A businessman may skip lunch and not realize until later that he is hungry. These and many more examples can readily be explained by Amsel's theory.

Although Amsel's theory is a very robust one, it has some limitations. By failing to incorporate the concept of intrinsic motivation, Amsel's theory has difficulty accounting for why an author may continue writing books even though he fails to find a publisher who is willing to publish even one of his manuscripts. The theory also fails to account adequately for the tendency of some people to shift tasks when they become successful or competent at their current task. According to Atkinson's theory, which I discuss next, such shifts are very predictable. Nevertheless, Amsel's theory can explain why people often do persist when it appears they should give up in the face of tremendous hardship and frustration.

Atkinson's Theory of Achievement Motivation

Atkinson's theory incorporates several cognitive concepts including expectations, incentive, and value. It is a theory that has had an enormous impact on people interested in achievement motivation.

One of Atkinson's important contributions to work on achievement motivation was his suggestion that the need to achieve is always tempered by another fundamental need, the need to avoid failure. That is, one cannot set out to achieve a goal without considering the consequences of failure. Atkinson's theory recognizes that people may differ in the strength of these two motives, but in the final analysis, goal-directed behavior is determined by the joint action of the two motives. It is assumed that if the motive to succeed is greater than the motive to avoid failure, a person will strive to attain a particular goal; if the motive to avoid failure is greater than the motive to succeed, the person will select goals that minimize the chance of failure. In other words, fear of failure may alter the goals a person selects. Rather than selecting a goal that would bring the greatest satisfaction, a person may prefer a second-best goal if that goal involves less risk of failure.

It is convenient to discuss the two conflicting motives—the hope of success and the fear of failure—as separate motives. It will then be shown how the two separate motives interact to produce various types of achievement-oriented behaviors. I will start by discussing the first of these two, the hope of success.

Hope of success. According to Atkinson's theory (1957), hope of success can be expressed as a quantity. Theoretically, hope of success can be calculated for a variety of tasks, so that it is possible to predict which task a person will select. There are three factors, or values, that need to be determined in order to arrive at this quantity. First, it is necessary to obtain a measure of the general personality disposition that motivates a person to succeed (M_S). As we have noted, the TAT has been adapted for this purpose. Second, it is necessary to determine the difficulty of the task. This can be expressed as the probability of success (P_S). If success is certain, P_S is 1; if failure is certain, P_S is 0. Finally, it is necessary to assess the pleasure or pride that a person may experience following success. This factor has been called the incentive value of success (In_S). For both theoretical and empirical reasons, it is assumed that In_S is simply $1-P_S$. That is, when the task is difficult (the probability of success is low), the incentive value is high; and when the task is easy (the probability of success is high), the incentive value is low. Atkinson assumes that the three factors operate in a multiplicative fashion according to the following formula:

$$T_S = M_S \times P_S \times In_S$$

where

T_S = tendency to achieve success, or simply hope of success

M_S = motive to achieve success

P_S = perceived probability of success

In_S = incentive value of success ($1-P_S$)

Fear of failure. As we have noted, hope of success does not by itself predict final performance. It is assumed that fear of failure, or the tendency to avoid failure ($T-f$), also plays an important role. It is assumed that fear of failure can also be expressed as a quantity. Again, three factors are assumed to be involved. First, it is assumed that there is a general personality disposition, or motive, to avoid failure (M_F). Atkinson has, for purposes of obtaining a measure of this tendency, used the Test Anxiety Questionnaire (Mandler & Cohen, 1958; Mandler & Sarason, 1952). There is good evidence that situations designed to evaluate performance are likely to arouse this particular motive. Accordingly, the way a person normally responds to tests provides a reasonably good measure of this motive. As in the case of hope of success, task difficulty and incentive are assumed to play important roles in fear of failure. Again, it is assumed that these three factors operate in a multiplicative fashion according to the following formula:

$$T-f = M_F \times P_f \times In_f$$

where

$T-f$ = tendency to avoid failure

M_F = motive to avoid failure

P_f = probability of failure ($1-P_S$)

In_f = negative incentive value of failure

Resultant achievement motivation. Whereas success can lead to feelings of pride and satisfaction, failure can lead to feelings of shame. The expectations of success and failure, acting together, lead a person to undertake or not to undertake a given task. Atkinson maintains that these two motives are additive. The way they combine to produce resultant (total) motivation can be expressed as follows:

$$T_S + T-f = (M_S \times P_S \times In_S) + (M_F \times P_f \times In_f)$$

Since In_f is negative, motivation to undertake a task can be positive, negative, or zero, depending on whether hope of success is stronger than fear of failure, fear of failure is stronger than hope of success, or the two are equal. To illustrate this fact, different values have been substituted into the above equation. Table

Table 13-2. Calculations of T_s and T_{-f} for five levels of task difficulty when $M_S > M_F$, when $M_F > M_S$, and when $M_S = M_F$. (From J. W. Atkinson, "Motivational Determinants of Risk-Taking Behavior." *Psychological Review*, 1957, 64, 359,-327. Copyright ©1957 by the American Psychological Association. Reprinted with permission.)

	Task (P_s)	$(M_S \times P_s \times In_s)$	+	$(M_F \times P_f \times In_f)$	=	$T_s + T_{-f}$
$M_S > M_F$,	A (0.9)	(5 × 0.9 × 0.1)	+	(1 × 0.1 × –0.9)	=	0.36
where $M_S = 5$ and $M_F = 1$	B (0.7)	(5 × 0.7 × 0.3)	+	(1 × 0.3 × –0.7)	=	0.84
	C (0.5)	(5 × 0.5 × 0.5)	+	(1 × 0.5 × –0.5)	=	1.00
	D (0.3)	(5 × 0.3 × 0.7)	+	(1 × 0.7 × –0.3)	=	0.84
	E (0.1)	(5 × 0.1 × 0.9)	+	(1 × 0.9 × –0.1)	=	0.36
$M_F > M_S$,	A (0.9)	(1 × 0.9 × 0.1)	+	(3 × 0.1 × –0.9)	=	–0.18
where $M_F = 3$ and $M_s = 1$	B (0.7)	(1 × 0.7 × 0.3)	+	(3 × 0.3 × –0.7)	=	–0.42
	C (0.5)	(1 × 0.5 × 0.5)	+	(3 × 0.5 × –0.5)	=	–0.50
	D (0.3)	(1 × 0.3 × 0.7)	+	(3 × 0.7 × –0.3)	=	–0.42
	E (0.1)	(1 × 0.1 × 0.9)	+	(3 × 0.9 × –0.1)	=	–0.18
$M_S = M_F$,	A (0.9)	(5 × 0.9 × 0.1)	+	(5 × 0.1 × –0.9)	=	0
where $M_S = 5$ and $M_F = 5$	B (0.7)	(5 × 0.7 × 0.3)	+	(5 × 0.3 × –0.7)	=	0
	C (0.5)	(5 × 0.5 × 0.5)	+	(5 × 0.5 × –0.5)	=	0
	D (0.3)	(5 × 0.3 × 0.7)	+	(5 × 0.7 × –0.3)	=	0
	E (0.1)	(5 × 0.1 × 0.9)	+	(5 × 0.9 × –0.1)	=	0

13-2 shows the outcome when $M_S > M_F$, when $M_F > M_S$, and when $M_S = M_F$.

The important thing to note in Table 13-2 is that when $M_S > M_F$, the maximum motivation is predicted to occur for tasks with a 0.5 difficulty level. These are tasks at which success and failure are equally likely. In contrast, when $M_F > M_S$, the maximum motivation is predicted to occur for tasks with either a 0.1 or 0.9 level of difficulty. Interestingly, the theory predicts that a person in whom $M_F > M_S$ will select either a task at which he is almost sure to succeed or, paradoxically, a task at which he is likely to fail. Atkinson has suggested that this paradoxical prediction can be understood if we consider the psychological consequences of failing at a very difficult task. Failing at a very difficult task does not produce shame to the same degree as failing at an easy task—perhaps none at all. The reason is that no one would expect a person to succeed at a very difficult task. For a person who had played tennis only a few times, losing a tennis match to the current world champion would be no disgrace.

Tests of Atkinson's Theory

Vocational choice and achievement motivation. The real test of any theory is whether it predicts real-world behavior. One of the obvious challenges to achievement motivation theory is how well it predicts vocational choice. In one very good study of this question, Mahone (1960) predicted that people in whom $M_S > M_F$ should make more realistic vocational choices than people in whom $M_F > M_S$. He reasoned that people in whom $M_S > M_F$ will select goals that are more consistent with their ability, whereas those in whom $M_F > M_S$ are more likely to select goals that are either too easy or too difficult. To test this hypothesis, Mahone asked a group of college students to indicate their vocational goals. Mahone then had clinical psychologists rate these goals for their degree of realism. In order to make their evaluations, the clinical psychologists were given the students' grade-point averages, college entrance examination scores, and other relevant information. Table 13-3 shows the relation between the

Table 13-3. Clinical Judgments of Realism of Vocational Choice in 135 Students as a Function of Need for Achievement (nAch) and Debilitating Anxiety. (From C. Mahone, "Fear of Unrealistic Vocational Aspiration." *Journal of Abnormal and Social Psychology*, 1960, *60*, 253-261. Copyright © 1961 by the American Psychological Association. Reprinted with permission.)

		Clinical Judgments (%)	
nAch	Anxiety	Realistic	Unrealistic
High	High	48	52
High	Low	75*	25*
Low	High	39*	61*
Low	Low	68	32

*$\chi^2 = 7.96$, $p < 0.003$

clinical judgments and the resultant achievement motivation of the subjects. As Mahone predicted, subjects in whom $M_S > M_F$ displayed more realism than those in whom $M_F > M_S$. These results are, of course, consistent with Atkinson's theory. People in whom $M_F > M_S$ tend to select tasks that are either too easy or too difficult.

Mahone also had the students estimate their own ability in relation to other students. These estimates were compared with the objective percentile scores obtained on college entrance exams. Mahone found that students low in resultant achievement motivation were the most inaccurate in estimating their own abilities; students high in resultant achievement motivation were the most accurate. This finding, together with those reported above, indicates that people high in resultant achievement motivation not only have different risk preferences than people low in resultant achievement motivation, but have different perceptions of their own abilities. Morris (1966) has also collected evidence that people high in resultant achievement motivation are more likely to select jobs consistent with their ability, whereas people low in resultant achievement motivation are more likely to select either overly easy or overly difficult jobs.

Persistence and Achievement Motivation

Atkinson's theory predicts the level of task difficulty a person will select. The question arises whether a person will persist at those tasks he initially chooses to work at. The answer is a qualified yes. Norman Feather (1961, 1963) showed, for example, that when the initial P_S was 0.7, subjects in whom $M_S > M_F$ showed greater persistence than subjects in whom $M_F > M_S$. (Recall from Table 13-3 that $M_S > M_F$ subjects should be attracted to such tasks and $M_F > M_S$ subjects should tend to avoid them.) Feather further showed that when the initial P_S was 0.5, persistence was greater among those in whom $M_F > M_S$ than for those in whom $M_S > M_F$. (Again, $M_F > M_S$ subjects are expected to select tasks with a low probability of success.)

An important factor in determining whether a person will continue working is the difficulty level of an alternative activity. The problem in the real world is predicting when the alternative activity will become more desirable than the activity initially selected. It seems reasonable to assume that a person's skill will improve as he works at a given task. As skill increases, the perceived P_S value should increase in direct proportion. This means that the person may abandon a task in midstream if an alternative activity becomes available that is nearer his preferred level. This is one explanation of why business executives switch jobs so often. Once they have mastered the operations of one company, they may be motivated by the new challenges offered by another.

Bernard Weiner's Explanatory Style Theory of Achievement

Bernard Weiner's theory grows out of the observation that people have different explanations for success and failure (Weiner, 1972, 1991). He postulated that success and failure at achievement tasks may be attributed to any of four factors: ability, effort, task difficulty, and luck (see also Weiner et al., 1971). These four factors can be classified along two dimensions: locus of control (internal or external) and stability (stable or unstable). This classification scheme is shown in Table 13-4. Internals believe their successes and failures result from their own actions. Whether they succeed or fail, they attribute the outcome to their ability (or lack of it) or to the effort they did or did not put forth. Externals, in contrast, tend to believe that success or failure is something that happens to them; it is beyond their control. When they succeed, it is because they had an easy task or they were lucky. When they fail, it is because they had a difficult task or had bad luck. Sometimes they win and sometimes they don't.

The stable/unstable classification pertains to the fact that some things are stable over time while others are not. Ability is, for the most part, relatively stable. While it may change over the long run, it typically does not change in the short run. Abilities take time to develop. Effort, in contrast, is not at all stable. Some days we work very hard at a task and on other days we do not. Task difficulty is also stable over time whereas luck is not. If we return to the same task day after day, the difficulty of that task does not change. Luck, on the other hand, is much more capricious. Sometimes things go our way, sometimes they don't. The best we can do with luck is to take advantage of it when it comes.

Attribution styles of people high and low in resultant achievement motivation. Although it is interesting to see how people in general perceive the causes of success and failure, a more interesting question is how people high and low in resultant achievement motivation perceive why they succeed and fail. This is especially interesting in view of the fact that it appears that people high in resultant achievement motivation are motivated by failure whereas people low in resultant achievement motivation are motivated by success.

Weiner and Kukla (1970) found that people high in resultant achievement motivation perceived success as due to ability and effort and failure as due to lack of effort. People low in resultant achievement motivation perceived success as due to task difficulty or luck and failure as due to lack of ability. These rather complicated findings might seem incomprehensible at first glance. They can be readily understood, however, if we consider that people high in resultant achievement motivation see themselves as high in ability, whereas people low in resultant achievement motivation see themselves as low in ability (Weiner & Potepan, 1970).

Table 13-4. Attributions for Success and Failure

| | Locus of Control | |
	Internal	External
Stable	Ability	Task difficulty
Unstable	Effort	Luck

Weiner (1972) has suggested that because people high in achievement motivation perceive themselves as high in ability, they tend to account for variability in performance as due to effort. Thus, when they fail, they perceive their failure as due to lack of effort. Failure, therefore, motivates them to work harder. (Failure may also challenge their view that they are high in ability and may thereby motivate them to reaffirm this view by trying harder.) Curiously, success reduces their motivation. Weiner suggests that following success they tend to relax. As a consequence, their performance tends to diminish on subsequent attempts or tasks.

Because people low in resultant achievement motivation perceive themselves as low in ability, they easily account for failure. It is simply due to lack of ability. Clearly, it is useless to work harder if one lacks the basic ability. How does such a person account for success? Obviously, if one lacks ability, it would be illogical to attribute success to ability. Because effort is closely linked to ability, it would also be illogical to ascribe success to effort. That is, since effort is the energy for an action while ability provides the direction for that energy, one cannot succeed merely by increasing effort. Success, therefore, must have occurred because the task was easy or the person was lucky.

Why should success motivate the person low in resultant achievement motivation when he perceives that his performance is due to luck? It may simply be that such people want to take advantage of a "run of good luck." This suggestion is consistent with the findings of Weiner and Kukla (1970) that male pupils high in resultant achievement needs are more likely to ascribe success to themselves whereas males low in resultant achievement needs are more likely to ascribe their success to external factors. If success is due to such exter-

PRACTICAL APPLICATION 13.2

Getting People to Accept Challenges

People with high resultant achievement motivation tend to accept challenges. They will take on difficult tasks, but not ones that are impossible. Once they have committed themselves to a course of action, they persist. The question that many people have asked is how we can get people with low resultant achievement motivation also to accept challenges and take on difficult tasks. In short, how can we motivate people who are not now motivated? At least three approaches have been suggested.

Reducing the Negative Affect Associated with Failure

It has been found repeatedly that people who are high in resultant achievement motivation (success-oriented people) experience pride when they succeed but relatively little shame or guilt when they fail, whereas people low in resultant achievement motivation (fear-oriented people) experience guilt and shame when they fail but relatively little pride when they succeed (Sorrentino & Hewitt, 1984). Rather than pride, fear-oriented people seem to experience something akin to relief. Success means they do not have to deal with the guilt and shame that come with failure.

At this point we do not have a clear understanding of why the affect associated with success and fear is asymmetrical. There are several possibilities. It may simply be that the individual was punished for failure in the past, and therefore shame and guilt have become conditioned rejection or punishment responses. Another possibility grows out of the work of Herbert S. Terrace (1969), who found that when he taught pigeons to make discriminations without errors, they became very emotional when they were transferred to a more difficult task at which they did make errors. Terrace's work has led to the suggestion that people may react to negative feedback (failure) with an unlearned emotional response when

they have not previously been exposed to failure. In short, people may become hypersensitive to failure if they have previously known nothing but success.

How do you treat people who are hypersensitive to failure? One obvious procedure is to try to desensitize them. It has been suggested that people who are allowed to fail from time to time in the course of learning automatically become desensitized to failure, and not to failure in that task alone but to failure in general. People who are hypersensitive would have to be introduced to failure under very supportive conditions. They then might come to realize that they have nothing to fear when they fail. The idea here is that if people no longer fear failure, they will be more inclined to try difficult or challenging tasks.

Motivating People with Difficult Tasks

A second approach is to require people to work at a difficult task (Locke & Latham, 1990). Give them no choice, in other words; simply tell them to do it. This approach is designed to capitalize on the attributional process that takes place in such situations. When people succeed at difficult tasks, they tend to take credit for their success (self-serving bias), whereas when they succeed at an easy task, they tend to attribute their success to the fact that the task was not difficult. When the task is difficult, they say to themselves, "Since I did that pretty well, I must be pretty good"; when the task is easy, they say to themselves, "Well, of course I did it well—any fool could have done that." As we have noted, one of the reasons people tend to put forth effort is that they perceive themselves to have ability. It makes no sense, as I have pointed out, for people to work hard at a task for which they think they have no ability.

The second reason for giving people a difficult task lies in the way they respond to failure at easy and difficult tasks. People who fail at a difficult task tend to attribute their failure to the difficulty of the task ("Of course I couldn't do that—I'm not Superman"). A response of this sort, of course, does not undermine their perceptions of their ability. When they fail at an easy task, though, they tend to blame their own lack of ability. Since it takes little or no effort to do an easy task, it is hard to avoid the conclusion that failure can be due to nothing but lack of skill. And of course when people perceive themselves to be lacking in ability, they are reluctant to put forth effort. One variant of this approach is to give people an easy task at which they are likely to succeed and tell them that this task will predict future performance. It has been shown that people then treat that task as providing them with an estimate of their ability (for example, Brickman, Linsenmeier, & McCareins, 1976; Feldman & Bernstein, 1978; Vreven & Nuttin, 1976).

Attributional Retraining

A third approach is to alter people's perceptions of their ability. If people expect to do poorly because of their sex, age, education, race, or whatever, they are not going to put forth effort. The problem here is to change their expectations. It is important to demonstrate that the factor to which they attribute their failure to perform well, whatever it may be, is not a problem. Often providing examples can help to eliminate the stereotypes to which people cling. If one sees that someone else of the same sex or age or whatever has succeeded, the belief that such factors are important is effectively undermined.

Another important thing to emphasize is the role of effort and persistence (Ostrove, 1978). Sometimes people are simply not aware of the factors that differentiate successful and unsuccessful people. If they can be made aware of those factors, they are more likely to adopt a strategy that will help them succeed.

Once they begin to experience success, they will be more likely to repeat the behaviors that lead to success.

Still another approach is simply to make people aware of the fact that performance is often unstable and not necessarily a good predictor of future performance. In one study, college freshmen were given information suggesting that the factors that lead to low grades in the first year are temporary. This suggestion led to improved performance on sample items of the Graduate Record Exam and to improved grades the following semester (Wilson & Linville, 1985). The effects were greater among women than among men, a finding that is consistent with the idea that women have a greater tendency to adopt the entity model of intelligence and ability.

It should be noted that programs designed to provide children with continuous success by giving them relatively easy tasks is not an effective way of producing stable confidence, challenge seeking, and persistence (Relich, 1983). In fact, it has been found that such procedures can backfire and lower children's confidence in their ability (Meyer, 1982). A young child who is always given easy tasks to ensure success may interpret this to mean that the parent or the teacher has no confidence in his or her ability. When people are incompetent, you give them easy things to do. Further, the child may come to the conclusion that it is bad to fail. When people make sure that you avoid something, you are likely to conclude that there must be something bad about that thing you are being protected from. What does this train of thought do for self-esteem? If you have so little ability that you can't be permitted to choose a challenging task for yourself because you would fail and feel bad, you're not likely to have much self-esteem left to protect. A major ingredient of self-esteem is the belief that you have ability.

nal factors as luck, then it is important to take advantage of such situations.

The Work of J. T. Spence

In recent years, Janet Spence and her colleagues have provided a multidimensional view of achievement that has grown out of their work with the Work and Family Orientation (WOFO) Questionnaire. Two main concerns have guided this work. First, how similar are men and women when it comes to achievement motivation? Is achievement motivation structurally the same or structurally different in men and women? Second, what are some of the real-world outlets for the achievement motive? Often women's accomplishments have been dismissed or simply overlooked. Their achievements as they pertain to the family, for example, have received very little attention. Most research pertaining to achievement motivation has focused on academic and vocational achievement. How does the achievement motive find expression in everyday activities?

Definition of achievement motivation. Spence and Helmreich (1983, p. 12) suggest that "achievement is task-oriented behavior that allows the individual's performance to be evaluated according to some internally or externally imposed criteria that involve the individual in competing with others, or that otherwise involves some standard of excellence." As they point out, while achievement-oriented individuals often express their achievement in conventional job- and school-related activities, they also find outlets for their achievement striving in other voluntary activities. The *Guinness Book of World Records* is testimony to the fact that humans voluntarily attempt to achieve, master, or compete in a wide range of activities for no other reason than to see if what they have in mind can be done.

The Work and Family Orientation (WOFO) Questionnaire. The WOFO consists of two parts. The first consists of items that measure attitudes toward achievement-related activities (see Table 13-5). The second consists of items that inquire about people's educational aspira-

tions; the relative importance of work versus marriage as anticipated sources of life satisfaction; and extrinsic and intrinsic goals, such as the desire for pay, prestige, and job advancement (see Helmreich & Spence, 1978).

The first part of the scale focuses on three factors: work, mastery, and competitiveness. The interesting thing about the factor structure is that the same three factors emerge for both men and women—good evidence that the structure of achievement is the same in both sexes.

Results from large samples of university students indicated that men score significantly higher than women on the mastery and competitiveness subscales, while women score higher than men on the work subscale. Subsequent studies involving varsity athletes, businesspeople, and academic psychologists obtained the same pattern of results. Though the differences are fairly small, they are significant, and they are found consistently (Spence & Helmreich, 1983).

Ability of WOFO to predict overall GPA. In order to see whether the scale could predict academic achievement as indicated by a student's cumulative GPA, Spence and Helmreich (1983) administered the WOFO to more than 1300 students. The results pointed to an interaction of GPA with the three subscales. As work and mastery scores were similarly related to GPA, these two scores were combined into a single work-mastery score. In order to show how the students with higher GPAs differed from those with lower GPAs, the investigators divided each sex into two groups, one consisting of the half with GPAs above the median (high GPA group) and the other of the half with GPAs below the median (the low GPA group). Thus they now had four groups. The results, shown in Figure 13-1, indicate that students with low grades were low in both work-mastery and competitiveness. The finding is not surprising. What was surprising was the finding that the people with high GPAs were high in work-mastery but low in competitiveness. Those who were high in both work-mastery and competitiveness did not do so well academically. Men who were high in work-mastery and high in competitiveness had the lowest GPAs. While it is too early to explain exactly why this should be the case, the findings are obviously very important.

Table 13-5. Items from the first part of the WOFO scale. The items are to be answered using a four-point scale that goes from *Not at all like me* to *Very much like me*. The items that measure Competitiveness, Mastery, and Work are labeled with the letters C, M, and W. Items that are to be reverse-scored are marked with an asterisk (*). (From J. T. Spence and R. L. Helmreich, "Achievement-Related Motives and Behavior." In *Achievement and Achievement Motivations*, J. T. Spence (Ed.), 1983. W. H. Freeman, San Francisco. Reprinted with permission.)

1. I would rather do something at which I feel confident and relaxed than something which is challenging and difficult. (M)*
2. It is important to me to do my work as well as I can even if it isn't popular with co-workers. (W)
3. I enjoy working in situations involving competition with others. (C)
4. When a group I belong to plans an activity, I would rather direct it myself than just help out and have someone else organize it. (M)
5. I would rather learn easy fun games than difficult thought games. (M)*
6. I find satisfaction in working as well as I can. (W)
7. It is important to me to perform better than others on a task. (C)
8. If I am not good at something, I would rather keep struggling to master it than move on to something I may be good at. (M)
9. There is satisfaction in a job well done. (M)
10. I feel that winning is important in both work and games. (C)
11. Once I undertake a task, I persist. (W)
12. I find satisfaction in exceeding my previous performance even if I don't outperform others. (M)
13. It annoys me when other people perform better than I do. (C)
14. I prefer to work in situations that require a high level of skill. (M)
15. I like to work hard. (W)
16. I try harder when I'm in competition with other people. (C)
17. I more often attempt tasks that I am not sure I can do than tasks that I believe I can do. (M)
18. Part of my enjoyment in doing things is improving my past performance. (M)
19. I like to be busy at all times. (W)

Ability of WOFO to predict annual income. Annual income is often taken as an indication of achievement in the business world. In order to explain the possibility that competitiveness is detrimental not only to academic achievement but to performance in the business world (at least as measured by income), a group of businesspeople were given the WOFO (Saunders, 1978). Businesspeople tend to score relatively high on the competitiveness scale, a finding that is consistent with the idea that in order to survive in the business world, you need to be competitive. If we look at who makes the most money (Figure 13-2), however, we can see that competitiveness has a detrimental effect. People who make the most money are those high in

work-mastery and low in competitiveness. Again, while there is no ready explanation for these results, they are obviously important.

Ability of WOFO to predict scientific productivity. If the WOFO scale is a measure of achievement, it follows that it should predict whether or not a person is likely to make a contribution to scientific knowledge. One way of measuring the worth of a scientific contribution is to count the number of times a scientific article has been cited by other scientists in their publications. This is called a citation index.

A study of the citation indices of academic psychologists suggests that the WOFO can indeed predict

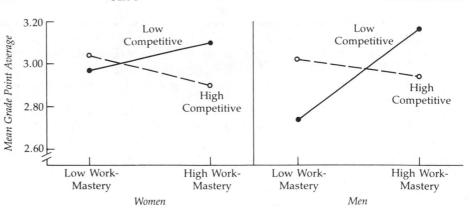

Figure 13-1 Mean grade point average in the four achievement-motive groups of male and female undergraduates. (From J. T. Spence and R. L. Helmreich, "Achievement-Related Motives and Behavior." In *Achievement and Achievement Motivations*, J. T. Spence (Ed.), 1983. Copyright © 1983 by W. H. Freeman, San Francisco. Reprinted with permission.)

scientific attainment (Helmreich et al., 1978, 1980). People who make the most contributions are those who are high in work-mastery and low in competitiveness (Figure 13-3). What makes these findings especially interesting is the fact that they parallel the findings in regard to GPAs and annual salaries. The question that all of these studies raise is why interpersonal competitiveness reduces rather than augments the tendency towards work and mastery. Most of us tend to assume that competitiveness is a kind of energizer. Possibly it is, but rather than helping people to persist (work) and master the tasks before them, it directs behavior in a somewhat different direction.

Summary

The initial impetus for work on achievement motivation came from Henry Murray, who recognized that people vary in their desire or tendency to "overcome obstacles, to exercise power, to strive to do something difficult as well as and as quickly as possible." In order to measure the achievement motive with more precision, McClelland and his colleagues adapted the TAT and developed a precise method of scoring the achievement motive.

Learning theorists who have examined the question of persistence have concluded that the principles of learning can indeed explain why people will often persist in situations in which reward is infrequent or frustration is present. Amsel has argued that when a person performs a response in the presence of frustrat-

ing or disrupting cues, those cues become conditioned to the response. As a result, the cues come to support, rather than disrupt, behavior in those situations. Further, the person will persist in the presence of cues that would normally disrupt behavior. Withholding a reward for a correct response has also been shown to produce persistence. Amsel argues that the absence of a reward that a person has come to expect normally produces frustration. Performing a response in the presence of the frustration cue of absence of reward will result in the conditioning of this cue to the ongoing behavior. As a result, a person will learn to persist, at least for a time, in the absence of a reward.

One of Atkinson's important and fundamental contributions was his suggestion that the need to achieve is always tempered by another fundamental need, the need to avoid failure. According to Atkinson's theory, resultant achievement motivation is determined by two factors, or quantities, referred to as hope of success and fear of failure. Hope of success is made up of three factors, or values: motive to succeed, probability of success, and the incentive value of success. Similarly, fear of failure is made up of three values: motive to avoid failure, probability of failure, and the incentive value of failure. According to the theory, people in whom the motive to succeed is greater than the motive to avoid failure $(M_S > M_F)$ will choose tasks with an intermediate (0.5) level of difficulty, while people in whom the motive to avoid failure is greater than the motive to succeed $(M_F > M_S)$ will choose tasks that are very easy (0.1) or very difficult (0.9).

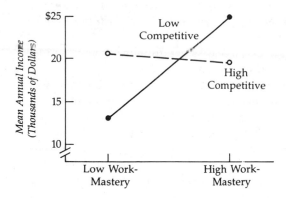

Figure 13-2. Income in four achievement-motive groups of businessmen corrected for years of experience. (From J. T. Spence and R. L. Helmreich, "Achievement-Related Motives and Behavior." In *Achievement and Achievement Motivations*, J. T. Spence (Ed.), 1983. Copyright © 1983 by W. H. Freeman, San Francisco. Reprinted with permission of the editor.)

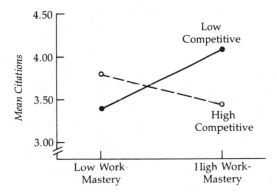

Figure 13-3. Citations to published research in four achievement-motive groups of male academic scientists. (From R. L. Helmreich, W. E. Beane, G. W. Lucker, and J. T. Spence, "Achievement Motivation and Scientific Attainment." *Personality and Social Psychology Bulletin*, 1978, *4*, No. 2, 222-226. Copyright © 1978 by Sage Publications, Inc. Reprinted with permission.)

Tests of Atkinson's theory with male subjects have generally provided results consistent with the theory. For example, it has been shown that people in whom $M_S > M_F$ tend to select jobs consistent with their ability, whereas people in whom $M_F > M_S$ tend to make unrealistic vocational choices. Atkinson's theory has also been shown to predict persistence. In general, people tend to persist at those tasks that they initially selected.

Weiner has suggested that there are four basic perceived causes of success and failure at achievement tasks: ability, effort, task difficulty, and luck. People who are high and low in resultant achievement motivation respond quite differently to success and failure; the question is how to account for this difference. Weiner and Kukla found that people high in resultant achievement motivation perceived success as due to ability or effort and failure as due to lack of effort, while people low in resultant achievement motivation perceived success as due to task difficulty or luck and failure as due to lack of ability. The key to understanding these findings is that people high in resultant achievement motivation perceive themselves as high in ability, whereas people low in resultant achievement motivation see themselves as low in ability.

Janet Spence and her colleagues have constructed the Work and Family Orientation (WOFO) Questionnaire, which has three subscales: work, mastery, and competitiveness. Men tend to score higher on the mastery and competitiveness subscales while women tend to score higher on the work subscale. The WOFO scale has been successful in predicting a variety of indices of achievement behavior, such as GPA, annual salary, and scientific productivity. In each of these cases, it has been shown that people who are high in work-mastery and low in competitiveness perform the best. It appears that a high level of interpersonal competitiveness reduces performance.

Self-Esteem and Self-Worth

The concepts of self-esteem and self-worth are closely linked, even interchangeable according to some researchers. While it has been argued that the need for maintaining good self-esteem is innate (e.g., Maslow), not all people experience good self-esteem. Whether they do or not is determined by such things as whether or not they experienced conditional versus unconditional love (e.g., Rogers), and whether or not they have learned to take pride in their accomplishments. There is a strong cognitive component to self-esteem that appears to be motivated by the need for people to maintain good self-esteem.

Definition of Self-Esteem and Self-Worth

It has been suggested that self-esteem can be defined as *pride in oneself in which one becomes aware and accepting of one's imperfections while cherishing one's inherent strengths and positive qualities* (proposed by Andrea Parecki as quoted in Lazarus, 1991). Like other definitions, this one contains the idea that people engage in a process of self-evaluation. What this definition does not immediately convey is the feelings that people experience as a result of engaging in self-evaluation. The concept of self-worth is often employed to capture the idea that the outcome of this process can produce profoundly positive or profoundly negative feelings. To the degree that people can accept their weaknesses and faults while simultaneously recognizing their strengths, they can experience strong self-worth. Alternatively, if they are unable to accept their weaknesses, or they do not see themselves as having any strengths or positive qualities, they can experience an absence of self-worth.

It has been suggested that self-esteem is not a global attribute that cuts across all situations but rather is specific to certain situations (domains). Susan Harter prefers to use the word *global self-worth* to emphasize the idea that self-esteem is multidimensional

and that feelings of self-worth come from competencies that people experience in different domains (Harter, 1990).

At least three distinct domains have been identified: performance, social, and appearance (Heatherton & Polivy, 1991). Research using a scale designed to measure these domains showed that people's self-esteem for each of these domains often drops momentarily when they experience "private" failure on a task (performance self-esteem), when they experience "public" failure on a task (social self-esteem), and when they have concerns about their physical appearance (physical self-esteem). Other research suggests there are many more domains and that they change with age (Harter, 1990). What seems to determine a domain is what is important to an individual at various stages in his or her life.

Even though it can be shown that self-esteem often drops momentarily as the result of some type of negative feedback, different people seem to have different levels of self-esteem for each of these domains that seem to be relatively stable over time. Most researchers emphasize the role of early experiences in establishing these relatively stable levels of self-esteem, a conclusion that is consistent with the work of Coopersmith.

Are People Born with the Need to Experience High Self-Esteem?

Various psychologists have suggested that people are born with a need to experience good self-esteem. Maslow, for example, suggested that after people have satisfied their need for belongingness, they would strive to satisfy their esteem needs. He suggested that all people in our society have a need or desire to have a good opinion of themselves. Maslow suggests that there are two subsidiary sets of esteem needs. First, there are the desires for strength, for achievement, for adequacy, and for mastery and competence. Second, there is the need for reputation and prestige, status, fame, glory, dominance, recognition, attention, importance, dignity, or appreciation. Satisfaction of the esteem needs, Maslow has argued, leads to feelings of self-confidence, worth, strength, and capacity, together with the feeling of being useful. Failure to satisfy the esteem needs leads to feelings of inferiority, weakness, and helplessness.

Competence and Feelings of Self-Esteem

Feelings of self-esteem and beliefs about competence are closely linked. In this section I will discuss two theories which address this relationship.

Weiner's Theory

A frequently asked question is whether competence leads to improved self-esteem, or conversely, whether good self-esteem will lead to improved competence. Weiner (1979, 1991) has suggested that self-esteem has to do with the way we feel about ourselves when the locus of control for an event is perceived as internal. Specifically, he notes that internal people are likely to experience feelings not only of pride but of competence when they succeed, and they are likely to experience feelings of shame and incompetence when they fail. Because these feelings are linked to internal self-attributions (ability and effort), Weiner believes, these feelings have a great deal to do with a person's tendency to persist or not to persist. As we noted previously, people with high nAch not only tend to view themselves as high in ability but tend to persist at tasks that challenge that ability. As we also noted previously, the main factor in changing achievement behavior is to change people's ability or their perceptions of their ability. Apparently, when people have a good opinion of their ability, they are inclined to put forth effort. Once they have put forth effort and succeeded, feelings of self-esteem emerge. Thus, esteem feelings become the factor that mediates persistence (Weiner, 1979). To the degree that persistence is a necessary requirement for developing competence, then self-esteem plays an important role in producing competence.

What about the person who holds an external frame of reference? Because, according to Weiner's analysis, such people tend to view success and failure as due to luck or chance, succeeding or failing will not tend to alter their perceptions of their ability or effort.

As a result, they will not be inclined to have either a particularly good or particularly bad view of themselves, nor will they be inclined to persist at a task. To the degree that persistence is an important requirement for developing competence, such people will tend not to become highly competent. In summary, Weiner's position is that when a person has a good opinion of his or her ability (and perceives the environment as essentially controllable), he or she will be inclined to put forth effort. To the degree that effort is fundamental to developing skills, such a person will become competent.

Coopersmith's Work

In an extensive study of self-esteem, Stanley Coopersmith (1967) has concluded that people who enjoy high self-esteem (have a good opinion of themselves) differ in a number of important ways from people with low self-esteem. They set higher goals, are less troubled by anxiety, experience less stress together with fewer psychosomatic symptoms, are less sensitive to failure and criticism, experience greater feelings of control (and suffer less from feelings of helplessness), tend to be more enterprising in approaching problems, and tend to explore more (show more curiosity toward themselves and their environment). They are, in a basic sense, intrinsically motivated people who not only tend to be competent but have a positive attitude toward themselves.

Coopersmith's findings concerning the antecedents of self-esteem are particularly interesting. Extensive data collected on the parents of high- and low-self-esteem children indicate that parents play a primary role in determining whether a child experiences positive or negative self-esteem. Parents of children who experience high self-esteem are characterized by their total acceptance of and respect for the child, by their tendency to set clearly understandable limits on what the child is permitted and not permitted to do, and by their tendency to allow the child great latitude to explore and test within those limits. Coopersmith argues that parents of high-self-esteem children create a climate that frees the child from anxiety and doubt. Within such an environment the child can freely explore the environment and in doing so gain competence in dealing with it. Coopersmith notes that parents of high-self-esteem children not only encourage the children to become responsible and competent but to accept the independence and diversity of expression that often accompany the emergence of such behavior. In other words, the child is informed by the parent (a significant giver of acceptance and love) that he or she is an important individual who can expect to continue being accepted not only by the parents but by society at large even if he or she occasionally fails or if his or her behavior deviates somewhat from the norm. The child reacts to that signal, Coopersmith finds, by continuing to set high goals and to work hard to attain them.

Coopersmith's work indicates that self-esteem may mediate, in part, the tendency to achieve. His work suggests that individual differences in self-esteem are acquired early in life. As we noted earlier, one of the reasons it is difficult to change achievement behavior is that to change achievement it is necessary to change a person's perception of his or her ability. If self-esteem affects one's perception of one's ability (competence), then it becomes necessary to alter self-esteem as well. At this point we run into the chicken-and-egg problem of what to focus on first. The work on changing achievement motivation suggests that we need to focus on both self-esteem and perception of ability so that they can influence each other.

Self-Esteem and Reactions to Success and Failure

Whether one has a good opinion of oneself (high self-esteem) or a poor opinion of oneself (low self-esteem) has for some time been regarded as a major determinant of such things as achievement behavior. For example, Shrauger (1972) reported that low-self-esteem people do significantly worse in achievement settings than high-self-esteem people. The question arises whether high- and low-self-esteem subjects are differentially affected by success and failure. In a study to examine the reactions of high- and low-self-esteem people, Brockner (1979) found that whereas high-self-esteem people performed equally well following success and failure, low-self-esteem people performed significantly worse following failure (but just as well as high-self-esteem people in the success condition), but only under self-focusing stimulus conditions. That is, when subjects were encouraged to focus on their performance or simply tended to be self-conscious about their performance, low-self-esteem subjects tended to perform poorly if they had previously failed. These findings are consistent with Carver's (1979) model, which suggests that if fear or anxiety cues become salient, they will disrupt performance. According to Carver, when such cues become salient the person is inclined to assess the likelihood of completing the task. Subjects whose expectations are positive (as they are after success) will be motivated to match their behavior against the standard. If they begin to think they will not be able to complete the task, however, they will respond with passivity and withdrawal. Since low-self-esteem subjects tend to have a low opinion of their ability, they will be more inclined to respond to failure with reduced motivation. Tests of this model have shown that positive expectations indeed lead to greater persistence or performance than negative expectations, but only when there is self-focused attention (Carver, Blaney, & Scheier, 1979a, 1979b).

Pride, Self-Esteem, and the Self-Concept

It has been suggested that pride is a positive emotion that can be grouped with such emotions as triumphant, victorious, accomplished, special, brave, and courageous (Storm & Storm, 1987). Lazarus (1991) suggests that the core relational theme for pride is *enhancement of one's ego-identity by taking credit for a valued object or achievement, either our own or that of someone or some group with whom we identify*. This emphasizes the idea that pride plays an important role in the emergence of the self both as an individual and as a member of a group. Like Lazarus, others have suggested that pride is important for the emergence of such traits as confidence, independence, curiosity, and initiative—qualities that characterize people with high self-esteem (see Harter, 1990). It is from being able to experience pride (take credit) that people gain a strong sense of their own power and agency. It provides them with the unshakable belief that they can effect change and thereby cope.

Achieving a milestone is a powerful way of enhancing self-esteem and developing a positive selft-concept.

Pride can be viewed as the emotion that can help sustain goal-directed behavior. When people encounter adversity they need to believe that they can and will succeed if they simply exercise their skills and persist. There are many examples of people who, in the face of adversity, are able to sustain themselves because they are convinced their actions will eventually make a difference. Persistence is not something that just happens in a vacuum. It is something that is learned. It is based on developing an unshakable belief that over the long haul one's abilities and persistence will make a difference. As Snyder et al. have argued, it is people who have a sense of agency and pathways that become optimists. As we saw earlier, it is the optimists who persist and succeed.

Children need to experience pride because it gives them a sense of autonomy, power, and self-confidence. The question that we might ask, therefore, is can anyone prevent them from experiencing pride? The answer seems to be yes. Sometimes parents or teachers will take credit for things children have done and thereby rob them of this powerful emotion. Sometimes children are raised in environments that prevent them from doing things on their own. What seems to nurture pride is allowing people to make their own choices and giving them full credit for their accomplishments while not blaming them for their shortcomings. Coopersmith's work is a good example of how to maximize feelings of pride in children and, in the process, of how to nurture good self-esteem. When children are viewed as independent, autonomous, and capable of making choices, they learn they can effect change or simply be agents. In their own small way, children learn they can be victorious and triumphant and that is what gives them the confidence later in life to accept challenge.

One's Self-Concept and Self-Esteem

There is a great deal of evidence that the self-concept of people with high and low self esteem is very different. It appears that as the result of certain early experiences, people develop or construct a self-concept that is cither good at enhancing and maintaining their self-esteem or is flawed. In this section I will examine some of the research which shows how the self-concept of high- and low-self-esteem people differ. Later I will talk about how these differences may have emerged as the result of certain early experiences. Finally I will talk about how the self-concept can be restructured so that people can better maintain good self-esteem.

Having a Clearly Differentiated (Complex) Self-Concept

A great deal of research points to the idea that people who have good self-esteem have a clearly differentiated self-concept (Campbell, 1990; Markus & Nurius, 1986). Among other things, that means they have a clear idea of which life domains are important to them and they have a clear idea of their strengths and weak-

PRACTICAL APPLICATION 13.3

Learning to Manage Self-Doubt Following Failure: Using Downward Comparison

One of the things most likely to undermine goal-directed behavior is failure. Both high- and low-self-esteem people experience self-doubt following failure, and both tend to reduce their efforts markedly as a result. While low-self-esteem people are still licking their wounds, high-self-esteem people can be seen working hard to achieve their goals. In short, they seem to bounce back as though nothing happened.

When you ask both high- and low-self-esteem people what they thought about following failure, they provide an interesting insight into how some people have learned to manage their thinking so that it does not undermine their ability to carry on in the face of adversity. What the high-self-esteem people do is to lower their expectations, at least momentarily. Specifically, they shift from comparing themselves to people who are high performers (people who have already achieved difficult goals) to people who are low performers (people who they have already passed on the road to success). As a result of

shifting their comparison from high to low performers, they feel much better about themselves. Instead of seeing themselves as in the bottom of the high group they see themselves as being in the top of the low group. In short, they see themselves as winners. They take credit for what they have already achieved and take pride in that fact.

Low-self-esteem people, in contrast, are not inclined to do this. They continue to compare themselves with people in the high-performance group. In continuing to make this comparison they come to the realization that, relative to these top performers, they have not achieved that much. As a result they cannot take pride in their past accomplishments and they begin to see themselves as losers (e.g., Gibbons & McCoy, 1991; Wills, 1981, 1991).

The immediate question is why would either the high- or low-self-esteem people ever select the high-performance group as a standard of comparison in the first place? Why not select the low group and

nesses in these domains. As a result, they have a clear and stable view of themselves. This enables them to deal with virtually all types of feedback, both positive and negative. Low-self-esteem people, in contrast, do not seem to have a clearly defined idea of what life domains are important to them, nor do they seem to have a clear idea of their strengths and weaknesses in these domains. As a result, they are unable to deal with feedback that is negative.

It is important to remember that good self-esteem involves learning to acknowledge and accept one's weaknesses. This seems to immunize us to some extent from the impact of negative feedback. As Baumgardner (1990) has pointed out, "To know oneself is to like oneself." When people know themselves they can maximize out-

comes because they know what they can and cannot do. One of the strategies of people with low self-esteem or unstable self-esteem (a positive but fragile view of themselves) is to resist or ward off evaluative feedback (Kernis, Grannemann, & Barclay,1989). While this is a protective device that can help people avoid negative feedback, it also robs them of a clear idea of who they are. It also robs them of valuable information they need to improve their behavior. It is when people learn to be open to evaluation (seek out criticism and help) that they are more likely to learn and therefore develop.

Self-Perpetuating Quality of Poor Self-Esteem

There is a great deal of data to suggest that people with

maintain that group as one's standard of comparison? Wouldn't this serve to ensure that one always had good self-esteem?

The answer is no. This doesn't work for most people because self-esteem is much more complex than simply comparing oneself with poorer performers. There are at least two reasons. First, people are normally well aware of the fact that they are part of a larger society and that they have a position in this larger society. Thus, in the long run, people know they are going to be judged in terms of what the larger group has done. Second, people take a great deal of satisfaction in maximizing their skills and becoming the best. In order to know how far they can go and what it means to be the best, people look to others around them. Just why they are inclined to do this is not that clear. It may be that we have been taught to be the best we can or that humans are endowed with a drive to be their best. Both positions have their advocates. Whatever the reason, we know that certain people, usually those we call high achievers, are motivated by a desire to excel.

From studying the behavior of high- and low-self-esteem people, especially those who are high achievers to begin with, we know that in time both will again select the high performers as their standard of comparison. The reason they do this is that the high performers serve to motivate them to develop their skills. It is similar to why difficult tasks motivate people. What the high-self-esteem people have learned is simply how to get themselves through those times of self-doubt.

It is important to recognize that there are people who never do select the the high-performance group as their standard. Usually, it is the low achievers who select so-called low performers as their standard of comparison. This obviously serves to help them to maintain their self-esteem. To select the high performers would be devastating for such people.

poor self-esteem engage in behaviors that serve to perpetuate low self-esteem. To understand why they do this we need to start by pointing out that people with low self-esteem often feel threatened. Their self-esteem is already low and the possibility of receiving any further negative information about themselves is often too overwhelming for them to face. As a result they often attempt to resist all forms of evaluation. This means they screen out not only the bad but the good. One obvious implication is that by screening out all feedback they screen out the very information they need to form a highly differentiated self. As a result they attempt to operate with an amorphous self-concept that is characterized by lack of differentiation, lack of clarity, and lack of certainty.

Overgeneralization. The tendency of people with low self-esteem to overgeneralize following failure illustrates the problem that can result from lack of differentiation. Overgeneralization refers to the tendency of negative outcomes to trigger other feelings of personal inadequacy in domains that are unrelated to the initial negative outcome (Kernis, Brockner, & Frankel, 1989). What this means is that when people experience negative outcomes, such as at work, they are inclined to generalize that negative outcome to other domains in their life such as their social relations, appearance, and intelligence. The net effect is that being criticized for something they did at work not only leads them to question whether they have the ability to do their job but leads them to question such things as their general intelligence, their appearance, and their ability to maintain good social relationships. It may even lead to the breakup of a social relationship that is undergoing some turbulence because they reason that their failure at work is indicative of their overall inability to maintain good social relations. The process seems to involve rumination. As they think about what they did wrong, they begin looking for other examples of where they failed in their life. They may come to the conclusion, based on the examples they dredge up while ruminating, that they are not worthy of good self-regard. As a result their self-worth plummets. Remember that the term *self-worth* is often used to denote how we feel about ourselves in a number of different domains.

What do high-self-esteem people do when they receive negative feedback? First, presumably because they have highly differentiated self-concepts, the negative feedback does not cross over into other domains of their lives. As a result, it remains highly compartmentalized. If the work domain is itself highly differentiated, the high-self-esteem person may be able to further compartmentalize the negative feedback into a subcategory of that domain. The net result is that high-self-esteem people simply reconfirm something they already knew about themselves before they received negative feedback.

The important thing to note here is that high-self-esteem people and low-self-esteem people are alike in that negative feedback creates self-doubt in both. The difference is that high-self-esteem people do not overgeneralize when this happens. It is the tendency to overgeneralize that is the source of the problem. This is reminiscent of the antecedents of pessimism and depression.

Compartmentalization of the Self into Positive and Negative

Some people compartmentalize their knowledge about the self in terms of positive and negative categories. According to compartmentalization theory, if people activate one of these categories, access to the other is temporarily blocked. As a result, if people active the positive category they will feel good about themselves,

and if they activate the negative category they will feel bad about themselves. In general, high-self-esteem people tend to have a bias towards perceiving their positive qualities or strengths. As a result they tend to feel good about themselves most of the time. Low-self-esteem people, in contrast, tend to have a bias towards perceiving their negative qualities or their weaknesses. As a result they tend to feel bad about themselves much of the time (Showers, 1992).

What happens when the self-concept tends to be more differentiated or more complex? Having a highly differentiated self-concept (many distinct categories) tends to reduce the impact of negative feedback (Showers, 1992). This is exactly what one would expect based on the research we have just reviewed. Thus, it can be argued that it is good for people to have highly differentiated self-concepts.

Origins of a Good Self-Concept: Coming Full Circle

The development of a good self-concept requires that people engage in a process of self-evaluation that does not bias them towards inaction. The thing that is most characteristic of people with good self-esteem is their willingness to take action in order to make things better. If they do not have a good self-concept, they are inclined to say to themselves, "Why should I take action, because I lack the skills or the strengths to make a difference."

White's analysis of effectance motivation suggests that people learn to develop a self-concept that is characterized by a tendency to take action—something called a tendency towards mastery. He suggests that what rewards the tendency towards mastery is *feelings of efficacy*. When people realize they can change the environment for better or for worse, they gain a sense of being an effective agent. Such feelings, White argues, act as a reward that strengthens people's belief in their capacity to make still further changes. In that sense, feelings of efficacy are the same as feelings of pride. When people are victorious or triumphant, they experience feelings of efficacy or feelings of pride. They realize they have the power to change things. When people perceive themselves as effective agents they typically experience good self-esteem. Ultimately, good self-esteem grows out of the perception that one has the strengths, skills or even the persistence to make things better. Another word that we might use in this context is self-confidence. Self-confident people are willing to "stick their necks out" because they are confident they can make a difference.

Summary

Self-esteem can be defined as *pride in oneself in which one becomes aware and accepting of one's imperfections while cherishing one's inherent strengths and positive qualities.* Susan Harter uses the term *global self-worth* as opposed to self-esteem to emphasize the idea that self-esteem is multidimensional and that feelings of self-worth come from competencies that people experience in different domains. Maslow has suggested that people are born with a need to experience good self-esteem.

Weiner has examined the relation between feelings of self-esteem and competence. He has observed that when people perceive the locus of control as internal, they are more likely to experience feelings of pride and competence when they succeed and to experience feelings of shame and incompetence when they fail. Coopersmith states that people who enjoy high self-esteem set higher goals, are less troubled by anxiety, experience less stress (together with fewer psychosomatic symptoms), are less sensitive to failure, experience greater feelings of control, tend to be more enterprising, and tend to explore more.

People with high self-esteem are less affected by failure than those with low self-esteem. Further, low-self-esteem people are affected more by self-focusing instructions, a finding that is consistent with Carver's model, which suggests that if fear and anxiety cues are made salient, performance will be disrupted.

The core relational theme for pride, according to Lazarus, *is enhancement of one's ego-identity by taking credit for a valued object or achievement, either our own or that of someone or some group with whom we identify.* When children experience pride they gain a sense of autonomy, power, curiosity, and self-confidence. This is the basis for seeing themselves as agents capable of initiating change.

A great deal of research points to the idea that people who have good self-esteem have a clearly differentiated self-concept. It has been suggested that "To know oneself is to like oneself." When people know themselves they can maximize outcomes because they know what they can and cannot do. Acknowledging the fact that we are complex—made up of conflicting impulses and needs—may be the first step in producing the differentiation of the self that has been linked to good self-esteem.

People with poor self-esteem often engage in behaviors that serve to perpetuate their low self-esteem. In order to avoid any further threats to their already fragile self-esteem, they resist all forms of evaluation. In the process, they screen out not only negative feedback but positive feedback as well. By screening out all evaluation they deprive themselves of the information they need to develop a highly differentiated self-concept.

People with good self-esteem are characterized by their willingness to take action in order to make things better. White's analysis of effectance motivation suggests that people come to develop a self-concept that is characterized by a sense of mastery, and that it is out of this sense of mastery that people attempt to effect change.

Finally, people with high self-esteem are more inclined to make a downward comparison, a strategy that serves to enhance their self-esteem.

Main Points

1. Competence is skill, ability, capacity, proficiency, or fitness.

2. According to White's theory of competence, feelings of efficacy reward the development of competence.

3. Piaget argues that competence develops out of the child's need to interact with his or her environment.

4. People have different implicit theories of intelligence. According to an attentional model, implicit theories tend to focus people's attention on certain aspects of the environment rather than on others, and this results in the development of certain cognitive structures as opposed to others.

5. Lay persons view intelligence as made up of three components: *problem-solving ability, verbal ability,* and *social competence.*

6. Sternberg conceptualizes intelligence as involving problem-solving skills. His triarchic theory of intelligence involves three components: *analytical, synthetic,* and *contextual.*

7. Some people see intelligence as fixed—an entity view of intelligence, while other see intelligence as changeable—an incremental view of intelligence.

8. People who believe in the entity model of intelligence are motivated to select goals that will put them in a favorable light, whereas people who hold to the incremental model of intelligence tend to set a goal that will increase their competence.

9. Outcome expectations are defined as "a person's estimate that a given behavior will lead to certain outcomes." Self-efficacy refers to personal judgments and beliefs about capabilities of performing a specified behavior in a particular situation.

10. The need to achieve was originally defined by Murray as the desire or tendency to "overcome obstacles, to exercise power, to strive to do something difficult as well as and as quickly as possible."

11. McClelland has argued that the achievement motive grows out of a more basic incentive to "do something better," not to gain approval or any other kind of external reward, but "for its own sake."

12. Amsel argues that the absence of a reward that a person has come to expect normally produces frustration, and that frustration cues can be conditioned to the ongoing goal-directed behavior.

13. According to Atkinson, resultant achievement motivation is a joint function of the need to achieve and the need to avoid failure.

14. Because the strengths of these two motives appear to vary independently, Atkinson says that the need or motive to achieve may be stronger than the need or motive to avoid failure ($M_S > M_F$), they may be equal ($M_S = M_F$), or the motive to avoid failure may be stronger than the need or motive to succeed ($M_F > M_S$).

15. According to Atkinson's theory, people in whom $M_S > M_F$ tend to select tasks of intermediate difficulty, whereas people in whom $M_F > M_S$ tend to select either very easy or very difficult tasks.

16. Research conducted with male subjects has generally provided support for Atkinson's theory.

17. Subjects in whom $M_S > M_F$ display more realism in regard to vocational choice than subjects in whom $M_F > M_S$.

18. People attribute success and failure to four factors: ability, effort, task difficulty, and luck.

19. People high in resultant achievement motivation attribute success to ability and effort, and failure to lack of effort; people low in resultant achievement motivation attribute success to task difficulty and luck, and failure to lack of ability.

20. Getting people to accept challenges is important, and there are at least three things that can help: reduce the negative affect associated with failure, motivate people with difficult tasks, and give people attributional retraining.

21. Janet Spence and her colleagues, using the Work and Family Orientation (WOFO) Questionnaire, have found three aspects or dimensions of achievement: work, mastery, and competitiveness.

22. Men tend to score higher than women on the mastery and competitiveness subscales, whereas women tend to score higher on the work subscale.

23. In a variety of situations it has been found that high levels of achievement are associated with high levels of work and mastery and low levels of competitiveness.

24. It has been suggested that self-esteem can be defined as *pride in oneself in which one becomes aware and accepting of one's imperfections while cherishing one's inherent strengths and positive qualities.*

25.   It has been suggested that self-esteem is not a global attribute that cuts across all domains.

26.   At least three domains have been identified: performance, social, and appearance.

27.   Weiner has suggested that self-esteem has to do with the way we feel about ourselves when the locus of control for an event is perceived as internal.

28.   Acceptance by parents, having limits, and having the opportunity to explore are three factors that appear to be important in the development of self-esteem, which Coopersmith suggests influences a child's tendency to achieve.

29.   High-self-esteem people perform equally well following success and failure, while low-self-esteem people perform significantly worse following failure, but only under self-focusing stimulus conditions.

30.   Lazarus suggests that the core relational theme for pride is *enhancement of one's ego-identity by taking credit for a valued object or achievement, either our own or that of someone or some group with whom we identify.*

31.   Pride can be viewed as an emotion that helps sustain goal-directed behavior.

32.   People with good self-esteem typically have a clearly differentiated self-concept.

33.   It has been suggested that "to know oneself is to like oneself."

34. Low-self-esteem people are inclined to resist all forms of evaluation.

35.   Overgeneralization refers to the tendency of negative outcomes to trigger other feelings of personal inadequacy in domains that are unrelated to the initial negative outcome.

36.   High-self-esteem people tend to have a bias towards perceiving their positive qualities or strengths, whereas low-self-esteem people, in contrast, tend to have a bias towards perceiving their negative qualities or their weaknesses.

37.   Some people compartmentalize their knowledge about the self in terms of positive and negative categories.

38.   Some people learn to manage self-doubt following failure by engaging in downward comparisons.

39.   The development of a good self-concept requires that people engage in a process of self-evaluation that leads to action as opposed to inaction.

40.   This tendency towards action has been referred to as a tendency towards mastery.

Chapter Fourteen

Achieving Personal Success: The Self-Regulation of Motivation

- Do people need a good self-concept to succeed?
- Are we predestined to do one thing in life or are people really free to choose?
- Is it important for people to have dreams?
- Should people select easy or difficult goals for themselves?
- Is ability or motivation more important for succeeding?

- Does everybody experience self-doubt from time to time?
- What can people do who have low self-esteem?
- How does one learn to maintain an optimistic outlook when things are going bad?
- Can people change their self-concepts?
- Can people become optimists?

Introduction

There have been four major developments, many of which have occurred in the last decade, that have made this chapter possible. First, there is a great deal of research which shows that the self-concept is, perhaps, the basis for all motivated behavior. It is the self-concept that gives rise to possible selves, and it is possible selves that create the motivation for behavior. It is not just wanting or desiring something that creates motivation, but it is the belief that one can actually achieve a particular goal that leads people to put forth effort. When people believe in the incremental theory of intelligence versus the entity theory of intelligence, for example (Chapter 13), they are inclined to work to attain a goal. It is the belief that creates a possible self which in turn creates the dynamics that lead to action. Second, there is a great deal of research which shows that goals are necessary for creating action. Without goals people never get started. Goals also serve to give direction to behavior. For a variety of reasons, it has been suggested that it is important for people to set difficult but attainable goals. Whether or not people will do so, however, is linked to their self-concept, or more precisely, to their feelings of self-esteem. When self-esteem is low people frequently set easy goals for themselves. Third, there is a growing body of research which shows that self-regulation of behavior is important if goals are to be attained. While some people are inclined to give up the instant they first experience failure or adversity, others are not. Research shows that it is the people who persist that succeed. Thus, learning how to adjust one's behavior or change one's plan is important. It is also important to learn how to manage one's emotions, since they can undermine even the best-laid plans. There are many people who have the potential to become athletes, musicians, actors, entrepreneurs, but because they have not learned the process of self-regulation they are lacking an important ingredient necessary to develop that talent. As Albert Bandura has pointed out: "Talent is only as good as its execution" (Bandura, 1991). Fourth, there is a growing body of research which indicates that it is possible to change the self-concept. Self-change is not something that people can will but rather it depends on the process of self-reflection. Through self-reflection, people often come to view themselves in a new, more powerful way, and it is through this new, more powerful way of viewing the self that people can develop new possible selves.

From Needs to Goals to Action

Motivation theory has grown out of idea that humans have needs (Murray, 1938). For some time psychologists have speculated on just how needs are translated into action. At one point, it was thought that needs lead directly to action. In recent years it has been suggested that needs do not lead directly to action but rather that needs give rise to *dispositions* within individuals that dispose them to strive to approach a particular class of positive incentives (goals) or avoid a particular class of negative incentives (threats) (Atkinson & Birch, 1978; Weiner, 1974). It has been suggested that *possible selves* provide the bridge to action. Possible selves provide the cognitive representation of the motives or end states (goals and threat), the plans and pathways for achieving them, and the values associated with them (Markus & Nurius, 1986). Thus, two individuals who have an equally strong need to achieve may not be equally inclined to achieve a goal. Without clearly defined possible selves, one never sets the goals that are necessary for action.

A Flow Diagram for the Self-Regulation of Motivation

In order to help the reader understand the role of various processes in achieving personal success, I have constructed a flow chart that shows each of the various components involved in personal success (boxes) and how these components are linked (arrows). This flow chart is presented in Figure 14-1. The processes, represented by arrows, are not predetermined but rather can be learned. That means there are several points at which people can intervene to alter or speed up this process. I will start by presenting an overview of this model and then systematically discuss each of the various components of this model.

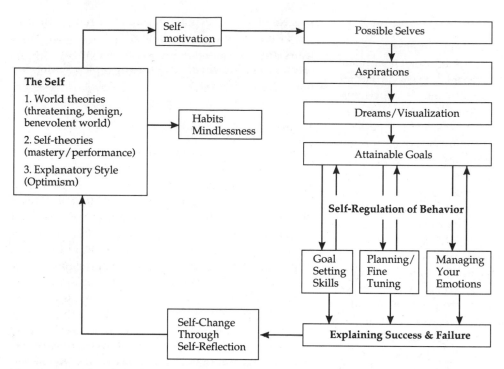

Figure 14–1. This flow chart represents the various components that are involved in achieving personal success (box), together with the various processes (arrows) that are involved in linking these various components. People repeat this cycle over and over.

The box on the left represents the self-concept. Everything begins and ends with the self. The self is a relatively static thing that can lead to action by generating possible selves. The self contains our implicit theories of reality (Epstein, 1990). It contains theories about the world and our ability to deal with the world.

The right side of the model represents action. As we move from the top (possible selves) downward to attainable goals we move from the more abstract to the more concrete. Possible selves represent the possibilities or alternatives available to people. It is necessary, however, for people to choose among those alternatives, since it would be difficult to pursue all the possible selves simultaneously. When people make a choice by selecting one or more of those possible selves to pursue, they create aspirations for themselves. People aspire to such things as becoming an actor, a doctor, an athlete. In order to make their aspirations more personal or more real, people often create dreams or visions in which they can see themselves engaging in a specific activity related to their aspirations such as playing the part of a gangster in a movie, performing a heart operation, or winning a Gold Medal in swimming. Assuming that dreams can create desire, people still need to set specific goals for themselves because without them there still will not be action. Action comes when there is a discrepancy between where I am now and where I want to be. Also, goals give direction.

While goals create the initial impetus for action, it is difficult but attainable goals that sustain that action. Without difficult goals people are never fully mobilized. However, if the goals are unattainable (extremely difficult, for example), they do not have the capacity to create or sustain action. It has been suggested that people need to learn the art of setting goals. This so-called art falls under the process of self-regulation. By learning how to set goals people can learn how to fully mobilize themselves to put forth maximum effort. It is also important that people learn how to make plans and how to adjust their behavior as well as their plans when they encounter failure and adversity. Again, this is something that can be learned and therefore falls under self-regulaton. Finally, many people give up under conditions of failure and adversity because it leads to self-doubt. People who succeed have learned how to manage their self-doubt as well as other emotions that can undermine behavior. This is another example of self-regulation.

The double arrows linking each of these processes to goals are there to indicate that these are feedback loops. If people don't do it right the first time, they can simply make adjustments until they discover the right way. People are always learning how to regulate such things as goals, plans, and emotions in order to ensure that they reach their goals.

By reflecting on their behavior people can learn to change their perceptions of themselves. When they succeed, for example, they can incorporate that fact into their self-concept. As we will see, a positive self-concept grows out of the perception that we are competent.

The box named *self-motivation* (half-way between the static on the left and the dynamic on the right) links the self to action. People can learn to create action by creating possible selves. The box named *self-change through self-reflection* (half-way between the static on the left and the dynamic on the right) links feedback from actions to the self. By learning to think about success and failures in certain ways people can change their self-concepts. Among other things, they can learn to become optimists. Optimism, it has been shown, comes from learning to attribute success and failure to their proper place within the self-concept.

Defining the Self-Concept

The term *self-concept* is typically used to embrace how we think about the external world and how we think about our ability to deal with it. It grows out of our at-

tempts to make sense of our own behavior. It represents the past, present, and the future. It determines such diverse things as how we process information, the feelings we experience, the dreams we have, our motivation to act, our reactions to feedback, how we reflect on such things as success and failure (Deci & Ryan, 1991; Dweck, 1991; Markus & Wurf, 1987).

The self-concept may or may not be conscious, meaning that we may or may not be aware of the principles by which it operates. For example, we may or may not be aware of the fact that we ascribe to an entity theory of intelligence or an incremental theory of intelligence. Nevertheless, because we have decided at some level of consciousness to endorse one or the other, our actions are highly predictable. If we believe in an incremental theory, for example, we will be more inclined to put forth effort.

The "I" and the "Me" of Self

Going back to William James (1890), people have made a distinction between the "I" and the "me" of the self. Deci and Ryan (1991) have argued that the self is both an agent and repository (a storage place) of societies' values. The repository part of the self (the "me") involves values (e.g., family, justice, sharing) and regulatory processes (e.g., persisting, following rules, abstaining from aggression). We internalize both values and regulatory processes because, as social beings, we have a need for relatedness. To gain that sense of relatedness or acceptance we internalize the beliefs of people who are important to us such as our parents and friends. The agent side (the "I") is the autonomous side of the self that needs to be in control. When the autonomous side of the self is allowed to develop skills and competence by mastering the environment, the individual gains a sense of self-determination. The agent side (the "I") is responsible for actively integrating information (as opposed to absorbing it) as well as for generating rules and principles to guide our actions. According to this distinction, the "me" is actively constructed by the "I." Over time I will change my values and my self-regulatory processes so they will be congruent with the self-determined "I" part of the self. "I" may decide, for example, to give up the idea that I

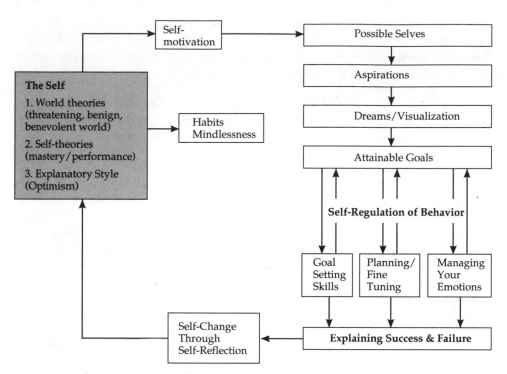

Figure 14–2. The Self is the home of World Theories, Self-Theories, and such things as the explanatory style that people use to explain events that happen to them.

must have children because it is inconsistent with my desire to pursue a certain lifestyle I have selected for myself, such as sailing around the world.

In the model I have presented, the "I" part of the self uses self-reflection to construct the "me." By becoming mindful of what I enjoy and what brings me happiness, for example, the "I" constructs values and ideals that will bring even greater happiness in the future. Self-reflection is more than just feedback. To become good self-reflectors people need to have the skills of knowing what to look for. What is important is often hidden or disguised, and therefore people need to learn how to uncover what is important by carefully putting their own behavior under a microscope. It is like becoming a skilled researcher who learns how to isolate the critical variable that gives rise to happiness and satisfaction.

The Tendency to View the World as Threatening, Benevolent, or Benign

A number of self-theorists suggest that everyone develops an implicit theory of reality (e.g., Epstein, 1990; Dweck & Leggett, 1988). It appears that people not only have a world theory and a self-theory, but that they have beliefs and ideas about the relationship between these two sets of themes. They may believe, for example, that because they live in a bad world they cannot control most things that happen to them, or, alternatively, that because it is a good world events are controllable (Epstein, 1990). In this section I will present three prototypes of how people conceptualize the world and how their conceptualization of the external world determines what they think they can or should do or what they cannot or should not do. I call these *prototypes* because they represent at least three more or less distinct ways that people can view the world. Each of these ways has been described by different theorists who have pursued somewhat different lines of research.

Prototype 1: The World as Threatening or Malevolent

A number of researchers have pointed out that some people are inclined to view the world in negative terms (Epstein, 1990; Watson & Clark, 1984). They see the world as threatening or malevolent. There are many people who wake up each morning dreading to enter the world that lies outside their front doors; they see it as hostile and threatening. Apprehensive that the world is going to inflict harm on them, their bodies go into a stress mode, preparing for the fight or flight. Their hearts may speed up and their blood pressure may rise. Sometimes these people are angry. In a world that is threatening and hostile the best defense, they tacitly say to themselves, is an offense. Alternatively, these people may become very passive, hoping that by being submissive they will be left alone.

These people are pessimists. They expect bad things to happen and sometimes seem to take satisfaction from seeing bad things happen to other people. It confirms their view that the world is indeed hostile and threatening and that their approach to it is the right one. For these people the sense of "I" is virtually undeveloped. They are reactive people who feel they have little control. Their tacit description of life is "This is a dog-eat-dog world" or "It is survival of the fittest." There are at least two dimensions that characterize this perception of the world.

First, these people tend to have what Watson and Clark called a "disposition towards negative affectivity." All their experiences are focused around "deprivation and defeat." They are anxious, fearful, unhappy and distressed. Watson and Clark (1984) have argued a wide variety of personality scales that purport to measure trait anxiety, neuroticism, repression-sensitization, ego strength, and general maladjustment appear to measure the same underlying personality trait—a trait that they have called a disposition toward *nega-*

tive affectivity. Following up on this work, it has been suggested that people who are anxious and fearful tend to view the world as threatening (Franken, Gibson & Rowland, 1992). The concept of threatening grows out of the observation that these people are inclined to limit their interactions with the world because that world is a source of danger, a threat to their physical and psychological well-being.

It is worth noting in this context that people who are anxious tend to have low self-esteem (Franken, Gibson & Rowland, 1992). For example, they are easily discouraged, they are inclined to give up when things aren't working, they get nervous in new situations, they have poor opinions of themselves, they do not see life as satisfying, they often wish they were someone else, and so forth.

The second thing that characterizes people who view the world as threatening is their tendency to view it in terms of *limited possibilities* as opposed to unlimited possibilities. Evidence for this comes from a variety of sources. For example, it has been observed for some time that people who are anxious do not select new or different activities but rather select activities that are more familiar to them (e.g. Berlyne, 1960; White, 1959). There is also evidence that people who can be characterized as fearful perceive more activities as dangerous and risky and therefore psychologically unavailable to them (Franken, Gibson, & Rowland, 1992).

Prototype 2: The World as Benevolent

In recent years a number of researchers have pointed out that some people have the disposition to view the world in positive terms (Seligman, 1990; Scheier & Carver, 1985, 1988; Snyder et al., 1991).They see the world as benevolent; a world that is good and generous. These are people who wake up in the morning convinced that good things are going to happen to them. They exude confidence and seem unaffected by setbacks. These people are optimists. The sense of "I" is highly developed in these people. They respond to the world with a sense of having the ability to find the right path to claim their rightful reward. Their tacit description of life is "This is my day" or "Something good is going to happen to me today." Again, there are two dimensions that characterize these people.

First, people who see the world as benevolent have a disposition to experience positive affect. They see themselves as not only succesful but as happy people. Martin Seligman (1990) views optimism as being the opposite of depression. While depression is characterized by negative mood and negative affect, optimism is characterized by positive mood and positive affect.

The second thing that characterizes this view of the world is that the world offers many positive opportunities or *possibilities*. Evidence for this again comes from a variety of sources, including the evidence that people who are low in anxiety as compared to high in anxiety are more inclined to explore their environment, more inclined to respond to new and different stimulation, and more inclined to try new and different activities (e.g. Berlyne, 1960; White, 1959). There is also evidence from the work on optimism which shows that optimists are open to new experiences and challenges (Seligman, 1990). There is also evidence from the work on hope (Snyder et al., 1991). People who are hopeful tend to have a strong sense of agency (goal-directed determination) and have pathways (can plan routes to goals). Research with hopeful people has shown, among other things, that hopeful people set more goals and more difficult goals. Still further evidence comes from the work on sensation seeking. Sensation seekers are people who are motivated by the need for novel and complex stimulation and who view the external world as a place where they can experience such stimulation (Zuckerman, 1979).

We did a study with sensation seekers to explore their tendency to take risks. Risk is defined by Webster's dictionary as the *possibility of loss or injury*. If an activity is perceived to be risky it follows that one should avoid such activities. But what makes something risky? Is there some objective measure of risk? Perhaps everything we do is risky if viewed from a certain perspective. It is clear from our research that people do not agree that activities traditionally labeled as dangerous should be necessarily avoided. It is important to remember that the labeling of something as dangerous or risky is based on norms. If we were to use only anxious people to define what is risky, then the

norms for what is risky would be very different than if we used nonanxious people or sensation seekers. Perhaps leaving one's house would be viewed as a risky activity if we used only very anxious people. The fact that some people are willing to engage in activities that have traditionally been labeled as risky while others are not is interesting and is something that we wanted to explore. In our study we gave participants Zuckerman's Sensation Seeking Scale, the Wolpe and Lange's Fear Schedule Survey, a Danger Assessment Questionnaire, and an Attitudes Towards Risk Questionnaire. The Attitudes Toward Risk Questionnaire asked people to indicate on a 5-point scale whether items were "Like me" or "Not like me." A factor analysis of this scale indicated there were two distinct factors: one that pertained to taking psychological risks and another to taking physical risks. We called the first factor "disregard of social approval" and the second factor "disregard of danger." The items for the two factors are presented in Table 14-1.

What we found was that people who are high in the sensation seeking motive tended to be less fearful, tended to perceive a variety of activities as less dangerous, and indicated that they like to take both physical and psychological risks. Among other things, these results indicate that such things as fear, danger, and risk are perhaps "in the eye of the beholder." Let me explain.

The Self-Actualized Person

The self-actualized person is perhaps a good example of someone who sees the world as benevolent. In Chapter 11 I discussed Maslow's self-actualization theory but said little about that part of the theory for which Maslow is best known, his ideas on becoming self-actualized (Maslow, 1943, 1959, 1971). He suggested that before people can become self-actualized they must satisfy the four classes of needs (deficiency needs) that are at the bottom of the hierarchy (physiological needs, safety needs, love and belongingness needs, and self-esteem needs). When these needs have been reasonably satisfied they are motivated by a whole new set of needs called *being needs*. These are what provide meaning to the life of the self-actualized

Table 14-1. Items from the Attitudes Towards Risk Questionnaire. It should be noted that in the original scale administered to the participants in the study the items were mixed together. They have been rank-ordered in this table according to which item loaded greatest on that particular factor. (From R. E. Franken, "Sensation Seeking and the Tendency to View the World as Threatening." *Personality and Individual Differences*, 1992, 13, 31-38 (Appendix 3, p. 37). Copyright © 1992. Reprinted with kind permission from Pergamon Press Ltd, Headington Hill Hall, Oxford OX3 OBW, UK.).

Factor 1: Psychological Risks: Disregard of social approval

1. While I don't deliberately seek out situations or activities that society disapproves of, I find that I often end up doing things that society disapproves of.
2. I often do things that I know my parents would disapprove of.
3. I often think about doing things that are illegal.
4. I do not let the fact that something is considered immoral stop me from doing it.
5. I often think about doing things that I know my friends would disapprove of.
6. I often seek out situations or activities that society does not approve of.
7. I do not let the fact that something is illegal stop me from doing it.
8. I often think about doing things that I know my parents would disapprove of.
9. I often think about doing things that I know society would disapprove of.
10. I often think about doing things that are considered immoral.

Factor 2: Physical Risks: Disregard of danger

11. I like the feeling that comes with taking physical risks.
12. I consider myself a risk-taker.
13. Being afraid of doing something new often makes it more fun in the end.
14. The greater the risk the more fun the activity.
15. I like to do things that almost paralyze me with fear.
16. I like the feeling that comes with taking psychological or social risks.
17. While I don't deliberately seek out situations or activities that involve physical risk, I often end up doing things that involve physical risk.
18. I like the feeling that comes from entering a new situation.
19. I often think about doing activities that involve physical risk.
20. I often think about doing things that would arouse a great deal of fear or anxiety in me.

person and are based on values such as truth, honesty, beauty, and goodness.

There are several things that characterize the self-actualized person. First, they are people who tend to be *problem-focused*. By that I mean they approach life in terms of things that need to be done or things that need to be accomplished. The problems they focus on are often determined by the values they hold to be important. For example, if they believe that it is important for people to be able to enjoy beauty, they may spend their time attempting to create more beauty through their own creative efforts or through an organization devoted to promoting the arts. In this context it is important to note that the self-actualized person tends to be intrinsically motivated as opposed to extrinsically motivated. They find that self-satisfaction comes from doing things they value as opposed to things that bring monetary reward.

Another thing that characterizes the self-actualized person is their *ongoing freshness* of appreciation, almost childlike, of all that life has to offer. Maslow often talks in his writings about the self-actualized person never growing tired of the basic experiences in life (often sensory) such as smelling a flower, watching a bird bring worms to its offspring, tasting a fresh apple pie, the caressing feel that may come from a warm summer breeze.

A third characteristic of self-actualized persons is their concern for growth, something that Maslow called *growth motivation*. Having satisfied their basic deficiency needs they strive to solve problems that lie outside themselves. These people can often be seen working on the problems faced by other people or by society. They seem to gain self-satisfaction from using and developing their skills to address the welfare of the larger world in which they live.

A fourth characteristic of self-actualized persons is their ability to have what Maslow calls *peak experiences*. These are sometimes called *mystic experiences* or *oceanic experiences* because they involve a momentary transcendence of the present including feelings of there being unlimited horizons or possibilities, feelings of being both powerful and weak, feelings of being freed from the bonds of both time and space. He notes that these experiences can be triggered by a number of things including sexual orgasm and music.

Prototype 3: The World as Benign

There are people who view the world as neither threatening nor benevolent. It is what you do with the world that is important. What brings pleasure and satisfaction is not the result of something good happening or preventing something bad from happening to them but rather from their own actions, or more precisely from exercising competence. These are people who wake up in the morning with a goal they want to accomplish. They may have decided they want a bigger house in a new location so they buy an old house, tear it down, and build their dream house.

The word *benign* is defined by Webster's dictionary as *of a gentle disposition*. People who view the world as benign approach it with the view that the world can be molded or shaped into something that can bring them pleasure. The world as it exists now is not an im-

mediate source of pleasure or satisfaction. Pleasure comes from operating on the world in some way and changing it. In order to operate on the world one must develop skills or competence. It is through one's skills and competence that one can shape the world into something new and different, and it is through exercising skills and competence that one experiences satisfaction. It isn't that the world needs to be changed so much, but that people need to exercise competence. The world simply provides the raw material. Their tacit description of life is, "I will develop the skills so that I can make it into what I want" or "I want to be free to do it my way."

This view of the world has its origins in the philosophy of individualism. According to this philosophy, people should be treated as autonomous and self-reliant. Further, they must be given freedom to exploit the world because it is through exercising one's skills and changing things that people gain happiness.

One current theory that seems to closely reflect the idea that some people view the world as benign can be found in the theory of Deci and Ryan (1991). Instead of the words *autonomy* and *self-reliance*, they use the words *autonomy* and *self-determination*. They suggest that people are born with three needs: the need for autonomy, the need for competence, and the need for relatedness. It is the satisfaction of these needs that brings happiness and satisfaction.

What about the dimensions of affect and possibilities that I suggested could be used to characterize the other two world theories? People who view the world as benign do not see it as the source of either positive or negative affect. Positive and negative affect come from one's actions which, in turn, are a product of one's goals. The main positive emotion that Deci and Ryan talk about is the emotion of pride. Pride results from exercising competence or gaining mastery. Negative affect comes from not being able to experience autonomy and self-determination. Frustration would be one of the main negative emotions. They also talk about the need for relatedness and suggest that this need provides the primary impetus for internalizing values and regulatory processes.

What about possibilities? Possibilities come from within the self and have little or no direct link to the external world. The self acts on the world and creates something new by molding or shaping the world according to one's needs or desires. The basis for all possibilities is eventually linked to competence. With competence anything is possible but without competence nothing is possible.

Does this mean that people who view the world as benign have nothing to fear, or that they gain no pleasure from the external world? The answer to that is no. Deci and Ryan recognize that the external world can be a source both of pleasure and pain, although they do not see this as the focus of the self. It may be unfortunate that one has to deal with such things as crime, pollution, and divorce in the course of exercising competence, but these are not the things that are of central concern to the self. They are more peripheral to the self. They are things that one must learn to deal with on an ad hoc basis or regulate in some way. The self is concerned with autonomy, self-determination and relatedness.

Self-Theories: Individual Strategies/Orientations

In order to understand how people view the self we need to observe how they cope, adapt, shape, or embrace the external world. The different ways that people cope, adapt, shape, mold, or embrace the external world can be called strategies. Strategies refer to the methods or plans that people use. Most people do not merely react to the external world, they respond. By that I mean they employ carefully devised strategies. Reacting can be thought of as a short-term, often ad hoc way of dealing with a situation. Responding can be thought of as carefully devised plans that people use in a wide variety of situations.

While there are many strategies that people use, there are two that seem to be very pervasive across many situations. They have been identified as the *mastery strategy* and the *performance strategy* or, alternatively, the *mastery orientation* and the *performance orientation*. I like the word orientation because it implies that people are not locked into one or the other but rather are inclined to *use* one or the other. Orientation, therefore, is like *disposition* in that it points

you in a certain direction. In the final analysis what elicits a particular strategy is the situation.

The mastery strategy and the performance strategy have been discussed by various theorists. Most notable among these has been Dweck (Dweck, 1991; Dweck & Leggett, 1988). They have their roots in the early literature on the mastery motive (e.g. White, 1959) and in Rogers's work on conditional and unconditional love (Rogers, 1959).

When I use the word *strategy* I do not mean to imply that these are rational or conscious. Rather, they are implicit theories that people have developed as a result of such processes as modeling and instruction as well as construction. We are not locked into one strategy or another and can learn to change our orientation by adjusting our focus.

The Mastery Strategy

The mastery strategy can be defined in terms of a general belief system that involves three interrelated beliefs. It involves the belief that one can acquire the skills that will make it possible for them to survive, the belief that one can control the environment through the development of skills, and the belief that one has the capacity to create happiness and health. In Dweck's theory (Dweck, 1991), the mastery strategy grows out of the belief that intelligence is incremental. Through work and effort people can change their intelligence or, alternatively, their ability to adapt to the world.

Sometimes people who talk or write about the mastery motive or mastery orientation fail to emphasize the fact that people with strong mastery motive are typically very skilled people. In addition to believing they can control things, they actually have a large repertoire of skills that enables them to control things. They often have, for example, the ability to acquire the information they need, they know how to organize the information they acquire, they know how to apply that information, they have the social skills necessary to be truly effective in the highly social environment in which we live, and so forth. The mastery motive, in other words, involves both attitudes/beliefs combined with a set of generalized skills. It is the belief that one can do something or learn something that will enable them to adapt.

People who develop a mastery strategy are those who learn to take credit for their actions. Further, they come to develop a generalized belief that they can affect change through their ability to learn and develop new skills. The thing that sustains (rewards) them in their continued development of new skills is feelings of self-efficacy that come with the development of each new skill. The emotion that is typically experienced is a feeling of pride.

The Performance Strategy

The performance strategy can be defined in terms of a belief system in which people have three interrelated beliefs: that one can achieve for oneself what one wants by learning the rules for winning, that winning is an acceptable way to get ahead, and that happiness is the result of winning. The performance-oriented person tends to be concerned with the outcome. This is very different from the mastery orientation which is concerned with the process. Since this is a very important distinction, let me spend a little time talking about it.

Outcome-oriented versus process-oriented. As I indicated above, what sustains (rewards) mastery type individuals is feelings of self-efficacy they receive from effectively dealing with the world in which they live. In short, they can take credit for their successes. For them it is the process of being in control that seems to be the source of their motivation. What sustains the performance types, in contrast, is winning. Winning is an outcome. While skills can be and often are involved in winning, people with a performance-orientation do not view themselves as necessarily having skills. Rather, they see themselves as using tactics, such as undermining other people. As a result it is more difficult for them to take credit for their successes.

This distinction does not mean that mastery types do not like to win nor that performance types are not interested in experiencing the feelings of self-efficacy that come from being able to take credit for one's behavior. Rather, it is a matter of focus or emphasis.

There is a great deal of evidence that the more powerful motivator of behavior in the long run is experiencing feelings of efficacy (Deci & Ryan, 1991).

Since mastery-oriented individuals have skills, they are in a good position to take credit for their behavior. Performance-oriented individuals, in contrast, lacking such a backlog of skills, are not in a good position to take credit for their behavior. They must, therefore, look to winning as a source of satisfaction.

The Relationship between World Theories and Self-Theories

What is the relationship between world theories and self-theories? Epstein (1990) has suggested that people have propositions that link these two subdivisions of the self. What is the nature of these propositions? As yet we do not have a clear idea of how to characterize them. All we really know is that there seem to be world theories that vary independently from self-theories. That is, knowing that one has adopted the view that the world is threatening does not allow us to predict whether or not one has adopted a mastery orientation versus a performance orientation. It seems intuitively obvious that they should be congruent. I suggested earlier that people have ideas and beliefs about the relationship between their world theories and self-theories. At this point we only have a superficial idea about the nature of these ideas or beliefs (something Epstein calls "propositions"). Perhaps these ideas and beliefs can be conceptualized as superordinate categories. Ask yourself what your guiding phrase is for your life. Perhaps in that phrase you can link your self-theory with your world theory. For example, if your guiding phrase is "I want to make this a better world," you might see the world as a source of pain, at least for some people, and attempt to change it for them by creating a new drug that would alleviate a persisting problem. In other words, you might link your perceptions of a threatening world with a mastery strategy.

The Need for a Positive Self-Concept

All of us are born with the need to develop a positive

self-concept. Among other things, that means to be loved and respected by others. We initially seek love and respect from our parents. The performance orientation may have its roots in something that Rogers calls unconditional love. Let me explain why.

Rogers's Concept of Conditional and Unconditional Love

Rogers's main contribution to humanistic theory is the "self-concept." The self-concept represents the thoughts and perceptions that we all have about ourselves. Rogers assumed that we are innately motivated to develop a positive self-concept. He further assumed that we are motivated to realize our potential. The road to a positive self-concept and to self-actualization, however, is filled with obstacles that may block our progress.

A very early experience that often prevents us from developing a positive self-concept is "conditional love." Conditional love is love that is dependent on our acting in an acceptable way. Instead of being loved for who we are or for what we believe, we are loved for what we do or what we accomplish. According to Rogers, this kind of love often produces a negative self-image. When parents or other significant people in our lives emphasize the importance of achieving important goals or acting in a certain prescribed way, we develop unrealistic ideas or beliefs about what we must do before we can think positively about ourselves. According to Rogers, if we are to be able to think positively about ourselves, we need to have a sense of worth that is not conditional on a specific behavior. All of us make mistakes; we all fail sometimes. Faced with this reality, we often develop a sense of conditional worth: "When I succeed or when I act in a certain way, I am worthy, but when I don't succeed or act in a certain way, I am not worthy." Conditional worth eventually leads to a negative self-concept. According to Rogers, the realization that I can never achieve certain goals or act in certain ways leads to a sense of futility. I can never be that good person that I perceive is my ideal.

Unconditional love, in contrast, leads to a sense of positive self-regard. Since love is not dependent on act-

ing in prescribed ways, it doesn't matter if I sometimes fail or make mistakes. According to Rogers, when mistakes and failures are not linked directly to feelings of worth, they can be viewed in a more realistic and less destructive way. We can view our mistakes simply as part of the process of maturing or as feedback about our progress. When parents withdraw love in order to indicate their disapproval, it creates a great deal of anxiety in the child, as it should, given that the parent is their primary means of survival. If, on the other hand, parents do not withdraw their love when they disapprove, the child is not overpowered with feelings of anxiety.

Summary

The self-concept is determined both by how one views the external world and how one views one's ability to deal with the external world. These correspond to the repository side of the self ("me") and the agent part of the self ("I").

At least three prototypes have been discussed in the psychological literature describing how people view the external world. People who perceive the world as threatening (Prototype 1) tend to view it in negative terms. These people are dispositionally inclined to experience negative affect and to see the world as limited in opportunities or simply limited in possibilities. Anxious and neurotic people are examples of this prototype. People who view the world as benevolent (Prototype 2) view it in positive terms. They are dispositionally inclined to experience positive affect and tend to view the world as offering many opportunities or simply many possibilities. Examples of this type are the optimists and the hopeful people. The self-actualized person, as described by Maslow, would be an example of the person who sees the world in benevolent terms. People who view the world as benign tend to view the external world as more neutral (Prototype 3). What is important for this type is autonomy and self-determination. It is through autonomy and self-determination that people can shape or mold the external world and in the process experience the pleasure that comes with exercising competence. The outside world, in other words, is neither a source of pleasure nor pain, nor is it a source of opportunity or lack thereof. People who embrace the philosophy of individualism are examples of this type. Finally, a distinction was made between people who hold a mastery orientation and those who hold a performance orientation. Whereas the mastery orientation is motivated by the process (feelings of efficacy that come from exercising skills), the performance orientation is motivated by outcome. Rogers's concept of conditional and unconditional love is one way of understanding why some people develop a mastery orientation and some people develop a performance orientation.

Epstein's Cognitive-Experiential Self-Theory (CEST)

In order to understand the importance of the self-concept in a wide range of motivated behaviors, I have decided to discuss Epstein's theory of the self, which is a comprehensive theory that addresses a number of important issues related to achieving success, health, and happiness.

Epstein's Cognitive-Experiential Self-Theory (CEST) grew out of his observations that academic intelligence is not a good predictor of such things as mental health, physical health, romantic relations, family relations and success in work. If academic intelligence is not a good predictor, what *would* be a good predictor? In attempting to answer this question, it seemed to Epstein that there must be a separate system, one that was designed to help us deal with everyday-life situations.

Two Semi-Independent Systems for Processing Information

Epstein (1990, 1991, 1992) has proposed a theory of the self that is based on the idea that people possess two semi-independent systems for processing information: a rational system and an experiential system. The *rational system* operates according to socially accepted rules of logic and evidence and functions at the conscious level. The *experiential system* is a more emotional/holistic system (see Table 14-2) that operates at the level of the preconscious. It is a system that has

evolved over millions of years and is the same system used by other higher order animals to adjust to their environments. It is oriented towards immediate and decisive action and processes information rapidly and more crudely than the rational system (Epstein, Lipson, Holstein & Huh, 1992). The fact that it operates at a preconscious level means that we are not completely aware of why we do things when we are operating by this system. Our actions, in other words, tend to be more automatic. In the rational system, there is often a break or pause between thought and action. To act we need to make the conscious decision to act.

Constructive Thinking Inventory

In order to find a measure that might tap this domain of competence, Epstein developed the *Constructive Thinking Inventory*, an inventory that measures such things as emotional coping, behavioral coping, categorical thinking, personal superstitious thinking, esoteric thinking, and naive optimism (see Chapter 9). The inventory that eventually emerged (using factor analytic techniques) was one that it has been shown can, indeed, predict such a things as satisfactory romantic and social relationships, mental and physical well-being, and success in the workplace (Epstein & Meier, 1989). You might want to go back to Chapter 9 where Epstein's Constructive Thinking Inventory is discussed in greater detail to refresh your memory about the nature of this scale.

Constructive Thinking and Coping

Consistent with the idea that good constructive thinkers should be good at dealing with stress, it was shown in an experiment that manipulated stress that good as compared to poor constructive thinkers had fewer negative thoughts, related and unrelated to the experiment, and less negative affect throughout the experiment. The results suggest that poor constructive thinkers contribute to their own stress in two ways. They spontaneously generate negative thoughts in the absence of external stressors and they are inclined to appraise external stressors as more threatening (Katz & Epstein, 1991).

Table 14-2. Comparison of The Experiential and Rational Systems. (From S. Epstein, A. Holstein, and E. Huth, "Irrational Reactions to Negative Oꞵoutcomes: Evidence for Two Conceptual Systems."*Journal of Personality and Social Psychology*, 1992, *62*, 328-339. Copyright © 1992 by the American Psychological Association. Reprinted with permission.)

Experiential System	*Rational System*
Holistic	Analytic
Emotional: pleasure/pain oriented (what feels good)	Logical: reason oriented (what is sensible)
Associationistic connections	Cause and effect connections
More outcome oriented	More process oriented
Behavior mediated by "vibes" from past experiences	Behavioral mediated by conscious appraisal of events
Encodes reality in concrete images, metaphors, and narratives	Encodes reality in abstract symbols: words and numbers
More rapid processing: oriented towards immediate action	Slower processing: oriented towards delayed action
Slower to change: changes with repetitive or intense experience	Changes more rapidly: changes with speed of thought
More crudely differentiated: broad generalization gradient, categorical thinking	More highly differentiated, dimensional thinking
More crudely integrated: dissociative, organized into emotional complexes (cognitive-affective modules)	More highly integrated
Experienced passively and preconsciously: we are seized by our emotions	Experienced actively and consciously: we are in control of our thoughts
Self-evident valid: "experiencing is believing"	Requires justification via logic and evidence

Epstein (1992) has shown that poor constructive thinkers have a tendency to make unfavorable overgeneralizations about themselves following negative outcomes. People with low self-esteem also tend to overgeneralize about the self following unfavorable outcomes. We talked about this same phenomenon in Chapter 13.

Can People Learn to Become Good Constructive Thinkers?

As I suggested in Chapter 9, in order for people to change from being poor constructive thinkers to good constructive thinkers they must change their implicit self-theories. Not only must people learn to see themselves as competent in dealing with life's problems, but they need to see the world as less threatening.

Summary

Epstein has proposed a self-theory that is based on the idea that people possess two semi-independent systems for processing information. The *rational system* operates according to socially accepted rules of logic and evidence and functions at the conscious level, while the *experiential system* is a more emotional/holistic system that operates at the level of the preconscious. Epstein developed the *Constructive Thinking Inventory*, an inventory that measures such things as emotional coping, behavioral coping, categorical thinking, personal superstitious thinking, esoteric thinking, and naive optimism. The inventory has been shown to predict such things as satisfactory romantic and social relationships, mental and physical well-being, and success in the workplace.

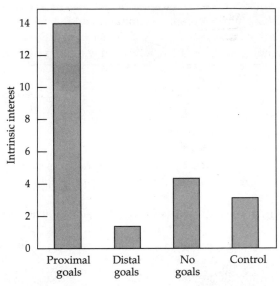

Figure 14–3. Level of intrinsic interest in arithmetic activities shown by children in different goal conditions when given free choice of activities. (From A. Bandura & D. H. Schunk, " Cultivating Competence, Self-Efficacy and Intrinsic Interest through Proximal Self-Motivation." *Journal of Personality and Social Psychology*, 1981, *41*, 586-598. Copyright © 1981 by the American Psychological Association. Reprinted by permission.)

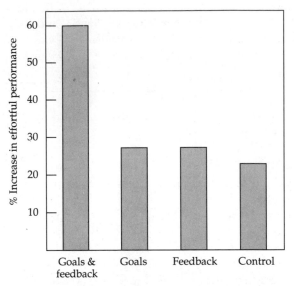

Figure 14–4. Mean percentage change in level of motivation under conditions combining goals with performance feedback, goals alone, feedback alone, or none of these factors. (From A. Bandura & D. Cervone, "Self-Evaluative and Self- Efficacy Mechanisms Governing the Motivational Effects of Goal Systems." *Journal of Personality and Social Psychology*, 1983, *45*, 1017-1028. Copyright © 1983 by the American Psychological Association. Reprinted with permission.)

The Process of Self-Motivation: Having and Setting Goals

As I indicated in the beginning of this chapter, the current position is that the self gives rise to thoughts and images but not to actions. Actions, it has been suggested, come from the setting of goals (Locke & Latham, 1990). Without goals you never do anything or accomplish anything. Goals are what give the focus that is necessary for success. Goals are the basis for self-discipline. Goals are what maintain our interest.

Evidence from a wide variety of sources attests to the importance of having immediate goals. Figure 14-3 shows the level of intrinsic interest in arithmetic activities of children in different goal conditions when given free choice of activities. Bandura argues that proximal or subgoals generate self-satisfaction that results from the personal accomplishment that individ-

uals experience. These immediate subgoals offer a continuing source of motivation quite apart from the loftier superordinate goals called aspirations.

One of the main reasons why people may not set goals for themselves is that they are fearful of the regret that may come from not achieving those goals, especially if the goals are risky. The best way to avoid regret, therefore, is simply not to decide on a goal. To put it another way, the reason people do not set goals for themselves is that they are motivated to protect their self-esteem. Research has shown that it is people with low self-esteem who are inclined to make decisions that minimize choices that may result in regret (Josephs, Larrick, Steele, & Nisbett, 1992). One way around this dilemma is to set goals that are less threatening to one's self-esteem. Another way is to learn how to self-regulate one's thinking, a topic I will discuss in the next section.

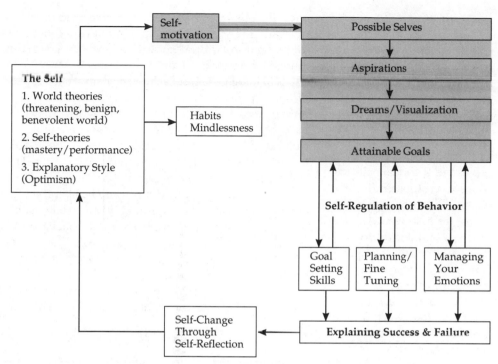

Figure 14–5. The process of self-motivation involves the setting of attainable goals. There are several intervening processes including the creation of possible selves, formulating aspirations, and dreaming and visualization.

Feedback and self-efficacy. Within Bandura's theory feedback is essential if motivation is to be maintained at a high level. Figure 14-4 shows what happens to motivation when people do not have feedback to accompany their goals. These results are consistent with the idea that people are motivated to meet a certain standard of performance that they have set for themselves. Unless you have feedback, it is impossible to determine how well you are doing. That in turn makes it difficult or even impossible to determine such things if you need to put forth more effort, need to persevere, or even need to analyze your behavior.

Summary

The current position is that the self gives rise to thoughts and images (cognitions) but not to actions. Actions, it has been suggested, come from the setting of goals. Evidence suggests that it is immediate as opposed to long-term goals that create action. Bandura's theory has addressed the question of goal-setting. The key to self-motivation, within Bandura's theory, is setting immediate attainable goals. Within Bandura's theory feedback is essential if motivation is to be maintained at a high level.

Links Between the Self and Goals: Possible Selves, Aspirations and Dreams

There are a number of processes that have been hypothesized to intervene between the self-concept and goals. There are three that I would like to discuss. These are the concepts of possible selves, aspirations and dreams.

Possible Selves

It has been suggested that *possible selves* are what links the self-concept to goals (Markus & Nurius, 1986; Markus, Cross, & Wurf,1990). As Markus and Nurius state:

> The inclusion of a sense of what is possible within the self-concept allows it to become dynamic.

Possible selves are the future-oriented component of the self-concept. Possible selves are the ideal self that we would like to become: the successful self, the creative self, the rich self, the thin self, the loved self, the respected self. Possible selves are also what we are afraid we might become: the alone self, the depressed self, the incompetent self, the alcoholic self, the unemployed self. Because a person is aware that he or she enjoys using drugs, for example, a possible self might be that of a drug addict. Because a person is aware of the fact that he or she cannot make decisions, for example, a possible self might be that of a person who depends on others to get them through life.

The Role of Self-Knowledge

Self-knowledge, by itself, does not automatically lead to growth and development. That is why Markus and Nurius (1986) have argued that we need to think in terms of possible selves. It is the possible selves that create motivation and therefore are the basis for change. Possible selves, however, are closely linked to the self-concept. When we think about what we might become we draw heavily upon self-knowledge. We ask ourselves, for example, whether or not we have the skill or ability to do something, whether or not we can develop that skill or ability, whether or not we have the motivation (are willing to put forth the effort and persist), whether or not we are willing to give up other activities. In other words, possible selves are not simply images that we arbitrarily draw out of the air but rather are images that we create from information contained in the self.

Possible selves are created selectively on the basis of one's experience in a given domain of expertise. As one becomes aware of one's own abilities or talents, one develops an enduring sensitivity to tasks in which those abilities or talents might be relevant (Nicholls, 1990). If an individual knows he or she is "smart" in school, for example, he or she will remain sensitive to issues of intelligence and achievement in school. If people know they are good at dealing with others they will remain sensitive to occupations in which they can make use of those talents. The self also contains sociocultural and historical information (Stryker, 1984). This information can be both liberating and limiting. The knowledge that someone from a poor background became President or Prime Minister can be liberating for others from a similar background because they realize that even though they are from a poor background they do not have to set limits on their goals. The knowledge that no one from their family has ever experienced great success, on the other hand, could be limiting because a person may unconsciously draw the unwarranted conclusion that this means he or she cannot hope for success.

Functions of the Self-Concept

Provide information. One of the functions of the self-concept is to provide information that will enable people to make judgments about what they can or cannot do. The information contained in the self-concept, however, is not always well-grounded in reality nor has a great deal of it been confirmed by social experience (Markus & Nurius, 1986). There are numerous examples of people who have self-concepts that underestimate their skills and talents. As a result, these people are often prevented from constructing possible selves that involve high levels of accomplishment. A person who believes in the entity theory of intelligence, for example, could be viewed as having a limiting self-concept. Because one holds to an entity theory one is unable to see oneself as developing the skills to become a great artist and therefore fails to put forth effort.

Provide context. Another function of the self is to provide context. Humans are inclined to view feedback from their behavior in terms of their enduring aspirations and goals. Receiving a grade of B has very different implications for someone whose only wish is to graduate versus someone who wants to be admitted to medical school. Similarly, a broken lunch date may have very different implications for someone fearful of being lonely versus someone who is simply trying to gain new information from someone they perceive as being able to provide that information.

The self-concept, in other words, is not only a storehouse of information about the self but provides the global integration of that information. It is from that integration of information that we come to have a sense of what has been called identity. As Erikson (1950) points out, the sense of identity provides people with the ability to experience the self as something that has both continuity and sameness. Interestingly, it is because people have developed a sense of continuity and sameness that they often have difficulty changing. To change means one must give up, at least momentarily, that sense of who one is.

Context comes from the themes that people use to characterize their interactions with the world. Themes, such as "the world is threatening" or "the world is benevolent," allow people to explain what happened to them. Interestingly, the structure or themes that people use serve to perpetuate those themes. If a person's theme is that the world is threatening or bad, they tend to keep track of bad things that happen to them. However, if a person's theme is that the world is benevolent, then they tend to keep track of good things that happen to them. As a result, people tend to maintain continuity, even if that continuity is characterized by bias.

What Kind of Self-Concept Do People Need for Developing Diverse Possible Selves?

Because possible selves are so closely linked to the self-concept, one of the ultimate goals of people who wish to achieve great things is to develop a self-concept that will then lead to the development of possible selves. As Markus and Nurius (1986) point out, possible selves do not simply happen; rather, they grow out of a well-defined self-concept. But what does such a self-concept look like? There are at least three things that characterize a well-defined self-concept.

1. It Must be a Highly Differentiated Self-Concept

As I indicated in the previous chapter, numerous writers and researchers have suggested that people who have highly differentiated or diverse self-concepts tend to be more likely to achieve difficult goals. Markus and Nurius (1986) suggest that people who view themselves as having *numerous categories* for the self (numerous possible selves), are able to achieve more goals because they perceive that they can assume more roles. Linville (1987) has suggested that people who have *diverse conceptions* of their identity, something called *self-complexity*, are better able to achieve goals as well as deal with a wide variety of negative events. It is because they can see themselves in a wide variety of situations that they can rise to new challenges and cope with new situations. Jennifer Campbell (1990) argues that people with high self-esteem have greater *clarity* of the self-concept. Using confidence measures, she has found that people with high self-esteem were more certain of self-attributes. Baumgardner(1990) suggests that it is important to have *depth* or *certainty* about a particular trait dimension. Being certain that one is athletic or creative is important, she argues, because it is the basis for self-esteem which, in turn, is the basis for attempting new and different things. As I have indicated before, her research indicates that "to know oneself is to like oneself" (p. 1062). She argues that a strong self-concept, one characterized by depth or certainty, promotes a sense of control over future outcomes and thus leads to positive affect and self-confidence.

2. It Must be A Positive Self-Concept

Not only must the self-concept be highly differentiated, it must be positive in nature. The fact that high-self-esteem people describe themselves with more positive attributes is well-known (Campbell, 1990). A great deal of research has shown that people with high self-esteem not only possess attributes that are linked to success but tend to cope well with change and stress. It has been found, for example, that children who have been identified as having high self-esteem are characterized by two sets of attributes: (1) confident, curious, independent and self-initiating, and (2) having the ability to adapt to change and stress. Low-self-esteem children, in contrast, are characterized by (1) failure to show con-

PRACTICAL APPLICATION 14.1

The Art of Creating Possible Selves

Sometimes people get into a rut. Because their parents told them they should become a doctor like their great Uncle George, they never entertain any other alternative. Years ago I had a friend who had decided, with encouragement from his parents, to pursue a career in engineering like that of his uncle. Not having the aptitude he struggled and he failed. It was at this point that he had to face, for the first time in his life, that his chosen career might not be right for him. When he began to explore other possibilities, he suddenly realized his interests were in the social sciences. One success followed another and eventually, after graduating from Oxford, he went on to set up his own research institute.

How do you go about creating possible selves without having to wait for failure? Start by making a list of things that you are good at doing or things that you have done well. Make sure this list contains things that are not part of your school experiences, such as good at bargaining, good at making friends, and so forth. Also, write down some of the skills that you think you might acquire with a modest amount of effort or even great effort. You might say to yourself, for example, that even though you have never repaired a bicycle, you think you could learn how to do it or that you could readily learn how to play another instrument.

Next, find the category under which such a skill could be found. For example, if you have worked at a swimming pool and been left in charge from time to time, then you would call that "manager." If you said that you had organized a school dance you would call that "producer" or "organizer." If you have won an athletic contest you would call that "winning athlete." Take each of these category names and put them into a new list. The purpose of this exercise is

---

fidence, curiosity, independence and initiative, and (2) inability to adapt to change (Harter, 1990). One of the consistent themes in the self-concept literature is the finding that when people have good self-concepts they are motivated by challenges and can deal with stress (e.g., Epstein, 1992). Another common theme in the experimental literature is that people with good self-esteem tend to be react positively to new challenges (Seligman, 1990). There is a great deal of evidence which suggests that in order to be positive people need to view the world as benevolent. It is in a benevolent world that people can embrace the world and take risks.

3. It Must be Closely Linked to Perceptions of Competencies

It has been suggested that ultimately the self-concept is linked to competencies (Nicholls, 1990) and perceptions of competencies (Langer & Park, 1990). When people have a clear perception that they are compe-

tent in a given domain, they are likely to set more difficult goals for themselves, a topic that we covered in Chapter 13. There is some reason to believe that taking an optimistic view of one's competencies is, perhaps, a good idea (Seligman, 1990). When people think they can do something they will often try, and in the process of trying they will often succeed. That is what it means to be an optimist.

The Self-Concept Is Created/Constructed and so Are Possible Selves

It is important to emphasize the idea that possible selves can be viewed as an act of creativity. Possible selves do not just happen. They result from combining and recombining elements of the self in new and different ways. Sometimes they emerge from acts of fantasy in which people entertain a wide variety of images where they see themselves doing a variety of different things. Possible selves are also constructed. By that I

to get you to think in broader terms. When you do that a whole new world will open up for you. You will say to yourself, I am a manager, an organizer, an athlete. Often people do not realize that the skills they acquired in one task will generalize to other situations. Armed with these new categories, you can suddenly see yourself doing many things.

With this new list, think of things that you might do. Make sure you write down all those things you could do even if they wouldn't make money or make you famous. Over the next weeks or even month, write down other things that come to mind. From this list, generate as many possible selves as you can. It is not important whether or not you actually want to pursue them. The point of this exercise is to make you aware of the fact there are many possibilities. You might be surprised to find that there are many options that you had never considered before.

A very good technique is to ask your friends what they think a person with such skills (using the category list) might do. We are often blind to new alternatives because our self-concept works hard to prevent us from entertaining new alternatives. In fact, when you suggest a new alternative to people they often react by saying "That isn't me." Nevertheless, when people make suggestions we tend to incorporate those ideas into our unconscious. It is amazing how a simple act of encouragement can alter someone's motivation. If someone else can believe you can do it, why can't you? Psychologists have known about this phenomenon for some time and systematically use suggestions and encouragement to get people to try new things. Often when people try new things they succeed, which is the basis for further strivings.

mean that people often make decisions about what they should or should not do, perhaps based on values they hold or principles that they have come to accept as important. The act of deciding that living long as opposed to well, for example, can affect the selection of such things as occupations (Kendall, Learner, & Craighead, 1984; Learner, 1982).

The idea that possible selves are creative and constructed offers some exciting possibilities for people who are interested in self-change. If possible selves are created and constructed then people can take personal responsibility for motivating themselves to change. Many theorists take the position that such things as possible selves are only the beginning point for change. In the final analysis people need to set clearly defined goals for themselves. This is not to negate the importance of constructing possible selves. Quite the contrary. There is a great deal of evidence that people need to set goals that are congruent with things they value, and that if they don't it is likely they will not achieve those goals. A

study by Langer and Thompson (cited in Langer, 1989) illustrates that people find it difficult if not impossible to change behaviors that they value. They had people select from a list of negative traits—such as rigid, grim, gullible, and the like—and asked them whether they had tried to change these behaviors and if they had succeeded or failed. Later, they asked these people how much they valued such traits as consistency, seriousness, trust, and so on. They found that people had difficulty changing certain negatively phrased traits if it was a trait they valued. For example, people generally do not like to see themselves as *rigid* but if they value *consistency* they may find it difficult to become *spontaneous*. Similarly, people generally do not like to see themselves as *gullible*, but if they value *trust* they may have difficulty becoming *suspicious* or *cynical*.

Despite the fact that possible selves are closely linked to your self-concept, you can begin to create new possible selves. In the accompanying practical application I suggest one possible way for you to do this.

Aspirations

Many current theorists conceptualize motivation as coming from a discrepancy or incongruity between goals and aspirations (e.g., Bandura, 1991). Therefore, in order for people to become motivated they have to experience some type of discrepancy between what they are now and what they would like to be in the future (possible selves). Possible selves represent all the possible alternatives from which we can choose. In the final analysis, people need to select one of more of those alternatives. The selection of an alternative is what creates aspirations. In other words, I can do many things but until I make a choice or selection, those alternatives are mere possibilities.

The impetus that pushes us from possible selves to creating aspirations may be as simple as a word of encouragement from another person. It can be as complex as carefully weighing the pros and cons. In the final analysis, it boils down to making a selection or decision.

The process by which people achieve or realize their aspirations is *concept-matching* (Bandura, 1991). In our minds we conceptualize what is needed to develop or realize one of our possible selves. By systematically setting goals we create the behaviors that are necessary to achieve that aspiration.

Aspirations can and should be translated into clear mental images. Unlike possible selves, which tend to be broad and free of constraints, aspirations are more limited and focused. Aspirations are the bridge that is necessary for moving from possible selves to goals. When we have a clear idea of our aspirations we are in a position to set goals. Aspirations are important but they are still not sufficient to create the focus that is necessary to succeed. That comes with goal-setting.

Dreams and Visualization

Nuttin (1984) has criticized psychology for talking about the impersonal, instinctual or unconscious nature of human motivation. He has argued that personalized motivation transforms the activity of goal-setting into concrete intentions and plans. Dreams and visualization are one way of personalizing motivation. They also make things seem real. But dreams and visualization may do more. They may serve to access those systems that are directly concerned with creating action, such as the experiential system proposed by Epstein.

Dreams and Visualization as a Means of Personalizing Motivation

In talking about what motivates people in their lives, Levinson (1978) used the word *dream* to describe the imagined possibilities of the self. He conceptualized the *dream* as an "imagined self" associated with a variety of goals, aspirations, and values. He suggested that as people mature the dream becomes cognitively refined and more motivationally powerful. As Markus and Nurius (1986) point out, when people think about goals they rarely think in terms of abstractions. When people think about getting a B.A., for example, they think "I am getting a B.A." It is a very personal thing in which I am the central character.

Dreams and Visualization as a Means of Making Goals Real

Shelly Taylor (1983) has described the need for people to gain a sense of mastery as they come to grips with life-threatening situations such as cancer. Her research has shown that when people can a gain a sense of mastery, their ability to cope improves and their health improves. How is this sense of mastery represented in the self-system? Markus and Nurius (1986) suggest that simply having a desire is probably not sufficient. They suggest that this desire must be translated into a "vision of the self as healthy, active, and strong and must be accompanied by specific plans and strategies for becoming these possible selves" (p. 961). In other words, people need to create an image that is both focused (specific) and real (pertaining to one's needs).

Dreams and Visualization as a Means of Accessing Action-Based Motivation Systems

Some people believe that the process of motivation is not governed by the rational thought system but rather comes out of a system that is more image-based (such as visual or auditory images) or perhaps emotion-based (pleasure/pain) such as in the experiential system proposed by Epstein. When people distinguish between these two hypothetical systems they often suggest that the rational system uses abstract symbols, words, and numbers whereas the experiential system uses concrete images, metaphors, and narratives (Epstein, 1990).

People who have worked with mental images have argued that one of the best ways for people to attain their goals is to give their brains clear, realistic mental images, preferably visual images, of the goals they want to attain (e.g., Cratty, 1990). The image should be as detailed as possible, incorporating as many senses as possible (Samuels & Samuels, 1975). Recently Crick and Koch (1992) have provided evidence for the idea that when people create mental images they actually stimulate neurons in the brain to fire. Their research grows out of the observation that people often fill in missing information when presented with visual stimulation that is incomplete or has parts missing. They argue that when people "fill in" missing information they draw on memories to supply the missing information. Their work provides evidence for the position that when people create mental images, these images are real as opposed to illusionary because neurons in the brain are actually firing in response to those images. Hobson, as we noted in Chapter 6, has argued that dreams are produced by memories that fire neurons in the brain. In other words, visualization helps make ideas and possibilities *real*.

Summary

It has been suggested that possible selves are what links the self-concept to goals. The first step of self-motivation, therefore, is to create possible selves. Possible selves are the future part of our self-concept. Possible selves, however, are closely linked to the self-concept and therefore self-knowledge plays an important role in the creation of possible selves. Possible selves are created selectively on the basis of one's experience in a given domain of expertise, but they also contain sociocultural and historical information which provides the context for creating possible selves. The function of the self-concept is not only to provide information but context. Having a diverse set of possible selves is important because it provides the individual with a great choice of alternatives from which to choose. Three things are important for the creation of diverse possible selves: a highly differentiated self, a positive self-concept, and a self that is linked closely to perceptions of competencies. Theorists believe that the self , as well as possible selves, are constructed.

Many current theorists conceptualize motivation as coming from a discrepancy or incongruity between goals and aspirations. It is when people select one of the possible selves that aspirations arise. Dreams and/or visualization can be important in three ways: They can personalize aspirations, they can make aspirations seem more real, and they act as a means for activating those systems of the self that have to do with motivation (goal-directed behavior) such as suggested in Epstein's theory of the self.

The Self-Regulation of Behavior

In order to achieve goals, we need to learn how to set attainable goals, how to acquire the skills we need, and how to manage our emotions including self-doubt. In the flow chart (Figure 14-6) I have connected each of these components to goals with a set of double arrows. These double arrows represent feedback loops. The idea behind feedback loops is that if you do not succeed on your first try you can adjust something or do something that will correct the situation.

There are three things that people need to learn to regulate: the nature and difficulty of their goals, the plans they have devised to achieve their goals, and their emotions.

Self-Regulation Process #1: Setting Difficult but Attainable Goals

According to Locke and Latham (1990), people should set difficult goals for themselves. The general rule of thumb is that the goal should be difficult but also attainable. For the most part, people have the capacity to determine if they can or cannot do something. Once they have decided they can they need to push them-

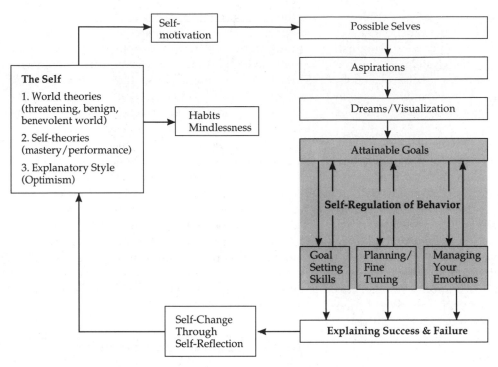

Figure 14–6. The achievement of goals is not something that should be left to chance. People need to learn how to carefully set goals, how to fine tune their behavior so that they can achieve these goals, and finally, how to manage their emotions.

selves to do it fast and well so that they will extend their perceptions of what constitutes an upper limit for themselves. I have heard it suggested that if you don't feel that you are slightly over your head you are not pushing yourself hard enough.

Should people find themselves in over their heads they should immediately reduce their goals so they can manage. On the other hand, if people find they are bored, they should increase the demands of the task. Finding the right difficulty level is not easy. It is something that people need to work at. Figure 14-7 shows what happens when people do not have goals and then spontaneously set low or high goals for themselves. Clearly, setting high goals is the best strategy.

One of the things that prevents people from selecting a difficult task is their own ego-defense system. As a general rule, people do not like to be put in a posi-

tion where they might be viewed as lacking in competence. To avoid that possibility, they select only easy tasks. While this puts off having to deal with the question of their competence, at least for another day, they fail to do what is most important for developing a sense of competence, and that is to stretch themselves. People with an entity theory of intelligence tend to select easy tasks. These people are strongly motivated to avoid tasks in which they might fail because to fail would further undermine their already fragile perceptions of being competent.

Self-Regulation Process #2: Making Plans and Making Adjustments

Designing routes to goals. Making plans is one of the most important things that people need to do if they hope to achieve their goals. Part of any plan is time management. That means, among other things, setting aside the time necessary to accomplish certain goals. Planning also involves breaking down goals into manageable units or subgoals. It is the subgoals that become the focus of attention. In other words, people need immediate goals.

Miller, Galanter, and Pribram (1960) have suggested the TOTE model as a way of conceptualizing how people gain congruence between a goal (an ideal) and a behavior (Figure 14-8).

According to their model, an individual creates a plan, activates the plan, and then monitors feedback to determine whether or not there is congruity or incongruity. If there is congruity with an ideal goal state (there is a conceptual match) the individual exits (ready to devise a new plan); otherwise he or she adjusts behavior to eliminate the incongruity.

Adjustment and fine-tuning. Most contemporary researchers (e.g., Campion & Lord, 1982; Carver & Scheier, 1981) view plans as adjustable and subject to frequent modification. In other words, the plan is as likely to change as the individual's action sequence. People who succeed rarely do so on the first try, so they change, in some way, what they are doing. Colonel Sanders, the founder of Kentucky Fried Chicken, is said to have knocked on more than 1600 doors before he could find a buyer for his famous chicken recipe. What often differentiates people who succeed and those who do not is persistence. I don't mean blind persistence but rather the kind of persistence in which people systematically change one thing and then another until they have achieved their goal. The Japanese have created a concept that is called "continuous improvement." According to this process, they keep searching for ways to improve their products by 1% here and 1% there. In other words, rather than trying to do something totally different, they attempt to improve something that is already good. When some people do not succeed the first time, they totally abandon their goal and move on to something else. Had Thomas Edison used that approach, he never would have invented the light bulb and many other things for which he is famous. The top athletes

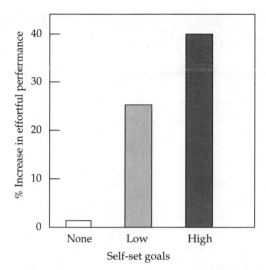

Figure 14–7. Mean increases in motivational level under conditions of performance feedback alone depending on whether people continue to perform the activity without goals or spontaneously set low or high goals for themselves. (From A. Bandura, "Self-Regulation of Motivation through Anticipatory and Self-Reactive Mechanisms." In R. A. Dienstbier (Ed.), *Perspectives of Motivation,* 1991, 69-164 (Figure 6). Nebraska Symposium on Motivation, Lincoln: University of Nebraska Press. Copyright © 1991. Reprinted with permission.)

do the same thing as Thomas Edison did. They work to improve one small thing, thereby creating an edge over their competitors. The best way to change something is to decide in advance what needs to be changed and then to search for a route to achieve that change. When people have a clear concept of what they want to achieve it is much easier for them to make the necessary adjustments.

Using mental rehearsal. In athletics, the use of mental rehearsal has become commonplace. One of my favorite examples (one I referred to in Chapter 3) is Greg Louganis who won the gold medal for diving in the 1988 Olympics. In order to learn a new dive Greg first attempted to visualize himself doing that dive. This is not a simple process; in order to get a clear image of that dive he rehearsed it over and over in his mind.

PRACTICAL APPLICATION 14.2

Learning to Become a Risk-Taker

Unless you take some risk in life you can never expect great things to happen to you. Setting risky goals, however, tends to threaten self-esteem because people (especially low-self-esteem people) are fearful of the regret they may experience if they do not achieve their goals. Research has shown that when you remove the threat, low-self-esteem people no longer show this tendency and behave like high-self-esteem individuals (Josephs, Larrick, Steele, & Nisbett, 1992). Given that taking risks is not only adaptive but necessary if one is to make any significant achievements, the question is how do people learn to deal with this problem?

According to the principles of self-regulation, people can learn to structure their thinking in such a way as to minimize feeling of risk (or perhaps social disapproval). The problem here is one of focus or emphasis. If you are inclined to focus only on negative possibilities then, of course, you will be overwhelmed by feelings of failure or simply social disapproval. What you need to do is learn to focus on the regret you would experience if you had not taken the chance. What if you had the chance of becoming an actor at one point in your life and you turned down the opportunity?

I have a good friend who is a very successful businessman and likes to recall how people used to call him "crazy Johnny" behind his back in the earlier days when he was building his business. The reason they called him crazy Johnny was that he did things which other people thought were risky. As he likes to point out with pride, nobody calls him "crazy Johnny" anymore. In fact, many of the people who reportedly called him "crazy Johnny" now seek his advice. While they were content with the status quo, he was breaking new ground. He takes great satisfaction in the fact that he not only succeeded but that he earned the respect of many people in the process. He isn't suffering from any low self-esteem these days.

It is important to remember that people also make fun of people who didn't take those chances that would have changed their lives forever. I know many people who live lives of quiet self-regret. When they had a chance to do something great, they got bogged down in indecision and lost forever a great opportunity. Interestingly, we never laugh at people who fail as long as they end up on their feet. Like "crazy Johnny," make sure you get the last laugh.

Once he had a clear image he would mount the ladder and try the dive. At the precise moment he left the board he would run the mental image in his mind, letting the image guide his behavior. Initially his attempts to match his behavior to the image were less than perfect, a common observation that has been made by other athletes. However, with successive attempts he found that he could quickly match his behavior to the mental image he had created. This is a good example of a feedback loop.

Many if not most athletes use imagery in much the same way that Greg Louganis did. In order to understand why imagery works we need to understand that any response is made up of many smaller components, and that when we think of each of these components they fire a neural process in the brain that is responsible for that component. There is even evidence that when we think about certain things blood flows to that area of the brain. By repeatedly creating the same image we force the brain to connect these various neural firings into a sequence. In this way, the behavior takes on an automatic quality.

Elizabeth Manley, who won the silver medal for figure skating in the 1988 Winter Olympics, was considered at best to be a distant contender for third place. Just days before the competition, she she had a breakthrough in her mental imagery. For the first time in some time, she could see herself performing her rou-

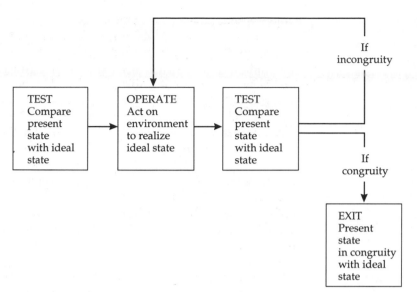

Figure 14–8. Schematic of the TOTE unit. The TOTE model suggests that people are inclined to compare their present state with an ideal state (TEST) to determine if there is need for action. If there is a discrepancy, they are motivated to act on the environment (OPERATE). If the discrepancy remains (if there is incongruity), they will be motivated to continue acting on the environment to realize the ideal state. Once the discrepancy is removed (there is congruity), they will cease acting on the environment (EXIT). (From *Understanding Motivation and Emotion* by John Marshall Reeve, p. 182. Copyright © 1992 by Holt Rinehart Winston. Reprinted with permission of the publisher.)

tine flawlessly. When it came time for her to perform, she did just that.

The problem for athletes is that they often want to do different things (e.g., different dives) involving different sequences of the same basic components. In order to instruct the brain, the easiest thing for the athlete to do is to rehearse the image corresponding to the desired behavior just before attempting the behavior. This is precisely what Jack Nicklaus, the golfer, does before making a shot. If he merely walked up to the ball without mentally rehearsing the shot, the brain would not necessarily know which neural pattern to run.

Using advisors and coaches. It is not surprising, I suppose, that so many successful people have advisors. In order to perfect something you need to understand exactly what it is that you should be doing. Asking experts is a very good way of determining whether or not you are doing something correctly. Harvey McKay, the CEO of a large company, has acquired a number of skills. He has transformed himself into a marathon runner, has written a best-selling book entitled *Swim With the Sharks Without Being Eaten Alive*, and currently is on the international speakers tour. One of the interesting things about Harvey McKay is that each time he set out to accomplish yet another goal he first located the best experts he could find and asked them to coach him. It makes good sense that if you are going for the top, you contact people who are there or who have been there. They can help you break down a larger goal into manageable subgoals which are at the heart of learning any complex skill.

Self-Regulation Process #3: Managing Your Emotions, Moods, and Self-Doubt

Moods and self-efficacy. Not only are self-efficacy beliefs affected by momentary changes in performance, but they can also be affected by mood. Kavanaugh and Bower (1985) demonstrated that self-efficacy beliefs tend to change quite dramatically as a result of people being in a positive, neutral or negative mood state (Figure 14-9). According to Bower's affective priming theory, past successes and failures are stored as memories along with affect. When a particular mood is aroused the memories associated with that mood are also aroused. These memories serve as the data base for making judgments about such things as the likelihood of succeeding (i.e., self-efficacy judgments). Managing your moods, therefore, is an important consideration. Among other things, it means you need to work on becoming more optimistic.

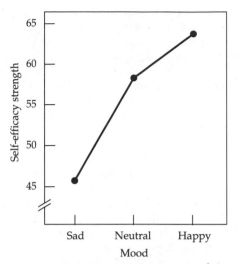

Figure 14–9. Mean strength of self-perceived efficacy across heterosexual, social, and athletic domains of functioning when efficacy judgments were made in a positive, neutral, or negative mood state. (From D. J. Kavanagh and G. H. Bower, "Mood and Self-Efficacy: Impact of Job and Sadness on Perceived Capabilities." *Cognitive Therapy and Research*, 1985, *9*, 507-525. Copyright © 1985 by Plenum Publishing. Reprinted with permission.)

Virtually everybody suffers from self-doubt. Some people, however, are able to manage it and not let it overwhelm them. This idea is summed up in the proverb: "You cannot prevent the birds of worry and care from flying over your head. But you can stop them from building a nest in your head" (Bandura, 1989).

Self-doubt as intrusive thinking. Self-doubt often results when you cannot turn off negative thoughts that intrude into your thinking. In his work on test anxiety, Sarason (1975) has found that one of the major components of test anxiety is intrusive thinking. As a result of such intrusive thinking, people are unable to focus their attention on the task at hand. It is not the intrusive thinking per se nor the frequency per se that most peo-

ple find is a source of stress but rather the inability to turn them off (Churchill & McMurray, 1990; cited in Bandura, 1991; Kent, 1987). Evidence from many sources indicates that when people dwell on their coping deficiencies they not only distress themselves but they impair their level of functioning (Bandura, 1988; Lazarus & Folkman, 1984; Meichenbaum, 1977). The net result is that intrusive thinking, if left unmanaged, leads to a deterioration in performance. The failure to control intrusive thinking can also result in depressive rumination. Depressive rumination not only impairs performance but diminishes perceptions of competency. Since I have already discussed depressive rumination in Chapter 10, I won't elaborate further on it here.

Self-doubt and self-efficacy. The interesting thing about coping self-efficacy beliefs is that when people have strong coping self-efficacy beliefs they are less troubled by self-doubt, they tend to handle adversity better, and they tend to organize their thinking better. In other words, when people have strong feelings of efficacy they do not need to spend as much time managing negative thinking that undermines performance.

Within Bandura's theory there is a dual route to emotional control. On the one hand, people perceive they have the ability or skills to cope with a specific situation. In addition, people perceive they can deal with intrusive negative thoughts. This dual route to emotional control is illustrated in a study by Ozer and Bandura (1990) that I talked about in Chapter 11. Since women must live with the possibility of potential sexual assault, Ozer and Bandura set out to empower women to prevent and control sexual abuse should the occasion arise. The training involved having women participate in a mastery modeling program in which they mastered the physical skills to defend themselves successfully against unarmed sexual assailants. Their results showed that mastery modeling not only enhanced perceived coping ability but it increased perceived ability to control negative intrusive thinking. The increased ability to exercise control over negative intrusive thoughts was viewed as an important benefit since one of the things that is a source of stress and worry for women are thoughts that intrude into their thinking about their sexual safety.

Three Methods of Dealing with Self-Doubt

Various methods have been suggested as ways of giving people control over negative intrusive thoughts. Ellis and Greiger (1977) have suggested three methods: self-talk, cognitive restructuring, and substituting other thoughts.

Self-talk. It is generally acknowledged that people often engage in self-talk when they are trying to accomplish a task (Helmstetter, 1986). They say to themselves such things as: "This is too hard for me"; "I'm never going to make it"; "If I can just get around the next corner I am home free"; "I think I am going to win this one"; and so forth. Where does this self-talk come from and what does it mean? It obviously comes from our assessment of our abilities relative to the difficulty of the task. Since self-talk changes quite dramatically as we proceed from the beginning to the end of a task, self-talk is obviously not a stable estimate of our abilities but rather a momentary or transient estimate. For example, people will start by saying "I think I am going to do well," then when things get tough say, " I don't think I can do this," and towards the end say, "If I can just hang in there I will make it." All of us have probably said something very similar to ourselves at one time or another.

Motivation is obviously at a low point when our self-talk becomes negative. That is, when the discrepancy between our abilities and our goals is no longer optimal we are inclined to give up. The question, therefore, is can we learn to control our self-talk in order to prevent our motivation from dropping off? A number of people believe the answer is yes. It grows out of the work of sports psychology and is based on a distinction that often invokes the words *conscious* (images and thoughts) and *unconscious* (the source of behavioral programs). I don't think these are necessarily the best words. The distinction that people are making has to do with systems in the brain that pro-

duce the response (output system) and separate systems in the brain that evaluate how well we are doing (evaluative system). According to this interpretation, when people provide the output system with an image of what they need, it attempts to find the program (the pattern of neuron connections) that will produce the desired response (see Crick & Koch, 1992). When a baseball pitcher visualizes throwing a curve ball, for example, the brain activates the motor program necessary for that behavior. If, perchance, the manager says to the pitcher "Don't throw a fast ball because he will hit it out of the park", the image given the pitcher's brain is that of a fastball. Not surprisingly, the pitcher throws a fastball which is then hit out of the park as predicted.

The distinction between two separate systems for output and evaluation means that if I can override my "natural" tendency to give up when I feel some discomfort, my output system will continue to activate the desired response. The reason we have an evaluative system, it has been argued, is to prevent us from injuring ourselves or from taking too great risks. For many of us, we are inclined to shut down well before we have put ourselves in danger. What this means is that I need to become mindful of the tendency to engage in self-talk, especially when things get tough, and to consciously engage in positive self-talk to counteract negative self-talk.

Cognitive restructuring. The obvious next step, once you have learned to substitute positive for negative self-talk, is to become aware of the dynamics of success. If you are aware of the fact, for example, that when you push yourself you tend to experience self-doubts, you can reflect on this event as an indication that you are indeed pushing yourself to new heights. The motto "No pain, no gain" is an apt description of this concept. Athletes, especially body builders, often use this motto to help them overcome plateaus. We are becoming more and more aware of the fact that we all create limits for ourselves that are purely psychological. Once Roger Bannister broke the four-minute mile, many other athletes followed within a short period of time. Obviously, it wasn't their bodies that were limiting them, but their minds.

PRACTICAL APPLICATION 14.3

Preparing Yourself for the Setbacks and Hard Work Ahead

It is exciting to decide on a dream. It is a far different matter to make the commitment to do whatever is necessary to achieve that dream. One of the things that we often fail to appreciate is that people who have succeeded experienced periods of self-doubt, often thought about quitting, experienced failure along the way, or wondered whether the time they were putting in was worth it. The best way I know to help prepare yourself for such events is to collect stories about the struggles that the people you admire went through. A good starting point would be to read John White's (1982) book titled *Rejection*. In this book White recounts numerous stories about eminent people who experienced many rejections but prevailed just the same. Gertrude Stein submitted poems to editors for 20 years before she had one accepted. James Joyce's book titled *Dubliners* was rejected by 22 publishers. Van Gogh sold only one painting during his lifetime. Rodin was repeatedly rejected by the Ecole des Beaux-Arts. Decca Records turned down the Beatles. In the academic world there are numerous examples. John Garcia, whose pioneering work demonstrated that there are "limitations to learning," was once told by a reviewer of his oft-rejected manuscripts that one is no more likely to find the phenomenon he discovered than bird droppings in a cuckoo clock (Bandura, 1989). When Martin Seligman first attempted to report his pioneering research on learned helplessness, he was told by a senior professor in his department, a person who had been editor of the *Journal of Experimental Psychology* for twenty years, that the article made him "physically sick."

Start collecting your own stories and examine these stories for what made it possible for these people to prevail in spite of overwhelming odds. Things don't just happen. Success isn't an accident. Success comes from learning to deal with adversity.

Humans are often inclined to assume that other people succeed because they are more intelligent, more talented, or luckier. The fact is that what makes the difference is one's ability to prevail. In one study, people were asked to judge the intelligence of scientists who had made an important discovery. One group was told about the process the scientists went through that led them to their discovery while the other group was not. Those subjects that were told about the process judged the scientists as less intelligent (Langer & Thompson, 1987). Once you understand that achievement simply involves systematically approaching a goal and then prevailing, you won't become overwhelmed by the oft-mistaken belief that in order to succeed you need to be talented or gifted. Zig Zigler tells the story of a janitor he met with an I.Q. of 160. Unless you set goals and prevail, it doesn't matter how gifted you are.

Substituting other thoughts. One reason competing against other people can push us to new levels is that our attention gets diverted away from our pain and fatigue and towards the idea of winning. There is a great deal of evidence that indicates when we are thinking pleasant thoughts, our body reacts accordingly (see Chapter 9). The trick is to learn to control our thinking so that we do not fall prey to lower motivation.

Managing Anxiety and Arousal

Even professional athletes find from time to time that they are plagued with high levels of anxiety or arousal. Knowing that such high levels of anxiety or arousal can interfere with their performance, they use techniques that enable them to bring their anxiety and arousal under control. The most prevalent method is to use some type of relaxation procedure (see Chapter 9).

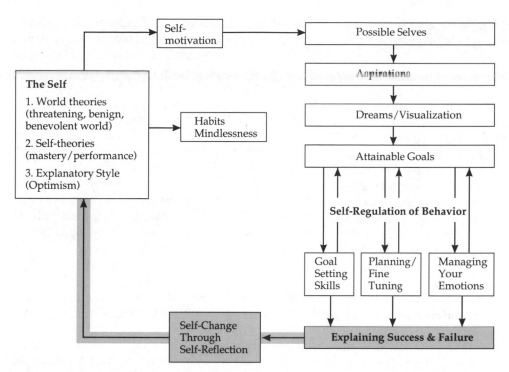

Figure 14–10. In order to achieve success people need to develop a self-concept that is resilient in the face of failure and capitalizes on success. The process by which people develop such a self-concept is called self-reflection. The essence of positive self-reflection is learning to adapt the explanatory style for success and failure that characterizes optimists.

Alternatively, some people use a form of meditation or thought distraction. When we divert our thinking away from the problem, our body often returns to a more normal way of functioning. Since I have already discussed relaxation in the chapter on stress, I will simply refer the reader to that chapter.

Athletes often find that by simply focusing their attention on the mental image that guides their behavior, they can manage arousal and anxiety. Focusing on a mental image would serve to maintain feelings of competency while simultaneously making sure that there is no room for potentially negative intrusive thoughts.

Summary

The process of self-regulation involves: (1) learning to set goals that are attainable, (2) learning to plan routes to goals and to fine tune, and (3) learning to manage your emotions. Various theorists have argued that the motivation to act and become competent results from the discrepancy between aspirations and goals. One of the objects of goal setting is to learn how to set goals that create an optimal discrepancy. Planning routes to goals involves not only planning the things you need to do but setting aside the time for actually accomplishing those plans. Mental images are a useful technique for planning routes to goals. Seeking out experts is a good way to learn to break tasks down into their components. Three methods have been put forth to manage self defeating thoughts: self-talk, cognitive restructuring, and substituting other thoughts. Various relaxation procedures have been suggested for dealing with high anxiety and arousal. Some athletes have simply learned to focus on positive mental images as a way of maintaining feelings of competency and ensuring that there is no room for potentially negative intrusive thoughts.

Self-Reflection: The Basis for Self-Change

Ultimately, people need to develop a self-concept that will enable them to achieve success. Specifically, they need to develop the agent part of the self or the "I." The agent part of the self determines what information people process about the environment (as opposed to passively absorbing it) and the rules and principles that will guide their actions. According to Deci and Ryan (1991), the motivation for developing the "I" or the agent part of the self comes from the need for autonomy and control which translates into self-determination. They argue that the need for self-determination is not learned but emerges in the course of development. It typically emerges when we have received positive feedback from our initial attempts to master our environment. The problem for many people is not understanding how to do what their heart tells them they should do. In this section I will provide some ways of developing a positive or winning self-concept. It comes from learning to think positively.

The process I will be talking about is called self-reflection. In order to acquire new habits that will replace old habits, people need to uncover the thinking that underlies their old habits and then replace that old thinking with new thinking habits. One of the keys to this process is becoming aware of how you think and then changing the way you think. Pop motivational speakers often suggest that you start by deciding to think positively. That is easier said than done. That may be especially difficult for people who have been trained to be cautious and analytical. In order to learn any new habit you need to engage in behaviors that will produce a positive outcome (reward). When you can see that your new way of thinking produces more success/self-satisfaction, you are ready to make that new way of thinking a part of your life. What I want to show you is that if you practice becoming aware of the way you think, you will learn to think about your

actions (reflect on your actions) and you will learn how to uncover your thinking style. Having done that, you will then be in a position to try new ways of thinking and to see if they lead to greater self-satisfaction. If they do, then you have the basis for substituting new habits for old habits.

One of the things that people need to learn to do if they hope to achieve success is to accept challenges. It is through accepting challenges that people stretch themselves and develop competency. Many people learn, often as children, to view the world in ways that make it very difficult for them to accept challenges. When people are sensitized, for example, to perceive that making mistakes is the same as failure and that failure is a reason for being rejected or even humiliated, they will naturally avoid any activity that might result in making mistakes. Young children, for example, often discover that parents and teachers are more likely to point out what they have done wrong than what they have done right, and that doing something wrong is grounds for punishment and humiliation. I remember one day watching a father as he pitched balls to his 6-year-old son. Whenever his son missed one of his pitches, which he did most of the time, his father yelled at him such phrases as "Pay attention," or "You don't listen to a thing I say." Finally, in exasperation, I heard him yell, his face red with anger, "You really are stupid, aren't you?" I was amazed at his reaction but perhaps I shouldn't have been. Over the years I have observed over and over again similar examples of this behavior, not only by parents but by teachers and coaches, who think it is motivating to say such things as: "Are you stupid or something?" or "Can't you do anything right?" or "Don't you ever listen?" No wonder some children learn to avoid certain activities or challenging tasks in which they might make a mistake. One of the byproducts of this process is self-reproach. We learn to say to ourselves "I really must be stupid" or "I can't do anything right."

Behavior Results from Thinking Habits

The reason for getting people to engage in self-reflection is to break bad thinking habits. It is important to recognize that indeed these are habits and nothing more. As Martin Seligman has noted in his book *Learned Optimism*:

> Habits of thinking need not be forever. One of the most significant findings in psychology in the last twenty years is that individuals can choose the way they think" (Seligman, 1990, p. 8).

Reflection and Mindfulness

Ellen Langer (1990) has made a similar point in her book titled *Mindfulness*. She has argued that indeed people often do things out of habit. When we no longer know why we are doing something these habits take on a mindless quality. While there is nothing wrong with doing things out of habit, in order to change a habit we need to become mindful of why we are doing it. Ellen Langer talk about habits that we have acquired directly through our own experiences and those that are the product of belief systems that we have acquired and stored somewhere in our unconscious. These habits can be thought of as concepts or pictures that we have stored in our brain. In her research she has been able to show that one reason people act old, such as not making decisions or not carrying heavy things, is not because their bodies force them to act this way but rather because these people have stored mental images of how old people act and then base their actions on these mental images. She was able to show that when she induced people to think of themselves as younger, not only did many outward changes occur, such as a younger posture and gait, but more basic changes occurred, including improved eyesight, better mental functioning, and improved memory (Langer, 1989).

In the flow chart I included mindlessness with habits. While the effect is often the same, it is important to remember that they often have somewhat different origins. Even if we haven't been actively taught to think in certain ways, we learn thinking habits by modeling other people. Bandura (1991) argues that we do not simply absorb standards or conduct from whatever influences happen to impinge upon us. Rather, he suggests that we construct generic standards from numerous evaluative rules that are prescribed, taught or modeled. In other words, we need not think in certain ways. We can change the generic rules by which we evaluate our own behavior. We can change rules by developing a strong sense of agency.

There are several other causes of mindlessness, all of which involve in one way or another that failure to consider that there are other alternatives. Anyone wanting to more fully explore the power of becoming mindful should read Ellen Langer's book titled *Mindfulness*. The point I want to make is that we do not have to act mindlessly, as we often do. We become mindful by reflecting on our own behavior.

Self-Confidence: Harmonizing Feelings of Perceived Competency and Optimism

Self-confidence. Ultimately, the way to achieve personal success is to develop self-confidence. Self-confidence is not something that just happens; self-confidence is something people learn to nurture and develop. There are two things that you need to develop lasting self-confidence: a sense of competency or self-determination (or more precisely an understanding of the process by which competency or self-determination are achieved), and a sense of optimism (or more precisely how to effectively deal with adversity). Let me start with competency.

Developing your sense of competency. One of the most important things you can learn is that competency isn't something you have or don't have, or that it is something that just happens one day. Rather, competency is something people develop. While there are obvious biological limitations, they account for much less than people often think. In a study done by Langer, she asked her students to evaluate the intelligence of scientists who had achieved an "impressive" intellectual outcome (such as discovering a new planet or inventing a new drug). When she described the achievement in terms of a series of steps that characterize most achievements, they judged the scientists as less intelligent than when the achievement was just named. When people can see the steps, accomplishment does not seem that difficult. The key to self-confidence is recognizing there are a series of well-defined steps to every accomplishment and that if you can just discover those steps you too can do great things.

Learn to focus on process. Most achievement involves a series of steps. The Japanese have made great strides in manufacturing quality products such as cars and electronic equipment that are in demand around the world. It wasn't that long ago that the phrase "Made in Japan" was an immediate reason for rejecting a Japanese product. Now it is just the reverse. How did they achieve this reversal? The Japanese have learned to approach manufacturing systematically, conceptualizing manufacturing as a process that is made up of many components that need to be linked. Instead of trying to improve the overall product by inventing something new, their strategy has been to focus their energy on trying to improve each of the components as well as improving the linking of those components. Whenever they learn how to produce a better part or component, they introduce the change as soon as possible rather than wait for a model change (which has been a North American tendency). As a result, they always tend to be slightly ahead of their competition. This approach, as I indicated earlier, has come to be called the "continuous improvement" approach.

The concept of the continuous improvement approach to manufacturing is a good metaphor for creating personal competency. Like manufacturing cars, competency is made up of a series of components. Each of these components can be improved and then reintroduced into the chain that makes up a skill or competency. Athletes often approach the development of athletic skills in this way. For a period of time they work on one component. Once having perfected that component, they reintroduce it into the chain to ensure that it fits or harmonizes with the other components. Next they work on another component and then reintroduce that component into the chain. This process is repeated over and over. While there is no dramatic change in the short run, it is often very dramatic over the long run.

The ability to break things down into components and then reassemble them in various ways makes it possible for athletes to create a wide variety of skills out of a few basic components. It is this ability to reassemble various components that has made Greg Louganis a great diver, Martina Navratilova a great tennis player, Wayne Gretsky a great hockey player, and Barbra Streisand a great singer. Standup comics often use a similar approach. They have a series of components (skits, jokes) that they can string together in various ways depending on the nature of their audience or the feedback they get from their audience.

Learned Optimism

No matter how skilled you are or how carefully you plan to reach your goal, you will encounter frustrations and setbacks. That is the reason you need to learn to become an optimist. I have already talked at some length in Chapters 10 and 11 about the different ways optimists and pessimists react to success and adversity and how people can learn to become optimists.

Coming Full Circle

As you become aware of the process by which skills are acquired and of the fact that there are ways of dealing with obstacles and setbacks that will enable you to succeed, you will develop greater self-confidence. With increased self-confidence you will be able to create new possible selves, create new aspirations, and set more difficult goals. What often prevents people from moving forward is the fear that they will not have the skills to handle a new situation or that they will not be able to deal with adversity. If, however, they know that they can develop new skills and that they have the skills to deal with adversity, the fear will be less and they will be able to move forward with the confidence that they have the resources to deal with the unknown.

An Overview: The Key to Personal Success Is Becoming a Process-Oriented as Opposed to a Goal-Oriented Person

Most current motivation theorists hold the view that people need to learn to focus on the process as opposed

Many people have discovered that one of the most rewarding things they can do is to help others to achieve their full potential. Mothers have traditionally played an important role in helping their children to develop the self-confidence they need to achieve success and happiness.

to the goal if they want to succeed. Virtually all of the work that I have presented in this chapter stresses the importance of the process as opposed to the outcome. By focusing on the process, personal success is available to virtually anyone who is willing to follow the flow chart that I outlined. Further, it is the process of achieving goals that seems to provide the motivation for success as well as the satisfaction that comes with setting goals. In his book entitled *Flow*, Csikszentmihalyi (1990) argues that optimal experience occurs when we undertake challenging tasks with clear goals and immediate feedback. In such situations, he argues, we lose all self-doubt and experience a sense of being in control. The experience is so strong, he argues, that we are more than willing to put forth the effort needed to develop the skills that we require.

Getting There or Being There

The difference between dreams and goals are often the difference between being there or getting there. Many

motivation writers have argued that the main reward or pleasure that comes with achievement is not in reaching the goal but in working towards the goal. When Torvil and Dean won their gold medal in the Olympics for pair figure skating, Dean described how he felt at that moment by saying he felt that he had achieved his dream. It was wonderful. In the next sentence he talked about how difficult it was to go back to work. While achieving a dream can be and often is exciting, the pleasure is often short-lived. In order to continue enjoying life one needs new dreams to sustain one. In writing about Steve Jobs, author Jeffrey Young titled his book *Steve Jobs: The Journey is the Reward*. For many people like Steve Jobs, it is working towards the dream that provides the real pleasure and excitement.

Mother Teresa is perhaps one of the best examples of a person who has leaned the importance of creating something that transcends ourselves.

Main Points

1. In recent years it has been suggested that needs do not give rise to actions but rather to dispositions, and that possible selves translates these dispositions to action.

2. The term *self-concept* is typically used to describe how people think about the external world and how they think about their ability to deal with it.

3. The repository side of self (the "me") involves values and regulatory processes whereas the agent side of the self (the "I") is the autonomous side that needs to be in control.

4. The three different prototypes of self/environmental awareness are: (1) the world is hostile and threatening, (2) the world is benevolent, and (3) the world is benign.

5. People develop different strategies or orientations for dealing with the world.

6. People with a mastery strategy learn to deal with the world by developing competency. Feelings of efficacy are what reward the development of competency.

7.   People with a performance strategy learn to deal with the world by learning the rules of winning.

8.   Mastery type individuals tend to be process-oriented; performance types tend to be outcome-oriented.

9.   The ideal situation is one in which you not only win but can take credit for the win.

10.   According to Rogers, we are born with a need to develop a positive self-concept.

11.   One of the things that prevents us from developing a positive self-concept, according to Rogers, comes from being raised with conditional love. People who have been raised with conditional love often do not feel worthy.

12.   Unconditional love, in contrast, leads to a sense of positive self-regard.

13.   Conditional love also leads to the development of anxiety. In order to reduce anxiety, people learn to engage in behaviors that will elicit signs of approval.

14.   Epstein has proposed a theory of the self based on the idea that people possess two semi-independent systems for processing information: a rational system and an experiential system.

15.   The rational system operates according to socially accepted logic and evidence and functions at the conscious level.

16.   The experiential system is a more emotional/holistic system that operates at the level of the preconscious.

17.   Epstein has found that poor constructive thinkers have a tendency to make unfavorable overgeneralizations about themselves following negative outcomes.

18.   Actions come from the setting of goals.

19.   Evidence from a wide variety of sources attests to the importance of having immediate goals.

20.   The key to self-motivation within Bandura's theory is setting attainable goals.

21.   Outcome expectations within Bandura's theory are defined as "a person's estimate that a given behavior will lead to certain outcomes."

22.   Self-efficacy is defined as "the conviction that one can successfully execute the behavior required to produce the outcomes."

23.   Feelings of self-efficacy come from past performance.

24.   Within Bandura's theory, feedback is essential for maintaining motivation.

25.   Possible selves link the self-concept to goals.

26.   Possible selves are the future-oriented component of the self-concept. By creating new selves we force the brain to entertain new possibilities.

27.   Possible selves are closely linked to the self concept.

28.   The self-concept is based on one's experiences in a given domain and also reflect sociocultural and historical information.

29.   The self-concept provides both information and context.

30.   The three qualities of the self-concept that are likely to lead to diverse possible selves are: a highly differentiated self-concept, a positive self-concept, and a self-concept that is closely linked to perceptions of competency.

31.   It has been suggested that the self-concept is created and constructed.

32.   Aspirations result from making a choice among one or more of the possible selves.

33.   Aspirations create the discrepancy that has been hypothesized to motivate behavior.

34.   Dreams and visualization are a means of personalizing motivation, as a way of making goals real, and perhaps as a means of assessing the sensory/emotional motivation system.

35.   It is important to learn to set difficult but attainable goals.

36.   It is important not only to make plans but to learn how to adjust behavior to ensure that behavior is congruent with the plans.

37.   It is also important to learn to change one's plan when the plan does not work. Blind persistence is not the way to succeed.

38.   Many people make use of mental rehearsal to create a plan in their minds.

39.   It is sometimes advisable to make use of advisors and coaches.

40.   Since mood can affect feelings of self-efficacy it is important to learn how to manage your moods.

41.   Learning to manage self-doubt is important because self-doubt tends to undermine feelings of self-efficacy.

42.   Within Bandura's theory there is a dual route to increasing emotional control: perceived ability to cope and perceived ability to control negative intrusive thoughts.

43.   When people learn coping skills they are less troubled by adversity and they tend to organize their thinking better.

44.   Self-doubt often occurs when people are unable to turn off negative thoughts that intrude into their thinking.

45.   Three methods have been suggested to deal with self-doubt: self-talk, cognitive restructuring, and substituting other thoughts.

46.   The process of self-reflection is the first step towards the process of self-change.

47.   Through self-reflection we can learn to change our thinking habits.

48.   Langer's work shows how important it is for us to become mindful of our thoughts and decisions.

49.   Self-confidence is the result of learning to harmonize feelings of perceived competency with optimism.

50.   Competency is something you can learn to develop by learning to focus on the process.

51.   The key to personal success is becoming a process-oriented individual.

References

AARONS, L. Sleep-assisted instruction. *Psychological Bulletin*, 1976, *83*, 1-40.

ABBOTT, R. A., & CARVER, C. S. Dispositional optimism and recovery from coronary artery bypass surgery: The beneficial effects of physical and psychological well-being. *Journal of Personality and Social Psychology*, 1989, *57*, 1024-1040.

ABELSON, H., COHEN, R., HEATON, E., & SUDER, C. National survey of public attitudes toward and experience with erotic materials. In *Technical Report of the Commission on Obscenity and Pornography* (Vol. 6). Washington, D.C.: Government Printing Office, 1971.

ABPLANALP, J. Premenstrual syndrome: A selective review. *Women and Health*, 1983, *8*, 107-124.

ABRAMSON, L. Y., METALSKY, G. I., & ALLOY, L. B. Hopelessness depression: A theory-based process-oriented subtype of depression. *Psychological Review*, 1989, *96*, 358-372.

ABRAMSON, L. Y., SELIGMAN, M. E. P., & TEASDALE, J. D. Learned helplessness in humans: Critique and reformulation. *Journal of Abnormal Psychology*, 1978, *87*, 49-74.

ADELSON, S. F. Changes in diets of households, 1955 to 1965. *Journal of Home Economics*, 1968, *60*, 448-455.

ADLER, T. Neurochemistry linked with anorexia, bulimia. *APA Monitor*, October, 19, 1989.

AINSWORTH, M. D. S., BLEHAR, M. C., WATER, E., & WALL, S. *Patterns of Attachment: A Psychological Study of the Strange Situation*. Hillsdale, N.J.: Erlbaum, 1978.

AKIL, H., MADDEN, J., IV, PATRICK, R. L., & BARCHAS, J. D. Stress induced increase in endogenous opiate peptides: Concurrent analgesia and its partial reversal by naloxone. In H. W. Kosterlitz (Ed.), *Opiates and endogenous opiate peptides*. Amsterdam: Elsevier North-Holland, 1976.

AKISKAL, H. S., & MCKINNEY, W. T., JR. Psychiatry and pseudopsychiatry. *Archives of General Psychiatry*, 1973, *28*, 367-373.

ALCOCK, J. *Animal behavior: An evolutionary approach*. Sunderland, Mass.: Sinauer, 1979.

ALEXANDER, B. K., PEELE, S., HADAWAY, P. F., MORSE, S. J., BRODSKY, A., & BEYERSTEIN, B. L. Adult, infant, and animal addiction. In S. Peele, *The meaning of addiction*. Lexington, Mass.: Lexington Books, 1985.

ALEXANDER, R., & EPSTEIN, S. Reactivity to heteromodal stimulation as a function of stimulus intensity and inner arousal. *Psychophysiology*, 1978, *15*, 387-393.

ALLEN, L. S., & GORSKI, R. A. Sexual dimorphism of the anterior commissure and massa intermedia of the human brain. *Journal of Comparative Neurology*, 1991, *312*, 97-104.

ALLEN, L. S., RICHEY, M. F., CHAI, Y. M., & GORSKI, R. A. Sex differences in the corpus callosum of the living human being. *Journal of Neuroscience*, 1991, *11*, 933-942.

ALLISON, T. S., & ALLISON, S. L. Time-out from reinforcement: Effect on sibling aggression. *Psychological Record*, 1971, *21*, 81-86.

ALLOY, L. B., & ABRAMSON, L. Y. Judgement of contingency in depressed and nondepressed students: Sadder but wiser. *Journal of Experimental Psychology: General*, 1979, 108, 441-485.

ALLOY, L. B., & ABRAMSON, L. Y. Learned helplessness, depression, and the illusion of control. *Journal of Personality and Social Psychology*, 1982, *42*, 1114-1126.

ALLPORT, G. W. *Personality: A psychological interpretation*. New York: Holt, 1937.

ALLRED, K. D., & SMITH, T. The hardy personality: Cognitive and physiological responses to evaluative threat. *Journal of Personality and Social Psychology*, 1989, *56*, 257-266.

AMERICAN PSYCHIATRIC ASSOCIATION. *Diagnostic and statistical manual of mental disorders* (3rd edition-Rev). Washington, D. C.: Author, 1987.

AMERICAN PSYCHIATRIC ASSOCIATION. *Diagnostic and statistical manual of mental disorders* (3rd ed.). Washington, D.C., 1980.

AMSEL, A. Behavioral habituation, counterconditioning, and a general theory of persistence. In A. H. Black & W. F. Prokasy (Eds.), *Classical conditioning II: Current research and theory. New York:* Appleton-Century-Crofts, 1972.

AMSEL, A. Frustrative nonreward in partial reinforcement and discrimination learning: Some recent history and a theoretical extension. *Psychological Review*, 1962, *69*, 306-328.

AMSEL, A. The role of frustrative nonreward in noncontinuous reward situations. *Psychological Bulletin*, 1958, *55*, 102-119.

ANDERSON, J. R. The role of hope in appraisal, goal-setting, expectancy, and coping. Unpublished doctoral dissertation. University of Kansas, Lawrence, 1988.

ANDERSON, K. J. Arousal and the Inverted-U hypothesis: A critique of Neiss's "Reconceptualizing Arousal." *Psychological Bulletin*, 1990, *107*, 96-100.

ANDREWS, F. M. Social and psychological factors that influence the creative process. In I. A. Taylor and J. W. Getzels (Eds.), *Perspective in creativity*. Chicago: Aldine, 1975, pp. 117-145.

ANDS, D. E. Further studies on endocrine treatment in adolescence and early-adult life. *Journal of Mental Science*, 1954, *100*, 211-219.

ANGELL, M. Disease as a reflection of the psyche. *New England Journal of Medicine*, 1985, *312*, 1570-1572.

APFELBAUM, M. Influence of level of energy intake on energy expenditure in man: Effects of spontaneous intake, experimental starvation, and experimental overeating. In G. A. Bray et al. (Eds.), *Obesity in perspective*, DHEW Publication no. NIH 75-708 (Vol. 2). Washington, D.C.: U.S. Government Printing Office, 1975.

APPLEY, M. H. Motivation, equilibrium, and stress. In R. A. Dienstbier (Ed.), *Perspectives on Motivation*. Nebraska Symposium on Motivation. Lincoln: University of Nebraska Press, 1991.

APTER, M. J. *The experience of motivation: Theory of psychological reversals*. New York: Academic Press, 1982.

ARKES, H. R., & BOYKIN, A. W. Analysis of complexity preference in Head Start and nursery school children. *Perceptual and Motor Skills*, 1971, *33*, 1131-1137.

ARKIN, A. M., ANTROBUS, J. S., ELLMAN, S. J., & FARBER, J. Sleep mentation as affected by REMP deprivation. In A. M. Arkin, J. S. Antrobus, & S. J. Ellman (Eds.), *The mind in sleep: Psychology and psychophysiology*. Hillsdale, N.J.: Erlbaum, 1978.

ARKKELIN, D., OAKLEY, T., & MYNATT, C. Effects of controllable versus uncontrollable factors on responsibility attributions: A single-subject approach. *Journal of Personality and Social Psychology*, 1979, *37*, 110-115.

ARMITAGE, A. K., HALL, G. H., & SELLERS, C. M. Effects of nicotine on electrocortical activity and acetylcholine release from the cat cerebral cortex. *British Journal of Pharmacology*, 1969, *35*, 152-160.

ARNOLD, M. B. *Emotion and personality* (2 vols.). New York: Columbia University Press, 1960.

ARNOLD, M. B. Perennial problems in the field of emotions. In M. B. Arnold (Ed.), *Feelings and emotions: The Loyola Symposium*. New York: Academic Press, 1970.

ARONFREED, J. *Conduct and conscience: The socialization of internalized control over behavior*. New York: Academic Press, 1968.

ASCHOFF, J. (ED.) *Circadian clocks*. Amsterdam: North-Holland, 1965.

ASERINSKY, E., & KLEITMAN, N. Regularly occurring periods of eye mobility and concomitant phenomena during sleep. *Science*, 1953, *118*, 273-274.

ASKEVOLD, F. Measuring body image. *Psychotherapy and Psychosomatics*, 1975, *26*, 71-77.

ATHANASIOU, R., SHAVER, P., & TAVRIS, C. Sex. *Psychology Today*, July 1970, pp. 37-52.

ATKINSON, J. W. The achievement motive and recall of interrupted and completed tasks. *Journal of Experimental Psychology*, 1953, *46*, 381-390.

ATKINSON, J. W. Motivational determinants of risk-taking behavior. *Psychological Review*, 1957, *64*, 359-372.

ATKINSON, J. W., & BIRCH, D. *An Introduction to Motivation* (Rev. Ed.). New York: Van Nostrand, 1978.

AUSTIN, W. Sex differences in bystander intervention in a theft. *Journal of Personality and Social Psychology*, 1979, *37*, 2110-2120.

AVERILL, J. R., & BOOTHROYD, P. On falling in love in conformance with the romantic ideal. *Motivation and Emotion*, 1977, *1*, 235-247.

AX, A. F. The physiological differentiation between fear and anger in humans. *Psychosomatic Medicine*, 1953, *15*, 433-442.

ÅNKERSTEDT, T., TORSVALL, L., & GILLBERG, M. Sleepiness and shift work: Field studies. *Sleep*, 1982, *5*, S95-S106.

BAEKELAND, F. Exercise deprivation: Sleep and psychological reactions. *Archives of General Psychiatry*, 1970, *22*, 365-369.

BAEKELAND, F., & LASKY, R. Exercise and sleep patterns in college athletes. *Perceptual and Motor Skills*, 1966, *23*, 1203-1207.

BAILEY, J.M., & PILLARD, R. C. A genetic study of male homosexual orientation. *Archives of General Psychiatry*, 1991, *48*, 1089-1097.

BAILEY, J. M., PILLARD, R. C., NEALE, M. C. I., & AGYEI, Y. Heritable factors influence sexual orientation in women. *Archives of General Psychiatry*, 1993, *50*, 217-223.

BAKER, J. W., II, & SCHAIE, K. W. Effects of aggressing ``alone'' or ``with another'' on physiological and psychological arousal. *Journal of Personality and Social Psychology*, 1969, *12*, 80-96.

BALES, R. F. Cultural differences in the rate of alcoholism. *Quarterly Journal of Studies on Alcohol*, 1946, *6*, 380-499.

BANAJI, M. R., & STEELE, C. M. The social cognition of alcohol use. *Social Cognition*, 1989, *7*, 137-151.

BANCROFT, J. A physiological approach. In J. H. Geer & W. T. O'Donohue (Eds.), *Theories of human sexuality* (pp. 411-421). New York: Plenum, 1987.

BANDURA, A. *Aggression: A social learning analysis*. Englewood Cliffs, N.J.: Prentice-Hall, 1973.

BANDURA, A. Human agency in social cognitive theory. *American Psychologist*, 1989, *44*, 1175-1184.

BANDURA, A. Self-efficacy conceptions of anxiety. *Anxiety Research*, 1988, *1*, 77-98.

BANDURA, A. Self-regulation of motivation through anticipatory and self reactive mechanisms. In R. A. Dienstbier (Ed.), *Perspectives on Motivation*. Nebraska Symposium on Motivation. Lincoln: University of Nebraska Press, 1991.

BANDURA, A. *Social Foundations of Thought and Action: A Social Cognitive Theory*. Englewood Cliffs, N.J.: Prentice-Hall, 1986.

BANDURA, A., CIOFFI, D., TAYLOR, C. B., & BROUILLARD, M. E. Perceived self-efficacy in coping with cognitive stressors and opiod addiction. *Journal of Personality and Social Psychology*, 1988, *55*, 479-488.

BANDURA, A., & JOURDEN, F. J. Self-regulatory mechanisms governing the impact of social comparison on complex decision making. *Journal of Personality and Social Psychology*, 1991, *60*, 941-951.

BANDURA, A., TAYLOR, C. B., WILLIAMS, S. L., MEFFORD, I. N., & BARCHAS, J. D. Catecholamine secretion as a function of perceived coping self-efficacy. *Journal of Consulting and Clinical Psychology*, 1985, *53*, 406,414.

BARASH, D. P. *Sociobiology and behavior*. New York: Elsevier North-Holland, 1977.

BARD, P. A diencephalic mechanism for the expression of rage with special reference to the sympathetic nervous system. *American Journal of Physiology*, 1928, *84*, 490-515.

BARE, J. K. The specific hunger for sodium chloride in normal and adrenalectomized white rats. *Journal of Comparative and Physiological Psychology*, 1949, *42*, 242-253.

BAREFOOT, J. C., DAHLSTROM, W. G., & WILLIAMS, R. B. Hostility, CHD incidence, and total mortality: A 25-year follow-up study of 255 physicians. *Psychosomatic Medicine*, 1983, *45*, 59-64.

BARKER, R. G. *The stream of behavior*. New York: Appleton-Century-Crofts, 1963.

BARNES, G. E., MALAMUTH, N. M., & CHECK, J. V. P. Personality and sexuality. *Personality and Individual Differences*, 1984, *5*, 159-172.

BARON, J. The effect of normative beliefs on anticipated emotions. *Journal of Personality and Social Psychology*, 1992, *63*, 320-330.

BARON, R. A. *Human aggression*. New York: Plenum, 1977.

BARON, R. A. Threatened retaliation from the victim as an inhibitor of physical aggression. *Journal of Research in Personality*, 1973, *7*, 103-115.

BARON, R. A., & BELL, P. A. Effects of heightened sexual arousal on physical aggression. *Proceedings of the American Psychological Association 81st Annual Convention*, 1973, 171-172.

BARON, R. A., & EGGLESTON, R. J. Performance on the ``aggression machine'': Motivation to help or harm? *Psychonomic Science*, 1972, *26*, 321-322.

BARR, T. *Psychopharmacology*. Baltimore: Williams & Wilkins, 1969.

BARRON, F., & HARRINGTON, D. M. Creativity, intelligence, and personality. In M. R. Rosenzweig & L. W. Porter (Eds.), *Annual review of psychology*. Palo Alto, California: Annual Reviews, 1981, pp. 439-476.

BARRY, H., III, WAGNER, A. R., & MILLER, N. E. Effects of alcohol and amobarbital on performance inhibited by experimental extinction. *Journal of Comparative and Physiological Psychology*, 1962, *55*, 464-468.

BARSALOU, L. W. Ad hoc categories. *Memory and Cognition*, 1993, *11*, 211-227.

BASH, K. W. Contributions to a theory of the hunger drive. *Journal of Comparative Psychology*, 1939, *28*, 137-160.

BASOW, S. A. *Stereotypes and Roles (3rd Edition)*. Pacific Grove, California: Brooks/Cole Publishing, 1992.

BATSON, C. D. How social an animal? The human capacity for caring. *American Psychologist*, 1990, *45*, 336-346.

BAUM, A., & SINGER, J. E. (EDS.). *Advances in environmental psychology* (Vol. 2): *Applications of personal control*. Hillsdale, N.J.: Erlbaum, 1980.

BAUMGARDNER, A. H. To know oneself is to like oneself: Self-certainty and self-affect. *Journal of Personality and Social Psychology*, 1990, *58*, 1062-1072.

BEACH, F. A. Hormonal control of sex-related behavior. In F. A. Beach (Ed.), *Human sexuality in four perspectives*. Baltimore: Johns Hopkins University Press, 1976.

BEARY, J. F., BENSON, H., & KLEMCHUK, H. P. A simple psychophysiologic technique which elicits the hypometabolic changes in the relaxation response. *Psychosomatic Medicine*, 1974, *36*, 115-120.

BECHTEL, W. , & ABRAHAMSEN, A. *Connectionism and the mind: An introduction to parallel processing in networks*. Cambridge, MA: Basil Blackwell, 1991.

BECK, A. T. *Cognitive theory and emotional disorders*. New York: International Universities Press, 1976.

BECK, A. T. Cognitive therapy: A 30-year retrospective. *American Psychologist*, 1991, *46*, 368-375.

BECK, A. T. Cognitive therapy of depression: New approaches. In P. Clayton & J. Barrett (Eds.), *Treatment of Depression: Old and New Approaches* (pp. 265-290). New York: Raven Press, 1983.

BECK, A. T. *Depression: Clinical, experimental, and theoretical aspects*. New York: Harper & Row, 1967.

BECK, A. T., WEISSMAN, A., & KOVACS, M. Alcoholism, hopelessness, and suicidal behavior. *Journal of Studies on Alcohol*, 1976, *37*, 66-77.

BECK, A. T., & YOUNG, J. E. College blues. *Psychology Today*, 1978, *12* (4), 80-92.

BECKER, M. (ED.). *The health belief model and personal health behavior*. Thorofare, N.J.: Charles B. Slack, 1974.

BELL, A., & WEINBERG, M. S. *Homosexualities: A Study of Human Diversity*. New York: Simon and Schuster, 1978.

BELL, A., WEINBERG, M. S., & HAMMERSMITH, S. K. *Sexual preference: Its development in men and women*. Bloomington: Indiana University Press, 1981.

BELL, P. A., & BYRNE, D. Repression-sensitization. In H. London & J. E. Exner, Jr. (Eds.), *Dimensions of personality*. New York: Wiley, 1978.

BELL, R. Q. Stimulus control of parent or caretaker behavior by offspring. *Developmental Psychology*, 1971, *4*, 63-72.

BELL, R. Q., & HARPER, L. V. *Child effects on adults*. Hillsdale, N.J.: Erlbaum, 1977.

BELLAH, R. N., MADSEN, R., SULLIVAN, W. M., SWIDLER, A., & TIPTON, S. M. *Habits of the Heart*. New York: Harper and Row, 1985.

BELLER, A. S. *Fat and thin: A natural history of obesity*. New York: McGraw-Hill, 1978.

BEMIS, K. M. Current approaches to the etiology and treatment of anorexia nervosa. *Psychological Bulletin*, 1978, *85*, 593-617.

BEN-TOVIM, D., WHITEHEAD, J., & CRISP, A. H. A controlled study of the perception of body width in anorexia nervosa. *Journal of Psychosomatic Research*, 1979, *23*, 267-272.

BENASSI, V. A., & MAHLER, H. I. M. Contingency judgments by depressed college students: Sadder but not always wiser. *Journal of Personality and Social Psychology*, 1985, *49*, 1323-1329.

BENBOW, C. P., & STANLEY, J. C. Sex differences in mathematical ability; Fact or artifact? *Science*, 1980, *210*, 1029-1031.

BENBOW, C. P., & STANLEY J. C. Sex differences in mathematical reasoning ability: More facts. *Science*, 1983, *222*, 1029-1031.

BENSON, H. *Your Maximum Mind*. New York: Avon Books, 1987.

BENSON, H. *The Relaxation Response*. New York: Avon Books, 1975.

BENSON, H., & WALLACE, R. K. Decreased blood pressure in hypertensive subjects who practiced meditation. *Circulation*, 1972, Suppl. 2, 516.

BERGMAN, J., KAMIEN, J. B., AND SPEALMAN, R. D. Antagonism of cocaine self-administration by selective dopamine D1 and D2 antagonists. *Behavioural Pharmacology*, 1990, *1*, 355-363.

BERKMAN, J. M. Anorexia nervosa, anterior pituitary insufficiency, Simmonds' cachexia, and Sheehan's disease. *Postgraduate Medicine*, 1948, *3*, 237-246.

BERKOWITZ, L. *Aggression: A social psychological analysis*. New York: McGraw-Hill, 1962.

BERKOWITZ, L. Aggressive cues in aggressive behavior and hostility catharsis. *Psychological Review*, 1964, *71*, 104-122.

BERKOWITZ, L. Frustration-aggression hypothesis: Examination and reformulation. *Psychological Bulletin*, 1989, *106*, 59-73.

BERKOWITZ, L. The frustration-aggression hypothesis revised. In L. Berkowitz (Ed.), *Roots of aggression*. New York: Atherton Press, 1969.

BERKOWITZ, L. On the formation and regulation of anger and aggression: a cognitive-neoassociationistic analysis. *American Psychologist*, 1990, *45*, 494-503.

BERKOWITZ, L. Some determinants of impulsive aggression: Role of mediated associations with reinforcements for aggression. *Psychological Review*, 1974, *81*, 165-176.

BERKOWITZ, L., & DANIELS, L. R. Affecting the salience of the social responsibility norm: Effects of past help on the response of dependency relationships. *Journal of Abnormal and Social Psychology*, 1964, *68*, 275-281.

BERKOWITZ, L., & GEEN, R. G. Film violence and the cue properties of available targets. *Journal of Personality and Social Psychology*, 1966, *3*, 525-530.

BERLYNE, D. E. *Aesthetics and psychobiology*. New York: Appleton-Century-Crofts, 1971.

BERLYNE, D. E. *Conflict, arousal, and curiosity*. New York: McGraw-Hill, 1960.

BERLYNE, D. E. The influence of complexity and novelty in visual figures on orienting responses. *Journal of Experimental Psychology*, 1958, *55*, 289-296.

BERLYNE, D. E. Novelty, complexity and hedonic value. *Perception and Psychophysics*, 1970, *8*, 279-286.

BERLYNE, D. E. The reward value of indifferent stimulation. In J. T. Tapp (Ed.), *Reinforcement and behavior*. New York: Academic Press, 1969.

BERLYNE, D. E., KOENIG, I. D. V., & HIROTA, T. Novelty, arousal, and the reinforcement of diversive exploration in the rat. *Journal of Comparative and Physiological Psychology*, 1966, *62*, 222-226.

BERMANT, G., & DAVIDSON, J. M. *Biological bases of sexual behavior*. New York: Harper & Row, 1974.

BERNSTEIN, A. S. Electrodermal lability and the OR: Reply to O'Gorman and further exposition of the significance hypothesis. *Australian Journal of Psychology*, 1973, *25*, 147-154.

BERNSTEIN, A. S. The orienting response as novelty and significance detector: Reply to O'Gorman. *Psychophysiology*, 1979, *16*, 263.

BERNSTEIN, A. S., TAYLOR, K. W., & WEINSTEIN, E. The phasic electrodermal response as a differentiated complex reflecting stimulus significance. *Psychophysiology*, 1975, *12*, 158-169.

BERREBI, A. S., FITCH, R. H., RALPHE, D. L., DENENBERG, J. O., FRIEDRICH JR., V. L., & DENENBERG, V. H. Corpus-callosum: Region-specific effects of sex, early experience and age. *Brain Research*, 1988, *438*, 216-224.

BEXTON, W. H., HERON, W., & SCOTT, T. H. Effects of decreased variation in the sensory environment. *Canadian Journal of Psychology*, 1954, *8*, 70-76.

BHANJI, S., & THOMPSON, J. Operant conditioning in the treatment of anorexia nervosa: A review and retrospective study of 11 cases. *British Journal of Psychiatry*, 1974, *124*, 166-172.

BIEBER, I., DAIN, H. J., DINCE, P. R., DRELLICH, M. G., GRAND, H. G., GUNLACH, R. H., KREMERS, M. V., WILBUR, C. B., & BIEBER, T. B. *Homosexuality: A Psychoanalytic Study*. New York: Vintage, 1962.

BINDRA, D. A. Motivational view of learning, performance, and behavior modification. *Psychological Review*, 1974, *81*, 199-213.

BIRNEY, R. C., BURDICK, H., & TEEVAN, R. C. *Fear of failure*. New York: Van Nostrand, 1969.

BIXLER, E. O., KALES, A., SOLDATOS, C. R., VELA-BUENO, A., JACOBY, J. A., & SCARONE, S. Sleep apnea in a normal population. *Research Communications in Chemical Pathology and Pharmacology*, 1982, *36*, 141-152.

BLANCHARD, R. J., BLANCHARD, D. C., & FIAL, R. A. Hippocampal lesions in rats and their effects on activity, avoidance, and aggression. *Journal of Comparative and Physiological Psychology*, 1970, *71*, 92-102.

BLAÜMCHEN (Eds.). *Biochemical bases of coronary heart disease* (pp. 99-105). New York: Carger, 1983.

BLISS, E. L., & BRANCH, C. H. H. *Anorexia nervosa: Its history, psychology, and biology*. New York: Paul Hoeber, 1960.

BLOOM, G., VON EULER, U. S., & FRANKENHAEUSER, M. Catecholamine excretion and personality traits in paratroop trainees. *Acta Physiologica Scandinavica*, 1963, *58*, 77-89.

BLOOMFIELD, H. H., CAIN, M. P., JAFFE, D. T., & KORY, R. B. *TM: Discovering inner energy and overcoming stress.* New York: Dell, 1975.

BLUM, K., HAMILTON, M. L., & WALLACE, J. E. Alcohol and opiates: A review of common neurochemical and behavioral mechanisms. In K. Blum (Ed.), *Alcohol and opiates: Neurochemical and behavioral mechanisms.* New York: Academic Press, 1977.

BOLGER, N. Coping as a personality process: A prospective study. *Journal of Personality and Social Psychology,* 1990, *59,* 525-537.

BOLGER, N., & ECKENROLE, J. Social relationships. personality, and anxiety during a major stressful event. *Journal of Personality and Social Psychology,* 1991, *61,* 440-449.

BOLLES, R. C. Species-specific defense reactions and avoidance learning. *Psychological Review,* 1970, *77,* 32-48.

BOLLES, R. C., & FANSELOW, M. S. Endorphins and behavior. *Annual Review of Psychology,* 1982, *33,* 87-101.

BONANNO, G. A., & SINGER, J. L. Repressive personality style: Theoretical and methodological implications for health and pathology. In J. L. Singer (Ed.), *Repression and dissociation* (pp. 435-470). Chicago: University of Chicago Press, 1990.

BONNET, M. H. Effect of sleep disruption on sleep, performance, and mood. *Sleep,* 1985, *8,* 11-19.

BONNET, M. H., & ROSA, R. R. Sleep and performance in young adults and older normals and insomniacs during sleep loss and recovery. *Biological Psychology,* 1987, *25,* 153-172.

BONVALLET, M., & ALLEN, M. B., JR. Prolonged spontaneous and evoked reticular activation following discrete bulbar lesions. *Electroencephalography and Clinical Neurophysiology,* 1963, *15,* 969-988.

BORDEN, R. J., BOWEN, R., & TAYLOR, S. P. Shock-setting behavior as a function of physical attack and extrinsic reward. *Perceptual and Motor Skills,* 1971, *33,* 563-568.

BORING, E. G. *A history of experimental psychology* (2nd ed.). New York: Appleton-Century-Crofts, 1950.

BOWLBY, J. *Attachment and Loss: Vol. 1. Attachment.* New York: Basic Books, 1969.

BOWLBY, J. *Attachment and Loss: Vol. 2. Separation: Anxiety and Anger.* New York: Basic Books, 1973.

BOWLBY, J. *Attachment and Loss: Vol. 3. Loss: Sadness and Depression.* New York: Basic Books, 1980.

BOZARTH, M. A., & WISE, R. A. Toxicity associated with long-term intravenous heroin and cocaine self-administration in the rat. *Journal of the American Medical Association,* 1985, *253,* 81-83.

BRADLEY, G. W. Self-serving biases in the attribution process: A reexamination of the fact or fiction question. *Journal of Personality and Social Psychology,* 1978, *36,* 56-71.

BRADY, J. V. Emotion and sensitivity of psychoendocrine systems. In D. C. Glass (Ed.), *Neurophysiology and emotion.* New York: Rockefeller University Press, 1967.

BRADY, J. V. Towards a behavioral biology of emotion. In L. Levi (Ed.), *Emotions: Their parameters and measurement.* New York: Raven Press, 1975.

BRAIN, P. F. *Hormones and aggression,* Vol. 1. Montreal: Eden Press, 1977.

BRAIN, P. F., & NOWELL, N. W. Isolation versus grouping effects on adrenal and gonadal functions in albino mice: I. The male. *General and Comparative Endocrinology,* 1971, *16,* 149-154.

BRAUCHT, G. N., BRAKARSH, D., FOLLINGSTAD, D., & BERRY, K. L. Deviant drug use in adolescence: A review of psychological correlates. *Psychological Bulletin,* 1975, *79,* 92-106.

BREHM, J. W. Postdecision changes in the desirability of alternatives. *Journal of Abnormal and Social Psychology,* 1956, *52,* 384-389.

BREMER, J. *Asexualization: A follow-up study of 244 cases.* New York: Macmillan, 1959.

BRICKMAN, P., LINSENMEIER, J. A. W., & MCCAREINS, A. G. Performance enhancement by relevant success and irrelevant failure. *Journal of Personality and Social Psychology,* 1976, *33,* 149-160.

BRINKERHOFF, M. B., & LUPRI, M. B. Interspousal violence. *Canadian Journal of Sociology,* 1988, *13,* 407-435.

BROBECK, J. R. Food and temperature. *Recent Progress in Hormone Research,* 1960, *16,* 439-466.

BROCKNER, J. The effects of self-esteem, success-failure, and self consciousness on task performance. *Journal of Personality and Social Psychology,* 1979, *37,* 1732-1741.

BROOKS-GUNN, J., & FURSTENBERG, F. F., JR. Adolescent sexual behavior. *American Psychologist,* 1989, *44,* 249-257.

BROTHERS, L. A biological perspective on empathy. *American Journal of Psychiatry,* 1989, *146,* 10-19.

BROWN, G. M. Endocrine alterations in anorexia nervosa. In P. L. Darby, P. E. Garfinkel, D. M. Garner, & D. V. Coscina, *Anorexia nervosa: Recent developments in research* (pp. 231-247). New York: Alan R. Liss, Inc., 1983.

BROWN, J. D. Staying fit and staying well: Physical fitness as a moderator of life stress. *Journal of Personality and Social Psychology,* 1991, *60,* 555-561.

BROWNELL, K.D., GREENWOOD, M.R.C., STELLAR, E., & STRAGER, E.E. The effects of repeated cycles of weight loss and regain in rats. *Physiology and Behavior,* 1986, *38,* 459-464.

BROWNMILLER, S. *Femininity.* New York: Linden Press/Simon & Schuster, 1984.

BRUCH, H. *Eating disorders: Obesity, anorexia nervosa, and the person within.* New York: Basic Books, 1973.

BRUNER, J. Another look at New Look 1. *American Psychologist,* 1992, *47,* 780-783.

BRUNER, J. S., MATTER, J., & PAPANEK, M. L. Breadth of learning as a function of drive level and mechanization. *Psychological Review,* 1955, *62,* 1-10.

BRYSON, J. B., & DRIVER, M. J. Cognitive complexity, introversion, and preference for complexity. *Journal of Personality and Social Psychology,* 1972, *23,* 320-327.

BUCHSBAUM, M. S., GERNER, R., & POST, R. M. The effects of sleep deprivation on average evoked potentials in depressed patients and normals. *Biological Psychiatry,* 1981, *16,* 351-363.

BUCK, R. *Human motivation and emotion.* New York: Wiley, 1976.

BURNAND, G., HUNTER, H., & HOGGART, K. Some psychological test characteristics of Klinefelter's syndrome. *British Journal of Psychiatry,* 1967, *113,* 1019-1096.

BURNSTEIN, E., & WORCHEL, P. Arbitrariness of frustration and its consequences for aggression in a social situation. *Journal of Personality,* 1962, *30,* 528-540.

BUSS, A. H. Physical aggression in relation to different frustrations. *Journal of Abnormal and Social Psychology,* 1963, *67,* 1-7.

BUSS, A. H., & PERRY, M. The aggression questionnaire. *Journal of Personality and Social Psychology,* 1992, *63,* 452-459.

BUTLER, R. A. Discrimination learning by rhesus monkeys to visual-exploration motivation. *Journal of Comparative and Physiological Psychology,* 1953, *46,* 95-98.

BYRNE, D. Social psychology and the study of sexual behavior. *Personality and Social Psychology Bulletin,* 1977, *3,* 3-30.

CACIOPPO, J. T., UCHINO, B. N., CRITES, S. L., SNYDERSMITH, M. A., SMITH, G., BERNTSON, G. G., & LANG, P. J. Relationship between facial expressiveness and sympathetic activation in emotion: A critical review, with emphasis on modeling underlying the mechanism and individual differences. *Journal of Personality and Social Psychology,* 1992, *62,* 110-128.

CAHALAN, D., & ROOM, R. *Problem drinking among American men.* Monograph 7. New Brunswick, N.J.: Rutgers Center of Alcohol Studies, 1974.

CAMPBELL, J. B., & HAWLEY, C. W. Study habits and Eysenck's theory of extraversion-introversion. *Journal of Research in Personality,* 1982, *16,* 139-146.

CAMPBELL, J. D. Self-esteem and clarity of the self-concept. *Journal of Personality and Social Psychology,* 1990, *59,* 538-549.

CAMPION, M. A., & LORD, R. G. A control systems conceptualization of the goal-setting and changing process. *Organization Behavior and Performance,* 1982, *30,* 265-287.

CANNON, W. B. The James-Lange theory of emotions: A critical examination and an alternative theory. *American Journal of Psychology,* 1927, *39,* 106-124.

CARLSON, E. R., & COLEMAN, C. E. H. Experiential and motivational determinants of the richness of an induced sexual fantasy. *Journal of Personality*, 1977, *45*, 528-542.

CARLSON, M., CHARLIN, V., & MILLER, N. Positive mood and helping behavior: a test of six hypotheses. *Journal of Personality and Social Psychology*, 1988, *55*, 211-229.

CARROLL, J. L. The relationship between humor appreciation and perceived physical health. *Psychology*, 1992, *27*, 34-37.

CARROLL, J. L, & SHMIDT, J. L. JR. Correlation between humorous coping style and health. *Psychological Reports*, 1990, *70*, 402.

CARSKADON, M. A., & DEMENT, W. C. Cumulative effects of sleep restriction on daytime sleepiness. *Psychophysiology*, 1981, *18*, 107-113.

CARSKADON, M. A., & DEMENT, W. C. Sleepiness and sleep state on a 90-min schedule. *Psychophysiology*, 1977, *14*, 127-133.

CARTWRIGHT, R. D., LLOYD, S., BUTTERS, E., WEINER, L., MC-CARTHY, L., & HANCOCK, J. Effects of REM time on what is recalled. *Psychophysiology*, 1975, *12*, 561-568.

CARTWRIGHT, R. D., MONROE, L. J., & PALMER, C. Individual differences in response to REM deprivation. *Archives of General Psychiatry*, 1967, *16*, 297-303.

CARTWRIGHT, R. D., & RATZEL, R. Effects of dream loss on waking behaviors. *Archives of General Psychiatry*, 1972, *27*, 277-280.

CARVER, C. S. A cybernetic model of self-attention processes. *Journal of Personality and Social Psychology*, 1979, *37*, 1251-1281.

CARVER, C. S., BLANEY, P. H., & SCHEIER, M. F. Focus of attention, chronic expectancy, and responses to a feared stimulus. *Journal of Personality and Social Psychology*, 1979, *37*, 1186-1195. (a)

CARVER, C. S., BLANEY, P. H., & SCHEIER, M. F. Reassertion and giving up: The interactive role of self-directed attention and outcome expectancy. *Journal of Personality and Social Psychology*, 1979, *37*, 1859-1870. (b)

CARVER, C. S., & SCHEIER, M. F. *Attention and self-regulation: A control-theory approach to human behavior.* Chicago: Springer-Verlag, 1981.

CASS, V. C. The implication of homosexual identity formation for the Kinsey model and scale of sexual preference. In McWhiter, D. P., Sanders, S. A., and Reinisch, J. M. (Eds.), *Homosexuality/Heterosexuality: Concepts of Sexual Orientation* (pp. 239-266). New York: Oxford University Press, 1990.

CASTALDO, V., & KRYNICKI, V. Sleep patterns and intelligence in functional mental retardation. *Journal of Mental Deficiency Research*, 1973, *17*, 231-235.

CASTALDO, V., KRYNICKI, V., & GOLDSTEIN, J. Sleep stages and verbal memory. *Perceptual and Motor Skills*, 1974, *39*, 1023-1030.

CATTELL, R. B. *Abilities: Their structure, growth and action.* Boston, MA; Houghton Mifflin, 1971.

CAUL, W. F., BUCHANAN, D. C., & HAYS, R. C. Effects of unpredictability of shock on incidence of gastric lesions and heart rate in immobilized rats. *Physiology and Behavior*, 1972, *8*, 669-672.

CAUTHEN, N. R., & PRYMAK, C. A. Meditation versus relaxation: An examination of the physiological effects of relaxation training and of different levels of experience with transcendental meditation. *Journal of Consulting and Clinical Psychology*, 1977, *45*, 496-497.

CHAIKEN, S., & PLINER, P. *Women, but not men, are what they eat: The effect of meal size and gender on perceived femininity and masculinity.* Unpublished manuscript, Vanderbilt University, 1984.

CHAMBLESS, D. L., & GRACELY, E. J. Fear of fear and the anxiety disorders. *Cognitive Therapy and Research*, 1989, *13*, 9-20.

CHASSLER, S. What teen boys think about sex. *Parade Magazine*, pp. 16-17, December, 1988.

CHOMSKY, N. *Language and mind* (Enl. ed.). New York: Harcourt Brace Jovanovich, 1972.

CHURCHILL, A. C., & MCMURRAY, N. E. (1990). *Self-efficacy and unpleasant intrusive thought.* Manuscript submitted for publication.

CIALDINI, R. B. & KENRICK, D. T. Altruism as hedonism: A social development perspective on the relationship of negative mood to state and helping. *Journal of Personality and Social Psychology*, 1976, *34*, 907-914.

CIBA FOUNDATION SYMPOSIUM. *Sex hormones and behavior.* Amsterdam: Excerpta Medica, 1979.

CLARK, K. B. Empathy: A neglected topic in psychological research. *American Psychologist*, 1980, *35*, 187-190.

CLARKE, D. H. *Exercise physiology.* Englewood Cliffs, N.J.: Prentice-Hall, 1975.

COBB, S., & ROSE, R. M. Hypertension, peptic ulcer, and diabetes in air traffic controllers. *Journal of the American Medical Association*, 1973, *224*, 489-492.

COHEN, D. B. Dysphoric affect and REM sleep. *Journal of Abnormal Psychology*, 1979, *88*, 73-77.

COHEN, D. B. Neuroticism and dreaming sleep: A case for interactionism in personality research. *British Journal of Social and Clinical Psychology*, 1977, *16*, 153-163.

COHEN, S., LICHTENSTEIN, E., PROCHASKA, J. O., ROSSI, J. S., GRITZ, E. R., CARR, C. R., ORLEANS, C. T., SCHOENBACH, V. J., BIENER, L., ABRAMS, D., DICLEMENTE, C., CURRY, S., MARLATT, G. A., CUMMINGS, K. M., EMONT, S. L., GIOVINO, G., & OSSIP-KLEIN, D. Debunking myths about self-quitting: Evidence from 10 prospective studies of persons who attempt to quit smoking by themselves. *American Psychologist*, 1989, *44*, 1355-1365.

COHEN, S., & MCKAY, G. Social support, stress and the buffering hypothesis: A theoretical analysis. In A. Baum, J. E. Singer, & S. E. Taylor (Eds.), *Handbook of Psychology and Health* (Vol. 4, pp. 253-267). Hillsdale, N.J.: Erlbaum, 1984.

COHEN, S., & WILLIAMSON, G. M. Stress and infectious disease in humans. *Psychological Bulletin*, 1991, *109*, 5-24.

COLEMAN, M. Serotonin levels in whole blood of hyperactive children. *Journal of Pediatrics*, 1971, *78*, 985-990.

COLEMAN, R. M. *Wide Awake at 3:00 A. M.: By Choice or By Chance.* New York; W. H. Freeman, 1986.

COLLINS, D. L., BAUM, A., & SINGER, J. E. Coping with chronic stress at Three Mile Island: Psychological and biochemical evidence. *Health Psychology*, 1983, *2*, 149-166.

CONDRY, J. C. Enemies of exploration: Self-initiated versus other-initiated learning. *Journal of Personality and Social Psychology*, 1977, *35*, 459-477.

CONDRY, J. C., & CHAMBERS, J. Intrinsic motivation and the process of learning. In M. R. Lepper & D. Greene (Eds.), *The hidden costs of rewards: New perspectives on the psychology of human motivation.* Hillsdale, N.J.: Erlbaum, 1978.

CONGER, J. J. Reinforcement theory and the dynamics of alcoholism. *Quarterly Journal of Studies on Alcohol*, 1956, *17*, 296-305.

CONNERS, M.E., & JOHNSON, C.L. Epidemiology of bulimia and bulimic behaviors. *Addictive Behaviors*, 1987, *12*, 165-179.

COOPER, J. R., BLOOM, F. E., & ROTH, B. H. *The biochemical basis of neuropharmacology* (4th ed.). New York: Oxford University Press, 1982.

COOPERSMITH, S. *The antecedents of self-esteem.* San Francisco: W. H. Freeman, 1967.

COSCINA, D. V., & DIXON, L. M. Body weight regulation in anorexia nervosa: Insight from an animal model. In P. L. Darby, P. E. Garfinkel, D. M. Garner, & D. V. Coscina (Eds.), *Anorexia nervosa: Recent developments* (pp. 207-220). New York: Alan R. Liss, Inc., 1983.

COSTELLO, C. G. A critical review of Seligman's laboratory experiments on learned helplessness and depression in humans. *Journal of Abnormal Psychology*, 1978, *87*, 21-31.

COSTELLO, C. G. *Anxiety and depression: The adaptive emotions.* Montreal: McGill-Queens University Press, 1976.

COX, W. M., & KLINGER, E. A motivational model of alcohol use. *Journal of Abnormal Psychology*, 1988, *97*, 168-180.

COYNE, J. C., & LAZARUS, R. S. Cognitive style, stress perception, and coping. In I. L. Kutash & L. B. Schlesinger (Eds.), *Handbook on stress and anxiety: Contemporary knowledge, theory, and treatment* (pp. 144-158). San Francisco: Jossey-Bass, 1980.

CRANDALL, C.S. Social contagion of binge eating. *Journal of Personality and Social Psychology*, 1988, *55*, 588-598.

CRATTY, B. J. *Psychology in Contemporary Sport.* Englewood Cliffs, N.J.: Prentice Hall, 1989.

CRICK, F., & KOCH, C. The problem of consciousness. *Scientific American*, September, 1992, 153-159.

CRICK, C., & MITCHISON, G. The function of dream sleep. *Nature*, 1983, *304*, 111-114.

CRICK, C., & MITCHISON, G. REM sleep and neural nets. *The Journal of Mind and Behavior*, 1986, *7*, 229-250.

1992CRISP, A. H., & KALUCY, R. S. Aspects of the perceptual disorder in anorexia nervosa. *British Journal of Medical Psychology*, 1974, *47*, 349-361.

CROWLEY, W. R., O'DONOHUE, T. L., & JACOBOWITZ, D. M. Changes in catecholamine content in discrete brain nuclei during the estrous cycle of the rat. *Brain Research*, 1978, *147*, 315-326.

CROWTHER, J. H., LINGSWILER, V. M., & STEPHENS, M. A. P. The topology of binge eating. *Addictive Behaviors*, 1984, *9*, 299-303.

CROYLE, R. T., & COOPER, J. Dissonance arousal: Physiological evidence. *Journal of Personality and Social Psychology*, 1983, *45*, 782-791.

CSIKSZENTMIHALYI, M. *Flow: The Psychology of Optimal Experience*. New York: Harper and Row, 1990.

CUTHBERT, B., KRISTELLER, J., SIMONS, R., HODES, R., & LANG, P. J. Strategies of arousal control: Biofeedback, meditation, and motivation. *Journal of Experimental Psychology: General*, 1981, *110*, 518-546.

CZAYA, J., KRAMER, M., & ROTH, T. *Changes in dream quality as a function of time into REM*. Paper presented at the meeting of the Association for the Psychophysiological Study of Sleep, San Diego, 1973.

D'EMILIO, J., & FREEDMAN, E. B. *Intimate Matters: A History of Sexuality in America*. New York: Harper & Row, 1988.

DABBS, J. M., JR, FRADY, R. L., CARR, T. S., & BESCH, N. F. Saliva testosterone and criminal violence in young adult prison inmates. *Psychosomatic Medicine*, 1987, *49*, 174-182.

DALLY, P. J. Anorexia nervosa. New York: Grune & Stratton, 1969.

DALTON, K. Menstruation and crime. *British Medical Journal*, 1961, *3*, 1752-1753.

DALTON, K. *The pre-menstrual syndrome*. Springfield, Ill.: Charles C Thomas, 1964.

DALTON, K. *The premenstrual syndrome and progesterone therapy*. London: Heinman, 1977.

DALTON, K. Schoolgirls' misbehaviour and menstruation. *British Medical Journal*, 1960, *2*, 1647-1649.

DALY, E. M., LANCEE, W. J., & POLIVY, J. A canonical model for the taxonomy of emotional experience. *Journal of Personality and Social Psychology*, 1983, *45*, 443-457.

DANK, B. Coming out in the gay world. *Psychiatry*, 1971, *34*, 180-197.

DANOWSKI, T. S., LIVSTONE, E., GONZALES, A. R., JUNG, Y., & KHURANA, R. C. Fractional and partial hypopituitarism in anorexia nervosa. *Hormones*, 1972, *3*, 105-118.

DARWIN, C. *The expression of emotions in man and animals*. London: Murray, 1872.

DARWIN, C. *The expression of emotions in man and animals*. Chicago: University of Chicago Press, 1965. (Originally published, Philadelphia: R. West, 1873.)

DARWIN, C. *The origin of species*. New York: Modern Library, 1936. (Originally published, 1859.)

DAVIDS, A. An objective instrument for assessing hyperkinesis in children. *Journal of Learning Disabilities*, 1971, *4*, 35-37.

DAVIS, B. *Norepinephrine and epinephrine secretions following rest and exercise in trained and untrained males*. Unpublished doctoral dissertation, University of Illinois at Urbana-Champaign, 1973.

DAVIS, C. M. Self selection of diet by newly weaned infants. *American Journal of Diseases of Children*, 1928, *36*, 651-679.

DAVIS, D. H., GOODWIN, D. W., & ROBINS, L. N. Drinking amid abundant illicit drugs. *Archives of General Psychiatry*, 1975, *32*, 230-233.

DAVIS, V. E., & WALSH, M. J. Alcohol, amines, and alkaloids: A possible biochemical basis for alcohol addiction. *Science*, 1970, *167*, 1005-1007.

DE RIVERA, T. *A Structural Theory of Emotions*. New York: International University Press, 1982.

DE TOCQUEVILLE, A. *Democracy in America*, trans. G. Lawrence, J.P. Mayer (Ed.) N.Y.: Doubleday, Anchor Books, 1969.

DE WIED, D. Inhibitory effects of ACTH and related peptides on extinction of conditioned avoidance behavior in rats. *Proceedings of the Society for Experimental Biology and Medicine*, 1966, *122*, 28-32.

DE WIED, D. Opposite effects of ACTH and glucocorticoids on extinction of conditioned emotional behavior. In L. Martini, F. Fraschini, & M. Motta (Eds.), *Proceedings of the Second International Congress on Hormonal Steroids*. Amsterdam and New York: Excerpta Medica, 1967.

DE WIED, D. Pituitary-adrenal system hormones and behavior. In H. Selye (Ed.), *Selye's guide to stress research* (Vol. 1). New York: Van Nostrand Reinhold, 1980.

DEBONO, E. *Lateral Thinking*. London: Penguin Books, 1970.

DEBONO, E. *Six Thinking Hats*. New York: Penguin Books, 1987.

DECI, E. L. Effects of externally mediated rewards on intrinsic motivation. *Journal of Personality and Social Psychology*, 1972, *22*, 113-120.

DECI, E. L. *Intrinsic motivation*. New York: Plenum, 1975.

DECI, E. L., & RYAN, R. M. *Intrinsic Motivation and Self-Determination in Human Behavior*. New York: Plenum, 1985.

DECI, E. L., & RYAN, R. M. A motivational approach to self: Integration in Personality. In R. A. Dienstbier (Ed.) *Perspectives on Motivation*. Nebraska Symposium on Motivation. Lincoln: University of Nebraska Press, 1991.

DELGADO, J. M. R. Aggressive behavior evoked by radio stimulation in monkey colonies. *American Zoologist*, 1966, *6*, 669-681.

DELGADO, J. M. R. Cerebral heterostimulation in a monkey colony. *Science*, 1963, *141*, 161-163.

DELGADO, J. M. R. Inhibitory systems and emotions. In L. Levi (Ed.), *Emotions: Their parameters and measurement*. New York: Raven Press, 1975.

DELGADO, J. M. R. Social rank and radio-stimulated aggressiveness in monkeys. *Journal of Nervous and Mental Disease*, 1967, *144*, 383-390.

DEMBER, W. N. Response by the rat to environmental change. *Journal of Comparative and Physiological Psychology*, 1956, *49*, 93-95.

DEMBER, W. N., & EARL, R. W. Analysis of exploratory, manipulatory, and curiosity behaviors. *Psychological Review*, 1957, *64*, 91-96.

DEMBROSKI, T. M., & COSTA, P. T. Coronary prone behavior: Components of the Type A pattern and hostility. *Journal of Personality*, 1987, *55*, 212-235.

DEMBROSKI, T. M., MACDOUGALL, J. M., COSTA, P. T., JR., & GRANDITS, G. A. Components of hostility as predictors of sudden death and myocardial infarction in the multiple risk factor intervention trial. *Psychosomatic Medicine*, 1989, *51*, 514-522.

DEMBROSKI, T. M., MACDOUGALL, J. M., WILLIAMS, R. B., HANEY, T. L., & BLUMENTHAL, J. A. Components of Type A, hostility, and anger-in: Relationship to angiographic findings. *Psychosomatic Medicine*, 1985, *47*, 219-233.

DEMENT, W. C. The biological role of REM sleep (circa 1968). In A. Kales (Ed.), *Sleep: Physiology and pathology*. Philadelphia: Lippincott, 1969.

DEMENT, W. C. The effect of dream deprivation. *Science*, 1960, *131*, 1705-1707.

DEMENT, W. C. *Some must watch while some must sleep*. San Francisco: W. H. Freeman, 1972.

DEMENT, W. C., & CARSKADON, M. A. Current perspectives on daytime sleepiness. *Sleep*, 1982, *5*, S56-S66.

DEMENT, W. C., & VILLABLANCA, J. Clinical disorders in man and animal model experiments. In O. Petre-Ouadens & J. Schlag (Eds.), *Basic sleep mechanisms*. New York: Academic Press, 1974.

DENENBERG, V. H. Stimulation in infancy, emotional reactivity, and exploratory behavior. In D. C. Glass (Ed.), *Neurophysiology and emotion*. New York: Rockefeller University Press and Russell Sage Foundation, 1967.

DENGERINK, H. A. Anxiety, aggression, and physiological arousal. *Journal of Experimental Research in Personality*, 1971, *5*, 223-232.

DENGERINK, H. A., & BERTILSON, H. S. The reduction of attack instigated aggression. *Journal of Research in Personality*, 1974, *8*, 254-262.

DENGERINK, H. A., & LEVENDUSKY, P. G. Effects of massive retaliation and balance of power on aggression. *Journal of Experimental Research in Personality*, 1972, *6*, 230-236.

DENGERINK, H. A., O'LEARY, M. R., & KASNER, K. H. Individual differences in aggressive responses to attack: Internal-external locus of control and field dependence-independence. *Journal of Research in Personality*, 1975, *9*, 191-199.

DERRYBERRY, D., & TUCKER, D. M. The Adaptive Base of the Neural Hierarchy: Elementary motivational controls on network function. In R. A. Dienstbier (Ed.), *Perspectives on Motivation*. Nebraska Symposium on Motivation. Lincoln: University of Nebraska Press, 1991.

DEY, F. Auditory fatigue and predicted permanent hearing defects from rock-and-roll music. *New England Journal of Medicine*, 1970, *282*, 467-469.

DIAMOND, M. C. The interaction between sex hormones and environment. In M. C. Diamond (Ed.), *Enriching Heredity*. New York: Free Press, 1988, pp. 115-177.

DIAMOND, M. Sexual identity, monozygotic twins reared in discordant sex roles. A BBC follow-up. *Archives of Sexual Behavior*, 1982, *11*, 181-186.

DIAMOND, M. C., DOWLING, G. A., & JOHNSON, R. E. Morphologic cerebral cortical asymmetry in male and female rats. *Experimental Neurology*, 1981, *71*, 261-268.

DILALLA, L. F., & GOTTESMAN, I. I. Biological and genetic contributions to violence –Widom's untold tale. *Psychological Bulletin*, 1991, *109*, 125-129.

DINGES, D. F. The nature and timing of sleep. *Transactions & Studies of the College of Physicians of Philadelphia*, 1984, *6*, 177-206.

DINGES, D. F. The nature of sleepiness: cause, contexts, and consequences. In A. J. Stunkard & A. Baum (Eds.) *Persepectives in Behavioral Medicine: Eating, Sleeping, and Sex*. Hillsdale, N. J.: Lawrence Erlbaum Associates, pp. 147-179, 1989.

DINGES, D. F. , & KRIBBS, N. B. Performing while sleepy: effects of experimentally induced sleepiness. In T. M. Monk (Ed.), *Sleep, Sleepiness and Performance*. New York: Wiley, pp. 97-127, 1991.

DOHLER, K-D., COQUELIN, A., DAVIS, F., et al. Pre- and postnatal influence of testosterone propionate and diethylstilbestrol on differentiation of the sexually dimorphic nucleus of the preoptic area in male and female rats. *Brain Research*, 1984, *302*, 291-295.

DOLE, V. P. Addictive behavior. *Scientific American*, 1980, *243(6)*, 138-154.

DOLE, V. P. A relation between non-esterified fatty acids in plasma and the metabolism of glucose. *Journal of Clinical Investigations*, 1956, *35*, 150-152.

DOMINICK, J. R., & GREENBERG, B. S. Attitudes toward violence: The interaction of television exposure, family attitudes, and social class. In G. A. Comstock & E. A. Rubinstein (Eds.), *Television and social behavior* (Vol. 3): *Television and adolescent aggressiveness*. Washington, D.C.: Government Printing Office, 1971.

DOMINO, G. Creativity and the home environment. *Gifted Child Quarterly*, 1979, *23*, 818-828.

DONNERSTEIN, E., DONNERSTEIN, M., & EVANS, R. Erotic stimuli and aggression: Facilitation or inhibition. *Journal of Personality and Social Psychology*, 1975, *32*, 237-244.

DONNERSTEIN, E. I., & LINZ, D. G. The question of pornography. *Psychology Today*, 1986, *20*, 56-59.

DONNERSTEIN, E., & WILSON, D. W. Effects of noise and perceived control on ongoing and subsequent aggressive behavior. *Journal of Personality and Social Psychology*, 1976, *34*, 774-781.

DOOB, A. N., & CLIMIE, R. J. Delay of measurement and the effects of film violence. *Journal of Experimental Social Psychology*, 1972, *8*, 136-142.

DORFMAN, D. D. Esthetic preference as a function of pattern information. *Psychonomic Science*, 1965, *3*, 85-86.

DORSKY, F. S., & TAYLOR, S. P. Physical aggression as a function of manifest anxiety. *Psychonomic Science*, 1972, *27*, 103-104.

DOWLING, C. *Perfect Women: Daughters Who Love Their Mothers But Don't Love Themselves*. Pocket Books, 1989.

DÖRNER, G. Hormone-dependent brain development. *Psychoneuroendocrinology*, 1983, *8*, 205-212.

DURDEN-SMITH, J., & DE SIMONE, D. *Sex and the Brain*. New York: Warner, 1983.

DWECK, C. S. Motivational processes affecting learning. *American Psychologist*, 1986, *41*, 1040-1048.

DWECK, C. S. Self-theories and goals: Their role in motivation, personality, and development. In R. A. Dienstbier (Ed.), *Perspectives on Motivation*. Nebraska Symposium on Motivation,1990. Lincoln: University of Nebraska Press, 1991.

DWECK, C. S., & LEGGETT, E. L. A social-cognitive approach to motivation and personality. *Psychological Review*, 1988, *95*, 256-273.

DWECK, C. S., & LICHT, B. Learned helplessness and intellectual achievement. In J. Garber and M. Seligman (Eds.). *Learned Helplessness: Theory and Application*, 1990, pp. 197-222.

DYKSTRA, L. Drug Action.. In J. Grabowski and G.R. Vanden Bos (Eds.), *Psychopharmacology: Basic Mechanisms and Applied Interventions,* Washington, D. C.: American Psychological Association, 1992, pp. 59–66.

EAGLY, A. H., & STEFFEN, V. J. Gender and aggressive behavior: A meta-analytic review of the social psychological literature. *Psychological Bulletin*, 1986, *100*, 309-330.

EARL, R. W. *Problem solving and motor skill behaviors under conditions of free-choice*. Unpublished doctoral dissertation, University of Michigan, 1957.

EASTERBROOK, J. A. The effect of emotion on cue utilization and the organization of behavior. *Psychological Review*, 1959, *66*, 183-201.

EDEN, A. *Growing up thin*. New York: David McKay, 1975.

EGGER, M. D., & FLYNN, J. P. Effects of electrical stimulation of the amygdala on hypothalamically elicited attack behavior in cats. *Journal of Neurophysiology*, 1963, *26*, 705-720.

EHRENKRANZ, J., BLISS, E., & SHEARD, M. H. Plasma testosterone: Correlation with aggressive behavior and social dominance in man. *Psychosomatic Medicine*, 1974, *36*, 469-475.

EHRHARDT, A. A., & MEYER-BAHLBURG, H. F. L. Effects of prenatal sex hormones on gender-related behavior. *Science*, 1981, *211*, 1312-1318.

EHRHARDT, A. A., MEYER-BAHLBURG, H. F. L., & ROSEN, L. R., FELDMAN, J. F., VERIDIANO, N.P., ZIMMERMAN, I., & MCEWEN, B. S. Sexual orientation after prenatal exposure to exogenous estrogen. *Archives of Sexual Behavior*, 1985, *14*, 57-77.

EKMAN, P. The argument and evidence about universals in facial expression of emotions. In H. Wagner & A. Manstead (Eds.), *Handbook of social psychophysiology* (pp. 143-163). New York: Wiley, 1989.

EKMAN, P., LEVENSON, R. W., & FRIESEN, W. V. Autonomic nervous system activity distinguishes among emotions. *Science*, 1983, *221*, 1208-1210.

ELLIOTT, E. E., & DWECK, C. S. Goals: an approach to motivation and achievement. *Journal of Personality and Social Psychology*,1988, *54*, 5-12.

ELLIS, A., & GRIEGER, R. *Handbook of rational emotive therapy*. New York: Springer, 1977.

ELLMAN, S, J., SPIELMAN, A. J., LUCK, D., STEINER, S. S., & HALPERIN, R. REM Deprivation: A Review. In S. J. Ellman and J. S. Antrobus (Eds.), *The Mind in Sleep: Psychology and Psychophysiology* (2nd Edition). New York: Wiley (pp. 329-376), 1991.

ELLMAN, S.J., & STEINER, S.S. The effect of electrical self-stimulation on REM rebound. Paper presented at the meeting of the Association for the Psychophysiological Study of Sleep, Boston, 1969a.

ELLMAN, S.J., & STEINER, S.S. The effect of REM deprivation on intracranial self-stimulation. Paper presented at the meeting of the Association for the Psychophysiological Study of Sleep, Boston, 1969b.

ELLMAN, S, J. , & WEINSTEIN, L. N. REM sleep and dream formation: A theoretical integration. In S. J. Ellman and J. S. Antrobus (Eds.) *The Mind in Sleep: Psychology and Psychophysiology* (2nd Edition). New York: Wiley (pp 466 - 488), 1991.

EMMONS, R. A. The repressive personality social support. In H. S. Friedman (Ed.), *Hostility, Coping and Health*. Washington, D. C.: American Psychological Association, 1992, pp. 141-150.

EMRICK, C. D., & HANSEN, J. Assertions regarding effectiveness of treatment of alcoholism: Fact or fantasy. *American Psychologist*, 1983, *38*, 1078-1088.

ENDLER, N. S., PARKER, J. D. A., BAGBY, R. M., & COX, B. J. Multidimensionality of state and trait anxiety: Factor structure of the Endler Multidimensional Anxiety Scales. *Journal of Personality and Social Psychology*, 1991, *60*, 919-926.

ENGLE, K. B., & WILLIAMS, T. K. Effect of an ounce of vodka on alcoholics' desire for alcohol. *Quarterly Journal of Studies on Alcohol*, 1972, *33*, 1099-1105.

EPSTEIN, S. Cognitive-experiential self-theory. In L. A. Pervin (Ed.), *Handbook of Personality: Theory and Research*. New York: Guilford Press, 1990, pp. 165-191).

EPSTEIN, S. Cognitive-experiential self-theory: an integrative theory of personality. In R. Curtis (Ed.), *The Relational Self: Convergences in Psychoanalysis and Social Psychology*. New York: Guilford Press, 1991, pp. 111-137.

EPSTEIN, S. Coping ability, negative self-evaluation, and overgeneralization. Experiment and theory. *Journal of Personality and Social Psychology*, 1992, 62, 826-836.

EPSTEIN, S. The nature of anxiety with emphasis upon its relationship to expectancy. In C. D. Spielberger (Ed.), *Anxiety: Current trends in theory and research*. New York: Academic Press, 1972.

EPSTEIN, S., LIPSON, A., HOLSTEIN, C., & HUH, E. Irrational reactions to negative outcomes: Evidence for two conceptual systems. *Journal of Personality and Social Psychology*, 1992, 62, 328-339.

EPSTEIN, S. & MEIER, P. Constructive thinking: A broad coping variable with specific components. *Journal of Personality and Social Psychology*, 1989, 57, 332-350.

ERDMANN, G., & JANKE, W. Interaction between physiological and cognitive determinants of emotions: Experimental studies on Schachter's theory of emotions. *Biological Psychology*, 1978, 6, 61-74.

ERIKSON, E. H. *Childhood and Society*. New York: Norton, 1950.

ERIKSON, E. H. *Identity and the Life Cycle*. New York: Norton, 1980.

ERIKSON, E. H. *Identity: Youth and Crisis*. New York: Norton, 1968.

ERON, L. D., HUESMANN, L. R., LEFKOWITZ, M. M., & WALDER, L. Q. Does television violence cause aggression? *American Psychologist*, 1972, 27, 253-263.

EYSENCK, H. J. *The biological basis of personality*. Springfield, Ill.: Charles C Thomas, 1967.

EYSENCK, H. J. *Dimensions of personality*. London: Routledge & Kegan Paul, 1947.

EYSENCK, H. J. Introverts, extraverts, and sex. *Psychology Today*, January 1971, pp. 48-51; 82.

EYSENCK, H. J. Personality and stress as causal factors in cancer and coronary heart disease. In M. P. Janisse (Ed.), *Individual differences, stress, and health psychology*. New York: Springler-Verlag, 1988.

EYSENCK, H. J. Personality and the maintenance of the smoking habit. In W. L. Dunn (Ed.), *Smoking behavior: Motives and incentives*. Washington, D.C.: Winston, 1973.

EYSENCK, H. J. *Sex and personality*. London: Open Books, 1976.

FAIRBORN, C. A cognitive behavioural approach to the treatment of bulimia. *Psychological Medicine*, 1981, 11, 707-711.

FAIRBORN, C. G. Self-induced vomiting. *Journal of Psychosomatic Research*, 1980, 24, 193-197.

FAIRBORN, C. G., & COOPER, P. J. Self-induced vomiting and bulimia nervosa: An undetected problem. *British Medical Journal*, 1982, 284, 1153-1155.

FALK, J. L. Drug dependence: Myth or motive? *Pharmacology Biochemistry and Behavior*, 1983, 19, 385-391.

FARKAS, G. M., & ROSEN, R. C. Effect of alcohol on elicited male sexual response. *Journal of Studies on Alcohol*, 1976, 37, 265-272.

FARLEY, F. H. The big T in personality. *Psychology Today*, May 1986, pp. 44-52.

FAUSTO-STERLING, A. *Myths of Gender: Biological Theories About Women and Men*. New York: Basic Books, 1985.

FAVA, M., COPELAND, P.M., SCHWEIGER, U. & HERZOG, D. B. Neurochemical abnormalities of anorexia nervosa and bulimia nervosa. *American Journal of Psychiatry*, 1989, 146, 963-971.

FEATHER, N. T. Reactions to male and female success and failure at sex-linked occupations: Effects of sex and socio-economic status of respondents. *Australian Journal of Psychology*, 1978, 30, 21-40.

FEATHER, N. T. The relationship of expectation of success to reported probability, task structure, and achievement-related motivation. *Journal of Abnormal and Social Psychology*, 1963, 66, 231-238.

FEATHER, N. T. The relationship of persistence at a task to expectation of success and achievement-related motives. *Journal of Abnormal and Social Psychology*, 1961, 63, 552-561.

FEINBERG, I., KORESKO, R. L., HELLER, N., & STEINBERG, H. R. Sleep EEG and eye-movement patterns in young and aged normal subjects and in patients with chronic brain syndrome. In W. B. Webb (Ed.), *Sleep: An active process*. Glenview, Ill.: Scott, Foresman, 1973.

FEINSTEIN, D., & KRIPPNER, S. *Personal Mythology*. Los Angeles: Jeremy P. Tarcher, Inc., 1988.

FELDMAN, R. S., & BERNSTEIN, A. G. Primacy effects in self-attribution of ability. *Journal of Personality*, 1978, 46, 732-742.

FENIGSTEIN, A. Does aggression cause a preference for viewing media violence? *Journal of Personality and Social Psychology*, 1979, 37, 2307-2317.

FENWICK, P. B., DONALDSON, S., GILLIS, L., BUSHMAN, J., FENTON, G. W., PERRY, I., TILSLEY, C., & SERAFINOWICZ, H. Metabolic and EEG changes during transcendental meditation: An explanation. *Biological Psychology*, 1977, 5, 101-118.

FERGUSON, T. J., & RULE, B. G. An attributional perspective on anger and aggression. In R. G. Geen and E. Donnerstein (Eds), *Aggression: Theoretical and Empirical Reviews, Vol. I: Theoretical and Methodological Issues*. New York: Academic Press, pp. 41-74, 1983.

FERN, R. W. Hearing loss caused by amplified pop music. *Journal of Sound and Vibration*, 1976, 46, 462-464.

FESHBACH, N. D. Parental empathy and child adjustment/maladjustment. In N. Eisenberg & J. Strayer (Eds.), *Empathy and Its Development* (pp. 271-291). New York: Cambridge University Press, 1987.

FESHBACH, S. The function of aggression and the regulation of aggression. *Psychological Review*, 1964, 71, 257-272.

FESTINGER, L. *A theory of cognitive dissonance*. Evanston, Ill.: Row, Peterson, 1957.

FESTINGER, L., PEPITONE, A., & NEWCOMB, T. Some consequences of de-individuation in a group. *Journal of Abnormal and Social Psychology*, 1952, 47, 382-389.

FEY, S. G., & LINDHOLM, E. Biofeedback and progressive relaxation: Effects on systolic and diastolic blood pressure and heart rate. *Psychophysiology*, 1978, 15, 239-247.

FINCHER, J. Natural opiates in the brain. *Human Behavior*, January 1979, pp. 28-32.

FISCHMAN, J. Type A on trial. *Psychology Today*, February 1987, 42-50.

FISHER, C., & DEMENT, W. *Dreams and psychosis*. Paper presented at the meeting of the Western New England Psychoanalytic Society, New Haven, Conn., 1962.

FISHER, H. *Anatomy of Love: The Natural History of Monogamy, Adultery and Divorce*. New York: Norton, 1992.

FISHER, W. A., & BYRNE, D. Sex differences in response to erotica? Love versus lust. *Journal of Personality and Social Psychology*, 1978, 36, 117-125.

FISHMAN, S. M., & SHEEHAN, D. V. Anxiety and panic: Their cause and treatment. *Psychology Today*, April 1985, pp. 26-32.

FOLKMAN, S. Personal control and stress and coping processes: A theoretical analysis. *Journal of Personality and Social Psychology*, 1984, 46, 839-852.

FOLKMAN, S., & LAZARUS, R. S. If it changes it must be a process: Study of emotion and coping during three stages of a college examination. *Journal of Personality and Social Psychology*, 1985, 46, 839-852.

FOLKMAN, S., LAZARUS, R. S., DUNKEL-SCHETTER, C., DELONGIS, A., & GRUEN, R. J. Dynamics of a stressful encounter: Cognitive appraisal, coping, and encounter outcomes. *Journal of Personality and Social Psychology*, 1986, 50, 992-1003.

FOLKMAN, S., SCHAEFER, C., & LAZARUS, R. S. Cognitive processes as mediators of stress and coping. In V. Hamilton & D. M. Warburton (Eds.), *Human stress and cognition: An information processing approach* (pp. 265-298). New York: Wiley, 1979.

FOOTE, R. M. Diethylstilbestrol and the management of psychological states in males. *Journal of Nervous and Mental Disease*, 1944, 99, 928-935.

FORD, C. S., & BEACH, F. A. *Pattern of sexual behavior*. New York: Harper, 1951.

FORGAS, J.P., & BOWER, G. Mood effect on person-perception judgments. *Journal of Personality and Social Psychology*, 1987, 53, 53-60

FOULKES, D. Dream reports from different stages of sleep. *Journal of Abnormal and Social Psychology*, 1962, 65, 14-25.

FOULKES, D. *The psychology of sleep*. New York: Scribner's, 1966.

FOULKES, D., SPEAR, P. S., & SYMONDS, J. D. Individual differences in mental activity at sleep onset. *Journal of Abnormal Psychology*, 1966, 71, 280-286.

FOULKES, D., & VOGEL, G. Mental activity at sleep onset. *Journal of Abnormal Psychology*, 1965, *70*, 231-243.

FRANKEN, R. E. *Sensation seeking and beliefs and attitudes.* Unpublished research, 1987.

FRANKEN, R. E. Sensation seeking and keeping your options open. *Personality and Individual Differences*,1993, *14*, 247-249.

FRANKEN, R. E. Sensation seeking, decision making styles, and preference for individual responsibility. *Personality and Individual Differences*, 1988, *9*, 139-146.

FRANKEN, R. E. Thinking styles of sensation seekers. Unpublished research. University of Calgary, 1990.

FRANKEN, R. E., GIBSON, K., & MOHAN, P. Sensation seeking and disclosure to close and casual friends. *Personality and Individual Differences*, 1990, *11*, 829-832.

FRANKEN, R. E., GIBSON, K. J., & ROWLAND, G. L. Sensation seeking and the tendency to view the world as threatening. *Personality and Individual Differences*, 1992, *13*, 31-38.

FRANKEN, R. E., GIBSON, K. J., & ROWLAND, G. L. *Sensation seeking, drug use, and attitudes toward drug use.* Unpublished research, 1986.

FRANKEN, R. E., & STRAIN, A. Effect of increased arousal on response to stimulus change in a complex maze. *Perceptual and Motor Skills*, 1974, *39*, 1076-1078.

FRANKENHAEUSER, M., DUNNE, E., & LUNDBERG, U. Sex differences in sympathetic-adrenal medullary reactions induced by different stressors. *Psychopharmacology*, 1976, *476*, 1-5.

FRANKENHAEUSER, M., & JOHANSSON, G. Task demand as reflected in catecholamine excretion and hear rate. *Journal of Human Stress*, 1976, *2*, 15-23.

FRANKENHAEUSER, M., LUNDBERG, U., & FORSMAN, L. Dissociation between sympathetic-adrenal and pituitary-adrenal responses to an achievement situation characterized by high controllability: Comparison between Type A and Type B males and females. *Biological Psychology*, 1980, *10*, 79-91.

FREEDMAN, D. G. *Human sociobiology.* New York: Free Press, 1979.

FREEDMAN, J. L. Effect of television violence on aggressiveness. *Psychological Bulletin*,1984, *96*, 227-246.

FREEDMAN, J. L. Television violence and aggression: A rejoinder. *Psychological Bulletin*, 1986, *100*, 372-378.

FREEDMAN, J. L., LEVY, A. S., BUCHANAN, R. W., & PRICE, J. Crowding and human aggressiveness. *Journal of Experimental Social Psychology*, 1972, *8*, 528-548.

FRENCH, E. G. Motivation as a variable in work-partner selection. *Journal of Abnormal and Social Psychology*, 1956, *53*, 96-99.

FREUD, S. The ego and the id. In *The standard edition of the complete psychological works of Sigmund Freud* (Vol. 19). London: Hogarth Press, 1947. (Originally published, 1923.)

FREUD, S. Formulations regarding the two principles of mental functioning. In *Collected papers of Sigmund Freud* (Vol. 4). London: Hogarth Press, 1949. (Originally published, 1911.)

FREUD, S. *A general introduction to psychoanalysis.* New York: Washington Square Press, 1934. (Originally published, 1915.)

FREUD, S. Instincts and their vicissitudes. In *Collected papers of Sigmund Freud* (Vol. 4). London: Hogarth Press, 1949. (Originally published, 1915.)

FREUD, S. *The interpretation of dreams.* London: Hogarth Press, 1953. (Originally published, 1900.)

FRIEDMAN, H. S. *Self-Healing Personality. Why Some People Achieve Health and Others Succumb to Illness.* New York: Henry Holt, 1991.

FRIEDMAN, H. S. Understanding hostility, coping, and health. In H. S. Friedman (Ed.) *Hostility, Coping and Health.* Washington, D. C.: American Psychological Association, 1992, pp. 3-9.

FRIEDMAN, M. Toward a reconceptualization of guilt. *Contemporary Psychoanalysis*, 1985, *21*, 501-547.

FRIEDMAN, M., & ROSENMAN, R. H. *Type A behavior and your heart.* New York: Knopf, 1974.

FRIEDMAN, M. I., & STRICKER, E. M. The physiological psychology of hunger: A physiological perspective. *Psychological Review*, 1976, *83*, 409-431.

FRIEDMANN, J., GLOBUS, G., HUNTLEY, A., MULLANEY, D., NAITOH, P., & JOHNSON, L. Performance and mood during and after gradual sleep reduction. *Psychophysiology*, 1977, *14*, 245-250.

FRIJDA, N. H. , KUIPERS, P., & TER SCHURE, E. Relations among emotion, appraisal, and emotional action readiness. *Journal of Personality and Social Psychology*, 1989, *57*, 212-228.

FRIJDA, N. H. The laws of emotion. *American Psychologist*, 1988, *43*, 349-353.

FRODI, A. Experiential and physiological responses associated with anger and aggression in women and men. *Journal of Research in Personality*, 1978, *12*, 335-349.

FROHMAN, L. A., GOLDMAN, J. K., & BERNARDIS, L. L. Metabolism of intravenously injected 14C-glucose in weanling rats with hypothalamic obesity. *Metabolism: Clinical and Experimental*, 1972, *21*, 799-805.

FROST, R. O., BURISH, T. G. & HOLMES, D. S. Stress and EEG alpha. 1978.

FROST, R. O., GOOLKASIAN, G. A., ELY, R. J., & BLANCHARDS, F. A. Depression, restraint, and eating behavior. *Behavioral Research and Therapy*, 1982, *20*, 113-121.

FUNKENSTEIN, D. H. The physiology of fear and anger. *Scientific American*, 1955, *192*(5), 74-80.

FUNKENSTEIN, D. H., KING, S. H., & DROLETTE, M. E. The direction of anger during a laboratory stress-inducing situation. *Psychosomatic Medicine*, 1974, *16*, 404-413.

FUSTER, J. M. Effects of stimulation of brain stem on tachistoscopic perception. *Science*, 1958, *127*, 150.

GACKENBACH, J., & BOSVELD, J. *Control Your Dreams.* New York: Harper and Row, 1989.

GACKENBACH, J., & BOSVELD, J. Take control of your dreams. *Psychology Today*, (Oct.), 27-32, 1989.

GAGNON, J. H. *Human Sexualities.* Glenview, Illinois: Scott Foresman, 1977.

GAGNON, J. H. Scripts and the coordination of sexual conduct. In J. K. Cole & R. Diensteiber (Eds.), *Nebraska Symposium Motivation* (Vol. 21, pp. 27-59). Lincoln: University of Nebraska Press, 1974.

GAGNON, J., DE KONINCK, J., & BROUGHTON, R. Reappearance of electroencephalogram slow waves in extended sleep with delayed bedtime. *Sleep*, 1985, *8*, 118-128.

GALE, A., COLES, M., & BLAYDON, J. Extraversion-introversion and the EEG. *British Journal of Psychology*, 1969, *60*, 209-223.

GAMBARO, S., & RABIN, A. I. Diastolic blood pressure responses following direct and displaced aggression after anger arousal in high- and low-guilt subjects. *Journal of Personality and Social Psychology*, 1969, *12*, 87-94.

GANELLEN, R. J., & BLANEY, P. H. Hardiness and social support as moderators of the effects of life stress. *Journal of Personality and Social Psychology*, 1984, *47*, 156-163.

GARCIA, J., & KOELLING, R. A. Relation of cue to consequence in avoidance learning. *Psychonomic Science*, 1966, *4*, 123-124.

GARCIA, J., MCGOWAN, B. K., ERVIN, F. R., & KOELLING, R. A. Cues: Their relative effectiveness as a function of the reinforcer. *Science*, 1968, *160*, 794-795.

GARDINER, R. J., MARTIN, F., & JUKIER, L. Anorexia nervosa: Endocrine studies of two distinct clinical populations. In P. L. Darby, P. E. Garfinkel, D. M. Garner, & D. V. Coscina, *Anorexia nervosa: Recent developments in research* (pp. 285-289). New York: Alan R. Liss, Inc., 1983.

GARFINKEL, P. E., & GARNER, D. M. *Anorexia nervosa: A multidimensional perspective.* New York: Brunner/Mazel, 1982.

GARFINKEL, P. E., MOLDOFSKY, H., GARNER, D. M., STANCER, H. C., & COSCINA, D. V. Body awareness in anorexia nervosa: Disturbances in ``body image'' and ``satiety.'' *Psychosomatic Medicine*, 1978, *40*, 487-498.

GARN, S. M., & CLARK, D. C. Trends in fatness and the origins of obesity. *Pediatric*,. 1976, *57*, 443-455.

GARRITY, T. F., STALLONES, L., MARX, M. B., & JOHNSON, T. P. Pet ownership and attachment as supportive factors in the health of the elderly. *Anthrozoos*, 1989, *3*, 35-44.

GARROW, D. J. S., CRISP, A. H., JORDON, H. A., MEYER, J. E., RUSSELL, G. F. M., SILVERSTONE, T., STUNKARD, A. J., & VAN ITALLIE, T. B. Pathology of eating, group report. In T. Silverstone (Ed.), *Dahlem Konferenzen, Life Sciences Research Report 2*. Berlin, 1975.

GARROW, J. The regulation of energy expenditure. In G. A. Bray (Ed.), *Recent Advances in Obesity Research* (Vol. 2). London: Newman, 1978.

GEBHARD, P. H. Sex differences in sexual responses. *Archives of Sexual Behavior*, 1973, 2, 201-203.

GEEN, R. G. Effects of attack and uncontrollable noise on aggression. *Journal of Research in Personality*, 1978, 12, 15-19.

GEEN, R. G. Effects of frustration, attack, and prior training in aggressiveness upon aggressive behavior. *Journal of Personality and Social Psychology*, 1968, 9, 316-321.

GEEN, R. G. *Human Aggression*. Pacific Grove, California: Brooks/Cole Publishing, 1990.

GEEN, R. G. Observing violence in the mass media: Implications of basic research. In R. G. Geen & E. C. O'Neal (Eds.), *Perspectives on aggression*. New York: Academic Press, 1976.

GEEN, R. G. Preferred stimulation levels in introverts and extraverts: Effects on arousal and performance. *Journal of Personality and Social Psychology*, 1984, 46, 1303-1312.

GEEN, R. G., & O'NEAL, E. C. Activation of cue-elicited aggression by general arousal. *Journal of Personality and Social Psychology*, 1969, 11, 289-292.

GEEN, R. G., & STONER, D. Effects of aggressiveness habit strength on behavior in the presence of aggression-related stimuli. *Journal of Personality and Social Psychology*, 1971, 17, 149-153.

GEEN, R. G., STONER, D., & SHOPE, G. L. The facilitation of aggression by aggression: Evidence against the catharsis hypothesis. *Journal of Personality and Social Psychology*, 1975, 31, 721-726.

GEER, J. H., & BROUSSARD, D. B. Scaling sexual behavior and arousal:consistency and sex differences. *Journal of Personality and Social Psychology*, 1990, 58, 664-671.

GEER, J. H., DAVISON, G. C., & GATCHEL, R. J. Reduction of stress in humans through nonveridical perceived control of aversive stimulation. *Journal of Personality and Social Psychology*, 1970, 16, 731-738.

GEISELMAN, P. J., & NOVIN, D. Sugar infusion can enhance feeding. *Science*, 1982, 218, 490-491.

GELLER, E., RITVO, E. R., FREEMAN, B. J., & YUWILER, A. Preliminary observations of the effect of flenfluramine on blood serotonin and symptoms in three autistic boys. *New England Journal of Medicine*, 1982, 307, 165-169.

GENTRY, W. D. Relationship of anger-coping styles and blood pressure among black Americans. In M. A. Chesney and R. H. Rosenman (Eds.), *Anger and Hostility in Cardiovascular and Behavioral Disorders*. Washington, D. C.: Hemisphere, pp. 139-147, 1985.

GENTRY, W. D., CHESNEY, A. P., GARY, H. E., HALL, R. P., & HARBURG, E. Habitual anger-coping styles: I. Effect on men's blood pressure and risk for essential hypertension. *Psychosomatic Medicine*, 1982, 44, 195-202.

GERNER, R. H., POST, R. M., GILLIN, J. C., & BUNNEY, W. E. Biological and behavioral effects of one night's sleep deprivation in depressed patients and normals. *Journal of Psychiatric Research*, 1979, 15, 21.

GERRARD, M. Sex, sex guilt, and contraceptive use revisited: The 1980s. *Journal of Personality and Social Psychology*, 1987, 52, 975-980.

GESCHWIND, N., & BEHAN, P. Left-handedness: Association with immune disease, migraine, and developmental learning disorder. *Proceedings of the National Academy of Science*, 1982, 79, 5097-5100.

GETZELS, J. W., & JACKSON, P. W. *Creativity and intelligence. Exploration with gifted students*. New York: Wiley, 1962.

GIBBONS, F. X., & MCCOY, S. B. Self-esteem, similarity, and reactions to active versus passive downward comparison. *Journal of Personality and Social Psychology*, 1991, 60, 414-424.

GIBBS, F. A., & MALTBY, G. L. Effect on the electrical activity of the cortex of certain depressant and stimulant drugs—barbiturates, morphine, caffeine, Benzedrine, and adrenalin. *Journal of Pharmacology and Experimental Therapeutics*, 1943, 78, 1-10.

GIBSON, K. J., FRANKEN, R. E., & ROWLAND, G. L. Sensation seeking and marital adjustment. *Journal of Sex and Marital Therapy*, 1989, 15, 57-61.

GIESE, H., & SCHMIDT, A. *Student sexualität*. Hamburg: Rowohlt, 1968.

GILBERT, D. G. Paradoxical tranquillizing and emotion-reducing effects of nicotine. *Psychological Bulletin*, 1979, 86, 643-661.

GILBERT, R. M. Drug abuse as an excessive behavior. In H. Shaeffer and M. E. Burglass, *Classic contributions in the addictions*. New York: Brunner/Mazel, 1981.

GILLBERG, M., & ÅKERSTEDT, T. Body temperature and sleep at different times of day. *Sleep*, 1982, 5, 378-388.

GILLIN, J. C., & WYATT, R. J. Schizophrenia: Perchance a dream. *International Review of Neurobiology*, 1975, 17, 297-342.

GLADUE, B. A. Aggressive behavioral characteristics, hormones, and sexual orientation in man and women. *Aggressive Behavior*, 1991, 17, 313-326.

GLANZER, M. The role of stimulus satiation in spontaneous alternation. *Journal of Experimental Psychology*, 1953, 45, 387-393.

GLASS, D. C. *Behavior patterns, stress, and coronary disease*. Hillsdale, N.J.: Erlbaum, 1977. (a)

GLASS, D. C. Stress, behavior patterns, and coronary disease. *American Scientist*, 1977, 65, 177-187. (b)

GLASS, D. C. Stress, competition, and heart attacks. *Psychology Today*, December 1976, pp. 55-57; 134.

GLASS, D. C., & SINGER, J. E. *Urban stress*. New York: Academic Press, 1972.

GLASSER, W. *Positive addiction*. New York: Harper & Row, 1976.

GLASSMAN, A. Indolamines and affective disorder. *Psychosomatic Medicine*, 1969, 31, 107-114.

GLAUBMAN, H., ORBACH, I., GROSS, Y., AVIRAM, O., FRIEDER, I., FRIEMAN, M., & PELLED, O. The effect of presleep focal attention load on subsequent sleep patterns. *Psychophysiology*, 1979, 16, 467-470.

GLAUBMAN, R. REM deprivation and divergent thinking. *Psychophysiology*, 1978, 15, 75-79.

GLICKMAN, S. E., & SCHIFF, B. B. A biological theory of reinforcement. *Psychological Review*, 1967, 74, 81-109.

GOLDFARB, A. I., & BERMAN, S. Alcoholism as a psychosomatic disorder: I. Endocrine pathology of animals and man excessively exposed to alcohol; Its possible relation to behavioral pathology. *Quarterly Journal of Studies on Alcohol*, 1949, 10, 415-429.

GOLDFOOT, D. A., WESTERBORG-VAN LOON, H., GROENVELD, W., & SLOB, A. K. Behavioral and physiological evidence of sexual climax in the female stump-tailed Macaque *(Macaca arctoides)*. *Science*, 1980, 208, 1477-1479.

GOLDMAN, R. F., HAISMAN, M. F., BYNUM, G., HORTON, E. S., & SIMS, E. A. H. Experimental obesity in man: Metabolic rate in relation to dietary intake. In G. A. Bray, G. F. Cahill, E. S. Horton, H. A. Jordan, F. R. McCrumb, Jr., L. B. Salans, & E. A. H. Sims (Eds.), *Obesity in perspective*. Washington, D.C.: Government Printing Office, 1975.

GOLDMAN, R., JAFFA, M., & SCHACHTER, S. Yom Kippur, Air France, dormitory food, and eating behavior of obese and normal persons. *Journal of Personality and Social Psychology*, 1968, 10, 117-123.

GOLDMAN, J. K., SCHNATZ, J. D., BERNARDIS, L. L., & FROHMAN, L. A. Adipose tissue metabolism of weanling rats after destruction of ventromedial hypothalamic nuclei: Effect of hypophysectomy and growth hormone. *Metabolism: Clinical and Experimental*, 1970, 19, 995-1005.

GOLDMAN, J. K., SCHNATZ, J. D., BERNARDIS, L. L., & FROHMAN, L. A. Effects of ventromedial hypothalamic destruction in rats with preexisting streptozotocin-induced diabetes. *Metabolism: Clinical and Experimental*, 1972, 21, 132-136. (a)

GOLDMAN, J. K., SCHNATZ, J. D., BERNARDIS, L. L., & FROHMAN, L. A. The vivo and in vitro metabolism in hypothalamic obesity. *Diabetologia*, 1972, 8, 160-164. (b)

GOLEMAN, D. Meditation helps break the stress spiral. *Psychology Today*, February 1976, pp. 82-86; 93.

GOMEZ, J., & DALLY, P. Psychometric ratings in the assessment of progress in anorexia nervosa. *British Journal of Psychiatry*, 1980, 136, 290-296.

GOODENOUGH, D. R. Field dependence. In H. London & J. E. Exner, Jr. (Eds.), *Dimensions of personality*. New York: Wiley, 1978.

GOODNER, C. J., & RUSSELL, J. A. Pancreas. In T. C. Ruch & H. D. Patton (Eds.), *Physiology and biophysics*. Philadelphia: Saunders, 1965.

GOODSITT, A. Letter: Anorexia nervosa. *Journal of the American Medical Association*, 1974, 230, 372.

GOODWIN, F. K. Cerebrospinal fluid norephinerine in affective illness. *American Journal of Psychiatry*, 1978, 135, 907-912.

GORSKI, R. A. Hormone-induced sex differences in hypothalamic structure. *In Bull TMIN*, 16, Suppl 3, 67-90, 1988.

GORSKI, R. A. Sexual differentiation of the endocrine brain and its control. In M. Motta (Ed.), *Brain Endocrinology* (2nd Edition), pp. 71-104, 1991.

GORSKI, R. A. The neuroendocrine regulation of sexual behavior. In G. Newton and A. H. Riesen (Eds.), *Advances in Psychobiology, Vol. II*. New York: Wiley, pp. 1-58, 1974.

GORSKI, R. A. Sexual dimorphisms of the brain. *Journal of Animal Science*, 1985, 61, 38-61.

GORSUCH, R. L., & BUTLER, M. C. Initial drug abuse: A review of predisposing social psychological factors. *Psychological Bulletin*, 1976, 83, 120-137.

GOUGH, H. G. Studying creativity by means of word association tests. *Journal of Applied Psychology*, 1976, 61, 348-353.

GOY, R. W., & McEWEN, B. S. *Sexual differentiation of the brain*. Cambridge, Mass.: M.I.T. Press, 1980.

GREEN, R. Variant forms of human sexual behavior. In C. R. Austin & R. V. Short (Eds.), *Reproduction in mammals (Vol. 8: Human sexuality)*. Cambridge: Cambridge University Press, 1980.

GREENBERG, R., & PEARLMAN, C. A. Cutting the REM nerve: An approach to the adaptive role of REM sleep. *Perspectives in Biology and Medicine*, 1974, 17, 513-521.

GREENBERG, R., PILLARD, R., & PEARLMAN, C. The effect of dream (stage REM) deprivation on adaptation to stress. *Psychosomatic Medicine*, 1972, 34, 257-262.

GREENE, D., & LEPPER, M. R. Effects of extrinsic rewards on children's subsequent intrinsic interest. *Child Development*, 1974, 45, 1141-1145.

GREENE, R., & DALTON, K. The premenstrual syndrome. *British Medical Journal*, 1953, 1, 1007-1014.

GREENWELL, J., & DENGERINK, H. A. The role of perceived versus actual attack in human physical aggression. *Journal of Personality and Social Psychology*, 1973, 26, 66-71.

GREGORY, W. L. Locus of control for positive and negative outcomes. *Journal of Personality and Social Psychology*, 1978, 36, 840-849.

GREISER, C., GREENBERG, R., & HARRISON, R. H. The adaptive function of sleep: The differential effects of sleep and dreaming on recall. *Journal of Abnormal Psychology*, 1972, 80, 280-286.

GREIST, J. H., KLEIN, M. H., EISCHENS, R. R., FARIS, J., GURMAN, A. S., & MORGAN, W. P. Running as treatment for depression. *Comprehensive Psychiatry*, 1979, 20, 41-54.

GRIFFIN, S. J., & TRINDLER, J. Physical fitness, exercise, and human sleep. *Psychophysiology*, 1978, 15, 447-450.

GRIFFITH, W., MAY, J., & VEITCH, R. Sexual stimulation and interpersonal behavior: Heterosexual evaluative responses, visual behavior, and physical proximity. *Journal of Personality and Social Psychology*, 1974, 30, 367-377.

GRINSPOON, L., & HEDBLOM, P. *The speed culture: Amphetamine use and abuse in America*. Cambridge, Mass.: Harvard University Press, 1975.

GROSS, J., STITZER, M.L., & MALDONADO, J. Nicotine replacement: Effects on postcessation weight gain. *Journal of Consulting and Clinical Psychology*, 1989, 57, 87-92.

GROSSMAN, S. P. *A textbook of physiological psychology*. New York: Wiley, 1967.

GROSVENOR, A., & LACK, L. C. The effect of sleep before or after learning on memory. *Sleep*, 1984, 7, 155-167.

GRUNBERG, N. E., & STRAUB, R. O. The role of gender and taste class in the effects of stress on eating. *Health Psychology*, 1992, 11, 97-100.

GUILFORD, J. P. *The nature of human intelligence*. New York: McGraw-Hill, 1967.

GUR, R. Brain Sex. Televsion documentary. Canadian Broadcasting Company, 1992.

GUY, R. F., RANKIN, B. A., & NORVELL, M. J. The relation of sex-role stereotyping to body image. *Journal of Psychology*, 1980, 105, 167-173.

HADAWAY, P. F., ALEXANDER, B. K., COAMBS, R. B., & BEYERSTEIN, B. The effect of housing and gender on preference for morphine-sucrose solution in rats. *Psychopharmacology*, 1979, 66, 87-91.

HADDAD, N. F., McCULLERS, J. C., & MORAN, J. D. Satiation and the detrimental effects of material rewards. *Child Development*, 1976, 47, 547-551.

HAESSLER, H. A., & CRAWFORD, J. D. Fatty acid composition and metabolic activity of depot fat in experimental obesity. *American Journal of Physiology*, 1967, 213, 255-261.

HALL, J. B., & BROWN, D. A. Plasma glucose and lactic acid alterations in response to a stressful exam. *Biological Psychology*, 1979, 8, 179-188.

HALMI, K. A., POWERS, P., & CUNNINGHAM, S. Treatment of anorexia nervosa with behavior modification. *Archives of General Psychiatry*, 1975, 32, 93-96.

HAMBURG, D. A. Recent research on hormonal factors relevant to human aggressiveness. *International Social Science Journal*, 1971, 23, 36-47.

HAMILTON, P., HOCKEY, B., & REJMAN, M. The place of the concept of activation in human information processing theory: An integrative approach. In S. Dornic (Ed.), *Attention and performance VI*. Hillsdale, N.J.: Erlbaum, 1977.

HAMNER, W. C. Reinforcement theory and contingency management in organizational settings. In H. L. Tosi & W. C. Hamner (Eds.), *Organizational behavior and management: A contingency approach*. Chicago: St. Clair Press, 1974.

HANSEN, J. R., STØA, K. F., BLIX, A. S., & URSIN, H. Urinary levels of epinephrine and norepinephrine in parachutist trainees. In H. Ursin, E. Baade, and S. Levine (Eds.), *Psychobiology of stress: A study of coping men*. New York: Academic Press, 1978.

HARBURG, E., BLAKELOCK, E. H., & ROEPER, P. J. Resentful and reflective coping with arbitrary authority and blood pressure. *Psychosomatic Medicine*, 1979, 41, 189-202.

HARLOW, H. F. Mice, monkeys, men, and motives. *Psychological Review*, 1953, 60, 23-32.

HARLOW, H. F., & HARLOW, M. K. Effects of various mother-infant relationships on rhesus monkey behaviors. In B. M. Foss (Ed.), *Determinants of infant behavior* (Vol. 4). London: Methuen, 1969.

HARRIMAN, A. E. The effect of a preoperative preference for sugar over salt upon compensatory salt selection by adrenalectomized rats. *Journal of Nutrition*, 1955, 57, 271-276.

HARRINGTON, D. M. Creativity, analogical thinking and muscular metaphors. *Journal of Mental Imagery*, 1981, 6, 121-126.

HARRINGTON, D. M., & ANDERSEN, S. M. Creativity, masculinity, femininity, and three models of psychological androgyny. *Journal of Personality and Social Psychology*, 1981, 41, 744-757.

HARRIS, C. B. Hope: Construct definition and the development of an individual differences scale. Unpublished doctoral dissertation, University of Kansas, Lawrence, 1988.

HARTER, S. Causes, correlates, and the functional role of global self-worth: A life-span perspective. In R. J. Sternberg & J. Kolligian, Jr. (Eds.), Competence Considered. New Haven: Yale University Press, 1990, pp. 67-97.

HARTMANN, E. L. *The functions of sleep*. New Haven, Conn.: Yale University Press, 1973.

HARTMANN, E. L. The functions of sleep. *Annual of Psychoanalysis*, 1974, 2, 271-289.

HARTMANN, E. L., BAEKELAND, F., & ZWILLING, G. R. Psychological differences between long and short sleepers. *Archives of General Psychiatry*, 1972, 26, 463-468.

HARTMANN, E. L., & STERN, W. C. Desynchronized sleep deprivation: Learning deficit and its reversal by increased catecholamines. *Physiology and Behavior*, 1972, 8, 585-587.

HARTSE, K. M., ROTH, T., & ZORICK, F. J. Daytime sleepiness and daytime wakefulness: The effect of instruction. *Sleep*, 1982, 5, S107-S118.

HASELTINE, F. P., & OHNO, S. Mechanisms of gonadal differentiation. *Science*, 1981, 211, 1272-1278.

HASHIM, S. A., & VAN ITALLIE, T. B. Studies in normal and obese subjects with a monitored food dispensory device. *Annals of the New York Academy of Science*, 1965, *131*, 654-661.

HAWKE, C. C. Castration and sex crimes. *American Journal of Mental Deficiency*, 1950, *55*, 220-226.

HAWKINS, R. C., JR., TURELL, S., & JACKSON, L. J. Desirable and undesirable masculine and feminine traits in relation to students' dietary tendencies and body image dissatisfaction. *Sex Roles*, 1983, *9*, 705-724.

HAYWOOD, H. C. Individual difference in motivational orientations: A trait approach. In H. Day, D. E. Berlyne, & D. E. Hunt (Eds.), *Intrinsic motivation: A new direction in education.* Toronto: Holt, Rinehart & Winston, 1971.

HEATH, R. G. Electrical self-stimulation of the brain in man. *American Journal of Psychiatry*, 1963, *120*, 571-577.

HEATHER, N., WINTON, M., & ROLLNICK, S. An empirical test of ``a cultural delusion of alcoholics.'' *Psychological Reports*, 1982, *50*, 379-382.

HEATHERON, T.F., & BAUMEISTER, R.F. (in press) Binge-Eating as Escape from Self-Awareness, *Psychological Bulletin.*

HEATHERTON, T.F., & POLIVY, J. Chronic dieting and eating disorders: A spiral model. In J.H. Crowther, S.E. Hobfall, M.A.P. Stephens, & D.L. Tennenbaum (Eds.), *The Etiology of Bulimia: The Individual and Familial Context.* Washington, D.C.: Hemisphere Publishers.

HEATHERTON, T. F., & POLIVY, J. Development and validation of a scale to measuring state self-esteem. *Journal of Personality and Social Psychology*, 1991, *60*, 895-910.

HEBB, D. O. Drive and the C.N.S. (conceptual nervous system). *Psychological Review*, 1955, *62*, 243-254.

HEBB, D. O. *The organization of behavior.* New York: Wiley, 1949.

HECKHAUSEN, H. *The anatomy of achievement motivation.* New York: Academic Press, 1967.

HEIDER, F. Attitudes and cognitive organization. *Journal of Psychology*, 1946, *21*, 107-112.

HEIDER, F. *The psychology of interpersonal relations.* New York: Wiley, 1958.

HEILMAN, M. E., & SARUWATARI, L. R. When beauty is beastly: The effects of appearance and sex on evaluations of job applicants for managerial and non-managerial jobs. *Organizational Behavior and Human Performance*, 1979, *23*, 360-372.

HEIMAN, J. R. A psychophysiological exploration of sexual arousal patterns in females and males. *Psychophysiology*, 1977, *14*, 266-274.

HEIMAN, J. R. Women's sexual arousal. *Psychology Today*, April 1975, pp. 91-94.

HEIMBURGER, R. F., WHITLOCK, C. C., & KALSBECK, J. E. Stereotaxic amygdalotomy for epilepsy with aggressive behavior. *Journal of the American Medical Association*, 1966, *198*, 165-169.

HELMREICH, R. L., BEANE, W. E., LUCKER, G. W., & SPENCE, J. T. Achievement motivation and scientific attainment. *Personality and Social Psychology Bulletin*, 1978, *4*, 222-226.

HELMREICH, R. L., & SPENCE, J. T. The Work and Family Orientation Questionnaire: An objective instrument to assess components of achievement motivation and attitudes toward family and career. *JSAS Catalog of Selected Documents in Psychology*, 1978, *8*, 35.

HELMREICH, R. L., SPENCE, J. T., BEANE, W. E., LUCKER, G. W., & MATTHEWS, K. A. Making it in academic psychology: Demographic and personality correlates of attainment. *Journal of Personality and Social Psychology*, 1980, *39*, 896-908.

HELMSTETTER, S. *What To Say When You Talk To Yourself.* New York: Simon and Schuster, 1986.

HERMAN, C. P. External and internal cues as determinants of smoking behavior of light and heavy smokers. *Journal of Personality and Social Psychology*, 1974, *30*, 664-672.

HERMAN, C. P., & MACK, D. Restrained and unrestrained eating. *Journal of Personality*, 1975, *43*, 646-660.

HERMAN, C. P., & POLIVY, J. A boundary model for the regulation of eating. In A. J. Stunkard & E. Stellar (Eds.), *Eating and its disorders.* New York: Raven Press, 1984.

HERMAN, C. P., & POLIVY, J. *Breaking the diet habit.* New York: Basic Books, 1983.

HERMANN, M. G. Assessing the personalities of Soviet Politburo members. *Personality and Social Psychology Bulletin*, 1980, *6*, 332-352.

HERON, W. The pathology of boredom. *Scientific American,196*, 52-56, 1957.

HERRENKOHL, L. Prenatal stress reduces fertility and fecundity in female offspring. *Science, 1979, 206*, 1097-1099.

HERTZ, M. M., PAULSON, O. B., BARRY, D. I., et al. Insulin increases transfer across the blood/brain barrier in man. *Journal of Clinical Investigation*, 1981, *67*, 595-604.

HERZOG, D. B. Bulimia in the adolescent. *American Journal of Diseases of Children*, 1982, *136*, 985-989. (b)

HERZOG, D. B. Bulimia: The secretive syndrome. *Psychosomatics*, 1982, *23*, 481-487. (a)

HESS, W. R. Stammgarglien-reizversuche. *Berichte über die Gesamte Physiologie und Experimentelle Pharmakologie*, 1928, *42*, 554.

HESS, W. R., & BRUGGER, M. Das subkortikale zentrum der afektiven abwehrreaktion. *Helvetica Physiologica et Pharmacologia Acta*, 1943, *1*, 33-52.

HINDE, R. A., & STEVENSON-HINDE, J. (Eds.). *Constraints on learning.* New York: Academic Press, 1973.

HINES, M., ALLEN, L. S., & GORSKI, R. A. Sex differences in subregions of the medial nucleus of the amygdala and the bed nucleus of the stia terminalis of the rat. *Brain Research*, *579*, 321-326.

HINES, M., ALSUM, P., ROY, M. et al. Estrogenic contribution to sexual differentiation in the female guinea pig: Influences of diethylstibestrol and tamoxifen on neural, behavior and ovarian development. *Hormones and Behavior*, 1987, *21*, 402-417.

HINES, M., CHIU, L., MCADAMS, L. A., BENTLER, P. M., & LIPCAMON, J. Cognition and the corpus callosum: Verbal fluency, visuospatial ability, and language lateralization related to midsagittal surface areas of the callosal subregions. *Behavioral Neurosciences*, 1992, *106*, 3-14.

HINES, M., and GREEN, R. Human Hormonal and neural correlated of sex-typed behaviors. *Review of Psychiatry*, 1991, *10*, 536-555.

HINZ, L.D., & WILLIAMSON, D.A. A review of the affective variant hypothesis. *Psychological Bulletin*, 1987, *102*, 150-158.

HIROTO, D. S. Locus of control and learned helplessness. *Journal of Experimental Psychology*, 1974, *102*, 187-193.

HIROTO, D. S., & SELIGMAN, M. E. P. Generality of learned helplessness in man. *Journal of Personality and Social Psychology*, 1975, *31*, 311-327.

HIRSCH, J., KNITTLE, J. L., & SALANS, L. B. Cell lipid content and cell number in obese and nonobese human adipose tissue. *Journal of Clinical Investigation*, 1966, *45*, 1023

HIRSCHMAN, R., & HAWK, G. Emotional responsivity to nonveridical heart rate feedback. *Journal of Research in Personality*, 1978, *12*, 235-242.

HITE, S. *The Hite Report: A Nationwide Survey of Female Sexuality.* New York: Macmillan, 1976.

HOBSON, J. A. *The Dreaming Brain.* New York: Basic Books, 1988.

HOCKEY, G. R. J., DAVIES, S., & GRAY, M. M. Forgetting as a function of sleep at different times of day. *Quarterly Journal of Experimental Psychology*, 1972, *24*, 386-393.

HOFFMAN, M. Homosexual. *Psychology Today*, July 1969, pp. 43-45; 70.

HOFFMAN, M. Homosexuality. In F. A. Beach (Ed.), *Human sexuality in four perspectives.* Baltimore: Johns Hopkins University Press, 1976.

HOFFMAN, M. L. Conscience, personality, and socialization techniques. *Human Development*, 1970b, *13*, 90-126.

HOFFMAN, M. L. *Development of prosocial behavior.* New York: Academic Press, 1982.

HOFFMAN, M. L. Moral development. In P. H. Mussen (Ed.), *Handbook of child psychology* (Vol. 2) (3rd ed.). New York: Wiley, 1970a.

HOKANSON, J. E. Psychophysiological evaluation of the catharsis hypothesis. In E. I. Megargee & J. E. Hokanson (Eds.), *The dynamics of aggression: Individual, group and international analyses.* New York: Harper & Row, 1970.

HOKANSON, J. E., BURGESS, M., & COHEN, M. F. Effects of displaced aggression on systolic blood pressure. *Journal of Abnormal and Social Psychology*, 1963, *67*, 214-218.

HOKANSON, J. E., & BURGESS, M. The effects of status, type of frustration, and aggression on vascular processes. *Journal of Abnormal and Social Psychology*, 1962, *65*, 232-237. (b)

HOKANSON, J. E., & BURGESS, M. The effects of three types of aggression on vascular processes. *Journal of Abnormal and Social Psychology*, 1962, *64*, 446-449. (a)

HOKANSON, J. E., & BUTLER, A. C. Cluster analysis of depressed college students' social behaviors. *Journal of Personality and Social Psychology*, 1992, *62*, 273-280.

HOKANSON, J. E., DEGOOD, D. E., FORREST, M. S., & BRITTAIN, T. M. Availability of avoidance behaviors in modulating vascular-stress responses. *Journal of Personality and Social Psychology*, 1971, *19*, 60-68.

HOKANSON, J. E., & EDELMAN, R. Effects of three social responses on vascular processes. *Journal of Personality and Social Psychology*, 1966, *3*, 442-447.

HOKANSON, J. E., & SHETLER, S. The effect of overt aggression on physiological arousal. *Journal of Abnormal and Social Psychology*, 1961, *63*, 446-448.

HOKANSON, J. E., WILLERS, K. R., & KOROPSAK, E. The modification of autonomic responses during aggressive interchange. *Journal of Personality*, 1968, *36*, 386-404.

HOLLON, S. D., DERUBEIS, R. J., & EVANS, M. D. Combined cognitive therapy and pharmacology in the treatment of depression. In D. Manning and A. Francis (Eds.), *Combination Drug and Psychotherapy in Depression*. Washington D. C.: American Psychiatric Press, 1978.

HOLMES, D. S. Effects of overt aggression on level of physiological arousal. *Journal of Personality and Social Psychology*, 1966, *4*, 189-194.

HOLMES, D. S. Meditation and somatic arousal reduction. *American Psychologist*, 1984, *39*, 1-10.

HOOKER, E. The adjustment of the male overt homosexual. *Journal of Projective Techniques*, 1957, *21*, 18-31.

HOON, P. W., WINCZE, J. P., & HOON, E. F. A test of reciprocal inhibition: Are anxiety and sexual arousal in women mutually inhibitory? *Journal of Abnormal Psychology*, 1977, *86*, 65-74.

HOPSON, J. A pleasure chemistry. *Psychology Today*, July/Aug, 28-33, 1988.

HOPSON, J. L. Boys will be boys, girls will be... *Psychology Today*, August 1987, pp. 60-66.

HOROWITZ, M. J. Psychological response to serious life events. In V. Hamilton & D. Warburton (Eds.), *Human stress and cognition: An information processing approach*. New York: Wiley, 1979.

HOROWITZ, M. J. *Stress response syndromes*. New York: Jacob Aronson, 1976.

HOTH, C. C., REYNOLDS, C. F., HOUCK, P. R., HALL, F., et al. Predicting mortality in mixed depression and dementia using EEG sleep variables. *Journal of Neuropsychiatry and Clinical Neurosciences*, 1989, *14*, 366-371.

HOWLEY, E. T. The effect of different intensities of exercise on the excretion of epinephrine and norepinephrine. *Medicine and Science in Sports*, 1976, *8*, 219-222.

HOYENGA, K. B., & HOYENGA, K. T. *The question of sex differences: Psychological, cultural, and biological issues*. Boston: Little, Brown, 1979.

HOYT, M. F., & SINGER, J. L. Psychological effects of REM (``dream'') deprivation upon waking mentation. In A. M. Arkin, J. S. Antrobus, and S. J. Ellman (Eds.). *The mind in sleep: Psychology and psychophysiology*. Hillsdale, N.J.: Erlbaum, 1978.

HUBA, G. J., NEWCOMB, M. D., & BENTLER, P. M. Comparison of canonical correlation and interbattery factor analysis on sensation seeking and drug use domains. *Applied Psychological Measurement*, 1981, *5*, 291-306.

HUBEL, D. H. The visual cortex of normal and deprived monkeys. *American Scientist*, 1979, *67*, 532-543.

HUBEL, D. H., & WIESEL, T. N. Brain mechanisms of vision. *Scientific American*, September 1979, pp. 150-162.

HULL, C. L. *Principles of behavior*. New York: Appleton-Century-Crofts, 1943.

HULL, J. G., & BOND, C. F. Social and behavioral consequences of alcohol consumption and expectancy: A meta-analysis. *Psychological Bulletin*, 1986, *99*, 347-360.

HULL, J. G., VAN TREUREN, R. R., & VIRNELLI, S. Hardiness and health: A critique and alternative approach. *Journal of Personality and Social Psychology*, 1987, *53*, 518-530.

HUTT, C. Exploration and play in children. In P. A. Jewell & C. Loizos (Eds.), *Play, exploration, and territory in mammals*. Symposia of the Zoological Society of London, No. 18. New York: Academic Press, 1966.

HUXLEY, J. S. *Evolution: The modern synthesis*. London: Allen & Unwin, 1942.

HYDE, J. S. Gender differences in aggression. In J. S Hyde & M. C. Linn (Eds.), *The Psychology of Gender: Advances Through Meta-Analysis* (pp. 51-66). Baltimore: Johns Hopkins University Press, 1986.

HYDE, J. S., FENNEMA, E., & LAMON, S. J. Gender differences in mathematics performance: A meta-analysis. *Psychological Bulletin*, 1990, *107*, 139-155.

HYDE, J. S., & LINN, M. Gender differences in ability: A meta-analysis. *Psychological Bulletin*, 1988, *104*, 53-69.

IMPERATO-MCGINLEY, J., GUERRERO, L., GAUTIER, T., et al. Steroid 5 alpha reductase deficiency in man: An inherited form of male pseudo-hermaphorditism. *Science*, 1974, *186*, 1213-1215.

ISEN, A. M., DAUBMAN, K. A., & NOWICKI, G. P. Positive affect facilitates creative problem solving. *Journal of Personality and Social Psychology*, 1987, *52*, 1122-1131.

ISRAEL, N. R. Leveling-sharpening and anticipatory cardiac response. *Psychosomatic Medicine*, 1969, *31*, 499-509.

IVEY, M. E., & BARDWICK, J. M. Patterns of affective fluctuation in the menstrual cycle. *Psychosomatic Medicine*, 1968, *30*, 336-345.

IZARD, C. E. Facial expressions and the regulation of emotions. *Journal of Personality and Social Psychology*, 1990, *58*, 487-498.

IZARD, C. E. *Human emotions*. New York: Plenum, 1977.

IZARD, C. E., &. TOMKINS, S. S. Affect and behavior: Anxiety as negative affect. In C. D. Spielberger (Ed.), *Anxiety and behavior*. New York: Academic Press, 1966.

JACOBS, B. L. How hallucinogenic drugs work. *American Scientist*, 1987, *75*, 386-392.

JACOBS, B. L., & TRULSON, M. E. Mechanisms of action of LSD. *American Scientist*, 1979, *67*, 396-404.

JACOBSON, R. C., & ZINBERG, N. E. *The social basis of drug prevention*. Publication SS-5. Washington, D.C.: Drug Abuse Council, 1975.

JAFFE, J. H., & MARTIN, W. R. Opiod Analgesics and Antagonists. In A. G. GILMAN, T. W. RALL, A. S. NIES, & P. TAYLOR (Eds.) *Goodman and Gilman's The Pharmacological Basis of Therapeutics* (pp. 485-521). New York: Pergamon Press, 1990.

JAKOBOVITS, C., HALSTEAD, P., KELLY, L., ROE, D., & YOUNG, C. Eating habits and nutrient intake of college women over a thirty year period. *Journal of the American Dietic Association*, 1977, *71*, 405-411.

JAMES, W. The Principles of Psychology. New York: Holt, 1890.

JAMES, W. What is an emotion? *Mind*, 1884, *9*, 188-205.

JASPER, H. H. Electroencephalography. In W. Penfield & T. C. Erickson (Eds.), *Epilepsy and cerebral localization*. Springfield, Ill.: Charles C Thomas, 1941.

JEFFREY, D. B., & KATZ, R. G. *Take it off and keep it off*. Englewood Cliffs, N.J.: Prentice-Hall, 1977.

JESSOR, R. Marijuana: A review of recent psychosocial research. In R. L. Dupont, A. Goldstein, and J. O'Donnell (Eds.), *Handbook on drug abuse*. Rockville, Md.: National Institute on Drug Abuse, 1979.

JEVNING, R., WILSON, A. F., & DAVIDSON, J. M. Adrenocortical activity during meditation. *Hormones and Behavior*, 1978, *10*, 54-60.

JOHNSON, E. H., SPIELBERGER, C. D., WORDEN, T. J., & JACOBS, G. A. Emotional and familial determinants of elevated blood pressure in black and white adolescent males. *Journal of Psychosomatic Research*, 1987, *31*, 287-300.

JOHNSON, J. H., & SARASON, I. G. Life stress, depression, and anxiety: Internal-external control as a moderator variable. *Journal of Psychosomatic Research*, 1978, *22*, 205-208.

JOHNSON, J. H., & SARASON, I. G. Moderator variables in life stress research. In I. Sarason and C. Spielberger (Eds.), *Stress and anxiety* (Vol. 6, pp. 151-167). New York: Halstead, 1979.

JOSEPHS, R. A., LARRICK, R. P., STEELE, C. M., & NISBETT, R. E. Protecting the self from the negative consequences of risky decisions. *Journal of Personality and Social Psychology*: 1992, *62*, 26-37.

Journal of Abnormal Psychology. *Special Issue: Models of Addiction*, 1988, *97*, 115-245.

JOUVET, M. The states of sleep. *Scientific American,* February 1967, pp. 62-72.

JOYCE, C. R. B. Cannabis. *British Journal of Hospital Medicine,* 1970, *4,* 162-166.

JULIEN, R. M. *A primer of drug action.* San Francisco:W. H. Freeman, 1975.

JURASKA, J. M., & KOPCIK, J. R. Sex and environmental influences on the size and ultrastructure of the rat corpus callosum. *Brain Research,* 1988, *450,* 1-8.

KAGAN, J. Temperamental contributions to social behavior. *American Psychologist,* 1989, *44,* 668-674.

KAGAN, J. *Establishing a morality: The nature of the child.* New York: Basic Books, 1984.

KAHA, C. W. The creative mind: Form and process. *Journal of Creative Behavior,* 1983, *17,* 84-94.

KAHN, R. L. Stress: From 9 to 5. *Psychology Today,* September 1969, pp. 34-38.

KAHN, R. L., WOLFE, D. M., QUINN, R. P., SNOEK, J. D., & ROSENTHAL, R. A. *Organizational stress: Studies in role conflict and ambiguity.* New York: Wiley, 1964.

KAHNEMAN, D. *Attention and effort.* Englewood Cliffs, N.J.: Prentice-Hall, 1973.

KALANT, O. J. *The amphetamines: Toxicity and addiction* (2nd ed.). Toronto: University of Toronto Press, 1973.

KALES, A., BIXLER, E. O., SOLDATOS, C. R., VELA-BUENO, A., CALDWELL, A. B., & CADIEUX, R. J. Role of sleep apnea and nocturnal myoclonus. *Psychosomatics,* 1982, *23,* 589-595, 600.

KALLMANN, F. J. A. A comparative twin study on the genetic aspects of male homosexuality. *Journal of Nervous and Mental Disease,* 1952, *115,* 283-298.

KANDEL, D. B. Marijuana users in young adulthood. *Archives of General Psychiatry,* 1984, *41,* 200-209.

KANDEL, D. B., KESSLER, R. C., & MARGULIES, R. Z. Antecedents of adolescent initiation into stages of drug use: A developmental analysis. In D. B. Kandel (Ed.), *Longitudinal research on drug abuse.* Washington, D.C.: Hemisphere, 1978.

KANFER, F. H. Personal control, social control, and altruism. *American Psychologist,* 1979, *34,* 231-239.

KAPLAN, R. M. Behavior as the central outcome in health care. *American Psychologist,* 1990, *45,* 1211-1220.

KARLI, P., & VERGNES, M. Rôle des différentes composantes du complexe nucléaire amygdalien dans la facilitation de l'aggressivité interspécifique du rat. *Comptes Rendus des Séances de la Société Biologie,* 1965, *159,* 754.

KATZ, J. Hormonal abnormality found in patients with anorexia nervosa. *Journal of the American Medical Association,* 1975, *232,* 9-11.

KATZ, J. L. Testimony to Maryland Governor's Prescription Drug Commission, 1990.

KATZ, L., & EPSTEIN, S. Constructive thinking and coping with laboratory-induced stress. *Journal of Personality and Social Psychology,* 1991, *61,* 789-800.

KAVANAUGH, D.J., & BOWER, G. H. Mood and self-efficacy: Impact of job and sadness on perceived capabilities. *Cognitive Therapy and Research,* 1985, *9,* 507-525.

KAZDIN, A. E. *History of behavior modification: Experimental foundations of contemporary research.* Baltimore: University Park Press, 1978.

KEESEY, R. E., & POWLEY, T. L. Hypothalamic regulation of body weight. *American Scientist,* 1975, *63,* 558-565.

KEINAN, G. Decision making under stress: Scanning of alternative under controllable and uncontrollable treats. *Journal of Personality and Social Psychology,* 1987, *52,* 639-644.

KELLER, M. The great Jewish drink mystery. *British Journal of Addiction,* 1970, *64,* 287-295.

KELLY, J. A., & WORRELL, L. Parent behaviors related to masculine, feminine, and androgynous sex role orientations. *Journal of Consulting and Clinical Psychology,* 1976, *44,* 843-851.

KEMLER, D., & SHEPP, B. The learning and transfer of dimensional relevance and irrelevance in children. *Journal of Experimental Psychology,* 1971, *90,* 120-127.

KENDALL, P. C., LEARNER, R. M., & CRAIGHEAD, W. E. Human development and intervention in childhood psychotherapy. *Child Development,* 1984, *55,* 71-82.

KENDLER, K. S., HEATH, A., MARTIN, N. G., & EAVES, L. J. Symptoms of anxiety and depression in a volunteer population. *Archives of General Psychiatry,* 1986, *43,* 213-221.

KENT, G. Self-efficacious control lover reported physiological, cognitive and behavioural symptoms of anxiety. *Behaviour Research and Therapy,* 1987, *25,* 341-347.

KERNIS, M. H., BROCKNER, J., & FRANKEL, B. S. Self-esteem and reactions to failure: The mediating role of overgeneralization. *Journal of Personality and Social Psychology,* 1989, *57,* 707-714.

KERNIS, M. H., GANNEMANN, B. D., & BARCLAY, L. C. *Journal of Personality and Social Psychology,* 1989, *56,* 1013-1022.

KESSLER, S., & MOOS, R. H. The XYY karyotype and criminality: A review. *Journal of Psychiatric Research,* 1970, *7,* 153-170.

KEYS, A. B., BROZEK, J., HENSCHEL, A., MICHELSEN, O., & TAYLOR, H. L. *The biology of human starvation.* Minneapolis: University of Minnesota Press, 1950.

KIESLER, C. A., & PALLAK, M. S. Arousal properties of dissonance manipulations. *Psychological Bulletin,* 1976, *83,* 1014-1025.

KIMURA, D. Sex differences in the brain. *Scientific American,* 1992, *267,* 118-125.

KINSEY, A. C., POMEROY, W. B., & MARTIN, C. E. *Sexual behavior in the human female.* Philadelphia: Saunders, 1953.

KINSEY, A. C., POMEROY, W. B., & MARTIN, C. E. *Sexual behavior in the human male.* Philadelphia: Saunders, 1948.

KIRSCH, I. Response expectancy as a determinant of experience and behavior. *American Psychologist,* 1985, *40,* 1189-1202.

KLAUSNER, S. Z., FOULKES, E. F., & MOORE, M. H. *The Inupiat: Economics and alcohol on the Alaskan North Slope.* Philadelphia: Center for Research on the Acts of Man, University of Pennsylvania, 1980.

KLÜVER, H., & BUCY, P. C. An analysis of certain effects of bilateral temporal lobectomy in the rhesus monkey with special reference to "psychic blindness." *Journal of Psychology,* 1938, *5,* 33-54.

KLÜVER, H., & BUCY, P. C. Preliminary analysis of the function of the temporal lobe in monkeys. *Archives of Neurology and Psychiatry,* 1939, *42,* 979-1000.

KLECK, R. E., & RUBENSTEIN, C. Physical attractiveness, perceived attitude similarity, and interpersonal attraction in an opposite-sex encounter. *Journal of Personality and Social Psychology,* 1975, *31,* 107-114.

KLEIN, R., & ARMITAGE, R. Rhythms in human performance: 1½ hour oscillation in cognitive style. *Science,* 1979, *204,* 1326-1328.

KLEIN, R. F., BOGDONOFF, M. D., ESTES, E. H., JR., & SHAW, D. M. Analysis of the factors affecting the resting FAA level in normal man. *Circulation,* 1960, *20,* 772.

KLEINGINNA, P. R., JR., & KLEINGINNA, A. M. A categorized list of motivation definitions, with suggestions for a consensual definition. *Motivation and Emotion,* 1981, *5,* 263-291. (a)

KLEINGINNA, P. R., JR., & KLEINGINNA, A. M. A categorized list of emotion definitions, with suggestions for a consensual definition. *Motivation and Emotion,* 1981, *5,* 345-379. (b)

KLESGES, R.C, MEYERS, A.W., KLESGES, L.M. & LAVASQUE, M.E. Smoking, body weight, and their effects on smoking behavior: A comprehensive review of the literature. *Psychological Bulletin,* 106, 204-230.

KNOTT, P. D., LASATER, L., & SHUMAN, R. Aggression-guilt and conditionability for aggressiveness. *Journal of Personality,* 1974, *42,* 332-344.

KOBASA, S. C. Commitment and coping in stress among lawyers. *Journal of Personality and Social Psychology,* 1982, *42,* 707-717.

KOBASA, S. C. Personality and resistance to illness. *American Journal of Community Psychology,* 1979, *7,* 413-423. (b)

KOBASA, S. C. Stressful life events, personality, and health: An inquiry into hardiness. *Journal of Personality and Social Psychology,* 1979, *37,* 1-11. (a)

KOBASA, S. C., MADDI, S. R., & KAHN, S. Hardiness and health: A prospective study. *Journal of Personality and Social Psychology,* 1982, *42,* 168-177.

KOBASA, S. C., & PUCCETTI, M. C. Personality and social resources in stress-resistance. *Journal of Personality and Social Psychology*, 1983, *45*, 839-850.

KOLATA, G. Brain receptors for appetite discovered. *Science*, 1982, *218*, 460-461.

KOLB, L. *Drug addiction, a medical problem*. Springfield, Ill.: Charles C Thomas, 1962.

KONEČNI, V. J. Annoyance, type and duration of postannoyance activity, and aggression: The cathartic effect. *Journal of Experimental Psychology: General*, 1975, *104*, 76-102. (a)

KOOP, C. E. Report of the Surgeon General's Workshop on pornography and public health. *American Psychologist*, 1987, *42*, 944-945.

KOOPMANS, H. S. Satiety signals from the gastrointestinal tract. *American Journal of Clinical Nutrition*, 1985, *42*, 1044-1049.

KORIDZE, M. G., & NEMSADZE, N. D. Effect of deprivation of paradoxical sleep on the formation and differentiation of conditioned reflexes. *Neuroscience and Behavioral Physiology*, 1983, *82*, 369-373.

KOULACK, D., PREVOST, F., & DE KONINCK, J. Sleep, dreaming, and adaptation to a stressful intellectual activity. *Sleep*, 1985, *8*, 244-253.

KOVACS, M., RUSH, A. J., BECK, A. T., & HOLLON, S. D. Depressed outpatients treated with cognitive therapy or pharmacotherapy. *Archives of Psychiatry*, 1981, *38*, 33-39.

KRAINES, S. H. *Mental depressives and their treatment*. New York: Macmillan, 1957.

KRAMER, M., CZAYA, J., ARAND, D., & ROTH, T. *The development of psychological content across the REMP*. Paper presented at the meeting of the Association for the Psychophysiological Study of Sleep, Jackson Hole, Wyo., 1974.

KRAMER, S. & WILLIAMS, L. Health: Forget about losing those last five kilos. *Time Magazine*, July 8, 1991, pp. 40-41.

KRANTZ, D. S., & SCHULZ, R. A model of life crisis, control, and health outcomes: Cardiac rehabilitation and relocation of the elderly. In A. Baum & J. E. Singer (Eds.), *Advances in environmental psychology (Vol. 2: Applications of personal control.)* Hillsdale, N.J.: Erlbaum, 1980.

KRAUT, R. Two components of happiness. *Philosophical Review*, 1979, *87*, 167-196.

KREUZ, L. E., & ROSE, R. M. Assessment of aggressive behavior and plasma testosterone in a young criminal population. *Psychosomatic Medicine*, 1972, *34*, 321-332.

KUHL, J. Motivational and functional helplessness: The moderating effect of state versus action-orientation. *Journal of Personality and Social Psychology*, 1981, *40*, 155-170.

KUHN, D. Z., MADSEN, C. H., & BECKER. W. C. Effects of exposure to an aggressive model and ``frustration'' on children's aggressive behavior. *Child Development*, 1967, *38*, 739-745.

LA CROIX, A. Z., & HAYNES, S. G. Gender differences in the health place. In R. C. Barnett, L. Biener, and G. K. Baruch (Eds.), *Gender and Stress*. New York: Free Press,1987, pp. 96-121.

LABERGE, S. *Lucid Dreaming*. New York: Ballantine Books, 1985.

LACEY, B. C., & LACEY, J. I. Two-way communication between the heart and the brain: Significance of time within the cardiac cycle. *American Psychologist*, 1978, *33*, 99-113.

LACEY, J. I., KAGAN, J., LACEY, B. C., & MOSS, H. A. The visceral level: Situational determinants and behavioral correlates of autonomic response. In P. Knapp (Ed.), *Expression of the emotions in man*. New York: International Universities Press, 1963.

LACEY, J. I., & LACEY, B. C. Some autonomic-central nervous system interrelationships. In P. Black (Ed.), *Physiological correlates of emotion*. New York: Academic Press, 1970.

LAGERSPETZ, K. Studies on the aggressive behavior of mice. *Annales Academiae Scientiarum Fennicae*, Series B, 1964, *131*, 1-131.

LANG, A. R., SEARLES, J., LAUERMAN, R., & ADESSO, V. Expectancy, alcohol, and sex guilt as determinants of interest in and reaction to sexual stimuli. *Journal of Abnormal Psychology*, 1980, *89*, 644-653.

LANGAN, P. A., & INNES, C. A. *The risk of violent crime* (Bureau of Justice Statistics Special Report, NCJ-97119). Washington, D.C.: U.S. Government Printing Office, 1985.

LANGELLE, C. An assessment of hope in a community sample. Unpublished master's thesis. University of Kansas, Lawrence, 1989.

LANGER, E., & RODIN, J. The effects of enhanced personal responsibility for the aged: A field experiment in an institutionalized setting. *Journal of Personality and Social Psychology*, 1934, 191-198.

LANGER E., & THOMPSON *Mindlessness and self-esteem: The observers perspective*. Harvard University, 1987.

LANGER, E. J. *Mindfulness*. Reading, Massachusetts: Addison Wesley, 1989.

LANGER, E. J., & PARK, K. Incompetence: A conceptual consideration. In R. J. Sternberg and J. Kolligian, Jr., *Competence Considered*. New Haven: Yale University Press, 1990.

LANGLEY, P. W., SIMON, H. A., BRADSHAW, G. F., & ZYTKOW, J. M. *Scientific discovery: computational exploration of the creative process*. Cambridge, MA: MIT Press, 1986.

LARSON, L. A., & MICHELMAN, H. *International guide to fitness and health: A world survey of experiments in science and medicine applied to daily living*. New York: Crown, 1973.

LASAGNA, L., MOSTELLER, F., VON FELSINGER, J. M., & BEECHER, H. K. A study of the placebo response. *American Journal of Medicine*, 1954, *16*, 770-779.

LAUDENSLAGER, M. A., RYAN, S. M., DRUGAN, R. C., HYSON, R. L., & MAIER, S. E. Coping and immunosuppression, inescapable but not escapable shock suppresses lymphocyte proliferation. *Science*, 1983, *221*, 568-570.

LAZARUS, A. A. Behavioral rehearsal vs. non-directive therapy vs. advice in effective behavior change. *Behavior Research and Therapy*, 1966, *4*, 95-97.

LAZARUS, R. S. Cognition and Motivation in Emotion. *American Psychologist*, 1991, *46*, 352-367.

LAZARUS, R. S. The self-regulation of emotion. In L. Levi (Ed.), *Emotions: Their parameters and measurement*. New York: Raven Press, 1975.

LAZARUS, R. S. The stress and coping paradigm. In C. Eisdorfer, D. Cohen, A. Kleinman, & P. Maxim (Eds.), *Models for clinical psychopathology* (pp. 177-214). New York: Spectrum, 1981.

LAZARUS, R. S., & FOLKMAN, S. *Stress, appraisal, and coping*. New York: Springer, 1984.

LAZARUS, R. S., & LAUNIER, R. Stress-related transactions between person and environment. In L. A. Pervin & M. Lewis (Eds.), *Perspectives in interactional psychology*. New York: Plenum, 1978.

LEARNER, R. M. Children and adolescents as producers of their own development. *Developmental Review*, 1982, *2*, 342-370.

LEDWIDGE, B. Run for your mind: Aerobic exercise as a means of alleviating anxiety and depression. *Canadian Journal of Behavioural Science*, 1980, *12*, 126-140.

LEFCOURT, H. M., MARTIN, R. A., & SALEH, W. E. Locus of control and social support: Interactive moderator of stress. *Journal of Personality and Social Psychology*, 1984, *47*, 378-389.

LEFCOURT, H. M., MILLER, R. S., WARE, E. E., & SHERK, D. Locus of control as a modifier of the relationship between stressors and moods. *Journal of Personality and Social Psychology*, 1981, *41*, 357-369.

LEGGETT, E. *Children's entity and incremental theories of intelligence: Relationships to achievement behavior*. Paper presented at meeting of Eastern Psychological Association, Boston, March 1985.

LEHMAN, H. C. The most creative years of engineers and other technologists. *Journal of Genetic Psychology*, 1966, *108*, 263-270.

LEON, G. R. Current directions in the treatment of obesity. *Psychological Bulletin*, 1976, *83*, 557-578.

LEPPER, M. R., & GREENE, D. Turning play into work: Effects of adult surveillance and extrinsic rewards on children's intrinsic motivation. *Journal of Personality and Social Psychology*, 1975, *31*, 479-486.

LEPPER, M. R., GREENE, D., & NISBETT, R. E. Undermining children's intrinsic interest with extrinsic reward: A test of the ``overjustification'' hypothesis. *Journal of Personality and Social Psychology*, 1973, *28*, 129-137.

LERNER, M. J. The desire for justice and reactions to victims. In J. Macaulay & L. Berkowitz (Eds.), *Altruism and helping behavior*. New York: Academic Press, 1970.

LERNER, M. J. The justice motive: Some hypotheses as to its origin and forms. *Journal of Personality*, 1977, *45*, 1-52.

LERNER, M. J., & MILLER, D. T. Just world research and the attribution process: Looking back and ahead. *Psychological Bulletin*, 1978, *85*, 1030-1051.

LERNER, M. J., & SIMMONS, C. H. Observers' reaction to the ``innocent victim'': Compassion or rejection? *Journal of Personality and Social Psychology*, 1966, *4*, 203-210.

LERNER, R. M. *On the nature of human plasticity*. New York: Cambridge Press, 1984.

LESTER, J. T. Stress: On Mount Everest. *Psychology Today*, September 1969, pp. 30-32; 62.

LEVAY, S. A difference in hypothalamic structure between heterosexual and homosexual men. *Science*, 1991, *253*, 1034-1037.

LEVENSON, R. W., & RUEF, A. M. Empathy: A physiological substrate. *Journal of Personality and Social Psychology*, 1992, *63*, 234-246.

LEVINSON, D. J. *The seasons of a man's life*. New York: Ballantine, 1978.

LEVINE, S. Stimulation in infancy. *Scientific American*, May 1960, pp. 80-86.

LEVINE, S. Stress and behavior. *Scientific American*, January 1971, pp. 26-31.

LEVY, J. Lateral differences in the human brain in cognition and behavioral control. In P. Buser (Ed.), *Cerebral correlates of conscious experience*. New York: North-Holland, 1978.

LEWIN, I., & GLAUBMAN, H. The effect of REM deprivation: Is it detrimental, beneficial, or neutral? *Psychophysiology*, 1975, *12*, 349-353.

LIEBERMAN, P. *The Biology and Evolution of Language*. Cambridge, MA: Harvard University Press.

LIEBHART, E. H. Effects of false heart rate feedback and task instructions on information search, attributions, and stimulus ratings. *Psychological Research*, 1977, *39*, 185-202.

LIND, S. K., & MUMFORD, M. D. *Values as predictor of job performance and advancement potential*. Paper presented at the meetings of the Southeastern Psychological Association, Atlanta, Georgia, March, 1987.

LINDSLEY, D. B. Attention, consciousness, sleep, and wakefulness. In J. Field (Ed.), *Handbook of physiology: Neurophysiology* (Vol. 3). Baltimore: Williams & Wilkins, 1960.

LINDSLEY, D. B. Psychological phenomena and the electroencephalogram. *Electroencephalography and Clinical Neurophysiology*, 1952, *4*, 443-456.

LINDSLEY, D. B., & HENRY, C. E. The effect of drugs on behavior and the electroencephalograms of children with behavior disorders. *Psychosomatic Medicine*, 1942, *4*, 140-149.

LINSENMEIER, J. A. W., & BRICKMAN, P. Advantages of difficult tasks. *Journal of Personality*, 1978, *46*, 96-112.

LINVILLE, P. W. Self-complexity as a cognitive buffer against stress-related illness and depression. *Journal of Personality and Social Psychology*, 1987, *52*, 663-676.

LINZ, D., DONNERSTEIN, E., & PENROD, S. The findings and the recommendations of the Attorney General's Commission on Pornography. *American Psychologist*, 1987, *42*, 946-953.

LLOYD, C. W. Problems associated with the menstrual cycle. In C. W. Lloyd (Ed.), *Human reproduction and sexual behavior*. Philadelphia: Lea & Febiger, 1964.

LLOYD, R. W., JR., & SALZBERG, H. C. Controlled social drinking: An alternative to abstinence as a treatment goal for some alcohol abusers. *Psychological Bulletin*, 1975, *82*, 815-842.

LOCKE, E. A., & LATHAM, G. P. *A Theory of Goal Setting and Task Performance*. Englewood Cliffs, N.J.: Prentice Hall, 1990.

LONG, G. T., & LERNER, M. J. Deserving, the ``personal contract'' and altruistic behavior by children. *Journal of Personality and Social Psychology*, 1974, *29*, 551-556.

LOO, C. M. The effects of spatial density on the social behavior of children. *Journal of Applied Social Psychology*, 1972, *2*, 372-381.

LORE, R. K., & SCHULTZ, L. A. Control of human aggression. *American Psychologist*, 1993, *48*, 16-25.

LORENZ, K. *On Aggression*. N.Y.: Harcourt Brace Jovanovich, 1966.

LORENZ, K. Z. *On aggression*. London: Methuen, 1966.

LORENZ, K. Z. Innate bases of learning. In K. H. Pribram (Ed.), *On the biology of learning*. New York: Harcourt, Brace & World, 1969.

LORO, A. D., & ORLEANS, C. S. Binge eating in society: Preliminary findings and guidelines for behavioral analysis and treatment. *Addictive Behaviors*, 1981, *6*, 155-166.

LOVEJOY, C. O. The origin of man. *Science*, 1981, *211*, 341-350.

LOWELL, E. L. The effect of need for achievement on learning and spread of performance. *Journal of Psychology*, 1952, *33*, 31-40.

LOWTHER, W. Marriage running down. *Maclean's*, August 6, 1979, p. 43.

LUCKHARDT, A. B., & CARLSON, A. J. Contributions to the physiology of the stomach: XVII. On the chemical control of the gastric hunger mechanism. *American Journal of Physiology*, 1915, *36*, 37-46.

LUNDBERG, O., & WALINDER, J. Anorexia nervosa and signs of brain damage. *International Journal of Neuropsychiatry*, 1967, *3*, 167-173.

LUNDBERG, U., & FRANKENHAEUSER, M. Psychophysiological reactions to noise as modified by personal control over noise intensity. *Biological Psychology*, 1978, *6*, 51-59.

LYNN, R. *Attention, arousal, and the orientation reaction*. Oxford: Pergamon Press, 1966.

MACANDREW, C., & EDGERTON, R. B. *Drunken comportment: A social explanation*. London: Nelson, 1970.

MACCOBY, E. E., & JACKLIN, C. N. *The psychology of sex differences*. Stanford: Stanford University Press, 1974.

MACKINNON, D. W. The nature and nurture of creative talent. *American Psychologist*, 1962, *17*, 484-495.

MACKWORTH, N. H. The breakdown of vigilance during prolonged visual search. *Quarterly Journal of Experimental Psychology*, 1948, *1*, 6-21.

MACLEAN, P. D. Sensory and perceptive factors in emotional functions of the triune brain. In L. Levi (Ed.), *Emotions: Their parameters and measurement*. New York: Raven Press, 1975.

MACON, D. A. (1987, March). *Age, climate and personality as predictors of scientific productivity*. Paper presented at the meeting of the Southern Psychological Association, Atlanta, Georgia.

MAEHR, M. L., & STALLINGS, W. M. Freedom from external evaluation. *Child Development*, 1972, *43*, 177-185.

MAHONE, C. H. Fear of failure and unrealistic vocational aspiration. *Journal of Abnormal and Social Psychology*, 1960, *60*, 253-261.

MAHONEY, M. J., & MAHONEY, K. *Permanent weight control*. New York: W. W. Norton, 1976.

MAIER, S. F. Failure to escape traumatic shock: Incompatible skeletal motor responses or learned helplessness? *Learning and Motivation*, 1970, *1*, 157-170.

MAIER, S. F., & LAUDENSLAGER, M. Stress and health: Exploring the links. *Psychology Today*, 1985, *19*, 44-49.

MAIER, S. F., LAUDENSLAGER, M., & RYAN, S. M. Stressor controllability, immune function, and endogenous opiates. In F. R. Brush and J. B. Overmier (Eds.), *Affect, Conditioning, and Cognition: Essays on the Determinants of Behavior*. Hillsdale, N.J.: Erlbaum, 1985.

MAIER, S. F., SELIGMAN, M. E. P., & SOLOMON, R. L. Pavlovian fear conditioning and learned helplessness. In B. A. Campbell & R. M. Church (Eds.), *Punishment*. New York: Appleton-Century-Crofts, 1969.

MALAMUTH, N. M., & DONNERSTEIN, E. *Pornography and sexual aggression*. New York: Academic Press, 1984.

MALTZMAN, I. Orienting reflexes and significance: A reply to O'Gorman. *Psychophysiology*, 1979, *16*, 274-282.

MANDERLINK, G., & HARACKIEWICZ, J. M. Proximal versus distal goal setting and intrinsic motivation. *Journal of Personality and Social Psychology*, 1984, *47*, 918-928.

MANDLER, G., & COHEN, J. E. Test anxiety questionnaires. *Journal of Consulting Psychology*, 1958, *22*, 228-229.

MANDLER, G., & SARASON, S. B. A study of anxiety and learning. *Journal of Abnormal and Social Psychology*, 1952, *47*, 166-173.

MARANTO, G. Coke: The random killer. *Discover*, March 1985, 16-21.

MARGULES, D. L. Beta-endorphin and endoloxone: Hormones of the autonomic nervous system for the conservation or expenditure of bodily resources and energy in anticipation of famine or feast. *Neuroscience and Biochemical Reviews*, 1979, *3*, 155-162.

MARGULES, D. L., MOISSET, B., LEWIS, M. J., SHIBUYA, H., & PERT, C. B. Beta-endorphin is associated with overeating in genetically obese mice (ob/ob) and rats (fa/fa). *Science*, 1978, *202*, 988-991.

MARK, V. H., & ERVIN, F. R. *Violence and the brain.* New York: Harper & Row, 1970.

MARKUS, H. On splitting the universe. *Psychological Science,* 1990, *1,* 181-185.

MARKUS, H., CROSS, S., & WURF, E. The role of the self system in competence. In R. J. Sternberg & J. Kolligian, Jr. (Eds.), *Competence Considered.* New Haven: Yale University Press, 1990, pp. 205-225.

MARKUS, H., & NURIUS, P. Possible selves. *American Psychologist,* 1986, *41,* 954-969.

MARKUS, H., & WOLF, E. The dynamic self-concept: A social psychological perspective. *Annual Review of Psychology,* 1987, *38,* 299-337.

MARLER, P. Birdsong and speech development: Could there be parallels? *American Scientist,* 1970, *58,* 669-673.

MARSHALL, G. D., & ZIMBARDO, P. G. Affective consequence of inadequately explaining physiological arousal. *Journal of Personality and Social Psychology,* 1979, *37,* 970-988.

MARSHALL, G. N., & LANG, E. L. Optimism, self mastery, and symptoms of depression in women professionals. *Journal of Personality and Social Psychology,* 1990, *59,* 132-139.

MARSHALL, G. N., WORTMAN, C. B., KUSULAS, J. W., HERVIG, L. K., & VICKERS, R. R. JR. Distinguishing optimism from pessimism: Relations to fundamental dimensions of mood and personality. *Journal of Personality and Social Psychology,* 1992, *62,* 1067-1074.

MARTIN, R. A., & LEFCOURT, H. M. The sense of humor as a moderator of the relation between stressors and moods. *Journal of Personality and Social Psychology,* 1983, *45,* 1313-1324.

MARTINDALE: *The extra pharmacopoeia* (A. Wade & J. E. F. Reynolds, Eds.). London: Pharmaceutical Press, 1977.

MASLACH, C. Negative emotional biasing of unexplained arousal. *Journal of Personality and Social Psychology,* 1979, *37,* 953-969.

MASLOW, A. H. *The farther reaches of human nature.* New York. Viking, 1971.

MASLOW, A. H. *Motivation and personality.* New York: Harper & Row, 1954.

MASLOW, A. H. *Motivation and personality* (2nd ed.). New York: Harper & Row, 1970.

MASLOW, A. H. *New knowledge in human values.* New York: Harper & Row, 1959.

MASLOW, A. H. A theory of human motivation. *Psychological Review,* 1943, *50,* 370-396.

MASON, J. W. Emotions as reflected in patterns of endocrine integration. In L. Levi (Ed.), *Emotions: Their parameters and measurement.* New York: Raven Press, 1975.

MASON, J. W., BRADY, J. V., & TOLSON, W. W. Behavioral adaptations and endocrine activity. In R. Levine (Ed.), *Endocrines and the central nervous system: Proceedings of the Association for Research in Nervous and Mental Diseases.* Baltimore: Williams & Wilkins, 1966.

MASON, J. W., MAHER, J. T., HARTLEY, L. H., MOUGEY, E. H., PERLOW, M. J., & JONES, L. G. Selectivity of corticosteroid and catecholamine responses to various natural stimuli. In G. Serban (Ed.), *Psychopathology of human adaptation.* New York: Plenum, 1976.

MASSERMAN, J. H., & YUM, K. S. An analysis of the influence of alcohol on experimental neuroses in cats. *Psychosomatic Medicine,* 1946, *8,* 36-52.

MASTERS, W. H., & JOHNSON, V. E. *Homosexuality in perspective.* Boston: Little, Brown, 1979.

MASTERS, W. H., & JOHNSON, V. E. *Human sexual inadequacy.* Boston: Little, Brown, 1970.

MASTERS, W. H., & JOHNSON, V. E. *Human sexual response.* Boston: Little, Brown, 1966.

MASTERS, W. H., & JOHNSON, V. E. *The pleasure bond: A new look at sexuality and commitment.* Boston: Little, Brown, 1975.

MATTHEWS, K. A. Coronary heart disease and Type A behaviors: Update on the alternative to the Booth-Kewley and Friedman (1987) quantitative review. *Psychological Bulletin,* 1988, *104,* 373-380.

MATTHEWS, K. A. Psychological perspectives on the Type A behavior pattern. *Psychological Bulletin,* 1982, *91,* 293-320.

MATTHEWS, K. A., & BRUNSON, B. I. Allocation of attention and the Type A coronary-prone behavior pattern. *Journal of Personality and Social Psychology,* 1979, *37,* 2081-2090.

MATTHEWS, K. A., GLASS, D. C., ROSENMAN, R. H., & BORTNER, R. W. Competitive drive, pattern A, and coronary heart disease: A further analysis of some data from the Western Collaborative Group Study. *Journal of Chronic Disease,* 1977, *30,* 489-498.

MASLOW, A. H. *Motivation and personality* (2nd ed.). New York: Harper & Row, 1970.MASLOW, A. H. *Motivation and personality* (2nd ed.). New York: Harper & Row, 1970.

MAY, R. *The meaning of anxiety.* New York:Norton, 1983.

MAY, R. B. Stimulus selection of preschool children under conditions of free choice. *Perceptual and Motor Skills,* 1963, *16,* 203-206.

MASLOW, A. H. *Motivation and personality* (2nd ed.). New York: Harper & Row, 1970.

MAYER, J. Regulation of energy intake and the body weight: The glucostatic theory and lipostatic hypothesis. *Annals of the New York Academy of Sciences,* 1955, *63,* 15-43.

MAYR, E. Behavior programs and evolutionary strategies. *American Scientist,* 1974, *62,* 650-659.

McARDLE, W. D., KATCH, F. I., & KATCH, V. L. *Exercise Physiology.* Philadelphia: Lea & Febiger, 1991.

McCARTY, D., & KAYE, M. Reasons for drinking: Motivational patterns and alcohol use among college students. *Addictive Behaviors,* 1984, *9,* 185-188.

McCRAE, R. R., & COSTA, P. T., JR. Validation of the five-factor model of personality across instruments and observers. *Journal of Personality and Social Psychology,* 1987, *52,* 81-90

McCLELLAND, D. C. *Human motivation.* Glenview, Ill.: Scott, Foresman, 1985.

McCLELLAND, D. C. Motivational factors in health and disease. *American Psychologist,* 1989, *44,* 675-683.

McCLELLAND, D. C., ATKINSON, J. W., CLARK, R. A., & LOWELL, E. L. *The achievement motive.* New York: Appleton-Century-Crofts, 1953.

McCLELLAND, D. C., DAVIS, W. N., KALIN, R., & WANNER, E. *The drinking man.* New York: Free Press, 1972.

McCLELLAND, D. C., ROSS, G., & PATEL, V. The effect of an academic examination on salivary norepinephrine and immunoglobulin levels. *Journal of Human Stress,* 1985, *11,* 52-59.

McCLELLAND, J. L., & RUMELHART, D. E. *Parallel distributed processing* (Vol. 2). Cambridge MA: MIT Press, 1986.

MCCRAE, R. R. Creativity, Divergent thinking and Openness to Experience. *Journal of Personality and Social Psychology,* 1987, *52,* 1258-1265.

McDOUGALL, W. *An introduction to social psychology* (30th ed.). London: Methuen, 1950. (Originally published, 1908.)

McEWEN, B. S. Neural gonadal steroid actions. *Science,* 1981, *211,* 1303-1311.

McFARLAND, C., ROSS, M., & DE COURVILLE, N. Women's theories of menstruation and biases in recall of menstrual symptoms. *Journal of Personality and Social Psychology,* 1989, *57,* 522-531.

McGRATH, M. J., & COHEN, D. B. REM sleep facilitation of adaptive waking behavior: A review of the literature. *Psychological Bulletin,* 1978, *85,* 24-57.

McGRAW, K. O., & McCULLERS, J. C. The distracting effect of material reward: An alternative explanation for superior performance of reward groups in probability learning. *Journal of Experimental Child Psychology,* 1974, *18,* 149-158.

McGRAW, K. O., & McCULLERS, J. C. *Some detrimental effects of reward on laboratory task performance.* Paper presented at the meeting of the American Psychological Association, Chicago, September 1975.

McGUINNESS, D. *When children don't learn: Understanding the biology and psychology of learning disabilities.* New York: Basic Books, 1985.

McLEARN, G. E. Biological bases of social behavior with particular reference to violent behavior. In D. J. Mulvihill, M. M. Tumin, & L. A. Curtis (Eds.), *Crimes of Violence* (Vol. 13). Staff report submitted to the National Commission on the Causes and Prevention of Violence. Washington, D. C.: Government Printing Office, 1969.

McPARTLAND, R. J., & KUPFER, D. J. Rapid eye movement sleep cycle, clock time, and sleep onset. *Electroencephalography and Clinical Neurophysiology*, 1978, *45*, 178-185.

MECKLENBURG, R. S., LORIAUX, D. L., THOMPSON, R. H., ANDERSON, A. E., & LIPSETT, M. B. Hypothalamic dysfunction in patients with anorexia nervosa. *Medicine*, 1974, *53*, 147-159.

MEICHENBAUM, D. H. *Cognitive-behavior modification: An integrative approach*. New York: Plenum Press, 1977.

MEYER, L. B. *Emotion and Meaning in Music*. Chicago: University of Chicago Press, 1961.

MEYER, W. U. Indirect communications about perceived ability estimates. *Journal of Educational Psychology*, 1982, *74*, 888-897.

MEYER-BAHLBURG, H. F. Sex hormones and male homosexuality in comparative perspective. *Archives of Sexual Behavior*, 1977, *6*, 297-325.

MEYER-BAHLBURG, H. F. L., & EHRHARDT, A. A. Prenatal sex hormones and human aggression: A review, and new data on progestogen effects. *Aggressive Behavior*, 1982, *8*, 39-62.

MEYERS, W. U. Indirect communications about perceived ability estimates. *Journal of Educational Psychology*, 1982, *74*, 888-897.

MILGRAM, S. Behavioral study of obedience. *Journal of Abnormal and Social Psychology*, 1963, *67*, 371-378.

MILGRAM, S. *Obedience to authority*. New York: Harper & Row, 1974.

MILLER, D. G., GROSSMAN, Z. D., RICHARDSON, R. L., WISTOW, B. W., & THOMAS, F. D. Effect of signaled versus unsignaled stress on rat myocardium. *Psychosomatic Medicine*, 1978, *40*, 432-434.

MILLER, D. T. Ego involvement and attributions for success and failure. *Journal of Personality and Social Psychology*, 1976, *34*, 901-906.

MILLER, D. T. Personal deserving versus justice for others: An exploration of the justice motive. *Journal of Experimental Social Psychology*, 1977, *13*, 1-13.

MILLER, G. A. The magical number seven, plus or minus two: Some limits on our capacity for processing information. *Psychological Review*, 1956, *63*, 81-97.

MILLER, G. A., GALANTER, E., & PRIBRAM, K. H. *Plans and structure of behavior*. New York: Holt, 1960.

MILLER, I. W., III, & NORMAN, W. H. Learned helplessness in humans: A review and attribution-theory model. *Psychological Bulletin*, 1979, *86*, 93-118.

MILLER, L. B., & ESTES, B. W. Monetary reward and motivation in discrimination learning. *Journal of Experimental Psychology*, 1961, *61*, 501-504.

MILLER, N. E. Effects of learning on physical symptoms produced by psychological stress. In H. Selye (Ed.), *Selye's guide to stress research* (Vol. 1). New York: Van Nostrand Reinhold, 1980.

MILLER, N. E. The frustration-aggression hypothesis. *Psychological Review*, 1941, *48*, 337-342.

MILLER, N. E. Learnable drives and rewards. In S. S. Stevens (Ed.), *Handbook of experimental psychology* (pp. 435-472). New York: Wiley, 1951.

MILLER, N. E. Learning resistance to pain and fear: Effects of overlearning, exposure, and rewarded exposure in context. *Journal of Experimental Psychology*, 1960, *60*, 137-145.

MILLER, P. A., & EISENBERG, N. The relation of empathy to aggressive and externalizing/antisocial behavior. *Psychological Bulletin*, 1988, *103*, 324-344.

MILLER, W. R. Controlled drinking: A history and critical review. *Journal of Studies on Alcohol*, 1983, *44*, 68-83.

MILLER, W.. R., & MUÑOZ, R. F. *How to control your drinking*. Englewood Cliffs, N.J.: Prentice-Hall, 1976.

MILLER, W. R., & SELIGMAN, M. E. P. Depression and learned helplessness in man. *Journal of Abnormal Psychology*, 1975, *84*, 228-238.

MILLS, J. H. Effects of noise on young and old people. In D. M. Lipscomb (Ed.), *Noise and Audiology*. Baltimore: University Park Press, 1978.

MILLS, J. H. Noise and children: A review of literature. *Journal of Acoustical Society of America*, 1975, *58*, 767-779.

MILSTEIN, R. M. Responsiveness in newborn infants of overweight and normal weight parents. *Appetite*, 1980, *1*, 65-74.

MINEKA, S. Animal models of anxiety-based disorders: Their usefulness and limitations. In A. Tuma & J. Maser (Eds.), *Anxiety and anxiety disorders*. (pp. 199-244). Hillsdale, N. J.: Erlbaum, 1985.

MISCHEL, W. Delay of gratification, need for achievement, and acquiescence in another culture. *Journal of Abnormal and Social Psychology*, 1961, *62*, 543-552.

MOISEEVA, N. I. The significance of different sleep states for the regulation of electrical brain activity in man. *Electroencephalography and Clinical Neurophysiology*, 1979, *46*, 371-381.

MOLDOFSKY, H., & GARFINKEL, P. E. Problems of treatment of anorexia nervosa. *Canadian Psychiatric Association Journal*, 1974, *19*, 169-175.

MONEY, J. Propaedeutics of diecious G-I/R: Theoretical foundations for understanding dimorphic gender-identity/role. In Reinisch, J., Rosenblum, L. A., & Sanders, S. A. (Eds.), *Masculinity/femininity: Basic Perspectives* (pp. 13-28). New York: Oxford University Press, 1987.

MONEY, J. Sex hormones and other variables in human eroticism. In W. C. Young (Ed.), *Sex and internal secretions*. Baltimore: Williams & Wilkins, 1961.

MONEY, J. Sin, sickness, or status: Homosexual gender identity and psychoneuroendocrinology. *American Psychologist*, 1987, *42*, 384-399.

MONEY, J. *Venuses penuses: Sexology, sexosophy, and exigency theory*. Buffalo, NY: Prometheus, 1986.

MONEY, J., & EHRHARDT, A. A. *Man and woman, boy and girl: The differentiation and dimorphism of gender identity from conception to maturity*. Baltimore: Johns Hopkins University Press, 1972.

MONEY, J. , SCHWARTZ , M., & LEWIS, V. Adult erotosexual status and fetal hormonal masculinization and demasculinization: 46 XX congenital virilizing adrenal hyperphasia and 46 XY androgen-insensitivity syndrome compared. *Psychoneuroendocrinology*, 1984, *9*, 203-207.

MOOK, D. G. Oral and postingestional determinants of the intake of various solutions in rats with esophageal fistulas. *Journal of Comparative and Physiological Psychology*, 1963, *56*, 645-659.

MORGAN, E. *The descent of woman*. New York: Stein and Day/Bantam, 1972.

MORGAN, W. P., & HORSTMAN, D. H. Anxiety reduction following acute physical activity. *Medicine and Science in Sports*, 1976, *8*, 62.

MORGANE, P. J., & STERN, W. C. The role of serotonin and norepinephrine in sleep-waking activity. *National Institute on Drug Abuse, Research Monograph Series*, 1975, *No. 3*, 37-61.

MORRIS, D. *The naked ape*. New York: Dell, 1969.

MORRIS, J. L. Propensity for risk taking as a determinant of vocational choice: An extension of the theory of achievement motivation. *Journal of Personality and Social Psychology*, 1966, *3*, 328-335.

MORRISON, A. R. A window on the sleeping brain. *Scientific American*, 1983, *248*, 94-102.

MORSE, D. R., MARTIN, J. S., FURST, M. L., & DUBIN, L. L. A physiological and subjective evaluation of meditation, hypnosis, and relaxation. *Psychosomatic Medicine*, 1977, *39*, 304-324.

MORTON, J. H., ADDITION, H., ADDISON, R. G., HUNT, L., & SULLIVAN, J. J. A clinical study of premenstrual tension. *American Journal of Obstetrics and Gynecology*, 1953, *65*, 1182-1191.

MORUZZI, G., & MAGOUN, H. W. Brain stem reticular formation and activation of the EEG. *Electroencephalography and Clinical Neurophysiology*, 1949, *1*, 455-473.

MOSES, J. M., JOHNSON, L. C., NAITOH, P., & LUBIN, A. Sleep stage deprivation and total sleep loss: Effects on sleep behavior. *Psychophysiology*, 1975, *12*, 141-146.

MOSES, J. M., LUBIN, A., NAITOH, P., & JOHNSON, L. C. Circadian variation in performance, subjective sleepiness, sleep, and oral temperature during an altered sleep-wake schedule. *Biological Psychology*, 1978, *6*, 301-308.

MOSES, J. M., NAITOH, P., & JOHNSON, L. C. The REM cycle in altered sleep/wake schedules. *Psychophysiology*, 1978, *15*, 569-575.

MOSHER, D. L., & ABRAMSON, P. R. Subjective sexual arousal to films of masturbation. *Journal of Consulting and Clinical Psychology*, 1977, *45*, 796-807.

MOSSHOLDER, K. W. Effects of externally mediated goals setting on intrinsic motivation: A laboratory experiment. *Journal of Applied Psychology*, 1980, *65*, 202-210.

MOUNT, G. R., WALTERS, S. R., ROWLAND, R. W., BARNES, P. R., & PAYTON, T. I. The effects of relaxation techniques on normal blood pressure. *Behavioral Engineering*, 1978, *5(1)*, 1-4.

MOWDAY, R. T. Equity theory predictions of behavior in organizations. In R. M. Steers & L. W. Porter (Eds.), *Motivation and work behavior*. New York: McGraw-Hill, 1979.

MOWRER, O. H. A stimulus-response analysis of anxiety and its role as a reinforcing agent. *Psychological Review*, 1939, *46*, 553-565.

MOYER, J. A., HERRENKOHL, L. R., & JACOBWITZ, D. M. Stress during pregnancy: Effects on catecholamines in discrete brain regions of offspring as adults. *Brain Research*, 1978, *144*, 173-178.

MOYER, K. E. *The psychobiology of aggression*. New York: Harper & Row, 1976.

MULLANEY, D. J., JOHNSON, L. C., NAITOH, P., FRIEDMANN, J. K., & GLOBUS, G. G. Sleep during and after gradual sleep reduction. *Psychophysiology*, 1977, *14*, 237-244.

MUMFORD, M. D., & GUSTAFSON, S. B. Creativity syndrome: Integration, Application, and Innovation. *Psychological Bulletin*, 1988, *103*, 27-43.

MUNSINGER, H., & KESSEN, W. Uncertainty, structure, and preference. *Psychological Monographs*, 1964, *78* (9, Whole No. 586).

MURRAY, H. A. *Explorations in personality*. New York: Oxford University Press, 1938.

NACHMAN, M. Learned taste and temperature aversions due to lithium chloride sickness after temporal delays. *Journal of Comparative and Physiological Psychology*, 1970, *73*, 22-30.

NAKAZAWA, Y., KOTORII, M., KOTORII, T., TACHIBANA, H., & NAKANO, T. Individual differences in compensatory rebound of REM sleep with particular reference to their relationship to personality and behavioral characteristics. *Journal of Nervous and Mental Disease*, 1975, *161*, 18-25.

NARABAYASHI, H. Stereotaxic amygdalectomy. In B. Eleftheriou (Ed.), *The neurobiology of the amygdala*. New York: Plenum, 1972.

NASH, S. C. Sex role as a mediator of intellectual functioning. In M. A. Wittag & A. C. Petersen (Eds.), *Sex-related differences in cognitive functioning* (pp. 263-302). New York: Academic Press, 1979.

NATHAN, P. E., & LISMAN, S. A. Behavioral and motivational patterns of chronic alcoholics. In R. E. Tarter & A. A. Sugerman (Eds.), *Alcoholism: Interdisciplinary approaches to an enduring problem*. Reading, Mass.: Addison-Wesley, 1976.

NATIONAL COMMISSION ON THE CAUSES AND PREVENTION OF VIOLENCE. DC: U.S. Government Printing Office Crime, 1970.

NEISS, R. Ending arousal's reign of error: A reply to Anderson. *Psychological Bulletin*, 1990, *107*, 101-105.

NEISS, R. Reconceptualizing arousal: Psychological states in motor performance. *Psychological Bulletin*, 1988, *103*, 345-366.

NEZU, A. M., NEZU, C. M, & BLISSETT, S. E. Sense of humor as a moderator of the relation between stressful events and psychological distress: A prospective analysis. *Journal of Personality and Social Psychology*, 1988, *54*, 520-525.

NIAURA, R. S., ROHSENOW, D. J., BINKOFF, J. A., MONTI, P.M., PEDRAZA, M., & ABRAMS, D. B. Relevance of cue reactivity to understanding alcohol and smoking relapse. *Journal of Abnormal Psychology*, 1988, *97*, 133-153.

NICHOLLS, J. G. The development of the concepts of effort and ability, perception of academic attainment, and the understanding that difficult tasks require more ability. *Child Development*, 1978, *49*, 800-814.

NICHOLLS, J. G. What is ability and why are we mindful of it? A Developmental perspective. In R. J. Sternberg & J. Kolligian, Jr. (Eds.) *Competence Considered*. New Haven: Yale University Press, 1990, pp. 11-40.

NICHOLS, J. R. The children of drug addicts: What do they inherit? *Annals of the New York Academy of Science*, 1972, *197*, 60-65.

NICHOLS, J. R. How opiates change behavior. *Scientific American*, 1965, *212(2)*, 80-88.

NISBETT, R. E. Hunger, obesity, and the ventromedial hypothalamus. *Psychological Review*, 1972, *79*, 433-453.

NISBETT, R. E. Taste, deprivation, and weight determinants of eating behavior. *Journal of Personality and Social Psychology*, 1968, *10*, 107-116.

NISBETT, R. E., & SCHACHTER, S. Cognitive manipulation of pain. *Journal of Experimental Social Psychology*, 1966, *2*, 227-236.

NISHIHARA, K., MORI, K., ENDO, S., OHTA, T., & KENSHIRO, O. Relationship between sleep efficiency and urinary excretions of catecholamines in bed-rested humans. *Sleep*, 1985, *8*, 110-117.

NOLEN-HOEKSEMA, S. *Sex Differences in Depression*. Stanford: Stanford University Press, 1990.

NOLEN-HOEKSEMA, S. Sex differences in depression: Theory and evidence. *Psychological Bulletin*, 1987, *101*, 259-282.

NOTTEBOHM, F., & ARNOLD, A. P. Sexual dimorphism in vocal control areas of the songbird brain. *Science*, 1976, *194*, 211-213.

NOVACO, R. W. Anger and its therapeutic regulation. In M. A. Chesney and R. H. Rosenman (Eds.), *Anger and Hostility in Cardiovascular and Behavioral Disorders*. Washington, D. C.: Hemisphere, pp. 139-147, 1985.

NUTTIN, J. R. *Motivation, planning and action: A relational theory of behavior dynamics*. Hillsdale, N.J.: Erlbaum, 1984.

O'BRIEN, C. P., NACE, E. P., MINTZ, J., MEYERS, A. L., & REAM, N. Follow-up of Vietnam veterans. I. Relapse to drug use after Vietnam service. *Drug and Alcohol Dependence*, 1980, *5*, 333-340.

O'LEARY, A. Stress, emotion, and human immune function. *Psychological Bulletin*, 1990, *108*, 363-382.

O'LEARY, M. R., & DENGERINK, H. A. Aggression as a function of the intensity and pattern of attack. *Journal of Experimental Research in Personality*, 1973, *7*, 61-70.

OLDS, J., & MILNER, P. Positive reinforcement produced by electrical stimulation of the septal area and other regions of the rat brain. *Journal of Comparative and Physiological Psychology*, 1954, *47*, 419-427.

OLWEUS, D., MATTSSON, A., SCHALLING, D., & LOW, H. Testosterone, aggression, physical, and personality dimensions in normal adolescent males. *Psychosomatic Medicine*, 1980, *42*, 253-269.

ONIANI, T. N. Does paradoxical sleep deprivation disturb memory trace consolidation? *Physiology and Behavior*, 1984, *33*, 687-692.

ORNE, M. T., & PASKEWITZ, D. A. Aversive situational effects on alpha feed-back training. *Science*, 1974, *186*, 458-460.

ORNSTEIN, R., & SOBEL, D. The healing brain. *Psychology Today*, March 1987, 48-52.

ORY, M., & GOLDBERG, E. Pet ownership and life satisfaction in elderly women. In A. H. Katcher & A. Beck (Eds.), *New Perspectives on Our Life with Companion Animals* (pp. 803-817). Philadelphia: University of Pennsylvania Press, 1983.

OSBORN, C. A., & POLLACK, R. H. The effects of two types of erotic literature on physiological and verbal measures of female sexual arousal. *Journal of Sex Research*, 1977, *13*, 250-256.

OSTROVE, N. Expectations for success on effort-determined tasks as a function of incentive and performance feedback. *Journal of Personality and Social Psychology*, 1978, *36*, 909-916.

OVERMIER, J. B., & SELIGMAN, M. E. P. Effects of inescapable shock on subsequent escape and avoidance responding. *Journal of Comparative and Physiological Psychology*, 1967, *63*, 28-33.

OWENS, W. A. Cognitive, noncognitive and environmental correlates of mechanical ingenuity. *Journal of Applied Psychology*, 1969, *53*, 199-208.

OZER, E., & BANDURA, A. Mechanisms governing empowerment effects: A self-efficacy analysis. *Journal of Personality and Social Psychology*, 1990, *58*, 472-486.

PADILLA, A. M., PADILLA, C., KETTERER, T., & GIACALONE, D. Inescapable shocks and subsequent escape/avoidance conditioning in goldfish *(Carassius auratus)*. *Psychonomic Science*, 1970, *20*, 295-296.

PANKSEPP, J. The neurochemistry of behavior. *Annual Review of Psychology*, 1986, *37*, 77-107.

PARKER, S. J., & BARRETT, D. E. Maternal Type A behavior during pregnancy, neonatal crying, and early infant temperament: Do Type A women have Type A babies?, *Pediatrics*, 1992, *89*, 474-479.

PARKES, K. R. Locus of control, cognitive appraisal, and coping in stressful episodes. *Journal of Personality and Social Psychology*, 1984, *46*, 655-668.

PARLEE, M. B. The premenstrual syndrome. *Psychological Bulletin*, 1973, *80*, 454-465.

PARMEGGIANI, P. L. Interaction between sleep and thermoregulation. *Waking and Sleeping*, 1977, *1(2)*, 123-132.

PATON, W. D. M., & CROWN, J. (Eds.) *Cannabis and its derivatives: Pharmacology and experimental psychology—Symposium proceedings.* London: Oxford University Press, 1972.

PATTERSON, G. R. Mothers: The Unacknowledged Victims. *Monograph of the Society for Research in Child Development.* no. 45, 1980.

PATTERSON, G. R. The aggressive child: Victim and architect of a coercive system. In E. J. Mash, L. A. Hamerlynck, & L. C. Handy (Eds.), *Behavior modification and families.* New York: Brunner/Mazel, 1976.

PAVLOV, I. P. *Conditioned reflexes* (G. V. Anrep, trans.). New York: Dover, 1927.

PECK, M. S. *The Different Drum: Community Making and Peace.* Simon and Schuster, 1988.

PEELE, S. The cultural context of psychological approaches to alcoholism. *American Psychologist,* 1984, *39,* 1337-1351.

PEELE, S. *Diseasing of America: Addiction Treatment Out of Control.* Lexington, Mass.: Lexington, 1989.

PEELE, S. Love, sex, drugs and other magical solutions to life. *Journal of Psychoactive Drugs,* 1982, *14,* 125-131.

PEELE, S. *The meaning of addiction.* Lexington, Mass.: Lexington Books, 1985.

PEELE, S. Out of the habit trap. *American Health,* September/October 1983, 42-47.

PEELE, S. Redefining addiction. I: Making addiction a scientifically and socially useful concept. *International Journal of Health Services,* 1977, *7,* 103-124.

PEELE, S., & BRODSKY, A. *The truth about addiction and recovery.* New York: Fireside, 1991.

PENDERY, M. L., MALTZMAN, I. M., & WEST, L. J. Controlled drinking by alcoholics?: Findings and a reevaluation of a major affirmative study. *Science,* 1982, *217,* 160-175.

PENNEBAKER, J. W. Confession, inhibition, and disease. In L. Berkowitz (Ed.), *Advances in Experimental Social Psychology* (Vol. 22, pp. 211-244). Orlando, Florida: Academic Press, 1989.

PENNEBAKER, J. W. Inhibition as the linchpin. In H. S. Friedman (Ed.), *Hostility, Coping and Health.* Washington, D. C.: American Psychological Association, 1992, pp. 127-139.

PERLIN, L. I., SCHOOLER, C. The structure of coping. *Journal of Health and Social Behavior,* 1978, *19,* 2-21.

PERSKY, H., SMITH, K. D., & BASU, G. K. Relation of psychologic measures of aggression and hostility to testosterone production in man. *Psychosomatic Medicine,* 1971, *33,* 265-277.

PERVIN, L. A. (Ed.). Goal concepts in personality and social psychology. Hillsdale, N.J.: Erlbaum, 1989.

PETERSEN, A. C., COMPAS, B. E., BROOKS-GUNN, J., STEMMLER, M., EY, S., & GRANT, K. E. Depression in adolescence. *American Psychologist,* 1993, *48,* 155-168.

PETERSEN, S. E., FOX, P. T., POSNER, M. I., MINTUN, M., RAICHLE, M. E. Positron emission tomography studies of the cortical anatomy of single-world processing. *Nature,* 1988, *331,* 585-589.

PETERSEN, C. Explanatory style as a risk factor for illness. *Cognitive Therapy and Research,* 1988, *12,* 117-130.

PETERSEN, C., & SELIGMAN, M. Causal explanations as a risk factor for depression: Theory and evidence. *Psychological Review,* 1984, *91,* 347-374.

PETERSON, C., SELIGMAN, M., & VAILLANT, G. Pessimistic explanatory style as a risk factor for physical illness: A thirty-five-year longitudinal study. *Journal of Personality and Social Psychology,* 1988, *55,* 23-27.

PFAFFMAN, C. The pleasures of sensation. *Psychological Review,* 1960, *67,* 253-268.

PHILLIP, J. D., JR., & BOONE, D. C. Effects of adrenaline supplement on the production of stress induced ulcers in adrenal sympathectomized male rats. *Proceedings of the 76th Annual Convention of the American Psychological Association,* 1968, *3,* 261-262 (Summary).

PIAGET, J. *The origins of intelligence in children.* New York: International Universities Press, 1952.

PIAGET, J. Piaget's theory. In P. H. Mussen (Ed.), *Carmichael's manual of child psychology* (Vol. 1, 3rd ed.). New York: Wiley, 1970.

PIAGET, J., & INHELDER, B. *The psychology of the child.* New York: Basic Books, 1969.

PICKENS, R. Self administration of stimulants by rats. *International Journal of Addiction,* 1968, *3,* 215-221.

PIETROPINTO, A., & SIMENAUER, J. *Beyond the Male Myth: What Women Want to Know About Men's Sexuality.* New York: Times Books, 1977.

PITTS, F. N., JR. The biochemistry of anxiety. *Scientific American,* 1969, *220*(2), 69 75.

PIVIK, T., & FOULKES, D. Dream deprivation: Effects on dream content. *Science,* 1966, *153,* 1282-1284.

PLOTKIN, W. B. Long-term eyes-closed alpha-enhancement training: Effects on alpha amplitudes and on experiential state. *Psychophysiology,* 1978, *15,* 40-52.

POLIVY, J. Perception of calories and regulation of intake in restrained and unrestrained subjects. *Addictive Behavior,* 1976, *1,* 237-243.

POLIVY, J., & HERMAN, C. P. *Breaking the diet habit: The natural weight alternative.* New York: Basic Books, 1983.

POLIVY, J., & HERMAN, C.P. Diagnosis and treatment of normal eating. *Journal of Consulting Psychology,* 1987, *55,* 635-644.

POLIVY, J., & HERMAN, C. P. Dieting and binging: A causal analysis. *American Psychologist,* 1985, *40,* 193-201.

POLIVY, J., HERMAN, C. P., HACKETT, R., & KULESHNYK, I. The effects of self-attention and public attention on eating in restrained and unrestrained subjects. *Journal of Personality and Social Psychology,* 1986, *50,* 1253-1260.

POLIVY, J., SCHUENEMAN, A. L., & CARLSON, K. Alcohol and tension reduction: Cognitive and physiological effects. *Journal of Abnormal Psychology,* 1976, *85,* 595-600.

POSNER, M. I., PETERSON, S.E., FOX, P.T., RAICHLE, M. E. Localization of cognitive operations in the human brain. *Science,* 1988, *240,* 1627-1631.

POST, R. M., LAKE, C. R., JIMERSON, D. C., BUNNEY, W. E., WOOD, J. H., ZIEGLER, M. G., & POWERS, P. S. Obesity: Psychosomatic illness review: No. 2. *Psychosomatics,* 1982, *23,* 1027-1039.

PRIBRAM, K. H. Self-consciousness and intentionality. In G. E. Schwartz & D. Shapiro (Eds.), *Consciousness and self-regulation: Advances in research* (Vol. 1). New York: Plenum, 1976.

QUADAGNO, D. M., BRISCO, R., & QUADAGNO, J. S. Effects of perinatal gonadal hormones on selected nonsexual behavior patterns: A critical assessment of the nonhuman and human literature. *Psychological Bulletin,* 1977, *82,* 62-80.

QUAY, H. C. Psychopathic behavior: Reflection on its nature, origins and treatment. In F. Weizman & I. Uzfiris (Eds.), *The structure of experience.* New York: Plenum, 1977.

QUIRCE, C. M., ODIO, M., & SOLANO, J. M. The effects of predictable and unpredictable schedules of physical restraint upon rats. *Life Sciences,* 1981, *28,* 1897-1902.

RABINOWITZ, D., & ZIERLER, K. L. Forearm metabolism in obesity and its response to intra-arterial insulin: Characterization of insulin resistance and evidence for adaptive hyperinsulinism. *Journal of Clinical Investigation,* 1962, *41,* 2173-2181.

RADA, R. T., LAWS, D. R., & KELLNER, R. Plasma testosterone levels in the rapist. *Psychosomatic Medicine,* 1976, *38,* 257-268.

RADLOFF, R., & HELMREICH, R. Stress: Under the sea. *Psychology Today,* 1969, *3*(4), 28-29.

RAHE, R. H., HERVIG, L., & ROSENMAN, R. H. Heritability of Type A behavior. *Psychosomatic Medicine,* 1978, *40,* 478-486.

RAICHLE, M. I. Modern imaging approaches to human learning and memory: Establishing a basis for understanding the damaged brain. *Plasticity and Pathology in the Damaged Brain.* The Second Annual Bristol-Myers Squibb Symposium on Neuroscience Research. University of California, San Diego. Raven Health Care Communications, 1988.

RAMIREZ, E., MALDONADO, A., & MARTOS, R. Attributions moderate immunization against learned helplessness in humans. *Journal of Personality and Social Psychology,* 1992, *62,* 139-146.

RAPOPORT, J. L. The Biology of Obsessions and Compulsions. *Scientific American,* (March), 1989.

RAPOPORT, J. L. *The Boy Who Couldn't Stop Washing: The Experience and Treatment of Obsessive-Compulsive Disorder.* E.P. Dutton, 1989.

RAYNOR, J. O. Future orientation in the study of achievement motivation. In J. W. Atkinson & J. O. Raynor (Eds.), *Motivation and achievement.* Washington, D. C.: Winston, 1974, pp. 121-154.

REICHE, R., & DANNECKER, M. Male homosexuality in West Germany — A sociological investigation. *Journal of Sex Research,* 1977, *13,* 35-53.

REID, J. B. Social-interactional patterns in families of abused and nonabused children. In C. Zahn-Waxler, E. M. Cummings, & R. Iannotti (Eds.), *Altruism and aggression: Biological and social origins* (pp. 238-255). Cambridge: Cambridge University Press, 1986.

REID, R. L., & YEN, S. S. Premenstrual syndrome. *American Journal of Obstetrics and Gynecology,* 1983, *139,* 85-104.

REISENZEIN, R. The Schachter theory of emotions: Two decades later. *Psychological Bulletin,* 1983, *94,* 239-264.

RELICH, J. D. *Attribution and its relation to other affective variables in predicting and inducing arithmetic achievement.* Unpublished doctoral dissertation, University of Sydney (Australia), 1983.

RESCORLA, R. A. Pavlovian conditioning: It's not what you think it is. *American Psychologist,* 1988, *43,* 151-169.

RESHAM, S. C., AGNEW, H. W., JR., & WILLIAMS, R. L. The sleep of depressed patients. *Archives of General Psychiatry,* 1965, *13,* 503-507.

RICHARDSON, G. S., CARSKADON, M. A., ORAV, E. J., & DEMENT, W. C. Circadian variations in elderly and young adult subjects. *Sleep,* 1982, *5,* S82-S94.

ROBERTS, W. W., & KIESS, H. O. Motivational properties of hypothalamic aggression in cats. *Journal of Comparative and Physiological Psychology,* 1964, *58,* 187-193.

ROBERTS, W. W., STEINBERG, M. L., & MEANS, L. W. Hypothalamic mechanisms for sexual, aggressive, and other motivated behaviors in the opossum (*Didelphis virginiana*). *Journal of Comparative and Physiological Psychology,* 1967, *64,* 1-15.

ROBINS, L. N., DAVIS, D. H., & GOODWIN, D. W. Drug use by U.S. Army enlisted men in Vietnam: A follow-up on their return home. *American Journal of Epidemiology,* 1974, *99,* 235-249.

ROBINS, L. N., HELZER, J. E., & DAVIS, D. H. Narcotics use in Southeast Asia and afterward. *Archives of General Psychiatry,* 1975, *32,* 955-961.

ROBINS, L. N., HELZER, J. E., HESSELBROCK, M., & WISH, E. Vietnam veterans three years after Vietnam: How our study changed our view of heroin. In L. Brill & C. Winick (Eds.), *The yearbook of substance use and abuse* (Vol. 2). New York: Human Sciences Press, 1980.

RODGERS, W. L. Specificity of specific hungers. *Journal of Comparative and Physiological Psychology,* 1967, *64,* 49-58.

RODIN, J. Current status of the internal-external hypothesis for obesity. *American Psychologist,* 1981, *36,* 361-372.

RODIN, J. Effects of food choice on amount of food eaten in a subsequent meal: Implications for weight gain. In J. Hirsch and T. B. Van Itallie (Eds.), *Recent advances in obesity research* (Vol. 4). Lancaster, Penn.: Technomic, 1984.

RODIN, J. *Obesity theory and behavior therapy: An uneasy couple.* Unpublished manuscript, 1980.

RODIN, J., & LANGER, E. J. Long-term effects of a control-relevant intervention with the institutionalized aged. *Journal of Personality and Social Psychology,* 1977, *35,* 897-902.

RODIN, J., & SLOCHOWER, J. Externality in the nonobese: Effects of environmental responsiveness on weight. *Journal of Personality and Social Psychology,* 1976, *33,* 338-344.

RODIN, J., SLOCHOWER, J., & FLEMING, B. Effects of degree of obesity, age of onset, and weight loss on responsiveness to sensory and external stimuli. *Journal of Comparative and Physiological Psychology,* 1977, *91,* 586-597.

RODIN, J., WACK, J., FERRANNINI, E., & DEFRONZO, R. A. Effect of insulin and glucose on feeding behavior. *Metabolism,* 1985, *34,* 826-831.

ROEBUCK, J. B., & KESSLER, R. G. *The etiology of alcoholics: Constitutional, psychological, and sociological approaches.* Springfield, Ill.: Charles C Thomas, 1972.

ROGERS, C. R. *Client-centered therapy: Its current practice, implications, and theory.* Boston: Houghton Mifflin, 1951.

ROGERS, C. R. A theory of therapy, personality, and interpersonal relationships, as developed in the client-centered framework. In S. Koch (Ed.), *Psychology: A study of a science. Study 1: Conceptual and systematic* (Vol. 3: *Formulations of the person and the social context*). New York: McGraw-Hill, 1959.

ROKEACH, M. Some unresolved issues in theories of beliefs, attitudes and values. In *Nebraska Symposium on Motivation.* (Vol. 28, pp. 261-304). Lincoln: University of Nebraska Press, 1980.

ROOS, P. E., & COHEN, L. H. Sex roles and social support as moderators of life stress adjustment. *Journal of Personality and Social Psychology,* 1987, *52,* 576-585.

ROSE, G. A., & WILLIAMS, R. T. Metabolic studies on large and small eaters. *British Journal of Nutrition,* 1961, *15,* 1-9.

ROSEN, J. C., & LEITENBERG, H. Bulimia nervosa: Treatment with exposure and response prevention. *Behavior Therapy,* 1982, *13,* 117-124.

ROSENFELD, A. H. Depression: Dispelling despair. *Psychology Today,* 1985, *85,* 29-34.

ROSENMAN, R. H., BRAND, R. J., JENKINS, C. D., FRIEDMAN, M., STRAUS, R., & WURM, M. Coronary heart disease in the Western Collaborative Group Study: Final follow-up experience of 8½ years. *Journal of the American Medical Association,* 1975, *233,* 872-877.

ROSENMAN, R. H., FRIEDMAN, M., STRAUS, R., JENKINS, C. D., ZYZANSKI, S. J., & WURM, M. Coronary heart disease in the Western Collaborative Group Study: A follow-up experience of 4½ years. *Journal of Chronic Disease,* 1970, *23,* 173-190.

ROSENMAN, R. H., FRIEDMAN, M., STRAUS, R., WURM, M., JENKINS, D., & MESSINGER, H. B. Coronary heart disease in the Western Collaborative Group Study: A follow-up experience of two years. *Journal of the American Medical Association,* 1966, *195,* 86-92.

ROSENTHAL, R. H., & ALLEN, T. W. An examination of attention, arousal, and learning dysfunctions of hyperkinetic children. *Psychological Bulletin,* 1978, *85,* 689-715.

ROSLER, A., & KOHN, G. Male pseudohermaphorditism due to 17B-hydroxysteroid dehydrogenase deficiency. *Journal of Steroid Biochemistry,* 1983, *19,* 663-674.

ROSMAN, B. L., MINUCHIN, S., LIEBMAN, R., & BAKER, L. Input and outcome of family therapy in anorexia nervosa. In *Adolescent psychiatry* (Vol. 5). New York: Jason Aronson, 1977.

ROSSIER, J., BLOOM, F. E., & GUILLEMIN, R. Endorphins and stress. In H. Selye (Ed.), *Selye's guide to stress research* (Vol. 1). New York: Van Nostrand Reinhold, 1980.

ROSVOLD, H. E., MIRSKY, A. F., & PRIBRAM, K. H. Influence of amygdalectomy on social behavior in monkeys. *Journal of Comparative and Physiological Psychology,* 1954, *47,* 173-178.

ROTH, T., KRAMER, M., & LUTZ, T. The effects of sleep deprivation on mood. *Psychiatric Journal of the University of Ottawa,* 1976, *1,* 136-139.

ROTTER, J. B. Generalized expectancies for internal versus external control of reinforcement. *Psychological Monographs,* 1966, *80*(1, Whole No. 609).

ROTTER, J. B. An introduction to social learning theory. In J. B. Rotter, J. E. Chance, & E. J. Phares (Eds.), *Applications of a social learning theory of personality.* New York: Holt, Rinehart & Winston, 1972.

ROUTTENBERG, A. The reward system of the brain. *Scientific American,* November 1978, 154-164.

ROUTTENBERG, A. The two-arousal hypothesis: Reticular formation and limbic system. *Psychological Review,* 1968, *75,* 51-80.

ROWLAND, G. L., FRANKEN, R. E., & HARRISON, K. Sensation seeking and participation in sporting activities. *Journal of Sports Psychology,* 1986, *8,* 212-220.

ROZIN, P. Specific aversions as a component of specific hungers. *Journal of Comparative and Physiological Psychology,* 1967, *64,* 237-242.

ROZIN, P. Specific hunger for thiamine: Recovery from deficiency and thiamine preference. *Journal of Comparative and Physiological Psychology,* 1965, *59,* 98-101.

RUBIN, M. A., MALAMUD, W., & HOPE, J. M. The electroencephalogram and psychopathological manifestations in schizophrenia as influenced by drugs. *Psychosomatic Medicine,* 1942, *4,* 355-361.

RUBIN, R. T., REINISCH, J. M., & HASKETT, R. F. Postnatal gonadal steroid effects on human behavior. *Science,* 1981, *211,* 1318-1324.

RUDERMAN, A. J. Dietary restraint: A theoretical and empirical review. *Psychological Bulletin,* 1986, *99,* 247-262.

RULE, B. G., & NESDALE, A. R. Differing functions of aggression. *Journal of Personality,* 1974, *42,* 467-481.

RUMELHART, D. E., & MCCLELLAND, J. L. *Parallel distributed processing* (Vol. 1). Cambridge, MA: MIT Press, 1986.

RUSSEK, M. Participation of hepatic glucoreceptors in the control of food. *Nature*, 1963, *197*, 79-80.

RUSSELL, J. A., & STEIGER, J. H. The structure in persons' implicit taxonomy of emotions. *Journal of Research in Personality*, 1982, *16*, 447-469.

SACKETT, G. P. Effects of rearing conditions upon the behavior of rhesus monkeys (Macaca mulata). *Child Development*, 1965, *36*, 855-868.

SADAVA, S. W. Towards a molar interactional psychology. *Canadian Journal of Behavioral Science*, 1980, *12*, 33-51.

SALANCIK, G. R., & PFEFFER, J. An examination of need-satisfaction models of job attitudes. *Administrative Science Quarterly*, 1977, *22*, 427-456.

SALKOVSKIS, P. M., CLARK, D. M., & HACKMANN, A. Treatment of panic attacks using cognitive therapy with exposure or breathing restraining. *Behavior Research and Therapy*, 1991, *29*, 161-166.

SALTUS, R. Sleep. *Calgary Herald*, July 6, 1990.

SAMUELS, M., & SAMUELS, N. *Seeing With the Mind's Eye*. New York: Random House, 1975.

SARASON, B. R., PIERCE, G. R., & SARASON, I. G. Social support: The sense of acceptance and the role of relationships. In B. R. Sarason, I. G. Sarason, & G. R. Pierce (Eds.), *Social Support: An Interactional View*. New York: Wiley, 1990, pp. 97-128.

SARASON, B. R., SARASON, I. G., & PIERCE, G. R. *Social Support: An Interactional View*. New York: Wiley, 1990.

SARASON, I. G. Stress, anxiety, and cognitive interference: Reactions to tests. *Journal of Personality and Social Psychology*, 1984, *46*, 929-938.

SAUNDERS, D. *The relationship of attitude variables and explanations of perceived and actual career attainment in male and female businesspersons*. Unpublished doctoral dissertation, University of Texas at Austin, 1978.

SCARAMELLA, T. J., & BROWN, W. A. Serum testosterone and aggressiveness in hockey players. *Psychosomatic Medicine*, 1978, *40*, 262-265.

SCHACHTER, J. Pain, fear, and anger in hypertensives and normotensives. *Psychosomatic Medicine*, 1957, *19*, 17-29.

SCHACHTER, S. *Emotion, obesity, and crime*. New York: Academic Press, 1971. (a)

SCHACHTER, S. Nicotine regulation in heavy and light smokers. *Journal of Experimental Psychology: General*, 1977, *106*, 5-12.

SCHACHTER, S. Some extraordinary facts about obese humans and rats. *American Psychologist*, 1971, *26*, 129-144. (b)

SCHACHTER, S., GOLDMAN, R., & GORDON, A. Effects of fear, food deprivation, and obesity on eating. *Journal of Personality and Social Psychology*, 1968, *10*, 91-97.

SCHACHTER, S., & GROSS, L. P. Manipulated time and eating behavior. *Journal of Personality and Psychology*, 1968, *10*, 98-106.

SCHACHTER, S., KOZLOWSKI, L. T., & SILVERSTEIN, B. Effects of urinary pH on cigarette smoking. *Journal of Experimental Psychology: General*, 1977, *106*, 13-19.

SCHACHTER, S., & RODIN, J. *Obese Humans and Rats*. Erlbaum.

SCHACHTER, S., SILVERSTEIN, B., KOZLOWSKI, L. T., PERLICK, D., HERMAN, C. P., & LIEBLING, B. Studies of the interaction of psychological and pharmacological determinants of smoking. *Journal of Experimental Psychology: General*, 1977, *106*, 3-4.

SCHACHTER, S., SILVERSTEIN, B., & PERLICK, D. Psychological and pharmacological explanations of smoking under stress. *Journal of Experimental Psychology: General*, 1977, *106*, 31-40.

SCHACHTER, S., & SINGER, J. E. Cognitive, social, and physiological determinants of emotional states. *Psychological Review*, 1962, *69*, 379-399.

SCHACHTER, S., & SINGER, J. E. Comments on the Maslach and Marshall-Zimbardo experiments. *Journal of Personality and Social Psychology*, 1979, *37*, 989-995.

SCHACHTER, S., & WHEELER, L. Epinephrine, chlorpromazine, and amusement. *Journal of Abnormal and Social Psychology*, 1962, *65*, 121-128.

SCHAEFER, C., COYNE, J. C., & LAZARUS, R. S. The health-related functions of social support. *Journal of Behavioral Medicine*, 1981, *4*, 381-406.

SCHEIER, M. F., & CARVER, C. S. A model of behavioral self-regulation: Translating intention into action. In L. Berkowitz (Ed.), *Advances in Experimental Social Psychology* . New York: Academic Press, 1988, *21*, 303-346.

SCHEIER, M. F., & CARVER, C. S. Optimism, coping and health: Assessment and implications of generalized outcomes expectancies. *Health Psychology*, 1985, *4*, 210-247.

SCHEIER, M. F., MATTHEWS, K. A., OWENS, J. F., MAGOVERN, S. J. SR., LEFEBVRE, R. C., & SCHIFF, S. R. Conditioned dopaminergic activity. *Biological Psychiatry*, 1982, *17*, 135-154.

SCHILDKRAUT, J. J., & KETY, S. S. Biogenic amines and emotion. *Science*, 1967, *156*, 21-30.

SCHLEISER-STROPP, B. Bulimia: A review of the literature. *Psychological Bulletin*, 1984, *95*, 247-257.

SCHUCK, J., & PISOR, K. Evaluating an aggression experiment by use of simulating subjects. *Journal of Personality and Social Psychology*, 1974, *29*, 181-186.

SCHULL, W. J., & SCHULSINGER, F. *An adoption study of human obesity*. Unpublished manuscript. University of Pennsylvania, 1985.

SCHWARTZ, G. E. The facts of transcendental meditation: Part II. TM relaxes some people and makes them feel better. *Psychology Today*, April 1974, pp. 39-44.

SCHWARTZ, G. E., DAVIDSON, R. J., & GOLEMAN, D. J. Patterning of cognitive and somatic processes in the self-regulation of anxiety: Effects of meditation versus exercise. *Psychosomatic Medicine*, 1978, *40*, 321-328.

SCRIMA, L. Isolated REM sleep facilitates recall of complex associative information. *Psychophysiology*, 1982, *19*, 252-259.

SCRIMA, L., BROUDY, M., NAY, K. N., & COHN, M. A. Increased severity of obstructive sleep apnea after bedtime alcohol ingestion: Diagnostic potential and proposed mechanism of action. *Sleep*, 1982, *5*, 318-328.

SELIGMAN, M. E. P. Boomer blues. *Psychology Today*, 1988, October, 50-55.

SELIGMAN, M. E. P. *Helplessness: On depression, development, and death*. San Francisco: W. H. Freeman, 1975.

SELIGMAN, M. E. P. *Learned Optimism*. New York: Alfred A. Knopf, 1990.

SELIGMAN, M. E. P. Why is there so much depression today? The waxing of the individual and the waning of the commons. G. *Stanley Hall Lecture Series, 9*. Washington D.C.: American Psychological Association, 1989.

SELIGMAN, M. E. P., & MAIER, S. F. Failure to escape shock. *Journal of Experimental Psychology*, 1967, *74*, 1-9.

SELIGMAN, M. E. P., MAIER, S. F., & SOLOMON, R. L. Unpredictable and uncontrollable aversive events. In F. R. Brush (Ed.), *Aversive conditioning and learning*. New York: Academic Press, 1971.

SELIGMAN, M. E. P., & SCHULMAN, P. Explanatory style as a predictor of performance as a life insurance agent. *Journal of Personality and Social Psychology*, 1986, *50*, 832-838.

SELYE, H. On the real benefits of eustress. *Psychology Today*, March 1978, pp. 60-63; 69-70.

SELYE, H. Stress: It's a G.A.S. *Psychology Today*, September 1969, pp. 25-26; 56.

SELYE, H. *The stress of life* (Rev. ed.). New York: McGraw-Hill, 1976.

SELYE, H. *Stress without distress*. Philadelphia: Lippincott, 1974.

SENNECKER, P., & HENDRICK, C. Androgyny and helping behavior. *Journal of Personality and Social Psychology*, 1983, *45*, 916-925.

SEWITCH, T. S. *A multi-method assessment of test anxiety in an actual course examination*. Unpublished doctoral dissertation, University of Connecticut, Storrs, 1984.

SHAINESS, N. A. A reevaluation of some aspects of femininity through a study of menstruation: A preliminary report. *Comprehensive Psychiatry*, 1961, *2*, 20-26.

SHAW, J. Psychological androgyny and stressful life events. *Journal of Personality and Social Psychology*, 1982, *43*, 145-153.

SHEDLER, J., & BLOCK, J. Adolescent drug use and psychological health. *American Psychologist*, 1990, *45*, 612-630.

SHEPPARD, C., FRACCHIA, J., RICCA, E., & MERLIS, S. Indications of psychopathology in male narcotic abusers, their effects and relation to treatment effectiveness. *Journal of Psychology*, 1972, *81*, 351-360.

SHERMAN, I. W., & SHERMAN, V. G. *Biology: A Human Approach*. N.Y.: Oxford University Press, 1989.

SHOPE, G. L., HEDRICK, T. E., & GEEN, R. G. Physical/verbal aggression: Sex differences in style. *Journal of Personality*, 1978, *46*, 23-42.

SHORTELL, J., EPSTEIN, S., & TAYLOR, S. P. Instigation to aggression as a function of degree of defeat and capacity for massive retaliation. *Journal of Personality*, 1970, *38*, 313-328.

SHOWERS, C. Compartmentalization of positive and negative self-knowledge: Keeping bad apples out of the bunch. *Journal of Personality and Social Psychology*, 1992, *62*, 1036-1049.

SHRAUGER, J. S. Self-esteem and reactions to being observed by others. *Journal of Personality and Social Psychology*, 1972, *23*, 192-200.

SIEGEL, A., & FLYNN, J. P. Differential effects of electrical stimulation and lesions of the hippocampus and adjacent regions upon attack behavior in cats. *Brain Research*, 1968, *7*, 252-267.

SIEGEL, J. M. Anger and cardiovascular disease. In H. S. Friedman (Ed.), *Hostility, Coping and Health*. Washington, D. C.: American Psychological Association, 1992, pp. 49-64.

SIEGEL, J. M. Reticular formation activity and REM sleep. In R. Drucker-Colin, M. Shkurovich, & M. B. Sterman (Eds.), *The functions of sleep*. New York: Academic Press, 1979.

SIEGEL, J. M. Stressful life events and use of physician services among the elderly: The moderating role of pet ownership. *Journal of Personality and Social Psychology*, 1990, *58*, 1081-1086.

SIEGEL, S. Classical conditioning, drug tolerance, and drug dependence. In R. G. Smart, F. B. Glasser, Y. Israel, H. Kalant, R. E. Popham, and W. Schmidt (Eds.), *Research advances in alcohol and drug problems*. New York: Plenum, 1983.

SIEGEL, S. The role of conditioning in drug tolerance and addiction. In J. D. Keehn (Ed.), *Psychopathology in animals: Research and clinical implications*. New York: Academic Press, 1979.

SIGMON, S. T., & SNYDER, C. R. Positive and negative affect as a counter-explanation for the relationship between hope and coping strategies. Unpublished manuscript, University of Kansas, Department of Psychology, Lawrence, 1990.

SIGNORELLA, M. L., & JAMISON, W. Masculinity, femininity, androgyny, and cognitive performance: A meta-analysis. *Psychological Bulletin*, 1986, *100*, 207-228.

SILVERSTEIN, B., KOZLOWSKI, L. T., & SCHACHTER, S. Social life, cigarette smoking, and urinary pH. *Journal of Experimental Psychology: General*, 1977, *106*, 20-23.

SIMON, N. G., & WHALEN, R. E. Hormonal regulation of aggression; Evidence for a relationship between, receptor binding, and behavioral sensitivity to androgen and estrogen. *Aggressive Behavior*, 1986, *12*, 255-267, 1986.

SIMON, W., & GAGNON, J. H. Sexual scripts: Permanence and change. *Archives of Sexual Behavior*, 1986, *15*, 97-120.

SIMS, E. A. H., GOLDMAN, R. F., GLUCK, C. M., HORTON, E. S., KELLEHER, P. C., & ROWE, D. W. Experimental obesity in man. *Transcripts of the Association of American Physicians*, 1968, *81*, 153-170.

SKINNER, B. F. *The behavior of organisms: An experimental analysis*. New York: Appleton-Century-Crofts, 1938.

SKINNER, H. A., GLASER, F. B., & ANNIS, H. M. Crossing the threshold: Factors in self-identification as an alcoholic. *British Journal of Addiction*, 1982, *77*, 51-64.

SLADE, P. D., & RUSSELL, G. F. M. Awareness of body dimensions in anorexia nervosa: Cross-sectional and longitudinal studies. *Psychological Medicine*, 1973, *3*, 188-199.

SLADECZEK, I., & DOMINO, G. Creativity, sleep and primary process thinking in dreams. *Journal of Creative Behavior*, 1985, *19*, 38-46.

SMART, R. G. Effects of alcohol on conflict and avoidance behavior. *Quarterly Journal of Studies on Alcohol*, 1965, *26*, 187-205.

SMITH, C., & BUTLER, S. Paradoxical sleep at selective times following training is necessary for learning. *Physiology and Behavior*, 1982, *29*, 469-473.

SMITH, C., & YOUNG, J. Reversal of paradoxical sleep deprivation by amygdaloid stimulation during learning. *Physiology and Behavior*, 1980, *24*, 1035-1039.

SMITH, G. F., & DORFMAN, D. D. The effect of stimulus uncertainty on the relationship between frequency of exposure and liking. *Journal of Personality and Social Psychology*, 1975, *31*, 150-155.

SMITH, J. E., CO, C., FREEMAN, M. E., SANDS, M. P., & LANE, J. D. Neurotransmitter turnover in rat striatum is correlated with morphine self-administration. *Nature*, 1980, *287*, 152-154.

SMITH, R. E., PTACEK, J. T., & SMOLL, F. L. Sensation seeking, stress, and adolescent injuries: A test of stress-buffering, risk-taking, and coping skills hypothesis. *Journal of Personality and Social Psychology*, 1992, *62*, 1016-1024.

SMITH, T. W., & FROHM, K. D. What's so unhealthy about hostility? Construct validity and psychosocial correlates of the Cook and Medely Ho Scale. *Health Psychology*, 1985, *4*, 503-520.

SNYDER, C. R., HARRIS, C., ANDERSON, J. R., HOLLERAN, S. A., IRVING, L. M., SIGMON, S. T., YOSHINOBU, L., GIBB, J., LANGELLE, C., & HARNEY, P. The will and the ways: Development and validation of an individual-differences measure of hope. *Journal of Personality and Social Psychology*, 1991, *60*, 570-585.

SNYDER, F., SCOTT, J., KARACAN, I., & ANDERSON, D. Presumptive evidence on REMS deprivation in depressive illness. *Psychophysiology*, 1968, *4*, 382.

SNYDER, M., SIMPSON, J. A., & GANGESTAD, S. Personality and sexual relations. *Journal of Personality and Social Psychology*, 1986, *51*, 181-190.

SNYDER, S. The brain's own opiates. *Chemical and Engineering News*, 1977, *55 (48)*, 26-35; 266-271 (a).

SNYDER, S. Opiate receptors and internal opiates. *Scientific American*, 1977, *236 (3)*, 44-56.

SOBELL, M. B., & SOBELL, L. C. Behavior treatment of alcohol problems: A concept coming of age. In K. R. Blankstein and J. Polivy (Eds.), *Self-Control and Self-Modification of Emotional Behaviors*. New York: Plenum, 1982.

SOBELL, M. B., & SOBELL, L. C. *Behavioral Treatment of Alcohol Problems: Individualized Therapy and Controlled Drinking*. New York: Plenum, 1978.

SOBELL, M. B., & SOBELL, L. C. Second year treatment outcome of alcoholics treated by individualized behavior therapy: Results. *Behavior Research Therapy*, 1976, *14*, 195-215.

SOLOMON, R. L. The opponent-process theory of acquired motivation: The costs of pleasure and the benefits of pain. *American Psychologist*, 1980, *35*, 691-712.

SOLOMON, R. L., & CORBIT, J. D. An opponent process theory of motivation: I. Temporal dynamics of affect. *Psychological Review*, 1974, *81*, 119-145.

SOLOMON, R. L., & WYNNE, L. C. Traumatic avoidance learning: The principles of anxiety conservation and partial irreversibility. *Psychological Review*, 1954, *61*, 353-385.

SORRENTINO, R. M., & HEWITT, E. C. The uncertainty-reducing properties of achievement tasks revisited. *Journal of Personality and Social Psychology*, 1984, *47*, 884-899.

SOURS, J. A. The anorexia nervosa syndrome. *International Journal of Psycho-Analysis*, 1974, *55*, 567-576.

SPEALMAN, R. D., MADRAS, B. K., & BERGMAN, J. Effects of cocaine and related drugs in nonhuman primates. II. Stimulant effects on schedule-controlled behavior. *Journal of Pharmacology and Experimental Therapeutics*, 1989, *251*, 142-149.

SPEILBERGER, C. D. *Manual for the State-Trait Anxiety Inventory*. (Form V). Palo Alto, CA: Consulting Psychologists Press, 1983.

SPENCE, J. T. The distracting effects of material reinforcers in the discrimination learning of lower- and middle-class children. *Child Development*, 1970, *41*, 103-111.

SPENCE, J. T. Masculinity, femininity, and gender-related traits: A conceptual analysis and critique of current literature. In B. A. Maher and W. B. Maher (Eds.), *Progress in experimental personality research* (vol. 13, pp. 1-97). New York: Academic Press, 1984.

SPENCE, J. T., & HELMREICH, R. L. Achievement-related motives and behavior. In J. T. Spence, *Achievement and achievement motives*. San Francisco: W. H. Freeman, 1983.

SPENCE, J. T., & HELMREICH, R. L. *Masculinity and femininity: Their psychological dimensions, correlates, and antecedents*. Austin: University of Texas Press, 1978.

SPENCE, J. T., HELMREICH, R. L., & STAPP, J. A. A short version of the Attitudes Towards Women Scale (AWS). *Bulletin of the Psychonomic Society*, 1973, *2*, 219-220.

SPERRY, R. W. The great cerebral commissure. *Scientific American*, 1964, *210*(1), 42-52.

SPIELBERGER, C., KRASNER, S. S., & SOLOMON, E. P. The experience, expression, and control of anger. In M.P. Janisse (Ed.), *Health Psychology: Individual Differences and Stress*. N.Y.: Springer-Verlag, 1988.

SPINKS, J. A., BLOWERS, G. H., & SHEK, D. T. L. The role of the orienting response in the anticipation of information: A skin conductance response study. *Psychophysiology*, 1985, *22*, 385-394.

SPRAGUE, J., & QUADAGNO, D. Gender and sexual motivation: An explanation of two assumptions. *Journal of Personality and Human Sexuality*, 1987, *2*, 57-76.

STACY, A. W., WIDAMAN, K. F., & MARLATT, G. A. Expectancy models of alcohol use. *Journal of Personality and Social Psychology*, 1990, 918-928.

STEELE, C. I. Weight loss among teenage girls: An adolescent crisis. *Adolescence*, 1980, *15*, 823-829.

STEELE, C. M. What happens when you drink too much? *Psychology Today*, January 1986, pp. 48-52.

STEELE, C. M., & JOSEPHS, R. A. Alcohol myopia: Its prized and dangerous effects. *American Psychologist*, 1990, *45*, 921-933.

STEELE, C. M., SOUTHWICK, L., & PAGANO, R. Drinking your troubles away: The role of activity in mediating alcohol's reduction of psychological stress. *Journal of Abnormal Psychology*, 1986, *95*, 173-180.

STEELE, R. S. Psychoanalysis and hermeneutics. *International Review of Psychoanalysis*, 1979, *6*, 389-411.

STEIN, L. The chemistry of reward. In A. Routtenberg (Ed.), *Biology of reinforcement: Facets of brain stimulation reward*. New York: Academic Press, 1980.

STEIN, M. I. Creativity. In F. Bogarta & W. W. Lambert (Eds.), *Handbook of personality theory and research* Chicago: Rand McNally, 1968, pp. 67-89.

STELLAR, E. The physiology of motivation. *Psychological Review*, 1954, *61*, 5-22.

STEPANSKI, E., LAMPHERE, J., BADIA, P., ZORICK, F., & ROTH, T. Sleep fragmentation and daytime sleepiness. *Sleep*, 1984, *7*, 18-26.

STERNBERG, R. J. *Love:The Way You Want It*. New York: Bantam, 1991.

STERNBERG, R. J. Prototypes of competence and incompetence. In R. J. Sternberg and J. Kolligian, Jr. (Eds.), *Competence Considered*. New Haven: Yale University Press, 1990, pp. 67-97.

STERNBERG, R. J. *The Triarchic Mind: A Theory of Human Intelligence*. New York: Penguin Books, 1988.

STEWART, J., & KOLB, B. Cerebral asymmetry and sex. *Behavior and Neural Biology*, 1988, *49*, 344-360.

STOKOLS, D. Conflict-prone and conflict-resistant organizations. In H. S. Friedman (Ed.), *Hostility, Coping and Health*. Washington D. C.: American Psychological Association, 1992.

STOKOLS, D. Establishing and maintaining healthy environments. *American Psychologist*, 1992, 47, 6-22.

STORM, C., & STORM, T. A taxonomic study of the vocabulary of emotions. *Journal of Personality and Social Psychology*, 1987, *53*, 805-816.

STRAUB, R. O., SINGER, J. E., & GRUNBERG, N. E. Toward an animal model of Type A behavior. *Health Psychology*, 1986, *5*, 71-85.

STRAUS, M., GELLES, R., & STEINMETZ, S. K. *Behind Closed Doors: Violence in the American Family*. Garden City. N.Y: Anchor Press, 1980.

STRICKLAND, B. R. Internal-external control expectancies: From contingency to creativity. *American Psychologist*, 1989, *44*, 1-12.

STRIEGEL-MOORE, R. H., SILBERSTEIN, L. R., & RODIN, J. Toward an understanding of risk factors for bulimia. *American Psychologist*, 1986, *41*, 246-263.

STRYKER, S. Identity theory: Developments and extensions. In (Chair), *Self and social structure*. *Conference on self and identity*. Symposium conducted at the meeting of the British Psychological Society, University College, Cardiff, Wales, 1984.

STUART, R. B. *Act thin, stay thin*. New York: Norton, 1978.

STUNKARD, A. J. Obesity and the denial of hunger. *Psychosomatic Medicine*, 1959, *21*, 281-289.

STUNKARD, A. J., FOCH, T. T., & HRUBEC, Z. *A twin study*

STUNKARD, A. J., SORENSON, T. I. A., HANIS, C., TEASDALE, T. W., CHAKRABORTY, R., & STURUP, G. K. Correctional treatment and the criminal sexual offender. *Canadian Journal of Corrections*, 1961, *3*, 250-265.

SUEDFELD, P. The benefits of boredom: Sensory deprivation reconsidered. *American Scientist*, 1975, *63*, 60-69.

SUEDFELD, P., & KRISTELLER, J. L. Stimulus reduction as a technique in health psychology. *Health Psychology*, 1982, *1*, 337-357.

SUGIYAMA, Y. Social organization of hanuman langurs. In S. Altmann (Ed.), *Social communication among primates*. Chicago: University of Chicago Press, 1967.

SUOMI, S. J., & HARLOW, H. F. Monkeys at play. *Play, A Natural History Magazine Supplement*, December 1971, pp. 72-77.

SVEBAK, S., & MURGATROYD, S. Metamotivational dominance: A multimethod validation of reversal theory constructs. *Personality and Social Psychology*, 1985, *48*, 107-116.

SWAAB, D. F., & FLIERS, E. A. A sexually dimorphic nucleus in the human brain. *Science*, 1985, *228*, 1112-1115.

SWEENEY, P., ANDERSON, K., & BAILEY, S. Attributional style in depression: A meta-analytic review. *Journal of Personality and Social Psychology*, 1986, *50*, 974-991.

SWINSON, R. P., & EAVES, D. *Alcoholism and addiction*. Estover, Plymouth, England: MacDonald and Evans, 1978.

SWITZKY, H. N., & HAYWOOD, H. C. Motivational orientation and the relative efficacy of self-monitored and externally imposed reinforcement systems in children. *Journal of Personality and Social Psychology*, 1974, *30*, 360-366.

SYLVA, K., BRUNER, J. S., & GENOVA, P. The role of play in the problemsolving of children 3-5 years old. In J. S. Bruner, A. Jolly, & K. Sylva (Eds.), *Play: Its role in development and evolution*. New York: Penguin, 1976.

SYMONS, D. *The evolution of human sexuality*. New York: Oxford University Press, 1979.

TAGGART, P., CARRUTHERS, M. E., & SOMERVILLE, W. Electrocardiogram, plasma catecholamines and lipids, and their modification by oxprenolol when speaking before an audience. *Lancet*, 1973, *2*, 341-346.

TAKASAWA, N. Change in the amount of performance and change of physiological activity level. *Journal of Child Development*, 1978, *14*, 1-15.

TALLMAN, J. F., PAUL, S.M., SKOLNICK, P., & GALLAGER, D. W. Receptors for the age of anxiety: Pharmacology of the benzodiazepines. *Science*, 1980, *207*, 274-281.

TANNER, O. *Stress*. New York: Time-Life, 1976.

TARLER-BENLOLO, L. The role of relaxation in biofeedback training: A critical review of the literature. *Psychological Bulletin*, 1978, *85*, 727-755.

TAUB, J. M. Behavioral and psychological correlates of a difference in chronic sleep duration. *Biological Psychology*, 1977, *5*, 29-45.

TAUB, J. M., HAWKINS, D. R., & VAN DE CASTLE, R. L. Personality characteristics associated with sustained variations in the adult human sleep/wakefulness rhythm. *Waking and Sleeping*, 1978, *2*(1), 7-15.

TAVRIS, C. *Anger: The misunderstood emotion*. N. Y.: Simon and Schuster, 1989.

TAVRIS, C. *The Mismeasure of Woman*. New York: Simon and Schuster, 1992.

TAVRIS, C., & WADE, C. *The longest war: Sex differences in perspective*. (2nd ed.). San Diego: Harcourt Brace Jovanovich, 1984.

TAYLOR, C. W. Can organizations be creative too? In C. W. Taylor (Ed.), *Climate for creativity* (pp. 1-15). New York: Pergamon Press, 1972.

TAYLOR, S. *Positive Illusions: Creative self-deception and the healthy mind*. New York: Basic Books, 1989.

TAYLOR, S. E. Adjustment to threatening events: A theory of cognitive adaptation. *American Psychologist*, 1983, *38*, 1161-1173.

TAYLOR, S. E. Health psychology: The science and the field. *American Psychologist*, 1990, *45*, 40-50.

TAYLOR, S. E. *Positive Illusions: Creating Self-Deception and the Healthy Mind*. New York: Basic Books, 1986.

TAYLOR, S. E., KEMENY, M. E., ASPINWALL, L. G., SCHNEIDER, S. G., RODRIGUEZ, R., & HERBERT, M. Optimism, coping, psychological distress, and high-risk sexual behavior among men at risk for acquired immunodeficiency syndrome (AIDS). *Journal of Personality and Social Psychology*, 1992, *63*, 460-473.

TAYLOR, S. P. Aggressive behavior and physiological arousal as a function of provocation and the tendency to inhibit aggression. *Journal of Personality*, 1967, *35*, 297-310.

TAYLOR, S. P., & PISANO, R. Physical aggression as a function of frustration and physical attack. *Journal of Social Psychology*, 1971, *84*, 261-267.

TEFLER, E. *Happiness*. New York: St. Martin's Press, 1980.

TEITELBAUM, P. Disturbances in feeding and drinking behavior after hypothalamic lesions. In M. R. Jones (Ed.), *Nebraska Symposium on Motivation* (Vol. 9). Lincoln: University of Nebraska Press, 1961.

TEMPLER, D. I. Anorexic humans and rats. *American Psychologist*, 1971, *26*, 935.

TEMPLETON, R. D., & QUIGLEY, J. P. The action of insulin on the motility of the gastrointestinal tract. *American Journal of Physiology*, 1930, *91*, 467-474.

TERRACE, H. S. Extinction of a discriminative operant following discrimination learning with and without errors. *Journal of the Experimental Analysis of Behavior*, 1969, *12*, 571-582.

TERZIAN, H., & ORE, G. D. Syndrome of Klüver and Bucy: Reproduced in man by bilateral removal of the temporal lobes. *Neurology*, 1955, *5*, 373-380.

TESSER, A., & PAULHUS, D. L. Toward a causal model of love. *Journal of Personality and Social Psychology*, 1976, *34*, 1095-1105.

THARP, G. D. The role of glucocorticoids in exercise. *Medicine and Science in Sports*, 1975, *7*, 6-11.

THOMAS, A., CHESS, S., & BIRCH, H. G. The origins of personality. *Scientific American*, August 1970, pp. 102-109.

THOMAS, H. Preference for random shapes: Ages six through nineteen years. *Child Development*, 1966, *37*, 843-859.

THOMPSON, R. A. Emotion and self-regulation. *Nebraska Symposium on Motivation 1988: Socioemotional development*. Lincoln, Nebraska: University of Nebraska Press, 1990.

TIENARI, P. Psychiatric illness in identical twins. *Acta Psychiatrica Scandinavica*, 1963, *39*, Suppl. No. 171, 1-195.

TIGER, L. *Optimism: The biology of hope*. New York: Simon & Schuster, 1979.

TILLEY, A. J. Recovery sleep at different times of the night following loss of the last four hours of sleep. *Sleep*, 1985, *8*, 129-136.

TILLICH, P. The right to hope. *The University of Chicago Magazine*, 1965, *58*, 16-22.

TOCH, H. *Violent men*. Chicago: Aldine, 1969.

TOMPOROWSKI, P. D., & ELLIS, N. R. Effects of Exercise on Cognitive Processes: A Review. *Psychological Bulletin*, 1986, *99*, 338-346.

TORRENCE, E. P. *Rewarding creative behavior*. Englewood Cliffs, N.J.: Prentice-Hall, 1965.

TOWBES, L. C., COHEN, L. H., & GLYSHAW, K. Instrumentality as a life-stress moderator for early versus middle adolescents. *Journal of Personality and Social Psychology*, 1989, *57*, 109-119.

TRACY, R. L., & TRACY, L. N. Reports of mental activity from sleep stages 2 and 4. *Perceptual and Motor Skills*, 1974, *38*, 647-648.

TRAVAGLINI, P., BECK-PECCOZ, P., FERRARI, C., AMBROSI, B., PARACCHI, A., SEVERGNINI, A., SPADA, A., & FAGLIA, G. Some aspects of hypothalamic-pituitary function in patients with anorexia nervosa. *Acta Endocrinologica*, 1976, *81*, 252-262.

TROLLINGER, L. M. A study of the biographical and personality factors of creative women in music. Doctoral dissertation, Temple University, Philadelphia, PA, 1979.

TROPE, Y. Uncertainty-reducing properties of achievement tasks. *Journal of Personality and Social Psychology*, 1979, *37*, 1505-1518.

TSUDA, A., & HIRAI, H. Effects of the amount of required coping response tasks on gastrointestinal lesions in rats. *Japanese Psychological Research*, 1975, *17*, 119-132.

TYLER, L. E. *Individuality*. San Francisco: Jossey-Bass, 1978.

ULEMAN, J. S. *A new TAT measure of the need for power*. Unpublished doctoral dissertation. Harvard University, 1966.

ULRICH, R. E., WOLFE, M., & DULANEY, S. Punishment of shock-induced aggression. *Journal of Experimental Analysis of Behavior*, 1969, *12*, 1009-1015.

UNGER, R. K. Personal appearance and social control. In M. Safir, M. Mednick, I. Dafna, & J. Bernard (Eds.), *Women's worlds: From the new scholarship* (pp. 142-151). New York: Praeger, 1985.

U.S. DEPARTMENT OF JUSTICE. *Intimate Victims: A Study of Violence Among Friends and Relatives*. Washington, D. C.: U.S. Government Printing Office, 1980.

VAILLANT, G. E. *The natural history of alcoholism*. Cambridge: Harvard University Press, 1983.

VAILLANT, G. L. *Adaptation to life*, New York: Wiley, 1977.

VALENSTEIN, E. S., COX, V. C., & KAKOLEWSKI, J. W. Reexamination of the role of the hypothalamus in motivation. *Psychological Review*, 1970, *77*, 16-31.

VALINS, S. Cognitive effects of false heart-rate feedback. *Journal of Personality and Social Psychology*, 1966, *4*, 400-408.

VALINS, S. Emotionality and information concerning internal reactions. *Journal of Personality and Social Psychology*, 1967, *6*, 458-463.

VALLARDARES, H., & CORBALAN, V. Temporal lobe and human behavior. 1st International Congress, *Neurological Science*, 1959, 201-203.

VAN DYKE, C., & BYCK, R. Cocaine. *Scientific American*, 1982, *246*, 128-141.

VANTRESS, F. E., & WILLIAMS, C. B. The effect of the presence of the provocator and the opportunity to counteraggress on systolic blood pressure. *Journal of General Psychology*, 1972, *86*, 63-68.

VEREBY, V., & BLUM, K. Alcohol euphoria, possible mediation via endorphinergic mechanisms. *Journal of Psychedelic Drugs*, 1979, *11*, 305-311.

VERNIKOS-DANELLIS, J., & HEYBACH, J. P. Psychophysiologic mechanisms regulating the hypothalamic-pituitary-adrenal response to stress. In H. Selye (Ed.), *Selye's guide to stress research* (Vol. 1). New York: Van Nostrand Reinhold, 1980.

VEZINA, P., KALIVAS, P. W., & STEWART, J. Sensitization occurs to the locomotor effects of morphine and the specific μ opioid receptor agonist DAGO, administered repeatedly to the ventral tegmental area but not to the nucleus accumbens. *Brain Research*, 1987, *417*, 51-58.

VISINTAINER, M., VOLPICELLI, J., & SELIGMAN, M. Tumor rejection in rats after inescapable and escapable shock. *Science*, 1982, *216*, 437-439.

VITIELLO, M. V. Conditioned insulin secretion and meal feeding in rats. *Journal of Comparative and Physiological Psychology*, 1977, *91*, 128-133.

VITZ, P. Affect as a function of stimulus variation. *Journal of Experimental Psychology*, 1966, *71*, 74-79. (a)

VITZ, P. Preference for different amounts of stimulus complexity. *Behavioral Science*, 1966, *11*, 105-114. (b)

VOGEL, G. W. A motivational function of REM sleep. In R. Drucker-Colin, M. Shkurovich, & M. B. Sterman (Eds.), *The functions of sleep*. New York: Academic Press, 1979.

VOGEL, G. W. A review of REM sleep deprivation. *Archives of General Psychiatry*, 1975, *32*, 749-761.

VOGEL, G. W. Sleep-onset mentation. In A. M. Arkin, J. S. Antrobus, & S. J. Ellman (Eds.), *The mind in sleep: Psychology and psychophysiology*. Hillsdale, N.J.: Erlbaum, 1978.

VOLPICELLI, J. R. Uncontrollable events and alcohol drinking. *British Journal of Addiction*, 1987, *82*, 385-396.

VON EULER, U. S. *Noradrenaline*. Springfield, Ill.: Charles C Thomas, 1956.

VREVEN, R., & NUTTIN, J. R. Frequency perception of successes as a function of results previously obtained by others and by oneself. *Journal of Personality and Social Psychology*, 1976, *34*, 734-745.

WALKER, E. L. Psychological complexity and aesthetics, or the hedgehog as an aesthetic mediator (HAM). Invited address to American Psychological Association convention, New Orleans, September 1974.

WALKER, E. L. *Psychological complexity and preference: A hedgehog theory of behavior*. Pacific Grove, Calif.: Brooks/Cole, 1980.

WALKER, L. E. A. Psychology and violence against women. *American Psychologist*, 1989, *44*, 695-702.

WALLACE, R. K., & BENSON, H. The physiology of meditation. *Scientific American*, February 1972, pp. 84-90.

WALLACE, R. K., BENSON, H., & WILSON, A. F. A wakeful hypometabolic physiologic state. *American Journal of Physiology*, 1971, *221*, 795-799.

WALSH, A. The Science of Love and Its Effects on Mind and Body. Buffalo N. Y.: Prometheus Books, 1991.

WALTERS, J., APTER, M. J., & SVEBAK, S. Color preference, arousal, and the theory of psychological reversals. *Motivation and Emotion*, 1982, *6*, 193-215.

WARM, J. S., & DEMBER, W. N. Awake at the switch. *Psychology Today*, April 1986, pp. 46-53.

WARREN, M. P., & VANDEWIELE, R. L. Clinical and metabolic features of anorexia nervosa. *American Journal of Obstetrics and Gynecology*, 1973, *117*, 435-449.

WATERMAN, A. S. Two conceptions of happiness:Contrasts of Personal Expressiveness (Eudiaimonia) and hedonic enjoyment. *Journal of Personality and Social Psychology*, 1993, *64*, 678-691.

WATERS, W. F., McDONALD, D. G., & KORESKO, R. L. Habituation of the orienting response: A gating mechanism subserving selective attention. *Psychophysiology*, 1977, *14*, 228-236.

WATSON, D., & CLARK, L. A. Negative affectivity: The disposition to experience aversive emotional states. *Psychological Bulletin*, 1984, *96*, 465-490.

WATSON, J. B., & MORGAN, J. J. B. Emotional reactions and psychological experimentation. *American Journal of Psychology*, 1917, *28*, 163-174.

WEBB, W. B. A further analysis of age and sleep deprivation effects. *Psychophysiology*, 1985, *22*, 156-161.

WEBB, W. B. *Sleep: The gentle tyrant*. Englewood Cliffs, N. J.: Prentice-Hall, 1975.

WEBB, W. B. Theories of sleep functions and some clinical implications. In R. Drucker-Colin, M. Shkurovich, & M. B. Sterman (Eds.), *The functions of sleep*. New York: Academic Press, 1979.

WEBB, W. B., & AGNEW, H. W., JR. Analysis of the sleep stages in sleep-wakefulness regimens of varied length. *Psychophysiology*, 1977, *14*, 445-450.

WEBB, W. B., & AGNEW, H. W., JR. Are we chronically sleep deprived? *Bulletin of the Psychonomic Society*, 1975, *6*, 47-48. (a)

WEBB, W. B., & AGNEW, H. W., JR. Sleep efficiency for sleep-wake cycles of varied length. *Psychophysiology*, 1975, *12*, 637-641. (b)

WEBB, W. B., & FRIEL, J. Sleep stage and personality characteristics of ``natural'' long and short sleepers. *Science*, 1971, *171*, 587-588.

WEBB, W. B., & LEVY, C. M. Age, sleep deprivation, and performance. *Psychophysiology*, 1982, *19*, 272-276.

WEBER, M. *The Protestant ethic and the spirt of capitalism* (T. Parsons, trans.). New York: University of Nebraska Press, 1964.

WEIDNER, G., SEXTON, G., MCLELLARN, R., CONNOR, S. L. & MATARAZZO, J. D. The role of Type A behavior and hostility in an elevation of plasma lipids in adult women and men. *Psychosomatic Medicine*, 1987, *49*, 136-145.

WEINER, B. (Ed.). *Achievement Motivation and Attribution Theory*: Morristown, N. J.: General Learning Press, 1974.

WEINER, B. Achievement motivation as conceptualized by an attribution theorist. In B. Weiner (Ed.), *Achievement Motivation and Attribution Theory*. Morristown, N. J.: General Learning Press, 1974.

WEINER, B. (Ed.). *Attribution: Perceiving the causes of behavior*. Morristown, N.J.: General Learning Press, 1972.

WEINER, B. An attributional theory of achievement motivation and emotion. *Psychological Review*, 1985, *92*, 548-573.

WEINER, B. On perceiving the other as responsible. In R. A. Dienstbier (Ed.), *Nebraska Symposium on Motivation (1990): Perspectives on Motivation*. Lincoln Nebraska, University of Nebraska Press, 1991.

WEINER, B. On perceiving the other as responsible. In R. A. Dienstbier (Ed.), *Perspectives on Motivation*. Nebraska Symposium on Motivation Lincoln: University of Nebraska Press, 1991.

WEINER, B. *Theories of motivation: From mechanism to cognition*. Chicago: Markham, 1972.

WEINER, B. A theory of motivation for some classroom experiences. *Journal of Educational Psychology*, 1979, *71*, 3-25.

WEINER, B., FRIEZE, I., KUKLA, A., REED, L., REST, S., & ROSENBAUM, R. M. *Perceiving the Causes of Success and Failure*. Morristown N.J.: General Learning Press, 1971.

WEINER, B., FRIEZE, I., KUKLA, A., REED, L., REST, S., & ROSENBAUM, R. M. Perceiving the causes of success and failure. In E. E. Jones, D. E. Kanouse, H. H. Kelly, R. E. Nisbett, S. Valins, and B. Weiner (Eds.), *Attribution: Perceiving the causes of behavior*. Morristown, N.J.: General Learning Press, 1971.

WEINER, B., & KUKLA, A. An attributional analysis of achievement motivation. *Journal of Personality and Social Psychology*, 1970, *15*, 1-20.

WEINER, B., & POTEPAN, P. A. Personality characteristics and affective reactions towards exams of superior and failing college students. *Journal of Educational Psychology*, 1970, *61*, 144-151.

WEINER, H., & KATZ, J. L. The hypothalamic-pituitary-adrenal axis in anorexia nervosa: A reassessment. In P. L. Darby, P. E. Garfinkel, D. M. Garner, & D. V. Coscina, *Anorexia nervosa: Recent developments in research* (pp. 249-270). New York: Alan R. Liss, Inc., 1983.

WEINGBERGER, D. A. The construct validity of the repressive coping style. In J. L. Singer (Ed.), *Repression and dissociation*. Chicago: University of Chicago Press, 1990, pp. 337-386.

WEISS, J. M. Effects of coping behavior in different warning signal conditions on stress pathology in rats. *Journal of Comparative and Physiological Psychology*, 1971, *77*, 1-13. (a)

WEISS, J. M. Effects of coping behavior with and without a feedback signal on stress pathology in rats. *Journal of Comparative and Physiological Psychology*, 1971, *77*, 22-30. (c)

WEISS, J. M. Effects of coping responses on stress. *Journal of Comparative and Physiological Psychology*, 1968, *65*, 251-260.

WEISS, J. M. Effects of punishing the coping response (conflict) on stress pathology in rats. *Journal of Comparative and Physiological Psychology*, 1971, *77*, 14-21. (b)

WEISS, J. M. Somatic effects of predictable and unpredictable shock. *Psychosomatic Medicine*, 1970, *32*, 397-408.

WEISS, J. M., GLAZER, H. I., & POHORECKY, L. A. Coping behavior and neurochemical changes: An alternative explanation of the original ``learned helplessness'' experiments. In G. Serban & A. Kling (Eds.), *Animal models in human psychobiology*. New York: Plenum, 1976.

WEISS, J. M., GLAZER, H. I., POHORECKY, L. A., BRICK, J., & MILLER, N. E. Effects of chronic exposure to stressors on avoidance-escape behavior and on brain norepinephrine. *Psychosomatic Medicine*, 1975, *37*, 522-534.

WEISS, J. M., STONE, E. A., & HARRELL, N. W. Coping behavior and brain norepinephrine level in rats. *Journal of Comparative and Physiological Psychology*, 1970, *72*, 153-160.

WEISS, M. Alcohol as a depressant of psychological conflict in rats. *Quarterly Journal of Studies on Alcohol*, 1958, *19*, 226-237.

WEISSMAN, M. M., LEAR, P. F., HOLZER, C. E., III, MEYERS, J. K., & TISCHLER, G. L. The epidemiology of depression: An update on sex differences in rates. *Journal of Affective Disorders*, 1984, *7*, 179-188.

WENDER, P. H., KETY, S. S., ROSENTHAL, D., SCHULSINGER, F., ORTMANN, J., & LUNDE, I. Psychiatric disorders in the biological and adoptive families of adopted individuals with affective disorders. *Archives of General Psychiatry*, 1986, *43*, 923-929.

WESTON, J. The pathology of child abuse. In R. Helfer & L. Kempe (Eds.) *The battered child*. Chicago: University of Chicago Press, 1968.

WHALEN, R. E. Brain mechanisms controlling sexual behavior. In F. A. Beach (Ed.), *Human sexuality in four perspectives*. Baltimore: Johns Hopkins University Press, 1976.

WHITAKER, L. H. Oestrogen and psychosexual disorders. *Medical Journal of Australia*, 1959, *2*, 547-549.

WHITAM, F. L. The homosexual role. A reconsideration. *Journal of Sex Research*, 1977, *13*, 1-11.

WHITAM, F. L., & MATHY, R. M. *Male homosexuality in four societies*. New York: Praeger, 1986.

WHITE, A., HANDLER, P., & SMITH, E. L. *Principles of biochemistry* (3rd ed.). New York: McGraw-Hill, 1964.

WHITE, G. D., NIELSEN, G., & JOHNSON, S. M. Timeout duration and the suppression of deviant behavior in children. *Journal of Applied Behavior Analysis*, 1972, *5*, 111-120.

WHITE, J. *Rejection*. Reading MA.:Addison-Wesley, 1982.

WHITE, J. A., ISMAIL, A. H., & BOTTOMS, G. D. Effects of physical fitness on the adrenocortical response to exercise stress. *Medicine and Science in Sports*, 1976, *8*, 113-118.

WHITE, R. W. Motivation reconsidered: The concept of competence. *Psychological Review*, 1959, *66*, 297-333.

WIDOM, C. S. Does violence beget violence? A critical examination of the literature. *Psychological Bulletin*, 1989, *106*, 3-28.

WIDOM, C. S. A tail on an untold tale: Response to "Biological and genetic contributions to violence - Widom's untold tale." *Psychological Bulletin,* 1991, *109,* 130-132.

WIEBE, D. J. Hardiness and stress moderation: A test of proposed mechanisms. *Journal of Personality and Social Psychology,* 1989, *60,* 89-99.

WIEDEKING, C., LAKE, R., ZIEGLER, M., KOWARSKI, A. A., & MONEY, J. Plasma noradrenaline and dopamine-beta-hydroxylase during sexual activity. *Psychosomatic Medicine,* 1977, *39,* 143-148.

WIKLER, A. *Opioid dependence.* New York: Plenum, 1980.

WILCOXIN, H. C., DRAGOIN, W. B., & KRAL, P. A. Illness-induced aversions in rat and quail: Relative salience of visual and gustatory cues. *Science,* 1971, *171,* 826-828.

WILLIAMS, R. *The Trusting Heart: Great News About Type A Behavior.* N. Y.: Random House, 1989.

WILLIAMS, R. H. Hypoglycemosis. In R. H. Williams (Ed.), *Diabetes.* New York: Hoeber, 1960.

WILLS, T. Downward comparison principles in social psychology. *Psychological Bulletin,* 1981, *90,* 245-271.

WILLS, T. Similarity and downward comparison. In J. Suls & T. Wills (Eds.), *Social Comparison: Contemporary Theory and Research* (pp. 51-78). Hillsdale, NJ: Erlbaum, 1991.

WILM, E. C. *The theories of instinct: A study of the history of psychology.* New Haven, Conn.: Yale University Press, 1925.

WILSON, E. O. *Sociobiology, the new synthesis.* Cambridge, Mass.: Harvard University Press, 1975.

WILSON, G. T. The effect of alcohol on human sexual behavior. In N. Mello (Ed.), *Advances in substance abuse: Behavioral and biological research.* Greenwich, Conn.: JAI Press, 1981.

WILSON, G. T., & LAWSON, D. M. Expectancies, alcohol, and sexual arousal in women. *Journal of Abnormal Psychology,* 1978, *87,* 358-367.

WILSON, J. D., GEORGE, F. W., GRIFFIN, J. E., et al. The hormonal control of sexual development. *Science,* 1981, *211,* 1285-1294.

WILSON, T. D., & LINVILLE, P. W. Improving the performance of college freshmen with attributional techniques. *Journal of Personality and Social Psychology,* 1985, *49,* 287-293.

WILSON, T. D., & SCHOOLER, J. W. Thinking too much: Introspection can reduce the quality of preferences and decisions. *Journal of Personality and Social Psychology,* 1991, *60,* 181-192.

WING, L. *Autistic children: A guide for parents.* London: Constable, 1971.

WINOKUR, G. Unipolar depression. *Archives of Psychiatry,* 1979, *36,* 47-52.

WISE, C. D., & STEIN, L. Facilitation of brain self-stimulation by central administration of norepinephrine. *Science,* 1969, *163,* 299-301.

WISE, R. A. The neurobiology of craving: Implications for the understanding and treatment of addiction. *Journal of Abnormal Psychology,* 1988, *97,* 118-132.

WISE, R. A., & BOZARTH, M. A. A psychomotor stimulant theory of addiction. *Psychological Review,* 1987, *94,* 469-492.

WOLPE, J. *The practice of behavior theory.* New York: Pergamon Press, 1969.

WONNOCOTT, S. (1992) Bath University, England.

WOOD, J. V., SALTZBERG, J. A., NEALE, J. M., STONE, A. A. & RACH-MIEL, T. B. Self-focused attention, coping responses, and distressed mood in everyday life. *Journal of Personality and Social Psychology,* 1990, *58,* 1027-1036.

WOODS, J. H., KATZ, J. L., & WINGER, G. Abuse liability of benzodiazepines. *Pharmacological Review,* 1987, *39,* 251-413.

WOODS, S. C., VASSELLI, J. R., KAESTNER, E., SZAKMARY, G. A., MILBURN, P., & WOOLEY, S. C., WOOLEY, O. W., & DYRENFORTH, S. R. Theoretical, practical, and applied social issues in behavioral treatments of obesity. *Journal of Applied Behavioral Analysis,* 1979, *12,* 3-25.

WORCHEL, P. The effect of three types of arbitrary thwarting on the instigation to aggression. *Journal of Personality,* 1974, *42,* 301-318.

WORICK, W. W., & SCHALLER, W. E. *Alcohol, tobacco, and drugs: Their uses and abuses.* Englewood Cliffs, N.J.: Prentice-Hall, 1977.

WORK IN AMERICA: Report of a special task force to the U.S. Department of Health, Education, and Welfare. Cambridge, Mass.: MIT Press, 1973.

WRIGHT, R. A., TOI, M., & BREHM, J. W. Difficulty and interpersonal attraction. *Motivation and Emotion,* 1984, *8,* 327-341.

WURTMAN, R. J. Nutrients that modify brain function. *Scientific American,* 1982, *246,* 50-59.

WYNNE, L. C., & SOLOMON, R. L. Traumatic avoidance learning: Acquisition and extinction of dogs deprived of normal peripheral autonomic function. *Genetic Psychology Monographs,* 1955, *52,* 241-284.

YERKES, R. M. & DODSON, J. D. The relation of strength of stimulus to rapidity of habit-formation. *Journal of Comparative Neurological Psychology,* 1908, *18,* 459-482.

YOSHINOBU, L. R. Construct validation of the Hope Scale: Agency and pathways components. University of Kansas, Lawrence, 1989.

YOUNG, J. S. *Steve Jobs: The Journey is the Reward.* Glenview Illinois: Scott, Foresman and Company, 1988.

YOUNG, P. T. *Understanding your feeling and emotions.* Englewoods Cliffs, N. J.:

YOUNG, P. T., & CHAPLIN, J. P. Studies of food preference, appetite, and dietary habit: III. Palatability and appetite in relation to body need. *Comparative Psychology Monographs,* 1945, *18*(3), 1-45.

ZAHN-WAXLER, C., & KOCHANSKA, G. The origins of guilt. *Nebraska Symposium on Motivation 1988: Socioemotional Development.* Lincoln, Nebraska: University of Nebraska Press, 1990.

ZEKI, S. The visual image in mind and brain. *Scientific American,* September, 1992, 69-76.

ZENTALL, S. S., & ZENTALL, T. R. Optimal stimulation: A model of disordered activity and performance in normal and deviant children. *Psychological Bulletin,* 1983, *94,* 446-471.

ZILBERGELD, B. *Male sexuality: A Guide to Sexual Fulfillment.* Boston: Little Brown, 1978.

ZILLMANN, D. Arousal and aggression. In R. Geen & E. Donnerstein, (Eds.), *Aggression: Theoretical and empirical reviews: Vol. 1* (pp. 75-102). N. Y.: Academic Press, 1983.

ZILLMAN, D., KATCHER, A. H., & MILAVSKY, B. Excitation transfer from physical exercise to subsequent aggressive behavior. *Journal of Experimental Social Psychology,* 1972, *8,* 247-259.

ZIMBARDO, P. G. The human choice: Individuation, reason, and order versus deindividuation, impulse, and chaos. In W. J. Arnold & D. Levine (Eds.), *Nebraska Symposium on Motivation* (Vol. 17). Lincoln: University of Nebraska Press, 1972.

ZIMBARDO, P. G. Pathology of imprisonment. *Society,* 1972, *9,* 4-8.

ZINBERG, N. E., & ROBERTSON, J. A. *Drugs and the public.* New York: Simon & Schuster, 1972.

ZUBEK, J. P. (Ed.) *Sensory deprivation.* New York: John Wiley, 1969.

ZUCKERMAN, H. The scientific elite: Nobel laureates' mutual influence. In R. S. Albert (Ed.) *Genius and eminence.* New York: Pergamon Press, 1974, pp. 171-186.

ZUCKERMAN, M. *Biological bases of sensation seeking, impulsivity, and anxiety.* Hillsdale, N.J.: Erlbaum, 1983.

ZUCKERMAN, M. The search for high sensation. *Psychology Today,* February 1978, pp. 38-46; 96-99. (a)

ZUCKERMAN, M. Sensation seeking. In H. London & J. E. Exner, Jr. (Eds.), *Dimensions of personality.* New York: Wiley, 1978. (b)

ZUCKERMAN, M. *Sensation seeking: Beyond the optimal level of arousal.* Hillsdale, N.J.: Erlbaum, 1979.

ZUCKERMAN, M., BUCHSBAUM, M. S., & MURPHY, D. L. Sensation-seeking and its biological correlates. *Psychological Bulletin,* 1980, *88,* 187-214.

Author Index

Aarons, L. , 149
Abbott, R. A., 351
Abelson, H., 117
Abplanalp, J., 235
Abrahamsen, A., 30, 31
Abrams, D. B. , 204
Abramson, L. Y., 117, 319, 350, 359
Agnew, H. W., Jr. , 150, 152, 164, 174
Agyei, Y. , 135
Ainsworth, M. D. S., 364
Akil, H., 268
Alcock, J., 21
Alexander, B. K., 190
Alexander, R., 59
Allen, L S., 131, 132, 134
Allen, M. B., Jr., 60
Allen, T. W. , 63
Allison, S. L. , 237
Allison, T. S., 237
Alloy, L. B., 3509
Allport, G. W. , 15
Allred, K. D., 291
Amsel, A. , 258, 304, 418
Åkerstedt, T., 150, 153
Anderson, J. R., 350, 359, 445, 446
Anderson, K. J. , 60
Andrews, F. M., 397
Angell, M., 366
Annis, H. M., 211
Apfelbaum, M., 97
Apter, M. J., 71, 72
Arkes, H. R., 376, 377
Arkin, A. M., 172
Arkkelin, D., 242
Armitage, A. K., 202
Armitage, R., 151
Arnold, M. B., 73
Aserinsky, E., 147
Askevold, F., 106
Aspinwall, L. G., 294
Atkinson, J. W., 19, 258, 417, 419-421, 441
Averill, J. R., 124, 271

Ax, A. F., 245, 252
Baekeland, F., 42, 152
Bagby, R. M., 307
Bailey, J. M., 134, 135
Baker, J. W., Ii, 246
Bales, R., 212
Banaji, M. R., 184, 209
Bancroft, J. A., 129
Bandura, A., 19, 186, 214, 251, 258, 341, 343-345, 348, 359, 415, 416, 441, 459, 465, 466
Barash, D. P., 20
Barchas, J. D., 345
Barclay, L. C., 434
Bard, P., 73, 227
Bardwick, J. M., 234
Barefoot, J. C., 281
Barker, R. G., 3
Barnes, G. E., 121
Baron, J., 307
Baron, R. A., 220, 221, 223, 248, 252
Barr, T., 193
Barrett, D. E., 283
Barron, F., 397
Barry, H., Iii, 206
Barsalou, L. W., 402
Bash, K. W., 81
Basow, S. A., 120
Basu, G. K., 234
Batson, C. D., 367
Baum, A., 276
Baumgardner, A. H., 306, 434, 457
Beach, F. A., 130, 136
Beary, J. F., 290
Bechtel, W., 30, 31
Beck, A. T., 323, 324, 330, 333
Becker, M., 213
Becker. W. C., 248
Bell, A., 136, 137
Bell, P. A., 163, 252
Bellah, R. N., 310
Beller, A. S., 99

Bemis, K. M., 106
Ben-Tovim, D., 106
Benbow, C. P., 143
Benson, H., 67, 290, 291, 295
Bentler, P. M., 131, 184, 392
Bergman, J., 193
Berkowitz, L., 15, 238, 248, 250, 252
Berlyne, D. E., 3, 46, 59, 63, 258, 338, 377, 378, 379, 380, 382, 394, 397, 445, 446
Bernardis, L. L., 88
Bernstein, A. G., 66, 425
Berntson, G. G., 368
Berrebi, A. S., 131
Bertilson, H. S., 222
Besch, N. F., 234
Bexton, W. H., 57
Bhanji, S., 106
Bieber, I., 137
Biener, L.
Bindra, D. A., 194
Binkoff, J. A., 204
Birch, D., 19, 258
Birch, H. G., 383, 441
Birney, R. C., 213
Bixler, E. O., 175
Blakelock, E. H., 245
Blanchard, D. C., 228
Blanchard, R. J., 228
Blaney, P. H., 432
Blehar, M. C., 364
Bliss, E., 234
Bliss, E. L., 106
Blissett, S. E., 294
Blix, A. S., 339
Block, J., 200
Bloom, F. E., 196, 268, 303
Bloom, G., 272
Bloomfield, H. H., 288
Blowers, G. H., 62
Blum, K., 205
Bolger, N., 276, 277, 285
Bolles, R. C., 189, 269, 317

Bond, C. F., 207
Bonnet, M. H., 155
Bonvallet, M., 60
Boone, D. C., 278
Boothroyd, P., 124
Borden, R. J., 222
Boring, E. G., 7, 8
Bosveld, J., 169
Bottoms, G. D. , 42
Bowen, R., 222
Bower, G. H., 465
Bowlby, J., 364
Boykin, A. W. , 376, 377
Bozarth, M. A., 202
Bradshaw, G. F. , 399
Brady, J. V., 271, 318, 341, 343, 343
Branch, C. H. H., 106
Braucht, G. N., 185
Brehm, J. W. , 124
Bremer, J., 234
Brickman, P., 425
Brinkerhoff, M. B., 225, 246
Brisco, R., 135
Brockner, J., 432
Brodsky, A., 191
Brooks-Gunn, J., 120, 312
Brothers, L., 367
Broughton, R., 151
Brouillard, M. E., 186, 344
Broussard, D. B., 119
Brown, J. D., 290
Brown, W. A., 234
Brownell, K.D., 105
Brownmiller, S. , 107
Bruch, H., 106
Brugger, M., 227
Bruner, J. S., 35, 385, 386
Bryson, J. B., 383
Buchanan, D. C., 270
Buchsbaum, M. S., 157, 194
Bucy, P. C., 228
Burdick, H., 213
Burgess, M., 246
Burish, T. G., 59
Burnstein, E., 248
Buss, A. H., 244, 248, 254
Butler, A. C., 326
Butler, M. C., 185
Butler, R. A., 375
Byck, R., 193
Byrne, D., 117, 120, 163
Cacioppo, J. T., 368
Cahalan, D., 210
Campbell, J. B., 71

Campbell, J. D., 433, 457
Campion, M. A., 463
Cannon, W. B., 73, 75, 77
Carlson, A. J., 81
Carlson, E. R., 117
Carlson, M., 309
Carr, T. S., 234
Carroll, J. L., 27
Carruthers, M. E., 282, 339
Carskadon, M. A., 152, 153, 159
Cartwright, R. D., 162, 172
Carver, C. S., 350, 351, 358, 359, 360, 432, 445, 463
Cass, V. C., 140,
Castaldo, V., 162
Cattell, R. B., 394
Caul, W. F., 270
Cauthen, N. R., 290
Chai, Y. M., 131
Chaiken, S., 107
Chambers, J., 388
Chambless, D. L., 307
Chassler, S., 120
Check, J. V. P., 121
Chess, S., 383
Chomsky, N., 20, 21
Churchill, A. C., 466
Cialdini, 15
Cioffi, D., 186, 344
Clark, D. C., 90
Clark, D. M., 307
Clark, K. B., 368
Clark, L. A., 445
Clarke, D. H., 42
Climie, R. J., 251
Cobb, S., 278
Cohen, D. B., 156, 160, 163, 169
Cohen, J. E., 420
Cohen, L. H., 293
Cohen, M. F., 246
Cohen, S., 214, 215, 266, 363
Coleman, C. E. H., 117
Coleman, M., 63
Coleman, R. M., 154, 155
Collins, D. L.,276
Compas, B. E., 312
Condry, J. C., 386, 388
Conger, J. J., 206
Conners, M.E., 102, 103
Connor, S. L., 281
Cooper, J. R., 196, 303
Cooper, P. J., 104
Coopersmith, S., 431
Copeland, P.M., 105

Corbalan, V., 229
Corbit, J. D., 31, 43, 181, 182
Coscina, D. V., 102
Costa, P. T., 245, 281
Costello, C. G., 314
Cox, B. J., 307
Cox, V. C., 25
Cox, W. M., 207, 212, 215
Coyne, J. C., 273, 284
Craighead, W. E., 458,
Crandall, C.S., 103
Cratty, B. J., 69, 463
Crawford, J. D., 89
Crick, C., 166
Crick, F., 27, 31, 33, 461, 467
Crisp, A. H., 106
Crites, S. L., 368
Cross, S., 455
Crown, J., 198
Crowther, J. H., 102
Csikszentmihalyi, M., 4, 472
Cunningham, S., 106
Cuthbert, B., 290
Czaya, J., 170
D'emilio, J., 120
Dabbs, J. M., Jr, 234
Dally, P., 106
Dalton, K., 234, 235
Daly, E. M., 260
Dank, B., 137
Dannecker, M., 137
Darwin, C., 17
Daubman, K. A., 397
Davids, A., 62
Davidson, J. M., 290
Davis, B., 194
Davis, C. M., 83, 85
Davis, D. H., 191, 210
Davis, V. E., 205
Davison, G. C., 285
De Courville, N., 235
De Koninck, J., 151, 163
De Rivera, T., 19, 258
De Simone, D., 129
De Tocqueville, A., 310
De Wied, D., 268
Debono, E., 394, 395, 400, 401
Deci, E. L., 33, 311, 384, 443, 448, 450, 469
Delgado, J. M. R. , 231
Dember, W. N., 4, 66, 67, 374, 376, 409
Dembroski, T. M., 245, 281
Dement, W. C., 147, 152, 153, 159, 174
Denenberg, J. O.
Denenberg, V. H., 383

Dengerink, H. A., 222, 223, 240, 241, 252, 253
Derubeis, R. J., 312, 322
Dey, F., 45
Diamond, M., 139
Diamond, M. C. 130, 139
Dilalla, L. F. , 237
Dinges, D. F., 153, 154, 155, 156
Dixon, L. M. , 102
Dohler, K-D., 135
Dole, V. P., 82, 187, 190
Dominick, J. R., 251
Domino, G., 401
Donnerstein, E. I., 250, 251
Doob, A. N., 251
Dorfman, D. D., 377, 380, 381
Dorsky, F. S., 253
Dowling, C., 107
Dowling, G. A., 130
Dörner, G., 136
Driver, M. J., 383
Drolette, M. E., 245
Dulaney, S., 237
Dunne, E., 344
Durden-Smith, J., 129
Dweck, C. S., 35, 352, 413, 414, 415, 443, 444, 449
Dykstra, L., 186, 196
Dyrenforth, S. R., 99
Eagly, A. H., 221, 225, 244
Earl, R. W., 4, 374, 375, 376, 409
Easterbrook, J. A., 59, 64, 67, 273, 386
Eaves, D., 180, 181, 193, 198, 204, 206, 207
Eaves, L. J., 311
Eckenrole, J., 276, 285
Edelman, R., 237, 246
Eden, A., 90
Egger, M. D., 227
Eggleston, R. J., 221
Ehrenkranz, J., 234
Ehrhardt, A. A., 135, 141
Eibl-Eibesfeldt, 8
Eisenberg, N., 253
Ekman, P., 259, 294
Elliott, E. E., 414
Ellis, A., 466
Ellis, N. R., 43
Ellman, S. J., 158, 160
Emmons, R. A., 285
Emrick, C. D., 211
Endler, N. S., 307
Engle, K. B., 207
Epstein, S., 35, 59, 223, 224, 264, 285-288, 302, 332, 333, 442, 443, 445, 450, 452,

457, 461
Erdmann, G., 75,
Erikson, E. H., 456
Ervin, F. R., 227
Estes, B. W., 388
Evans, M. D., 312, 322
Ey, S., 312
Eysenck, H. J., 43, 69, 70, 76, 121, 122, 184, 201, 202, 206, 285, 346, 383
Fairborn, C. G. 104, 105
Falk, J. L., 191
Fanselow, M. S., 189, 269
Farkas, G. M., 206
Farley, F. H., 338, 391, 392
Fausto-Sterling, A., 136, 235
Fava, M., 105, 106, 189
Feather, N. T., 422
Feinberg, I., 162
Feldman, R. S., 425
Fenigstein, A., 251
Fennema, E., 143
Fenwick, P. B., 290
Ferguson T. J., 241, 242
Fern, R. W., 45
Feshbach, N. D., 253
Feshbach, S., 224
Festinger, L., 35, 243, 387, 395
Fey, S. G., 290
Fial, R. A., 228
Fincher, J., 186
Fischman, J. , 282, 283
Fisher, C., 159
Fisher, H., 123
Fisher, W. A., 117
Fishman, S. M., 197
Fleming, B., 94
Fliers, E. A., 130
Flynn, J. P., 227, 229
Foch, T. T., 87,
Folkman, S., 273, 274, 275, 466
Foote, R. M., 234
Ford, C. S., 136
Forgas, J.P., 309
Forsman, L., 267
Foulkes, D., 159, 163, 169, 170
Foulkes, E. F., 213
Fox, P. T., 52
Frady, R. L., 234
Franken, R. E., 125, 293, 381, 382, 391, 392, 393, 397, 398, 445
Frankenhaeuser, M., 267, 272, 292, 344
Freedman, E. B., 120
Freedman, J. L., 251
Freeman, A., 354

French, E. G., 277, 417
Freud, S., 11, 16
Friedman, H. S., 265, 266
Friedman, M., 280, 328
Friedman, M. I., 79, 80
Friel, J., 152
Friesen, W. V. , 294
Frieze, I., 319, 422
Frijda, N. H., 258, 260, 261, 263, 264, 325, 333
Frodi, A., 247
Frohm, K. D., 282
Frohman, L. A., 88
Frost, R. O., 59, 91
Funkenstein, D. H., 245
Furstenberg, F. F., Jr., 120
Fuster, J. M., 57
Gackenbach, J., 169
Gagnon, J. H., 117, 118
Gagnon, P., 151
Galanter, E., 463
Gallager, D. W., 303
Gambaro, S., 246
Gangestad, S., 122
Garcia, J., 85
Garfinkel, P. E., 106
Garn, S. M., 90
Garner, D. M., 106
Garrity, T. F., 286
Garrow, D. J. S., 97
Gatchel, R. J., 285
Gebhard, P. H., 117
Geen, R. G., 71, 220, 224, 247, 248, 251, 282
Geer, J. H., 119, 285
Geiselman, P. J., 82
Geller, E., 63
Genova, P., 385, 386
Gentry, W. D., 245
Gerner, R., 157
Gerner, R. H., 157
Getzels, J. W., 398
Gibb, J., 350, 445, 446
Gibbons, F. X., 393, 434
Gibson, K. J., 125, 293, 393, 445
Giese, H., 121
Gilbert, D. G., 202
Gilbert, R. M., 213
Gillberg, M., 150, 153
Gillin, J. C., 162
Gladue, B. A. , 234, 236
Glanzer, M., 374
Glaser, F. B., 211
Glass, D. C., 282, 283
Glasser, W., 180

Glassman, A., 312
Glaubman, H., 149, 162
Glazer, H. I., 271
Glickman, S. E., 24
Goldberg, E., 286
Goldfoot, D. A., 115
Goldman, J. K., 88
Goldman, R., 93, 94, 99
Goleman, D., 288, 290
Gomez, J., 106
Goodenough, D. R., 162
Goodner, C. J., 79
Goodsitt, A., 106
Goodwin, D. W., 191
Gordon, A., 93, 94
Gorski, R. A., 130, 131, 132, 134
Gorsuch, R. L., 185
Gottesman, I. I., 237
Gough, H. G., 401
Goy, R. W., 129, 136
Gracely, E. J., 307
Grannemann, B. D., 434
Grant, K. E., 312
Green, R., 235
Greenberg, B. S., 165, 251
Greenberg, R., 163
Greene, R., 388
Greenwell, J., 252
Greenwood, M.R.C., 105
Greiser, C., 163
Grieger, R., 466
Griffin, J. E., 42
Grinspoon, L., 192, 193
Gross, J., 101
Grossman, S. P., 228
Grosvenor, A., 160
Grunberg, N. E., 91, 283
Guilford, J. P., 394
Guillemin, R., 268
Gustafson, S. B., 394, 397, 398
Guy, R. F., 107
Hackmann, A., 307
Haddad, N. F., 388
Haessler, H. A., 89
Hall, F., 155
Hall, G. H., 202
Halmi, K. A., 106
Halstead, P., 103
Hamburg, D. A., 231
Hamilton, M. L., 205
Hamilton, P., 64, 65
Hammersmith, S. K., 137
Handler, P., 268
Hansen, J., 211

Hansen, J. R., 339, 344
Harackiewicz, J. M., 386
Harburg, E., 245
Harlow, H. F., 338, 375, 384
Harney, P., 350
Harrell, N. W., 342
Harrington, D. M. , 397
Harris, C., 350, 445, 446
Harris, C. B., 359
Harrison, K., 391
Harrison, R. H., 163
Harter, S., 430, 432, 457
Hartmann, E. L., 152, 164, 173
Hartse, K. M., 153
Haseltine, F. P., 129, 130, 132, 134
Hashim, S. A., 85
Hawk, G., 75
Hawke, C. C., 234
Hawkins, D. R., 151
Hawkins, R. C., Jr, 103, 107
Hawley, C. W., 71
Haynes, S. G., 278
Hays, R. C., 270
Haywood, H. C., 388
Heath, A., 311
Heath, R. G., 339
Heather, N., 211
Heatherton, T. F., 430
Hebb, D. O. , 46, 57, 60, 73, 303
Hedblom, P. , 192, 193
Hedrick, T. E. , 247
Heider, F. , 38
Heilman, M. E., 107
Heiman, J. R., 117
Heimburger, R. F., 229
Helmreich, R. L., 426, 427
Helmstetter, S., 466
Helzer, J. E., 210
Herbert, M., 294
Herman, C. P., 94, 95, 96, 102, 103, 202
Heron, W., 57, 58
Hervig, L., 283
Hervig, L. K., 351
Herzog, D. B., 103, 104, 105
Hess, W. R., 227
Hewitt, E. C., 424
Heybach, J. P., 268
Hinde, R. A., 20
Hines, M., 131, 132, 135
Hinz, L.D., 104
Hirai, H., 271
Hirota, T., 380, 382
Hiroto, D. S., 316-318
Hirsch, J., 90

Hirschman, R., 75
Hite, S., 119
Hobson, J. A., 167, 168, 399, 400
Hockey, B., 64, 65
Hoffman, M. L., 327, 329
Hokanson, J. E., 237, 246, 318, 326
Holleran, S. A., 350, 445, 446
Hollon, S. D., 312, 322, 354
Holmes, D. S., 59, 246, 290
Holstein, C., 333, 452
Holzer, C. E., Iii, 311
Hooker, E., 137
Hopson, J., A., 188, 189
Hopson, J. L., 236
Horowitz, M. J., 62, 285, 291
Horstman, D. H., 42
Hoth, C. C., 155
Houck, P. R., 155
Howley, E. T., 42, 194
Hoyenga, K. B., 128
Hoyenga, K. T., 128
Hoyt, M. F., 172
Hrubec, Z., 87
Huba, G. J., 184, 392
Huh, E., 333, 452
Hull, C. L., 258, 374
Hull, J. G.. 207
Hunt, L., 45
Hutt, C., 375
Hyde, J. S., 143, 244
Imperato-Mcginley, J., 138
Inhelder, B., 409
Innes, C. A., 221
Irving, L. M., 350, 445, 446
Isen, A. M., 397
Ismail, A. H., 42
Israel, N. R., 60
Ivey, M. E., 234
Izard, C. E. , 259, 311, 328, 367
Jackson, L. J., 103, 107
Jackson, P. W., 398
Jacobs, B. L., 198
Jacobson, R. C., 212
Jaffe, J. H., 186
James, W., 33, 72, 73, 75, 77, 443
Janke, W., 75
Jasper, H. H., 51
Jeffrey, D. B., 100
Jessor, R., 213
Jevning, R., 290
Johnson, C.L., 102, 103
Johnson, E. H., 245
Johnson, L. C., 151
Johnson, R. E., 130

Johnson, S. M., 237
Johnson, V.E., 112, 113, 114, 116, 117, 122
Josephs, R. A., 184, 207, 454, 464
Jourden, F. J., 416
Jouvet, M. , 54, 148, 149
Joyce, C. R. B., 198
Julien, R. M., 185
Juraska, J. M., 131
Kagan, J., 327
Kaha, C. W., 400
Kahn, R. L., 277
Kahn, S., 291
Kahneman, D., 59, 65
Kakolewski, J. W., 25
Kalant, O. J., 195
Kales, A., 175
Kalsbeck, J. E., 229
Kalucy, R. S., 106
Kamien, J. B., 193
Kandel, D. B., 201, 212, 213
Kaplan, R. M.. 364
Karli, P., 229
Kasner, K. H., 240, 241
Katch, F. I., 101
Katch, V. L., 101
Katz, J., 106
Katz, J. L., 195
Katz, L., 288, 452
Katz, R. G., 100
Kavanaugh, D.J., 465
Kaye, M., 184
Kazdin, A. E., 305
Keesey, R. E., 88, 89
Keller, M., 212
Kellner, R., 234
Kelly, L., 103
Kemeny, M. E., 294
Kemler, D., 318
Kendall, P. C., 458
Kendler, K. S., 311
Kent, G., 466
Kernis, M. H., 434
Kessen, W., 376, 377, 383
Kessler, R. C.. 212
Kessler, R. G., 185
Kety, S. S., 42, 43, 311, 312, 343
Keys, A. B., 102
Kiesler, C. A., 163
Kiess, H. O., 228
Kimura, D., 130, 131, 135, 141, 143
King, S. H., 245
Kinsey, A. C., 1212
Kirsch, I., 207
Klausner, S. Z., 213

Kleck, R. E., 124
Klein, R., 151
Klein, R. F., 82
Kleinginna, A. M., 19, 260
Kleinginna, P. R., Jr., 19, 260
Kleitman, N., 147, 176
Klemchuk, H. P., 290
Klesges, L.M., 101
Klesges, R. C., 101
Klinger, E., 207, 212, 215, 314
Klüver, H., 228
Knittle, J. L., 90
Kobasa, S. C., 291, 292, 349, 364, 367
Koch, C., 27, 31, 33, 461, 467
Kochanska, G., 326, 327, 329
Koelling, R. A., 85
Koenig, I. D. V., 380, 382
Kohn, G., 238
Kolata, 82
Kolb, B., 130
Kolb, L., 184
Koopmans, H. S., 82
Kopcik, J. R., 131
Koresko, R. L., 66
Koropsak, E., 246
Koulack, D., 163
Kowarski, A. A., 115
Kozlowski, L. T., 202
Kraines, S. H., 42
Kramer, M., 156, 170
Krantz, D. S., 285
Krasner, S. S., 245
Kraut, R., 340
Kreuz, L. E., 234
Kribbs, N. B., 153, 156
Kristeller, J. L., 62
Krynicki, V., 162
Kuhl, J., 322
Kuhn, D. Z., 248
Kuipers, P., 261
Kukla, A., 319, 422, 423
Kupfer, D. J., 151
Kusulas, J. W., 351
La Croix, A. Z., 278
Laberge, S., 169, 170
Lacey, B. C., 64
Lacey, J. I., 60, 64
Lack, L. C., 160
Lacosta, 130
Lagerspetz, K., 226
Lake, R.. 115
Lalivas, P. W., 195
Lamon, S. J., 143
Lancee, W. J., 260

Lang, E. L., 360
Lang, P. J., 368
Langan, P. A., 221
Lange, 72. 73
Langelle, C., 350, 359, 445, 446
Langer, E. J., 34, 36, 203, 276, 295, 364, 395,
    400, 458, 459, 468, 470
Langley, P. W., 394
Larrick, R. P., 454, 464
Larson, L. A., 42
Lasagna, L., 189
Lasky, R., 42
Latham, G. P., 258, 344, 453, 461
Laudenslager, M., 284, 366
Launier, R., 273, 349
Lavasque, M.E., 101
Laws, D. R., 234
Lazarus, R. S., 75, 258, 259, 273, 274, 275,
    276, 284, 302, 306, 327, 330, 332, 338,
    340, 341, 342, 346, 349, 430, 432
Lear, P. F., 311
Learner, R. M., 34, 458,
Ledwidge, B., 42, 195
Lefcourt, H. M., 291, 294
Lefebvre, R. C., 351
Leggett, E. L., 413, 414, 444, 449
Leitenberg, H., 104, 105
Leon, G. R., 102
Lepper, M. R., 388
Lerner, M. J., 368, 369
Levay, S., 130, 134
Levendusky, P. G., 223
Levenson, R. W., 294, 367
Levinson, D., 460
Lewin, I., 162
Lewis, V., 135
Licht, B., 352
Liebhart, E. H., 75
Lind, S. K.. 397
Lindholm, E., 290
Lindsley, D. B., 51, 56
Lingswiler, V. M., 102
Linsenmeier, J. A. W., 425
Linville, P. W., 425, 457
Linz, D. G., 250
Lipcamon, J., 131
Lipson, A., 333, 452
Lisman, S. A., 184
Lloyd, C. W., 235
Locke, E. A., 258, 344, 453, 461
Lord, R. G., 463
Lore, R. K., 252
Lorenz, K., 20
Loro, A. D., 103

Low, H., 231
Lowell, E. L., 417
Lowther, W., 44
Luckhardt, A. B., 81
Lundberg, U., 267, 292, 344,
Lunde, I., 311
Lupri, M. B., 225, 246
Lutz, T., 156
Lynn, R., 65
Mack, D., 96
Mackinnon, D. W., 391, 401
Mackworth, N. H., 66
Maclean, P. D., 25
Macon, D. A., 402
Maddi, S. R., 291,
Madras, B. K., 193
Madsen, C. H., 248
Madsen, R., 310
Maehr, M. L., 388
Magoun, H. W., 24. 50
Magovern, S. J. Sr., 351
Mahone, C. H., 422
Mahoney, K., 100
Mahoney, M. J., 100
Maier, S.F., 284, 314, 315, 316, 366
Malamuth, N. M., 121, 250
Maldonado, A., 318
Maltzman, I., 66
Maltzman, I. M., 212
Manderlink, G., 386
Mandler, G., 251, 420
Margules, D. L., 89
Margulies, R. Z. , 212
Mark, V. H., 227
Markus, H., 19, 433, 441, 443, 455, 456, 457
Marlatt, G. A., 207
Marler, P., 21
Marshall, G. D., 75
Marshall, G. N., 351, 360
Martin, N. G., 311
Martin, R. A., 292, 294
Martin, W. R., 186
Martindale, 187
Maslach, C., 75
Maslow, A. H., 12, 14, 17, 361, 362, 363,
    396, 429, 446, 448
Mason, J. W., 270, 341, 343
Masserman, J. H., 206
Masters, W. H., 112, 113, 114, 116, 117, 122
Matarazzo, J. D., 281
Mathy, R. M., 136
Matter, J., 386
Matthews, K. A., 281, 282, 351
Mattsson, A., 231

May, R., 302
May, R. B., 376
Mayer, J., 79
Mayr, E., 20
Mcadams, 131
Mccardle, W. D., 101
Mccareins, A. G., 425
Mccarty, D., 184
Mcclelland, J. L., 30
Mcclelland, D. C., 31, 277, 363, 417, 418
Mccoy, S. B., 434
Mccrae, R. R., 397
Mccullers, J. C., 388
Mcdonald, D. G., 66
Mcdougall, W., 7-9
Mcewen, B. S., 129, 136
Mcfarland, C., 235
Mcgrath, M. J., 160
Mcgraw, K. O., 388
Mcguinness, D., 59
Mckay, G., 363
Mclearn, G. E., 226
Mclellarn, R., 281
Mcmurray, N. E., 466
Mcpartland, R. J., 151
Means, L. W., 228
Mefford, I. N., 345
Meichenbaum, D. H., 466
Meier, P., 285, 286, 288, 452
Meyer, L. B., 45
Meyer-Bahlburg, H. F., 135
Meyers, A.W., 101
Meyers, J. K., 311
Meyers, W. U., 425
Michelman, H., 42
Milgram, S., 222
Miller, D. G., 270
Miller, D. T., 369
Miller, G. A., 59, 411, 463
Miller, I. W., Iii, 319
Miller, L. B., 388
Miller, N. E., 206, 248, 272, 302, 304
Miller, P. A., 253
Miller, W. R., 207, 211
Mills, J. H., 45
Milner, P., 339
Milstein, R. M., 87
Mineka, S., 303
Mintun, M., 52
Mirsky, A. F., 231
Mischel, W., 417
Mitchison, G., 166
Mohan, P., 125
Moiseeva, N. I., 173

Moldofsky, H., 106
Money, J., 115, 134, 135, 138, 139, 141
Monroe, L. J., 162, 172
Monti, P.M., 204
Mook, D. G., 79
Moore, M. H., 213
Moran, J. D., 388
Morgan, J. J. B., 8
Morgan, W. P., 42
Morgane, P. J., 148
Morris, D., 114, 116
Morris, J. L., 422
Morrison, A. R., 149
Morse, D. R., 290
Morton, J. H., 235
Moruzzi, G., 24, 50
Moses, J. M., 150, 151, 164
Mossholder, K. W., 386
Mount, G. R., 290
Mowrer, O. H., 304
Moyer, K. E., 226, 228, 231
Mullaney, D. J., 152
Mumford, M. D., 394, 397, 398
Munsinger, H., 376, 377, 383
Muñoz, R. F., 207, 211
Murgatroyd, S., 72
Murphy, D. L., 194
Murray, H. A., 417
Myers, 222
Nachman, M., 85
Naitoh, P., 151
Nakazawa, Y., 163
Narabayashi, H., 229
Nathan, P. E., 184
Neale, J. M., 298
Neale, M. C. I., 136
Neiss, R., 60
Nesdale, A. R., 221
Newcomb, M. D., 184, 392
Newcomb, T., 243
Nezu, A. M., 294
Niaura, R. S., 204
Nicholls, J. G., 456
Nichols, J. R., 190, 210, 458
Nielsen, G., 237
Nisbett, R. E., 37, 85, 103, 388, 454, 464
Nishihara, K., 150
Nolen-Hoeksema, S., 322, 323
Norman, W. H., 319
Norvell, M. J., 107
Novin, D., 82
Nowicki, G. P., 397
Nurius, P., 19, 433, 441, 455, 456, 457
Nuttin, J. R., 425

O'brien, C. P., 188
O'leary, M. R., 222, 240, 241, 252, 284
Odio, M., 270
Ohno, S., 129, 130, 132, 134
Olds, J., 23, 339
Olweus, D., 231
O'neal, E. C., 251,
Ore, G. D., 229
Orleans, C. S., 103
Orne, M. T., 59
Ornstein, R., 366
Ortmann, J., 311
Ory, M., 286
Osborn, C. A., 117
Ostrove, N., 425
Overmier, J. B., 314
Owens, J. F., 351
Ozer, E., 345, 348, 416, 466
Pallak, M. S., 163
Palmer, C., 162, 172
Panksepp, J., 189
Papanek, M. L., 386
Park, K., 458
Parker, J. D. A., 307
Parker, S. J., 283
Parkes, K. R., 292
Parlee, M. B., 235
Parmeggiani, P. L., 150
Paskewitz, D. A., 59
Patel, V., 277
Paton, W. D. M., 198
Patterson, G. R., 220, 223, 224, 237
Paul, S.M., 303
Paulhus, D. L., 124
Pavlov, I. P., 27
Pearlman, C., 165
Peck, M. S., 361
Pedraza, M., 204
Peele, S., 33, 189, 191, 195, 210, 212-215
Pendery, M. L., 212
Pennebaker, J. W., 291
Penrod, S., 250
Pepitone, A., 243
Perlick, D., 202
Perlin, L. I., 359
Perry, M., 244, 254
Persky, H., 234
Pervin, L. A., 258
Petersen, S. E., 52
Peterson, C., 295, 353
Pfaffman, C., 338
Phillip, J. D., Jr., 278
Piaget, J., 383, 409
Pickens, R., 194

Pierce, G. R., 284, 361
Pietropinto, A., 120
Pillard, R. C., 134, 135
Pisano, R., 248
Pisor, K., 252
Pitts, F. N., Jr., 42
Pivik, T., 163
Pliner, P., 107
Plotkin, W. B., 62
Pohorecky, L. A., 271
Polivy, J., 94-97, 102, 103, 260, 430,
Pollack, R. H., 117
Posner, M. I., 52
Post, R. M., 42, 157
Potepan, P. A., 423
Powers, P., 106
Powers, P. S., 87,
Powley, T. L., 88, 89
Prevost, F., 163
Pribram, K. H., 40, 59, 231, 232, 233, 463
Prymak, C. A., 290
Ptacek, J. T., 293
Puccetti, M. C., 291
Quadagno, D., 120
Quadagno, D. M. 135
Quay, H. C., 63
Quigley, J. P., 81
Quirce, C. M., 270
Rabin, A. I., 246
Rabinowitz, D., 81, 98
Rachmiel, T. B., 298
Rada, R. T., 234
Rahe, R. H., 283
Raichle, M. E., 52
Ramírez, E., 318
Rankin, B. A., 107
Rapoport, J. L., 22
Ratzel, R., 172
Raynor, J. O., 19, 258
Reed, L., 319, 422
Reiche, R., 137
Reid, R. L., 225, 235
Reisenzein, R., 75
Rejman, M., 64, 65
Relich, J. D., 425
Rescorla, R. A., 30
Rest, S., 319, 422
Reynolds, C. F., 155
Richey, M. F., 131
Roberts, W. W., 228
Robertson, J. A., 210
Robins, L. N., 184, 191, 210
Rodin, J., 81, 94, 98, 100, 104, 276
Rodriguez, R., 294

Roe, D., 103
Roebuck, J. B., 185
Roeper, P. J. , 245
Rogers, C. R., 12, 13, 14, 17, 430, 449, 451
Rohsenow, D. J., 204
Rollnick, S., 211
Room, R., 210
Roos, P. E., 293
Rosa, R. R., 155
Rose, G. A., 90
Rose, R. M. , 234, 278
Rosen, J. C., 104, 105
Rosen, R. C., 206
Rosenfield, 45
Rosenfeld, A. H. 309
Rosenbaum, R. M., 319, 422
Rosenman, R. H., 63, 280, 281, 283
Rosenthal, D., 311
Rosler, A., 138
Ross, G., 277
Ross, M., 235
Rossier, J., 268
Rosvold, H. E., 231
Roth, B. H., 196, 303
Roth, T., 153, 156, 170
Rotter, J. B., 224, 240, 316
Routtenberg, A., 194, 339
Rowland, G. L., 391, 393, 445
Rozin, P., 15
Rubenstein, C., 124
Ruderman, A. J., 97
Ruef, A. M., 367
Rule, B. G., 221, 241, 242
Rumelhart, D. E., 30
Russek, M., 81
Russell, G. F. M., 106
Russell, J. A., 79, 260
Ryan, R. M., 33, 311, 387, 443, 448, 450, 469
Ryan, S. M. , 366
Sackett, G. P., 377
Salans, L. B. , 90
Saleh, W. E., 292
Salkovskis, P. M., 307
Saltus, R. S., 155
Saltzberg, J. A., 298
Samuels, M., 461
Samuels, N., 461
Sands, M. P., 234
Sarason, B. R., 361
Sarason, I, G., 277, 284, 361, 465
Sarason, S. B., 251, 284, 420
Saruwatari, L. R., 107
Saunders, D., 427
Scaramella, T. J., 234

Schachter, J., 245, 252
Schachter, S., 10, 37, 46, 73, 74, 75, 84, 85,
    93, 94, 201, 202, 203
Schaefer, C., 273, 284
Schaie, K. W., 246
Schaller, W. E., 180
Schalling, D., 231
Scheier, M. F., 350, 351, 358, 359, 360, 432,
    445, 463
Schiff, B. B., 24
Schildkraut, J. J., 42, 43, 312, 343
Schleiser-Stropp, B., 103, 104
Schneider, S. G., 294
Schooler, C., 359
Schooler, J. W., 401
Schulman, P., 352
Schulsinger, F., 311
Schultz, L. A., 252
Schulz, R. A., 285
Schwartz , M., 135
Schwartz, G. E., 288, 290
Schweiger, U., 105
Scott, T. H., 57
Scrima, L., 160, 175
Seligman, M. E. P., 11, 27, 37, 198, 258,
    285, 293, 295, 303, 306, 398, 309, 310,
    314, 315-319, 321, 324, 333, 352, 353,
    355, 358, 359, 398, 445, 446, 457, 458,
    470,
Sellers, C. M., 202
Selye, H., 269, 270, 349
Sexton, G., 281
Shainess, N. A., 234
Shaw, J., 293
Sheard, M. H., 234
Sheehan, D. V., 197
Shek, D. T. L., 62
Shepp, B. , 318
Sheppard, C., 185
Sherman, I. W., 80, 81
Sherman, V. G., 80, 81
Shetler, S., 246
Shmidt, J. L. Jr., 27, 121
Shope, G. L., 247
Shortell, J., 223, 224
Showers, C., 436
Shrauger, J. S., 105, 432
Siegel, A., 229
Siegel, J. M., 148, 286
Siegel, S., 187
Sigmon, S. T., 350. 359, 445, 446
Silberstein, L. R., 98, 104
Silverstein, B., 202
Simenauer, J., 120

Simon, H. A., 399
Simon, N. G., 234
Simon, W., 117, 118
Simpson, J. A., 122, 282
Singer, J. E., 46, 73, 74, 75, 276, 283
Singer, J. L., 172
Skinner, B. F., 10
Skinner, H. A., 211
Skolnick, P., 303
Slade, P. D., 106
Sladeczek, I., 401
Slochower, J., 94
Smith, E. L., 268
Smith, G., 368
Smith, G. F., 377, 380, 381
Smith, J. E., 268
Smith, K. D., 234
Smith, R. E., 293
Smith, T., 291
Smith, T. W., 282
Smoll, F. L., 293
Snyder, C. R., 258, 350, 351, 358, 359, 445,
    446
Snyder, F., 159
Snyder, M., 122
Snyder, S., 186
Snydersmith, M. A., 368
Sobel, D., 366
Sobell, L. C., 211, 212
Sobell, M. B., 211, 212
Solano, J. M., 270
Solomon, E. P. , 245
Solomon, R. L., 31, 32, 43, 181-184, 305,
    346
Sorrentino, R. M., 424
Sours, J. A., 106
Spealman, R. D., 193
Speilberger, C. D., 307
Spence, J. T., 388, 423, 426, 427
Spielberger, C., 245
Spinks, J. A., 62
Sprague, J., 120
Stacy. A. W., 207
Stallings, W. M., 388
Stanley J. C., 143
Steele, C. I., 107
Steele, C. M., 184, 207, 209, 454, 464
Steele, R. A., 184
Steffen, V. J., 221, 225, 244
Steiger, J. H., 260
Stein, L., 194, 339
Stein, M. I., 398
Steinberg, M. L., 228
Steiner, S.S., 158

Stellar, E., 25, 105
Stemmler, M., 312
Stepanski, E., 175
Stern, W. C., 148, 173
Sternberg, R. J., 124, 125, 411, 412
Stewart, J., 130, 195
Stoa, K. F., 389
Stokols, D., 278, 364
Stone, A. A., 298
Stone, E. A., 342
Storm, C., 432
Storm, T., 432
Strain, A., 381, 382
Straub, R. O., 91, 283
Stricker, E. M., 78, 80
Strickland, B. R., 397, 400
Striegel-Moore, R. H., 98, 104
Stryker, S., 456
Stuart, R. B., 100
Stunkard, A. J., 87
Sturup, G. K., 234
Suedfeld, P., 26, 62
Sullivan, W. M., 310
Suomi, S. J., 384
Svebak, S., 72
Swaab, D. F., 130
Swidler, A., 310
Swinson, R. P., 180, 181, 193, 198, 204, 206,
    207
Switzky, H. N., 388
Sylva, K., 385, 386
Symons, D., 115
Taggart, P., 339
Takasawa, N., 59
Tallman, J. F., 196, 303
Tanner, O., 277, 303
Tarler-Benlolo, L., 290
Taub, J. M., 150, 151
Tavris, C., 128, 132, 138, 245, 254, 255
Taylor, C. B., 186, 344, 345
Taylor, C. W., 397
Taylor, K. W., 66
Taylor, S., 293
Taylor, S. E., 294, 350, 363, 364, 366, 460
Taylor, S. P., 222, 223, 224, 240, 248, 253
Teasdale, J. D., 319, 359
Teevan, R. C., 213
Tefler, E., 340
Teitelbaum, 88
Templeton, R. D., 81
Ter Schure, E., 261
Terrace, H. S., 424
Terzian, H., 229
Tesser, A., 124

Tharp, G. D., 42
Thomas, A., 383
Thomas, H., 376
Thompson, 468
Thompson, J., 106
Thompson, R. A., 327
Tiger, L., 188, 351
Tilley, A. J., 164
Tillich, P., 350
Tipton, S. M., 310
Tischler, G. L., 311
Toch, H., 224
Toi, M., 124
Tolson, W. W., 341, 343
Tomporowski, P. D., 43
Torrence, E. P., 397
Torsvall, L., 153
Tracy, L. N., 171
Tracy, R. L., 171
Trollinger, L. M., 398
Tinbergen, 19, 20
Trulson, M. E., 199
Tschukitschew, 81
Tsuda, A., 271
Turell, S., 103, 107
Tyler, L. E., 394
Uchino, B. N., 368
Ulrich, R. E., 237
Unger, R. K., 107
Ursin, H., 339
Vaillant, G. E., 184, 206, 212, 214, 353, 401
Valenstein, E. S., 25
Valiant, G., 295
Valins, S., 10, 75
Vallardares, H., 229
Van De Castle, R. L., 151
Van Dyke, C., 193
Van Itallie, T. B., 85
Vantress, F. E., 246
Vereby, V., 205
Vergnes, M., 229
Vernikos-Danellis, J., 268
Vezina, P., 195
Vickers, R. R. Jr., 351
Villablanca, J., 174
Visintainer, M., 11, 353
Vitz, P., 377
Vogel, G., 159
Vogel, G. W., 147, 159, 160, 162, 170, 172,
Volpicelli, J., 11, 353
Volpicelli, J. R., 189
Von Euler, U. S., 51, 272
Vreven, R., 425
Wade, C., 138

Wagner, A. R., 206
Walker, E. L., 4, 45
Walker, L. E. A., 225
Wall, S., 364
Wallace, J. E., 205
Wallace, R. K., 290, 291
Walsh, A., 123
Walsh, M. J., 205
Walters, S. R., 72
Warm, J. S., 66, 67
Water, E., 364
Waterman, A. S., 340, 392
Waters, W. F., 66
Watson, D., 308, 445
Webb, W. B., 147, 150, 152, 157, 164, 174
Weidner, G., 245, 281
Weinberg, M. S., 136, 137
Weiner, B., 242, 258, 319, 422, 423, 431, 441
Weingberger, D. A., 285
Weinstein, E., 66
Weinstein, L. N., 158, 159
Weiss, J. M., 268, 270, 271, 272, 278, 313,
318, 342
Weiss, M., 206
Weissman, M. M., 311
Wender, P. H., 311
West, L. J., 212
Whalen, R. E., 128, 234
Whitaker, L. H., 234
Whitam, F. L., 136, 137
White, A., 268
White, G. D., 237
White, J., 468
White, J. A., 42
White, R. W., 3, 31, 383, 409, 410, 445, 446,
449
Whitehead, J., 106
Whitlock, C. C., 229
Widaman, K. F., 207
Widom, C. S., 221, 227
Wiebe, D. J., 291
Wiedeking, C., 115,
Wikler, A., 187, 188
Willers, K. R., 246
Williams, C. B., 246
Williams, R., 283
Williams, R. T., 90
Williams, S. L., 345
Williams, T. K., 207
Williamson, D. A., 104
Williamson, G. M., 266
Wills, T., 434
Wilson, A. F., 290
Wilson, D. W., 251

Wilson, E. O., 20
Wilson, J. D., 129, 130, 132, 134
Wilson, T. D., 401, 425
Wing, L., 63
Winton, M., 211
Wise, C, D., 194
Wise, R. A., 184, 195, 203
Wolfe, M., 237
Wolpe, 12
Wonnocott, S., 202
Wood, J. V., 298
Woods, J. H., 196
Wooley, O. W., 99
Wooley, S. C., 99
Worchel, P., 248
Worick, W. W., 180
Wortman, C. B., 351
Wright, R. A., 124
Wurf, E., 443, 455
Wurtman, R. J., 80
Wyatt, R. J., 162
Yen, S. S., 235
Yoshinobu, L., 350, 445, 446
Yoshinobu, L. R., 359
Young, C., 103
Young, P. T., 338
Yum, K. S., 206
Zahn-Waxler, C., 326, 327, 329
Zeki, S., 30, 52, 68
Zentall, S. S., 62
Zentall, T. R., 62
Ziegler, M., 115
Zierler, K. L., 81, 98
Zilbergeld, B., 119
Zillmann, D., 15
Zimbardo, P. G., 75, 238, 243
Zinberg, N. E., 210, 212
Zubek, J. P., 59
Zuckerman, H., 398
Zuckerman, M., 125, 184, 194, 200, 339,
346, 347, 388, 389, 392, 393, 396, 446
Zwilling, G. R., 152
Zytkow, J. M., 399
Zyzanski, S. J.

Subject Index

Ability, 424-425, 427-428, 433, 458
Accommodation, 411
Accomplishment, 434
Achievement, 29, 31, 120, 213, 399-400, 419-430
Achievement, *see also* need for achievement
Acquired motives, 25-27
Action, 19, 259, 455, 462
Acts of Commission, 329, 332, 336
Acts of Omission, 329, 332, 336
Adaptation, 378
Addictive personality, 184
Adipose tissue, 80, 88
Adrenal cortex, 269
Adrenal glands, 56, 128, 271
Adrenal medulla, 270
Adrenocortical response, 42
Adrenocorticotropic hormone, (ACTH), 269
Adventure, 120
Adventure seeking, 292
Adversity, 356-360, 365-366, 434
Affect, 347, 380, 447
Affect, *see also* Hedonic tone
Affective aggression, 223-224
Affective disorder, 314
Affective disorder, and eating, 104
Agency, 259, 410, 434, 448
Aggression, 25, 219-256, 387
Aggression, and anxiety, 252
Aggression, and social disapproval, 252
Aggression, definition of, 220
Aging, 355
Alarm reaction, 270
Alcohol use, and depression, 205
Alcohol use, and quitting, 213-215
Alcohol use, beliefs about control, 211
Alcohol use, cultural differences, 210
Alcohol use, moderators, 212-215
Alcohol use, situational factors, 210
Alcohol, 80, 184, 189, 204-215

Alcoholic, 33
Alienation, 142
Alprazolam, 305
Alternation behavior, 375
Alternatives, 405
Alternatives, *see also* possibilities
Altruism, 369
Ambiguity, 278, 309, 394
Amino acids, 80
Amphetamines, 42, 148, 192-195, 341
Amygdala, 134
Amygdala, *see also* Limbic system
Anabolism, 97
Analytical ability, 414
Androgens, 128-130
Androstenedione, and aggression, 235-236
Anger, 223-224, 245-246, 260, 279, 283
Anonymity, 243
Anorexia Nervosa, 79, 88-89, 97, 105-107
Antianxiety drugs, 195-198
Anticipatory bodily preparation, 55
Antidepressant, 324
Antidepressants, 311, 314
Antitraditional orientation, 199
Anxiety, 42, 60, 72, 75, 118, 142, 184, 187, 196-197, 260, 278, 304-310, 330, 344, 346, 389, 399, 412, 433, 447, 453, 469
Anxiety, state, 308-309
Anxiety, trait, 308-309
Appraisal, 260-261, 275
Appreciation, 432
Arousal, 2, 15-16, 42, 45, 53, 56, 59, 64-68, 70, 75, 150, 202, 283, 305, 340, 346, 348, 350, 369, 380, 382, 384-385, 390, 411, 420, 469
Aspirations, 444, 461-462, 474
Aspirin, 80
Assimilation, 411
Attachment, 362-369
Attention, 52, 62, 64-67, 149, 150, 156, 388, 412, 432, 468
Attention, see also vigilance

Attention/rejection model, 60-61
Attitudes, 34
Attraction, 124
Attribution theory, 37-38
Attribution, and aggression, 241-243
Attribution, and depression, 321
Attribution, and self-change, 445
Autism, 62-63
Automatic thoughts, 326
Automatic, 274, 405, 466
Autonomic Nervous System (ANS), 50, 52, 292
Autonomous types, 325-326
Autonomous, 399-400, 445, 450-451, 472
Autonomy, *see* autonomous
Avoidance learning, 306-307, 318

Basal Metabolism Rate (BMR), 87
Being needs, 448
Belief and self-control, 191
Beliefs, 34, 356-360
Beliefs, and alcohol, 207
Belongingness, 362-369
Benevolent, 447-450
Benign, 310, 450-451
Benzodiazepines, 196-197, 305
Binge eating, 102-103
Biogenic amines, 148
Bisexual, 136-138
Blame, 427
Blood pressure, 114, 116, 246, 291, 293, 296, 447
Boredom, 72, 376, 393
Boundary theory, 94
Brain differentiation, 132-134
Brave, 434
Bulimia, 79, 103-104, 107

Caloric thrift, *see* Anabolism
Caloric waste, *see* Catabolism
Calories, 87
Cancer, 355

Cannabis, *see* Hallucinogenics
Carbohydrates, 79-81
Cardiovascular disorders, 248
Catabolism, 97-98
Catecholamine hypothesis, 314
Catecholamines, 194, 273, 283, 343, 347, 348, 350, 368
Categories, 33
Catnaps, 154-155
Cerebral cortex, 53, 133
Certainty, 404, 437, 458
Challenge, 126, 266, 293, 299, 351, 416, 433, 458, 472
Chance meeting, 123
Chloriazepoxide, 195
Chlorpromazine, 74, 341
Choice, 386, 435, 456
Choice, *see also* decisions
Circadian Rhythm, 150, 152
Clarity, 437, 458
Classical conditioning, 9, 27-29
Claustrophobia, 28
Clitoris, 113, 114, 129
Cocaine, 192-195
Cognitive dissonance, 34, 55, 389, 397
Cognitive incongruity, 304
Cognitive restructuring, 469
Cognitive, definition, 32
Cognitive-experiential self-theory (CEST), 288
Collative variables, 381
Commitment, 124-127, 293, 394-395
Communicate, 260, 396
Community, 362-369
Compartmentalization, 438
Compassion, 260
Competence, 410-418, 433, 445, 450, 460, 472-473
Competitive, 279, 282
Competitiveness, 427-431
Complexity, 45, 156, 377-385, 390, 396, 399, 411, 435
Compliance, 224
Concept-matching, 462
Concerns, 265
Conditional love, 453
Confidence, 434
Conflict, 380-381, 399
Conflict-prone, 279, 281
Conflict-resistant, 279, 281
Congenital adrenal hyperphasis (CAH), 137
Connectionism, 30-31
Conscious, 35

Consistency, 405
Constructive thinking, 288-290, 296, 454-455
Consummate love, 126-127
Context, 414-415, 458-459
Continuous improvement, 465, 473
Control, 120
Control, 308, 317, 320, 346, 433, 447, 472
Control, and aggression, 224
Control, and power, 225
Control, and stress, 275, 277, 283, 293, 299
Control, *see also* controllability
Controllability, *see* control
Controllable, *see* control
Conventional, 399
Coping, 266-269, 308, 340, 343, 346
Core relational themes, 260, 329, 342, 434
Core sexual identity, 140, 143
Coronary heart disease (CHD), 279, 280, 282
Corpus callosum, 133
Cortical activity, 55, 147
Cortical activity, *see also* EEG activity
Corticosteroids, 368
Corticosterone, 271, 272
Corticotropin-releasing factor (CRF), 269
Cortisone, 271
Counterconditioning, 307, 420
Courageous, 434
Creativity, 394, 396-406, 460
Criticism, 433
Curiosity, 375-385, 411, 433-434
Cynical hostility, 283-284
Cynical, 461

Danger, 309, 448
Danger, *see also* fear, threat
Decisions, 274, 367, 394, 403
Deindividuation, 243
Delinquency, 394
Dependency, 181
Depression and eating disorders, 91
Depression, 26, 42, 142, 159-160, 182-184, 308, 310-328, 361, 364
Desensitize, 307, 426
Destructive thinking, 287
Diabetes, 81
Diazepam, 195
Diethylstibestrol-affected (DES), 137
Differentiated, *see* differentiation
Differentiation, 412, 413, 435, 437, 459
Differentiation, *see also* brain differentiation
Difficulty, 417, 424-425

Dignity, 432
Dihydrotestosterone, 129, 140
Direction, 2, 259
Discipline, 331
Discrepancy, 381, 464
Discrimination, 271
Disease, and stress, 269
Diseases of adaptation, unpredictable, 271
Disgust, 260
Disinhibited eater, 96
Disinhibition, 206, 393-394, 399
Disposition, 19, 443
Disputation, 357-360
Dissonance, *see* cognitive dissonance
Distraction, 325-326, 357-360, 470
Distress, 266-300
Divergent thinking, 399
Dominance hierarchy, 233
Dominance, 432
Dopamine system, 193-194
Dopamine, 42-43, 115, 123, 314
Dopanergic system, 204
Doubt, 433
Dreaming, theories of, 165-168
Dreams, 142, 462-463
Drive, 375
Drug addiction, definition, 180
Dualism, 5, 27

EEG activity, 51-52, 56, 147-149, 158, 202
EEG activity, *see also* cortical activity
Effectance motivation, 31, 438
Effectance motivation, 411
Effeminate, 141
Effort, 424-425, 427-428, 433, 458
Ego strength, 447
Elavil, 314
Emotion, 75, 258, 318, 320
Emotion-focused, 275, 289-292
Emotionality, 385, 389
Emotions, dimensions of, 261
Emotions, theories of, 72-75
Empathetic-distress, 329, 335
Empathetic-guilt, 331
Empathy, 253, 329, 369-371
Empowerment, 169, 466
Empty calories, 80
Endocrine system, 52
Endogenous morphine, *see* Endorphins
Endorphins, 123, 186, 188-189, 205, 270, 296, 349, 368
Energy, 3, 259
Entity theory, 415-417
Envy, 260

Epinephrine, 53, 74, 279, 345, 347, 348
Escape learning, 306, 318-319
Esteem needs, 364-365
Estradiol, 128-129
Estrogen, and aggression, 234
Estrogens, 128-129
Ethology, 8
Euphoria, 182-184, 269
Evolution, 7, 40
Excitement, 72
Exercise, 42, 46, 188, 291-292
Expectations, 417, 422
Experience *see*king, 393
Experiential system, 288, 454-455, 463
Experimental neurosis, 206
Explanatory style, 321-324, 335, 352, 353-355
Exploration, *see* exploratory behavior
Exploratory behavior, 375-385, 411, 433
External, 38, 87, 240, 318, 320, 322-323, 424-425
External, *see also* Internal-External
Externality, *see* External
Extinction, 29
Extraversion, 70-71, 121, 151
Extrinsic motivation, 388-390

Facial expression, 260, 330, 370
Failure, 387, 433
Falling in love, 118, 123
Fame, 432
Famine hypothesis, 89
Fantasy, 117, 142
Fat cells, *see* Adipose tissue
Fatigue, 152
Fats, 79-80, 99
Fatty acids, 269, 271
Fear of failing, 420
Fear, 8, 28, 304-307, 330, 390, 399, 426, 447, 448, 456
Fear-based guilt, 331
Feedback, 66, 156, 346, 360, 436, 445, 456, 474
Feelings of efficacy, 3, 411, 417-418, 438, 452
Fight/flight, 267
Fixed action patterns, 22
Flexibility, 394
Flooding, 307
Flow, 3-4
Follicle-stimulating hormone (FSH), 128-129
Food preference, 85
Fright, 260

Fructose, 102
Frustration, 248, 420-421, 450

GABA (Gamma-amino butyric acid), 196, 305
Gastrointestinal tract, 79, 82
Gender schema, 142
Gender-identity, 135
General Adaptation Syndrome (G.A.S.), 270
Genetic Programs, 20-21
Genital, 113
Glory, 432
Glucocorticoids, 267, 269, 271
Glucose, 79-82, 102, 269, 271
Glycogen, 80
Goal, *see also* goal-directed
Goal-directed, 259, 261, 310, 361
Goals, 265, 351, 361, 375, 389, 416, 434, 443-445, 455, 463-465, 474
Goals, paratelic, 72
Goals, telic, 72
Gonadotropic hormones, 128
Growth motivation, 450
Guilt, 12, 260, 328-336, 426

Habits, 472
Habitual, 405
Habitual, *see also* automatic
Habituate, 307, 335
Hallucinations, 58, 148
Hallucinogenics, 198-201
Happiness, 37, 260, 340-351
Hard-wired, 21
Hardiness, 280
Hardy personality, 293, 366
Harm, 241
Health, 11, 27, 169, 189, 200, 287, 295, 296, 353, 366-367, 454
Heart rate, 114, 116
Hedonic enjoyment, 350
Hedonic happiness, 350
Hedonic tone, 70, 380, 382
Hedonism, 4, 184, 340-351
Helplessness, 11, 355, 410, 416, 432-433
Helplessness, *see also* learned helplessness
Heroin, 186-192
Hippocampus, *see* Limbic system
Homeostasis, 24
Homologous, 5
Homophobia, 142
Homosexuality, 135-143
Hope of success, 421-423
Hope of success, *see also* need to achieve

Hope, 260, 352-362
Hopeful, 276
Hopelessness, 410
Hostile, 279, 366
Hostile, *see also* hostility
Hostility, 245-246, 330
Humanistic theories, 12-14
Humor, 295
Hunger, 79
Hungers, theories of, 81-82
Hyperactivity, 62-63
Hyperinsulin response, 98
Hypertension, 281
Hypothalamus, 25, 53, 79, 132, 134-136, 150, 227

Images, 400, 466
Imitation, and aggression, 237
Immune response, 285, 293, 295-296
Immune system, 189, 355, 365, 368
Immunization, 320
Implicit theories, 35, 261, 446
Importance, 432
Impulsivity, 62
Incentive, 422
Incongruity, 380-381
Incremental theory, 415-417
Incubation, 404
Independence, 399-400, 433, 434
Individualism, 312-313, 450
Induction, 331
Inescapable shock, 317-319, 344
Inescapable, 317
Inferiority, 432
Information, 382-383, 394, 400, 402
Initiative, 434
Inner dialogue, 327
Inner dialogue, *see also* self-talk
Insecurity, 308
Insomnia, 174-175
Instinct, 5-8
Instrumental aggression, 223-224, 237
Instrumental learning, 9
Instrumentality, 294
Insulin, 79, 81, 94
Insults, 252
Intelligence, 288, 413-417
Intercourse, 118-122
Internal, 38, 240, 318, 320, 322-323, 424-425, 432
Internal, *see also* Internal-External
Internal-External, 294
Internal-External, and obesity

Internal-External, *see also* Locus of control
Interpersonal Violence, 225
Interspousal abuse, 225
Intimacy, 115, 120, 124-127, 395
Intrinsic motivation, 388-390, 412, 433
Introversion, 70-71, 121, 151
Intrusive thinking, 278, 351, 467-468
Intuition, 399

Jealousy, 260
Jet lag, 153
Justice motive, 370

Knowledge, 400

Labels, 33, 74
Lateral hypothalamus (LH), 88-89
Lateral thinking, 400
Laughter, 189
Laws of emotions, 262-264
Learned helplessness, 316-318
Lesbian, 135-143
Leuteinizing hormone, (LH), 128
Levelers, 60-61
Librium, 195, 305
Limbic system, 24, 53, 199, 228-233
Lipids, 88
Locus coeruleus, 54, 56, 148, 314, 315
Locus of control Theory, 38
Loneliness, 364
Love withdrawal, 331
Love, 8, 120, 122-127, 260
Lucid dreaming, 169
Lysegic Acid Diethylamide (LSD),
    see Hallucinogenics

Magic mushrooms, *see* Hallucinogenics
Malnutrition, 84
Management of anger, 254-255
Manic-depressive, 314
Marijuana, *see* Hallucinogenics
Maritial satisfaction, 395
Masculination, 134-138
Massive retaliation, 223
Mastery strategy/orientation, 449-450
Mastery, 11, 31, 355, 361, 416, 427-431, 445,
    450
Masturbation, 118, 121
Mathematical abilities, 131
Meditation, 290
Memory, 152
Menopause, 129
Mental Images, 68-69
Mental rehearsal, 465

Metabolism, 87-90, 99, 202, 291
Methadone, 187
Microsleeps, 152
Migraine headaches, 291
Mindfulness, 36, 299, 366-367, 397, 472-473
Mindlessness, *see* mindfulness
Mineralcorticoids, 267, 271
Modeling, 117, 237, 370, 399, 473
Monoamine oxidase (MAO), 314, 349, 391-
    392
Monoamine oxidase inhibitors (MAOI),
    314
Morphine, 186-192
Morphine, *see* Heroin
Motives, 265
Myopia, and alcohol, 207-210
Mystic, 450

Naloxone opiate receptors, 187
Narcolepsy, 149
Nardil, 314
Narplan, 314
Need to achieve, 419, 421-424, 433
Need to avoid failure, 421-423
Need to avoid failure,
    see also fear of failing
Need to communicate, *see* communicate
Needs, 12, 19, 259, 443
Negative evaluation, 151
Neural networks, 30-31
Neurotic, 12, 363
Neuroticism, 447
Neurotransmitters, 341
Nicotine, 201-204
Noradrenergic system, 105
Norepinephrine, 42, 43, 51, 53-54, 80, 115,
    123, 148, 273, 314-315, 343, 344, 347,
    348, 391
Novelty, 375-385, 390, 396
NREM dreams, 151
NREM, 151, 169-173
Nutrition, 84-85

Obesity, 15, 79, 86-91
Obsessive compulsive, 22
Openness, 400
Opponent process theory, 31, 182-184, 348
Optimal arousal, 59, 71
Optimal arousal, *see also* arousal
Optimal experience, 4
Optimal stimulation, 62
Optimism, 11, 37, 126, 280, 294, 352-362,
    445, 460, 473, 447
Orgasm, 113, 114, 115, 118, 119

Orientation reaction, 65-66
Outcome orientation, 452
Ovaries, 236
Overgeneralization, 437
Overstimulation, 304-305
Overweight, *see* Obesity
Oxytocin, 123

Pacer, 378
Pair-bonding, 115, 116
Panic, 309
Parallel processing, 30
Parnate, 314
Partial reinforcement effect, 421
Passion, 125-127
Pathways, 360, 410, 448
Patterns, 30, 396-397, 400
Peak experiences, 448
Penis, 116
Perceptual speed, 130
Performance strategy/orientation, 416,
    432, 452
Permanence, 321
Persistence, 2, 15, 259, 416, 420-421, 424,
    427-428, 433, 464
Personal control, 346, 361
Personalization, 322-323
Pervasiveness, 322
Pessimism, 11, 294, 310-328, 447
Pet ownership, 287
Petting, 118
Phenylethylanine (PEA), 123
Phobia, 305
Physical activity, 87
Physical activity, *see also* exercise
Pituitary Adrenal Response, 269
Pituitary, 56
Plasma lipids, 283
Play, 386-387
Pleasure bond, 115
Pornographic, 117, 250
Positive Emission Tomography (PET), 52
Positive self-regard, 13, 453
Possibilities, 415, 447-448, 450
Possibilities, *see also* alternatives
Possible selves, 443-444, 457-461, 462
Power, 120,
Power, 370, 434
Predictability, 404, 405
Premenstrual syndrome (PMS), 234
Prestige, 432
Prewired, 8
Pride, 260, 410, 426, 433, 434-438, 450

Problem solving, 52, 126, 130, 276, 354, 396, 414,
Problem-focused, 275, 297-298, 449
Process-orientation, 327, 452, 473
Progesterone, and aggression, 234
Progestins, 128
Promiscuity, 122, 141
Proteins, 79-80
Prototypes, 447-451
Prozac, 314
Psilocybin, *see* Hallucinogenics
Psychoactive, 181
Psychoanalytic Theory, 11, 139, 330
Punishment, 426

Rage, 8, 238-239
Raphe Nuclei, 54, 56, 148
Rational system, 288, 335, 454-455, 463
Reactive inhibition, 376
Recognition, 432
Redundancy, 402
Relatedness, 450-451
Relaxation response, 67, 291, 296, 297, 299, 470
Relaxed awareness, 26, 189
Releasing Stimuli, 9
Relief, 260
REM deprivation, 158-163
REM deprivation, *see also* REM sleep
REM dreams, 151-152
REM rebound, 159
REM sleep, and adaptation to stress, 161
REM sleep, and consolidation of learning, 163
REM sleep, and creativity, 161-162
REM sleep, and field independence/dependence,162
REM sleep, and individual differences, 162
REM sleep, and learning, 160-161
REM sleep, and neuroticism, 163
REM sleep, *see also* REM deprivation
REM, and dreams, 168
REM, and paralysis, 149
REM, theories of, 158-163
Remote associations, 403
Repression-sensitization, 447
Repressive personality, 286
Repressors, 286
Reputation, 432
Response unavailability, 304
Responsibility, 323
Restrained eater, 95-96

Restricted environmental stimulation, 62, 391
Restricted orientation, 121-122
Retaliation in like kind, 222
Reticular Activating System (RAS), 24, 50-51, 53, 56, 60, 148, 198
Reward Centers, 23-24
Rigidity, 399
Risk, 189, 340, 345, 351, 390, 448, 466
Rock music, 44-47
Role playing, 370
Romantic, 117, 122, 125
Rumination, 324-325, 335, 404, 437
Running, 41-44

Sadness, 260
Satiation, *see also* stimulus satiation
Satiety, 79, 82
Scrotum, 116,
Self-actualized, 448-449
Self-awareness, and eating, 104
Self-certainty, 308
Self-change, 445, 460, 471-474
Self-concept, 352, 433-434, 443-475
Self-confidence, 44, 365, 399-400, 438, 473-474
Self-determination, 389, 445, 450-451, 472-473
Self-disclosure, 124
Self-doubt, 259, 299, 445, 467, 470
Self-efficacy, 344, 347, 350, 456, *see also* feelings of efficacy
Self-esteem, 278, 280, 410, 430-438, , 4413-444, 448, 455
Self-image, 142
Self-image, 399
Self-initiated, 387
self-injury, 188
Self-knowledge, 458
Self-limiting, 326
Self-monitor, 121-122
Self-motivation, 445
Self-referent, *see* self-reflection,
Self-reflection, 332, 403, 443-446, 471-474
Self-regulation, 19, 259, 443-475
Self-reliant, 450
Self-satisfaction, 472
Self-serving bias, 426
Self-statements, 293
Self-statements, *see also* self-talk
Self-talk, 468
Self-worth, 363, 410, 431-438
Sensation *see*king, 124, 184, 295, 390-395, 448

Sensitizer, 309
Sensory deprivation, 26, 57-59
Sensory overload, 59, 66, 413
Sensory-narrative based system, 335
Septum, *see* Limbic system
Serotonergic system, 105
Serotonin, 22, 54, 63, 80, 148, 199, 314
Set-point Theory, 89
Sex hormones, 127-130
Sex-assignment, 139-141
Sexual arousal, 112-120, 128
Sexual dimorphism, 132-134
Sexual orientation, 21,135-143
Sexual scripts, 117-120
Shame, 260, 328-336, 426, 433
Sharpeners, 60-61
Shift work, 154
Signaled, 272
Sleep deprivation, and mood, 156
Sleep deprivation, 151, 157
Sleep disorders, 174-175
Sleep patterns, 157
Sleep reduction, 153, 156
Sleep reduction, *see also* sleep deprivation
Sleepiness, 152
Slow wave sleep (SWS), 151
Social relationships, 277
Social support, 285, 286, 365-367
Sociotropic types, 325-326
Softwired, 21
Spatial abilities, 130-131
Species-specific, 25
Specific dynamic action (SDA), 87
Spiral model of eating disorder, 107
Stage of resistance, 271
Status, 432
Stereotype, 34, 121, 141, 367
Stimulus change, 376
Stimulus satiation, 376
Strategies, 451, 464
Stress, 69, 266-300, 433, 447, 454, 458, 468
Substance abuse, definition, 180
Substitution, 469
Suicide, 142, 311-312
Supervision clarity, 279
Suppression of aggression, 252
Surprisingness, 379-381
Suspicious, 461
Sympathetic adrenal response, 267-268
Sympathetic nervous system, 54, 56
Synthesis, 401-402, 414

Tactile, 112-113
Task difficulty, 427-428

Teacher-learner paradigm, 221-222, 247
Temporal lobes, 228-230
Temporary, 321
Testes, 116, 236
Testosterone, 128-130, 393
Testosterone, 129-130, 133-134, 138, 140
Testosterone, and aggression, 233-234
Threat, 198, 266, 274, 294-296, 310, 330,
    346, 351, 366, 436, 443, 447, 452, 454,
    459, 466
Thrill-*seek*ing , 340, 341, 348, 393
Tofranil, 314
Tolerance, 181
Tricyclic antidepressants, and hunger, 82
Triumphant, 434
Truth, 449
Type A, 282-286

Ulcers, 272, 278, 279
Ultradian rhythms, 151
Uncertainty, 345, 380-381
Uncertainty, *see also* unpredictable
Unconditional love, 453
Unconscious, 35
Uncontrollable, 314, 345
Unconventional, 394, 400
Undependable, 394
Universal, 322
Unpredictability, 394
Unrestrained eater, 95-96
Unrestricted orientation, 121-122
Urinary acidity, 202

Vagina, 114
Valium, 181, 195, 305

Values, 34
Varied, *see* complexity
Variety, *see* complexity
Vasocongestion, 114, 116
Ventromedial nuclei (VMN), 88-89
Victim derogation, 371
Victorious, 434
Vigilance, 66-67, 156
Violence, 250-251
Visual Images, 27
Visualization, 462-463

Withdrawal symptoms, Heroin, 187, 190
Work, 427-431

Yo-Yo effect, 89-90